RESEARCHERS AT WORK

Highlights the process of experimentation and hypothesis testing.

☑ Researchers at Work

Henry was able to form new memories for some tasks

Figure 9.18 Henry's Performance on a Mirror-Tracing Task

■ **Question:** Was Henry able to learn anything new?

■ **Hypothesis:** Henry's deficit after the surgery made it impossible for him to form new memories of any sort.

■ **Test:** Psychologist Brenda Milner (1965) gave Henry a mirror-tracing task (**Figure 9.18A**) and asked him to do it ten times for several successive days.

(A) Henry was given this mirror-tracing task to test motor skill.

■ **Result:** In fact, Henry improved considerably over the course of ten trials the first day (Milner, 1965). The next day when the test was presented again, Henry did not remember having ever done it before. Yet his performance was better than at the start of the first day. Over three successive days, Henry never recognized the task, but his performance improved steadily (**Figure 9.18B**).

(B) Although Henry never recognized the task, his performance progressively improved over successive days, demonstrating a type of long-term memory.

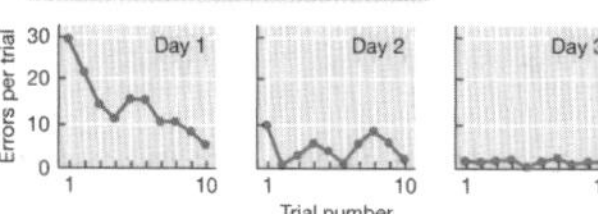

■ **Conclusion:** Even though Henry did not recognize having done the task before, his improved performance from one day to the next demonstrated a kind of memory in the form of motor skill. The fact that Henry could learn a new skill, without ever being aware that he had done it before, suggested that his deficit was restricted to a particular kind of memory.

SECTION SUMMARIES AND REVIEW QUESTIONS

Review what you've learned from the text.

4.5 SUMMARY

- Exposure to stress increases the probability that a person will develop schizophrenia. Complications at birth that deprive the newborn of oxygen, or growing up in a big city with its stresses, make a person more vulnerable to schizophrenia.
- Home movies of monozygotic twins as children indicate that the twin who later developed schizophrenia moved in more disorganized, jerkier fashion than the twin that remained well.
- Observations suggest that someday it may be possible to identify babies carrying genes that put them at risk for schizophrenia and protect them from the stresses that would lead them to develop the disorder.
- In rats, maternal neglect can epigenetically imprint certain genes in the pups to cause them to be more anxious in adulthood, and there is evidence that this same gene is affected by early neglect in humans.

REVIEW QUESTIONS

1. Describe the evidence that stress plays a role in the development of schizophrenia.
2. What do old home movies of monozygotic twins tell us about the origins of schizophrenia?
3. Does growing up in a big city increase or decrease the probability of developing schizophrenia?

THINGS TO LEARN

Provides learning objectives.

Things to Learn

- Sequential nature of stages of motor development
- How experience can affect motor development
- Development of sensory system
- Ways to test infant mental development
- Development of memory in infants
- Piaget's stages of cognitive development
- Temperament and anxiety in children
- Importance of love for proper development
- Attachment styles in infants

MARGINAL GLOSSARY

Helps you identify and learn key terminology as you read.

homeostasis The process of keeping a constant, stable internal environment in the body.

set point A particular value that a system keeps returning to.

negative feedback A signal to a system to decrease activity.

hypothalamus A part of the brain that maintains the constant internal environment in the body.

the furnace eventually turn **feedback**, when the result *back is found in all homeos*

In our bodies, temperat called the **hypothalamus** (hypothalamus carefully mea pothalamus directs the bod cool down (for example, by its set point (about 98.6°F) thermostat. We saw anoth reduction model) when we (such as eating) reduces the

FOOD FOR THOUGHT

Requires integration and application of materials just read.

Food for Thought

Do you think John B. Watson was correct in his bold declaration that he could mold any infant to fulfill any human occupation as an adult?

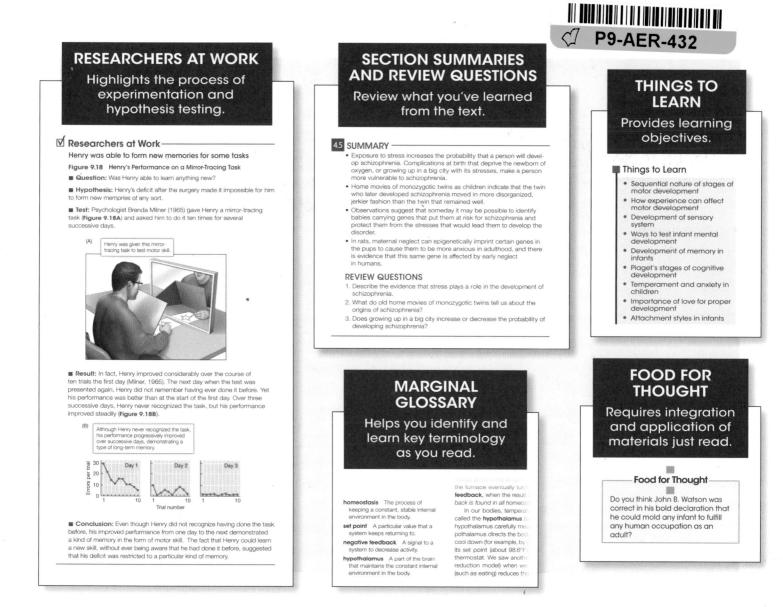

More Support to Help You Learn

■ ■ ■

Companion Website

www.oup.com/us/breedlove

Available at no additional cost, the open-access Companion Website provides you with the following review resources:

- **Chapter Outlines:** Detailed outlines that give an overview of each chapter.
- **Chapter Summaries:** Full summaries of each chapter provide a thorough review of the important facts and concepts covered.
- **Flashcards:** Interactive flashcard activities are an effective way for you to learn and review all of the important terminology.
- **Practice Quizzes:** For each chapter, a 25-question practice quiz is provided. You can use this quiz as a self-review exercise, to help check your understanding of the chapter's material.

The Four Principles of Psychology

Four key principles are used to emphasize that psychology is a science. These principles offer a framework to discuss proven concepts, research-based investigations and experiments, and critical-thinking skills.

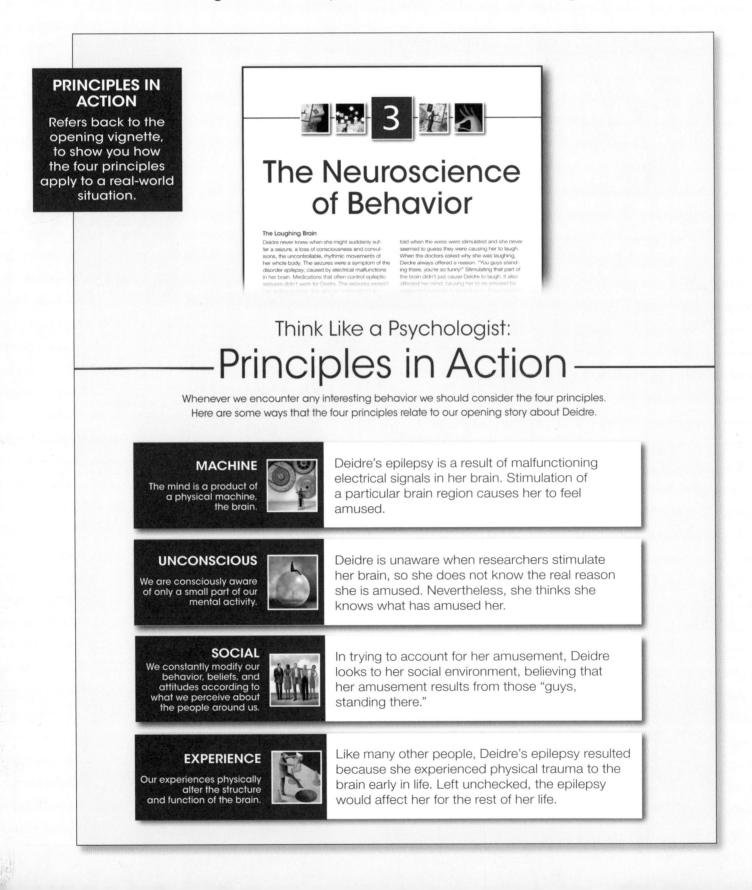

PRINCIPLES IN ACTION

Refers back to the opening vignette, to show you how the four principles apply to a real-world situation.

The Neuroscience of Behavior

The Laughing Brain

Deidre never knew when she might suddenly suffer a *seizure*, a loss of consciousness and convulsions, the uncontrollable, rhythmic movements of her whole body. The seizures were a symptom of the disorder *epilepsy*, caused by electrical malfunctions in her brain. Medications that often control epileptic seizures didn't work for Deidre. The seizures weren't

told when the wires were stimulated and she never seemed to guess they were causing her to laugh. When the doctors asked why she was laughing, Deidre always offered a reason. "You guys standing there, you're so funny!" Stimulating that part of the brain didn't just cause Deidre to laugh, it also affected her *mind*, causing her to be *amused* by

Think Like a Psychologist:

Principles in Action

Whenever we encounter any interesting behavior we should consider the four principles. Here are some ways that the four principles relate to our opening story about Deidre.

MACHINE The mind is a product of a physical machine, the brain. 	Deidre's epilepsy is a result of malfunctioning electrical signals in her brain. Stimulation of a particular brain region causes her to feel amused.
UNCONSCIOUS We are consciously aware of only a small part of our mental activity. 	Deidre is unaware when researchers stimulate her brain, so she does not know the real reason she is amused. Nevertheless, she thinks she knows what has amused her.
SOCIAL We constantly modify our behavior, beliefs, and attitudes according to what we perceive about the people around us. 	In trying to account for her amusement, Deidre looks to her social environment, believing that her amusement results from those "guys, standing there."
EXPERIENCE Our experiences physically alter the structure and function of the brain. 	Like many other people, Deidre's epilepsy resulted because she experienced physical trauma to the brain early in life. Left unchecked, the epilepsy would affect her for the rest of her life.

Principles of Psychology

Principles of Psychology

S. Marc Breedlove
Michigan State University

Sinauer Associates, Inc. Publishers
Sunderland, Massachusetts

New York Oxford
Oxford University Press

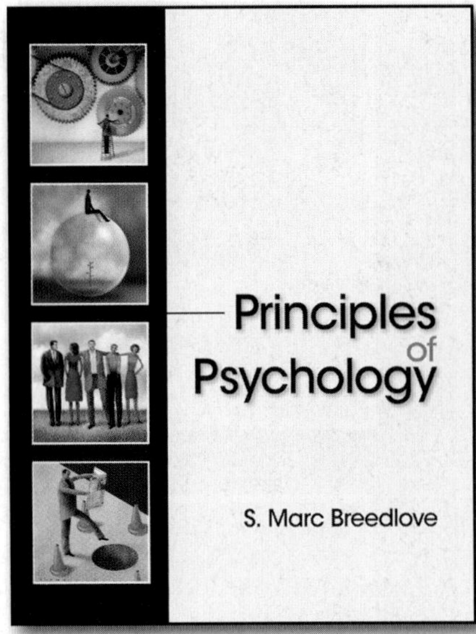

About the cover

The four images on the cover were chosen to represent the four principles: machine, unconscious, social, and experience. All images ©Dave Cutler.

Principles of Psychology

Copyright © 2015 by Sinauer Associates, Inc.
All rights reserved. This book may not be reproduced in whole or in part without permission from the publisher.

Address editorial correspondence to:
Sinauer Associates, Inc.,
P. O. Box 407
Sunderland, MA 01375 U.S.A.
www.sinauer.com
publish@sinauer.com

Address orders, sales, license, permissions, and translation inquiries to:
Oxford University Press U.S.A.
198 Madison Avenue
New York, NY 10016
Orders: 1-800-445-9714

Library of Congress Cataloging-in-Publication Data
Breedlove, S. Marc.
Principles of psychology / S. Marc Breedlove, Michigan State University.
pages cm
ISBN 978-0-1993-2936-6
1. Psychology. I. Title.
BF121.B636 2015
150—dc23
2014040616

Printed in U.S.A.
10 9 8 7 6 5 4 3 2 1

For my children

Ben, who taught me about love
Nick, who taught me about family
Tessa, who taught me about hope
Kit, who taught me about courage

Brief Contents

Contents

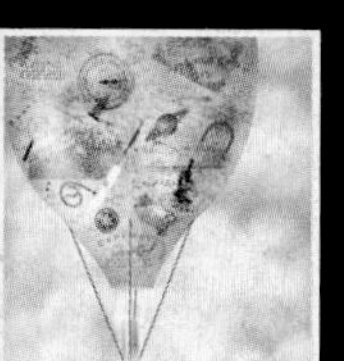

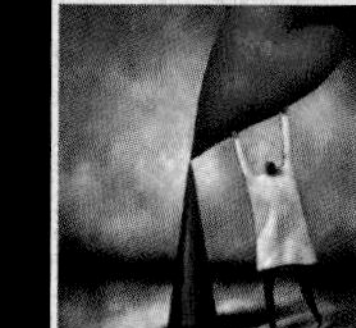

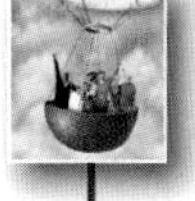

Chapter 7 Consciousness 247

Chapter 8 Learning 307

Chapter 9
Memory 351

Chapter 10 Language and Cognition 397

Chapter 11 Intelligence 451

Chapter 12
Motivation and the Regulation of Behavior 499

Chapter 13
Emotions, Stress, and Health 549

Chapter 14
Personality 597

Chapter 16 Clinical Psychology 693

Preface

I've written this textbook as an affectionate kick in the pants to the field of psychology. For several years when I taught Psychology 101 at the University of California, Berkeley I invited guest lecturers from different sub-disciplines in the field to join me to chat informally with the students about "What's the big picture?" of their research. The goal was to distill concepts that come up in many different experiments, conducted in widely different areas of psychology. These talks also revolved around how to think critically about the concepts of psychology and how research can contradict our day-to-day impressions about human behavior.

These experiences taught me that psychology as a field needs to be more effective in communicating the hard-won findings of our *research-based science*. Relatively few of our fellow citizens know, for example, that:

- Bias shapes every human judgment.
- Genes influence *all* human behavior but *determine* only the simplest of human behaviors (like color blindness).
- No human has ever been formally *taught* her or his first language, although almost everyone learns one.
- People can sincerely, even vividly, remember events that never happened.
- Our sensory systems actively distort information about our surroundings.
- No one really understands why antidepressant or antipsychotic drugs work.
- There is no cure for schizophrenia, but young adults who develop schizophrenia often recover.

Many scientific observations support each of these ideas, but plenty of adults in our society would disbelieve most of them, *even those who previously took a college course in Introductory Psychology*. How have psychologists failed to get our messages out to the public?

I think introductory textbooks are overly focused on details and minor points that should be addressed in later, more advanced courses. What's needed in an introductory textbook is a broad framework upon which you can hang details that come your way to help you gain a solid understanding of our hard-won knowledge. I think this can be made easier by emphasizing a few important principles that relate to almost any behavior.

The Four Principles

Principles of Psychology is organized around the following four important, well-established principles:

- The mind is a product of a physical machine, the brain.
- We are consciously aware of only a small part of our mental activity.
- We constantly modify our behavior, beliefs, and attitudes according to what we perceive about the people around us.
- Experience physically alters the structure and function of the brain.

These principles may sound simple and uncontroversial, but each gives rise to surprising revelations (including many of the counterintuitive findings listed above) and can serve as touchstones, or a framework, for the field as a whole. They help emphasize proven concepts, support research-based investigations and experiments, and encourage critical thinking, thereby encouraging you to see the "big picture."

Vignettes and Principles in Action

Because we all love and readily remember narratives, I begin each chapter with a vignette, an instance when behavior has a big impact on someone's life. The chapter returns to the vignette several times as we cover findings that relate to that particular case. To close the chapter, I show how the four principles relate to the vignette, with a feature called "Think Like a Psychologist: Principles in Action." I even offer a mnemonic, **MUSE** (**M**achine-like brain, **U**nconscious processes, **S**ocial influences, **E**xperience matters) so that, for the rest of your life, whenever you encounter any interesting behavior, you can recall the four principles to consider how they might apply to this instance. If you do that, you will indeed be thinking like a psychologist.

Psychology Is a Research-Based Science

Among other things, the fact that psychology is a science means I'm not going to shrink away from presenting what other sciences tell us about human behavior. I explore concepts and discoveries from all areas of psychology, as well as evolutionary biology, genetics, and neuroscience. Cognizant of you, the student, nothing I've written about these topics assumes any prior biology background is needed to understand the interplay between the sciences and behavior. I want the science to excite you and broaden your understanding of human behavior.

Nature vs. Nurture

Understanding psychology as a research-based science also helps deal with one of the biggest questions facing individuals and society: the nature vs. nurture question. Given our society's confusion about genes and experience, I think few people grasp how these two factors can really interact to affect behavior. For this reason I devote Chapter 4 *Genes, Environment, and Behavior* to explain why *every* behavior is affected by *both* genes and experience, with examples that you can incorporate into your thinking. Rather than just say that genes and the environment "interact," without providing an explanation of what that means, I show you *how* they interact. We'll see that experience affects when and where genes are expressed—so it's not just which genes you inherited, but *how those genes are used* that matters. Experience-driven gene expression can affect the structure of the brain, which affects behavior, which affects experience to start the whole cycle over again. While these are awesome and important ideas, they are not mystical and there's no reason why anyone can't grasp them to understand the nature vs. nurture debate.

Critical Thinking

Psychology's important mission is to teach people how to think critically about human behavior, to apply the same hard-nosed attitude that scientists display in other fields. You will spend the rest of your life observing human behavior and trying to make sense of it. So I created two features to help you think critically about behavior, including your own, to better understand the human mind: "Researchers at Work" and "Skeptic at Large."

Researchers at Work

Each chapter offers one or two examples of hypothesis testing to show you the logic of scientific thinking. Following the progress of a successful line of research that provides a conclusion that has withstood the test of time teaches critical thinking without leaving you confused about what we do know. "Researchers at Work" includes the Question that prompted the study, the specific Hypothesis that was being tested, then the Test, the Results of the test, and the Conclusion drawn from the result. We also have terrific figures illustrating the results, and I hope the combination of step-by-step narrative and pictures makes the logic of these experiments clear, and helps drive home the critical thinking skills of a research-based science of behavior.

Skeptic at Large

To reinforce the critical thinking needed to see through the hooey that's presented to us over the Web every day, Chapter 1 offers several psychological myths, including at least one relevant to each subsequent chapter, and briefly previews how we'll disprove them along the way. Most chapters have a box, "Skeptic at Large," that takes on a widespread notion and demonstrates how research disproves it. These particular instances of critical thinking should help you see the danger of our current "misinformation age" and the power of experimentation, reinforcing the "Researchers at Work" feature.

The Cutting Edge

Psychology is a living, research-based science and I want you to know that we are still exploring the frontiers. Thus each chapter ends with "The Cutting Edge," which explores an exciting report of recent research on the very edge of what we know. How does the grooming provided by a rat mother affect the specific genes in the pups' brain? How do eye-tracking systems determine, with over 90% accuracy, people who have been diagnosed with schizophrenia? Are people suffering from eating disorders more sensitive to photos of fattening foods than control participants? Showing these vibrant frontiers will emphasize that psychology research is abundant and thriving.

Final Thoughts

The aim of this text is to present you with a more unified message to emphasize how a few principles are at work in many findings. Without apology, I write for you, the students. I want you to read, understand, and (if at all possible) be entertained by what I'm saying. Of course, I want to be precise—to impart what I really mean. But I have no desire to use long words or complicated sentence structures for their own sake.

I wrote this book in a conversational style and tried to use the power of storytelling—the human mind loves narratives and we will recall their details more fully. In addition to the vignettes, sometimes I offer personal stories to illustrate psychological phenomenon, certain you will better remember the finding because of the story. I want you to remember the stories and the principles long after the examinations are over and your course grades are posted. No matter how many details you've forgotten, if what you read here helps you to think like a psychologist, then you'll carry this course with you for life.

Acknowledgments

When I began work on this book, I thought I knew what I was getting into. After all, I'd been a co-author or co-editor for two other college-level textbooks. While the dates on my earliest Word files for this book are dated 1996, I didn't really begin in earnest until 2005. If I'd known then that it would take nearly 10 years to complete the book, I honestly doubt that I would have started. Of course, I am enormously proud of the final product, but also totally humbled. So many people have brought talent, effort, and perseverance to bear on producing this book that it literally makes me laugh out loud to think how inadequate my contributions alone would have been.

My first thanks go to Andy Sinauer, who has gathered and nurtured a wonderful cadre of talent that keeps producing, year after year, the most beautiful textbooks I've ever seen—an enduring testament to his vision and his team. Andy's personal encouragement was critical in starting this project, and I am so grateful for his steadfast belief in this undertaking.

Sinauer Associates Editor Sydney Carroll has been an amazing bedrock of guidance and support. Not only has she been a tremendous resource for ideas and problem-solving, Syd has somehow kept the entire juggernaut of editors, reviewers, designers, artists, and a sometimes unbelievably cranky author moving along. Each time I thought we'd hit an unmovable roadblock, Syd found a way forward. What's funny is how, after each detour, the book came into better focus, so that the crystallization of the book in many ways is as much a reflection of Syd's mind as mine. No matter whose name is on the front of the book, this has been a partnership, and I have been so glad to have such a capable, tireless, genial colleague.

Syd's predecessor, Editor Graig Donini persuaded me to take the plunge in the first place, so I want to thank (blame?) him for his encouragement and faith that I could see it through. Graig's support and creative insights in the early stages were absolutely critical. The formation of the book also benefitted enormously from several editors guided first by Graig and then by Syd, including Development editors Annie Reid and Carol Pritchard-Martinez. Each brought unique strengths to bear on the text, from the first stage to the last, and I feel so grateful for their collective guidance.

Once the actual production of the book began, yet another team of talented people came to bear. Copy editor Liz Pierson made so many improvements on every page, with a tireless attention to detail. Toward the end of the process Copy editor Lou Doucette read the text with a fine-tooth comb and was remarkably good at catching places where changing a few words could avoid misunderstandings, and also caught several flat-out mistakes (all of them mine)! Christine Lofgren was also a tremendous help with the writing of the Glossary and the Quiz Yourself questions and answers.

In Sinauer's production department, Chris Small was so important to the process of bringing the book into focus, and has so many great ideas about future editions that I'm excited to see what we come up with next. With her elegant vision and grace, compositor and designer Joanne Delphia did an amazing job of taking the deluge of words, jumbled images, and diverse features and somehow getting them to simply flow across the pages that follow. It was like watching someone pour a messy, lumpy batter into a pan and then somehow pull a beautiful, delicious pastry out of the oven. Photo researcher David McIntyre continues to amaze me with his ability to find the perfect photos and images to complement the text. He brings a terrific eye and a great sense of humor, as well as an amazingly broad store of knowledge, to the process. Thank you to Jason Dirks and his team of editors in the Media and Supplements department for their patience and skill in creating a compelling and useful supplements package. Stephanie Bonner, Production Editor, also deserves a special thank you for all of her work and efforts to help tidy up the book. Mike Demaray and Helen Wortham at Dragonfly Media Group are incomparable with their ability to coalesce complex, sometimes dense scientific concepts into spare, elegant, beautiful simplicity in the illustrations. There is no doubt in my mind that they are the finest scientific illustrators on Earth.

Production Editor Kathaleen Emerson was tireless in her efforts to keep me on track, and her ability to keep tabs on the illustrations, photos, editors, and hundreds of draft files is nothing short of preternatural. Kath's patience with me was also preternatural, as the thousands of emails between us prove. She has been much more than midwife to the birth of this child; more like a genetic engineer.

I also want to thank the folks in the Higher Education Department at Oxford University Press. As our co-publisher in this project, they have been enthusiastic throughout, offering invaluable advice and suggestions. The have been our "partner" in the truest sense of the word. Special thanks go to John Challice, VP and Publisher, Higher Education; Patrick Lynch, Editorial Director; Jane Potter, Psychology Senior Acquisitions Editor. Further thanks go to Jolene Howard, Director of Market Development; and Eden Kram-Gingold: Marketing Manager; thank you both for your well-orchestrated campaign and your fervor for this book.

Finally, I want to warmly thank the many reviewers who took the time from their busy lives to offer reactions and feedback to the (many, many, many) drafts of every chapter. I learned a lot in doing the research to write this book, but I learned a lot more from the collective knowledge of these remarkably informed, wise people. The reviewers taught me so much. Not only did they catch mistakes that made me blush, but they pushed me to think harder about many issues, and I know the book is so much better because of their selfless efforts. Nevertheless, if there are shortcomings or mistakes in what follows, I have to take full responsibility for them.

Reviewers

The following reviewers have read, critiqued, or class-tested many iterations of this book. We wish to thank them for their time and extraordinarily thoughtful and helpful comments; the book is greatly improved because of their input.

Eileen Achorn, *University of Texas at San Antonio*
Rachel Albert, *University of Wisconsin-Stevens Point*
George Alder, *Simon Fraser University*
Nancy Alwood, *University of Arkansas*
Sandra Arntz, *Carroll University*
Diane Ashe, *Valencia College, Winter Park*
Pamela Auburn, *University Houston-Downtown*
Kevin Autry, *University of Arkansas*
Angela Bahns, *Wellesley College*
Steve Balsis, *Texas A & M University, College Station*
Jonathan Banks, *Nova Southeastern University*
Dave Baskind, *Delta College*
Kiersten Baughman, *Ball State University*
Gwyneth Beagley, *Alma College*
Holly Beard, *Midlands Technical College*
Burton Beck, Jr., *Pensacola State University*
Felice Bedford, *University of Arizona*
Jennifer Bellingtier, *University of Northern Iowa*
Michael Benhar, *Suffolk County Community College*
Melissa Berry, *University of Dayton*
Bakhtawar Bhadha, *Pasadena City College*
Julia Blau, *State University of New York, College at Oneonta*
Tim Bono, *Washington University of St. Louis*
Carol Borden, *St. Cloud State University*
Louis Boudreau, *University of Connecticut*
Jessica Boyette-Davis, *York College of Pennsylvania*
Debi Brannan, *Western Oregon University*
Eric Bressler, *Westfield State University*
Thomas Brothen, *University of Minnesota*
Trina Brown, *Savannah College of Art & Design*
Brad Brubaker, *Indiana State University*
Josh Burk, *College of William and Mary*
Laura Byers, *Grand Rapids Community College*
Aimee Callender, *Auburn University*
Ken Callis, *Southeast Missouri State University*
Michele Camden, *Stetson University*
J. Timothy Cannon, *University of Scranton*

Bernardo Carducci, *Indiana University Southeast*
Marie Cassar, *Saginaw Valley State University*
Amber Chenoweth, *Hiram College*
Sheryl Civjan, *Holyoke Community College*
Wanda Clark, *South Plains College*
James Collins, *Carson-Newman University*
Jessamy Comer, *Rochester Institute of Technology*
Sheree Dukes Conrad, *University of Massachusetts, Boston*
Shaun Cook, *Millersville University*
Erin Cooper, *College of the Canyons*
Kristi Cordell-McNulty, *Angelo State University*
Justin Couchman, *Albright College*
Verne Cox, *University of Texas at Arlington*
Howard Casey Cromwell, *Bowling Green State University*
Craig Cummings, *Auburn University*
Brian Cusato, *Centre College*
Thomas Daniel, *Auburn University*
Natalie Dautovich, *University of Alabama, Tuscaloosa*
Samuel Day, *Susquehanna University*
Scott Debb, *Norfolk State University*
Stacie Craft DeFreitas, *University of Houston-Downtown*
Casey Dexter, *Berry College*
Matt Diggs, *Collin College*
Stephanie Ding, *Del Mar College*
Maureen Donegan, *Delta College*
Dale Doty, *Monroe Community College*
Kari Dudley, *University of New Hampshire*
Kimberley Duff, *Cerritos College*
Felecia Terry Dunson, *Valencia College, Winter Park*
Erin Dupuis, *Loyola University of New Orleans*
Ramani Durvasula, *California State University, Los Angeles*
Jennifer Dyck, *State University of New York at Fredonia*
April Dye, *Carson-Newman University*
John Edlund, *Rochester Institute of Technology*
Robert Egbert, *Walla Walla University*
Christine Feeley, *Suffolk County Community College*
Keith Feigenson, *Albright College*
Kimberly Fenn, *Michigan State University*
Annette Feravich, *Oakland University*
Thomas Fischer, *Wayne State University*
Julia Fisher, *Coker College*
Faith Florer, *Manhattan College*
Andrea Flynn, *DePaul University*
Johnathan Forbey, *Ball State University*
Catherine Forte, *Tacoma Community College*
Charles Fox, *Worcester State University*
Michael Foy, *Loyola Marymount University*
Christopher France, *Cleveland State University*
Denise Frank, *Mercy College*
Michael Frank, *Stockton College*
Rebecca Fraser-Thill, *Bates College*
Alexandra Frazer, *Muhlenberg College*
Michael Frederick, *University of Baltimore*
Sara Frederick-Holton, *Capella University*
Linda Freeman, *Valencia College, Winter Park*
Karyn Frick, *University of Wisconsin, Milwaukee*
William Fry, *Youngstown State University*
April Fugett, *Marshall University*
Philip Gable, *University of Alabama*
Christopher Gade, *University of California, Berkeley*
Danielle Gagne, *Alfred University*
Chad Galuska, *College of Charleston*
Janet Gebelt, *Westfield State University*
Caroline Gee, *Saddleback College*
Shriradha Geigerman, *Georgia Institute of Technology*
Seth Gillihan, *Haverford University*
Amanda Gingerich, *Butler University*
Melissa Glenn, *Colby College*
William Goggin, *University of Southern Mississippi*
Rudy Goldstein, *University of Kansas*
Adam Goodie, *University of Georgia*
Joel Goodin, *Florida State University*
Jennifer Grabski, *Alfred University*
Peter Gram, *Pensacola State College*
Daniel Greenberg, *College of Charleston*
Gary Greenberg, *Wichita State College, emeritus*
Donnell Griffin, *Davidson County Community College*
Azriel Grysman, *Hamilton College*
Fay Guarraci, *Southwestern University*
Jill Haasch, *Elizabeth City State University*
Chuck Hallock, *Pima Community College*
Sidney Hardyway, *Volunteer State Community College*
John Haworth, *Chattanooga State Community College*
Mark Hicks, *Lorain County Community College*
Heidi Higgins, *Brigham Young University-Idaho*
Amy Holmes, *Davidson County Community College*
Kevin Holmes, *Colorado College*
Allen Huffcutt, *Bradley University*
Kelly Huffman, *University of California, Riverside*
Trevor Hyde, *Cardinal Stritch University*
Malgorzata Ilkowska, *Georgia Institute of Technology*
Steven Isonio, *Golden West College*
Darren Iwamoto, *Chaminade University of Honolulu*
James Jakubow, *Florida Atlantic University*
Benjamin Jee, *Rhode Island College*
Elizabeth Jenkins, *Collin College*
Steve Jenkins, *Wagner College*
Susan Jenks, *The Sage Colleges*
Andrew Johnson, *Park University*
John Johnson, *Pennsylvania State University*
David Jones, *Westminster College of Missouri*
Matthew Kailey, *Red Rocks Community College*
Hilary Kalagher, *Drew University*
Theodora Kanellopoulos, *Queens College, City University of New York*
Kiesa Kelly, *Tennessee State University*
Abigail Kerr, *Illinois Wesleyan University*
Andrew Kim, *Citrus College*

Michael Kitchens, *Lebanon Valley College*
Kristina Klassen, *North Idaho College*
David Kreiner, *University of Central Missouri*
Michelle LaBrie, *College of the Canyons*
Alan Lambert, *Washington University of St. Louis*
Jean Lamont, *Bucknell University*
Franki Larrabee, *Chippewa Valley Technical College*
Cindy Lausberg, *University of Pittsburgh*
Shannon Layman, *University of Texas at Arlington*
Jennifer Lee, *Cabrillo College*
Jonathan Lewis, *University of North Texas*
Richard Lewis, *Pomona College*
Sam Ling, *Boston University*
Paul Locasto, *Quinnipiac University*
Christine Lofgren, *University of California, Irvine*
Greg Loviscky, *Pennsylvania State University, University Park*
John Lu, *Concordia University Irvine*
Wade Lueck, *Pima Community College*
Agnes Ly, *University of Delaware*
Margaret Lynch, *San Francisco State University*
Mike Mangan, *University of New Hampshire*
Alisha Marciano, *Lynchburg College*
Jillian Marshall, *Connecticut College*
Diane Martichuski, *University of Colorado, Boulder*
Robert Martinez, *University of the Incarnate Word*
Amy Masnick, *Hofstra University*
Mark Mattson, *Fordham University*
John Mavromatis, *St. John Fisher College*
Nicolle Mayo, *Mansfield University*
Christopher Mazurek, *Columbia College*
Jennifer McCabe, *Goucher College*
Patsy McCall, *Angelo State University*
Kristin McCombs, *Zane State College*
Daniel McConnell, *University of Central Florida*
Jason McCoy, *Cape Fear Community College*
Julie McIntyre, *The Sage Colleges*
Emalinda McSpadden, *Bronx Community College*
Julian Megosa, *Walla Walla University*
Michael Melville, *University of New Hampshire*
Tracy Meyer, *Collin College*
Dennis Miller, *University of Missouri*
Marty Milligan, *San Bernardino Valley College*
Darlene Mosley, *Pensacola State College*
Courtney Mozo, *Old Dominion University*
Paige Muellerleile, *Marshall University*
Angela Neal, *University of New Hampshire*
Katy Neidhardt, *Cuesta College*
Todd Nelson, *California State University, Stanislaus*
Jeffrey Nettle, *Housatonic Community College*
Christopher Niemiec, *University of Rochester*
Bonnie Nolan, *Rutgers University, New Brunswick*
Brian Nolan, *Quincy University*
Nicholaus Noles, *Michigan State University*
Sadie Oates, *Pitt Community College*
Kathryn Oleson, *Reed College*
Lynn Olzak, *Miami University of Ohio*
Kristen Onos, *University of New Hampshire*
Barbara Oswald, *Miami University of Ohio*
Monica Overton, *Illinois Wesleyan University*
Justin Peer, *University of Michigan, Dearborn*
Marion Perlmutter, *University of Michigan*
Linda Perrotti, *University of Texas at Arlington*
Daniel Peterson, *Knox College*
Doug Peterson, *University of South Dakota*
Terry Pettijohn, *The Ohio State University at Marion*
Kathy Phillippi-Immel, *University of Wisconsin-Fox Valley*
Leslie Phillmore, *Dalhousie University*
Jamie Pierson, *Miami University*
Kellie Pierson, *Northern Kentucky University*
Mark Plonsky, *University of Wisconsin-Stevens Point*
Christy Porter, *College of William and Mary*
Tracy Powell, *Western Oregon University*
Brian Rabinovitz, *American University*
Lisa Raskin, *Amherst College*
Meera Rastogi, *University Cincinnati*
Neelam Rattan, *San Jose State University*
Ann Renken, *University of Southern California*
Harvey Richman, *Columbus State University*
Robert Rieske, *Louisiana State University*
Sheldon Rifkin, *Kennesaw State University*
Jill Rinzel, *University of Wisconsin-Waukesha*
Vicki Ritts, *St. Louis Community College-Meramec*
Kelley Rogers, *Valencia College*
Matt Rossano, *Southeastern Louisiana University*
Ann Rost, *Missouri State University*
Lawrence Rudiger, *University of Vermont*
Jeff Rudski, *Muhlenberg College*
Ramon Russe, *Lake-Sumpter State College*
David Ryan, *East Tennessee State University*
Lawrence Ryan, *Oregon State University*
Kara Sage, *Hamilton College*
Sharleen Sakai, *Michigan State University*
Heather Schellinck, *Dalhousie University*
Jim Schirillo, *Wake Forest University*
Steve Schuetz, *University of Central Missouri*
Joseph Sclafani, *University of Tampa*
Ines Segert, *University of Missouri*
Colleen Seifert, *University of Michigan*
Fred Shaffer, *Truman State University*
Keith Shafritz, *Hofstra University*
Steven Shatz, *Hofstra University*
Stuart Silverberg, *Westmoreland County Community College*
Patricia Simone, *Santa Clara University*
Sheldon Siporin, *Pace University*
Brenda Smith, *Westmont College*
Melissa Smith, *University of North Carolina, Ashville*
Ken Sobel, *University of Central Arkansas*
Jennifer Spychalski, *College of Charleston*

Tamara Stachowicz, *Davenport University*
Jeannine Stamatakis, *Lincoln University*
Emily Stark, *Minnesota State University, Mankato*
Lyra Stein, *Rutgers University*
Barry Stennett, *University of North Georgia-Oconee*
Courtney Stevens, *Willamette University*
Julia Strand, *Carleton College*
Jutta Street, *Campbell University*
Helen T. Sullivan, *Rider University*
Elizabeth Swenson, *John Carroll University*
Michael Swett, *Portland Community College*
Lorey Takahashi, *University of Hawaii at Manoa*
Shawn Talbot, *Kellogg Community College*
Kathleen Taylor, *Columbia University*
Brian Thomas, *Baldwin Wallace College*
Lisa Thomassen, *Indiana University-Bloomington*
Clarissa Thompson, *University of Oklahoma*
Albert Toh, *University of Arkansas at Pine Bluff*
Natasha Tokowicz, *University of Pittsburgh*
Michelle Tomaszycki, *Wayne State University*
Terry Trepper, *Purdue University Calumet*
Alexa Tullett, *University of Alabama*
Joseph Vielbig, *Arizona Western College*
Rita Smith Wade-El, *Millersville University*
Jeffrey Wagman, *Illinois State University*
Kurt Wallen, *Neumann University*
Linda Walsh, *University of Northern Iowa*
Jason Warnick, *Arkansas Tech University*
Lynn Washington, *Arkansas Tech University*
Mark Watman, *South Suburban College*
Nicole Weekes, *Pomona College*
Christine Weinkauff, *California State University, San Bernardino*
Becky Weldon, *George Washington University*
David Widman, *Juniata College*
Judith Wightman, *Kirkwood Community College*
Patrick Williams, *University Houston-Downtown*
Laura Wilson, *University of Mary Washington*
Patrick Wise, *Monroe County Community College*
Marc Wolpoff, *Riverside City College*
Erin Wood, *Catawba College*
James Woodson, *University of Tampa*
Thomas Wrobel, *University of Michigan-Flint*
Rick Wynn, *County College of Morris*
Jennifer Yates, *Ohio Wesleyan University*
Anthony Zoccolillo, *Texas A & M University-Corpus Christi*

About the Author

S. Marc Breedlove, the Barnett Rosenberg Professor of Neuroscience at Michigan State University, has written over 100 scientific articles investigating the role of hormones in shaping the developing and adult nervous system, publishing in journals including *Science*, *Nature*, *Nature Neuroscience*, and the *Proceedings of the National Academy of Science*. He has been widely interviewed about his research by periodicals including the *San Francisco Chronicle*, *Los Angeles Times*, *New York Times*, and *Newsweek*, as well as broadcast programs such as *All Things Considered*, *Good Morning America*, and *Sixty Minutes*. He has active grant support from the National Institute of Neurological Disorders and Stroke, the National Institute of Mental Health, and the National Science Foundation. Dr. Breedlove is a Fellow of the American Association for the Advancement of Science, and the Association for Psychological Science.

Dr. Breedlove is also a co-author of two biological psychology textbooks: *Biological Psychology*, Seventh Edition by Breedlove and Neil V. Watson; and the recently published *The Mind's Machine: Foundations of Brain and Behavior*, by Watson and Breedlove.

Media and Supplements

to accompany ***Principles of Psychology***

For Students

Companion Website

www.oup.com/us/breedlove

Available at no additional cost, the Companion Website provides students with the following review resources:

- **Chapter Outlines:** Detailed outlines that give an overview of each chapter.
- **Chapter Summaries:** Full summaries of each chapter provide a thorough review of the important facts and concepts covered.
- **Flashcards:** Interactive flashcard activities are an effective way for students to learn and review all of the important terminology.
- **Practice Quizzes:** Each chapter includes a 25-question practice quiz, which students can use as a self-review exercise, to check their understanding.

For Instructors

An extensive and thoughtful supplements program offers instructors everything they need to prepare their course and lectures, and assess student progress.

Ancillary Resource Center (ARC)

(For more information, go to www.oup.com/us/breedlove)

Available online exclusively to adopters, the Ancillary Resource Center (ARC) includes all of the instructor resources that accompany *Principles of Psychology*.

- **Psychology News Feed:** Continuously updated by Marc Breedlove, this news feed brings instructors interesting news stories from the field of psychology. Great as a resource for lecture starters or reading assignments. (Also available in Dashboard.)
- **Instructor's Manual:** For each chapter of the textbook, the Instructor's Manual includes the following:
  - Chapter Overview
  - Learning Outcomes
  - Chapter Outline
  - In-Class Discussion Questions
  - Suggested Online Resources
- **Textbook Figures & Tables:** All of the textbook's figures and tables are provided in a variety of formats, including: high- and low-resolution, with and without balloon captions, and unlabeled (all balloon captions, labels, and leaders removed).

- **PowerPoint Resources:**
  - *Figures & Tables*: This presentation includes all of the figures and tables (all formats) from the chapter, with titles.
  - *Lecture*: A complete lecture outline, ready for use in class. Includes coverage of all important facts and concepts presented in the chapter, along with selected figures and tables.
- **Animations:** All of the animations from Dashboard are available in the ARC for download, making it easy to include them in lecture presentations and online course materials. (Also available in Dashboard.)
- **Videos:** A collection of videos selected to accompany each chapter helps bring some of the key concepts from the textbook to life. Ideal for use as lecture starters or paired with assignments.
- **Test Bank:** A complete test bank provides instructors with a wide range of test items for each chapter, including multiple choice, fill-in-the-blank, short answer, and essay questions. All questions from the Dashboard and Companion Website quizzes (see below) are also included. Each question is referenced to a specific textbook section, a Bloom's Taxonomy level, and an APA Learning Outcome.
- **Computerized Test Bank:** The Test Bank is also provided in Blackboard Diploma format (software included). Diploma makes it easy to create quizzes and exams using any combination of publisher-provided questions and an instructor's own questions, and to export those assessments for print or online delivery in a wide range of learning management system formats.

Dashboard

(For more information, go to www.oup.com/us/dashboard)

Oxford's Dashboard learning management system features a streamlined interface that connects instructors and students with the functions that they perform most often, simplifying the learning experience in order to save instructors time and put students' progress first. Dashboard's pre-built assessments were created specifically to accompany *Principles of Psychology*, and are automatically graded so that instructors can see student progress instantly. Dashboard includes the following resources:

- **Quizzes:** For each chapter of the textbook:
  - A pre-lecture formative quiz designed to be used as an initial assessment of basic student comprehension of the important facts and concepts introduced in the chapter.
  - A post-lecture summative quiz designed to be used as an assessment of student mastery of the important facts and concepts introduced in the chapter, after the student has read the chapter and attended the relevant lecture/class period/discussion section.
- **Animations:** A set of detailed animations help students understand some of the book's more complex topics and processes by presenting them in a clear, easy-to-follow narrative.
- **Matching Exercises:** These fully assignable questions assess student understanding of important structures and concepts through image- and text-based matching exercises.
- **Psychology News Feed:** Continuously updated by Marc Breedlove, this news feed brings you interesting news stories from the field of psychology. Great as a resource for lecture starters or reading assignments.

LMS Course Cartridges

For those instructors who wish to use their campus learning management system, a course cartridge containing all of the Dashboard resources is available for a variety of e-learning environments. (For more information, please contact your local Oxford representative.)

Principles of Psychology

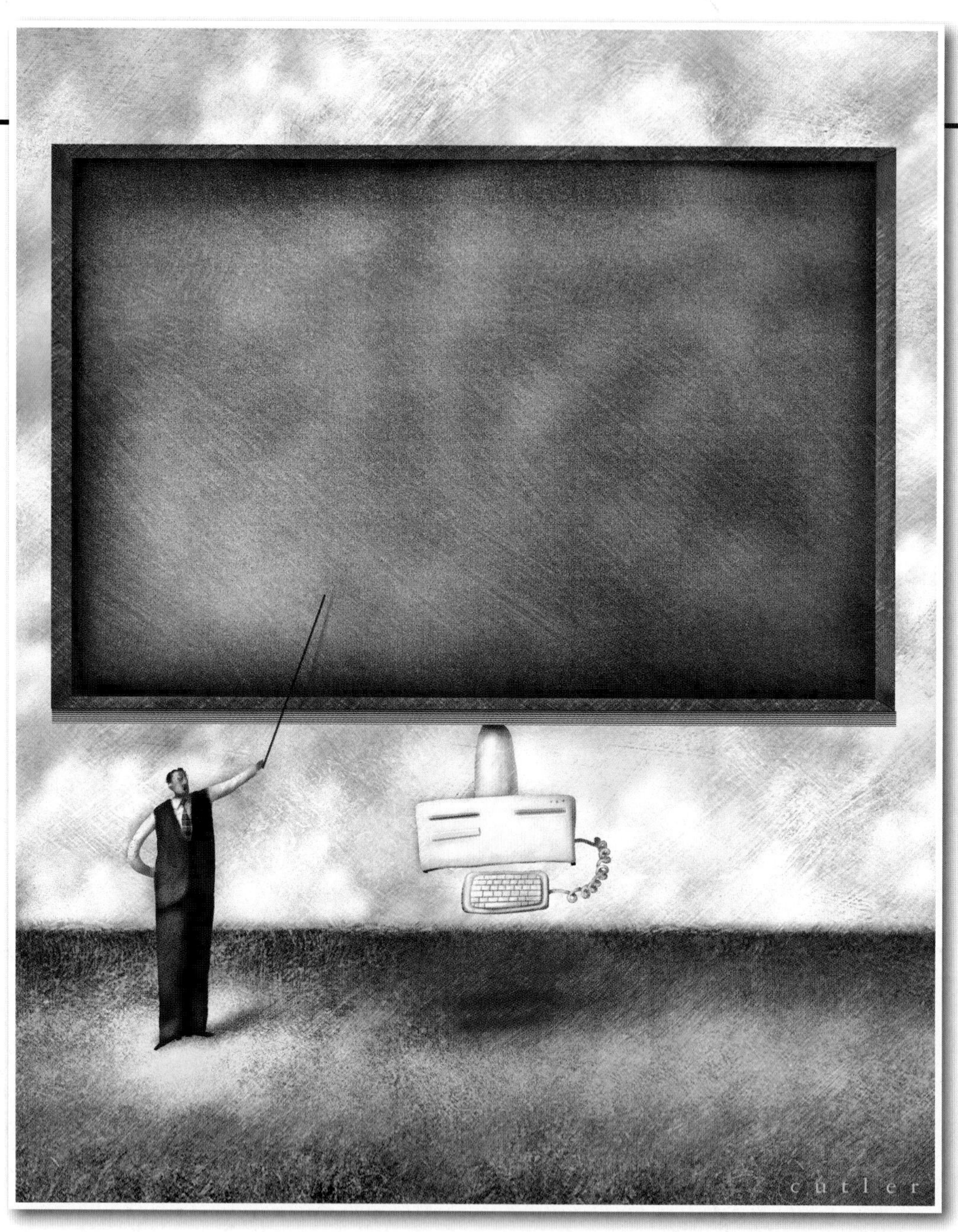
cutler

Introduction: Principles of Psychology

The Wages of Fear

We'll never fully understand what happened on that hot August day in 2014 when 18-year-old Michael Brown, an unarmed African American with no criminal record, was shot and killed by a white police officer in Ferguson, Missouri. The officer stopped Michael and another black youth because they were walking down the street rather than on the sidewalk. Somehow things went horribly wrong after that, but accounts vary in the details. As one official said, "This is a difficult and complex situation. There are many sides to the story" (Bosman & Goode, 2014). The police said Michael charged the patrol car, attacked the officer though the window, and tried to get his gun. Other witnesses offered conflicting accounts, raising various questions about what really happened. Was Michael holding up his hands or running away when he was shot? The fatal shot entered the top of Michael's head—was he charging the officer or falling down? What we do know is that the population of Ferguson is two-thirds black while its police department is over 90% white, and that the town has a history of racial tension. Many people assume racial stereotypes played a role, at least in the ways the two men responded to each other. Did Michael feel persecuted and angry when a white officer stopped him for jaywalking? Would the officer have been as likely to stop a middle-aged white couple jogging in the street? Fear may well have influenced how the officer behaved (Wines & Robles, 2014). Might the officer have been less afraid, less likely to shoot, if Michael, who was 6 feet, 4 inches tall, had been shorter? Or white? Or female?

No college course can explain Michael's death. But **psychology**, the study of the mind and behavior, is the science that strives to understand why people behave the way they do, including behaviors that lead to tragedy as they did in Ferguson. In this book we will examine many different influences on behavior. We'll learn that we are not always consciously aware of why we do what we do, that we are remarkably sensitive to what the people around us are doing, and that our previous experience in life leaves an imprint on our brain that can make a tremendous difference to our future behavior. Even if the facts never completely emerge, and we never know what happened when Michael died, we can at least understand some of the forces that led up to that day.

Chapter Preview

psychology The scientific study of the mind and behavior.

To understand today's science of psychology, we have to know something about its past. The first two sections of this chapter will review the human quest to understand behavior. Section 1.1 will discuss the earliest studies of behavior up to Darwin's revolutionary discovery that behaviors, like physical traits, are subject to evolution through natural selection. Section 1.2 will review the rise of psychology as an experimental science, and the use of scientific methods and careful manipulations and measurements to understand behavior. The last section will discuss some myths of psychology that, to the annoyance of psychology instructors everywhere, persist to this very day. We'll conclude by introducing four important principles of psychology that you will see at work in every chapter and that will, I hope, provide you with a framework on which to hang all that you are about to learn.

Things to Learn

- Importance of observing and anticipating the behavior of others
- Social brain hypothesis
- Early philosophers' distrust of the senses
- Empiricist philosopher John Locke's concept of a *tabula rasa*
- Darwin's impact on the new field of psychology

1.1 Psychology's Roots

What is behavior? Can we define certain behaviors that are intrinsically human—behaviors that have characterized people since the earliest times? Of course, we have no written records about how prehistoric people explained the behavior of themselves and other animals, but we can make educated guesses about their behavior based on our understanding of human evolution and the study of preliterate societies. In this section we'll consider some of the earliest human behaviors and some of the first written discussions of human behavior, including the question asked by ancient and renaissance philosophers concerning how it is possible that we can ever come to know anything. We'll see how Charles Darwin's discovery of evolution revolutionized our understanding of the roots of all behaviors, including those that are said to be exclusively human.

Our ancestors had to pay attention to the behavior of people and other animals

Those of us living in cities may not realize how modern life separates us from other animals. Unlike our human ancestors, who spread across the plains of Africa despite having very few physical advantages, people today pay little attention to other animals. Modern conveniences—electricity, television, refrigeration, automobiles, running water—have put us in an entirely different environment than the rest of the animal world. In order to survive, we don't need to know the habits of the animals that live around us, as our ancestors did; these animals are not our primary food source, nor in most cases are they a source of danger.

There are no reliable descriptions of what life was like a million years ago, but we do have firsthand descriptions from scientists and observers studying preliterate human groups, including a few that survive even today in remote parts of the world. People in such groups are remarkably knowledgeable about the animals living around them. For example, the first Western biologist to systematically classify bird species in New Guinea in the 1930s found 137 different species in one area. This diversity of bird life was no surprise to the local inhabitants, because they had 136 different names for them (Gould, 1979). In Chapter 10 we'll learn about people living in the Amazonian jungle whose only words for numbers translate as "one," "two," and "many," which might suggest they are "primitive" in their thinking. Indeed, when they trade goods with outsiders, they may occasionally be cheated because of their indifference to quantity (appar-

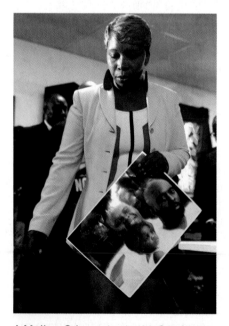

A Mother Grieves Lesley McSpadden's son, Michael Brown, died on the street in Ferguson, Missouri.

ently 8, 12, and 15 are all about the same to them). But as one of the Americans studying them noted, "they know the usefulness and location of all important plants in their area; they understand the behavior of local animals and how to catch and avoid them; and they can walk into the jungle naked, with no tools or weapons, and walk out three days later with baskets of fruit, nuts, and small game" (Colapinto, 2007, p. 131). Such skill in the natural world requires a keen understanding of animal behavior. In that sense, the people in these communities are amateur psychologists trying to understand the behavior of other animals, and it seems likely that early humans were too.

Living Close to Nature The people of New Guinea had a specific name for each of the many bird species that were first cataloged by western biologists in the 1930s.

Whether on the prehistoric plains of Africa or the modern-day streets of Manhattan, our survival is promoted by being a member of a group: more pairs of eyes are better at spotting food and predators, and more hands are better able to protect and serve. In group situations it is important to get along with others, at least to some degree; a solid understanding of human behavior may sometimes mean the difference between life and death, even today. People benefit by understanding the personalities of the people in their group, and by keeping track of whether they've been helpful or hurtful in the past. Who owes you a favor? Who holds a grudge against you? Anthropologists have theorized that the human mind can keep track of about 150 different human relationships (Dunbar 2012; Dunbar & Shultz, 2007), noting that preliterate groups are rarely any bigger than that. In what has been dubbed the "social brain hypothesis," they speculate that perhaps the human brain can't effectively deal with social interactions with more than 150 people.

If modern life separates us from other animals, it bombards us with people. It was once a rare event for a human to encounter a stranger, but today many of us may see hundreds of strangers every day. If, as the social brain hypothesis suggests, we can only keep track of about 150 people on an ongoing basis, we may often interact with people about whom we know nothing. Sometimes that lack of personal history, or dealing with a complete unknown, can be deadly. If Michael Brown and the police officer who shot him had been part of a group of 150 people who had known each other all their lives, perhaps their confrontation would have been resolved smoothly, with no escalation to violence and death. Instead, it seems likely that they were suspicious and afraid of one another.

Most of us do not yearn to return to simpler times when we would never meet a stranger, but it's interesting to think about how behavior evolved in that context. How has human behavior changed in the context of modern times? Let's consider this question by examining some of the earliest scientific writing about human behavior, which dates from about the time that people first began living in large, anonymous cities.

Early philosophers wrestled with questions about knowledge and reality

As civilization developed, people no longer had to work all day just to gather enough food to survive. Some people had time to specialize in a trade or profession. The ancient Greek **Aristotle** (384–322 BCE) earned a living by tutoring young people (including a lad called Alexander the Great) in the basic letters and science of his day. Many of Aristotle's writings have survived, including many observations of the behavior of animals and humans. He

Aristotle (384–322 BCE) An ancient Greek teacher who was a keen observer of animals and humans and was interested in sensory illusions.

Figure 1.1 Illusory Movement Aristotle noted that if you stare at a waterfall for a few minutes and then look at a stationary object, the stationary object will appear to move. This waterfall illusion, sometimes called the motion aftereffect, illustrates how our senses may deceive us. You can recreate this illusion (without a waterfall) to see an "expanding Buddha" at www.michaelbach.de/ot/mot-adapt/index.html.

Plato (428–347 BCE) An ancient Greek philosopher who was skeptical of our senses and stressed reliance on logic and reasoning.

noted that castrating young roosters made them less aggressive as adults, that many children whose mothers drank alcohol during pregnancy were mentally disabled, and that pregnant women were more likely to suffer morning sickness if they carried girls than boys—all observations that were confirmed by later scientists (Berthold, 1849; Schiff et al., 2004; Streissguth et al., 1980). Of course, he was also wrong about some things, but in general he was a keen observer. Among other things, Aristotle described optical illusions, circumstances in which our senses give us a distorted view of reality (**Figure 1.1**). As we'll see in Chapter 6, psychologists today are still working to understand why our senses sometimes distort reality in optical illusions and other circumstances.

The ancient Greek **Plato** (428–347 BCE) shared Aristotle's interest in sensory illusions and developed a healthy skepticism about our senses. Plato knew that under certain circumstances people may hallucinate entire events that never happened. In his famous parable of the cave, Plato proposed a "thought experiment." What if people were raised in a cave with a fire constantly blazing in the mouth? Imagine these people were chained to a rock such that the only thing they ever saw was a wall in front of them on which were cast shadows of people and animals passing in front of the fire behind them (**Figure 1.2**). Plato asserted

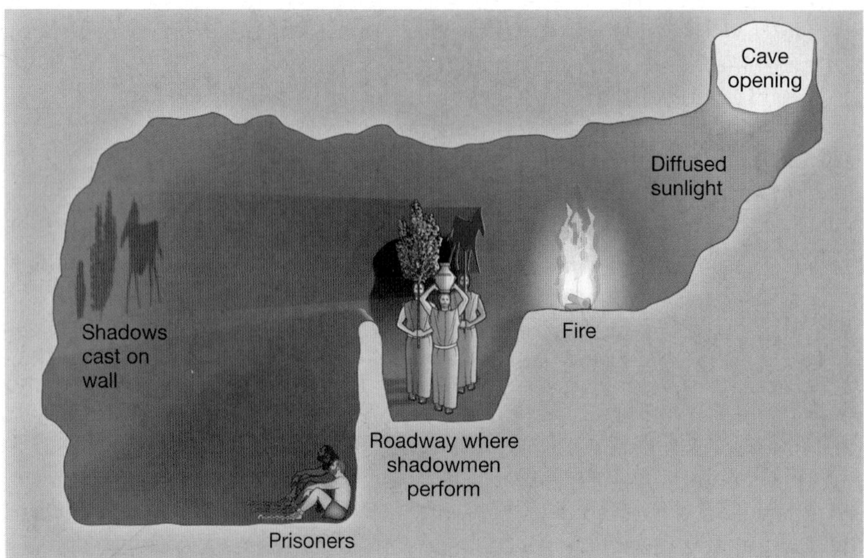

Figure 1.2 Plato's Parable of the Cave A person raised in such circumstances might come to see the shadows as reality, and would be shocked at the actual nature of the world. Is there a reality that our senses gloss over?

that such people would believe the shadows represented all there is in the world. If one of them was unchained and allowed to see the fire at the mouth of the cave, and the three-dimensional people and animals passing by the fire and casting shadows on the wall, he would be astonished at this deeper reality. Returned to chains, that person would forever have a different concept about reality, and would probably have a hard time convincing any of his neighbors that the shadows were mere outlines, not reality itself.

Skepticism about the reliability of the senses led Plato to rely, whenever possible, on logic and reasoning rather than observations alone, since they can be misleading. Nearly 2,000 years later, Renaissance thinkers in Europe, deeply schooled in the writings of Aristotle and Plato, continued having doubts about the reliability of our senses. When the French mathematician **René Descartes** (1596–1650) asserted, "I think, therefore I am," he was seeking a foundation of certain knowledge, a system of knowing about reality that did not rely on our fallible senses. Descartes's introspective approach would inspire the first scientific movement in psychology, *psychophysics*, which we'll discuss later in this chapter. Descartes was also a pioneer in thinking about the ways in which the nervous system is like a machine, noting, for example, how we reflexively withdraw our foot from a fire. Descartes struggled to reconcile the notion of the brain as a mere machine with the religious concept of a spiritual self, the soul. We'll discuss Descartes's unsatisfactory proposal, dualism, in more detail in Chapter 3 (see Box 3.1).

In the late 1600s, a group of British **empiricist philosophers** objected to the view of Descartes and classical philosophers that the only true knowledge comes from within, insisting that, however unreliable our senses may at times be, we are utterly dependent on them for learning what we need to know about the world. Among them, **John Locke** (1632–1704) believed that the mind of a newborn baby is a blank slate (in Latin, a *tabula rasa*) that learns through the various senses what the world is like and how to behave. From this perspective, with the proper training, any baby could grow up to perform the duties of a doctor, lawyer, philosopher, or king. Such thinking would come to dominate psychology in the mid-twentieth century.

René Descartes (1596–1650) A Renaissance philosopher who built a system of knowing about reality that does not rely on our fallible senses.

empiricist philosophers A group of British philosophers, including John Locke, who believed we are dependent on our unreliable senses to learn about the world.

John Locke (1632–1704) A seventeenth-century British empiricist philosopher who believed that the mind of a newborn baby is a *tabula rasa* that is molded by experience.

Charles Darwin (1809–1882) The discoverer of evolution by natural selection who argued that all human behaviors must have had beginnings in earlier ancestors.

Margaret Floy Washburn (1871–1939) A psychologist who described the behavior of many animals, relating them to the human mind.

Darwin taught us that there is a continuum of behavior from animals to humans

Today it may be difficult for us to grasp how much **Charles Darwin** (1809–1882) and his text *On the Origin of Species* astonished the world. Darwin's intended audience was not other scientists but ordinary people, and when his book went on sale in 1859, it was an instant bestseller, and is still in print today. Many readers were fascinated by the idea that humans had a shared ancestor with other animals. Thirteen years later, Darwin published *The Expression of the Emotions in Man and Animals* (1872) in which he explicitly argued that all human behaviors, including our emotional behaviors, must have had beginnings in earlier ancestors. That is, Darwin believed that our closest animal relatives, such as monkeys and apes, display at least some emotional behaviors. He asserted that just as there is a continuum of physical traits across animal species, there is a continuum of behaviors as well. Darwin described many instances of non-human animals displaying behaviors we associate with emotions, including facial expressions. Many of Darwin's ideas about emotion have been amply confirmed, as we will see in Chapter 13. *The Expression of the Emotions in Man and Animals* is Darwin's chief contribution to psychology and had a big impact on the field, which was only just becoming recognized (the first psychology research laboratory would not be established until 7 years later). Early in the twentieth century, psychologist **Margaret Floy Washburn** further illuminated relationships between human

Charles Darwin (1809-1882) Darwin insisted that behaviors, like physical traits, could evolve over time by natural selection.

Margaret Floy Washburn (1871–1939) A gifted scientist despite the barriers to women in science, her views on animal behavior are widely held in psychology today.

natural selection The process by which mutations that improve survival and reproduction accumulate in subsequent generations, changing a species over time.

and animal behavior. Her book *The Animal Mind* (1908) described behaviors of over 100 species of animals, exerting an enormous influence on the young science of psychology. Her accomplishments were the more remarkable because society in her day presented so many barriers to women in science.

The recognition that humans are part of a continuum of species, and that our behavioral traits developed by **natural selection**, spurred enduring interest in studying the behavior of non-humans. In every chapter of this book we will discuss concepts that were originally demonstrated in experiments with non-human animals, mostly rats and mice. Many introductory psychology textbooks have glossed over these contributions from animal research, or have presented conclusions as though they had been derived from the study of humans (Domjan & Purdy, 1995; Eaton & Sleigh, 2002). Animal studies are sometimes underemphasized to avoid criticism from those who oppose animal research. As someone who has published research on both humans and animals, I am of course concerned with the issues of ethical research, which are discussed in Chapter 2.

By the mid-twentieth century, many psychologists were studying learning in rats and pigeons, confident that the basic rules uncovered in these species would apply to humans as well. To a great extent, that confidence was amply confirmed, reinforcing the point that the ability to learn evolved long before the common ancestor to all the mammals, and that ability is shared by them all. We'll find in Chapter 8, for example, that some processes that underlie learning in the mammalian brain are also at work in sea slugs (Hawkins, 2013). Given how shocked people of the Victorian era were to learn that all life on Earth is related, imagine how startled they would have been to hear that slugs learn about the world in much the same way we do!

1.1 SUMMARY

- The survival of early humans was dependent on familiarity with animal behaviors.
- Early humans had to know enough about the behavior of other people to remain safely in the group. Some researchers have speculated that the human brain can only manage social relations with about 150 people.
- Philosophers like *Plato* and *René Descartes* believed the senses offered an unreliable understanding of the world and believed knowledge should be based on logic and reason.
- *Empiricist philosophers* like *John Locke* insisted that we get vital information from our senses, and posited that a person's mind at birth is a tabula rasa that experience can mold to support a wide range of behavior.
- *Charles Darwin* and his followers proposed that behaviors evolved by *natural selection* and that the behavior of animals offered important insights into the human mind.

REVIEW QUESTIONS

1. Why did early humans need to pay careful attention to the behavior of others?
2. What were the views of Plato and Descartes about the reliability of our senses for understanding the world?
3. What does the phrase *tabula rasa* mean, and what philosopher is associated with applying this notion to the human mind?
4. What was Charles Darwin's contribution to the science of psychology?

Food for Thought

The social brain hypothesis suggests that our mind can only keep track of about 150 people. Does the number of friends you have on Facebook confirm or refute this notion?

1.2 The Rise of Empiricism

By the middle of the nineteenth century, psychology began to mature as a science. There was widespread agreement that behavior could be studied, in both humans and other species, in an objective way, and this was viewed as an important enterprise that could better humanity. From that background, several forces shaped the psychology we know today. The science of psychology formally began in Germany in the late 1800s and quickly spread around the world. American psychologists spearheaded the next two shifts in the field, first insisting on the importance of function for understanding behavior, and then for a time forbidding any study of mental activity that cannot be observed directly. By the second half of the twentieth century, all mental activities, including emotions and consciousness, were again embraced as appropriate for psychological research.

Things to Learn

- Rise of German psychophysics in the 1800s
- Psychological school of structuralism
- Functionalism's emphasis on adaptive significance and practical study
- Dominance of behaviorism in much of the twentieth century
- "Cognitive revolution" in psychology and the rise of neuroscience
- Contributions of women and people of color despite societal barriers

German thinkers brought keen observation and structure to psychology

An emphasis on careful measurement of behavior, which is a hallmark of modern psychological science, bloomed in nineteenth-century Germany as physicists, physiologists, and philosophers began testing the limits of human senses. Just how good are we at detecting lights and sounds? How well can we tell which of two books is heaviest to hold? How soft a touch can we detect on our fingertips or on our leg? Answering such questions became the mission of **psychophysics**, the study of how physical events, such as lights and sounds, affect our senses (see Chapter 6). This program of research required careful physical measurements of lights, sounds, and touches, which in the nineteenth century meant researchers had to build and assemble equipment themselves (which is how physicists came to be involved). The German fascination and facility with precision engineering during that era is probably one reason why psychophysics first flourished there.

psychophysics The study of how physical events, such as lights and sounds, affect our senses.

Wilhelm Wundt (1832–1920) A German physiologist who established the first research laboratory in psychology and wrote the first psychology textbook.

Building on the accomplishments of previous psychophysicists, the German physiologist **Wilhelm Wundt** (pronounced "voondt"; 1832–1920) established the first laboratory explicitly designed for psychology experiments in 1879 at the University of Leipzig. For many historians, Wundt's lab represents the formal beginning of modern psychology as a science (King et al., 2013). Wundt was one of the first scientists to consider himself a "psychologist." (The word "psychology" first appears in English in a 1654 medical book [Partlitz, 1654, p. 168], where it was defined as "the knowledge of the Soul" [psyche].) Wundt wrote the first psychology textbook, translated as *Principles of Physiological Psychology,* in 1874. A prodigious author over a 65-year career, Wundt published an estimated 53,000 pages, including a ten-volume work covering every branch of psychology and much of what is today considered anthropology.

Among his many contributions, Wundt was interested in visual illusions, such as that in **Figure 1.3A**, sometimes called the "Wundt illusion" (although others described it first), in which background drawings can make perfectly straight lines appear to be curved. He was meticulous in measuring such perceptual distortions. For example, in **Figure 1.3B** most people see the vertical line as being longer than the horizontal line,

(A) Wundt illusion

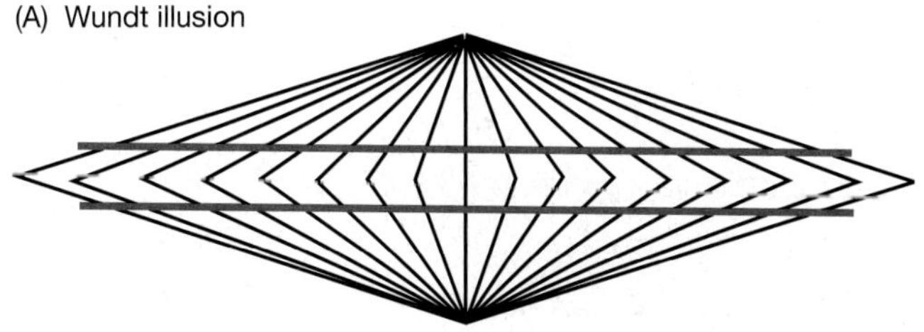

(B)

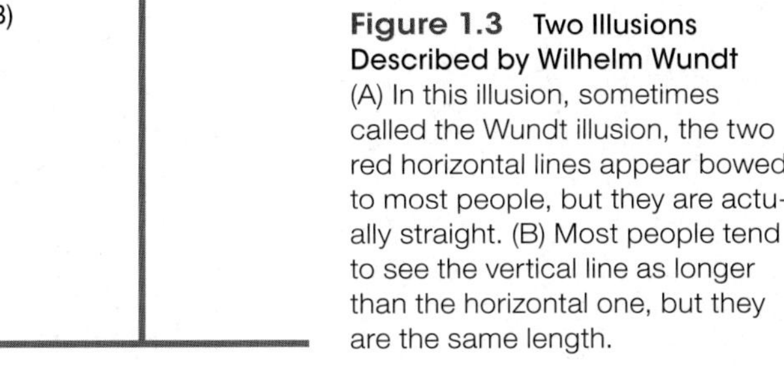

Figure 1.3 Two Illusions Described by Wilhelm Wundt (A) In this illusion, sometimes called the Wundt illusion, the two red horizontal lines appear bowed to most people, but they are actually straight. (B) Most people tend to see the vertical line as longer than the horizontal one, but they are the same length.

structuralism The introspective analysis of the human mind by breaking it down into the simplest kinds of experience, and then asking how these simple experiences come together to produce more complex experiences.

William James (1842–1910) An American psychologist who emphasized the adaptive function of behaviors and mental processes to help survival and reproduction.

functionalism A broad school of thought in psychology that insisted that mental processes like consciousness must serve a practical, adaptive purpose.

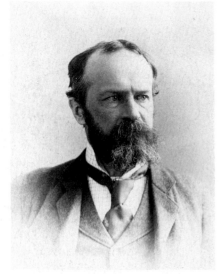

when in fact they are the same length (Kunnapas, 1955). When Wundt asked people to estimate the lengths of the horizontal and vertical lines, he found that on average they saw the vertical line as 25% longer than the horizontal one. In this way, he could quantify just how much the placement of the two lines in that position distorted their appearance in our mind. For example, if he varied the angle between the two lines, the distortion varied as well, reaching its maximum when the angle was 90 degrees.

Wundt insisted that psychology was a natural science, like chemistry or physics. He believed that psychology and biology were two different perspectives to study the same processes, just as chemistry and physics could provide different viewpoints in studying the same object, such as a crystal. "Nothing occurs in our consciousness that does not find its sensible foundation in certain physical processes," and all psychological events "are accompanied by physiological nerve-actions" in the brain (Wundt, 1893, p. 644; tr. Kim, 2006). We'll discuss this thoroughly modern view of psychology later in this chapter.

One of Wundt's students, Edward Titchener (1867–1927), immigrated to the United States as a tireless advocate for Wundt's ideas. Titchener developed and extended those ideas into what came to be called **structuralism**, the analysis of the human mind by breaking it down into the simplest kinds of experience (like particular sensations), and then asking how these simple experiences come together to produce more complex experiences (such as emotions). This program of study required *introspection*, close attention to what one is experiencing at any one time. Dominant for a time, structuralism was eventually abandoned for a broader view of psychology called functionalism, which we'll take up next.

William James emphasized functionalism and the "brain as machine"

A few years before Wundt opened the first lab for conducting psychological *research* in Leipzig, Professor **William James** (1842–1910) assembled equipment for *teaching* psychological phenomena at Harvard (King et al., 2013). James had a massive influence on psychology, beginning with his two-volume *Principles of Psychology* (1890), which instantly became the leading textbook in the new field. Trained as a physiologist, James was also keenly interested in the biological underpinnings of psychology and, like Wundt, thought psychology as a natural science would one day understand how particular conditions in the brain underlie "various sorts of thought or feeling" (James, 1890, p. vi). His contributions to psychology are still felt today as his ideas about consciousness, attention, memory, and emotions, among others, are still actively pursued by psychologists around the world. We'll encounter James's ideas on each of those topics in later chapters.

In addition to these scientific contributions, James served as a highly respected leader, which gave legitimacy to the new academic field. Like James, the first psychology professors were hired into physiology and philosophy departments. The first psychology doctoral degree awarded in the United States was to a Harvard student, G. Stanley Hall, working under James, in 1878. Due in large part to William James's prominence and leadership, the twentieth century saw, at university after university, small groups of faculty migrate from other departments to establish separate psychology departments.

James was dissatisfied with the structuralist idea that conscious experience could be broken down into constituent parts. To him, consciousness was a single, continuous flow, which he termed a "stream of consciousness." James also embraced Charles Darwin's ideas on the evolution of behaviors such as emotions. These ideas led James to emphasize the *adaptive function* of behaviors and mental processes to help survival and reproduction as being at least as important as the physical, structural mechanisms underlying them. Thus the thinking of James and his followers is often called **functionalism**, a broad school

William James (1842–1910) His comprehensive textbook, *Principles of Psychology*, published in 1890, helped shape the field.

of thought that insists that mental processes like consciousness must serve a practical, adaptive function. In some ways, modern *evolutionary psychology* (see Chapter 15) is a descendant of functionalism.

Among other things, the emphasis on function focused on ways the mind changes and adapts to different situations and different environments. Thus functionalism was also concerned with practical questions, such as how to help children learn in school, so functionalists were eager to measure the behavior of other people in varying situations. You can see how that is a departure from structuralism's sole emphasis on introspection. Instead of sitting still and focusing on inner thoughts through introspection, functionalist psychologists carefully observed, timed, and measured the behaviors of others. Functionalism was a response to the narrow focus of structuralism, and effectively replaced that system in psychology.

Functionalism's emphasis on accurately measuring people's behavior while performing a task under various circumstances became a defining characteristic of psychology that is still with us today. But some researchers, dissatisfied with other functionalist goals of studying internal mental processes like consciousness, insisted that psychology must deal only with readily measured, observable behaviors, which led to a new phase in the science of psychology called *behaviorism*.

behaviorism The perspective that psychologists should study only observable behavior and not subjective mental events.

Ivan Pavlov (1849–1936) A Russian physiologist who described classical conditioning, such as how ringing a bell before giving food to a dog would eventually result in the dog learning to salivate at just the sound of the bell.

Edward Thorndike (1874–1949) A behaviorist who studied how dogs and cats learn to escape from puzzle boxes.

John B. Watson (1878–1958) A behaviorist who insisted that psychology should be an objective experimental branch of natural science concerned only with observable behavior.

Behaviorism revealed the rules of learning, but only a limited understanding of behavior

The study of learning at the end of the nineteenth century formed the roots of **behaviorism**, the doctrine that psychologists should only study *observable behavior*, actions that can be objectively and accurately measured, not subjective mental events like consciousness or emotion. This perspective promoted psychology as the science of behavior, not of the mind, and de-emphasized what happens inside the brain. Assuming that nearly all behavior is learned, behaviorists asserted that an individual can be taught how to behave, and that any unacceptable behaviors can be unlearned.

Ivan Pavlov (1849–1936) demonstrated how repeatedly exposing a dog to the sound of a bell and then giving it some food would eventually cause the dog to salivate in response to the bell alone. The dog learned that food often followed the ringing of the bell. Such learning came to be known as classical conditioning (see Chapter 8). **Edward Thorndike** (1874–1949) (also discussed in Chapter 8) studied how cats and dogs learned to escape from puzzle boxes he built (Thorndike, 1898). These studies and those that followed showed the value of controlling exactly what happens to the animal, and carefully measuring the time it takes for the animal to learn something. Much of what was discovered about learning in animal subjects was soon found to apply to humans as well.

These early studies of learning, firmly anchored in the functionalism that dominated psychology at that time, were simply a small part of a large field. But in 1913, a brash young scientist named **John B. Watson** (1878–1958) published what came to be known as the "behaviorist manifesto," confidently asserting that "psychology must discard all references to consciousness" and be "a purely objective experimental branch of natural science" (Watson, 1913) by concerning itself only with observable behavior. Watson's formal academic career was cut short by a scandal. Forced to switch careers in his mid-forties, Watson moved to advertising, which quickly made him a wealthy man. But Watson continued to influence psychology by writing persuasive articles and books to promote behaviorism. Despite his bravado, the initial response to Watson's manifesto from most psychologists was "meh." Fifteen years later, Watson complained that the professors of psychology attacked his views but that "younger students seem to be accepting behaviorism" (Watson, 1928, p. 507).

John B. Watson (1878–1958) His "behaviorist manifesto" would eventually pervade twentieth-century psychology.

Behaviorist psychology

Figure 1.4 The Black Box in Behaviorism Behaviorists were not concerned with interior mental processes but rather with outward behaviors. For behaviorists, the goal of psychology was to determine how various experiences could result in different behaviors.

Watson's hope was well founded, as behaviorism came to dominate psychology through the 1940s and 1950s, with many scientists studying learning, in both humans and non-humans, in great detail. The leader of behaviorism during that era was **B. F. Skinner** (1904–1990), who in addition to publishing many detailed studies of learning in rats, pigeons, and humans, wrote widely popular articles and books, even novels, about how behaviorism could help society. Like Watson, Skinner insisted that psychologists should study only observable behavior, because it can be reliably and accurately measured.

B. F. Skinner (1904–1990) A behaviorist who rejected the study of any mental events and felt that the brain fell outside the field of psychology.

Gestalt psychologists A group of German psychologists who insisted that the entire perception we experience is more than just the sum of the parts.

Max Wertheimer (1880–1943) An influential pioneer in Gestalt psychology.

Wolfgang Köhler (1887–1967) An influential pioneer in Gestalt psychology.

Skinner himself noted that his approach, considering only what is happening around an individual, and how that environment leads to changes in his or her behavior, was sometimes characterized as treating the individual as a "black box" (Skinner, 1989, p. 18). His concern was with what went in, and what behavior came out, not with what was inside the black box itself (**Figure 1.4**). He felt the interior of the box was the concern of "brain science," not psychology (Skinner, 1989). These days that distinction between psychology and what is now called neuroscience has faded away. Many neuroscientists carefully measure behavior, and many psychologists directly study brain function. And both types of scientists may hold degrees in psychology or neuroscience or some other field entirely. The number of colleges and universities that offer undergraduate majors in neuroscience is rapidly growing, typically drawing on faculty from both psychology and biology departments, as well as chemistry and physics.

While behaviorism dominated psychology for several decades, eventually the field became disenchanted with this approach, for several reasons. First, behaviorism was a victim of its own success. With many labs carefully varying one condition or another when teaching an animal or person some task, eventually most psychologists came to feel that we had uncovered all we needed to know about how to optimize the learning of an individual rat, pigeon, or person, especially in the context of what Skinner called a "teaching machine," and everyone else called a "Skinner box." Even within that thriving community of learning psychologists, many began resisting the narrow focus on all behavior being learned through a series of punishments and rewards. In Chapter 8 we'll see that rats roaming around a maze are in fact learning a lot even when there are no apparent punishments or rewards.

Back in Germany, psychologists studying perception also rebelled against the American behaviorist movement's presumption that learning, and observable behaviors, were the only important phenomena in psychology. These scientists, including **Max Wertheimer** (1880–1943) and **Wolfgang Köhler** (1887–1967), became fascinated by the ways our mind seems to "fill in" certain visual scenes, as in **Figure 1.5A**. They and other **Gestalt psychologists** insisted that the entire perception we experience is more than just the sum of the parts (in German, *Gestalt* means "shape" or "form," referring to our perception of an overall pattern). Likewise, when we see an ambiguous picture like that in **Figure 1.5B**, we perceive a whole Wolverine, or a complete scene of two Batmen looking at each other—we don't perceive a mixture of those two scenes. We'll learn about Gestalt principles of perception in Chapter 6. In the current historical context, the Gestalt psychologists served to undercut the behaviorist insistence that only observable behaviors were worthy of study. That meant many other areas of human experience—including emotions, insight, and consciousness—were ignored by behaviorists as unimportant and outside the realm of psychology as a science. Eventually psychologists became convinced that we could scientifically study mental events, effectively overthrowing behaviorism (Staddon, 1993), as we'll see next in our discussion of cognitive science.

Figure 1.5 Gestalt Psychology Rebels against Behaviorism Gestalt psychologists insisted that our perception of the world is more than just the sum of the parts presented. (A) Here we readily complete the picture to see a panda from blobs of black and white. (B) In an ambiguous picture like this one, we readily see either two Batmen or a single Wolverine but find it difficult to see both at once. Our minds perceive one whole scene or another, but not a blend of the two. Again, our experience of the whole cannot be explained by just summing up the parts of the picture. (B courtesy of Olly Moss, Ollymoss.com.)

Modern psychology is a cognitive science that discerns processes in the machine at work

cognitive psychology The study of internal mental processes, specifically how we acquire and process information and gain knowledge.

Even at the height of behaviorism's dominance, some theorists were interested in the roles of perception and thinking processes, which they termed "cognitive psychology," in learning (Hilgard, 1948, p. i). For example, experiments we'll review in Chapter 8 led psychologists to propose that rats form a "cognitive map" that allows them to efficiently navigate from one place to another in a maze. In the 1950s, a few researchers speculated about the limitations of the human mind to hold and process information (Miller, 1956). But it was the publication of Ulric Neisser's *Cognitive Psychology* in 1967 that marked the widespread recognition that this was a separate subfield of psychology. Today we can define **cognitive psychology** as the study of internal mental processes, specifically how we acquire and process information and gain knowledge. The big distinction from behaviorism is the emphasis on *internal* mental processes, as opposed to externally visible behavior alone.

The early cognitive psychologists were fascinated by computers, which were just coming on the scene. In many ways, computers were also like a "black box," with information going in and being processed by the computer, which then sent information out (**Figure 1.6**). Simple as that description of a computer may seem, cognitive psychologists saw the power of what this information-processing device could achieve. Since they could understand how human-made computers work, it gave them hope that they could understand how the human mind works to take in information, process it, and then produce behavior (Von Neumann, 1951). They also had an everyday confirmation that by varying the input to a computer and carefully noting the output, it was possible to understand what was happening inside the black box itself. For example, when a cognitive psychologist wrote a program to run on the computer, sometimes she or he didn't get the expected output because of

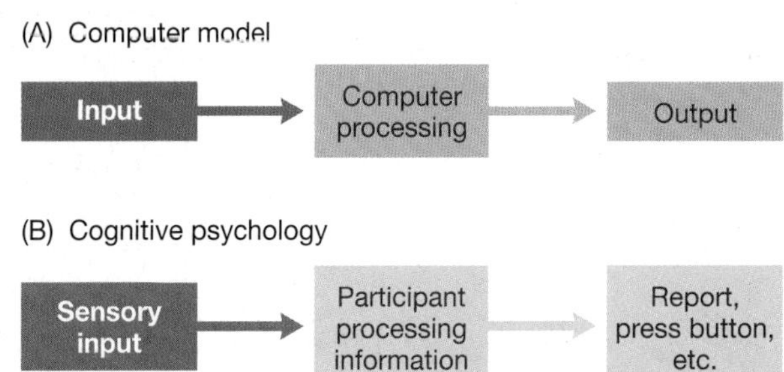

Figure 1.6 Black Boxes in Various Forms (A) Cognitive psychology was inspired by the model of computer processing, where information goes in, is processed, and then information comes out. (B) Most cognitive psychology experiments consist of carefully controlling sensory input, asking the participant to process that information in a particular fashion, and observing the person's response.

an error in the program. In these cases, varying the input in a systematic fashion and noting whether the expected output was given could sometimes give clues to what the program was doing wrong and pinpoint how to correct it. So in fact, you could learn about the processes going on *inside the black box* without opening up the box itself. If that black box happened to be the human brain, then you would be learning about how the mind works. In some ways, this remains the approach of most cognitive psychologists, carefully controlling sensory information available to participants, asking them to process that information in a particular way, and then reporting the participants' "output," either verbally or by pressing a button, for example (see Chapter 10).

In many ways, cognitive psychology represents the core of the field today, so people talk about the "cognitive revolution" that happened in psychology (Miller, 2003). Among other things, this means that cognitive approaches have spilled into almost every other subfield of psychology. When we describe social psychology (see Chapter 15), personality psychology (see Chapter 14), and clinical psychology (see Chapter 16), we'll see many examples of studies using the cognitive psychology approach and methods to reveal important principles. Once cognitive psychologists began revealing the different steps in information processing, they naturally became interested in how that processing was done inside the brain. This led the field to be interested in studying events inside the "black box" directly, which leads us to neuroscience.

Neuroscience aims to explore the brain and its workings directly, peering inside the "black box"

Skinner asserted that looking inside the "black box," the animal's brain, fell outside the charge of psychology and instead belonged to "brain science." Today we call that field **neuroscience**, the study of the nervous system, which includes the brain and spinal cord and all of their connections to the body. Among neuroscience's many contributions to psychology, we can include the discovery that one side of the brain controls most of our language abilities, a greater understanding of the changes taking place in the brain during learning, and techniques to monitor the activity of the brain in awake, healthy people (**Figure 1.7**). We'll review these and many details about modern neuroscience in Chapter 3.

neuroscience The study of the nervous system, which includes the brain and spinal cord and all of their connections to the body.

Neuroscience is one of the fastest-growing scientific fields, in part because it is a profoundly interdisciplinary field that has always attracted many psy-

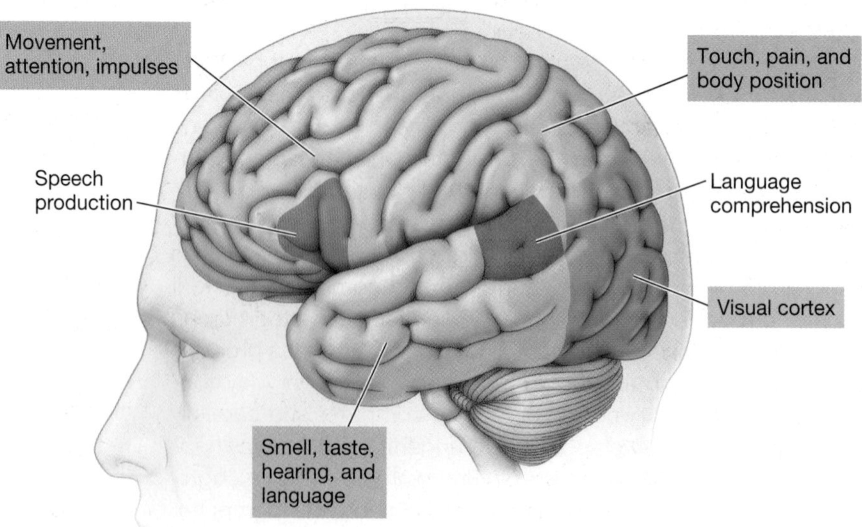

Figure 1.7 **Brain Activity** We'll discuss the anatomical terms for these brain regions in Chapter 3 (see Figures 3.18 and 3.19).

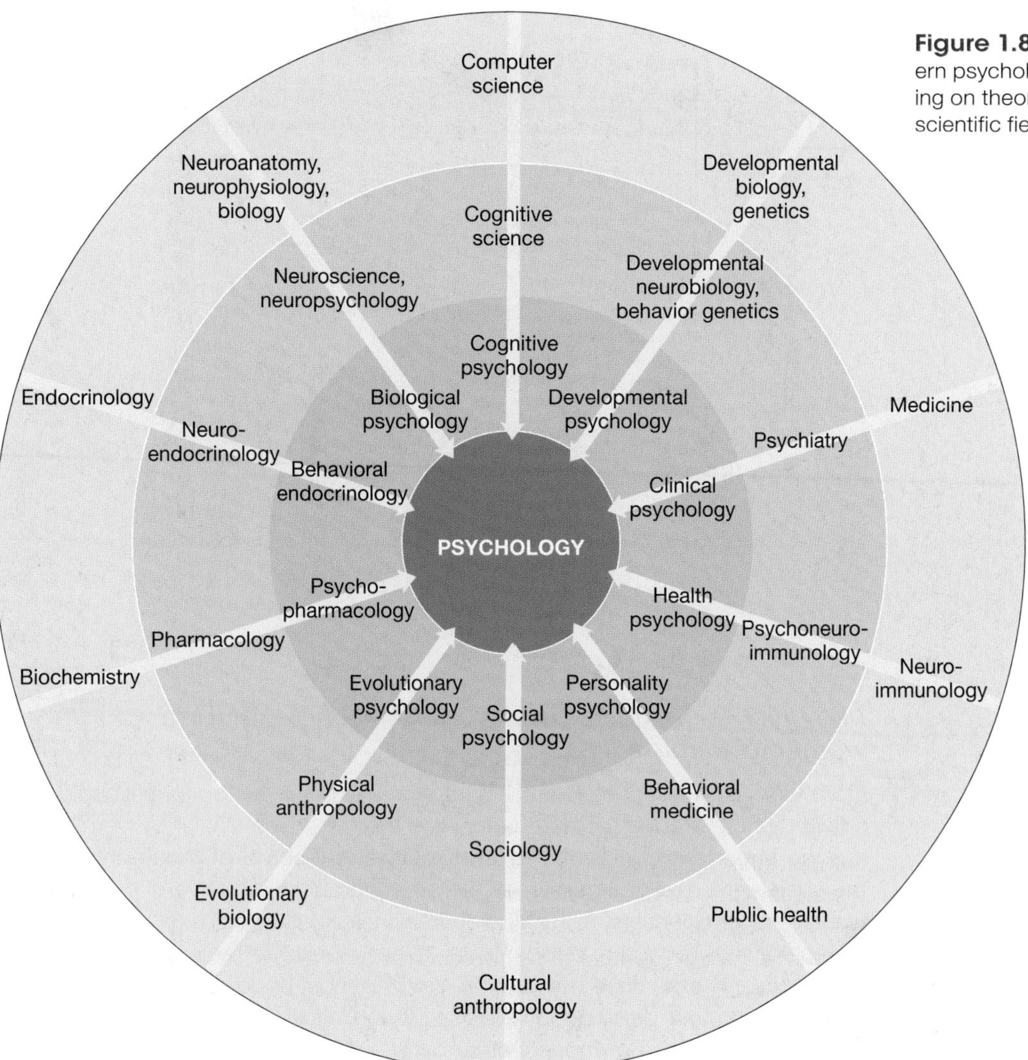

Figure 1.8 What's in a Name? Modern psychology is interdisciplinary, drawing on theories developed in many other scientific fields.

chologists, who go by various descriptions, including *biological psychologists* and *physiological psychologists*. Neuroscience also includes many cognitive psychologists who often use imaging methods to measure activity in different brain regions when a participant is engaged in a particular information-processing task. These scientists are often referred to as *cognitive neuroscientists*, demonstrating how thoroughly the two subfields blend into one another. Psychology also benefits from vibrant subfields of developmental, social, personality, and clinical psychology, as we'll see in future chapters. Thus the modern science of psychology brings together many different fields of science, all bringing particular perspectives and methods to bear on the study of behavior (**Figure 1.8**).

There is no doubt that psychology is an exciting, growing field. Today so much scientific research is being published in psychology that no one, not even textbook authors, can hope to keep up with it all. Given the size of this book, you may find the idea of reading it rather daunting. (Certainly I was daunted by the idea of writing it!) Even so, we can only skim the surface of what psychology has accomplished. If you take further courses in psychology, or decide to become a psychologist yourself, you'll find a depth in our understanding that I think would impress even as prolific a researcher as Wilhelm Wundt (**Figure 1.9**).

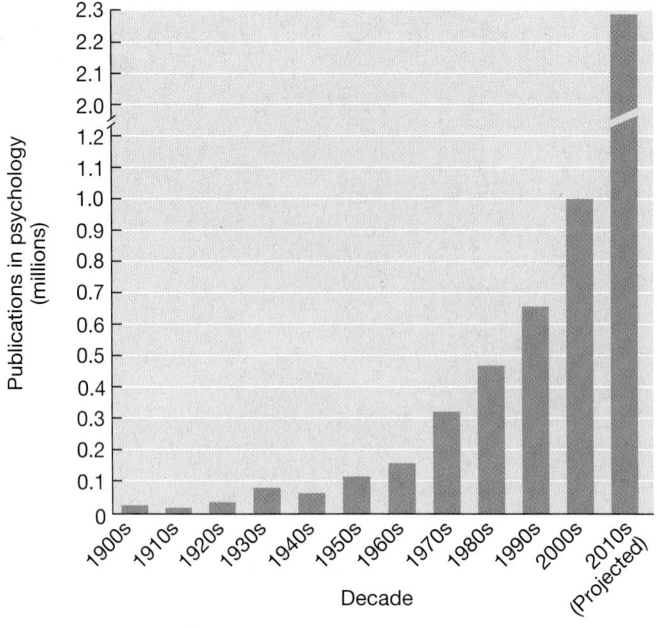

Figure 1.9 Psychology Is a Vibrant, Growing Field There has been exponential growth in psychology research. (Data from PsycInfo and PsycArticles databases.)

Like most scientific fields, psychology long excluded women and minorities

From today's perspective, there is a gaping hole in this history of psychology as a field—where are the women, where are the minorities? Women were indeed making important contributions, and we'll review some of those shortly. But the social attitudes of those times were remarkably dismissive of women who wanted to be scientists, in psychology and every other field, to an extent that may be difficult for young people today to appreciate. At the start of the twentieth century, women were denied admission to most undergraduate institutions, a stance the most prestigious colleges in the United States would not change until the late 1960s. For those women who did manage to get an undergraduate degree somewhere, most universities would not consider them for doctoral programs as the twentieth century began. We'll never know how many more contributions women might have made to psychology's beginning had they not been systematically excluded from the field.

Thus it is hardly surprising that the origins of psychology from the 1880s to the 1930s involved few women—as *scientists*. Women were, however, involved as *participants* in early psychology experiments. Sigmund Freud, for example, examined many women in his studies of **hysteria**, a mental disorder believed at the time to be caused by a malfunctioning uterus (the term derives from the Greek *hysteria*, meaning "womb" or "uterus"). While today we would probably classify the symptoms of hysteria as reflections of anxiety, in that era men lacked the anatomy to be even considered for a diagnosis of hysteria. Surgical removal of the uterus (hysterectomy) was sometimes recommended as a treatment and was reported (by the men who had recommended it) to provide relief of the symptoms (Chodoff & Roy, 1982; Gilman et al., 1993). The notion that women were afflicted with an organ that triggered disordered, irrational thinking was just one reason why they were considered "unsuitable" to become scientists.

Nevertheless, several women overcame the societal obstacles, through determination and talent, to make important contributions to early psychology. We've already noted the contribution of Margaret Floy Washburn (1871–1939). She wasn't allowed to apply for graduate studies at Columbia, so she went to Cornell where she was the first American woman to earn a PhD in psychology, in 1894. She then became a professor of psychology at Vassar (her undergradu-

hysteria A mental disorder diagnosed until the 1930s, believed to be caused by a malfunctioning uterus.

Mary Whiton Calkins (1863–1930) The first female president of the American Psychological Association and a professor at Wellesley College. She completed the requirements for a doctorate at Harvard but was never awarded the degree.

Mary Cover Jones (1897–1987) An early psychologist who studied the development of children and pioneered the technique of desensitization for phobias.

Francis Sumner (1895–1954) The first African American awarded a doctorate in psychology, in 1920 from Clark University. He went on to chair the psychology department at Howard University.

Kenneth Clark (1914–2005) A pioneering African American psychologist who developed the Clark Doll Test along with his wife, Mamie Phipps Clark.

Mamie Phipps Clark (1917–1983) A pioneering African American psychologist who developed the Clark Doll Test along with her husband, Kenneth Clark.

ate alma mater), where she was famous for her outstanding lectures (Scarborough, 2000). Washburn was an early leader in the study of animal behavior, and her groundbreaking book *The Animal Mind* (Washburn, 1908) remained in print for almost 30 years and is still regarded as a classic. An admirer of Darwin, Washburn agreed that there was a continuum of mental phenomena across species, and she was very interested in the extent to which animals have consciousness. She also advocated a rigorous, skeptical attitude and warned against projecting human emotions and reasoning onto other species. She became the second woman to be president of the American Psychological Association (APA) and the second to be inducted into the National Academy of Sciences of the United States.

Kenneth Clark (1914–2005) Kenneth Clark was the first black president of the American Psychological Association.

The *first* woman president of the APA was **Mary Whiton Calkins** (1863–1930), who had to get special permission from Harvard just to sit in and listen to William James's lectures. She was eventually admitted as a "guest," not a student, in 1892. When she submitted a doctoral thesis 3 years later that was unanimously approved by the psychology faculty (including James) as having "satisfied all customary requirements" for the degree, the Harvard administration refused to grant her a degree and, despite her illustrious career, never wavered from that stance (Furumoto, 1980). Despite having no graduate degree, Calkins became a professor at Wellesley College, where she taught for over 30 years. She published several influential books, including *An Introduction to Psychology* (Calkins, 1901).

Inspired by the work of the behaviorist John B. Watson, **Mary Cover Jones** (1897–1987) developed a technique for treating phobias (irrational fears) called *desensitization*, which involved repeatedly exposing the patient (in this case, a boy who was afraid of rabbits) to stimuli that were gradually more and more like the feared object (Jones, 1924). Although largely ignored at the time, desensitization remains in wide use for treating phobias today (Rutherford, 2006) (see Chapter 16). In 1926, Cover Jones earned her doctorate at Columbia University, which had softened its policies toward women since refusing admission to Margaret Floy Washburn. Cover Jones went on to publish many studies of developing children, including long-term studies of emotional development and puberty.

Happily, in the modern era there are fewer barriers to women entering science. By the twenty-first century, over two-thirds of PhDs awarded in psychology were earned by women (**Figure 1.10**). Thus in later chapters we'll meet many famous female psychologists.

The young field of psychology was no more welcoming to people of color than to women, and in this way, too, psychology was like the other sciences in those days. The first African American to earn a doctorate in psychology, in 1920 from Clark University, was **Francis Sumner** (1895–1954). He went on to chair the psychology department at historically black Howard University for nearly 25 years, and trained many people who themselves became influential psychologists. For example, after getting undergraduate degrees in psychology at Howard University, **Kenneth Clark** (1914–2005) and his wife, **Mamie Phipps Clark** (1917–1983), entered the doctoral program at Columbia. They were the first and second African Americans awarded doctorates in psychology from Columbia, in 1940 (Kenneth) and 1943 (Mamie). Together they developed the Clark Doll Test where children were shown two dolls that were identical except one was white and the other black. When asked which was the "nice" doll and which was the "bad" doll, most children, even black children, identified the white doll as the "nice" one, the one they would most prefer to have and the one that most closely resembled themselves (Clark & Clark, 1947). When the U.S. Supreme Court was deliberating on whether to require schools to integrate black and white children together, the Clarks offered evidence that black children in segregated schools are even more likely to

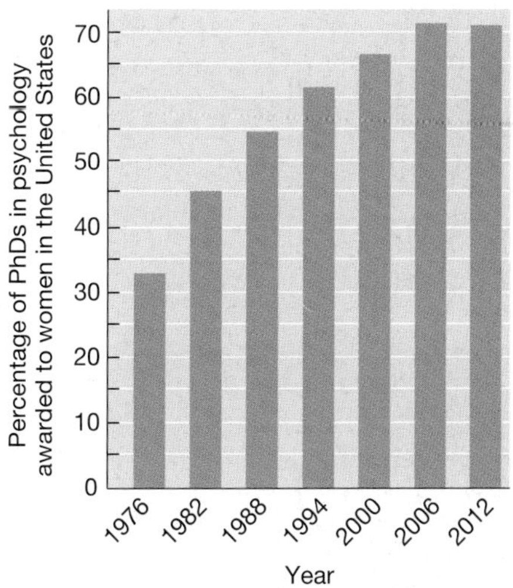

Figure 1.10 Women Predominate in Psychology Degrees Today (Data from Committee on Women in Psychology.)

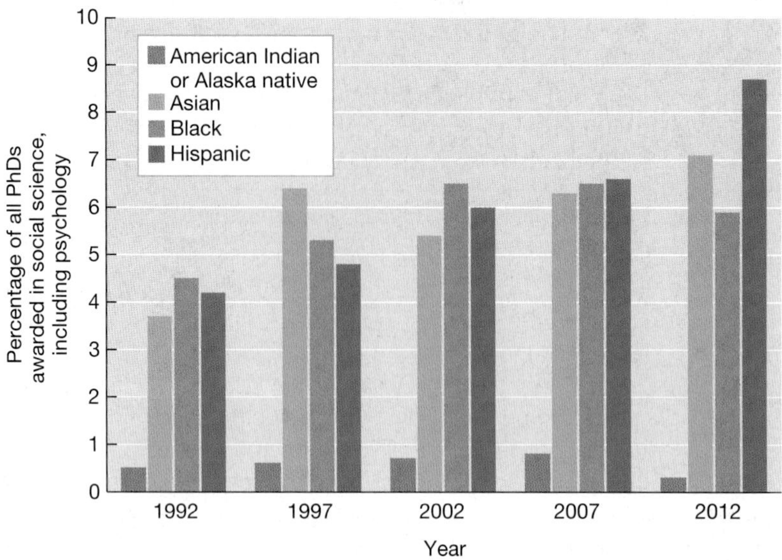

Figure 1.11 The Modern Rise in People from Various Races and Ethnicities Earning PhDs While the percentage of people from underrepresented groups who are getting PhDs has risen, especially compared with the mid-twentieth century, it is still not proportional to the composition of the overall U.S. population. (After National Science Foundation, 2012.)

prefer white dolls over black dolls. Kenneth Clark was the first black president of the APA. While the number of people from underrepresented groups getting doctorates in social sciences, including psychology, continues to rise in the United States, it is still well below the proportions of those groups in the total population (**Figure 1.11**).

1.2 SUMMARY

- The largely German field of *psychophysics* in the nineteenth century strove to measure the limits of human sensory detection, demonstrating the power of careful measurement of human behavior.
- *Wilhelm Wundt* established the first laboratory for psychology research in Leipzig, Germany, in 1879. He and his students formed the *structuralist* school of psychology, using introspection to discover the structure of the mind.
- In America, *William James* and his colleagues rejected purely introspective investigation and formed *functionalism*, the school of psychology emphasizing the adaptive function of behavior and the careful measurement of the behavior of other people and animals.
- *Behaviorism*, led by *John B. Watson* and *B. F. Skinner*, further emphasized the careful measurement of behavior, specifically when organisms are learning, and rejected the study of any mental phenomena, like emotions and consciousness, that could not be directly observed.
- *Gestalt psychologists,* including *Max Wertheimer* and *Wolfgang Köhler*, studied perception, noting that our perception of any observed scene was more than just the sum of its parts, thus demonstrating that mental functions that could not be directly observed could nevertheless be studied.
- In the dawn of computers, *cognitive psychologists* also rejected behaviorism's restrictive vision, demonstrating that human information processing could be understood by carefully controlling sensory

information, asking the participants to perform some mental task, and then noting their behavioral output, to discern processes at work in the mind.

- The resulting "cognitive revolution" influenced every area of psychology and encouraged the growth of *neuroscience* to directly monitor brain activities underlying behavior.
- Until recently, prevalent social attitudes largely excluded women and minorities from most scientific fields, including psychology. Nevertheless, women like *Margaret Floy Washburn, Mary Whiton Calkins, Mary Cover Jones,* and *Mamie Phipps Clark* made important contributions to the new field.

REVIEW QUESTIONS

1. From psychology's beginnings, what were the three major schools of thought before the "cognitive revolution"? Who were some leaders of each school of thought?
2. In what ways do behaviorists and cognitive psychologists regard organisms as a "black box"? How did the arrival of computers affect the perspectives of cognitive psychologists?
3. Who were some of the women who, despite many societal obstacles, managed to make important contributions to the early days of psychology? What were some of their contributions?

Food for Thought

The human mind is often referred to as a machine, similar to a computer. Considering this, do you think we will one day have computers that achieve consciousness? How would you know if a computer were conscious?

1.3 Psychological Myths and Four Principles of Psychology

Things to Learn

- Enduring psychological myths
- Four principles a psychologist should always consider

The science of psychology has come a long way in the past 150 years. What's more, introductory psychology has one of the largest enrollments of any college course, so you would think that the hard-won understanding we've gained about the science of behavior would be widely known. But in fact, many now thoroughly discredited ideas about psychology—some of which were abandoned by the field decades ago—are still widely held by our friends and neighbors. For someone like me who makes a living by teaching psychology, that's pretty depressing.

Here we'll discuss a few of the more famous myths of psychology, offering some suggestions about why particular ideas seem to persist, like zombies, no matter how often they've been debunked. Then we'll talk briefly about four principles of psychology that will be revisited in every chapter. These principles will, I hope, leave you with a bedrock of understanding about psychology.

Despite great progress, many psychological myths endure

Certain myths about psychology seem to persist in our culture, no matter how often they have been disputed. In fact, the very title of one terrific book, *50 Great Myths of Popular Psychology* (Lilienfeld et al., 2009), gives you an idea of how many such misconceptions color the general public's (mis)understanding of psychology. For over 80 years psychology professors have remarked on the prevalence of psychology misconceptions among students in introductory courses (Kuhle et al., 2009; Nixon, 1925). There are probably many reasons why these myths endure. Some of these ideas have been forcefully portrayed in popular media so often that they've become tropes, and so people think they are well established. But in each case, careful experimental work has disproven these notions, despite their popularity. One of my aims in this book is to arm you with the understanding needed to think critically about these myths, and to show you how we proved them to be false. On the next page are some of the psychological myths that we'll discuss and disprove—at least one from each chapter.

Psychological Myths

Sigmund Freud was a great pioneer in psychology who discovered the unconscious.

While not the first person to recognize the importance of the unconscious, Freud was wildly successful at *popularizing* notions about the unconscious in Western culture. Unfortunately, most of his personal notions about the unconscious are untestable—that is, Freudian theory is not grounded in science (see Box 2.1). This is why, in reviewing the history of psychology as a *science* thus far, the only mention of Freud was his discredited ideas about hysteria. His ideas live on mostly in literature and popular entertainment. Freud's ideas will come up in several chapters, but mostly to explain why mainstream psychology has retained almost none of them (see Chapters 1, 5, 16).

Scientific ability can be objectively assessed, so the best applicants get jobs in the lab.

Scientists, even women scientists, prefer hiring a man for a lab position over an equally qualified woman, and will suggest paying him more than her (see Chapter 2).

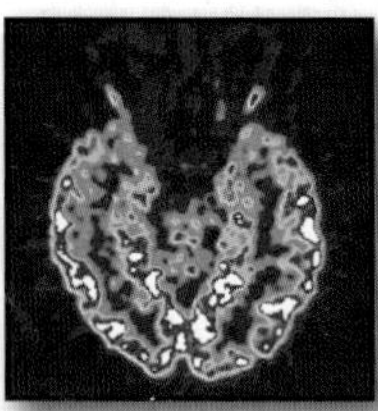

We only use 10% of our brain.

It's astonishing how this myth persists when there have never been any data behind it (Beyerstein, 1999; Boyd, 2008). About two-thirds of Americans believe this "factoid" (Harris Interactive, 2013). Despite tremendous strides in the field throughout the twentieth century, nearly a third of psychology majors also believed this misguided idea (Higbee & Clay, 1998)! We'll see that, in fact, scientists attempting to monitor brain function must "subtract out" the continuous activity that is occurring throughout the brain even when we are "vegging out." Almost all of the brain is active almost all of the time (see Chapter 3).

Heritable traits, such as mental disorders and IQ, cannot be altered by experience.

Experiences, especially early in life, can profoundly alter the likelihood that heritable mental disorders will appear (see Chapters 4 and 16) and can affect IQ (see Chapter 11).

Newborn babies can focus their vision only on objects that are nearby.

Newborns can in fact focus their vision on distant objects, but because connections between the eye and the brain are immature, they have relatively low resolution in visualizing objects, however far away they are (see Chapter 5).

We use red, blue, and green detectors in our eyes to distinguish colors.

Most of us do indeed have three different kinds of color detectors in our eyes, but all three of them can respond to light of almost any color. None of the three responds exclusively to one of those colors (see Chapter 6).

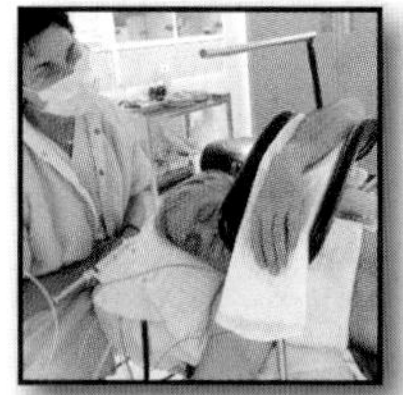

Hypnosis is a fundamentally different state of consciousness that can be used to help recover memories.

There is no evidence that hypnosis is any more an "altered" state of consciousness than when you change from daydreaming to, say, reading a book. And while hypnosis can help control pain, it consistently fails to help memory recall when tested in the lab. Outside the lab, several cases of memories "recovered" under hypnosis, which sent people to prison, were later proven to be false (see Chapter 7).

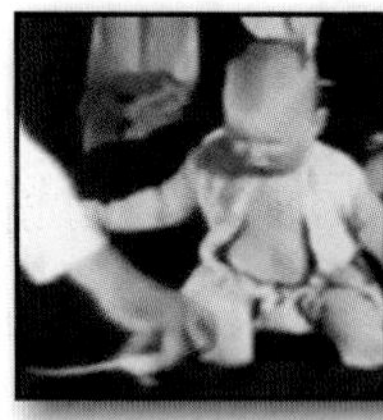

A baby named Little Albert was taught to be afraid of furry objects and grew up to have a phobia about Santa Claus.

While there's still some question over who Little Albert was, he either died young or grew up with few notable phobias except, perhaps, to dogs (see Chapter 8).

People with amnesia don't remember their own name or recognize their family.

People with amnesia typically forget the events that happened a few hours or days before some head trauma, but they still know their name and recognize their family. The few people who act fully aware of their surroundings and yet claim to not know their name or where they come from are probably pretending (see Chapter 9).

Subliminal messages can get you to buy things you wouldn't otherwise buy.

While there are plenty of cases where we know someone received information displayed on a screen without being aware of it, there's no evidence that such signals can get someone to buy anything (see Chapter 10).

Having kids listen to Mozart will make them smarter.

This idea, strongly promoted by people hoping to sell books, CDs, and DVDs, has been tested repeatedly and fails to work as advertised (see Chapter 11).

Some people choose to have a homosexual orientation.

While this notion is slowly fading in Western societies, there was never any scientific evidence to support it. In contrast, a host of studies have identified events occurring before birth (sometimes years before birth) that influence whether a baby will grow up to be gay or straight (see Chapter 12).

A polygraph test can accurately detect when someone is lying.

Polygraph tests are reasonably good at detecting when a person is feeling *stressed*, but they are lousy at detecting when someone is lying. In laboratory tests, they are accurate only about half the time. Would you want to stake your job or your freedom on the flip of a coin? (See Chapter 13.)

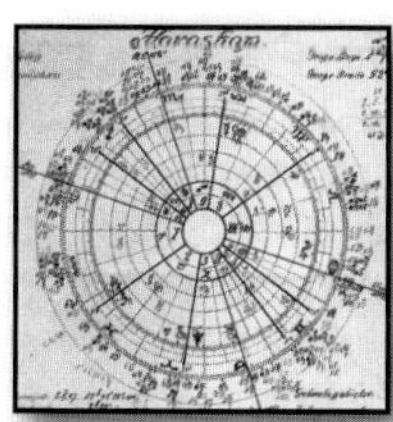

Astrological signs provide a hint of a person's personality.

The idea that a person's astrological sign will give any clue to their personality has been repeatedly disproven. Yet many people reading descriptions of the personality that supposedly matches their sign think it's accurate (see Chapter 14).

Many people heard or saw a woman being murdered in New York City, but none of them tried to help her.

While it's true that some of the neighbors who heard or saw the murder of Kitty Genovese taking place did nothing, several people tried to help (Cook, 2014). In fact, Kitty died in the arms of a woman who resided in her apartment building (see Chapter 15).

There is more crime and craziness around the full moon.

Police records show no peak of crime or arrests during the full moon. Despite the widespread belief of medical staff that there is a peak in emergency room activity around the full moon, hospital records disprove the idea (see Chapter 16).

People who develop schizophrenia never recover.

We'll see that many people who develop schizophrenia eventually return to happy, productive lives (sometimes without medication). By the way, your chances of recovery from schizophrenia are only about half as good if you live in the United States rather than in an economically less developed country like India (see Chapter 16).

Taking introductory psychology is a waste of time because "all they teach you is stuff everybody already knows."

But if that is so, why do so many people believe one or more of the myths above? If you're thinking now that you already knew those were all myths, then good for you. But we'll learn in Chapter 10 that, now that you've read that these are all myths, you may be fooling yourself about what you believed before you read this material.

Each of these myths was disproven by the application of critical thinking skills and careful experimentation, which are the hallmarks of psychology as a science, and the driving force behind this book. If the only achievement of psychology as a science were to disprove many long-cherished ideas about human behavior, that would still be a huge accomplishment. But psychology has also made active progress in identifying certain processes that do seem to make a difference in human behavior. The attempt to distill this hard-won knowledge into a small number of principles, which I hope you will remember long after your course is over, is also a theme in this book, as we'll discuss next.

Think like a psychologist: There are four important principles to consider for any behavior

To try and combat the enduring myth that everything taught in introductory psychology courses is "stuff everybody already knows," as well as the myths we just discussed, I've written this book around four important principles that have emerged in the field of psychology over the years and are considered by psychologists when analyzing any behavior. Though they may seem simple and uncontroversial, these principles will help you stay focused on the big issues I'm trying to convey and can also inform your judgments in the future, throughout your everyday life. Each principle and how it can illuminate findings in psychology, sometimes in ways that may seem counterintuitive, is described next:

1. **The mind is a product of a physical machine, the brain.** The brain is a physical machine that uses electricity and chemicals rather than gears and pulleys. The mind is a *product* of the brain. Since genes are used to construct that machine, genes influence every human behavior (yes, even television viewing habits).
2. **We are consciously aware of only a small part of our mental activity.** We will see many, many examples of events in the environment that affect a person's behavior without that person ever being aware of it. For example, later in this chapter we'll see a case where people are affected by seeing an African American face they were unaware of. Chapter 2 offers several examples of unconscious bias in judgment, which we'll discuss in detail in Chapter 10.
3. **We constantly modify our behavior, beliefs, and attitudes according to what we perceive about the people around us**. As we noted earlier in the chapter, we are and have always been profoundly social beings. In following chapters we'll see that we not only change our behavior based on what other people around us are doing, we also change our beliefs and may also change our remembrance of past events, because of the activity of people around us. We'll describe this in most detail in Chapter 15, but we'll see evidence of social influences on behavior in every chapter.
4. **Experience physically alters the structure and function of the brain.** We'll study this fact in detail in Chapter 9 when we find that learning changes the structure and function of the brain. The whole point of reading this book and taking this course is to physically alter your brain so that in the future this information will be of use to you (and no, I don't just mean for the final exam). In Chapter 4 we'll learn that one important process affected by experience is when and where you actually use the genes you inherited from your parents.

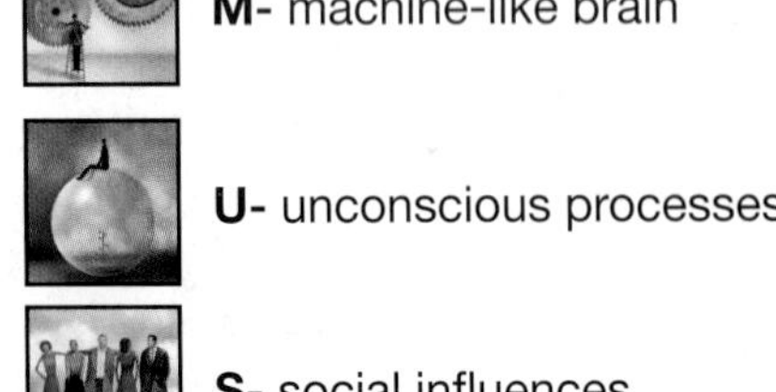

M- machine-like brain
U- unconscious processes
S- social influences
E- experience matters

Psychology's MUSE Our ability to remember is a subject that has always interested psychologists. Mnemonics are "tricks" that help people remember certain pieces of information. This mnemonic for the four principles and the images that accompany them may help you remember them.

THINK LIKE A PSYCHOLOGIST: THE PRINCIPLES IN ACTION Each chapter of this book opens with a vignette, or case study, describing some interesting behavior related to that chapter's topic. As each chapter unfolds, we'll refer back to the vignette several times as findings shed light on the case. We'll close each chapter with a feature "Think Like a Psychologist: The Principles in Action," where we'll relate the four principles to the vignette and demonstrate how to apply some of what we've learned in the chapter. We'll see an example of this at the end of this chapter.

RESEARCHERS AT WORK For another example of how to think like a psychologist and to show you how psychologists conduct science, the Researchers at Work feature highlights important psychological discoveries and demonstrates the scientific process—asking a question, experimentation, and hypothesis testing. Over the course of this book, the progression of experiments provides an increasingly sharper picture of the factors shaping behavior. Below is our first Researchers at Work, which may shed light on what happened to Michael Brown, whom we met at the beginning of the chapter (**Figure 1.12**).

subliminal Referring to a stimulus that a person is unaware of having perceived.

Researchers at Work

Detecting racial associations with crime

Figure 1.12 Looking for Trouble (After Eberhardt et al., 2004)

■ **Question:** Do ideas about race affect our visual perception?

■ **Hypothesis:** People's tendency to identify weapons in a blurry picture may be affected if they are reminded of African Americans.

■ **Test:** Have white college students look at a screen with images of objects that are either crime relevant (like a handgun) or crime irrelevant (like a book). For each object, the first image is so blurry it is unrecognizable. The image gets progressively clearer across 40 different frames until the students correctly identify it. But before the students do this task, you ask them to look for a flash on the screen. Unknown to the students, during this task they are shown a photo of a black face, a white face, or an abstract line drawing for fifty-thousandths of a second (50 milliseconds). Pilot studies indicate that people are unaware of seeing a face when it is shown so briefly, so when the students are asked later, none of them will be aware of having seen a face. In other words, these "flashes" are **subliminal** images, meaning people are not aware of having seen them (see Chapter 10). The question is whether seeing a black or white face, even without being aware of it, influences the students' ability to identify the objects.

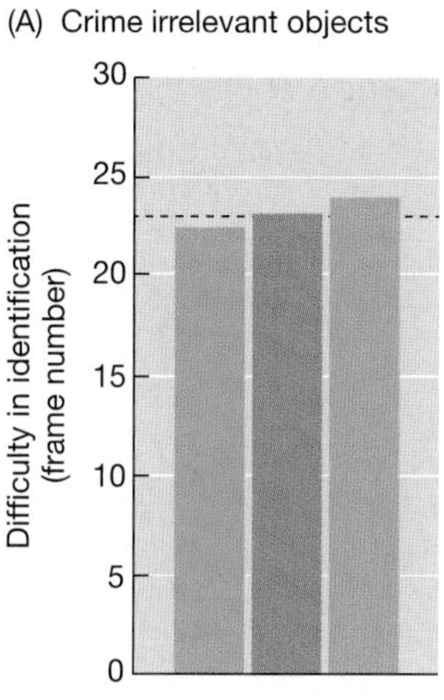

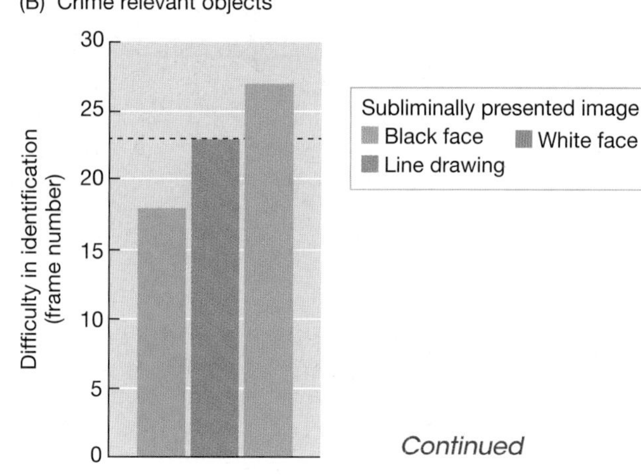

Continued

Researchers at Work *Continued*

■ **Results:** Of the 40 progressively clearer frames for each object, participants typically identified crime-irrelevant objects by about frame 23. This performance was the same no matter which subliminal image they were shown beforehand (**Figure 1.12A**). However, in identifying *crime-relevant objects*, students who had been subliminally exposed to an African American face identified the objects sooner than those shown an abstract drawing. Students shown a subliminal image of a white face needed *more* frames before they could identify crime-relevant objects than did those shown an abstract drawing (**Figure 1.12B**).

■ **Conclusion:** Reminding people of a black face, even if they are unaware of it, improves their ability to visually identify crime-relevant objects like a handgun. Seeing a white face actually makes people worse at identifying crime-relevant objects (Eberhardt et al., 2004). These results suggest that the cultural association of African Americans with crime may predispose us to perceive crime-relevant objects more readily in the presence of African Americans.

By itself, this study is interesting, but like many good studies, it raises more questions than it answers. Was there something about the faces used, apart from race, that caused the participants to identify crime-relevant objects more quickly? For example, would the results be affected if all the white faces were of choirboys and all the black faces were of convicted felons? In fact, all the faces were of undergraduate students at Stanford University. The only known difference between them was race. The participants in the study were white. Would the results be different if the participants were African Americans rather than whites? (A second run of the experiment with African American participants would answer this question.) Perhaps the most important question, which may also be the most difficult to answer, is whether these effects found in the lab have any significance for the real world (Blanton et al., 2009; Fazio et al., 1995; Greenwald et al., 2009). In real life, are policemen more likely to perceive a weapon if they are seeing a black person than a white person? We'll need to consider the relevance of lab work to real life repeatedly in this book. At this point, it is reasonable to say that the effects found in this lab study *may* reflect real-world interactions between police and citizens, and that unconscious racial bias may have played a role in Michael Brown's death.

In the pages that follow, we'll encounter many more instances of real-life dramatic events that raise questions about human behavior. Psychology is the science that can some day answer these questions. It's true that in some ways psychology has a long history: We've seen that philosophers from ancient times through the Renaissance pondered how we can know anything. Darwin's discovery that our behaviors evolved along with our physical traits also provided tremendous insight into human behavior. But as I'm writing this, only 135 years have passed since Wundt opened his laboratory, ushering in the age of *psychology as an experimental science*, carefully manipulating conditions to see how they affect behavior. In Chapter 2 we'll see how powerful this experimental approach can be for understanding psychology. In this chapter's Researchers at Work, we reviewed an experiment asking whether people are more likely to see crime-related objects when they've (unknowingly) glimpsed a black face, and we'll see more examples of experiments in the Researchers at Work in every chapter. Among other things, psychology has taught us about the interplay of the four principles of MUSE: our mind is a process at work in a material machine, yet we are unaware of much of that processing, which is acutely sensitive to our social world and constantly shaped by experience. We'll revisit these four themes throughout the book.

I hope you enjoy the chapters that follow. As I was writing, I imagined that you and I were friends having a conversation. I hope this relatively informal approach makes it easier for you to follow the thread of our chat. When I discuss what we know about one topic, I want you to be prompted to ask the next question, which I have tried to anticipate. Of course, I'm limited in terms of how much psychology knows, how much I know, and how many pages I can expect you to read. But there is always a next question. My deepest wish is that you will spend the rest of your life asking the next question, and that reading this book helps you do that.

1.3 SUMMARY

- Critical thinking and skepticism have dismantled and refuted many long-held psychological myths.
- We will repeatedly encounter four important principles of psychology:
  1. The mind is a product of a physical machine, the brain.
  2. We are consciously aware of only a small part of our mental activity.
  3. We constantly modify our behavior, beliefs, and attitudes according to what we perceive about the people around us.
  4. Experience physically alters the structure and function of the brain.

REVIEW QUESTIONS

1. What are some of the persistent myths of psychology?
2. What four principles of psychology will be emphasized in this book (hint: MUSE)?
3. Can you relate each of the four principles to some past behavior of your own? Or of someone you know?

Food for Thought

Can you think of reasons why some particular psychological myth continues to be perpetuated?

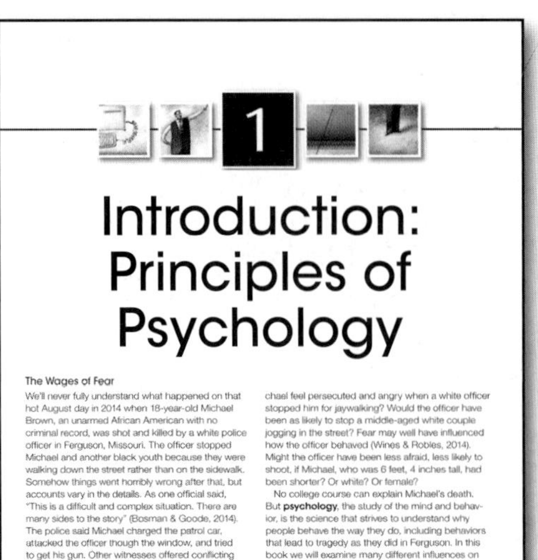

1

Introduction: Principles of Psychology

The Wages of Fear

We'll never fully understand what happened on that hot August day in 2014 when 18-year-old Michael Brown, an unarmed African American with no criminal record, was shot and killed by a white police officer in Ferguson, Missouri. The officer stopped Michael and another black youth because they were walking down the street rather than on the sidewalk. Somehow things went horribly wrong after that, but accounts vary in the details. As one official said, "This is a difficult and complex situation. There are many sides to the story" (Bosman & Goode, 2014). The police said Michael charged the patrol car, attacked the officer though the window, and tried to get his gun. Other witnesses offered conflicting accounts, raising various questions about what really happened. Was Michael holding up his hands chael feel persecuted and angry when a white officer stopped him for jaywalking? Would the officer have been as likely to stop a middle-aged white couple jogging in the street? Fear may well have influenced how the officer behaved (Wines & Robles, 2014). Might the officer have been less afraid, less likely to shoot, if Michael, who was 6 feet, 4 inches tall, had been shorter? Or white? Or female?

No college course can explain Michael's death. But **psychology**, the study of the mind and behavior, is the science that strives to understand why people behave the way they do, including behaviors that lead to tragedy as they did in Ferguson. In this book we will examine many different influences on behavior. We'll learn that we are not always consciously aware of why we do what we do, that we

Think Like a Psychologist:

Principles in Action

Whenever we encounter any interesting behavior we should consider the four principles. Here are some ways that the four principles relate to our opening story about Michael.

M
(Machine-like brain)
The mind is a product of a physical machine, the brain.

One expert declared that the police officer "may have been pulling the trigger out of pure adrenaline, because he was in fear" (Wines & Robles, 2014). If this speculation is true, then the surge of adrenaline may have tipped the scales, causing the circuits in the officer's brain to pull that trigger when he otherwise would not.

U
(Unconscious processes)
We are consciously aware of only a small part of our mental activity.

Even if the officer had never behaved in an overtly racist fashion, and had never considered himself prejudiced, unconscious bias must be considered. Most people, even most African Americans, have an unconscious bias to associate white faces with positive characteristics, and to associate African American faces with negative characteristics (see Chapter 15).

S
(Social influences)
We constantly modify our behavior, beliefs, and attitudes according to what we perceive about the people around us.

The encounter between the officer and Michael was, of course, a social encounter. How much did the officer's belonging to an almost exclusively white police force affect his attitudes? To what extent did being with a friend when he encountered the officer affect Michael's behavior?

E
(Experience matters)
Our experiences physically alter the structure and function of the brain.

Surely Michael's upbringing in a racially tense community, and coming of age during an era when the economy offered few jobs, affected his attitudes and behaviors that day. Did the officer's experiences earlier in life with African Americans tinge his attitudes and behaviors toward those two black teenagers? How did that accumulated experience affect his brain, and therefore his mind?

KEY TERMS

Aristotle, 5
behaviorism, 11
Mary Whiton Calkins, 16
Kenneth Clark, 16
Mamie Phipps Clark, 16
cognitive psychology, 13
Charles Darwin, 7
René Descartes, 7
empiricist philosophers, 7
functionalism, 10
Gestalt psychologists, 12
hysteria, 16
William James, 10
Mary Cover Jones, 16
Wolfgang Köhler, 12
John Locke, 7
natural selection, 8
neuroscience, 14
Ivan Pavlov, 11
Plato, 6
psychology, 4
psychophysics, 9
B. F. Skinner, 12
structuralism, 10
subliminal, 23
Francis Sumner, 16
Edward Thorndike, 11
Margaret Floy Washburn, 7
John B. Watson, 11
Max Wertheimer, 12
Wilhelm Wundt, 9

QUIZ YOURSELF

1. Being a member of a group is an important part of human survival. Anthropologists have theorized that humans can keep track of about ________ different human relationships.
   a. 50
   b. 100
   c. 150
   d. 200
2. Wilhelm Wundt established the first laboratory explicitly designed for psychology experiments. The foundation of the type of rigorous scientific approach he used there originated in ________, or the study of how physical events affect our senses.
   a. structuralism
   b. cognitive empiricism
   c. sensory analysis
   d. psychophysics
3. The group of psychologists who insisted that the perception we experience is more than the sum of the parts were known as the ______ psychologists.
   a. Gestalt
   b. behaviorist
   c. psychoanalytic
   d. functionalist
4. What mental disorder did Sigmund Freud attribute to a malfunctioning uterus?
   a. Phobia
   b. Hysteria
   c. Homosexuality
   d. Fixation
5. A scientist who studied only observable behavior and stressed the roles of punishments and rewards in learning was
   a. Wilhelm Wundt.
   b. Margaret Floy Washburn.
   c. William James.
   d. B. F. Skinner.
6. Plato used a parable to illustrate his skepticism about our senses. In this, he proposed people may see only the ________ of the events occurring in the world.
7. ________ was the mechanism of evolution that Darwin proposed for both animal and human behavior.
8. The school of psychology that promoted analysis of the human mind by breaking it down into the simplest kinds of experience was known as ________. The school of psychology that stressed the practical adaptive purpose of mental process was known as ________.
9. To remember the four principles of psychology used in our textbook, the author recommends a memory trick using the word MUSE. Using this trick, the four principles are ________, ________, ________, and ________.
10. When the U.S. Supreme Court considered school integration, findings from the ________ were used to provide evidence regarding racial preferences in children?

1. c; 2. d; 3. a; 4. b; 5. d; 6. shadows; 7. Natural selection; 8. structuralism; functionalism; 9. machine-like brain; unconscious processes; social influences; experience matters; 10. Clark Doll Test

Imagine
Molecules
atoms
SCIENCE
Experiment
DISCOVER!
atoms
EXPLORE
cutler

Psychology as a Science

Are women musicians inferior?

The world of professional musicians is intensely competitive. Typically there are over 100 passionate musicians auditioning for every position with a major symphony orchestra, all hoping to spend the rest of their lives making the music they love. With so few positions, only the best of the best have any hope of being hired.

For most of the twentieth century, a glance at any of the "big five" U.S. orchestras would have suggested that men must be better musicians than women, because only about 5% of the players were female. Among the experts in charge of screening applicants, men were deemed to be better musicians—because they were more passionate, or more dedicated, or more innately talented than women (Simon, 1967). An editorial titled "Why women musicians are inferior" summed up the prevalent attitude in 1938: "The woman musician was never born capable of sending anyone further than the nearest exit" ("Why," 1938).

But an odd thing happened in the 1960s when several orchestras made a simple change in the auditioning process—having the musicians play behind a screen. Then the committee judges, told only the musician's application number, were free to concentrate on the sound produced, without any visual distractions. Upon establishment of the process of these "blind" auditions, the hiring of women musicians for symphony orchestras rose dramatically, so that by 2000 nearly half the new hires were women (Goldin & Rouse, 2000). It would appear that before blind auditions, the committee found women musicians inferior *because committee members knew they were women*. That is, the hiring process was skewed by *bias*.

You might think bias would be found only in the arts, where judgments may seem more subjective than in, say, science. But when researchers asked a group of scientists to rate the qualifications of someone applying for a job as a laboratory manager, it turned out that an applicant named "John" was rated significantly more competent than an applicant named "Jennifer," even though the resumes were otherwise identical. What's more, the scientists suggested a starting salary $4,000 higher for John than for Jennifer (Moss-Racusin et al., 2012). Even *female scientists* preferred John over Jennifer. What's going on here?

Chapter Preview

In the real-world example of women musicians described above, the increase in hiring women after blind auditions (**Figure 2.1**) could, in theory, have been mere coincidence—maybe women had really gotten better (or the men had gotten worse) over that 40-year period, or maybe a lot more women auditioned. But in the case of the scientists rating an applicant, the only thing different about the two versions of the resume was the first name of the applicant, so it seems inescapable that the scientists' judgment was colored by whether they *thought* the applicant was a man or a woman. We can be more confident of what factor was affecting the scientists' rating the job applicant because researchers conducting the experiment had great control over the situation. The researchers carefully constructed the experiment to focus on a single difference. Careful control of experimental conditions in research on behavior is of utmost importance, and is the very essence of psychology as a science, permeating every page of this book.

This chapter is divided into two sections. The first will deal with the method that is used in any scientific field, although we will emphasize examples from psychology. Using that grounding in the scientific method, the second section will deal with approaches and issues that are particularly prominent in the scientific study of behavior.

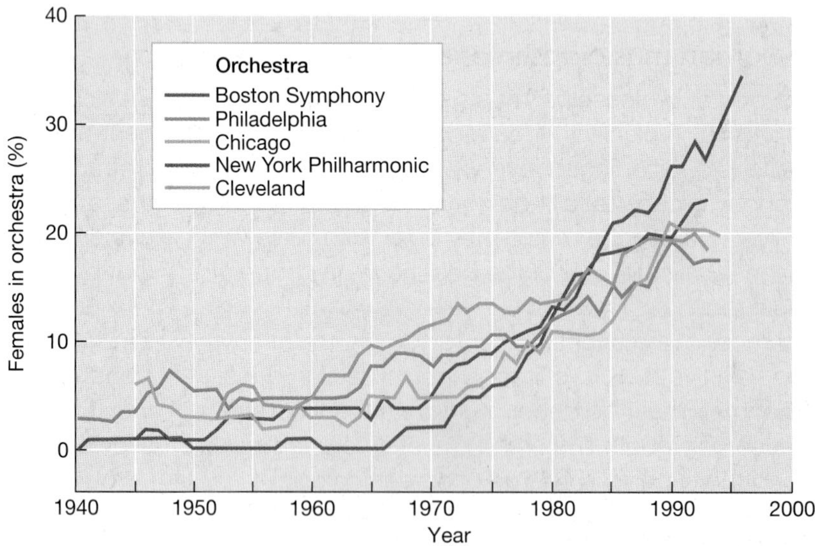

Figure 2.1 Did Women Musicians Get That Much Better? After the introduction of "blind" auditions in the late 1960s, the number of women playing in major symphony orchestras increased dramatically. (After Goldin & Rouse, 2000.)

Things to Learn

- Three kinds of scientific observation
- Correlation does not prove causation
- Confounding variables
- Occam's razor and Clever Hans
- Independent and dependent variables
- Hypotheses and strong inference
- Replication and meta-analysis

2.1 What Constitutes a Science?

Science is not just an endeavor practiced by a few people in lab coats. Rather, science is a way of looking at the world to make sense of what we see. Some might regard science as just the collection of all the facts that scientists have proven to be true. But the best scientists have a healthy skepticism concerning so-called proven facts, knowing that *we can never prove anything to be true.*

Rather, we get closer to the truth by *disproving* false explanations for the events around us. If eventually we can think of only one explanation that has not yet been disproven, that doesn't mean the explanation is true. For all we know, that explanation will be thoroughly disproven tomorrow. Thus science is more of a journey, the shedding of wrong ideas, than an arrival at the destination, "the truth."

The scientific process, in psychology or any other field, typically progresses in stages, and in this section we'll discuss those stages in turn. First we have to *observe* and carefully measure the events that have caught our interest, such as behaviors. Then we look for **variables**—either events in the environment or other behaviors, which often change along with the behavior of interest. We come up with *hypotheses* to explain why those variables and the behavior might vary together (*covary*). Then we devise experiments *to disprove as many of these explanations as we can*. Once we have a collection of hypotheses that have survived (so far), we may try to relate them to one another to form a *theory*, which can provoke another set of hypotheses to be tested.

variables Factors, either events in the environment or other behaviors, that often change along with the behavior of interest.

observation The careful noting and recording of events that occur over time.

descriptive method Making observations with the goal of accurately and impartially describing and cataloging behaviors without any attempt to influence them.

Science begins with the careful observation of phenomena

All science begins with **observation**, the careful noting and recording of events that occur over time. In psychology the events of interest are the behaviors and mental processes of people and other animals. The initial stages of research are simply to observe how individuals normally behave, measuring as carefully as possible the frequency of different behaviors, when they occur, how they vary across individuals, how they change when the environment changes, and so on. This is often called the **descriptive method**, when the goal is to accurately and impartially describe and catalog behaviors without any attempt to influence them. In this way the descriptive method contrasts with experimentation, which involves deliberately manipulating the situation, as we'll discuss later.

Descriptive studies require impartial observation and cataloging of behavior. Researchers can draw on a variety of techniques for collecting data, including direct observation, which may involve equipment such as cameras and timers or machines that record physiological responses; the administration of questionnaires, interviews, and standardized tests; and examination of historical records. Data collection can sometimes be accomplished in a day—and sometimes takes years. A brief overview of three methods used in descriptive studies follows.

NATURALISTIC OBSERVATION Descriptive studies of behavior of a species in its natural environment are sometimes called *naturalistic observation*, especially when studying non-human animals. A famous example is Jane Goodall's decades of observing the behaviors of chimpanzees in Africa. Scientists also sometimes observe humans in their habitat, say children on a playground, or adults in a singles' bar (Moore, 1985). The main advantage of naturalistic observation is that you know this behavior is taking place in "real life" and not something that happens only in a laboratory. One important concern about naturalistic research is whether the presence of an observer might be affecting the behavior of the individuals. To avoid that, Goodall spent so much time around the chimps that eventually they lost interest in her. Naturalistic observation of humans can often be done without any of the people becoming aware that they are under study, as

The Descriptive Method of Naturalistic Observation How do people behave in shopping malls? Do they travel singly or in groups? Where do they congregate? How much of their time is spent talking to other people versus quietly looking at store window displays?

case study A careful, intensive observation of one or a few individuals, typically people who display a particular behavior.

surveys A means of gathering data about behavior by having people answer questions about their behavior, thoughts, or opinions.

in a crowded public space. The second important concern about naturalistic studies is whether the particular individuals being observed, and the environment they are in, are truly representative of everyone of that species, wherever they occur. If the circumstances surrounding these particular chimpanzees, or children or adults, are unusual, then what you learn from these particular individuals may not apply to others.

CASE STUDIES A **case study** is a careful, intensive observation of one or a few individuals, typically people who display a particular behavior (Yin, 2013). Often the behavior is one that poses a problem either for that person or for other people, and so has come to the attention of a psychologist or psychiatrist. Usually there is an attempt to help the person avoid or overcome the problem, and those attempts are also part of the case study. Because case studies often include treatments, they may not be purely descriptive; they typically report what treatment the person was provided or urged to try. Case studies often include face-to-face interviews and may involve asking the person to fill out a questionnaire or take some tests.

For example, in 1965 a surgical accident severely damaged the penis of a baby boy. Physicians and psychologists were consulted and eventually recommended that the baby be surgically altered to look like a girl and be raised as a girl. Later reports indicated that the child grew up to be a well-adjusted girl on her way to becoming a young woman. For years this case study was presented as a demonstration that only social rearing determines whether a person feels like a boy or girl, a man or woman. As we'll see in Chapter 12, however, later events suggested a very different conclusion.

In later chapters we'll learn about case studies of identical quadruplets who all developed schizophrenia (see Chapter 4), a girl who was horribly neglected by her parents (see Chapter 5), a man who couldn't learn new facts (see Chapter 9), and a man who survived an accident in which a steel rod passed through his skull (see Chapter 14). Each of these case studies provided compelling demonstrations about what can happen, but it's probably safe to say that their biggest contributions were in raising questions rather than providing conclusive answers. Some case studies, such as that of the boy who was reported to be happy when raised as a girl, and a woman said to have multiple personalities (see Box 16.2), are perhaps more compelling than true, which may impede progress in psychology.

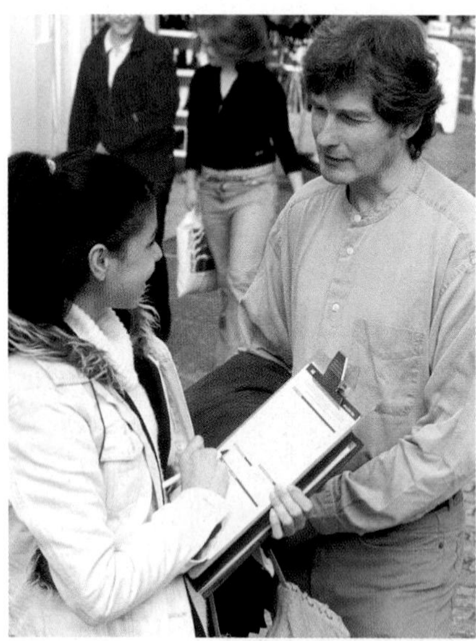

Survey Methods We can learn about attitudes and behavior by asking people to answer questions, either in person as here, or over the phone or the Internet. Surveys can also be conducted anonymously, to encourage people to be candid.

SURVEYS **Surveys**, having people answer questions about their behavior, thoughts, or opinions, are another way to gather data about behavior (Statistics Canada, 2010). Usually participants answer on paper or through the Internet, but surveys may also be conducted in face-to-face interviews or over the phone. An advantage of surveys is the ability to gather information from many people in a relatively short amount of time. Through the use of the Internet, survey answers can be gathered from lots of people from around the globe in a relatively short time, at a relatively low cost. An important consideration in survey research is whether the individuals we choose to interview are truly representative of everyone, an issue we'll return to later in this chapter.

A disadvantage of surveys is that there may be a difference between what people *report* about their behavior and how they actually behave. People may be reluctant to admit to behaviors or feelings that are frowned on by society. Thus for sensitive topics it may be important to let people know their responses will be anonymous so they may answer more truthfully. Also, surveys may ask the same question in several different ways to gauge whether the respondents are being truthful. But even then, surveys of peoples' past behavior depend on their having accurate memories, and as we'll see in Chapter 9, our memory, even for our own past behavior, is not always accurate. Surveys that ask people for their opinions are probably less subject to distortions of memory. After all, people should know what opinion they have at this moment, right? For example, surveys indicate that a growing proportion of people believe that "society should accept homosexuality"—the majority of people now hold this view in North America, Europe, and Latin America (Pew Research Center, 2013). While only a minority of people hold this view in Africa, Asia, and the Middle East, even there surveys indicate that acceptance is rising.

An important consideration in surveys is the care that must be taken in the wording of the question to avoid ambiguity. Also, it turns out that the opinion that people endorse for a given topic can sometimes depend heavily on how we frame the question. As we'll see in Chapter 10, people's strong preference between two alternative courses of action can be completely reversed just by how those alternatives are presented.

For all observational methods—naturalistic, case study, or survey—we always consider whether what we observed these particular individuals doing in this particular place and time will *generalize*, meaning it will also describe how other individuals behave in other places and times.

No behavior occurs in complete isolation. As we observe and measure behavior, we may note things that are happening in the environment or the way people respond to each other. Noticing these other variables may suggest patterns that can be explored statistically, as we'll discuss next.

We can measure how closely two variables vary together

Sometimes when we keep track of two different variables in a group of people, we may notice that when one variable is high, the other one tends to be high too. For example, we may note that children with large vocabularies tend to have parents with more years of education. Or we may observe that when one variable is high, the other tends to be low. For example, maybe children who watch a lot of TV don't tend to read very much. When the two variables vary together in a predictable fashion, we say they **covary**, or that they exhibit *covariance*.

covary Vary together in a predictable fashion; generally said of two variables.

correlation coefficient A quantitative, statistical measure of how closely two variables fluctuate together.

Another example might be to compare how much time students spend studying and what grade they get on an exam. We can get a sense of whether two variables covary by plotting them on a graph where individuals are represented by dots placed such that an individual's score for one measure, say hours spent studying, is indicated on the *x*-axis and the other measure, say the exam score, is indicated on the *y*-axis. This type of graph is called a scatterplot, because we can see how the individuals are "scattered" across the graph (**Figure 2.2**). In this case, just looking, you can see there seems to be a relationship between time spent studying and exam score. For example, the person who studied the least got a very low score, and the one who studied the most got the highest score.

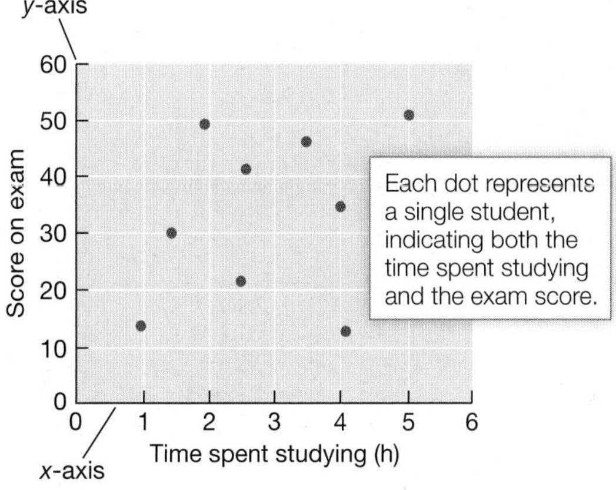

Figure 2.2 A Scattering of Scores In this scatterplot, we're looking at nine students who studied for an exam, each indicated by a single dot. It appears that, in general, those who studied more did better on the exam, but there are exceptions.

When two variables fluctuate together like this, we also say they *correlate*. The **correlation coefficient** is a quantitative, statistical measure of how closely two variables fluctuate together. There are several ways to measure correlation, but psychologists typically use *Pearson's correlation coefficient*, usually symbolized by the letter *r*. This measure of correlation ranges from a low of –1.0 to a high of +1.0. If two variables fluctuate completely independently of one another, we say they are not correlated. In such cases, the correlation coefficient *r* will be around zero (**Figure 2.3A**). If two

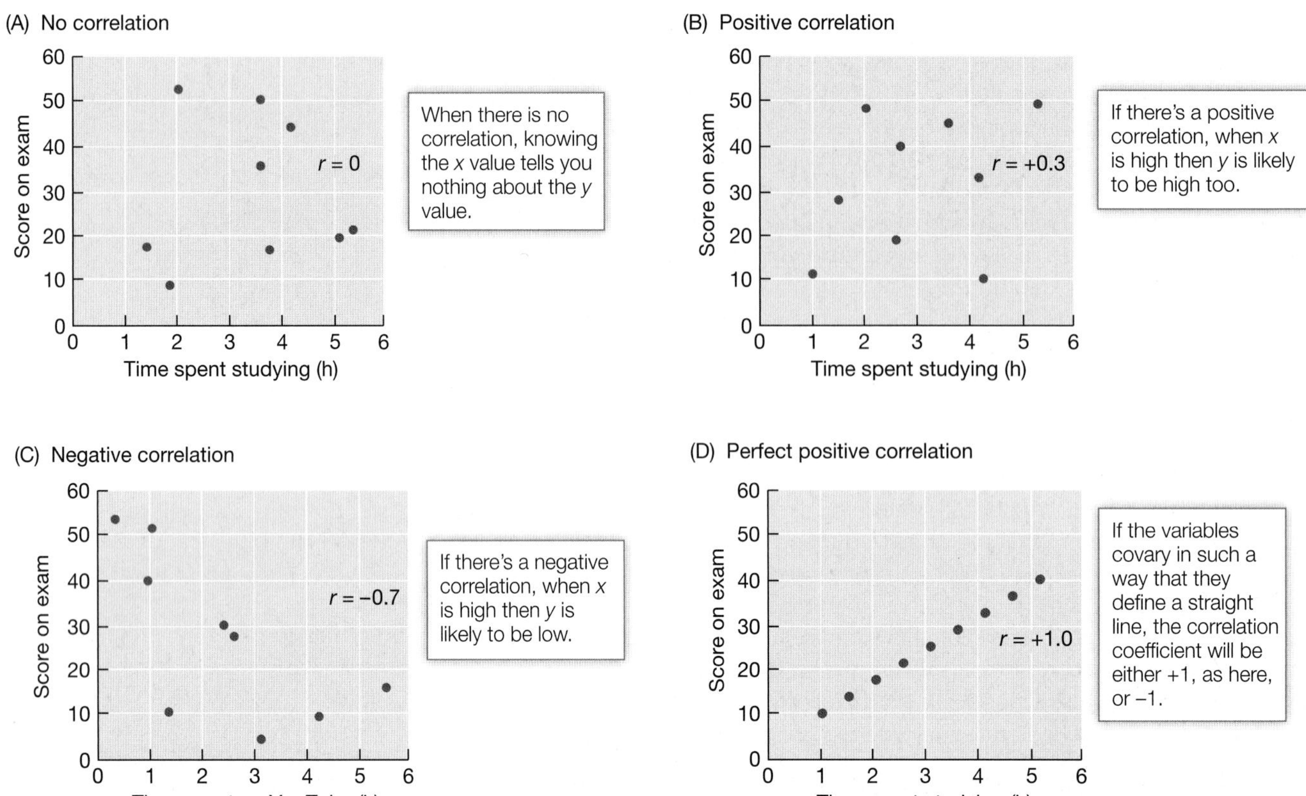

Figure 2.3 Examples of Correlation between Two Variables (A) No correlation. (B) Positive correlation. (C) Negative correlation. (D) Perfect correlation.

variables tend to go up and down together, the correlation coefficient will be positive, meaning greater than zero, so we call that a positive correlation (**Figure 2.3B**). If one of the variables goes up when the other goes down, they still correlate, but we call that a negative correlation and *r* will be less than zero (**Figure 2.3C**). For example, hours spent watching YouTube videos the week before a test might negatively correlate with exam scores.

The stronger the relationship between the two variables, the greater the absolute value of *r* will be. A correlation of +0.7 or –0.7 indicates a tighter relationship between the two variables than correlations of +0.3 or –0.3. If the correlation between two variables is perfect, then *r* will be either +1.0 or –1.0, and knowing the value of *x* lets you predict *exactly* the value of *y*. In that case, knowing how many hours a student studied would allow you to predict exactly his or her score. **Figure 2.3D** presents an example of a perfect correlation that is positive, so the correlation coefficient is +1.00. Even a glance tells you that the dots form a straight line, and if that's so then the correlation must be perfect. The extent to which some dots fail to fall on a straight line tells you how much the correlation falls below 1.00. If the dots seem to form no line at all, but form a round cloud, then the correlation will be around zero (see Figure 2.3A). In that case, knowing a person's score on one variable doesn't offer any prediction about her score on the other variable.

A crucial point to keep in mind whenever you see a correlation, either depicted in graphs or reported by a correlation coefficient, is that just because two variables correlate, that doesn't mean one has any effect on the other. In other words, there may be no causal relationship between the two. This point is often summarized as *correlation does not prove causation*. This is true even if the correlation is perfect or near perfect. In fact you can find many examples of variables that are strongly correlated where you can be pretty sure there is no causal relationship between the two. For example, **Figure 2.4A** shows a strong

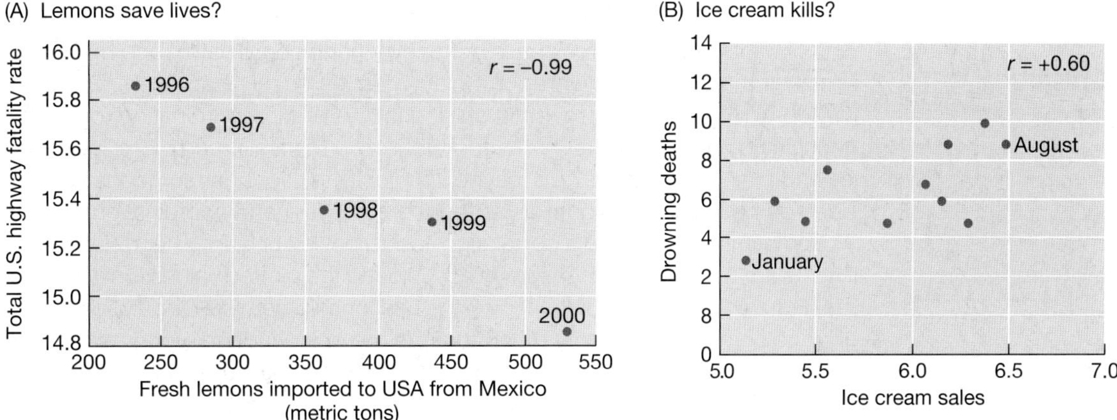

Figure 2.4 **Correlation Does Not Prove Causation** Here are two strong correlations, but in both cases we can be reasonably sure that neither variable was affecting the other one. (A after Johnson, 2008; B after Moore, 1993.)

negative correlation between the number of highway fatalities in the United States each year and the amount of lemons imported to the United States from Mexico (Johnson, 2008). Do you suppose this means a reduction in traffic fatalities results in more people surviving who like Mexican lemons? Or that increased import of lemons causes more people to stay home making lemonade rather than going for a spin on the highway? Do not fall for statistical "tricks" that imply relationships when there are none. It is not true that global warming over the centuries has been caused by the decline of pirates (Andersen, 2012). Another famous example is the correlation between sales of ice cream and deaths by drowning in the first 8 months of the year (**Figure 2.4B**).

These are examples of **spurious correlations**: instances when two variables covary not because there is any causal relationship between them, but because they are both being affected by some other variable. The U.S. traffic statistic reflects historical trends of increases in traffic safety measures, while the Mexican lemon import statistic reflects simultaneous trends in international trade. It is often the case that a host of variables change over time that have no other relationship to one another. As temperatures rise from January to August, people eat more ice cream and go swimming more often, which means there will be more drownings. Temperature is a **confounding variable**, a third factor that affects both variables of interest, causing them to covary even though neither has any causal effect on the other (**Figure 2.5**). I chose those correlations so it would be obvious that there's no causal relationship between them, but in science it isn't always so obvi-

spurious correlations Instances when two variables covary not because there is any causal relationship between them, but because they are both being affected by some other variable.

confounding variable A third factor that affects both variables of interest, causing them to covary even though neither has any causal effect on the other.

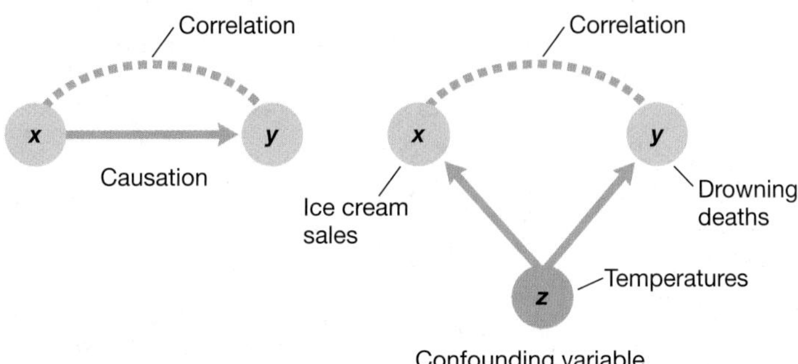

Figure 2.5 **Confounding Variables Can Result in Spurious Correlations**

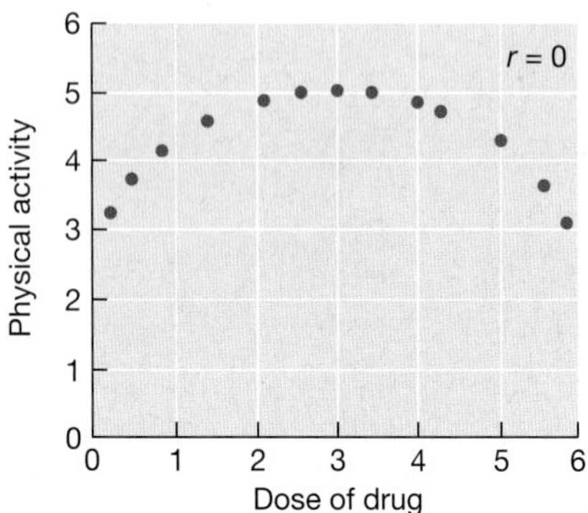

Figure 2.6 When Not to Use a Correlation Coefficient In this case, knowing the value of *x* gives a very accurate prediction about the value of *y*, but because the dots don't even come close to forming a straight line, the correlation coefficient is zero. More advanced statistical tools can more accurately describe this covariation.

ous that a correlation is spurious. For example, maybe you notice that surgeons who play lots of video games have better eye–hand coordination and make fewer mistakes than surgeons who don't play video games (Rosser et al., 2007). Did playing video games improve the surgeons' eye–hand coordination, or are surgeons who have good eye–hand coordination in the first place more likely to enjoy and play video games? Or maybe it's mostly the younger surgeons who play video games, and their youth gives them better eye–hand coordination.

Sometimes calculating a correlation coefficient is not helpful. Correlation coefficients are technically a measure of how closely the plotted values form a straight line. **Figure 2.6**, for example, shows the relationship between the dose of a drug given to some rats and how much the rats move around in an open space. You can see that knowing the dose of the drug lets you predict exactly how much the animal will move around. But this is not a *linear* relationship—in fact, the correlation coefficient is zero. If all you look for is a linear relationship, you may fail to see that a close relationship between the two variables does exist. This is why it's always a good idea to look closely at your data. A glance at the data in Figure 2.6 tells you that the correlation coefficient is zero, but shows a distinct pattern that implies some sort of relationship between the two variables. More advanced statistical methods could be employed to explore that relationship.

Correlation coefficients don't always tell the whole story if the investigation involves a relationship between variables in two different kinds of participants. For example, say you want to test the hypothesis that the hormone testosterone makes people aggressive. One way to go about this would be to measure participants' testosterone levels and then ask them questions that might reveal how physically aggressive they are. Gathering a sample of men and women, you might get results as in **Figure 2.7**. Notice that there is a cluster of data points for men, and another cluster of data points for women. In each group, there is no obvious correlation between the hormone and aggression, but because of the way the data fall by gender, it appears that there is a strong correlation overall. If you were to calculate the value of *r*, you might conclude that the two variables (aggression and testosterone) covary, and speculate that testosterone drives aggression. This happens, however, to be a spurious correlation because when you examine the data for just men or just women, no relationship between the two variables is apparent. A confounding variable, gender, affects both measures when the groups are considered together.

If correlation cannot demonstrate a causal relationship between two variables, it may seem to be of limited value in explaining behavior. But there are many instances in which correlation is useful as an observational tool. Ideas about behavior can be disproven through description or correlation. For example, per-

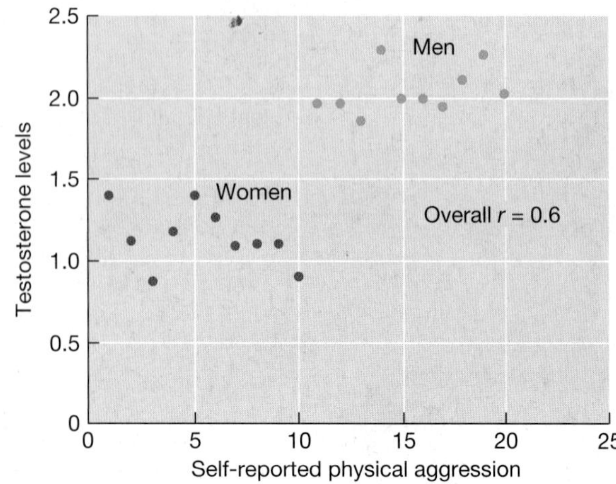

Figure 2.7 Another Instance Where a Correlation Coefficient Is Misleading Although there is no correlation between circulating testosterone levels and aggression in either men or women, because those factors differ, on average, between the sexes, computing a correlation coefficient across both sexes results in a highly positive value. Puts and colleagues (2012) did not present this correlation in their excellent paper. They sent me the data so I could show you an example of a confounding variable, in this case, gender.

haps you've heard that people are depressed around the Christmas holidays; a count of calls to suicide prevention hotlines in different months of the year will quickly disprove that idea (see Chapter 16). Or take the notion that college education makes people happier; you could look for a correlation between years of education and people's reported contentment with life. If there's no correlation, or if less-educated people report being happier than more-educated people, the idea would seem dubious. In fact, happiness *is* positively correlated with amount of education (Pew Research Center, 2011), so that possibility was not disproven by the correlation. But a positive correlation between education and happiness does not prove that education causes happiness. Could other variables be at play? Suppose children who are born healthier, or come from wealthier families, are more likely to seek higher education. Could it be that health and/or wealth are the factors that lead to happiness—whether these children went to college or not? Even if there is a causal relationship between the two variables, you don't know the *direction* of causation. Does going to college make people happy, or do happy people tend to go to college?

Because correlation cannot tell us whether two variables actually affect each other, scientists often prefer experimental over descriptive methods. Experiments allow researchers to manipulate one variable to see if it affects the other, as we'll discuss next.

Observations of behavior may generate hypotheses to be tested

Careful behavioral observations, either of individuals in their natural settings or of case studies, not only inform us about what people and animals actually do, but may also suggest a hypothesis. A **hypothesis** (plural *hypotheses*) is a tentative explanation for a relationship between two or more variables, and in psychology at least one of those variables is usually a behavior. So you might want to understand what conditions in the environment make someone more or less likely to display a behavior, or whether some behaviors often precede another, or why some people display the behavior more often than others.

Hypotheses arise when we are genuinely curious about what's happening and when we have considered hypotheses about behavior that other people have suggested and tested, say by taking a course in introductory psychology! One useful rule of thumb in evaluating hypotheses is the principle of **Occam's razor**, which states that when choosing between competing hypotheses, the simpler one, requiring the fewest assumptions, is usually better. Occam was a medieval scholar who applied this principle often, and later scholars referred to it as a razor that "cuts away" explanations that require a lot of unnecessary assumptions.

hypothesis A tentative explanation for a relationship between two or more variables.

Occam's razor A principle that when choosing between competing hypotheses, the simpler one, requiring the fewest assumptions, is usually better.

Occam's Razor Usually the simpler explanation is more likely to be true.

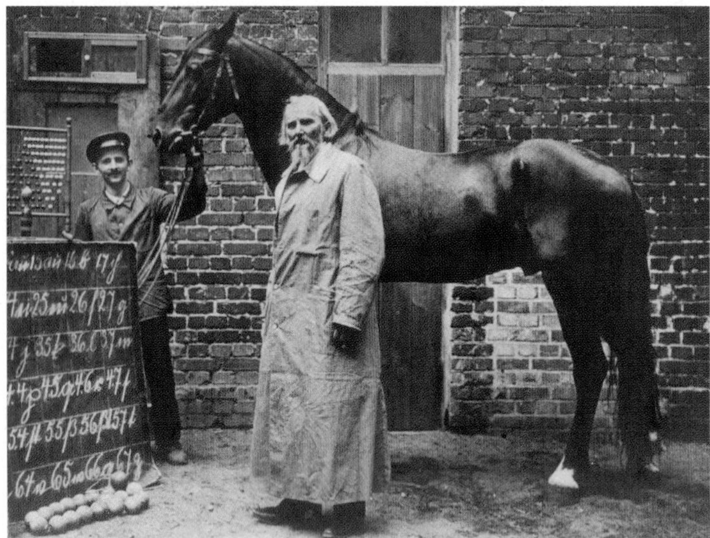

Figure 2.8 Clever Hans The elderly gentleman standing in front is Hans's owner, Wilhelm von Osten.

We can see Occam's razor at work in the famous case study of **Clever Hans**, a horse in early-twentieth-century Berlin that seemed to understand mathematics (**Figure 2.8**). In response to mathematical problems that people posed, Hans would almost always indicate the correct answer by tapping his right front hoof on the ground (Pfungst, 1907/1911). He answered questions on many other topics by nodding his head for yes or shaking his head for no. An article in *The New York Times* seemed to accept that a horse could understand mathematics, but a simpler explanation would be that a human was telling Hans the answers.

Intrigued by reports of Hans's intelligence, researchers came to test the horse. When they asked Hans questions that his elderly owner couldn't answer, neither could Hans. Through careful experimentation, researchers found that Hans was also unable to answer correctly if his owner wasn't nearby. Observing horse and owner together suggested that the owner unknowingly cued Hans to begin tapping by leaning forward to count the taps, and the horse knew to stop when, having reached the correct number of taps, his owner stood erect again. With the owner out of sight, one investigator could provide such body cues to make the horse provide any desired number of taps (Pfungst, 1907/1911). The principle of Occam's razor favors the simpler explanation that the horse attended cues from people over explanations that entailed a lot of additional assumptions: that a horse can understand German, or count hoofbeats, or do arithmetic.

Clever Hans A horse in early-twentieth-century Berlin that seemed to understand mathematics, but was actually using cues from his owner to answer questions.

experimentation A scientific approach of deliberately manipulating a variable to then observe whether and how other variables are altered in response.

independent variable The variable that is deliberately manipulated in an experiment.

While Occam's razor is useful for evaluating hypotheses, it is not infallible. Sometimes explanations that require fewer assumptions turn out to be false. For example, in a world where people "knew" that men were better musicians, that hypothesis seemed simpler than assuming that experts were biased against women. As we'll see next, experimentation can help us sort through hypotheses, no matter how unlikely they may seem.

Experimentation can reveal cause-and-effect relationships between variables

Experimentation is a scientific approach of deliberately manipulating a variable to then observe whether and how other variables are altered in response. We've seen the limits of correlation, which cannot address whether one of the two correlated variables is actually having any influence over the other. With experimentation, we deliberately manipulate one variable to see if that affects the other. Let's consider two different questions we might ask.

1. A correlation has been observed between people who play lots of video games and good eye–hand coordination. Does playing video games improve eye–hand coordination, or are people with good eye–hand coordination attracted to video games?
2. Does a newly developed drug relieve depression?

In each case, we want to know whether one variable (games, a drug) affects another (eye–hand coordination, depression).

If changing one variable reliably changes the other, it is reasonable to believe there is a *causal relationship* between the two. In experiments of this sort, the variable that we deliberately manipulate is called the **independent variable**. It's said to be independent because it is *free* to be manipulated, made higher or lower, weaker or stronger, by the scientist. For our two questions, we could manipulate the independent variable by having people play video games, or take our drug. The other variable, the one that we suspect might be affected when we manipulate the independent variable, is called the **dependent variable** because we suspect that it may *depend* on that other variable. For our questions the dependent variables would be eye–hand coordination or depression, respectively.

In an experiment testing the effectiveness of antidepressant medication, it is pretty clear that the medication is the independent variable because it can be manipulated in various ways: we could try giving several different doses of the medication: 5 milligrams, or 10 or 15. We are "free" to manipulate the amount of drug, and we hypothesize that relief from depression may "depend" on that dose. In such experiments we refer to the people who are getting a particular treatment as the **experimental group** (or *treatment group*)—the group of individuals for whom we are manipulating the independent variable (video games or drug). To know what difference the independent variable makes, the experimental result needs to be compared with that from a **control group** (or *comparison group*)—a group of individuals who closely resemble those in the experimental group, but who are not receiving the experimental treatment (no game playing, no drug). By striving to have individuals in the control group as similar as possible to those in the experimental group, we are trying to arrange things so that any difference between the experimental outcomes in the two groups is due to the independent variable we are manipulating and not to some other factor. To investigate the effect of video game experience on eye–hand coordination, we would ask the experimental group to play video games and the control group to do something else, maybe watch a TV show.

When we are not giving an explicit treatment, we typically don't use the terms *experimental group* and *control group*, but we still compare groups. Returning to the study of scientists evaluating applicants named "Jennifer" or "John," it doesn't matter which group—the female applicants or the male applicants—is considered the experimental group. We could frame the question either way: "Are female applicants undervalued?" or "Are male applicants favored?" and we'll get the same result. In either case, what's crucial is to ensure that everything about the two applications is exactly the same except for the first name, so that any difference in the evaluations would have to be due to that perceived difference in gender. Gender had a big effect on the scientists' evaluation.

The Jennifer–John study points out the advantage of experimentation relative to merely describing or measuring correlation. It was already widely known that there are more men than women in science, especially in senior positions. There were many plausible explanations for why that had happened, without assuming bias in hiring or evaluating applicants. And indeed, those factors may play a role. But by deliberately manipulating gender of the applicants, and carefully keeping everything else about their applications the same, experimenters could disprove the hypothesis that both sexes are treated equally at the start of their career. Thus experimentation allows us to isolate factors that seem to affect behavior. In fact, there is evidence that playing video games not only improves eye–hand coordination (Bavelier et al., 2012) but also affects brain structure (Kühn et al., 2013).

It is important that scientists strive to publish their results so that other researchers can be aware of what's already been done and so that the results may one day prove useful. Experiments investigating the potential effects of drugs such as antidepressants have to be rigorously conducted, given that their findings may be extremely important to the well-being of many people. Experiments that have significant implications are usually subject to **replication**: various labs repeat an experiment to see if they can get results comparable to the original finding. This is an important part of the scientific process. Sometimes the labs cooperate and try to see whether they were doing something a little

dependent variable The variable that you suspect might be affected when you manipulate the independent variable in an experiment.

experimental group The group of individuals for whom you have manipulated the independent variable in an experiment.

control group A group of individuals who closely resemble those in the experimental group but did not receive the experimental manipulation.

replication The repeating of an experiment to determine if results are comparable to the original finding.

meta-analysis A careful review of many studies that tries to gauge whether there really is an effect of the manipulation on the behavior of interest.

differently that led to different results. But sometimes the conflicting findings are just out there, unresolved.

Eventually there may be many published studies, some trying to do the exact same experiment while others deliberately alter one or more aspects of the study. Such cases may lead to a **meta-analysis**, a careful review of many studies that tries to gauge whether there really is an effect of the manipulation on the behavior of interest. We'll end this chapter describing an important meta-analysis that suggests that many people taking antidepressant medication would do as well taking sugar pills.

The closing years of the twentieth century saw a marked increase in the number of women entering graduate programs in the sciences. You might think that this influx of women into the field would result in a fading away of any bias favoring men in the sciences. On the other hand, the study of how scientists rate "John" versus "Jennifer" suggests that gender bias is still with us. Recently researchers came up with another test for whether professors in various scholarly fields encourage men and women equally, as we'll see next (**Figure 2.9**).

☑ Researchers at Work

Is gender bias in science a thing of the past?

Figure 2.9 The Old (White) Boys Club (After Milkman et al., 2014.)

■ **Question:** Does gender bias persist in various scholarly fields?

■ **Hypothesis:** Professors will encourage women and men equally to enter their respective fields of study.

■ **Test:** Send hundreds of college professors a fake e-mail, supposedly from a student, asking for mentoring. Have the e-mails be identical except for whether they are signed by a male or female first name, and a "white"- or "nonwhite"-sounding last name.

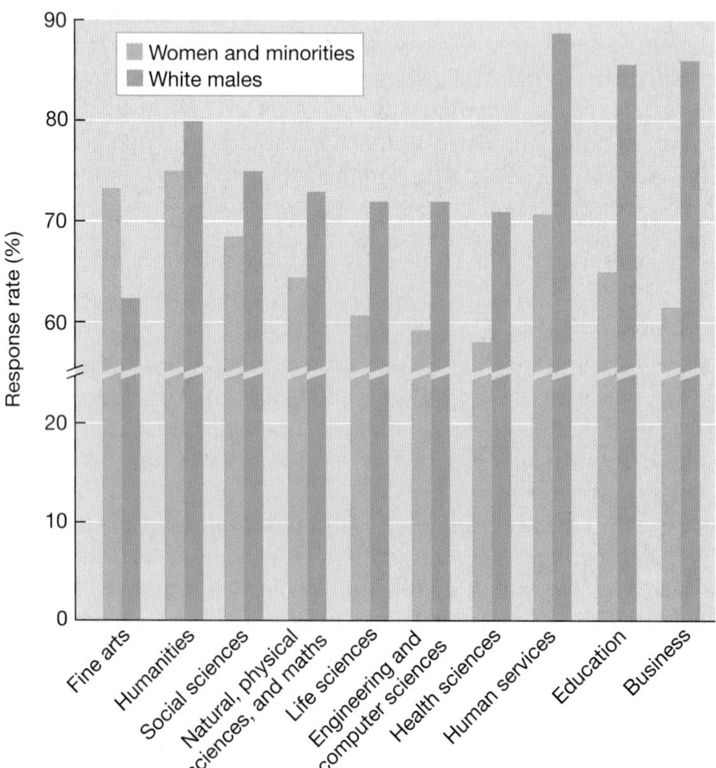

■ **Results:** In most fields of study, e-mails that appeared to be from women and minorities got significantly fewer responses than those appearing to be from white males.

■ **Conclusion:** These results contradict the hypothesis that professors are equally encouraging to men and women, or to "white" versus "nonwhite" students. Apparently professors, on average, are more encouraging to white men than to other groups.

Of course, some of these professors did reply to women and to students with "nonwhite"-sounding names, so no one is suggesting that all professors display bias. But it does appear that white men contacting professors are more likely than other groups to be encouraged to enter most fields, including the sciences. Perhaps the increasing numbers of women and people of diverse races and ethnicity entering graduate programs in the sciences will eventually shift this bias in the future.

Strong inference is the process of disproving as many plausible hypotheses as possible

For as long as there have been people, they have surely tried to understand the behavior of the people and animals around them. These efforts resulted in "folk psychology" or "commonsense psychology," which varies considerably across cultures and is passed from generation to generation (Ravenscroft, 2010). Sometimes there seems to be a kernel of truth behind these ideas, often captured in sayings such as "Absence makes the heart grow fonder," but you can often think of contradictory phrases like "Out of sight, out of mind" (Pellegrini, 1977). These old sayings can't all be true, or at least not in every situation. Does misery love company, and does practice make perfect, really? Happily for psychologists, a scientific method has arisen that we can use to discard wrong hypotheses, in our case hypotheses about behavior.

This isn't the place to review the history of how science as a field evolved as an effective and efficient way of learning about the world. Today most scientists agree on how scientific inquiry should proceed, at least in theory, to understand any phenomena, in any field of study. Described as **strong inference** (Fudge, 2014; Platt, 1964), it consists of four steps:

1. Come up with alternative hypotheses to explain your observations.
2. Design an experiment that could have several different outcomes, some of which would disprove a hypothesis.
3. Carry out the experiment to see which outcome you get, and therefore which hypotheses have survived.
4. Then go back to the beginning.

The power of this approach is that each time you eliminate a hypothesis, you keep going back to step 1 to think of a way to test, and eventually eliminate, other, often more specific, hypotheses (**Figure 2.10**). As this method keeps eliminating as many plausible explanations as possible, any surviving explanation has at least the potential to be true.

The experiment above (see Figure 2.9) disproved the hypothesis that professors encourage women and men equally. Scientists tested and disproved the hypothesis that Clever Hans could answer questions correctly without his owner being present. Then they hypothesized that the owner was cuing the horse by tensing his body, but they could not prove this was *true*. For all we know, Clever Hans paid no attention to his owner's body posture but was instead cluing in on the owner's mouth or eyes. We could test those hypotheses in turn, covering the owner's eyes in some trials, or his mouth in others.

strong inference A prescribed method for conducting scientific inquiry that consists of repeatedly disproving hypotheses.

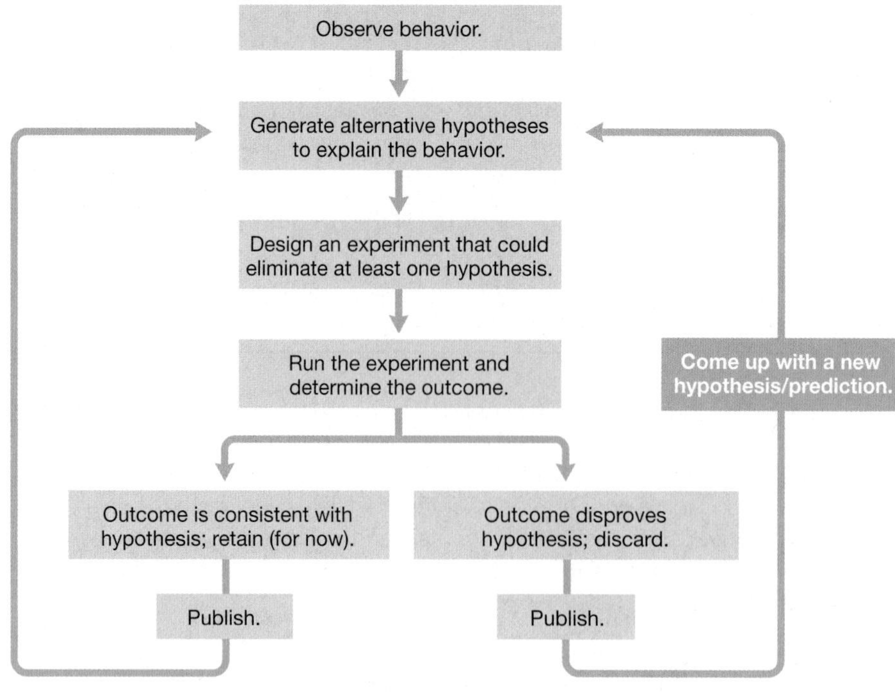

Figure 2.10 The Scientific Process of Strong Inference This process can never prove a hypothesis to be true. Even if every prediction of the hypothesis you've tested so far has been confirmed, tomorrow you (or someone else!) might find another prediction of the hypothesis that is not confirmed.

theory A group of hypotheses about a particular phenomenon that have survived all current testing and that are all compatible with one another.

Note that while we can sometimes *disprove* a hypothesis, we can never *prove* it is true (Popper, 1959). No matter how many tests fail to disprove the hypothesis, it's always possible that tomorrow someone will think of a test that thoroughly disproves it. If that happens, we'll have to come up with another explanation for what's happening, and kick off the next set of attempts to disprove this new hypothesis.

It sometimes happens that several different hypotheses about a particular topic, such as how infants learn language (see Chapter 10), have so far withstood the process of strong inference. In that case, researchers may try to fit these surviving hypotheses together to form a more coherent explanation of what's going on. This can be the origin of a **theory**, a group of hypotheses about a particular phenomenon that have survived testing (so far) and that are all compatible with one another.

In psychology, the phenomena that theories address are behavior and/or mental processes. There are theories about why we forget (see Chapter 9), how children become progressively more sophisticated in their thinking (see Chapter 5), how the two sides of the brain differ in function (see Chapter 10), and so on.

Once a lot of hypotheses come together to form a more or less coherent theory, it usually happens that this resulting theory in turn suggests yet more hypotheses to be tested (**Figure 2.11**). For example, in Chapter 8 we'll see how theories of animal learning suggested testable hypotheses about how humans learn, which for the most part survived the test. In Chapter 14 we'll see that when that same theory of animal learning suggested hypotheses about human personality, they were for the most part disproven.

Note that both hypotheses and theories are, at heart, possible explanations for whatever phenomenon we are observing. In general, a theory should apply to a larger range of phenomena than a hypothesis, but it may not be easy to judge where that dividing line is. Another important distinction is that we usually apply the term *hypothesis* to an explanation that might be readily disproven with a single or only a few experiments. A theory, in contrast, usually explains so many different phenomena that disproving its prediction for one particular case might not be enough to persuade people to abandon the theory altogether. On the other hand, if enough hypotheses generated by a particular theory are disproven, eventually scientists start questioning the current theory and begin casting about for another theory that better fits what's been seen so far (Koestler, 1959; Kuhn, 1962).

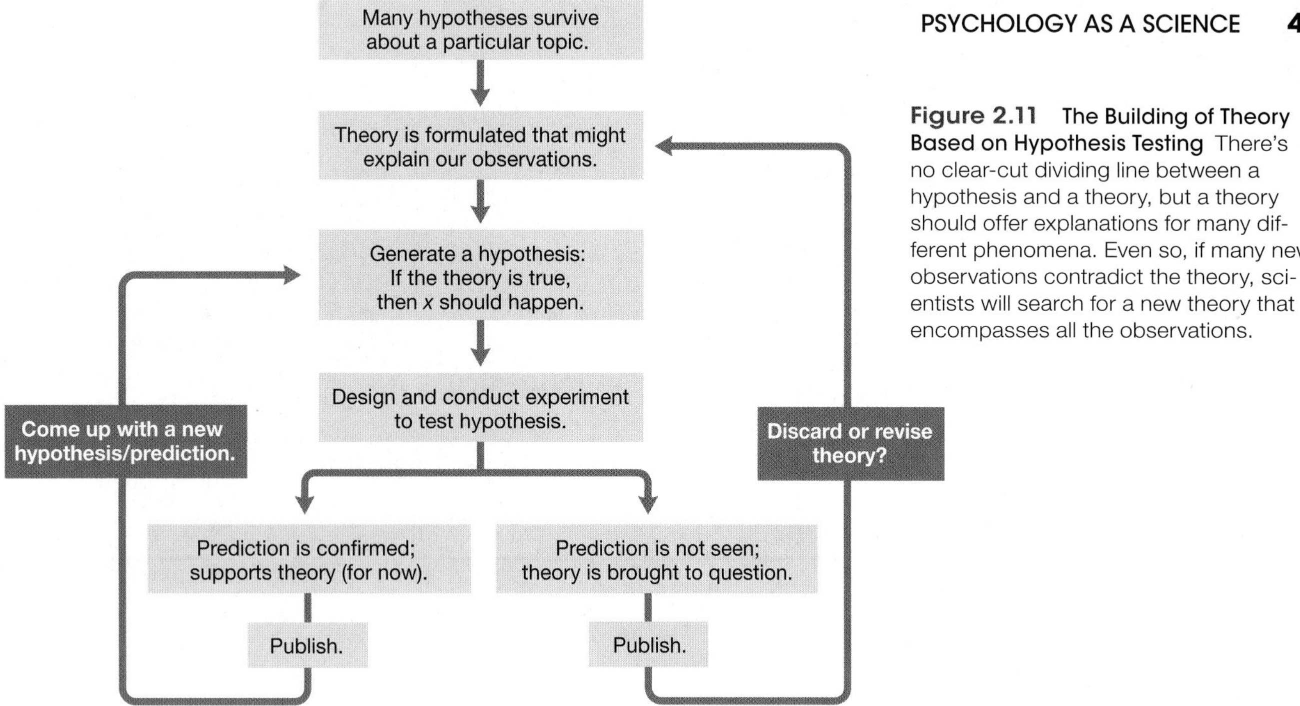

Figure 2.11 The Building of Theory Based on Hypothesis Testing There's no clear-cut dividing line between a hypothesis and a theory, but a theory should offer explanations for many different phenomena. Even so, if many new observations contradict the theory, scientists will search for a new theory that encompasses all the observations.

Understanding that science progresses only by disproving many hypotheses, subjecting any surviving hypotheses to more and more critical tests, helps us see the limits of science. As we discuss in **Box 2.1**, any theories or systems of ideas that are, by their very nature, impossible to disprove are immune to the scientific process.

Having discussed how the scientific method works generally, we'll take up some of the specific problems facing the science of psychology in the next section.

Skeptic at Large

BOX 2.1

Theories That Cannot Be Disproven Fall outside the Realm of Science

I don't mean to alarm you, but it is possible that the world that you think is around you does not, in fact, exist. Maybe you are playing a very sophisticated virtual reality game such that all your sensory processes, including the reading of this "book," are simply manufactured sensory information fed to your brain. As in the *Matrix* movies (see figure), your body might be tucked out of the way somewhere, taking in this information and thinking it is moving about in a real world. To take it further, maybe you don't actually have any body at all, no hands, feet, eyes, or ears, but are just a brain being fed information to make you *think* you are walking around, seeing the world and reading a book. For that matter, maybe you're not even a brain, but a complex computer program running in a very elaborate virtual world. As any experiment you perform in this virtual world would give precisely the results that have been programmed to happen in this world, you can never disprove this hypothesis. It might be true, but it cannot be addressed by the scientific method, and so science has nothing to say about it.

Similarly, the extreme versions of creationism, which insist that the world is only a few thousand years old, that the fossils we find in the earth and all other physical evidence we have about evolution were planted about 6,000 years ago, cannot possibly be disproven. If you accept that any and all physical evidence, anything that you can find and measure, may have been artificially provided to mislead us about the true nature of the universe, then there's no point in doing science to understand the universe. Clearly science can no more disprove this idea than it can disprove the idea that we live in a virtual reality in a computer somewhere. Again, the theory may be true, but it isn't science.

Unfortunately, the field of psychology has a history of brilliant, charismatic people who proposed highly

Continued

BOX 2.1

elaborate theories about the mind that are, by their very nature, impossible to disprove. The most prominent example is Sigmund Freud (1856–1939), who at the start of the twentieth century founded *psychoanalysis*, a method of understanding people's psychological problems and trying to help them overcome them. Because his way of thinking became so immensely popular, having a profound impact well outside the realm of science, influencing theory and practice in all of the arts, including literature and movies, we cannot discuss psychology without discussing Freud. Every student has heard of him. So we have to talk about him, but it will almost always be to say that despite the popularity of his ideas in our culture, they had virtually no impact on psychology as a science because they are impossible to disprove.

In the areas of developmental psychology (see Chapter 5), as well as consciousness (see Chapter 7), personality (see Chapter 14), and clinical psychology (see Chapter 16), we will discuss Freudian ideas to which many people have been exposed—and then will go on to explain why most psychologists today consider them unimportant (except for historical context). In each of those areas of psychology, Freud's theories were so elaborate that there was always a ready explanation for any case that seemed to contradict his ideas. So they could not be disproven. Likewise, every religion based on an all-powerful, invisible force that can do absolutely anything is impossible to disprove and therefore outside the boundaries of science.

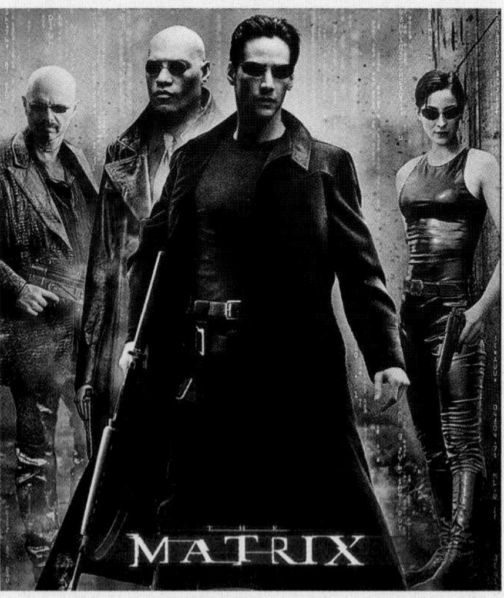

Maybe It's True… We have no way of disproving the hypothesis that our universe is a simulation runnning in a computer.

2.1 SUMMARY

- The *descriptive method* of accurately and impartially recording behavior includes naturalistic observations, intensive *case studies* of particular individuals, and *surveys* asking people about their attitudes and behaviors.
- The *correlation coefficient*, abbreviated as *r*, quantifies covariance between two *variables*. Positively correlated variables tend to go up and down together. If one variable tends to go down when the other goes up, they are negatively correlated.
- The value of *r* varies from –1.0, for variables displaying perfect negative correlation, to +1.0, for variables displaying perfect positive correlation. If there's no correlation, *r* will be about zero.
- Although two variables may be strongly correlated, that does not prove that either actually affects the other. Correlation does not prove causation.
- A *hypothesis* is a tentative explanation for a relationship between two or more variables.
- *Occam's razor* is a principle suggesting that among competing hypotheses, the one requiring the fewest assumptions should be favored.
- *Experimentation* is the process of manipulating an *independent variable* to look for changes in one or more *dependent variables.*
- The individuals subjected to manipulation of the independent variable are referred to as the *experimental group*, while those not subjected to the manipulation are in the *control group*. We look for differences between these groups to test hypotheses.
- *Strong inference* is the scientific process of proposing many different hypotheses to explain a relationship between variables and devising experiments that may disprove as many hypotheses as possible. Hypotheses that survive such tests are retained for further testing.

- If several different hypotheses about a particular set of phenomena have survived testing and seem compatible with one another, they may form a *theory*, a broader explanation of several closely related phenomena.

REVIEW QUESTIONS

1. Describe the major types of descriptive methods, identifying the strengths and concerns of each.
2. What are correlations, and why are they of limited value in understanding behavior?
3. Describe experimentation in terms of independent and dependent variables, and in terms of experimental and control groups.
4. What are the steps in strong inference? Is the aim to prove that a hypothesis is true?

Food for Thought

A good scientist is skeptical about everything, including her own hypotheses. What are the dangers if a scientist comes to feel emotionally attached to a particular hypothesis?

2.2 How Do We Scientifically Study Behavior?

Applying the scientific method to the study of the mind and behavior can be challenging for several reasons. For example, there is so much variability in the way people behave that we have to think carefully about how to gather groups of people to study. That same variability means we must rely on statistical tools to tell us whether, for example, two groups of people are actually different from one another. Also, for many of the things we care about, such as anxiety, visual experience, or intelligence, we have to devise ways to measure processes that we cannot directly observe. Furthermore, because people are so sensitive, responding to so many different influences, it can be difficult to isolate just one possible influence to test how it affects behavior. Finally, there are ethical constraints on the experiments we can do with people and animals that aren't an issue for scientists who study minerals or plants, for example.

Things to Learn

- Definition of random sampling
- Three measures of central tendency
- Inferential statistics
- Measuring variability and detecting differences
- Reliability and validity of psychological measures
- Controlling unconscious bias
- Tuskegee syphilis study
- Modern boards for ethical research

Random sampling is absolutely crucial in psychology, and surprisingly difficult to do

Humans can vary widely in how they think or behave. So if our goal is to understand human behavior, we can't just study one person and expect to understand humans. But on the other hand, it's not as though we can study *every* human, either. Instead, we study a tiny subset of humans, and hope that we can learn something that will be relevant to people generally.

Sometimes we might be asking about all humans, but more commonly we are testing a hypothesis about particular categories of people, such as newborn babies, or teenage girls, or college students, or adult men, or new parents. We refer to that entire set of individuals we want to learn about as the **population**, while the subset we select for actual study is the **sample**. Not just any sample will do. To safely generalize about the population we're interested in, we have to gather a **representative sample**, a sample that accurately reflects the total population we are interested in. How do we know whether a sample is representative of the whole population, if the point of gathering a sample is that we can't measure the whole population? At some level, we can never be sure our sample is truly representative of the population, so good researchers worry about this problem. Among other things, that means they are careful to avoid feeling too confident about their results—it's always possible that another sample would give very different results.

While we can never be certain that our sample is truly representative, there are steps we can take to maximize our chances for a representative sample. **Random samples** are ones in which every member of the population has an equal chance of being selected, and the selection of one person has no influence on who is selected next. It's easy to understand the first part of that definition, that everyone has an equal chance of being selected. You can probably see how that would lead to random selection. But you might not understand the importance of the second

population The entire set of individuals we want to understand.

sample The subset of the population selected for actual study.

representative sample A sample that accurately reflects the total population of interest.

random samples Samples in which every member of the population has an equal chance of being selected, and the selection of one person has no influence on who is selected next.

study population The group from which we can actually draw our sample.

part of the definition—that the selection of one person should have no influence on who's selected next. For example, if I am sampling people at random and the first person chosen is a woman, it is important that the next person selected be just as likely to be a woman as before. No matter who is in my sample already, everyone in the population must still have an equal chance of being selected next. Random sampling is required by statistical tools used to analyze data.

Let's look a little closer at the process of random sampling. The website www.random.org will generate a random string of integers 0 through 9, meaning every integer has an equal chance of being selected. I just went there and got this:

77885489180533373788075656654618398957489052526090

Some people looking at this string would say it doesn't look very random: it starts with a pattern of two 7s and two 8s—that doesn't look random, does it? But in fact, if the numbers are truly chosen randomly, then even though a 7 was chosen first, that in no way affects the probability that a 7 will be chosen next. So when I draw a 7 first, there's still a one out of ten chance that I'll draw another 7. Therefore in any string of random numbers, there will usually be several repeated digits.

If your aim is to look for a difference between people who vary in some characteristic, say men versus women, or 18-year-olds versus 14-year-olds, gathering random samples of each means the two groups of participants are likely to be equivalent in every other way except for that characteristic. In other words, your samples of men and women should be more or less equal in terms of age, or income, or race. Still, as you gather the samples, it's a good idea to look at such characteristics to be sure the luck of the draw didn't result in samples that differ in some other way (because unusual things do occur).

In other cases, you may draw a random sample of people with the intent of assigning them to either an experimental group or a control group to test a hypothesis. In that case, not only should you draw a random sample of people to participate, but you should be sure those people are then *randomly assigned* to either group. Again, random assignment helps avoid having the two groups of participants be different before you've even had a chance to perform whatever manipulation you've got in mind. You want the two groups to be equivalent before you perform your manipulation, as a fair test of whether that manipulation actually has an effect.

In practice, psychologists rarely have the ability to randomly sample from everyone in the population of interest. You can only get access to people in a certain geographical area, for example. Or perhaps you can only find people who have registered to vote, or gotten a driver's license. In many cases, the only participants you can get access to are college students who have to participate to pass their course in psychology. So you have to make a distinction between the *theoretical* population you are interested in and the **study population**, the group from which you can actually draw your sample (**Figure 2.12**).

Then how do you actually gather the sample from that study population? Have a computer randomly draw names from voter polls? Find a school that agrees to let you study the children? Have college students sign up online? The method of drawing your sample is sometimes called the *sampling frame*, the way you select individuals from the study population.

Theoretical population

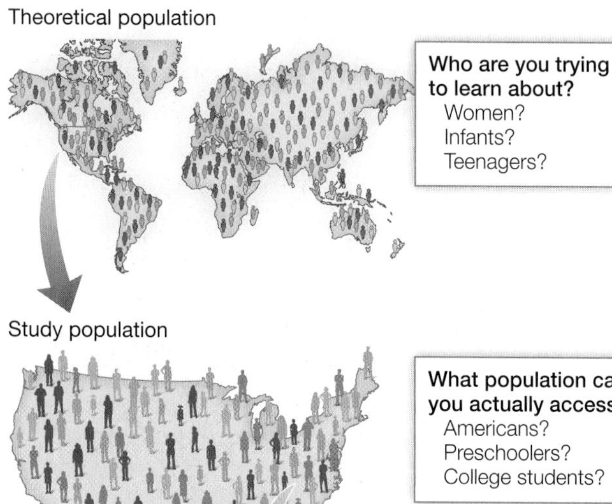

Who are you trying to learn about?
Women?
Infants?
Teenagers?
Study population
What population can you actually access?
Americans?
Preschoolers?
College students?

Sampling frame

How can you choose from among them?
Voter records?
Preschool records?
Intro psych students?
Sample
Who did you end up studying?

Figure 2.12 The Theory and Practice of Sampling

So you have gathered random samples, performed your manipulation, and then measured the behavior of the experimental group and the control group. To gauge whether that measure is different in the two groups, you'll need to harness the power of statistics.

We use measures of central tendency to gauge differences between groups

The generalization might be made that all of science comes down to *asking whether there are differences*. Sometimes we look for differences across time, as when we ask whether behavior changes after we administer a drug, or as children grow up, or after some dramatic event like the 9/11 attacks. Other times we look for differences between groups, comparing people given a drug with those given sugar pills, or people who went to college with those who didn't, or younger children versus older children. In each case, if we see a difference across time or between groups, we'll reach one conclusion, and if we see no difference, we'll reach another conclusion.

To look for a difference between two groups, the first step is usually to compare their average scores. You probably already know that you calculate the average measure for a group by adding up all the scores and dividing that sum by the number of individuals in the group. Because there are several different definitions of the English word *average*, scientists typically call this the **mean** (or the *arithmetic mean*). If the means for the experimental and control group differ, then perhaps your manipulation had an effect.

You may have an intuitive sense of what a mean or average represents about the scores in a sample. If you distribute all the scores from each participant in a sample from highest to lowest, the mean typically falls somewhere in the middle of the range. For this reason, scientists refer to the mean as a **measure of central tendency**, that is, an indication of where the scores cluster. You might conceptualize the arithmetic mean by thinking of a giant seesaw (**Figure 2.13A**). Assume each person has the same weight. Now have the participants stand

mean The average measure for a group calculated by adding up all the scores and dividing that sum by the number of individuals in the group.

measure of central tendency An indication of where the scores in a sample cluster.

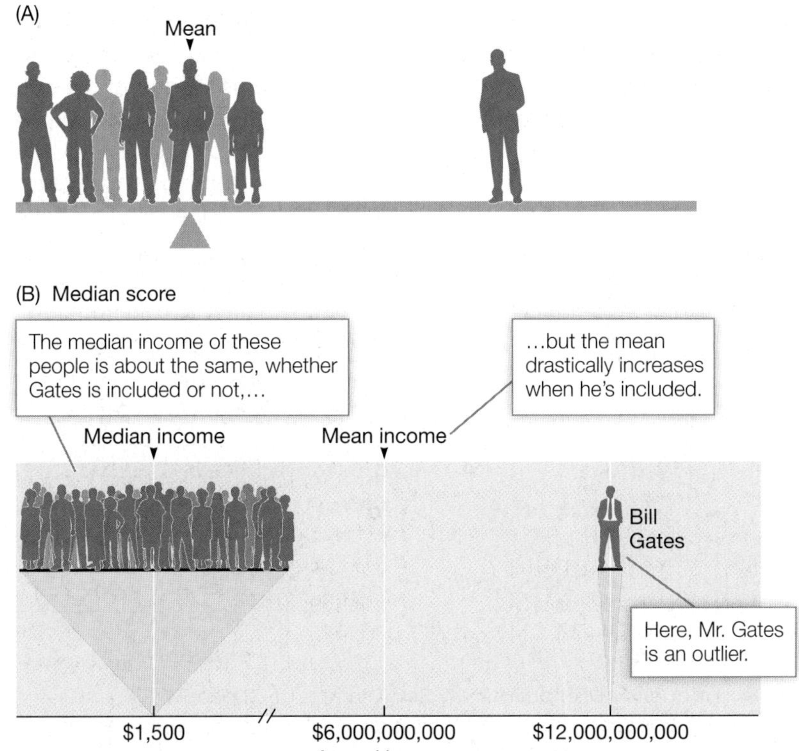
(A)
Mean
(B) Median score
The median income of these people is about the same, whether Gates is included or not,...
...but the mean drastically increases when he's included.
Median income
Mean income
Bill Gates
Here, Mr. Gates is an outlier.
$1,500
$6,000,000,000
$12,000,000,000
Annual income

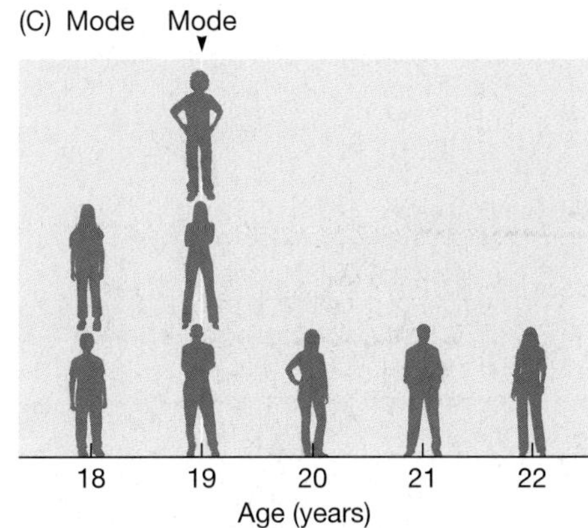
(C) Mode
Mode
18
19
20
21
22
Age (years)

Figure 2.13 Measures of Central Tendency (A) The mean, or average, is the value that exactly balances all the scores so that if this were a seesaw, it could be balanced there. (B) The median score is the one that falls in the middle, with half the other scores lower and the other half higher. (C) The mode is the single score that is seen more often than any other.

outlier A score that is either much greater or much smaller than the others.

median A measure of central tendency that is the value that falls in the middle of all the scores, such that half the scores are higher and half are lower.

mode A measure of central tendency that is the single score that is most commonly found among the participants.

frequency distributions Graphs in which a score is noted on the *x*-axis while the number of people who have each score is noted on the *y*-axis.

along a length of a board so that each person stands on the part of the board representing his or her score. If two people have the same score, one stands on the shoulders of the other. The mean would be that point along the board where you could stick a wedge beneath that would perfectly balance all those people.

While the mean is the most commonly used measure of central tendency, there are times when it might not paint a very accurate picture of what's going on. For example, if billionaire Bill Gates moved to a small village of 100 cattle farmers in Sudan, the average annual income of the village would be over a million. But would that give an accurate idea of what life is like for most of the people there? This example shows a shortcoming of the mean as a measure of central tendency—it can be shifted a lot by just one **outlier**, a score that is either much greater or much smaller than the others. In this case, another measure of central tendency would better convey the typical income of the villagers: the median. The **median** is the value that falls in the middle of all the scores, such that half the scores are higher and half are lower (**Figure 2.13B**). In this case, it would be whichever farmer's income is greater than that of 50 people in the village and lower than that of another 50 people (one of whom is Mr. Gates). If Mr. Gates lost so much wealth that he had only $1 billion, the mean income of the village would drop dramatically (by millions!), but the median income in that village would be *exactly the same*. Since 100 of the 101 people in that village would have exactly the same income as before Mr. Gates lost his billions, the unvarying median more accurately portrays the village as a whole.

Sometimes what you want to know from a sample is which score is the most common. If the scores range from 0 to 100 and there are more scores of 39 than any other score, then that suggests that the scores cluster around that value. This measure of central tendency is the **mode**: the single score that is most commonly found among the participants (**Figure 2.13C**). The mode may be relatively easy to determine if there aren't lots of scores. For example, in a college classroom you could ask for a show of hands of people who are 18 years old, or 19, or 20, and so on. Whichever age produced the most hands would be the modal age.

To help visualize these measures of central tendency, we can consider **frequency distributions**, graphs in which some score is noted on the *x*-axis while the number of people who have each score is noted on the *y*-axis (**Figure 2.14**). Psychologists often think about frequency distributions, as when considering different people's scores on IQ tests (see Chapter 11), or hours spent on the Internet, or time needed to solve a puzzle.

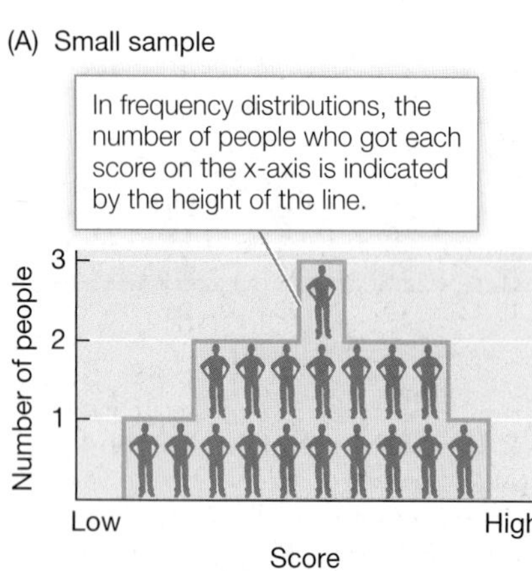
(A) Small sample
In frequency distributions, the number of people who got each score on the x-axis is indicated by the height of the line.
Number of people
3
2
1
Low
High
Score

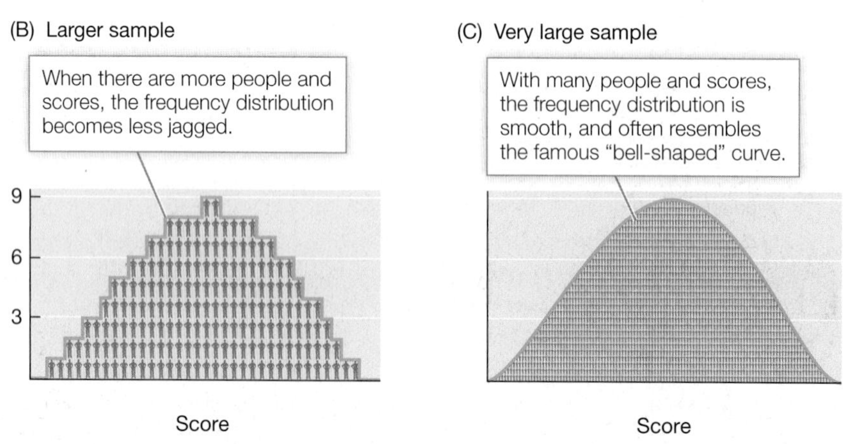
(B) Larger sample
When there are more people and scores, the frequency distribution becomes less jagged.
9
6
3
Score
(C) Very large sample
With many people and scores, the frequency distribution is smooth, and often resembles the famous "bell-shaped" curve.
Score

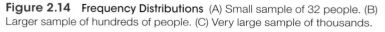

Figure 2.14 Frequency Distributions (A) Small sample of 32 people. (B) Larger sample of hundreds of people. (C) Very large sample of thousands.

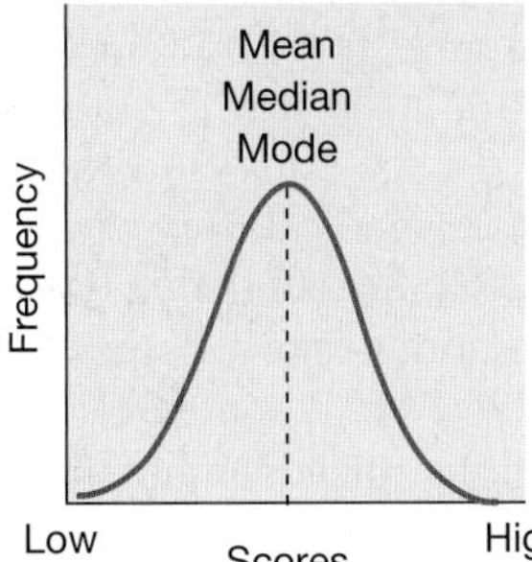

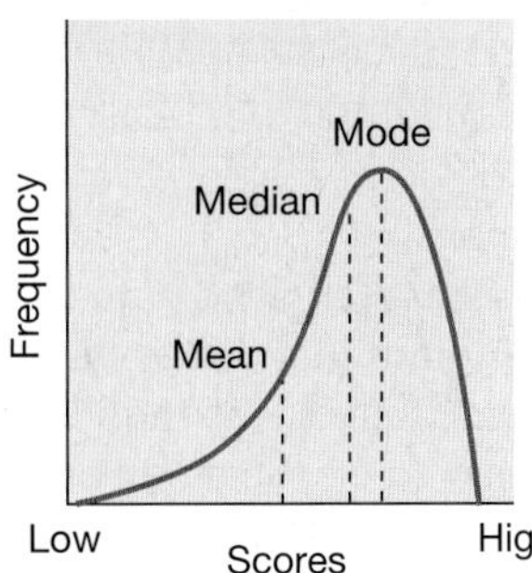

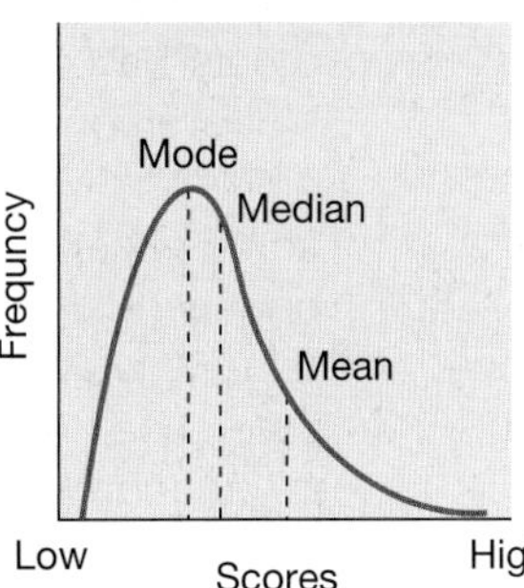

Figure 2.15 Comparing the Mean, Median, and Mode (A) In normal symmetrical distributions, the mean, median, and mode are identical. (B) In a negatively skewed distribution of more very low scores than very high scores, the distribution will not be symmetrical, and the measures of central tendency will differ. The outliers, the very low scores, pull the mean down considerably more than the median or mode. (C) A positively skewed distribution with many very high scores will have a higher mean. Note that here and in (B), the median falls somewhere between the mode and the mean.

When we gather scores from a large number of people, the frequency distribution often forms what is called a bell-shaped curve (statisticians call it the *normal* curve). In a normal frequency distribution, the mode is always easy to see, as it is the score on the *x*-axis that has the highest *y* value, in other words, the peak of the curve. That's the score that more people had than any other.

When a curve is symmetrical, as in **Figure 2.15A**, all three measures of central tendency will be the same. But sometimes scores are not distributed evenly, and so the shape of frequency distribution is not symmetrical, but *skewed* (**Figure 2.15B,C**). In those cases, the mode is still obvious—the *x* value where the curve is highest. But the median may be shifted by outliers, and the mean will be shifted even more (as in the case of Mr. Gates in the village).

Psychologists love statistics because we have to

So far we've talked as if when searching for differences, either across time or between experimental and control groups, it would be obvious that they exist. This may have been the case in the early days of science, when our understanding of the world was so primitive. In 1847, having doctors wash their hands between patients so dramatically reduced the spread of disease that the effect was obvious (Nuland, 2004). But in modern psychological research it's not always obvious whether measures taken from two different groups of people are truly different from one another. At least two factors make it difficult to tell whether the behavior of two groups of participants really differs. One is the "luck of the draw" when we select our participants in the first place, and the other is the tremendous variability in behavior across people (or animal subjects).

Despite our precaution to use random sampling to maximize our chances for a representative sample, it's rare that any two samples are exactly alike. If we gather ten random samples from the same population, and measure a particular behavior in the people in those samples, the ten means will probably differ at least somewhat across the samples. But if we really did gather the samples randomly from the same population, we can attribute those differences in sample means to random differences, the sort of variability that is due to pure chance alone. Maybe one random sample happened to include one or two people who are very unlike most other people. Having such people in the sample might make that group mean different from the other group means.

inferential statistics Mathematical procedures to help infer what the population is like based on a sample.

range The highest and lowest scores, used as a rough gauge of variability.

variance A statistical measure of the amount of variability in a population or sample.

standard deviation The average amount that each individual score falls above or below the mean, used to express variance.

Another problem is that modern psychologists are testing for more subtle influences than, say, whether eating fruit prevents scurvy. Psychology experiments have to take into account considerable variability in human behaviors. Not everyone in the experimental group will respond the same way to our manipulation. We will see different results from different groups subjected to the same experiment. In other words, there is a lot of variability in our participants and therefore in the measurements we gather from them. So how do we determine whether two groups are truly different from one another, or whether the difference between them is just due to random chance?

To address this question, scientists rely on **inferential statistics**, mathematical procedures to help infer what the population is like based on the sample we've gathered. In most of psychology, this means trying to estimate whether apparent differences between two samples are likely to represent genuine differences between the two populations the samples came from. The question is usually framed like this: How likely is it that this much of a difference in our two samples could be due to pure chance alone? In other words, if we gathered two samples from the very same population, how often would they differ by this much?

For example, to see if a drug helps relieve depression, we can draw random samples of 50 people with depression, and ask half of them to take the drug each day and the other half to take a sugar pill each day (as we'll discuss at the end of the chapter, we'll be careful not to let them know which treatment they are receiving). A month later we can test and see that the average depression score for the people given the drug is indeed lower than that of the people given the sugar pill. Could a difference between the means of that size happen by chance alone, or does this difference indicate that the drug actually works?

To determine if the two samples might be that different by chance alone, we need to have some idea of how much variability there is in the measure of interest. If there is a lot of variability in the measure, then group means that differ by 10 points might be common and could easily happen by chance alone. But if there is little variability, then mean differences of 10 points might indicate that the two groups really did differ. One way to gauge variability is the **range**, the lowest and highest scores we see. A very wide range indicates a lot of variability. A narrow range indicates little variability.

A more versatile measure is **variance**, a statistical measure of the amount of variability in a population or sample. The most common way of expressing variance is the **standard deviation**, the average amount that each individual differs from (*deviates* from) the mean (**Figure 2.16**). We can readily see that if there is a lot of variance in the population, then there will be a lot of variance in samples too. If there's a lot of variance across samples from the same population, then the means of those samples may differ quite a lot due to chance alone. In that case, we would need to see a larger difference in means before we'd consider two samples to be genuinely different from one another.

To talk about how big a difference is between groups, we typically talk about how different the two means are from one another in terms of number of standard deviations, sometimes referred to as *effect size*. If the mean score for women is 2 standard deviations greater than the mean score for men, that indicates a bigger difference than if they differ by only ½ a standard deviation.

Inferential statistics takes into account the standard deviation from two samples to estimate the probability that the differences in their means could be due to chance alone. If that big a difference in the means is unlikely to happen by chance, then the two groups may really differ. That outcome would suggest that our manipulation of the independent variable actually caused a change in the dependent variable. So perhaps the drug actually helped relieve depression, or playing video games improved eye–hand coordination. On the other hand, if the difference be-

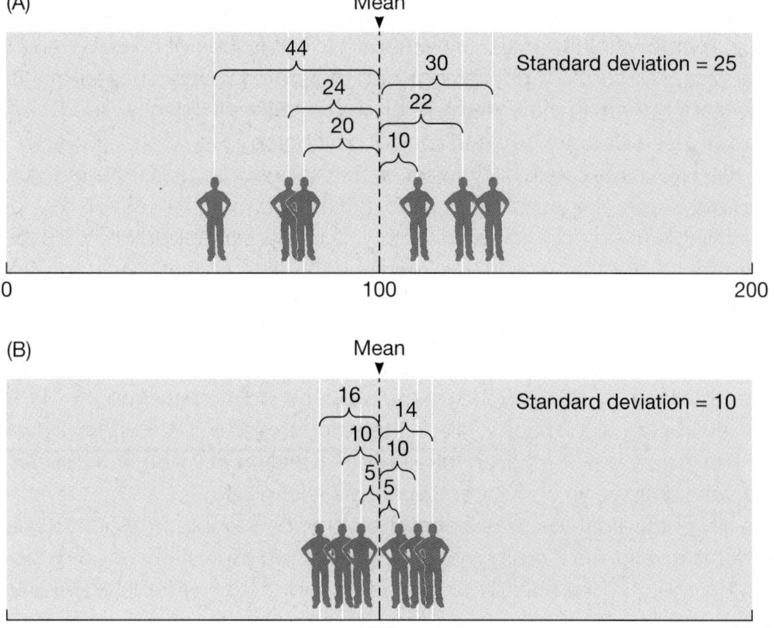

Figure 2.16 The Standard Deviation Is a Measure of Variance (A) In this sample, individuals deviate from the mean, on average, by 25 points. Note that whether their score is above or below the mean does not affect how far they deviate from the mean. (B) There is less variance in this sample, so the standard deviation is smaller, as individuals differ from the mean by 10 points on average.

tween the two sample means is no bigger than we could expect by chance alone, then our manipulation of the independent variable apparently had no effect on the dependent variable. Maybe the drug doesn't affect depression.

There are many inferential statistical tests for estimating the probability that a difference between two samples could be due to chance alone. These days, when computer programs do all the mathematical work for us, the most difficult aspect of inferential statistics is knowing which is the appropriate statistical test for the question we are asking. Assuming we apply the correct statistical test, it will calculate the ***p*-value**, the probability that the two samples could be this different due to chance alone. In the social and life sciences, there is a convention that if p is less than 0.05, then we will (tentatively) conclude that the two groups are different. A p-value of 0.05 ($p = 0.05$) means there is a 5% chance, or 1 chance in 20, that two samples from the very same population could be that different by pure chance alone. When p is less than 0.05, we say the difference between the two groups is **statistically significant**. Just because a difference is *statistically* significant, that doesn't mean it is significant in the sense of being important, or likely to make a big difference in how we see the world. It just means the difference is not likely to be due to pure chance or a random outcome.

In psychology experiments, we are often comparing whether two groups differ in their behavior, as measured by some test. For our conclusions to have any relevance to real life, it is important that those tests actually measure what we think they do, a topic we'll take up next.

***p*-value** The probability that the difference between two samples could occur by chance alone.

statistically significant A p-value chosen by convention as indicating that the differences are not likely due to chance. In psychology, this is generally that p is less than 0.05.

reliability The degree to which your measurement tool produces consistent, repeatable results.

validity The extent to which a test actually measures the trait it is intended to measure.

Psychological measures should be both reliable and valid

Two crucial issues for all sciences are **reliability**, the degree to which your measurement tool produces consistent, *repeatable* results, and **validity**, the degree to which your measurement tool actually measures what it's supposed to measure. A good measurement tool is both reliable and valid.

Reliability and validity are especially important for psychology, because unlike the speed of a falling object, or the amount of light coming from a star, or the amount of heat generated by a chemical reaction, most psychological processes cannot be directly observed. So in those cases we have to try to devise a

psychological test A way of measuring a psychological event or process.

unconscious bias Also called *implicit bias*. An inclination to prefer one type of person, object, or idea over others without being consciously aware of that preference.

psychological test, a way of measuring a psychological event or process, such as love, memory, intelligence, or personality. The issues of reliability and validity are important throughout psychology and therefore in every chapter of this book, but we'll apply them in more detail when we discuss intelligence (see Chapter 11), personality (see Chapter 14), and clinical psychology (see Chapter 16).

Of the two issues, reliability is an easier concept to understand and is also easier to evaluate in a psychological test. If a psychological test of, say, personality is reliable, then every time we apply it to a particular person, we should get similar results. In other words, the results should be repeatable, consistent. For example, if a bathroom scale reports a different weight every time we place the same bag of sugar on it, then the scale is not reliable. If the same person taking a psychological test gets wildly different scores at different times, then either the test is unreliable or the psychological process we're measuring is not stable. These examples also make it clear that an *unreliable test cannot possibly be valid*. That's why we don't even take up the question of whether a psychological test is valid until we've convinced ourselves it is reliable.

If a psychological test has been shown to be reliable, the next question is whether it is *valid*—is it really measuring what we think it is? For psychological tests, it is much more difficult to evaluate validity than reliability. Perfectly reasonable, intelligent psychologists may disagree on this issue, even if they are all considering the same information. We'll see this difficulty most clearly in Chapter 11 when we consider the issue of whether IQ tests actually measure "intelligence." The answer to this question depends on what we mean by "intelligence," and different experts have different ideas about what "intelligence" is or is not. Like all scientists, psychologists must always be concerned about whether their measures and tests are valid.

Assuming you have reliable and valid measures of behavior, how can you use those measures to gain a better understanding of behavior and mental processes?

Psychologists strive to avoid bias by withholding information

As we saw at the start of the chapter, even experts in musical performance or scientific aptitude can have their judgment biased by gender. The opposite of bias is to be open-minded or neutral. In this book we are concerned about bias in psychological judgments, so it is sometimes referred to as *psychological bias* or *cognitive bias*. A Wikipedia page on "list of cognitive biases" offers over 100 different examples that have been documented (so far), several of which we'll discuss in Chapter 10. Most important, these are biases that the person making the judgment is not consciously aware of. So each is sometimes referred to as an **unconscious bias** (or *implicit bias*), an inclination to prefer one type of person, object, or idea over others without being consciously aware of that preference. In other words, if we were to ask the female scientists whether they are aware of a conscious bias favoring male job applicants, most of them would answer no, even though, as a group, they clearly favored "John" over "Jennifer" for the position. In Chapter 15 we'll review compelling evidence that judges and juries are more likely to choose the death penalty for men convicted of murder if the men are African Americans, especially if their skin is darker. This is almost certainly an unconscious bias for most of the jurors—if asked, they would surely deny choosing the death penalty because the accused was black. Such a bias is in contrast to *explicit bias*, when people are aware that they prefer one type of person over another. A famous bias, without any serious consequence, is the preference of most Americans for Coke over Pepsi, as we discuss in **Box 2.2**.

Given the prevalence of biases that have been documented repeatedly in laboratories, I think most psychologists would agree that all human judgments are biased. The main issue is how profound the biases are and how much they

Skeptic at Large

BOX 2.2

The Pepsi Paradox

In the 1970s, an advertising campaign for Pepsi claimed that in blind taste tests, most people preferred Pepsi over Coca-Cola. I was a graduate student at UCLA during this campaign, which offered a great experimental opportunity in our undergraduate lab classes. Students were asked whether they preferred Coke or Pepsi. Then they were asked to taste from unlabeled cups of colas and state their preferences. Just as the campaign indicated, most people, even those who claimed they strongly preferred Coke, preferred Pepsi in the blind taste test. In lab section after lab section, year after year, the results were always the same. Yet at that time, and still today, many more people buy Coke than Pepsi.

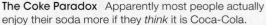

The Coke Paradox Apparently most people actually enjoy their soda more if they *think* it is Coca-Cola.

This is sometimes called the "Pepsi paradox" because people reliably prefer Coke only when they can see the branding information. One interpretation is that people are biased to choose Coke over Pepsi. The strong advertising campaigns have tricked them into drinking Coca-Cola even though they would get more enjoyment if they drank Pepsi. But wait a minute. Another interpretation is that, because of all that advertising, people *actually get more enjoyment by drinking from a bottle labeled Coke* than they would get drinking from a bottle labeled Pepsi. And indeed, having a Coke or Pepsi label on the bottle significantly affects people's stated preferences, no matter which cola is actually in the bottle (Woolfolk et al., 1983). Notice that both interpretations indicate that advertising really works—either it tricks you into choosing a cola that brings you less pleasure, or it provides you more pleasure by triggering reactions that go beyond the actual taste of the cola.

At least some brain imaging studies provide support for the latter explanation. In blind taste tests, most participants once again preferred Pepsi over Coke. But of course not everyone preferred Pepsi in the blind tests. Interestingly, whichever cola the participants preferred in these unlabeled trials also triggered greater activity in a brain region associated with flavors. In later tests, participants sampled two colas, one identified as either Coke or Pepsi, and the other left unidentified. In these tests, there was more activity in a particular part of the brain when people *knew they were drinking Coke* than during any other condition, including drinking *unlabeled* Coke (McClure et al., 2004). Knowing they were drinking Pepsi provided no boost to activity in that brain region. Later studies showed that people with damage to that same brain region had no preference for drinks labeled as Coke (Koenigs & Tranel, 2008). These results suggest that people really do enjoy their cola more as long as they *think* it is Coke. Why? Perhaps thinking we are drinking Coke triggers associations with advertising imagery and cultural ideas about drinking Coke. It makes us part of the in-crowd. It's an odd way to think about Coca-Cola's multimillion-dollar advertising budget. All that money really does bring you more enjoyment when you drink from a can displaying the Coke label.

vary from individual to individual. The only certain way to prevent humans from displaying an unconscious bias favoring a particular characteristic is to *withhold that information from them*. Thus in the case of orchestra auditions, judges were not allowed to see whether the musicians were men or women. Musical experts who are certain older violins are superior in fact like new violins just as well if they play them blindfolded (Fritz et al., 2014).

Nowhere is the importance of withholding information to control bias more prominent than in the testing of medicine. It has been repeatedly shown that when people are given a **placebo**, a pill or other treatment that has no known physiological effect, and are told to expect particular effects, they are likely to report having exactly those effects. The most common placebo is a sugar pill. Placebos have powerful effects on many conditions you might consider purely "physical,"

placebo A pill or other treatment that has no known medical effect.

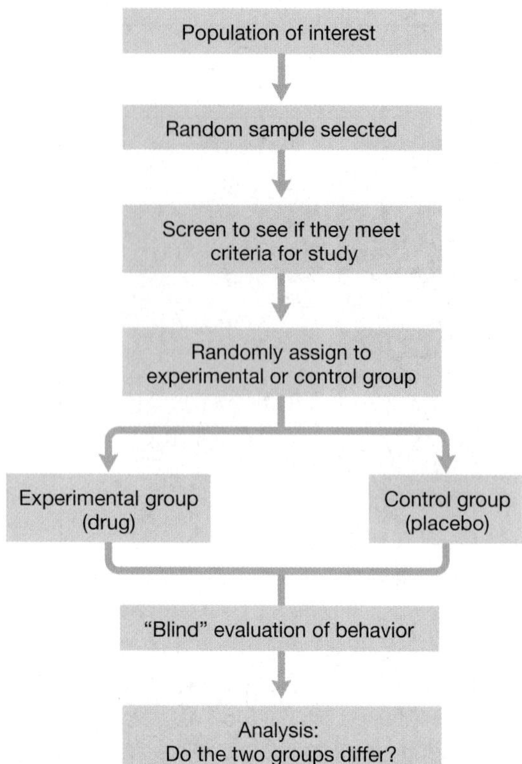

Figure 2.17 **Randomized, Double-Blind, Placebo-Controlled Studies** Such studies are the gold standard for evaluating medical and psychological treatments.

like arthritis pain (Zhang et al., 2008), high blood pressure (Asmar et al., 2001), insomnia (Huedo-Medina et al., 2012), and Parkinson's disease (Lidstone et al., 2010). It seems clear that it is the patient's *expectation* that makes the placebo effective, since large pills are more effective placebos than small pills (Buckalew & Ross, 1981) and expensive pills are more effective placebos than cheap pills (Waber et al., 2008).

This means that whenever we are asking whether a drug is effective for treating any ailment, we need to compare how well the drug works compared with a placebo. Such comparisons are called *placebo-controlled trials*. If drug and placebo are equally effective, then it makes no sense to approve use of the drug, which may have unanticipated harmful side effects.

For placebo-controlled trials to be maximally effective, it is important that the people receiving treatment be unaware of whether they are getting the drug or the placebo. If the person knows he's just getting a sugar pill, he won't have the expectation of improvement and so won't respond. Not only is it important for participants to be unaware of which pill they're taking, it's also important that the *physician* be unaware of which pill each participant is taking. After all, if the doctor knows that someone is taking a placebo, the doctor may have an unconscious bias to see less of a response in the patient's symptoms, or may be less effective at reassuring the patient that the drug might work (Gracely et al., 1985). When both the patient and the doctor are "blind" to the patient's treatment, the study is called a *double-blind trial*. Finally, the strongest test of the drug versus the placebo is to be sure the patients in the two groups are as similar as possible in the severity of their ailment, their susceptibility to placebos, and so on. The best way to ensure that is to have the assignment of each patient be entirely *random*. Thus the gold standard for evaluating drug effectiveness is the **randomized, double-blind, placebo-controlled trial**, where patients are randomly assigned to either the drug or placebo treatment, and neither the patient nor the person evaluating his progress knows which group he is in until the study is over (**Figure 2.17**). We'll discuss the importance of such trials for evaluating antidepression medication at the end of this chapter.

randomized, double-blind, placebo-controlled trial The best form of assessment for evaluating drug effectiveness, in which patients are randomly assigned to either the drug or placebo treatment, and neither the patient nor the person evaluating his progress knows which group he is in.

Recognizing the hazards of bias distorting judgment, good scientists work hard to avoid the possibility of their own biases when measuring behavior. This is why in clinical trials of drug effects on depression or schizophrenia, it's important for the scientist to be in the dark about whether the patient being evaluated is on the drug or the placebo. Similarly, a researcher asking if a certain experience makes a person more empathetic, or a certain hormone makes a rat more anxious, must be careful when she is evaluating the behavior of either the person or the rat. If the researcher knows which person was given the experience, or which rat was given the hormone, her expectations about the outcome might color her evaluation of the behavior. So in the best studies, the person evaluating an individual's behavior is unaware of which treatment the individual received. In that case we say the researcher was "blind" to which treatment the individual received. These days, blind evaluation of behavior is often accomplished by videotaping the individual's behavior. Then two or more researchers who are uninformed about the individual's treatment can independently score the behavior to get unbiased measures. (This is also a common test for whether the behavioral measure is reliable—do different judges come up with similar scores when they watch the same video?)

Now that you've seen a wider range of psychological research, you can see the progression from describing behavior to noting changes in variables, testing hypotheses to explain the behavior, and evaluating which findings withstand the test of time. This progression is detailed in **Table 2.1**.

■ TABLE 2.1 Typical Stages of Psychological Research

	Research stage			
	Descriptive (Observe and measure behavior.)	Correlational (Find commonalities, make predictions.)	Experimental (Test hypotheses to explain the behavior.)	Public discourse (Test the reliability of the findings.)
ACTIVITY	Naturalistic observations, case studies, surveys	Statistical analysis to look for two or more behaviors that covary	Experiments manipulating an independent variable to test its effect on a dependent variable	Can other labs replicate the findings? Are there enough reports for a meta-analysis?
EXAMPLE	Playing video games and doing surgery both require good eye-hand coordination.	Those surgeons who play more video games make fewer mistakes in surgery.	People randomly assigned to play video games show improved eye-hand coordination and changes in brain structure compared with control groups.	Other labs get similar results, suggesting video game play really does improve eye-hand coordination.

There are standards of ethical conduct in human and animal experimentation

There are times when the interests of scientists asking a question may be in conflict with the interests of the people being studied. Perhaps the most infamous example is the **Tuskegee** (Tuss-KEE-gee) **syphilis study**, when the U.S. Public Health Service and the federal Centers for Disease Control and Prevention carefully followed the progression of the sexually transmitted disease syphilis in hundreds of poor African American men in Tuskegee, Alabama, for 40 years. The science was straightforward: compare an experimental group of men who had contracted syphilis with a control group of men who did not have syphilis to estimate the effect of the disease on health. When the study began in 1932, known treatments for the disease were ineffective, and so this research design made sense. But by 1947 it was widely known that a standard regimen of penicillin would cure syphilis. Yet the scientists *continued the study for another 25 years, never telling the infected men that they had the disease and taking no steps to get them effective treatment.* In fact, because the study supplied the men with free medical care, they were unlikely to see an outside doctor who, upon diagnosing the disease, would have cured them (Centers for Disease Control and Prevention, 2013). In those 25 years, many of the men died of the disease, some spread the disease to their wives, and some had children born with the disease. When these details were leaked to the public in 1972, the scandal led to the enactment of regulations to protect humans involved in scientific experiments (**Figure 2.18**). Within a few years Congress passed the National Research Act, creating guidelines for the ethical conduct of research.

Tuskegee syphilis study A study in which the U.S. Public Health Service and the Centers for Disease Control and Prevention followed the progression of syphilis in hundreds of poor African American men in Tuskegee, Alabama, without providing them with a known cure for the disease.

Institutional Review Board (IRB) A group of individuals convened by an institution to ensure studies involving humans meet ethical standards.

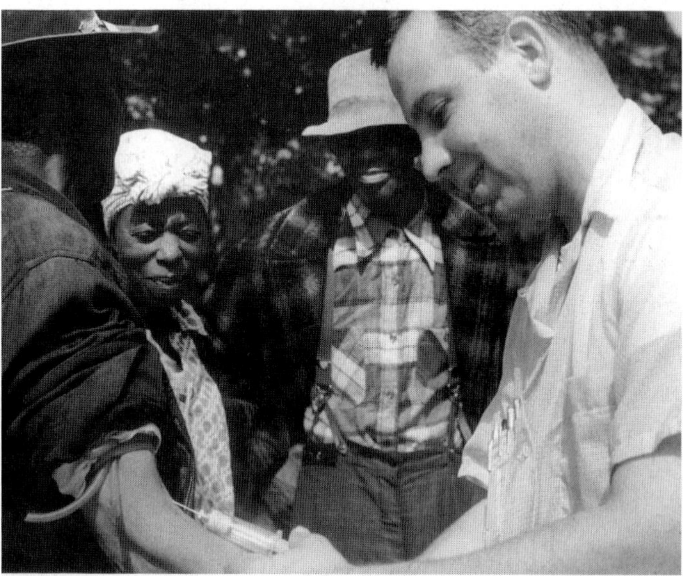

Figure 2.18 The Tuskegee Syphilis Study Most of the people conducting the study were middle-class white men, while all of the participants were poor African American men.

Today scientists are required to get approval from their institution before they can even begin any research on humans or other vertebrate species. Research on humans must be approved by an **Institutional Review Board (IRB)**. The composition and reviewing function of the IRB is dictated by a code of regulations (http://www.hhs.gov/ohrp/humansubjects/guidance/45cfr46.html). All research universities con-

informed consent The process of informing participants in a study about what they'll be doing and any risks they face, then getting their active agreement beforehand. This is required by IRBs.

Institutional Animal Care and Use Committee (IACUC) A group of individuals convened by an institution to review and approve the proposed research with animals before it can begin.

vene IRBs, required to include at least one community member who has no financial ties to the institution, that must approve any research. Researchers must fully describe the proposed research and satisfy the IRB that it will meet ethical standards before they can even begin the study. The primary concern of the IRB is the safety of participants, so the IRB must consider any *adverse events* that might occur. In Chapter 15 we'll see examples of old experiments that IRBs would probably not approve today for fear of the psychological harm they might cause participants. The IRB also considers the privacy of participants and any concerns about confidential information that might be revealed to others. Among other things, IRBs require **informed consent**, the process of informing participants about what they'll be doing and any risks they face, then getting their active agreement beforehand. If, as is often the case in psychology research, some information must be withheld from the participants, the investigator is required to *debrief* them afterward, informing them what the study was about, and revealing any deception that was involved and why it was necessary.

For research with animals, an **Institutional Animal Care and Use Committee (IACUC)** must review and approve the proposed research before it can begin. As with IRBs, every IACUC must have at least one community member who has no connection to the institution so he or she can feel free to voice objections to any proposed research without fear of reprisal. The mandate of the IACUC is to evaluate the scientific rationale for the proposed study and to avoid or minimize any discomfort, stress, or pain to the animals, consistent with the Animal Welfare Act and guidelines of the National Institutes of Health (NIH). The IACUC inspects all animal-use facilities twice a year, and both the IACUC and the facilities are subject to surprise visits from the U.S. Department of Agriculture (USDA) to ensure compliance with all federal guidelines.

The review process, whether by an IRB or IACUC, is typically a multistep process. It is rare that a proposal is approved the first time an investigator submits it. Usually the board asks for more information from the investigator, and often the board may require the investigator to modify the proposed research to ensure it meets ethical standards. As the investigator cannot start the study until she receives approval, she either satisfies the board or abandons the study. Almost always, the investigator finds a way to conduct the study in such a way that the board can approve it. There's no way for the investigator to get around this process if the results are to be published one day.

Among researchers there is a continuing discussion about whether the people we study should be referred to as "subjects," as had been the convention throughout the twentieth century. Because people in studies should have informed consent before deciding to participate, some researchers feel they should be considered "participants" (Boynton, 1998), not subjects. Among other things, there is the concern that scientists who consider these people "subjects" may accord them less dignity and respect. In other words, they may subject people to treatment they would not offer to a voluntary participant. In the United States, all federal regulations regarding experimentation with people still refer to them as *subjects*, and so other researchers think it is important to use that term in scientific publications to be consistent with those regulations (Resnik & Bond, 2007). While the publication manual of the American Psychological Association asserts that the term "subject" can be applied to humans (American Psychological Association, 2010), there seems to be a trend to refer to people in studies as participants. Following that lead, this book will refer to animal *subjects* (they don't give consent) and human *participants*.

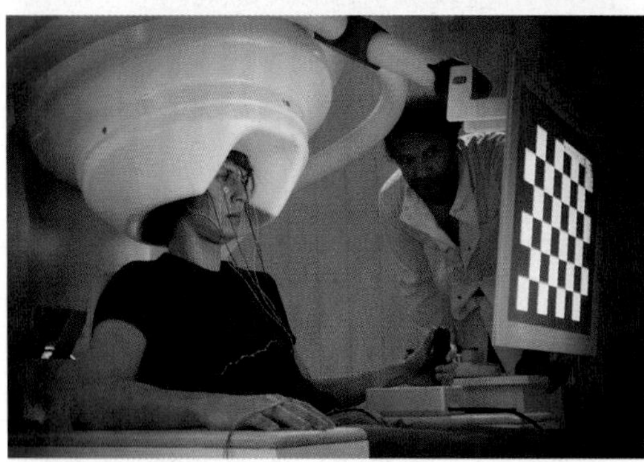

A Subject and a Participant Ethical standards require people to be informed participants in any study.

Another issue concerning ethical scientific behavior is whether researchers should be required to report *all* results, including those that do not support their favored hypotheses. We'll examine the consequences of selective reporting next to conclude the chapter.

The Cutting Edge

Meta-Analysis Casts Doubt on Antidepressant Drugs

Perhaps the most controversial placebo effect in psychology concerns antidepressants. As we'll discuss in detail in Chapter 16, the currently most effective antidepressants are part of a class of drugs called selective serotonin reuptake inhibitors (SSRIs). In randomized, double-blind, placebo-controlled trials of SSRI drugs, about a third of the people suffering depression who were given placebos reported improvement (Khan et al., 2012). So presumably some of the people given the antidepressant drug improved not because of anything the drug did, but because, like the people given the placebo, they expected the pill to work, or because they were going to get better anyway.

One problem plaguing the interpretation of these studies is that the pharmaceutical companies conducting the trials may choose to not publish the results. Hoping to sell the drug someday, they often fail to report those trials where the drug was no better than the placebo. Rather, they do several trials and tend to publish, and publicize, only those that show an effect. Obviously such practices work to exaggerate the effectiveness of the antidepressants. So researchers used the Freedom of Information Act to gain access to the unreported trials for SSRI drugs and conducted a meta-analysis (Fournier et al., 2010), asking whether, when all the trials, not just the published trials, were examined, the drugs worked any better than the placebo? They also went back and got information about the severity of depression in many of the patients.

Their analysis indicated that for people with mild to moderate depression, which constituted the vast majority of cases (approximately 87%), the placebo was just as effective as the antidepressant medication (**Figure 2.19**).

They concluded that only a minority of people with the most severe cases of depression benefitted from SSRI medication more than if they had received placebos. Thus most people currently taking SSRI medication apparently receive no more benefit than if they were taking placebos.

While this meta-analysis remains controversial, there is little dispute that many people taking SSRIs are benefitting because of the placebo effect rather than the drug itself. However, given the potentially fatal consequences of depression posed by the threat of suicide, there is no easy answer to the question of whether a person who has been diagnosed with depression should try medication. Even taking a placebo might save his life.

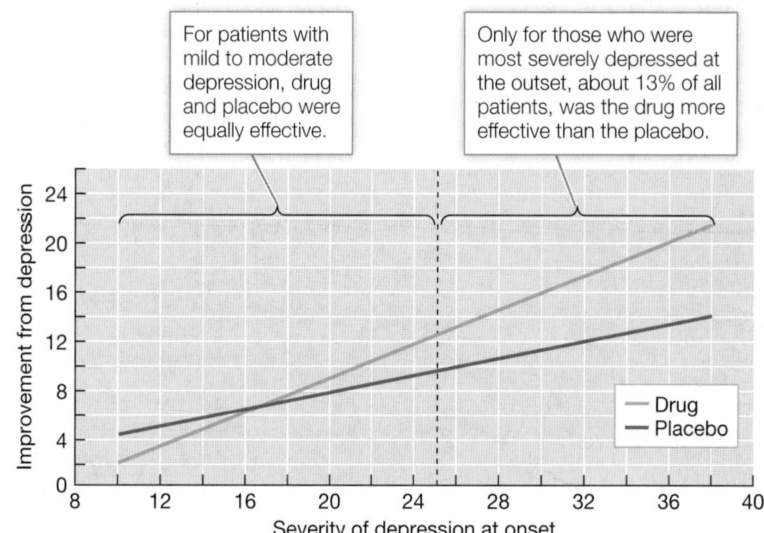
For patients with mild to moderate depression, drug and placebo were equally effective.
Only for those who were most severely depressed at the outset, about 13% of all patients, was the drug more effective than the placebo.
Improvement from depression
0
4
8
12
16
20
24
8
12
16
20
24
28
32
36
40
Severity of depression at onset
Drug
Placebo

Figure 2.19 **Are Antidepressants More Effective Than Placebos?** (After Fournier et al., 2010.)

2.2 SUMMARY

- We study *samples* of individuals in hopes of understanding the behavior of the *population* they are drawn from.
- In a *random sample*, every member of the population has an equal chance of being selected, and selection of one individual has no effect on who is selected next. A random sample offers the best chance for a *representative sample*.
- *Measures of central tendency* include the *mean* (or average), the *median* (the middle score, which is greater than half the scores and lower than the other half), and the *mode* (the single most common score).
- *Variance* is a statistical measure of variability, usually expressed as the *standard deviation*, the average difference, in either direction, of the scores from the mean.
- *Inferential statistics* provides information on the reliability of information derived from samples, including their means and standard deviations, to help researchers calculate the probability that the populations the samples were derived from truly differ. This is usually reported as a *p*-value, the probability that two samples could differ this much by pure chance alone.
- By convention, psychologists say the difference between two groups is *statistically significant* if the *p*-value is less than 0.05, meaning one would expect a difference that large only 5 times in 100 if the two populations were actually equivalent.
- Psychological measures should exhibit both *reliability*, meaning they provide consistent, repeatable results, and *validity*, meaning they actually measure what they are said to measure.
- Experiments have revealed many cognitive biases, inclinations to reach unfair or inaccurate judgments. An example is the *placebo* effect, the tendency of people to report that pills had the expected effect even if they were merely sugar pills. Thus the gold standard for evaluating medical or psychological treatments is the *randomized, double-blind, placebo-controlled trial*.
- To ensure that studies involving humans and animals meet ethical standards, researchers must submit detailed plans for any experiment to review by either an *Institutional Review Board* (*IRB*) in the case of studies of humans, or an *Institutional Animal Care and Use Committee* (*IACUC*) for animal studies. IRBs strive to ensure the safety and privacy of any people being studied, and require that participants be provided *informed consent*.
- IACUCs require that investigators avoid or minimize any discomfort, stress, or pain to animals as mandated by federal guidelines.

REVIEW QUESTIONS

1. Explain how random sampling improves our chances of drawing a representative sample.
2. What are advantages and disadvantages of each of the three measures of central tendency?
3. How do inferential statistics guide us in the process of testing hypotheses?
4. Describe reliability and validity and how they apply to psychological measures.
5. What is a placebo, and how do modern studies use placebos to evaluate the effectiveness of treatments?
6. What are the boards that must approve experiments on humans or other animals before they can begin, and what are the goals of that review process?

Food for Thought

Do you think an ethical lapse as large as in the Tuskegee syphilis study could happen today? Why or why not?

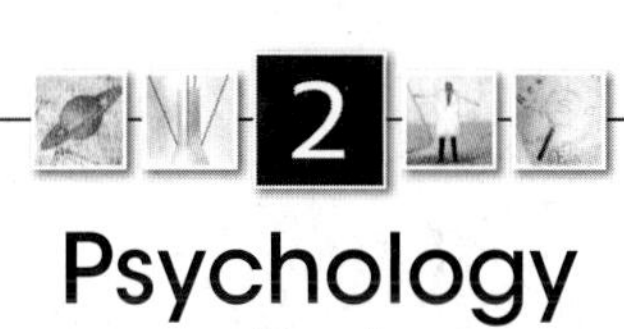

Psychology as a Science

Are women musicians inferior?

The world of professional musicians is intensely competitive. Typically there are over 100 passionate musicians auditioning for every position with a major symphony orchestra, all hoping to spend the rest of their lives making the music they love. With so few positions, only the best of the best have any hope of being hired.

For most of the twentieth century, a glance at any of the "big five" U.S. orchestras would have suggested that men must be better musicians than women, because only about 5% of the players were female. Among the experts in charge of screening applicants, men were deemed to be better musicians, either because they were more passionate, or more dedicated, or more innately talented than women (Simon, 1967). An editorial titled "Why women musicians are inferior" summed up the prevalent attitude in 1938: "The woman musician was never born capable of sending anyone further than the nearest exit" (*Down Beat*, 1938).

But an odd thing happened in the 1960s when several orchestras made a simple change in the auditioning process—having the musicians play behind a screen. Then the committee judges, told only the musician's application number, were free to concentrate on the sound produced, without any visual distractions. Upon establishment of the process of these "blind" auditions, the hiring of women musicians for symphony orchestras rose dramatically, so that by the year 2000 nearly half the new hires were women (Goldin & Rouse, 2001). It would appear that before blind auditions, the committee found women musicians inferior *because committee members knew they were women*. That is, the hiring process was skewed by *bias*.

You might think bias would be found only in the arts, where judgments may seem more subjective than in, say, science. But when researchers asked a group of scientists to rate the qualifications of someone applying for a job as a laboratory manager, it turned out that an applicant named "John" was rated significantly more competent than an applicant named "Jennifer," even though the resumes were otherwise identical. What's more, the scientists suggested a starting salary $4,000 higher for John than for Jennifer (Moss-Racusin et al., 2012). Even *female scientists* preferred John over Jennifer. What's going on here?

Think Like a Psychologist:

Principles in Action

Whenever we encounter any interesting behavior we should consider the four principles. Here are some ways that the four principles relate to our opening story about women applicants for a lab job.

MACHINE

The mind is a product of a physical machine, the brain.

We can detect the influence of bias on the workings of the brain. In Chapter 15 we'll learn about the Implicit Association Test (IAT), which reveals that the brain needs a little more time to associate jobs in science with women than with men.

UNCONSCIOUS

We are consciously aware of only a small part of our mental activity.

The scientists evaluating Jennifer's and John's applications were unconsciously biased against women, and the musical judges probably were too. If left unaware of how much this bias can affect their judgment, they might never consider taking steps to neutralize it.

SOCIAL

We constantly modify our behavior, beliefs, and attitudes according to what we perceive about the people around us.

The beliefs that one sex has a greater aptitude for music or for science originated in our culture and are perpetuated by social interactions. We can only speculate about where those attitudes originally arose in our history, and whether they will fade away in the future.

EXPERIENCE

Our experiences physically alter the structure and function of the brain.

Both the music judges and the scientists absorbed the ideas about gender differences in aptitude in the course of growing up in our culture, an experience that affected their developing brains enough to instill a bias in their judgment. Withholding information about gender would prevent that bias from affecting decisions.

KEY TERMS

case study, 32
Clever Hans, 38
confounding variable, 35
control group, 39
correlation coefficient, 33
covary, 33
dependent variable, 39
descriptive method, 31
experimental group, 39
experimentation, 38
frequency distributions, 48
hypothesis, 37
independent variable, 38
inferential statistics, 50
informed consent, 56
Institutional Animal Care and Use Committee (IACUC), 56
Institutional Review Board (IRB), 55
mean, 47
measure of central tendency, 47
median, 48
meta-analysis, 40
mode, 48
observation, 31
Occam's razor, 37
outlier, 48
placebo, 53
population, 45
psychological test, 52
***p*-value,** 51
randomized, double-blind, placebo-controlled trial, 54
random samples, 45
range, 50
reliability, 51
replication, 39
representative sample, 45
sample, 45
spurious correlations, 35
standard deviation, 50
statistically significant, 51
strong inference, 41
study population, 46
surveys, 32
theory, 42
Tuskegee syphilis study, 55
unconscious bias, 52
validity, 51
variables, 31
variance, 50

QUIZ YOURSELF

1. What is a quantitative, statistical measure of how closely two variables fluctuate together?
   a. Correlation coefficient
   b. Frequency distribution
   c. Arithmetic mean
   d. Expected value
2. A third factor that affects both variables of interest, causing them to covary even though there is no causal relationship between them, is
   a. an independent variable.
   b. a confounding variable.
   c. a dependent variable.
   d. a manipulated variable.
3. The statistical measure of variability that is the average amount by which scores differ from the mean is
   a. range.
   b. arithmetic mean.
   c. standard deviation.
   d. median.
4. In the social and life sciences, the convention for concluding that two groups are actually different is that
   a. $r > 0.75$.
   b. $r < 0.0$.
   c. $p > 0.10$.
   d. $p < 0.05$.
5. An inclination to prefer one type of person, object, or idea over others without being consciously aware of that preference is
   a. an unconscious bias.
   b. the placebo effect.
   c. a logical fallacy.
   d. a weak inference.
6. A ________ is a group of hypotheses about a particular set of phenomena that have survived testing and that are compatible with each other.
7. A rule of thumb when evaluating hypotheses is the principle of ________, which states that when choosing between competing hypotheses, the simpler one is usually better.
8. A ________ is a careful review of many studies that tries to gauge whether there really is an effect of the manipulation on the behavior of interest.
9. The entire set of individuals we want to study is the ________, while the subset we actually study is the ________.
10. The ________ is a study where patients are randomly assigned to either the drug or placebo treatment and neither the patient nor the person evaluating his progress knows which group he is in.

1. a; 2. b; 3. c; 4. d; 5. a; 6. theory; 7. Occam's razor; 8. meta-analysis; 9. population, sample; 10. randomized, double-blind, placebo-controlled trial

http://
CUTLER

The Neuroscience of Behavior

The Laughing Brain

Deidre never knew when she might suddenly suffer a *seizure,* a loss of consciousness and convulsions, the uncontrollable, rhythmic movements of her whole body. The seizures were a symptom of the disorder *epilepsy*, caused by electrical malfunctions in her brain. Medications that often control epileptic seizures didn't work for Deidre. The seizures weren't just embarrassing—they left her vulnerable to accidents. How would she ever be able to drive safely? So Deidre agreed to try something drastic—letting doctors implant tiny wires through her skull to pinpoint exactly where in her brain the electrical problems began. From this information the doctors could decide whether to remove that part of the brain, which should stop the seizures.

When the doctors carefully passed a tiny electrical current through each wire in turn, they found that stimulating the wire to a particular part of the brain elicited a reliable change in Deidre's behavior—she laughed. You might think that Deidre would be puzzled by her own sudden laughter, but she wasn't told when the wires were stimulated and she never seemed to guess they were causing her to laugh. When the doctors asked why she was laughing, Deidre always offered a reason. "You guys standing there, you're so funny!" Stimulating that part of the brain didn't just cause Deidre to laugh, it also affected her *mind*, causing her to be *amused* by whatever happened to be going on. If two doctors were standing there in lab coats, she interpreted their behavior as humorous. Presumably this same part of her brain was normally active when Deidre heard a funny joke.

Deidre's behavior demonstrated that even a mental process as elusive as humor is a product of a machine: give the machine a tiny zap of electricity and Deidre would feel amused without even hearing a joke. Deidre's epilepsy was also a result of electrical activity—uncontrolled electrical activity—in that marvelously complex machine between her ears. Why does electrical activity in the brain affect behavior so profoundly? In this chapter we'll find out.

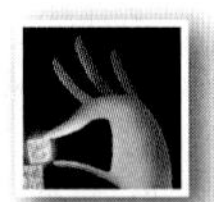

Chapter Preview

mind A process going on in the brain that includes all thoughts and feelings.

neuroscience The study of the nervous system.

neurons Also called *nerve cells*. Cells specialized to process information, making up the nervous system.

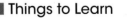

Does Deidre's reaction to electrical stimulation of her brain surprise you? You may think that you are entirely in charge of what you do and that your sense of humor is central to who you are as a person. So what does it mean if someone could stick a wire in your head and cause you to find something funny by applying a little current with an AA battery? It's surprising to find that our interactions with the world could be so profoundly altered by a tiny trickle of electricity. Yet electrical stimulation of one part of the brain may cause a person to laugh, while stimulating another part may induce fear, or make the eyes blink, or make the person stand up and remove some clothes.

These and many other experiments that we'll encounter in this book demonstrate that the brain is indeed a machine. As we'll see in this chapter, this machine relies on electricity and chemicals to work, so that's why tampering with electrical or chemical processes in the brain can affect our vision, emotion, or memory. To understand how we feel, think, and behave, we need to learn what this remarkable machine is made of and how it works.

Our goal in this chapter is to explain how the brain is structured and how it functions. In effect, you'll be learning about the machine we call the brain and the way its parts are connected to one another. This machine allows us to interpret the world around us and react to it. Let's define the **mind** as a *process* going on in the brain that includes all thoughts and feelings: experiencing the world through all our senses, reasoning, paying attention, remembering, feeling emotions, deciding what to do next, imagining, and even giving us the *self-awareness* of these thoughts and feelings. The mind isn't an object that we can pick up or see; it is a complicated *process* going on in the brain machine. We can learn some things about the process by studying the machine.

The brain is part of a broader biological system called the nervous system, which is the subject of the field called **neuroscience**. We'll start our study of neuroscience by examining the microscopic parts of the nervous system and communication among those parts. We'll find that the brain is made up of billions of cells known as **neurons** (or *nerve cells*), and that each one is a tiny information processor. These tiny processors are busily communicating with each other, using chemicals and tiny trickles of electricity. Next we'll see how putting billions of neurons together makes the nervous system, how different parts of the nervous system control different behaviors, and then how we can study brain mechanisms of behavior. Once we've covered this material, we'll see that some traditional distinctions between psychology and biology seem rather blurry, indicating that in fact psychology and biology are simply two different scientific approaches to understand the same thing.

Things to Learn

- Different parts of a neuron
- How neurons communicate with other cells
- Some important neurotransmitters
- Three functional classes of neurons
- Reflexes versus neural networks

3.1 The Structure of the Nervous System: A Microscopic View

In the 1600s scientists began using microscopes to examine organisms and discovered that the basic structural and functional unit of all life is the *cell*, a small packet of fluid called *cytoplasm* that is enclosed in a *membrane*. Within the cytoplasm are many tiny structures, including a spherical *nucleus* (**Figure 3.1A**), which we now know contains the tightly wound strands of DNA, called chromosomes, that we will discuss in Chapter 4.

Neurons in the brain are specialized to process information and use chemicals to communicate with one another, which is why a wide variety of drugs af-

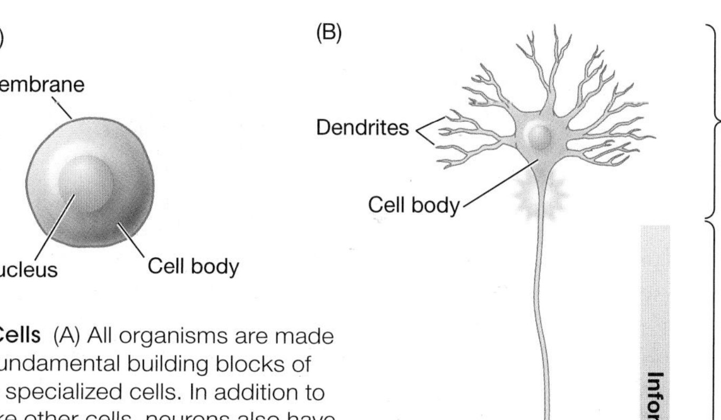

...and travels down the axon.

Figure 3.1 **Neurons, or Nerve Cells** (A) All organisms are made up of microscopic cells, the most fundamental building blocks of life. (B) Neurons, or nerve cells, are specialized cells. In addition to having a cell body and a nucleus like other cells, neurons also have extensions called dendrites, which receive information, and an extension called an axon, which passes information on to other cells.

fect our mind. Brain cells also use electricity to analyze these chemical signals, which is why tiny electrical currents in certain spots in Deidre's brain made her feel amused. Once you've learned more about individual brain cells and how they communicate with each other, we'll see how they work together to make a functional brain.

The brain contains billions of neurons, or nerve cells

Your brain contains nearly 100 billion neurons (Herculano-Houzel, 2012). Neurons vary in size and shape, but almost all have certain common structures in addition to cytoplasm and a nucleus within a membrane. The part of a cell surrounding the nucleus is called the **cell body** or *soma,* but unlike other cells, neurons have long extensions coming off the cell body (**Figure 3.1B**). If you think of an ordinary cell as a round ball, neurons are more like an inflated rubber glove with fingers sticking out.

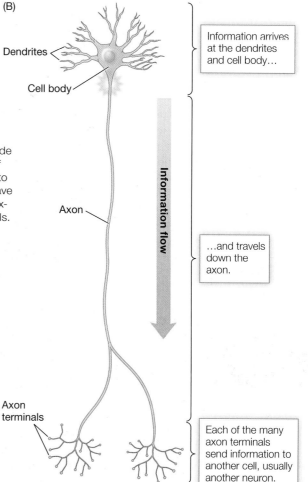

Neurons use these fingerlike extensions to communicate with one another. The extensions come in two types: one to receive information and one to send information. The branchlike extensions that *receive* signals from other cells are called **dendrites**, and most neurons have several dendrites. Each neuron also *sends* signals to other cells through a single **axon**, a cylinder that is usually thinner than a dendrite. Only one axon extends from the neuronal cell body, but the tips of the axon usually branch into many different endings called **axon terminals**, which pass messages to other cells. Because axon terminals spread out a bit at the very tip, forming a buttonlike shape, they are sometimes called *terminal buttons*.

In addition to neurons, the brain is also made up of smaller cells called **glia** (or *glial cells*). The name glia derives from the Latin word for "glue," because scientists once thought these cells acted like glue to keep clumps of neurons together. Today we know that glia are quite active, regulating the strength of connections between neurons. Nevertheless, most of what we know about brain function comes from the study of neurons, so we will discuss neurons for most of this chapter.

Each neuron uses an internal electrical system to sum up all the inputs arriving at its dendrites from other neurons. If the sum of the inputs is strong enough, the neuron will then send an electrical signal, called an *action potential* or nerve impulse, down its axon and each of its many branches. We'll discuss these electrical signals in more detail in Section 3.2, after you've learned more about

cell body Also called *soma*. The part of a cell surrounding the nucleus.

dendrite One of the extensions of a neuron's cell body that receives information.

axon A single extension from the nerve cell that carries nerve impulses from the cell body to other cells.

axon terminal Also called *terminal button*. The end of an axon that passes information to other cells.

glia Also called *glial cells*. Brain cells that regulate the strength of connections between neurons.

neurotransmitter Also called *transmitter*. The chemical used by a neuron to transmit information to another cell.

synapse A specialized junction where the axon terminal of a neuron communicates with another cell.

synaptic cleft The tiny, fluid-filled gap between a neuron's axon terminal and another cell.

vesicles Microscopic spheres in a neuron that contain neurotransmitter molecules to be released into the synaptic cleft.

neurotransmitter receptors Also called *receptors*. Large protein molecules, embedded in the cell membrane, to which neurotransmitters can bind.

neuron structures. When the action potential arrives at the end of a branch, the axon terminal releases a chemical called a **neurotransmitter** (or simply a *transmitter*). While sometimes the release of neurotransmitter activates some part of the body (for example, making a muscle twitch), most neurons release the chemical to send a message to another neuron, as we'll discuss next.

Neurons communicate with each other at synapses

We've defined dendrites as neuronal extensions that gather information and the axon as a neuronal extension that sends information to other neurons. Right now, in your brain, billions of axons are sending information to billions of dendrites (try not to get dizzy). How is the information transmitted?

The short answer is that one neuron sends information to another using tiny amounts of a chemical neurotransmitter. To really answer this question, let's consider an axon terminal of one neuron that ends right next to the dendrite of another neuron, as shown in **Figure 3.2A**. The axon tip and the dendrite are very close together (less than a millionth of an inch). The place where an axon of one neuron meets a dendrite of another is called a **synapse**, a specialized junction where the axon terminal of a neuron communicates with another cell. The tiny, fluid-filled gap between the axon terminal and the dendrite is called the **synaptic cleft** (or gap). The axon terminal releases minute amounts of neurotransmitter into the synaptic cleft (**Figure 3.2B**). The neurotransmitter molecules are packaged inside the axon terminal in microscopic spheres called **vesicles**. When the axon terminal releases neurotransmitter, many vesicles empty their contents at once into the synaptic cleft.

The released neurotransmitter quickly reaches the other side of the synaptic cleft, where it binds briefly to **neurotransmitter receptors** on the membrane of the other neuron. The receptors are said to be on the membrane of the *post*-synaptic neuron whereas the neuron that is sending the signal is known as the *pre*-synaptic neuron. Once the neurotransmitter makes contact with the post-synaptic neuron, the signal from the axon of the other neuron is complete. Note that information passes in only *one direction* at the synapse: one neuron's axon tip releases a chemical, and the receptors of another neuron respond to it. There are many different neurotransmitters in the brain, and some scientists have proposed that disorders such as schizophrenia and depression are caused by the release of too much or too little neurotransmitter (as will be discussed in Chapter 16).

Axons usually synapse on dendrites, but sometimes they synapse on the cell body of a neuron, and sometimes axons synapse on cells other than neurons. For example, axons from your spinal cord synapse on your muscles. When those axons release neurotransmitter onto a muscle, it contracts, moving your hand, foot, or elbow, depending on which muscle received the signal.

The human brain has an estimated 10^{15} synapses (Pakkenberg et al., 2003). This is a remarkably large number: a "1" with 15 zeros after it. If you gathered that many grains of sand, each 1 mm across, they would fill a cube with each side longer than an American football field. Such vast networks of connections are responsible for all of humanity's achievements.

Neurotransmitters transfer information across synapses

How does the released neurotransmitter affect the target cell? As mentioned above, on the receiving portion of a cell, such as a dendrite, are large molecules called neurotransmitter receptors (or simply, *receptors*) that detect a specific neurotransmitter (**Figure 3.2C**). Receptors are embedded in the cell membrane. Part of each receptor molecule sticks *outside* the cell, and another part of the molecule passes through the membrane and is *inside* the cell.

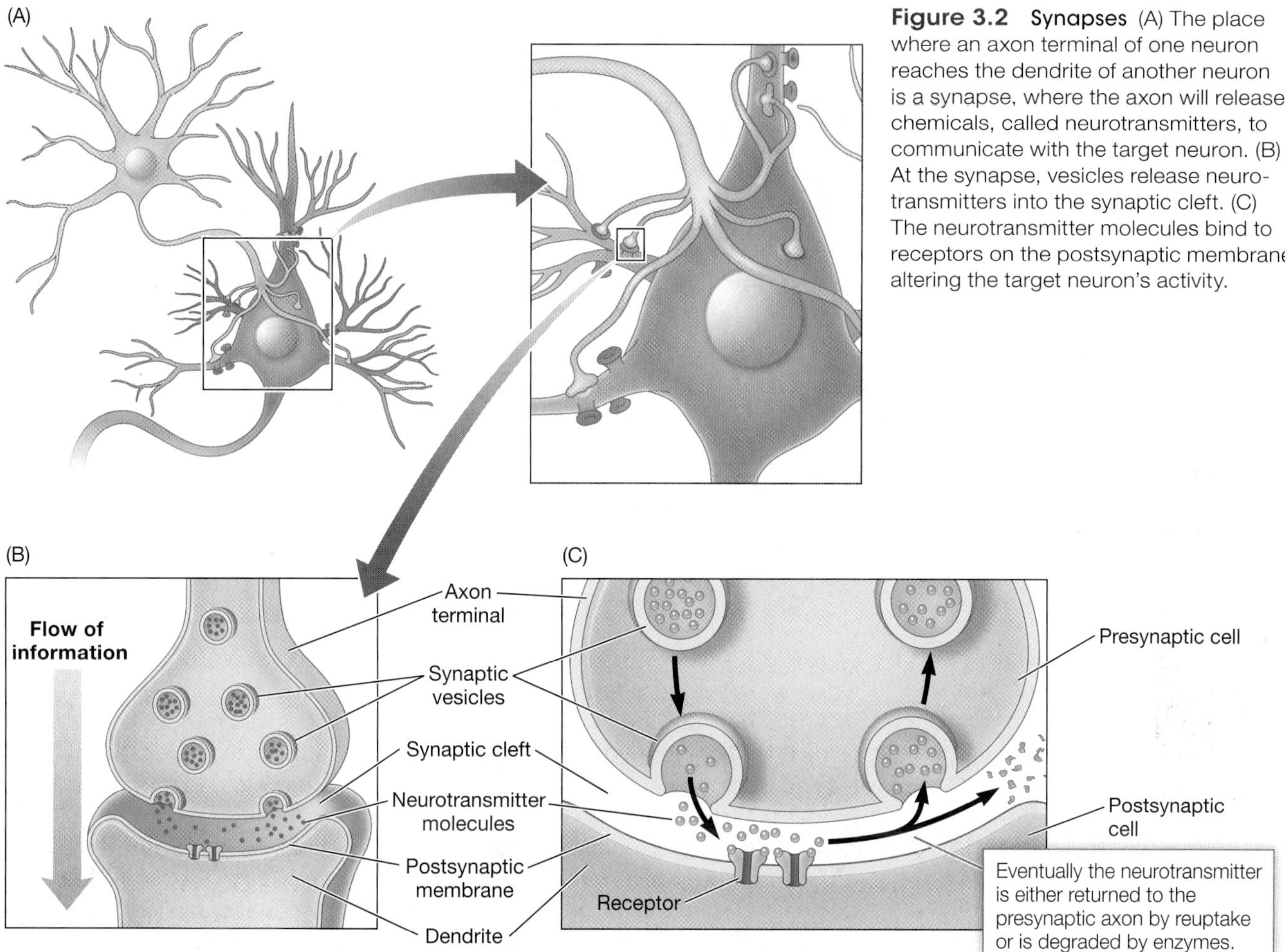

Figure 3.2 Synapses (A) The place where an axon terminal of one neuron reaches the dendrite of another neuron is a synapse, where the axon will release chemicals, called neurotransmitters, to communicate with the target neuron. (B) At the synapse, vesicles release neurotransmitters into the synaptic cleft. (C) The neurotransmitter molecules bind to receptors on the postsynaptic membrane, altering the target neuron's activity.

The shape of a neurotransmitter is specific to its target receptor; the neurotransmitter molecule fits into a part of the receptor molecule much like a key fits into a lock, or like the last piece fits into a jigsaw puzzle. Each of the various neurotransmitters has a different shape, and each fits a different type of receptor. When the neurotransmitter fits into the receptor, it causes the rest of the receptor to change shape. (Imagine a jigsaw puzzle that shifts around a bit as you fit in the last piece.) As the receptor shape is transformed, a chemical reaction is triggered by the part of the receptor that extends inside the cell. Thus, while the neurotransmitter molecule never *enters* the target cell, it nevertheless affects the interior of that cell by affecting the receptor that spans the target cell's membrane. The neurotransmitter doesn't stay bound to the receptor for long—after about a thousandth of a second (a *millisecond*, or *ms*) it drifts away again, allowing the receptor to return to its original shape.

There are probably more than 100 different chemicals that serve as neurotransmitters in the brain, so each neuron is surrounded by a "soup" of neurotransmitter chemicals that are carrying information from many other neurons:

- **Acetylcholine**, the first neurotransmitter discovered, is used by many parts of the nervous system. Some neurons release acetylcholine onto the heart to slow its beating. Other neurons release acetylcholine onto muscles to make them contract.
- **Glutamate** is one of the most common neurotransmitters in the brain. Glutamate is used in almost every sensory system, from pain to vision, and almost always causes neurons to be more active.

acetylcholine A neurotransmitter used by many parts of the nervous system.

glutamate A common neurotransmitter in the brain that usually causes neurons to be more active.

■ **TABLE 3.1 Some Common Neurotransmitters**

Name	Examples of function
Acetylcholine	Contracts muscles, slows heart rate and breathing
Norepinephrine	Speeds heart rate and breathing
Glutamate	Usually excites neurons
GABA	Usually inhibits neurons
Serotonin	Affects mood (enhancing serotonin signaling relieves depression in some people)
Dopamine	Motor control, reward systems (interfering with dopamine signaling relieves some symptoms of schizophrenia)
Endorphins	Reduce the perception of pain

- **GABA** (an acronym for ***g***amma ***a***mino***b***utyric ***a***cid) is a neurotransmitter that, in contrast to glutamate, usually reduces the activity of neurons.
- **Endorphins** Several neurotransmitters are classified as endorphins, because they seem to act as "***endo***genous (internal) m***orphin***e" to damp down pain signals.
- **Serotonin** is a neurotransmitter made by neurons in the base of the brain that send their axons throughout the brain and spinal cord. Serotonin excites some neurons and inhibits others.
- **Norepinephrine** (also known as noradrenaline) is released by certain neurons to speed heart rate, breathing, and neuronal activity as part of the "fight or flight" response.
- **Dopamine** is a neurotransmitter important in the brain's control of movement, and also in signaling pleasure from a wide variety of stimuli, including food, sex, and drugs. Drugs that interfere with dopamine signaling in the brain relieve some of the symptoms of schizophrenia.

GABA An acronym for *gamma-aminobutyric acid*. A neurotransmitter that usually reduces the activity of neurons.

endorphins Neurotransmitters that seem to act as "***endo***genous (internal) m***orphin***e" to damp down pain signals.

serotonin A neurotransmitter made by neurons in the base of the brain that send their axons throughout the brain and spinal cord.

norepinephrine A neurotransmitter that speeds heart rate, breathing, and neuronal activity as part of the "fight or flight" response.

dopamine A neurotransmitter involved in movement and in signaling pleasure.

reuptake The process by which axon terminals take back neurotransmitter molecules from the synaptic cleft.

motor neuron A type of neuron that sends commands to make muscles move, using acetylcholine as a neurotransmitter.

Table 3.1 lists some of the neurotransmitters and some of their functions, which we will discuss further in Chapter 7.

As mentioned earlier, neurotransmitter molecules do not remain in the synaptic cleft for long, for two reasons. First, the axon terminal that releases the neurotransmitter molecules soon actively gathers them up to use again later. This process of taking back neurotransmitter molecules is called **reuptake**. (Certain drugs exploit the process of reuptake. For example, modern antidepressant drugs make serotonin synapses more effective by inhibiting the reuptake of serotonin, thus prolonging the time that the neurotransmitter can affect the receptors in the target cell [see Chapter 16].) Second, chemicals called *degradative enzymes* in the synaptic cleft quickly dismantle any transmitter molecules that were not picked up by reuptake.

Why do reuptake and degradation of transmitter molecules occur? Why the big hurry to get rid of the signal that one cell is providing to the other? It's important to clear the synaptic cleft of neurotransmitter molecules so that another signal can cross the cleft in the near future. In this way, a fresh barrage of neurotransmitters can communicate across the synapse every thousandth of a second or so. To see why a brief signal can make the synapse more useful, consider how worthless a doorbell would be if the first time someone pushed the button it rang forever. It could only send one message, one time. But you could use that doorbell to send a lot more information if you could ring it anywhere between 1,000 times per second (Hurry up and answer the door, I really need to talk to you!) and once per second (Take your time, I was bored at my place and thought I'd just hang out here).

We can classify neurons into three functional types

No matter which neurotransmitter a neuron uses, we can classify the neuron as belonging to one of three functional classes, based on what it does. **Motor neurons** release their neurotransmitter, which happens to be acetylcholine, onto muscles, making them contract to produce movement (**Figure 3.3A**). Any movement we make, whether walking up stairs, throwing a basketball, or writing a note, occurs because various motor neurons have stimulated our muscles to contract in a particular sequence to produce that behavior. Other motor neurons stimulate various glands in the body to contract and release substances, usually without our being aware of it.

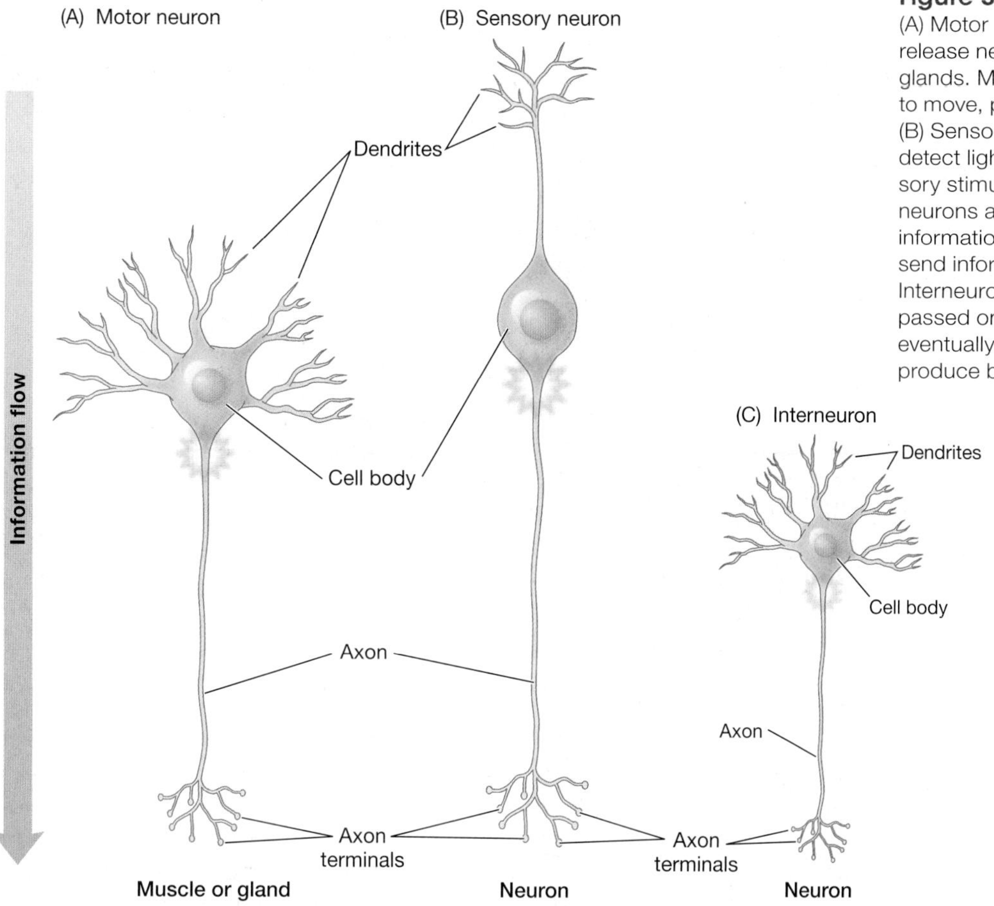

Figure 3.3 Three Kinds of Neurons (A) Motor neurons have axons that release neurotransmitter on muscles or glands. Motor neurons cause muscles to move, producing all of our behavior. (B) Sensory neurons are specialized to detect light, sound, touch, or other sensory stimuli. (C) The vast majority of brain neurons are interneurons, which receive information only from other neurons, and send information only to other neurons. Interneurons process the information passed on from sensory neurons and eventually command motor neurons to produce behavior.

Sensory neurons, such as those in our eyes, are sensitive to physical events, such as light reaching them (**Figure 3.3B**). Different sensory neurons detect sound, touch, taste, light, and smells, and send information about those events to the brain. Most sensory neurons use glutamate as a neurotransmitter to tell the brain about all the things happening around us.

The vast majority of neurons in our brain receive signals only from other neurons, and in turn release neurotransmitters only to other neurons. We call them **interneurons**, because they only listen to and talk to other neurons (**Figure 3.3C**). Interneurons rely on a wide variety of different neurotransmitters. Interneurons are not just idlers, gossiping away with each other while sensory neurons gather all the information and motor neurons do all the work. The interneurons *analyze* that sensory information and *make decisions* about what behavior the motor neurons should produce.

Let's look at how sensory neurons, interneurons, and motor neurons work in the simplest unit of behavior, a reflex. A **reflex** is a simple behavior that is automatically triggered by a particular stimulation, without our conscious effort. A famous reflex we've all experienced takes place when we accidentally put a hand on a hot surface. Sensory neurons in our skin detect the stimulation—a hot surface. They then release neurotransmitters onto interneurons in the spinal cord, and these interneurons command motor neurons to jerk our hand back. This can happen even before we're aware of the pain—our conscious effort isn't needed for the reflex to happen (**Figure 3.4**).

Only a few interneurons are needed to make simple decisions in reflexes, but when you make a complex decision, like whether to lie down for a nap,

sensory neuron A type of neuron that is sensitive to physical events and sends information to the brain about them, typically using glutamate as a neurotransmitter.

interneuron A neuron that receives input from and sends output to other neurons.

reflex A simple behavior that is automatically triggered by a particular stimulation, without our conscious effort.

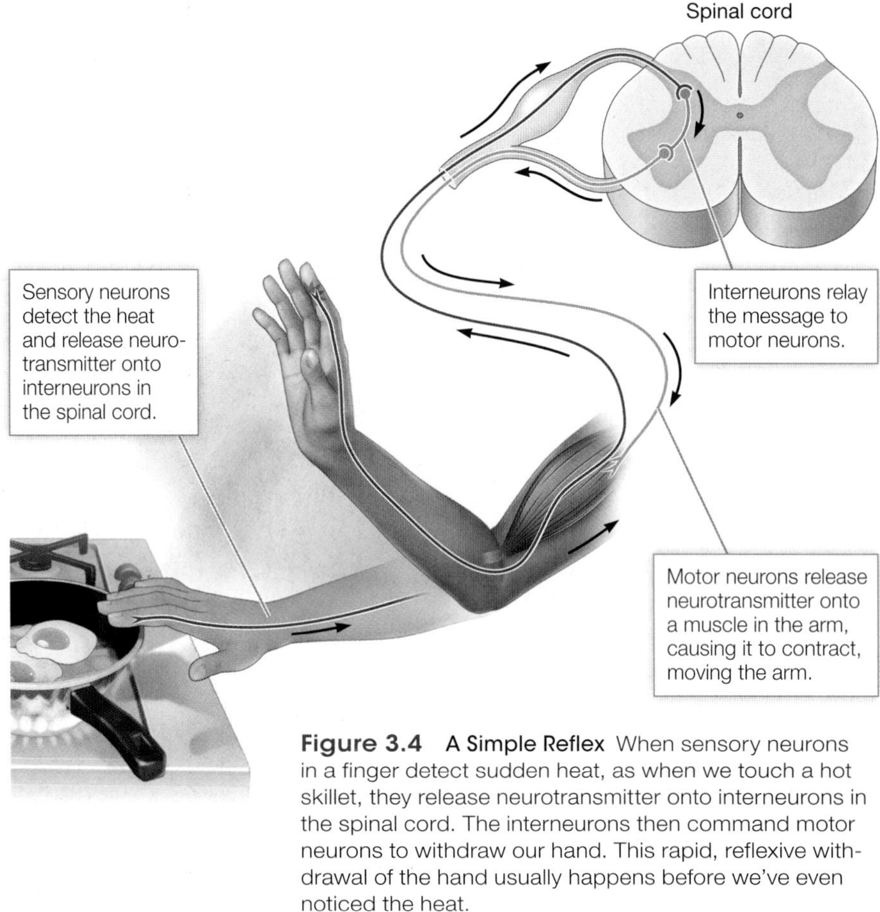

Spinal cord
Sensory neurons detect the heat and release neuro-transmitter onto interneurons in the spinal cord.
Interneurons relay the message to motor neurons.
Motor neurons release neurotransmitter onto a muscle in the arm, causing it to contract, moving the arm.

Figure 3.4 A Simple Reflex When sensory neurons in a finger detect sudden heat, as when we touch a hot skillet, they release neurotransmitter onto interneurons in the spinal cord. The interneurons then command motor neurons to withdraw our hand. This rapid, reflexive withdrawal of the hand usually happens before we've even noticed the heat.

read a book, or call a friend, you are using your billions of interneurons to carefully sift through all incoming sensory information, memories about the past, and plans for the future to make that decision. Without those billions of interneurons weighing options and making decisions about what your body will do next, you would produce only simple, reflexive behaviors.

Any reasonably complex behavior—that is, behavior more complicated than simple sensory detection or reflexes—is controlled by a **neural network**: a wide-ranging scattering of many interneurons communicating with one another to process information. Sensory neurons send information into the network, which then reaches a decision and sends commands out to motor neurons so that you stick out your tongue, make a fist, go to bed, or laugh. Other networks gather information about sounds and decode them into language, and yet other networks gather information about nutrients in your body to decide when you should eat. All these networks of neurons in the brain communicate with each other by releasing neurotransmitters at synapses.

That networks of neurons are responsible for all of our thoughts and actions underscores the machinelike property of the brain. The notion that the mind is a product of a physical machine means that we don't need to resort to supernatural ideas, such as a soul, to explain why we yearn, learn, and remember. This is a good thing for the scientific enterprise, because no matter how attractive the idea of souls or spirits may be, they are beyond the grasp of scientific investigation (**Box 3.1**). Studying the machinelike aspects of the brain may start us thinking about the question of free will—if our brain is just a machine, how can we *choose* for that machine to do one thing rather than another? We'll take up that question in Section 7.1.

In the next section you'll learn how each neuron uses electricity to monitor neurotransmitter activity at the thousands of synapses on its dendrites, and to decide whether to release neurotransmitter from its own axon.

neural network A wide-ranging scattering of many interneurons communicating with one another to process information.

Psychology in Everyday Life

BOX 3.1

Dualism and Descartes's Error

One of the smartest people who ever lived was René Descartes (1596–1650), the famous French mathematician who once declared, "I think, therefore I am." Consciousness was the one thing of which he was absolutely certain, and from this foundation he built an entire philosophy. He was also the first person to convincingly argue that animals might be understood as very complicated machines. Why does a man jerk his foot away from a fire? Because the heat triggers machinery to pull the foot back (**Figure A**; compare with our modern understanding as portrayed in Figure 3.4). Descartes was wrong about the details of the machinery, but he realized that a complicated machine could do what animals do.

(A)

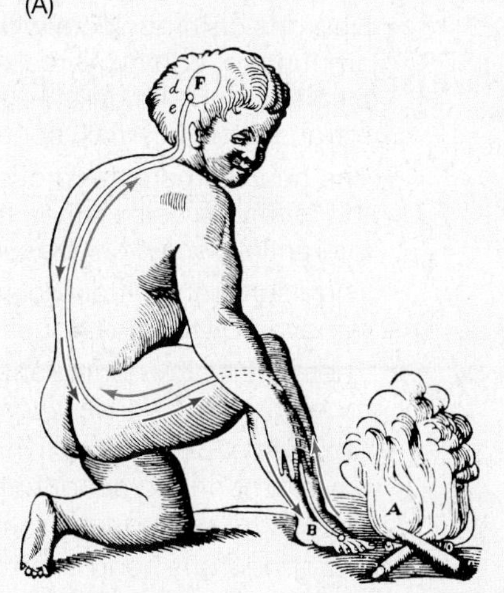

(B)

Material or Spiritual? (A) Descartes's speculation about what happens when a man pulls his foot from a fire. A tube (blue) sends information about heat to the brain, where it is reflected down a tube (red) to move the foot. (B) In this scene from the movie *Ghost*, Patrick Swayze (who plays the ghost) is somehow able to mold clay on a potter's wheel.

But when it came to humans, Descartes faltered. He could accept that much of our body is mechanical, like the jerking of our foot from the fire, but surely not our minds? If the mind were just a complex mechanism, he reasoned, then we could no more hold people responsible for what they did than we could blame a rock for falling when we dropped it. Following the prevailing Christian thought of his time and place, Descartes believed we each have a soul (but that animals do not), and he decided that our soul is not mechanical or material, but is a spirit that probably sits inside the brain. Descartes's notion that we consist of two completely different substances, material and spiritual, is known as *dualism.* The picture we get is of the spiritual soul inside the brain, watching through our eyes and listening through our ears, pulling levers and pushing buttons to make our body do what our soul wants.

One problem with dualism is that it simply puts off the tough questions. If we want to understand how a person can see, hear, and talk, it doesn't help much to imagine a tiny little person inside the head who sees, hears, and talks for him. Now we still have to ask how *the little person* can see, hear, and talk.

Another problem with dualism: How could the immaterial soul and the material body ever interact with each other? You've probably seen movies where ghosts pass through walls one moment, then throw pots and pans the next. How could that really work? If bullets and people pass right through us, how would we ever be able to pick anything up? For that matter, how could we walk across the floor if our feet just passed through? Outside of Hollywood scripts, that could never work (**Figure B**). Likewise, there's no way for an entirely immaterial soul to affect the very material brain. Virtually no psychologists or neuroscientists accept Descartes's dualism today.

Damage to specific parts of the brain causes very specific losses of behavior, such as speech, hearing, or vision. If all the speaking, hearing, and seeing were being done by some nonmaterial spirit roaming around inside the brain, we'd expect it either to be present and able to do everything, or to be gone altogether. We won't talk about souls in this book because our interest here is in science, and science offers no expertise in religion or tools to study religious ideas such as a soul. But if there is any part of us that observes the world around us and decides what we should do next, it's not some wispy, wimpy thing *inside* the brain, it *is* the brain.

3.1 SUMMARY

- *Neurons* are cells specialized to process information. Neurons have extensions called *dendrites* that receive information, usually from other neurons, and an extension called an *axon* that sends information to other cells.
- Neurons communicate with each other when an axon releases small amounts of chemicals called *neurotransmitters* onto another cell at a specialized site called a *synapse*. The *axon terminal* stores neurotransmitter in small, spherical *vesicles*.
- The neurotransmitter crosses the *synaptic cleft* but does not enter the receiving cell. Rather, the neurotransmitter affects that cell by interacting with *neurotransmitter receptors* on the cell's surface.
- The neurotransmitter molecules are either degraded by enzymes or removed by *reuptake* back into the axon terminal.
- There are many neurotransmitters, each affecting a different type of receptor, and each is involved in many different behaviors.
- *Sensory neurons* detect information about the external and internal environment and send that information to the brain, usually using *glutamate* as a neurotransmitter.
- *Motor neurons* send commands to make muscles move, using *acetylcholine* as a neurotransmitter.
- The vast majority of neurons in the brain are *interneurons*, communicating exclusively with other neurons, using a wide variety of neurotransmitters.
- While simple, automatic behaviors such as *reflexes* may involve only a few interneurons, all complex behavior results from the interaction of billions of interneurons forming *neural networks* in the brain.

REVIEW QUESTIONS

1. What are the different parts of a neuron, and what do they do?
2. What are the three types of neurons, based on function, and what roles do they play? Which type is most common in the brain?
3. What is a neurotransmitter, and how does it pass information from one neuron to another?
4. What two processes halt the effect of neurotransmitter molecules once they've been released?
5. Name three neurotransmitters and give an example of a function each is known to play.

Food for Thought

While we don't yet know the total number, it's clear that there are many different neurotransmitters, probably more than 100. What do you think is gained by having so many neurotransmitters at work rather than just one or two?

3.2 The Nervous System at Work: The Body Electric

Things to Learn

- Electrical properties of neurons
- Mechanism underlying action potentials
- How neurons sum information from many synapses
- Why drugs and hormones can affect mental function

Now you know some of the basics of the different parts of neurons and how they communicate with one another. One neuron releases neurotransmitter molecules to talk to other neurons, or to muscles or other body organs. In addition to that chemical signaling *between* neurons, there is also electrical signaling at work *within* each neuron, which is our next topic. You'll learn that a neuron uses electrical signals to sum up all the inputs it receives to make a decision: fire a nerve impulse or not? If the neuron is excited enough, it will send a nerve impulse down the axon to every tip, and each tip will release neurotransmitter to pass information to another cell. An overabundance of nerve impulses in Deidre's brain caused seizures. Passing electrical current through a tiny wire in her brain affected Deidre's mind because it excited particular neurons to send nerve impulses down their axons.

Every cell in your body is a tiny battery

The brain isn't normally stimulated by electrical wires, as Deidre's was when doctors investigated her epilepsy. Instead, nerve cells are usually stimulated by other nerve cells releasing neurotransmitter onto them. Then each neuron responds to those chemical signals by producing electrical signals, as we mentioned briefly before. How does a neuron use electricity to receive signals and send messages?

Small electrically charged particles are called *ions*. Some ions are negatively charged, and some are positively charged. Neurons have more negative charges inside them than the body fluids surrounding them. Why? Because the cells are full of proteins, which tend to be negatively charged. Also, neurons are constantly working to push out some positively charged ions. Any difference in charged particles is called a polarization, so we say that cells are **polarized** (**Figure 3.5**). If we make a hole in the cell membrane, positively charged ions will be pulled in because opposite charges attract, and there are more negative charges inside the cell than outside. The more negatively charged the interior, the more positive ions will be pulled in.

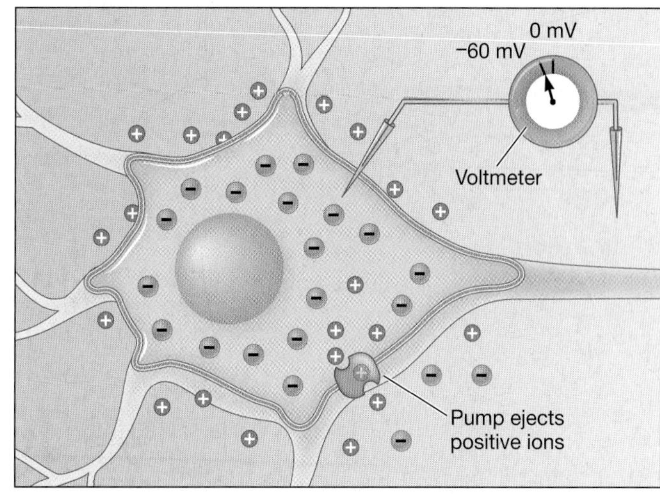

Figure 3.5 The Cell as a Battery Like batteries, neurons are polarized: they have more negative charges inside the cell than outside the cell. Neurons use a lot of energy to constantly pump out some positive ions.

We measure this tendency, or *potential*, for charged particles to move from one place (outside the cell) to another (inside the cell) as a **potential difference in charge**. It is measured in units called *volts* (*V*) by a device called a *voltmeter* (see Figure 3.5). The greater the voltage difference between two places, the more readily charged particles will flow from one place to the other. For example, the potential for negatively charged electrons to flow from one end of an AA battery to the other is 1.5 V. When we put both ends of the battery in contact with a flashlight, electrons flow from one end of the battery through the bulb (making light for us to see) then back through the other end of the battery.

In neurons, the potential difference in charge across the cell membrane, called the *membrane potential*, means that every neuron acts like a tiny battery. While an AA battery has a negative end and a positive end, with a potential difference of 1.5 V between them, a neuron has a negative interior and a positive exterior, with a much smaller potential difference between them. If you take a voltmeter and put one of its wires (called an *electrode*) inside the neuron and the other electrode in the fluid outside the neuron, you'll find that the inside is about 60-thousandths of a volt, or 60 *millivolts* (*mV*), more negative than the outside (see Figure 3.5). We always measure cell voltages in comparison with the outside, so we say the cell has a membrane potential of –60 mV because it's more negative inside than outside.

When neurons are not being stimulated by other neurons (or by wires from outside the brain), they have a **resting potential** (the membrane potential of a neuron at rest) of about –60 mV. What determines the resting potential? The insides of neurons have a high concentration of potassium ions (K^+), which normally can pass freely across the neuronal membrane, and are attracted to the negative interior. All ions tend to move away from an area of high concentration to an area of low concentration, as if spreading themselves out. In this case, the K^+ ions concentrated inside the neuron pass outside until the neuron has a negative potential of about –60 mV. The K^+ ions are still more concentrated inside the neuron, but now that negative charge pulling them in exactly balances their tendency to move outside. "Resting" potential may sound relaxing, but as we'll see next, the neuron's membrane potential is constantly shifting above and below the resting potential.

polarized Having a positive or negative charge.

potential difference in charge The measure of the tendency for charged particles to move from one place to another, usually reported in volts.

resting potential The membrane potential of a neuron when it is not being stimulated.

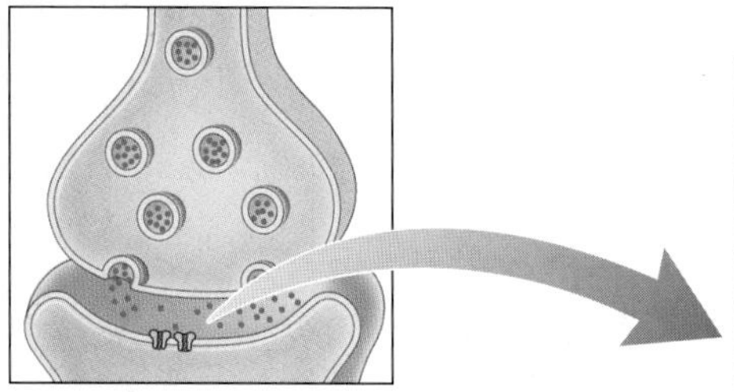

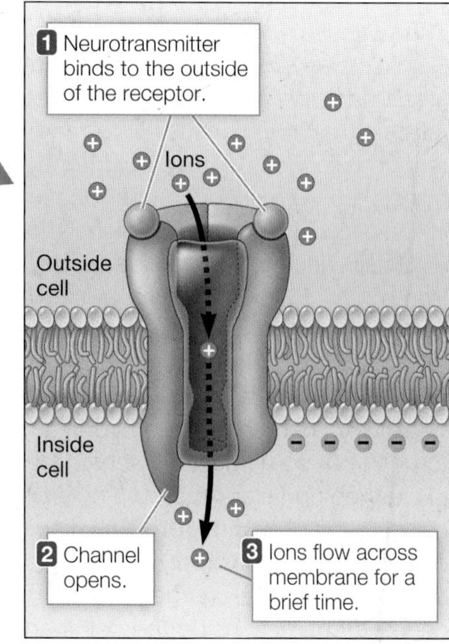

1 Neurotransmitter binds to the outside of the receptor.
Ions
Outside cell
Inside cell
2 Channel opens.
3 Ions flow across membrane for a brief time.

Figure 3.6 Ions Flow for Electrical Signaling in Neurons When opened by the action of a neurotransmitter, ion channels in a neuron's membrane allow positively charged ions such as sodium (Na^+) to enter the neuron.

Neurons use electrical signals to summarize information from many synapses

Now let's see how that difference in charge across the membrane of a cell provides a way for neurons to translate the chemical, neurotransmitter signal from a synapse into a tiny electrical signal. We'll see that the neuron summarizes tiny electrical signals from thousands of synapses. Then in the next section we'll see what determines whether a neuron passes information down its axon to the next cell.

In most cells of the body, the voltage difference across the membrane remains constant, but in neurons the voltage difference across the membrane changes constantly. We mentioned earlier that K^+ ions normally flow readily across the neuron's membrane, and are more concentrated inside the neuron than outside. Another positive ion, sodium (Na^+), is more concentrated *outside* the cell than inside and, is thus attracted to the negative interior of the neuron. But unlike K^+ ions, Na^+ ions normally cannot cross the membrane. Na+ ions can only cross the membrane through *gated ion channels* that open only when a specific neurotransmitter molecule attaches to a receptor on the channel. You can think of an *ion channel* as a tiny tunnel or pore running through the cell membrane that allows ions such as Na^+ to cross the membrane. Once the ion channel opens, positive Na^+ ions flow into the neuron, attracted to its negative interior (**Figure 3.6**). This inflow of Na^+ ions may change the voltage difference across the neuron's membrane from –60 mV to, say, –50 mV. The ion channel stays open only for a millisecond or so. Then the channel closes again, allowing the neuron to return to its resting potential.

A single neurotransmitter molecule has hardly any effect, but a neuron's voltage fluctuates widely due to the combined effect of thousands of neurotransmitter molecules, at each of thousands of receptors, at each of thousands of synapses on the same neuron. If this sounds chaotic, don't worry. Even if many synapses are active at the same time, the neuron is structured such that its voltage returns to the resting potential in just a few milliseconds. What's more, each neuron is constantly pushing Na^+ ions out to maintain the resting potential (see Figure 3.5).

The fluctuating voltage of a neuron isn't just random chatter. Rather, the constantly fluctuating membrane potential of a neuron is an efficient way to add together and summarize what's happening at all those thousands of synapses. The more synapses are active at any given moment, the more the neuron's voltage will waver for a brief time. If no synapses are active, then the neuron's potential will hold steady. In this way, the neuron's potential reflects the average activity of thousands of synapses. In other words, the neuron is summarizing (or

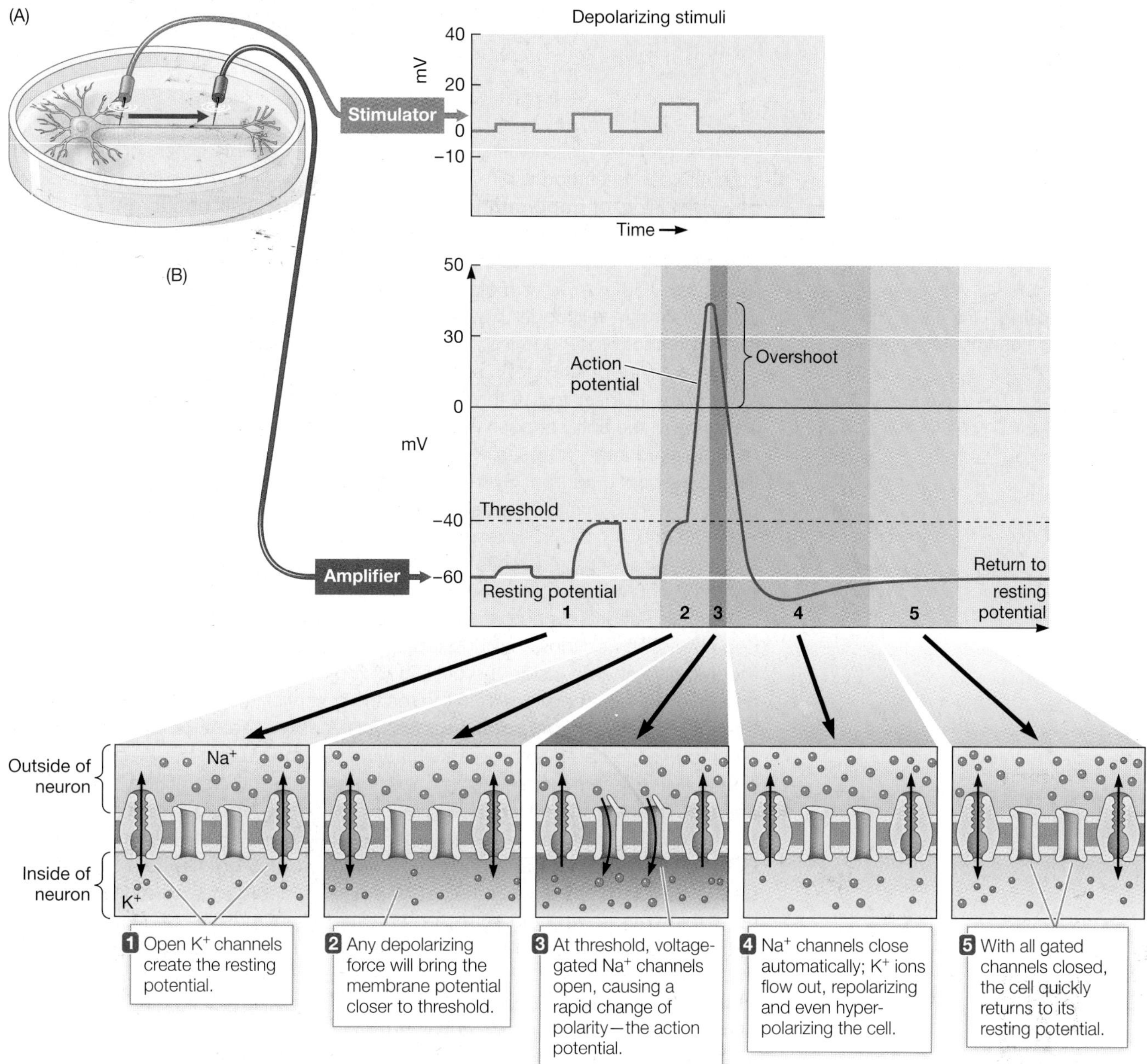

Figure 3.7 **The Action Potential** (A) If we stimulate an axon with a tiny electrical charge, it will be briefly depolarized and then return to the resting potential. (B) But if we keep increasing our stimulation, reaching threshold, the axon will suddenly show a dramatic change called the action potential. The electrical changes in the neuron are caused by the opening and closing of voltage-gated sodium channels.

integrating) information from thousands of inputs (synapses) and updating that average every few milliseconds. Next we'll see how some synapses make the neuron more likely to pass along information, while other synapses inhibit the neuron from passing along information.

Synaptic input determines whether a neuron will produce an action potential

So far we've seen how a neuron *receives* information, but a neuron *sends* information as well. To do that, neurons briefly reverse their potential to send an electrical message from the cell body out to the very tips of the axon. This special signal is called an **action potential** (or *nerve impulse*), and it consists of a brief reversal of an axon's potential, making the inside of the axon more electrically positive than the fluid surrounding it for less than 1 millisecond (ms) (**Figure 3.7A**). Once the action potential begins, it spreads down the axon to all the axon terminals, as we'll discuss in the next section.

action potential Also called *nerve impulse*. The electrical message of a neuron that travels along the axon to the axon terminals.

depolarizing Reducing the polarization of a neuron, making it more likely to fire.

threshold The size of depolarization necessary to trigger an action potential.

hyperpolarizing Increasing the polarity of a neuron, making it less likely to fire.

axon hillock The widest part of an axon where it originates from the cell body.

What causes this sudden, brief change in the axon's potential? An action potential can be triggered in an axon by deliberately making the neuron less negative inside, or **depolarizing** it. It may seem odd to talk about "de" polarizing the cell, but it makes sense because at rest the neuron is "polarized," being about 60 mV more negative inside than outside. If we change the potential from –60 mV to –50 mV, we've made the neuron *less* polarized. Only depolarizations of a certain size will trigger the action potential, and we say that this certain size is the **threshold** for triggering an action potential (**Figure 3.7B**).

The entry of positive ions such as Na^+ at synapses depolarizes the neuron and brings it closer to the threshold, which triggers an action potential, so we can think of the entry of positive ions as exciting the neuron. The neurotransmitters released into synapses work by allowing charged particles (ions) to enter the postsynaptic neuron. Synapses that allow positive ions to enter the neuron are *excitatory synapses* because they bring the neuron closer to threshold, when an action potential is triggered.

Other synapses are *inhibitory* because they allow *negatively* charged ions to enter the neuron. (If you're wondering why negatively charged ions would enter a negatively charged neuron, that's a good question. The answer is that these negatively charged ions are bunched up outside the cell, so they push in despite the negative charge inside the cell.) Inhibitory synapses make the inside of the neuron even more negative than the resting potential, taking it further away from threshold, so it is **hyperpolarized**. For this reason, the neuron becomes *less* likely to produce an action potential, so we say the neuron has been *inhibited*. The activity of all synapses, some excitatory and some inhibitory, constantly changes the neuron's potential above and below the resting potential.

The axon is the part of the neuron that produces action potentials. Why? Because, unlike other parts of the neuron, axon membranes have large numbers of special ion channels that allow positively charged sodium (Na^+) ions to enter the axon. During the action potential, so many positive Na^+ ions from the outside fluid enter that the inside of the axon briefly becomes more positive than the outside. Then the potential quickly returns to the usual –60 mV as K^+ ions move out. You might wonder if eventually so many Na^+ ions enter that it might affect the neuron's resting potential, but recall that neurons use special pumps to constantly push Na^+ ions back out (see Figure 3.5).

In effect, these Na^+ channels act as tiny voltmeters, carefully measuring how polarized the axon is. Only when the neuron becomes depolarized enough to reach threshold do the channels open to let sodium enter. For this reason, the Na^+ channels are called *voltage-gated sodium channels*: the gate to the channel opens in response to changes in voltage, specifically depolarization (see Figure 3.7B). These voltage-gated Na^+ channels are found only on axons, starting at the widest part of the axon where it joins the cell body. When this region, called the **axon hillock** ("little hill"), reaches threshold, the sodium channels open to begin an action potential.

Once begun, action potentials travel down the axon

Having started at the axon hillock, the action potential travels at speeds between 1 and 250 miles per hour down the axon to its tip. If, as is common, the axon splits into many different branches, the action potential will travel down each of those branches and reach every axon tip or terminal.

The voltage-gated sodium channels ensure that once an action potential begins, it spreads all the way down to the tip—or tips—of the axon. As the action potential occurs in one part of the axon, the inrush of sodium ions depolarizes the neighboring sodium channels until *they* reach threshold and start the whole process over again in the next patch of axon (**Figure 3.8**).

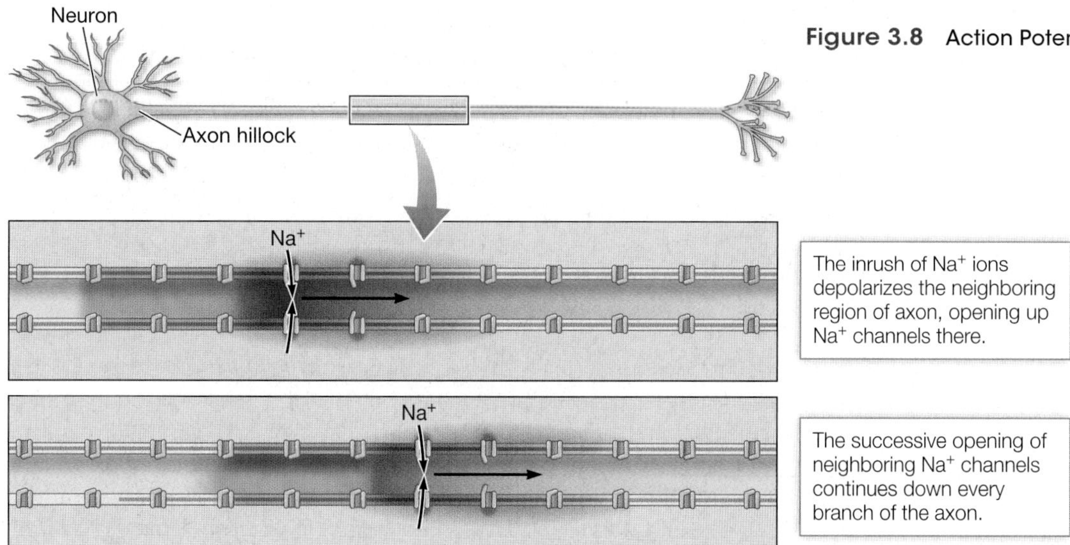

Neuron
Axon hillock
Na^+
Na^+
The inrush of Na^+ ions depolarizes the neighboring region of axon, opening up Na^+ channels there.
The successive opening of neighboring Na^+ channels continues down every branch of the axon.

Figure 3.8 Action Potential Propagation

What's more, the change in electrical potential in the axon is just as large at the axon tip as at the start of the axon. This is because the same voltage-gated sodium channels are found throughout the axon, so the same change in potential occurs.

For the same reason, every action potential a neuron produces is the same size in terms of voltage change. We say that action potentials are an **all-or-none property** of neurons because a given neuron produces action potentials that are always the same size. The neuron either produces an action potential or not, and when it does, the action potential is always the same size. These properties of the action potential have led some people to liken them to the flushing of a toilet.

all-or-none property The fact that size of the action potential is independent of the size of the stimulus.

Action potentials work like a flushing toilet

A flushing toilet may seem like an odd analogy in a psychology text, but it is useful for understanding how neurons use electrical signals to process information. If you gently push the lever on a toilet, nothing much happens. If you gradually increase the force you apply to the lever, you eventually find the threshold: the amount of force that is just enough to trigger a flush. Likewise, the neuron has a threshold: the amount of synaptic excitation that is just enough to trigger an action potential at the start of an axon, the hillock (**Figure 3.9**).

Once you're past the threshold, it doesn't matter how hard you pushed the toilet lever—the flush will always be the same. Similarly, once the neuron is pushed past threshold, the action potential will be the same. This is the all-or-none property of action potentials.

Also notice that when a properly working toilet flushes, the water always goes in the

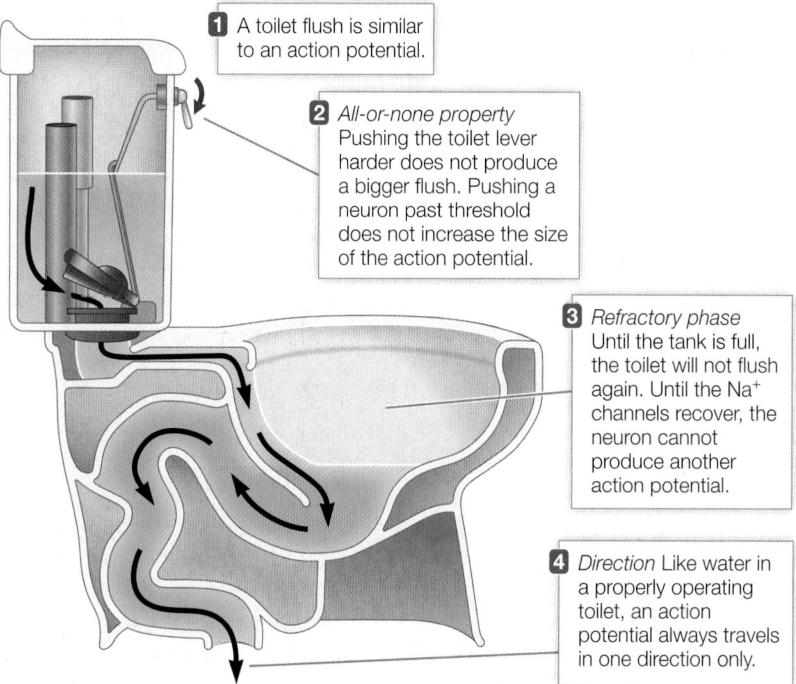

1 A toilet flush is similar to an action potential.
2 *All-or-none property* Pushing the toilet lever harder does not produce a bigger flush. Pushing a neuron past threshold does not increase the size of the action potential.
3 *Refractory phase* Until the tank is full, the toilet will not flush again. Until the Na^+ channels recover, the neuron cannot produce another action potential.
4 *Direction* Like water in a properly operating toilet, an action potential always travels in one direction only.

Figure 3.9 The Flushing Toilet Analogy for Action Potentials

TABLE 3.2 Comparison of Axons and Dendrites

Property	Axon	Dendrite
Information flow	Away from neuron	Into neuron
Diameter	Thin, uniform	Thick, variable
Number per neuron	One (but may have branches)	Many
Voltage changes	All-or-none	Variable, graded

same direction (no one is interested in buying a toilet that sometimes flushes backward). Likewise, the neuron's action potential goes in only one direction down the axon, from the end attached to the cell body to the axon terminals.

After a toilet has flushed, it takes a while (about a minute) before it can flush again. After a neuron fires, it takes a while (about a millisecond) before it can fire again. So the toilet has a period of time after a flush, about 1 minute, when it can't flush again. Likewise, the neuron has a period of time, about 1 ms, when it can't produce another action potential. During this time the neuron is said to be *refractory*, which means "stubborn" or "unresponsive," so we call this time the **refractory phase**.

Why do neurons have a refractory phase for action potentials? Because, if you remember, the voltage-gated sodium channels always close for a while after they open, no matter what the membrane potential is. Until that time is up, the sodium channels won't open again. If the situation is urgent, we can flush our toilet about 60 times per hour or fire our neurons about 1,000 times per second. If things are *really* urgent, we do both.

Of course, neurons are different from toilets in many ways. The outflow of a toilet goes only to the single sewer line leaving a house, but an action potential may flow down to many axon branches, to communicate with hundreds of other neurons. Voltage-gated sodium channels on the axon branches ensure that the action potential is just as large in each branch, so it's not diminished by spreading out among branches. A toilet has only one lever, but each neuron has hundreds or thousands of synapses, and some synapses make the neuron more likely to reach threshold, while others make it less likely. This excitation–inhibition capacity of neurons makes them good at summarizing information from many synapses.

The all-or-none property of action potentials is very different from the changes in potential at a synapse. There are many different kinds of synapses, excitatory and inhibitory, and some synapses are stronger than others, causing a greater change in the target neuron's potential. These changes at synapses are graded, rather than all-or-none like action potentials.

Now that you know more about the parts of neurons and how they communicate, we can summarize the differences between dendrites, which receive information from synapses, and axons, which send information via action potentials, in **Table 3.2**.

Myelin speeds up action potentials

The speed of the action potential, as it travels from the cell body to the axon tip, depends on several factors. One factor is the axon's diameter: the action potential travels faster in thick axons than in thin ones. If the axon is thick, the depolarization caused by the opening of sodium channels in one patch of axon spreads more readily through the inside of the axon to open up the next patch of sodium channels.

Another factor affecting the speed of action potential travel is whether the axon is wrapped in **myelin**, a fatty substance that provides electrical insulation. The myelin sheath is composed of specialized glial cells, and is tightly wrapped

refractory phase A period during and immediately after a nerve impulse when a neuron cannot produce another action potential.

myelin The fatty insulation around an axon, formed by glial cells, which increases the speed of conduction of nerve impulses.

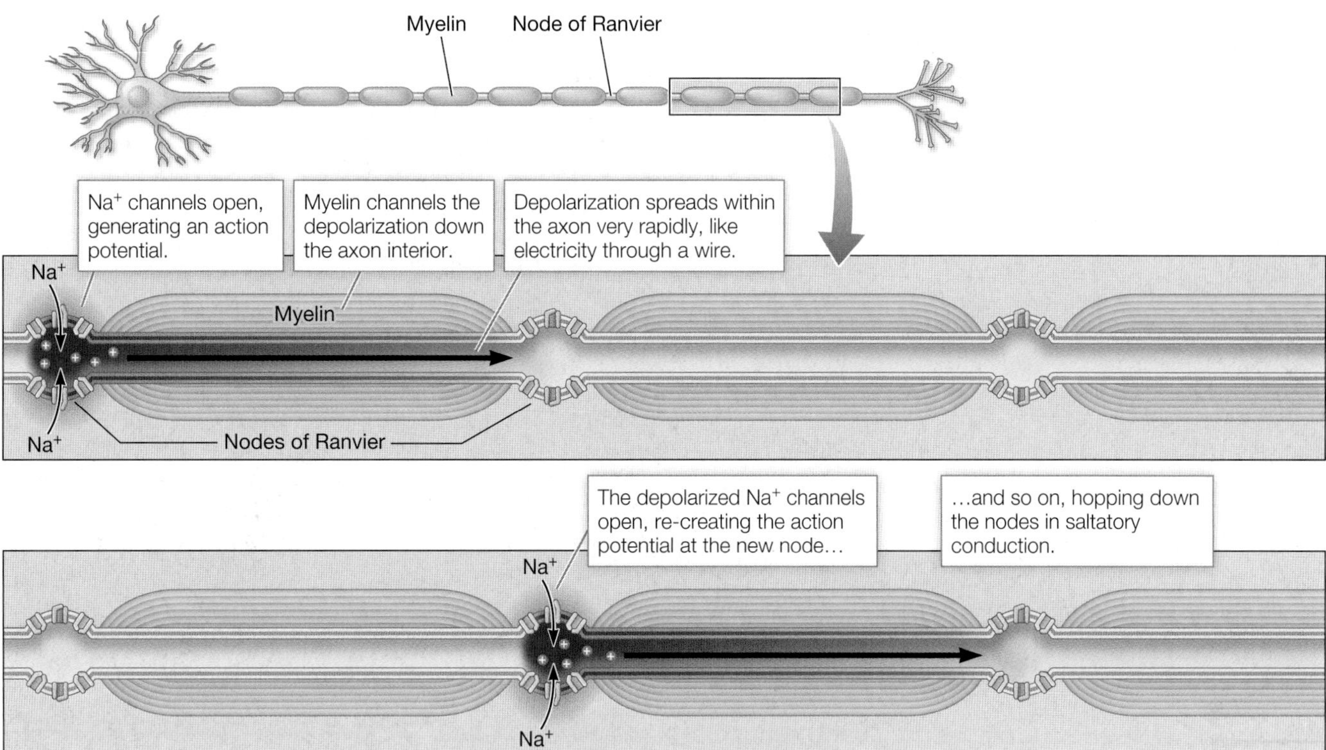

Myelin
Node of Ranvier
Na+ channels open, generating an action potential.
Myelin channels the depolarization down the axon interior.
Depolarization spreads within the axon very rapidly, like electricity through a wire.
Na+
Myelin
Na+
Nodes of Ranvier
The depolarized Na+ channels open, re-creating the action potential at the new node...
...and so on, hopping down the nodes in saltatory conduction.
Na+
Na+

Figure 3.10 Myelin Increases the Speed of an Action Potential The insulating properties of myelin force the electrical current to rapidly reach the next node, triggering an action potential there. In this way, action potentials travel much faster down myelinated axons than down unmyelinated axons.

around the axon. Regularly spaced along the axon's length are breaks in the myelin called the **nodes of Ranvier** (**Figure 3.10**). In myelinated axons, the action potential travels much faster because insulation provided by the myelin sheath forces electrical current to flow down the interior of the axon rather than spread outside the axon. For this reason, the depolarization in a myelinated axon spreads very quickly inside the axon from one node of Ranvier to the next, triggering action potentials at each node. Because the action potential seems to jump quickly from one node to the next, the process is called **saltatory conduction** ("saltatory" means "jumping").

nodes of Ranvier Regularly spaced breaks in the myelin sheath of an axon.

saltatory conduction The form of conduction in which the action potential "jumps" from one node of Ranvier to the next.

Because different axons vary in size and not all are myelinated, the speed with which action potentials travel from the cell body down the axon can vary tremendously. Action potentials travel down small, unmyelinated axons at about 1 mile per hour, while they zoom at 250 miles per hour down large axons that are myelinated.

There is little myelin in our brains at birth, so an important part of growing up is *myelination*: the spread of myelin sheathings on axons to let the brain function properly. Babies and children need at least some fat in their diet to support myelination. Fat molecules are light in color (think of shortening), so parts of the brain packed with myelinated axons are referred to as *white matter*. In contrast, brain regions filled with neuronal cell bodies look darker and are called *gray matter*.

But all the effort of neurons in the gray matter may count for little if the white matter over their axons isn't functioning properly to get their message out. In *multiple sclerosis* (*MS*), the immune system attacks myelin, disrupting action potential conduction and causing various sensory and motor problems. People with MS may be unable to walk, may lose vision or hearing, or may experience any combination of such symptoms.

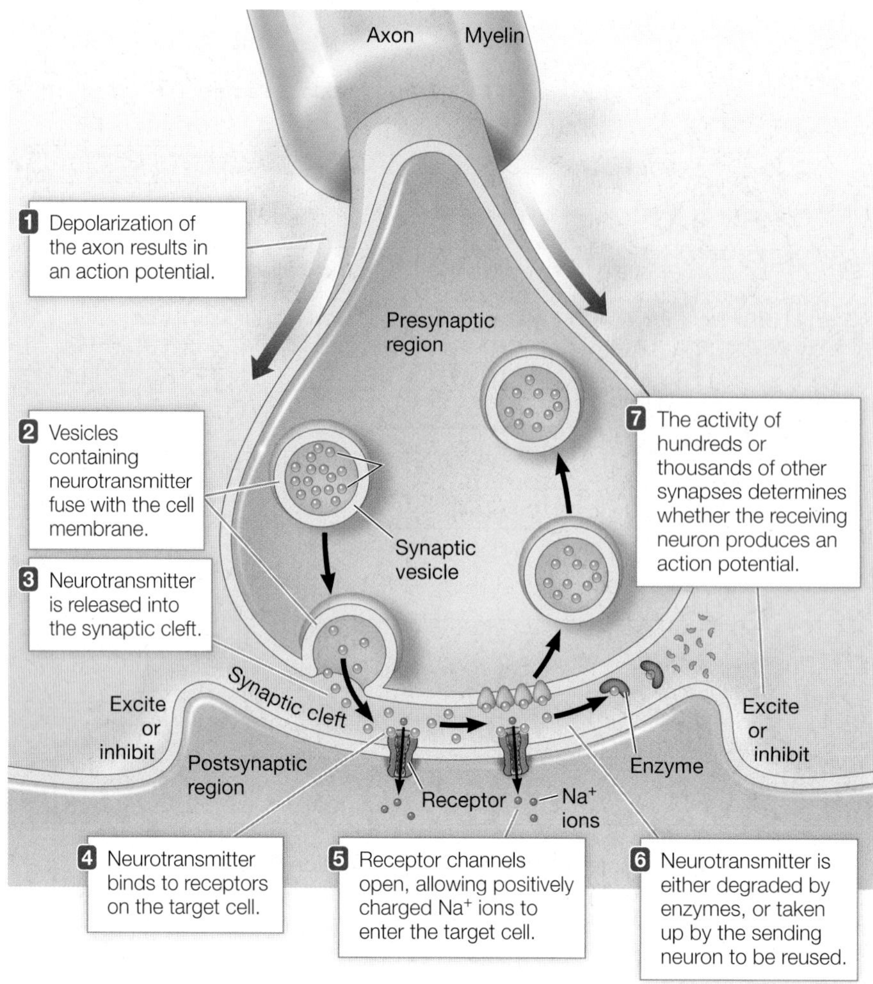

Axon
Myelin
1 Depolarization of the axon results in an action potential.
Presynaptic region
2 Vesicles containing neurotransmitter fuse with the cell membrane.
Synaptic vesicle
7 The activity of hundreds or thousands of other synapses determines whether the receiving neuron produces an action potential.
3 Neurotransmitter is released into the synaptic cleft.
Synaptic cleft
Excite or inhibit
Postsynaptic region
Receptor
Na+ ions
Enzyme
Excite or inhibit
4 Neurotransmitter binds to receptors on the target cell.
5 Receptor channels open, allowing positively charged Na+ ions to enter the target cell.
6 Neurotransmitter is either degraded by enzymes, or taken up by the sending neuron to be reused.

Figure 3.11 Summary of Steps in Communication at Synapses

If everything is working properly, the action potential arrives at the axon terminal and communicates with another cell, as we'll discuss next.

What happens when the action potential reaches the end of an axon?

As we have seen, the arrival of the action potential causes the axon terminal to release neurotransmitter into the synapse. Usually this neurotransmitter finds the dendrite of another neuron on the other side of the synapse and either excites or inhibits that neuron. In this way, the transmitting neuron's action potential makes the receiving neuron either more or less likely to produce an action potential of its own. In other cases, the axon terminal synapses with muscle fibers, making them contract, causing movement. If the synapse is on an internal organ, the neurotransmitter may cause the organ to squeeze harder or grow larger. **Figure 3.11** summarizes the overall process of synaptic communication.

Now you've seen how the brain uses both chemical and electrical signals. Every synapse converts an electrical signal (the action potential) into a chemical signal (a neurotransmitter) and then converts it back into an electrical signal again (as the receiving cell is electrically excited or inhibited by the entry of either positive or negative ions).

Because this conversion from electrical to chemical signals and back again happens in the tiny space of a synapse, early scientists had a difficult time deciding whether the nervous system uses electrical or chemical signals. When Otto Loewi ("LOW-ee") went to sleep one night in 1921, scientists all over the world were trying to figure out how a neuron communicated with other neurons.

Did each neuron release a chemical into the "soup" surrounding other neurons? Or did the neuron send an electrical signal, a "spark," across the synapse?

In the night Loewi dreamed of an experiment to answer this question, woke up, scribbled down some notes, and fell back to sleep. The next day he remembered dreaming but couldn't recall the details of the experiment, nor could he decipher what his notes meant. When he had the dream again and woke up at 3 AM, Loewi got right out of bed and marched to the lab to perform the experiment before he could forget again.

Loewi's wonderful experiment, illustrating the power of experimental reasoning, proved that both signals were at work, as we'll discuss next (**Figure 3.12**).

☑ Researchers At Work

The telltale frog heart: Loewi's marvelous dream

Figure 3.12 Otto Loewi's Dream Experiment

■ **Question:** Do neurons release a chemical to communicate with other cells, or is the communication based on electrical signals?

■ **Hypothesis:** If a chemical is released from presynaptic terminals, it should be possible to gather those chemicals to affect another target cell.

■ **Test:** Electrically stimulate a nerve called the vagus, which is known to slow down heartbeats, in a frog. Collect fluid from around the slowed heart and apply that fluid to the heart of a second frog.

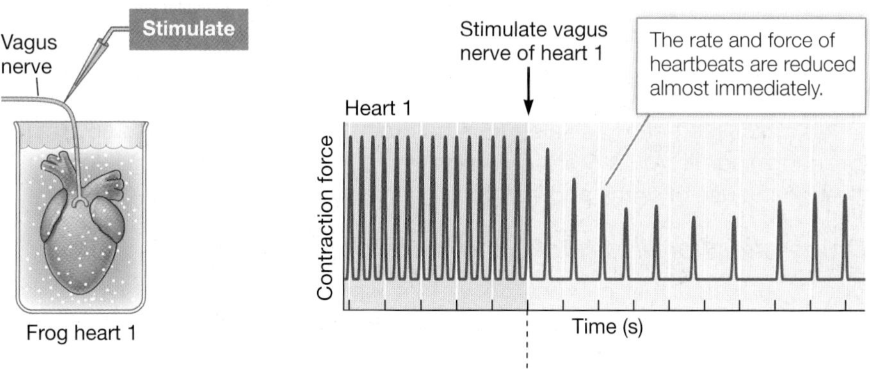

■ **Result:** When exposed to fluid from the first heart, the second heart also slowed.

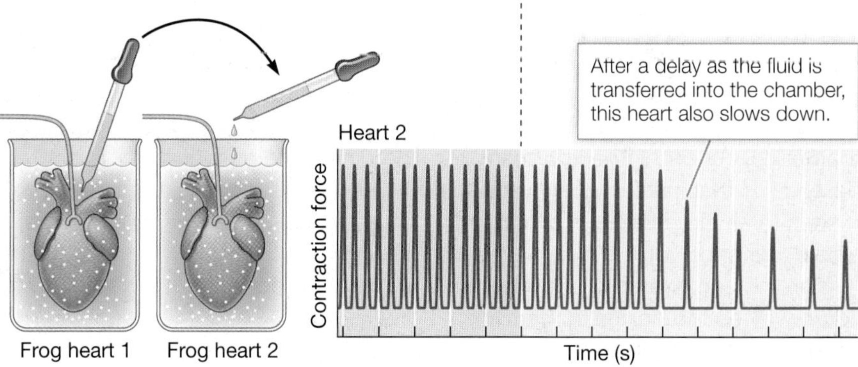

■ **Conclusion:** The vagus nerve uses a chemical neurotransmitter, not a direct electrical connection, to communicate to cells of the heart and cause it to slow down.

Loewi's elegant, simple experiment convinced scientists that neurons release chemicals, which we now call neurotransmitters, to communicate with other cells. In this case, the neurotransmitter released by the frog's nerve was acetylcholine (see Table 3.1). Today we know that many nerves communicating with various organs and glands release this same neurotransmitter. In 1936 Loewi was awarded the Nobel Prize in Physiology or Medicine for his breakthrough discovery that other scientists only "dreamed of."

Today we know that scientists in both camps, the "soups" and the "sparks," were correct. A neuron uses electrical signals to sum up all the excitatory and inhibitory inputs it receives to make a decision (fire a nerve impulse or not?). It then uses an action potential to send that decision down the axon to every tip. Each tip then releases a chemical to pass information to the next neuron. Our brain—the machine in our skull—is both an electrical *and* a chemical device. Interfering with either the electrical or chemical function of this machinery affects the ongoing process called our mind.

Now you can see why providing a tiny electrical stimulation to Deidre's brain could affect her perception. Her brain machine used electricity as part of that process she experienced as her mind. The doctors' electrical stimulation triggered hundreds of axons to produce action potentials. These action potentials swept down axons, reached the axon terminals, and caused neurotransmitters to be released. These neurotransmitters then stimulated other neurons, until eventually Deidre had the sense that what was happening around her was funny. She then attributed her amusement to the two experimenters nearby ("You guys [are] so funny"). Where in the brain are those places that gave her this experience? Nobody knows. Because neurons make so many synaptic connections, probably hundreds of different parts of her brain were affected by this one tiny electrical stimulation.

It is difficult to get wires safely into the brain to affect the machine and therefore the mind. A much more common way to interfere with brain function is through the use of drugs and hormones, which we'll discuss next.

Drugs affect brain signals and therefore the mind

Once you realize that neurons do all that work inside your skull by sending chemical signals to one another, it's easy to appreciate how introducing a new chemical into the "soup" could affect the brain. Every drug that affects your mood or thinking process is a chemical that gets to the brain and affects neurotransmitter communication.

For example, drugs of abuse, such as heroin, enter the brain and stimulate billions of synapses. Why does heroin activate receptors in those synapses? A heroin molecule is very similar to certain other molecules—the neurotransmitters we mentioned earlier called endorphins, which your brain normally uses to stimulate receptors in a careful, controlled way. The heroin molecule is enough like endorphin molecules that it affects the receptors as well as, or even better than, the natural endorphin neurotransmitter. The difference between heroin and endorphins is that instead of activating a few thousand synapses at a time, heroin rushes to all the millions of synapses at once, producing an incredibly pleasurable experience you can't achieve normally.

Heroin is an example of an **agonist**, a drug that activates a receptor in the same way as the normal neurotransmitter (**Figure 3.13A**). Other drugs are **antagonists**—they bind the receptor but do *not* activate it, preventing the normal neurotransmitter from having an effect (**Figure 3.13B**). You'll be introduced to certain agonists and antagonists in chapters to come. For example, you'll learn in Chapter 16 that most drugs that suppress symptoms of schizophrenia are antagonists for one class of dopamine receptors.

agonist A drug that activates a receptor in the same way as the normal neurotransmitter.

antagonist A drug molecule that interferes with neuronal signaling by preventing a neurotransmitter from binding to its receptor.

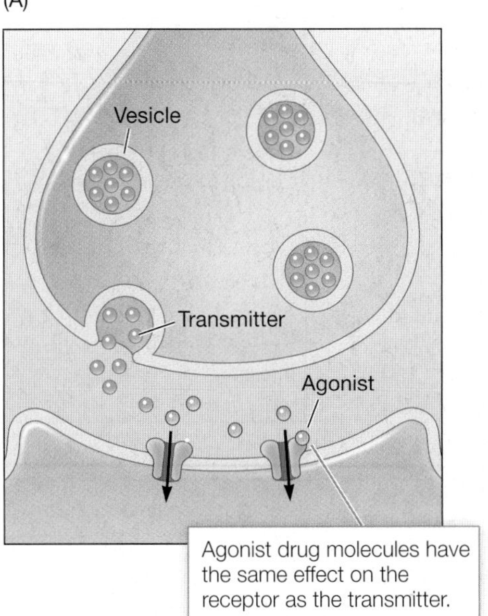
(A)
Vesicle
Transmitter
Agonist
Agonist drug molecules have the same effect on the receptor as the transmitter.

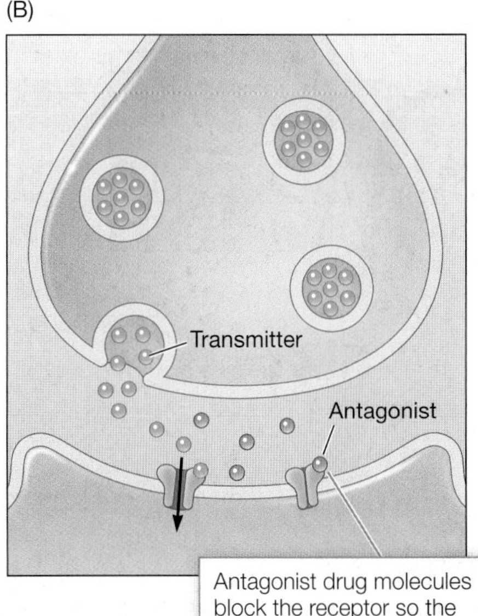
(B)
Transmitter
Antagonist
Antagonist drug molecules block the receptor so the transmitter cannot affect it.

Figure 3.13 **Mechanism of Drug Action in the Nervous System** (A) Agonist. (B) Antagonist.

Different drugs produce different reactions because they act on different receptors. Heroin acts on one type of receptors, while the active molecule in marijuana is an agonist that acts on a different class of receptors, and alcohol molecules affect yet another type, GABA receptors (covered in Section 7.4). The different receptors are found on different neurons, which normally have different functions, so the drug-induced experience depends on which neurons are activated.

The same heroin molecules that make a person feel great also inhibit neurons that normally transmit pain. If related drugs such as morphine are taken carefully and gradually, they can help people suffering from pain. Of course, other drugs affect the brain in ways that are useful beyond making you feel great for a few minutes. As mentioned earlier, most antidepressant drugs have their effect because they interfere with reuptake of serotonin, making those synapses more effective.

Some drugs that reduce anxiety make a certain class of receptors much more sensitive to the transmitter GABA (see Table 3.1). GABA tends to inhibit neurons from firing, so these drugs exaggerate that effect, reducing the firing of many neurons in the brain. By increasing the strength of this chemical signaling in the brain machine, we reduce anxiety in the mind and therefore physiological signs of anxiety as well. We will talk in greater depth about how drugs affect behavior in Section 7.4.

hormones Chemicals released from one part of the body that enter the bloodstream and affect other parts of the body.

pituitary gland An endocrine gland that releases hormones that affect virtually all other endocrine glands.

Hormones affect the brain too

The body uses other chemicals besides neurotransmitters to communicate with the brain. **Hormones** are chemicals released from one part of the body that enter the bloodstream and affect other parts of the body. Almost all the hormones that are released by various glands enter the brain and have effects there. Glands that release hormones are called *endocrine glands* because they release material inside the body ("endo" meaning "internal") rather than outside (think of sweat glands).

As with all other processes in our body, the brain carefully monitors and controls all endocrine glands, regulating their release of hormones. The **pituitary gland** is sometimes called the "master gland" because it releases hormones

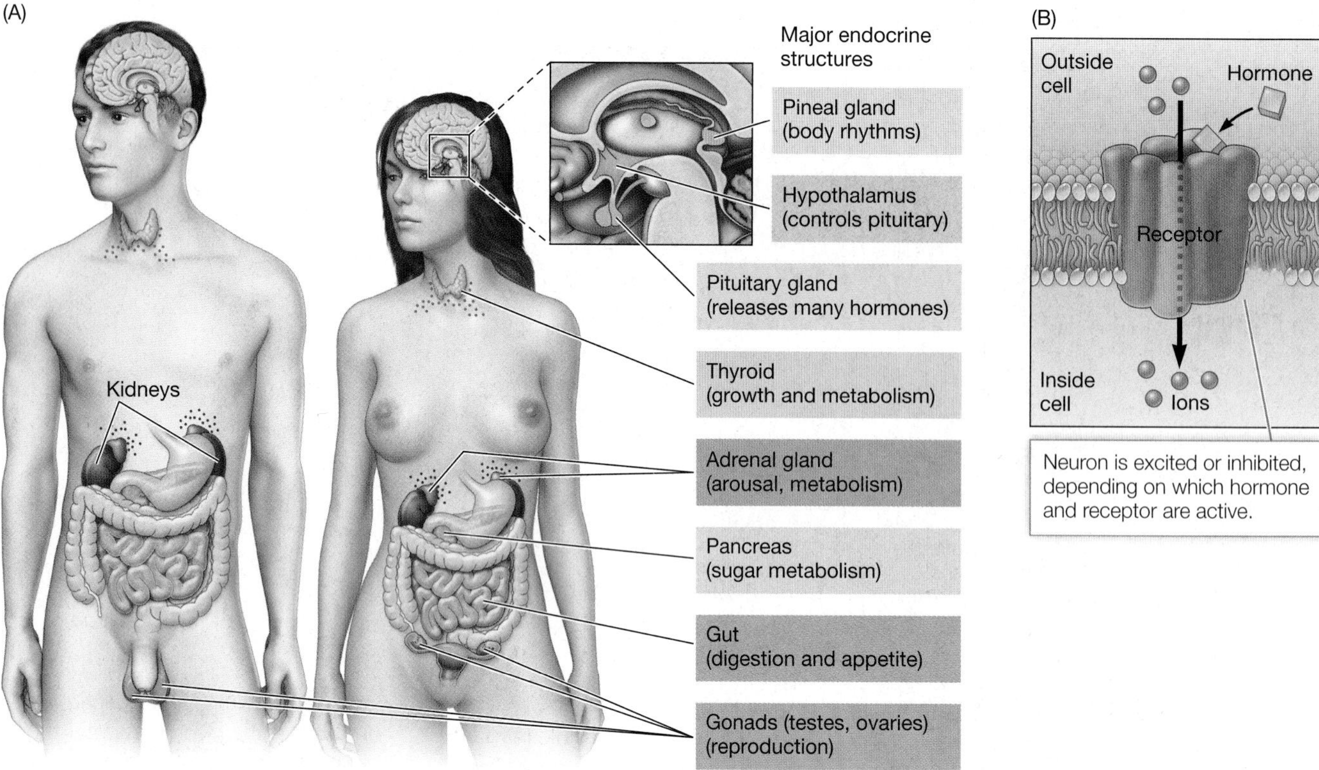

Figure 3.14 Hormone Action in the Body and Brain (A) Endocrine glands throughout the body release hormones into the bloodstream. (B) When the hormones arrive at target neurons, they interact with receptors that may make the neurons more or less likely to produce an action potential.

that affect every other endocrine gland. But this "master" gland is itself entirely controlled by the brain lying just above it. One of our brain's many jobs is to monitor our environment—what's the temperature, what time of day is this, what time of year is this, how old am I, are there any suitable mates nearby—to decide exactly which hormones we need. Note that although our brain determines which hormones to call on, we are unaware of the final decision and unable to consciously affect the outcome (**Figure 3.14A**).

Whenever hormones affect neurons, they may also affect behavior. For example, hormones from the adrenal glands may make us feel anxious, while some hormones from the pituitary are thought to make us more likely to trust other people. The hormone *testosterone*, which builds up muscles, also makes a male more likely to be aggressive and more likely to seek out a mate. Likewise, hormones known as *estrogens* released from the ovary prepare the female's body for pregnancy and make her more receptive to a male that approaches her.

In animals, these effects of hormones on behavior are fairly reliable, but in humans they tend to be very subtle. That means researchers have to use very careful experimental design to see the effects of the hormone, and these effects change the probability of behavior only a little. Nevertheless, the consistency of effects across species, including our own, paints a coherent picture. The hormones act as coordinators, regulating many different processes in many different parts of the body. It happens that the brain is just one more part of the body responding to these coordinating signals (**Figure 3.14B**).

Just as drugs can affect behavior by acting on neurotransmitter receptors, hormones that we take can affect behavior by stimulating those brain regions that normally respond to the natural hormones that our body makes. For this reason, athletes who take steroid hormones such as testosterone may build up their muscles, but they may also become more irritable and aggressive. We'll discuss in greater detail how hormones affect behavior in Section 12.3.

3.2 SUMMARY

- Neurons are *polarized*, having more negatively charged particles inside than outside.
- The difference in electric potential between the interior and the exterior of a biological cell is called the *potential difference*.
- The *resting potential* of a neuron is about –60 mV, but the arrival of neurotransmitter at synapses on the dendrites and cell body can open up ion channels and move the neuron away from its resting potential.
- Excitatory synapses allow positively charged ions in, *depolarizing* the neuron.
- Inhibitory synapses allow negatively charged ions to enter, *hyperpolarizing* the neuron.
- If the neuron is depolarized enough to reach *threshold*, its axon produces an *action potential*, an influx of positive sodium ions that briefly makes the inside of the axon more positive than the outside. Each action potential lasts about 1 ms, so a neuron can produce at most about 1,000 action potentials per second.
- Once generated, the action potential continues down the length of the axon in an *all-or-none* fashion, without getting smaller as it invades each branch of the axon.
- Some axons have insulating sheaths of the fatty substance *myelin*, which speeds up action potential travel down the axon.
- Communication among neurons consists of chemical signals (neurotransmitters) that pass between neurons at synapses, and electrical signals within each neuron that summarize the activity of many synapses and then produce an action potential to release neurotransmitter onto the next cell.
- Electrical stimulation of the brain, as in Deidre's case, triggers action potentials that mimic normal neuronal activity, affecting the mind.
- Drugs affect mental function by acting on receptors in synapses, making neurons more or less likely to produce action potentials.
- In addition to receiving synaptic stimulation, some neurons have receptors that allow them to respond to *hormone* signals from endocrine glands, which can also affect mental function and behavior.

REVIEW QUESTIONS

1. How does an individual neuron sum up all the synaptic input it receives?
2. What changes in the membrane potential make a neuron more likely to produce an action potential? What changes in its membrane potential make a neuron less likely to produce an action potential?
3. How does the neuronal production of action potentials resemble the flushing of a toilet? In what ways do the two processes differ?

Food for Thought

Electrical stimulation at some brain sites causes people to experience intense pleasure.

Should society allow people to get wires installed in their brain to stimulate themselves electronically? Would this be acceptable in some cases and not others?

3.3 Understanding the Nervous System: Divide and Conquer

We've described how neurons gather information from many synapses and summarize that information to decide whether to produce an action potential to communicate with other neurons. We noted earlier that sensory neurons are specialized to detect stimuli such as light or sound or odors to inform the brain about what's happening around us, while motor neurons are specialized to activate our muscles and organs, producing behavior (see Figure 3.3). We'll discuss sensory neurons and motor neurons in detail in later chapters.

Things to Learn

- Divisions of the nervous system
- Four lobes of the cortex and their functions
- How the left side of the brain controls the right side of the body
- Divisions and functions of the autonomic nervous system

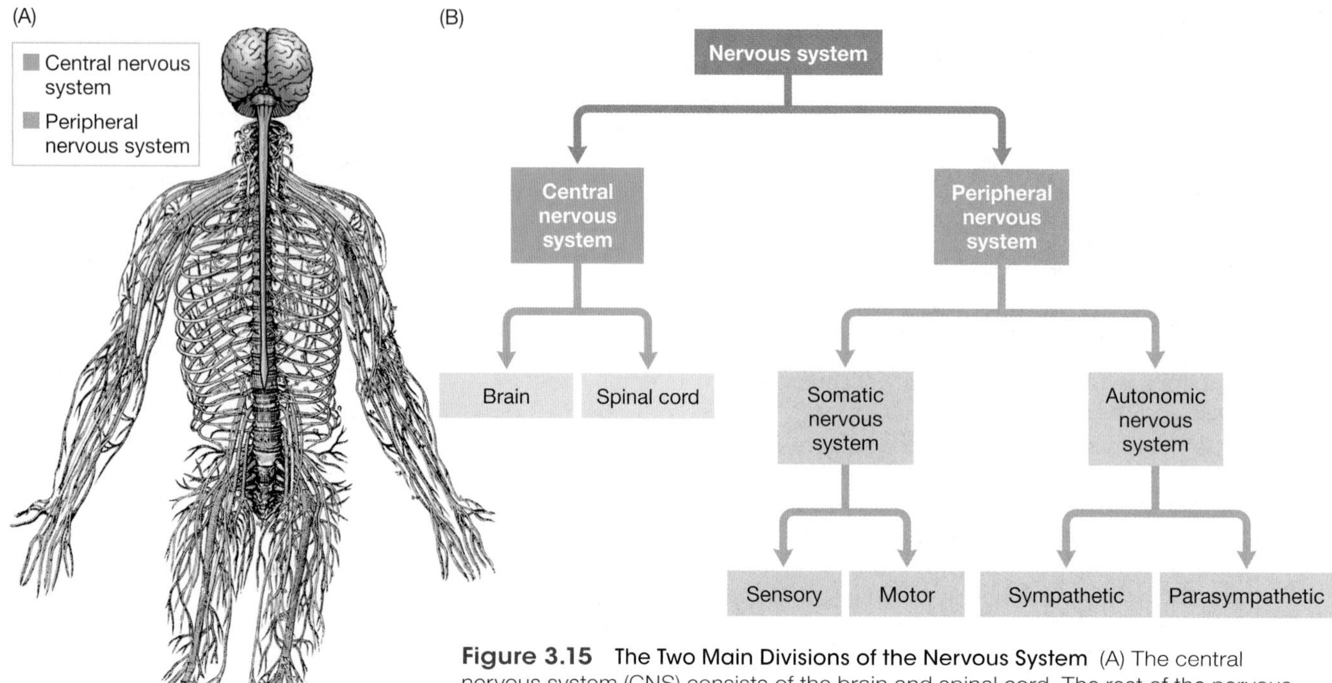

Figure 3.15 The Two Main Divisions of the Nervous System (A) The central nervous system (CNS) consists of the brain and spinal cord. The rest of the nervous system, called the peripheral nervous system (PNS), carries information to the CNS, and also carries commands from the CNS to muscles and organs. (B) Divisions of the nervous system that we will discuss in this section.

For now, let's discuss those many billions of interneurons that listen to sensory neurons and command motor neurons. When put together, these billions of neurons, sending action potentials along axons and communicating through synapses, form a complex communications network in your body called the **nervous system**. The primary center of the nervous system is the **brain**, an organ that coordinates and regulates all body processes, gathers sensory information, makes decisions about what you should do next, then sends commands to every part of your body to produce that behavior.

Like any other machine, the nervous system has a distinctive structure. Neurons are not just distributed haphazardly around the brain. There are many brain regions where collections of neurons are packed closely together. During the Renaissance, early anatomists identified these distinctive parts of the human brain that appear in every person and even, in many cases, in other animals. They gave these parts Latin names, which we still use today, but they had few clues about how they worked. They used the term **nucleus** (plural *nuclei*) to refer to any collection of neuron cell bodies in the brain or spinal cord. It can be confusing that today the same word is also the name for the spherical center of a cell that contains DNA. Think of it this way: the brain has many collections of neurons called nuclei (and each neuron has a nucleus inside).

Early anatomists studying the brain speculated that the various brain nuclei represented functional units, although they had no idea what the functions might be. Neuroscientists have since discovered that various nuclei in the brain do indeed control different behavioral functions. For example, some nuclei play a role in movement control while others are active during stressful or emotional times, as we'll see. In Deidre's case, her doctors were trying to find out which part of her brain was electrically malfunctioning to cause seizures. To decide whether she would be better off having that part of her brain removed, they needed to know what functions were controlled there. If that part of the brain turned out to be important for speech, for example, she might be better off tolerating the seizures than risking the loss of her speech.

nervous system The complex communication network of the body that is composed of all the neurons.

brain The center of the nervous system that coordinates and regulates all body processes.

nucleus The term used by anatomists to refer to any collection of neuron cell bodies in the brain or spinal cord.

The nervous system is vast and complicated. We'll break it into parts, and then subdivide those parts. As a preview, **Figure 3.15A** shows the divisions we'll discuss in this section. When we're done, we'll reassemble the various pieces to understand how the entire nervous system operates.

central nervous system (CNS) The brain and spinal cord.

spinal cord A cylindrical bundle of neurons and axons connected to the base of the brain.

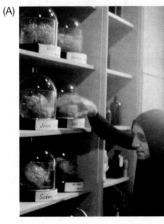

The central nervous system gathers information and makes the big decisions

The first division of the nervous system we'll consider is the **central nervous system** (**CNS**): the brain and spinal cord, which process and control everything we experience and do. Later we'll discuss the *peripheral nervous system*, which carries information between the CNS and the rest of our body (**Figure 3.15B**).

SPINAL CORD About the thickness of your little finger, the **spinal cord** is a cylindrical bundle of neurons and axons connected to the base of the brain. In many ways, the spinal cord acts as a messenger between your brain and body. The brain directly controls only a few muscles, in your head and upper neck. To control your many other muscles, your brain sends commands to the spinal cord. The spinal cord then sends commands to your muscles, for example, to raise your hand or kick your foot out.

Likewise, sensory information from much of the rest of your body, including touch, pain, and the sense of what your muscles are up to, must first pass into the spinal cord. (The brain gets some sensory information directly from your eyes, ears, nose, and tongue.) The spinal cord then tells the brain what has happened. In this way, the brain and spinal cord are constantly swapping information and commands. This is how your brain is aware of what happens to your body and decides what your body will do next.

Damage to the upper part of the spinal cord breaks this communication link between brain and spinal cord, as happened to the late actor Christopher Reeve (famous for his film role as Superman) when he was thrown from his horse. That's why he was unable to move his body below the neck or feel sensation from his body or breathe on his own. Just as the brain is protected by the bony skull, the spinal cord is protected by the bones of the spinal column or backbone, to avoid such injuries. Reeve's spinal cord was damaged when his backbone was broken.

BRAIN Even if your only source of information is science fiction movies, you have some idea of what the human brain looks like (**Figure 3.16A**). Movie makers seem to think that the brain is pink, but in fact the living brain is a light gray organ, tinged with pink because of the extensive network of blood vessels running through it (**Figure 3.16B**). You've probably never seen a living brain, because a thick, bony skull normally protects it.

(A) (B)

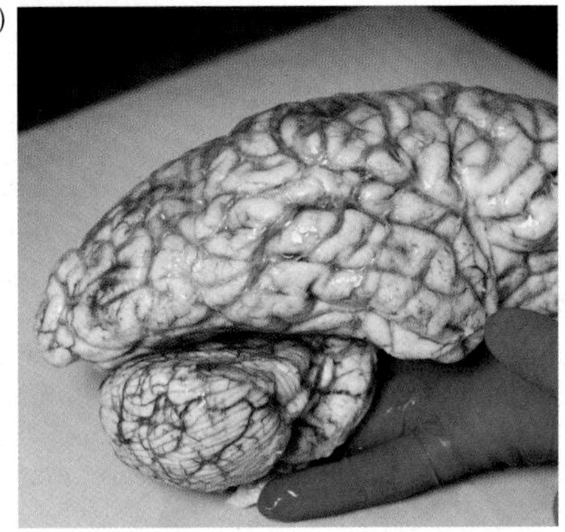

Figure 3.16 Brains in Fiction and in Real Life (A) The only brains most people ever see are fake brains in movies. (B) It is true that the human brain has lots of bumps and ridges on its surface, and requires an extensive blood supply.

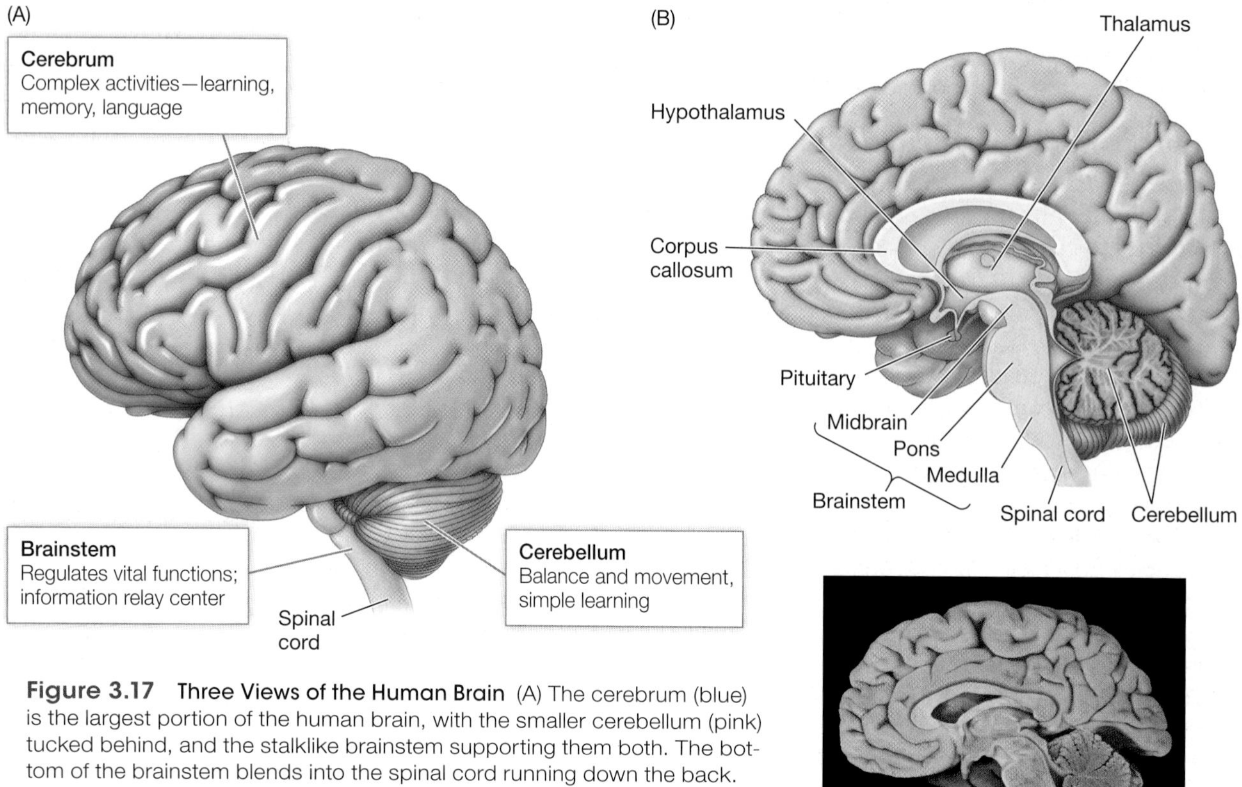

Figure 3.17 Three Views of the Human Brain (A) The cerebrum (blue) is the largest portion of the human brain, with the smaller cerebellum (pink) tucked behind, and the stalklike brainstem supporting them both. The bottom of the brainstem blends into the spinal cord running down the back. The brain and spinal cord together make up the central nervous system, or CNS. (B) If we cut the brain open at the midline and look at the inner surface, we can see the brainstem embedded in the cerebrum, and the cerebellum attached to the brainstem. (C) The brain consists of two hemispheres joined together by the corpus callosum (see part [B]), which sends information back and forth between the right and left halves of the brain.

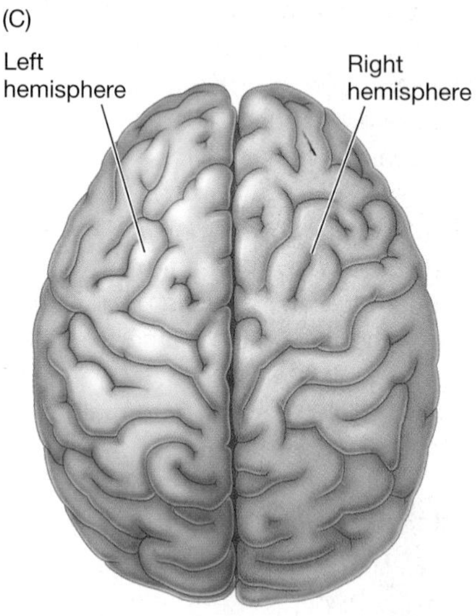

The brain has three main parts: the brainstem, cerebellum, and cerebrum (**Figure 3.17A**). Let's consider each in turn.

brainstem The stalk-like core of the brain that controls vital functions and transfers information between the cerebrum, cerebellum, and spinal cord.

Brainstem When the spinal cord reaches the skull, it merges with a part of the brain called the **brainstem**, the stalklike core of the brain that controls vital functions such as breathing and heart rate, and that transfers information between the cerebrum, cerebellum, and spinal cord. The top of the brainstem, buried deep within the cerebrum, is called the **thalamus** (**Figure 3.17B**). Almost all sensory information from our body, including from our eyes and ears, is first sent to the thalamus. Axons then carry this information back and forth to the cerebrum. The cerebrum decides which sensory information is important, and tells the thalamus to keep sending some information while suppressing other information. This is one way in which we ignore unimportant signals, such as the low buzz that may come from overhead lights.

Just beneath the thalamus is a part of the brainstem called the **hypothalamus** ("hypo" means "below" or "sub," so this name describes its position under the thalamus; see Figure 3.17B). The hypothalamus is tiny but vitally important to such basic brain functions as thirst, hunger, body temperature, and sexual drive. The hypothalamus also controls the nearby pituitary gland, which, as we noted earlier, regulates almost all hormones.

The region of the brainstem beneath the hypothalamus is more or less tubular in shape and can be divided into three parts: the midbrain, pons, and medulla, each containing many brain structures (see Figure 3.17B). A network of neurons in the brainstem, called the *reticular formation*, is crucial for arousing the brain, as we'll discuss in Section 7.2. The brainstem controls many vital functions, such as breathing, heart rate, blood pressure, and the workings of the digestive system. For this reason, damage to the brainstem is often fatal. Axons from neurons in the ears enter the brain through the brainstem, where the first steps in processing sound take place. Brainstem neurons also control many reflexes, such as making the pupil smaller when light hits the eye.

Cerebellum Perched on top of the brainstem, but tucked beneath and at the back of the cerebrum, is what looks like a separate little brain (see Figure 3.17B). The **cerebellum**, which means "little brain," controls balance and coordinates movements of the body. The cerebellum isn't really independent of the rest of the brain. The cerebellum and the rest of the brain are extensively joined together and constantly communicate. People with damage to the cerebellum have difficulty moving smoothly. In recent years it has become clear that the cerebellum is also involved in many other functions in addition to movement, including simple types of learning and sensory processing. Another indication of how many functions are carried out in the cerebellum is that it has been implicated in three apparently very diverse disorders: autism, dyslexia, and attention deficit disorder. We'll discuss each of these disorders in later chapters.

Cerebrum The **cerebrum** is the largest, most complicated part of the brain, sitting atop the rest of the nervous system in humans (see Figure 3.17). It is responsible for all of our most complicated mental processes, including the analysis of sensory information, decision making, and language. The cerebrum is the most important part of the brain for controlling complex behavior.

A deep fissure divides the brain into two halves called the right and left **cerebral hemispheres** (**Figure 3.17C**). The outer part of the cerebrum is called the **cerebral cortex** or just *cortex*. The anatomical word *cortex*, meaning "outer portion," comes from the same root as the word *cork*. The wood for cork comes from the outer layer, the bark, of trees. So cortex can mean the outer layer of any body structure, but in neuroscience the term *cortex* means the cerebral cortex. Now let's look at the cerebrum in more detail.

The cerebral surface is divided into lobes

The cerebrum is wrinkled, like a walnut, with lots of hills, called *gyri* (singular *gyrus*), and valleys, called *sulci* (singular *sulcus*). Renaissance anatomists noticed that prominent valleys, or fissures, divide each of the two cerebral hemispheres into four lobes, shown in **Figure 3.18**.

thalamus The brain region at the top of the brainstem that trades information with the cerebrum.

hypothalamus A part of the brainstem beneath the thalamus that regulates many physiological processes, including hunger, thirst, and temperature.

cerebellum A brain region attached to the brainstem that is involved in the regulation of movement.

cerebrum The brain region atop the brainstem that controls higher mental functions.

cerebral hemispheres The left and right halves of the brain.

cerebral cortex Also called *cortex*. The outer covering of the cerebral hemispheres that consists largely of nerve cell bodies and their branches.

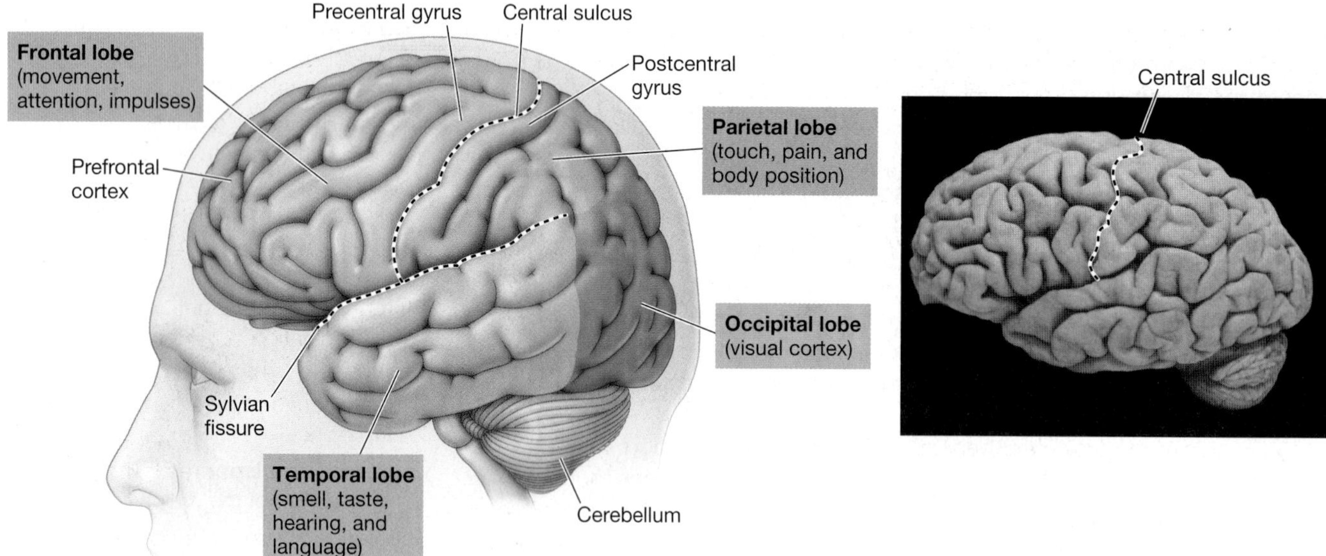

Figure 3.18 Divide and Conquer the Brain The cerebral hemispheres can each be divided into four lobes (shown in different colors). Different functions are associated with each of the four lobes.

In front, just above and behind the eyes, are the appropriately named **frontal lobes** of the cortex. The very front-most part of the frontal lobes, directly above the eyes, is called the **prefrontal cortex**, which is involved in many of our most complex behaviors. A simplified view of the prefrontal cortex is that this region helps us in decision making and impulse control. In Section 5.1 we'll learn that frontal cortex is one of the last regions to mature, in our early twenties, which may relate to poor impulse control in some teenagers and young adults. The frontal lobes are also the brain region that controls movement. The back-most strip of the frontal cortex is called **motor cortex**, where electrical stimulation reliably causes movements of particular parts of the body (the green strip in **Figure 3.19A**). A nearby portion of the frontal lobe, *Broca's area*, is crucial for our ability to speak. Damage here can cause a person to be unable to speak, even though he may still understand others. Curiously enough, Broca's area is found in the left hemisphere; damage to the same region in the right frontal lobe rarely affects language (discussed in Section 10.1).

Behind the frontal lobes are the **parietal lobes** (see Figure 3.18), which analyze information from our skin to give us the sense of touch, pain, and body sense: information about what our body is doing from moment to moment. In the **somatosensory cortex** ("somato" refers to "body"), nerve cells are activated by sensors for touch that are at different parts of the body. As with the motor cortex, the somatosensory cortex displays an orderly organization in which touch signals from neighboring parts of the body arrive at neighboring parts of somatosensory cortex (the purple strip in Figure 3.19A).

Mapping is a technique to determine the role of a particular brain area. Mapping of the motor cortex involves stimulating regions of motor cortex to cause movement in specific parts of the body, resulting in our understanding which parts of the motor cortex innervate certain parts of the body. Similarly, we can touch different parts of the body, and observe which parts of the frontal cortex are stimulated in response to get an idea of what parts of the somatosensory cortex are associated with what parts of the body. Mapping of the cortex has lead to the concept of a *homunculus,* which means "little man," whose body parts are proportional to the amount of brain cortex devoted to

frontal lobes The section of the cerebrum in front, just above and behind the eyes.

prefrontal cortex The frontmost part of the frontal lobes, which is involved in many of our most complex behaviors.

motor cortex The backmost strip of the frontal cortex; it controls movement.

parietal lobes Regions of cortex behind the frontal lobes; they are involved in touch, pain, and sense of body position.

somatosensory cortex The frontmost strip of parietal cortex that receives touch information.

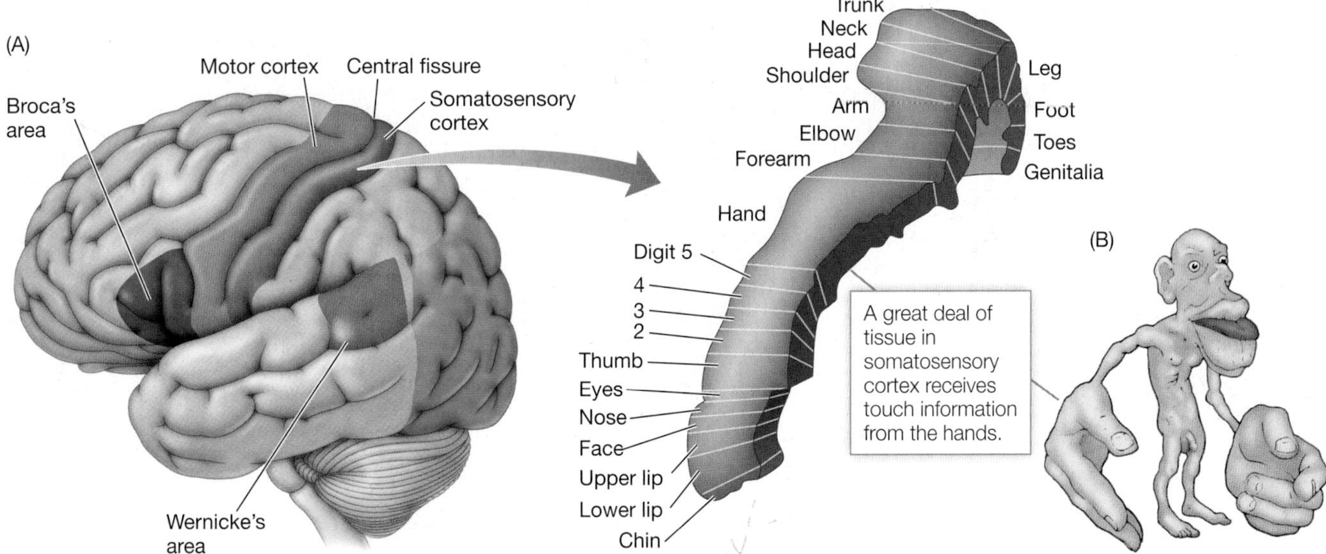

Figure 3.19 The Representation of the Body in the Brain (A) Motor cortex is in the frontal lobe. Somatosensory cortex is in the parietal lobe, just behind motor cortex. Brain cells that send motor commands to a particular part of the body are just across the central fissure from brain cells that receive sensory information from that same part of the body. (B) The size of various body parts in the homunculus reflects how much cortical tissue is devoted to either sending motor commands to that part of the body (motor cortex) or processing sensory information from that part of the body (somatosensory cortex). The homunculus shown here has been mapped from the somatosensory cortex.

them. **Figure 3.19B** shows the homunculus corresponding to the mapping of the somatosensory cortex. The homunculus's body appears distorted because some small parts of the body, such as the lower lip and hands, have many more touch receptors than do some other, larger parts of the body. There is also a map of the body, another homunculus, in the adjacent motor cortex (green strip in Figure 3.19), which corresponds roughly with the somatosensory map.

Returning to Figure 3.18, notice that the **occipital lobes** are at the very back of the brain. This region of the cerebrum receives information from our eyes to give us our sense of vision, so it is sometimes referred to as *visual cortex*. A blow to the back of the head can damage the occipital lobe and leave a person either partially or wholly blind, even if the eyes are undamaged.

In the middle of the brain and to the side are the **temporal lobes** (think of them as next to your temples). The temporal lobes receive information about smell, taste, and sound. The temporal lobes are also crucial for us to understand language. We already noted that Broca's area, which is crucial for *producing* speech, is found only in the left frontal lobe. Similarly, it is the left temporal lobe that processes our *understanding* of speech, in a region called *Wernicke's area* (see Figure 3.19A). In Section 10.1 we'll talk about what happens to language when Broca's area or Wernicke's area is damaged, and later in this chapter we'll see how they become active in the healthy brain during language tasks.

Note that each type of sensation—touch, vision, hearing, taste, smell—reaches a separate part of the cortex. While only a small portion of cortex is motor cortex controlling movement, there are many different regions of **sensory cortex**, devoted to analyzing sensory information. We've just seen that the visual cortex is in the occipital lobe, the auditory (hearing) cortex is in the temporal lobe, and the somatosensory cortex in is the parietal lobe (see Figure 3.18).

occipital lobes Also called *visual cortex*. Regions of cortex at the back of the brain, which receive information from the eyes.

temporal lobes Regions of cortex on the sides of the brain, which receive information about smell, taste, sound, and are critical for understanding language.

sensory cortex Several different regions of cortex devoted to analyzing sensory information.

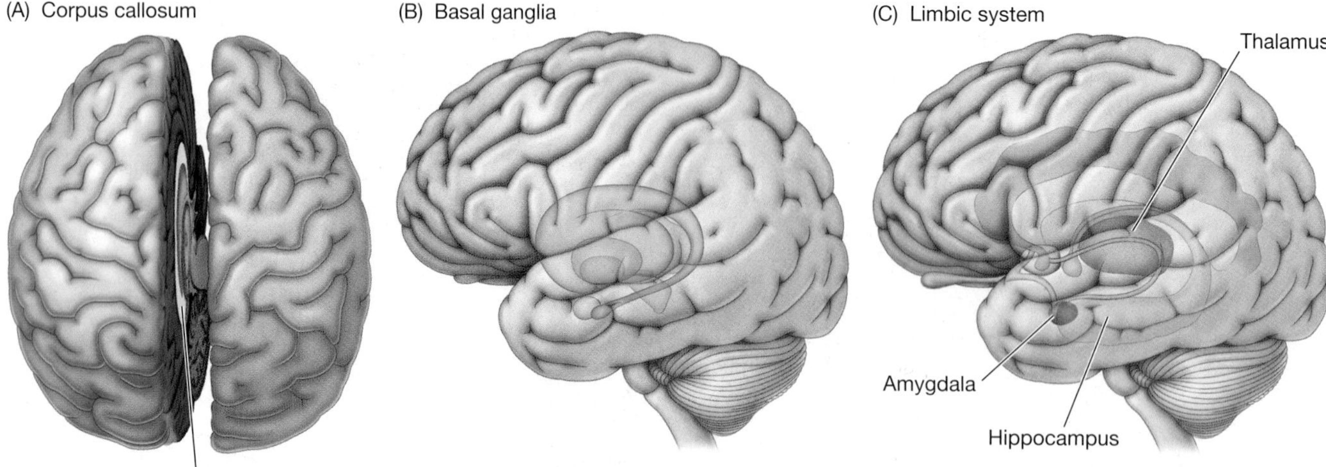

Figure 3.20 Corpus Callosum, Basal Ganglia, and Limbic System (A) The corpus callosum consists of millions of axons communicating information from one cerebral hemisphere to the other. (B) The basal ganglia (blue) are important in motor control. (C) The limbic system consists of different brain regions that are involved in many functions, including memory, emotions, and sensory processing.

Beneath the surface of the cerebral cortex are orderly clusters of cells

So far we've described the outer surface of the cerebrum, the cortex. Under the surface, the **corpus callosum** consists of millions of axons sending action potentials, and therefore conducting information, between the left and right hemispheres (**Figure 3.20A**; see also Figure 3.17B). Also beneath the surface are other brain structures that extensively exchange information with the cerebral cortex. One of these is the **basal ganglia**, a collection of interconnecting nuclei that together help control movement of the body (**Figure 3.20B**). *Parkinson's disease*, which causes the hands or head to show a tremor at rest, is due to a loss of neurons in one part of the basal ganglia. The loss of these neurons happens gradually in all of us, but for some reason it happens faster in some people than in others. Also, some illegal drugs accelerate this loss and with just one dose can "freeze" people, making them unable to move for the rest of their lives. No one makes or sells these toxic drugs on purpose, but sometimes drug dealers manufacture them by accident.

Another collection of regions under the cerebral cortex is known as the **limbic system** (**Figure 3.20C**). The limbic system has many parts. One is the **hippocampus**, which is shaped like a sea horse (*hippocampus* is Latin for "sea horse"). The hippocampus and other parts of the limbic system are crucial for allowing us to form permanent memories (see Section 9.3). Another part of the limbic system is the **amygdala** (from the Greek for "almond," because it's shaped like one). The amygdala, along with other portions of the limbic system, is important in many emotions, especially fear (see Section 13.1). The thalamus, mentioned earlier as the very top of the brainstem, is also part of the limbic system (see Figure 3.17B). Recall its role in swapping sensory information with the cortex. In later chapters we will discuss these structures again. For now, remember that the limbic system includes the hippocampus, amygdala, and thalamus, and that the limbic system as a whole tends to be involved in memory, emotions, and sensory processing.

Having covered many brain regions and many functions, you may want to review by studying **Table 3.3**. Next we'll discuss how each side of the brain relates to the body.

TABLE 3.3 Functions Associated with Major Brain Regions

Brain region	Function	Refer to
Brainstem	Relays sensory and motor information between spinal cord and brain, controls heart rate and breathing	Figure 3.17A
Thalamus	Exchanges sensory information with cortex	Figure 3.17B
Hypothalamus	Many physiological processes, including hunger, thirst, temperature, hormones	Figure 3.17B
Cerebellum	Motor coordination, balance	Figure 3.17A
Frontal lobe	Motor control and higher mental processes	Figure 3.18
Parietal lobe	Somatosensory information	Figure 3.18
Occipital lobe	Visual cortex	Figure 3.18
Temporal lobe	Hearing, language, taste and smell	Figure 3.18
Basal ganglia	Motor coordination	Figure 3.20
Limbic system	Many functions, including learning and emotions	Figure 3.20

Each side of the brain controls the opposite side of the body

Somewhere in our evolutionary history, the common ancestor of all the *vertebrates* (animals with a backbone, including humans and all other mammals, birds, reptiles, amphibians, and fish) already had a central nervous system consisting of a brain and spinal cord. All modern vertebrates inherited a brain and spinal cord from this ancestor. In addition, vertebrates share another aspect of the brain: the left side of the brain controls the right side of the body, and the right side of the brain controls the left side of the body (**Figure 3.21**).

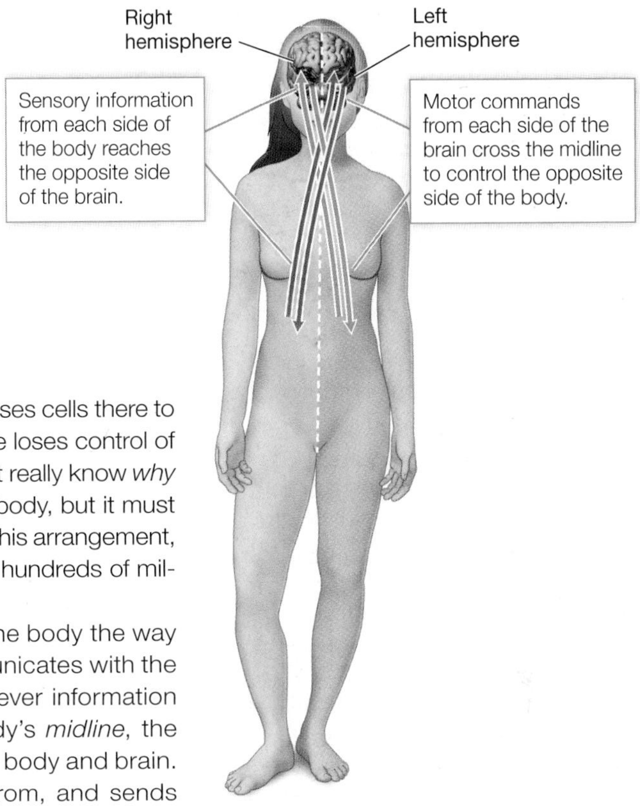

A *stroke* is a loss of blood supply to a part of the brain that causes cells there to die. If someone suffers a stroke on the right side of the brain, she loses control of the left side of the body, or loses sensation from the left. We don't really know *why* the two sides of the brain each control the opposite side of the body, but it must be an arrangement that works well because all vertebrates have this arrangement, and they have successfully survived in every corner of Earth for hundreds of millions of years.

The spinal cord does not command the opposite side of the body the way the brain does. Instead, the left side of the spinal cord communicates with the left side of the body, the right side with the right. But whenever information from the spinal cord travels to the brain, it crosses the body's *midline*, the imaginary line that runs between the left and right sides of the body and brain. For this reason the left side of the brain gets information from, and sends commands to, the right side of the spinal cord. That means that each hemisphere of the brain receives all the sensory information, such as vision, hearing, and touch, from the opposite side of the body, and also sends motor commands to the opposite side of the body.

As noted earlier when we discussed Broca's area and Wernicke's area, in most people the left cortex analyzes language and controls speech. This is an example of **hemispheric specialization** (or *hemispheric lateralization*), the tendency for one side of the brain or the other to perform certain complex tasks. While the left side of the brain handles language and speech, the right side often plays a larger role in emotional processing and in spatial skills such as geometry. This "left-brain, right-brain" specialization, which is often touted in popular books, is not an absolute distinction: both sides normally play a role in language—it's just that the left side normally plays a bigger role than the right for this task. What's more, normally the two sides of the brain are constantly trading information back and forth through the millions of axons that make up the corpus callosum.

In so-called *split-brain patients*, people who have had their corpus callosum cut to control seizures like those Deidre had, only the left hemisphere can talk to us about what it's thinking (Gazzaniga, 2005). We'll discuss split-brain patients in detail in Sections 7.1 and 10.1.

You may have read that the right side of the brain controls speech in left-handed people, but this is not true. Most left-handers, who are using the right side of the brain to control their dominant (left) hand, nevertheless control speech from the left side of the brain, just like right-handers (see Figure 10.14). No one knows why most people are right-handed.

The peripheral nervous system carries information between the body and the central nervous system

Information from our senses and from inside our body is continually flowing into our brain and spinal cord. In response, our brain and spinal cord send out millions of commands, controlling our movements, heartbeats, speech, and just

Right hemisphere
Left hemisphere
Sensory information from each side of the body reaches the opposite side of the brain.
Motor commands from each side of the brain cross the midline to control the opposite side of the body.

Figure 3.21 Switching Sides
A schematic representation of information crossing the midline of the body and brain.

corpus callosum The main band of axons communicating between the two cerebral hemispheres.

basal ganglia A collection of interconnecting nuclei under the cerebral cortex that help control movement of the body.

limbic system A collection of brain nuclei under the cerebral cortex that play a key role in learning, emotions, and sensory processing.

hippocampus Part of the limbic system that is crucial in the formation of permanent memories.

amygdala A group of nuclei, one in each temporal lobe, that is key in producing and recognizing fear.

hemispheric specialization Also called *hemispheric lateralization*. The tendency for one side of the brain or the other to perform certain complex tasks.

nerves Bundles of axons that carry information to and commands from the central nervous system (CNS) to the rest of the body.

peripheral nervous system (PNS) The portion of the nervous system that includes all the nerves and neurons outside the brain and spinal cord.

somatic nervous system The part of the PNS that carries sensory information from the body to the CNS and motor commands from the CNS to the body.

autonomic nervous system A part of the nervous system that is not under our conscious control, consisting of the sympathetic and parasympathetic nervous systems.

sympathetic nervous system The part of the autonomic nervous system that activates the body for action (the "fight or flight" response).

parasympathetic nervous system The part of the autonomic nervous system that prepares the body to relax and recuperate.

about everything our body does. How does the spinal cord communicate with the body? **Nerves** are bundles of axons that send information from all parts of the body into the central nervous system (CNS), or send commands from the CNS to all parts of the body. These nerves are part of the other half of the nervous system, the **peripheral nervous system** (**PNS**), an amazingly elaborate network of nerves that penetrate every inch of our body (see Figure 3.15A). Some nerves contain axons that carry motor information from the brain or spinal cord to muscles. Others have axons that carry sensory information from a part of the body, such as the eyes, to the brain or spinal cord.

The peripheral nervous system itself can be divided into two parts: the somatic nervous system and the autonomic nervous system (see Figure 3.15B). The **somatic nervous system** consists of those millions of nerves that bring us sensory information we are aware of, and the millions more nerves that we use to consciously control our muscles. For this reason, we can say that the somatic nervous system has a *sensory component* that sends information into the central nervous system, and a *motor component* that carries commands from the central nervous system to our muscles. One characteristic of the somatic nervous system is that we are aware of what the sensory component tells us, and we consciously control the commands flowing out to the motor component.

The autonomic nervous system is out of our control

In contrast to the somatic nervous system, the other part of the peripheral nervous system, the **autonomic nervous system**, is an extensive network of nerves that gather information about our body and control countless internal processes *without* our being aware of it or being able to consciously control it. That's why it's called the "autonomic" system—it runs by itself without our having to attend to it, controlling blood pressure, heart rate, sweating, blushing, and hundreds of other processes. Even if we wanted to consciously control our autonomic nervous system, we can't. We cannot tell our autonomic nervous system to lower our blood pressure, or make the left side of our face blush. Damage to the brain or spinal cord can disrupt CNS control of the autonomic nervous system, resulting in sweating and a racing heart at inappropriate times.

There are some processes, such as breathing and urinating, where normally the autonomic nervous system is in charge, but we also have some control. That's because muscles we control through our somatic nervous system can affect those processes. Note that we can always use our somatic nervous system to *indirectly* affect the autonomic nervous system. If we decide to run a few laps, for example, we'll cause our autonomic nervous system to increase our heart rate, breathing, and the like. If we use our somatic nervous system to get on a roller coaster, we'll give our autonomic nervous system a real workout.

We are not aware of the autonomic nervous system regulating bodily processes, but that doesn't mean it is independent of the central nervous system. The autonomic nervous system constantly sends information about bodily processes to the brain and spinal cord. What's more, the brain and spinal cord closely control the activity of the autonomic nervous system. It's simply that we are unable to consciously *control* or be *aware* of those parts of our brain that communicate with the autonomic nervous system. In Sections 7.3 and 13.2 we'll talk about how people use meditation to affect autonomic functions indirectly.

The autonomic nervous system itself can be divided into two parts (**Figure 3.22**). The part of the autonomic nervous system called the **sympathetic nervous system** pumps up physiological processes to prepare your body for action. The sympathetic nervous system causes your heart to beat faster, your breathing to speed up, your blood pressure to rise, the pupil of your eye to open wide.

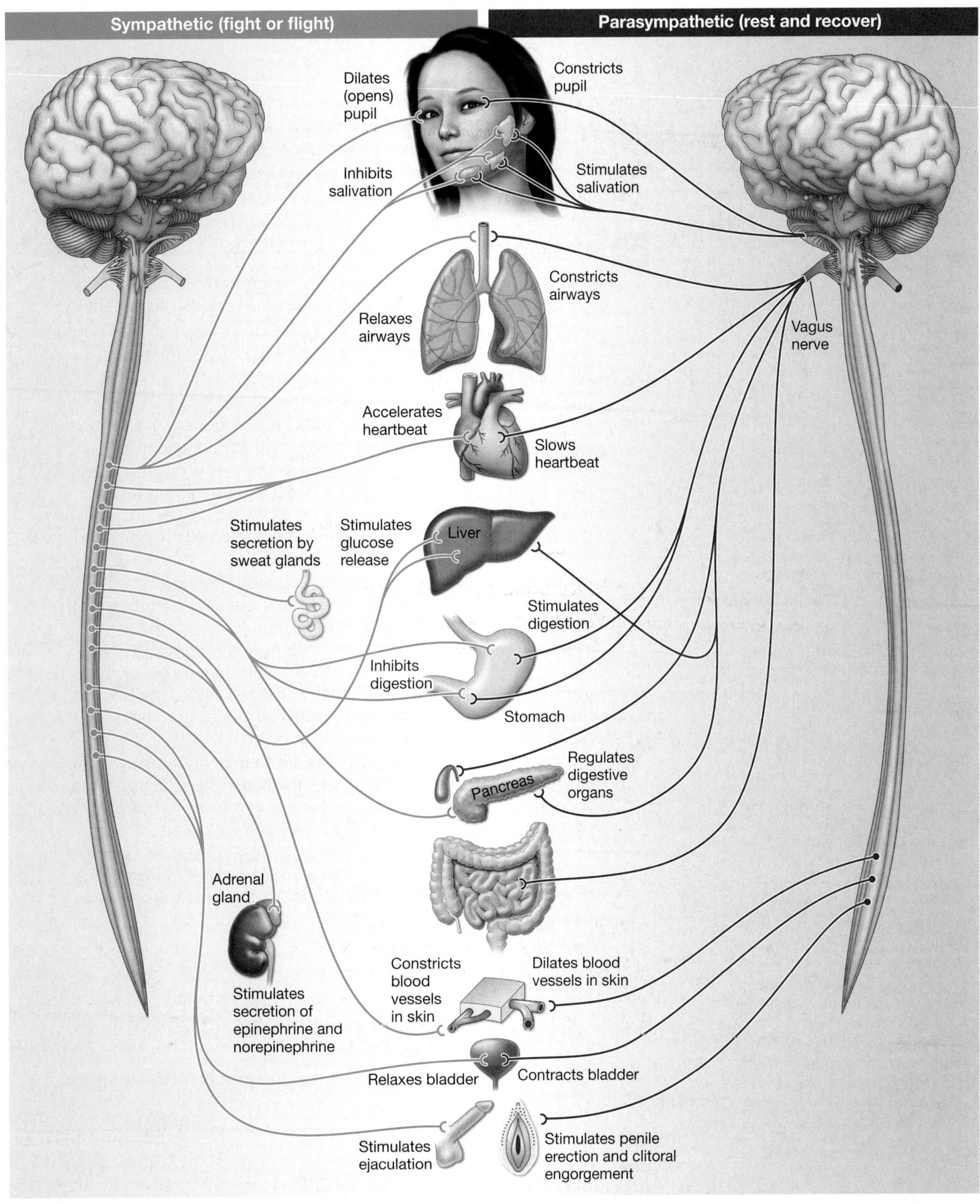

Figure 3.22 The Autonomic Nervous System In general, the sympathetic portion of the autonomic nervous system prepares the body for action, while the parasympathetic portion prepares the body for rest.

This series of changes prepares you to either meet a challenge or run away, so it's sometimes called the "fight or flight" response.

In contrast, the other part of the autonomic nervous system, the **parasympathetic nervous system**, triggers physiological responses to put the body at rest: slowing heart rate and breathing, lowering blood pressure, and shrinking the pupil of the eye. Parasympathetic function is sometimes simplified as "rest and recover" (see Figure 13.1). Notice in Figure 3.22 that the sympathetic and parasympathetic nervous systems use different nerves, coming from different parts of the CNS, even when controlling the same organ, such as the heart or stomach.

Now that we've repeatedly divided and subdivided the nervous system, spend a little time reviewing all the pieces and see how they fit together by consulting again Figure 3.15B.

3.3 SUMMARY

- The *brain* and *spinal cord* make up the *central nervous system* (*CNS*), which analyzes sensory information and controls behavior.
- The *brainstem* is attached to the spinal cord, and includes neurons that are crucial for basic life functions such as breathing.
- Attached to the brainstem is the *cerebellum*, which coordinates motor behaviors.
- Atop the brainstem is the *cerebrum*, which controls higher mental functions, including decision making and language.
- The outer layer of the cerebrum, called *cortex*, is divided into four pairs of lobes. The *frontal lobes* control judgment and decision making, as well as body movement, while the *parietal lobes* analyze touch and pain, the *temporal lobes* analyze smell, taste, sound, and speech, and the *occipital lobes* analyze vision.
- Under the cerebral cortex, the *basal ganglia* are crucial for motor coordination while the *limbic system* plays a key role in learning, emotions, and sensory processing.
- The *peripheral nervous system* (*PNS*) consists of the *somatic nervous system*, which carries sensory information from the body to the CNS and motor commands from the CNS to the body, and the *autonomic nervous system*, which regulates countless internal processes.
- We cannot consciously control the autonomic nervous system, which consists of the *sympathetic nervous system*, preparing the body for "fight or flight," and the *parasympathetic nervous system*, which prepares the body to "rest and recover."
- The left side of the brain receives sensory information from the right side of the body, and controls movement of the right side of the body, but the two sides of the brain normally communicate with each other through a bundle of axons called the *corpus callosum*.

REVIEW QUESTIONS

1. Describe the subdivisions of the CNS and the PNS.
2. Name the major parts of the brain, including the four cortical lobes and some of the structures beneath them.
3. Describe a function that is associated with each of the cortical lobes.

Food for Thought

Somatosensory cortex is organized as a "map," such that neighboring parts of the body send sensory information to neighboring parts of the somatosensory cortex.

What do you think the map of the somatosensory cortex would look like in a person who was born without legs or lost his legs? Would there be a gap in cortex where sensory information from the legs should arrive?

3.4 How We Study the Brain

Things to Learn

- Ways to disrupt brain function
- How EEGs work
- What mirror neurons are
- How to get detailed images of a living brain
- Methods for monitoring brain activity

Because medication was not effective at controlling Deidre's epilepsy, she and her doctors explored the possibility of removing the part of her brain where the electrical overexcitation began. Removing that part of the brain would prevent the overexcitation from spreading to the rest of the brain. That meant Deidre and her doctors needed to find out what functions that part of her brain normally served. Then she could decide whether to risk losing that function for a chance to stop the seizures.

Deidre and her team of neuroscientists were like mechanics, trying to figure out what was going on when this brain machine worked properly and improperly. An auto mechanic can look up detailed descriptions of how a car was manufactured and how it was designed to work, but neuroscientists have to figure out for themselves how the brain works. Let's explore some of the ways in which neuroscientists tinker with the brain to understand behavior.

lesion An area of tissue damage.

transcranial magnetic stimulation (TMS) The temporary, localized disruption of the functioning of a brain region produced by the application of strong magnetic fields.

Lesions and electrical stimulation can map brain functions

Before the twentieth century, the only way to puzzle out the function of different brain regions was the *lesion method*. A **lesion** is an area of damage. In humans, a stroke or a blow to the head may cause brain lesions. As we'll see soon, today technology allows us to see exactly which parts of the brain have been damaged in a living patient. In the past, scientists could learn which part of the brain was damaged only after the patient had died and the brain was removed for examination. Then the researchers tried to associate the patient's symptoms with damage to brain parts. From such cases, early scientists learned that vision depends on the back of the brain (the occipital lobe), that strokes on the left side of the brain often disrupt language, that damage to the brainstem is almost always fatal, and many of the other things we've discussed so far in this chapter.

An infamous use of lesioning was in *lobotomy*, the deliberate cutting of connections in the frontal lobe, which was used to treat schizophrenia, depression, and even, as we'll see in Chapter 16, unruly teenage behavior! This now discredited treatment, widely used in Europe and the United States until the 1960s, did not actually help any of those disorders. But many people alive today who had a lobotomy show deficits in attention or arousal, so these lesions are one source of evidence that the frontal lobes are important for directing attention.

Today it is possible to inhibit the activity of a small patch of brain temporarily, like a reversible lesion. **Transcranial magnetic stimulation (TMS)** uses a coil of wire placed over the skull. By rapidly changing the electrical current in the coil, researchers can generate a changing magnetic field that disrupts functioning in the brain region underneath the coil (**Figure 3.23**). Placing the coil over the left temple, and therefore over the left temporal cortex, can disrupt a person's ability to understand speech for a short while. No one knows exactly how TMS disrupts brain function. It probably affects electrical signals, but we don't know the details. We don't know why the effect is temporary, but TMS is being tested as a treatment for a variety of disorders, like depression. For now, TMS is typically used experimentally to locate brain regions that influence specific behaviors.

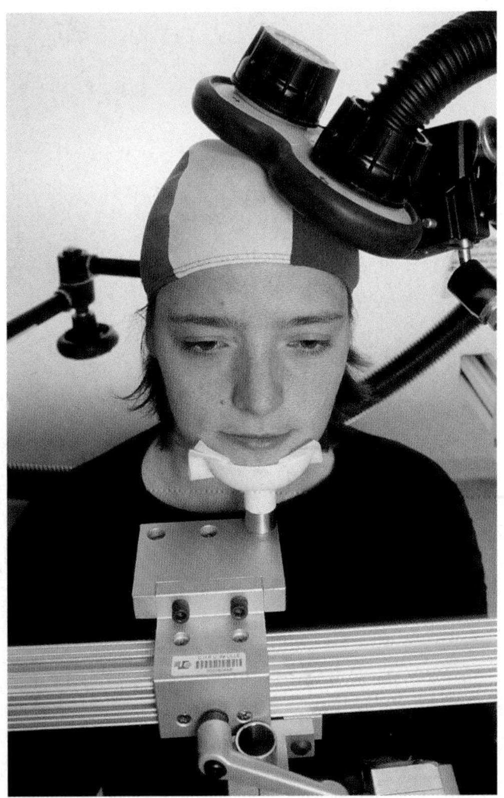

Figure 3.23 Transcranial Magnetic Stimulation (TMS) A rapidly changing magnetic field can affect electrical activity in a targeted region of the brain, temporarily disrupting synaptic processes there.

All lesion studies have limitations. Just because destruction or disruption of a given brain region disrupts a particular behavior doesn't mean that it is the *only* brain region responsible for that behavior. It is likely that other brain regions also contribute to that behavior. Studies of brain activity during behavior, using methods we'll discuss shortly, confirm that many brain regions are active during any behavior. So when lesions disrupt a behavior, that result indicates that this particular brain region is one of several brain parts involved in the behavior. Also, it is possible that a lesion in a brain region X is just disrupting the exchange of information between two other brain regions, Y and Z, that are really doing all the important work for a behavior. In some ways, we learn the most from lesion studies when the behavior is *not* affected. Massive damage to the right hemisphere has only a small effect on language, so we can conclude that the right hemisphere is not essential to language.

Instead of destroying or inhibiting a brain region to see which behaviors are disrupted, we can take another strategy and ask what behaviors occur when we electrically stimulate different brain parts. We've already seen how electrical stimulation of Deidre's brain gave us some idea of the function of different brain regions. Stimulating some parts of the brain makes a person move, stimulating other regions makes a person hear sounds that aren't really there, and stimulating yet other regions causes a person to see lights, or to find something really funny.

Most lesion and electrical stimulation experiments use non-human subjects, but in general the results are remarkably consistent with what has been seen in humans. For example, whether the subject is a person, rat, or lizard:

- Stimulating the left frontal cortex will cause movement on the right side of the body.
- Stroking the skin on the right side of the body will cause neurons in the left parietal lobe to fire action potentials.
- Lesioning the left occipital lobe will disrupt vision on the right.

These and *many other commonalities* revealed by lesion and stimulation studies remind us that other animals really are our distant cousins, and that we all inherited these aspects of brain organization from common ancestors.

Scientists can eavesdrop on electrical signals within the brain

You've seen that neurons use two different kinds of electrical signaling: (1) tiny fluctuations in voltage around synapses when neurotransmitters bind to receptors and, if enough of these voltage changes reach the axon, (2) action potentials that carry information from the neuron's cell body to its axon tips. You probably won't be surprised to learn that devices can detect this electrical activity to give us some idea of what's happening in the brain. Early in the twentieth century, as the machines for measuring voltage became more sensitive and accurate, scientists sought to determine the difference in voltage between two places on the scalp. The idea was to eavesdrop, detecting electrical signals in the brain underneath the scalp. These machines are called electroencephalographs, and these days their output is displayed on a computer screen (**Figure 3.24**).

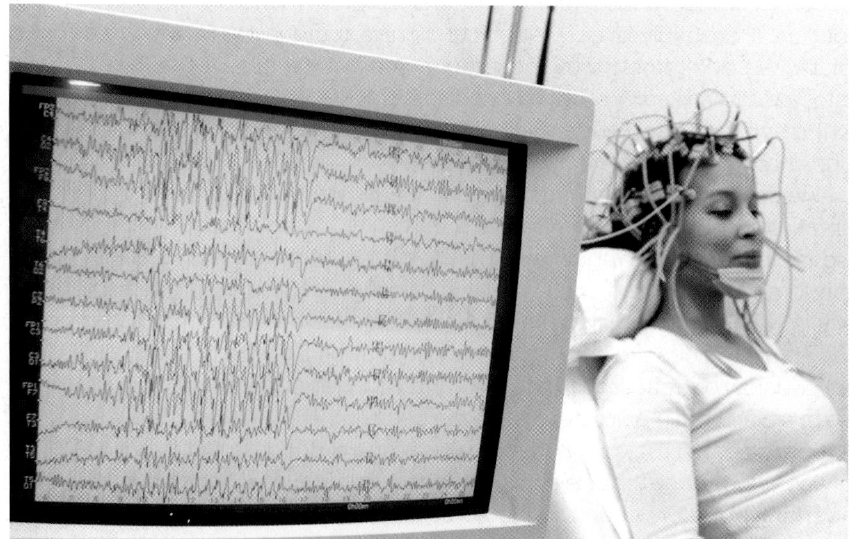

Figure 3.24 Electroencephalogram (EEG) The EEG tracings on the left side of the computer screen include large, synchronous discharges of a seizure.

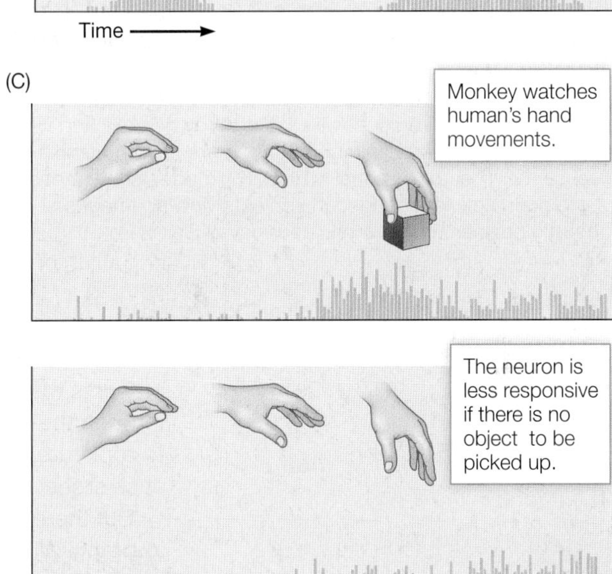

Figure 3.25 Eavesdropping on Neuronal Activity (A) In this portion of the cortex many mirror neurons are found. (B) This neuron fires just before the monkey reaches for the raisin, or when the monkey observes a human experimenter reaching for the raisin in the same manner. (C) This mirror neuron fired when the monkey observed a human reaching for a box (top). The mirror neuron also fires, but much less vigorously, if there is no box for the human to grasp. (After Rizzolatti et al., 2006; Umiltá et al., 2001.)

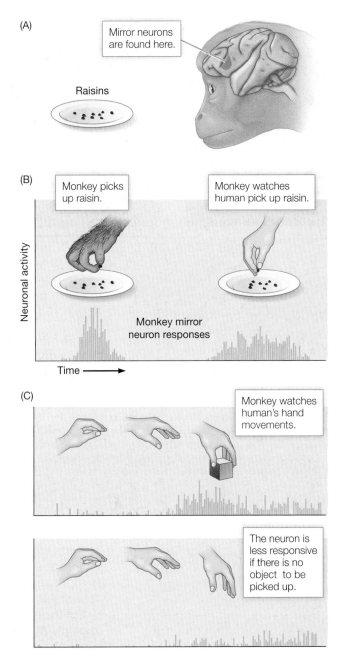

The resulting **electroencephalogram** (**EEG**) reveals, for example, that the electrical activity measured from the brain is different if a person is awake or asleep. The EEG can also detect electrical storms during epileptic seizures such as those Deidre had. By comparing EEG signals from many different pairs of wires on the scalp, it's sometimes possible to locate where a seizure begins and to monitor its spread across the brain. EEG recordings are important for detecting different sleep states, as we'll learn in Section 7.2.

In animal subjects, we can eavesdrop on the electrical activity of individual neurons, and there are times when these studies offer tantalizing glimpses into how the human brain may work. For example, scientists implanted tiny wires in the brains of monkeys to detect action potentials of individual neurons in a portion of the frontal cortex known to be important for motor control of the hand. So they were not too surprised to detect neurons that fired whenever the monkey made a particular gesture, such as picking up a raisin. But they were surprised to see that the same neurons also fired whenever the monkey saw *someone else* pick up a raisin in the same way (**Figure 3.25**; Umiltà et al., 2001). Many such neurons have been found in this particular region of the frontal cortex; they are called **mirror neurons** because they are active whenever the subject performs a particular act or watches someone else mirror that same behavior. There is great interest in mirror neurons because they seem to provide a neural basis for imitating other individual's behavior, or for understanding someone else's action. Perhaps they will prove relevant to human disorders, such as autism (see Section 5.2), where people have difficulty understanding the behavior of others (Hamilton, 2013). Scientists have found evidence of mirror neurons in humans too (Press et al., 2012), using imaging technology that we'll discuss next.

Today's imaging technology reveals the brain's interior structure and function

The past few decades have changed the way we study the mind at work. If X-rays are pointed at your forehead, detectors placed behind your head will show differences in how many X-ray particles come out the other side. More X-rays will come out the other side if they pass through fluid-filled spaces than through solid brain. If we circle the entire brain, directing X-rays at many different angles, we can use computers to analyze how well the rays passed through from each angle. From this information, we can then reconstruct a three-dimensional view of where the fluid is and detect differences between really dense brain tissue

electroencephalogram (EEG) A recording of fluctuating potentials taking place in the brain, made by an electroencephalograph.

mirror neuron Neuron that is active both when an individual makes a particular movement and when that individual sees another individual make that same movement.

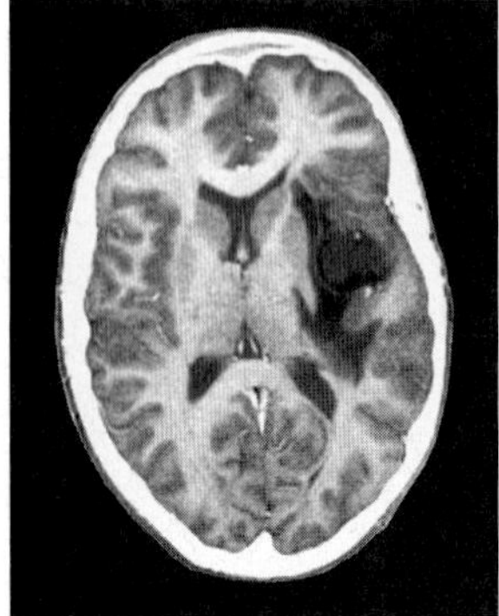

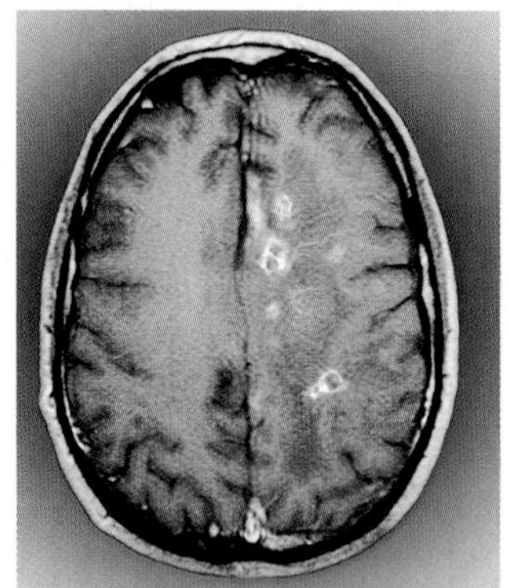

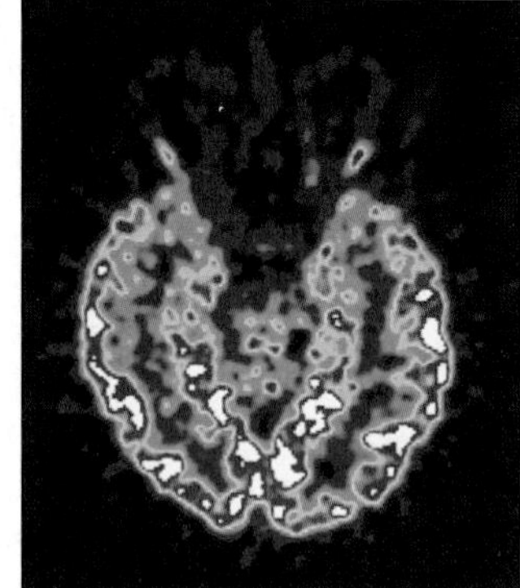

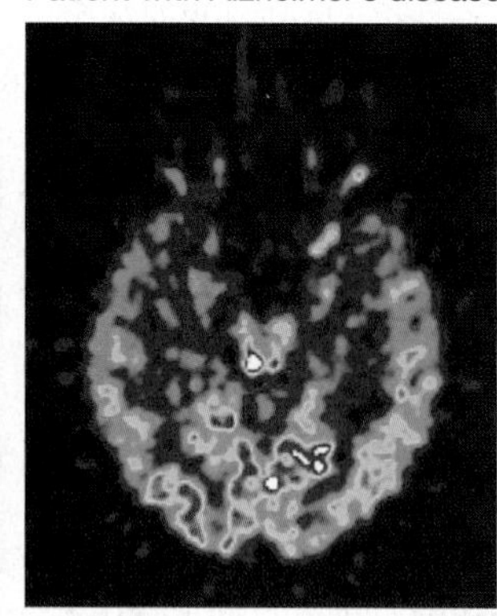

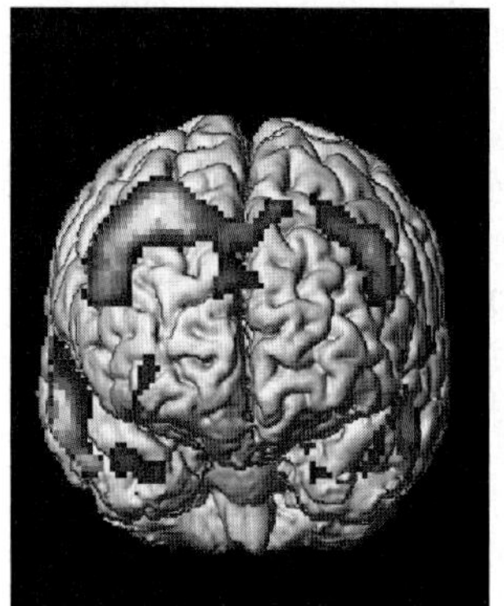

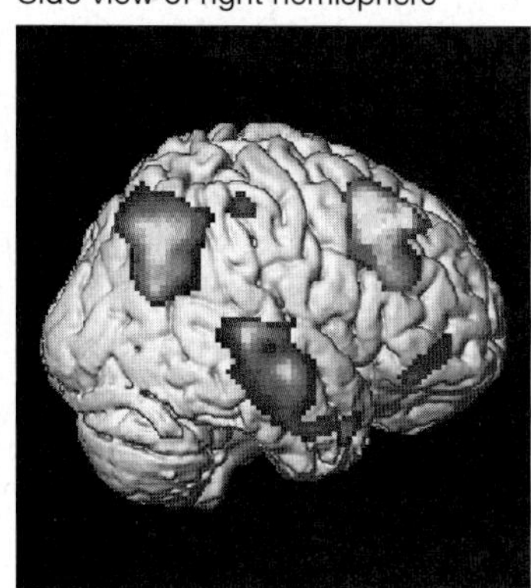

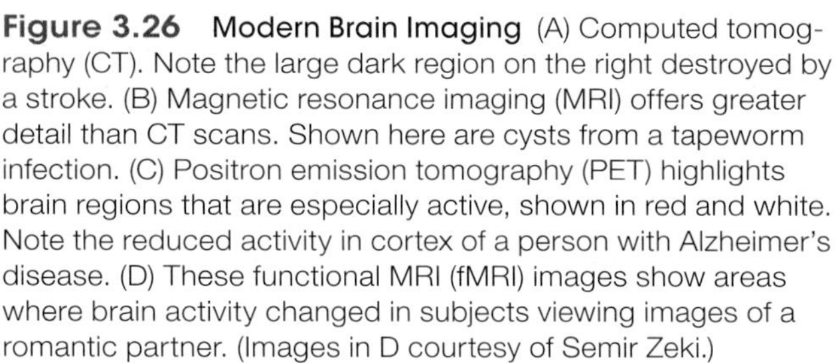

Figure 3.26 **Modern Brain Imaging** (A) Computed tomography (CT). Note the large dark region on the right destroyed by a stroke. (B) Magnetic resonance imaging (MRI) offers greater detail than CT scans. Shown here are cysts from a tapeworm infection. (C) Positron emission tomography (PET) highlights brain regions that are especially active, shown in red and white. Note the reduced activity in cortex of a person with Alzheimer's disease. (D) These functional MRI (fMRI) images show areas where brain activity changed in subjects viewing images of a romantic partner. (Images in D courtesy of Semir Zeki.)

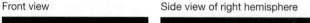

and less dense tissue. This technique, called **computed tomography** (**CT**), presents much more detailed images than old-fashioned X-rays that pass once through the brain to reach a plate of film on the other side. "Tomography" refers to a picture made by putting together lots of different "slices" of brain, in this case slices revealed by the various beams of particles (**Figure 3.26A**).

But there's a better way to see the brain than with CT. **Magnetic resonance imaging** (**MRI**) provides a more detailed view of brain structure, and a better sense of varying density of brain tissue, than CT does (**Figure 3.26B**). Instead of passing X-rays through the head, MRI subjects the head to a magnetic field thousands of times stronger than Earth's magnetic field. The patient doesn't notice it, but the protons in water molecules in the head are pulled by the magnetic field. If the field is then turned off, the protons jump back (physicists say they "resonate") and in doing so send radio frequency signals out of the head at all angles. Detectors keep track of all these signals coming out, and computers reconstruct the three-dimensional structure of the brain.

CT and MRI allow us to see a *brain*, but how can we watch a *mind* at work? For that, we have to go beyond brain *structure* and monitor brain *process*. There is a way to estimate brain process. The brain requires so much energy to work (think of all those ion channels opening and closing, ions pumping out of cells, assembly of neurotransmitters, and recycling of vesicles) that blood flow is carefully controlled for every brain region. When one brain region is active, blood flow increases to that area to provide the oxygen and nutrients needed. So if we can trace the blood flow in various brain regions, we'll know

computed tomography (CT) A technique for examining brain structure through computer analysis of X-ray particles passing through the head from several different positions.

magnetic resonance imaging (MRI) A technique that uses magnetic fields to generate images revealing structural details in the living brain.

which parts of the brain are working hard during a particular task and which parts are less active.

One way to do this is to add a radioactive marker to the blood and use particle detectors and computers to find where most of the radioactive markers in the blood are going. The more radioactivity in a region, the more blood is there and therefore the more that brain region must be working. The radioactive molecules emit particles, called positrons, which produce rays that pass through the skull and are detected. That's why this method is called **positron emission tomography (PET)** (**Figure 3.26C**). If the radioactive marker is part of a chemical that binds to particular neurotransmitter receptors, PET can even reveal how those receptors are distributed in the brain.

MRI can also tell us how blood is flowing inside the brain, without injecting radioactive fluid or anything else into the bloodstream. This method, called **functional MRI (fMRI)**, requires rapidly turning on and off a magnetic field around the whole head (**Figure 3.26D**). The signals released from iron in the oxygen-carrying molecules in the blood differ depending on whether an oxygen molecule is present. So by keeping track of these two different signals (oxygen or no oxygen) from billions of individual molecules, we can determine how much oxygen is present. The blood vessels in the brain bring more oxygen to those regions that are doing more work. fMRI can detect which brain regions are active when a person is looking at colors, moving a finger, or reading a book. As you will see many fMRI images in this book and in the popular press, it is important for you to understand how they are made, which we'll explain next.

positron emission tomography (PET) A technique for examining brain function using injections of radioactive substances used by the brain. Particle detectors and computers are used to find where most of the radioactive markers gather in the brain.

functional MRI (fMRI) Magnetic resonance imaging that detects changes in blood flow and oxygen content, identifying regions of the brain that are particularly active during a given task.

We infer brain function by comparing different mental activities

In Chapter 1 we discussed that absurd myth that "we only use 10% of our brain." This pseudo-fact has circulated for at least 60 years. In fact, fMRI shows that the *entire brain is active whenever we are awake*, even if we're doing something as boring as staring at a dot on a blank screen. The question is which parts of the brain become *more* active when we're doing one task rather than another. Scientists have used this strategy to figure out which parts of the brain are particularly involved in different mental processes, as is described in **Figure 3.27**.

☑ Researchers At Work

Mental subtraction

Figure 3.27 Isolating Specific Brain Activity

■ **Question:** Are different parts of the brain active during different mental processes?

■ **Hypothesis:** Brain regions engaged in a specific mental process, like visual processing, can be isolated by subtracting resting scans from scans during that activity.

■ **Test:** Participants are scanned twice—once while looking at a blank screen, and once while looking at a test stimulus. The control scan is then subtracted from the test scan.

■ **Results:** By repeating the process and averaging the results across several people, a stable "difference image" showing activation of just a few brain regions is formed.

Continued

Researchers at Work *Continued*

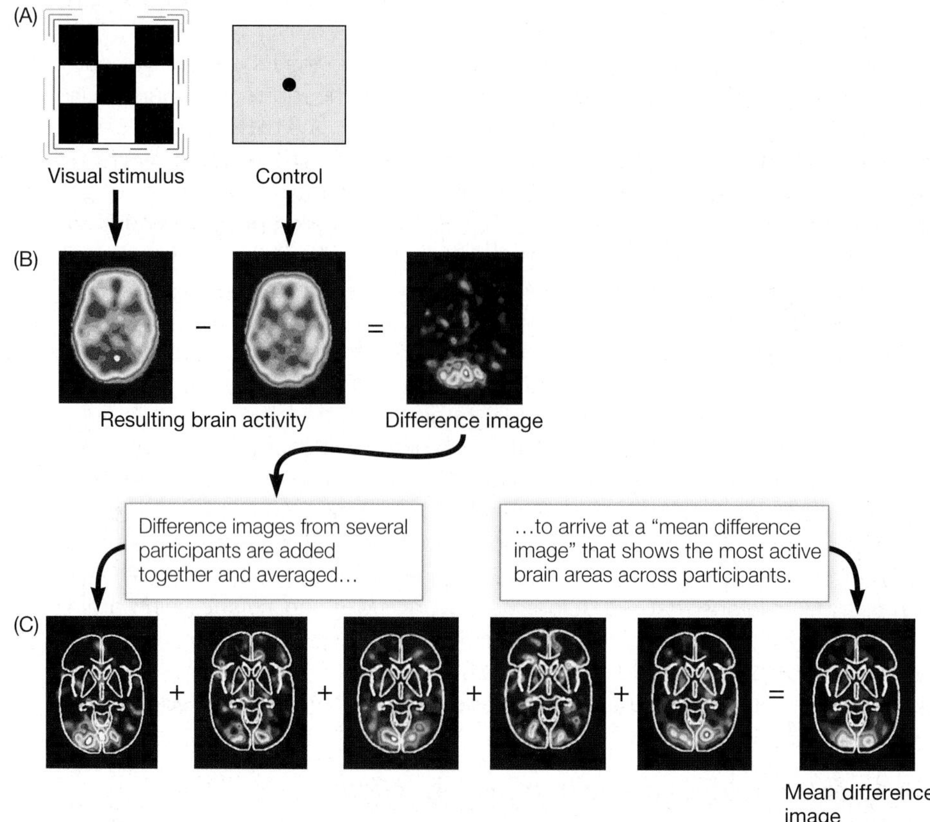
(A)
Visual stimulus
Control
(B)
Resulting brain activity
Difference image
Difference images from several participants are added together and averaged…
…to arrive at a "mean difference image" that shows the most active brain areas across participants.
(C)
Mean difference image

■ **Conclusion:** The activated brain regions in the difference image—in this case, the occipital cortex—are involved in the mental activity of visual processing. This result conforms with many other reports, using other methods, that occipital cortex is crucial for vision.

The process used in Figure 3.27, in which a baseline image is subtracted from an image of a mental activity, can be used to study many behaviors—for example, which brain regions are especially active when we are simply seeing words, rather than listening to them, saying them out loud, or reasoning about their meaning. Such studies confirm what we told you earlier, that Wernicke's area, in the temporal lobe on the left side (but not the right) is active when we are understanding language, and Broca's area in the left frontal lobe is important when we are producing speech.

For someone like Deidre, who was considering having surgery to open her skull and remove the part of her brain that started seizures, noninvasive imaging methods are a big help. The surgeon can have an excellent, detailed picture of what that particular patient's brain looks like before surgery. Sometimes it is even possible to see the small damaged region that is starting the seizure.

These new methods of keeping track of which brain regions are active during different behaviors are constantly improving, giving us more detail about smaller and smaller parts of the brain and about rapid changes in brain activity. We can now ask: Which part of the brain is especially active when we are solving math problems in our head, navigating through complex city streets in a video game, or listening to someone speaking English versus Spanish? It turns out that different tasks activate different brain regions, and each of those different brain regions is in about the same place in every person. These new approaches represent our best hope for one day understanding how a machine called the brain can produce the miraculous process we call the mind.

Psychology and biology use two different vocabularies to describe the same thing

In this chapter we've seen many instances in which the brain is like a machine. It's made of neurons, glia, and other cells rather than gears and pulleys, or chips and motherboards. But just like gears and pulleys, the cells in the brain interact with each other *physically*, swapping chemical transmitters, triggering electrical signals, and eventually commanding muscles to move. When Deidre had a seizure, it wasn't because some devil invaded her body, as some ancient peoples thought, but because some neurons became overexcited and that overexcitement spread across her brain. There's no ghost inside us providing a mind in addition to physical interactions. Rather, the mind is a process generated by those physical interactions. So we can describe anything the mind does either in terms of process or machinery.

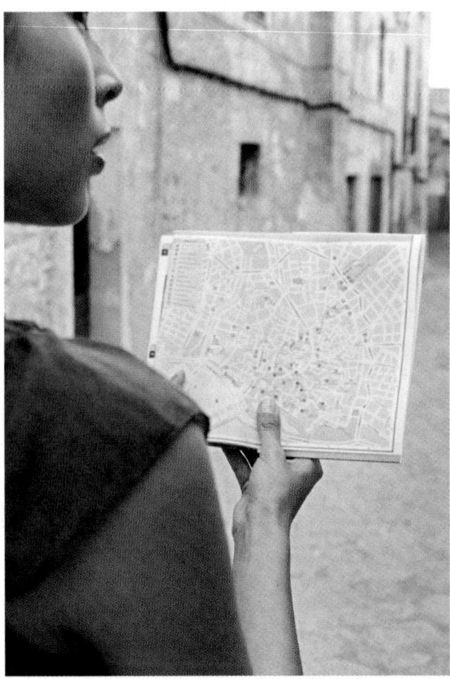

The Brain at Work Which parts of the brain are active when a person is reading a map?

This may be a new way of thinking about yourself, but if you consider it you'll realize that anything you experience—joy, pain, or remembrance—can be described in two fundamentally different ways. You can talk about the feelings as you experience them (process), or if you know enough, you can talk about what the various nerve cells of the brain are doing (machine) during joy, pain, or remembrance. You can use different terminologies, either psychological descriptors (joy, pain, remembrance) or biological descriptors (nerves, synapses, electrical currents). In other words, psychology and biology use two different vocabularies to describe the exact same thing.

We've talked about the structure of the brain in general terms, but in fact your brain is constantly changing. It's never the same from one minute to the next. Everything that happened to you to change your future behavior has left a physical change in your brain (otherwise your behavior wouldn't have changed). The brain machine displays **plasticity** (or *neural plasticity*), which means it can change easily (plastic materials were named "plastic" in the first place because they're easily molded to any shape). You remember that nice thing that happened to you last week because the experience altered the structure of your brain to allow you to remember it! What changed in your brain? We'll discuss these ideas about plasticity in Section 9.3.

plasticity Also called *neural plasticity.* The ability of the brain to change in structure or function.

After surgery removed the part of her brain that was triggering seizures, Deidre was free to pursue the rest of her life. Maybe one day she was having a picnic by a lake when she suddenly remembered a picnic long ago with a family friend who is now dead. We can describe that experience in purely psychological terms:

1. Deidre experienced a gentle breeze, the sunshine, a checkered tablecloth on grass, the blue lake.
2. These experiences reminded her of the earlier picnic there, and she remembered something the friend said that day.
3. She felt sad, and tears pricked her eyes.

These psychological terms all relate to the *process*: Deidre's mind experiencing these events. Perhaps one day we will be able to describe the same scene in biological terms:

1. Light from the lake, tablecloth, and grass excited neurons in Deidre's eyes, and neurons under her skin were activated by the breeze.
2. This information reached her brain, and because it was similar to the earlier event, it activated neurons that stored the information from that previous picnic, her friend, and his subsequent death.
3. The activation of these neurons in turn activated another network of neurons that gave Deidre the experience of sadness the day her friend died, activating the autonomic nervous system to release tears.

Notice that the biological description is vague. We know a lot about how visual scenes activate the retina, but we don't really know much about which neurons are active when we're sad. Probably the limbic system plays a role in sadness. We know that the autonomic nervous system triggers the tears, but we don't know what determines when that trigger gets pulled. In short, there's a lot we don't know about the biology of conscious life. On the other hand, people have been talking about such events in *psychological* terms for thousands of years (maybe a million years). Plus, because each of us has had experiences like these, it's easy for us to relate to them in psychological terms.

In contrast, our biological understanding of the brain is fairly new and primitive. Will there come a time when we can describe exactly what happens in the brain, in biological terms? A major international effort to expand our understanding of neuroscience, described next, is intended to help reach that goal.

The Cutting Edge

Mapping the Connectome in the Human Brain

The estimated number of synapses in the human brain that we mentioned earlier is so vast (10^{15}) that it's difficult to grasp. Yet there are two major, multibillion-dollar efforts to understand those connections. The Human Brain Project (www.humanbrainproject.eu) is supported by the European Union, while the U.S.-supported project is called the BRAIN Initiative (http://www.nih.gov/science/brain/). Everyone agrees that the idea of mapping all the connections (sometimes called the connectome) and all the activity of a human brain is incredibly ambitious, and plenty of neuroscientists are skeptical that it can be done (Waldrop, 2012).

(A)

(B)

Figure 3.28 The Jam-Packed, Highly Connected Brain Neurons are encased in a dense matrix of other axons, dendrites, and glia. (A) A reconstruction of what a tiny cube of the brain is really like, using different colors to identify the different cells involved. Ten of these cubes placed side by side would be about the width of an average human hair. (B) A human brain map would also have to keep track of long-distance connections, a tiny fraction of which are shown here. (Part A courtesy of Daniel Berger and Jeff Lichtman.)

To further appreciate how daunting this task really is, you need to realize that illustrations of neurons in textbooks (including this one) are necessarily misleading in one regard: To convey the parts and functions of a neuron, we illustrate one or only a few cells as if they were alone. But in reality, neurons are encased in a dense matrix of other axons, dendrites, and glia. **Figure 3.28A** shows a reconstruction of what a tiny cube of the brain is really like. At many points where two different-colored cell parts come together, one or more synapses are present. Imagine how difficult it would be to untangle all those parts to figure out who's communicating with whom. In addition to that challenge, some axons stretch out tremendous distances, so a human brain map would also have to keep track of those long-distance connections, which are revealed by a brain imaging technique called **diffusion tensor imaging** (**DTI**). A tiny fraction of these "axonal highways" are shown in **Figure 3.28B**.

Of course, just because it's daunting doesn't mean we can't try. At least one of the goals of these projects is to discover new technologies to make the seemingly impossible possible. But the next step seems even more daunting. Even if we are able to catalog all the synapses in the brain, and to map all the differences in activity of 100 billion neurons, will we be able to understand how that activity relates to the mind? Obviously I don't know, but I'm certainly eager to stick around and see.

diffusion tensor imaging (DTI) A brain imaging technique that reveals axonal connections.

3.4 SUMMARY

- One way to study brain function is to examine behavior after the brain has incurred a *lesion*, an area of damage caused by a stroke, a blow to the head, or an experimental procedure.
- *Transcranial magnetic stimulation* (*TMS*) allows scientists to temporarily disrupt function in a brain region through the skull, without surgery.
- Electrical stimulation of different brain regions elicits different behaviors or mental states, indicating that those particular brain regions play some role in those particular behaviors.
- *Electroencephalograms* (*EEGs*) record signals from electrodes placed on the surface of the scalp to detect electrical signals generated by the activation of synapses in the brain. EEGs can detect different sleep states and epileptic seizures.
- Brain imaging techniques include *computed tomography* (*CT*) and *magnetic resonance imaging* (*MRI*), which offer detailed views of the human brain, while *functional MRI* (*fMRI*) and *positron emission tomography* (*PET*) reflect the mind at work by showing which brain regions are especially active when a person is performing a particular task.
- Imaging techniques indicate a close relationship between the function of our brain as a (very complicated) machine and our mental state. This modern picture of the mind refutes Descartes's concept of dualism, that the mind is independent of physical forces.
- We may one day be able to understand any behavior using either the vocabulary of psychology (experience, motives, emotions, etc.) or the vocabulary of biology (neural growth, activity, hormones, etc.), as we now understand that these two disciplines offer separate means of describing the same events.

REVIEW QUESTIONS

1. By what methods can a living human brain be examined without requiring surgery, and how do they differ?
2. We sometimes gain insight into the importance of a certain region of the brain by examining the behavior of someone who has suffered a stroke that has damaged that region. This is an example of what type of method? What makes interpreting such reports tricky?
3. How do modern studies of brain activity refute the myth that "we only use 10% of our brain"?

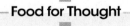

Food for Thought

When Deidre was considering surgery to remove the part of her brain that was causing seizures, what if it had turned out that the seizures began in the same brain region where stimulation caused her to be amused? What if it were you, and the surgeon said you might lose your sense of humor if the part of your brain that causes your seizures were removed. Would you opt for the surgery?

The Neuroscience of Behavior

The Laughing Brain

Deidre never knew when she might suddenly suffer a *seizure*, a loss of consciousness and convulsions, the uncontrollable, rhythmic movements of her whole body. The seizures were a symptom of the disorder *epilepsy*, caused by electrical malfunctions in her brain. Medications that often control epileptic seizures didn't work for Deidre. The seizures weren't just embarrassing—they left her vulnerable to accidents. How would she ever be able to drive safely? So Deidre agreed to try something drastic—letting doctors implant tiny wires through her skull to pinpoint exactly where in her brain the electrical problems began. From this information the doctors could decide whether to remove that part of the brain, which should stop the seizures.

When the doctors carefully passed a tiny electrical current through each wire in turn, they found that stimulating the wire to a particular part of the brain elicited a reliable change in Deidre's behavior—she laughed. You might think that Deidre would be puzzled by her own sudden laughter, but she wasn't told when the wires were stimulated and she never seemed to guess they were causing her to laugh. When the doctors asked why she was laughing, Deidre always offered a reason. "You guys standing there, you're so funny!" Stimulating that part of the brain didn't just cause Deidre to laugh, it also affected her *mind*, causing her to be *amused* by whatever happened to be going on. If two doctors were standing there in lab coats, she interpreted their behavior as humorous. Presumably this same part of her brain was normally active when Deidre heard a funny joke.

Deidre's behavior demonstrated that even a mental process as elusive as humor is a product of a machine: give the machine a tiny zap of electricity and Deidre would feel amused without even hearing a joke. Deidre's epilepsy was also a result of electrical activity—uncontrolled electrical activity—in that marvelously complex machine between her ears. Why does electrical activity in the brain affect behavior so profoundly? In this chapter we'll find out.

Think Like a Psychologist:

Principles in Action

Whenever we encounter any interesting behavior we should consider the four principles. Here are some ways that the four principles relate to our opening story about Deidre.

MACHINE

The mind is a product of a physical machine, the brain.

Deidre's epilepsy is a result of malfunctioning electrical signals in her brain. Stimulation of a particular brain region causes her to feel amused.

UNCONSCIOUS

We are consciously aware of only a small part of our mental activity.

Deidre is unaware when researchers stimulate her brain, so she does not know the real reason she is amused. Nevertheless, she thinks she knows what has amused her.

SOCIAL

We constantly modify our behavior, beliefs, and attitudes according to what we perceive about the people around us.

In trying to account for her amusement, Deidre looks to her social environment, believing that her amusement results from those "guys, standing there."

EXPERIENCE

Our experiences physically alter the structure and function of the brain.

Like many people with epilepsy, Deidre's disorder resulted because she experienced physical trauma to the brain early in life. Left unchecked, the epilepsy would affect her for the rest of her life.

KEY TERMS

acetylcholine, 67
action potential, 75
agonist, 82
all-or-none property, 77
amygdala, 93
antagonists, 82
autonomic nervous system, 94
axon, 65
axon hillock, 76
axon terminals, 65
basal ganglia, 93
brainstem, 88
brain, 86
cell body, 65
central nervous system (CNS), 87
cerebellum, 89
cerebral cortex, 89
cerebral hemispheres, 89
cerebrum, 89
computed tomography (CT), 100
corpus callosum, 93
dendrite, 65
depolarizing, 76
diffusion tensor imaging (DTI), 104
dopamine, 68
electroencephalogram (EEG), 99
endorphins, 68
frontal lobes, 90
functional MRI (fMRI), 101
GABA, 68
glia, 65
glutamate, 67
hemispheric specialization, 93
hippocampus, 93
hormones, 83
hyperpolarizing, 76
hypothalamus, 89
interneurons, 69
lesion, 97
limbic system, 93
magnetic resonance imaging (MRI), 100
mind, 64
mirror neurons, 99
motor cortex, 90
motor neurons, 68
myelin, 78
nerves, 94
nervous system, 86
neural network, 70
neurons, 64
neuroscience, 64
neurotransmitter, 66
neurotransmitter receptors, 66
nodes of Ranvier, 79
norepinephrine, 68
nucleus, 86
occipital lobes, 91
parasympathetic nervous system, 94
parietal lobes, 90
peripheral nervous system (PNS), 94
pituitary gland, 83
plasticity, 103
polarized, 73
positron emission tomography (PET), 101
potential difference in charge, 73
prefrontal cortex, 90
reflex, 69
refractory phase, 78
resting potential, 73
reuptake, 68
saltatory conduction, 79
sensory cortex, 91
sensory neurons, 69
serotonin, 68
somatic nervous system, 94s
somatosensory cortex, 90
spinal cord, 87
sympathetic nervous system, 94
synapse, 66
synaptic cleft, 66
temporal lobes, 91
thalamus, 89
threshold, 76
transcranial magnetic stimulation (TMS), 97
vesicles, 66

QUIZ YOURSELF

1. Neurons that receive signals only from other neurons and release neurotransmitters only to other neurons are
   a. interneurons.
   b. sensory neurons.
   c. motor neurons.
   d. mirror neurons.
2. Communication between neurons involves ________ signaling, while the signaling within each neuron is ________.
   a. network; mechanical
   b. chemical; electrical
   c. automatic; voluntary
   d. mechanical; automatic
3. When a neuron is ________ it is more likely to fire, so we say it is ________.
   a. hyperpolarized; inhibited
   b. hyperpolarized; excited
   c. depolarized; inhibited
   d. depolarized; excited
4. A method that acts as a reversible lesion is
   a. EEG (electroencephalogram).
   b. CT (computerized tomography).
   c. MRI (magnetic resonance imaging).
   d. TMS (transcranial magnetic stimulation).
5. ________ are cells specialized to process information. They have extensions called ________ that receive information from other cells and extensions called ________ to send information to other cells.
6. The part of the brainstem that receives the sensory information is the ________. The part of the brainstem that controls basic brain functions such as thirst, hunger, and sexual drive is the ________.
7. The brain region that is associated with learning and emotional behaviors is the ________. The seahorse-shaped part of this system that is active in forming new memories is the ________. (The almond-shaped part of the system that is important in many emotions is the ________.)
8. The central nervous system is made up of the ________ and ________. The ________ is made up of the autonomic nervous system and the somatic nervous system.
9. The fatty substance that provides electrical insulation along the axon serving to speed up the action potential is ________.

1. a; 2. b; 3. d; 4. d; 5. Neurons; dendrites; axons; 6. thalamus; hypothalamus; 7. limbic system; hippocampus; amygdala; 8. brain; spinal cord; peripheral nervous system; 9. myelin

CUTLER

4 Genes, Environment, and Behavior

Non-Identical Identical Sisters

These days medical technology has made multiple births relatively common, so the media take notice only for extreme cases like "Octo-Mom." But in the 1930s, when a set of quadruplets was delivered in a midwestern U.S. hospital, it was big news, especially because the four girls were genetically identical. They became instant celebrities, as the public was eager to watch the progress of these four cute little blonde girls. Before they were teenagers, they were in show business, singing, tap-dancing, and doing comedy routines in three states.

But there was a dark side of the girls' lives that the public did not see. Eventually all four would be diagnosed with a mental disorder, *schizophrenia*, gaining the attention of researchers at the National Institute of Mental Health (NIMH), who studied them extensively. The findings were published using the pseudonym "Genain" for their last name and Nora, Iris, Myra, and Hester (N.I.M.H.) as their disguised first names, reflecting their order of birth (Rosenthal, 1963).

For 50 years now, the fact that all four Genain quadruplets developed schizophrenia has been cited in textbooks and classrooms as evidence of a strong genetic component to the disease. But while the girls were genetically identical (Segal, 2001), they were quite different from one another in terms of the severity of disease. The last born sister, "Hester," developed symptoms at age 11 and by high school had to be hospitalized. She was the only sister to never finish high school, and she spent much of her life in institutions. In contrast, "Myra's" first symptoms came on suddenly at the age of 24, but she eventually recovered, working as a secretary, marrying and raising two sons. The other two sisters' outcomes were somewhere in between, recovering enough to work and support themselves, although they never married. So if schizophrenia is simply a result of what genes you inherit, why weren't the sisters affected to the same degree?

Identical twins confirm a genetic influence on schizophrenia: if one twin has the condition, the other is much more likely to have the disorder than someone from the general population. However, in about half the cases when one identical twin develops schizophrenia, *the other twin never does*. So something in the environment must matter, too. In this chapter, we'll try to understand how both genes and the environment influence schizophrenia and all human behaviors.

Chapter Preview

genetic determinism The belief that genes determine everything about us, including our behavior.

nature One side of a philosophical debate that attributes our behavior to genetics.

nurture One side of a philosophical debate that attributes our behavior to environmental influences.

Every day, newspapers, magazines, and Internet links talk about genes. We are told that genes have been found for diseases such as cancer and for conditions such as schizophrenia, homosexuality, or aggressiveness. These stories rarely provide you with enough information to understand what genes are, how they work, or how they can affect behavior. It's easy for some people to come away from such reports believing in **genetic determinism**—the idea that genes alone determine everything about us, including what behaviors we display. In this view, Hester was doomed by her genes to become schizophrenic. But that can't be right, because her identical twins, with the same genes, were much less severely affected. And there are many pairs of identical twins in which one has schizophrenia while the other does not. To understand why the idea of genetic determinism of behavior is wrong, we need to understand some basic principles of how genes work and how they affect behavior.

The question of how much genes affect behavior is often described as the "nature versus nurture debate." How much of what we do is the result of **nature**, meaning our genes and strictly biological influences, versus **nurture**, meaning the way we are raised and influenced by our environment (**Table 4.1**)? But this way of framing the issue, as a "debate" about nature "versus" nurture, is misleading because it assumes that nature and nurture are two distinct influences. In fact, we'll see in this chapter that nature and nurture are inseparable. Even though genes influence all of our behaviors, our behavior is not genetically determined. Our learning experiences and social interactions are critically important influences on our future behavior, not because genes are unimportant but because *learning experiences and social interactions affect how we use the genes we inherited.* This means that stress, including the stress of unhappy relationships with other people, may activate genes in unfortunate ways—in the case of schizophrenia, causing a breakdown in brain function that may lead to hallucinations and delusions.

TABLE 4.1 What Is Nature and What Is Nurture?

Nurture (Influences found outside your body)	Nature (Influences found inside your body)
Entertainment	Genes
Education	Brain circuits
Warmth	Sensory systems
Climate	Hormones
Water	Growth factors
Food	Neurons
Social interactions	Cells
	Tissues
	Organs

We will begin by describing what genes are and how they work. Then we'll see that even though we can't change which genes we carry, our life experiences greatly affect when, how, and where we use those genes. We'll see that genes affect all behaviors, but that nearly all behaviors are the result of nurture as well. Thus we'll see that genes *influence* every human behavior, but that no gene *determines* behavior.

trait A physical or behavioral characteristic feature displayed by an individual.

protein A long string of amino acids. The basic building material of organisms.

nucleus The spherical central structure of a cell that contains the chromosomes.

chromosomes Condensed strands of DNA and associated molecules found in the nucleus of cells.

4.1 Genes at Work

Who we are and how we behave depends on our characteristics, or **traits**, some of which we inherited from our parents. Before we consider how much of our behavior results from nature, or genes, and how much environment, or nurture, influences us, we need to know just how our genetic blueprint works. In this section we look at genes and their function and at the way genes are passed on from parents to children.

The genes we inherit provide "recipes" for making proteins

Our bodies consist of billions of cells, each made up of molecules called **proteins**, the building blocks of life on Earth. Proteins form structures inside our cells and regulate all the processes that keep our cells alive and functioning properly.

Within each cell's cytoplasm, the protein-rich fluid inside our cells, is a spherical structure called the **nucleus** (**Figure 4.1**). Each cell's nucleus contains rod-shaped structures called **chromosomes**. In humans, each nucleus has 23 pairs

Things to Learn

- Structural basis of heredity
- Why we all carry mutations
- Dominant versus recessive genes

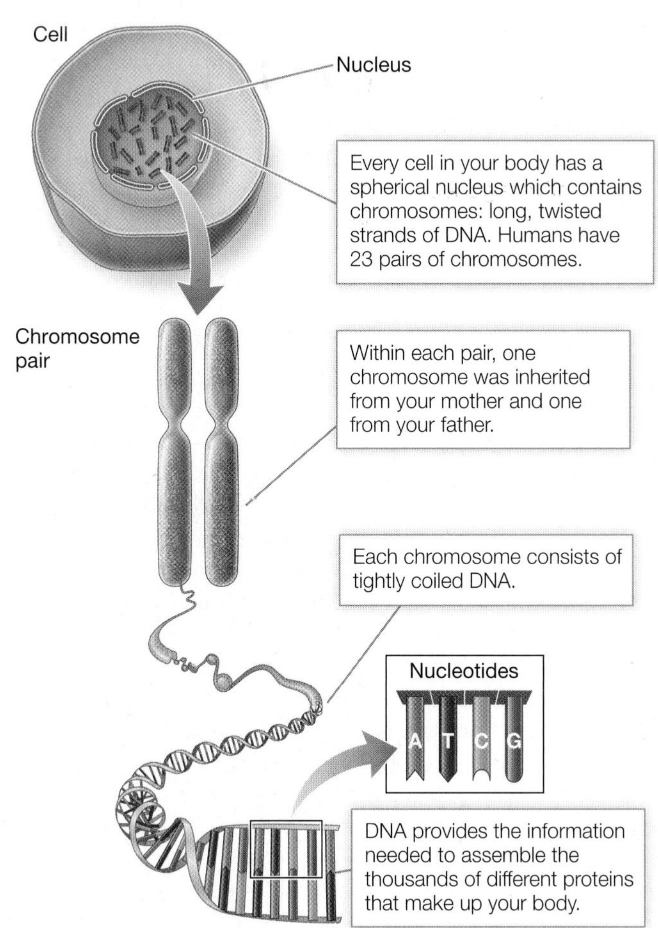

Cell
Nucleus
Every cell in your body has a spherical nucleus which contains chromosomes: long, twisted strands of DNA. Humans have 23 pairs of chromosomes.
Chromosome pair
Within each pair, one chromosome was inherited from your mother and one from your father.
Each chromosome consists of tightly coiled DNA.
Nucleotides
A
T
C
G
DNA provides the information needed to assemble the thousands of different proteins that make up your body.

Figure 4.1 Each Cell Carries Genetic Information

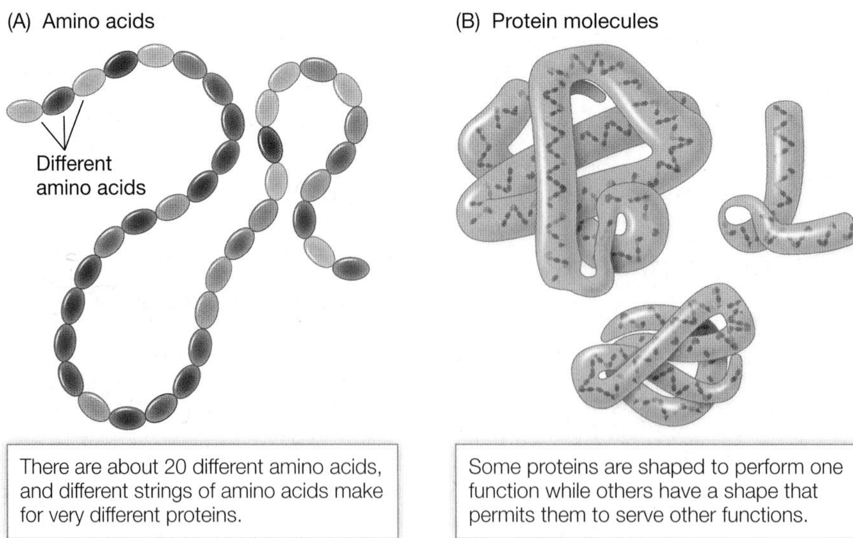

(A) Amino acids
(B) Protein molecules
Different amino acids
There are about 20 different amino acids, and different strings of amino acids make for very different proteins.
Some proteins are shaped to perform one function while others have a shape that permits them to serve other functions.

Figure 4.2 Protein Molecules Make up Your Body Protein consists of a strand of amino acids (A). Protein molecules (B) make between 25,000 and 100,000 different proteins.

DNA A long molecule that encodes hereditary information, coiled up to form chromosomes in the nucleus of cells.

gene A length of DNA that encodes the information for making a protein.

nucleotides Four subunits of DNA that combine in different ways to specify which protein the cell will make.

amino acids Subunits of proteins, strung together in a sequence that forms a particular protein molecule.

fertilization The fusion of sperm and egg.

of chromosomes, for a total of 46. Each chromosome is made up of a very long molecule of **DNA**, which stands for ***d***eoxyribo***n***ucleic ***a***cid (see Figure 4.1). Organisms store inherited information in these DNA molecules in units we call genes. For our purposes we can define a **gene** as a specific length of DNA that carries the information needed to make one or more of the proteins required for the body to function properly. It's estimated that humans have about 20,000 genes (International Human Genome Sequencing Consortium, 2004.)

To understand how the information in our genes affects our body and brain, we need to know a bit more about the makeup of DNA and proteins. DNA itself is composed of subunits called **nucleotides**. There are four different nucleotides, abbreviated A, T, C, and G (for ***a***denine, ***t***hymine, ***c***ytosine, and ***g***uanine), and DNA consists of long stretches of these nucleotides, one after the other—for example, ATTGGCTATGCT. The sequence of nucleotides is not random; it specifies exactly which protein a cell will make.

Proteins are composed of smaller subunits called **amino acids**, which are strung together rather like beads on a string. There are 20 different amino acids, and cells make different proteins by varying the amino acids and the order in which they are strung together, as shown in **Figure 4.2A**. Some proteins, such as various neurotransmitter receptors, are very large and may consist of hundreds or thousands of amino acids. The different combinations of the 20 amino acids can produce an enormous number of possible proteins (**Figure 4.2B**).

In order to function properly, a cell uses the information from genes to string together the right sequence of amino acids to make each protein. We can think of a gene as a "recipe" (or a set of instructions) for the sequence of amino acids in a particular protein (**Figure 4.3**). If the correct amino acids are strung together in the correct order, the protein will have the right shape to do its job. But if the amino acids are strung together in the wrong order, or an incorrect amino acid is inserted, the protein may have the wrong shape and may not work the way it should. For example, several kinds of proteins in our eyes change their shape when hit by light, and this information about light eventually reaches our brain. In some cases, replacing just one amino acid will prevent a protein from making this change in response to light. In such cases, the person may not be able to see, or may be unable to see certain colors, as we'll discuss later.

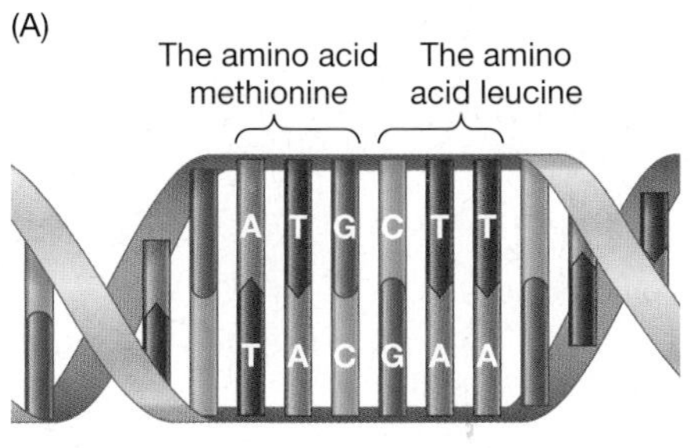

A stretch of DNA that encodes for a particular protein is called a gene. The sequence of nucleotides specifies the order in which amino acids are assembled to make a particular protein.

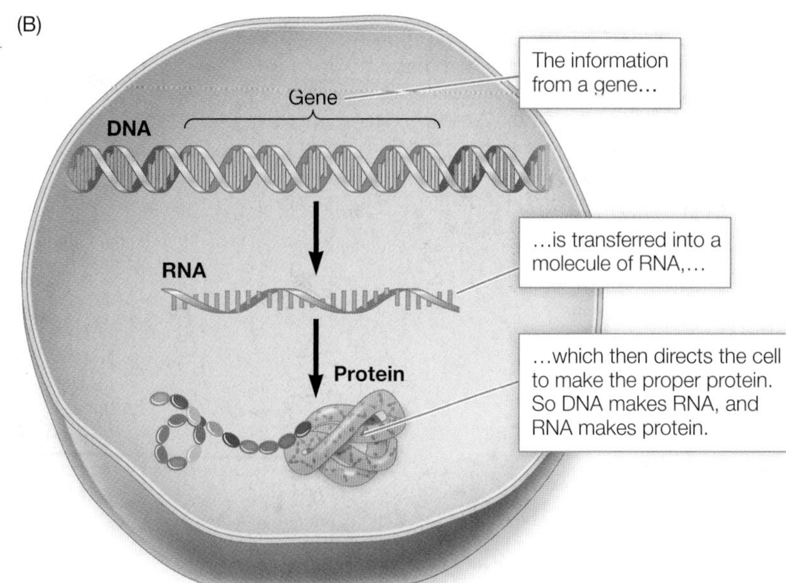

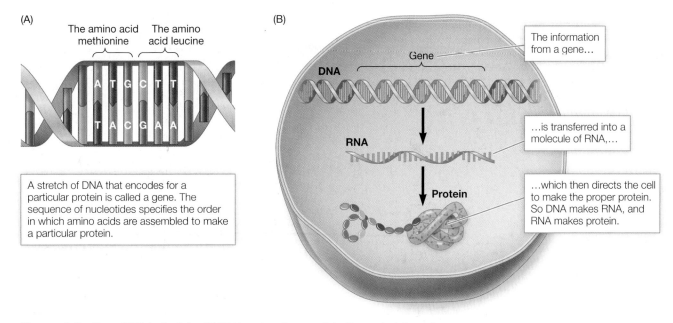

Figure 4.3 From DNA to Protein (A) DNA molecules consist of long stretches of nucleotides that specify the sequence of amino acids needed to make a protein molecule. There are only 4 different kinds of nucleotides, but the particular sequence of nucleotides will call for a particular sequence of amino acids to be joined together. (B) Information from the gene determines the structure of the protein.

Similarly, many thousands of different proteins are produced and used in the brain, enabling it to work. The construction of our entire body and brain requires the proper production of thousands of different proteins, each one with a distinct sequence of amino acids. In short, genes on chromosomes specify which amino acids will be joined together, and in what order, to make each particular protein.

alleles One of two or more different versions of a gene.

But how did our cells get these genetic instructions? They were passed on from our parents, in a process we describe next.

Our mother and father give us slightly different "recipes" for each protein

Your first cell started making proteins when your father's sperm fused with your mother's egg in the process of **fertilization**, or conception. The sperm contained one set of 23 chromosomes and the egg contained another set of 23, so that at fertilization your first cell received the full complement of 23 pairs of chromosomes, for a total of 46.

In general, we get one particular "recipe" for making each protein from our father's chromosomes, and another particular recipe for that protein from our mother's chromosomes. But the recipes from our two parents are rarely identical, even though they are for the same protein. Think of it as if one recipe for French toast calls for cinnamon while another calls for nutmeg. In the case of proteins, the differences in "recipes" are different amino acids. Maybe your mother's instructions called for one amino acid in the 200th spot on the protein, while your dad's called for a different amino acid in that spot. In many cases, small differences like this have no appreciable effect on how well the finished protein works, so over the eons slightly different recipes have arisen and been kept in the population.

More Than a Passing Resemblance Some of the genes we inherit from our parents will affect our outward appearance, and some will affect our behavior.

Genes with slightly different instructions for making the same protein are called **alleles**. Except in those rare cases where your mother and father gave you exactly the same instructions for a protein, you have two different alleles for each of your thousands of genes. For most genes, many different alleles exist in any population

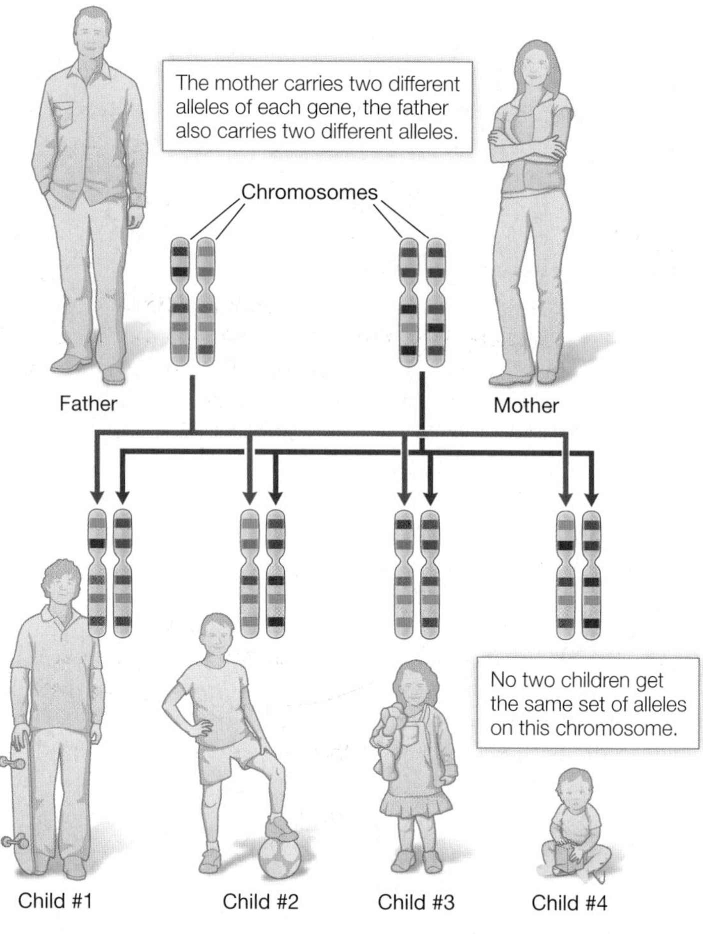

The mother carries two different alleles of each gene, the father also carries two different alleles.
Chromosomes
Father
Mother
No two children get the same set of alleles on this chromosome.
Child #1
Child #2
Child #3
Child #4

Figure 4.4 Differing Alleles Result in Different Versions of a Protein Note that the chromosome donated by each parent can carry a mix of genes from the grandmother and the grandfather. While we depict only five different genes here, in fact each of the 23 pairs of chromosomes carries nearly a thousand different genes. Thus a single pair of parents can generate a staggeringly large number of genetically distinct offspring.

mutation A change in the nucleotide sequence of a gene as a result of unfaithful replication.

of humans, but each individual has only two of them (**Figure 4.4**). The diversity of alleles is one reason humans are so diverse.

How did so many different alleles come about? Sometimes when eggs or sperm are made, the DNA from the parent is not copied properly. We say the miscopied gene is a **mutation**: a change in DNA sequence resulting in changes in the instructions for making a protein. Many mutations are minor and have no effect on how well the final protein works, and we all carry some mutations (Leroi, 2003). For example, maybe several different amino acids will work equally well at a certain place in the protein. But some alleles encode instructions for a protein that just doesn't work. Everyone has some alleles that don't produce a functional protein (**Box 4.1**). But in most cases your body still functions normally, as we'll explain next.

Sons by the Dozen While all of these 12 brothers bear some resemblance to one another, each has a distinct face.

If we get a nonfunctional allele from one parent, the other allele usually spares us from harm

You have two alleles for every gene, one from each of your two biological parents. If your father gave you a bad allele for a particular protein, say protein Z, then that protein Z might not work. But your mother also gave you an allele for protein Z, and it is almost certainly different from the allele your father supplied. So if your father's allele for protein Z doesn't work, you're OK because your mother's allele has instructions for a working version of it (see Figure 4.4).

Because you're here, we can say with certainty that you inherited at least one functional allele for all the proteins essential for life, either from your mother or father. Living humans are exceedingly complex, even as embryos, so if you were

Psychology in Everyday Life

BOX 4.1

Natural Selection Favors Beneficial Alleles

Mutations are common fare in science fiction. The X-Men of comics and movies have mutations that give them spectacular powers beyond those of normal humans. This glamorous view of mutations as beneficial is, alas, almost entirely fictional. Mutations change the structure of DNA, and they usually result from a mistake in copying DNA when a parent makes an egg or sperm. In other words, when your father's sperm was made, an allele was accidentally made that was just a tiny bit different from his own. The wrong nucleotide got put in one spot, so a different amino acid was placed in the corresponding part of a protein (see Figure 4.3). Many such mutations are harmless. But some mutations are harmful—the substitution of one or more amino acids can disrupt the ability of the protein to function properly. Most of these harmful mutations are not deadly, however. They simply result in proteins that don't work as well as they should.

While most mutations are unhelpful, and some even harmful, once in a great while a mutation occurs that actually makes a protein function better than before. There are even occasions when the mutation produces a protein that can serve some new, beneficial function for our bodies. These sorts of beneficial mutations are so rare that each one arose for the first time in a different individual. Probably no one embryo has ever been lucky enough to get two really beneficial mutations. But when rare beneficial mutations do arise, if they help the individual to reproduce, they may be passed to offspring and eventually become more common in the population (see Figure).

Note that once a new allele is passed on to other individuals, we no longer call it a mutation. Now it is simply a new allele for that gene.

Eventually, more and more of these beneficial mutations, each of which arose for the first time in a different individual, get brought together in future generations. This accumulation of more and more beneficial mutations is one way to describe evolution by **natural selection**. New species (including humans) arise as natural selection works for billions of years, favoring beneficial mutations and working against harmful mutations.

natural selection The process by which mutations that improve survival and reproduction accumulate in subsequent generations, changing a species over time.

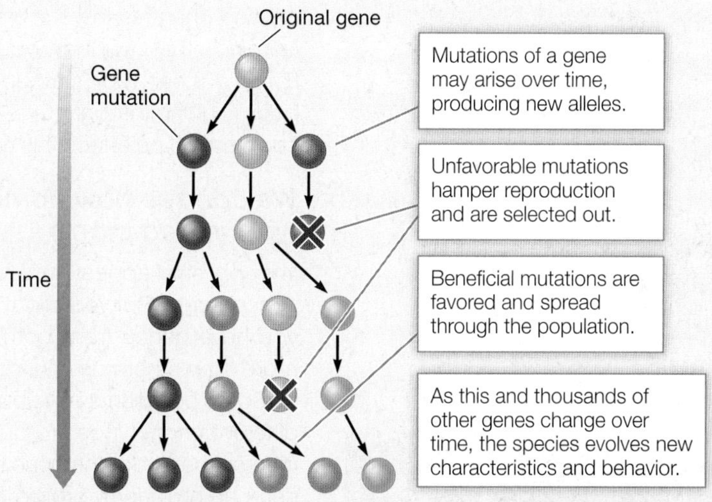

Original gene
Gene mutation
Time
Mutations of a gene may arise over time, producing new alleles.
Unfavorable mutations hamper reproduction and are selected out.
Beneficial mutations are favored and spread through the population.
As this and thousands of other genes change over time, the species evolves new characteristics and behavior.

Genes and Evolution Because natural selection favors genetic mutations that help reproduction, species evolve over time.

missing a key protein altogether, chances are you would not have survived. What differs among us is which of the many different alleles we carry for various genes. Almost all alleles work—they each make a functional protein—but the proteins may work slightly differently from one another, and that may make a difference.

The term **genotype** describes the genetic information you received from your parents. Your genotype was set at the instant of fertilization. For the rest of your life, your genotype will remain the same. But there's more to you than your genotype.

Many things have happened to your body and brain over the years. Your **phenotype** is the sum total of all the physical characteristics and processes going on

genotype All the genetic information that one specific individual has inherited.

phenotype The sum of an individual's physical characteristics at one particular time.

Figure 4.5 Genotype versus Phenotype

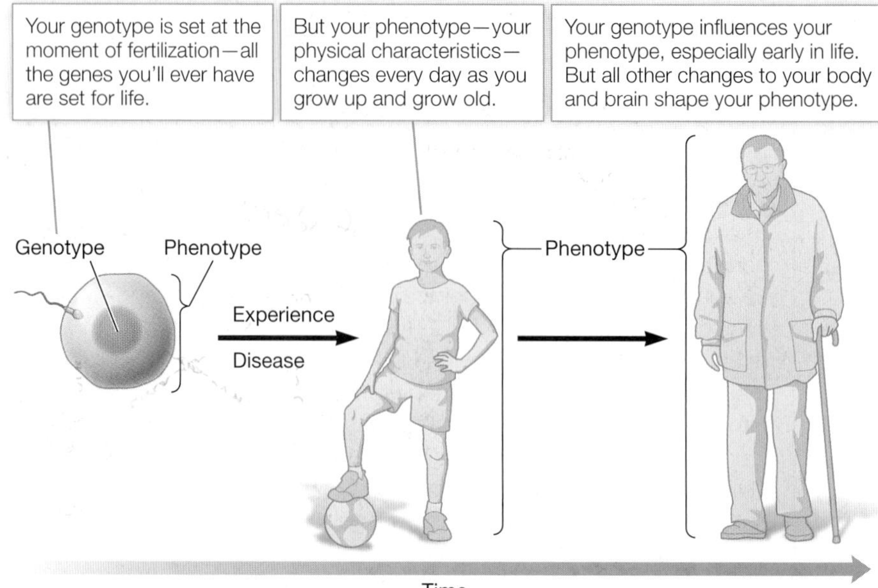

Your genotype is set at the moment of fertilization—all the genes you'll ever have are set for life.
But your phenotype—your physical characteristics—changes every day as you grow up and grow old.
Your genotype influences your phenotype, especially early in life. But all other changes to your body and brain shape your phenotype.
Genotype
Phenotype
Experience
Disease
Phenotype
Time

dominant In the context of heredity, an allele that affects an individual's phenotype regardless of the other allele carried for that gene.

within you at a particular time. It includes your hair color, your intelligence, and your tendency to get the hiccups. Note that while your genotype never changes, your phenotype never stays the same. Your body changes every day—even, in a subtle way, from breath to breath (**Figure 4.5**). For example, reading this paragraph has caused changes in your brain—a subtle alteration of your phenotype known as *learning*—that may help you perform better on an exam sometime in the future. Even your behavior is a part of your phenotype, since behavior is a process your body is going through. One objective of this chapter is to demonstrate how a person's genotype affects his or her behavioral phenotype.

We can see how dominant and recessive alleles work in pea plants

Your physical appearance and behavior depend on the genes you inherited from your parents. But you might look more like one parent than the other, even though you have genes from both. That's because some genes influence phenotype more than others do. We can explain this idea using pea plants as an example.

Some pea plants have purple flowers and others have white flowers. These two different phenotypes are due to differences in the plants' genotypes—they carry different alleles for the gene that controls flower color. Plants making purple flowers carry an allele for a protein needed to make a purple pigment (**Figure 4.6A**). The plants making white flowers have a different allele for this gene, and that protein doesn't work. So the flowers are white because all the other proteins in the blossom are white and no purple pigment has been added (**Figure 4.6B**).

Purple and White Pea Blossoms

What happens if we crossbreed a white-flowering pea plant with a purple-flowering plant? (Yes, plants have sex.) As it turns out, all of the offspring will have purple flowers. The purple color appears because each offspring has two different alleles of the gene—one from each parent. One allele produces a purple pigment, but the other does not. Consequently, all the flowers make some purple pigment and end up purple (**Figure 4.6C**). In this case we say that the purple allele is *dominant*. An allele for a gene is **dominant** when it affects the individual's phenotype no matter what other allele the individual carries for that gene. In this case, the purple allele dominates the other, white allele. Later we'll learn about some brain disorders that are inherited in a dominant fashion—if someone inherits just one allele for Huntington's disease, for example, that person will eventually develop the disorder. The protein made by that allele damages the brain by middle age.

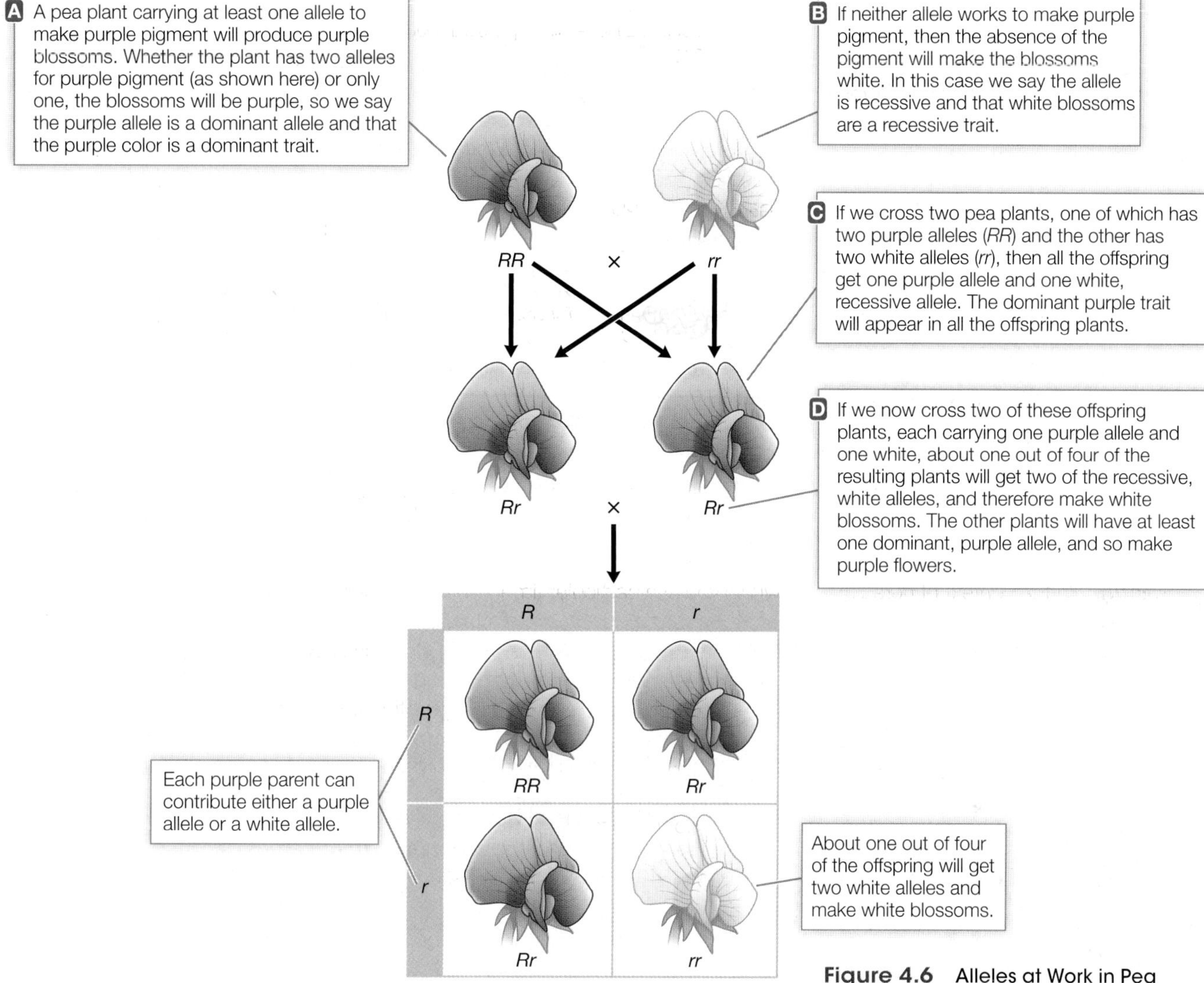

A A pea plant carrying at least one allele to make purple pigment will produce purple blossoms. Whether the plant has two alleles for purple pigment (as shown here) or only one, the blossoms will be purple, so we say the purple allele is a dominant allele and that the purple color is a dominant trait.
B If neither allele works to make purple pigment, then the absence of the pigment will make the blossoms white. In this case we say the allele is recessive and that white blossoms are a recessive trait.
C If we cross two pea plants, one of which has two purple alleles (RR) and the other has two white alleles (rr), then all the offspring get one purple allele and one white, recessive allele. The dominant purple trait will appear in all the offspring plants.
D If we now cross two of these offspring plants, each carrying one purple allele and one white, about one out of four of the resulting plants will get two of the recessive, white alleles, and therefore make white blossoms. The other plants will have at least one dominant, purple allele, and so make purple flowers.
RR
×
rr
Rr
×
Rr
R
r
R
r
RR
Rr
Rr
rr
Each purple parent can contribute either a purple allele or a white allele.
About one out of four of the offspring will get two white alleles and make white blossoms.

Figure 4.6 Alleles at Work in Pea Flower Blossoms

The white flower color, by contrast, appears only if the individual plant carries two white alleles (one from each parent). This allele is said to be *recessive*, and the white flower color is said to be a *recessive trait*. A **recessive** allele affects the individual's phenotype only when it is present on *both chromosomes*. If a dominant allele is present on one chromosome, then the recessive trait does not show up. Later we'll learn about intellectual disabilities that result when a child inherits two alleles for a particular protein that are both dysfunctional. The brain doesn't develop properly unless that protein works properly.

recessive In the context of heredity, an allele that affects an individual's phenotype only when it is present on both chromosomes.

Suppose we now crossbreed two of the offspring from our original pea plants. Each of these offspring carries one white allele and one purple allele, and each has purple flowers. When we cross these purple-flowering plants with one another, we find that their offspring are not all the same. Many of them have purple flowers, but a few have white flowers. How did this happen?

Variations in phenotype are observed in crossbred pea plants because each parent carries both a white allele and a purple allele. Any of their offspring that got at least one purple allele produced purple flowers. But a few of their offspring happened to get two recessive, white alleles (**Figure 4.6D**). These plants made only white flowers. If we cross these white-flowering plants together, their offspring produce only white flowers, because there's no purple allele that can be passed on.

Now that we have seen what genes are, how they contain instructions for making proteins, how we inherit them, and how some genes have a greater effect than others, we can look at how individual cells make use of genes. We'll see that many factors, including experience and the environment, influence whether a particular gene is used.

4.1 SUMMARY

- *Genes* carry information, specifically about the sequence of *amino acids* that must be strung together to form a *protein*.
- *Packed* as a set of *chromosomes* inside every cell's *nucleus*, tens of thousands of genes allow you to make the many proteins needed to live and grow.
- For each gene, you carry two different versions called *alleles*, one from your mother and one from your father.
- Some alleles carry a *mutation* that makes a nonfunctional protein, but if the other allele makes a protein that works, you can still make functional protein.
- The sum of your genes, your *genotype*, was determined when your mother's egg was *fertilized* by your father's sperm, but your *phenotype*—all of your physical characteristics and processes—is constantly changing as experience and the environment affect your development throughout your life.
- Some alleles are *dominant*, meaning even a single copy will have an effect on the phenotype. Other alleles are *recessive*, meaning they affect the phenotype only if the individual carries two copies of that allele.

REVIEW QUESTIONS

1. How do genes carry information from parents to offspring?
2. What are alleles, and why are some dominant while others are recessive?
1. Compare and contrast genotype and phenotype.

Food for Thought

You inherited tens of thousands of genes, and in most cases you have two different alleles for each. They carried the "recipes" for thousands of different proteins, all of which work together.

If you could instantly swap all of the molecules of one of your proteins with another version of that protein, would that affect the function of other proteins?

4.2 The Regulation of Genes

Things to Learn

- Meaning of gene expression
- Experience regulates gene expression
- Epigenetic regulation
- Examples of gene–environment interaction

Genes have a powerful effect on our phenotype, including our behavior. Since our genotype remains the same from birth to death, and since genes affect phenotype, it may seem as if our behavior is fixed. But behavior is not as simple as that. Our behavior never changes our genotype, never alters which alleles we inherited from our parents—but experience influences our genes by changing *where, and when, and how we use the genes* we inherited. In this section we discuss how individual cells "decide" which genes to use and how the environment can influence that decision, shaping the influence of genes.

Different genes are used at different times in different cells

Every cell carries a full set of genes, but most cells use only a subset of those genes. Liver cells use all the genes necessary to make the proteins that liver cells need to do their job. The proteins a brain cell needs differ from those used in liver cells, so brain cells use a different subset of genes. Lung cells use yet a different set of genes. When a cell uses a gene to make a particular protein we refer to it as **gene expression**. Liver cells express one set of genes, brain cells express another set, lung cells yet another set (**Figure 4.7A**).

gene expression A process by which a cell directs a gene to make its protein.

Gene expression is not an all-or-none process. In certain circumstances, a cell may increase expression of some genes, making more of those genes' pro-

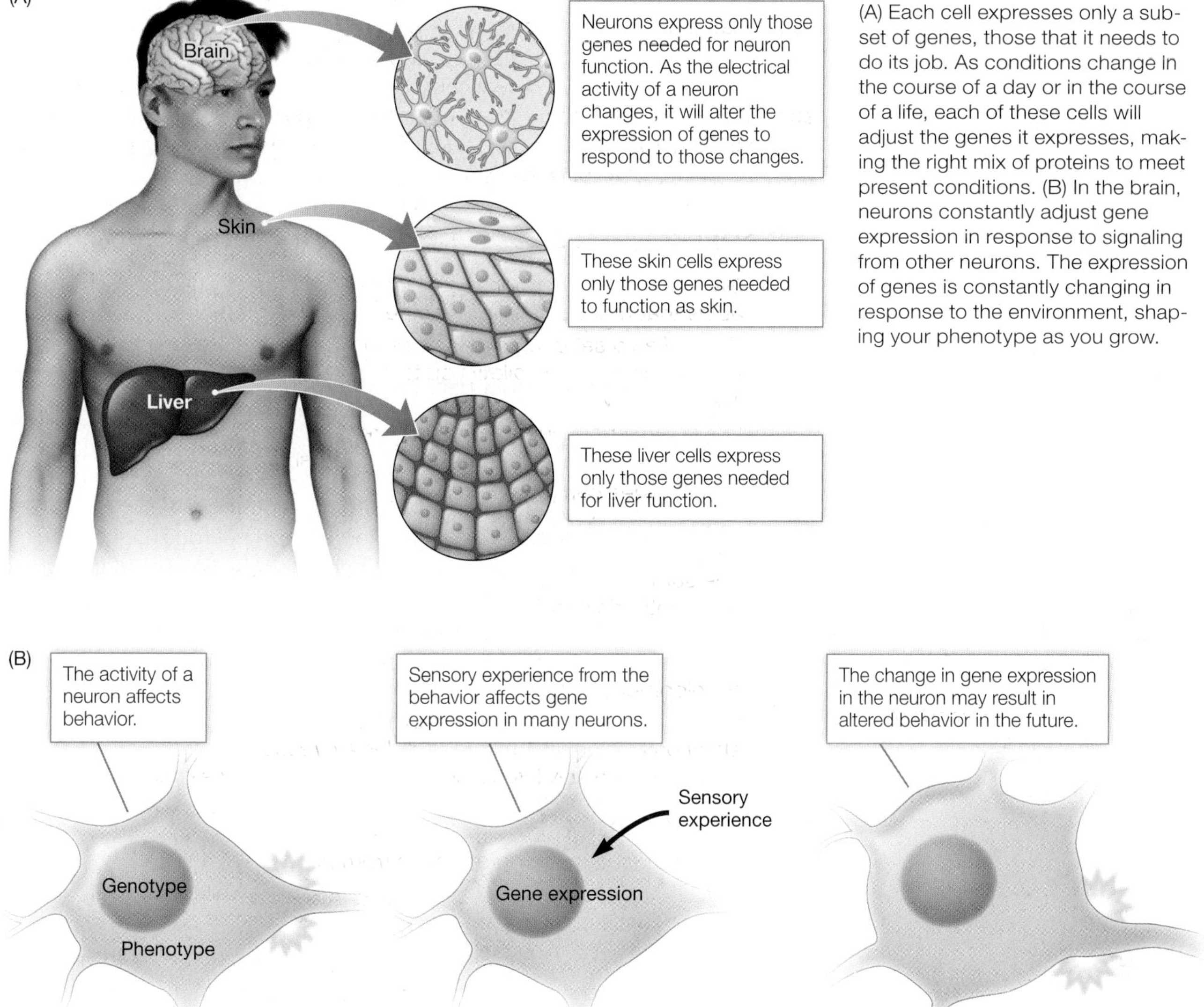

(A)
Brain
Skin
Liver
Neurons express only those genes needed for neuron function. As the electrical activity of a neuron changes, it will alter the expression of genes to respond to those changes.
These skin cells express only those genes needed to function as skin.
These liver cells express only those genes needed for liver function.
(B)
The activity of a neuron affects behavior.
Sensory experience from the behavior affects gene expression in many neurons.
The change in gene expression in the neuron may result in altered behavior in the future.
Sensory experience
Genotype
Phenotype
Gene expression
Time

Figure 4.7 Gene Expression (A) Each cell expresses only a subset of genes, those that it needs to do its job. As conditions change in the course of a day or in the course of a life, each of these cells will adjust the genes it expresses, making the right mix of proteins to meet present conditions. (B) In the brain, neurons constantly adjust gene expression in response to signaling from other neurons. The expression of genes is constantly changing in response to the environment, shaping your phenotype as you grow.

teins. In other circumstances the cell may decrease expression of those same genes, for example, if environmental changes reduce the need for that particular protein (**Figure 4.7B**).

To understand how cells control gene expression, we need to refine our description of DNA. We stated that DNA is a very long molecule that contains information, specifically instructions about which particular amino acids to string together to make up proteins. Recall that a gene is a stretch of DNA that provides the instructions for a particular protein. But there are also long stretches of DNA *between* genes. These lengths of DNA do not code for amino acids to make a protein. Rather, much of the DNA between genes determines whether the neighboring genes will be expressed. This DNA next to a gene controls which cells will express that gene, when the gene will be expressed, and how strongly it will be expressed. Let's look at an example.

No matter what you've been told, two blue-eyed people *can* have a brown-eyed child (Sturm & Larsson, 2009). The various shades of green, blue, and brown eye colors that arose in prehistoric Europe do not result from different pigment proteins. Rather, one pigment is present to some extent in the colored portion—the iris—of almost all eyes, but different eye colors result from *how much* of this pigment is present, and which cells produce it. Three different alleles of this pigment gene exist, and they differ not in terms of what pigment they make, but in terms of *how much* pigment they make and where it is made. The three alleles differ in the DNA *next* to the gene, not in the gene itself or in the structure of the pigment it makes. Each person inherits stretches of DNA from both parents, which contributes to wide variation in the amount of pigment and hence wide variation in eye color. The alleles differ in terms of how they are *expressed* and therefore *how much* pigment protein they produce.

Why do psychologists care about gene expression? Because experience, including learning, affects gene expression, as we'll explore next.

Sensory experience and learning affect gene expression

To appreciate how genes affect behavior, it's important to know that the relationship between genes and behavior is reciprocal. Not only do genes affect brain function and behavior, but *behaviors affect gene expression in the brain*. Basically, any change in the activity of neurons, such as the production of action potentials (see Chapter 3), will affect gene expression (**Figure 4.8**). Let's look at how sensory experience affects gene expression in neurons. Light striking a cell in your eye starts a chain of events that brings information about the light to your brain. The cell in your eye also changes its gene expression in response to its encounter with that light, increasing the expression of some genes, making more of their proteins, and decreasing the expression of other genes. In addition, when that same cell releases neurotransmitter to communicate information to a neuron, the neuron in turn changes its gene expression as a response to that signal. From the first cell that encounters the light all the way to the brain, as information about that light passes through neurons, the neurons also alter their gene expression.

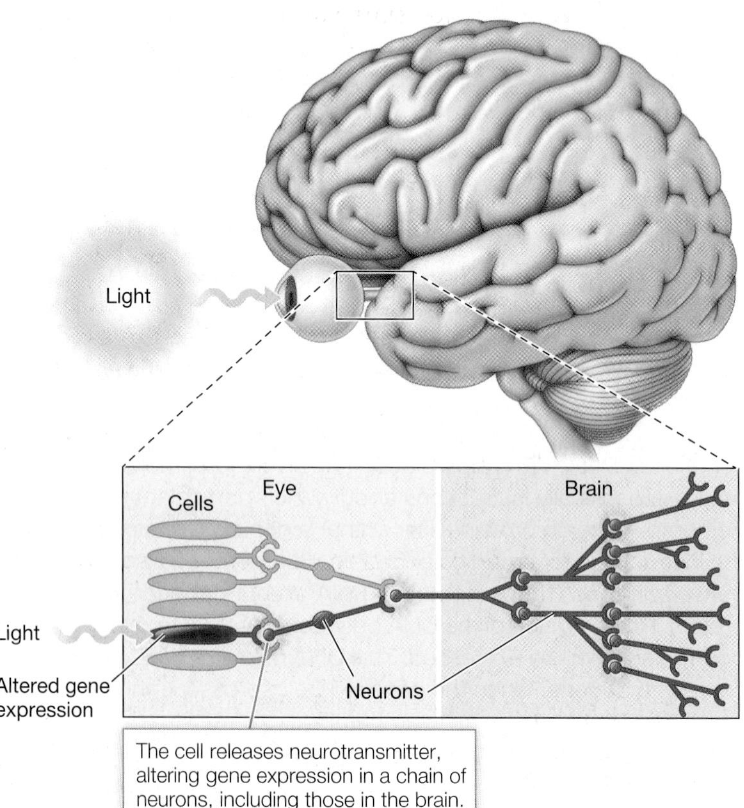
Light
Eye
Cells
Brain
Light
Altered gene expression
Neurons
The cell releases neurotransmitter, altering gene expression in a chain of neurons, including those in the brain.

Figure 4.8 Chains of Gene Expression
Changes in the electrical activity of a neuron will lead the cell to alter gene expression. That means that as information enters the nervous system, all the neurons carrying and analyzing that information will adjust gene expression in response. So reading this caption and examining this figure is changing the expression of many different genes in thousands of neurons in your brain right now.

For most people, this is a new way to think about genes. Genes are not a simple, constant influence. All the cells in your body are changing, from second to second, as particular genes are being expressed. In the brain, one factor that constantly affects gene expression is experience. What did you see this morning, what did you hear, what did you learn? Was your walk to class pleasant, or did you see a cyclist get hurt in an accident? All of those events altered gene expression in millions of neurons in your brain, changing your phenotype.

The fact that gene expression in the brain changes constantly in response to experience explains why both nature and nurture influence human behavior. Both genes and experience are important because *experience affects gene expression*. What matters is not just what genes you inherited, but also how those genes are expressed in response to experience. Experiences early in life have an especially profound and long-lasting effect on gene expression in the brain—and hence on behavior.

epigenetics The study of factors that affect gene expression.

Genes and experience interact

Epigenetics is the study of factors that affect gene expression. If the sequence of nucleotides in a gene represents the recipe for a protein, epigenetics asks: When in life and where in the body is that recipe actually used and the protein actually made? This knowledge will help us better understand development of the body and brain.

Epigenetics is important for a discussion of genes and behavior because experience and the environment are epigenetic factors, determining whether a gene is turned on (expressed) or off (not expressed), or how strongly it is expressed in the brain. As an example, many researchers work with strains of laboratory mice in which every individual mouse carries the same alleles for about 99.9% of all its genes. Male and female mice differ slightly from one another (males carry a Y chromosome that females do not), so researchers typically use either all males or all females in a particular study.

Males from different inbred strains show reliable differences in behavior—for example, in how readily they explore when placed in a large open space. But are the behavioral differences between the mouse strains entirely due to differences in their genes, or does the environment matter, too? One big environmental factor early in life is what sort of mother carries you before birth, and what sort of mother takes care of you after birth. Experiments revealed that both genes and these early environmental conditions affected behavior, as we'll see in **Figure 4.9**.

☑ Researchers at Work

Mothers matter

Figure 4.9 Epigenetic Influences on Behavior

■ **Question:** Are the average differences in behavior between males of two different inbred strains of mice due to the different genes they carry, or do environmental factors contribute as well?

■ **Hypothesis:** Altering early environmental conditions, namely the type of mother that carries the males before birth, and the type of mother that cares for the males after birth, may affect behavior.

■ **Test:** Gather mouse embryos of a particular strain, called Black6 (full name C57Black6) a few days after fertilization. Implant those genetically identical embryos into either a mouse mother of the same strain, or a mouse mother from a different, albino strain. At birth, take some offspring (called pups) and switch them to a mother of the other strain, which will nurse and raise them. Let other pups remain with a mother of the same strain.

Continued

Researchers at Work *Continued*

In the end, this produces four groups of genetically identical male mice that have experienced different environments. Some mice will be just like all of the mice from the original Black 6 strain—they will have a mother of their own strain that carried them prenatally and raised them after birth. But other mice will have been carried and raised by a mother from a different strain, and two other groups of mice will have been carried by a mother of one strain and then raised by a mother of the other strain. After the Black6 males grow up, compare their behaviors.

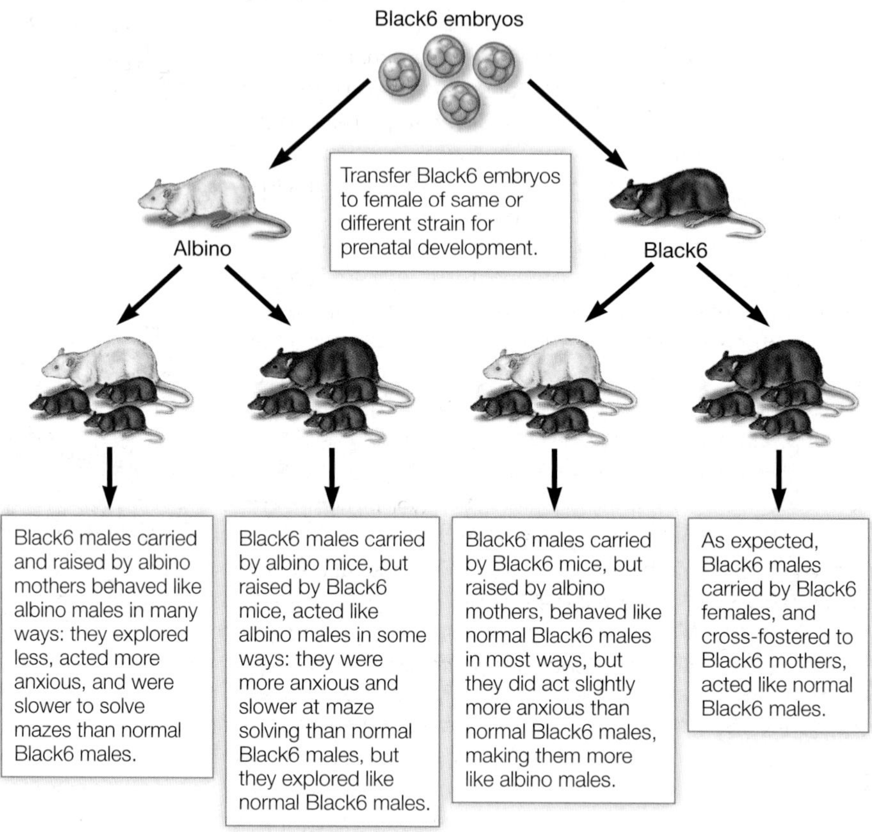

Black6 embryos
Transfer Black6 embryos to female of same or different strain for prenatal development.
Albino
Black6
Black6 males carried and raised by albino mothers behaved like albino males in many ways: they explored less, acted more anxious, and were slower to solve mazes than normal Black6 males.
Black6 males carried by albino mice, but raised by Black6 mice, acted like albino males in some ways: they were more anxious and slower at maze solving than normal Black6 males, but they explored like normal Black6 males.
Black6 males carried by Black6 mice, but raised by albino mothers, behaved like normal Black6 males in most ways, but they did act slightly more anxious than normal Black6 males, making them more like albino males.
As expected, Black6 males carried by Black6 females, and cross-fostered to Black6 mothers, acted like normal Black6 males.

■ **Results:** Males carried and raised by a mother of the opposite strain showed differences in exploratory behavior, in how anxiously they behaved, and in how quickly they solved a maze (Francis et al., 2003). What's more, these males nurtured by a mother of a different strain now behaved like males of their adopted strain. In other words, these Black6 males behaved the way albino males normally behave.

■ **Conclusion:** Some of the behavioral differences between the Black6 and albino strains are *not* genetic, but arise from the strain of mother that nurtured the males before and after birth. Even though the males within each strain were genetically identical, and the two strains showed different behavior, the differences in the two strains' genes were *not* the cause of all differences in their behavior. Something about the environment before birth and early in life has an epigenetic effect so that the genetically identical mice do not express their genes identically. Some behavioral differences between the two strains—including a difference in startle response to loud sounds—remained, no matter which prenatal environment or rearing environment they were given. For those few behaviors, the genotype of the males seemed to determine the differences in how they behaved.

Those genetically identical Black6 males that were raised by albino mothers displayed different behaviors because they were expressing their identical genes in different ways. This is an example of **gene-environment interaction**: when the environment determines whether a gene will affect behavior, in this case by affecting expression of that gene. Note that we could as easily define gene–environment interaction as a case when genes determine whether an environmental factor will affect behavior. These two definitions are equivalent, because they describe two different perspectives on the same process.

gene-environment interaction The effect of the environment on gene expression.

The classic illustration of a gene–environment interaction comes from a famous attempt to selectively breed rats for intelligence. The researcher deliberately chose male and female rats that were good at learning to navigate a maze and bred them (Tryon, 1940). He also chose rats that were poor at maze learning and bred them. After about six generations of this selective breeding, the offspring of the "maze-bright" line of rats consistently solved mazes faster than the "maze-dull" rats (**Figure 4.10A**). This result showed that genes influence maze-learning abilities.

But later researchers found gene–environment interactions also at work (Cooper & Zubek, 1958). Altering the animals' rearing conditions (**Figure 4.10B**) could also affect maze performance. If rats from the two lines were raised in an "enriched" environment where they were given more space and new toys to explore every day, the "dull" rats improved at maze running until they were as fast as the "bright" rats. Conversely, if the rats were raised in "impoverished" conditions—in small cages with no toys and few companions—then the performance of the "bright" rats declined so that they were no better at solving mazes than the "dull" rats (**Figure 4.10C**). So the genes carried by the two strains of rats did affect maze learning, but only in a particular environment (the standard lab cage). In other environments, the different genes carried by the two lines made no difference to maze learning.

We've seen how the environment and experience can affect gene expression and influence behavior in other animals. To explore the interaction of genes and experience in human behavior, we'll start by considering the rare cases where a single gene has a big effect on a particular behavior, yet the environment and experience can play a role too. When we later consider the more common cases where many genes are responsible for a behavior disorder, we'll find an even greater role for experience.

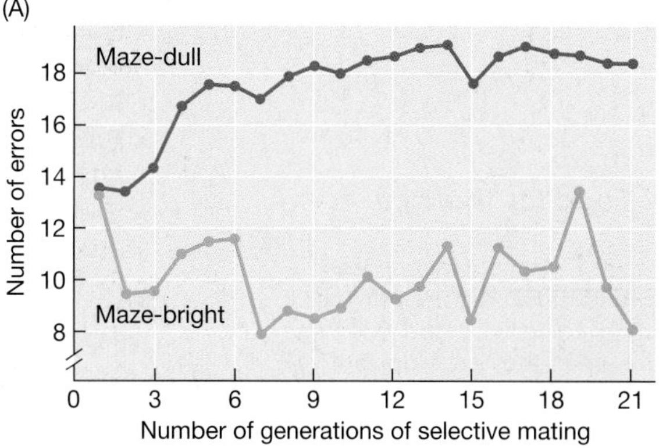

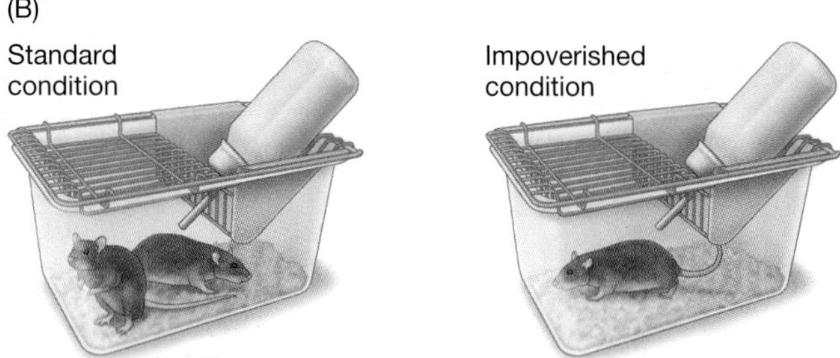

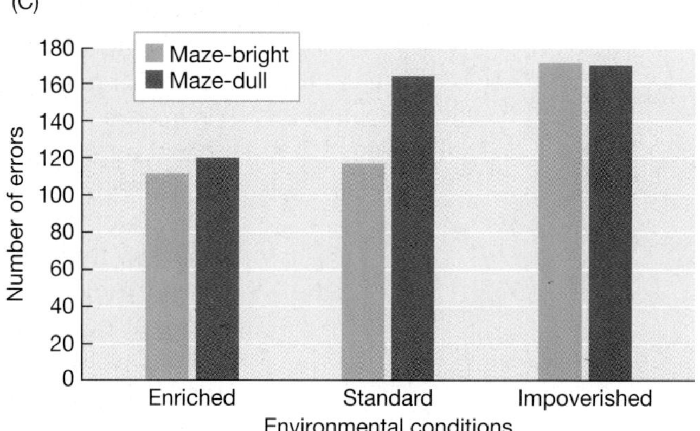

Figure 4.10 Gene-Environment Interactions (A) Rats selected for fast or slow maze learning were bred together to make "maze-bright" and "maze-dull" lines. (B) Different groups of rats were raised in different conditions. (C) If rats from the two lines were raised in special, enriched conditions, they both performed well. When the rats were raised in impoverished conditions, with little chance to explore, the lines scored equally poorly on the mazes. (After Cooper & Zubek, 1958.)

4.2 SUMMARY

- Cells carefully control which proteins they produce, and how much of each protein they produce, by closely regulating how genes are expressed.
- *Gene expression* is affected by many factors, including the environment.
- Because gene expression in neurons is especially sensitive to how active the neuron is, sensory experiences affect gene expression in the brain.
- *Epigenetic* effects occur when environmental conditions influence gene expression.
- Studies have demonstrated that environmental influences such as enriching experiences and maternal care significantly modify the effects of genes on behavior and accomplishment.

REVIEW QUESTIONS

1. Why is it important that different types of cells express different subsets of genes, and why do they need to carefully regulate how much of each kind of protein they make?
2. Explain the gene–environment interaction revealed when maze-bright and maze-dull rats were raised in different conditions.
3. Give examples of how the environment has influenced your genes and affected your behavior.

Food for Thought

Genetically identical mice raised by mothers of two different strains are reliably different in the way they behave when they grow up. But we could ask why mothers from the two strains differ in their maternal behaviors.

How would we test whether that difference in mothering behavior is due to differences in the genes the mothers carry or to differences in their own experience?

4.3 Single Gene Effects on Behavior

Things to Learn

- Two classes of single gene effects on behavior
- Why some mutations are disastrous
- Mutations that affect sensory systems

For almost any complex behavior, no single gene is responsible for the differences in behavior we see in people. Rather, many genes each have a small effect, which in combination with the differences in individuals' past experiences causes people to behave differently from one another. However, there are some exceptions: cases in which a single gene, acting either as a recessive allele (the same allele is present on both chromosomes) or a dominant allele (only one allele needs to be present), is the cause of certain behaviors. In these cases, the behavioral difference among individuals really is determined by the differences in the genes they carry. These cases fall into two basic categories: (1) destructive processes, and (2) sensory defects.

Genes that severely disrupt brain function have a strong, direct, and disastrous effect on behavior

We all carry some alleles that don't make a functional protein, and as we said earlier, if our other allele works properly, we can still function normally. But some alleles cause a disastrously abnormal protein to be made—one that not only doesn't do its job but actually does damage. The destructive protein acts like a poison, harming the very cells that make it. The person carrying such an allele is in trouble even if the other allele is functional. Even if the person is making some good versions of the protein, the bad versions still do harm.

In many cases, fetuses with alleles producing harmful proteins do not survive. In other cases, an allele may make harmful protein, but not so harmful that the fetus dies. Such alleles may, however, cause problems later in life. One example is a particular allele of the gene called *huntingtin*. Most people have at least one functional allele of the *huntingtin* gene and so have no problem. But there is one allele of *huntingtin* that works satisfactorily only for a time. The embryo survives and the person grows up without symptoms. Then, in middle age, the abnormal, toxic protein begins to kill certain neurons

(A) Brain loss in Huntington's

In Huntington's disease, neurons in this part of the brain (striatum) begin dying.

Patient with Huntington's disease

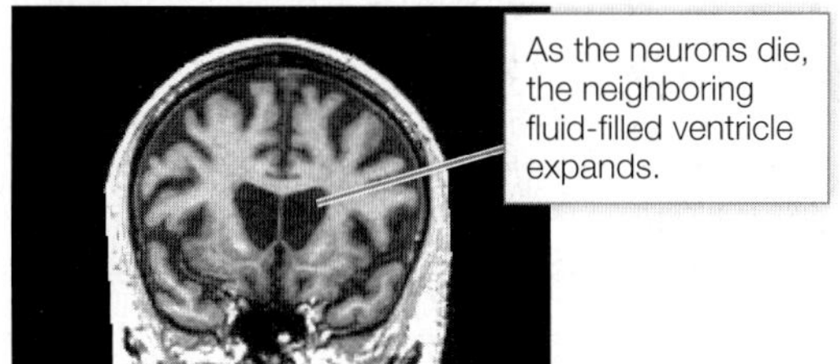

As the neurons die, the neighboring fluid-filled ventricle expands.

(B) Patient with Huntington's

(C) Inheriting Huntington's disease

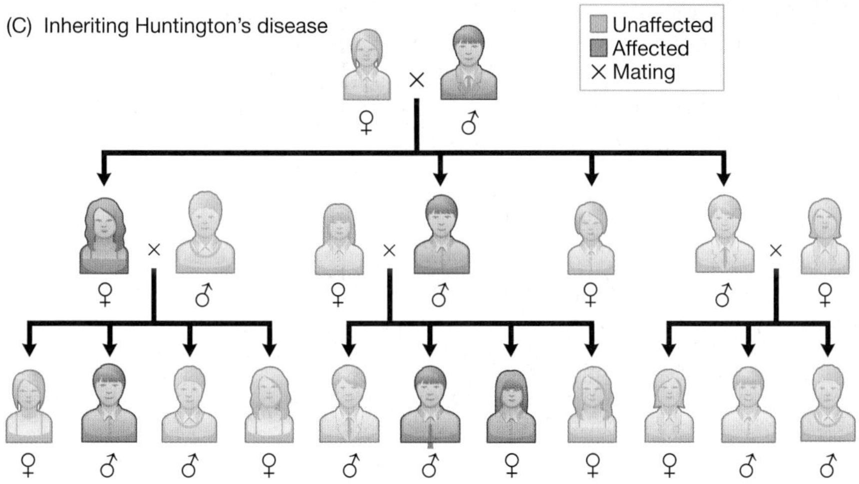

Figure 4.11 A Destructive Protein (A) People carrying a defective allele for the *huntingtin* gene show no symptoms early in life. But by middle-age, the abnormal protein causes neurons to die in a brain region known as the striatum. (B) As the cells there die, the person shows abnormal involuntary movements and disordered thinking and eventually dies. (C) Huntington's disease is a dominant trait, so a person carrying only one allele will display the disorder. This person has a 50-50 chance of passing that allele on to each child.

in the brain. The person gradually displays strange, sweeping motions of the arms and legs and loses touch with reality. This illness, called **Huntington's disease**, progresses, robbing afflicted individuals of their mental abilities and driving more and more bizarre movements and delusions until they die (**Figure 4.11**).

The harmful allele for *huntingtin* is dominant, wreaking its havoc no matter what allele the person carries for the gene on the other chromosome. Scientists do not yet understand why, but certain neurons in the brain, a part of the basal ganglia (see Figure 3.20B) called the striatum, are poisoned by the huntingtin protein they make, and die (see Figure 4.11A). As more and more of these neurons die, an individual's symptoms become progressively worse until he or she dies.

Harmful dominant alleles are not common, because the carrier usually does not survive to reproduce and pass on the allele. But Huntington's disease illustrates a rare case of an allele that does great harm *after* a person has had a chance to pass it on to the next generation. Each child of a person with Huntington's disease has a 50% chance of getting the disease, depending on whether he or she inherited the parent's abnormal allele or normal allele. Having watched her mother die of Huntington's disease, psychologist Nancy Wexler led a research team that discovered the *huntingtin* gene (Shelbourne et al., 2007). Now she and other children of people with Huntington's disease can choose to be tested to see if they carry the harmful allele.

Huntington's disease A progressive genetic disorder characterized by abrupt, involuntary movements and profound changes in mental functioning.

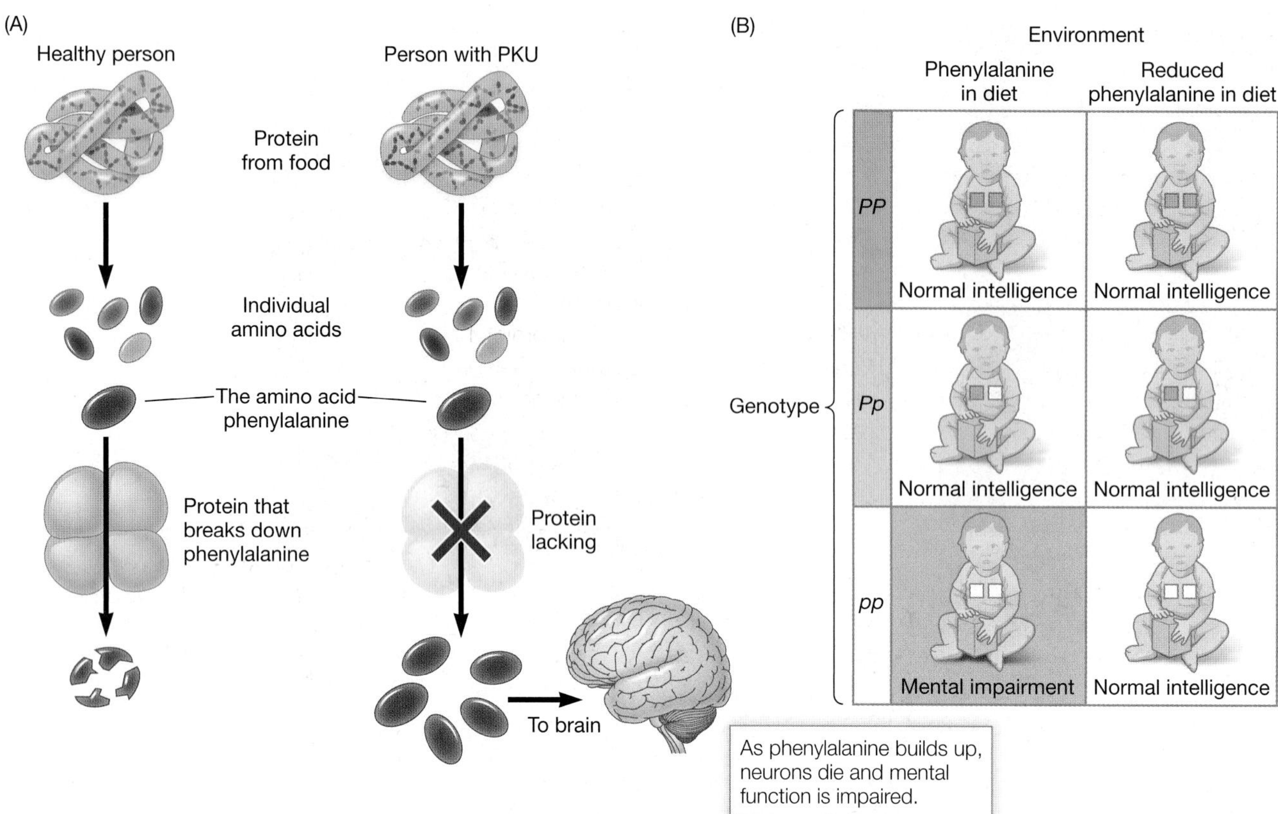

Figure 4.12 **Phenylketonuria (PKU)** (A) People carrying two copies of the recessive allele for PKU are unable to make a protein needed to break down phenylalanine. This leads to a buildup of phenylalanine that disrupts brain development, impairing mental development. However, simply reducing the intake of phenylalanine in food avoids the problem. (B) The gene causes mental impairment only in environments where phenylalanine is abundant in food.

A destructive process can also take place in the brain because of the *lack* of a functional protein. In such cases, the gene is recessive: only people who inherit two nonfunctioning alleles will have the disorder. **Phenylketonuria (PKU)** is a recessive hereditary disorder that at one time often resulted in mental impairment. Those afflicted with PKU lack a protein that breaks down phenylalanine, an amino acid that is present in many foods. Without a functional version of this protein, excess phenylalanine builds up in the blood and results in a disaster: brain cells die and mental functions falter (**Figure 4.12**).

The discovery of PKU marked the first time that a genetic problem was associated with mental disability. Today all babies are tested just a few days after birth to see if they have too much phenylalanine in their blood. Early detection is important because simply reducing phenylalanine in the diet prevents brain impairment. Food products containing phenylalanine are labeled so that people with PKU can avoid them. This dietary control is critical during the early years of life, especially before age 12.

PKU and its treatment offer another illuminating example of gene–environment interaction. Children carrying two PKU alleles will develop intellectual disability only if they eat significant amounts of phenylalanine. So even in this case of a powerful single-gene effect on behavior, the right environment can prevent the mental impairment. Conversely, a diet of phenylalanine causes no problem for brain development for most children. Put another way, the harmful effects of inheriting two PKU genes depend on the presence or absence of phenylalanine in the diet.

phenylketonuria (PKU) An inherited disorder of protein metabolism in which the absence of an enzyme leads to a toxic buildup of certain compounds, causing intellectual disability.

Genes that affect sensory systems can have a strong effect on behavior

There is one more class of exceptions to the rule that individual genes have only a small effect on behavior: cases in which an allele makes a protein that is vital for some sensory process, such as hearing or vision.

Every one of our sensory cells makes several highly specialized proteins that allow it to detect the physical events around us. Some sensory cells in our skin make specialized proteins that allow those cells to detect heat, others make a different protein that lets them detect cool temperatures, and yet others make a protein that detects damage to our skin (and sends a pain signal to our brain). In Chapter 6 we'll meet a girl who lacks a protein needed to perceive pain. Cells in our eyes make specialized proteins to detect light, and some proteins are specialized to respond to light of particular colors.

One highly specialized protein made in the eye makes it possible to distinguish green light from red light. Some people don't have a functional allele for this protein. About 1 out of every 11 human males does not make this protein and so cannot tell red from green. These individuals are sometimes said to be "color-blind," even though they can distinguish many colors—just not red from green (**Figure 4.13A**). This is not as big a problem as you might imagine. Many people with red-green color blindness grow up without ever noticing the deficiency. A test like that shown in **Figure 4.13B** can detect color blindness. Take a look yourself. Why is such color blindness more common in males than females? It is because the gene for one of the proteins for color vision is on the X chromosome, of which males have only one. This means males only receive one allele for that particular gene. If that allele doesn't make a functional protein, there's no other X chromosome to provide an allele to compensate.

Our ears use more than 100 different genes to work properly. If an individual inherits two dysfunctional alleles for any of those genes, that person will be born

Be Careful What You Eat This girl has phenylketonuria, so she eats fruit and protein-free rice and pasta (without cheese) for a diet low in phenylalanine.

(A)

(B)

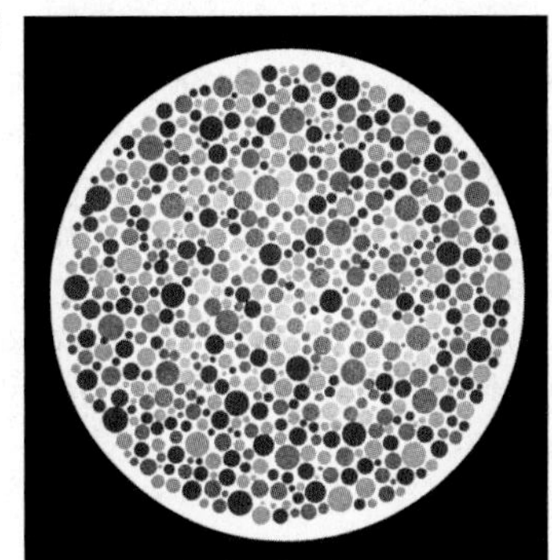

Figure 4.13 Simulating Color Blindness (A) The photograph on the right has been adjusted to simulate the experience of the most common form of color blindness in humans. For such individuals, the world's colors consist of blue and *not* blue. (B) Some people cannot see the differences in color needed to read the two numerals (74). The photo on the right (in A) was produced by software available from Vischeck (www.vischeck.com).

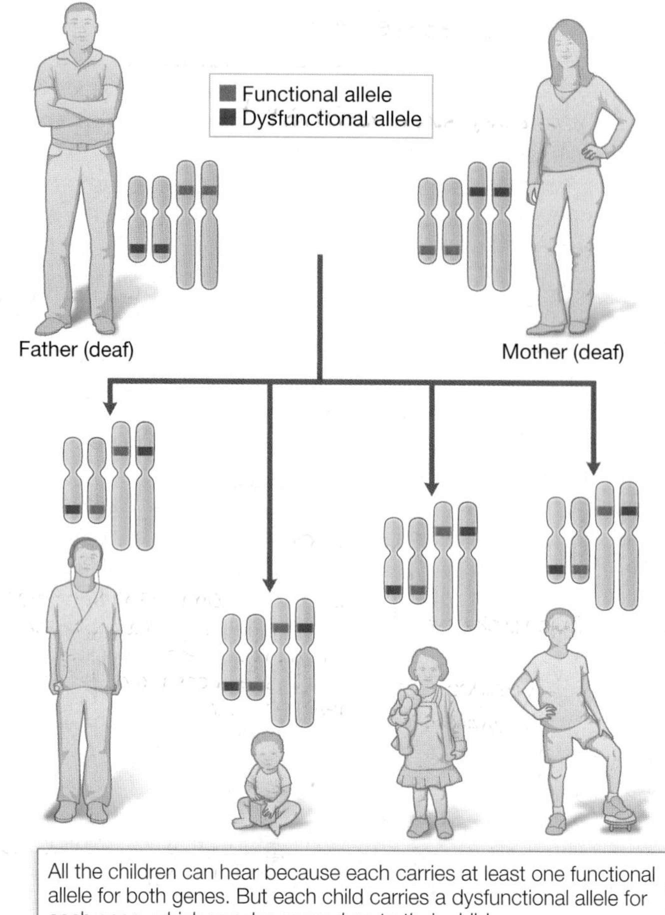
Functional allele
Dysfunctional allele
Father (deaf)
Mother (deaf)
All the children can hear because each carries at least one functional allele for both genes. But each child carries a dysfunctional allele for each gene, which may be passed on to their children.

Figure 4.14 Recessive Genes that Cause Deafness Because a functional ear requires many different proteins, there are many different genetic causes for deafness that are recessive traits. Only if the person inherits two dysfunctional alleles for the gene will he or she be deaf. Two unrelated people with inherited deafness are unlikely to be missing the same functional protein.

I See What You Mean People who are deaf can communicate through sign language.

deaf. Most cases of inherited deafness are the result of recessive genes. Because there are so many different recessive genes that cause deafness, however, the children of two deaf people usually have normal hearing. How does this happen? If the parents carry two dysfunctional alleles for two *different* genes, their offspring will inherit one functional and one dysfunctional allele for each of the two genes. That means they will have each of the proteins needed to hear. As shown in **Figure 4.14**, the children carry recessive alleles for deafness in two different genes and can pass these on to their children.

The important point to keep in mind is that traits affected by a single gene represent only a tiny fraction of all human characteristics. Single gene examples don't shed much light on how genes affect most behavior, including almost all complex behaviors such as language, athletic ability, and artistic expression. Single genes cause very few of the behavioral disorders that plague humans, no matter what we might read in newspapers or see on TV (**Box 4.2**).

Let's now examine those more complicated, and more common, instances where genes and the environment interact to mold our behavior, and not always for the better.

Skeptic at Large

BOX 4.2

Controlled by Our Genes?

(A)

| News | Sport | U.S. Showbiz | Femail | Health | Science | Money | Right

irectory | Health Boards | Diets | MyDish Recipe Finder

How switching off a fat gene may prevent weight-gain - EVEN if you eat a high-fat diet

- **Removing Plin2 gene made mice resistant to obesity**
- **Fat cells were 20% smaller and rodents also ate less**
- **Scientists think the effect could be duplicated in humans**

By CLAIRE BATES

PUBLISHED: 07:53 EST, 6 March 2013 | **UPDATED:** 09:02 EST, 6 March 2013

Share Tweet +1 Share 22 View comments

(B)

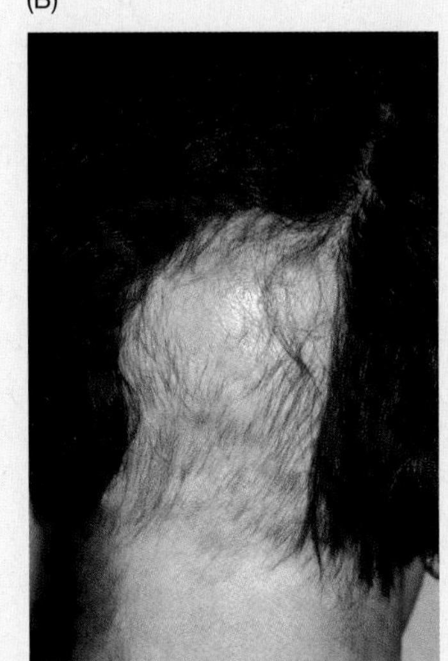

Looking for Simple Solutions (A) News outlets favor genetic explanations for behavior, even when the data are inconclusive. (B) Trichotillomania, the obsessive pulling of hair, has been featured on the TV show *Obsessed*.

It is almost impossible to open a newspaper or scan news reports on the Internet without reading about a new study claiming that genes are responsible for some type of human behavior. One week the gene that causes alcoholism is found, then the one that causes homosexuality, then the one that causes difficulty in reading. In subsequent weeks the media trumpet the discovery of genes that cause picky eaters, depression, schizophrenia, hair pulling, loneliness, or night owls. So many different genes have been reported to cause the childhood disorder known as autism (see Section 5.2) that you wonder if maybe every gene does. We've even been told that a gene was responsible for the famous Hatfield–McCoy feud that killed at least a dozen people over a hundred years of fighting in the Appalachian Mountains of the eastern United States. These reports of genetic breakthroughs are premature (Marchione, 2007; **Figure A**). What's going on?

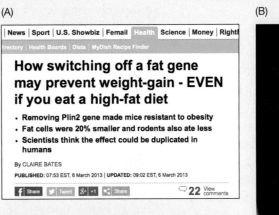

Some journalists have little scientific background and so may tend to overestimate the importance of a discovery. But it's also clear that our society is very receptive to hearing about the importance of genes for behavior. There's something fascinating, even seductive, about the idea of predestination—that we are born to behave in particular ways. But we can't just blame naive reporters and a receptive public for the overselling of genes and behavior.

What about the scientists? Are they lying about these findings? No. We know that genes really do influence alcoholism, schizophrenia, depression, sexual orientation, eating habits, sleeping habits, hair pulling, and autism. But for all of these behaviors, we also know that no single gene can account for all cases. Rather, many genes are at work, and each changes the *probability* that a person will show that particular behavior. If we get just one of those genes, our odds of avoiding the disorder are pretty good. But if we get several of those genes, and likewise, if we run into a lot of bumps in life, we may develop a problem. Of the behaviors mentioned above, only one has been shown to be caused by the action of a single gene: some people inherit a gene that causes them to compulsively pull at their hair until they may be almost bald (Browne et al., 2014; **Figure B**).

Aside from such rare cases, scientists are looking for one of the *many* genes involved in the behaviors. The objects of their search are one of the several genes that increase the probability that a person might develop those behaviors. It would be tremendously helpful to identify people who carry genes that make them more likely to abuse drugs, commit suicide, or develop schizophrenia. We could then make special efforts to help such people avoid those problems. Early intervention in the environment of children carrying these genes may be critical for making sure that none of us are controlled by our genes.

Of course, knowing a person's total genetic makeup carries some ethical risks. What sort of power does a doctor, corporation, or government have over us if every gene we carry is known and understood? For example, should employers be permitted to check out our genes before deciding whether to hire us? It is unfortunate that our society is unprepared for dealing with these important issues. This situation makes it that much more important that we all try to understand how genes really work.

4.3 SUMMARY

- Most human behaviors are influenced by many genes, each of which makes a subtle contribution, so that rarely does inheriting a particular gene reliably affect behavior.
- There are a few cases where inheriting a gene has a profound effect on behavior, no matter what the environment. For example, some alleles, such as that causing *Huntington's disease*, express a protein that is toxic, harming the cells that make it and leading to profound mental disorder and death.
- Sometimes the harmful effects of alleles can be averted, as when people inheriting two *phenylketonuria* (*PKU*) alleles are given diets with little phenylalanine.
- Many different proteins are crucial for sensory systems, so a nonfunctioning allele may result in a highly specific sensory deficit, such as the inability to distinguish red from green, or the inability to hear.

REVIEW QUESTIONS

1. How does a toxic allele lead to Huntington's disease?
2. What is phenylketonuria, and how can the harmful consequences of this condition be avoided?
2. Why is it that when two people who were both born deaf because of genetic disorders have children, their children usually can hear?

Food for Thought

If your mother or father had Huntington's disease, would you get the test to see if you're carrying the allele?

4.4 Multiple Gene Effects on Behavior

Things to Learn

- Logic of twin studies of heredity
- Meaning of heritability
- Limits of heritability estimates
- Power of twin adoption studies

Once we leave behind the examples of genes that directly affect sensory systems, or genes that make a toxic protein that cripples brain function, we encounter the far more common cases in which single genes cannot account for differences among people. We can learn about these more complicated influences of genes on behavior by focusing on schizophrenia.

Twin studies confirm a genetic contribution to schizophrenia

No human behavioral disorder has been more closely studied than schizophrenia, probably because it can have such devastating effects on both the people who have it and those around them. This and other disorders will be presented in more detail in Chapter 16, but for now we can define **schizophrenia** as a mental disorder characterized by hallucinations (usually hearing voices), delusions (beliefs in things that aren't true), disordered thinking, and emotional withdrawal from others. The Genain quadruplets considered at the start of this chapter suffered all these symptoms. Taken together, schizophrenia seems to be a universal human disorder. About 1% of the human population will exhibit the condition at some point in life, whether the population is the United States, China, or Argentina (Torrey, 2006).

When scientists started systematically researching schizophrenia, in the late 1800s, it seemed clear that it was inherited. People who have a close relative with schizophrenia are much more likely to develop the disorder than the general population. In fact, the more closely related a person is to someone with schizophrenia, the more likely he or she is to develop it (**Figure 4.15**). The siblings of someone with schizophrenia are more likely to get the disorder than are that person's first cousins, who are at greater risk than second cousins, and so on. This finding is a strong argument for a genetic component. The more genes someone shares with a person with schizophrenia, the more likely he or she is to develop the disorder.

But people who are closely related to each other share more than just genes. The more closely related we are, the more likely we are to grow up in the same household (for example, brothers and sisters tend to grow up together). So if there

schizophrenia A disabling mental disorder characterized by hallucinations, delusions, disordered thinking, and emotional withdrawal.

confounding variable A third factor that affects both variables of interest, causing them to covary even though neither has any causal effect on the other.

twin study Study of identical twins; used to estimate heritability of certain traits.

monozygotic twins Also called *identical twins*. Twins derived from a single fertilized egg.

dizygotic twins Also called *fraternal twins* or *non-identical twins*. Twins derived from two separate eggs.

were a toxin that causes schizophrenia, and if the toxin were present in a particular house, siblings of a person with schizophrenia would be more likely to develop the disorder than cousins would be. We have here **confounding variables** (or "confounders"): two variables that change together, making it difficult to know which one is at work (see Chapter 2). In this case, people who share similar genes also tend to share similar environments, so we don't know whether it is the shared genes or shared environments that make relatives of individuals with schizophrenia more likely to develop the disorder.

Twin studies are the most common method to tease out the confounding variable of similar environments shared by relatives. All twins share the same mother, so they develop in the same uterus, and are born within a few hours (if not minutes) of each other. Most twins also grow up in the same household, sharing the same family and environment. But not all twins are alike in how genetically related they are. Some twins are the result of a single fertilized egg that develops into an embryo that at some point splits into two individuals. These twins have the same genes and are called **monozygotic twins** because a fertilized egg is also called a *zygote* and they came from one zygote (**Figure 4.16A**). They are also called *identical twins* because they closely resemble each other.

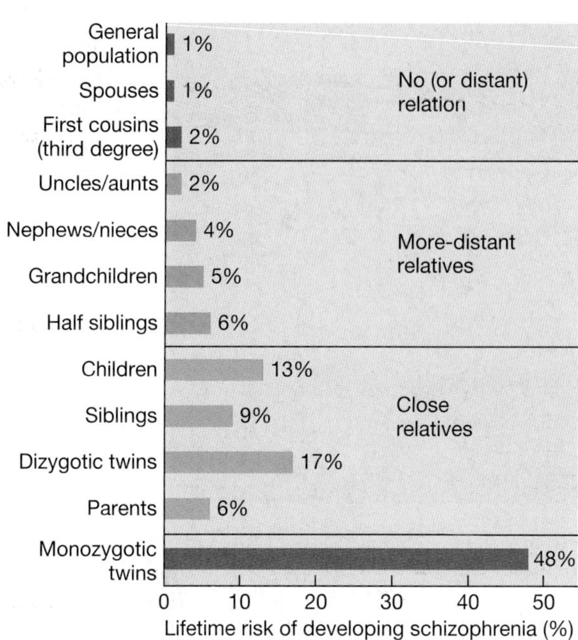

Figure 4.15 The Heritability of Schizophrenia The more closely related a person is to a patient with schizophrenia, the more likely that person is to develop schizophrenia at some point. (After Gottesman, 1991.)

Other twins result from two different sperm fertilizing two different eggs at about the same time. These twins, from two zygotes, are called **dizygotic twins**, *non-identical twins*, or in common usage, fraternal twins (**Figure 4.16B**). Dizygotic twins also tend to resemble each other, partly because they are the exact same age, and partly because most siblings resemble each other. But dizygotic twins are no more genetically related to each other than any other siblings are. For example, dizygotic twins may be a brother and sister, while monozygotic twins are always the same sex. On average, dizygotic twins share about half of their genes (as do all full siblings), whereas monozygotic twins share all of their genes.

Studies of monozygotic and dizygotic twins shed light on the relative effects of nature (genes) and nurture (environment) on the individual. A twin study examines pairs of people who grow up in the same household at the same time and therefore should have similar environments. Because monozygotic twins share more genes with each other than do dizygotic twins, it isn't surprising that monozygotic twins tend to be *more similar* to each other than dizygotic twins are for any characteristics that are affected by genes. For example, monozygotic twins tend to be closer together in height and weight than are dizygotic twins, evidence that genes affect those two characteristics. Monozygotic twins are more similar than dizygotic twins in many other characteristics, including blood type, eye color, and hair color (Segal, 2000). For these physical traits, monozygotic twins are always the same, whereas dizygotic twins may be the same or different.

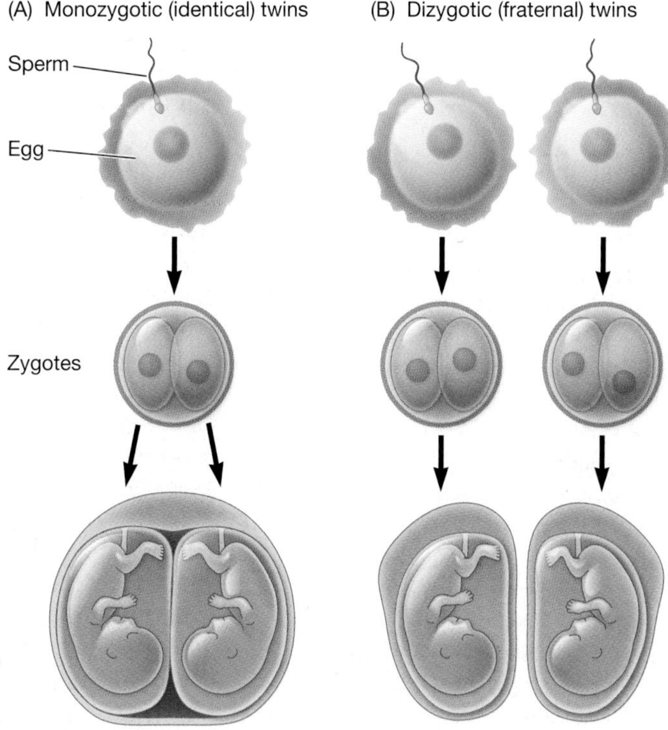

Figure 4.16 Monozygotic versus Dizygotic Twins (A) Monozygotic, or identical, twins arise from a single fertilized egg. (B) Dizygotic, or non-identical, twins arise from two separate fertilized eggs and are no more closely related than any other full siblings.

Figure 4.17 The Genain Quadruplets at Five Years Old Hester, who was always the smallest sister, is on the far right.

But what about behavior? Do monozygotic twins act more alike than dizygotic twins do? The answer, for many behaviors, is yes. Whether you ask about IQ test results, playing sports, choosing college majors, or watching TV, monozygotic twins are more alike than dizygotic twins, evidence again that genes affect all those behaviors (Segal, 2000). The extremely rare case of the Genains, monozygotic quadruplets discussed at the start of this chapter, offers strong evidence of the role genes play in the development of schizophrenia. As we noted, all four sisters eventually came down with the disorder (**Figure 4.17**).

In twin studies, we are interested in knowing if both twins share or do not share the same traits. Twins are **concordant** for a trait if both individuals have that trait. If both twins have schizophrenia, or both do not have schizophrenia, we say they are concordant for the disorder. Twins are **discordant** for a trait if one has it and the other does not. If one twin has schizophrenia and the other does not, they are discordant for schizophrenia.

Twin studies of behaviors, such as schizophrenia, find that monozygotic twins are more likely to be concordant than dizygotic twins are. For example, if 48% of monozygotic twins are concordant for a behavior but only 17% of dizygotic twins are concordant, then the greater concordance rate in the monozygotic twins must occur because they are more closely related genetically. If the additional 31% concordance is due to the monozygotic twins being twice as related as dizygotic twins (sharing all of their genes versus half), then, roughly speaking, this suggests that about 60% (31% × 2, because monozygotic twins share twice as many genes as dizygotic twins) of the variability in the instance of schizophrenia is due to differences in genes. These studies have been done many times, and slightly different studies get slightly different results (Sullivan et al., 2003). But taken together, they suggest that differences in genes account for about 60% of the differences between people in cases of schizophrenia. What does that mean?

What does it mean if a behavior is "heritable"?

Before anyone had ever heard of DNA or genes, the word "heritable" meant "something that is inherited." Today we say a trait is **heritable** if it is influenced by one or more genes inherited from the parents. The trait could be physical, such as height, or behavioral, such as IQ score or schizophrenia.

A more formal definition of **heritability** is an estimate of the *variation* of a trait in a population that arises from differences in people's genes. Heritability is a statistical estimate of what percentage of variation for that trait is caused by the various genotypes. Except for those traits in which single genes account entirely for a disorder, as in the case of color blindness or Huntington's disease, variation in genes accounts for 20%–70% of the variation in every human behavior (**Table 4.2**). Data like those in Table 4.2 underscore a principle of psychology of which we can be absolutely certain: genes influence all human behaviors.

While we now know that genes influence all behaviors, we also know that genes are not wholly in charge of behavior. Some 30%–80% of the variation in behaviors is not accounted for by variation in genes. The environment accounts for the rest of the variation. Estimates of heritability show us that genes are only part of the story, not the whole story. Experience also plays a role, which is why learning, for example, is so important.

There are several things that heritability does not mean

If the heritability estimate for schizophrenia is 0.60, that means that about 60% of all the variability in schizophrenia in the population is due to variability in the genes in that population. Heritability is a concept that is easily misunderstood. For this reason, let's learn what heritability estimates are *not*.

concordant Referring to any trait that is seen in both individuals of a pair of twins.

discordant Referring to any trait that is seen in only one individual of a pair of twins.

heritable A trait that is influenced by one or more genes inherited from one's parents.

heritability A statistical estimate of the extent to which individual differences in genes in a population contribute to individual differences in a trait.

1. The 0.60 estimate of heritability of schizophrenia does not mean that 60% of the people in the population have schizophrenia. Only about 1% of the population develops the disorder.
2. A heritability estimate of 60% does not mean that 60% of the people who have schizophrenia are that way because of genes, while the other 40% have schizophrenia because of nongenetic factors. It may be that genes play at least a small role in every case but that differences in people's genes alone cannot explain all the cases.

Heritability estimates only tell us about *populations* of people. We cannot use them to tell us anything about a *particular person*. When we meet someone who has schizophrenia, knowing that the heritability estimate of the disorder is about 60% tells us nothing about how this particular person came to have schizophrenia. He may have developed schizophrenia because of genes he inherited, because of stresses he encountered in life, or both. Heritability estimates are specific not only to the behavior measured, but also to the population in which they were measured. In Chapter 11 we'll learn that heritability estimates of intelligence differ quite a bit depending on whether the data are gathered from middle-class families or poor families. Although heritability estimates offer no predictive power about a particular individual, they make it clear that genes do matter.

TABLE 4.2 Estimates of Heritability for Various Behaviors in Humans

Trait	Heritability (%)
SOCIAL BEHAVIORS	
Aggression	40
Empathy	48
Leadership	40
Parental warmth	39
Prosocial behaviors	56
Risk-taking	39
Social responsiveness	45
Trust game	15
Ultimate game	41
SOCIAL ATTITUDES	
Conservatism	55
Religiousness	38
Specific religion	0
PERSONALITY	
Agreeableness	42
Conscientiousness	49
Extraversion	54
Neuroticism	48
Openness	57
PSYCHIATRIC CONDITIONS	
Alcoholism	55
Depression	37

Source: Bouchard, 2002; Ebstein et al., 2010.

Inferences about heritability from twin studies make several simplifying assumptions

Twin studies demonstrate that genes affect behavior, but note that all conclusions about heritability that come from comparing identical and non-identical twins rely on several assumptions that are probably not entirely correct. For example, is the environment of non-identical twins as similar as the environment of identical twins? Both kinds of twins grow up with someone exactly the same age, but non-identical twins may grow up with a same-age twin of the opposite sex. So if the behavior of non-identical twins is less similar than that of identical twins, maybe it's because the non-identical twins have less similar environments growing up.

Likewise, it seems clear that the *prenatal environment* is more similar in identical twins than in non-identical twins. If an embryo splits into two genetically identical individuals early in development, the resulting identical twins may share the same compartment in the uterus. If the split happens later, the twins may have one or even two membranes between them. In contrast, almost all non-identical twins develop in well-separated compartments within their mother's uterus (see Figure 4.16). Thus, in general monozygotic twins have a more similar prenatal environment than do dizygotic twins. This means *that estimates of heritability based on comparing monozygotic and dizygotic twins are going to overestimate the influence of genes.* How much does the greater similarity of prenatal environment in monozygotic twins inflate estimates of gene influence? No one really knows, and it is not easy to think how to go about estimating it.

We can't get around the fact that identical twins have a more similar prenatal environment than non-identical twins, but there are cases when the environment after birth is different for both kinds of twins, as we consider next.

Two of a Kind In fact, these actors are not natural "gingers"–their hair was dyed red for the "Harry Potter" movies.

Although rare, cases of identical twins who are reared apart offer powerful insights

A better test of the effects of genes on behavior would be to separate two identical twins at birth and raise them in completely different circumstances. In such **adoption studies**, if the twins still resemble each other behaviorally, even when raised apart, that resemblance suggests their shared genes are responsible for their similar behavior. Adoption of twins does happen, but it is not common. Furthermore, because only about 1% of the population will ever display schizophrenia, cases where a person who was raised apart from her or his twin later developed schizophrenia are rare. Nevertheless, researchers have found examples of monozygotic and dizygotic twins raised apart where one develops schizophrenia, and in such cases the other twin is much more likely to develop the disorder than the general population (Bouchard, 2002). In other words, more than 1% of those twins raised apart also developed schizophrenia. Furthermore, the concordance rate for schizophrenia is higher in monozygotic twins raised apart than in dizygotic twins raised apart. This greater concordance rate for monozygotic twins cannot be due to being raised in a more similar environment (including growing up with someone who looks almost like you).

Another piece of evidence supports the view that genes are responsible for the greater concordance for schizophrenia in identical versus non-identical twins. The *children* of identical twins discordant for schizophrenia are equally likely to develop the disorder whether their parent was the twin with schizophrenia or the one without (Gottesman, 1991). If the environment of the well twin keeps him from developing schizophrenia, then we'd expect the children of the well twin to be less likely to become ill than their cousins with a parent with schizophrenia. Rather, it appears the well twin is indeed carrying genes that make schizophrenia more likely, and passes some of those genes to the next generation. Despite carrying genes for schizophrenia, the well twin may have averted the disorder himself, but that doesn't change his genes. If his child inherits genes that increase the risk of schizophrenia, what will decide whether the child will develop schizophrenia?

If we set aside the single-gene effects we discussed earlier (sensory defects and destructive proteins), those estimates are never 100% (see Table 4.2). Rather, heritability is usually between 20% and 60%, no matter what behavior is studied. This means that the environment also has an important influence on all those behaviors. So we could next ask, what's important about the environment that is affecting the behavior?

adoption studies Studies of identical twins separated at birth.

4.4 SUMMARY

- If a behavior is influenced by genes, then the more closely related people are, the more similar they should be for the behavior.
- There is a *confounding variable* in some cases—more closely related people tend to have more similar home environments.
- One way to minimize this confounding variable is to use *twin studies*, comparing how often a pair of twins are *concordant* or *discordant* for a trait, such as *schizophrenia*. If the trait is influenced by genes, then *monozygotic twins* should be concordant more often than *dizygotic twins*.
- Measurements of similarities between monozygotic twins and dizygotic twins provide estimates of *heritability*, or how much of the variation of a trait in a population is due to differences in genes.
- Twin studies indicate a heritability of about 60% for schizophrenia, meaning a bit more than half the differences in the occurrence of schizophrenia in the population are due to differences in genes. It does *not* mean that half the cases of schizophrenia are due to genes.

- Twin studies probably overestimate the heritability of behavior.
- Still, monozygotic twins are more likely than dizygotic twins to be concordant for schizophrenia, even when raised apart, confirming that genes play a role in the disorder.

REVIEW QUESTIONS

1. What percentage of genes, on average, are shared between monozygotic twins? Between dizygotic twins?
2. How does comparing concordance in monozygotic versus dizygotic twins give an estimate of heritability?
3. What is heritability? What is it not?

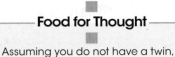

Food for Thought

Assuming you do not have a twin, have you imagined what it would be like to grow up with a twin? Would the constant presence of a twin have affected your behavior?

If you do have a twin, have you imagined how your behavior as a child might have been different without that presence in your environment?

4.5 The Interaction of Genes and Experience

Things to Learn

- Stress increases risk of heritable disorders
- Modern view of genes in schizophrenia
- Power of early experience for later behavior

Because heritability studies make it clear that genes alone cannot be the only factor in schizophrenia, there have been extensive studies trying to identify environmental factors that could lead to the disorder. Those studies have built up a clear picture that exposure to stress such as accident and disease can increase the likelihood of schizophrenia. In this example of the interaction of genes and experience, people who inherit genes that make them vulnerable to schizophrenia develop the disorder only if they are "pushed over the edge" by environmental stress.

Stress plays a role in the appearance of schizophrenia

Many findings indicate that different kinds of stress, such as disease, malnutrition, and neglect, increase the probability that a person will develop schizophrenia. For example, the proportion of people with schizophrenia is greater in cities than in rural areas, probably because city life is more stressful than rural life, as we'll discuss further in Chapter 16 (Pedersen & Mortensen, 2001). The proportion of people who develop schizophrenia also rises during times of social upheaval such as war. Another clue that stress plays a role is the time of life when schizophrenia appears. Most people who develop the disorder start displaying symptoms at the age when they must make the stressful transition from adolescence to adulthood. The four Genain sisters all developed symptoms by age 24, and many cases of schizophrenia appear when young people are adjusting to the stresses and strains of college life. If the challenges in this period become too great, they may push a person into schizophrenia. Yet that same person, with the same genes, might never develop schizophrenia if his environment were less stressful.

Perhaps the strongest evidence that stress plays a role in schizophrenia comes from the same twin studies that demonstrated the influence of genes for this disorder. Among the many cases of identical twins who are discordant for schizophrenia, we can ask whether the twin who developed schizophrenia was under more stress than the twin who did not. Many studies of identical twins discordant for schizophrenia indicate that the twin who developed schizophrenia was subjected to greater stress than the other twin. For example, the ill twin is more likely to have experienced complications during birth. This twin may have had the umbilical cord wrapped around her neck, and may have experienced more oxygen deprivation than the other twin. The ill twin usually had a lower birth weight and is also more likely to have shown evidence of an infection at birth, such as fever.

The Wear and Tear of City Life People who grow up in big cities are twice as likely to develop schizophrenia as people growing up in rural settings.

More evidence that the twin who developed schizophrenia was always the more vulnerable one comes from home movies. By examining old home movies of identical twins who are discordant for schizophrenia, observers can usually pick out which child, upon growing up, developed schizophrenia. This is the twin who shows more disorganized behavior. His or her movements are jerkier, less smooth. Even as babies, the child who will develop schizophrenia shows more abnormal crawling behavior (Walker & Lewine, 1990). Thus whatever has been different about the environment of the two twins (their genes, after all, were identical), it has an impact on motor behavior years before any schizophrenic symptoms appear. Scientists are increasingly starting to wonder whether small incidents early in life may make a crucial difference (Clarke et al., 2011). The challenges clear up and everything seems normal for a while, but they set the stage for the problems that may crop up years later.

The story of the Genain quads supports the idea that small stresses in early life can affect the later development of schizophrenia. The last-born sister, Hester, had the lowest birth weight and was the only one who needed to be kept in an incubator for her first few days of life. That might explain why she was the first to become ill, at age 11, and the only sister who spent much of her life in institutions. In contrast, Myra, who was always the healthiest, was the last to develop schizophrenia, at age 24, and she recovered enough to eventually work, marry, and raise two sons. The other two sisters, intermediate between Myra and Hester in health, had intermediate outcomes: they recovered to work as secretaries and support themselves, and they never married. Thus although all the sisters developed schizophrenia, and all would eventually receive medication to control it, they varied considerably in the severity of the disorder and in the consequences for their lives. Identical genes did not result in identical outcomes.

Because stress greatly increases the chances of developing schizophrenia, the Genain quads do not provide a compelling argument for the role of genes after all. Despite the public attention, few people knew that their irritable, controlling father was brutally abusive. A violent man who terrorized his entire family, he often carried a pistol in his pocket. Until the quads were over 20 years old, he insisted on sitting in their bedroom to watch them get dressed and undressed. Once the quads reached adolescence, their father would rub their buttocks and breasts and watch them change their feminine napkins (Rosenthal, 1963). His abuse was most often directed at Hester and Iris who, as children, were subjected to "female circumcision," surgical removal of the clitoris, supposedly to stop them from masturbating (Mirsky et al., 2000). They had their hands tied to the sides of the bed every night for a month afterward to prevent them from disturbing the stitches. These extra stresses may have had an effect far past adolescence, because Hester and Iris died when they were in their early seventies, a decade before their sisters who, as of this writing, are still alive. The horrific abuse heaped upon the Genain quads, not just early in life but well into their twenties, might have been enough to push anyone to schizophrenia.

Where does the theory that stress early in life and at adolescence leads to schizophrenia leave genetic theories? There is no contradiction. The estimates of heritability for schizophrenia might reflect that some people carry a gene or genes that make them more susceptible to stress, increasing the probability of schizophrenia (**Figure 4.18**).

This modern conception of schizophrenia, as a genetic susceptibility to various stresses and infections in life that lead to the disorder, offers many avenues of hope for treatment or cure. If we can someday identify the genes that make a child susceptible to schizophrenia in adulthood, it might be possible to intervene and shelter that child from the stresses and illnesses that promote the disorder (see Figure 16.20).

Genes and the environment constantly interact to affect our behaviors

With this understanding of the extensive interaction of genes and experience, we can offer a new perspective on the many influences on our behavior. Our genotype was indeed set at fertilization, and there is nothing we can do, at this point in our civilization, to change which genes we carry. Of course, technology may make that possible some day (Lewis, 2013). It is clear that genes

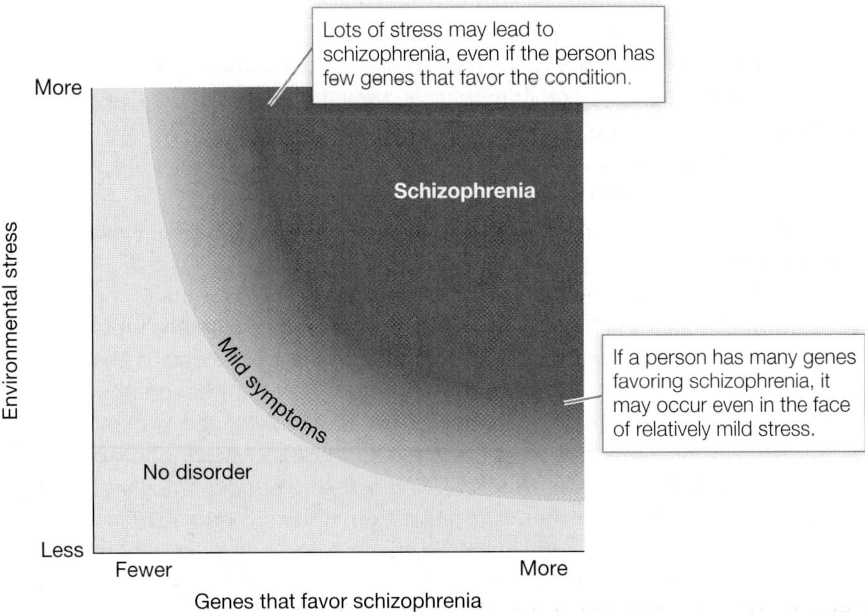

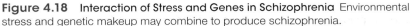

Figure 4.18 Interaction of Stress and Genes in Schizophrenia Environmental stress and genetic makeup may combine to produce schizophrenia.

have powerful effects on the way our body and brain are assembled. But the ways in which we *express* the genes we inherited are constantly changing in response to our environment. That means our time inside our mother's uterus; the way we were treated as an infant; our experiences in school; our conversations, work, and play with our peers; our arrival in college; even our reading of this book, have all affected the expression of our genes throughout our brain. As powerful as the effects of genes are, experiences that affect gene expression are just as powerful. Once we understand this interdependence of genes and experience in shaping the brain and therefore behavior, we no longer expect to find any simple cases where inheriting a single gene always leads to schizophrenia, depression, genius, athletic prowess, magnetic personality, a great sense of humor, or any other important human condition. Rather, all of these behaviors can be made more or less likely by particular sets of genes—*and* by particular sets of environments.

For Hester Genain, a series of circumstances seemed to act like a line of dominoes, each knocking down the next. Some small difference early in life tripped that first domino, causing her to be considerably smaller than her sisters at birth. Was there a problem in the tissues supporting her in the uterus? Was she subjected to an infection that her sisters were spared? We don't know. But it may be that her smaller size and poorer health brought her more abuse from her father, and may have made her a target for the horrific surgery, which must have made her adolescent transition terribly painful until she succumbed to schizophrenia before finishing high school. By age 66, Hester was the only one of the sisters so mentally confused that her behavior could no longer be tested (Mirsky et al., 2000). It is possible that if Hester's birth had been less complicated, or if she'd been sheltered from her father's abuse, or if she had been spared the horror of circumcision as a child, her schizophrenia might never have developed. In fact, we have to wonder whether, if they had been spared from extreme abuse as children, all four Genain girls might have grown up without ever suffering from schizophrenia.

With this understanding that genes matter, but are not all-powerful, and that the environment matters, especially for people carrying genes that put them at risk, we find ourselves with a great responsibility. Can we make a world where individuals are finally, truly in control of their lives, no matter what genes they inherited? We can't go back in time to provide those four little girls with a more nurturing family, so we'll never know whether early intervention might have spared them from schizophrenia.

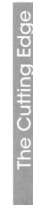

The Cutting Edge

Early Experience Epigenetically Affects the Stress Response in Adulthood

A compelling example of epigenetic regulation in animals appears to be important for humans too. A group of investigators noticed that some rat mothers are more attentive than others. The attentive mothers spend more time nursing their pups and more time licking them clean. Pups raised by more attentive mothers are less fearful in adulthood and show less dramatic responses to stress, including releasing smaller amounts of corticosterone, a stress hormone from the adrenal glands. Consequently, stress doesn't upset the health of these rats as much as it does those raised by inattentive mothers. No matter what genes the rat pups carry, if they are raised by attentive mothers they grow up to be less fearful and release less corticosterone in adulthood. If raised by less attentive mothers, they are more fearful and release more corticosterone (Weaver et al., 2005).

How does this happen? In the brain there are neurons that express the gene for a receptor to detect the stress hormones. When the hormone reaches these neuronal receptors, the brain instructs the adrenal glands to release less hormone in the future. In pups that are raised by an inattentive mother, the gene for the hormone receptor in the brain gets modified—chemicals called methyl groups are attached to the gene—so that less of the receptor gets made. When these pups grow up, because

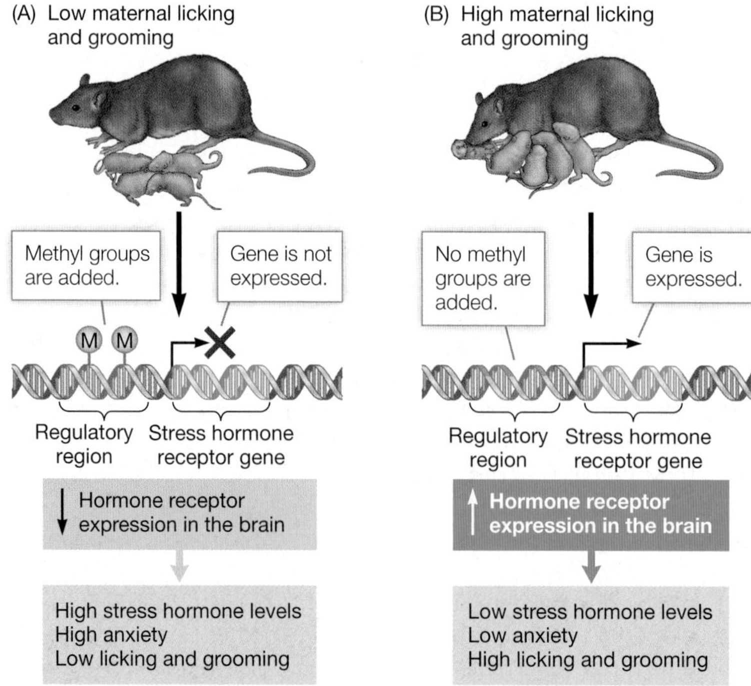

Figure 4.19 Early Experience Imprints Genes to Affect the Stress Response in Adulthood (After Hackman et al., 2010.)

they make less of the receptor in their brains, their adrenal glands release more stress hormones, they are more anxious, and the females are less likely to groom their own pups (**Figure 4.19A**)!

Conversely, when rat mothers groom their pups extensively, their behavior causes a protein cofactor to bind to the receptor gene, which prevents methyl groups from being attached (**Figure 4.19B**). These pups express the receptor gene more, making more hormone receptors and therefore producing less stress hormone as adults (Hackman et al., 2010). These pups are also less anxious and more likely to be attentive mothers when they grow up (Liu et al., 1997).

Does the fascinating mechanism of early neglect modifying a gene and thereby increasing its expression have any relevance for humans? Examination of the brains of suicide victims has revealed the same epigenetic changes—the addition of methyl groups on the gene for the stress hormone receptor—but only in victims who had been abused or neglected as children (McGowan et al., 2009). The implication is that early neglect epigenetically modified expression of the gene in these people, as it does in rats, making them less able to handle stress and therefore more likely to become depressed and commit suicide. The brains of suicide victims with no history of early abuse did not show the epigenetic changes, so their depression may have been a response to other influences.

Is this example of epigenetic effects due to genes or to the environment? Both are at work. The expression of genes for hormones plays a central role in the stress response, so genes are important. But having an inattentive mother affects the *expression* of those genes, so experience is important too. As we've seen, this interactive effect of the environment and genes on behavior is pervasive. In the next chapter we'll review other behavioral consequences of early neglect, and will have to wonder whether they, too, involve epigenetic regulation of gene expression.

4.5 SUMMARY

- Exposure to stress increases the probability that a person will develop schizophrenia. Complications at birth that deprive the newborn of oxygen, or growing up in a big city with its stresses, make a person more vulnerable to schizophrenia.
- Home movies of monozygotic twins as children indicate that the twin who later developed schizophrenia moved in more disorganized, jerkier fashion than the twin that remained well.
- Observations suggest that someday it may be possible to identify babies carrying genes that put them at risk for schizophrenia and protect them from the stresses that would lead them to develop the disorder.
- In rats, maternal neglect can epigenetically imprint certain genes in the pups to cause them to be more anxious in adulthood, and there is evidence that this same gene is affected by early neglect in humans.

REVIEW QUESTIONS

1. Describe the evidence that stress plays a role in the development of schizophrenia.
2. What do old home movies of monozygotic twins tell us about the origins of schizophrenia?
3. Does growing up in a big city increase or decrease the probability of developing schizophrenia?

Food for Thought

Perhaps one day we will identify a gene, or set of genes, that makes people more likely to develop schizophrenia if they are exposed to stress. If you were the parent of a baby carrying these genes, would you want to know? As the child grew up, would you want other people, such as schools and potential employers, to know?

4 Genes, Environment, and Behavior

Non-Identical Identical Sisters

These days medical technology has made multiple births relatively common, so the media take notice only for extreme cases like "Octo-Mom." But in the 1930s, when a set of quadruplets was delivered in a midwestern U.S. hospital, it was big news, especially because the four girls were genetically identical. They became instant celebrities, as the public was eager to watch the progress of these four cute little blonde girls. Before they were teenagers, they were in show business, singing, tap-dancing, and doing comedy routines in three states.

But there was a dark side of the girls' lives that the public did not see. Eventually all four would be diagnosed with a mental disorder, *schizophrenia*, gaining the attention of researchers at the National the girls were genetically identical (Segal, 2001), they were quite different from one another in terms of the severity of disease. The last born sister, "Hester," developed symptoms at age 11 and by high school had to be hospitalized. She was the only sister to never finish high school, and she spent much of her life in institutions. In contrast, "Myra's" first symptoms came on suddenly at the age of 24, but she eventually recovered, working as a secretary, marrying and raising two sons. The other two sisters' outcomes were somewhere in between, recovering enough to work and support themselves, although they never married. So if schizophrenia is simply a result of what genes you inherit, why weren't the sisters affected to the same degree?

Think Like a Psychologist:

Principles in Action

Whenever we encounter any interesting behavior we should consider the four principles. Here are some ways that the four principles relate to our opening story about the Genain quadruplets.

MACHINE

The mind is a product of a physical machine, the brain.

The Genain quadruplets probably inherited genes that put them at risk for schizophrenia, since all four were eventually diagnosed with the disorder, and both of their parents exhibited unstable behavior. Those genes would have affected the structure and/or functioning of their brains.

UNCONSCIOUS

We are consciously aware of only a small part of our mental activity.

Of course the quads were never consciously aware of the workings of those genes. Likewise, while they all experienced the stress of their parent's behavior, they could not know how those experiences were pushing them closer to the confusion and delusions of schizophrenia.

SOCIAL

We constantly modify our behavior, beliefs, and attitudes according to what we perceive about the people around us.

Most of the stress the quads were subjected to was from other people, primarily their abusive father. Among other things, he strictly limited their socializing with other people, and all four girls were deterred from getting to know schoolmates.

EXPERIENCE

Our experiences physically alter the structure and function of the brain.

All of the twins experienced the stress of their father's abuse, which must have increased their chances of developing schizophrenia. The youngest sister, Hester, the lightest at birth and the only sister to deal with an infection after birth, became ill at the youngest age and was the most debilitated.

KEY TERMS

adoption studies, 134
alleles, 113
amino acids, 112
chromosomes, 111
concordant, 132
confounding variables, 130
discordant, 132
dizygotic twins, 130
DNA, 112
dominant, 116
epigenetics, 121
fertilization, 113
gene, 112
gene-environment interaction, 123
gene expression, 118
genetic determinism, 110
genotype, 115
heritability, 132
heritable, 132
Huntington's disease, 125
monozygotic twins, 130
mutation, 114
natural selection, 115
nature, 110
nucleotides, 112
nucleus, 111
nurture, 110
phenotype, 115
phenylketonuria (PKU), 126
protein, 111
recessive, 117
schizophrenia, 130
trait, 111
twin study, 130

QUIZ YOURSELF

1. Two different versions of a gene to produce a particular protein are called
   a. amino acids.
   b. nucleotides.
   c. alleles.
   d. chromosomes.
2. Typically a recessive version of a gene encodes for a ________ protein.
   a. functional
   b. dysfunctional
   c. toxic
   d. epigenetic
3. Epigenetic factors alter the
   a. nucleotide sequence of a gene.
   b. position of a gene on the chromosome.
   c. number of versions of a gene.
   d. expression of a gene.
4. When two unrelated people with inherited forms of deafness have children, typically none of their children are ________ , but all will carry ________ dysfunctional gene(s) important for hearing.
   a. able to hear; one
   b. able to hear; two
   c. deaf; one
   d. deaf; two
5. ________ twins share all the same genes, while ____ twins, like any other full siblings, share only half their genes.
   a. Dizygotic; monozygotic
   b. Monozygotic; dizygotic
   c. Concordant; discordant
   d. Discordant; concordant
6. A stretch of ________ tthat encodes for a single protein is called a ________ .
7. Huntington's disease is caused by a ________ allele that results in damage to neurons in a brain region called the________.
8. While our________ is set at the moment of fertilization, our ________ changes throughout life.
9. Maze bright and maze dull strains of rats perform equally poorly if they are raised in ________ conditions, and perform equally well if they are raised in ________ conditions.

1. c; 2. b; 3. d; 4. d; 5. b; 6. DNA, gene; 7. dominant; striatum (or basal ganglia); 8. genotype; phenotype; 9. impoverished; enriched.

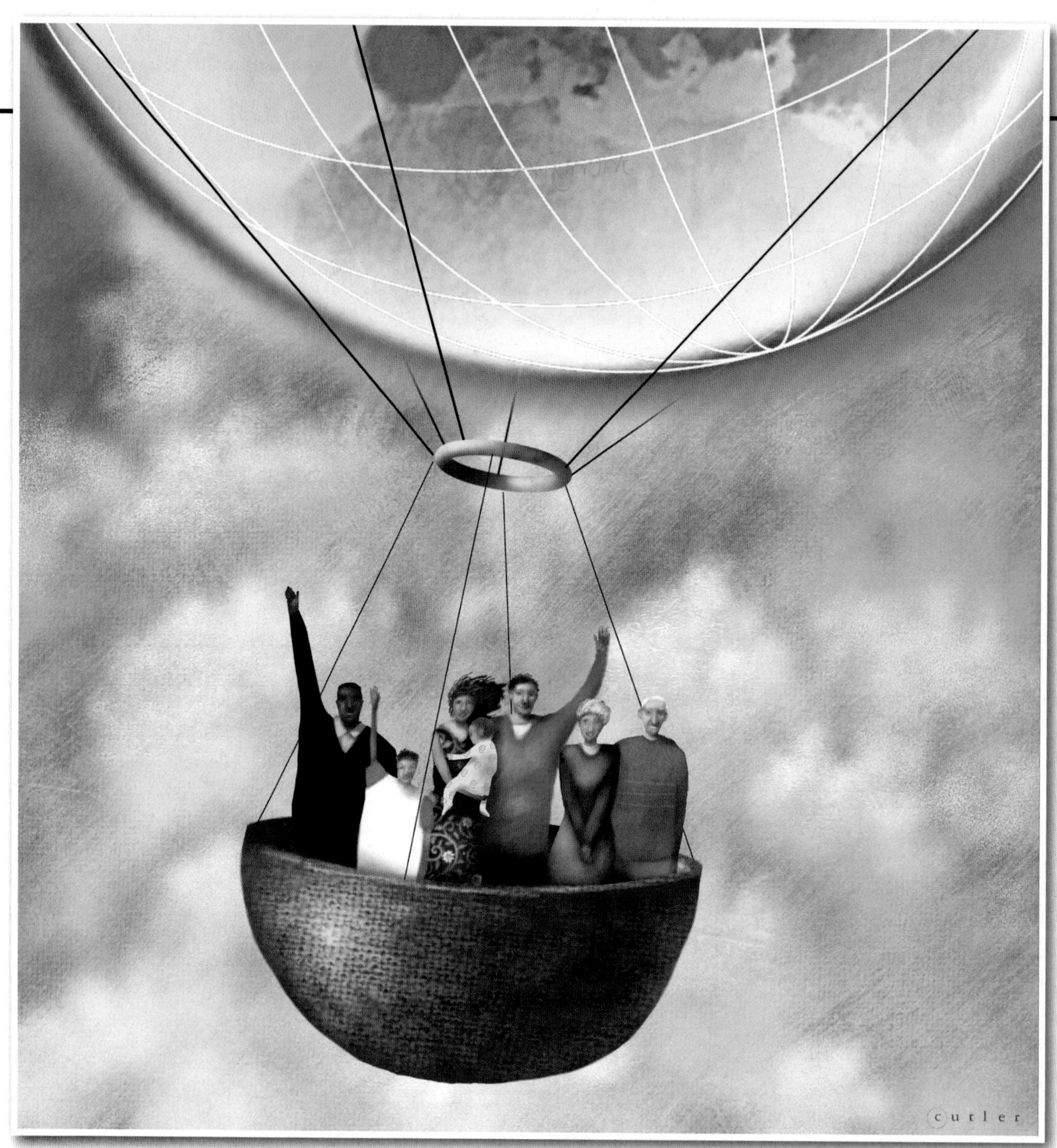
cutler

Developmental Psychology

Growing Up Alone

In the late 1790s, people in the small town of Aveyron in southern France found a naked boy in the woods who seemed to be wild, living on his own. His body had numerous scars, and townspeople guessed him to be about 12 years old. They called the boy Victor, and a local physician, Jean-Marc Itard, tried to teach the boy to behave in a civilized fashion. Victor learned to understand some speech but, despite years of effort, learned to say only "milk" and "oh God!" (in French, of course).

In 1970 a heartbreaking incident in Los Angeles echoed Victor's case. A social worker encountered a young girl, "Genie," who didn't talk or pay attention to any of the people in the office. She rocked her body and walked curiously, holding up her hands and hopping like a bunny. The horrible truth was that this tiny girl, who looked to be 6 or 7 years old, was actually 13. She had been living alone, locked in a room in the back of a house, eating the small amount of food that was tossed in to her. Genie had spent her days strapped, naked, to a potty chair. At night she was diapered and placed in a cage with a chicken-wire lid. Her father, who had enforced Genie's abuse, committed suicide before facing criminal charges.

Ironically, the week after the discovery of Genie, a movie about Victor premiered in Los Angeles. *The Wild Child* vividly portrayed Victor's inability to use speech. Aware of this tragic precedent, a team of therapists and scientists assembled around Genie to provide her with every opportunity to recover. With proper nutrition, Genie quickly gained weight and grew taller. But the bigger job was to rescue her mind. Genie had almost no language—the only words she said were "stop it" and "no more." In addition to her repetitive rocking and strange "bunny walk," Genie would sometimes erupt into silent rages, hitting and tearing at her own body. She drooled and spat constantly, and masturbated openly and excessively. Could Genie recover from such a nightmarish upbringing?

Chapter Preview

In this chapter we'll learn that just as a child's body develops in an orderly and predictable fashion, so too does a child's mind develop in progressive stages. Just as the body requires certain conditions, including nutrition and shelter, to grow properly, the mind also requires certain conditions, including experience and love, to grow properly. These findings will help us understand how Genie's early abuse shaped her behavior, and what an uphill battle she faced.

Developmental psychology is the study of how the mind and behavior progress as an individual grows up and grows old. A question commonly raised in developmental psychology is whether behavior develops in a slow, continuously gradual fashion or in a steplike fashion, jumping from one stage to the next. The answer, as you may have surmised, is that behavior develops in both fashions, and we'll see examples of both as the chapter unfolds. We'll also revisit the nature/nurture theme in this chapter, considering how behavioral development is influenced by both internal, biological factors such as genes and by external factors such as experience. You learned in Chapter 4 how experience affects when, where, and how we express the genes we inherited—including those in the developing brain. In this chapter we'll explain how experience guides the coming and going of synaptic connections between neurons.

There was a time when developmental psychologists were concerned only with babies, infants, and children. Once an individual reached adolescence, it seemed that developmental psychologists had nothing more to say. But today the transition from preadolescence to puberty and emerging adulthood is recognized as an incredibly important stage, and it is actively studied by many developmental psychologists. The field now embraces "lifespan development," recognizing that we never stop developing from our start as a single cell until the day we die.

We begin this chapter by exploring the development of the brain from a biological perspective. We'll learn that the developing brain is a hive of furious activity, with new cells being added at a dizzying rate; that normal development also involves the loss of cells and connections between cells; and that experience directs which connections will stay and which will be lost. Then we'll discuss the developing mind, looking at the unfolding of ever more complex motor, cognitive, and emotional functions as children grow. Here, too, experience plays a crucial role in allowing the mind to develop properly. After reviewing the critical transition from childhood to adulthood, we'll end the chapter by discussing the continued development of adult behavior, including the disturbing prospect of Alzheimer's disease and the challenge of facing our mortality.

developmental psychology The study of how the mind and behavior progress as an individual grows up and ages.

zygote A fertilized egg.

embryo An early developing individual, typically a sphere of dividing cells.

inner cell mass A clump of cells inside a mammalian embryo that will form the body.

fetus A developing individual at the stage where major organs and structures have formed. In humans, about the ninth week of development.

neural tube An early stage of the developing nervous system, which will eventually form the brain and spinal cord.

neurogenesis The division of cells that become neurons.

cell migration The stage of development when neurons and other cells migrate to their final position in the brain.

differentiation The process by which individual cells become more and more different from one another.

synaptogenesis The formation of synapses.

neuronal cell death A normal stage of development when some cells, including some neurons, die.

5.1 The Developing Brain

Things to Learn

- Six stages of neural development
- Massive growth of the fetal brain
- Dangers of prenatal alcohol
- Importance of experience for brain development

Let's first look at the developing brain from the biological point of view. It may surprise you to learn that brain development involves not just the steady adding of cells and connections between cells, but also the *loss* of neurons and synapses. Even more astonishing is the huge impact experience has on the biological development of the brain: *experience determines which cells and connections will be lost and which will be retained.* That is, experience shapes the developing brain, as well as that process going on within the brain—the mind.

There are six stages of neural development

Perhaps nothing in the world is quite so astounding as the development of the human brain. Consider for a moment that each of us began when a tiny egg was fertilized by an even tinier sperm—forming a single cell so small it could barely be seen without a microscope. Over the next 9 months or so, that tiny cell divided and grew to form a person with a brain, which is, as far as we know, the most complicated machine in the universe.

The fertilized egg is called a **zygote**, which quickly begins dividing to form a sphere of cells called an **embryo** (**Figure 5.1**). In mammals, which of course includes us, the outer layer of the sphere of dividing cells forms a *placenta*, which implants into the wall of the mother's uterus and provides nutrients and oxygen to the embryo. Inside the spherical embryo, a clump of cells called the **inner cell mass** divides and grows to form the entire body of this new person. The first thing the inner cell mass forms is a primitive gut. The next structure it forms is the nervous system.

Once the embryo forms the other major organ systems and structures, which in humans happens by about the ninth week of prenatal development, we call it a **fetus**. At this stage the heart, brain, eyes, and limbs are present but still tiny: the entire body is about an inch long. You would not be able to distinguish a 9-week-old human fetus from any other mammalian fetus by appearance alone. As fetal development continues, distinctive human features come into focus, including the brain.

The nervous system begins as a hollow tube, the **neural tube**. One end will become the brain, while the other end will form the spinal cord (see Figure 5.2). We can divide the cellular development of the brain into six stages. The first stage is the continued division of cells, some of which will become neurons, so we call this **neurogenesis** (**Figure 5.2A**). It is difficult to appreciate just how quickly the number of neurons increases: at one point, more than 250,000 neurons are added per minute! Researchers used to think that neurogenesis stopped shortly after birth, but we now know that some new neurons are formed in the brain throughout life. Just the same, the vast majority of the nearly 100 billion neurons in our brain were formed before we were born (Herculano-Houzel, 2012).

In the second stage of neural development, the many neurons that have been formed begin moving around, as if each were an independent slug, in a stage known as **cell migration** (**Figure 5.2B**). During this time the neurons scatter and begin to form the clumps of cells that will become brain regions. Once they reach their destination, neurons undergo the third phase of development, **differentiation** (**Figure 5.2C**), in which they become the type of neuron they are meant to be, growing the dendrites and body shape appropriate for their adult role in the brain. No other part of the body has so many different kinds of cells, with such vastly different shapes, as the brain. As the dendrites and axons of neurons grow, they begin the fourth phase of development, **synaptogenesis** (**Figure 5.2D**), the making of billions of connections, or *synapses*, with one another.

So far this description of brain development appears orderly and progressive: cells are made, arrange themselves, develop into neurons, and synapse with one another. But the next stage of development came as a surprise to biologists in the twentieth century, because it seemed like a step backward. In the fifth stage, called **neuronal cell death** (**Figure 5.2E**), many of the neurons that formed early in develop-

Zygote: The fertilized egg

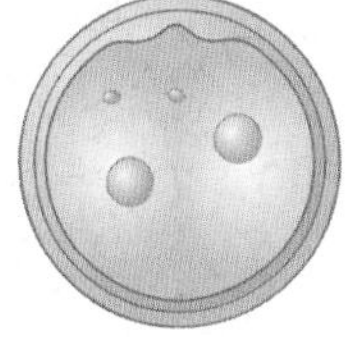

Embryo: Weeks 2–8

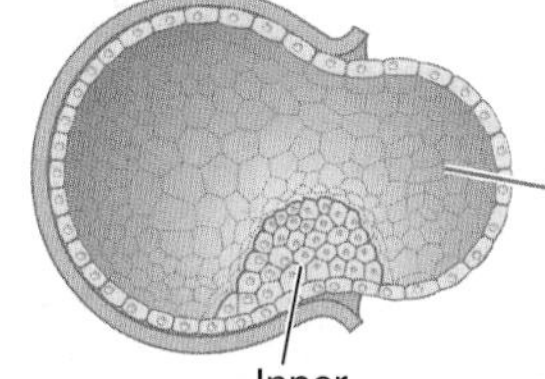

The body will arise from the inner cell mass, while the surrounding cells form the placenta.
Inner cell mass

Fetus: Weeks 8–38

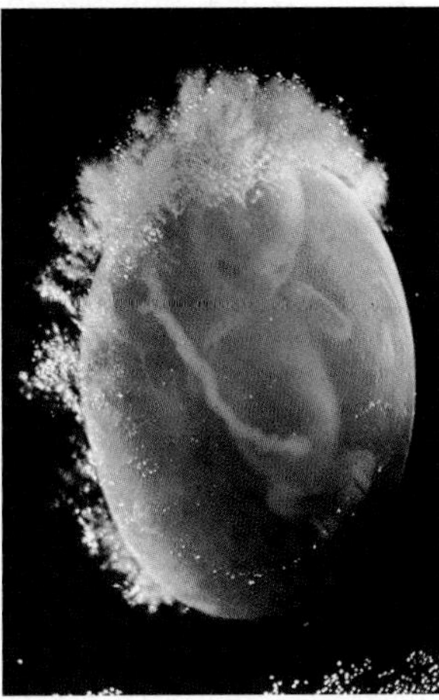

Figure 5.1 Stages of Prenatal Development The fertilized egg, or zygote, divides and grows to form an embryo. By the ninth week of development, the embryo has become a fetus, about 1 inch long and with all the major body structures and organ systems.

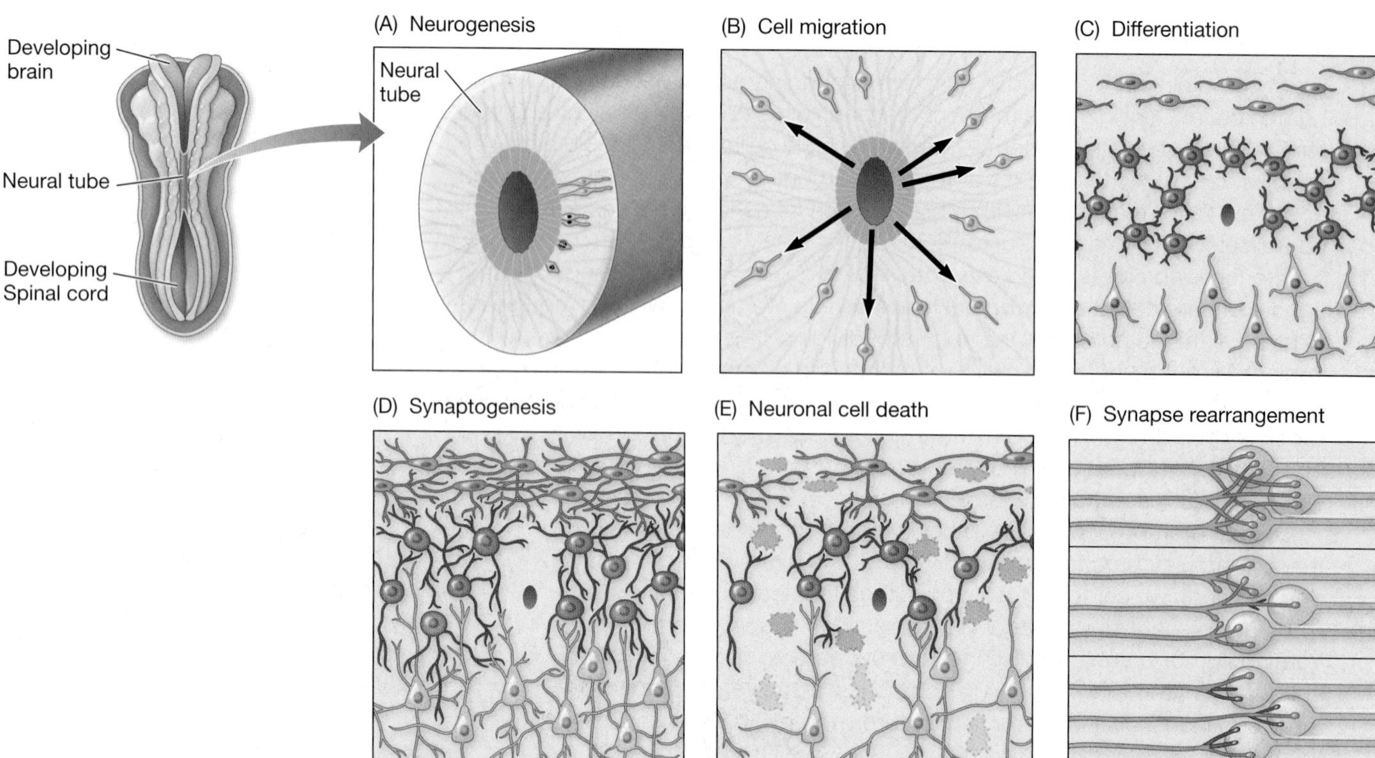

Figure 5.2 Six Stages of Cellular Development of the Brain

ment normally die. In many places in the brain, nearly half the neurons that form during prenatal development die before the individual is born. We don't know for sure why some cells die while others live, but the prevailing theory is that some make appropriate connections and so survive, while others do not and die. Normal neuronal cell death appears to cease before birth in mammals. Any loss of neurons after that point is due to injury or the slow loss with aging.

The sixth and final stage in the cellular development of the brain is **synapse rearrangement** (**Figure 5.2F**), when many synapses dissolve while new synapses form. Because some synapses are lost, this stage has also been called synapse elimination or synaptic pruning, which may sound like a step backward in development. However, reconfiguration of the synapses, which begins before birth and continues throughout life, serves to develop more efficient neural networks. In childhood many more synapses are gained than are lost, so there is in fact a net gain in the total number of synapses, making "synapse rearrangement" a better description (Huttenlocher et al., 1982). At puberty, synapse rearrangement will produce a net loss of synapses (Petanjak et al., 2011).

One sign of the increasing connectivity in the prenatal brain is the overall size of the brain (**Figure 5.3A**). The vast majority of neuronal cell death happens before birth, yet the overall size of the brain grows tremendously with the net gain of synapses and as individual neurons grow in size. The brain becomes more wrinkled as it grows because as the cortex expands, it buckles to fit inside the skull. By birth, the brain looks like that of an adult human brain in every way except size. A newborn's brain weighs about 400 grams, but by adulthood it will weigh about 1,400 grams (about 3 pounds). This tripling of brain weight after birth is one indication of how much the child must learn and grow to become an adult. Because most neurogenesis is completed before birth, this growth of the human brain after birth is caused primarily by the net gain of billions of synapses (**Figure 5.3B and C**). During this time, experiences—such as having people talk to the child—

synapse rearrangement The phenomenon of new synapses forming and old synapses retracting, especially prominent early in life.

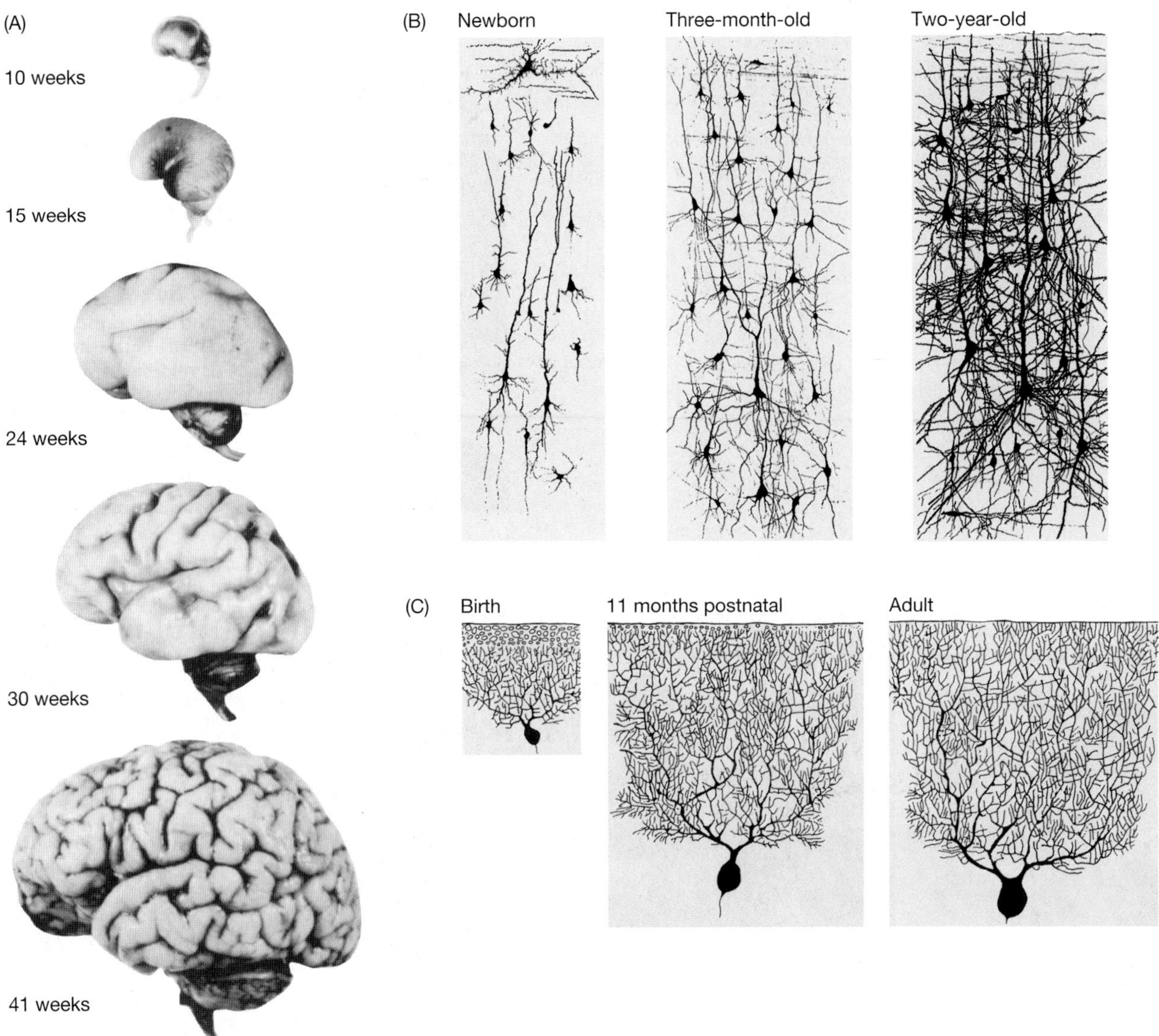

Figure 5.3 Development of the Human Brain (A) These side views of the human brain, shown at one-third their actual size, illustrate the dramatic growth of the brain before birth. (B) These representations of cerebral cortex show the extensive growth of dendrites as more and more synapses develop in the human brain after birth. (C) Neurons in the cerebellum also grow tremendously after birth. (A from Larroche, 1977; B from Conel, 1939, 1947, 1959; C after Zecevic & Rakic, 1976.)

have an enormous impact on the brain. If, like Genie, a child is deprived of these experiences, synaptic development will suffer.

Because the brain is growing so rapidly before birth, it is vulnerable to any disruption in nutrients or exposure to harmful chemicals, such as those delivered by smoking. Any substance that reaches an embryo or fetus and disrupts prenatal development is called a **teratogen**. There is growing concern that human-made chemicals in pollution may contaminate our food and act as teratogens, but probably the most common teratogen is deliberately ingested by pregnant mothers—alcohol. In ancient times, Aristotle noted that women who drank during pregnancy were likely to produce "foolish… languid" children. Children whose mothers drank while carrying them are at risk for **fetal alcohol syndrome** (**FAS**). Children with FAS have distinct facial features, including a

teratogen Any substance that reaches an embryo or fetus and disrupts prenatal development.

fetal alcohol syndrome (FAS) A condition in which children exposed to alcohol from their mother's drinking are born with distinct facial features and varying degrees of mental impairment.

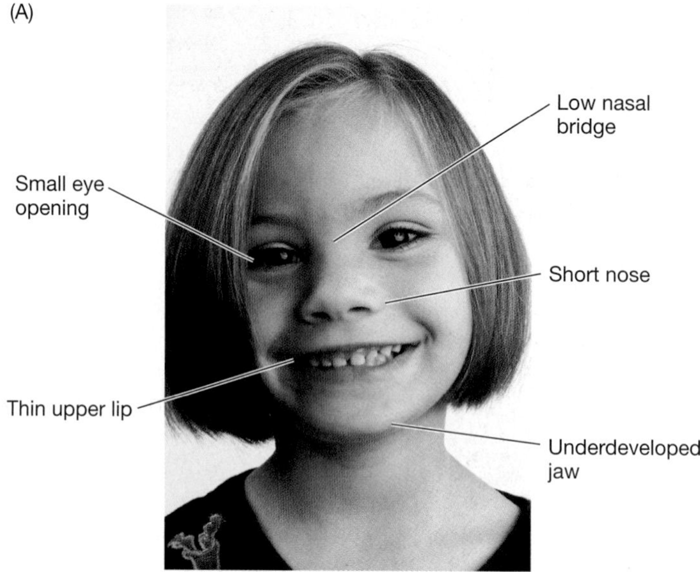

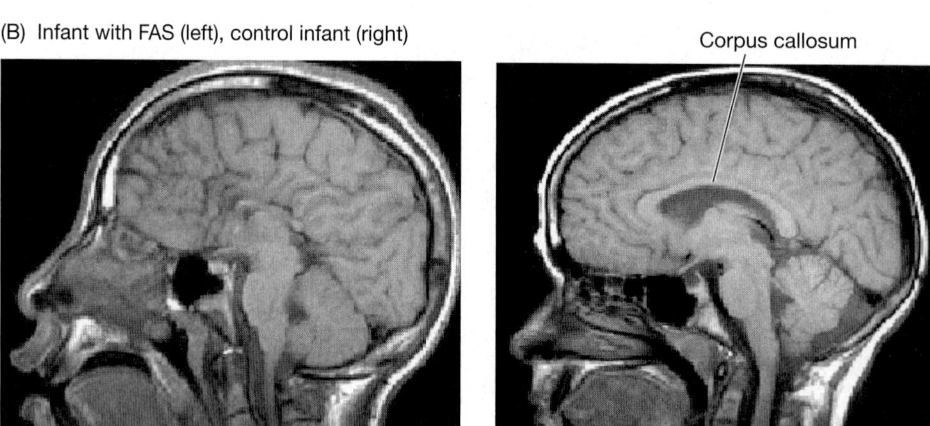

Figure 5.4 Fetal Alcohol Syndrome (FAS) (A) The typical facial features of fetal alcohol syndrome (FAS). (B) Fetal alcohol exposure can drastically affect brain development. On the left is the brain of an infant with FAS, showing a smaller brain with fewer wrinkles and the absence of a corpus callosum. On the right is the brain of a control infant of the same age. (B courtesy of E. Riley.)

sunken nasal bridge and altered shape of the nose and eyelid, as well as stunted growth (**Figure 5.4A**).

The main problem with FAS is not the appearance of the face, however, but mental impairment, which varies but can be severe. Some children with FAS fail to develop a corpus callosum, the wide bundle of neural fibers that connects the two cerebral hemispheres and allows them to communicate with one another (**Figure 5.4B**). Even when FAS is not diagnosed, prenatal exposure to alcohol is correlated with impairments in language and fine motor skills (Pruett et al., 2013) and with aggressive behaviors (Sood et al., 2001). There may be no such thing as a "safe" level of alcohol that a mother can drink without risking damage to her child. For this reason, the U.S. Surgeon General in 2005 went on record urging all pregnant women to abstain *entirely* from alcohol.

Experience guides brain development

Describing the development of the brain in terms of cellular events may give the impression that the young brain is simply following the instructions of genes, but this is far from true. In Chapter 4 we saw how the environment and experience can affect when, where, and how genes are expressed. The most dramatic demonstrations of how experience plays a role in guiding the young brain come from studies of the formation and loss of synapses in the developing visual system. These studies show that visual experiences influence synapse rearrangement so that we can see. In fact, unless we have enough visual experience early in life, we will never be able to see.

sensitive period A time during development when exposure to a stimulus has the greatest effect on a particular behavior.

plasticity Also called *neural plasticity*. The ability of the brain to change in structure or function.

Nobel Prize–winning research found that young kittens and monkeys have very few synaptic connections between the eye and the brain (Hubel & Wiesel, 1965). As the animals grow, more and more connections are formed, so that by maturity almost every neuron in the visual cortex normally gets information from both eyes. However, if researchers close one eyelid to prevent light from entering that eye, the synaptic connections from that eye to the brain are weakened. If the eye is deprived of light for too long, the synaptic connections are lost forever and the animal will be blind in that eye for the rest of its life.

Interestingly, depriving the adult eye of light has very little effect: when researchers reopen the eye, the animal can see just fine. It is only during development, when synapse rearrangement is at its peak, that visual deprivation causes blindness. Such research reinforced the notion of **sensitive periods** in development: times when events, such as visual deprivation, can have an especially large effect on brain development and later behavior.

The experiments on sensitive periods in visual development in animals help us understand the plight of some people who are born blind because they have *cataracts*—cloudy regions in the lens of the eye. In the twentieth century, as surgical techniques improved, it became possible to remove cataracts in adults who had been born with them. The surgeons expected these operations to finally give sight to people who had never seen, but the results were very disappointing. Even though the cataracts were completely removed, and a clear visual image was focused on the back of the eye, these people were never able to see. From the animal experiments, we now understand why: without early visual experience, the synapses from the eye to the brain were lost forever in these people (**Figure 5.5**). Nowadays when babies are born with cataracts, physicians know how important it is to remove them early in life so the babies can get the visual experience they need to develop full vision.

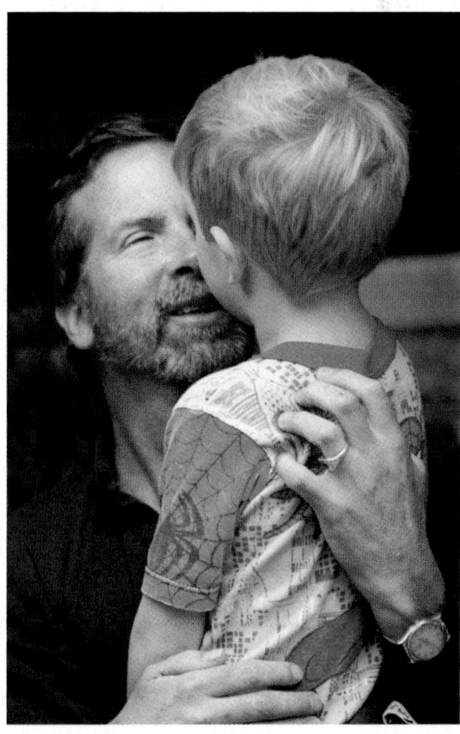

Figure 5.5 Learning to See Michael May lost his sight as a young boy but despite his blindness became an expert skier and founded his own successful company. An operation repaired one eye, but because of the absence of visual experience in a sensitive period of development he can't make much use of the information entering his eye. He keeps a blog of his experience since his surgery at www.senderogroup.com/mm/mike.htm. His story inspired the book and movie *Crashing Through*.

What is the basis of the sensitive period for visual experience? We've already mentioned that synapse rearrangement goes on throughout life, but the scale of rearrangement is much greater in young brains than in mature brains. And just as visual experience guides synaptic development in the visual cortex, experience in other sensory modalities guides synaptic development in other brain regions. As you may recall from Chapter 3, the ability of the brain to change is called **plasticity**, and it is clear that *developing brains are much more plastic than adult brains*, reflecting the greater amount of synapse rearrangement that goes on in young brains.

The amazing plasticity of the developing brain is seen in children's ability to recover from damage to the brain. When accident or disease damages a part of the adult brain, a behavioral function is typically disrupted. Which function is lost depends on which part of the brain is damaged. In adults, it is sometimes possible to recover some of the lost function through intensive therapy, and this recovery is probably due to the rearrangement of synapses in the remaining, healthy brain regions. But recovery in adults is modest at best, and often there is permanent loss of function. Children with brain damage, however, typically experience much greater recovery of brain function—a reflection of the greater plasticity in synapse rearrangement in the young brain.

infant A young child that has not yet learned to talk.

simple reflexes Unlearned, automatic responses to specific stimuli.

Perhaps the most dramatic examples of plasticity in the young brain are the cases when an entire cortical hemisphere is surgically removed in children to stop dangerous epileptic seizures. In adults, damage to an entire hemisphere causes widespread loss of functions that are never fully recovered. For example, if the left hemisphere is seriously damaged, an adult will probably never speak or understand language again. But when the left hemisphere is removed in children, they almost always recover language and eventually develop an IQ in the normal range (see Box 10.2).

5.1 SUMMARY

- The developing brain undergoes a sequence of six cellular events: *neurogenesis, cell migration, differentiation, synaptogenesis, neuronal cell death,* and *synapse rearrangement*. Most of these are complete by birth, but synapse rearrangement continues throughout life.
- Exposure of the developing brain to alcohol or other *teratogens* can severely affect these developmental processes, even going so far as to prevent development of major brain structures and permanently impair mental abilities.
- Although they depend on the action of many genes, these cellular processes are also coordinated and guided by the environment and by experience. For example, the developing brain must be stimulated by visual experience to properly form synapses between the eye and brain. Without visual experience early in life, during the *sensitive period*, the brain never makes the proper synaptic connections to interpret information from the eyes, leaving the individual blind.
- Sensitive periods in development and the ability of young children to recover from brain damage demonstrate that the young brain is much more *plastic* than the adult brain.

REVIEW QUESTIONS

1. What are the six stages of brain development, in order? (You can use logic to think about how some stages must precede others.)
2. Describe fetal alcohol syndrome.
3. Which stage of brain development continues throughout life, and how does experience guide this stage?

Food for Thought

Why do you think we lose so much neural plasticity when we grow up? Why have we not evolved to show greater brain plasticity throughout life?

Things to Learn

- Sequential nature of stages of motor development
- How experience can affect motor development
- Development of sensory system
- Ways to test infant mental development
- Development of memory in infants
- Piaget's stages of cognitive development
- Temperament and anxiety in children
- Importance of love for proper development
- Attachment styles in infants

5.2 The Developing Mind

We've seen how complicated brain development is in terms of cellular processes such as neurogenesis and synapse rearrangement. Meanwhile, as the brain develops, so does the mind. We can study the development of the mind using the terms and tests of psychology. Events occurring after birth offer many clues about how the mind develops. We'll begin by observing the **infant**, a young child who has not yet learned to talk, and will see how the mind continues to develop in childhood. We will again observe an orderly progression in development, this time in the unfolding of behavioral and cognitive abilities.

Developmental stages can be seen in motor and sensory development

Newborns display many organized behaviors that obviously could not have been taught to them. These are **simple reflexes**: unlearned, automatic responses to specific stimuli. For example, newborns will clasp any object placed in their hands (**Figure 5.6A**). This *grasping reflex* was probably important in early human evolution when mothers needed to carry their babies with them every-

(A) Grasping

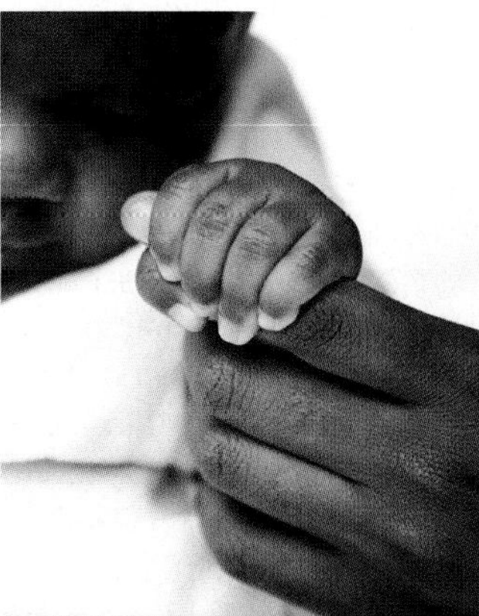

(B) Rooting

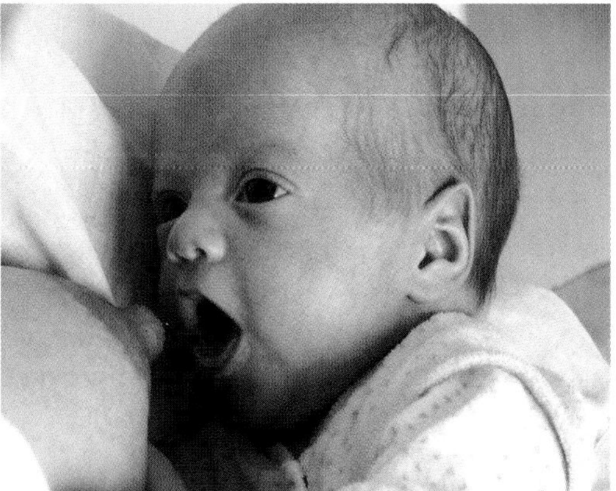

(C) Sucking

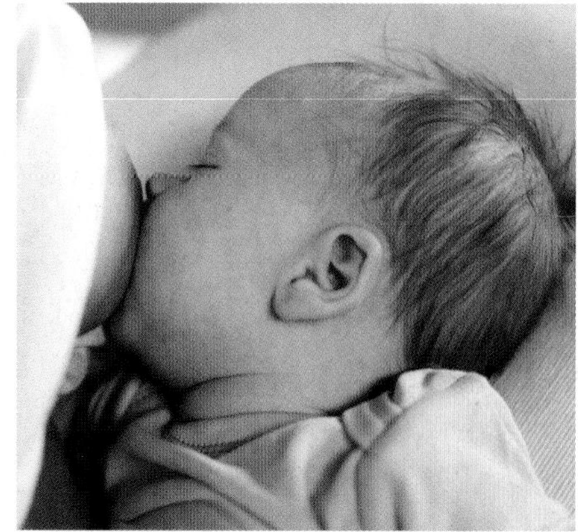

Figure 5.6 Newborn Infants' Reflexes (A) The grasping reflex is a response to items being placed in a baby's hand. (B) The rooting reflex normally helps the baby find the nipple for suckling. (C) Babies reflexively suck on objects placed in their mouth, which is normally their mother's breast offering them milk.

where. Another simple reflex is the *rooting reflex*, when a touch to the cheek causes the baby to turn her head toward the object, which normally is a nipple being offered for nourishment (**Figure 5.6B**). Similarly, babies exhibit the *sucking reflex* when almost any object is placed in their mouth, which normally is a nipple offering them milk (**Figure 5.6C**).

As babies grow, they show progressively more complex motor behaviors. Most babies show these behaviors in about the same order. These behaviors can be regarded as milestones in **motor development**. Although some of the progression is due to strengthening of muscles and fine-tuning of sensory systems (which we'll discuss soon), much of the progression reflects maturation of the brain. Also, some of the behaviors build on one another. For example, learning to stand while holding onto a table prepares a baby to walk while holding someone's hand, which is good training for learning to walk alone. **Figure 5.7** depicts some of the motor milestones of human infant development and the approximate ages at which most babies display them.

Scholars once debated whether the orderly progression of motor development milestones reflects an automatic, preprogrammed maturation of the body and brain or whether it is the result of progressive learning. We now know that the brain is constantly maturing and the baby is constantly learning, and that all development is affected by both genes and the environment; in short, that nature and nurture work together in development.

motor development The progressive increase in motor abilities displayed by growing babies.

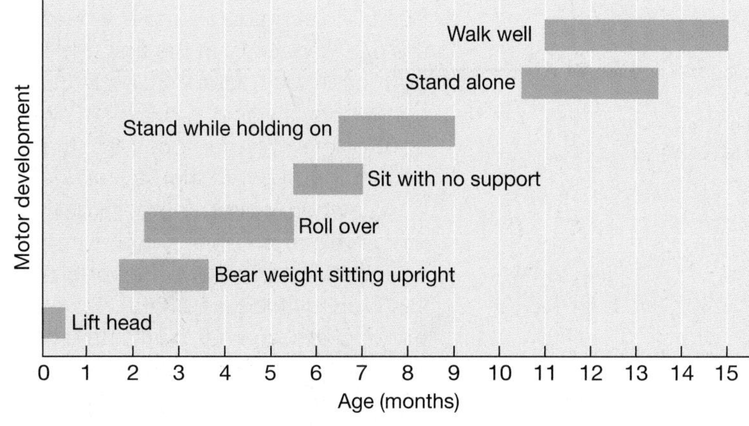

Figure 5.7 Milestones in Infant Motor Development Most infants achieve these motor stages in the displayed order, but notice that there is considerable variation in the time to reach each stage. (After Frankenburg et al., 1992.)

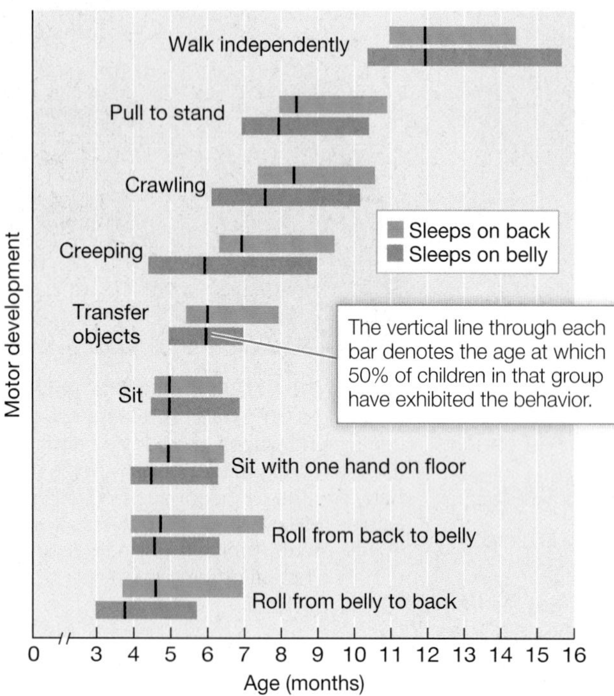

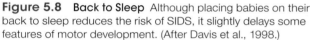

Figure 5.8 Back to Sleep Although placing babies on their back to sleep reduces the risk of SIDS, it slightly delays some features of motor development. (After Davis et al., 1998.)

The importance of *both* genetic forces and learning in motor development was confirmed in an unintended "experiment." A small percentage of babies die each year of **sudden infant death syndrome (SIDS)**, or *crib death*: a baby less than a year old simply stops breathing while asleep. We know almost nothing about why this happens, but several correlates have been discovered: babies are much more likely to die of SIDS if they live with a cigarette smoker, and babies placed to sleep on their tummies are more likely to die of SIDS than babies placed on their backs (Treyster & Gitterman, 2011). Armed with these correlates, the National Institutes of Health in the 1990s urged all parents to keep their homes smoke-free and launched the Back to Sleep campaign, advising that all babies be placed on their backs when sleeping. The campaign has been a big success, because the incidence of SIDS declined dramatically (Trachtenburg et al., 2012).

But interestingly, while the Back to Sleep campaign has saved many babies' lives, it slows progression of some motor milestones (Davis et al., 1998). Babies that sleep on their back take longer to creep (move while resting on their belly) and crawl (move while holding the body up on all four limbs) (**Figure 5.8**). Subsequent studies have found that the more "belly time" babies are provided while awake, the faster their motor skills advance (Majnemer & Barr, 2005; Robertson, 2011). Babies lying on their back have fewer chances to explore and experiment on their belly, and this reduced experience appears to slow their ability to creep and crawl. So despite the orderly, progressive unfolding of motor behaviors, which might suggest a programmed, genetically controlled development, experience also affects the pace of progress. Both genes and experience guide developing behavior.

sudden infant death syndrome (SIDS) Also called *crib death*. Death that occurs when a baby less than a year old simply stops breathing while asleep.

While the motor systems are developing, sensory systems are also maturing. Newborns can see, but their vision is rather poor—approximately 20/120 to 20/400—meaning that an object that an adult with good vision can see clearly from 120–400 feet away would have to be within 20 feet for the newborn to see it as clearly. Vision improves rapidly, so by 8 months of age the average baby has 20/30 vision, nearly as good as normal adult vision.

There is a lot of misinformation in circulation about why babies' vision is poor. One myth is that babies cannot focus on anything far away. While it is true that young babies do not have good control of the muscles used to focus the eye (especially in the first 2 months of life), in fact newborns can focus on both near and distant objects (Braddick & Atkinson, 2011). Another myth is that a baby's vision is "blurry." This description suggests that the parts in the front of the eye that focus an image on the back of the eye either have the wrong shape or are cloudy, but neither is true.

A newborn's vision is poor mostly because the neurons in the back of the eye (in the retina) and the synaptic connections to the brain are immature. Thus a newborn's brain receives fewer bits of information about the image, even when it is properly focused on the retina. It is like having a digital camera with only 5 million pixels whereas adults have 100 million pixels in each eye. So the vision of newborns is poor because they lack the resolution of adult vision (**Figure 5.9**), and this lack of resolution is due to inadequate connections between the eye and brain. This means that a newborn gets a lot more information about objects that are close than about objects that are distant (as do we all). An infant's vision improves as a result of the *maturation of neurons in the retina and connections between the retina and brain.*

Newborn's vision

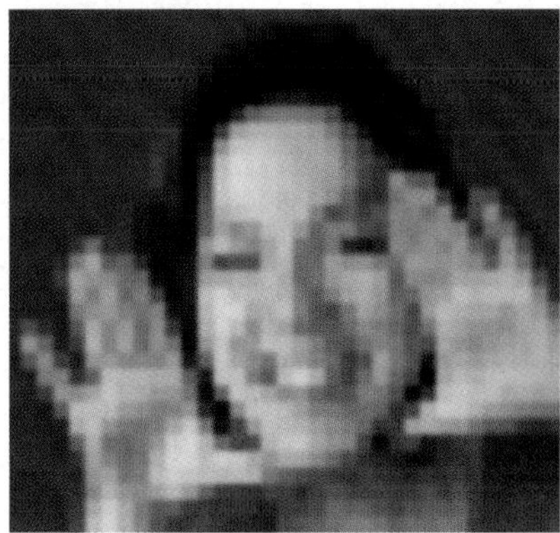

Four-month-old's vision

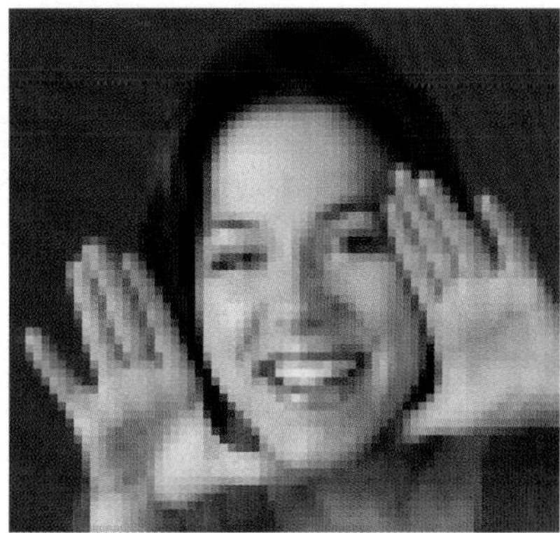

Eight-month-old's vision

Adult's vision

Figure 5.9 Infant Vision Rapidly Improves Newborns can focus a sharp image of both near and distant objects on the retina. However, because the retina and connections between the retina and brain are immature, newborns receive information about fewer bits of light and thus their vision is poor. With visual experience guiding the maturation of connections between the eye and the brain, vision improves rapidly.

Likewise, we know that by 2 months of age, babies can distinguish colors, despite what you might read on the labels of black-and-white toys sold for infants. Two-month-old babies can also distinguish shades of gray that differ by only 0.5% in brightness. We learned earlier in this chapter that visual experience is crucial for guiding the proper development of connections between the eye and brain in animals as well as in humans. That is why today when infants have cataracts—cloudy spots in the lens of the eye—physicians surgically correct them as soon as safely possible.

You might wonder how we know what infants can see when, by definition, they cannot speak, and we'll discuss that in some detail in the forthcoming Researchers at Work feature. Crawling infants dramatically demonstrate their use of vision by avoiding a **visual cliff**, an apparently steep drop in the floor that is actually covered by a sheet of glass or clear plastic (**Figure 5.10**). Although it would be perfectly safe for an infant to crawl over the glass to his mother, he will be reluctant to do so if he can see the drop. Some babies begin crawling at about 6 months of age, and by that time their vision is already good enough that the vast majority refuse to crawl onto the visual cliff. Even before they can crawl, 2-month-old babies show a change in heart rate when placed over the "deep" end of a visual cliff, but not the "shallow" end (Campos et al., 1970), showing that they can tell the two apart. So despite their poor vision, even 2-month-old babies have some depth perception.

As for hearing, even newborns will turn their head toward the source of a sound. In general, auditory systems seem to be more mature at birth than visual systems. This may be because the child has been receiving auditory stimulation while in the uterus (McMahon et al., 2012). By 6 months of age,

visual cliff An apparently steep drop in the floor that is actually covered by a clear surface.

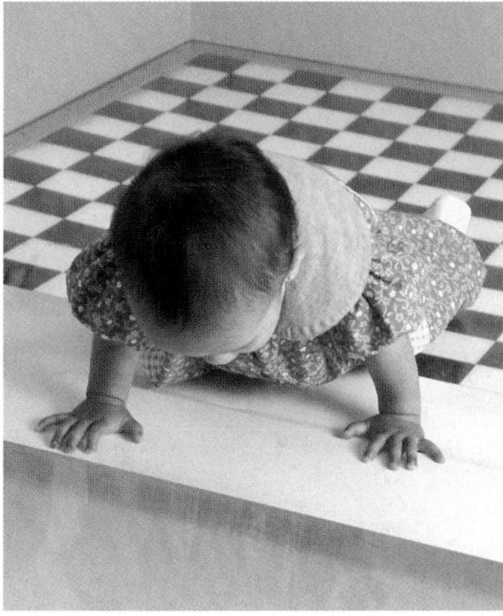

Figure 5.10 The Visual Cliff By the time babies begin to crawl, almost all of them can see the drop and will refuse to crawl onto the visual cliff.

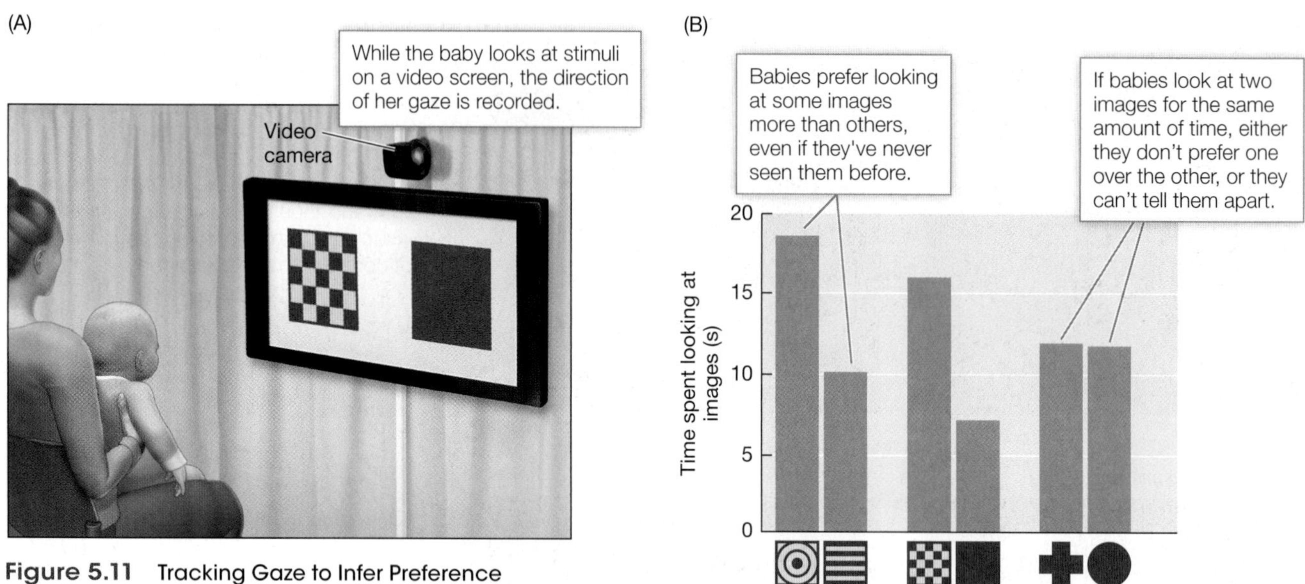

Figure 5.11 Tracking Gaze to Infer Preference (B after Fantz, 1965.)

most infants already have auditory sensitivity close to that of adults. Infants also prefer sounds that resemble speech, and this preference probably helps them acquire language. How do we know what sounds infants prefer to hear or what things a newborn can see? To answer that question, let's find out how psychologists can read babies' minds.

Psychologists have learned how to read babies' minds

In some ways, infants and non-human animals present a psychologist with the same problem—how can you tell what individuals see, hear, or remember if the individuals cannot communicate with you directly? The answer is to devise methods that allow the individuals' behavior to tell you what they do or don't know. In this way, you can "read their minds," not in the sense of ESP or some science fiction movie, but in the everyday sense that you can infer what others are thinking—from their behavior. For example, if you want to know whether a dog can distinguish red from green, you can arrange that a treat is always behind a green door, never a red door. Because dogs *can* learn to reliably find the treat (without cheating by smelling, for example), we know they can tell those colors apart. In this sense, we read a dog's mind. But teaching a dog or infant such tasks is time-consuming and demanding for the subject, so scientists have found a faster way to read an infant's mind.

One way to "read" someone's mind is to keep track of his or her eye movements. There are a variety of ways to use cameras and computers to accurately track exactly where an infant is looking when presented with a visual image (**Figure 5.11A**). When we apply such eye-tracking methods to infants, if they look at one stimulus longer than another, we can infer that they prefer that one over the other, or at least find it more interesting (**Figure 5.11B**). Using such methods, psychologists have learned that even very young infants prefer face-like images to almost anything else. The more an object looks like a face, the more time infants spend looking at it (Fantz, 1965). Even infants under 5 days old spend more time looking at a simple drawing of a face than at a bull's-eye, and as they grow older their preference gets stronger (**Figure 5.12**).

So if an infant looks at one picture more than another, we have "read her mind" and know two things: (1) she can tell the two pictures apart, and (2) she prefers looking at one over the other. If the infant looks at the two pictures for about the same amount of time, we don't know if that's because she can't dis-

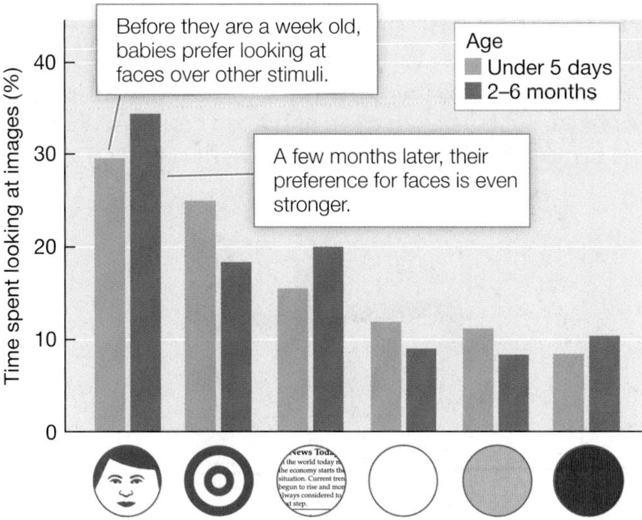

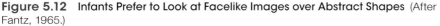

Figure 5.12 **Infants Prefer to Look at Facelike Images over Abstract Shapes** (After Fantz, 1965.)

tinguish them or because she doesn't prefer one over the other (see Figure 5.11B). But psychologists have found a way around that problem, which hinges on the fact that most of us, whether babies or adults, are interested in novelty. Like most people, infants prefer to look at things they haven't seen before. If you place a new picture in front of an infant and watch where she directs her gaze, you can see that preference.

The infant will look at the new picture quite avidly for a while, but eventually she must find it boring, because her gaze wanders off to other objects. The infant is displaying **habituation**, a decreased attention to a familiar stimulus. We can exploit habituation in babies by using the **habituation technique**. If the original picture and new picture are very different from each other, then the baby will much prefer to look at the new picture. But now we can systematically vary *how much* the two pictures differ from one another. If they are so much alike that the baby cannot tell them apart, then she will be equally habituated to them both. But if she can discriminate between the two, she'll show that by looking at the new picture longer. Without using any words, the infant has told us quite clearly that she can tell them apart. Let's see how scientists can use habituation to study mental development in **Figure 5.13**.

habituation A simple type of learning in which repeated presentation of a stimulus elicits a weaker and weaker response.

habituation technique A method of discerning individuals' recognition of a stimulus by determining whether they show evidence of habituating to that stimulus.

Researchers At Work

Habituation tests help researchers understand vision in infants

Figure 5.13 **The Habituation Technique for Testing an Infant's Visual System** (After Fantz, 1964.)

■ **Question:** Can infants tell two stimuli apart? If they look at two stimuli for the same amount of time, is it because they cannot tell them apart or because they simply don't prefer one over the other?

■ **Hypothesis:** Infants will habituate to one stimulus over the other. If so, then they can habituate to one stimulus and then come to prefer looking at the other.

Continued

Researchers at Work *Continued*

■ **Test:** Choose two stimuli that, when presented together, are gazed at equally by infants, such as a red circle and a red cross. At another session, present one stimulus until the infant looks away, suggesting she has lost interest.

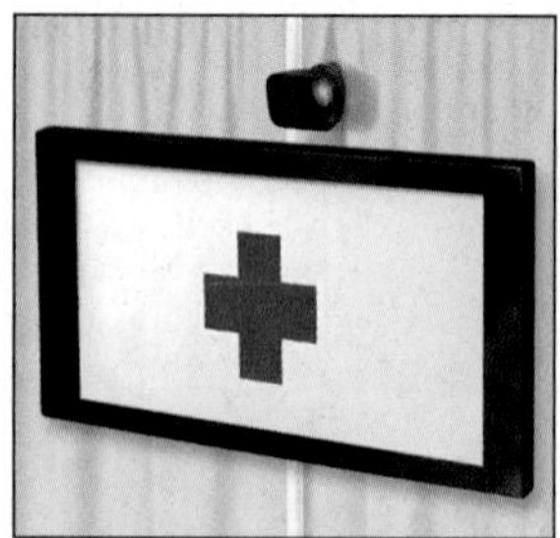

Two minutes later present both stimuli to see if the infant prefers looking at the new one.

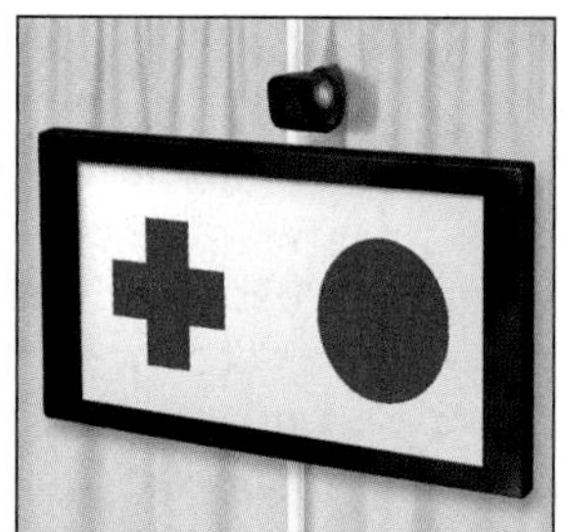

■ **Results:** The infant spends more time looking at the new stimulus (the circle), indicating that she had habituated to the old stimulus.

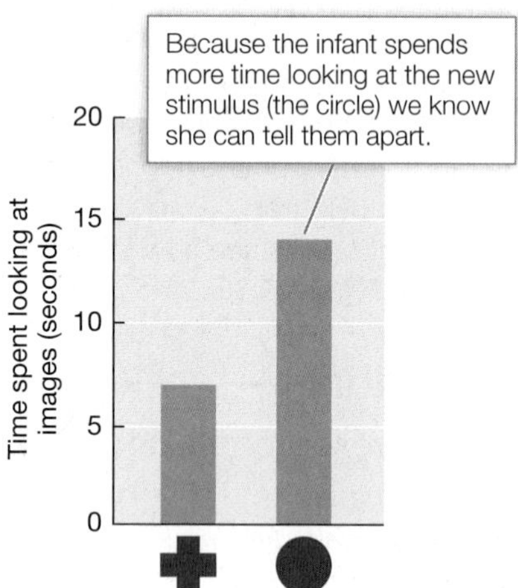
Because the infant spends more time looking at the new stimulus (the circle) we know she can tell them apart.
Time spent looking at images (seconds)
20
15
10
5
0

■ **Conclusion:** The infant must be able to distinguish the two stimuli, as she gazed longer at the new one. By studying many infants, having some habituate to the circle while others habituate to the cross, we can conclude that they can indeed distinguish these two stimuli at this age. Conducting further experiments with pairs of stimuli that are progressively more similar, we can determine the limits of vision in infants at various ages.

(A)

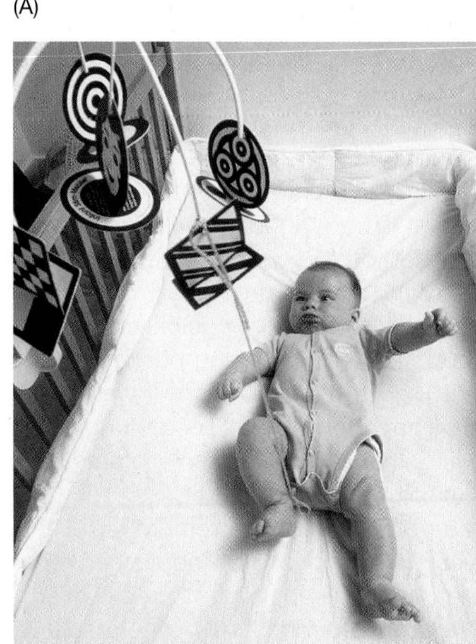

(B)

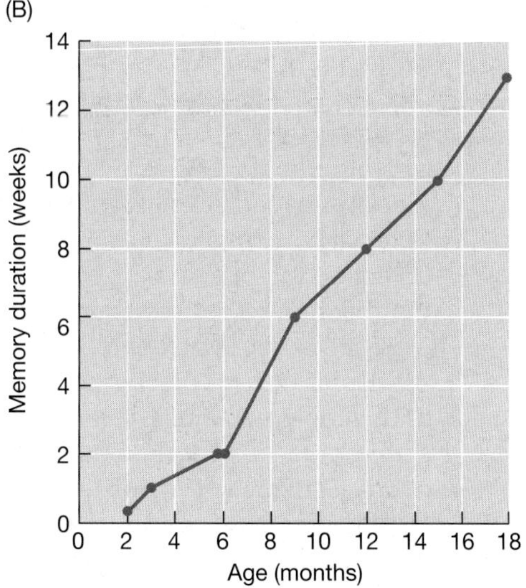

Figure 5.14 Testing Infant Memory (A) A baby soon learns that kicking one leg will cause the mobile overhead to move. If the baby is placed back in the crib a few weeks later *without* the ribbon attached to her foot, and if she remembers and recognizes the mobile, then she will kick her leg, even though it no longer moves the mobile. (B) As babies grow, they are able to remember the mobile (or toy train) after longer and longer periods. Notice the smooth progression of memory duration. (After Rovee-Collier, 2002.)

Memory develops steadily during infancy

How do we test a baby's memory? The habituation technique can also be used to measure how long a baby remembers a picture. The more time that passes between the first and second presentations of that original picture, the more likely it is that the baby will have forgotten about it. If the baby has forgotten the picture entirely, she'll spend as much time looking at it the second time as the first time. In other words, she'll show no evidence of habituation. All other things being equal, the more time she prefers looking at the new picture, the more she remembers and recognizes the old one. One way to test infant memory takes advantage of infants' interest in moving objects. Scientists connected a ribbon to one foot of a baby lying on its back in a crib. If the baby kicked that foot, it caused a mobile overhead to move (Rovee-Collier, 2002). Put in this situation, most babies learned to kick more and more to keep the mobile in motion (**Figure 5.14A**). For older infants, the baby sat in a parent's lap, and kicking the foot caused a toy train to light up and move.

After exposing the infant to such a situation, we can wait a few days and ask, Does the baby remember the mobile or train? If so, then when returned to the situation, she should begin kicking that foot right away, sooner than she did the first time she was in that situation. She'll also kick more than another infant, say a baby boy right next to her, who is looking at the same moving mobile or train but whose leg has had no influence on the movement.

An important control here is that when we return the infant to the crib, we do not connect the ribbon to her foot again. We measure how often she kicks her foot, but her kicks do not affect the mobile (or toy train). That way we know the kicks reflect her memory and not a relearning of the task. The more persistently the baby kicks, the more certain we can be that she remembers that kicking *used* to move the toy. Using these techniques, psychologists learned

infantile amnesia Relative inability of adults to recall events of their early childhood.

cognitive development The progressive increase in cognitive ability displayed by developing individuals.

that 2- to 3-month-old infants can remember this task for only about a week, but as babies get older, they are able to remember the task for more and more weeks (**Figure 5.14B**).

We can also use the habituation technique to discover what babies expect. If all other factors are equal, we spend more time looking at the unexpected than the expected. Given this tendency, experimenters have presented infants with scenes of objects moving about on a stage. Scenes showing an object on top of another object being pushed off the end have demonstrated that babies expect the top object to fall. How do we know that? They must expect the upper object to fall because when it does, they quickly lose interest. But if we use a trick, so that the upper object, on being pushed off the end, simply continues floating along through the air, infants will watch that scene much longer (just as we would). They look at that scene longer because it seems to defy the laws of physics. In this way, we know infants have a basic grasp of how objects move in space.

A peculiarity of early childhood is that most adults can remember events that happened when they were 5 or 6 years old, but very few adults can recall any memories before that time. This relative inability of adults to recall events of their early childhood is called **infantile amnesia**, and it has generated a lot of interest and attempts to account for the phenomenon. What is fascinating about infantile amnesia is that a 3-year-old can tell you detailed information about events that happened 6 months before, and yet as an adult, he will have no recollection of those events. So clearly the memory was there at some point and has been lost.

A modern hypothesis is that we depend heavily on language to encode and retrieve memories, so infantile memories, if stored without verbal information, may be less accessible. For example, when children report their earlier memories, they don't use any words that they did not know when the event happened (Simcock & Hayne, 2003). This result suggests that we rely heavily on language tags to store or retrieve memories, so our earliest events, before we have words to encode them, might be irretrievable. But perhaps the most plausible explanation is simply that younger children forget faster than older children or adults (Bauer, 2005; see Figure 5.14).

Another "mind-reading" method that can be applied to infants measures differences in heart rate associated with interest in an event. When we are calmly interested in some object or event, our parasympathetic nervous system is activated, which slows our heart rate. Say we want to assess how interested an infant is in various television images by seeing how long it takes to distract the child, making her look away from the TV. The more interested the infant is in an image, as measured by how long it takes to distract her, the more her heart rate decelerates (slows down; Lansink & Richards, 1997). We can use this technique to test whether a newborn remembers events before birth. Fetuses were exposed to a descending piano melody played through a speaker placed on the mother's belly a few weeks before birth. Six weeks later, the newborns showed a greater heart rate deceleration when hearing the descending melody than when hearing a reversed, ascending melody. Newborns who had not been exposed to the melody before birth showed an equal deceleration to both the ascending and descending melody (Granier-Deferre et al., 2011).

The ability to focus attention also matures as children get older, but some find it difficult to direct their attention effectively in school. Do these children actually have a disorder? What should be done about it (**Box 5.1**)?

Memory is but one of many capacities of the mind. We next consider **cognitive development**, a progressive increase in cognitive ability, embracing the development of reasoning and problem solving as well as language.

Skeptic at Large

BOX 5.1

Attention Deficit Hyperactivity Disorder

As most children get older, they are able to concentrate on a single task for longer and longer periods. Once they begin school, this ability to concentrate is exercised and extended through the grades. Yet some children find it difficult to fit this mold, and many things catch their attention, making them very distractible. In fact, children with **attention deficit hyperactivity disorder (ADHD)** have problems in *directing* attention and are impulsive, so they have difficulty following tasks to completion. There is no objective test for ADHD; it's typically diagnosed based on parent and teacher reports of hyperactivity.

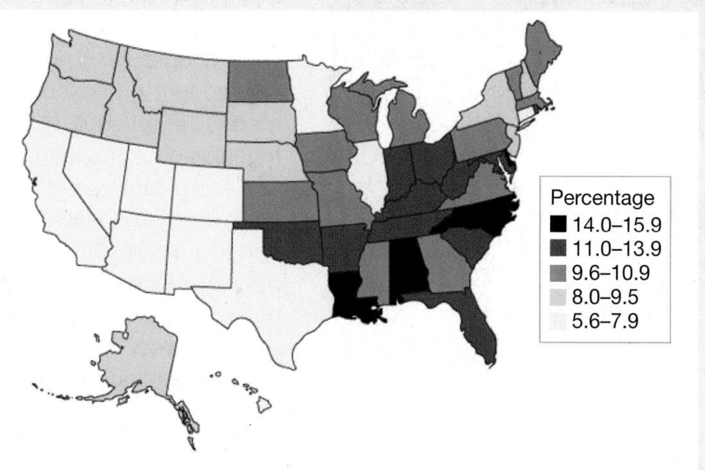

Prevalence of ADHD in the United States The rate of diagnosis for ADHD varies by state. Is ADHD really more common in the Southeast, or is the behavior more likely to be regarded as a problem?

But how do we define whether a child is "hyper" active? Surely different cultures would encourage different levels of activity in children, and who's to say which is the correct or "normal" level?

Would fewer children be diagnosed with ADHD if we simply provided longer recesses in school (Panksepp, 2007)? Boys are much more commonly diagnosed with ADHD than girls, in part because boys tend to be more active than girls. Indeed, young males engage in more active play than females in most mammalian species (mice, rats, monkeys), including ours. More active play in juvenile males is only a problem for mammals that go to school.

Might there have once been some benefit in ADHD from an evolutionary standpoint? Individuals who took notice of many different things in the environment, rather than focusing on just one thing for an extended period, may have benefitted by finding more food and detecting more predators.

Unfortunately, ADHD is labeled a disorder as if there were something wrong with the child, not a mismatch between the child and modern societal expectations. We don't know what causes ADHD, but there are clearly both genetic influences and environmental factors. The likelihood that a child will be diagnosed with ADHD (see figure) in the United States varies by region, which probably reflects regional differences in parents' and teachers' expectations for behavior and doctors' inclinations to reach the diagnosis. Children with ADHD appear delayed in terms of cortical maturation (Shaw et al., 2007), as seen in fMRI scans, suggesting that these children are not fundamentally different from other children, but simply take longer to reach the same ability to adapt to school. Thus controversy continues about whether these conditions should be called disorders at all (Mayes et al., 2008).

Children labeled with ADHD may feel stigmatized, and their self-esteem may suffer further than it already has from having failed to do well in school. So despite the risks of labeling, parents may be eager to get a diagnosis of ADHD to persuade schools to offer accommodations to help the child do better in the classroom. There is no cure for ADHD, but some medications help manage symptoms. **Methylphenidate** (also called *Ritalin*) is a nervous system stimulant (stronger than caffeine but weaker than amphetamine) that improves most symptoms of ADHD in some children. ADHD medication has consistently been found to be most effective when combined with psychosocial therapy, including summer programs to teach classroom coping skills (Pelham & Fabiano, 2008). No one knows the long-term consequences for brain development when children take stimulants for long periods, but so far there is no indication that the medications affect brain structure or make the children more likely to use illicit drugs (Mannuzza et al., 2008).

attention deficit hyperactivity disorder (ADHD) A problem in directing attention that is also accompanied by more physical activity and fidgeting.

methylphenidate Also called *Ritalin*. A nervous system stimulant used to treat ADHD.

Figure 5.15 Simple Genius Jean Piaget revolutionized ideas about the developing mind.

adaptation In Piaget's theory of cognitive development, the process by which an individual learns about the world and incorporates that information into his or her mental life.

assimilation In Piaget's theory of cognitive development, the process of taking in information about the external world.

accommodation In Piaget's theory of cognitive development, a change made in the mind as a result of taking in new information about the world.

constructivism The perspective that growing children are actively engaged in building their minds.

Piaget studied the stages of cognitive development

Swiss psychologist Jean Piaget (1896–1980) revolutionized the way scientists regarded children and the process of mental development (**Figure 5.15**). Piaget's crucial insight was that the mind of a young child is not simply an empty vessel, with an adult way of thinking, ready to learn whatever facts we wish to teach next. Rather, a child's mind is organized differently from an adult's, with its own, special logic. As she grows and interacts with the world, the child reorganizes her thought processes in successive stages of complexity, until she begins to reason like an adult. Albert Einstein declared this discovery "so simple that only a genius could have thought of it."

Several factors led Piaget to this outlook. The first was his own early experience. Ten-year-old Piaget resented a local librarian who treated him "like a child," and so he sent off for publication his observations of a rare albino sparrow in his neighborhood, hoping it would be published to prove that he was not just a child. When his observation appeared in print, the librarian began treating young Jean with respect. He continued publishing for the remaining 74 years of his life. He also continued his early work with non-human animals, which gave him an appreciation for alternative kinds of thinking and intelligence. But perhaps the biggest influence on Piaget's thinking came from his close study of his own three children as they grew. Observing and talking to his children, Piaget saw that their ideas about the world, which an adult would regard as incorrect, were perfectly consistent with what the child had learned so far. A child who thinks that the wind is generated by the waving of tree branches has been observing and correlating events she has seen, and given what she knows so far, her conclusions are perfectly reasonable.

Piaget's theory of how cognitive development unfolds embraces two key ideas. The first is that the child is an *active* participant who is engaged in **adaptation**: adapting to the world. The two processes driving adaptation are **assimilation**, the process of taking in information about the external world, and **accommodation**, or the change made in the mind as a result of taking in that new information (**Figure 5.16**). The idea that the growing child *actively builds* her own mind is sometimes known as **constructivism**. "Intelligence organizes the world by organizing itself" (Piaget, 1937/1954).

The second key idea in Piaget's theory is that there are distinct *stages of cognitive development* that a child must go through to think like an adult. Each successive stage builds on the previous one. Piaget believed that children must thoroughly accommodate one stage of thinking before they can properly assimi-

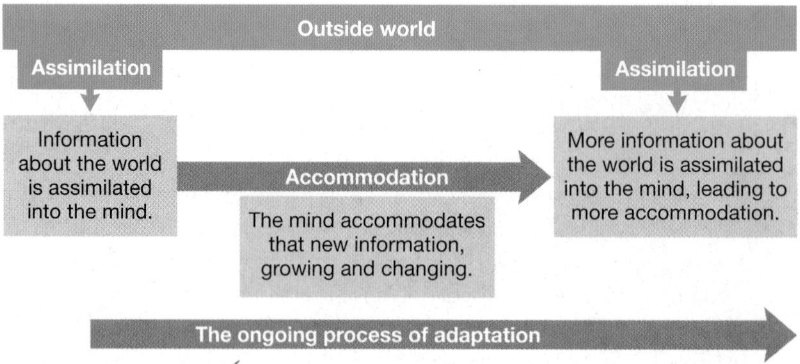

Figure 5.16 Piaget's Constructivist View of Mental Development in Children As the child assimilates new information, she accommodates that information to construct a new way of looking at the world. With this new mental apparatus, she can then assimilate more information.

late information for the next stage. "Children have real understanding only of that which they invent themselves, and each time that we try to teach them something too quickly, we keep them from reinventing it themselves" (Almy et al., 1966). One modern constructivist take on this view is that children, even very young children, are like scientists proposing hypotheses about how the world works, and then trying out various behaviors to test whether the hypothesis is correct: the "scientist in the crib" (Gopnik et al., 2000).

As we discussed earlier, a baby is born with reflexes that, by definition, are unlearned. To develop an adult mind, Piaget thought, the newborn must progress through four stages of cognitive development that can be described in terms of the concepts that a child learns at each stage.

sensorimotor stage The first stage of cognitive development in which individuals learn to use sensory and motor systems.

object permanence The concept that objects continue to exist even if we no longer perceive them.

schema In the context of Piaget's theory of cognitive development, a cognitive structure inside the mind.

THE SENSORIMOTOR STAGE Piaget called the first stage of cognitive development the **sensorimotor stage** because in the first 2 years or so of life we learn how to use the body's sensory and motor apparatus, learning how to use our senses and how to control our body. We learn to *distinguish ourselves from other things and people*. We learn to shake a rattle to make that sound, to hit a ball to set it rolling, to cry for a parent's attention. In other words, we learn that we are an *agent* that can affect the events around us. About midway through the sensorimotor stage, we learn about **object permanence**, the concept that objects continue to exist even if we can't see or hear them any longer. Before this stage is completed, a baby watching a toy train move behind a box may be surprised when the train reappears on the other side of the box (**Figure 5.17A**). But once the baby has understood object permanence, she will expect the train to reappear on the other side. We know this because the baby will shift her gaze to that other side of the box (**Figure 5.17B**) and will register surprise if the train doesn't appear (Charles & Rivera, 2009).

For Piaget, the principles learned at each stage of development reflected a cognitive structure inside the mind, which he called a **schema**. If the more familiar word "scheme" means an elaborate and systematic plan of action, then we can think of a schema as an elaborate and systematic way of thinking about the world. The newborn's schema is little more than reflexive behavior, but during the sensorimotor stage the infant learns to move toward and interact with objects and people and then progresses to the next stage.

(A)

(B)

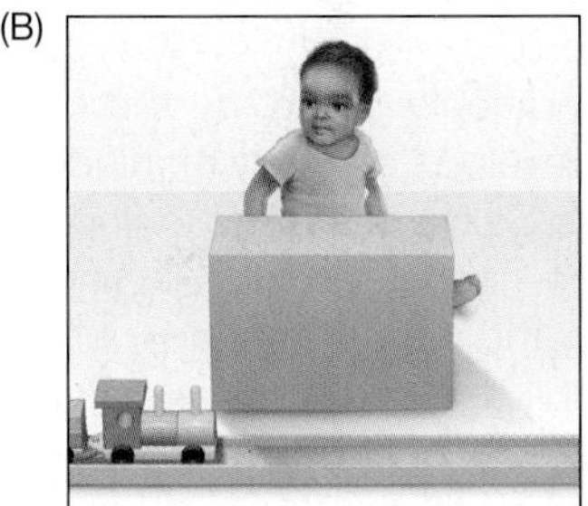

Figure 5.17 Object Permanence (A) When a moving object such as a toy train goes behind a box, a baby may be surprised when it reappears on the other side. (B) A baby who has grasped the concept of object permanence knows that the train still exists and expects it to reappear. The baby will act surprised if some other object comes out from behind the box.

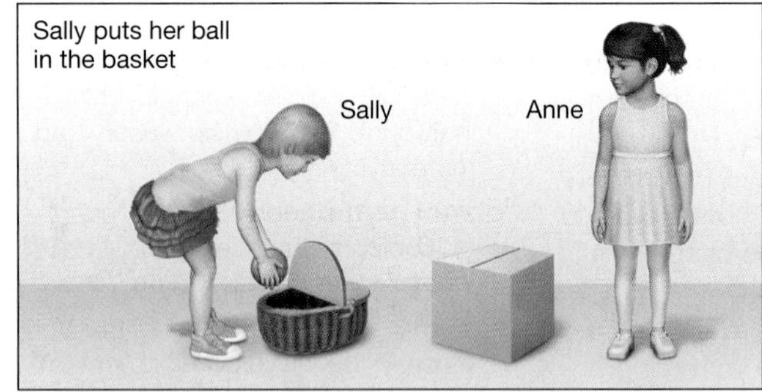
Sally puts her ball
in the basket
Sally
Anne

Sally goes away

Anne moves the ball
to the box

Where will Sally look
for the ball?

Figure 5.18 The Sally and Anne Test Preoperational children displaying egocentrism will expect Sally to know what they know, that the ball is in the box. By the end of the preoperational period, the child will have a theory of mind and will expect Sally to look in the wrong place, the basket.

preoperational stage The stage at which children learn to use language to represent objects and actions.

egocentrism In the context of cognitive development, the notion that everyone knows whatever you know.

theory of mind The understanding that other people may have different information, including inaccurate ideas.

THE PREOPERATIONAL STAGE During the **preoperational stage**, from about ages 2 to 7, the child learns to use language, using words as abstract representations of objects and actions. Learning a language is a remarkable accomplishment that almost all children achieve with apparent ease. We'll discuss that process in detail in Chapter 10. For now we'll simply point out that language acquisition is an important process going on during the preoperational stage, and children's ease in gaining a first language is another indication of how plastic the young brain is.

Preoperational children characteristically show **egocentrism**, the notion that everything revolves around them and that everyone knows what they know. For example, children at this age often assume that you can tell what *they* are thinking, yet they have a hard time seeing things from *your* perspective. If talking on the phone, they may hold up food to offer, unaware that the person on the other end of the line cannot eat it. Because children in the preoperational phase seem to assume that everyone sees and knows what they do, it is as though they do not yet have a **theory of mind**: the understanding that other people's minds are different from their own and may have different information.

One test of whether a child has a theory of (someone else's) mind is to see if the child understands that a person might have a false belief. In one famous example, children shown a Band-Aid box expect to see Band-Aids in it and are surprised when they are shown that it is full of crayons (Perner et al., 1989). Nevertheless, preoperational children, when asked afterward what *another* child will expect to see in the Band-Aid box, report that the *other child will expect to see crayons*. The preoperational child is too egocentric, with no theory of mind to understand that other people will expect to see Band-Aids in the box.

The **Sally and Anne test** offers another way to test whether a child has a theory of mind. You tell a child that the doll Sally has a shiny, new ball that she puts in her basket (Wimmer & Perner, 1983; Baron-Cohen et al., 1985). When Sally goes outside to play, another doll, Anne, moves the ball out of the basket and puts it in a box (**Figure 5.18**). At each stage you ask the child questions to make sure he understands what's happening. Now you say, "Sally comes back inside and wants to get her ball. Where will she look for it?" A young child without a theory of mind will think that Sally knows what he knows, and that she will look inside the box where Anne put the ball.

By the end of the preoperational stage, as the child sheds his egocentrism and develops a theory of mind, he will understand that of course Sally will *expect* to find the ball in the basket where she had placed it. He knows Sally will *not* expect to find the ball in the box where naughty Anne hid it. Some children seem to have a specific deficit in developing a theory of mind, which makes social relations very difficult for them. We explore this problem in **Box 5.2**.

Psychology in Everyday Life

BOX 5.2

Autism Is a Difficulty in Reading Other People's Minds

For the preoperational child who has difficulty with the Sally and Anne test (see Figure 5.18), the ability that most of us have to predict that Sally will look first in the basket for her ball must seem like magic—as if we'd read Sally's mind. In fact, that is exactly what we have done, but without any magic or supernatural forces. Using our theory of (Sally's) mind, we can sort out what Sally does and doesn't know, and so can infer what she will think. This ability to accurately guess what other people think is a crucial developmental milestone that allows us to readily interact with other people.

We can see how important the theory of mind is by examining a group of people who have a specific difficulty with this skill, long after they've mastered other cognitive skills. As the name indicates, *autism spectrum disorder* represents a continuum of disorders, but common to them all is a deficit in understanding what other people are thinking and feeling. The most severe form, called **autism**, is characterized by (1) impaired social interactions, (2) problems communicating, and (3) severely limited behavior and interests. These children may develop like other children, including early language, but then they regress, using less and less language until they may be completely silent. Children with autism fail to respond to other people's speech or gestures and avoid eye contact (see figure). They tend to focus on favorite objects, such as a toy, and show repetitive behaviors such as rocking their body or flapping their hands. Despite widespread rumors, it is quite clear that vaccines do *not* increase the incidence of autism (Hurley et al., 2010; Demichelli et al., 2012).

At the other end of the autism spectrum is "high functioning autism" sometimes called **Asperger's syndrome**. While clinicians have called for dropping the term Asperger's and regarding it as simply one end of the autism spectrum (see Chapter 16), some people identify with the term and want to retain it (Wallis, 2009; http://wrongplanet.net). Children with Asperger's syndrome have no difficulty with verbal communication—in fact they tend to be very articulate, giving the impression of a "little professor"—but they have great difficulty discerning what other people think and feel. Because they are so articulate, people with Asperger's syndrome can give us a sense of what it's like not to have a theory of mind. They find it difficult to look other people in the eyes because faces change so much and are so hard for them to understand. Because they can't read faces, children with Asperger's syndrome don't have the clues that other children have about what another person is feeling, and so they often misunderstand other people's intentions and wishes. Nevertheless, because they may also have strong talents in artistic or technical fields, many people with Asperger's syndrome have had happy, successful careers.

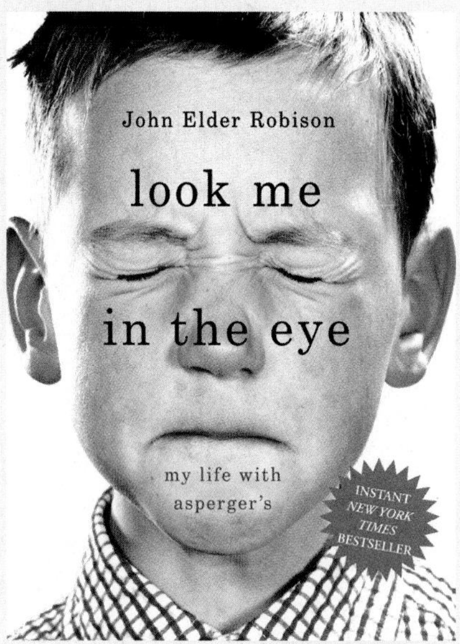

I Can't Look In his memoir, John Elder Robinson describes how he overcame his struggles with Asperger's syndrome to find his place in the world.

autism A spectrum of disorders characterized by impaired social interactions, problems communicating, and severely restricted behavior and interests.

Asperger's syndrome Also called *high functioning autism*. A part of the autism spectrum disorder in which individuals have no difficulty with verbal communication but still have difficulty discerning what others think and feel.

Despite having learned about object permanence during the sensorimotor stage, children at the preoperational stage still reason intuitively rather than logically. This intuitive reasoning is most famously seen when testing children on the concept of **conservation**: the physical laws that the volume and mass of an object remain the same—are conserved—no matter how you rearrange its parts. The classic example is to show a child two glasses, one taller than the other but of equal volume. If you ask the child which glass holds more, she will usually choose the taller glass. You can now fill the short glass with water and

Sally and Anne test A test to probe whether a child has a theory of other people's minds.

conservation The physical laws that volume and mass of objects are conserved no matter how they might be rearranged.

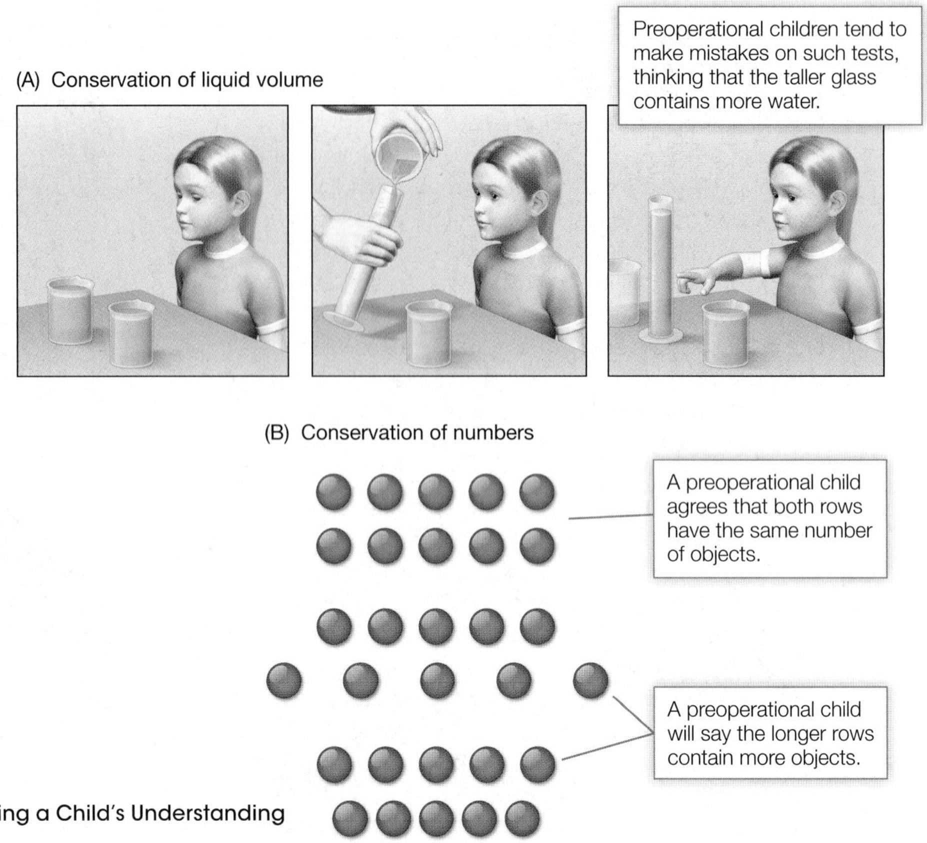

(A) Conservation of liquid volume

Preoperational children tend to make mistakes on such tests, thinking that the taller glass contains more water.

(B) Conservation of numbers

A preoperational child agrees that both rows have the same number of objects.

A preoperational child will say the longer rows contain more objects.

Figure 5.19 Testing a Child's Understanding of Conservation

then pour that water out into the tall glass, exactly filling it. But even after watching this demonstration, a child in the preoperational stage will still say the taller glass has more water (**Figure 5.19A**). Similar tests probe the child's understanding of the conservation of number, mass, and area (**Figure 5.19B**).

In sum, the accomplishments of the preoperational stage are (1) language, (2) theory of mind, and (3) understanding of physical conservation. Once children have acquired this schema, they can progress to the next stage.

THE CONCRETE OPERATIONAL STAGE In the **concrete operational stage**, from about age 7 to 11, children learn more formal logical skills (the term "operations" refers to logical operations or principles), but they tend to be very concrete in their thinking (hence the name). For example, they readily learn mathematical operations such as addition and multiplication, which require manipulating symbols (the numbers), but they have trouble with more abstract, theoretical questions such as whether adding 1 to an even number will always result in an even number or an odd number.

concrete operational stage The cognitive stage at which children acquire formal logical skills ("operations"), but tend to be very concrete in their thinking.

formal operational stage The cognitive stage at which children are able to consider many different theoretical possibilities for a condition, so they can solve complex, hypothetical problems using abstract ideas.

THE FORMAL OPERATIONAL STAGE Piaget's last stage of cognitive development is the **formal operational stage**, starting at about age 11. By this stage the child may quickly grasp that whenever you add 1 to an even number, the sum is always an odd number. Children in this stage are also able to consider many different theoretical possibilities for a condition. They can solve complex, hypothetical problems using abstract ideas and can engage in hypothesis testing, much like a scientist (so we've gone from "scientist in the crib" to "scientist in middle school"). Formal operational thinking also becomes concerned with the future and with ideological questions such as, Is killing always wrong?

(A)

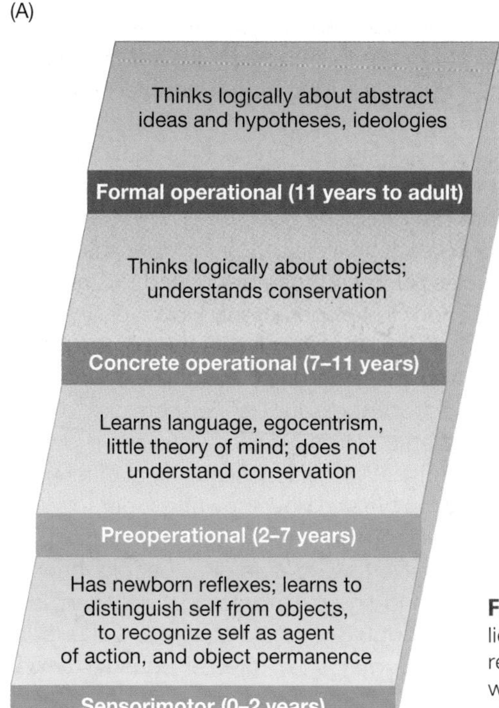

(B)

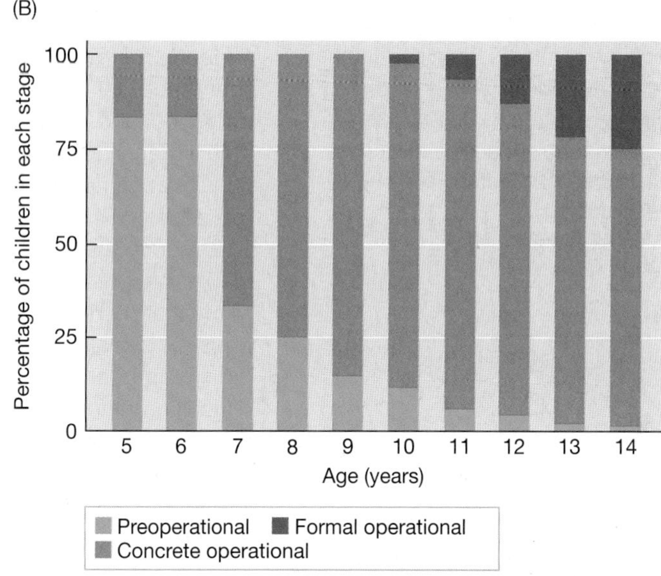

Figure 5.20 Piaget's Four Stages of Cognitive Development (A) Piaget believed that children need to assimilate and accommodate one stage of cognitive reasoning before they can reach the next stage. (B) Proportion of children age 5–14 who had reached each of the stages. Note that all of the 5-year-olds had already reached the preoperational stage. (After Renner et al., 1976.)

Figure 5.20 provides a summary of Piaget's four stages of cognitive development. While the stages are progressive, the transitions are not all-or-none. For example, while moving from one stage to the next, a child may think in a preoperational, egocentric fashion in some situations and in a concrete operational fashion in others. Or he may understand the conservation of volume before he understands the conservation of area. And although most of us reach the formal operational stage of thinking, there are plenty of complex questions that remain difficult to answer long after our college education is over. So despite the identified stages, development is still gradual and continuous.

Proper emotional and social development requires a warm, interactive adult

Of course the mind does not operate solely through logic. Emotional processes are at work too. **Temperament** refers to a person's emotional makeup, the way he or she generally responds to a variety of situations. It is considered a long-lasting aspect of personality and usually is thought of as inborn. (Originally the word "temperament" referred to the physical composition of an object, so the temperament of swords is steel.) Temperament can refer to many aspects of personality, but in developmental psychology it refers to differences in emotional response that are seen in infants and seem to persist throughout life.

Starting in the 1950s, a group of scientists began examining the temperaments of 2- to 3-month-old infants. About a third of the infants were difficult to classify in terms of emotional behavior, but the remaining infants showed consistent patterns of response. Some babies were *easy*: they woke up and got hungry at regular, predictable times, reacted cheerfully to new environments, and rarely acted fussy. *Difficult* babies fussed a good deal and responded irritably to new situations. *Slow-to-warm-up* babies were not very active and initially withdrew in response to new situations or people, but slowly accepted them with repeated exposure (Thomas & Chess, 1984). Sometimes difficult babies are described as "high reactive" and easy babies as "low reactive" (Kagan, 2002).

temperament A person's emotional makeup; the way the person generally responds to a variety of situations.

stranger anxiety The negative response of infants toward unfamiliar people.

imprinting The behavior by which birds are predisposed to follow any moving object that they see shortly after hatching.

These babies were reevaluated as they grew up, and the temperamental differences among them in infancy tended to persist in many ways. Easy infants (low reactives) usually became easy, cheerful children who adapted readily to preschool and school. Slow-to-warm-up babies tended to become shy, inhibited children who became shy, anxious teenagers. Difficult babies (high reactives) usually became children who had a harder time adjusting to school and were more likely to show aggressive behaviors (Caspi, 2000).

Because these differences arise so early in life, you might think that genes play a role in them, and indeed studies such as those discussed in Chapter 4 show that there is a heritable component to temperament. However, the environment can also affect temperament. Recall that about one-third of the babies did not fit neatly into any category, and most children, even those who were difficult as infants, learned to adjust to school and adult life. Furthermore, difficult infants became less difficult if their parents were able to respond in a patient, relaxed fashion to their children's demands. We'll discuss individual differences in temperament again in Chapter 14 when we see how they affect personality.

One milestone in infant emotional development is the onset of **stranger anxiety**, the negative response that infants have toward unfamiliar people: growing quiet and staring at the stranger, pouting and crying if the stranger gets too close. This fear of strangers usually arises at about 8–9 months of age (Brooker et al., 2013). As you might guess, difficult infants may show greater stranger anxiety than easy infants, but most infants display it to some degree. Unexpectedly, infants who are especially anxious around strangers spend *more* time looking at their eyes than less anxious infants do (Matsuda et al., 2013), perhaps looking for reassurance. Stranger anxiety typically fades by age 2, especially if a parent is calmly nearby when the stranger approaches. However, infants of anxious mothers tend to be more anxious, and remain anxious longer, than infants with non-anxious mothers (Murray et al., 2008).

It's easy to see how stranger anxiety might have been evolutionarily adaptive, as a way to encourage infants to avoid potentially harmful strangers. It also reminds us of behavior seen in the young of many animals, which stay close to parents and avoid unfamiliar individuals. Such behavior is especially prominent in many bird species, where the young avidly follow their mother as they search for food. In these cases, the young birds quickly learn to distinguish their mother from any other individual, usually within just an hour or so of hatching. The process of learning to recognize and follow a parent is called **imprinting** (**Figure 5.21**), which is a clearly adaptive response. Chicks will learn to follow any individual, even humans or inanimate objects that they see moving about in the first hours after hatching. As a 9-year-old growing up on a farm, I watched two rescued eggs hatch and was surprised that those two chicks eagerly followed me wherever I went, avoiding other people or nearby hens. They had imprinted on me and treated me as their mother.

Staying Close to Parents Starting about 8–9 months of age, most infants display stranger anxiety, becoming afraid of unfamiliar people, even if they appear to be a beloved figure like Santa Claus.

Scientists study love and attachment

Most mammals are unable to move about on their own right after birth, so we rarely see the sort of close following behavior that characterizes imprinting, but a series of experiments with rhesus monkeys conducted by the American psychologist Harry Harlow (1905–1981) in the 1950s–1970s powerfully demonstrated the drive that newborn rhesus monkeys have to recognize and stay close to a mother figure (Harlow et al., 1965). Harlow separated newborn monkeys from their mothers and raised them in clean, warm, safe environments with their nourishment provided by bottles placed in cloth-covered models of a

Figure 5.21 Following "Mom" These whooping cranes, having been imprinted on the ultralight aircraft as chicks, are following it to their winter feeding grounds. You can learn more about the procedure at operationmigration.org.

monkey mother (**Figure 5.22**). He found that the young monkeys would cling to the model not just when eating, but between meals as well. Several observations indicated that the monkeys drew comfort from the models. For one thing, if a monkey happened to be away from the model when an experimenter approached, it would run and cling to the model, in what resembled stranger anxiety in human infants. If a monkey was separated from the model, it would show behavioral signs of stress, such as sucking its thumb and rocking back and forth. When given the opportunity, it would quickly run back to the model.

What does the isolated infant monkey look for in a mother? Like human infants that prefer looking at faces rather than abstract shapes, infant monkeys prefer mother models with faces, even if they are crude models such as that in Figure 5.22 (Harlow, 1959). They also prefer models that offer nourishment in the form of a baby bottle, but what young monkeys really love is a soft mother model. When given the choice between a bare-wire model mother that gave milk or a soft, cloth-covered model that did not, Harlow's young monkeys choose the soft, cloth-covered model. Young monkeys love the feel of something soft, which would normally be their mother's belly.

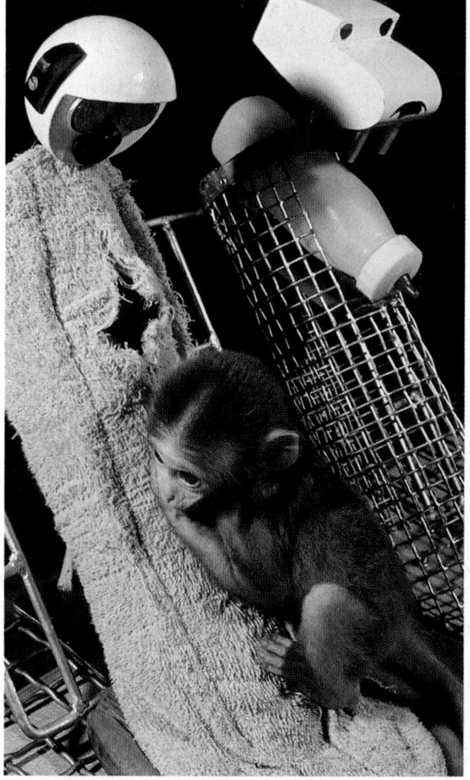

Figure 5.22 The Science of Love Harry Harlow found that infant rhesus monkeys separated from their mother would form a strong attachment to a mother model. When stressed, the monkeys would cling to the model and seemed to draw comfort from it. Soft, cuddly models were preferred over hard models, no matter which model provided milk.

Despite the comforts of the model, these motherless monkeys were permanently damaged by the absence of a real, interactive mother. As adults they could not get along with other monkeys, alternately running away from them and attacking them. This erratic behavior upset other monkeys, so that they often attacked the motherless monkeys. This abnormal social behavior meant, among other things, that the motherless monkeys were hopeless at having sexual relationships, never figuring out how to interact with a willing partner. More dramatically, females that had been raised without a real mother were themselves horrible mothers (Ruppenthal et al., 1976). They were artificially inseminated, and when their babies were born, the motherless mothers would neglect, attack, or even kill them. Just as these motherless mothers, when young, had yearned to hold onto their screen-and-cloth models, their own unfortunate offspring kept trying to return to their abusive mothers, in heartbreaking scenes.

What is fascinating is that much of the damage caused by being raised without a real mother could be avoided if the young monkeys were given regular exposure to similar-age peers (Harlow & Suomi, 1971; Suomi et al., 1976). Motherless monkeys that regularly played with their peers were much more socially adept as adults. These results suggest that the best therapy

attachment A strong emotional bond or tie between the infant and caregivers.

strange situation A test of attachment as revealed by a child's reaction to a temporary separation from the caregiver.

for abused children might be interaction with other, more supportively parented children.

These experiments were and remain controversial because of the obvious distress the young monkeys experienced. In today's world it may seem that the experiments were pointless, showing what we already know. But what we know today is very much a result of these experiments. When these studies began, many "experts" in child rearing urged parents not to get too close to their children. Spending too much time with children was thought to make them too emotionally dependent on their parents. For example, psychologist John Bowlby, whom we'll talk about shortly, was born in 1907 and raised by middle-class British parents who felt that children should see their parents once a day, at teatime, but otherwise be taken care of by a hired nanny. At age 7 he was sent away from his family to boarding school. Today we might find this type of rearing cold and damaging, but back then it was considered the ideal (if the family could afford it). Well into the 1950s and 1960s, many child-rearing books urged parents not to get too physically or emotionally close to children to avoid "spoiling" them (Blum, 2002). In this context, Harlow's results, including wrenching films of young motherless monkeys rocking with anxiety and curling into balls in withdrawal, shocked the world into realizing how important cuddling and emotional support are for proper social environment. Bucking the trend of psychologists of his day who felt science could only study behavior you could see and who were unwilling to use terms such as "mind" or "desire," Harlow insisted that he was studying *love*. Those isolated monkeys loved their cloth-model mothers, and normal monkeys loved their real mothers and benefitted enormously from the love those real mothers gave back to them. Harlow felt his experiments proved that *young individuals have a critical need for love,* and his graphic results convinced almost everyone.

INFANT ATTACHMENT Harlow's results were not lost on John Bowlby, who by then was a prominent child psychiatrist in London. Bowlby had been studying the effects of long-term hospitalization on children. If a child would need weeks of treatment in the hospital, "experts" at the time felt it was important for parents to leave quickly and to visit rarely, if at all. This was thought to help the child "settle in," which meant, in effect, be less trouble to the hospital staff. Bowlby thought that children who had settled in were in fact depressed because they were deprived of warm interaction with their parents (Bowlby, 1969). Bowlby proposed that human infants are born with the tendency to form an **attachment**, a strong emotional bond or tie between the infant and his or her caregivers (usually the mother), also known as the *attachment figures*. You might argue, and Harlow did, that what Bowlby and other Britons called "attachment" is what many other people, especially Americans, would call "love." Nevertheless, in the field the term "attachment" is used almost exclusively.

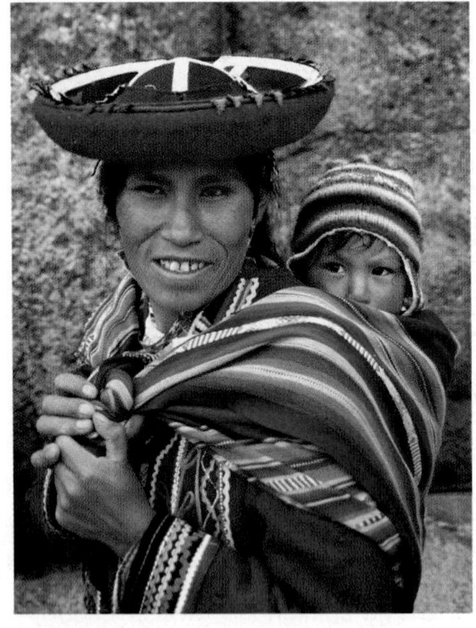

Attachment Behavior In many cultures, mothers keep their infants nearby at all times.

This attachment, which forms through the warm, supportive interaction with the parents, allows the child to use them as a "safe base" from which to explore the world. When upset or worried, a child can return to the mother or father as a haven. The child uses this early social interaction with his caregivers to build social relationships with other people. From Bowlby's perspective, the behavior of Harlow's young monkeys, pining to return to their mother model when separated, reflected their attachment to the models. The abnormal behavior of motherless monkeys as adults reflected the damage done by having an unmoving, inanimate object for an attachment figure instead of an active, supportive mother.

Inspired by the work of Bowlby and Harlow, American psychologist Mary Ainsworth devised the **strange situation**, a test of the attachment between child and parent as revealed by the child's reaction to separation from the

Secure attachment

Children with secure attachment were visibly upset when their parents left,...

...and clearly happy when their parents returned.

Avoidant attachment

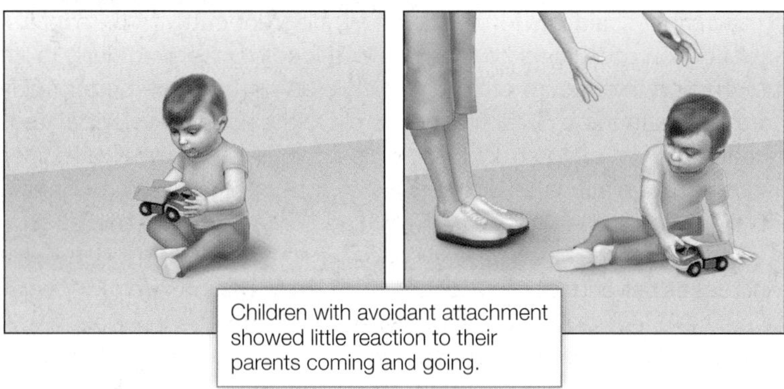
Children with avoidant attachment showed little reaction to their parents coming and going.

Ambivalent attachment

Children with ambivalent (or resistant) attachment were upset when their parents left,...

...but did not calm down with their parents return, and might even turn to a stranger.

Figure 5.23 Different Types of Attachment Styles

parent (Ainsworth et al., 1978). In this test, an infant or child is brought by a parent (usually the mother) to a laboratory room filled with toys and an unfamiliar person (an experimenter). In a carefully controlled script, the parent first leaves the child with the stranger for 3 minutes, then returns to be alone with the child in the room for 3 minutes, then leaves the child again, either alone or with the stranger, and finally the parent and child are reunited. During all these proceedings, the child's behavior is carefully monitored and measured through a one-way glass window.

The reaction of children to the strange situation tends to fall into one of three patterns, based on how they interact with the toys and stranger and on how they respond to separation and reunion with the parent (**Figure 5.23**). Most children play with the toys freely while Mom is in the room, are visibly upset when she leaves, have nothing to do with the stranger in Mom's absence, and welcome the reunion with Mom and are quickly comforted. This behavior fits Bowlby's

secure attachment A style of attachment in which the child is visibly upset when the caregiver leaves, rejects a stranger, and welcomes reunion with the caregiver.

avoidant attachment A style of attachment in which the child shows little or no distress when the caregiver leaves, shows little or no response upon reunion, and interacts very little with a stranger.

ambivalent attachment Also called *resistant attachment*. A style of attachment in which the child is upset when the caregiver leaves, may warm up to a stranger, and behave negatively toward the caregiver upon reuniting.

disorganized attachment A style of attachment in which the child shows an inconsistent pattern of response in the strange situation.

model of a **secure attachment** between child and parent. However, other children show little or no distress when Mom departs and little or no response to her return, and they interact very little with either toys or the stranger, displaying an **avoidant attachment** pattern. Yet other children display a complicated **ambivalent** (or *resistant*) **attachment**: they are upset when Mom leaves but behave negatively toward Mom on her return. The child might be angry at Mom, hitting her, or simply slow to warm up to her (Ainsworth et al., 1978).

In short, secure infants seek contact and connection with the parent, avoidant infants avoid the parent, and ambivalent infants show both positive and negative feelings toward the parent in the strange situation. While it's easiest for us to think of these categories as exclusive, there is in fact a continuum of attachment styles. Furthermore, a minority of babies don't neatly fit any of the three categories, as they behave inconsistently, a pattern that's been described as **disorganized attachment** (Main & Solomon, 1986).

Ainsworth and other scientists found that these different patterns of response to the strange situation correlate with many other aspects of behavior later in life. Children who showed the secure attachment style as infants have better social skills and more friends than do children who were avoidant or ambivalent. There's even evidence that the differing attachment styles of infants correlate with differences in their romantic relations as adults (Shaver et al., 1996). Still, many infants who are secure grow up to be socially awkward, and many avoidant babies grow up to have warm, close friendship. Having good interactions with peers while growing up increases the chances for positive adult relationships, even for people who were avoidant as children (Grossman et al., 2005; Simpson et al., 2007). Furthermore, these are only correlations, so we can't conclude that an avoidant attachment style caused later difficulties with social relations. Other factors (genes, prenatal conditions, early experiences) may have caused both the avoidant attachment and the awkward relations with other children in school.

The baby's response to the strange situation also correlates with the parent's behavior, specifically his or her parenting style. Secure infants tend to have warm, responsive parents, and avoidant infants tend to have unresponsive parents (**Table 5.1**). It's not clear, though, whether the adult's parenting style causes the baby to show a specific pattern of attachment, or whether the infant's attachment pattern shapes the parent's behavior. And because such correlations are far from perfect, we may conclude that a variety of factors affect both attachment and parenting style.

A sizeable body of research, emphasizing the importance of early infant–mother attachment, has explored the impact of day care on young children (**Box 5.3**). Considerable evidence supports the importance of warm, responsive caregivers, whether in a day care or in the home, for proper development.

And what of Genie, whom we met at the start of this chapter? Given her horrific upbringing, would she ever be able to have a normal life? Many of Genie's behaviors, such as rocking her body, masturbating openly, raging silently, and tearing and pulling at her body, are eerily reminiscent of Harlow's monkeys raised without a real mother. Yet many of the people who worked with Genie felt that, despite her limited language, she made real connections and bonds with other people. People were drawn to her and to the mission of helping her. So her capacity to form social bonds with other people was not entirely extinguished by her nightmarish childhood.

TABLE 5.1 Styles of Attachment

Infant attachment pattern	Caregiver parenting style[a]
Secure	Appropriate, prompt response, consistent with needs
Avoidant	Little or no response to distressed child, discouraging crying and encouraging independence, perhaps to the point of neglect
Ambivalent	Inconsistent between appropriate and neglectful responses
Disorganized	Frightened and frightening: withdrawn, negative, confused, poor at reading infant's emotions

[a]The behavior of the parent is correlated with the attachment patterns of the infant. Note that these are only modest correlations and that there are many exceptions to each.

Psychology in Everyday Life

BOX 5.3

What Are the Effects of Day Care on Children?

What happens to children when both parents work outside the home? The body of evidence concerning attachment of infants to their caregiver, who is usually their mother, brings up this question. It is especially relevant today when many 1-year-old children have two working parents. If the mother spends less time with the infant, will the infant develop a less secure attachment? Since most of these infants enter child-care facilities, how does that affect the baby's attachment to her or his mother?

Quality Matters The staff at quality day cares are emotionally attached to the children and stimulate their cognitive development.

As in most such questions about societal trends, the answer is complicated. First, there is evidence that infants in day care are slightly less likely to show a secure attachment pattern in the strange situation than infants kept at home full time (Thompson, 1991). However, the difference is rather small (29% of infants in day care versus 36% of infants kept at home), and it is possible that the children in day care are simply more used to separations from the mother in the presence of another adult and thus show fewer signs of attachment, such as being upset when the mother leaves and relieved when she returns (Belsky & Braungart, 1991). Even if infants in day care show less secure attachment than infants cared for by the mother at home full time, the important question is whether the two groups of infants differ in later success in school and in social interactions. There are reports that children who were in day care are more likely to be aggressive in school (Belsky, 2002), but again the differences are small and do not seem to persist.

Since 1990 the National Institute of Child Health and Human Development (NICHD) has supported long-range studies of various day cares and the effects of day care on infants and their later behavior. In general, these studies have not confirmed any difference in the security of attachment of children raised with some day care versus those raised exclusively in the home. Neither do they indicate that children raised with day care have a harder time getting along in school than children kept at home (NICHD, 2008). In fact, there is some evidence that children who have been in day care are more likely to be independent and outgoing.

However, all the researchers agree on one key point: the *quality of day care matters*. The strongest outcome seen so far from the NICDH study is that children in higher-quality day cares will do better, academically and emotionally, than children in low-quality day cares (Belsky et al., 2007). In fact, exclusive care by the mother did not predict most measures of school success, but higher-quality child care did (NICHD, 2006). What's the difference between a high-quality and a low-quality day care? At a high-quality day care (see figure), the staff are sensitive to the child even when she or he is not distressed, stimulate the child's cognitive development, have a positive regard for the child, and have an emotional attachment to the child.

Like Victor, the wild boy of Aveyron, Genie learned to understand some human speech, and she developed a much greater vocabulary, a few hundred words, which allowed her to communicate to some extent. However, she never learned to string more than two or three words together, and she showed no understanding of grammar (Curtiss, 1977). When we discuss the development of language in further detail in Chapter 10, we'll see that Genie's failure to develop a full, grammatical language capacity is one indication that humans must be exposed to language early in life, during a sensitive period, in order to learn it properly.

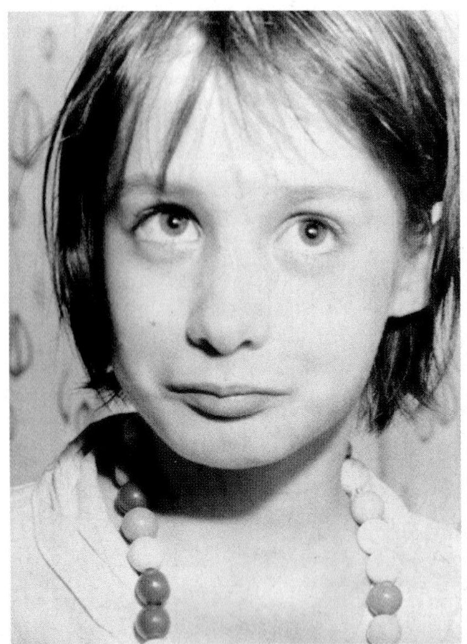
Genie

Was Genie mentally disabled from the beginning, as her abusive father believed? We'll never know for sure. The rapid growth in her vocabulary after her release makes it clear that she could have learned a lot more than she did while in captivity. Also, Genie's performance on IQ tests, while well below that of other children her age, continued to improve: every year her mental age increased by about a year. This is not what we would expect to see in someone who was mentally disabled. Yet in the end, Genie never achieved a normal IQ and, with her limited language, was never able to lead a normal, self-sufficient life. Eventually the funding to study Genie faded away and she became just another ward of the state. Her mother has since died. Now in her late fifties, Genie lives in an adult home for the mentally disabled.

Genie's case and others make it clear that environmental conditions are crucial for proper mental development. The only remaining questions are how important the environment is, what range of environments are best for development, and how much the variability in human intelligence is due to variability in the environment. We'll consider these questions in greater detail in Chapter 11, but for now it's important to note that early interventions, such as preschool education, have repeatedly been shown to make a difference in adult intelligence.

5.2 SUMMARY

- Babies are born with immature sensory systems and *simple reflexes*. In the first year they show an orderly, progressive increase in motor skills and fine-tuning of sensory capacity.
- The cognitive ability of *infants*, who by definition cannot yet use language, can be tested with methods such as *habituation techniques*, which rely on the time an infant spends looking at a scene to provide inferences about what she knows, or on behavioral techniques such as rewarding a baby's kicking by moving a mobile. Such methods show that memory steadily improves over the first years of life.
- Jean Piaget identified four stages in the *cognitive development* of children, who go from the *sensorimotor stage* of the first few years, when they learn about *object permanence* and develop a basic understanding of physics, to the *preoperational stage* where they learn language but tend to have *egocentric* thinking and have not yet learned about *conservation*.
- Young schoolchildren in the *concrete operational stage* understand conservation and many other logical principles but still tend to think in concrete rather than abstract terms.
- Later, starting about age 11 or so, children reach the adult, *formal operational stage* of reasoning and are able to reason about abstract and theoretical principles.
- Social relations also develop in an orderly, progressive fashion. Newborn babies already differ from one another in terms of *temperament*, but few display *stranger anxiety* until about 8–9 months of age. By that age they have formed an *attachment* to one or a few caregivers.
- Different infants display different attachment styles, which may form the model for future social relationships since there are correlations between infant attachment styles and later relations.
- It is clear that early social relationships have a critical impact on developing individuals. Experiments with monkeys have shown that growing up without a warm, caring caregiver results in highly abnormal social capacities at maturity. Similarly, children such as Genie who are deprived of love throughout childhood are unable to develop into mature, capable adults.

puberty The landmark event when an individual becomes capable of reproducing.

adolescence The process of transition from childhood to adulthood.

hormones (1) Chemicals released from one part of the body that enter the bloodstream and affect other parts of the body. (2) In the context of adolescent development, gonadal hormones such as estrogens and testosterone that drive sexual development.

secondary sex characteristics Physical characteristics that are typical of adults of one sex or the other.

menarche The time at which a girl has her first menstrual period.

REVIEW QUESTIONS

1. How do habituation techniques allow psychologists to measure sensory processes and learning in infants?
2. What are the four stages of cognitive development proposed by Piaget?
3. How is temperament evaluated in infants?
4. What are three types of attachment styles in young children, and how do those styles tend to correlate with later behaviors?

Food for Thought

Is ADHD really a disorder? Should children be medicated to fit in at school? Does long-term stimulant use harm the brain?

5.3 Adolescence: Developing Identity

Things to Learn

- Physical changes in adolescence
- Factors that affect age of first menstrual period
- Prolonged brain development, especially in frontal cortex
- Conflicts of adolescence and warnings of suicide
- Moral development

Puberty is the landmark period when an individual becomes capable of reproducing. For males, this is when live sperm are produced and for females it is when eggs are released. It may be hard to pinpoint when this happens exactly, but presumably the individual was incapable of reproducing one day and capable the next, so puberty is an *event* that happens. By contrast, **adolescence** is a *process* of transition, quite long in some species such as our own, from childhood to adulthood. We've already discussed another landmark event in cognitive development that takes place during adolescence: this is when most young people make the transition from concrete operational to formal operational reasoning. But there is still a tremendous amount of work to be done, as the body changes in response to hormones preparing for reproduction. First we'll review the changes in the body, brain, and mind as the child makes that transition to the adult world of independence and responsibility, and then we'll discuss how a sense of right and wrong develops as we grow up.

Adolescence is marked by physical changes that prepare boys and girls for adulthood

Physical growth of the body is greatest in the first 2 years of life. Then growth is relatively modest, an inch or two per year, until adolescence, when there is a brief but vigorous growth spurt of several centimeters per year (**Figure 5.24**) (Simm & Werther, 2005). This change in body size has many effects on behavior because it affects how other people relate to the individual. The body isn't just growing, of course, but also changing in many other ways. Boys begin to morph into the body proportions of men, and girls begin to morph into the body shape of women. **Hormones**, especially the gonadal hormones—estrogen from the ovaries and testosterone from the testes—drive the development of **secondary sex characteristics**: in girls, these include the wide hips, soft skin (including a layer of fat just under the skin), and breast development that are promoted by estrogens, whereas in boys, muscle growth, change in facial structure (including a wider jaw and thicker brow), and beard growth are promoted by testosterone. Hormones from the adrenal glands drive the development of pubic and underarm hair in both sexes. These many changes affect how other people relate to the individual, but the individual also notes the changes in his or her body in transition to adulthood.

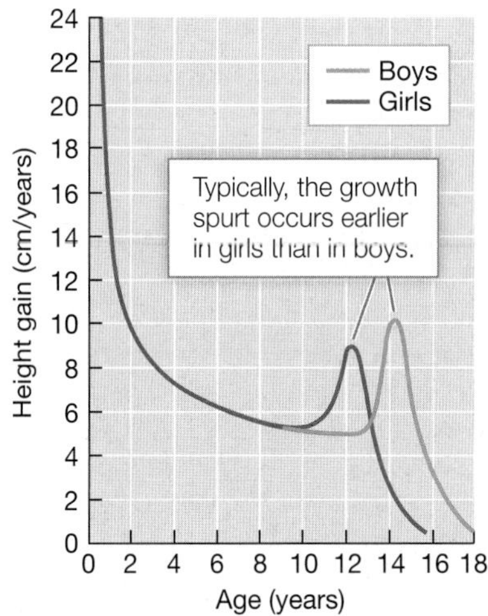

Figure 5.24 The Rate of Change in Height across Development After the dramatic growth of the first 2 years of life, a child's growth rate slows down until adolescence. (After Tanner et al., 1966.)

Many studies indicate that the transition to adolescence has accelerated in Western nations in the modern era, as children reach puberty at earlier ages than they used to. A convenient indicator of puberty in girls is **menarche**: the girl's first menstrual period. For example, historical records at maternity clinics in Norway show that the age of menarche declined from 1880 to 1960, in two distinct phases (**Figure 5.25A**; Brudevoll et al., 1979). The same trend is also apparent in other industrialized nations (**Figure 5.25B**; see also Talma et al., 2013).

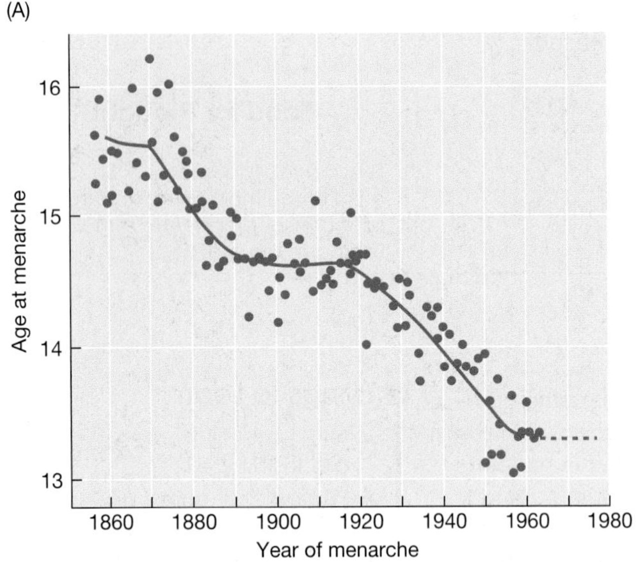

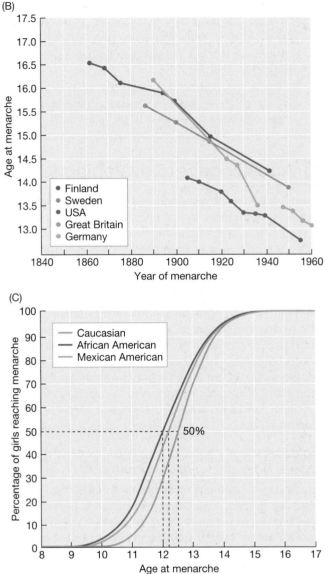

Figure 5.25 Historical Decline in Age of Menarche Over the past century, the age at which girls reach menarche has declined. (A) No one knows why the age of menarche in Norway declined in two waves, but the overall trend is clear. (B) The same trend is seen in other countries, although the records in these countries do not extend back as far. (C) In the modern-day United States, African American girls tend to reach menarche at an earlier age than Caucasian girls. These racial differences could be due to differences in stress during childhood, since childhood stress has been seen to lead to earlier menarche. (A after Brudevoll et al., 1979; B after Tanner et al., 1966; C after Chumlea et al., 2003.)

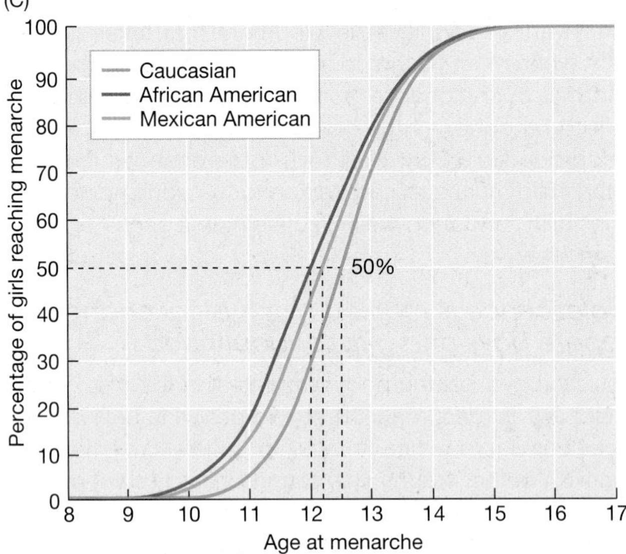

No one knows why girls are reaching puberty earlier in Western nations, but it could be due to improved nutrition or medical treatment, or to exposure to human-made chemicals in the environment. Increases in body fat may be one factor accelerating menarche (Morris et al., 2010). One theory is that the social experience of girls may be accelerating menarche. A host of studies has found that girls who are raised with a father enter menarche later than girls with an absent or mostly absent father (Surbey, 1990; Boothroyd et al., 2013a). The presence of the father during the first 10 years of the girl's life, well before menarche begins, has the greatest effect on the age of menarche, whereas the presence or absence of the mother seems to have no effect. Another reliable influence on the age of menarche is stress. The more stress a girl experiences, the more likely she is to reach menarche at a younger age. Presumably the absence of a father increases the stress on a family, and this may be why girls without a father present enter menarche sooner. Similarly, the modern acceleration of menarche could reflect the increased stress of growing up in a world where more and more demands are made on children. For another example, racial differences in menarche in the United States may reflect different levels of stress that girls of different races may experience in childhood. African American girls reach menarche at an earlier age than white girls, with Mexican American girls somewhere in between (**Figure 5.25C**; Chumlea et al., 2003). The important point here is that the social environment can have an effect on menarche, reminding us of the importance of our interactions with other people for so many aspects of development.

Sleep patterns also change at adolescence. Children entering adolescence start shifting their body clocks so that they stay up later, and sleep in later, than before (**Figure 5.26**; Roenneberg et al., 2004). This shift may also be socially driven. Perhaps teenagers eager to spend less time with their parents manage to do this by staying up later at night. That would make them want to sleep later in the morning. But the regularity of the shift over the course of development and the subtle sex differences suggest there is at least some biological factor at work. In any case, most teenagers have to go to school in the morning, and few school districts shift to later classes for high school.

Late risers
Early risers
Females
Males
10 20 30 40 50 60
Age (years)

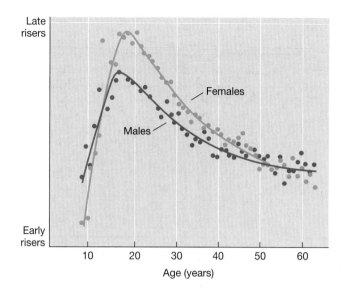

Figure 5.26 Oh, How I Hate to Get Up in the Morning The body clock shifts in most young people during adolescence, as they tend to get up later in the morning. (After Roenneberg et al., 2004.)

As the body is changing, so too is the brain (Steinberg, 2013). The stages of brain development we discussed earlier are mostly complete before puberty, except for myelination, which is completed by age 25 or so, and synapse rearrangement, which continues throughout life. We can see the consequence of both processes in a curious fashion: the top layer of cortex, which consists mostly of neuronal cell bodies, grows thinner. As there is little myelin in this region, the thinning of the top cortical layer reflects synapse rearrangement. Scientists who used scanners to monitor brain development during adolescence were surprised to discover the process is not complete until about age 20 (**Figure 5.27**; Gogtay et al., 2004). The greatest changes are in frontal cortex, which includes regions that are thought to be important for inhibiting behavior. The delayed maturation of inhibitory regions of frontal cortex may play a role in a sometimes troublesome characteristic of adolescent humans: problems in impulse control (Casey et al., 2008), which we will consider next.

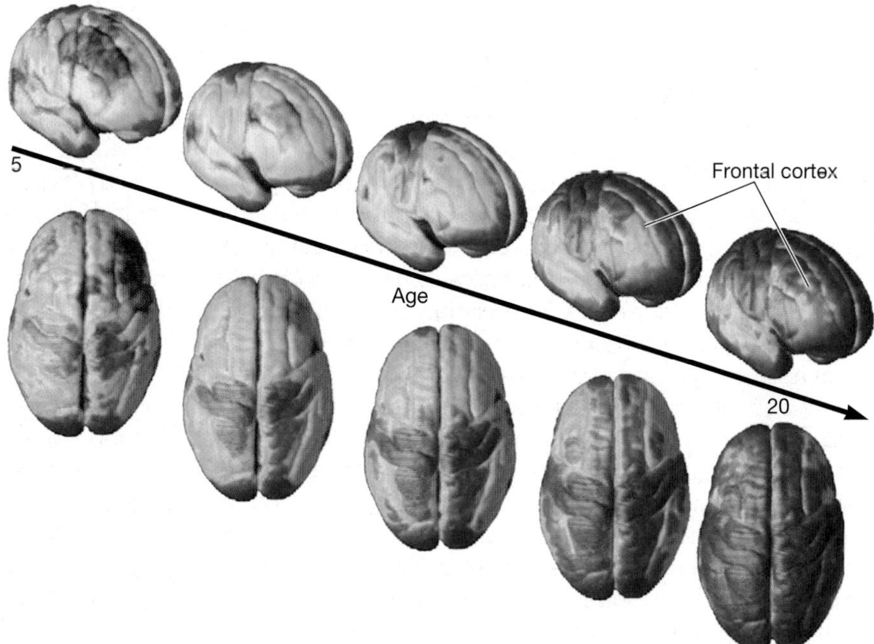

Figure 5.27 Cortical Thinning Continues throughout Adolescence Repeated measures from many people reveal that the top layer of cortex grows thinner during the transition from childhood to maturity, and is not complete until about age 20. Yellow and red colors represent cortical regions that are changing rapidly; blue and purple indicate regions that are undergoing little or no change. (From Gogtay et al., 2004, courtesy of Nitin Gogtay.)

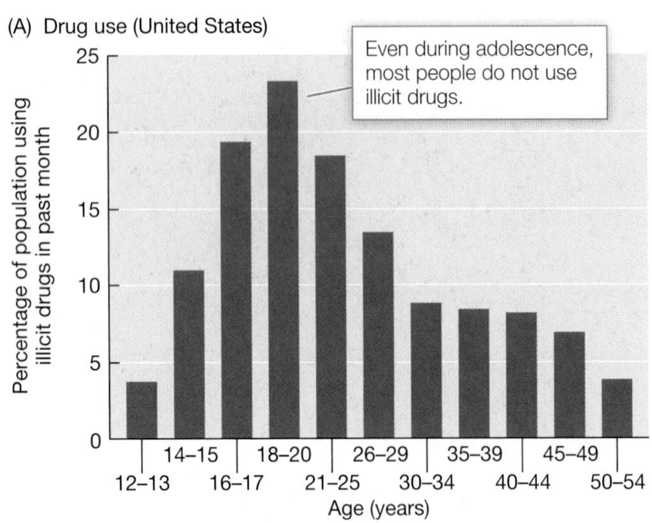

Figure 5.28 **Results of Risky Behavior in Adolescence** Although the vast majority of adolescents do not (A) use illicit drugs, (B) commit a major crime, or (C) get killed while driving a car, a person is more likely to engage in such behaviors during that period than at any other time in their lives. (A after Center for Mental Health Services, 2006; B after Blumstein, 1995; C after www.dft.gov.uk.)

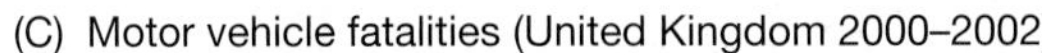

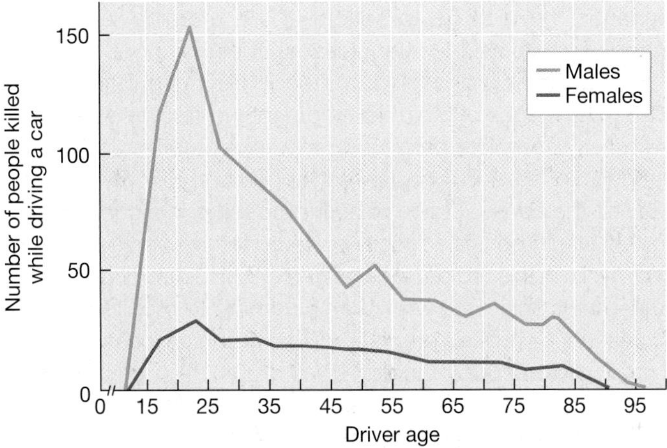

Adolescence can be a confusing and troubling time

Changes in the body and in legal status during adolescence present teenagers with ever greater independence and control. This greater autonomy is crucial for learning how to make good choices, which inevitably means teens have the opportunity to make poor choices, engaging in activity that is harmful or potentially harmful to themselves or others. Most adolescents never commit a crime, engage in risky sex, or have a major accident, but a person is more likely to engage in such behaviors during adolescence than at any other time in life (**Figure 5.28**; see also Lindberg et al., 2000). Laboratory studies suggest that teenagers make risky decisions in part because they underestimate how unpleasant some outcomes might be (Reyna & Brainerd, 2011). Perhaps they just haven't experienced enough negative outcomes in the "school of hard knocks"… yet.

A host of social changes accompany adolescence. Contrary to stereotype, most adolescents maintain good relationships with their parents (Arnett, 1999). However, most adolescents are also highly motivated to make friends and spend time with them. In some sense, this is a continuation of the attachment process we discussed earlier. The parent serves as a "safe base" to which the child returns after forays out into the world. With adolescence, those forays last longer and range farther. It is also somewhat similar to the way Harlow's young monkeys formed a vital, deep attachment to their mother (whether she was real or a model), and yet also sought out other young monkeys for playmates. The data from monkeys suggest that such peer interactions are valuable aids for social

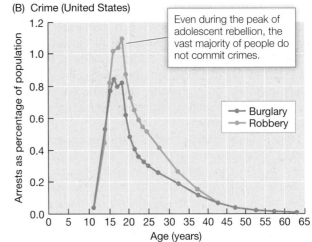

TABLE 5.2 Warning Signs of Suicide[a]

Threatening to hurt or kill oneself or talking about wanting to hurt or kill oneself
Looking for ways to kill oneself by seeking access to firearms, pills, or other means
Talking or writing about death, dying, or suicide when these actions are out of the ordinary for the person
Feeling hopeless
Feeling rage or uncontrolled anger or seeking revenge
Acting reckless or engaging in risky activities—seemingly without thinking
Feeling trapped—like there's no way out
Increasing alcohol or drug use
Withdrawing from friends, family, and society
Feeling anxious, agitated, or unable to sleep, or sleeping all the time
Experiencing dramatic mood changes
Seeing no reason for living or having no sense of purpose in life

Source: www.nimh.nih.gov/health/topics/suicide-prevention/suicide-prevention-studies/warning-signs-of-suicide.shtml

[a]Developed by the U.S. Department of Health and Human Services, these warning signs offer guidance about how to recognize someone at risk for suicide. If you or someone you know exhibits even a few of these signs, you can call the National Suicide Prevention Lifeline at 1-800-273-TALK (1-800-273-8255) at any time of day, any day of the year.

development. Even when a young monkey is raised by its real, nurturing mother, if it does not also have regular interactions with similar-age peers, it will have trouble getting along with other monkeys in adulthood. Almost all teens report that having good friends is important, in part because it helps them recover from setbacks in other parts of their life. Relations with their peers are also important for teenagers to form an identity, as we'll discuss in the next section. From this perspective, teenagers are walking a line between dependence and independence from their parents, learning to forge new relationships with their peers. Culture matters, too, of course. For example, adolescents in China spend less time with their peers, and more with their parents, than do teenagers in Western cultures (Chen & French, 2008).

Adolescents may experience mood swings that are more intense, on average, than at other stages of life. This may be one reason why some adolescents become depressed. Although it is true that many people recover on their own from adolescent depression, it nevertheless warrants attention since there is also a peak in suicide at these ages (Slama et al., 2009). Perhaps the saddest thing about suicide is that, even in people who have been depressed for some time, suicide is often an impulsive act. We know this because the few people who have survived an act that almost always leads to death, such as jumping off a bridge or building, almost always report that as soon as they had jumped they regretted following their impulse. Upon recovery, these individuals almost never attempt suicide again (Seiden, 1978). So intervention, preferably from warm and understanding parents as well as professionals, should always be considered. **Table 5.2** offers some warning signs of suicide that you can look out for in your friends (or in yourself), to help you decide when to intervene and potentially save someone's life.

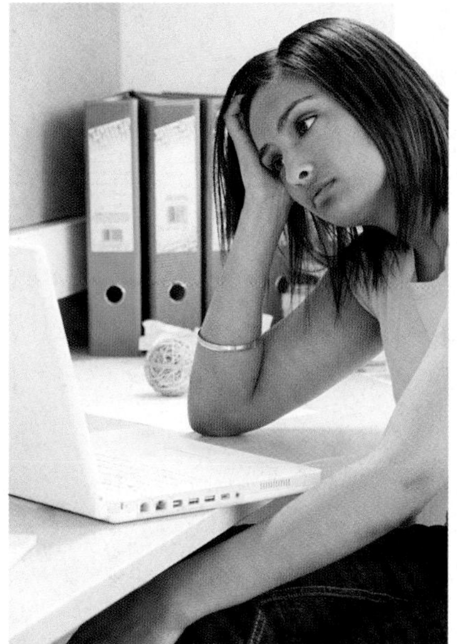

Depressed Teen Adolescence can be a challenging time of change that can sometimes be accompanied by depression.

If teenagers can work their way out of depression, their future prospects for avoiding depression are about the same as for anyone else. Unfortunately, it is not at all clear whether antidepressant drugs, which are modestly effective in adults, are effective in children and teenagers (Cox et al., 2012). Most double-blind studies find antidepressants to be no better than placebos at treating childhood and adolescent depression, as we discussed in Chapter 2. Furthermore, some studies indicate that adolescents taking antidepressants are more

morality A set of rules determining whether conduct is right or wrong.

likely to commit suicide than other depressed adolescents (Cox et al., 2012). One pitfall seems to be when teenagers who have been taking antidepressants decide on their own to quit. This can cause them to feel especially despondent and hopeless, which can lead to attempting suicide.

Many adolescents also experience growing conflicts with their families, as an adolescent's yearning for independence rubs against the parents' need to monitor and protect their children. The greater mood swings in adolescence seem to exacerbate the teen–parent conflicts. Just the same, most teenagers and their families manage to get along well enough to get through these trying years and emerge with strong, supportive relationships.

Adolescence is also a time of growing sexuality. As their bodies mature, taking on their adult form, including the capacity to reproduce, most young people take a greater interest in the opposite sex, both as friends and as romantic partners. We will discuss developing sexuality in some detail in Chapter 12, but for now note that while the hormones that arise at puberty clearly play a role in sexual drive, most people's sexual orientation (whether they are romantically attracted to the opposite sex or the same sex) arises well before puberty. If you ask people to recall the age at which they had their first "crush," a romantic attachment to a friend or entertainer, they report it was about age 10, so this cannot be driven by hormones (at least for the vast majority of people who begin adolescence after this age). Also, whichever sex was attractive to that person at age 10 is usually the sex they will be attracted to as adults, so sexual orientation seems to be set well before any overt sexual behavior arises (Herdt and Boxer, 1993).

We must learn to balance pleasing other people and defying them

Perhaps the biggest cognitive challenge for adolescence is the contuing development of a personal morality as they enter the adult world. **Morality** is a set of rules determining whether conduct is right or wrong, and for many people developing a personal morality is one of the most troublesome aspects of adolescence. There is no end of people telling adolescents what's right and wrong, but they don't all agree. In fact, sometimes authoritative, intelligent, responsible adults hold opposite views of what we should and should not do, so most people come to feel they have to work it out for themselves. Another difficult aspect of developing a personal morality is that sometimes there is a conflict of what we instantly and emotionally *feel* is the proper thing to do versus what seems proper when we try to use *reasoning*.

For American psychologist Lawrence Kohlberg (1927–1987), conflicting signals about right and wrong lie at the heart of a person's moral development. Kohlberg believed it is crucial that we each struggle with these questions if we are to achieve any lasting moral code. Just as Piaget felt there are distinct stages in cognitive reasoning that almost all children go through, Kohlberg felt there are distinct stages of moral reasoning that we all go through. And just as Piaget believed that children must master one stage of cognitive reasoning before they can reach the next, Kohlberg believed that we must achieve competence in each stage of moral reasoning before we can grasp the next.

To probe how people reason about moral questions, Kohlberg devised several hypothetical situations in which a fictitious person faces a moral dilemma. The following is one of Kohlberg's best-known dilemmas:

Heinz Steals the Drug

In Europe, a woman was near death from a special kind of cancer. There was one drug that the doctors thought might save her. It was a form of radium that a druggist in the same town had recently discovered. The drug was expensive to make, but the druggist was charging ten times what the drug cost him to make.

He paid $200 for the radium and charged $2,000 for a small dose of the drug. The sick woman's husband, Heinz, went to everyone he knew to borrow the money, but he could only get together about $1,000 which is half of what it cost. He told the druggist that his wife was dying and asked him to sell it cheaper or let him pay later. But the druggist said: "No, I discovered the drug and I'm going to make money from it." So Heinz got desperate and broke into the man's store to steal the drug for his wife. Should the husband have done that?

(Kohlberg, 1963, p. 19)

Kohlberg asked people what Heinz should do, and to explain why they felt that way. Whether they thought Heinz should steal the drug wasn't nearly as important to Kohlberg as the reasoning they used to reach their decision. Such interviews convinced him that there were progressive stages of moral reasoning.

Kohlberg proposed three levels of moral reasoning, achieved in stages (**Figure 5.29**). Young children use **preconventional moral reasoning**, based on personal consequences such as whether they'll be rewarded or punished. Kohlberg felt most adults develop **conventional moral reasoning**, which involves judging what's right and wrong based on society's expectations. Kohlberg held that few people achieve **postconventional moral reasoning** (sometimes called the "principled level"), in which rules are based on a social contract. At the highest level of moral reasoning, a person may reject rules even when the majority of citizens disagree.

Personal experience may have shaped Kohlberg's thinking, as we saw also with Piaget and Bowlby. During World War II, Kohlberg broke British laws by smuggling Jews who had fled Nazi Germany into Palestine (which was then ruled by Britain and would later become Israel). He made a leap to stage six reasoning in deciding the universal rights of individuals to escape unjust persecution overruled the laws that democratically governed Britain had devised to maintain order.

While Piaget felt that most children made the transition from one cognitive reasoning stage to the next at about the same age, Kohlberg believed people

preconventional moral reasoning Moral reasoning that weighs whether a behavior is "right" in terms of personal consequences.

conventional moral reasoning Moral reasoning that weighs whether a behavior is "right" in terms of what society expects people to do.

postconventional moral reasoning Moral reasoning, sometimes called the "principled level," in which rules and laws are part of a social contract, or that certain rules are universal, to be followed even if most people don't agree.

Moral stage	Should Heinz steal the drug?
Stage 6. Universal principles Even laws approved by the majority should be broken if they are unjust, violating universal rights of the individual.	No, the druggist has a right to charge what he likes for his efforts. Yes, Heinz's wife has a right to that medicine.
Stage 5. Social contract Laws should reflect what most people believe is right.	No, most people would say it is unjust to steal. Yes, the law should allow Heinz to take the medicine.
Postconventional ("principled") Are the laws just?	
Stage 4. Social order Society needs people to follow the rules, whatever they are.	No, we can't have people breaking into stores. Yes, we need people to survive cancer.
Stage 3. Conformity I want people to think well of me.	No, people would disapprove. Yes, people would think him heroic.
Conventional What does society expect?	
Stage 2. Seek reward I'll be nice to you so you'll be nice to me.	No, then he can go on TV and be famous because people will feel sorry for him. Yes, his wife will take care of him in return; she makes delicious pancakes.
Stage 1. Avoid punishment	No, he could go to jail. Yes, his children will hurt him if he doesn't.
Preconventional What are the personal consequences?	

Figure 5.29 Kohlberg's Six Stages of Moral Development

Justice versus Caring Even if you think it is fair for someone who doesn't work to be homeless, you may still want to reduce his suffering.

could make transitions in moral reasoning at just about any point in life. Kohlberg's depiction of moral development has been criticized. First, research has shown that whether a given child behaves according to preconventional or conventional morality can vary depending, for example, on whether an action would result in someone getting hurt, or simply be different from what other people do (Turiel, 2002). Second, some criticize Kohlberg's emphasis on *justice* as opposed to *caring* (Gilligan, 1982). From a caring orientation, the three stages of moral development can be seen as (1) what's good or bad for only *me*, (2) what's good or bad for *other people*, and (3) what's good or bad for *everyone*, including me? Sometimes orientations of justice (what is fair?) can be in conflict with orientations of caring (is someone suffering?). For example, you may think it is fair for people who don't work to be homeless, yet you may still want to reduce their suffering. There's no objective way to determine whether justice or caring is "more moral" than the other; they represent two different ways to guide our behavior.

5.3 SUMMARY

- During *adolescence* humans reach the landmark of *puberty*, when they become biologically capable of reproduction. *Hormones* secreted from the gonads at this stage drive the development of *secondary sex characteristics*, which signal the individual and the world that the person is entering the adult world.
- In modern times, the age of puberty has declined steadily, but no one knows why.
- Adolescence brings a final spurt of physical growth and changes in many physiological processes, such as sleep habits.
- The brain undergoes continued development in adolescence, especially in the frontal cortex. Some research indicates that immaturity of the frontal cortex may explain why adolescents are more likely to engage in risky, even life-threatening, behaviors.
- Peer relations are especially important to adolescents, in part because they are at an age when they are undergoing changes in moral reasoning.
- Kohlberg identified three levels of moral reasoning: *preconventional moral reasoning*, based on personal consequences; *conventional moral reasoning*, based on society's expectations; and *postconventional* (or principled) *moral reasoning*, which questions whether society's rules and laws are just.

REVIEW QUESTIONS

1. What changes happen in the body and brain during adolescence?
2. What factors have been proposed to affect the age of menarche?
3. Describe Kohlberg's six stages of moral development.

Food for Thought

The question in Kohlberg's hypothetical situation of what Heinz should do to save his wife has arisen recently in real life. Millions of people in Africa with AIDS would benefit from drugs that are prohibitively expensive for them.

Should drug companies be forced to give their drugs to poor people suffering from AIDS?

Things to Learn

- Erickson's stages of psychosocial development
- Effects of age on mental processes
- Loss of fluid intelligence coupled with gain in crystallized intelligence
- Risk factors and brain changes underlying Alzheimer's disease

5.4 Adulthood and Beyond

Reaching adulthood is certainly a milestone, but development doesn't stop there. We may bemoan the changes that happen to the body from this point on, but the mind continues to grow and, in many ways, improve as we grow older. Only in our elder years do we lose ground in some areas of cognition, although we'll see there are compensations in other areas. First we'll discuss Erikson's theory about how our relationships with other people change as we grow. This theory includes the entire life span, but we'll focus on the adult stages. Then we'll describe the changes in sensory systems, memory, and skill as adults age. Finally we'll review the psychological events of old age, which should be of special interest to you, as many of today's college students are projected to live to 100.

Erikson identified eight stages in the development of our relationships with others

Psychologist Erik Erikson (1902–1994) suggested that a human life could be divided into at least eight stages of development marked by shifts in our relationships with other people (Erikson, 1950) (**Table 5.3**). Erikson felt that these **stages of psychosocial development** were progressive—that experiencing one stage tended to lead to the next. However, as with Piaget's cognitive stages, where a child may use one level of reasoning for some problems and another level of reasoning for others, a person may show signs of being in one or more of the psychosocial stages at the same time, depending on which social relationship is under consideration.

Erikson describes the stages of psychosocial development as being characterized by tension: we are often torn between opposing ways of interacting with other people. For example, at the infant stage, a baby wavers between trusting and mistrusting her caregivers. We can't say which she *ought* to do, or which choice will be *best* for her, because that depends on the characteristics of her parents. If they are unreliable, then the baby might do well to note this. Erikson felt that the infant stage would successfully resolve when parents behave in a reliable, warm fashion so the baby learns that she can trust her caregivers, and that this lesson would help the baby in her future relationships. We've seen Erikson's prediction borne out in experiments demonstrating that infants with a secure attachment (caused in part by having a trustworthy caregiver) tend to have more satisfying friendships later in life. Similarly, for each subsequent psychosocial stage in which we are in tension between different ways of relating to people, successful resolution depends on finding the correct middle ground, which depends to some extent on the behavior of those around us. Take the time to review Table 5.3 before reading on.

One criticism of Erikson's theory is that it was not based on empirical studies, but inspired by study of biographies of famous people and by Sigmund Freud's

stages of psychosocial development Erik Erikson's proposed progressive stages of human development in which we decide how to behave with regard to others.

TABLE 5.3 Erikson's Eight Stages of Psychosocial Development

Stage	Age	Conflicting tendencies	Issue to resolve	Relationships
Infant	0–2	Trust versus distrust	Whom can I trust?	Mother, usually
Toddler	2–3	Autonomy versus shame	How can I do what I want without feeling bad about myself?	Parents
Preschooler	4–6	Initiative versus guilt	What can I do without causing trouble?	Family
Preadolescent	7–12	Industry versus inferiority	What activities am I good at? How do I compare with others?	Peers, family
Adolescent	13–19	Identity versus role confusion	Of all the social roles, which ones fit me and how can I develop a role that is uniquely my own?	Peers
Young adult	20s	Intimacy versus isolation	Whom can I trust with intimacy and love?	Peers, partner
Middle adult	30s–50s	Generativity versus stagnation	How can I continue to grow as a person?	Coworkers, family
Elder	60s+	Integrity versus despair	How can I feel content with my life, so I can face death calmly?	Family, community

Teenagers and Young Adults Are in the Process of Shaping Their Identity Many young people are working out the role they want to play, both in real life and in role-playing events.

theories (which were also based on anecdotes rather than experiments). However, the psychosocial stages have (so far) withstood the test of time, as they resonate with most people's personal experience of life. As we review them, see if you can relate them to your own life experience (so far).

At the second stage, Erikson describes the toddler as being pulled between autonomy (self-guidance) and shame as she moves about and interacts with the world. Too much autonomy, doing whatever she pleases, will strain her relationships with her parents, but finding it too shameful to take initiative and try something new will limit her development. Toddlers sometimes seem incredibly willful and hard to handle at this stage, which is why it is sometimes called "the terrible twos." They really dislike hearing the word "no" but really enjoy saying it!

In Erikson's third stage, preschoolers are described as being torn between initiative and guilt as they interact with their family and people outside the family. Preadolescents, in the fourth stage, have to deal with feelings of industry and competence versus feeling inferior as they learn about their own strengths and weaknesses while interacting with their peers, who are engaging in the same self-evaluation, and family.

Adolescents are in the fifth stage, torn between developing an **identity**, a consistent sense of who they are, and role confusion about what they should be. Adolescents may "try on" various social roles to see which fit them best. For this stage, the most important relationships are with peers. It is during adolescence that most people form a particular identity that seems to shape many of their subsequent decisions about how to conduct themselves and what to do with their lives. For Erikson, the *adolescent formation of identity is crucial* because it will continue to guide the individual's concept of self and therefore all future behavior, especially interactions with other people.

In Erikson's sixth stage the young adult is torn between seeking intimacy and isolation. At this stage most people seek out a partner in every sense of the word: a coworker in building a particular life as well as a sexual intimate. This is also the stage when people try to work out how they will earn a living. Young adulthood can be an anxious time of job seeking, trying to find one in which to excel and meet economic goals. Few people entering young adulthood have set realistic economic goals; many don't fully understand how much it costs to support themselves and just how difficult making money really is.

These days, the sixth stage that Erickson called young adulthood is sometimes referred to as **emerging adulthood** (Arnett, 2000), with its own stages: (1) deciding who you are and what you want; (2) moving away from home; (3) trying to make your own decisions about your future; (4) taking responsibility for yourself but still feeling "in-between," or not quite an adult; and (5) having a vision of what you want and feeling optimistic about life (Arnett, 2004).

By the time they have reached middle adulthood, many people have fairly stable lives. They may have an intimate partner, perhaps are starting a family, and have worked out a career. At this stage the challenge is to continue to grow as a person when so many life goals have been met. It is during this stage that people may experience a "midlife crisis" if they find they are dissatisfied with their job or partner, or worry that they have not accomplished enough in their careers. One response is to improve on those fronts, seeking challenges in one's career and strengthening relationships with one's partner and other people. Some people devote more time to children or to unrelated young people.

Erikson described quests for new relationships and challenges as a *generative response*, as in generating new life material. The opposite response is to *stagnate*: to persist in stale relationships, slog along on the job in the same old way. Stagnation can be self-centered, with a great deal of dissatisfaction with life, little effort to improve it, and little interest in the plight of other people. The generative response, in contrast, often involves investing in the next generation, helping along one's own children, younger colleagues at work, and/or

identity In this context, a consistent sense of who one is and should be.

emerging adulthood The transition from adolescence to full adulthood.

social institutions in the community. The eighth and final stage of life is to prepare for the inevitable end. The tension at this stage is between *despair*, giving up on life as we obsess over our coming death, and *integrity*, learning to be satisfied with our life, accepting its inevitable decline and focusing on those aspects of life that still have meaning and purpose for us. For Erikson this contentment with our life and sense that we have made a contribution is integrity, and offers the perspective of wisdom. This perspective brings an expanded sense of belonging, not just to the family and community, but to the world and humanity as a whole.

As you review these stages in Table 5.3, note that they also represent a progressive expansion in the sphere of social relations in the far-right column, "Relationships." The infant usually focuses on one primary caregiver, the toddler on both parents, younger children on the entire family, older children on schoolmates and family, and so on, until the final stages when a person may take an interest in the local and even global community. Another aspect to consider is that in the first stages of life a successful resolution depends very much on our environment, especially the behavior of others. As infants we can't learn to trust our parents if they aren't reliable, and as children we can't figure out our strengths and weaknesses if we are offered a poor education. But as we progress in life, successful resolution is less dependent on what *others* do and more dependent on what *we* do. For Erikson, one of the most important tasks for our psychosocial development is to become strong individuals who take charge of our lives.

menopause The time a woman's menstrual periods stop, around age 50.

The aging mind slows down but continues to grow

In many ways, young adulthood represents a peak in development, a time when our perceptual and motor skills are finely honed. These characteristics do fade with time. Yet we'll see that despite the decline of many abilities as we progress through the middle years, in terms of overall satisfaction with life, old age can be the most rewarding period of life.

There are definitely some drawbacks to physical aging. Our skin grows less supple, which is why older people may need to lick their fingers to pry pages apart when college students rarely do. Hair thins and grows gray. Muscles become weaker. Exercise can greatly combat this decline, but more and more exercise becomes necessary to postpone the inevitable. Reproductive systems begin to shut down, so in women the menstrual cycle stops, a process called **menopause**, at about age 50. With menopause comes the gradual decline of ovarian hormones such as estrogens and progesterone. These changes may cause "hot flashes," episodes when a woman's body suddenly feels uncomfortably warm. The emotional responses to menopause are extremely variable; some women report feeling irritable and agitated, whereas others report feeling calm and relieved, even energetic, after menopause. For men, the shutdown of the reproductive system is much more gradual but also begins at about age 50, as testosterone levels slowly decline. As our immune system ages, we become more susceptible to cancer and some infections such as pneumonia.

Ego Integrity The challenge of getting older is to celebrate your accomplishments and to feel fulfilled.

Things aren't much better when we consider sensory systems. Young adulthood certainly represents the peak in our sensory organ capabilities. For example, our hearing depends on the hair cells in the inner ear (see Chapter 6) that are mechanically stimulated so vigorously throughout life that sometimes they wear out and die. Because we mammals (unlike birds, for example) cannot make new hair cells in adulthood, our hearing can only go downhill after we reach adulthood (**Figure 5.30A**).

Similarly, vision fades beginning at middle age, as the lens of the eye ages and photoreceptors in the eye are lost. Cataracts impede and distort light entering the eye. Many people are drawn to brighter and brighter colors as they grow

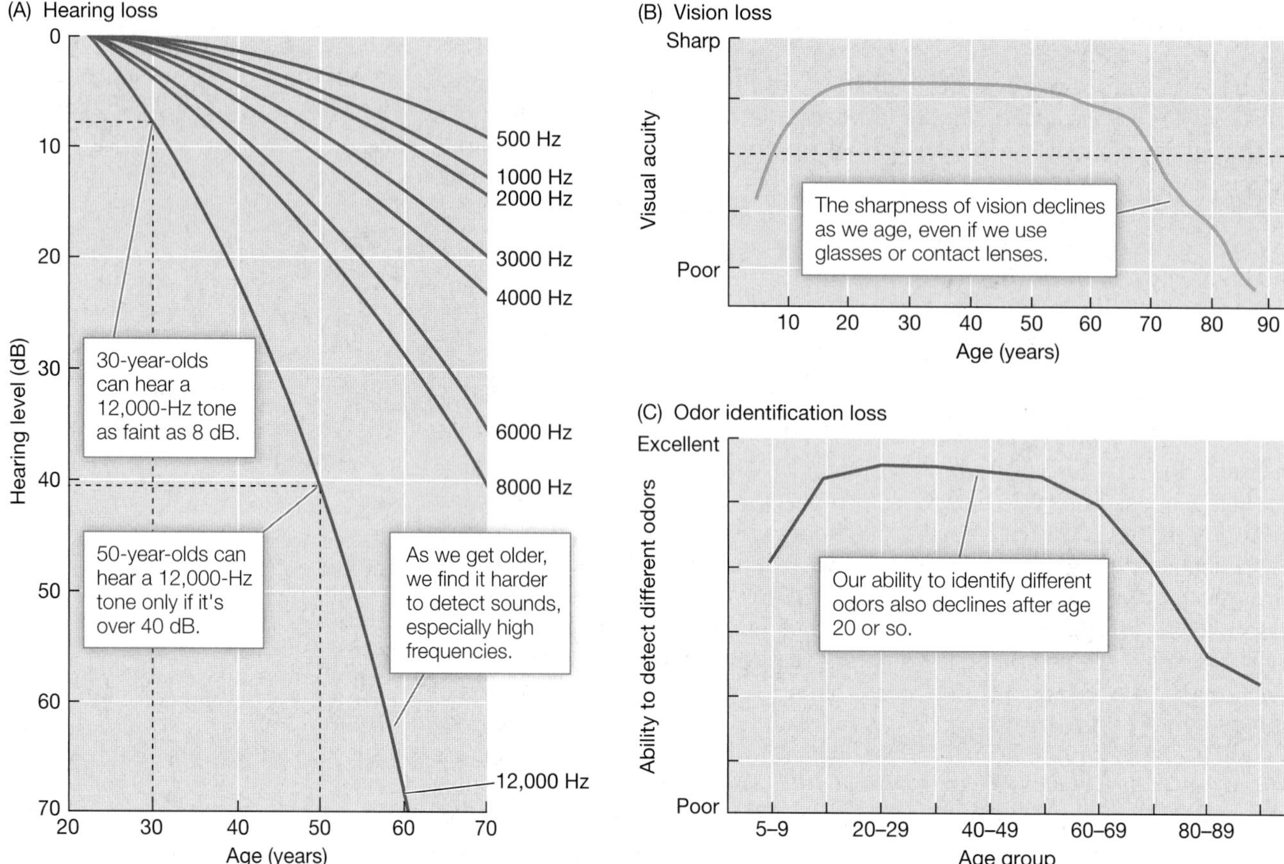

Figure 5.30 Progressive Loss of Sensory Capacity (A after Sound Research Laboratories, 1991; B, C after Doty et al., 1984.)

older, and this may reflect the dulling of colors by cataracts (**Figure 5.30B**); colors that older people find appealing may seem garish to younger people. Also, the proteins in the lens become progressively less flexible, so by age 40 most people find it difficult to focus on nearby objects, a condition called **presbyopia** ("aging" + "eyes"). People with presbyopia typically either hold menus and newspapers farther away or resort to reading glasses. Likewise, senses of taste and smell grow duller after middle age (**Figure 5.30C**). This change may be why some people are drawn to spicier foods as they age.

The wear on sensory and motor systems contributes to some declines in information processing, for example **reaction times**, such as the measure of how quickly a person can hit a button after seeing a light come on, or how quickly someone can hit a brake pedal after a light comes on (**Figure 5.31A**). This decline is probably one reason why drivers 75 and older are much more likely to have an automobile accident per mile driven (**Figure 5.31B**). There are also losses in the brain. We now know that some brain regions continue to gain new neurons in adults, but as we grow older more neurons are dying than are getting replaced, so many brain regions have a net loss of neurons. Likewise, the average length of dendrites grows shorter with aging, indicating that there is also a net loss of synapses as synapse rearrangement continues with age (Uylings & de Brabander, 2002). This means that overall brain weight peaks by about age 20 and shrinks by nearly 10% by age 90. Interestingly, some brain regions show more shrinkage than others, and we don't understand why. What we do know is that keeping physically and mentally active can slow down brain shrinkage as we grow old (Burns et al., 2008).

There is also a progressive decline in memory skills, such as recalling a list of words, either immediately after studying the list or after a delay. As with most

presbyopia A condition in which most people over 40 find it difficult to focus on nearby objects.

reaction time The amount of time it takes a subject to initiate some action after a predetermined signal.

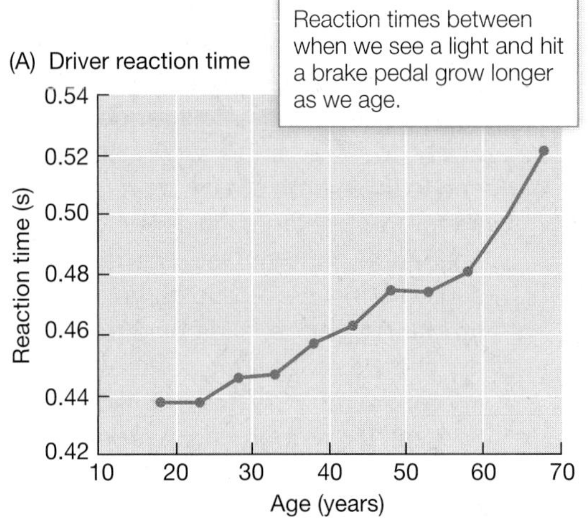

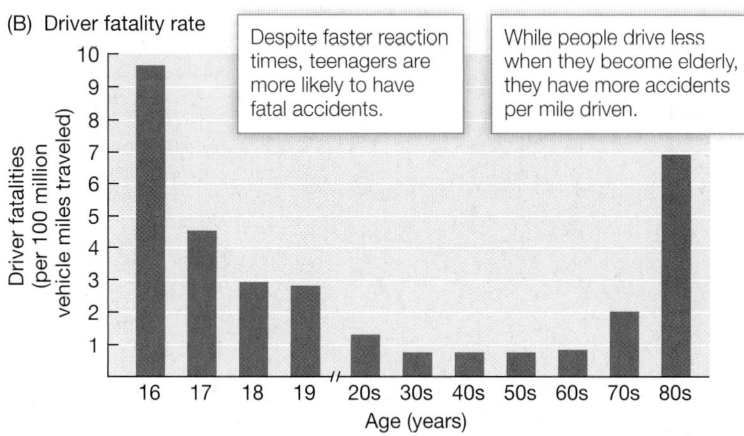

Figure 5.31 Reaction Times Go Up as We Age, and So Does Our Accident Rate Despite their greater risk per mile driven, elderly drivers are less likely to have fatal accidents (see Figure 5.28C), because they drive many fewer miles than younger drivers. (A after Olson, 1991; B after Fatality Analysis Reporting System of the National Highway Traffic Safety Administration, n.d.)

psychological characteristics, there is a great deal of variability, with some people showing memory declines at earlier ages than others. What we know is that in normally aging people there is a correlation between the strength of memory and the size of a brain region, the hippocampus, which is important for memory (see Chapter 9). The more the hippocampus shrinks, the faster memory declines (**Figure 5.32**). Those people who keep their mental edge as they age appear to do so by reorganizing brain circuits (Cabeza et al., 2002), an example of plasticity later in life.

This loss of brain tissue is probably responsible for the decline in cognitive processing tasks that do not depend on sharp eyes or fast muscles. For example, older people take longer than younger people to learn perceptual puzzles, to memorize lists of words, and to beat video games. Older adults also find it harder and harder to recall the names of people and objects, or the titles of books and movies, often having that frustrated feeling that the word is on the tip of their tongue. So clearly there are declines in some cognitive functions. But in other areas the elderly outperform younger adults, such as knowing the meanings of words, and general knowledge of historical events and how public institutions work. So is there a decline in intelligence with aging or not?

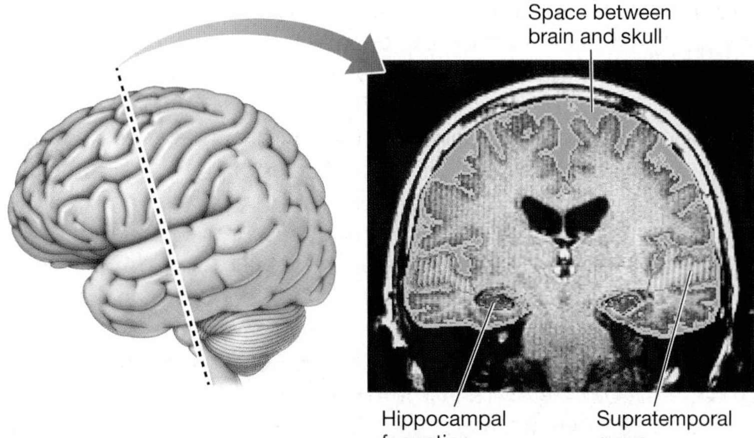

Figure 5.32 Hippocampal Shrinkage Correlates with Memory Decline in Normally Aging People Scientists measured the volume of three different variables: the space between the brain surface and the skull (green), a region called the supratemporal gyrus (orange), and the hippocampus (red). Only hippocampus volume correlated with memory performance. (From Golomb et al., 1994; MRI courtesy of James Golomb.)

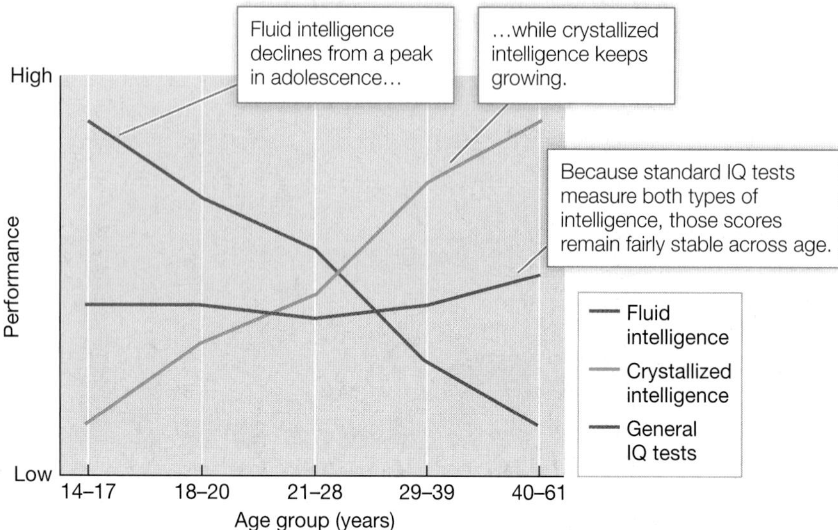

Figure 5.33 Changes in Intelligence with Age (After Horn, 1970.)

To resolve the paradox in how aging affects intelligence, psychologists realized that there are two different kinds of intelligence. **Fluid intelligence** is the ability to think and reason abstractly and to solve problems that are presented for the first time. Fluid intelligence is needed to perform well when first presented with a new video game. **Crystallized intelligence** is learning from past experience, based on a store of facts (Moran, 2013). Crystallized intelligence is great for recognizing words, faces, and historical references. If you're trying to solve a crossword puzzle, crystallized intelligence is more helpful than fluid intelligence. We will discuss these two kinds of intelligence further in Chapter 11.

fluid intelligence The capacity to reason logically and solve new problems, independent of what you know already.

crystallized intelligence The knowledge a person has acquired and the ability to use it appropriately.

perceptual speed How quickly we can detect and process stimuli.

Young adults have greater fluid intelligence than elderly people, but the elderly tend to have greater crystallized intelligence. Fluid intelligence peaks in adolescence but then begins to decline. In contrast, crystallized intelligence just keeps growing throughout adulthood (**Figure 5.33**). Only in extreme old age, or in the case of a pathology such as Alzheimer's disease (which we'll discuss shortly), does crystallized intelligence falter with age.

Over the past 50 years or so that psychologists have studied fluid and crystallized intelligence, the assumption has been that fluid intelligence somehow represented a core, essential feature of a person's brain, whereas crystallized intelligence could be influenced by many things in the environment: a warm and stimulating family, a quality education, an intellectually stimulating job. But there is a controversial report that at least some aspects of fluid intelligence can be improved with training (Jaeggi et al., 2008; Redick et al., 2013; see Section 11.3). Perhaps it is possible to regain some aspects of fluid intelligence in old age.

One of the remarkable things about memory, which we will discuss in detail in Chapter 9, is the seemingly limitless capacity that the brain has for storing bits of knowledge. Our ability to keep picking up more facts as we age, despite the gradual loss of neurons, dendrites, and synapses, attests to this remarkable storage capacity. But there's no denying that we lose our speed for processing new situations, solving new problems, or simply reacting to stimuli (see Figure 5.31A). Measures of **perceptual speed**—how quickly we can detect and process stimuli—steadily decline with age. For example, in visual tests where subjects have to find particular images on a page and compare them quickly and accurately, researchers found that younger adults do better than older adults (**Figure 5.34**; Schaie & Willis, 1993). These same researchers found that the deficit in fluid intelligence performance in elderly adults could be greatly relieved simply by making the tests untimed. When they had more time, elderly people performed as well as young adults, another indication that cognitive processing slows down with age.

So is life worth living with slower cognition? In fact, the elderly are as likely to be satisfied with their lives as young adults or middle-aged people are. No matter what age group you survey, about 80% of subjects are satisfied with their lives as a whole.

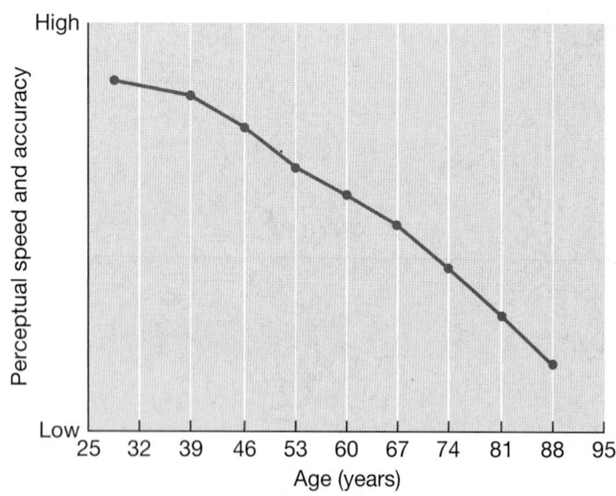

Figure 5.34 Perceptual Speed in Vision Declines with Age (After Schaie & Willis, 1993.)

■ **TABLE 5.4 Principles of a Good Death**

To know when death is coming, and to understand what can be expected
To be able to retain control of what happens
To be afforded dignity and privacy
To have control over pain relief and other symptom control
To have choice and control over where death occurs (at home or elsewhere)
To have access to information and expertise of whatever kind is necessary
To have access to any spiritual or emotional support required
To have access to hospice care in any location, not only in a hospital
To have control over who is present and who shares the end
To be able to issue advance directives which ensure wishes are respected
To have time to say goodbye, and control over other aspects of timing
To be able to leave when it is time to go, and not to have life prolonged pointlessly

Source: Smith, 2000.

For the elderly, this satisfaction withstands the gradually shrinking social circle as friends and family members die. Of course the death of a partner, child, or close friend has an impact, triggering grief and **bereavement**, the sense of loss and longing for someone who has died. There are no universal patterns of how people deal with bereavement, but people generally find the first year after losing a partner or child to be especially turbulent and dissatisfying. Yet most people recover from grief eventually and invest even more time in their remaining social contacts, which they find more rewarding than ever (Carstensen, 2006). You might be surprised to learn that the fear of death does not generally increase as people grow older. When asked, people are not more afraid of death as they grow elderly, but they do want a "good death": a death with dignity, love, and physical contact, and without pain (**Table 5.4**).

Paradoxically, despite all these losses with age, when asked, the population of people who report the most happiness are older people (Scheibe & Carstensen, 2010; Isaacowitz & Blanchard-Fields, 2012). Many elderly people say they are the happiest they have ever been, as we will discuss further in Chapter 13. For some people, old age also offers a hazard, as we discuss next.

The Cutting Edge

If We Are Lucky, We Face Aging and the Possibility of Alzheimer's Disease

As we've seen, elderly people remain satisfied with life, despite the slowing of cognitive processes and the increased difficulty of recalling names. So if we are lucky enough to avoid serious accidents or diseases, we will reach this stage of life. But some people begin to show signs of **dementia**, the progressive decline in cognitive function caused by damage or disease rather than normal aging. Dementia is not a disease, but a cluster of symptoms. It usually begins with forgetfulness, but forgetfulness alone is not dementia. In dementia, as the forgetfulness grows, several other problems arise, such as impairment in language, perception, or judgment, or a change in personality. As the memory decline progresses, the person with dementia will not be able to remember what he or she was doing just a few minutes ago, cannot follow a conversation, and may repeat the same thing over and over. With such severe memory impairment, the person may be easily confused, especially in unfamiliar settings.

A minority of cases of dementia are treatable if caused by a brain tumor or vitamin deficiency. But the two major causes of dementia, either a series of small strokes that destroy tissue in a broad range of brain regions or Alzheimer's disease, cannot be treated and tend to get worse with time. **Alzheimer's disease** (**AD**), the most common cause of dementia in older people, is the result of a buildup of abnormal clumps of dead and dying neurons called **neuritic plaques** in the brain. At present the only

bereavement The sense of loss and longing for someone who has died.

dementia The progressive decline in cognitive function caused by damage or disease rather than normal aging.

Alzheimer's disease (AD) The most common cause of dementia in older people.

neuritic plaques Abnormal clumps of dead and dying neurons seen in brains of people with AD.

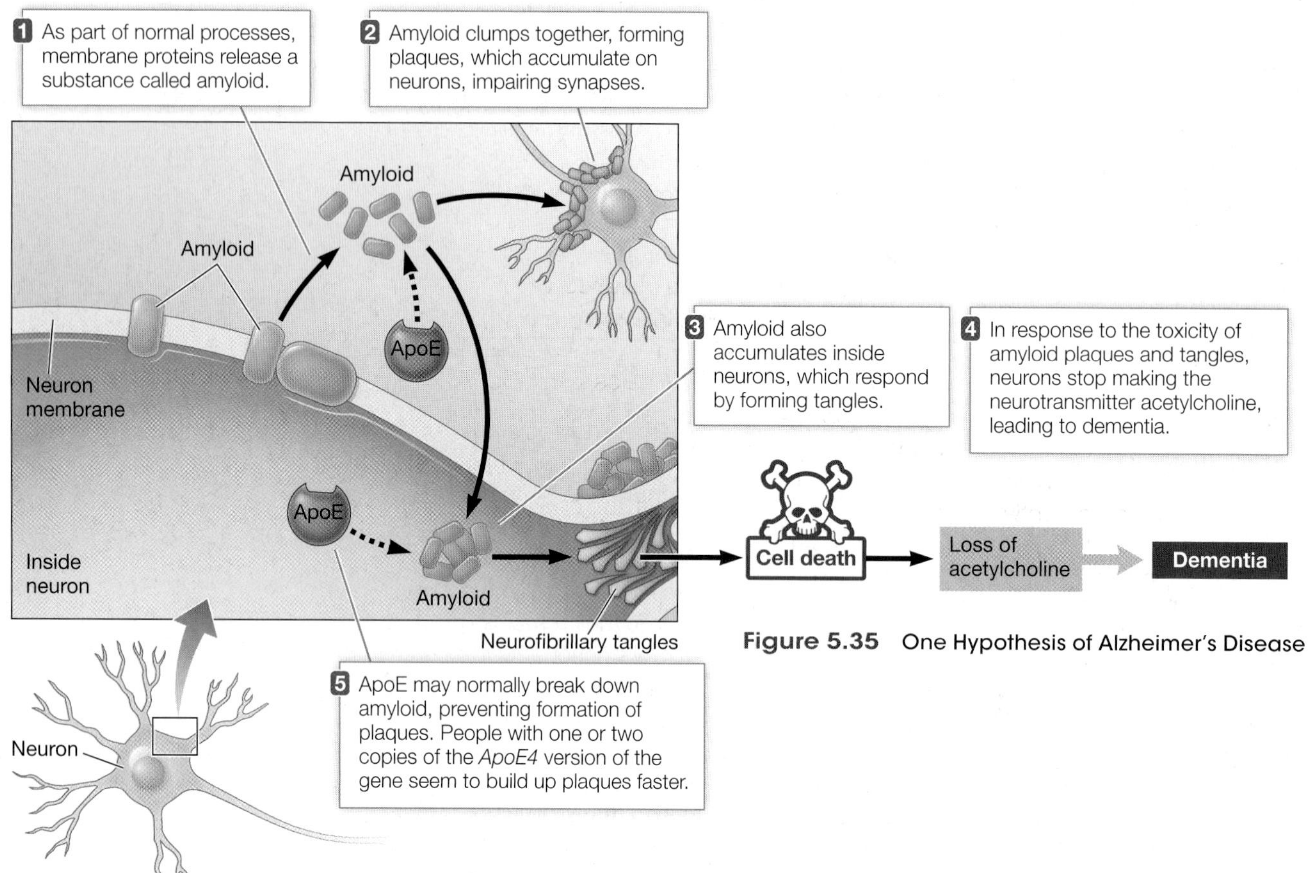
1 As part of normal processes, membrane proteins release a substance called amyloid.
2 Amyloid clumps together, forming plaques, which accumulate on neurons, impairing synapses.
Amyloid
Amyloid
ApoE
Neuron membrane
3 Amyloid also accumulates inside neurons, which respond by forming tangles.
4 In response to the toxicity of amyloid plaques and tangles, neurons stop making the neurotransmitter acetylcholine, leading to dementia.
ApoE
Inside neuron
Amyloid
Cell death
Loss of acetylcholine
Dementia
Neurofibrillary tangles
Neuron
5 ApoE may normally break down amyloid, preventing formation of plaques. People with one or two copies of the *ApoE4* version of the gene seem to build up plaques faster.

Figure 5.35 One Hypothesis of Alzheimer's Disease

way to be absolutely sure a person has AD is by seeing lots of these neuritic plaques in brain tissue after death. Short of that, an elderly person with progressive dementia and no other known causes (such as strokes) is presumed to have AD. Scientists know a lot about factors that lead to neuritic plaques: brain cells release a protein called **amyloid**, which accumulates in pockets and causes the plaques (**Figure 5.35**). We also know that there are strong genetic contributions. Some versions of a protein called presenilin cause more amyloid to be released, and the most common mutations associated with AD are in the gene for presenilin (Loy et al., 2013). Another protein, called ApoE, normally cleans up amyloid. There are at least four versions of the gene for this protein, and people who inherit a gene for the fourth version (*ApoE4*) are much more likely to develop AD. A person who inherits two copies of *ApoE4* is even more likely to develop AD and to develop the disorder earlier in life (Cosentino et al., 2008). There is no cure for AD, but there are some medications that delay the progressive dementia somewhat.

You might think that everyone who lives long enough would develop AD, but there's reason to think otherwise. First, sometimes AD appears before the age of 60, in so-called early onset AD. Also, while the chances of a person developing AD go up from the age of 60 to 85 or 90, people who reach 90 years of age without signs of dementia become increasingly *less* likely to develop AD (Breitner et al., 1999). These finding suggest that AD is not simply the wearing out of the brain, but a specific disease, to which some people are more susceptible than others.

But perhaps the best evidence that AD does not represent the wear and tear of a brain at work is the fact that many studies have shown that

amyloid A protein that accumulates to cause plaques in AD.

having an active brain makes you less likely to develop AD. We mentioned earlier that remaining physically active combats brain shrinkage with age. It also helps avoid AD. After just 6 months of a home-based program of mild physical activity, elderly people with memory impairment (but not dementia) showed improved memory performance (Lautenschlager et al., 2008). In one study, as little exercise as 20 minutes of walking, three times a week, significantly cut the risk of dementia and delayed the onset of symptoms. There is also excellent evidence that remaining intellectually active delays the onset of AD. For example, after controlling for other variables, including education, people who took part in leisure activities, especially intellectual activities such as playing bridge, being in a book group, or working crosswords, displayed a later onset of AD symptoms (Helzner et al., 2007). Finally, participating in social activities also helps preserve cognitive function in aging (Glei et al., 2005), probably because of the extensive intellectual stimulation provided by interacting with a complicated, active force—a human being. Unless a cure for AD arises, your best course of action to avoid dementia is to build up and maintain a rich, intellectually stimulating life. To that end, finding a compatible, outgoing, intellectually stimulating, physically active mate and/or circle of friends would be a good idea. You can't start thinking about these things too soon.

5.4 SUMMARY

- Erik Erikson's eight *stages of psychosocial development* emphasize the importance of social relations to the developing mind. At each stage we must choose between two different ways of interacting with others. Successful resolution of each stage depends to some extent on the social environment.
- During adolescence, successful resolution should lead to the development of an *identity*—the role in life that we take on—and will guide our decisions about mates and careers.
- The challenge of middle adulthood is to continue to grow and avoid stagnation, whereas in old age we must choose between despair and integrity, a satisfaction with a life well lived.
- There are many changes in the body with aging, including a dulling of the senses, loss of *perceptual speed*, slowing of *reaction times*, and a gradual decline in *fluid intelligence*.
- However, there is continuous growth in *crystallized intelligence* and continued satisfaction with life. Even into old age, people continue to build on crystallized intelligence and are satisfied with their lives.
- Some elderly people develop *dementia*, a progressive loss of cognitive function that is usually caused by *Alzheimer's disease*.
- Although there are genetic factors that affect the probability of developing Alzheimer's disease, physical activity and intellectual activity can help stave off this and other forms of dementia.

REVIEW QUESTIONS

1. Describe the tension between two ways of interacting with other people in Erikson's eight stages of psychosocial development.
2. What do we lose, and gain, as we grow old?
3. Describe the symptoms of Alzheimer's disease and the steps that have been shown to postpone the onset of those symptoms.

Food for Thought

Can you describe how an elderly person you know has managed to resolve the conflict between integrity and despair? What can you learn from their example that might sustain you one day when you grow old?

Developmental Psychology

Growing Up Alone

In the late 1790s, people in the small town of Aveyron in southern France found a naked boy in the woods who seemed to be wild, living on his own. His body had numerous scars, and townspeople guessed him to be about 12 years old. They called the boy Victor, and a local physician, Jean-Marc Itard, tried to teach the boy to behave in a civilized fashion. Victor learned to understand some speech but, despite years of effort, learned to say only "milk" and "oh God!" (in French, of course).

In 1970 a heartbreaking incident in Los Angeles echoed Victor's case. A social worker encountered a young girl, "Genie," who didn't talk or pay attention to any of the people in the office. She rocked her body and walked curiously, holding up her hands and hopping like a bunny. The horrible truth was that this tiny girl, who looked to be 6 or 7 years old, was actually 13. She had been living alone, locked in a room in the back of a house, eating the small amount of food that was tossed in to her. Genie had spent her days strapped, naked, to a potty chair. At night she was diapered and placed in a cage with a chicken-wire lid. Her father, who had enforced Genie's abuse, committed suicide before facing criminal charges.

Ironically, the week after the discovery of Genie, a movie about Victor premiered in Los Angeles. *The Wild Child* vividly portrayed Victor's inability to use speech. Aware of this tragic precedent, a team of therapists and scientists assembled around Genie to provide her with every opportunity to recover. With proper nutrition, Genie quickly gained weight and grew taller. But the bigger job was to rescue her mind. Genie had almost no language—the only words she said were "stop it" and "no more." In addition to her repetitive rocking and strange "bunny walk," Genie would sometimes erupt into silent rages, hitting and tearing at her own body. She drooled and spat constantly, and masturbated openly and excessively. Could Genie recover from such a nightmarish upbringing?

Think Like a Psychologist:

Principles in Action

Whenever we encounter any interesting behavior we should consider the four principles. Here are some ways that the four principles relate to our opening story about Genie.

MACHINE

The mind is a product of a physical machine, the brain.

Genie was severely malnourished, which had to impede the development of her brain. Once she was rescued and provided adequate nutrition, her body recovered somewhat but it may have been too late for much physical recovery for her brain.

UNCONSCIOUS

We are consciously aware of only a small part of our mental activity.

Infantile amnesia means we cannot consciously recall our early childhood years, despite their profound influence on development and adult behavior. Robbed of language, Genie cannot tell us what she remembers of the early ordeal that had such a crippling effect on her mind.

SOCIAL

We constantly modify our behavior, beliefs, and attitudes according to what we perceive about the people around us.

Genie suffered from severe lack of social stimulation, especially the warm, comforting parental care that Harlow called love. This forever impeded her ability to interact normally with others.

EXPERIENCE

Our experiences physically alter the structure and function of the brain.

In the absence of language stimulation early in life, Genie's language development was profoundly impaired, she never quite learned how to string more than a few words together or show an understanding of grammar.

KEY TERMS

accommodation, 160
adaptation, 160
adolescence, 172
Alzheimer's disease (AD), 187
ambivalent attachment, 170
amyloid, 188
Asperger's syndrome, 163
assimilation, 160
attachment, 168
attention deficit hyperactivity disorder (ADHD), 159
autism, 163
avoidant attachment, 170
bereavement, 187
cell migration, 144
cognitive development, 158
concrete operational stage, 164
conservation, 163
constructivism, 160
conventional moral reasoning, 179
crystallized intelligence, 186
dementia, 187
developmental psychology, 144
differentiation, 144
disorganized attachment, 170
egocentrism, 162
embryo, 144
emerging adulthood, 182
fetal alcohol syndrome (FAS), 147
fetus, 144
fluid intelligence, 186
formal operational stage, 164
habituation, 155
habituation technique, 155
hormones, 172
identity, 182
imprinting, 166
infant, 150
infantile amnesia, 158
inner cell mass, 144
menarche, 172
menopause, 183
methylphenidate, 159
morality, 178
motor development, 151
neural tube, 144
neuritic plaques, 187
neurogenesis, 144
neuronal cell death, 144
object permanence, 161
perceptual speed, 186
plasticity, 149
postconventional moral reasoning, 179
preconventional moral reasoning, 179
preoperational stage, 162
presbyopia, 184
puberty, 172
reaction time, 184
Sally and Anne test, 163
schema, 161
secondary sex characteristics, 172
secure attachment, 170
sensitive periods, 149
sensorimotor stage, 161
simple reflexes, 150
stages of psychosocial development, 181
stranger anxiety, 166
strange situation, 168
sudden infant death syndrome (SIDS), 152
synapse rearrangement, 146
synaptogenesis, 144
temperament, 165
teratogen, 147
theory of mind, 162
visual cliff, 153
zygote, 144

QUIZ YOURSELF

1. The process by which neurons in the developing brain make connections with one another is called
   a. neurogenesis.
   b. differentiation.
   c. apoptosis.
   d. synaptogenesis.
2. Substances, like alcohol, that cause malformations in developing embryos are called
   a. depressants.
   b. teratogens.
   c. hormones.
   d. myelins.
3. The main reason newborn humans have reduced vision is because
   a. their eyes do not focus a sharp image.
   b. they cannot move their eyes very well.
   c. synapses in the back of the eye are immature.
   d. the front of their eyes are cloudy.
4. The relative inability of adults to remember events from their first few years of life is called
   a. infantile regression.
   b. infantile amnesia.
   c. habituation.
   d. SIDS.
5. The first of Piaget's stages of cognitive development is called the ________ stage.
   a. preoperational
   b. sensorimotor
   c. egocentric
   d. concrete operational
6. The tendency of young animals to follow a parent is called
   a. temperament.
   b. egocentrism.
   c. imprinting.
   d. anxiety.
7. In the strange situation, an infant who is upset when his mother leaves and rejects her when she returns is said to have a(n) ________ attachment pattern.
   a. secure
   b. recessive
   c. avoidant
   d. ambivalent
8. For Kohlberg, people who think some rules are universal and must be followed even if they break the law are using ________ moral reasoning.
9. The ability of the brain, especially the developing brain, to change in response to experience or other aspects of the environment is called ________.

1. d; 2. b; 3. c; 4. b; 5. b; 6. c; 7. d; 8. postconventional (or principled); 9. plasticity (or neural plasticity)

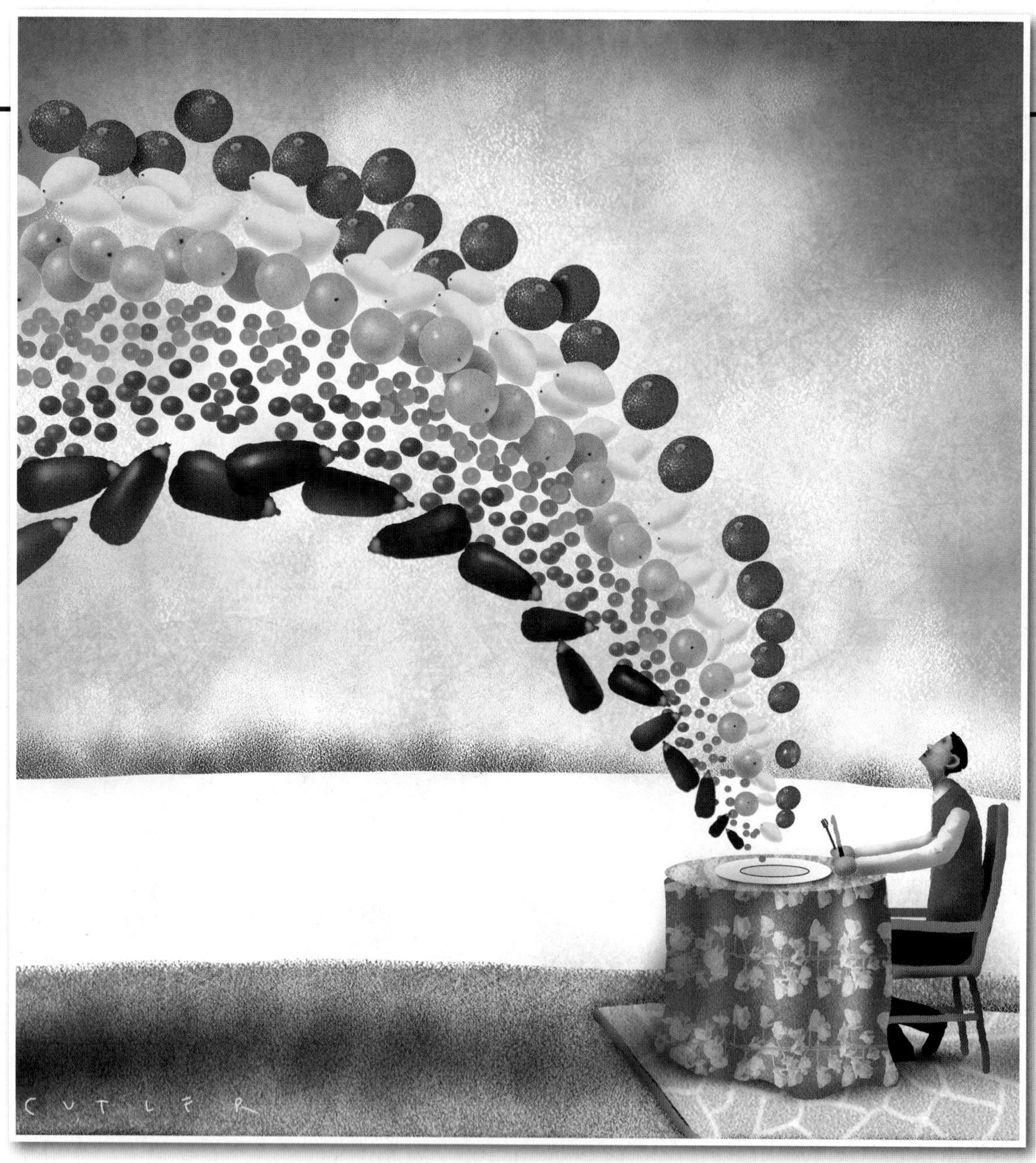
CUTLER

6 Sensation and Perception

No Pain, No Gain

Gail G. was a happy newborn. She slept easily and didn't cry much, but although her parents didn't know it at first, she had been born with a terrible, life-threatening condition—she cannot feel pain. Gail is now an active, happy teenager, but if you think a life without pain would be good, think again.

Gail has never been able to tell when she's hurting herself. As a baby, she would push her fingers into her eyes. Her parents tried restraints and putting goggles on her, but by the time she was 4, one eye was so severely damaged it had to be removed. When Gail's teeth came in, like most babies, she put her fingers in her mouth. But unlike other babies, Gail would bite her fingers to the bone, mutilating her fingers. Her parents had her baby teeth pulled (Gail didn't mind), reasoning that when her adult teeth came in, they could teach her to not bite herself. Gail's sister taught her to say "ouch" when she bumped something, so the family can make sure Gail's OK (Heckert, 2012). Unlike most people, when Gail injures herself, there's very little redness or swelling at the injury. This makes it even harder to tell when there's a problem. She broke her jaw as a toddler, and by the time the family found out, it was infected.

Gail's sensory problems are remarkably specific. On her skin she can still feel touch, heat, coolness, and vibrations. She just cannot feel pain. Perhaps this is why she has a generally sunny and happy disposition. You may be a cheerful person, but imagine how much cheerier you'd be if you'd never known pain, never felt ill. So on the one hand, her condition may shelter Gail from discomfort, but it may also keep her from ever being afraid. Does growing up without fear affect the developing mind?

Chapter Preview

sensation The process by which the nervous system detects the physical events around or inside us.

perception The experience we have as we process and interpret information from sensory cells.

percept The final interpretation of a stimulus.

stimulus (Pl. *stimuli*) Any physical event that affects a sensory receptor cell.

sensory receptor cells Also called *receptors*. Specialized sensory cells that detect stimuli.

In this chapter we'll find out how Gail came to have the dangerous disorder of painlessness. We'll also see that the experience of pain is complicated, because there are times when any one of us might feel no discomfort from an injury, even a life-threatening one. In these cases, we are not like Gail, who *never* feels pain (Heckert, 2012). Rather, in each situation our brain *determines* whether we will experience pain from an injury. This is not a conscious decision. Our brain normally has us experience pain upon injury because that is good for our long-term survival. But in some cases the brain spares us pain from a real injury, and in other cases the brain causes us pain when an injury isn't even there! We'll see that all pain is in our brain and, for the most part, pain is our friend.

We'll start this chapter by talking about principles seen in *all* sensory systems. We'll apply these general principles first to touch and pain, because in some ways these are the simplest sensory systems. Then we'll consider vision, which is so important that it makes use of nearly a third of the cortex. We'll follow that with a discussion about hearing, which is particularly helpful for communicating with other people. The chapter will conclude with the senses we use to detect chemicals in odors and tastes.

6.1 Sensory System Principles

Things to Learn

- Distinction between sensation and perception
- Characteristics of sensory receptor cells
- Principles of psychophysics, including absolute threshold
- Types of errors made when trying to detect signals amid noise
- Sensory adaptation

The world presents many opportunities and many hazards for every animal. You may stumble onto a tasty meal one moment, and meet some animal who thinks *you* are tasty the next. You may yearn for a mate, but you have to avoid bumping into a tree or walking off a cliff (or falling down a flight of stairs) as you search. Luckily, the world is full of physical events—sounds, odors, lights—that provide clues about what's going on around you. That is why natural selection has crafted remarkably sophisticated ways to detect nearby squeaks and far-off roars, hovering mosquitoes and distant mountains, fragrant fruits and repellent skunks. We rely heavily on our senses to make our way in the world. **Sensation** is the process by which the nervous system detects the physical events going on around us and inside us. We use sensory cells that are specialized to detect sounds, sights, and smells around us, as well as the position and movement of our body, and the aches and twinges inside us.

In psychology, sensation is distinguished from perception. **Perception** is the *experience* we have as we further process and *interpret* information from sensory cells. "We sense the presence of a stimulus, but we perceive *what* it is" (Levine & Shefner, 1981, p. 1). We can give a name to this final interpretation: it is an experience or a **percept**, our interpretation of sensory input.

As we'll see, in many cases the brain actually *distorts* sensory information, giving us perceptions that do not really reflect what's going on. Why? Because some bits of information are a lot more important than others. Before we explore this distinction between sensation and perception further, let's look carefully at sensation. We'll find that many aspects of sensation are the same for all the senses.

Sensation begins with a stimulus

A **stimulus** (plural *stimuli*) is any physical event that may affect a sensory cell. There are different stimuli for different senses. For example, sound waves are a stimulus for our hearing; light is a stimulus for our vision. A faint brushing of our arm is one stimulus for our skin, and a sharp slap is another one. The specialized sensory cells that detect stimuli are called **sensory receptor cells** or simply

receptors, because they "receive" the stimulus. Each kind of receptor cell is specialized to detect a particular kind of stimulus—sound wave, light, or odor, for example. Unfortunately, this same word *receptor* can also refer to the membrane-bound proteins that respond to neurotransmitters at a synapse. You have to rely on context to know which meaning of *receptor* we're using. In this chapter, when we say receptor we'll almost always mean a cell that detects stimuli.

Some sensory receptor cells are clustered together in one place in the body, such as in the eyes, ears, tongue, or nose. We call this clump of receptor cells, all detecting a particular kind of stimulus, a **sensory receptor organ** (**Figure 6.1**). Other types of receptor cells, such as those that detect touch, are spread out all over our body. Many terms for sensory processes are used in everyday life, such as *vision*, *taste*, and *touch*, but there are also specialized terms that you may not have heard before. For example, **audition** is the technical term for hearing; **olfaction** is the process of smelling odors. Psychologists refer to the different types of senses as different **modalities**.

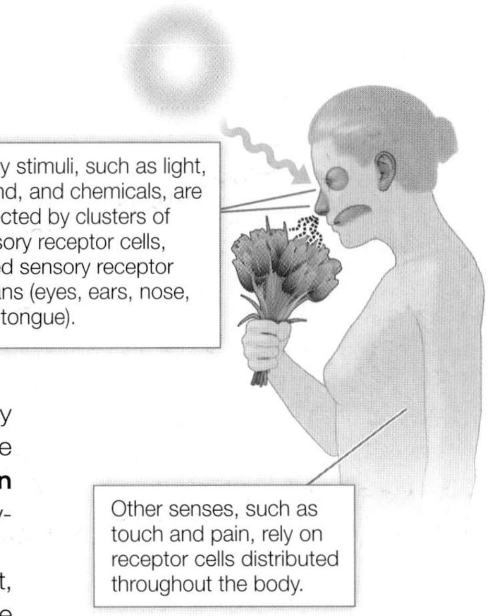

Many stimuli, such as light, sound, and chemicals, are detected by clusters of sensory receptor cells, called sensory receptor organs (eyes, ears, nose, and tongue).
Other senses, such as touch and pain, rely on receptor cells distributed throughout the body.

Figure 6.1 Sensory Receptor Organs

Receptor organs are specialized to detect a particular kind of physical event, such as the eye detecting light, but sometimes other events may also affect the receptor cell. For example, if you take your finger and *gently* press on your eyelid against your eye, you will notice a dark spot in your vision that moves as you gently move your fingertip. You may also get a blurring of your vision. In this case, the stimulus of light pressure has affected receptor cells in the eye that normally detect light. Both kinds of stimuli affect the cells, but because they normally detect light, we say that light is the **adequate stimulus** for the cells in the eye. Although pressure *can* also affect those cells, pressure is not considered the adequate stimulus for them. Of course, the pressure from your finger *is* the adequate stimulus for touch receptors in your eyelid, and that's why you felt that touch as well as saw that dark spot.

In addition to the traditional "five" senses, we are crucially dependent upon the *vestibular system*, which gives us our sense of balance, and *proprioception*, the information from sensory cells throughout muscle and skin reporting on the position and movement of our body. We tend to take these sensory systems for granted, but damage to either system can make even the simplest movements nearly impossible (Conte et al. 2013; Mast et al., 2014). Other species have specialized sensory systems that we humans lack altogether, for detecting magnetic or electrical fields, for example. **Table 6.1** summarizes the different modalities and their adequate stimuli.

sensory receptor organ A clump of receptor cells, all detecting a particular kind of stimulus.

audition The process of hearing.

olfaction The process of smelling odors.

sensory modalities The different types of senses. For example, vision, hearing, taste, touch, and smell.

adequate stimulus The type of stimulus for which a given sensory receptor organ is particularly adapted.

TABLE 6.1 Sensory Systems and Stimuli

Sensory system	Modality	Adequate stimuli
THE FIVE COMMONLY DESCRIBED SENSES		
Vision	Seeing	Light
Touch	Touch	Contact with the body surface
Audition	Hearing	Sounds (vibrations in air or water)
Olfaction	Smell	Chemicals in air or water
Gustation	Taste	Chemicals in the mouth
OTHER IMPORTANT HUMAN SENSES		
Vestibular	Balance	Position and movement of the head
Proprioception	Body sense	Position and movement of the body
SENSES THAT OTHER SPECIES HAVE BUT WE DO NOT		
Electrical	Electroreception	Changes in electrical currents (some fish)
Magnetic	Magnetoreception	Earth's magnetic field (some birds)

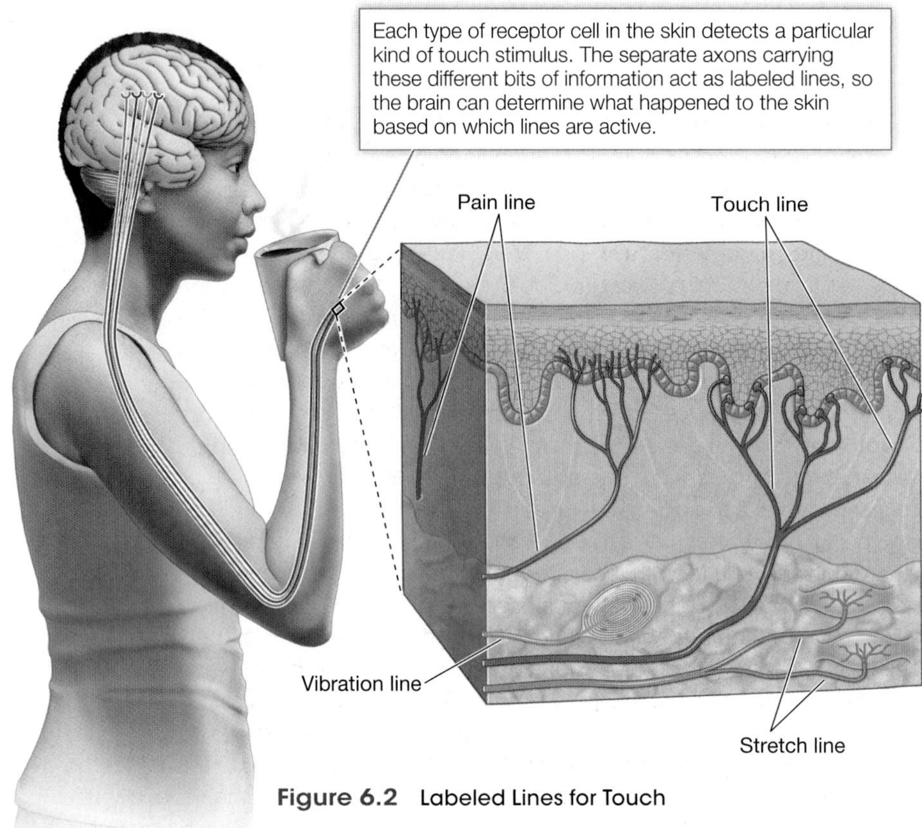

Each type of receptor cell in the skin detects a particular kind of touch stimulus. The separate axons carrying these different bits of information act as labeled lines, so the brain can determine what happened to the skin based on which lines are active.
Pain line
Touch line
Vibration line
Stretch line

Figure 6.2 Labeled Lines for Touch

labeled lines The concept that specific nerves are dedicated to relaying specific types of sensory information to the brain.

sensory code The relationship between stimuli and the action potentials they produce in sensory cells.

Early scientists speculated that maybe different parts of the body sent different types of energy to the brain, so pushing the eyeball sent "visual-type" energy to the brain, while pushing the skin sent "touch-type" energy to the brain (Müller, 1843). Today we know that these different types of energy don't exist. Rather, as you learned in Chapter 3, all neurons send only one type of "energy" to the brain: action potentials. But the brain *interprets* these action potentials very differently, depending on whether they are coming from the eye, the ear, or the skin. Action potentials from nerves from the eye are interpreted as visual events; action potentials from the ear are reporting about sounds; action potentials from the nose are about odors. In other words, the brain treats these different sources of information as **labeled lines**: the sensory modality is identified based on which nerves bring the information to the brain. That's why when you stimulate the receptor cells in your eye with gentle touch from your finger, you *see* something (the black spot) that isn't really there. Because your brain has received information coming across the "vision line" that normally carries information about light, it interprets it in the modality of vision. Labeled lines do not just convey information about the modality, of course; in the touch system, separate axons send information about light touch, while others report pain, or vibrations, or stretch (**Figure 6.2**).

All detection systems have thresholds

Each type of sensory stimulus can vary in intensity. Stimuli may be weak or strong. Light reflected from the moon, for example, is much weaker than light directly from the sun. Crying babies produce stronger sounds than buzzing mosquitoes do. In fact, some stimuli are so weak that we cannot detect them.

The concept of a **sensory code** revolves around the relationship between stimuli and the action potentials they produce in sensory cells. Let's consider a particular type of sensory receptor cell: a light touch receptor on your right pinky finger. How might we measure the intensity of a stimulus applied to this receptor? If we use some wires to record the action potentials coming from this receptor, we'll find that pressing a hair onto the skin above it will trigger a flurry of action potentials (**Figure 6.3A**). The more strongly we press against the skin, the more action potentials will be produced (**Figure 6.3B**). By keeping track of how many action potentials are produced, we can tell how strong a given stimulus is. In general, the stronger the stimulus, the more action potentials will be produced.

We can learn something by experimenting with weaker and weaker stimuli (maybe finer and finer hairs). The lighter the push against the skin, the fewer action potentials will be sent to the brain. If we keep reducing the pressure on the skin, eventually the receptor will no longer detect it, defining the threshold for this receptor. The **threshold** for a sensory cell is the weakest possible stimulus that still affects that cell's firing (**Figure 6.4**). Really weak stimuli are below threshold, so they have no effect on the receptor. Stronger stimuli are above threshold, affecting the receptor's signals to the brain. A stimulus that is just barely strong enough to affect the receptor is a *threshold stimulus*.

Since being aware of what's happening around you can be crucial for survival, you might think that the best sensory systems would be those that are as sensitive as possible, with the lowest possible threshold, to avoid missing any important stimuli. But that is not the case at all. It's true that *some* receptor cells are remarkably sensitive. Under the right conditions, some cells in your eye can detect a single photon, or particle of light. Because a single photon is the smallest amount of light energy, a threshold of a single photon is as low as possible. But consider: if human hearing systems were much more sensitive, you would be hearing the jostling of air molecules in your ear. *Most* sensory cells do not have the lowest possible threshold, and some have higher thresholds so they respond only to strong stimuli. In this way, you can detect the whole range of stimuli by detecting the weakest stimuli with some receptors and stronger stimuli with other receptors. What's remarkable about your eye, as we'll discuss later in this chapter, is that the receptor cells there are constantly changing their thresholds to match the lighting conditions around you.

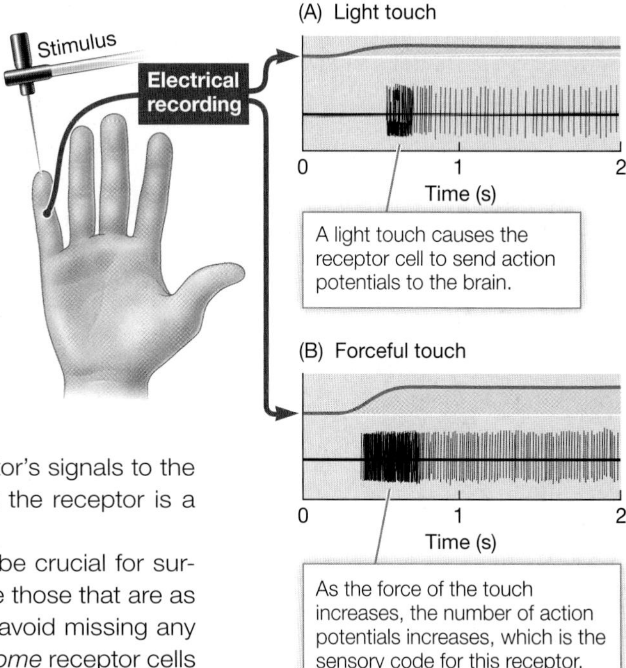

Figure 6.3 Sensory Code (After Knibestol & Valbo, 1970.)

threshold The weakest possible stimulus that still affects a sensory cell's firing.

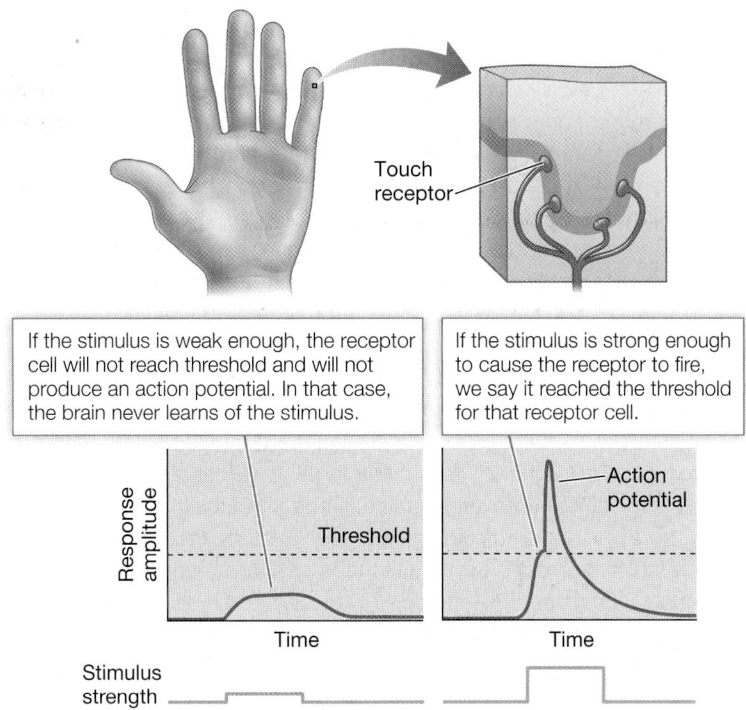

Touch receptor
If the stimulus is weak enough, the receptor cell will not reach threshold and will not produce an action potential. In that case, the brain never learns of the stimulus.
If the stimulus is strong enough to cause the receptor to fire, we say it reached the threshold for that receptor cell.
Action potential
Response amplitude
Threshold
Time
Time
Stimulus strength

Figure 6.4 Sensory Thresholds

Figure 6.5 Different Receptor Cell Thresholds Allow the Brain to Detect a Wide Range of Stimuli

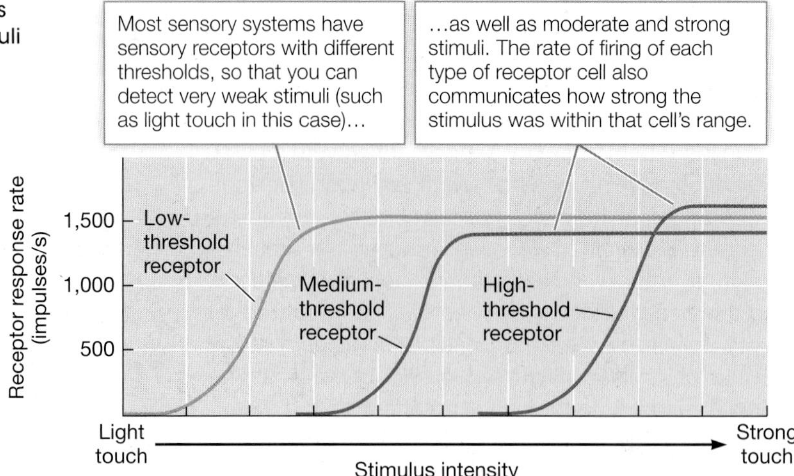
Most sensory systems have sensory receptors with different thresholds, so that you can detect very weak stimuli (such as light touch in this case)...
...as well as moderate and strong stimuli. The rate of firing of each type of receptor cell also communicates how strong the stimulus was within that cell's range.
Receptor response rate (impulses/s)
1,500
1,000
500
Low-threshold receptor
Medium-threshold receptor
High-threshold receptor
Light touch
Strong touch
Stimulus intensity

Why do you need receptor cells with high thresholds? Why not make all receptors as sensitive as possible? To understand the answer to this, remember that sensory neurons, like all neurons, can communicate only by sending action potentials, and every one is the same size. Because each action potential lasts nearly a thousandth of a second, there is a limit to how much information any neuron can signal. The neuron might only fire once every couple of seconds, or it can fire up to 1,500 times per second, but no more. So to be able to detect the entire range of stimulation, you need some receptors to be very sensitive to detect very light touch. But then a medium touch would maximize that receptor's firing rate (1,500 action potentials per second), and you'd have no way of detecting a stronger touch. So you have *other* touch receptors that have a higher threshold, receptor cells that ignore light touch and respond only to moderately strong touch. Your brain is told exactly how strong the touch was because the low-threshold, sensitive touch receptor is firing at the maximum rate, while the high-threshold, less sensitive receptor is firing moderately. By using many different receptors with different thresholds, our brain can detect a remarkable range of stimuli (**Figure 6.5**).

Psychophysics systematically analyzes perception

Psychophysics is the study of the relationship between a physical stimulus and our psychological experience of that stimulus. Typically, a psychophysicist will systematically change the intensity of a stimulus—such as the loudness of a sound—and then ask a participant to report how she or he experienced that sound at each intensity. For example, what's the softest sound that a person can detect? How bright does a light have to be for you to see it? It turns out that when presented with really weak stimuli, there comes a point when subjects sometimes do detect the stimulus, and sometimes don't. This happens even if the psychophysicist takes great care to make the stimulus exactly the same every time.

Psychophysicists systematically measure the frequency (what percentage of the time) at which a person can detect a stimulus of a given strength. The term **absolute threshold** is used to describe the lowest intensity of a stimulus that a person can detect half the time (**Figure 6.6**). If the stimulus is much stronger, the person will detect it every time, and the stimulus is said to be *above threshold*. If the stimulus is so weak that people detect it less than half the time, then it is *below threshold*. Of course, if the stimulus is really weak, people will never detect it. As you might expect, absolute threshold for a given task, like detecting light or sound or smells, can vary quite a bit from person to person. The com-

psychophysics The study of how physical events, such as lights and sounds, affect our senses.

absolute threshold The lowest intensity of a stimulus that can be detected half the time.

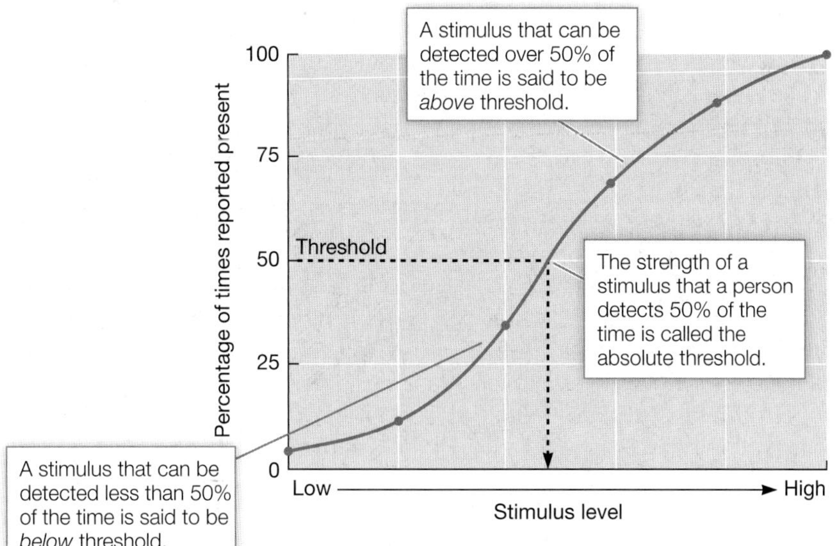

Figure 6.6 Absolute Threshold

parisons offered in **Table 6.2** are based on the average absolute thresholds taken from several healthy participants.

Psychophysicists also measure the **just noticeable difference** (**JND**; also sometimes called a "difference threshold")—how much a stimulus must change before a person can notice a difference between two stimuli. For example, how much louder do you have to make a sound before a person can tell "that sound is louder than the one before"? In a good sound system, each time you turn the volume knob another click, it should increase sound intensity by 1 JND. A system that boosts sound 100 JNDs every time you advance one click wouldn't give you much flexibility in adjusting volume. On the other hand, a system that requires several clicks to provide a single JND in volume would waste your time turning the knob more than you need to. You can determine the JND for any characteristic of a stimulus. For example, how much does the color of a light have to change before we can tell that it has changed? How much heavier does a weight have to be before we can tell?

Studies made by psychophysicists in the 1800s and 1900s revealed a number of surprising and important relationships between stimulation and sensation. Ernst Weber discovered a mathematical relationship between JNDs and a stimulus. **Weber's fraction** is the smallest change in the magnitude of a stimulus that can be detected, expressed as a proportion of the original stimulus (Fechner, 1860/1966). Weber's fraction to detect a difference in weight is 2%, meaning two weights have to differ by at least 2% for us to detect that difference. This

just noticeable difference (JND) Also called *difference threshold*. The smallest change in magnitude of a stimulus that can be detected.

Weber's fraction The smallest change in the magnitude of a stimulus that can be detected, expressed as a proportion of the original stimulus.

■ TABLE 6.2 Some Absolute Thresholds for Various Senses

Sense	Threshold
Vision	Stars at night, or a candle flame 30 miles away on a dark, clear night
Touch	The wing of a fly falling on your cheek from a height of 3 inches
Hearing	A ticking watch 20 feet away, with no other noises
Smell	A drop of perfume diffused across three rooms
Taste	A teaspoon of sugar in 2 gallons of water

Source: Galanter, 1962.

		Event: Signal	Event: Noise
Participant's response	Yes	**HIT** There was a signal, and I detected it.	**FALSE ALARM** I thought there was a signal, but there wasn't.
	No	**MISS** There was a signal I didn't detect.	**CORRECT REJECTION** I decided there was no signal, and I was right.

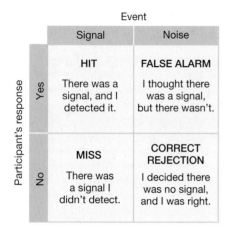

Figure 6.7 Outcomes for Detecting Signals in Noise

will be true whether the two objects are as small as pebbles or as large as suitcases. For detecting a JND in the loudness of sound, one sound must be about 10% louder than the other, while we can detect changes in the intensity of light of less than 1%.

Detection involves finding a signal in a background of noise

Because sensory systems are so sensitive, with such low absolute thresholds and the ability to detect very small JNDs, all organisms are faced with a problem. Sometimes a sensory cell may fire, signaling that something is out there, when in fact there was no stimulus at all. This is a *false alarm*—the sensory cell said a stimulus hit it when in fact there was no stimulus. In engineering, information reported by the system that is garbled or insignificant is called **noise**. All sensory systems have the problem of trying to detect signals and distinguish them from noise. Did I hear something hit the window? Was that my cell phone vibrating, or just some hum from my laptop?

Signal detection theory is concerned with measuring how we detect a signal in the midst of noise. Many factors affect how well we detect signals (Green & Swets, 1966). For example, if we are frightened, we will notice more sounds around us than when we feel safe. If we are expecting an important phone call, we will be more likely to hear it ringing if we are not engrossed in an activity. According to signal detection theory, our brains do not passively receive signals, but instead actively screen sensory input and determine whether each input is actually a signal or just noise. From this perspective, there are two ways in which a signal can be correctly detected: we may detect a signal that is real (a *hit*), or ignore noise that is unimportant (a *correct rejection*). There are also two ways we can be mistaken: we might ignore a true signal (a *miss*), or think there's a signal when really there's only noise (a *false alarm*; **Figure 6.7**).

In an ideal world, we would never make mistakes in detecting a signal. We would always detect the signal when it was really there, and never think we'd detected the signal when it was absent. For very easy detection tasks, we can come close to doing this. But in the real world, missing a signal can mean the difference between life and death, so maximally sensitive sensory systems have evolved. *Because sensory systems are so sensitive, mistakes are inevitable.* Signal detection theory teaches us that while mistakes are inevitable, there are things we can do to influence *which* mistake we will make: a miss or a false alarm.

In some cases, it may be better to have a false alarm than to miss a signal. A commonly used example is the person reading X-rays looking for signs of breast tumors. It isn't always easy to tell whether there's a tumor. The signs are quite subtle and variable. A false alarm (deciding there's a tumor present when there isn't) may do no more harm than sending the patient to the doctor for follow-up tests that correct the mistake. The other mistake, missing a tumor that's really there, could cost the patient her life. So in this case, you might adjust your criterion for whether there's a tumor so that you rarely miss a tumor, and you tolerate a lot of false alarms. What if there were no follow-up tests to decide? What if the only treatment was surgical removal of the breast? A false alarm would trigger an unnecessary major surgery. In that case, you might adjust your criterion so that you have fewer false alarms, but you would have to accept more cases where a tumor goes undetected.

In sensory systems, the key question is whether the stimulus you just received is *noise*, the random firing of sensory cells that are so sensitive they sometimes go off when nothing happened, or *signal*, an indication that something really is out there. In this case, the brain sets a criterion for deciding whether the stimulus is noise or signal. If the brain classifies the stimulus as noise, you'll never even perceive it. The brain may shift the criterion for whether the

noise The firing of a sensory cell without a stimulus or to an irrelevant stimulus.

signal detection theory A way to measure how well a real stimulus (a signal) is detected in the midst of irrelevant stimuli (noise).

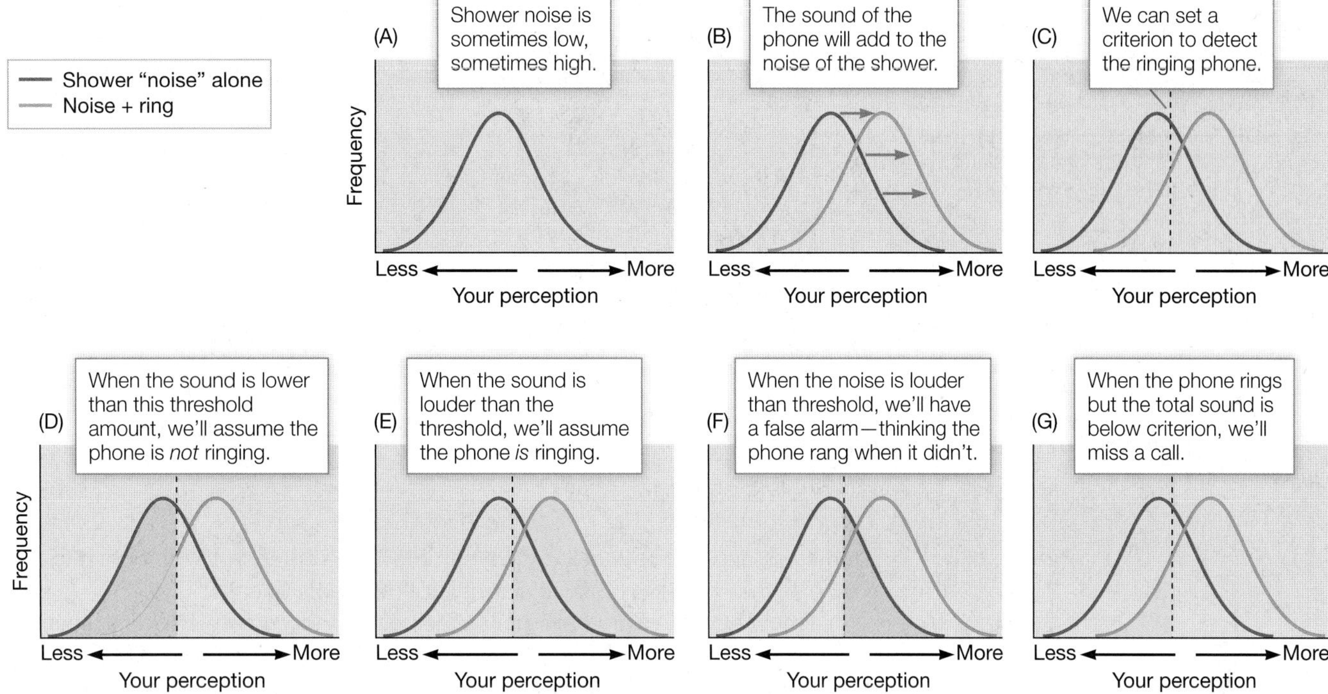
Shower "noise" alone
Noise + ring
(A)
Shower noise is sometimes low, sometimes high.
(B)
The sound of the phone will add to the noise of the shower.
(C)
We can set a criterion to detect the ringing phone.
(D)
When the sound is lower than this threshold amount, we'll assume the phone is not ringing.
(E)
When the sound is louder than the threshold, we'll assume the phone is ringing.
(F)
When the noise is louder than threshold, we'll have a false alarm—thinking the phone rang when it didn't.
(G)
When the phone rings but the total sound is below criterion, we'll miss a call.
Frequency
Less
More
Your perception

Figure 6.8 Signal Detection

stimulus is noise or signal, depending on which mistake is worse: a false alarm or a miss.

The concept of noise can be understood in the analogy of a person taking a shower who is listening for the phone (Wolfe et al., 2012). The noise from the shower varies, sometimes loud and sometimes soft (**Figure 6.8A**). If the phone rings, the sound of the ring is added to the noise (**Figure 6.8B**). Given this state of affairs, you have to set a criterion for how loud the total sound must be for you to get out of the shower. If the total sound is above that criterion, you will check the phone. If the total sound is quieter than that, you'll keep showering. Let's say you set your criterion where indicated by the dotted line in **Figure 6.8C**. Whenever the total sound is greater than that, to the right of the dotted line, you will get out of the shower to check the phone. If the total sound is less, to the left of the dotted line, you will scrub away. Here we can visualize how often we will make correct and incorrect decisions. The area under the red curve to the left of the dotted line (**Figure 6.8D**) represents those cases where we correctly reject the sound: there's no signal, no phone ringing. The larger that red area is, the more often we make that correct decision.

The blue area to the right of the line in **Figure 6.8E** represents the proportion of time we make another correct choice: times when we get out of the shower and find the phone really is ringing. But notice that there are times when we make a false alarm: we get out of the shower even though the phone's not ringing, represented by the red area in **Figure 6.8F**. Other times, represented by the blue area in **Figure 6.8G**, we miss a phone call, which is another mistake. Notice that *no matter where we set our criterion, we will make mistakes*. Our only choice is to decide which type of mistake is more acceptable: a miss or a false alarm.

When the signal from the phone is much greater than the noise of the shower—when the red and blue curves are really far apart—we will make few mistakes (**Figure 6.9A**). We might bring the phone into the bathroom for that reason. Even if we can't do that, we can still adjust the criterion to favor one outcome or the other. If we *really* don't want to miss that call, we might move our criterion, shifting the dotted line to the left (**Figure 6.9B**), so that we have many false

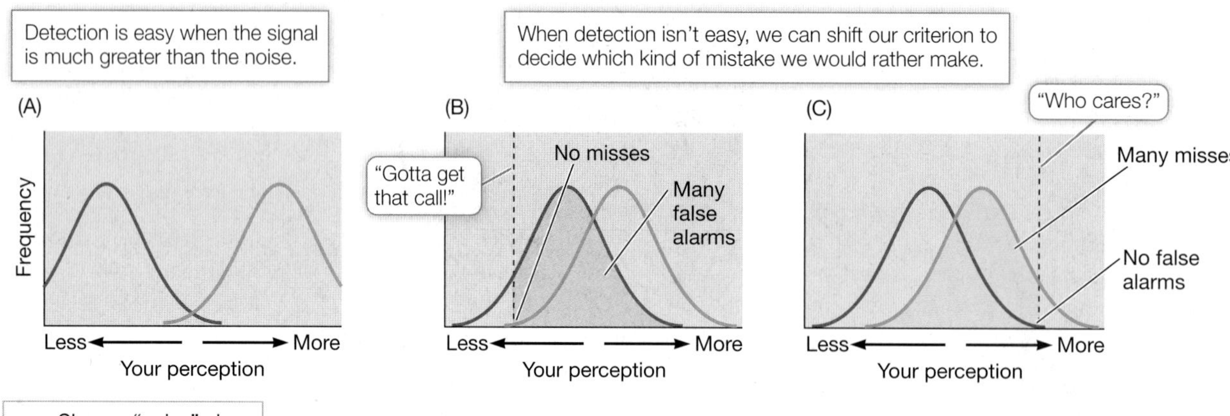

Figure 6.9 We Can Change Our Criterion Depending on Which Mistake We Prefer

alarms but never miss a call. Or we can move the criterion to the right (**Figure 6.9C**), so that we have no false alarms, but miss a lot of calls.

In almost any decision making, whether looking for tumors in X-rays, searching for enemy aircraft on radar screens, or doing an extra screening of a person at airport security, we have to choose which mistake is more tolerable—a miss or a false alarm. All other things being equal, reducing the likelihood of one mistake usually means increasing the likelihood of the other.

A stimulus that doesn't change is unimportant, so sensory systems ignore it

Sensory systems are not entirely faithful reporters about stimuli. If, while at the dinner table, you rest your leg against the chair, touch receptors in your leg will fire, telling you about that contact. But if you leave your leg there, soon the touch receptors stop firing. This is probably a good thing because you don't really want to be distracted from dinner by being reminded of where your leg is. Fact is, you're sitting on a lot of touch receptors throughout a meal, and they stop firing pretty soon, too.

Sensory adaptation is the progressive loss of responsiveness in sensory cells exposed to a constant stimulus. We can watch sensory adaptation at work by recording the electrical activity of a touch receptor (Knibestol & Valbo, 1970). Consider a touch receptor on your fingertip (see Figure 6.3). Notice that a weak stimulus, say a leaf landing on your finger, causes the touch receptor to fire. A stronger stimulus, say a hard push, causes the touch receptor to fire more rapidly. But in either case, in less than a second, the cell firing slows down. That is adaptation at work.

It's easy to see why adaptation is a good idea. Out in the wild, where life is harsh, every animal must be constantly alert, for either predators or prey, as well as for mates and children. If you think about it, in those circumstances, anything that stays constant is probably not too important. Fish don't need their skin constantly reporting "it sure is wet out here." But a new stimulus—a sudden touch on your shoulder, or a movement in the corner of your eye—needs your immediate attention. Also, your brain, marvelous as it is, can process only so much information at a time (D'Esposito & Postle, 2014). So it is far better for receptor systems to be selective, to report only on *changes* in stimuli.

sensory adaptation The progressive loss of responsiveness in sensory cells exposed to a constant stimulus.

Adaptation represents a very important way in which our sensory systems actually *distort* information, rather than faithfully reporting what's going on. As you think about vision, you may think that the receptors in your retina show little or no adaptation. After all, as you stare at a scene, say the front of your lecture hall with the professor standing there, you can look for a long time and still see everything. So the light receptors must not adapt, right? Wrong. In fact, retinal receptors adapt *very* quickly. The reason your vision does not fade as you stare at a scene is that, in fact, your eyes are constantly making very small movements, called *saccades*. You are not aware of these movements, and you cannot voluntarily stop them. And that's good, because the constant movement of your eyes means that your light receptors, which adapt very quickly, are exposed to a constantly shifting scene to avoid adaptation. That's why you continue to see. Why aren't you aware of these roving eyes? It is because your brain keeps careful track of the eye movements and constantly adjusts the input so you perceive a scene that stands still.

6.1 SUMMARY

- Sensory systems for each *modality* rely on *sensory receptor cells*, which are specialized to detect particular physical events, called *stimuli*.
- Different receptor cells and organs have different *thresholds* for detecting stimuli.
- *Psychophysicists* measure behavioral responses to stimuli to determine the *absolute threshold* for each modality and the *just noticeable difference* (*JND*) we can detect in stimulus intensity.
- For each modality, the JND is a fixed proportion so, for example, we can detect about a 2% difference in weight versus a 10% difference in loudness of sound.
- There are limits to how sensitive our sensory systems can be, and every stimulus we need to detect is embedded in many other, irrelevant stimuli. We are constantly trying to detect signals amid *noise*.
- Sensory systems help this process by adapting, diminishing reports from stimuli that don't change. *Sensory adaptation* helps us detect changing stimuli, as they are the most likely to be important for our health and survival.

REVIEW QUESTIONS

1. In psychology, what's the difference between sensation and perception?
2. How do labeled lines help us interpret sensory input?
3. Describe absolute threshold and how psychophysicists measure it.
4. Draw a 2 × 2 table to describe the four possible outcomes of any signal detection task. The table needs to specify when the signal *really is* present or not, and when you *decide* the signal is present or absent.
5. What is Weber's fraction, and how does it relate to JNDs?

Food for Thought

When you're sleeping, you ignore quiet noises. A person whispering random words may not wake you up.

But if the person whispers your *name* at the same level of loudness, you may wake up instantly. So was your brain, in fact, detecting the random words?

6.2 Touch and Pain

Things to Learn

- Kinds of touch receptor cells and their receptive fields
- Characteristics of pain receptors
- Nature and treatment of phantom limb pain

We'll start our discussion about modalities with touch and pain because some concepts we'll cover, such as *receptive fields*, are easier to understand for touch than other modalities and because pain offers an obvious distinction between sensation and perception that we've all experienced. We said earlier that sensation is the process by which the nervous system *detects* the physical events going on around us and inside us. On the other hand, perception is our *interpretation* or *experience* of the world, and this experience involves the further processing of sensory information. For example, if you stepped on a nail, sensory receptors would quickly signal your brain that something was wrong. If you were strolling across campus, you'd perceive the problem right away. In that case, sensation and perception are much the same. But if you were dashing like mad to get away from a lion that escaped from the zoo, you might not perceive the puncture at all. The receptors in the foot sent the same sensory information, but your brain built up a very different perception from that information. It might be an hour later, when you'd gotten to a safe spot, that you finally perceived your wound. (Am I bleeding? Ouch, my foot! How did that happen?) Let's consider touch in more detail, so we can consider further the difference between sensory processes and perception.

Our nerves provide information about a specific type of stimulation

Recall that in order to make sense of the various reports coming from nerves all over our body, the brain treats each nerve as a labeled line. Information coming along nerves from the eye must be about vision, so we experience a change in vision when a bird flies by or our finger presses on our eyelid. Information coming from a nerve in our skin isn't about vision, but about touch. There are at least four different types of touch receptors found in every part of our skin. Each of these receptors reports slightly different information. Some touch receptors report about vibration as our skin slides over a surface. Other receptors report about light touch, yet others report about temperature or damage to the skin (**Figure 6.10**). Our brain makes sense of this information by keeping track of the labeled lines—which kind of stimulus each axon is reporting.

Touch receptors vary in structure and function. For example, one type of touch receptor, called a *Meissner's corpuscle* after the scientist who discovered it, is a tiny round cell (*corpuscle* means "little body") that responds to touch. Another receptor, called a *Pacinian corpuscle*, which consists of onionlike layers of membrane, is sensitive to vibration, such as when you run your finger along a surface. The touch receptor called a *Merkel's disc,* often found just underneath one of the ridges that make up your fingerprints (see Figure 6.10), is sensitive to light touch that bends the ridges of your fingerprints. Nerves wrapped around

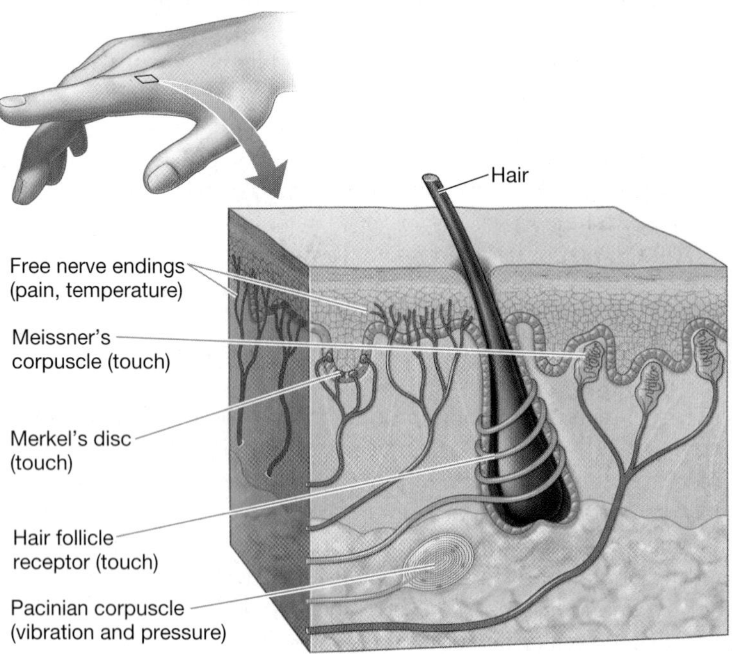

Figure 6.10 Different Touch Receptor Cells

hair follicles detect any bend of the hair. *Free nerve endings,* scattered throughout the skin, have various functions: some are finely attuned to detect damage and signal pain, while others are specialized to report temperature changes.

The brain gathers the different kinds of touch information that these and other receptors provide and keeps track of which "line" is providing which kind of information. By putting together all that information about light touch, vibration, and temperature, we gather a remarkable amount of information about whatever is touching our skin.

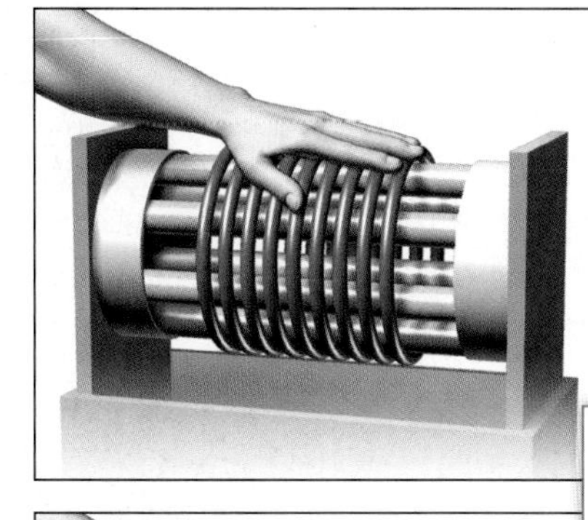

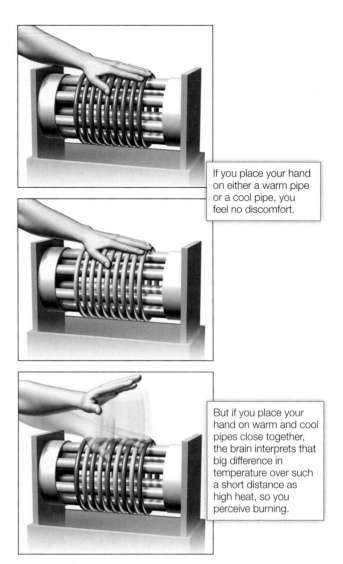

If you place your hand on either a warm pipe or a cool pipe, you feel no discomfort.

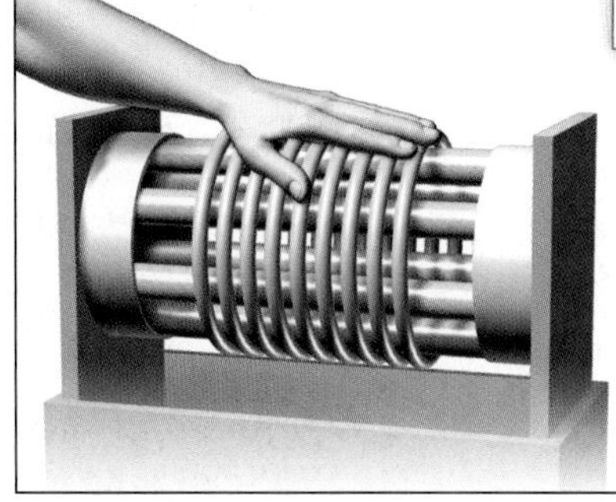

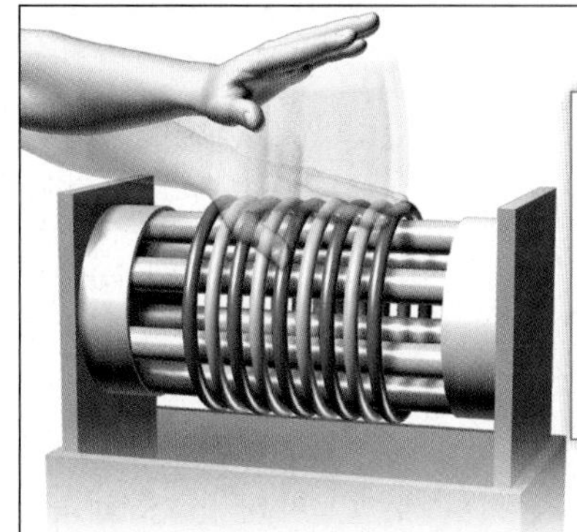

But if you place your hand on warm and cool pipes close together, the brain interprets that big difference in temperature over such a short distance as high heat, so you perceive burning.

Figure 6.11 The Thermal Grill Paradoxical Heat Illusion

Touch perception is more refined than you might think

Several illusions relating to touch show how our mind relies on knowing which nerve is transmitting which kind of information. The *paradoxical heat* illustration is sometimes demonstrated at science museums (**Figure 6.11**). The demonstration consists of two different copper pipes. One has warm (but not hot) water running through it. The other has cool (but not cold) water running through it. You can feel either pipe alone and detect the temperature, and neither will make your hand uncomfortable. But if the two kinds of pipes are running right next to each other, you can place your hand on both at once. This time the sensation is different—it feels like your hand is burning! You might jerk your hand away and look at it, but there will be no redness, no damage.

Why does your hand feel like it is burning? Here your brain is getting two different messages. Warm receptors are reporting warmth along one nerve, and cool receptors are reporting coolth (is that a word?) along another. But these two signals are coming from the same patch of skin, right next to each other. Normally the only way you would get such a big difference in temperature is if your hand were on something hot, so your brain interprets these signals as "that's hot," and you perceive pain (Harper & Hollins, 2014). Notice that I said you *perceive* pain. Here's a great example of the difference between sensation and perception. The touch receptors are faithfully reporting the *sensations* "warm" and "cool," but the brain puts the two together to come up with the *perception* of "burning." This illusion, like the visual illusions we'll discuss later, relies on putting together unusual sensations to give us a perception that is false, in the sense that it does not reflect reality.

Different receptor cells have different receptive fields

The **receptive field** of a sensory cell is that total region of space where stimuli will alter the cell's firing rate. For touch, the "region of space" refers to the parts of the body where the appropriate stimulus (deep pressure, vibration, light touch, heat) affects a given sensory cell's firing. If the sensory cell responds to warm stimuli applied only to your left ear, then we say the cell's receptive field is warmth to the left ear. The many different touch receptors have different receptive fields. Some receptive fields are large and some are small, and they often overlap (**Figure 6.12**).

receptive field The region of space where stimuli affect the activity of a cell in a sensory system.

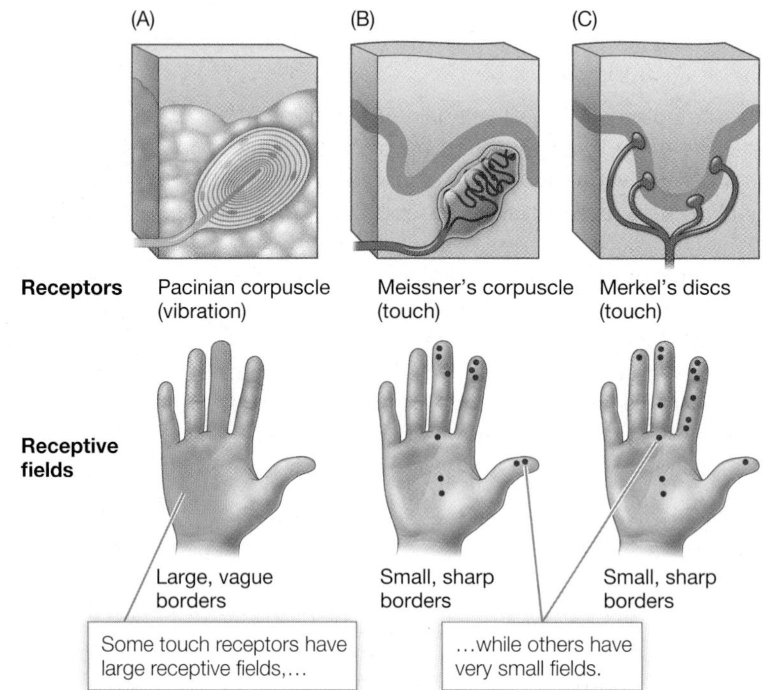

Figure 6.12 Receptive Fields of Touch Receptor Cells (After Johansson & Flanagan, 2009.)

Millions of touch receptors of each kind make a patchwork, covering every inch of your skin so that you can detect all kinds of stimuli from all over your body. Scientists map receptive fields by recording from the neuron and then applying stimuli to the body until they work out where the stimuli affect the firing rate (see Figure 6.3). For example, the scientist might insert tiny wires in the arm of a participant to record action potentials from a nerve. He could then take a small paintbrush and apply it gently until he finds a spot on the arm where lightly touching the skin causes that neuron to fire faster or slower. The scientist could then touch all around that point and, using a pen, mark out the boundaries of the receptive field for that particular neuron.

The concept of receptive field applies to neurons further down the line, away from the initial sensory receptor. For example, the touch receptor communicates with neurons in the spinal cord. The spinal cord neurons communicate with neurons in the brain. So the change in firing pattern caused by this stimulus will also alter the firing pattern of neurons in the spinal cord and brain. If we were to record from these brain neurons, we could map their receptive fields too. Everywhere on the body where touches affect the firing of a neuron, that's the receptive field for that neuron. This is true whether it is a sensory receptor cell or any other neuron.

Receptive fields for other modalities describe a different "region of space." For neurons in the visual system, the receptive field is that part of the visual field where light affects the neurons' firing. For the auditory system, the receptive field is the loudness, frequency, and location of sound that affect a given neuron's firing rate.

Your brain not only has to keep track of what modality is being reported in each nerve, and which *submodality* is being reported (light touch or vibration? deep pressure or warmth?), but it also has to note the receptive field of that nerve. This brings us to another touch illusion, described by Aristotle, that dupes us by exploiting how the brain keeps track of the receptive field of each touch receptor that is sending in reports (Benedetti, 1986; Gibson, 1966; Hayward, 2008). You can try it for yourself in **Figure 6.13**.

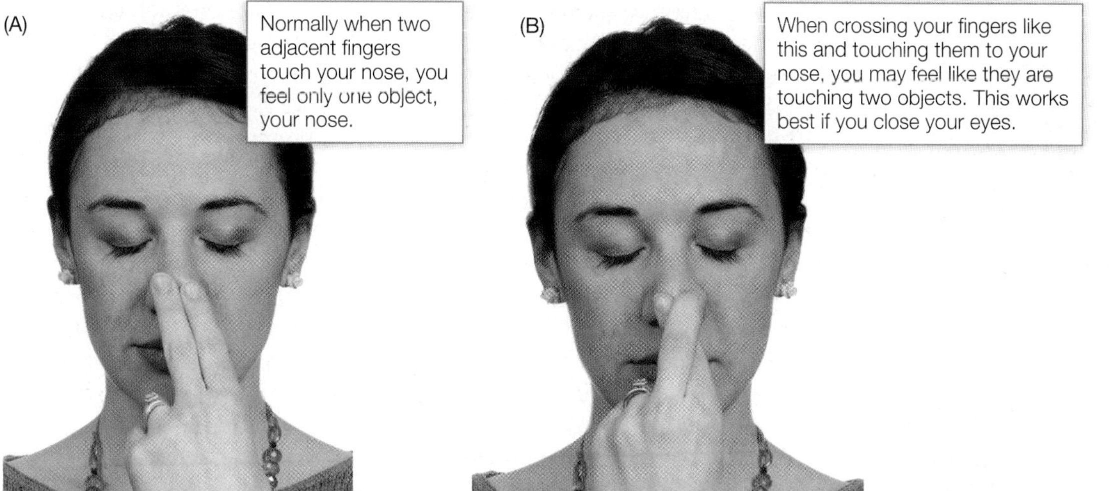

Normally when two adjacent fingers touch your nose, you feel only one object, your nose.

When crossing your fingers like this and touching them to your nose, you may feel like they are touching two objects. This works best if you close your eyes.

Figure 6.13 Aristotle's Touch Illusion

Painlessness is hazardous to your health

Among the many different receptors distributed throughout our skin, there are some that are specifically there to detect damage and report it to the brain. These specialized pain receptors are called **nociceptors** ("noxious" + "receptors"). Nociceptors are free nerve endings, where the axon shrinks to a very small diameter and breaks into several branches. This simple appearance is deceptive, however.

nociceptors Free nerve endings that are specialized pain receptors.

Sensation begins in nociceptors by special receptor proteins that span the membrane covering the nerve endings. A part of the receptor sticks out of the nerve that can detect a wide range of chemicals that are released when tissue is damaged (**Figure 6.14**). Contact with molecules released at the site of an injury causes changes in the shape of the receptor that let sodium ions (Na^+) in to trigger action potentials. How did we learn about these special receptor proteins for pain? For many years scientists could not agree whether there *were* skin receptors that were truly used *only* for pain sensation. Microscopic examinations of skin showed plenty of different receptors, but it was difficult to prove which, if any, reported pain information. The breakthrough that made identification of nociceptors possible came from the study of people like Gail, who have

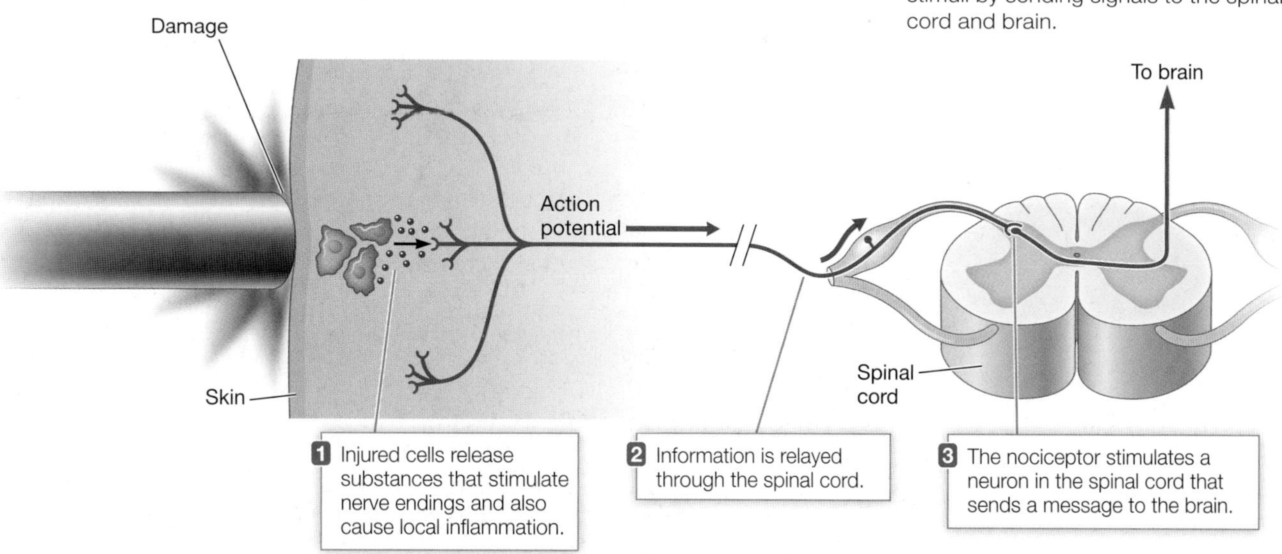

Damage
Skin
Action potential
To brain
Spinal cord
1 Injured cells release substances that stimulate nerve endings and also cause local inflammation.
2 Information is relayed through the spinal cord.
3 The nociceptor stimulates a neuron in the spinal cord that sends a message to the brain.

Figure 6.14 **Pain Receptors** Nociceptors respond to potentially damaging stimuli by sending signals to the spinal cord and brain.

THE HUMAN PINCUSHION WHO INCURS CONSTANT RISKS OF BLOOD POISONING.

Figure 6.15 Congenital Insensitivity to Pain (CIP) The earliest scientific report of a person with CIP was of a man working in the theater, like the man shown here, as a "human pincushion" (Dearborn, 1932).

congenital insensitivity to pain (CIP) A genetic condition that prevents the feeling of pain.

the condition called **congenital insensitivity to pain** (**CIP**), characterized by the ability to feel many sensations such as light touch, deep pressure, warmth, coolness, and vibration of the skin—but not pain. Gail's example shows you what a bad thing it is to never feel pain. People with CIP tend to live short, unhealthy lives (Goldberg et al., 2012). Never feeling pain, they never learn to avoid accidents, so they have lots of them. They damage their fingers and toes, arms and legs. Never ask a person with CIP to chop wood! Because the accident-prone tend to die young, few people with CIP have children to whom they can pass on their genes, so the incidence of CIP is very low.

Because people with CIP are born this way (*congenital* means "present at birth"), CIP was assumed to be the result of their genetic makeup. But it was difficult to figure out which gene was involved. Today we have the technology to determine the sequence of every gene in the human genome, but determining *which* gene is responsible for CIP is no easy task. That's why scientists were eager to study a Pakistani family with several members with CIP, including a boy who was earning his living doing pain-defying street performances (Cox et al., 2006).

The Pakistani boy could walk over coals (slowly), and could thread pins through his skin (like the gentleman with CIP in **Figure 6.15**), and even pushed knives through his arms. The audience would applaud and toss him coins. (It's a living, right?) But by the time the scientists got there, the boy was dead. He had wanted to impress his friends by jumping off a house. Apparently he did not feel any pain, but his injuries killed him just the same.

Although researchers were unable to study the boy with CIP, they were able to study the genetics underlying his condition by investigating genetic patterns in his surviving family, as described in **Figure 6.16**.

☑ Researchers at Work

Specialized receptors transmit information about pain

Figure 6.16 The Search for Painlessness (After Cox et al., 2006.)

■ **Question:** Why are some people born without the ability to feel pain?

■ **Hypothesis:** These individuals inherit a dysfunctional gene for a protein that is needed by nociceptors.

■ **Test:** Find a large family in which several individuals have CIP. Examine DNA from many family members to find a gene for which the people with CIP carry one version, while relatives without CIP carry another.

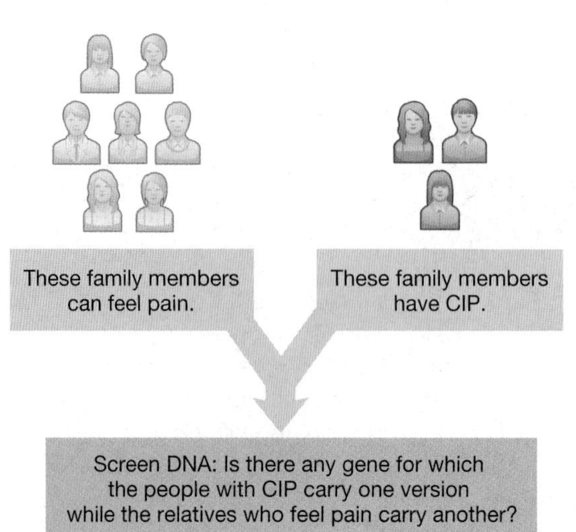

■ **Result:** One gene fit this criterion. When researchers determined the sequence of this gene, they recognized it as one that produces a sodium (Na^+) channel protein associated with free nerve endings. The version of this gene in the relatives with CIP had a mutation that made it dysfunctional. All the relatives with CIP carried two of these dysfunctional copies of the gene, while all the relatives who could feel pain had at least one functional version of the gene (Cox et al., 2006).

To prove that this gene associated with CIP was required for pain, the researchers deliberately disabled the same gene in mice (Nassar et al., 2004). They found that indeed, mice with two dysfunctional copies of this gene showed no sign of feeling pain.

■ **Conclusion:** A particular sodium channel is required for nociceptors to produce action potentials to inform the brain about pain. When the channel does not work properly, no nociceptor signals reach the brain and so no pain is perceived.

Overcoming Obstacles In addition to the challenge of learning to ski using only one leg, this person may also be dealing with phantom limb pain.

The Na^+ channel protein discovered by these studies appears to be crucial for free nerve endings to detect damage. Other touch receptors, including other free nerve endings, do not use this protein. That's why people like Gail, with two dysfunctional copies of the gene for the protein, can still detect other types of touch.

Once scientists learned that a single protein is involved in all pain sensation, the search was on for drugs that can *act directly on that protein to block pain*. If a drug could be developed that affects only that sodium channel protein, then we could stop pain without any other side effects. We have many excellent pain-killing drugs today, but they all have side effects, including the fact that many of them may lead to addicition. Thanks to people like Gail and the Pakistani family (and don't forget the laboratory mice), we may one day have nonaddictive pain-killers for people suffering from serious injuries and from diseases like cancer.

Pain illustrates the vast difference between sensation and perception

It is not always easy to measure pain, because there is a subjective component to pain. Sometimes the very same sensation—the firing of action potentials by a nociceptor next to damaged tissue—will elicit the perception of pain in one person but not another. Differences in the perception of pain are famously seen during combat. Before a big offensive, soldiers are afraid and tense. The coming battle could end a soldier's life. Getting wounded in battle, paradoxically, can *save* a soldier's life, because the wounded may be carried off for treatment—be sent to safety—and this is thought to explain why many soldiers with non-life-threatening wounds often report feeling little or no pain (Beecher, 1956). While the soldier's arm or leg may be damaged, and the soldier can feel that it is damaged, perhaps even feels some discomfort, he does not seem to be in agony. Outside of combat, however, people with similar wounds often have a very different *perception* of that same *sensation*: excruciating pain. Why is this so? Pain has a different meaning for the soldiers in combat (the outlook is good, they get to leave battle) than for the soldiers in the hospital (pain connotes a bad outcome, a threatening wound) (Bowman, 1997).

It is also possible to perceive pain without a stimulus. Consider, for example, the experience of **phantom limb pain**, when people with amputated limbs report that the missing part hurts. When accident or disease causes a person to lose a limb, tissue damage is, of course, very painful. But once the wound heals, the remaining tissues are healthy, yet the brain perceives pain (McCormick et al., 2013). Sometimes the person's perception is even more specific: "It feels as though my missing arm is twisted behind my back, and that's why it hurts" (**Figure 6.17A**).

phantom limb pain The perception of pain in a missing appendage.

Figure 6.17 Phantom Limb Pain (After Ramachandran & Rogers-Ramachandran, 2000.)

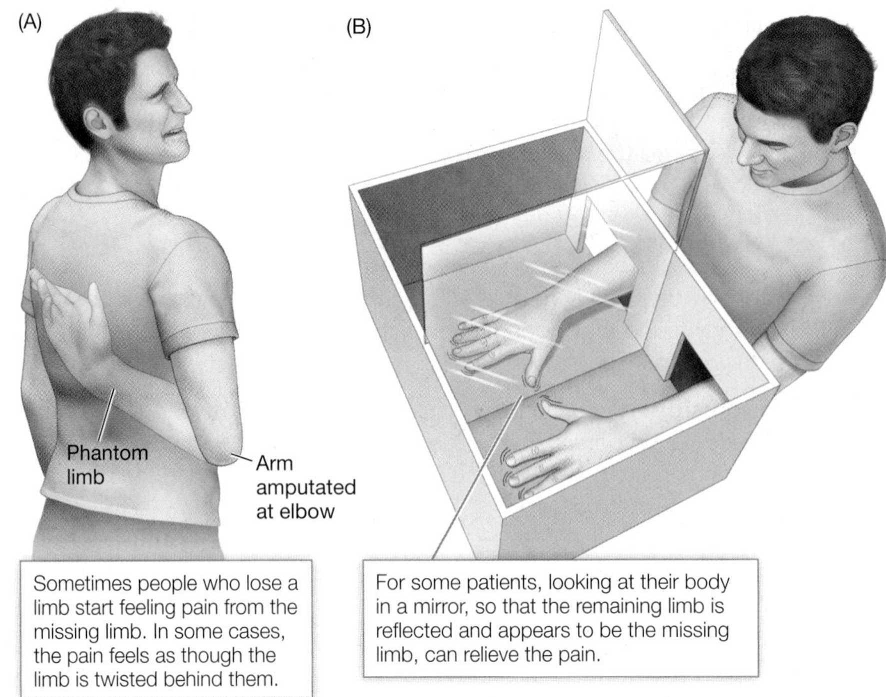
(A)
(B)
Phantom limb
Arm amputated at elbow
Sometimes people who lose a limb start feeling pain from the missing limb. In some cases, the pain feels as though the limb is twisted behind them.
For some patients, looking at their body in a mirror, so that the remaining limb is reflected and appears to be the missing limb, can relieve the pain.

neuropathic pain Pain caused by a damaged or malfunctioning nervous system.

It is not clear what's going on in phantom limb pain, but you might wonder if the nociceptors in the stump of the limb are somehow firing inappropriately, causing the pain sensation. That may be happening in a few cases, but in most cases, using drugs to silence nerves in the arm does not stop the pain (Foell et al., 2013). In those cases, the perception of pain is starting somewhere else, in either the spinal cord or brain. This is an example of **neuropathic pain**: pain caused by a damaged or malfunctioning nervous system. For over a century, physicians have tried to relieve neuropathic pain by injecting drugs to silence various parts of the nervous system, or even destroying parts of the nervous system. Sadly, these desperate measures may provide relief for a few months, but then the pain returns.

In a sense, phantom pain is pure perception without sensation. It isn't originating in any sensory information, because the sensory receptor cells, the nociceptors in the missing limb, aren't there. Yet the brain perceives pain. Here's another clue that phantom limb pain originates in the brain rather than in the damaged nerve endings of the stump—sometimes rubbing the stump relieves pain for a bit, but often rubbing the preserved hand on the *other* limb is more effective (Niraj & Niraj, 2014)!

The most provocative evidence that this sort of pain originates in the brain comes from studies asking people to imagine they have their limb back. A person with pain from a missing arm sits looking into a box with a mirror and puts the remaining hand into the box and looks down (**Figure 6.17B**). If the person looks at the right angle, the mirror image makes it looks as though both hands are there. Now the person is asked to imagine moving both limbs in mirror fashion while watching the "two" hands move. For many people missing a limb, the phantom pain is eased (Ramachandran & Rogers-Ramachandran, 1996; Deconinck et al., 2014). One theory is that the phantom pain is caused by the brain receiving disordered input from the body, and that by giving the brain cues that suggest the body is whole again, the input is reorganized and stops being painful. Sometimes just *imagining* moving the missing limb, without mirrors, can bring relief (Giraux & Sirigu, 2003). These findings demonstrate that "pain is in the brain": pain perception is *not* a simple reporting of sensory fibers from the body.

Are you now convinced that pain is, on the whole, good for you, even if it's never pleasant to experience? Indeed, the very point of pain is to make you uncomfortable. So let's leave unpleasant pain behind to study the glorious experience of vision.

6.2 SUMMARY

- The body is covered with nerve endings that are specialized to detect physical events on our skin and internal organs. Touch sensations are conveyed by various receptors for light touch, vibration, temperature, and tissue damage.
- Each sensory receptor has a different *receptive field*: the region of the body where stimuli of a particular type affect that neuron's firing.
- The brain keeps track of which nerves detect which types of stimuli and interprets what's happening and where.
- *Nociceptors* are specialized to detect damage to the skin. Detection of damage triggers action potentials that signal the brain to result in the perception of pain.
- Our perception of pain is very sensitive to context, so stimuli that are perceived as painful in one situation may go undetected in another.
- However unpleasant the experience, pain serves to maintain our health and survival.

REVIEW QUESTIONS

1. How are we able to perceive so many different kinds of stimuli (light touch, vibration, heat, cold, pain) from our skin?
2. Describe receptive fields and explain how a scientist can determine the receptive field of a neuron.
3. Give some examples to demonstrate that "pain is in the brain" and not simply the result of nociceptor activity.

Food for Thought

In Stieg Larsson's novel *The Girl Who Kicked the Hornet's Nest*, a villain congenitally insensitive to pain is said to have learned to be careful to avoid injury. But he is also particularly brutal to other people. Does it seem likely to you that such a person would have little sympathy for others?

6.3 Vision

Things to Learn

- How light is detected in the eye
- Cues we use for depth perception
- Mechanisms of color vision
- Principles of visual perception, including Gestalt rules

All our sensory systems are important, but for most people, vision is the most important and the most mysterious sensory system. Pain and touch detect events that happen close to us, but with vision we can see events unimaginable distances away, such as the stars at night. In the daytime, vision helps us maneuver around some objects and to use others for tools. With vision we detect myriad differences in color around us, which can be important for finding food or avoiding predators.

First we'll consider the remarkable sensory system in the eye with which our visual experience begins, and then we'll see how we use that sensory information to tell how far away an object is, and what color it is. We'll find that the visual system works rapidly by taking shortcuts and making assumptions about the world, and that some optical illusions work by taking advantage of those shortcuts. We'll conclude by discussing how the brain organizes these countless, disjointed percepts into a seamless experience of the world.

Reflected light arrives on the retina

Vision begins as light enters our eye, which is a very ingenious optical device. Take, for example, the round, transparent front of your eye, the **cornea**. Because the cornea is round, light rays are bent (or *refracted*) as they pass through it. Just behind the cornea is the **lens**, a flexible, transparent structure that further bends the light coming into the eye. The bending of light by the cornea and lens works to focus a sharp image onto the **retina**, the back of your eye's interior

cornea The round, transparent front of the eye.

lens The flexible, transparent structure in the eye that helps focus an image on the back of the eye's interior.

retina The surface at the back of the eye where the image from the lens and cornea is focused.

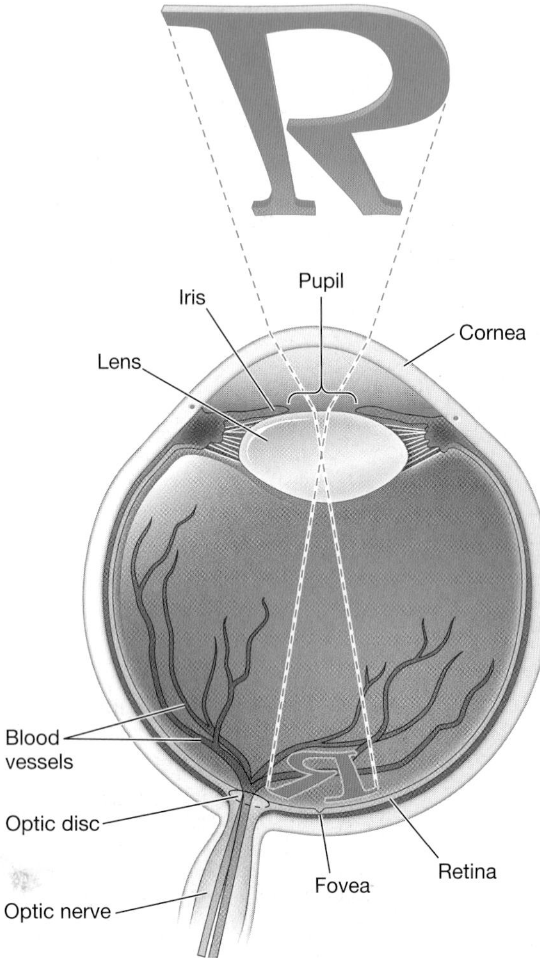

Figure 6.18 The Anatomy of the Eye

(**Figure 6.18**). The retina is an extension of the brain, complete with neurons and glia, which forms a layer on the back of the eye. The center of our gaze falls on the **fovea**, the part of our retina where our vision is sharpest.

Because of the shape of the lens, the image focused on the retina is upside down and reversed. The shape of the lens is similar to that of a magnifying glass. If you've ever played with a magnifying glass, you might have noticed that if you look through it while holding it out at arm's length, faraway scenes appear upside down and reversed. The same optic principle flips the image on our retinas.

Most of the refraction, or bending, of light that focuses an image on the retina is done by the outer layer, the cornea. In comparison, the lens hardly bends the light at all. The lens, however, can *change* its shape to fine-tune the refraction of light and to bring things into focus. To see this at work, hold out your hand in front of your face. If you close one eye and look at a fingertip, you can probably bring it into focus. But notice that as you focus on the fingertip, anything behind it in the distance gets blurred. Conversely, if you focus on things in the distance behind your finger, the image of the fingertip gets blurred. You are using your lens, making it thicker or thinner, to control which part of the view is in focus on your retina.

The light forming an image of the outside world that is focused on the retina passes through a layer of cells there and eventually lands on light-detecting neurons called **photoreceptors** (**Figure 6.19**). There are two basic kinds of photoreceptors, named after their shapes: rods and cones. **Rod** photoreceptors are extremely sensitive, so they can detect very low levels of light, such as on a starlit night. They respond about the same to light of any wavelength, which means they cannot help us distinguish colors. We rely heavily on our rods for night vision. In contrast, **cone** photoreceptors are relatively insensitive, so they work only when there is plenty of light, as when we are outdoors or in a well-lit room.

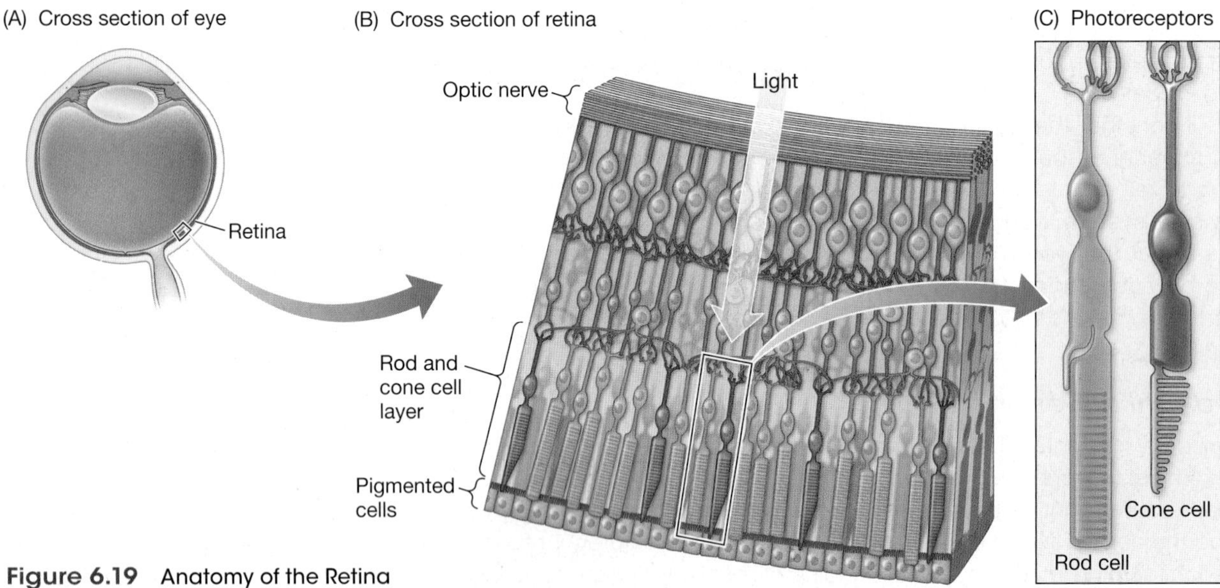

Figure 6.19 Anatomy of the Retina

TABLE 6.3 Rods and Cones Provide Different Information

Property	Cones	Rods
Approximate number of receptors per eye	4 million	100 million
Sensitivity	Low; needs relatively strong stimulation; used for day vision	High; can be stimulated by weak light intensity; used for night vision
Location in retina	Concentrated in and near fovea; less densely elsewhere	Outside fovea
Receptive field and visual acuity	Small in fovea, so acuity is high; larger outside fovea	Larger, so acuity is lower
Temporal responses	Relatively rapid	Slow

Cones are selectively sensitive to light of different wavelengths, so as we'll discuss later, they are crucial for allowing us to distinguish colors.

Rods and cones are so different that we can think of the visual system as consisting of two parts. **Table 6.3** compares some of the properties of the cone and rod systems. We've covered some of these differences between the two systems already, and we'll learn about some of the others later in this chapter.

While vision is caused by light entering our eye, it is often necessary to identify *where the light entering our eye is coming from.* The **visual field** is that part of space that we can see at any one time without moving our eyes. This is pretty much the same thing as that part of space from which light can enter our eyes, but as we'll see next, not all the light entering our eyes is detected.

photoreceptors Light-sensitive receptor cells in the retina.

rod A class of photoreceptors in the retina that can detect very low levels of light.

cone A class of photoreceptors in the retina that are responsible for color vision.

visual field The part of space that we can see at any one time.

optic disc The round area on the retina, lacking rods and cones, where axons exit the eye.

blind spots The parts of the visual fields that are missing because of the optic discs.

We all have our blind spots

A remarkable attribute of the retina is the blind spot. As you can see in Figure 6.18, the axons of neurons that send visual information to the brain all come together as they exit the eye in a round region called the **optic disc** (**Figure 6.20**). There are absolutely no rods or cones on the optic disc, which means we receive no sensory information from a significant part of the visual field. The areas in which we lack information from the visual field are called **blind spots**.

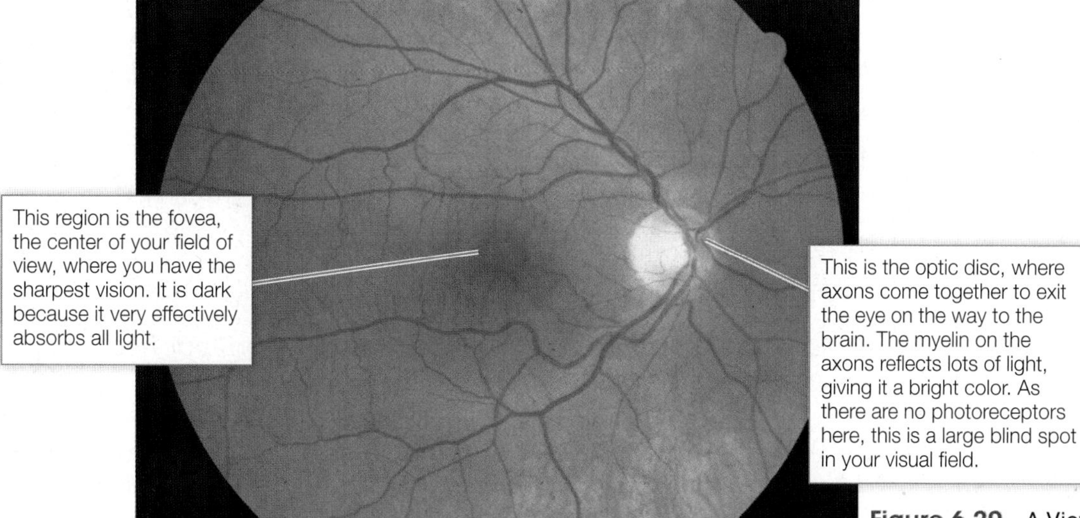

This region is the fovea, the center of your field of view, where you have the sharpest vision. It is dark because it very effectively absorbs all light.
This is the optic disc, where axons come together to exit the eye on the way to the brain. The myelin on the axons reflects lots of light, giving it a bright color. As there are no photoreceptors here, this is a large blind spot in your visual field.

Figure 6.20 A View of the Retina

(A)

Close your left eye, hold the book about a hand's width from your face, and fix your right eye on the F. Then move the book closer or farther until the red spot disappears.

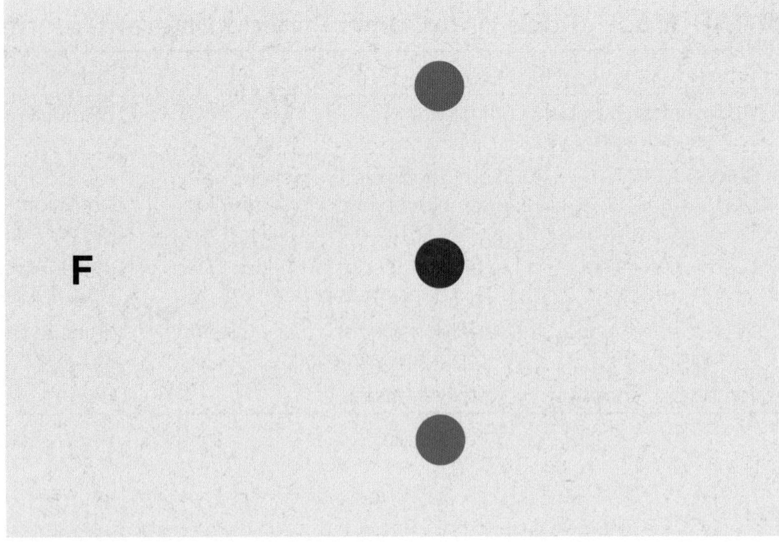

(B)

Again close your left eye and fix your gaze on the F. Now adjust the book's distance until the break in the red line seems to disappear. The blind spot you've just detected is always there, but you are not aware of it because your brain "fills in" that spot from the information surrounding it.

Figure 6.21 The Blind Spot

Look up from this book at the scene in front of you with one eye closed—do you notice a blank spot in the visual field? You can't see any empty spot, can you? Just the same, there is an empty spot in each eye, and **Figure 6.21** will help you prove that to yourself.

The blind spot offers another example of the difference between sensation and perception. There is absolutely no *sensory* information coming from those parts of the visual field, yet you *perceive* a whole visual field, without blank spots. Again, your brain distorts sensory information, filling in those gaps, to make you think you see more than you do. Now you might shrug off this fib as a small thing—maybe the blind spots are so tiny that this is why you have a hard time noticing them. But in fact when you close one eye, the blind spot in the open eye is nearly ten times larger than a full moon. And yet you cannot even notice the blind spot is there without some trick like that in Figure 6.21. Even with this figure, you can't make yourself *aware* of the blind spot. We cannot *experience* the blind spots in our vision. Popular demonstrations of what the world "looks like" to a bee fail to appreciate the crucial distinction between sensation and perception, as **Box 6.1** details.

Divide and conquer: How visual information reaches the two hemispheres of the brain

In Chapter 3 you learned that the right side of the brain receives information from the left side of the body, and vice versa. In the visual system, we can modify this principle a bit to say that the right side of the brain receives information about what you see in the left half of the visual field.

BOX 6.1

How Does a Flower Look to a Bee?

Insects have eyes that are quite similar to yours in some ways and quite different in others. Like you, insects have photoreceptor cells resting inside a fluid-filled compartment with a lens at one end to focus light onto the receptors. But while you have only two such compartments—your left and right eyes—insects have hundreds of them. Most of these "little eyes" are grouped together into two so-called compound eyes. The tiny little eyes within each compound eye are so tightly squeezed together that they have a six-sided, hexagonal shape.

Figure A A simple flower

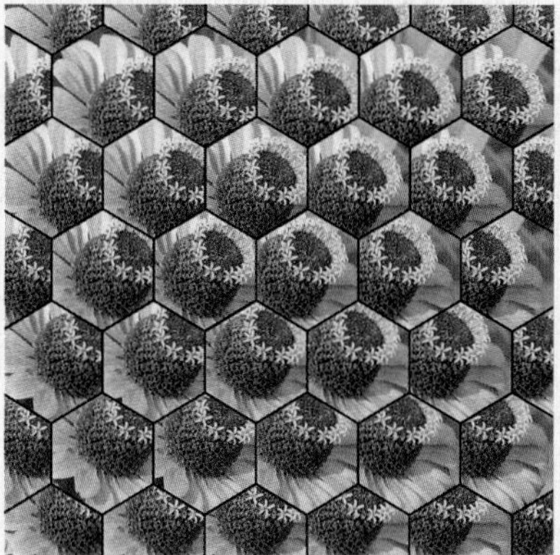

Figure B Is this how it looks to a bee?

You may have seen amusing photos of what a scene like that in **Figure A** looks like to insects, with the scene broken up into hundreds of hexagonal segments, each reproducing a large part of the scene, such as in **Figure B**. How would insects make sense of that scene?

Let's think a bit more critically about this. You might ask, is this photo *really* what the scene would look like to an insect? To answer this question, you'd want to find out a bit more about insects' eyes. You'd learn that each tiny "eye" in an insect's compound eye has only a few photoreceptors, most often only eight. With only eight photoreceptors, there's no way each little eye can report much information about the scene. Also, the lens of each little eye is pointed in a slightly different direction, meaning that each lens takes a somewhat different picture of the visual field, which is not what's portrayed in these photos. And you might also question why each little portion in Figure B is a hexagon. Yes, each little eye is hexagonal in shape, but the photoreceptors are more or less round. How could the activity of eight photoreceptors define six straight lines forming a hexagon, plus objects inside that hexagon? Consider what we know about human eyes. In the center of your retina, at the *fovea,* your photoreceptors are packed so closely together that they actually take on a hexagonal shape. But do you perceive a visual scene as a mosaic of hexagons? The suggestion made by the picture in Figure B is nonsense because it fails to take into account the process of perception. For a comparison, let's imagine that we are trying to make a similar photo based on the human visual system. Humans have two eyes pointed forward, which means that the visual fields of the two eyes overlap considerably. But the two eyes are in slightly different places, so the images from various objects in those two scenes will not line up the same. In essence, we poor humans are seeing double for most of the visual field! Most of our color-sensitive photoreceptors are trained on the center of the visual field, so color is perceived only there, not in the edges of the visual field. On top of these limitations, there are two large blind spots in the eyes where there are no photoreceptors, so those parts of the visual field are blank. What's worse, because the cornea and lens at the front of the eye reverse and flip images from the outside world, these pathetic humans eyes see everything upside down and backward! Does **Figure C** reflect how the world looks to you? Of course not—in fact our brains provide us with a percept like that in Figure A.

So how would that scene look to an insect? It's hard to say, since insects can't tell us how things look to them. Despite their different *sensory* apparatus, they probably *perceive* visual scenes much the same as we do, and certainly not as represented in Figure B.

Figure C Is this how it looks to a human?

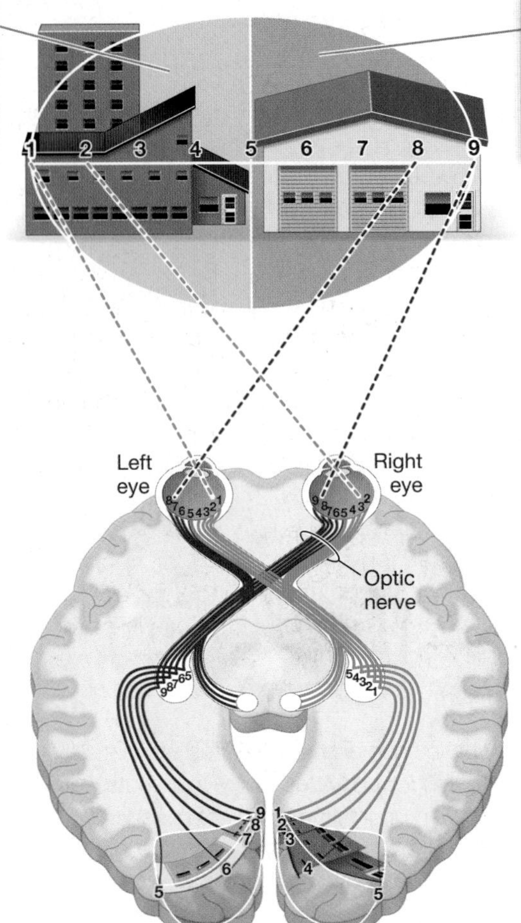
Light from the left visual field strikes the right sides of both retinas and converges in the right visual cortex.
Light from the right visual field strikes the left sides of both retinas and converges in the left visual cortex.
1 2 3 4 5 6 7 8 9
Left eye
Right eye
Optic nerve
Thus both eyes project to both sides of the brain, but left visual field goes to the right side of the brain, while the right visual field goes to the left hemisphere.

Figure 6.22 Visual Pathways to the Brain (After Frisby, 1980.)

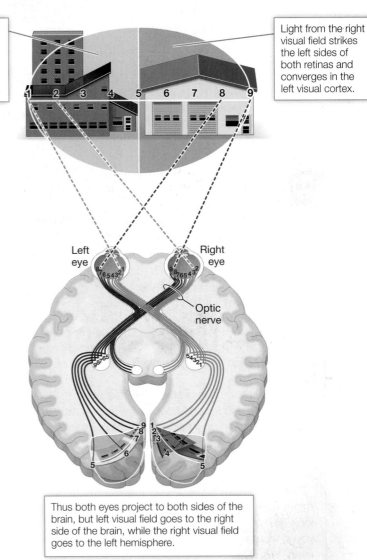

primary visual cortex (V1) The region of the occipital cortex where most visual information first arrives.

depth perception The ability to perceive distance.

binocular cues Information about distance provided by using two eyes.

binocular disparity The difference in the views from two eyes; this provides one important visual clue for depth perception.

Figure 6.22 shows you how this works. Light from the right visual field enters both eyes and hits their retinas. In the right eye, the light strikes the left half of the retina, near the nose. In the left eye, the light hits the left half of that retina, which in this case is near the temple. So the right visual field falls on the left halves of both retinas. The axons from these halves of the retinas then pass to the left side of the brain. Conversely, the right halves of the two eyes, which get information from the left visual field, project to the right side of the brain.

Axons from the retinas synapse in the brainstem region called the thalamus. Each thalamic neuron then sends their axons to **primary visual cortex** (sometimes called **V1**) in the occipital lobe. Almost every neuron in the visual cortex receives visual information from both eyes.

This process is easier to understand with a concrete example. Hold your right hand in front of you so that as you look out, it is to the right of center. If you look straight ahead and close first one eye and then the other, notice that you can see your hand with either eye. So both eyes get information about your hand and send that information to the opposite side of the brain, the left side. In the cortex, each neuron gets information about your hand from both eyes. In fact, there is a particular part of visual cortex that analyzes that part of visual space where your hand is. That cortical region does this by gathering information from both eyes, specifically from the portion of the left eye that is stimulated by that part of visual space and from the portion of the right eye stimulated by the same spot in visual space.

Remember from Chapter 3 that we can draw a map on the brain, showing how each part of the body sends touch information to a particular place on the somatosensory cortex. For the visual system, we can again draw a map on the visual cortex, but in this case our map would not be of one eye versus the other. Rather, the map on visual cortex would be a map of *visual space*, most of which is informed by both eyes. If you note the position of the numbers 1–9 in visual space on the retinas and visual cortex in Figure 6.22, you can see how particular regions of visual space are organized as inputs to particular regions of visual cortex.

Why does the brain blend this information from the two eyes? One reason is simply to get a better picture of the world out there. Having two eyes examine a particular part of visual space in most instances brings you more information than you could get from one eye. But if you close one eye for a few minutes, you probably won't be aware of much difference. In fact, people with only one functional eye get along pretty well. The main way in which vision is impaired by having only one eye is in telling how far away objects are, the topic we'll consider next.

Having two eyes helps bring us the world in 3D

Depth perception is the ability to perceive distance, or how near or far away an object is. Our visual system uses many features from a visual scene to provide us with depth perception. Much of our depth perception comes from **binocular cues**: information provided by our use of two eyes. Hold both hands out in front of your face again and this time hold up a finger from your left hand as far away as you can reach, while holding a finger of your right hand about half that distance away as in **Figure 6.23A**. Now close your left eye and align your fingers so that the finger of your right hand just blocks your view of the finger on your left hand, as in **Figure 6.23B**. Now open your left eye and close your right, and you'll see a very different image. Now the right finger no longer covers the left but seems to be well to the side (**Figure 6.23C**). Now keep both eyes open and hold the right finger so it blocks your view of some distant object, like a clock on a wall. If you now close first one eye and then the other, your experience may be that the object seems to move or the finger seems to move, or both. First of all, which eye still shows the finger over the object? For many people, it is the right eye, but for some people it is the left. Isn't it interesting how, when both eyes are open, it's difficult to actually experience the very different views that the two eyes provide? When both eyes are open, our brain automatically and seamlessly blends the two images to provide a single, coherent picture.

The two eyes get slightly different pictures simply because they are in slightly different places, about 6 centimeters apart. That means the relationship between a near object (your finger) and a distant object (say, a clock on the classroom wall) looks different from those two different vantage points. This difference in the views from two eyes is called **binocular disparity**: the difference in the apparent position of an object when seen from two different perspectives (**Figure 6.24**).

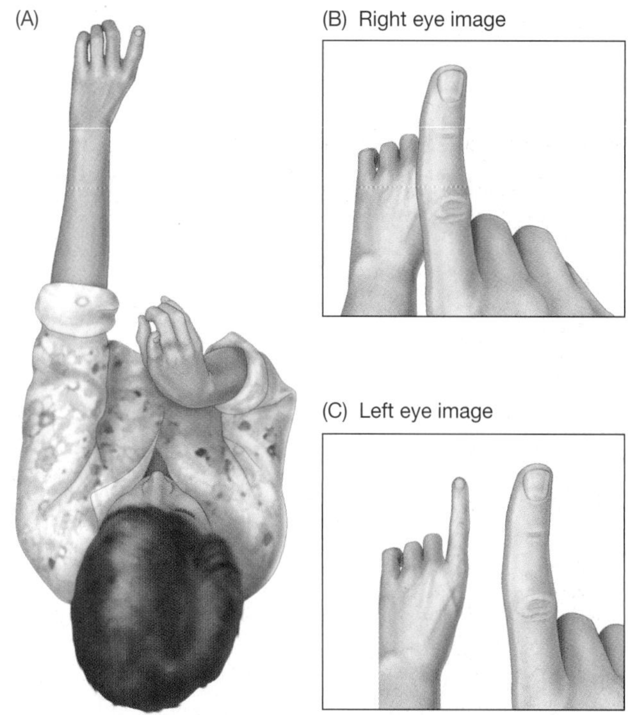

Figure 6.23 Binocular Vision Depends on Different Images on the Two Retinas Hold up two fingers as shown in (A) and, closing one eye, line them up so the tip of the nearer finger covers the tip of the farther one (B). Now if you close that eye and open the other, you get a very different view (C).

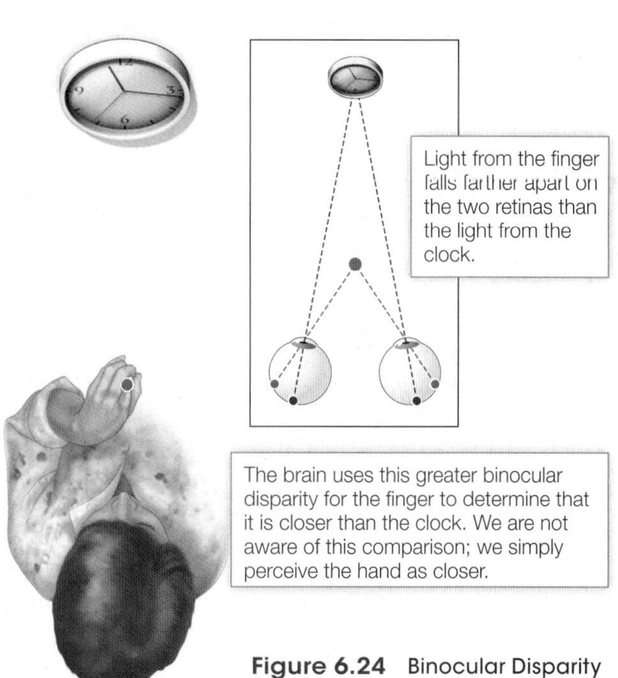

Light from the finger falls farther apart on the two retinas than the light from the clock.
The brain uses this greater binocular disparity for the finger to determine that it is closer than the clock. We are not aware of this comparison; we simply perceive the hand as closer.

Figure 6.24 Binocular Disparity

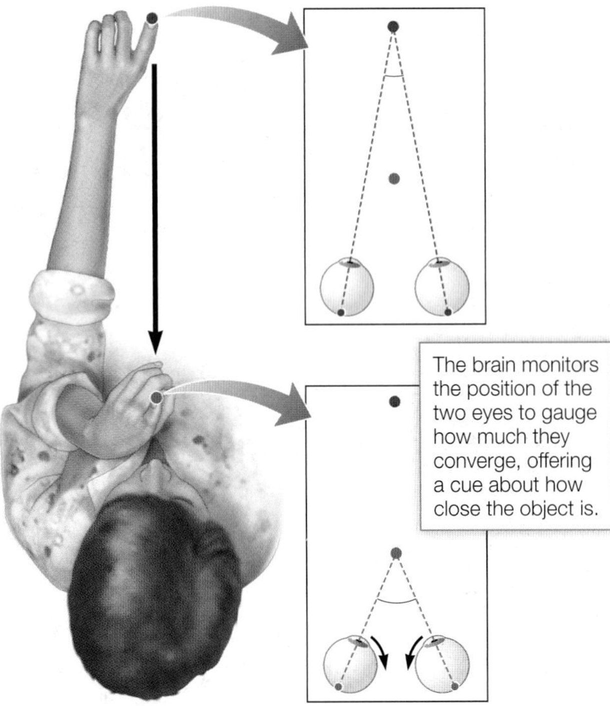

The brain monitors the position of the two eyes to gauge how much they converge, offering a cue about how close the object is.

Figure 6.25 Convergence Helps Gauge the Distance of Nearby Objects

Binocular disparity provides us with one important visual clue about whether objects are near or far: nearby objects provide a bigger difference to the two eyes than do distant objects. Prove this for yourself by moving your fingertip out of the way and looking at that distant object (such as a clock on the wall) while closing first one eye and then the other. The position of the object doesn't seem to move much, does it? But when you stick your hand out and look at your fingertip from each eye, you see a much bigger apparent "jump."

Normally when you look at a scene, your perception of whether objects are near or far away is provided by the brain analyzing whether objects are presenting a large or small binocular disparity. Near objects present a greater binocular disparity than distant objects. Of course, as in so many things, we are not *aware* that the brain is comparing binocular disparity for each object. We simply reap the benefit of that analysis by perceiving objects as near or far, more or less automatically.

Attempts to simulate depth perception, such as 3-D movies, exploit binocular disparity. For these systems to work, you must wear glasses that filter out some of what's on the screen, so that each eye gets a slightly different image. If it works well, the binocular disparity provided by the glasses will so closely match what happens when you're looking at a real scene that you'll perceive depth. Usually the film is made by having two cameras, carefully aligned about 6 centimeters apart (just like your eyes), film the scene simultaneously. By using the special glasses to deliver the two different images to your two eyes, you recreate binocular depth cues and perceive a three-dimensional scene.

convergence The binocular cue from the coming together of the two eyes to focus on really close objects.

monocular cues Depth cues that are available even to one eye.

When objects get really close to the eyes, we are provided with another binocular cue about distance. With both eyes open, hold that finger out in front of you again and now slowly move it toward your face until it touches your nose. As the finger gets close to your nose, you may be aware that you have to move your eyes to keep them both focused on the finger. Another person watching you will notice that your eyes come together, looking "crossed" by the time your finger touches your nose. This coming together of the two eyes to focus on really close objects is called **convergence** (the two eyes converge on the nearby object). Our brain monitors the movement of the eyeballs to converge on objects, and we automatically perceive them as really close (**Figure 6.25**).

While binocular cues such as binocular disparity and convergence provide most of our depth perception, they really only work for objects within about 4 meters. Any object farther away than that presents such a similar perspective to the two eyes (that is, no binocular disparity) that the brain cannot detect any difference. For objects farther away than 4 meters or so, we must use cues that are available even to one eye, so they are called **monocular cues** for depth. The simplest to understand is *occlusion*, when nearby objects block ("occlude") your view of more distant objects (**Figure 6.26**). Occlusion is the principle way artists inform you about depth in two-dimensional media, such as animated films, where no binocular cues are available (yes, you may be looking with two eyes, but they each get the same flat image).

Figure 6.26 Occlusion of Images Provides a Monocular Cue for Distance

Another important way to convey depth in two-dimensional media is controlling the size of an object in the picture. If everything else is equal, the far-

(A)

We perceive the smaller rabbits as farther away, in part because of the size cue.

(B)

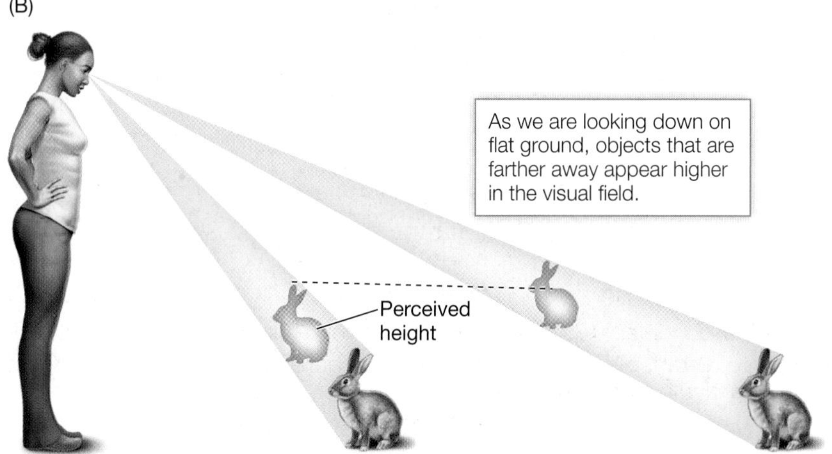

As we are looking down on flat ground, objects that are farther away appear higher in the visual field.
Perceived height

Figure 6.27 Size Cue and Relative Height

ther away an object is, the smaller it appears. This property that objects appear smaller when they are farther away is known as the **size cue** for depth (**Figure 6.27A**). Also, because we normally look down on a flat ground, the relative height of objects on the visual field provides another depth cue: the farther away the object, the higher it appears on the retina (**Figure 6.27B**).

When we look at a scene that includes straight lines, such as railroad tracks or the straight sides of buildings, another depth cue becomes apparent. This is the **linear perspective** depth cue: as the parallel lines move away from us, they appear to converge (grow closer together). The farther away they are, the more they converge (**Figure 6.28A**). Artists have used this cue to give a feeling of depth for centuries. It is also exploited in optical illusions such as you experience in **Figure 6.28B**. The railway lines make it clear that the person on top is farther away than the person on the bottom, so we perceive the upper person as bigger even though in fact the two people are the same size. (Don't believe they're the same size? Carefully cut out one figure and set it next to the other.)

size cue The property that objects appear smaller when they are farther away.

linear perspective The depth cue from parallel straight lines that converge with distance.

Figure 6.28 Linear Perspective

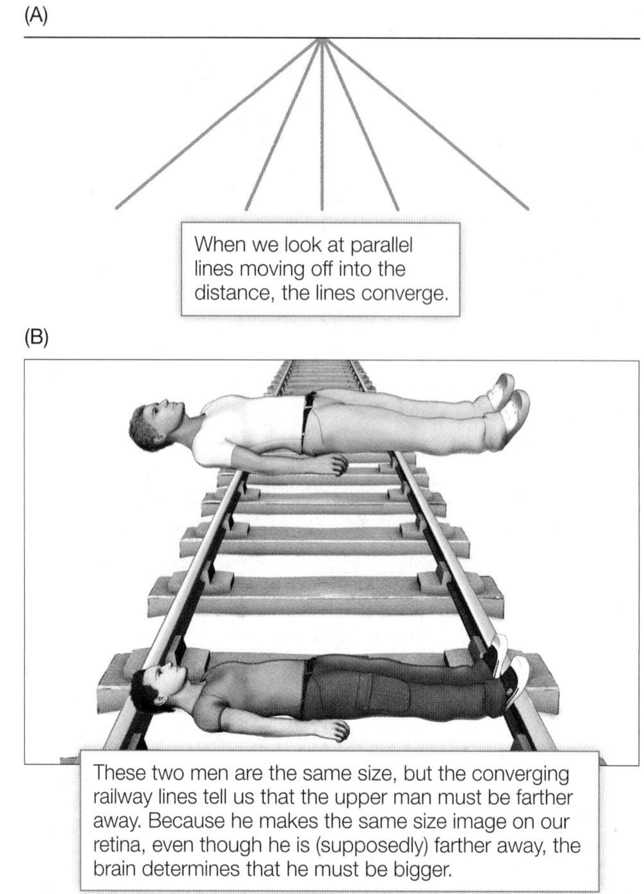
(A)
When we look at parallel lines moving off into the distance, the lines converge.
(B)
These two men are the same size, but the converging railway lines tell us that the upper man must be farther away. Because he makes the same size image on our retina, even though he is (supposedly) farther away, the brain determines that he must be bigger.

motion parallax A monocular depth cue from the shifting of a visual scene on the retina from head movement.

Another monocular depth cue is *distance fog*: the scattering of light in air makes more distant objects seem hazier than nearby objects. The farther away the object is, the foggier it appears (**Figure 6.29**).

Even if you use only one eye, there is a way to estimate how far away an object is—move your head. This monocular cue is **motion parallax**: the shifting of a visual scene on the retina as you move your head. Close one eye and extend your right arm out with the index finger blocking the view of some distant object, and then extend your left arm about halfway and line that index

Figure 6.29 A Distant Haze The increased fog overlying distant objects provides a monocular cue that they are farther away.

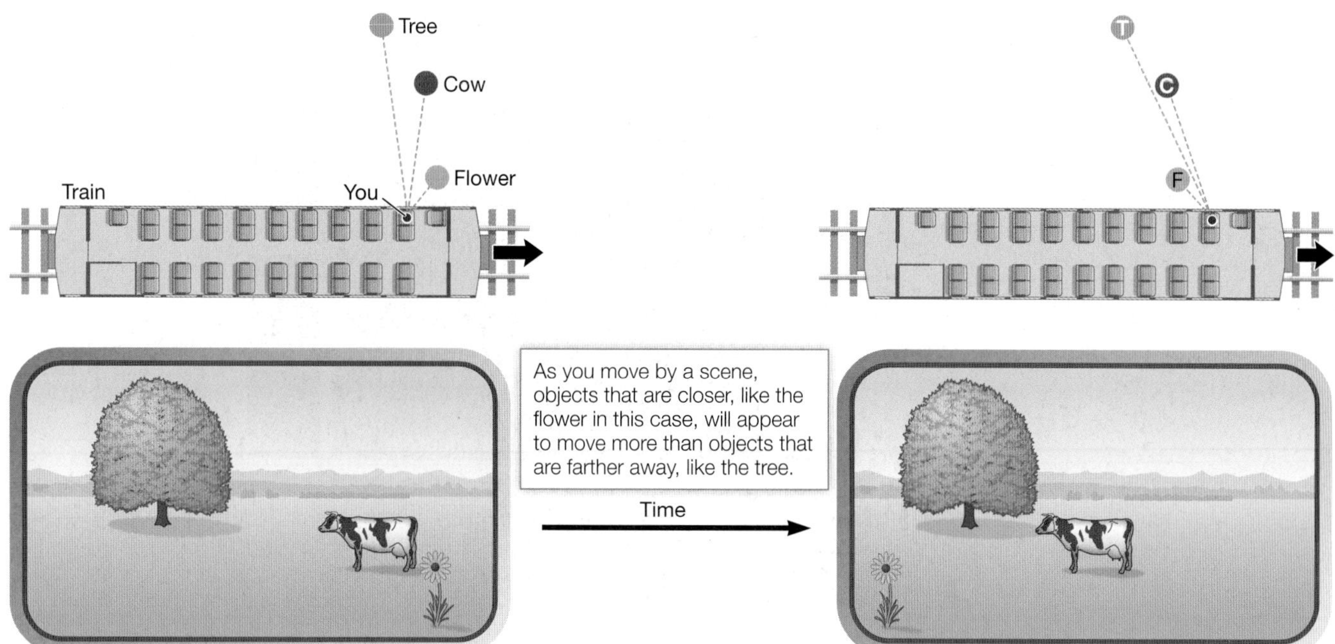

Figure 6.30 Motion Cues about Distance

finger up too. If you now move your head, notice that the fingers seem to move more than the distant object. In fact, the near finger seems to move more than the distant one. Likewise, if you're in a moving vehicle looking out the side, the position of nearby objects will appear to change more than that of distant objects (**Figure 6.30**).

Because of these many rich monocular cues for depth, you would have little problem driving a car or riding a bike even if you had use of only one eye. But for any activity that requires maneuvering around or manipulating nearby objects, you will do much better if you also have binocular depth cues.

iris The colored disc sitting just in front of the lens of the eye and that controls the amount of light entering the eye.

pupil The opening at the center of the iris.

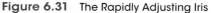

Our eyes adjust to massive changes in light intensity

Vision is so important to survival that natural selection has produced the ability to see over an astonishing range of light. We can see in a darkened theater, but we can also see in broad daylight, where it is over 10 billion times brighter! Until recently, no human-made devices could work over such a broad range of light.

Our eyes use two different processes to let us deal with such big differences in light. One process is readily visible at the front of the eye. The **iris** is the colored disc sitting just in front of the lens, and the opening in the center of the iris is the **pupil** (**Figure 6.31**). When we are in dim light, the iris opens up to make the pupil larger, letting more light in. If we move to brighter light, the iris may close down to make the pupil smaller, reducing how much light gets to the retina. This process works fast and is important, but the iris can only change the amount of light entering the eye by about 16-fold. So this process accounts for only a small fraction of our ability to see over large changes in light.

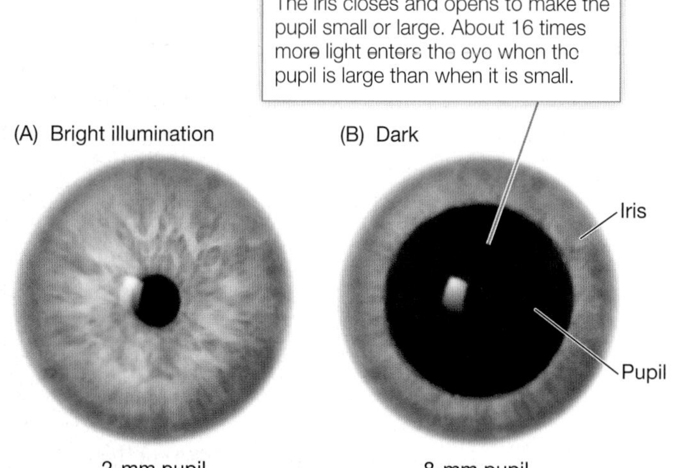

Figure 6.31 The Rapidly Adjusting Iris

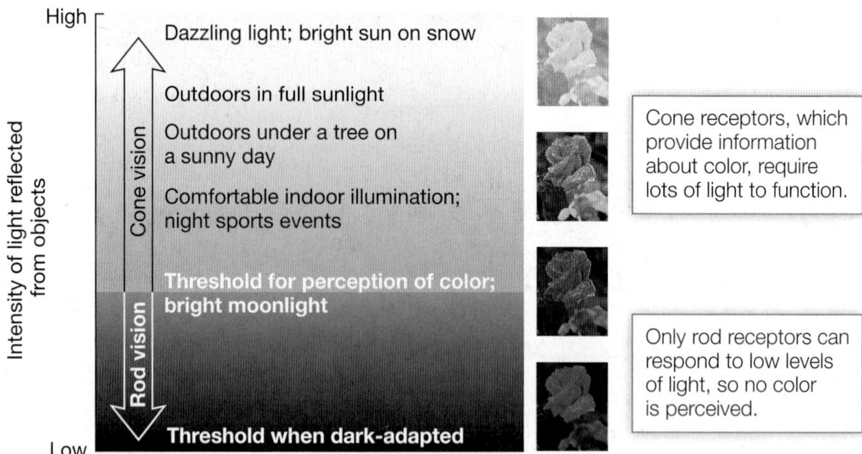

Figure 6.32 The Wide Range of Sensitivity to Light Intensity On a bright day there is more than 10 billion times more light than on a dark night, yet we can see in either condition. This wide range of sensitivity is possible because photoreceptors in the retina constantly change their sensitivity to light. This process takes much more time than changing the size of the pupil, but it provides a far greater range of sensitivity.

photoreceptor adaptation The ability of rods and cones to change their sensitivity.

The other process to control light sensitivity is slower, but it can work over a much broader range of illumination. **Photoreceptor adaptation** is the ability of rods and cones to change their sensitivity (Korenbrot, 2012). The photoreceptors may lower their threshold at one time, say when we've sat in a dark room for an hour, so that they can respond to a single photon, or particle, of light. Yet at another time, if we've been sitting on a park bench on a sunny day, those same photoreceptors may not respond until thousands of photons hit them (**Figure 6.32**).

Basically, photoreceptors adapt because the complicated chemical process that responds to light is carefully regulated inside the cells. As a result, the photoreceptors are always most sensitive to whatever light level they've been exposed to. Because this process is slow, it takes us a while to be able to see when we go from daylight into a darkened theater. The pupil opens up almost instantly, but until the photoreceptors have adapted, our eyes are too insensitive to let us see much.

The changes in our visual sensitivity to light bring up yet another difference between sensation and perception. The visual system is constantly detecting how much light enters our eyes. When we are reading a newspaper in a dimly lit room, less light is reflected from the black ink than from the surrounding paper, so we perceive the ink as black and the paper as white. That seems reasonable enough. But if we take that newspaper out into sunlight, a tremendous amount of light is bouncing off the ink now—at least 1,000-fold more light than when we were in the dim room. Yet we still *perceive* the ink as black. Why? Because our experience of "black" is not a purely sensory report of how much light hits the retina. Rather, our experience of "black" is a perception built up by comparing how much light bounces off the ink versus how much bounces off the surrounding paper. The perception of black requires the brain to take raw sensory information about the amount of light from the whole page and use it to calculate that the ink is black rather than gray or even white.

For an even more impressive example of when the brain must *calculate*, comparing the activity in many different sensory cells, let's talk about color next.

What is the physical nature of color?

To understand how we see colors, we first have to consider the very unintuitive nature of light. Sir Isaac Newton (1642–1727) was perhaps the first celebrity nerd (physicist Stephen Hawking presently holds Newton's old professorship). Newton shocked the world when he wrote that white light, such as that coming from the sun, is actually composed of many different colors combined: red-orange-yellow-green-blue-indigo-violet. Newton realized this by passing a beam of sunlight through a glass prism (**Figure 6.33A**). It must have been breathtaking for him when he realized that white light does not represent the *absence* of color, as probably every human mind for millions of years had thought, but instead is made up of *all* colors. This is so counterintuitive that only a great mind could have accepted the data and made sense of it.

Newton quickly realized why a colored object, such as a red apple, appears that color. When we shine a white light on it, the apple reflects back to our eyes only the red light that was hidden in the white light. Put another way, a red apple absorbs all the different colors in sunlight *except* the red component (**Figure 6.33B**). That red light is reflected, reaches our eyes, and causes us to experience a color we've come to call "red." What makes a white object white? It reflects all the colors in sunlight equally well. When a batch of light that contains a balanced mix of all colors hits our eyes, we experience that balanced blend as "white."

(A)

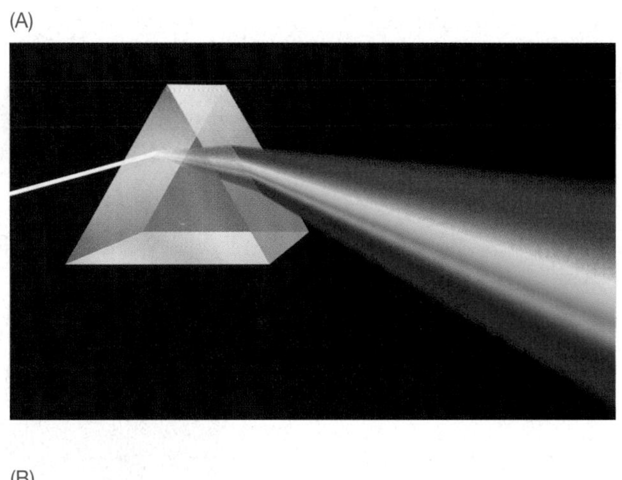

(B)

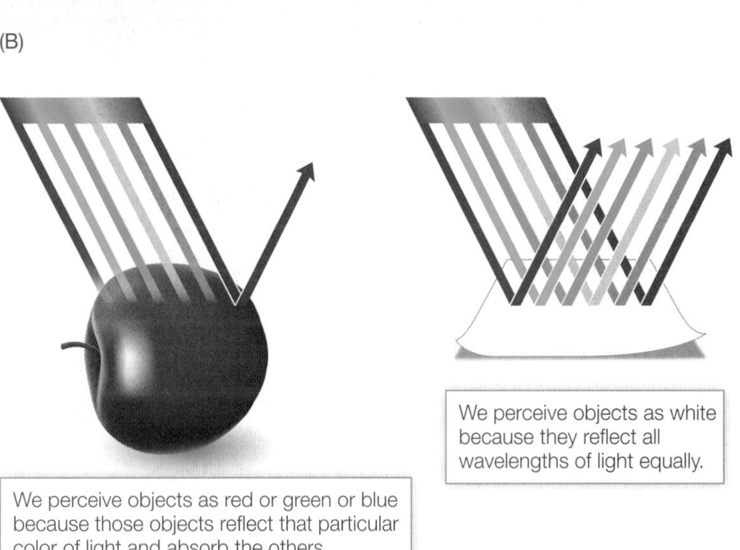

We perceive objects as white because they reflect all wavelengths of light equally.
We perceive objects as red or green or blue because those objects reflect that particular color of light and absorb the others.

Figure 6.33 White Light Contains Many Different Colors of Light

So what makes some light red and other light blue? The physical basis of colored light is about as counterintuitive as Newton's discovery. The tiniest particle of light is called a **photon**. Each photon behaves in many ways like a particle: a tiny bit of matter smaller than an atom. But photons also behave like waves, such as the ripples on the surface of water after you drop in a pebble. There is no easy way to reconcile these two properties of photons (both a particle and a wave), and modern physicists have had to abandon the attempt to understand it intuitively. They have just accepted that photons are both particles and waves, and have learned to predict how photons behave.

photon The smallest particle of light.

Happily, we can leave the paradoxes of physics for another class (philosophy?). Instead, we can visualize each photon as a single subatomic particle that also vibrates at a particular frequency as it moves through space. If the photon vibrates very fast, when it hits our eye we call the light violet. If the photon vibrates even faster, then our eye won't be able to detect it. Such light is called ultraviolet, or UV, and it has so much energy that it can damage our skin. It's the invisible UV light in sunlight that gives us sunburn. If a photon vibrates very slowly, we call it red. If the particle vibrates even more slowly, then our eye won't detect it. We call such really slow waves infrared, and although we can't see that kind of light, it is used in TV remote controls to let us change channels without getting off the couch. Infrared photons have so little energy that they are safe for

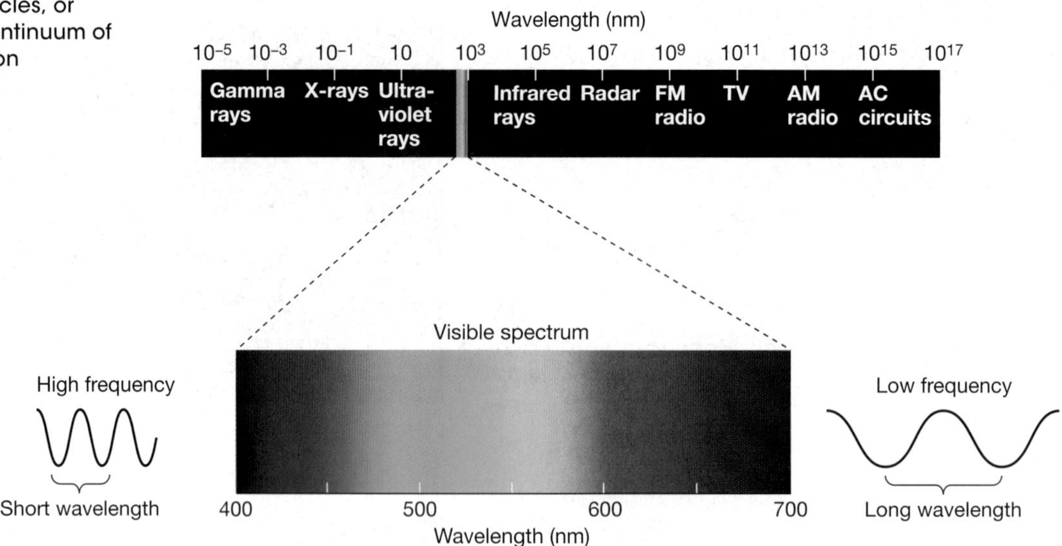

Figure 6.34 Light Particles, or Photons, Are Part of a Continuum of Electromagnetic Radiation

trichromatic theory The idea that color vision is based on receptors for three different colors.

even a toddler to shoot about the living room. No lamps will be broken (at least not by the infrared light coming from the remote). **Figure 6.34** indicates the frequencies of light that we can see and shows how these particles, which we call photons, are part of a continuum of electromagnetic radiation, including radio waves and microwaves. We can also think of light particles in terms of the frequency of the *wave* they produce as they vibrate through space.

Color is constructed by the brain

We mentioned earlier that the light receptors in the retina called rods detect light of any wavelength, and that the receptors called cones are used for detecting colors. You've probably heard before that we have different kinds of cones, each specialized to detect one color of light or another. The full story is a bit more complicated and, as so often is the case in discussions of vision, somewhat counterintuitive.

In the 1700s, scientists proposed the **trichromatic** ("three colors") **theory** that we see color because our eyes can distinguish between three primary colors: red, blue, and green. According to the trichromatic theory, we see all the other colors because they represent some blend of the primary colors, much as the primary colors of light can be blended to yield other colors of light. (Note that when you blend colors of *lights* you get very different results than when you blend colors of *paints*. Red and green light combine to make yellow light, which is not true for paints. Since vision is the detection of *light* bouncing off objects, the color-blending rules for light are relevant here.)

However, by the late 1800s several problems had been identified with this idea. For example, in addition to red, blue, and green, most of us also perceive yellow as a primary color: psychologically it seems distinct from the other three colors. More important, if you stare at a yellow object for a long time and look away, you'll see a faint blue spot, called an afterimage. Focus on the black dot in **Figure 6.35A** for at least 10 seconds under strong light, then look at **Figure 6.35B**. You'll see an afterimage, a faint version of the figure, but *all* the colors will be reversed. What is blue on the page looks yellow in the afterimage in the white circle in Figure 6.35B, while what was yellow on the page looks blue in the afterimage. Similarly, red on the page looks green, and vice versa. Also notice that

(A)

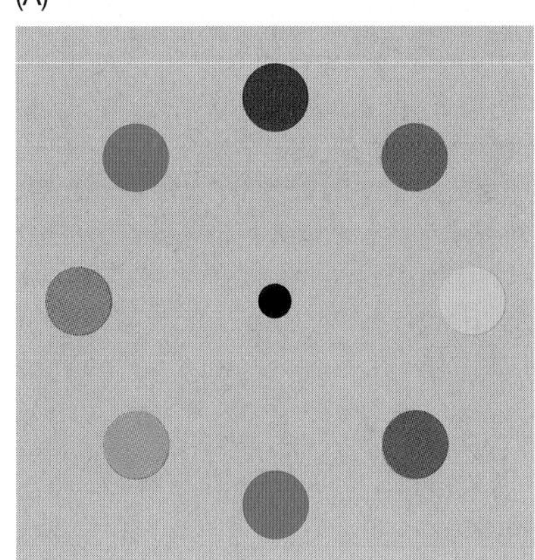

(B)

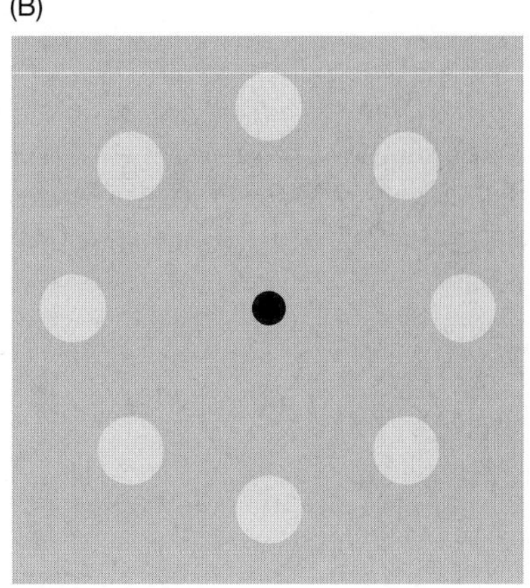

Figure 6.35 Afterimages Support a Color Opponent Theory Stare at the image in (A), focusing on the black dot in the center for at least 10 seconds. Then quickly shift your focus to the black dot in (B). The colors you see on the right are afterimages, and each is the opposite of the color on the left.

dark colors on the page look light in the afterimage, and vice versa. We already consider black and white to be opposites, but these results suggest that yellow and blue are also opposites, as are red and green.

Such experiments led to the development of the **color opponent theory** (sometimes referred to as *opponent–process theory*): color is detected by a system of *paired opposites* of color: blue versus yellow, red versus green, and black versus white. When we stare at Figure 6.35A, we tire out the blue detectors so that when we look at Figure 6.35B, the yellow detectors are more effective than the fatigued blue detectors. Our brain interprets the result as "there's something yellow there."

As in many other scientific conflicts, it has turned out that both the trichromatic and the color opponent theories are at least partly correct. As we'll see, we do indeed have three different receptors for color in the eye (as the trichromatic theory suggests), and the brain compares the activity of pairs of these receptors to analyze every color scene in terms of color opponency: blue–yellow, red–green, black–white (as the color opponent theory predicts). Let's see how both theories proved to be partly right.

Yes, most people have three different kinds of cones in the eye, and the cones differ in the wavelengths of light they respond to. Some cones are very good at detecting light of short wavelengths (and high frequency) like violet. Other cones are very good at detecting light of long wavelengths (and low frequency) like red. Cones of the third type are good at detecting light of intermediate wavelength (like yellows and greens). For now, let's call these three types of cones **short-**, **medium-**, and **long-wavelength cones**, often abbreviated as **S**, **M**, and **L cones**.

Figure 6.36 shows you how different wavelengths of light stimulate the three cones as well as the non-color-responsive rod photoreceptors. You may have been told that different cones detect only red, or only blue, or only green/yellow. But as you look at Figure 6.36, you can see that this is not true. In fact, the L cones not only respond to red light, but they respond to yellow and green and even blue light too! What's more, the M cones that respond to intermediate frequencies are stimulated

color opponent theory Also called *opponent–process theory*. The idea that color vision is based on a system of paired opposites of color.

short-wavelength cones Also called *S cones*. Cone photoreceptors that are best at detecting light of short wavelengths, such as violet.

medium-wavelength cones Also called *M cones*. Cone photoreceptors that are best at detecting light of intermediate wavelengths, such as yellows and greens.

long-wavelength cones Also called *L cones*. Cone photoreceptors that are best at detecting light of long wavelengths, such as red.

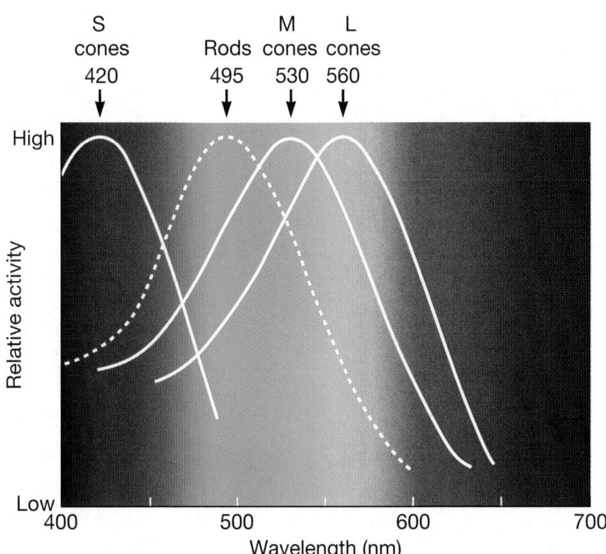

Figure 6.36 Photoreceptors Respond Differently to Light of Different Wavelengths Note that every photoreceptor responds at least somewhat to light of many different colors. We perceive each particular color based on the relative activity of at least two different cones.

Wonderful World of Color Using just three cones, each responding slightly differently to various wavelengths of light, we perceive a wide range of different hues.

by light of almost *any* color if it's bright enough. So the trichromatic theory was right to predict three color receptors, but wrong in predicting a receptor that sees only blue or only red. How can we understand this?

Figure 6.36 shows that what makes cones selective for color is that, when stimulated by *weak* light, they respond *best* to light of a particular frequency. But if the light is stronger, the cone will also respond to frequencies higher and lower than the optimal frequency. If you've been told that there are "red" cones, look at the graph showing how the L cone responds: it is most sensitive to yellow-green light, *not* red light. So when we see red (no, I don't mean when we're angry), it is not because red light reflected from that apple hit a cone that only responds to red light. Rather, the light stimulated the L cone quite a lot, the M cone a good bit, and the S cone not at all. By comparing the relative activity of these three cones (lots of L activity, some M activity, no S activity), the brain is able to infer what wavelength of light could produce that particular mix of activities. Of course, we are not aware of the mix of receptors being stimulated any more than we are aware of the existence of every color in pure sunlight. Rather, what we *experience* is simply the percept we call red.

In this way, the brain constructs for us the percept for every color, from red to violet, by comparing the *mixture of activity from all three cones*. For almost any color we're looking at, all three cones are stimulated to some degree. The only way to know exactly which color of light is coming into our eyes is to *compare* the activity of at least two different cones. That's why, no matter what you were taught before, there is no single class of "red" detectors or "blue" detectors, for example. For the most part, our information about color comes from *comparing* the activity of *different kinds of receptors*.

The rods contribute to color perception too. They respond broadly to light of almost any color except extreme red (see Figure 6.36). But by reporting to the brain how much total light is present, the rods also inform us about color. For example, if the rods are reporting lots of light total, then we'll experience the colors as brighter. Dim the lights in the room, and when the rods detect this, the colors—which reflect the various wavelengths of light the same as ever—will nevertheless look more faded. If we keep dimming the lights, eventually we will fall below the threshold for cones and will experience no colors at all. At this point, as the saying goes, "all cats look gray in the dark." Then only the rods are working, and by themselves they cannot discriminate any wavelengths of light.

Look again at Figure 6.36 and notice that the one color of light that does *not* stimulate rods much is red. This is why cars should use red light to illuminate the dashboard at night (but fashion calls for other colors). To keep your night vision, so you can see moving objects in dim light, you have to avoid having your rods adapt. If you glance at the red dashboard, the rods get virtually no stimulation at all. When you glance at a dashboard illuminated in white light, the rods adapt slightly, which may make it harder to see something out there in the dark.

By the way—it is because of our understanding of color opponency in our vision that lifeboats are yellow. To maximize the chance of spotting the lifeboat out on the vast blue ocean, they are intentionally colored the opposite of blue: yellow.

The visual system uses shortcuts to provide nearly instantaneous perception

In the natural world, almost all light comes from above, from either the sun in daytime or the moon and stars at night. So one thing that our brain automatically assumes when looking at a scene is that the light is falling from above. Only if we can actually see an alternative source, such as a flashlight on the ground, do we abandon this assumption. So when looking at **Figure 6.37A**, you probably see

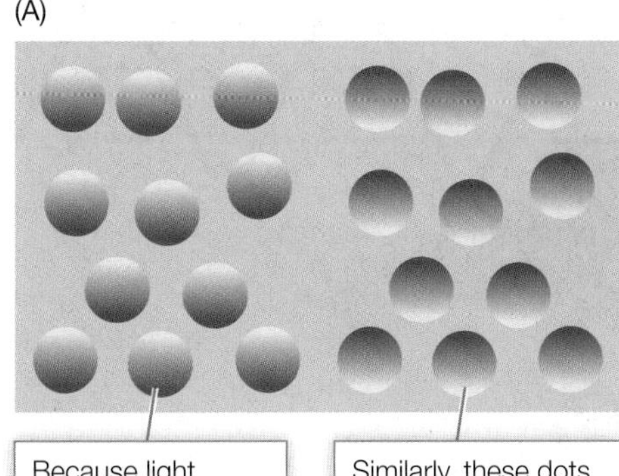

Similarly, these dots appear to be dented in, away from us. But if you hold the book upside down, the appearance of the dots will be reversed.

(B)
Shading around a patch of light affects the perception of brightness. For example, even though the tiles in the middle are the same shade of gray, one appears darker than the other. If you don't believe this, use your pinky finger to cover up the line where they meet. See?

Figure 6.37 Shadows Offer Cues (A) Note that whether you hold the book right-side up or upside down, the bumps look gray and the dents look blue. (B) Our perception of brightness is heavily dependent on context. (B from Purves & Lotto, 2010.)

the dots on the left as raised bumps on the surface, while the dots on the right look like round indentations. We have this perception because the shading on the dots, if light is coming from overhead, makes sense only if there are bumps on the left and dents on the right. But if you turn the book upside down, you'll see that what once looked like bumps now look like dents, and vice versa. You probably were not aware of this assumption of an overhead light when you examined the dots. You simply perceived that some dots are bumps and some are dents. By taking this shortcut, the brain can analyze the visual scene and make sense of it faster. Only in special cases, such as a tricky figure like **Figure 6.37B**, does our visual experience fail to match the stimulation on the retina.

Another shortcut used by the visual system is to assume that many nonliving objects don't change much. We expect objects to keep the same size, shape, and color, even though the *image* an object presents to the retina may change drastically. For example, when we see a bicycle tire from the side, a circular image hits our retina and of course we see a circle. But as we lie the tire down, the image hitting our retina changes from a perfect circle to an oval, yet we still *perceive* the object as a circle. This is an example of **shape constancy**: the visual perception that an object retains the same shape, no matter what angle we happen to see it from. For example, in **Figure 6.38** you perceive the bicycle tire as round, even though, if you trace the figure, it presents an oval shape. For all you know, it really is an oval seen head-on, but your experience of bicycle tires leads you to perceive it as a circle.

shape constancy The visual perception that an object retains the same shape, no matter what angle we happen to see it from.

size constancy The visual perception that an object does not change size, regardless of its distance away.

color constancy The visual perception that an object retains the same color, no matter what color light is shining on it.

Size constancy is the visual perception that an object does not change size, even as we get closer or farther away from it. In general, this is a safe assumption. Assuming the object remains the same size means that, as the image of the object gets smaller, we assume that it is moving farther away.

Color constancy is the visual perception that an object retains the same color, no matter what color light is shining on it. Again, in the natural world, few objects change color quickly, so if the color of light bouncing off an object and hitting our eyes changes over the course of a few seconds, we perceive the object as staying the same color and that the color of the light must have changed.

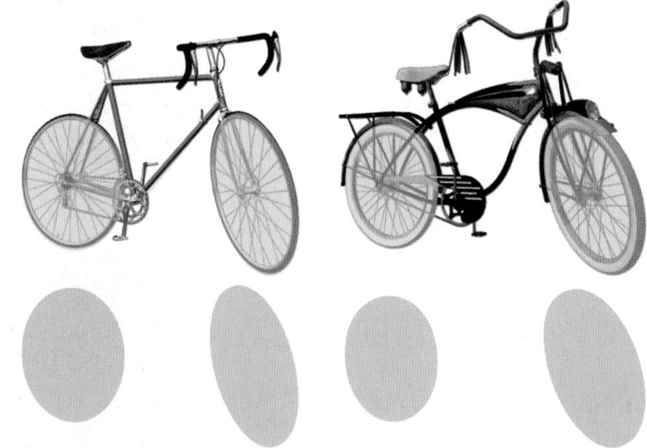

Figure 6.38 Shape Constancy Our knowledge of the world leads us to perceive all these bicycle tires as round, even though the shapes hitting our retinas vary considerably.

Figure 6.39 **The Ponzo Illusion** The two horizontal lines are the same length, but the upper one looks longer.

We can consider *optical illusions* as instances when our visual system analyzes a scene and makes a mistake, giving us a perception that does not quite fit reality. Now that you understand some of the properties of the visual system, you can understand how some optical illusions work.

For example, in the famous illusion in **Figure 6.39**, you probably perceive that the upper horizontal lines are longer than the lower ones, but in fact they are the same length. Optical illusions are not just amusing—they also offer us an opportunity to infer something about the process by which we see. For Figure 6.39, for example, we can ask: Why does adding those slanted lines on the sides cause us to perceive the horizontal line as longer or shorter, depending on which way the slanted lines are added? One idea is that we normally see such slanted lines in linear perspectives, as in Figure 6.28. In that case, the upper horizontal line must be farther away, so we perceive it as longer than the lower line, which is closer to us.

We noted that color perception is constructed by comparing the firing rate of two or more cones. But we automatically incorporate lots of other information about an object in constructing our percept of color. If an object is in shadow, like the middle center square of the Rubik's Cube in **Figure 6.40A**, we perceive

(A)

Three squares on the colored cube are exactly the same brown color, but we perceive them as lighter or darker depending on their surroundings. Because the middle square is in the shade, the equal intensity of light striking our retina is perceived as being due to that square being brighter. So we perceive it as brighter, almost orange.

(B)

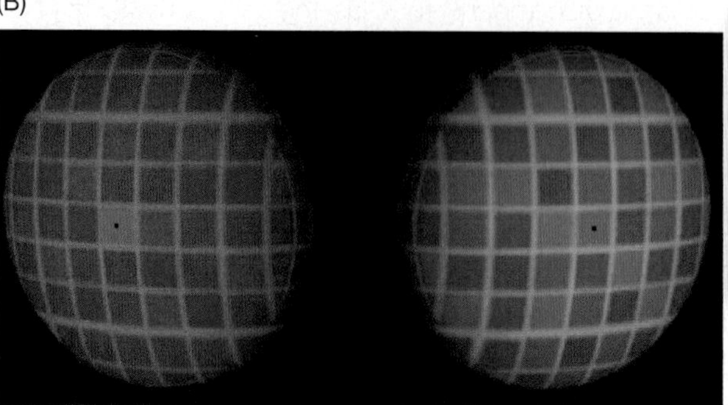

Because we perceive these two objects as being illuminated by different colors of light, we perceive the two center squares with dots as being different colors (green and yellow), but they are reflecting light of the same (greenish) color.

Figure 6.40 The Importance of Context for Color

it as a lighter color than the center square on top. But in fact they both reflect the same color of light to our eyes, stimulating cones in identical fashion. Similarly, in **Figure 6.40B** we infer that lights of two different colors are shining on the two buttons, so we perceive their center squares as different colors (but as you probably have guessed, they are identical). Just as pain is in the brain, so too is color. Our brain takes sensory information and distorts it to provide us with a perception that is usually accurate. In real life, these percepts are almost always accurate.

The visual system organizes perceptions of groups of objects

As we noted in Chapter 1, in the early twentieth century, a group of German psychologists founded **Gestalt psychology**, which emphasizes that the whole perception is more than just the sum of separate sensations. In German, *Gestalt* means, loosely, a unified or meaningful whole. The Gestalt psychologists insisted that the perceptual whole is greater than the sum of its parts. For example, if you look at **Figure 6.41A**, you will perceive a sphere with barbs sticking out of it, even though there are no lines forming a circle. Such figures are sometimes called *subjective contours* because you perceive lines that are not there.

Gestalt psychologists also noticed that looking at individual photos one after another relays a perception of movement, a notion exploited in motion pictures, which were a quite new invention at the time. We perceive a whole, meaningful, smooth movement when in fact there are simply a few unmoving images. Our tendency to see motion in these situations is sometimes called *apparent motion*.

The **Gestalt rules of perception** explain a number of ways in which vision organizes images. For example, the *rule of continuity* says that we tend to impart continuity, assuming that objects are permanent, which is why we see the sphere in Figure 6.41A and why we perceive a moving person rather than a person who pops up first in one place and then another on screen. The rule of continuity also explains why we perceive an uninterrupted visual field, when in fact we receive no sensory input from the blind spots in each eye (see Figure 6.21).

The Gestalt *rule of proximity* (*proximity* means "closeness") says that we have a tendency to perceive objects that are close to one another as part of a whole (**Figure 6.41B**). The closer they are to each other, and the farther they are from other objects, the more likely we are to think of them as part of a single object.

Gestalt psychology A German school of psychology that emphasizes that the whole perception is more than just the sum of separate sensations.

Gestalt rules of perception Tenets to explain many instances where vision organizes images.

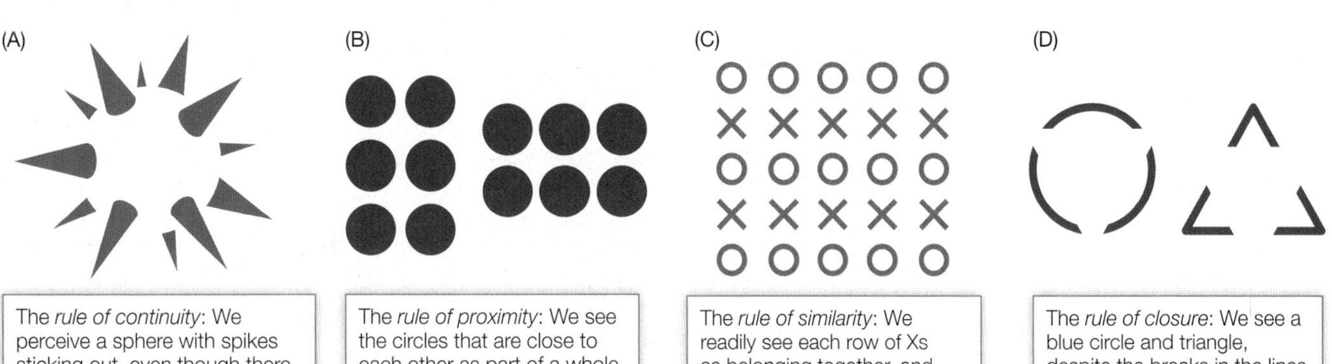

The *rule of continuity*: We perceive a sphere with spikes sticking out, even though there is no circle depicted.

The *rule of proximity*: We see the circles that are close to each other as part of a whole.

The *rule of similarity*: We readily see each row of Xs as belonging together, and each row of Os together.

The *rule of closure*: We see a blue circle and triangle, despite the breaks in the lines. We also "see" two white triangles.

Figure 6.41 Some Gestalt Rules of Perception

For most people, the perception switches back and forth from faces to a vase, and it is difficult to perceive both at once.

Figure 6.42 The Gestalt Rule of Symmetry

The Gestalt *rule of similarity* notes that the more figures resemble each other in color, texture, shape, and so on, the more likely we are to regard them as part of some whole (**Figure 6.41C**).

The *rule of closure* notes that our perception tends to fill in gaps, closing them off to perceive a whole object, such as the triangle and circle in **Figure 6.41D**. Note that the rule of closure is simply a special case of the rule of continuity—in this case we are imparting continuity across small breaks rather than large breaks.

The Gestalt *rule of symmetry* says that we perceive symmetrical lines as being part of a single object, so in **Figure 6.42** we may perceive a vase between the two faces. This is also known as the *figure-ground rule*, because we tend to perceive objects as either in the foreground or background. In this case, which object we perceive depends on which part of the picture we perceive as the background. This figure also illustrates another central point of Gestalt psychology: we perceive *either* a vase or two faces, and cannot perceive both at the same instant (see Figure 1.5B). The sensory input is the same, but our perception is something more than the sum of that sensory input.

Initially, Gestalt psychology was seen as an alternative view, rebelling against the notion that we could understand the mind simply by understanding sensory receptors. As sometimes happens with new and radical ideas that are basically correct, eventually many Gestalt ideas were incorporated into mainstream psychology. Gestalt psychologists were early and strong proponents of the distinction between sensation and perception that we introduced at the start of this chapter and that all psychologists recognize today.

6.3 SUMMARY

- Vision begins when light is refracted by the *cornea* and *lens* to focus an image on the *retina*.
- Two types of *photoreceptor* cells detect light: *rods* are extremely sensitive, so they work in low light, while *cones* require more light.
- Each eye has a large *blind spot*, but normally the brain "fills in" these regions, so we are not aware of them.
- The left *visual field* stimulates different parts of our two retinas and is reported to the right visual cortex, while the right visual field is reported to the left cortex.
- Differences in the visual images on the two eyes provide *binocular cues* to the distance of objects, giving us information about the depth of objects in a view.
- Many *monocular cues* about depth, including occlusion, *size cues*, *linear perspective*, and distance fog, supplement the binocular cues.
- We see over an enormous range of light intensities because the *pupil* can quickly change size to control the amount of light entering the eye, but it can adjust over only a small range.
- To adjust to greater changes in light, we must rely on *photoreceptor adaptation*, which can vary enormously but works more slowly than changes in pupil size.
- Color perception depends on the ability of different cones to respond differentially to light of various wavelengths. Most people have three different types of cones—*short-*, *medium-*, and *long-wavelength cones*—which together provide trichromatic vision as the *trichromatic theory* predicted.
- Our perception of color depends on the differential response of at least two different types of cones, as the *color opponent theory* predicted.
- The brain makes assumptions about the information from the eyes, such as the assumption that objects do not change shape or size,

and that light comes from overhead. Many optical illusions exploit these assumptions, providing special instances where we perceive something that isn't there because the assumptions do not apply.

- *Gestalt psychology* considers perception of the whole to be more than the sum of the parts. People tend to perceive continuities and recognize individual features that are close together or similar in shape to be part of a whole object.

REVIEW QUESTIONS

1. Describe the path of light entering each eye, and how information from the two retinas reaches the left and right cortex.
2. What are the two main types of photoreceptors, and what does each contribute to our overall vision?
3. What are the binocular cues and monocular cues to distance vision?
4. Describe the two processes that allow us to see over such a broad range of brightness. Which works faster? Which provides us with vision over a greater range of brightness?
5. Describe how the visual system constructs our perception of color.
6. Describe what some optical illusions tell us about assumptions the brain makes in visual perception.
7. What are the Gestalt rules of perception? Sketch some examples of each.

Food for Thought

Due to mutations in the genes for the pigments used in photoreceptors, some women have *four* different kinds of cones, each responding differently to various wavelengths of light. What do you think color perception might be like for these women?

6.4 Hearing

Things to Learn

- Nature of sound and its detection in the ear
- How the inner ear analyzes frequencies in sound
- Cues used for sound localization

As the descendants of people who lived on the plains of Africa, where a fast-running predator might suddenly appear on the horizon, or the presence of ripe fruit on a distant tree could signal a much-needed meal, we find vision powerful and immediate. Hearing can be just as important. For one thing, we use audition to communicate with people in public and on the phone. Before writing was invented, the only way people could communicate in any complex way was by listening to each other. Helen Keller, who was both deaf and blind, noted that blindness deprives you of contact with things, while deafness deprives you of contact with people. Two more things that make hearing valuable are that it works in the dark, and you can hear things that are out of sight, behind other objects.

We'll discuss what sounds are and how the ear detects them. Then we'll review how the brain interprets those sensations of sound to detect different pitches—how high or low a sound is—and to determine where a sound is coming from.

Sound is a pattern of pressure in the air (or water)

Sound can be understood as a result of a pattern of molecules bumping into each other. If I bang a drum in the lecture hall, the membrane of the drum vibrates like mad. When the membrane moves up, it pushes the air molecules that were next to the membrane up. Those air molecules bump more air molecules, which bump more, and so on. When the membrane moves down, it sucks some air molecules after it. If the membrane moves up and down thousands of times per second, then waves of air molecules will be bumping into each other thousands of times per second. Eventually the waves of bumping air molecules reach my ear and I hear a sound. Likewise, the singing of a whale may cause water molecules miles away to bump each other, and if my ear is in the water, I'll hear it.

Notice that none of the air molecules that were near the drum (or water molecules that were near the whale) ever reach my ear. Rather, those air molecules bump other air molecules that bump others, and so on, until eventually the air molecules that were next to my ear get bumped, and so on. Similarly, if you were to rudely push someone at the end of a line of people waiting to buy movie tick-

Figure 6.43 The Nature of Sound

(A)

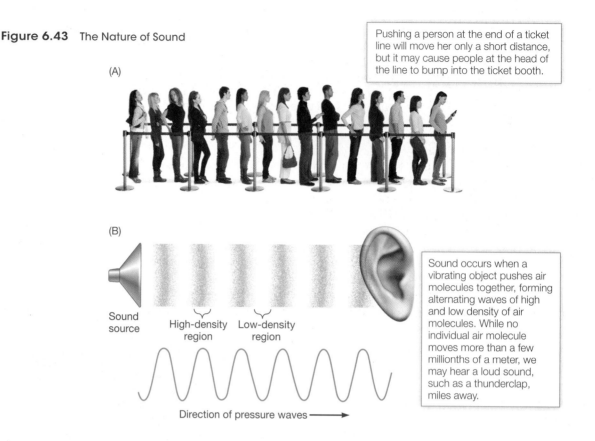

Pushing a person at the end of a ticket line will move her only a short distance, but it may cause people at the head of the line to bump into the ticket booth.

(B)

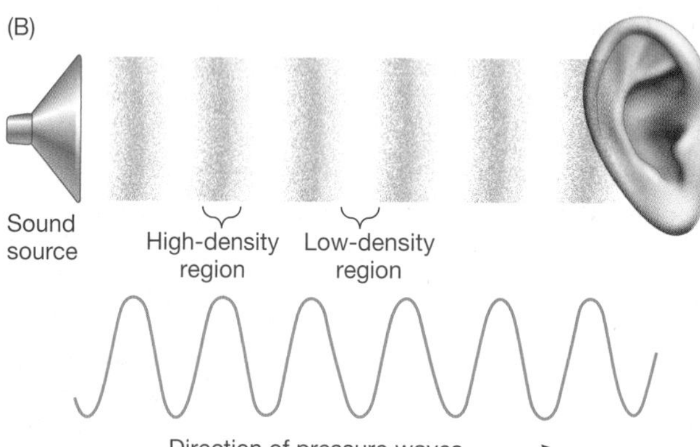

Sound occurs when a vibrating object pushes air molecules together, forming alternating waves of high and low density of air molecules. While no individual air molecule moves more than a few millionths of a meter, we may hear a loud sound, such as a thunderclap, miles away.

ets, she would bump into the person in front of her and the bump would continue up the line (**Figure 6.43A**). Your push might affect people at the other end of the line. Likewise, air molecules in motion bump against each other, resulting in alternating waves of high and low density called sound waves (**Figure 6.43B**). When these alternating waves of pressure hit our ears, we hear sound. If the waves of pressure are close together, arriving with a high frequency, we experience the sound as a high pitch. We experience low-frequency pressure waves as low in pitch.

The outer and middle ears funnel sound to the cochlea

The first job of the auditory system is to capture sound waves so they can be analyzed. The **outer ear** (technically known as a *pinna*) serves as a funnel, gathering sounds from a wide area around us and directing those sounds down a tunnel leading to the middle ear (**Figure 6.44A**). Many animals can move their outer ears around to gather sounds from a particular direction, but most humans cannot move their ears (although it's hilarious when they can). If we want to pay particular attention to sounds coming from a particular direction, we swivel our head to point our ears that way.

The **middle ear** consists of the *eardrum* (or *tympanum*), which vibrates in response to sounds gathered from the outer ear, and three tiny little bones that transmit the vibration to the inner ear (**Figure 6.44B**). These bones, called **ossicles** ("tiny bones"), vibrate along with the eardrum and push against a tiny oval window of the inner ear. The three middle ear ossicles are called the *malleus* ("hammer," because of its shape), the *incus* ("anvil," because the "hammer" pushes on it), and the *stapes* ("stirrup," because of its shape). The malleus is attached to the eardrum and picks up the vibrations there, and then transmits them to the incus. The incus in turn transmits the vibrations to the stapes, which passes them on to the inner ear.

outer ear Also called *pinna*. The visible part of the ear and the canal leading to the eardrum.

middle ear The eardrum and the three tiny bones for conducting sound.

ossicles The three tiny bones in the middle ear that amplify sounds.

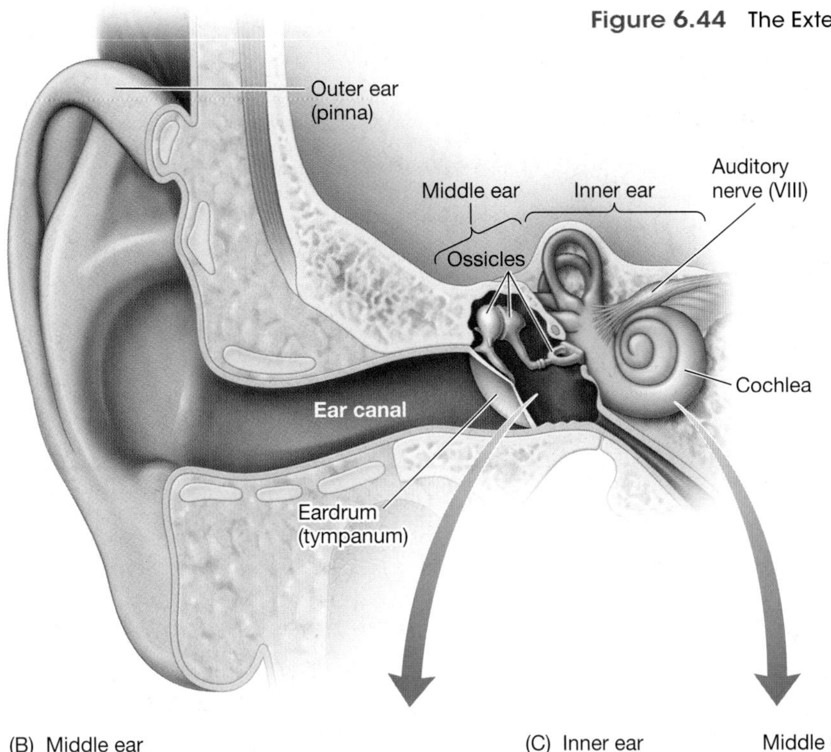

Figure 6.44 The External and Internal Ear

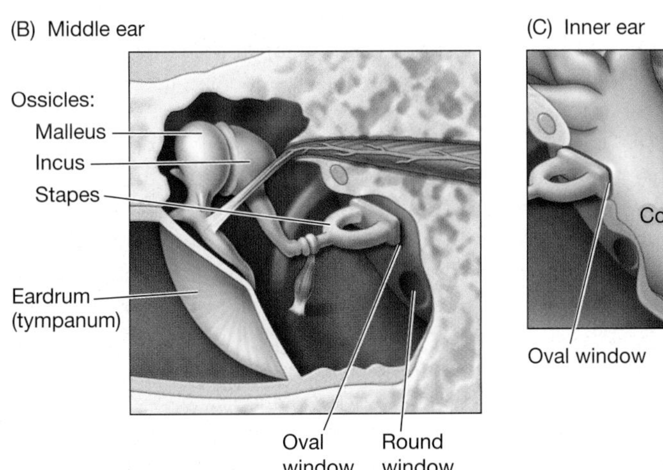

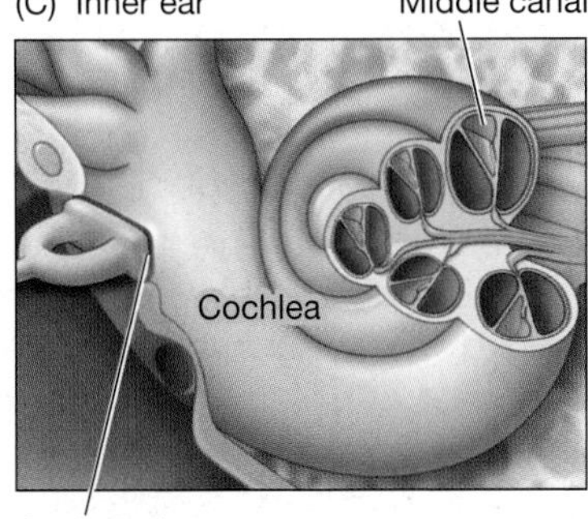

Because the eardrum is much larger than the oval window of the inner ear, the ossicles serve as an amplifier: the tiny vibrations of the large eardrum are transformed into stronger vibrations on the oval window. What's more, there are tiny muscles attached to the ossicles that can make the connections between them looser or stiffer. That means the amount of amplification from eardrum to inner ear can be adjusted. In response to a sudden loud sound, the muscles attached to the ossicles contract, dampening vibrations of the little bones. This action protects the inner ear somewhat from large vibrations that might cause damage.

The **inner ear** (**Figure 6.44C**) consists of a tiny snail-shaped organ called the cochlea that detects sounds, and some similar organs that are important for balance. The **cochlea** is a bony, fluid-filled, spiral-shaped tunnel that detects the vibrations transmitted by the ossicles. The outside of the cochlea is bony, to protect it from damage, but two regions of the cochlea next to the middle ear are covered with a membrane. One of these, the **oval window**, is attached to the foot of the stapes, and it is here where the vibrations picked up at the eardrum are passed on to the inner ear.

inner ear The tiny snail-shaped cochlea, and some similar organs that are important for balance.

cochlea A bony, fluid-filled, spiral-shaped tunnel of the inner ear that detects the vibrations transmitted from the tiny bones in the middle ear.

oval window The opening from the middle ear to the cochlea of the inner ear.

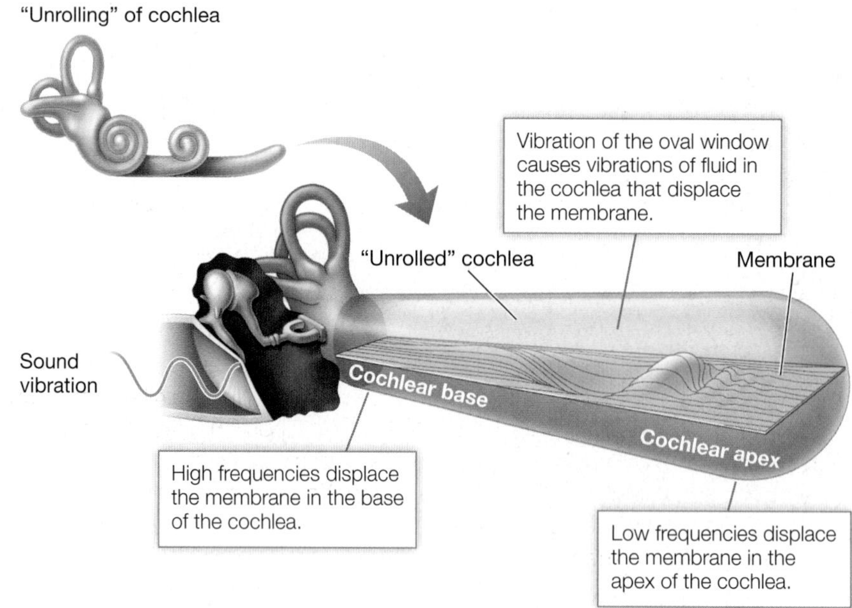

"Unrolling" of cochlea
Vibration of the oval window causes vibrations of fluid in the cochlea that displace the membrane.
"Unrolled" cochlea
Membrane
Sound vibration
Cochlear base
Cochlear apex
High frequencies displace the membrane in the base of the cochlea.
Low frequencies displace the membrane in the apex of the cochlea.

Figure 6.45 Cochlear Membrane Movement for Sounds of Different Frequencies

The cochlea detects the various frequencies of sound

Like a snail shell, the interior of the cochlea is hollow, but it is filled with fluid. Several membranes divide this corkscrew-shaped tunnel inside the cochlea into three compartments or canals, as shown in Figure 6.44C. Notice that each of these canals is also shaped like a corkscrew, running from the large start of the cochlea, where the middle ear ossicles connect, to the smaller tip of the spiral. The *middle canal* of the cochlea contains a complex device lined with auditory receptors that detect sound and report to the brain. The cochlea analyzes every sound, detecting which frequencies are present and how intense they are.

To understand how the cochlea works, it helps to imagine that we've unwound the snail-shaped cochlea so that we now have a long, straight tube (**Figure 6.45**). Membranes running the length of the fluid-filled tube divide it into the three parallel compartments (see Figure 6.44C). At one end of the cochlea is the oval window, where the ossicle called the stapes from the middle ear passes on vibrations from the eardrum. The vibrations from the stapes push on the oval window, sending vibrations into the fluid inside the cochlea.

The vibrating fluid inside the cochlea causes the membranes to vibrate too. The portion of the membranes nearest the oval window is called the base, and the opposite end is called the apex. In some ways this terminology is unfortunate, because in a triangle, say, the base is wide and the apex, or tip, is narrow. But in the cochlea, the base membrane near the oval window is narrower than the apex at the other end. As the fluid in the cochlea vibrates, it causes the membrane to vibrate, wobbling up and down. The gradual change in the width of the membrane means that high-frequency vibrations cause the narrow, base end to wobble more than the wide apex (see Figure 6.45). Conversely, low-frequency vibrations make the wide apex end wobble more. It may help you to remember that the narrow end of the membrane vibrates at high frequencies while the wide end vibrates with low frequencies if you reflect that, in general, small objects tend to vibrate faster than large objects. Tweety little flutes are a lot smaller than huge growling tubas, right?

If two different frequencies, one high and one low, are transmitted to the cochlea together, then two different parts of the membrane vibrate: one near the base and one near the apex. What's more, the louder the sound, the stronger the vibrations, and therefore the greater the wobbles in the membrane. So if we could just monitor exactly how much wobble there is at each segment of the membrane, from base to apex, we could reconstruct what particular mix of frequencies must have arrived at the eardrum. This is exactly what the cochlea does to tell the brain what jumbles of frequencies are in the sounds around us. When you realize that the snail-shaped cochlea, at about a third of an inch in diameter, is smaller than some real snails, this is a marvel of miniaturization. Let's find out how the cochlea does this.

The cochlea picks up good vibrations (and bad)

Let's take a closer look at the membranes that stretch from the base next to the oval window to the apex at the tip of the cochlea. The cochlea contains several rows of specialized receptor cells, each of which has little hairlike extensions pointing up away from one of those membranes. These **hair cells** detect the vibrations along the membrane and send that information to the brain.

How do the hair cells detect vibrations along the membrane? Their "hairs" jut up to touch the bottom of another membrane. As the membranes vibrate up and down, the upper membrane slightly bends the hairs of the hair cells. This produces an action potential in a neuron underneath the hair cell, which travels along the auditory nerve until it enters the brainstem, telling the brain that this particular part of the cochlea just wobbled. The person may then perceive a sound with a particular frequency, depending on just where along the cochlea that particular hair cell sat. The louder the sound, the more the hairs bend and the more action potentials travel along the auditory nerve. All this bouncing around may sound a bit violent to you, and indeed some hair cells are damaged inevitably as we age. Because we are not able to replace them, each lost hair cell reduces our ability to hear. Unfortunately, loud sounds can greatly accelerate this hair cell loss (Oesterle, 2013), so you really want to keep the volume low on your earphones.

In sum, the marvelous job that the cochlea manages is to analyze every sound and sort out just which frequencies are mixed together (based on which regions along the cochlea were wobbling) and how loud each frequency is (based on how large the wobble was at each point) and then to send that information to the brainstem. The brainstem then sends the information to higher parts of the brain, including the temporal cortex, to analyze that information further.

How do we know where a sound is coming from?

Over the course of evolution, animals that can localize *where* a sound is coming from, whether a roaring predator or a calling mate, enjoy a selective advantage over those that cannot. Natural selection's solution to the problem of **sound localization** is the evolution of two ears. Just as comparing the input to two eyes helps us determine where objects are in a scene, comparing the input to two ears helps us determine where a sound came from. Comparing input to the two ears provides several cues, collectively known as **binaural** (two ear) **cues** for sound localization. One binaural cue is the *intensity difference*: comparison of the intensities of sounds that reach the two ears. If I hear a sudden "bang" and it is louder in my left ear than my right, then the source of the sound is probably somewhere on my left.

In theory, having two ears anywhere on the body would give some cues about the source of a sound, but it turns out that having the ears on opposite sides of the head helps. A sound coming from my left enters my left ear unimpeded, but my head blocks some of that sound from getting to my right ear. We say that the head casts a *sound shadow*: the head absorbs some of the sound, lessening its intensity on the side opposite the sound source (**Figure 6.46**). The sound shadow cast by our head magnifies the intensity differences of sounds reaching the two ears.

hair cells Specialized receptor cells inside the cochlea.

sound localization The ability to perceive the source of a sound.

binaural cues Information about the location of sound found by comparing input to the two ears.

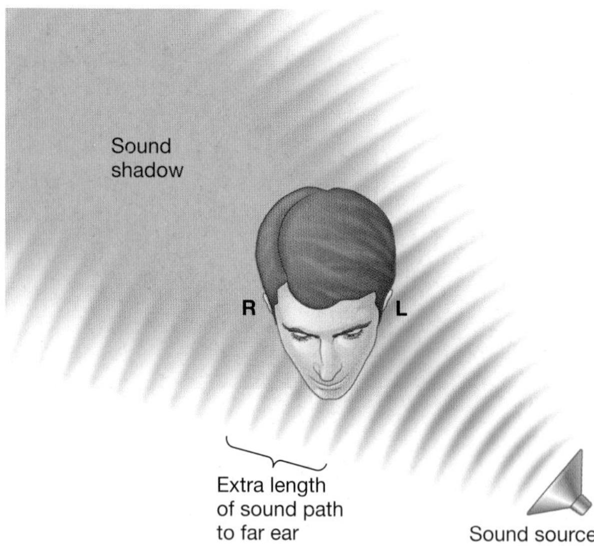

Figure 6.46 Binaural Hearing Helps Us Localize Sounds

Some sounds are not blocked very much by objects like your head. You've probably noticed when a car was driving near you with its windows rolled up and the sound system cranked up loud. Mostly all you could hear were the deep frequencies, the bass notes. So you probably heard the rhythmic, low-frequency *boom-boom-boom* of the drums but not the high-frequency vocals. That's because low-frequency sounds flow around and pass through objects, like heads and car windows, without much loss of intensity. So while the sound shadow and resulting intensity difference to the two ears are significant for medium- to high-frequency sounds, they don't help much to localize low-frequency sounds.

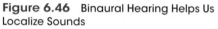

Another binaural cue is especially helpful for localizing low-frequency sounds. Psychologists refer to the time that it takes for something to happen as *latency*. In sound localization, the *latency difference* refers to the different times a sound arrives at the two ears. If the sound arrives at the left ear before the right, the source of the sound is probably on the left. There is a latency difference in the arrival of sounds at the two ears because sound waves move in air at about 340 meters per second (about 800 miles per hour). Because the openings of your ears are about one-eighth of a meter (5 inches) apart, a sound from your extreme left should enter your left ear about 300-millionths of a second (300 microseconds) before entering your right ear. If the source of the sound is directly in front of you, it should arrive at your two ears at about the same time. By comparing latency differences, the brain can gauge whether the sound is coming from the left or right of you.

Whether intensity differences or latency differences serve to localize sounds has been subject to some debate. The modern theory, called the **duplex theory**, is that we use *both* intensity differences (for medium to high frequencies) and latency differences (for low to medium frequencies) to localize sounds. In real life, most sounds are a mixture of both low and high frequencies, so both cues are normally available. And as always, we are not aware of this analysis going on in the brain. We simply perceive that the sound is coming from over here or over there.

duplex theory The idea that both intensity differences and latency differences are used to localize sound.

6.4 SUMMARY

- We detect waves of vibrating air molecules, called sound, when our *outer ear* (pinna) funnels the sound to the eardrum (tympanum).
- In the *middle ear*, three tiny bones (*ossicles*) transmit the vibrations of the eardrum to the *inner ear*, a snail-shaped structure called the *cochlea*. The vibrations of the ossicles are transmitted to the *oval window* of the fluid-filled cochlea. Inside the cochlea, the vibrations cause membranes to vibrate up and down.
- Sounds of different frequencies cause different areas of the cochlear membranes to vibrate. High frequencies stimulate the narrow end close to the oval window, and low frequencies affect the wider end at the tip.
- Cochlear membrane *hair cells* detect the movement and send signals about sound to the brain.
- We perceive the source of a sound by comparing the input to the two ears (*binaural cues*), comparing the latency and intensity of the sound. Sounds arriving to the left ear first originated from somewhere on our left. Sounds that are louder in the right ear originated from somewhere on our right.

Food for Thought

Specialized systems of hand gestures allow deaf people to communicate with one another, creating a "deaf culture." As electronic implants allow people to hear who would otherwise be deaf, should we be concerned that deaf culture may disappear?

REVIEW QUESTIONS

1. Follow the path of vibrations from a firing cannon to the inner ear of someone 1,000 meters away. Be sure to note whether air molecules, membranes, bones, fluid, or cells are vibrating.
2. How does the cochlea analyze a mixture of sounds?
3. What are binaural cues for localizing the source of a sound?

6.5 Taste and Smell

Things to Learn

- Biological mechanisms for detecting chemicals in odor and taste
- Detection of the five different tastes
- Mechanisms for detecting thousands of different odors

Our ancestors who lived in water evolved specialized *chemosensory systems* to detect chemicals. By detecting nutrients in the water around them, animals could find and follow a food source for a nice meal. Detecting chemicals secreted from a predator could help an animal avoid being a nice meal for someone else. The chemosensory systems all rely on specialized receptor proteins embedded in the cell membranes of receptor neurons. When the outside portion of the receptor protein encounters a molecule of the proper shape, the two bind together briefly, which causes the receptor protein to trigger changes inside the cell. Often the receptor opens up a channel that allows ions to flow, altering the electrical charge of the cell, which may trigger an action potential. In this way, chemosensory receptors are much like the neurotransmitter receptors we learned about earlier. Neurotransmitter receptors detect chemicals that serve as neurotransmitters, while chemosensory receptors detect chemicals that offer information about what's happening outside the cell.

Our nose and tongue are exquisitely sensitive chemical detectors

We have two chemosensory systems, the olfactory system in the nose for detecting odors, and the taste system on the tongue for detecting tastes. Both systems are remarkably sensitive, able to detect vanishingly small amounts of chemicals. Indeed, engineers are still struggling to make machines as effective as the human nose, and no one has yet made a machine as effective as a dog at detecting many different odors.

The olfactory and tastes systems are not as independent as you might think. Whenever you eat, both systems are actively responding, because chewing food not only exposes your tongue to the chemicals, but it also generates odors that reach your nose. What you might think of as the "taste" of food is more properly known as **flavor**: the combined stimulation provided to taste receptors in the mouth and olfactory receptors in your nose. As we'll see next, taste receptors provide rather limited amounts of information. It's the additional odor information that gives us the rich and varied flavors of food.

flavor The combined stimulation provided to taste receptors in the mouth and olfactory receptors in the nose while eating something.

Five taste receptors contribute to flavor

Our ability to distinguish tastes is called *gustation*, and it begins in **taste buds**: collections of 50–150 cells, including taste receptor cells and support cells (**Figure 6.47A**). Taste buds are distributed on the surface of your tongue, as well as on some of the soft tissue in the back and roof of your mouth. Each taste bud is roughly spherical in shape and has an opening, called the **taste pore**, at the surface of the tongue where chemicals in the mouth encounter the surface of taste receptor cells (**Figure 6.47B**). The **taste receptor cells** respond to their designated taste by stimulating axons in the base of the taste bud to send action potentials to the brain. A chemical that encounters the taste receptor cell and excites it is called a **tastant**.

You may have seen a popular demonstration that your nose is incredibly important for detecting flavors. A person who is blindfolded and holds his nose

taste buds Collections of 50–150 cells, including taste receptor cells and support cells, on the surface of the tongue, back of the mouth, and roof of the mouth.

taste pore An opening in a taste bud on the surface of the tongue, where chemicals in the mouth encounter the surface of taste receptor cells.

taste receptor cells Cells on the surface of the tongue that produce taste receptor proteins, which actually detect one of the five tastes.

tastant A chemical that encounters the taste receptor cell and excites it.

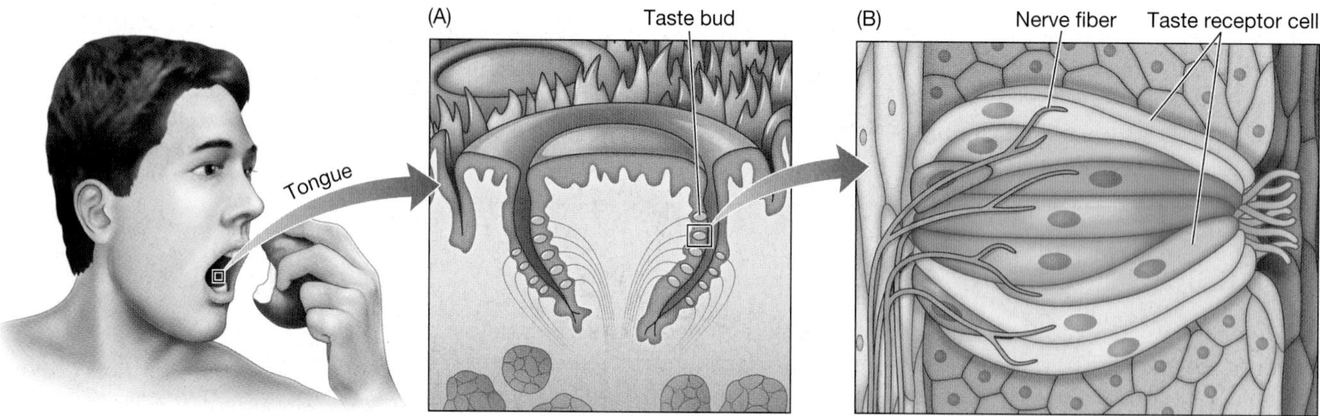

Figure 6.47 Taste Buds and Taste Receptor Cells (After McLaughlin et al. 1994.)

closed while chewing may not distinguish between a bit of apple and a bit of onion (Hänig, 1901). That's because the taste receptors in the mouth can only distinguish five different kinds of tastes: **sweet**, **sour**, **salty**, **bitter**, and **umami** (the Japanese word for "meaty"—this taste is also referred to as "savory"). All the other varieties of flavors, as mentioned earlier, derive from the combination of tasting and smelling the food. You can demonstrate this for yourself with a piece of chocolate. First, hold your nose firmly closed, then pop the chocolate in and begin chewing. You'll taste a mixture of sweet and bitter, but not much more. Now, while you're still chewing, let go of your nose and experience all that *flavor* provided by adding your sense of smell.

Five different kinds of taste receptor cells are each specialized to detect one of the five tastes. What distinguishes the five different taste receptor cells? Each produces a distinctive receptor protein that spans the cell's membrane. The portion of the protein that extends outside the membrane binds to the tastant, and this action triggers chemical reactions inside the cell that may result in an action potential being sent to the brain. In sum, there is a taste receptor *organ* (the tongue), which has on its surface taste receptor *cells*, which produce taste receptor *proteins* that actually detect the bitter, sour, sweet, salty, or meaty molecule.

There are several different taste receptor proteins for each class of taste. That is, each taste receptor cell has receptor proteins specific for a particular class of tastes. For example, a taste receptor cell that responds to bitter may make many of the different bitter receptor proteins, but it will not make receptor proteins for sweet, sour, or the other tastes.

Some tastes are relatively easy to understand because we can easily define which kinds of chemicals cause those tastes. For example, the receptor protein for detecting salty tastants depolarizes the receptor cell by allowing the positively charged sodium ions (remember that table salt is sodium chloride) to enter. Similarly, the sour receptor protein is thought to work by letting positively charged hydrogen ions enter the cell. Most sour tastes, such as vinegar, are chemically acidic, which means they have a surplus of hydrogen ions in solution.

There are several different taste receptor proteins that detect the many different kinds of sugar molecules: sucrose in table sugar, fructose in fruits, lactose in milk, and so on. Likewise, the few umami receptor proteins all detect amino acids (since meat consists mostly of protein, there are plenty of amino acids in meat). Umami receptor cells are especially sensitive to one amino acid, glutamate, which is why a sprinkling of monosodium glutamate (MSG) lends a savory taste to foods.

Responses of the bitter detectors are quite complex, responding to a broad range of chemicals that cannot be simply defined. There are at least 30 different

sweet One of the five different tastes, detected by taste receptor proteins that respond to sugar molecules.

sour One of the five different tastes, detected by taste receptor proteins that allow positively charged hydrogen ions to enter the cell.

salty One of the five different tastes, detected by taste receptor proteins that allow positively charged sodium ions to enter the cell.

bitter One of the five different tastes, detected by taste receptor proteins that respond to a wide range of chemicals.

umami One of the five different tastes, detected by taste receptor proteins that respond to amino acids.

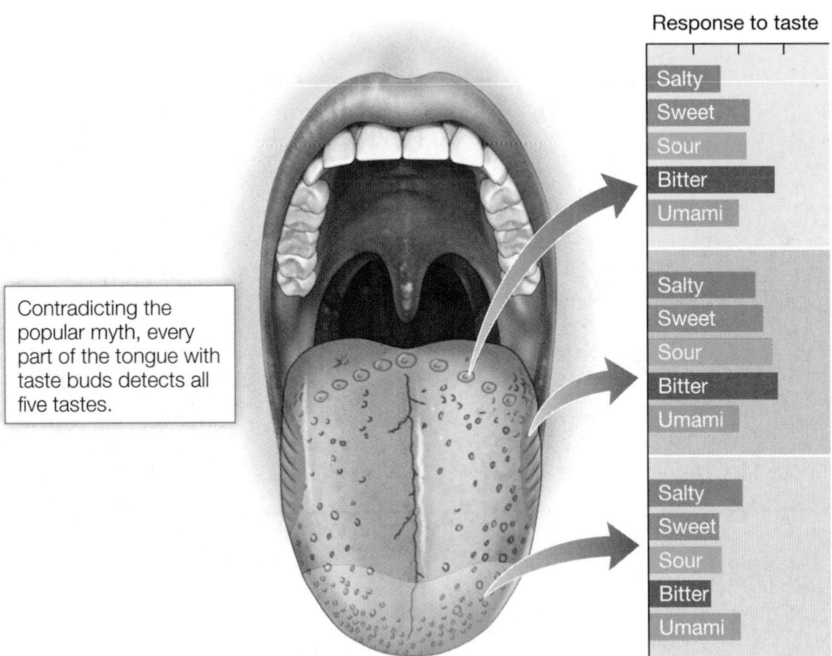

Figure 6.48 The Real Taste Map (After Bartoshuk, 1993, and Chandrashekar et al., 2006.)

bitter receptor proteins, which is why bitter is the most subtle of the classes of taste and the most difficult to describe. Receptors for bitter tastants are important for detecting poisons in food, as "spoiled" food usually tastes bitter (and sour) because of bacteria growing there. Those bacteria would probably make us sick. Bitter tastants also play an important role in providing the many nuances of food.

One interesting theory for why adults are more likely to appreciate bitter flavors such as coffee, green vegetables, alcoholic beverages, and dark chocolate is that some bitter receptor proteins are not expressed by taste receptor cells until maturity (Mennella, 2008; Mennella et al., 2010). Perhaps all bitter tastes are alike for children because they don't yet make the right receptor proteins to distinguish the bitter tastes in coffee and broccoli from those in a chemical like quinine. Maybe when you are young it is better to avoid all bitter foods, in case some are poisonous, until you gain some experience.

There is a small red berry, sometimes called the "miracle fruit," that contains a complex molecule that temporarily disables sour receptors. After chewing on the berry and rubbing the paste on your tongue, normally sour fruits like lime or lemon taste sweet. In this case, you perceive the sweet sugars (fructose, mostly) that are always present in such fruits but are normally overwhelmed by the tremendous sour taste. Block the sour receptors and the sweet taste comes through.

Taste buds are concentrated on the edges of the tongue, so you can't detect tastes very well in the center (**Figure 6.48**). But there is an enduring myth that different parts of the tongue detect different tastes (sweet at the tip, bitter at the back, and so on). This is nonsense. Any part of your tongue or mouth that can detect one taste can also detect the other four.

Some aspects of food are unrelated to taste buds and odors. Foods have textures that are detected by touch receptors in the mouth and tongue. Spicy foods contain chemicals that can cause a burning sensation. These chemicals actually affect temperature detectors in your mouth, causing them to signal a burning sensation even though the food may be cooler than your mouth. These chemicals evolved in plants to keep mammals from eating the seeds, and it works for most mammals. But many humans (I am one) have developed a love of those spices. Other chemicals, such as those found in menthol, activate touch receptors that normally register cool temperatures, so we perceive candies with menthol to feel cool.

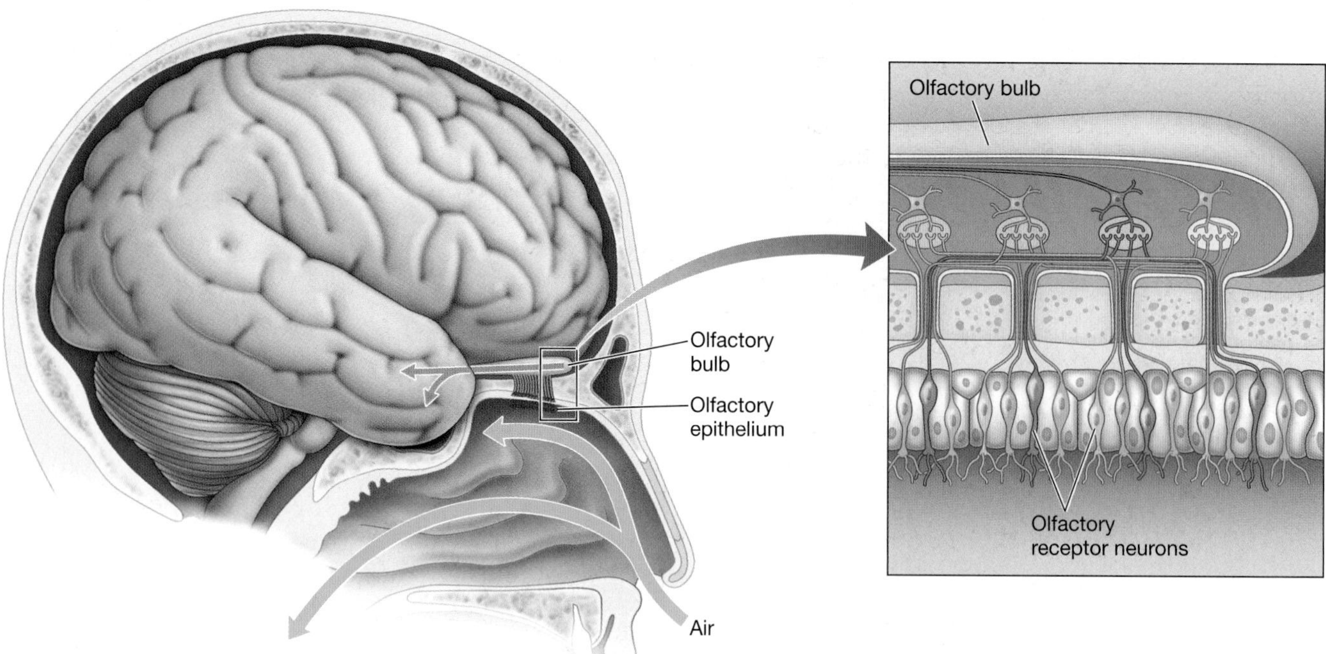

Figure 6.49 The Olfactory System

Thousands of different odor receptors bring us the richness of flavor

If you're disappointed to learn that we can detect only five tastes, let me console you with the fact that we can detect at least 10,000 different odors. By combining our abilities to detect five tastes and thousands of odors, we can appreciate an amazingly wide range of flavors. As mammals go, our odor discrimination is not at all impressive. No one has ever been able to find the limits of dogs' ability to detect different odors, but the performance of bloodhounds makes it clear that they are far more sensitive to odors than we are, and can distinguish many more odors than we can. As you learn about how the olfactory system works, you'll learn one important reason why dogs and mice are a lot better at detecting odors than we are.

Olfactory receptor neurons detect odors and are embedded in a sheet of cells, called the **olfactory epithelium**, lining the inside of the nose (**Figure 6.49**). Molecules that can be smelled are called **odorants**. As odorants enter the nose and land on the olfactory epithelium, they may bind to receptor proteins on the olfactory receptor neurons. The binding either excites or inhibits the firing of the receptor neuron. When these neurons fire, they send impulses along their axons, which pass through tiny holes in the skull, to stimulate neurons in the **olfactory bulb** of the brain.

We make hundreds of different kinds of olfactory receptor proteins, each specialized to bind with odorant molecules of a particular shape. Each olfactory receptor neuron makes only one kind of receptor protein to detect odorants. By comparing the activity of the hundreds of different kinds of olfactory receptors, the brain receives a very distinct signal for each of the thousands of odors we can distinguish.

Why can we detect more odors than there are receptors? Because a given odorant may excite one receptor neuron while inhibiting another. Or it may excite one type of receptor neuron much more than another. For this reason, our brain's ability to compare the relative activity of the hundreds of different olfactory receptor neurons gives us the ability to distinguish many more odors. Notice that this system is similar to the color detection system, where comparing the *relative activity* of three kinds of cones lets you detect four psychologically distinct colors (blue, yellow, red, green) and hundreds of intermediate hues.

olfactory receptor neurons Sensory neurons that detect odors and are found embedded in a sheet of cells lining the nose.

olfactory epithelium The sheet of cells lining the inside of the nose, in which the olfactory receptor neurons are embedded.

odorants Molecules that can be smelled.

olfactory bulb The part of the brain that receives impulses from the axons of the olfactory receptor neurons.

One reason other animals have a better sense of smell than we do is that they make many more olfactory receptor cells, and many more kinds of olfactory receptor proteins, than we do. We have about 400 different genes for making olfactory receptor proteins (Malnic et al., 2004). That means we have a few hundred different kinds of olfactory receptor neurons, and we compare their activity to distinguish lots of different odorants. But mice and dogs have over *1,000* different genes for olfactory receptor proteins, so they can distinguish many more odorants than we can (Quignon et al., 2005).

The Cutting Edge

Bionic Eyes

In both science fiction and real life, technology is making it possible for the deaf to hear and the blind to see. It is already routine to use *cochlear implants* to restore some hearing in adults who have lost hair cells in the cochlea, and to provide hearing for the first time in children born without hair cells. These devices rely on a microphone to pick up sound, then use electrodes surgically implanted in the cochlea (see Figure 6.44) to stimulate the auditory nerve directly.

The next frontier is to restore sight in people who have lost photoreceptors in the retina due to disease. Several devices are in production, and one, the Argus II Retinal Prosthesis System, was approved for use in the United States in 2013 (Stronks & Dagnelie, 2014). The device uses a camera mounted on a pair of glasses to record a visual scene. It then simplifies the image and simulates how that scene would have stimulated photoreceptors in the retina. Because a patient's own photoreceptors are gone or dysfunctional, the device uses an array of electrodes surgically implanted over the retina to stimulate neurons directly (**Figure 6.50**). The neurons then fire action potentials out the optic nerve to inform the brain about the visual scene.

The current Argus II model consists of an array of 60 electrodes on the retina, providing only 60 pixels. But that is enough to allow patients to walk around objects and go through doorways. Efforts are under way to produce a model with 1,000 electrodes, which is expected to make it possible to recognize faces. In theory, enough electrodes might restore normal vision. It's estimated that about 1 in 4,000 adults are blind because of degenerating retinal photoreceptors, so the potential impact of "bionic eyes" could be tremendous, especially for those people and their families.

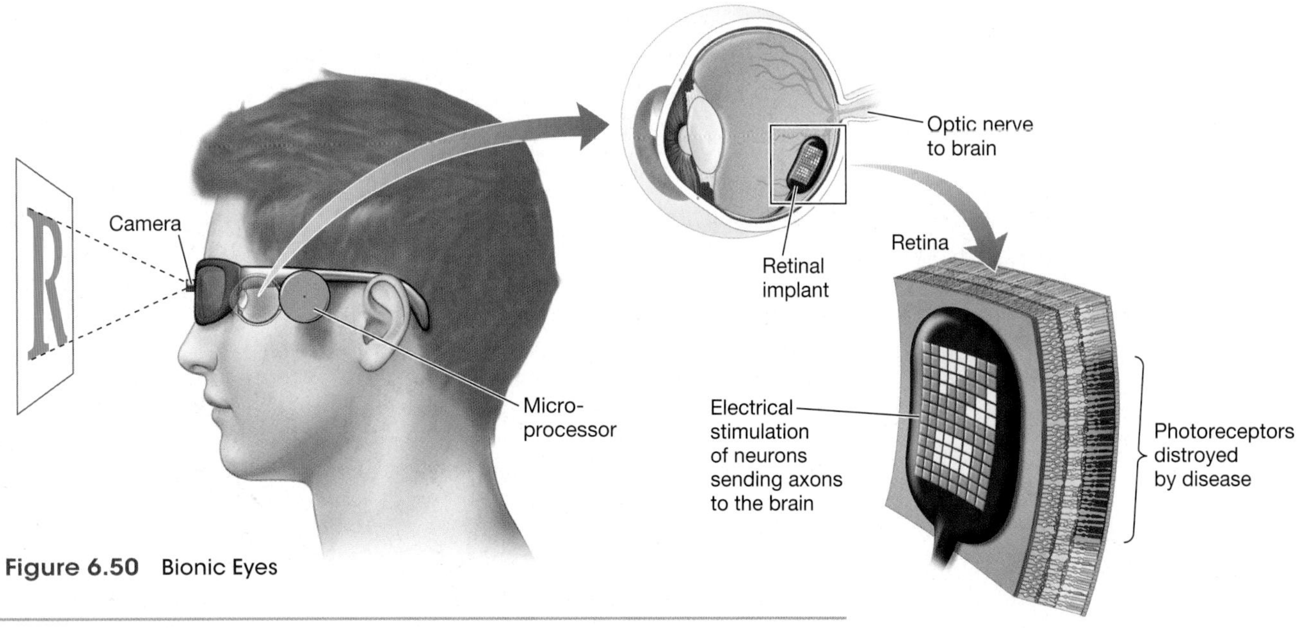

Figure 6.50 Bionic Eyes

6.5 SUMMARY

- Both taste and olfaction rely on sensory receptor cells with specialized membrane receptors that recognize chemicals and respond to them. Thus both systems rely on chemosensory receptors, and both contribute to the *flavor* of foods.
- *Taste buds* on the tongue are complex structures. Each contains one of five different kinds of *taste receptor cells* that detect *salty*, *bitter*, *sweet*, *sour*, or *umami* tastes. The center of the tongue has few taste buds, but all regions with taste buds can detect each of the five tastes.
- There are hundreds of different types of *olfactory receptor neurons*, all found in a sheet called the *olfactory epithelium* inside our nasal cavities.
- The olfactory receptor neurons have axons that pass through tiny holes in the skull to stimulate neurons in the *olfactory bulb* of the brain.
- We can distinguish thousands of different *odorants* by detecting the relative activity of many different kinds of olfactory receptors.

REVIEW QUESTIONS

1. What are the five basic kinds of taste receptors?
2. Of the two chemosensory systems that contribute to flavors, which contributes most to the experience, and why?
3. Describe how the olfactory system is able to distinguish thousands of different odors.

Food for Thought

Many people have reported that perceptions of odors and flavors have a more emotional aspect than visual or auditory perceptions. Is this true of your experience? If so, why do you think this might be so?

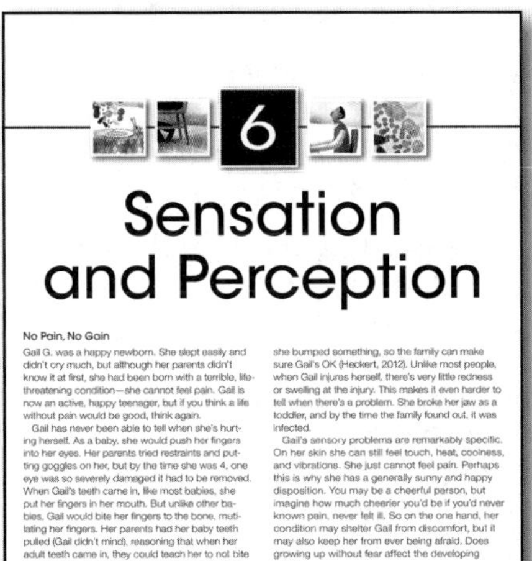

6

Sensation and Perception

No Pain, No Gain

Gail G. was a happy newborn. She slept easily and didn't cry much, but although her parents didn't know it at first, she had been born with a terrible, life-threatening condition—she cannot feel pain. Gail is now an active, happy teenager, but if you think a life without pain would be good, think again.

Gail has never been able to tell when she's hurting herself. As a baby, she would push her fingers into her eyes. Her parents tried restraints and putting goggles on her, but by the time she was 4, one eye was so severely damaged it had to be removed. When Gail's teeth came in, like most babies, she put her fingers in her mouth. But unlike other babies, Gail would bite her fingers to the bone, mutilating her fingers. Her parents had her baby teeth pulled (Gail didn't mind), reasoning that when her adult teeth came in, they could teach her to not bite herself. Gail's sister taught her to say "ouch" when she bumped something, so the family can make sure Gail's OK (Heckert, 2012). Unlike most people, when Gail injures herself, there's very little redness or swelling at the injury. This makes it even harder to tell when there's a problem. She broke her jaw as a toddler, and by the time the family found out, it was infected.

Gail's sensory problems are remarkably specific. On her skin she can still feel touch, heat, coolness, and vibrations. She just cannot feel pain. Perhaps this is why she has a generally sunny and happy disposition. You may be a cheerful person, but imagine how much cheerier you'd be if you'd never known pain, never felt ill. So on the one hand, her condition may shelter Gail from discomfort, but it may also keep her from ever being afraid. Does growing up without fear affect the developing mind?

Think Like a Psychologist:

Principles in Action

Whenever we encounter any interesting behavior we should consider the four principles. Here are some ways that the four principles relate to our opening story about Gail.

MACHINE

The mind is a product of a physical machine, the brain.

Because she lacks a functional version of a single protein, Gail can never feel pain. This has many consequences for her future, including the hazards of multiple injuries and undetected illness.

UNCONSCIOUS

We are consciously aware of only a small part of our mental activity.

Many unconscious reflexes that most of us display are absent in Gail. For instance, she may impulsively reach into a pot of boiling water to retrieve a spoon. In the absence of nociceptors, her hand is not immediately withdrawn; she has to realize she's made a mistake.

SOCIAL

We constantly modify our behavior, beliefs, and attitudes according to what we perceive about the people around us.

We have no reports that Gail lacks empathy for other people's suffering, but her painlessness could dampen such understanding. Her painlessness certainly means that Gail must rely on other people, her family and teachers, to help her avoid injuries.

EXPERIENCE

Our experiences physically alter the structure and function of the brain.

Despite her many injuries, including the loss of an eye, Gail has a cheery, sunny personality, which may reflect the fact that she's never experienced pain. Having never felt pain, can she feel as afraid as those of us who have experienced pain?

KEY TERMS

absolute threshold, 198
adequate stimulus, 195
audition, 195
binaural cues, 235
binocular cues, 216
binocular disparity, 216
bitter, 238
blind spots, 213
cochlea, 233
color constancy, 227
color opponent theory, 225
cone, 213
congenital insensitivity to pain (CIP), 208
convergence, 218
cornea, 211
depth perception, 216
duplex theory, 236
flavor, 237
Gestalt psychology, 229
Gestalt rules of perception, 229
hair cells, 235
inner ear, 233
iris, 221
just noticeable difference (JND), 199
labeled lines, 196
lens, 211
linear perspective, 219
long-wavelength cones, 225
medium-wavelength cones, 225
middle ear, 232
monocular cues, 218
motion parallax, 220
neuropathic pain, 210
nociceptors, 207
noise, 200
odorants, 240
olfaction, 195
olfactory bulb, 240
olfactory epithelium, 240
olfactory receptor neurons, 240
optic disc, 213
ossicles, 232
outer ear, 232
oval window, 233
perception, 194
percept, 194
phantom limb pain, 209
photon, 223
photoreceptor adaptation, 222
photoreceptors, 213
primary visual cortex (V1), 216
psychophysics, 198
pupil, 221
receptive field, 205
retina, 211
rod, 213
salty, 238
sensation, 194
sensory adaptation, 202
sensory code, 196
sensory modalities, 195
sensory receptor cells, 194
sensory receptor organ, 195
shape constancy, 227
short-wavelength cones, 225
signal detection theory, 200
size constancy, 227
size cue, 219
sound localization, 235
sour, 238
stimulus, 194
sweet, 238
tastant, 237
taste buds, 237
taste pore, 237
taste receptor cells, 237
threshold, 197
trichromatic theory, 224
umami, 238
visual field, 213
Weber's fraction, 199

QUIZ YOURSELF

1. In a signal detection task, the term for thinking there is a signal when there is only noise is
   a. false alarm.
   b. correct rejection.
   c. hit.
   d. miss.
2. Kim had to have his leg amputated after a motorcycle accident. He still feels pain in that leg, in spite of the fact that nociceptors of that leg are missing. This type of pain that originates in the brain is called
   a. congenital pain sensitivity.
   b. phantom limb pain.
   c. delayed pain.
   d. congenital pain.
3. Which of the following is *not* a monocular cue for depth?
   a. Occlusion
   b. Size
   c. Linear perspective
   d. Convergence
4. The bony, fluid-filled, spiral-shaped tunnel of the inner ear is the
   a. tympanum.
   b. malleus.
   c. oval window.
   d. cochlea.
5. The mechanism by which we can detect many more odors than there are odor receptors is similar to the mechanism by which we can detect many colors with only three types of cones. This mechanism is
   a. opponency.
   b. adaptation.
   c. relative activity.
   d. labeled lines.
6. ________ is the process by which the nervous system detects the physical events going on around us or inside us. ________ is the experience we have as we further process and interpret information from sensory cells.
7. The ________ of a sensory cell is that total region of space where stimuli will alter the cell's firing rate.
8. The parts of the visual fields that are missing because they correspond to the areas of the retina without rods or cones are called the ________ ________ .
9. Comparing input to the two ears provides two major cues to localize sound. Comparing loudness in your ears gives you the ________ difference cue. Comparing the times the sound arrives at the two ears gives you the ________ difference cue.
10. The five types of taste buds are ________, ________, ________, ________, and ________.

1. a; 2. b; 3. d; 4. d; 5. c; 6. Sensation, Perception; 7. receptive field; 8. blind spots; 9. intensity; latency; 10. sweet, sour, bitter, salty, umami (or meaty)

Cutler

7 Consciousness

Uncontrollable Sleep

Starting college always brings its share of new experiences and adjustments, but "Barry" knew something was wrong freshman year when he seemed to be sleepy all the time (S. Smith, 1997). Barry napped so often that his friends called him the hibernating bear. Of course, college can be exhausting, and many students seek refuge in long snooze sessions. But one day a strange thing happened to Barry: "I laughed really hard, and I kind of fell on my knees.... After that, about every week I'd have two or three episodes where if I'd laugh... my arm would fall down or my muscles in my face would get weak. Or if I was running around playing catch and someone said something, I would get weak in the knees. And there was a time there that my friends kinda used it as a joke. If they're going to throw me the ball and they didn't want me to catch it, they'd tell me a joke and I'd fall down and miss it."

It was as if any big surge in emotion in Barry might trigger a sudden, temporary paralysis lasting anywhere from a few seconds to a few minutes, affecting either a body part or his whole body. Romance became something of a challenge because sometimes during foreplay, Barry's body would just collapse. "Luckily, you're probably laying down, so it's not that big a deal. But it just puts a damper on the whole thing."

Sometimes Barry felt sleepy when he should be awake, and other times his body seemed to fall asleep when his head was awake. What was happening to Barry?

Chapter Preview

consciousness Our perception of what is going on in our minds.

French philosopher René Descartes's famous declaration in 1637, "I think, therefore I am," is, among other things, a report of his very personal experience. We relate to this quote because it speaks to our own experience of consciousness: an awareness that we are thinking. This chapter explores several perspectives on consciousness, including long-standing questions from philosophers concerning the nature of consciousness. We'll consider our nightly bouts of sleep during which, while we are mostly unconscious, the brain is nevertheless plenty busy. We'll discuss how hypnosis can help people focus their conscious awareness to reduce pain, but does not improve memory. We will conclude with a look at psychoactive drugs that can have profound effects on our consciousness, but sometimes at a terrible cost.

7.1 Consciousness

Things to Learn

- Philosophical problems of consciousness and free will
- Possible adaptive function of consciousness in humans and other animals
- Experiments that question the role of the conscious self in controlling behavior

Consciousness is one of those topics that prompts many students to enroll in psychology courses, yet defining consciousness is problematic. We all experience it, so we know what it is, but that experience is so personal, so subjective, that it's difficult to come up with an objective definition. We say people are conscious when they are awake (the opposite of unconscious), alert, and aware of their surroundings. But consciousness is more than being aware of our surroundings—we experience consciousness when we are dreaming, but are totally unaware of our (true) surroundings.

We can define **consciousness** as the state of being aware that we are conscious, and as our perception of what is going on in our minds. A lot of different activities are embedded in that phrase "perception of what is going on in our minds." It includes our perception of what's going on around us (in either the real world or a dream world), our sense of time passing, our sense of being aware, our recollection of events that happened in the past, and our imaginings about what might happen in the future.

One of the overarching principles of psychology is that much of what our brain is doing is outside of our awareness. In other words, we do not perceive some processes going on in our mind, and by definition they are *unconscious*. We can also talk about different *levels of awareness*: we are aware of some events, unaware of others, and sometimes we can be prompted to become aware of events that we had not noted before.

This section will consider both philosophical and biological theories about the nature of consciousness, pondering questions such as: What is the function of consciousness? Does it help individuals survive? Can consciousness evolve? It also reviews unsettling research that challenges our notions of consciousness, and raises questions about free will: studies suggesting that the brain can arrive at a decision *before our conscious self is aware of that decision*. Despite our powerful feeling that our conscious self, the part of our mind we are aware of, has made a decision, sometimes it was in fact made beforehand.

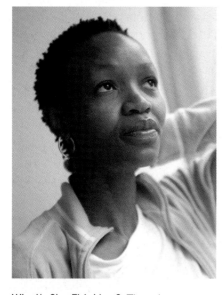

What's She Thinking? There is no way for someone else to discern her conscious experience.

It is difficult to assess consciousness

As we've noted, the hallmark of consciousness is that it is personal and subjective. You can get a sense of how personal consciousness is when you consider dreaming. When we are dreaming, we are not awake, alert, or aware of our real surroundings. But we are aware of the surroundings in our dream. I may even

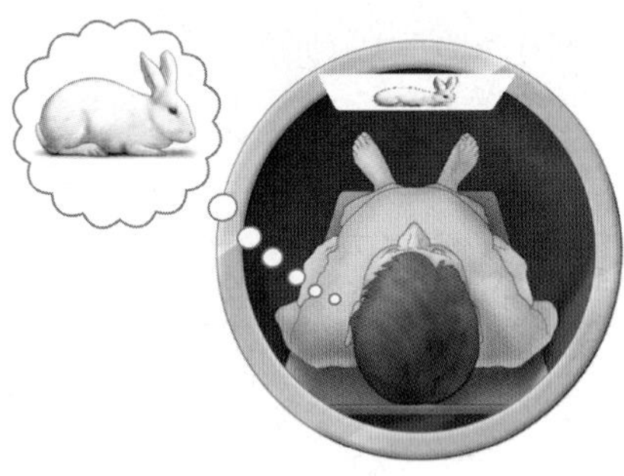

Participant in an fMRI machine viewing simple images

Researcher observing patterns of brain activity elicited as each image is viewed by the participant
"In the past, that pattern of brain activity only appeared when he was looking at the rabbit."

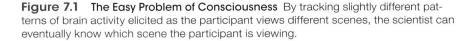

Figure 7.1 **The Easy Problem of Consciousness** By tracking slightly different patterns of brain activity elicited as the participant views different scenes, the scientist can eventually know which scene the participant is viewing.

become conscious of the fact that "I'm dreaming," yet no one else knows what I'm experiencing. Even when we are awake and moving about, it is difficult for others to know what, exactly, we are conscious of. I may be attending to the music playing, or remembering the time I first heard this song, or wondering whether a friend likes this type of music, or thinking about some problem that is totally unrelated to the music. In fact, my consciousness may pass through all those topics and more in the course of a single song. It is this fleeting, roaming nature of consciousness that moved psychology pioneer William James (1842–1910) to talk of the "stream of consciousness."

Scientists have tried to break into the personal experience of consciousness, to read a person's mind. These experiments called for a participant to view on a screen one of several natural scenes: landscapes, faces, animals, and so on, while scientists recorded activity in the person's visual cortex, using functional MRI (fMRI; see Figure 3.26). Using computers to track the differences in cortical activity during the viewing of different pictures, researchers discovered distinctive patterns of brain activity associated with each scene. Ultimately the scientists were able to predict which photo the participant was viewing, based on brain activity alone (Kay et al., 2008). That is, brain imaging and computer modeling gave researchers a window into the participant's mind. They could tell whether he was looking at a rabbit, a faded barn, or a vase of flowers (**Figure 7.1**).

In other experiments, scientists were able to determine from fMRI activity whether people were looking at a large cross, a circle, or some other crude shape (Kay & Gallant, 2009; Miyawaki et al., 2008). Scientists were even able to roughly reconstruct what YouTube video clip people were looking at by decoding their brain activity (Nishimoto et al., 2011). You might imagine that someday it may be possible to use brain imaging techniques to predict precisely what a person is seeing. No one has been able to do this yet, but because we can at least imagine how it could be done, philosophers refer to this as the **easy problem of consciousness**: finding out what particular pattern of brain activity underlies a relatively simple conscious experience, such as seeing a rabbit. We can also imagine how we might eventually use the specific pattern of brain activity to predict exactly what a person will do next, as we'll discuss at the end of this section.

easy problem of consciousness Also called the *mind–body problem*. The question of which particular pattern of brain activity underlies a particular conscious experience.

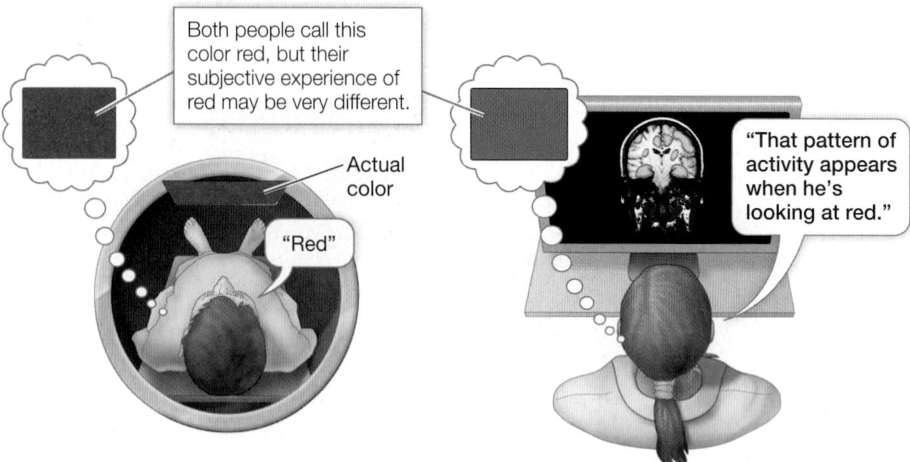

Figure 7.2 The Hard Problem of Consciousness The "hard" problem goes beyond predicting, from brain activity, what a person is seeing or thinking. The hard problem is to know what that person's subjective experience is like. For example, the scientist may know from brain activity that the person is looking at a red screen, but perhaps the color we all call red results in a different subjective experience, or qualia, for the participant than for the scientist.

As you might have guessed, if there is an "easy" problem of consciousness, there is also a contrasting *hard* problem of consciousness (Chalmers, 2010). A simple experiment illustrates the difference. Ask the participant to view a screen that is all red, or blue, or some other color. Observe which parts of the brain are active when the person is looking at each color, so that it is eventually possible to know just from brain activity alone whether the screen is red, blue, or some other color. This we would call an "easy" problem. But philosophers would be quick to point out that we don't know exactly how each person *experiences* red. It's easy to tell the person experiences a quality of "redness" that is different from the quality of "greenness" or "blueness," but it's hard to know if that experience is the same for each person. Psychologists refer to this aspect of a perception as **qualia**, the entirely subjective experience a person has with each perception (Ramachandran & Hubbard, 2001; Wright, 2008). All of us with normal color vision can agree that this apple is red and that pear is green, but how do we know whether what *you experience* when looking at objects we call red is the same as what *I experience* when I look at objects we call red? Maybe when you look at red apples you have the subjective experience, the same qualia of color, that I have when looking at green pears. We give the color the same name, but that color has a different qualia for you and me. For that matter, maybe no two people in the world experience the same qualia when looking at red, and no amount of talking would allow us to tell. Furthermore, even if the same brain regions are active when you look at red as when I look at red, we still can't be sure that you and I are *experiencing* the same qualia when looking at red.

This, then, is the **hard problem of consciousness**: how do we know what brain processes result in our personal conscious experience, for example, those that produce the particular qualia that someone experiences when they see the color red (**Figure 7.2**)? We not only lack the technology to ask this question, but we can't even imagine a technology that would allow an answer. A big problem is that we have no way of unambiguously communicating the qualia we are experiencing because, as we've seen, the fact that we use the same *word* for it is no guarantee that we have the same *experience*. Similarly, while we might agree that some colors are exciting and others are calming, does that prove we experience the same qualia for those colors? Maybe we find red exciting and green

qualia The entirely subjective experience a person has with a perception.

hard problem of consciousness The question of how brain processes result in our personal conscious experience (qualia).

calming because we've grown up associating the color we call red with blazing hot fires and the color we call green with peaceful meadows. There's just no way for me to slip inside your mind and see exactly what "red" looks like for you. Together, the easy and hard problems of consciousness are sometimes called the *mind–body problem* (see Box 3.1). Some neuroscientists think that we will never be able to solve the hard problem, and indeed the issue won't come up again in this book. There's plenty of work to be done trying to understand the so-called easy problems of consciousness.

The brain's activity is similar whether we imagine something or actually see it

Most of us can close our eyes and imagine seeing something that is not really present, like a faraway friend, or a strange alien described in a science fiction story. If we really concentrate, the experience of "seeing" the object in our imagination can be quite vivid. Here is another instance when we are consciously experiencing something that isn't real, showing that consciousness is more than simply "being awake and aware of our surroundings." Several experiments indicate that the parts of the brain that are active when we *imagine* seeing something are the same parts that are activated by *actually* seeing that thing (Kosslyn, 1994). No one is saying that the match is perfect, that precisely every neuron in my head that is active when I see Mount Rushmore is also active when I imagine Mount Rushmore. For one thing, we don't have anything close to the technology to test such an idea. Plus, you wouldn't expect that seeing an object and imagining an object would be *precisely* alike, since my experience in those circumstances isn't precisely alike. I have a pretty good imagination, but seeing Mount Rushmore gives me much more detail than I can imagine.

Still, these studies indicate that at least roughly the same brain regions are active when we imagine seeing something as when we actually see it. Such results suggest that the reason we have a similar subjective experience when seeing an object and when imagining seeing the object is because, when we are imagining, we somehow activate the brain regions that underlie the actual experience. This remarkable ability to re-create in our brains a specific experience, almost as if it were really happening, suggests a function for consciousness that we'll consider next.

What is the function of consciousness?

There can be no definitive answer to this question, but a compelling possibility is suggested by our ability to imagine events that might happen (Sperry, 1977). Consciousness offers a powerful tool for telling the future. We can use our mind's eye to enact a "simulation," imagining what would happen as the result of one behavior versus another. We can even imagine a complicated series of events. Running such simulations allows us to anticipate different consequences so that we can choose what to do. Even non-human animals, without the use of language, would benefit from being able to run such simulations in

Imagine That! A powerful function of consciousness is that we can imagine what consequences might follow if we were to do something. (Calvin and Hobbes ©1985 Watterson. Reprinted with permission of UNIVERSAL UCLICK. All rights reserved.)

Figure 7.3 Running a Simulation in the Mind's Eye? Our experience of "running a simulation," imagining what will happen next, does not seem to rely on words or language, so presumably other animals can also "run simulations" to guide their behavior. Perhaps border collies imagine the different outcomes of running to the left or right when deciding how best to herd sheep.

their minds. Will the predator chasing me be able to fit through this hole in the briar patch? Natural selection might favor the evolution of brain mechanisms supporting visual imagery in animals for problem solving. Indeed, in Section 9.1 we'll discuss visual imagery as an aspect of "working memory" that allows us to make use of what we've learned in the past. Of course, some animals have more sophisticated brains than others; determining which animals have brains complicated enough to support conscious awareness of visual simulations is an active area of study.

Consider how a dog herding sheep might benefit from running simulations in deciding what to do (**Figure 7.3**). "Let's see, if I run that way it will bring those two lambs back into the pack, but those three sheep on the other side may get too far away. If instead I run the other way to get those three sheep back into the flock, the whole flock will shift toward the lambs." Of course, the dog would not be thinking in *words*, but in *images* of what would happen in the two different scenarios. No one can say with certainty that these dogs run such simulations through consciousness, but it seems at least plausible. Similar simulations could prove useful for all the behaviors relevant to natural selection, such as finding mates and food, and avoiding predators. Thus natural selection would favor the evolution of consciousness with the capacity for complex visual imagery.

We humans are so very verbal—constantly talking, listening, and reading about the world around us—and our consciousness reflects this preoccupation with language. When I stop to think about it, I am aware of words passing through my mind. If I see a puzzling scene, I may think to myself, "What's going on here?" If I am waiting for someone who's late, I may think to myself, "I wonder if she's having car trouble," and so on. In these cases, it's as if I am talking to myself, thinking a sentence that I might say aloud if anyone were with me. This experience is sometimes called an **internal dialogue**, the words and sentences passing through our mind as a form of self-talk or inner speech. We may be even more aware of our internal dialogue when we are having a discussion. We may try out a sentence in our mind before we actually say it out loud to someone else (a very good practice that I sometimes skip, to my later regret). When you ask a

internal dialogue The words and sentences passing through your mind as a form of self-talk or inner speech.

question in class, for example, do you rehearse in your mind what you will say aloud if called upon? Perhaps that's the function of internal dialogue, to allow us to mentally rehearse what we'll say next. In Section 9.1 we'll talk about how such mental rehearsal aids working memory.

Is consciousness limited to such internal dialogue? If so, then can there be consciousness without language? What about newborn babies who have not yet learned language? Verbal though we are, most of us can have experiences, and be *consciously aware* that we are having that experience, without putting it into words. In fact, many traditions, such as Zen Buddhism and various meditation practices, discussed later in this chapter, strive to achieve a consciousness that is devoid of words, in pursuit of pure awareness, untainted by language. The prevailing view is that the complex language in our consciousness, the internal dialogue, is an augmentation or addition to consciousness. But perhaps the most compelling scientific evidence that consciousness is not entirely dependent on language comes from revolutionary studies of humans whose brains have been surgically split in two, as we'll discuss next.

Split-brain patients offer clues about consciousness without language

Evidence that language and consciousness can be separated comes from studies pioneered by psychologist Roger Sperry in people who had **split-brain** surgery, which cuts the **corpus callosum** (see Figure 3.17), a bundle of axons that connects the right and left cerebral cortex. Split-brain surgery interrupts communication between the two cerebral hemispheres. The surgery began to be performed in the early 1960s to control life-threatening epilepsy in patients who did not respond to medication. The surgery would prevent a seizure that begins in one cerebral hemisphere from passing through the corpus callosum to the other hemisphere. Because Sperry had done similar surgeries in cats in the 1950s to study brain function, he took an interest in split-brain patients.

Knowing that information from the left visual field is projected to the right cerebral hemisphere and vice versa, Sperry devised ways to show a picture to a split-brain patient's left or right hemisphere. Basically, participants were asked to stare at a dot, and then information was projected to either their left or right visual field. The information was flashed so quickly that the participants didn't have time to shift their gaze, so only the left or right visual field was stimulated. Sperry reasoned that, in participants without a corpus callosum, it would be hard for information that reached the right cerebral hemisphere to cross over to the left hemisphere. Because language is controlled by the left cerebral hemisphere (Chapter 10), which gets information only from the right visual field (see Figure 6.22), Sperry speculated that the split-brain patient might be unable to say what objects appeared in the left visual field. As depicted in **Figure 7.4A**, a person with an intact corpus callosum who sees a key in the left visual field can tell us what he sees. But a split-brain patient shown a key in the left visual field cannot tell us what is there. The split-brain person can talk to us only about objects he sees in the right visual field (**Figure 7.4B**).

Several ingenious experiments by Sperry and his colleagues established that the right hemisphere, the one that cannot initiate spoken language, can at least *understand* spoken language. If asked to look at a picture presented in the left visual field and to point out that object with the left hand, the split-brain patient performs fine. By choosing the correct object with the left hand, this hemisphere communicates with the scientists without using words. You can make the task a little more difficult, showing a scene to the left visual field and asking the person to pick out with his left hand which of several pictures belongs with the one displayed. If the split-brain patient is shown a scene of a snowbound home, his

split brain The result of a surgery that destroys the pathways of communication between the two cerebral hemispheres.

corpus callosum The main band of axons communicating between the two cerebral hemispheres.

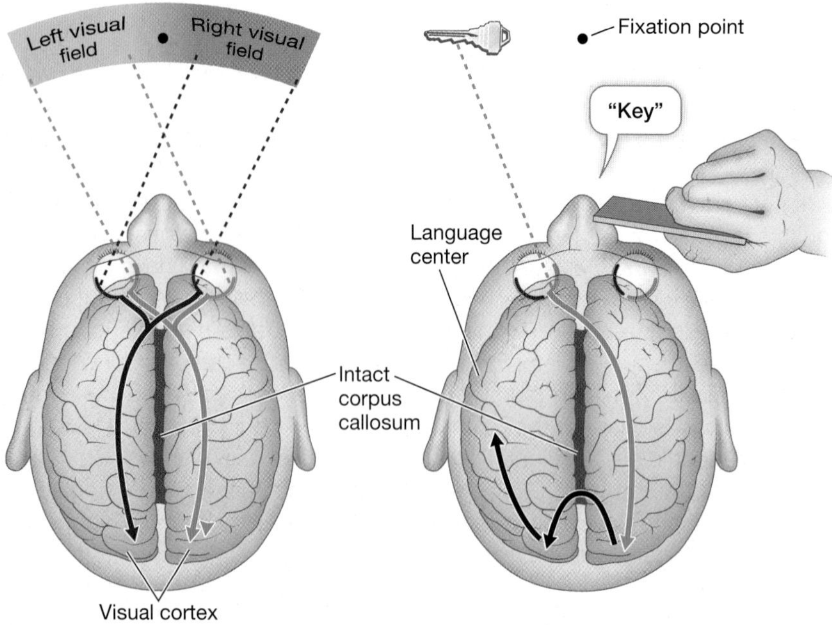

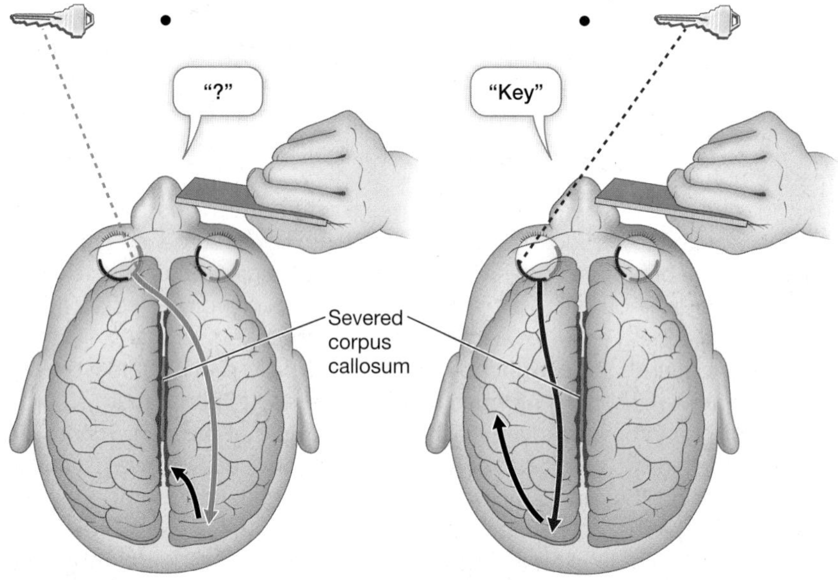

Figure 7.4 Testing of a Split-Brain Patient (A) Participants are asked to stare at the central dot, and then words or pictures are projected to one visual field or the other. Information in the left visual field reaches the right visual cortex. In people with an intact corpus callosum, information reaching the right hemisphere can pass through the corpus callosum to the left hemisphere, where language centers can report what the object is. (B) In split-brain participants, the severing of the corpus callosum prevents information from getting to the left hemisphere, so the patient cannot report what is there. The person can only report objects seen in the right visual field.

left hand may pick out a snow shovel. If the split-brain patient is presented simultaneously with different pictures in both visual fields, and is asked to point out related pictures with both hands, his two hands will point to two different pictures, each appropriate for the scene displayed to the corresponding hemisphere (**Figure 7.5**).

We readily assume that the split-brain person who reports seeing a key in his right visual field is a conscious person just like us. Likewise we assume that any person talking to us experiences consciousness. Interestingly, we cannot *prove* that this is true, as it's one more version of the hard problem. We give other people the benefit of the doubt, assuming they are conscious whether they're a split-brain patient or anyone else.

But what about the other hemisphere, which cannot talk to us—does it have consciousness too? Clearly the right hemisphere understands spoken instructions, like "Point to the object you saw." Do you need consciousness to understand simple commands like that? Or how about when the left hand correctly associates a snow shovel with the scene of a snowbound home? Doesn't that indicate a level of understanding (They're going to need to clear the snow at that house) that implies conscious deliberation? While we know the right hemisphere can understand language, since it follows simple instructions from the experimenters, we don't know whether the mind in the right hemisphere can use language to think. Does it think in words? Does it have an internal dialogue going on that never reaches the lips?

It's very strange to think about two different minds at work inside the same head. For those of us who have not had this rare split-brain surgery, our two hemispheres appear to work together seamlessly, forming a single mind. Even in split-brain patients, when outside the laboratory, the two minds are probably in synchrony most of the time. Simply moving the head and eyes, bringing the scene into both visual fields, probably keeps both hemispheres pretty well informed about events surrounding the patient. In fact, by moving the head and eyes, each hemisphere in the split-brain patient can also keep track of what the other hemisphere is doing. Presumably this helps split-brain patients do everyday tasks such as walking by coordinating the two legs, or eating a meal by coordinating the two arms. It might be like being conjoined twins, where each mind comes to understand and anticipate what the other mind will do next, so the two can coordinate body movements.

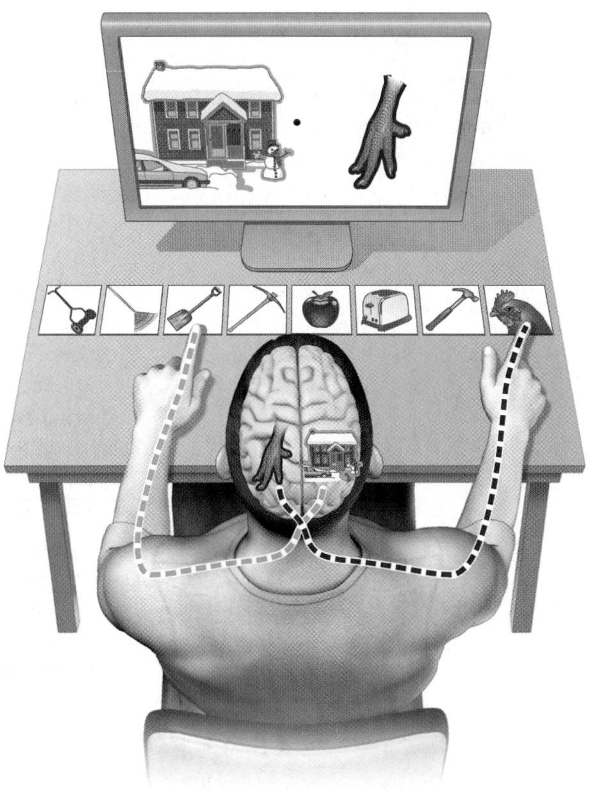

Figure 7.5 Evidence of Consciousness in the Right Cerebral Hemisphere If a split-brain patient is shown two different objects at the same time, one to the left visual field and another to the right, he will say that he sees only the object on the right (in this case, the chicken foot). However, when asked to point the hand at an image related to the image on the screen, his left hand will point to the snow shovel. (After Gazzaniga & LeDoux, 2013.)

In split-brain patients, the verbal mind tries to explain what the other mind is doing

One way we can determine what one hemisphere understands about the other would be to direct the right hemisphere, which cannot speak, to do something with the left hand and then ask the left hemisphere to tell us what's happening. It is in such tasks that split-brain patients really challenge our everyday experience of consciousness. For example, we can ask the two hands to pick out illustrated cards that belong to a scene, as we described before. As in Figure 7.5 we purposely show two different scenes to the two hemispheres. The left hemisphere sees a chicken foot while the right hemisphere sees a snowbound house. The left, talking hemisphere, correctly picks out a card depicting a chicken, while the right hemisphere correctly picks a card showing a snow shovel. If we ask the talking hemisphere why the left hand chose a snow shovel, an accurate response would be "I don't know." But when experimenters did this experiment, the patient had an answer ready: "Oh, that's simple. You need a shovel to clean out the chicken shed". In another test, a split-brain patient is shown a funny picture or just the word "laugh" and sometimes the patient laughs. When the experimenter asks the patient why she laughed, she will give a reason (Gazzaniga & LeDoux, 2013). But usually the reason is not very convincing. From this and similar experiments, it appears that the left brain is constantly trying to explain what the body just did. Sometimes the left, talking hemisphere engages in **confabulation**, filling in a gap in memory or understanding with a fabrication the person believes to be true. Confabulation is not lying—in confabulation the person actually believes what he or she is saying. The talking hemisphere came up with a (barely) plausible explanation for why the left hand chose a shovel, or why the person laughed.

Confabulation is also seen in people with memory problems, who can't remember something that happened a few minutes ago, as we'll discuss in some detail in Chapter 9. In Chapter 3 we met Deidre who, when given a tiny electrical

confabulation Filling in a gap in memory or understanding with a fabrication that the person believes to be true.

free will The power to make choices that are not constrained by supernatural, nonphysical forces.

stimulation in one part of her brain, laughed. When asked why she laughed, she always offered a reason, some event that was funny ("you two, standing over there"). Similar confabulation has been seen in other people who are induced to do something by electrical brain stimulation. "Why are you taking off your clothes?" "Because it's warm in here." People who find themselves doing something they don't understand usually confabulate an explanation.

We've described cases in which an outsider can see and understand why the person is confabulating—special cases in which people are not aware of why they are doing what they are doing, where confabulation helps them understand their own behavior. I don't have wires in my brain or a split corpus callosum (as far as I know). How might I know how much of *my* internal explanation for my everyday behavior is really confabulation?

I'm not the first person to doubt our understanding of why we do what we do. The philosopher Baruch Spinoza (1632–1677) suggested that while we know what we want to do next, we are usually unaware of *why* we want to do that. Spinoza speculated that if he threw a stone through the air, and the stone suddenly became conscious in mid-air, the stone would think "I want to go over there," and would believe it was going in that direction because of its desire. As we'll see next, experiments indicate that sometimes our conscious self really does think like Spinoza's stone.

We are not always aware of what our brain has decided to do

The concept of consciousness is inevitably bound up in the philosophical notion of **free will**: the power to make choices that are not constrained by supernatural, nonphysical forces such as fate, spirits, or gods. Here we are talking about which of an infinite number of possible behaviors a person chooses to display within the confines of the physical world. Even though you can't change the color of your skin like a chameleon, or fly by flapping your arms, you may still have free will. My conscious self, the one that is aware of the stream of mental events going on inside me, has the strong conviction that I have free will. I feel as though I decide whether to finish writing this paragraph, throw my hand in the air, or begin whistling a tune. As we'll see next, experiments suggest that in fact unconscious processes in my mind may make decisions about what I'm going to do before my conscious self is aware of it. Then we will have to ponder what such findings mean for the concept of free will.

An experiment made in the 1980s suggested that our conscious self may not be in charge of our decisions. Psychologists asked people to look at a clock with a second hand sweeping around a dial and, whenever they felt like it, to bend their wrist (Libet et al., 1983). The participants' only job was to notice where the clock's second hand was pointing when they first "felt the urge" to bend their wrist and to report the second hand's position at that time to the scientists (**Figure 7.6**). Scalp electrodes directly over participants' motor cortex measured electrical potentials during this task so scientists could observe a standard electrical signature, called the readiness potential (RP), that arises before a person begins moving. But here was the surprising finding: the scientists found that the RP arose from motor cortex *before* the person felt the urge to move! That meant that the motor cortex initiated the movement, and *then* the conscious self felt the urge to move, and then the movement happened. In these first experiments, the delay between when scientists knew the person was going to move and when the *person* knew he was going to move, was only a few hundreds of milliseconds. On the one hand, that's a fraction of a second. But on the other hand, if the decision to move came even a tiny fraction of a second before the person felt the urge to move, then in fact that person's conscious self did not decide to

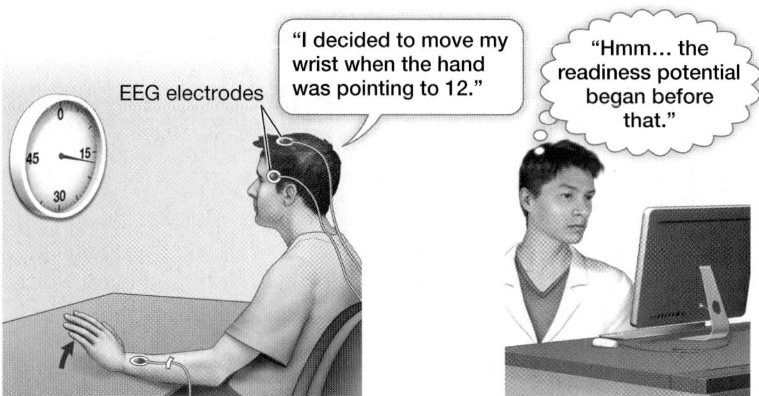

Figure 7.6 **Our Brain Decides What We'll Do before Our Conscious Self Is Aware of that Decision** Participants watched a moving hand on a clock and noted when they felt the urge to bend their wrist. The EEG electrodes on the scalp detected the readiness potential (RP) from motor cortex before the person reported feeling the urge to move. (After Libet et al., 1983.)

move. Rather, other parts of the brain decided to move and then the conscious self felt the urge. Some other process caused the person to move his wrist, and then that process led the conscious self to think that it had decided to move. That conscious self, mistakenly, thinks it started the process.

As brain imaging techniques have improved, scientists have gotten better and better at detecting signals that precede a movement. These improved techniques have made the conscious self appear to be even more of a latecomer to the decision process, as is illustrated in **Figure 7.7**.

☑ Researchers at Work

Who's in charge here?

Figure 7.7 **Decisions, Decisions** (After Soon et al., 2008.)

- **Question:** When do we become aware of a decision to do something?
- **Hypothesis:** Scientists will be able to predict which button a person will push before the participant is aware of the decision.
- **Test:** Have participants in an fMRI scanner look at a computer screen, watching a random series of letters flash across the screen. Instruct them to push one button with one hand or another button with the other, whenever they feel like it. Monitor their brain activity and look for patterns that precede pushing the left versus right button.

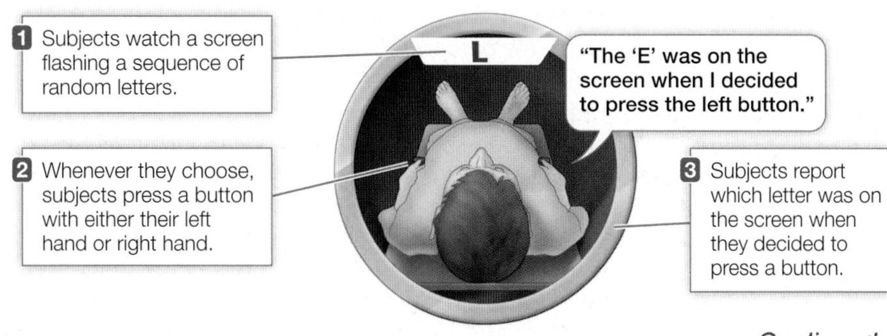

1 Subjects watch a screen flashing a sequence of random letters.
L
"The 'E' was on the screen when I decided to press the left button."
2 Whenever they choose, subjects press a button with either their left hand or right hand.
3 Subjects report which letter was on the screen when they decided to press a button.

Continued

Researchers at Work *Continued*

■ **Results:** Replicating Libet and colleagues' findings, scientists found that the readiness potential (RP) in motor cortex arose before the participant was aware of the "urge to push." But the fMRI detected the RP *5 full seconds* before the person was aware of a decision to push. What's more, the experimenters also found that other cortical regions, including prefrontal cortex, became active *5 seconds before that*. So the scientists knew when the participant had decided to push a button, and even which button he had decided to push, up to *10 seconds before the participant's conscious self was aware of the decision*.

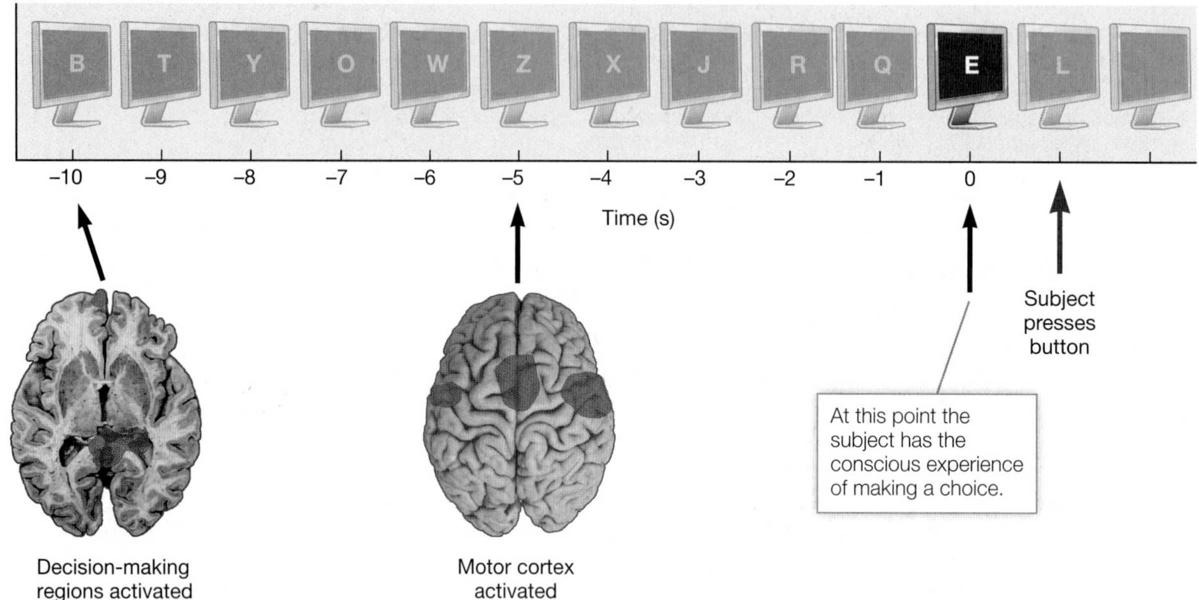

■ **Conclusion:** Participants conscious self becomes aware of the decision to push the left or right button rather late in the process.

Ten seconds is a long lag between when one part of my brain decided to push a button and when the part of my brain I'm aware of, my conscious self, became aware of the decision. But the worst of it is that I, the conscious self who's typing these words right now (uhm, I think), feels so strongly that *I'm the one* making these decisions. If these experiments on button pushing in a lab apply to everyday life, then this strong feeling my conscious self has, that it is making the decisions, could all be an illusion. And if the decision to do something like take a break from writing and go swimming is made before I think that "I" decided it, then what about my perceived reasons? "Oh, I'm feeling tired and the writing's not going smoothly now, so I might as well get some exercise." How do I know that's the *real* reason behind my decision if it was made before I was aware of it? Is my conscious self constantly confabulating reasons for what I do, like the left hemisphere of a split-brain person saying "You need a snow shovel to clean out the chicken shed"?

Popular media today point to some of the experiments we have just discussed and suggest they prove we have no free will. You'll find in **Box 7.1** that this notion does not withstand scrutiny.

Skeptic at Large

Is Free Will Illusory?

In the popular media, experiments showing that the brain decides before the conscious self is aware of the decision were widely reported as casting doubt on the existence of free will. How can a person really be free to decide to push a button if machines detect the decision before the person has made it? But in fact these experiments do not disprove the existence of free will if you untangle the two notions of free will and consciousness.

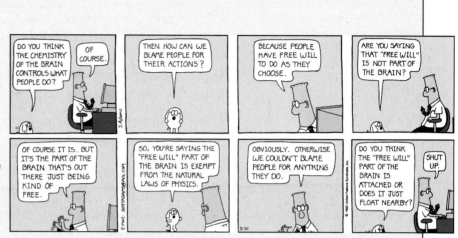

Free will? It's not easy to think about how free will might be possible in a material world (see Box 3.1). (DILBERT ©1993 Scott Adams. Used by permission of UNIVERSAL UCLICK. All rights reserved.)

When the scientist notes what decision I made before I was aware of it, that decision was nevertheless *made by me*. Yes, parts of my brain outside my consciousness actually made the decision before I was aware of it, but it's *my* brain, isn't it? So these experiments do not disprove the idea that we have free will, the ability to choose what, out of the infinite number of behaviors that are physically possible, we do next. Rather, they indicate that if we have free will, our consciousness may be unaware of some of the deliberations going on. Or, at least, our conscious self becomes aware of the outcome rather late in the decision-making process. Yes, perhaps my conscious self is mistaken in thinking that it made that decision, but such self-deception doesn't change the fact that it was still *my mind* that decided to do X rather than Y.

On the other hand, these experiments don't prove that we *do* have free will, either. It is always possible that whatever decision was reached by my unconscious mind is an inevitable reflex: the result of the physical state of my brain at that particular time, which might be simply the result of my particular brain's response to all that had happened to me before. In other words, if the only forces at work in the universe are physical forces like light hitting photoreceptors in the eye, action potentials running down axons, and neurotransmitters activating receptors on neurons, then perhaps the state of my mind is always an inevitable outcome of all those physical events that came before. I can't think of any way to disprove this possibility. Can you?

We noted earlier how consciousness may have evolved as a way to run simulations about future behavior to help make decisions. Perhaps the strong sense that this same conscious self is in charge of our behavior is a delusion, but it might be an adaptive delusion. Maybe having the sense that we are in complete control of our behavior is important to motivate us to get out of bed in the morning (or to come out of our burrow at night). If this is true, and I want to emphasize that I cannot say whether it is or not, then it reinforces my intuitive sense that my belief in free will is good for me.

The question of free will is often related to questions of morality, the issue of right versus wrong acts, whether we are free to choose between them, and whether we should be held responsible for what we do. Those philosophical and religious questions are outside the boundaries of psychology as a science, at least for now, because no one has been able to scientifically prove that we do or do not have free will. So we won't be considering these moral questions. Nevertheless, I predict you will find yourself pondering such questions as you review what we've learned about consciousness.

7.1 SUMMARY

- *Consciousness* is the state of being aware that we are conscious, and our perception of what is going on in our minds.
- The *easy problem of consciousness*, which is being actively pursued in many labs, is to determine the relationship between particular brain activity and particular experiences, such as being able to tell from brain activity whether a person is looking at a dog, listening to a song, or remembering a past event.
- The *hard problem of consciousness*, which may never be solved, is to understand the relationship between brain activity and the subjective experience, or *qualia*, of a perception, such as the experience of "red" versus "green."
- Consciousness may have evolved as a way to run complex simulations about what would happen if the individual did one thing or another, and the evolution of language has added the experience of an *internal dialogue* running in our mind.
- Experiments with *split-brain* patients indicate that they have two at least partially independent minds, only one of which can speak to us. These experiments also indicate that the speaking mind may engage in *confabulation* to explain the behavior of the other mind.
- Scientists monitoring brain recordings can predict when the participant is going to perform an act several seconds before he or she is aware of any such decision. These experiments call into question whether our conscious self is actually involved in our decisions or simply becomes aware of decisions other parts of our brain made. These experiments neither prove nor disprove whether we have *free will*.

REVIEW QUESTIONS

1. What are the easy and hard problems of consciousness?
2. What is confabulation, and how do instances of confabulation in humans seem to confirm Spinoza's speculation about a moving stone that gains consciousness?
3. Describe split-brain patients and the evidence that they have two minds at work in one head.
4. What do experiments measuring brain activity before people make decisions suggest about the importance of consciousness and free will?

Food for Thought

Should we be held responsible for our actions and speech during sleepwalking and sleeptalking, or awakening from anesthesia after surgery, if we later have no recollection of our behavior?

7.2 Sleep and Dreams

Things to Learn

- Brain mechanisms underlying biological rhythms
- Methods to monitor the stages of sleep
- Brain mechanisms controlling sleep and wakefulness
- Evolutionary functions of sleep
- Consequences of sleep deprivation and sleep disorders
- Changes in sleep as we grow up and grow old

Because all mammals sleep, it seems a safe bet that our ancestors in ancient Africa slept and were probably fascinated by sleep and dreams. The *Epic of Gilgamesh* from ancient Iraq may be the oldest written story on Earth (2,500 BCE or earlier), and dreams play a central role. In the poem, Gilgamesh has a series of dreams, which his comrade Enkidu interprets as foretelling the future. Over 1,000 years later, the Hebrew Bible was written, describing many instances of prophetic dreams. One, retold in the Koran, says an Egyptian pharaoh dreamed of seven fat cows being eaten by seven skinny cows. When the Hebrew slave Joseph interpreted the dream to mean that seven years of good harvests would be followed by seven years of famine, Pharaoh promoted Joseph and began storing food to prepare for the famine. Ancient Hindu scriptures from India describe different levels of wakefulness and sleep. This nearly universal fascination with sleep continues today, as thousands of websites offer to interpret your dreams to tell you what they really mean about your future or your mental state. Of course, few of these "experts" on dream imagery agree with one another.

In this section we'll find that many aspects of sleep remain a mystery. First we'll discuss the biological rhythms that have some animals sleeping at night and others during the day. Then we'll see that our vivid dreams take place during a particular type of sleep, and learn about various brain regions that regulate sleep and waking. We'll review theories about the function of sleep and the consequences of sleep deprivation. Finally, we'll discuss sleep disorders and how the qualities of sleep change as we grow up and grow old.

Gilgamesh Wrestling a Lion In the poem, Gilgamesh has prophetic dreams.

Biological rhythms enforce a sleep-wake cycle

If there is one thing that is constant about our world, it is the regular rotation of Earth that brings us night and day. With this backdrop, animals have evolved to be particularly adapted to being active during either the dark of night or the light of day. Most mammals are *nocturnal*, meaning they are active at night. They have many adaptations that help them survive nighttime forays, including vision that works well with little light, and keen senses of hearing and smell, which don't require any light at all. However, most monkeys and apes are *diurnal*, active during the daytime, like humans. Our vision is adapted to daylight hours, meaning we have excellent color vision but rather poor vision at night. We aren't as good at detecting odors as are nocturnal mammals.

Those of us who rely on alarm clocks and wristwatches to organize our activity might expect that other animals need to keep track of time, too, perhaps observing the sun to determine whether it is time to go to sleep or to explore. True enough, animals attend to the coming and going of daylight, but the story is a bit more complicated than that. For example, pretend for a moment that you're a hamster, a nocturnal creature. You sleep in a deep, dark underground burrow—how will you know when the sun goes down and it's time to get up? You need a bit of time to wake up fully, to stretch, groom, and maybe have a little snack before leaving the burrow, so ideally you want to wake up a little while *before* the sun goes down.

Because it is adaptive to predict when the sun will rise and set, animals have a built-in **biological clock**, a biological mechanism that keeps track of time. One way to see the biological clock in action is to bring animals, such as hamsters, into a windowless lab (**Figure 7.8A**). If you turn out the lights at a particular time every day, the hamsters soon become adjusted to the new schedule; they sleep while the lights are on and then, a few hours *before* the lights are scheduled to turn off, they begin rousing, stretching, and grooming in *anticipation* of the coming dark (**Figure 7.8B**). Their biological clock lets them know that the dark is coming.

The pattern animals display due to their biological clocks is called a **circadian rhythm**, an cycle of activity and rest lasting about one day (*circa* means "about" and *dian* refers to a day). In the lab, we can manipulate when hamsters will be active by adjusting when the lights are on. So clearly light is what cues the hamsters to be active.

If we keep the hamsters in constant dim light, we eliminate the cues by which they sense when it's time to be active or time to sleep. What happens then? Even without light cues, each hamster will show a daily pattern of activity, being active for about 12 hours and sleeping for about 12 hours, day after day! Under constant conditions, the hamster is said to *free-run*, showing a circadian pattern of activity that is not anchored by any external cue like sunset. Because their free-run cycle takes slightly more than 24 hours, the hamsters wake up just a little bit later each day, as if they were sleeping in a little longer each day (sounds nice, huh?).

biological clock A biological mechanism that keeps track of time.

circadian rhythm Animals' active–rest cycle with a duration of about one day.

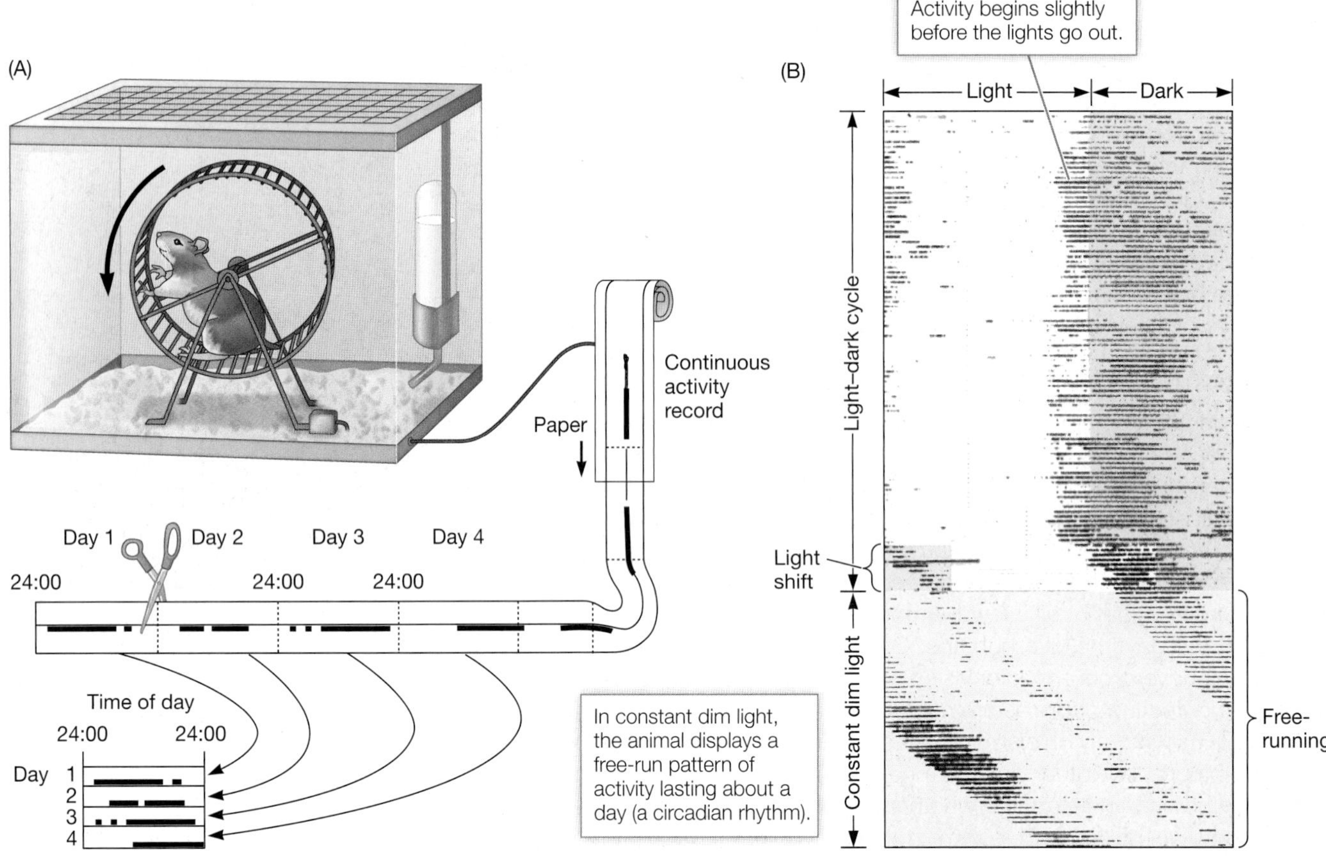

Figure 7.8 How Hamster Activity Is Measured in the Lab (A) A device measures how often the running wheel turns and keeps a continuous record of the activity for each day. (B) The animal becomes active a little bit before the lights go out each day, indicating that it has a good idea of the time of day. If we shift what time the lights go out, the animal soon reorganizes its activity to the new schedule. If we keep the hamster in constant dim light, it continues to show an activity pattern of about a day (a circadian rhythm). We say the animal is "free-running" because its activity is no longer anchored by any light cues. Because the free-run cycle takes slightly more than 24 hours, the animal becomes active a little bit later each day.

In an experiment in which human volunteers were asked to live in a cave, with no clocks and no external cues about time, they also were observed to free-run, and as in hamsters, their circadian rhythm ran just a bit longer than 24 hours (Weitzman et al., 1981). The volunteers were not aware that they were sleeping a bit later each day. By the end of the experiment, they had lost a few days, getting 74 "nights" of sleep over 77 days. When told the experiment was over, one volunteer was surprised because he thought he still had 3 days to go!

In theory, the biological clock underlying the circadian rhythms of activity might have been in almost any organ, but in fact the clock is in the brain. Tiny lesions in a part of the hypothalamus called the **suprachiasmatic nucleus (SCN)** inhibit animals' ability to show a circadian rhythm under constant dim light (**Figure 7.9**).

Because of our circadian clock, we often have a hard time adjusting when the periods of daylight and dark shift suddenly, as when you travel into a different time zone. **Jet lag** is caused by a loss of sleep and the uncomfortable disorganization of your body's physiology caused by a sudden shift in time zone. Only after several days of exposure to the light–dark cycle in the new location will your brain become synchronized to the light–dark periods of the new environment.

Most people suffer more from jet lag when they travel east than when they travel west. For example, if you began in New York and flew west to Los Ange-

suprachiasmatic nucleus (SCN) A small region of the hypothalamus that controls circadian rhythm.

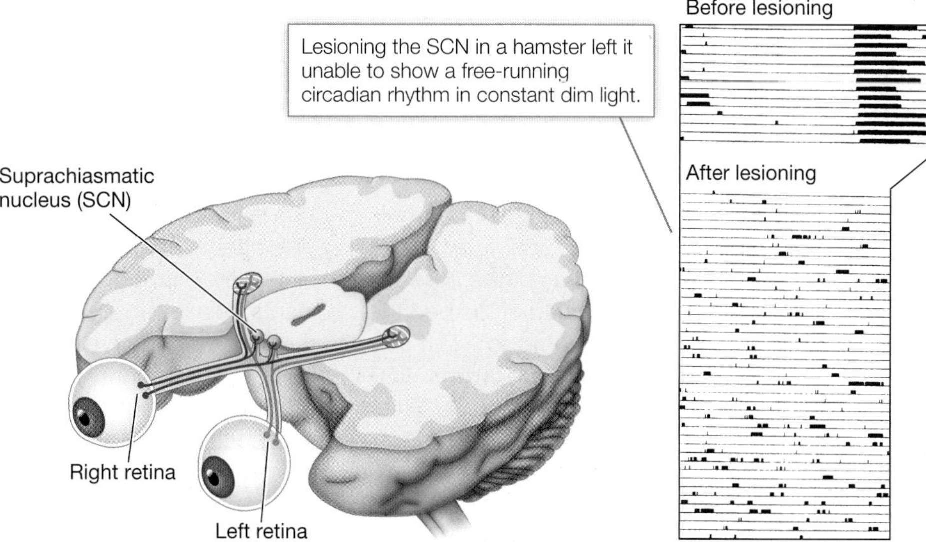

Figure 7.9 Damage to the SCN Abolishes Free-Running in Constant Conditions

les, you'd probably have no trouble falling asleep at 11 PM local time because that's 2 AM in New York. And when the alarm clock rings at 7 AM in Los Angeles, your SCN will act as if it's 10 AM—you got to sleep in!

jet lag The disruption of circadian rhythms caused by rapid travel across time zones.

The difference in jet lag effects from traveling east rather than west has been proven to make a difference in human performance. For example, when major league baseball teams travel west across time zones for a game, they are more likely to win than when they travel east across time zones (**Figure 7.10**) (Recht et al., 1995). Similarly, college football teams score fewer points when they travel east than when they travel west (Worthen & Wade, 1999).

There's lots of advice out there about how to combat jet lag, but it's almost impossible to escape this malady entirely when you travel across time zones. Your best bet is to try to get outside during daylight hours to get the new light-dark information to your SCN. No matter which direction you travel, most people have little trouble sleeping in synchrony with the new environment the first night, probably because they are slightly sleep-deprived and are tired from travel. Usually it's the next two to five nights when we have trouble getting to sleep, and here the direction of travel makes a big difference. If you decide to fly around the world, making lots of overnight stops, I recommend you fly west rather than east.

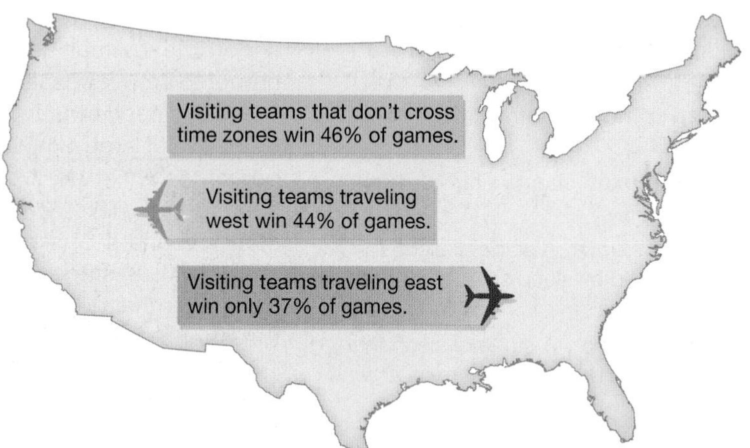

Visiting teams that don't cross time zones win 46% of games.
Visiting teams traveling west win 44% of games.
Visiting teams traveling east win only 37% of games.

Figure 7.10 Jet Lag Makes a Difference in Athletic Contests
Traveling east across time zones means having to wake up earlier than the brain expects, making it harder to get enough sleep. (After Recht et al., 1995.)

There are two different categories of sleep

Despite the millions of years that people have been sleeping and watching others sleep, it wasn't until 1953 that we learned that there are two fundamentally different kinds of sleep, as we will explain in this section. To understand these two different states of sleep, let's talk about techniques for monitoring human physiology, because these techniques were crucial for making this discovery.

A NIGHT IN THE SLEEP LAB To see how scientists study the mysteries of the night, let's follow what happens to a volunteer, Tessa, when

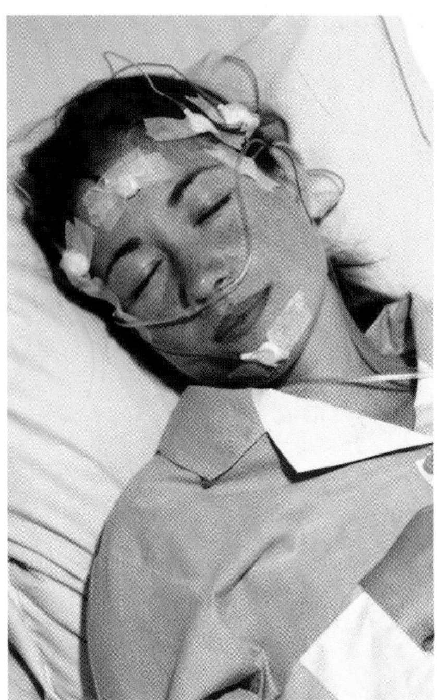

Figure 7.11 Ready for a Night's Sleep The wires pasted to this person's head are electrodes that detect rapidly fluctuating voltage changes in the brain. Connecting the electrodes to an electroencephalograph produces an EEG record of that activity, which changes in predictable patterns during the night's sleep.

she enters a sleep lab. Tessa shows up half an hour or so before her regular bedtime in comfy pajamas, and a technician begins attaching *electrodes* to her head and body. The wires at the other end of all these electrodes are then connected to a box at the head of the bed that connects them to an electroencephalograph in an adjacent room. The *electroencephalograph* is a machine that records **electroencephalograms** (**EEGs**), measures of rapidly fluctuating voltages taking place in the brain. Electrodes attached to Tessa's brain will record brain activity, while electrodes pasted on either side of Tessa's eyes monitor eye movements. Electrodes pasted on her arms will measure whether her muscles are tensed or relaxed. Despite looking like a cyborg with all these wires attached (**Figure 7.11**), Tessa soon stops noticing the wires and settles into bed.

Now let's take a look at Tessa's EEG in Figure 7.12. Before Tessa falls asleep and while she is still looking around, her EEG shows the typical pattern of wakefulness (**Figure 7.12A**). Because so many different parts of her brain are doing so many different tasks, a wide variety of voltage fluctuations are taking place in her brain. These thousands of different voltage fluctuations average out into a mix of high frequencies. The amplitude, or strength, of these fluctuations is relatively low because each center of brain activity is a relatively small region. A mix of many different high frequencies (greater than 15 to 20 cycles per second, or hertz [Hz]) with a low amplitude typical of wakefulness is called a **desynchronized EEG** (because no single frequency dominates). The term *beta activity* is also sometimes used to describe this pattern of wakefulness.

As Tessa closes her eyes and relaxes on her way to sleep, the EEG shows a regular oscillation of 8 to 12 Hz, known as the **alpha rhythm**. Tessa is still awake. We know this because she quickly answers if we quietly call her name. But soon the alpha rhythm in the EEG is joined by small, irregular waves and characteristic sharp waves called *vertex spikes* that define **stage 1 sleep** (**Figure 7.12B**). If we were to call Tessa's name now, we would have to say it more loudly and she might take longer to respond, although she might deny having been asleep. If we leave her alone, the EEG soon shows characteristic trains of spikes called **sleep spindles** and large single spikes of activity called **K complexes** that define **stage 2 sleep** (**Figure 7.12C**). It would be even harder to arouse Tessa now, although she might still deny having been asleep. Stage 2 sleep leads to (can you guess?) **stage 3 sleep**, defined by the appearance of large-amplitude, very slow waves called **delta waves** (about one per second) (**Figure 7.12D**). Eventually, delta waves may be present at least half the time. This period used to be known as *stage 4 sleep*, but because stages 3 and 4 of sleep are so much alike, many sleep labs simply regard them both as stage 3 sleep (Schulz, 2008). (Something that may help you remember that delta waves occur in deep sleep is that both terms begin with the letter *d*.)

Stage 3 sleep is also known as **slow-wave sleep** (**SWS**). Large, slow waves indicate that the hive of activity in the brain has quieted somewhat—instead of a multitude of different tasks being carried out by different regions, large areas of the brain are all working in synchrony. This synchronization has been likened to a room full of people who are all saying the same thing in unison.

electroencephalogram (EEG) A recording of fluctuating potentials taking place in the brain, made by an electroencephalograph.

desynchronized EEG Also called *beta activity*. A pattern of EEG activity comprising a mix of many different high frequencies, with no dominant frequency, and with low amplitude.

alpha rhythm Brain waves of 8–12 Hz that occur during relaxed wakefulness.

stage 1 sleep The initial stage of sleep in which the EEG shows small, irregular waves and characteristic sharp waves called vertex spikes.

sleep spindles A train of spikes in the EEG.

K complexes Large single spikes in the EEG.

stage 2 sleep A stage of sleep that is defined by sleep spindles and K complexes.

stage 3 sleep A stage of sleep that is defined by the presence of large-amplitude slow waves.

delta waves Large amplitude brain waves of 1 Hz, characteristic of stage 3 sleep.

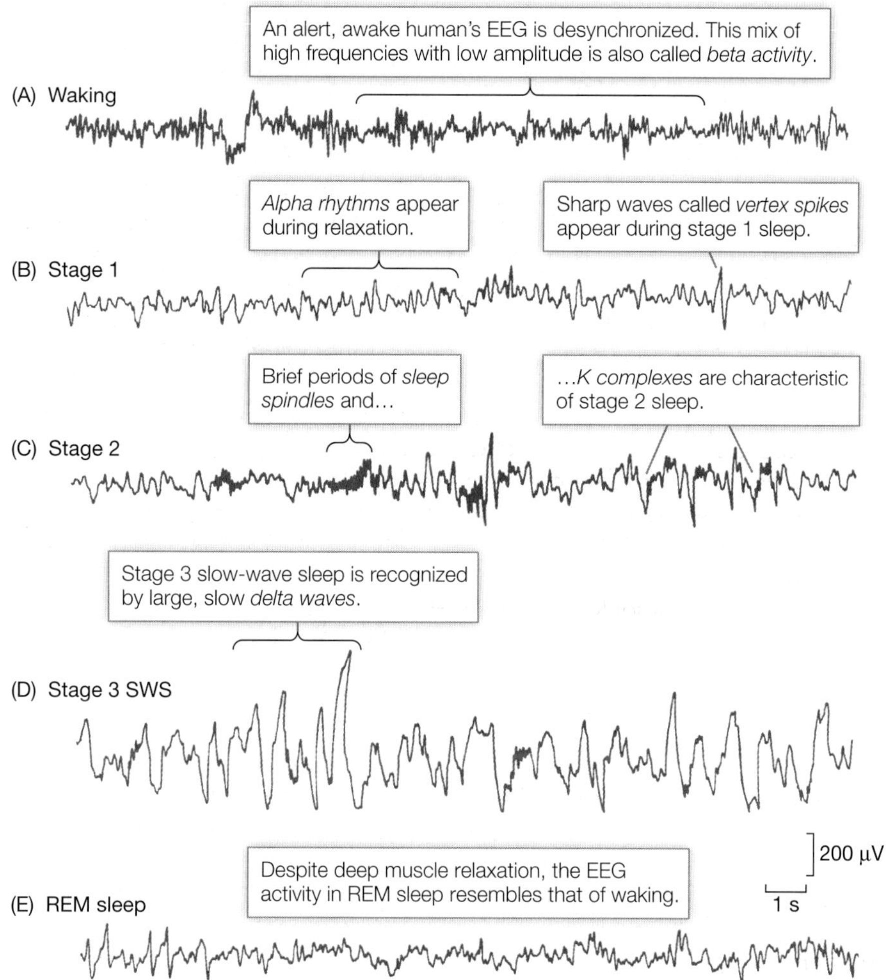
An alert, awake human's EEG is desynchronized. This mix of high frequencies with low amplitude is also called *beta activity*.
(A) Waking
Alpha rhythms appear during relaxation.
Sharp waves called *vertex spikes* appear during stage 1 sleep.
(B) Stage 1
Brief periods of *sleep spindles* and...
...*K complexes* are characteristic of stage 2 sleep.
(C) Stage 2
Stage 3 slow-wave sleep is recognized by large, slow *delta waves*.
(D) Stage 3 SWS
200 μV
1 s
Despite deep muscle relaxation, the EEG activity in REM sleep resembles that of waking.
(E) REM sleep

Figure 7.12 Electroencephalograms (EEGs) from the Various Stages of Sleep

From a distance you would hear the fall and rise of the cadence of speech in a slow rhythm. Just so, the EEG electrodes pick up a relatively slow fall and rise of brain electrical activity in unison. But if everyone in the room suddenly started having different conversations, all you would hear would be a low buzz, the rapid frequencies of many desynchronized speakers, no one of which would be loud enough to make out. This buzz is like the low-amplitude desynchronized EEG of wakefulness (see Figure 7.12A), when many brain parts are taking care of different tasks.

As Tessa continues to sleep, after about an hour or so she returns to stage 2 sleep, and then instead of cycling all the way back to stage 1, it looks as if she is awake again because her EEG has a low amplitude and fairly high frequency of desynchronized activity (**Figure 7.12E**). However, if we look at Tessa, we see that her eyes are still closed and she is still lying very still. In fact, her body looks completely limp, and the electrodes over her muscles indicate that they are much more relaxed than they are during wakefulness. The muscles are not just relaxed but *flaccid*. Stranger still, we can see that her eyes are darting back and forth, as if she were watching some scene under her eyelids. This pattern of desynchronized EEG, flaccid muscles, and rapid eye movements typifies **rapid-eye-movement sleep** (**REM sleep**) ("REM" rhymes with "gem"). REM sleep is also sometimes called "paradoxical sleep" because

slow-wave sleep (SWS) Sleep that is defined by the presence of slow-wave EEG activity (delta waves).

rapid-eye-movement (REM) sleep Also called *paradoxical sleep*. A stage of sleep characterized by desynchronized EEG, flaccid muscles, and rapid eye movements.

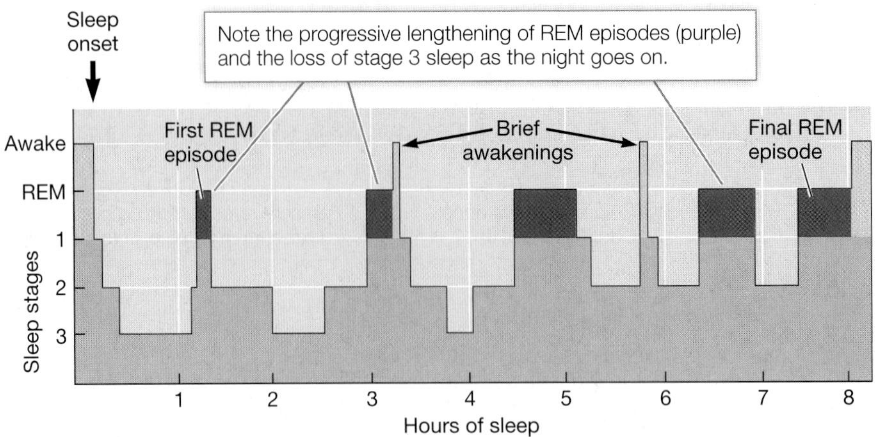

Figure 7.13 The Typical Night's Sleep for a Young Adult

non-REM (NREM) sleep Sleep stages 1, 2, and 3.

of the contrast between a very active brain and a very inactive body. We'll see later that in fact the body is *paralyzed* during REM and that if you could undo that paralysis, individuals would get up and start acting out their dreams.

Because REM sleep is so distinct from other sleep stages, scientists consider them two fundamentally different kinds of sleep: REM sleep versus **non-REM sleep** (**NREM sleep**), which consists of stages 1, 2, and 3. **Table 7.1** compares NREM and REM sleep. During the course of a night's sleep, people cycle through these various stages of sleep in a regular pattern (**Figure 7.13**).

VIVID DREAMS IN REM SLEEP Soon after researchers discovered REM sleep in the 1950s (Aserinsky & Kleitman, 1953), they found that sleepers aroused during REM sleep, when asked, often reported having vivid dreams. These dreams were very visual, with a story and the feeling that the dreamer "was there" experiencing sights, sounds, smells, acts, and thoughts (Moorcroft, 2013). In contrast, when people were aroused from other stages of sleep and asked what they had been doing, they tended to report more ordinary thinking about problems, the day's events, or tomorrow's plans, rather than experiencing events. The types of reports from REM sleep and SWS are so different that you can train other people to classify them correctly 90% of the time (Cartwright, 1979).

It is the extraordinarily vivid quality of dream experience that has made dreams fascinating to humans throughout history. It is easy to believe that these strange nightly quests mean *something*, and for thousands of years, as tales from the *Epic of Gilgamesh* and the Bible attest, people have tried to work out what dreams mean. At the start of the twentieth century, physician Sigmund Freud fell under the spell of dreams. A man of science, Freud dismissed the notion that dreams might tell the future in any supernatural fashion, but he felt that the content of dreams offered a glimpse into a person's mind, specifically the unconscious. For Freud, the key to understanding the meaning of dreams was to view them all as depicting *wish fulfillment*.

If our dreams revolve around our wishes (as Freud believed) why do we sometimes

TABLE 7.1 Comparison of NREM Sleep and REM Sleep

Property	NREM sleep	REM sleep
AUTONOMIC ACTIVITIES		
Heart rate	Slow	Variable with high bursts
Respiration	Slow	Variable with high bursts
Cerebral blood flow	Reduced	High
SKELETAL MUSCULAR SYSTEM		
Muscle tension	Progressively reduced	Eliminated
Twitches	Reduced	Increased
Eye movements	Infrequent, slow, uncoordinated	Rapid, coordinated
Cognitive state	Vague thoughts	Vivid dreams, well organized
NEURAL FIRING RATES		
Cerebral cortex activity	Many cells reduced	Increased firing rates

dream of dreadful things—the death of a friend, some calamity to the world—things we would not want to happen in real life? For Freud, many of these bad things that happened to other people were examples of what we *really* wish for, but are afraid to admit to the world (or ourselves). In other cases, Freud felt the mind purposely disguised our secret wishes so that we wouldn't recognize how selfish or cruel we really are. He contrasted the **manifest content**, what the dream *seemed* to depict, with the **latent content**, the *real* wishes that underlie the dream. He came up with a system for understanding how to see past the mind's distortions to reveal the true, latent content of dreams. For example, if you dream that a friend hurt you, then your *real* wish may be that you would hurt your friend, but your mind reverses roles to disguise your inner feelings.

manifest content According to Freud, what a dream seems to depict.

latent content According to Freud, the real wishes that underlie a dream

activation synthesis A theory that dreams result when the mind stitches together a narrative from images and sensations that were generated by random neural activity.

Freud's ideas about how to interpret dreams in order to understand a person's unconscious motives have not stood the test of time. One problem is that Freud's ideas about dreams are untestable. Given many distortions Freud suggested the mind could impose on dreams, *any* dream could mean *anything*. That means there's no objective way to tell which of the infinite number of possible interpretations is correct.

Probably the most important contribution Freud made to psychology as a field was his forceful, convincing demonstrations that we are not consciously aware of many of our brain's activities. This idea is now universally accepted and one of the foundations of modern behavioral research. But few scientists subscribe to Freud's ideas about the interpretation of dreams.

Today many scientists regard dreams as the result of the special quality of REM sleep, when the brain is quite active but receives little or no sensory input and no opportunity to move about (Hobson & Friston, 2012). The **activation synthesis** theory posits that our experiences in REM sleep are the more or less random result of which neurons happen to get activated. Our brain then strings together these disparate elements into a more or less coherent story, a narrative. Imagine a big roller cage, of the type used for lotteries or bingo games, filled with millions of different possible things we might see, hear, or feel. Different bits are drawn out at random, and with each new random experience we try to piece a story together that fits the experiences.

In some ways, trying to make a narrative from bits of random experience is an extension of what we discussed in the first section of this chapter. One part of my brain weighs many different factors to reach a decision about what to do next. Only later does my conscious self become aware of what that decision is. But I have the sense that "I" made the decision, and if you ask me why, I will offer a reason that may or may not be the real reason. The conscious me is trying to explain, after the fact, what my unconscious mind decided to do. When I awake, the conscious me is trying, after the fact, to piece together the random experiences of REM sleep into a coherent story.

If our consciousness is trying to make sense of a bunch of disconnected experiences we are having during REM sleep, then the main lesson to be learned from dreams may be to appreciate how inventive the mind can be at creating a narrative to explain whatever happens around us.

Two common sleep phenomena that you might think would be associated with dreaming actually happen outside of REM sleep. If you remember that the body is paralyzed in REM sleep, you'll realize that *sleepwalking* (or somnambulism) must happen during other stages. Indeed, if you wake up sleepwalkers (which, despite folklore, is perfectly safe to do), they usually act surprised to see what they're doing and have not been dreaming. Likewise, *night terrors*, when a person, usually a child, starts screaming as if in fear but typically does not wake up, also occur in SWS.

(A)

(B)

Postural Cues to Sleep States
The kitten in (A) must be in SWS, because its body is not limp, as it would be if it was in REM sleep, like the kitten in (B).

Do animals dream?

Examining sleep in other vertebrate species indicates that sleep is indeed crucial, because it is almost universal. The same kinds of physiological measures of the brain and body that are done in human sleep labs make it clear that all the other vertebrates sleep. What's more, all the mammals and birds that have been examined so far display both SWS and REM sleep, which indicates that these two kinds of sleep originated long ago in the common ancestor of birds and mammals. The widespread distribution of these two sleep states again indicates that sleep must be crucial for survival, otherwise we might expect some species to be sleepless. Other vertebrate species, such as lizards and fish, show clear signs of SWS, but it is not clear whether they ever show REM sleep.

Because our most vivid dreams are during REM sleep, and because other mammals display the same physiological signs of REM sleep that we do, does that mean that other animals dream? The strongest evidence supporting that view comes from experiments that tried to find brain centers for sleep. One approach to this question is to try lesioning various brain regions in animals and then to examine whether the animals' sleep is affected. The most startling results from such experiments came when a tiny region in the brainstem was lesioned in cats. The region is just below a structure called the *locus coeruleus* ("blue spot," because it has a slight bluish tinge), so the region is simply called the **subcoeruleus**. In the 1960s and 1970s, researchers found that lesioning the subcoeruleus caused cats to show strange behaviors (Morrison, 1983). These cats acted normally when awake, and went into SWS like normal cats. But when they might normally transition from SWS to REM sleep, these cats would stand up, shakily, and begin moving about. They would turn their head in such a way that they seemed to be visually tracking some moving object that wasn't there. They would take a forepaw and bat at something the experimenters could not see.

It soon became apparent that these animals were in REM sleep: their eyes tended to be closed, and the EEG gave signs of special waves that are normally seen only in REM sleep in cats. Yet these animals were moving around. During REM sleep, the subcoeruleus inhibits motor neurons, the cells that control muscles. That way, even though the brain is very active, and may be sending commands to motor neurons to move muscles, nothing happens because the motor neurons are too inhibited to fire. In these cats, lesioning the subcoeruleus stopped that profound inhibition so that the animals now acted out their dreams. This work was important in helping us understand how different brain regions control different aspects of sleep, a topic we will explore in depth shortly.

It wasn't until 20 years after this work with cats (which was later extended to rats) that doctors recognized that there are some people who show similar behavior (Schenk et al., 1986). These people tend to be men in middle age who start moving around at night. Their waking behavior and SWS seem normal, but then their eyes begin darting about under the lids, as in REM sleep, their hands start reaching out to grab things that aren't there, and unfortunately, they begin punching and kicking. Sometimes their bed partners become the inadvertent target of these aggressive behaviors. In other cases, the man may start running, all four limbs flailing about, while lying in bed (you can see a video of a man doing this on our website). If you wake the men, sometimes they remember dreams that seem to fit their behavior. No one knows why, but these men often dream of fighting or running away from some foe. This syndrome, called **REM behavior disorder** (**RBD**), can be controlled by several drugs that inhibit anxiety.

Today we know a great deal about how various brain regions, including the subcoeruleus, interact to control sleep states, which is our next topic.

subcoeruleus A region in the brainstem that inhibits motor neurons during REM sleep.

REM behavior disorder (RBD) A syndrome, primarily found in middle-aged men, that involves movements during REM sleep that seem to correspond to movements taking place in the current dream.

At least four brain regions regulate sleep states

Early in the twentieth century, scientists conducted some experiments that taught us important lessons about the brain centers for sleep, as we'll see next (**Figure 7.14**).

☑ Researchers at Work

Divide and conquer

Figure 7.14 The Stages of Sleep Are Controlled by the Brain (After Brémer, 1938; Siegel et al., 1986.)

■ **Question:** Which parts of the brain generate sleep and wakefulness?

■ **Hypothesis:** Dividing the brain into two parts—an upper part and a lower part—may reveal regions that generate different sleep states.

■ **Test:** First "isolate" the brain with an incision between the brainstem and the spinal cord. An "isolated brain" can no longer send commands to the spinal cord or receive information from the spinal cord. Observe the patterns of sleep and activity in the isolated brain. Then subdivide the brain to create an "isolated forebrain" by cutting all connections between the forebrain (cortex, thalamus, and hypothalamus) and the lower brainstem, including the midbrain and pons. Then observe signs of sleep and activity in the isolated forebrain.

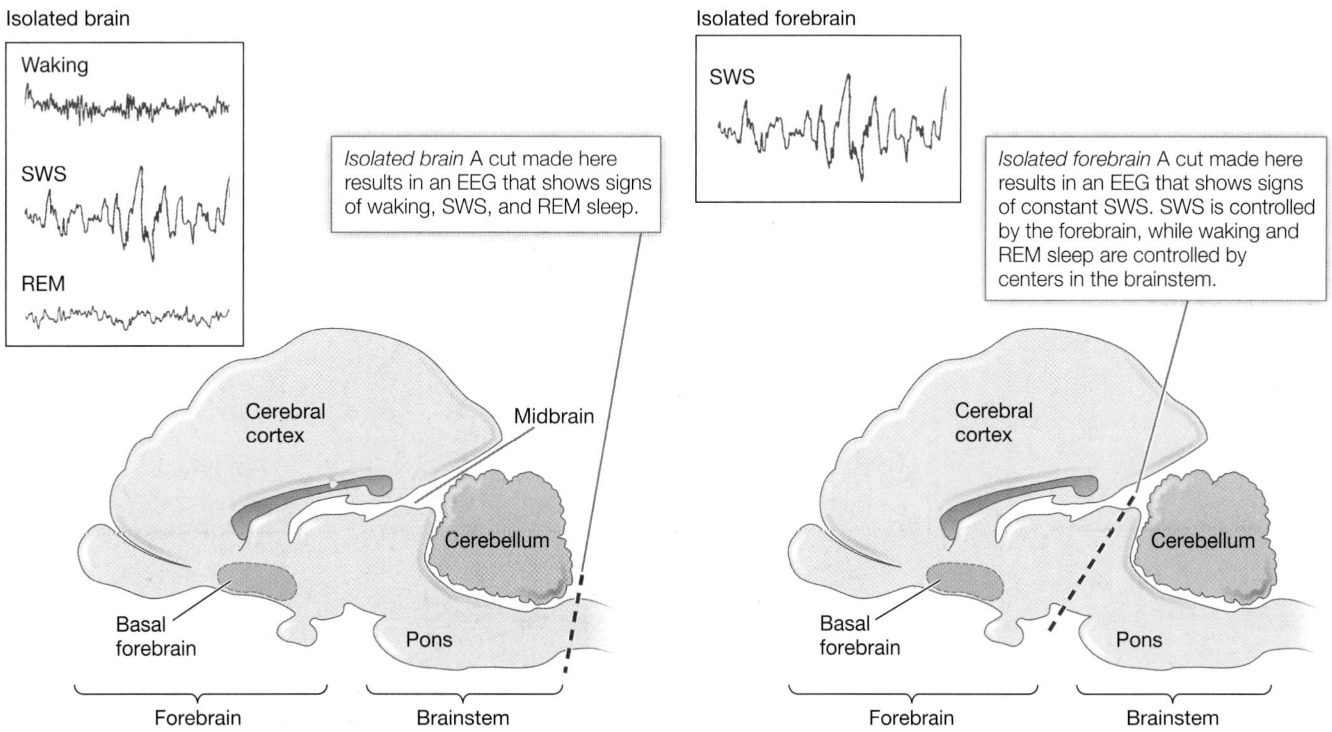
Isolated brain
Waking
SWS
REM
Isolated brain A cut made here results in an EEG that shows signs of waking, SWS, and REM sleep.
Cerebral cortex
Midbrain
Cerebellum
Basal forebrain
Pons
Forebrain
Brainstem
Isolated forebrain
SWS
Isolated forebrain A cut made here results in an EEG that shows signs of constant SWS. SWS is controlled by the forebrain, while waking and REM sleep are controlled by centers in the brainstem.
Cerebral cortex
Cerebellum
Basal forebrain
Pons
Forebrain
Brainstem

■ **Results:** The isolated brain continued to show signs of being awake at some times while being asleep at other times. In contrast, the isolated forebrain entered a state of constant SWS (Brémer, 1938).

Continued

Researchers at Work *Continued*

■ **Conclusion:** Because the isolated brain displays all three sleep states (waking, SWS, REM sleep), we conclude these states are entirely controlled by centers interacting within the brain. Because the isolated forebrain displays only SWS, the brain center(s) causing SWS must be in the forebrain. On the other hand, the center(s) causing wakefulness and REM sleep must be in the brainstem, somewhere between the cuts made to isolate the brain and to isolate the forebrain.

basal forebrain A region in the forebrain related to SWS sleep and insomnia.

reticular formation The area running through the middle of the brainstem, from medulla to midbrain, which is related to arousal from sleep.

These pioneering studies set the stage for later, more refined experiments that have given us a clear idea of how various brain centers interact to control whether we are awake, in SWS, or in REM sleep:

- The SWS center is in the forebrain, as the transection experiments above suggested, in a region called the **basal forebrain**. Electrical stimulation in this region induces SWS, while lesions in this region produce insomnia (**Figure 7.15**).
- The brainstem center that stirs the forebrain from slumber runs through the middle of the brainstem, up to the midbrain, and is called the **reticular formation**. Stimulation of this region quickly awakens a sleeping animal and increases arousal in an animal that's awake (see Figure 7.15).
- The brain center for REM sleep is in the subcoeruleus in the pons (see Figure 7.15). Recall that cats with a lesion of the subcoeruleus act out their dreams. The subcoeruleus inhibits motor neurons to keep them quiet, and therefore muscles flaccid, during REM sleep. It turns out that larger lesions around the subcoeruleus eliminate REM sleep altogether.

So far we have a SWS center in the basal forebrain, an arousal center in the brainstem called the reticular formation, and a REM sleep center in the pons. Each of these centers induces one of three states: NREM sleep (including SWS), waking, or REM sleep. But how is the action of these centers coordinated? It

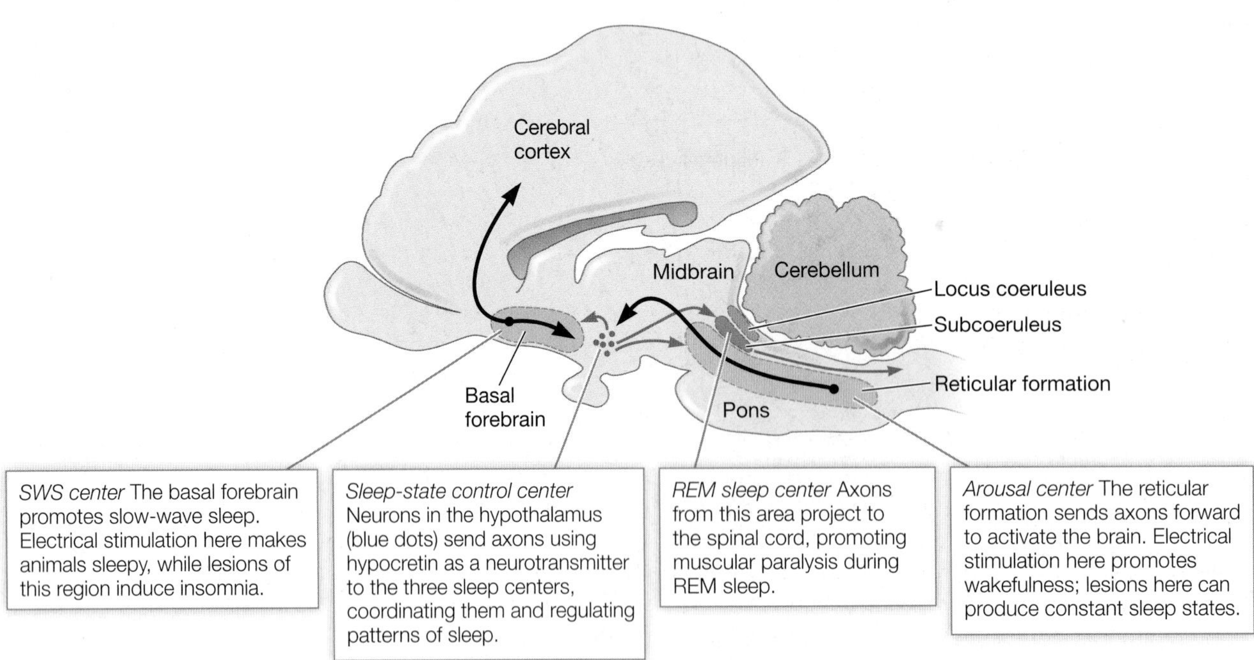
Cerebral cortex
Midbrain
Cerebellum
Locus coeruleus
Subcoeruleus
Reticular formation
Basal forebrain
Pons
SWS center The basal forebrain promotes slow-wave sleep. Electrical stimulation here makes animals sleepy, while lesions of this region induce insomnia.
Sleep-state control center Neurons in the hypothalamus (blue dots) send axons using hypocretin as a neurotransmitter to the three sleep centers, coordinating them and regulating patterns of sleep.
REM sleep center Axons from this area project to the spinal cord, promoting muscular paralysis during REM sleep.
Arousal center The reticular formation sends axons forward to activate the brain. Electrical stimulation here promotes wakefulness; lesions here can produce constant sleep states.

Figure 7.15 Brain Mechanisms Underlying Sleep

(1)

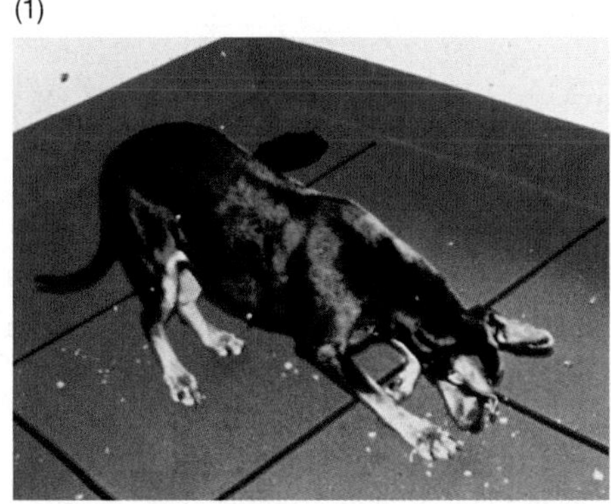

(2)

(3)

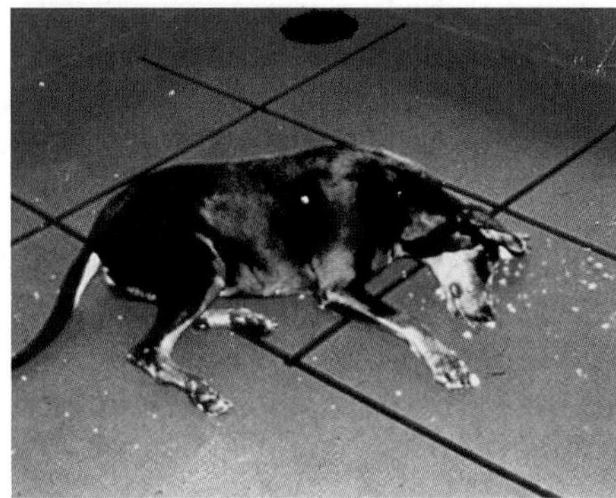

Figure 7.16 A Narcoleptic Dog A dog that suffers from narcolepsy (1) is offered a food treat, which is exciting, so (2) it becomes wobbly, and (3) finally falls limply to the floor. (Courtesy of Seiji Nishino.)

turns out that a fourth center—a *sleep-state control center*—plays a pivotal role, activating one or another of the other three centers to determine whether we are in NREM sleep, awake, or in REM sleep.

To understand how researchers discovered this sleep-state control center, let's return to Barry, whom we met at the beginning of this chapter. Barry suffers from **narcolepsy**, an unusual disorder causing a person to have intense attacks of sleep that last from 5 to 30 minutes during usual waking hours (Dantz et al., 1994). Most people display SWS for an hour or so before entering REM, but people with narcolepsy tend to enter REM sleep right away. Many people with narcolepsy also have Barry's sudden loss of muscle tone, leading to body collapse, without any loss of consciousness, a condition called *cataplexy*. Cataplexy can be triggered by sudden, intense emotions, including laughing and anger. Narcolepsy usually manifests itself between the ages of 15 and 25 and continues throughout life. Barry's case is typical in this regard, as his classic narcolepsy symptoms of excessive daytime sleepiness and cataplexy started his freshman year in college.

The breakthrough to understanding narcolepsy came from animal studies. Occasionally dogs are found to have narcolepsy (Aldrich, 1993). We recognize narcolepsy in dogs by the sudden loss of muscle tone whenever they get excited (**Figure 7.16**). This condition is inherited in these dogs, and researchers eventually isolated the gene involved (Lin et al., 1999). The gene encodes a receptor for a neurotransmitter called **hypocretin**, a neuropeptide found almost exclusively in the hypothalamus. When the gene for the hypocretin receptor was removed in mice, they displayed narcolepsy (Chemelli et al., 1999). When brains of humans with narcolepsy are examined after death, as many as 90% of the neurons with receptors for hypocretin are missing (**Figure 7.17**) (Thannickal et al., 2000). Because loss of hypocretin causes the

narcolepsy An unusual disorder causing a person to have intense attacks of sleep that last from 5 to 30 minutes during usual waking hours.

hypocretin A neuropeptide found almost exclusively in the hypothalamus, it coordinates the transition from one sleep state to another.

(A) Normal

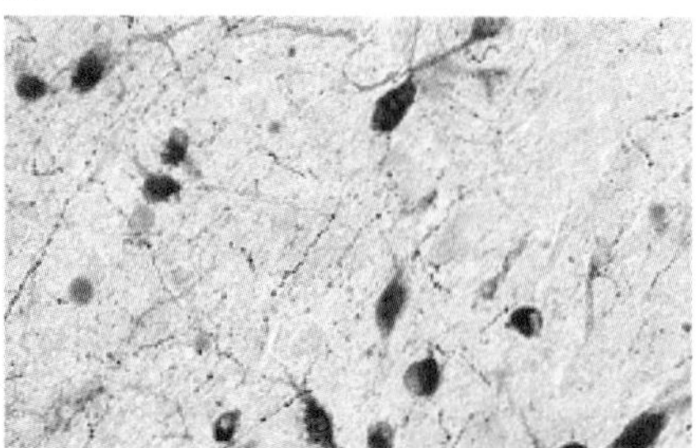

(B) Narcoleptic

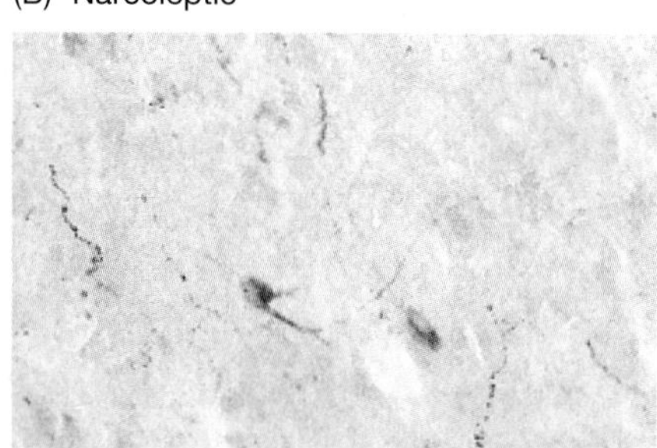

Figure 7.17 Loss of Hypocretin Neurons Leads to Narcolepsy Note the number of hypocretin-containing neurons (dark brown) from (A) the hypothalamus of a person who did not have narcolepsy and (B) that of a person who suffered from narcolepsy. (Courtesy of Jerome Siegel.)

sleep paralysis The temporary inability to move or talk either just before dropping off to sleep or just after waking.

uncontrolled switch from wakefulness to REM-like states in narcolepsy, it appears that hypocretin normally coordinates the transition from one sleep state to the other.

Where do hypocretin-releasing neurons in the hypothalamus send their axons? Not so coincidentally, they go to each of the three brain sleep regions we've discussed: the basal forebrain, the reticular formation, and the area near the locus coeruleus (Sutcliffe & de Lecea, 2002). Thus the hypocretin neurons of the hypothalamus seem to act as a switch (Saper et al., 2001), controlling whether we are awake, in NREM sleep, or in REM sleep (see Figure 7.15).

The problem in people with narcolepsy, such as Barry, is they seem to have a deficiency in the neurotransmitter that's used to control which sleep state we are in. Thus they suddenly feel sleepy in the middle of the day or, in the case of those with cataplexy, get the wrong combination of states: a wakeful brain with limp muscles. Most people with narcolepsy are able to control their sleepiness with stimulants, such as amphetamines or modafinil (Provigil). These drugs seem to combat cataplexy as well as daytime sleepiness. Barry eventually completed college and medical school. He is practicing medicine today.

Many people occasionally experience something like cataplexy. **Sleep paralysis** is the temporary inability to move or talk either just before dropping off to sleep or, more commonly, just after waking (Fukuda et al., 1998). For some people, the overwhelming feeling during sleep paralysis is of a heavy weight pressing on the chest, as famously portrayed in the painting *The Nightmare*. Some people may experience dreamlike hallucinations during such states (Cheyne, 2002). Sleep paralysis never lasts more than a few minutes, so it's best to relax and avoid panic.

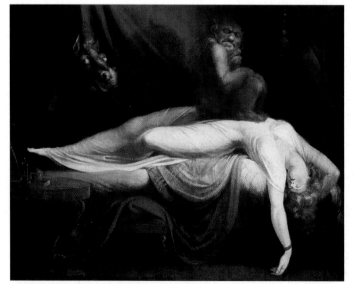

Nightmare While this painting is titled *The Nightmare*, it is also a great depiction of sleep paralysis, when the awakening sleeper may feel she cannot move, and may have trouble breathing.

We need sleep, but why?

We all have experienced what happens when we do without sleep—we get sleepy. We may ache all over, our eyelids feel heavy, our limbs feel weak, and our head nods as if our neck were a rubber band. But although feeling sleepy is unpleasant, it's not fatal. (Note that sometimes falling asleep is fatal, as when we are driving, but it's sleep, not sleepiness, that's the problem.) You may have heard that people who have been sleep-deprived for days will become crazy, but these stories are myths. In fact, for some conditions, like depression, sleep deprivation may counteract the symptoms, at least temporarily. If a person is already under stress or suffering a mental disorder, then sleep deprivation may exacerbate the problems that were already present, but healthy people deprived of sleep will be fine once they get some sleep. Why do we sleep? First we'll consider some of the theories about what sleep does for us; then we'll consider what happens when we do without sleep.

The four main theories about the function of sleep, which are not mutually exclusive, are:

1. Niche adaptation
2. Energy conservation
3. Memory consolidation
4. Body restoration

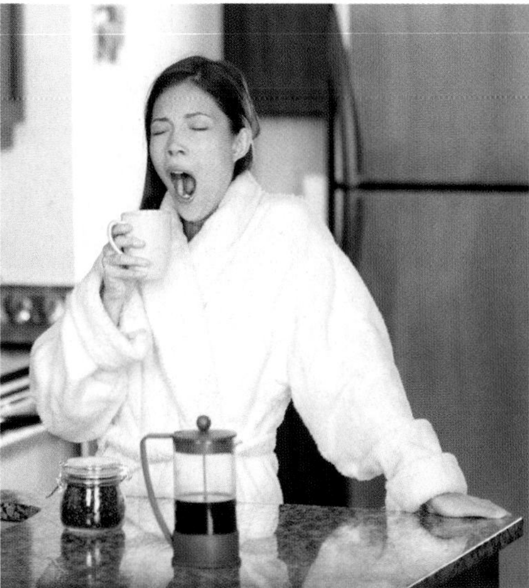

I Need Sleep! The most prominent result of sleep deprivation is that we feel sleepy. But are there more serious results of doing without sleep?

NICHE ADAPTATION Recall that almost all animals are either nocturnal or diurnal, and that each species has evolved many adaptations for daytime or nighttime activity. This adaptation to either daytime or nighttime activity is part of each species' *ecological niche*, the organism's way of life within an ecosystem. Natural selection favors species that become specialized to fill a particular ecological niche. Each species is better at gathering food either at night or in the daytime, and each species is also better at avoiding predators during either the day or night. If you're a nocturnal mammal like a mouse, you are adept at sneaking around in the dark, using acute hearing and smell to find your way around. Coming out in the daytime, when your vision is poor and predators like an eagle can see you from half a mile away, is a bad idea.

Each species searches for food, water, and mates during one time of day and spends the rest of the day holed up somewhere safe to stay away from predators. So one important function of sleep is to force the individual to conform to a particular ecological niche for which it is well adapted. A hypothesis associated with the niche adaptation theory is that the unpleasant feelings of sleepiness have evolved through natural selection to enforce a certain circadian rhythm.

ENERGY CONSERVATION Although sometimes the difference between the calories burned while we are asleep relative to when we are awake can be small, that small energy savings can be important. We use less energy when we are asleep because muscles relax, heart rate and breathing slow down, and body temperature falls slightly. In the wild, few individuals get all they want to eat, and many individuals are constantly on the verge of starvation, so conserving calories by sleeping is an adaptive strategy.

Sleep studies of many different mammals suggest that small savings in energy matter, especially for some animals. In general, the smaller the species, the more time it spends asleep each day. Rats sleep more than humans, who sleep more than cows. This finding suggests that sleep is important for conserving energy because small mammals have a hard time keeping their bodies warm. Why? Because small bodies cool off a lot faster than large ones. You've noticed this when you eat—scattered peas cool off a lot faster than a baked potato. This just reflects basic physics. A small body has more surface area relative to its total mass, so a proportionally bigger region is shedding heat. For the same reason, cows cool off more slowly than rats, so rats need to burn more energy per gram of body weight than cows do, just to maintain body temperature. In fact, the smallest mammals, shrews—tiny insect-eating animals that look like mice with pointy noses—sleep more than any other mammals examined so far (Allison et al., 1977).

No, I Really Need Sleep Tiny shrews lose body heat readily and spend a lot of time sleeping to conserve energy.

Finding Your Niche in Life Species that can sleep in secure circumstances tend to sleep more than other species.

Another general principle found when comparing sleep across mammals is that animals that have to sleep in "risky" environments (think of zebras sleeping out in the open) spend less time sleeping than species that have special "safe" places to sleep (think of a monkey sleeping up in a tree).

MEMORY CONSOLIDATION Another theory is that the brain somehow consolidates or "burns in" memories of things we've learned during waking hours so that we remember them better the next day. First, let me assure you that, despite ads you might read in the backs of magazines, you cannot learn new material *while* you are sleeping (Druckman & Bjork, 1994). Putting a speaker under your pillow to recite material you have to memorize for a final exam will not work unless you stay awake to listen. The question is whether sleep helps you learn or remember material or events experienced *before* you went to bed. For example, one of the earliest studies found that people who learned a verbal task just before going to sleep and were tested 8 hours later remembered more than people who learned the task in the morning and were tested 8 hours later (Jenkins & Dallenbach, 1924).

A surge of reports suggests that sleep helps consolidate memories in a wide variety of tasks, not just verbal memory tasks (Ellenbogen et al., 2007; Korman et al., 2007; Nishida & Walker, 2007). Some scientists, however, are skeptical that REM sleep is essential for learning (Siegel, 2001). Because sleep deprivation is necessarily accompanied by stress, it is hard to know whether stress might be the cause of memory disruption. Also, there is no correlation across species between time spent in REM sleep and obvious learning capacity. In humans, there is no correlation between the amount of REM sleep and either IQ or academic achievement (Borrow et al., 1980). At least one man whose brainstem injuries seemed to eliminate REM sleep was nevertheless able to learn, and he completed his college education (Lavie, 1993/1996). So even if REM sleep *aids* learning, clearly it is not absolutely *necessary* for learning.

BODY RESTORATION The body restoration theory suggests that sleep restores the body after waking activity takes a toll on it. Indeed, most of us have the experience of going to bed feeling tired, maybe a bit cranky, and waking up the next morning feeling rested and refreshed. If sleep has this restorative ability, you might expect that people would need to sleep longer after a day of strenuous activity versus a day of leisure, but that is not so. Studies of nonathletes show that exercise before bedtime may help them get to sleep sooner, but they may not sleep any *longer* (Chennaoui et al., 2014). Nevertheless, there is excellent evidence that sleep indeed restores the body in some way, and that evidence comes from studies of sleep deprivation, which we'll consider next. We'll find that although we don't know exactly what sleep is doing to restore the body, it must be doing something vital because total sleep deprivation is fatal.

Sleep deprivation has relatively mild effects, yet total sleep deprivation is fatal

Perhaps the most obvious support for the notion that we have a biological need for sleep is that when we lose sleep one night, we seem to need more sleep the next. This **sleep debt**, the increased feelings of sleepiness and tendency to sleep longer after a period of losing sleep, suggests that skipping a night's sleep leaves the body with an extra load of work to do. Then, the next night, we need to sleep longer to get that piled-up work completed. There may be some truth to this conjecture, but there is evidence that we apparently never fully recover all the sleep lost from skipping a night (Horne, 2011). When studied in the lab, a person who has gone without sleep one night will only sleep a few extra hours the next night or two. Of course it could be that

sleep debt The increased feelings of sleepiness and tendency to sleep longer after a period of losing sleep.

(A)

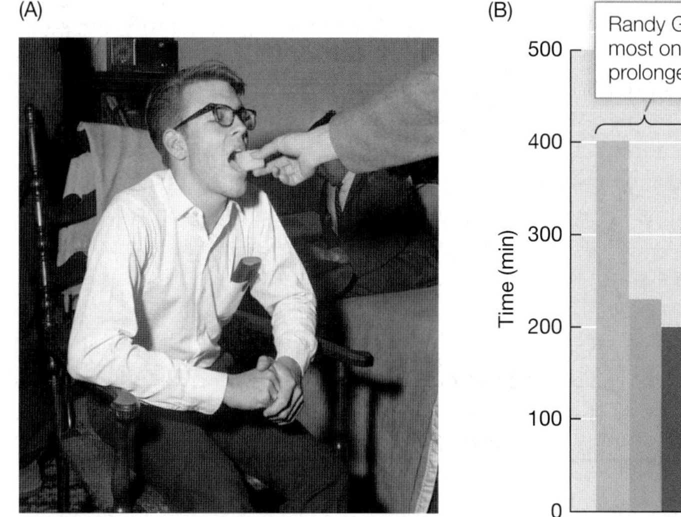

(B)

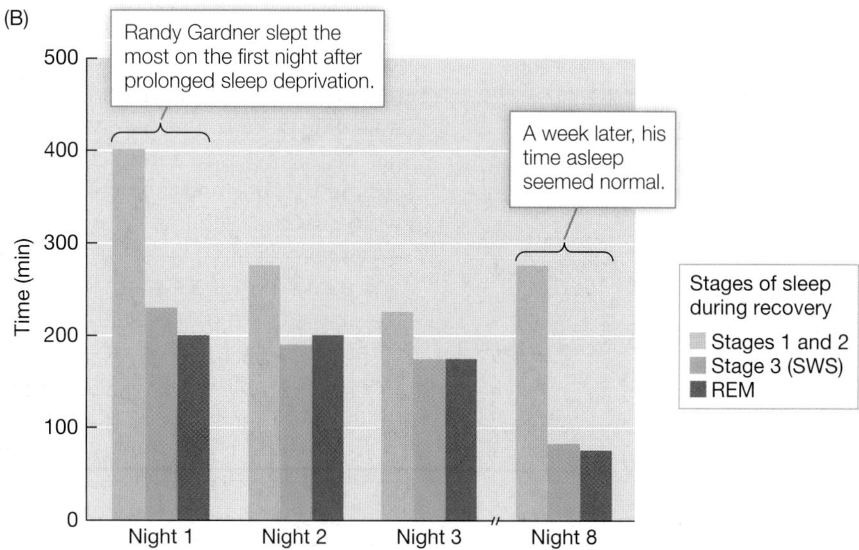

Figure 7.18 Randy Gardner's Sleep Experiment (A) Randy Gardner stayed awake for a long time without apparent harm. (B) Upon awakening from his first night's sleep after staying awake for 11 days, Randy appeared to be completely back to normal. (B after Gulevich et al., 1966.)

in those subsequent nights we are simply better at getting our "sleep work" done. To understand what that "sleep work" might be doing for us, let's ask what happens when we do without sleep.

You may be surprised to learn that when scientists test how well people perform various tasks after sleep deprivation, they don't note much of an effect. Only boring, repetitive tests requiring a lot of vigilance show a major decline in performance when people get sleepy. Several people have tried to stay awake for long periods, but perhaps the most famous and best-studied example is Randy Gardner, a high school student who in 1964 stayed awake for just over 11 days as part of a science fair project (**Figure 7.18A**). Sleep researchers learned about his project and began studying his behavior. Contrary to popular myths, Randy never had hallucinations or showed any other signs of mental disorder. On the contrary, his performance on arcade games remained quite good. Nevertheless, there were signs of his sleepiness: Randy's speech was sometimes halting or slurred, and he had trouble concentrating. Asked to count backward by sevens from 100 (100, 93, 86, 79,…), he sometimes had trouble even remembering what he was doing. At one point he was pretending to be a famous football star and may even have thought, for a bit, that he was that star. But on the final day of his project he handled himself quite well at a press conference, attending to questions and giving appropriate answers without any problems with his speech. When he finally went to bed, he slept for 15 hours, then awoke feeling refreshed and, apparently, completely normal. A week later his sleep was his normal 7 hours (**Figure 7.18B**), so Randy never got back the approximately 77 hours of sleep he had lost. In 2007 a British man beat Randy's record by a few hours, but unlike Randy, he used caffeine to help stay awake. Like Randy, this gentleman had difficulty with his speech when he was really feeling sleepy (as do we all), but was otherwise OK.

Just the same, complete loss of sleep for more than a few weeks appears to be fatal. The first indication of this came from experiments inspired by Gardner's project, where rats that were sleep-deprived for 11 days, like Randy, appeared to be OK. However, if the sleep deprivation continued, the animals began to lose weight, get a fever, break out in sores all over the body,

fatal familial insomnia (FFI) A fatal genetic human disorder that eliminates sleep at some point in midlife.

and within an average of 19 days, to die (Everson et al., 1989). If the rats were allowed to sleep, they recovered completely. The deaths were unexpected. In subsequent experiments the researchers avoided depriving animals of sleep until they died, but began asking what was going wrong beforehand. No single organ system seemed to be affected—heart, lungs, liver, kidneys all seemed to be functioning adequately. Rather, it appeared that the animals were infected with lots of bacteria, which caused the sores to break out and, eventually, death (Everson, 1993). Normally the bacteria involved are not fatal and a rat's immune system keeps them at bay, so the sleep deprivation seems to disable the immune system, making the animal vulnerable to invasions that it can normally handle just fine. This is one reason to think that sleep indeed restores the body (one of the four theories we discussed), specifically the immune system.

So are rats just different from people, or will people die from sleep deprivation that lasts 19 days or longer? It would be unethical to test this hypothesis with healthy people, but a very rare disease indicates that humans, like rats, will also die with prolonged sleep deprivation (Rodriguez-Martinez et al., 2008). It just takes longer. **Fatal familial insomnia** (**FFI**) is a human disorder caused by a gene that has no apparent effect in children or young adults, but at some point in midlife it eliminates sleep. At about age 50 or so, people carrying this gene begin showing symptoms. For the first few months they sleep less and less and may develop panic attacks and phobias. Next they become agitated, and may hallucinate over several months. In the third stage of FFI, they stop sleeping entirely and, like sleep-deprived rats, become feverish and lose weight. A few months later they become irrational, stop speaking, and die. Like rats that have been sleep-deprived for a few weeks, these people who have been without sleep for months lose weight and appear to succumb to diffuse bacterial infections rather than the failure of any particular organ system.

You might think that dolphins and whales, which are mammals that spend their entire lives in water and so must repeatedly come to the surface to breathe air, might not have a chance to sleep. In fact, for the first few weeks of life, baby whales may not sleep at all (Lyamin et al., 2008). But soon these animals display a neat trick—they sleep in one side of the brain at a time. When one side of a dolphin's brain is sleeping, the other side may be awake (Mukhametov, 1984). Some birds have also learned this trick of "unilateral sleep," probably to help look out for predators.

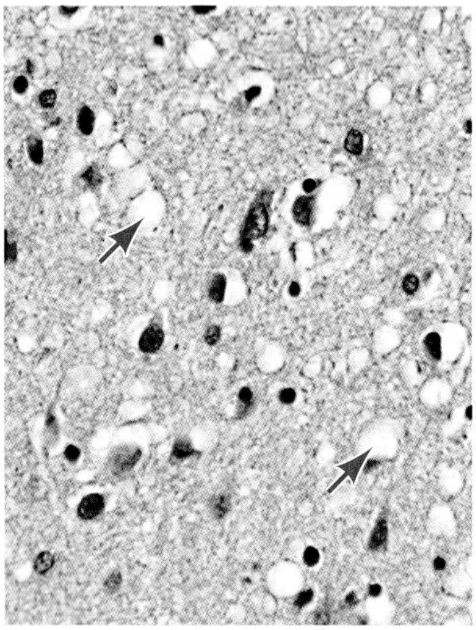

The fate of people with FFI seems to indicate that we cannot do without sleep altogether. But there are a few people who seem to need very little sleep—just 1 to 2 hours per night. They tend to have second jobs or hobbies to pass the time. The best-documented case was a retired nurse in England (**Figure 7.19**). To test her claim, scientists brought her into the lab and studied her in the way our fictional Tessa was studied earlier (Meddis, 1977). At first, the woman found everything so interesting that she couldn't get to sleep, but after a few nights she slept, as the EEGs and other equipment documented, for just an hour or two. She woke up feeling rested and refreshed. Despite having had only a few hours of sleep per night for decades, this woman seemed perfectly fit, despite her age, and had completed a demanding and successful career as a nurse.

Of the various hypotheses about the function of sleep, this nurse and other people like her seem to cast doubt on the importance of conserving energy. Apparently these folks save enough energy to do fine. Indeed, resting awake in bed probably uses about as few calories as sleeping. So whatever it is that sleep does that is crucial—restore our body, consolidate memory, maintain our immune response to invading microbes—these rare people who average only an hour or two of sleep per night must be more efficient at it than most

Holes in the Brain This section of frontal cortex shows the damage to brain tissue (arrows point to large holes) in a victim of FFI.

of us. It is important to note that no one has ever been documented to have absolutely *no* sleep, except those poor folks with FFI, who invariably die of it. Those of us who need 7 to 8 hours or more of sleep each night can be envious of these short sleepers—presumably they rarely have any trouble waking up in time for work or class.

Of course there are people who sleep little at night and are unhappy about that, who feel they are not getting the sleep they need. Let's consider this and other sleep disorders next.

Figure 7.19 **A Nonsleeper** This nurse slept only about an hour per night, yet she was a healthy and energetic person. Upon her death in her seventies, she had been awake for a total of 20 years longer than if she had slept 8 hours a night.

Sleep disorders can have mild effects or be devastating

We've already discussed several sleep disorders, including REM behavioral disorder, narcolepsy, sleep paralysis, and fatal familial insomnia. Except for sleep paralysis, these are fairly rare disorders. But other sleep disorders are quite common.

Perhaps the most common complaint about sleep is **insomnia**, difficulty getting the amount of sleep needed. Notice that this definition does not specify how much sleep a person needs each night because, as we've just seen, that can be very different for different people. For this reason, the definition of insomnia is inescapably subjective—if you feel you're getting enough sleep, then you are. We can divide insomnias into two types. Difficulty falling asleep is called *sleep-onset insomnia*. This type of insomnia is common, especially in people who are suffering from jet lag, which we discussed earlier, or from doing shift work or sleeping in a new environment (that hard hotel bed).

Interestingly, when brought to the sleep lab, some people complaining of sleep-onset insomnia appear to have another problem. People with **sleep state misperception** report that they didn't sleep even when their EEG shows signs of sleep and they failed to respond to stimuli (McCall & Edinger, 1992). They are sleeping without knowing it, and sometimes they are helped by having someone explain what's going on. Once they realize they really are sleeping, they sometimes relax and become more satisfied with their sleep.

Of course, many people reporting sleep-onset insomnia really do have a hard time getting to sleep, and they may be tempted to take *sleeping pills*. Most modern sleeping pills—including the benzodiazepine triazolam (Halcion) and its mimics Ambien, Sonata, and Lunesta—bind to GABA receptors (see Section 3.2 and Section 7.4 in this chapter), inhibiting broad regions of the brain. Unfortunately, none of these drugs provides a completely normal night of sleep in terms of time spent in various sleep states such as REM sleep. Current drugs fall far short of being a suitable remedy for insomnia for several reasons.

First, with continued use, sleeping pills lose their effectiveness (due to *tolerance*, which we'll discuss later in this chapter), and this declining ability to induce sleep often leads to increased self-prescribed dosages that can be dangerous (Rothschild, 1992). A second major drawback is that sleeping pills produce marked changes in the *pattern* of sleep, both while the drug is being used and for days afterward. During the initial phase of drug use, REM sleep is reduced, especially during the first half of a night of sleep. As drug use continues, REM sleep gradually returns. But withdrawal of sleeping pills results in a period of increased REM sleep with an intensity that may produce nightmares, which may lead to a return to reliance on sleeping pills.

Use of sleeping pills may also lead to a persistent "sleep drunkenness," coupled with drowsiness, that impairs waking activity, or leads to memory gaps about daily activity. Police report increasing cases of "the Ambien driver," a person who takes a sleeping pill and then gets up a few hours later to go for a spin, with sometimes disastrous results, while apparently asleep (Saul, 2006).

insomnia Difficulty getting the amount of sleep needed.

sleep state misperception A disorder in which people report not having been asleep when they actually were.

A Machine to Help Avoid Sleep Apnea This machine prevents the collapse of the airway that otherwise causes this man to stop breathing for a while several times each night. It also stops his snoring. (Courtesy of Christopher Breedlove.)

The treatment for insomnia that has the fewest side effects, and that is very effective for many people, is not to use any drug, but to develop a regular routine to exploit the body's circadian clock. Thus one sleep researcher suggests using an alarm clock to wake up faithfully at the same time each day and then simply going to bed when sleepy (Webb, 1992). A bedtime routine of quiet activities—get into pajamas, brush your teeth, read a book (this textbook if you like)—can also aid falling asleep (**Table 7.2**). Also, it's important to ignore preconceived notions about how much sleep you "need." If you get out of bed every day at 6 AM and don't feel sleepy until midnight, then your body is telling you that you need only 6 hours of sleep, no matter what various drug companies might say.

Difficulty remaining asleep through the night is *sleep-maintenance insomnia*. This type of insomnia, which is exacerbated by stress, also affects people who use drugs such as coffee, tobacco, or alcohol. As we'll see at the end of this section, it also affects many elderly people.

Some people who suffer from sleep-maintenance insomnia may be unaware of it. In these people, respiration becomes unreliable during sleep. Breathing may stop for a minute or so, or it may slow until blood levels of oxygen drop alarmingly. This syndrome, called **sleep apnea**, arises either from changes in neurons of the brainstem or from the progressive relaxation of muscles of the chest, diaphragm, or throat. In that case, relaxation of the throat obstructs the airway—a kind of self-choking. This kind of sleep apnea is common in people who are obese, but it also occurs, often undiagnosed, in people who are not obese. Sleep apnea is often accompanied by loud, interrupted snoring, so loud snorers should consult a physician about the possibility that they have sleep apnea. A machine (called a continuous positive airway pressure, or CPAP, machine) can maintain airway pressure to prevent collapse of the airway. Untreated sleep apnea can cause health problems, including high blood pressure (Wolk & Somers, 2003).

sleep apnea A sleep disorder in which respiration slows or stops periodically, waking the sufferer. Excessive daytime sleepiness may result from the frequent nocturnal awakening.

sudden infant death syndrome (SIDS) Also called *crib death*. Death that occurs when a baby less than a year old simply stops breathing while asleep.

Investigators have speculated that **sudden infant death syndrome** (**SIDS**, or crib death, see Section 5.2) in babies arises from sleep apnea as a result of immature brainstems that normally pace respiration, or from insufficient arousal mechanisms. While the cause is unknown, many factors are known to affect the likelihood of SIDS. It occurs only in babies less than a year old, is more common in boys than girls, and is more likely to happen to babies

TABLE 7.2 Dos and Don'ts of Getting a Good Night's Sleep

Do	Don't
Wake up about the same time each day (use an alarm clock if you have to)	Sleep too late on weekends (or on days when you have only late classes)
Go to bed when you feel sleepy	Stay up too late, even on weekends
Develop a calming bedtime routine	Drink caffeinated drinks after dinner
Find a quiet, dark place to sleep	Work shifts that require you to sleep in the daytime
Listen to your body	Listen to advertisements about how much sleep "everybody" needs

living in a home where someone smokes. Incidence of SIDS has been cut almost in half by the "Back to Sleep" campaign, which urges parents to place infants on their backs to sleep rather than on their stomachs. Placing the baby face down may lead to suffocation if the baby does not arouse properly.

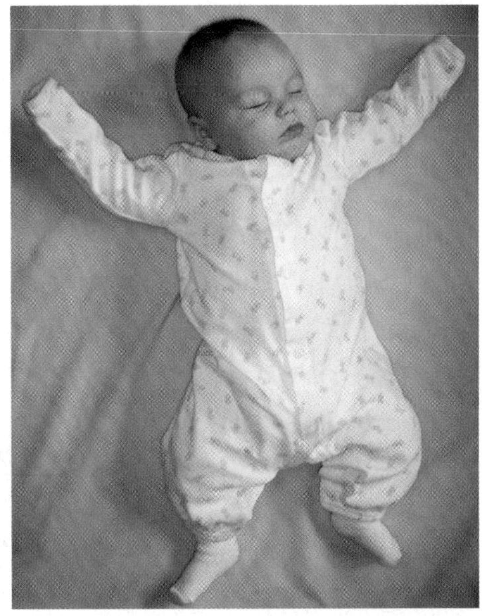

Safe to Sleep Placing babies on their back to sleep cuts the risk of sudden infant death in half.

Sleep patterns change across the life span

Newborn babies sleep a lot. Unfortunately for their parents, they seem to sleep at more or less random times of day (Kleitman & Engelmann, 1953). Newborn babies are also likely to be awake, and demanding attention, about any time of day. If you think about the dark environment in which the baby has spent the past 9 months, perhaps it's not surprising that she's not synchronized to day and night. Within a few months, most babies spend more time awake in the daytime than at night, with most babies fairly well synchronized to daytime activity by 4 or 5 months of age. There are still numerous daytime naps, occasional nighttime arousals, and predominance of sleep over waking.

The increased time awake grows gradually through development, reaching 16 hours per day during adolescence (**Figure 7.20**). Also note that about half the sleep in newborns is REM sleep. You can observe this preponderance of REM in newborns by watching one sleep—much of the time the baby's eyes are darting about, the fingers and mouth twitching. These hallmarks of REM sleep are even more prominent in newborns than in adults, as though the brainstem mechanisms that inhibit motor neurons to prevent movement aren't quite mature yet. Babies who are born prematurely spend even more time in REM sleep, suggesting that this state reflects immaturity of the brain. The proportion of sleep spent in REM gradually tapers off, making up 20% of total sleep by about the time children reach school age. This preponderance of REM early in life is nearly universal across mammalian species, so presumably REM sleep serves some important function in developing brains, but we still don't know what that function is. Scientists have speculated that REM sleep may be important for the dazzling pace with which new synapses arise in young mammals, which allows them to learn so much, so fast.

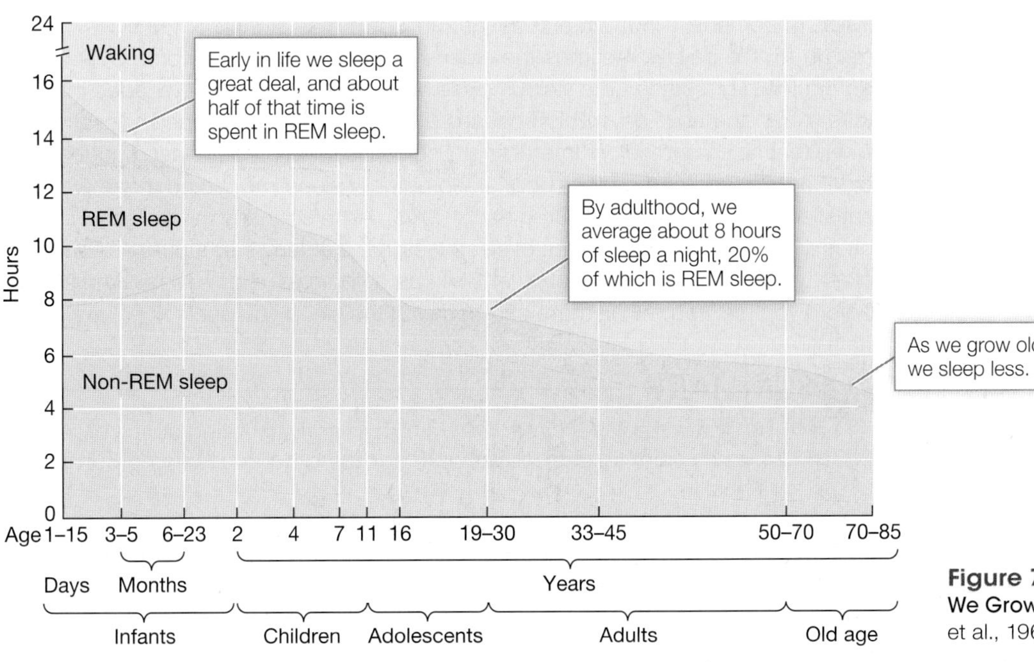

Figure 7.20 Changes in Sleep as We Grow Up and Grow Old (Roffwarg et al., 1966.)

Self-Defeating Behavior? Napping during the day may interfere with sleeping well at night.

Sleep is also important for growing children. As our earlier discussion about the importance of sleep for the immune system detailed, children need sleep to fight off the many microbes that they encounter each day. Young children tend to be early birds, waking up soon after daybreak, suggesting that they are very sensitive to light. But as children grow into adolescence, they tend to sleep later and later in the day (Roenneberg et al., 2004), as most parents trying to get teenagers to school on time have noticed. Perhaps you remember when your body shifted in this way, as it does for most people (see Figure 5.26). Also notice that after reaching a peak of late rising in young adulthood, most people start waking up earlier and earlier as they age. Some people might be tempted to explain the tendency of teenagers to sleep late by blaming them—they're just trying to avoid going to school. But the progressively earlier wake-up time from 30 years to 60 years cannot be readily ascribed to work habits. This shift suggests instead that some biological process underlies these changes in our circadian rhythms as we grow. Likewise, the sex difference in arousal time, which goes away in old age when sex differences in hormone secretions fade, also hints that the change in sleep patterns reflects some shift in physiology.

Not only do older people tend to wake up earlier in the day, but they also tend to get less total sleep. If you look back at Figure 7.20, you'll see that total time spent asleep each day continues to decline across the life span, from birth to old age. Note that the proportion of time spent in REM sleep also declines steadily, if more slowly, from young adulthood to old age. If we look at the breakdown of types of sleep a little more closely, we find that not only are old people spending less time in REM sleep, but they are also spending less time in stage 3. In addition to the decreased time in REM and stage 3, records show several awakenings through the night, which is also typical of sleep in the aged. This difficulty in *staying* asleep contrasts with the fact that most older people find it easy to *initiate* sleep.

The loss of stage 3 sleep is especially prominent in older adults. Stage 3 sleep is gone altogether by age 90 (Bliwise, 1989). Because growth hormone is released exclusively during stage 3 sleep, elderly people get little or no growth hormone, which may contribute to the cognitive decline with age. Boosting this idea is the finding that people suffering from senile dementia show an especially marked decline in stage 3 sleep.

Many older people complain about the disjointed, broken-up quality of sleep (Miles & Dement, 1980). An arousal at 2 or 3 am may stretch out until it's time to get up for the day. Sometimes the elderly make the condition worse by napping during the day, setting up a vicious cycle. A bad night's sleep persuades them to take a nap the next day, which causes them to have a shortened, dissatisfying sleep that night, and so on. Interestingly, objective measures of sleep suggest that older adults who complain of poor sleep actually sleep more than those who are satisfied with their sleep (McCrae et al., 2005). As in so many things, attitude may be important for the experience of sleep loss in the elderly. Perhaps if, as you grow older, you can regard waking up at 3 AM as a "bonus," a little more time awake before you die, you will be more satisfied with the sleep you get.

7.2 SUMMARY

- All animals display a *circadian rhythm* in activity, being active either during daylight (in diurnal species) or during darkness (in nocturnal species).
- A *biological clock* in the *suprachiasmatic nucleus* (*SCN*) of the hypothalamus allows animals to continue showing a rhythm of about 24 hours even in constant conditions.
- Normally information about light synchronizes the clock in the SCN to daylight.

- All mammals show two distinct kinds of sleep, *slow-wave sleep* (*SWS*) and *rapid-eye-movement sleep* (*REM sleep*), which can be distinguished by different patterns in an *electroencephalogram* (*EEG*) of the brain.
- We have our most vivid dreams during REM sleep, and there is evidence that other mammals dream during REM sleep too.
- SWS is triggered in the *basal forebrain*, while in the brainstem the *reticular formation* stimulates arousal, and a region of the pons in the *subcoeruleus* triggers REM sleep.
- Areas of the brain involved in sleep are innervated by hypothalamic neurons that release *hypocretin* to coordinate the transition from wakefulness to SWS to REM sleep.
- Loss of hypocretin signaling can cause inappropriate mixtures of sleep and wakefulness, such as the paralyzed body and wakeful brain (cataplexy) in people with *narcolepsy*.
- Sleep fulfills several functions: to ensure animals are active only during the time of day that suits their adaptations, to conserve energy, and to aid learning. Sleep also restores the body, in part by maintaining an effective immune system.
- Complete, prolonged sleep deprivation is fatal in both people and animals, yet doing without sleep for a few days seems to have little effect other than making one feel sleepy.
- The best treatment for most types of *insomnia* is to exploit the body's circadian rhythmicity by following a routine.
- Babies sleep a great deal and spend a greater proportion of time in REM sleep, but no one knows why.
- As we get older we sleep less, and the proportion of REM sleep decreases as well.

REVIEW QUESTIONS

1. What is the evidence that there is an internal biological clock in the brain?
2. Describe the stages of sleep and how they tend to appear in the course of a night's sleep.
3. What major ideas have been offered to explain why we sleep?
4. Describe the brain regions that promote different stages of sleep and wakefulness, including the region that seems to switch between these states.
5. Describe the various sleep disorders.

Food for Thought

We have all fantasized about how great it would be if we only needed to sleep an hour per night. If one day drugs are discovered that do for us whatever sleep does, so that we could choose to no longer sleep and never feel sleepy, would you use them? If many people did, how would it change our world?

7.3 Hypnosis and Meditation

Hypnosis and meditation are sometimes referred to as "altered states of consciousness," a phrase that implies that hypnosis and meditation are not just two "ordinary" states of mind, but that they are especially different from any other state. This is a slippery assertion that is difficult to test. What we can be sure of is that a person's conscious awareness changes when he or she is meditating or in a hypnotic state.

First we'll describe what hypnosis is like and dispel some of the many myths about it. Then we'll review the one great success story of hypnosis, which is in the control of pain. We'll also explore claims that hypnosis can improve recall, recovering lost memories, but we'll find there is virtually no evidence to support this idea and lots of evidence against it. We'll try to understand what's going on during hypnosis that makes it work, and conclude with another type of awareness, meditation.

Things to Learn

- History of hypnosis and its misuse
- Evidence that hypnosis can control pain
- Danger of hypnosis distorting memory
- Two main theories about mechanisms of hypnosis
- Beneficial effects of meditation and relaxation

Hypnosis is not what it's cracked up to be

hypnosis A process at work when one person, the hypnotist, suggests that another person will experience particular perceptions or engage in particular behaviors.

Hypnosis is a process at work when one person, the hypnotist, suggests that another person will experience particular perceptions or engage in particular behaviors. Notice that this definition immediately makes hypnosis a *social* interaction, and we'll see that there is growing sentiment that hypnosis is fundamentally about one person trying to conform to another person's requests. There is, unfortunately, much misinformation about hypnosis. Lurid portrayals of the hypnotic state in novels and movies provide a cheap way to get the audience's attention or turn the plot in a direction that could never happen in real life. So we begin our discussion of hypnosis by dispelling some of these myths.

No matter what you see on the screen, people cannot be hypnotized against their will. People under hypnosis cannot perform superhuman feats, and they will not do something they truly do not want to do (like reveal embarrassing personal secrets or hurt another person). While hypnotized people may show alpha rhythms in an EEG indicating a relaxed brain (Graffin et al., 1995), their EEG does not resemble that seen in sleep. Perhaps the most damaging myth, which we'll discuss in some detail later in this section, is that hypnosis improves recollection of memories. As we'll see, there is very little evidence that hypnosis *ever* improves recall and ample evidence that hypnosis can *distort* recall, planting false memories. To understand what hypnosis is (and is not), it's helpful to consider the history of hypnosis.

A Viennese physician, Franz Mesmer (1734–1815), began using magnets to treat patients for a wide variety of ailments, passing the magnet back and forth over the body part in question. While doing this he would talk to the patient in a soothing voice, explaining how the magnet would relieve the symptoms. Mesmer thought the magnets were increasing blood flow or stimulating nerves, but he soon learned that just passing his hands, without a magnet, over the body part could have the same effect. From this, you might have concluded that Mesmer's treatment had nothing to do with magnetism. Mesmer, however, concluded that his hands were magnets, sweeping the patient's body with healing waves of "animal magnetism." Mesmer moved to Paris where he was in great demand, but the scientists studying magnetism, including a committee chaired by Benjamin Franklin, tested his ideas about animal magnetism and, in 1784, dismissed them. The committee's report did not use the word "suggestion," but it is clear that the committee members felt that the hypnotist's assertion that the treatment would work tapped into a patient's "imagination" (Weitzenhoffer, 2000). Mesmer was discredited and died in poverty, but his procedures for getting people to relax and attend to someone's voice took hold. Eventually, "Mesmerism" was renamed "hypnosis" (from the Greek word for "sleep"), to distance the field from Mesmer's discredited ideas about magnets. From this point on, hypnosis has consisted of a hypnotist who speaks to a participant, suggesting that he or she will feel and do certain things.

Super Power? This seemingly "superhuman" task is not actually difficult to perform, whether you are hypnotized or not.

So what's it like to be hypnotized? First, you have to agree to listen to the hypnotist and agree to "see what happens." In other words, you have to be open to the experience. Hypnosis consists of two stages: first the *induction* of a hypnotic state, then the *suggestion* that you experience certain sensations or perform certain behaviors. It helps to withdraw to a calm, quiet room without distractions, and the first step is to relax the body. There are many different things the hypnotist might do to induce hypnosis, but usually the hypnotist, talking in a low, calm voice, asks you to look at a spot on a wall, and to concentrate on that spot while listening to his or her voice. After a while the hypnotist may assert that your eyes are getting tired (as indeed is likely if you've been staring at that spot for a while) and that your eyelids feel heavy. He may encourage you to close your eyes, and if you really are trying to cooperate, to see if you can be hypnotized, you will probably be glad to close your eyes. The hypnotist will then encourage you to relax deeply. Continuing to speak in a calm, low voice, urging you to pay attention to him, the hypnotist may now suggest you do certain things. "Now hold your arms out at shoulder height with the palm up. There, that's right.... Attend carefully to your left hand, how it feels. Imagine you're holding something heavy in that hand.... Maybe a heavy paperweight.... Now it seems to be getting heavier and heavier...." Indeed, your left hand may begin to sink slowly down. The hypnotist may go on to suggest a series of experiences you might feel. "Continue to relax with your eyes closed.... There's a mosquito flying around the room, and it's about to land on your right arm.... There, do you feel that?" For these and a series of other suggestions, you may actually feel as though your left hand is holding a heavy weight, or that a mosquito landed on your arm.

Animal Magnetism Franz Mesmer believed that magnetic fields from his hands could heal people with various ailments.

People vary in their susceptibility to hypnosis

An early finding in hypnosis research is that people vary quite a lot in how susceptible they are to hypnotic suggestions. Some people act as though they are holding something heavy in one hand, or they feel a mosquito land on their arm. In extreme cases, the participant may, as a result of hypnotic suggestion, report being unable to see in one or both eyes. On the other hand, some people seem very resistant to hypnosis, meaning they don't appear to experience any of the sensations or perform any of the behaviors the hypnotist suggests to them.

The **Stanford hypnotic susceptibility test** is used to estimate how readily a person can be hypnotized, basically by counting up how many hypnotic suggestions the participant follows (Weitzenhoffer & Hilgard, 1959). Many studies have surveyed what proportion of participants can reach various depths of suggestion using the Stanford and other scales. Such studies indicate that about half of the population is either not susceptible to hypnosis (14%) or only slightly susceptible (37%). The remaining half is about equally divided between being moderately susceptible or deeply susceptible to hypnotic suggestion (Weitzenhoffer, 2000).

If there is a single characteristic that indicates whether people will be susceptible to hypnosis, it is whether they have a good imagination (Spanos et al., 1993), echoing the conclusion of Franklin's committee in 1784. They are people who really get lost in a good book, who may not hear someone talking to them while reading or watching TV. They report having vivid imagery when they imagine a scene, and are good at concentrating on a task at hand (Council et al., 1996). Another way to describe such people is that they are *very good at directing their attention*, either into a book or movie, or onto some mental image they conjure up. If you are such a person, you may be wondering if you would be susceptible to hypnosis. I don't know the answer, but note that if you ever have the chance to be tested on the Stanford scale, you certainly won't respond to hypnotic suggestions *unless you are willing to try*. That is why neither you nor anyone else can be hypnotized against their will. So being susceptible to hypnosis is not a matter of being weak-willed or gullible, but a matter of whether you are open to new experiences and ideas.

In many ways, hypnosis is simply a matter of the participant focusing his or her attention in response to the hypnotist's suggestion. Sometimes it may be that the participant attends to the hypnotist's suggestions simply because of the mystique attached to the term "hypnosis."

To some extent hypnosis benefits from the *placebo effect*: if the participant thinks it works, it is more likely to work (recall the discussion of placebos in Section 2.2). The aura of mystery, and the idea that hypnotism is special, may make people more susceptible to the hypnotist's suggestions. Believing that

Stanford hypnotic susceptibility test A tool used to estimate how readily a person can be hypnotized.

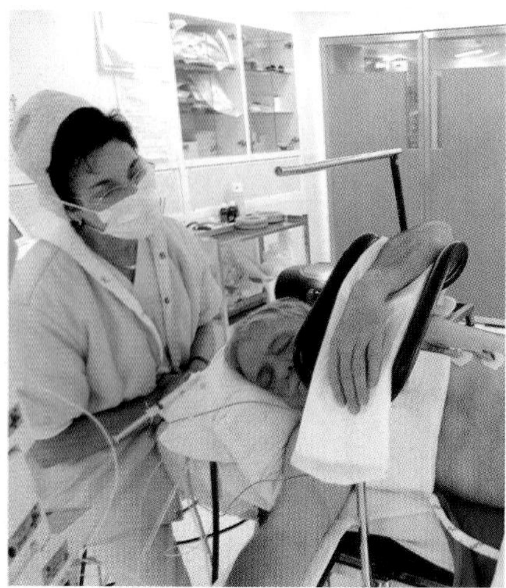

Invasive Surgery without Anesthesia
Hypnosis can reduce pain and the need for painkillers during minor surgeries.

hypnosis is special might make it more effective, in much the same way that a patient, believing that the pill provided by a doctor will relieve pain, may actually experience less pain, even if the pill is simply sugar.

In hypnosis, it is the participant who is doing most of the work, not the hypnotist. This is why some people can perform self-hypnosis, suggesting to themselves that they are feeling one way or another. Self-hypnosis can be a worthwhile skill to acquire; it can be used, for example, to reduce pain.

Hypnosis can reduce pain

Perhaps the most important use of hypnosis is in the control of pain (Hawkins, 2001; Patterson & Jensen, 2003; Stoelb et al., 2009). A few people who are especially sensitive to hypnosis can even undergo minor surgery, such as having a tooth removed or undergoing hand surgery using hypnosis, rather than chemical anesthesia. For the control of pain, hypnosis begins, as always, with the person agreeing to be open to the experience. The participant is encouraged to relax and attend carefully to the hypnotist in a calm, quiet setting. After the usual procedures of suggesting that the participant is experiencing heavy eyelids, heavy hands, and so on, the hypnotist will suggest to the person one of various ways to regard painful stimuli. There are many different strategies, but for the most part they hinge on distinguishing between whether the participant *feels* the pain versus whether the pain is *unpleasant*. In Section 6.2 we learned that one component of painful stimuli is the emotional experience, which by definition is unpleasant. The hypnotist may suggest to the person that the unpleasantness of the pain is reduced, or suggest that the participant regard the painful stimuli in a detached manner, as something that is being experienced by someone else. Hypnotic control of pain has been demonstrated in real-life situations, as we'll see next (**Figure 7.21**).

Researchers at Work

Talking away the pain

Figure 7.21 Benefits of Hypnosis during Surgery (After Lang et al., 2000.)

- **Question:** Can hypnosis control pain outside laboratory demonstrations?

- **Hypothesis:** Patients provided with the hypnotic suggestion to reduce pain will report less discomfort.

- **Test:** Patients having any of a variety of surgical procedures were awake during the surgery and, whenever they requested it, given intravenous painkillers. Importantly, patients were not screened for hypnotizability, but *randomly* assigned to receive hypnosis or not during the surgery.

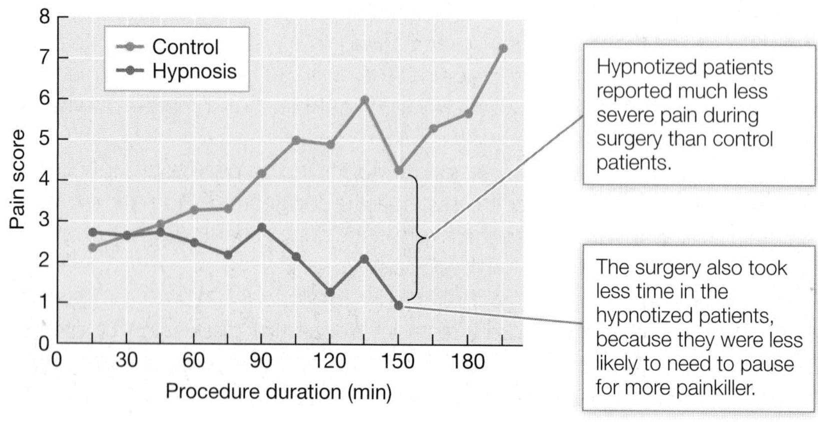

Control
Hypnosis
Pain score
0
1
2
3
4
5
6
7
8
0
30
60
90
120
150
180
Procedure duration (min)
Hypnotized patients reported much less severe pain during surgery than control patients.
The surgery also took less time in the hypnotized patients, because they were less likely to need to pause for more painkiller.

■ **Results:** On average, the patients who were hypnotized requested only half as much painkiller as the control group, and they reported much less severe pain. The hypnotized patients also reported much less anxiety than the non-hypnotized patients (Lang et al., 2000).

■ **Conclusion:** Hypnosis reduces the perception of pain not only in laboratory demonstrations, but also in real-life situations such as surgery. This hypnotic treatment can benefit patient and surgeon by allowing the surgery to proceed faster.

For people who are suffering from long-lasting, chronic pain, hypnosis is usually more effective if the hypnotist suggests that the pain is reduced to tolerable levels, rather than suggesting it is gone altogether (Stoelb et al., 2009). People can also learn to self-hypnotize, following the same hypnotic routine at home by themselves, perhaps aided by listening to a tape recording of a hypnotic session with a hypnotist. The Lamaze method of reducing pain perception during childbirth (Lothian, 2011) resembles hypnosis in that a coach (hypnotist?) encourages the mother giving birth to concentrate on patterns of breathing (to redirect attention?) and suggests that she can manage the pain.

Given the history of Mesmer's misguided use of magnets to relieve pain in "imaginative" patients, you may be wondering if hypnotized patients who are told to feel less pain might be tempted to report less pain simply to please the hypnotist. However, there are several indications that the pain relief is real (Schulz-Stübner et al., 2004). For example, a sample of participants who were moderately to very susceptible to hypnosis on the Stanford scale were asked to put their hand into a container of very warm water while having their brain activity scanned (Rainville et al., 1997). Before the scanning, participants were hypnotized and given the suggestion that they would find the water "neutral" or "painfully hot." In fact, the temperature of the water was carefully controlled to be exactly 117°F in every case. However, people hypnotized to expect the water to be painfully hot reported more pain than those expecting neutral temperatures. Furthermore, activation of touch-related cortical regions of the hand were equivalent in the two groups, but activation of the portion of the brain associated with *emotional* response to pain (the anterior cingulate cortex) showed greater activity in those participants expecting painfully hot water (**Figure 7.22**). Notice that

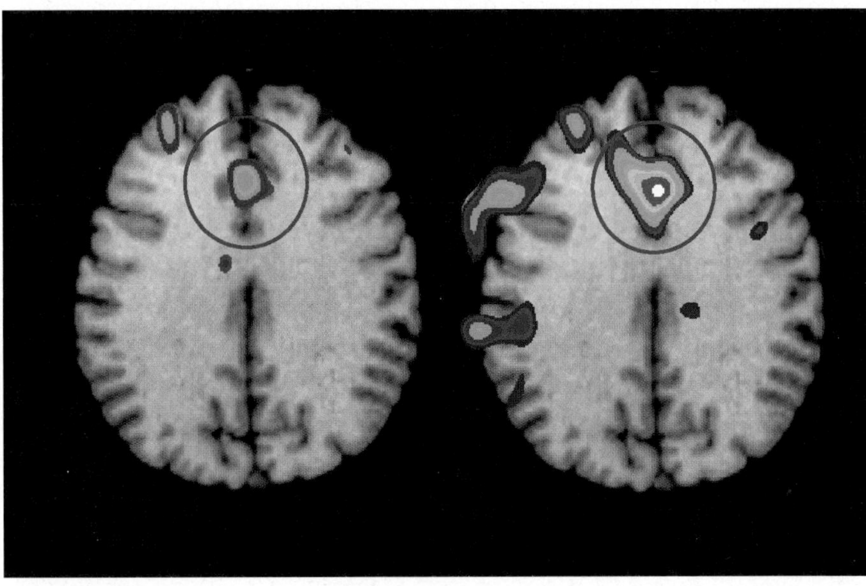

Figure 7.22 **The Pain in the Brain Is Mostly in the Gain** The brain of a participant told to expect only minor discomfort from putting a hand into 117°F water (left) showed less activation in the anterior cingulate cortex than did the brain of a participant expecting more discomfort from water of the same temperature (right). Areas of high activation are indicated by orange, red, and white. (From Rainville et al., 1997, courtesy of Pierre Rainville.)

this experiment gets at an "easy" question of consciousness we discussed in Section 7.1. The experimenters could have looked at the brain scans and predicted which group of participants was experiencing more pain.

Experiments have given us several insights into how hypnosis controls pain. The difference in brain activation observed in the hot water experiment described above, for example, indicates that the hypnotized people expecting water of a neutral temperature really were *experiencing* less pain, not just *reporting* less pain to please the hypnotist. It is also interesting that the brain regions activated directly by somatosensory stimuli were equivalent in the two groups, confirming the idea that there are two components of pain: the stimulus itself and the emotional response to that stimulus (see Section 6.2). Apparently hypnosis is effective because it dampens the *emotional* response to pain. You might wonder: In these cases does hypnosis cause the patients to release their own pain relievers (so-called opiates) in brain systems mediating pain, thereby reducing the intensity of the sensation? Drugs that block opiate receptors do not impair hypnotic pain reduction, so this is not the case. This is one way in which hypnosis is not like sugar pill placebos that the patient thinks are painkillers. Giving a person opiate blockers beforehand renders the placebo ineffective, but hypnosis still works (Goldstein & Hilgard, 1975).

Hypnosis has also been somewhat effective in helping people with obesity to eat less and exercise more to lose weight, but only if the hypnosis is in conjunction with a behavioral weight management program of exercise and low-fat diet (Allison & Faith, 1996; Pittler & Ernst, 2005). Hypnosis has not been very successful at helping people with drug addictions such as smoking cigarettes (Abbot et al., 2000; Mamtani & Cimino, 2002). As with many therapies, it may help some individuals, but on average hypnosis is not effective for addiction.

Hypnosis does not improve memory

One controversial use of hypnosis is for recovered memories. Many therapists, including Freud, claim that hypnosis can allow people to remember painful events that had been buried below consciousness. Indeed, testimony from patients who have recovered memories through hypnosis has been used to send people to prison. The problem is that when scientists try to demonstrate that hypnosis can recover memories, they find little or no evidence that it is effective. Rather, there is ample evidence that hypnosis can sometimes plant false memories.

AGE REGRESSION One early use of hypnosis to recover past memories, which seems to have originated from the entertainment world, is age regression, where hypnotized adults are asked to go back and become the children they were before. In such cases, the participants certainly act more like children. They may write with a childlike scrawl, draw crude sticklike figures, and speak in a childlike fashion. But when tested, the participants in fact know more than children, as shown by tests of logical reasoning, language comprehension, or personality traits (Nash, 1987). Most important, people who have been age regressed under hypnosis are no better at imitating children than are people who are simply asked to imitate children (Nash, 1987). Hypnotized participants during age regression may be asked to describe what they see and hear around them during some episode of their childhood, such as a day in first grade. While there are claims that people under hypnosis can remember details they could not before, there is no solid evidence that this is true. For example, if asked to go back to their fourth birthday, hypnotized participants may report vivid memories of the cake and events of the day, but their recollection of what day of the week it fell on is no better than it would be by chance (O'Connell et al., 1970). Yes, the person may report a newly remembered detail, and may even feel quite confident that it is true, but sometimes consulting with family members and records shows that the memory is incorrect.

WITNESS RECOLLECTION There are some cases in which hypnosis seemed to help witnesses recall details that proved worthwhile. The most famous example is of the school bus driver who under hypnosis was able to recall enough of a license plate number to lead to the capture of some kidnappers in 1976. But in the laboratory, hypnosis does not improve recall (Whitehouse et al., 2005). What laboratory studies show quite clearly is that hypnosis increases the number of *false* memories. For example, researchers staged a "crime reenactment" with participants as witnesses. In several of these experiments, those witnesses subjected to hypnosis had greater *confidence* in their memories, including those cases where they were mistaken, but in fact their memories were no more accurate than those of people who were not hypnotized (Spanos et al., 1991). This is, of course, a disastrous situation in the courtroom, where a hypnotized witness might swear to being very confident of a recollection that is false.

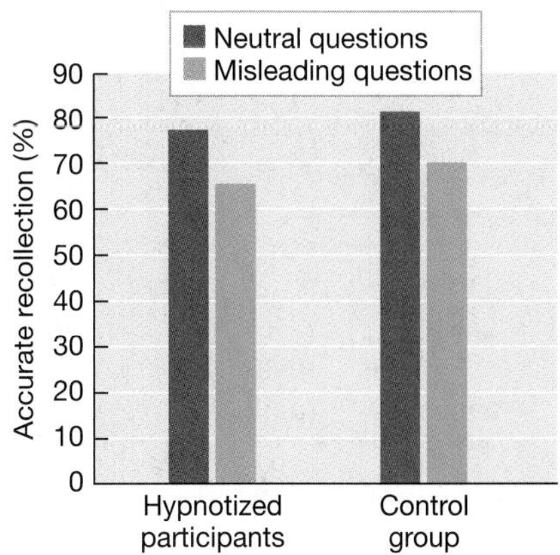

Figure 7.23 Hypnosis Does Not Improve Recall Both hypnosis and misleading questions reduce the accuracy of memory. (After Scoboria et al., 2002.)

So why was the bus driver able to remember those license plate numbers under hypnosis? First of all, it is possible that hypnosis does help some individuals to remember once in a while, even if it's not a reliable effect. But we have no way of knowing whether the witness would have recalled the details without hypnosis—sometimes it takes a while to retrieve detailed memories. Then there's the issue of selective reporting: when a witness *does* remember helpful information under hypnosis, it is big news. We rarely hear about the cases where hypnosis recovers a memory that provides a false lead, such as the hypnotized witness who recalled a robber's license plate number that turned out to belong to a university president (Orne, 1979)!

"RECOVERED" MEMORIES Another worrisome aspect of hypnotized witnesses in the courtroom is that their greater confidence in their memory makes them especially susceptible to misleading questions. For example, in one study participants listened to a story, then answered questions about events in the story while they were either hypnotized or not. As in many other studies, recall of hypnotized participants was *less* accurate than that of non-hypnotized participants. But some people were asked deliberately misleading questions ("Did the woman have one or two children?" rather than "Did the woman have any children?"). Not surprisingly, misleading questions reduced the accuracy of all participants, reducing the accuracy of hypnotized participants further (**Figure 7.23**) (Scoboria et al., 2002). Thus a police investigator asking a misleading question might inadvertently plant a wrong idea, which the hypnotized witness would confidently regard as a memory. Likewise, a clinical psychologist using hypnosis to "recover" damaging childhood memories might, by asking the wrong question ("Did your father ever abuse you?"), plant a false memory.

In one such case, a woman under hypnosis "remembered" being repeatedly raped by her father (a clergyman) and forced to self-abort two fetuses before she was 14. Her father lost his job, but luckily a medical exam showed that the woman was still a virgin at age 22 and had never been pregnant (Loftus, 1997), so he was not imprisoned. The woman, forced to realize she had confabulated the memories under her therapist's guidance, successfully sued the therapist.

An even more tragic case involved an 8-year-old girl who was kidnapped and murdered. One of her playmates, Eileen Franklin, *20 years later*, "recovered" the memory of watching her father, George, rape and murder the child. The father, based on his daughter's recovered memory alone, was sen-

Are Hypnotically Recovered Memories Reliable? Because her book is still in print, apparently Eileen Franklin still believes the memory she "recovered" under hypnosis, that her father raped and murdered two children when Eileen was eight. Eileen's father was convicted of murder and served over 6 years in prison. Ironically, the cover of Eileen's book shouts out that the case is "Mesmerizing."

tenced to life in prison. After he had served over 6 years, his conviction was overturned when the courts learned that the memory had been "recovered" under hypnosis (which would make it inadmissible evidence in California) and when newly available DNA evidence proved that the father was not responsible for another rape his daughter had "remembered." Given cases such as this and the repeated laboratory demonstrations that hypnosis can lead people to have confident, clear recollections of "memories" that are untrue, it's little wonder that many states, like California, forbid court testimony resulting from hypnosis. We'll discuss the unreliable nature of memory again in Section 9.2.

What is the boundary between being accommodating and being entranced?

I've purposely postponed talking about the theories that try to explain hypnosis until we have discussed what hypnosis can and cannot do. First there is that question from the start of this section, whether hypnosis is an "altered state of consciousness." The problem is one of defining terms: what is an "altered" state of consciousness versus a mere "changed" state of consciousness? If I'm daydreaming about scuba diving one moment, then answer the phone to talk with a friend the next, was my consciousness "altered"? Most people would say no. But if we looked at the EEG activity of my brain or put my head in an fMRI scanner, we would see that my brain activity was definitely different in those two states. For this reason, when someone points out that EEG activity or brain activation patterns are different in wakefulness versus hypnosis or meditation, that doesn't prove that these are special, "altered" states. It proves only that the mind is a process in a machine called the brain. Whenever we bend our mind to a different task, of course our brain activity is altered.

Theories to explain hypnosis fall into two classes. The **trance theory of hypnosis** proposes that hypnosis is a uniquely altered state of consciousness that allows people to be more flexible in their experience and behavior. The trance perspective posits that there is something special about the state of the participant's mind while in a hypnotic state that allows the participant to ignore stimuli or break bad habits. The **social theory of hypnosis** (or *role-playing theory*), on the other hand, posits that the hypnotized participant is simply trying to accommodate another person, the hypnotist, whom the participant trusts, so they can together accomplish some mutual goal. In the showbiz world, the shared goal is to entertain the audience. In the realm of therapy, the shared goal is to help the person avoid unpleasant experiences or unhelpful behaviors.

Several ideas have been put forward to explain why the hypnotic state is a special, trancelike condition. One of the pioneers of hypnosis research, Ernest Hilgard, suggested that people in a trance state experience a *division* (or "dissociation") *of consciousness*. Thus while one part of the mind might be aware of the painful stimulus, another part of the mind, which is reporting to the hypnotist, is not experiencing pain. Hilgard wrote of a "hidden observer," a part of the mind that is aware of everything that's happening, even if the hypnotized part of the mind is not. For example, when Hilgard asked participants to rate the pain of having their hand in ice water, those who had been hypnotized to feel less pain indeed reported less pain. But if he also had them press a key to rate the pain, they indicated that they were aware that the pain was greater than they were reporting (**Figure 7.24**). Hilgard thought the hidden observer was reporting the true state of events, so the person *was* aware of what was happening. Similarly, when people are hypnotized to be blind in one eye, or to not smell a strong smell, there's evidence that they actually can see, or smell, even if they report that they cannot. For example, participants who report they are deaf in one ear, in response to hypnotic suggestion, nevertheless show the effects of interference when words are played into that ear (Spanos et al., 1982). Likewise, people

trance theory of hypnosis A theory that hypnosis is a genuinely altered state of consciousness that allows people to be more flexible in their experience and behavior.

social theory of hypnosis Also called *role-playing theory*. Theory that the hypnotized participant is simply trying to accommodate another person, the hypnotist, whom the participant trusts.

who are blinded by hypnotic suggestion and presented with uncommon spellings of various words, demonstrate that they have in fact seen the words, because it affects their own spelling after the hypnotic episode (Bryant & McConkey, 1989). So the participants *report* not getting the sensory information, yet their *behavior* makes it clear that they do.

Hilgard's idea of a hidden observer is reminiscent of the split-brain patients we discussed earlier in the chapter. The talking half of the mind will perceive and relate an experience differently than the un-talking mind conveys using the left hand. Perhaps hypnosis is a special state where different parts of our mind separate, allowing our conscious self to experience less pain, or feel a mosquito land on our arm, without any surgical separation of brain regions.

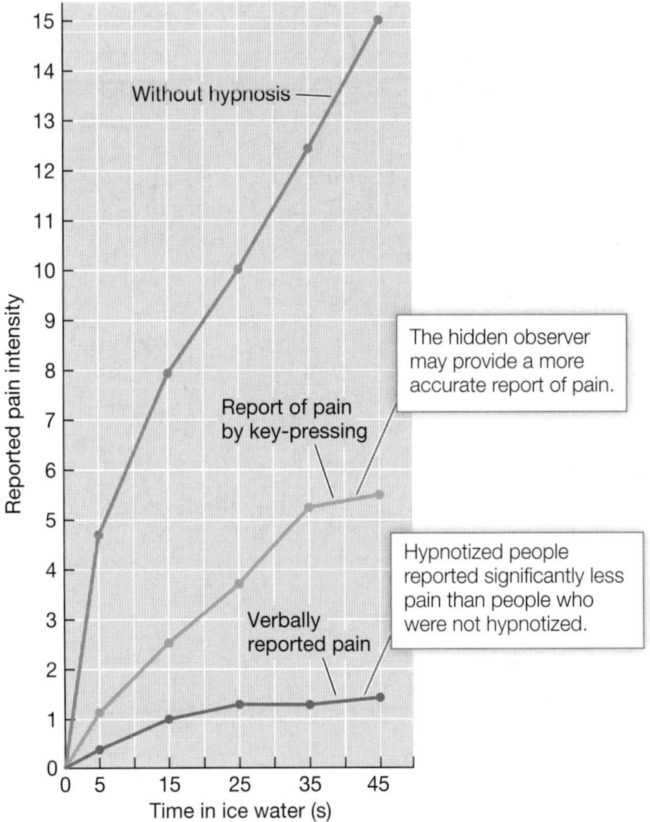

Figure 7.24 The "Hidden Observer" Reports Pain That the Hypnotized Person Denies (After Hilgard et al., 1975.)

Yet as the social theory suggests, it is undeniably true that hypnosis is a social interaction. It's difficult to know how much of the participant's behavior is due to a desire to cooperate and behave properly. Perhaps the most telling criticism of the trance theory is that if instead of hypnotizing people you ask them to *pretend* that they are hypnotized, they do all the things that hypnotized people do (Spanos, 1996). For example, a third person cannot distinguish between a person who is hypnotized to display age regression and a person who has been told to pretend they've been hypnotized to display age regression. Their speech, behavior, and mental abilities are equivalent (and, despite their best efforts at imitating children, are not quite like those of real children). If someone playing the role of a hypnotized person acts just like a hypnotized person, then it's possible the hypnotized participant is also just playing a role. This is not to suggest that the hypnotized participant is cheating or "faking it." The issue is whether the role-playing of the hypnotized participant is mistakenly attributed to some mysterious trance or "altered state."

The two explanations of hypnosis just discussed converge on several points. We've seen that any change in consciousness will be accompanied by a change in brain activity. That is, the state of hypnosis is marked by the same change in brain activity regardless of how it is reached. As in so many instances of controversy in psychology, the difference between the trance theory and the role-playing theory of hypnosis may be a result of failure to have a clear notion of what these terms mean. What is a "trance" exactly? If you can't find any characteristic that guarantees the person is in a trance, then maybe "trance" isn't a very useful concept. And just because we associate the word *role-playing* with drama and pretend play, where characters act as though things are different than they really are, that doesn't mean that all role-playing is false or ineffective. Hypnotized people who feel reduced pain, even if it's because they believe they are supposed to feel less pain, are nevertheless benefitting from hypnosis.

The research indicates that hypnosis is *both* a result of social influences *and* a change in consciousness (Rossi, 2002). Whether that change in consciousness is so great that it should be called an "altered state" is hard to say—there is no objective definition of an "altered state" of consciousness. But if the history of Dr. Mesmer's brainchild has taught us anything, it is that misconceptions and controversies about hypnosis will continue.

A Mandala for Meditation Some people look at a repeating, regular pattern such as this to focus their attention during meditation.

Meditation resembles self-hypnosis

For centuries, many traditions, particularly in Buddhist and Hindu cultures, have promoted the practice of taking a few minutes every day to relax the body and concentrate the mind in a calm, relaxing fashion. There are many variations of this activity, and it goes by many different names, but we may regard **meditation** as the practice of focusing attention in order to relax the body and mind, and to reduce stress. As with hypnosis, meditation begins by relaxing the body and focusing attention. But while hypnosis relies on another person to suggest how to direct your attention, in meditation *you* decide where to direct your attention. Depending on the type of meditation, you might concentrate your attention on an external object, such as a beautiful mandala, or on your own breathing, or on a *mantra*, a particular sound or phrase that is repeated, either aloud or in your mind, over and over (such as "om" or "om mani padme hum"). In each case, one goal of concentrating all of your attention on a single, simple object or process is to try to empty the mind of any other content. It is as if you are trying to stop, or drown out, the mind's "internal dialogue," simplifying mental content in order to relax and avoid troublesome thoughts.

In several traditions, meditation is seen as a method of spiritual growth or a way to gain religious insight, and we have no scientific tools to measure whether it is effective in that regard. But it is clear that meditation works as a means of relaxing the body, reducing stress, and improving health. Physiological measures demonstrate that people who are meditating show a reduction in breathing rate, heart rate, and blood pressure, and an increase in the appearance of alpha rhythms in EEG (Travis et al., 2002) that characterizes relaxed wakefulness. There is also good evidence that a program of meditation can improve health. For example, in one study people with heart disease were *randomly* assigned to either meditation training or, as a control, health education. Four months later, the people who had been meditating showed greater improvements in blood pressure, heart rate, and blood sugar than the control participants (Paul-Labrador et al., 2006).

As we will discuss in Section 13.2, while meditation clearly carries all these benefits, it is not clear whether the benefits result from the mental activity involved or the relaxation of the body that comes along with it. For example, the physiological changes that occur during meditation, including increased alpha rhythms in the EEG, are also seen in people who are taught to simply relax the body (Holmes, 1987).

There have also been reports that people who practice meditation for a significant portion of their lives have improved health, or even differences in brain structure: Zen Buddhist meditators do not show as much shrinkage of the brain with age as non-meditators do (Pagnoni & Cekic, 2007). But these studies don't prove that meditation prevents brain shrinkage, because we can't rule out the possibility that the sort of people who choose a long-term program of meditation may have been different from control participants even before they meditated. Perhaps they are more likely to choose a simpler, less stressful lifestyle and that is what provides them with better health. At the very least, we can say this about meditation: there is no evidence that it does harm, and there is evidence that it is good for your health, either because of the relaxation that is at the core of the practice or because of the mental exercise of attention that it provides.

As with hypnosis, people have wasted time debating about whether meditation is an "altered state." The altered EEG of people who are meditating proves only that they are relaxing, not that they are in some superspecial, spiritual state. Whether meditation represents an "altered state" depends solely on how you define that term, and on that there is little agreement.

meditation The practice of focusing attention in order to relax the body and mind, and to reduce stress.

psychoactive drugs Drugs (chemical substances) that alter mental function, affecting consciousness.

7.3 SUMMARY

- *Hypnosis* is a condition during which a hypnotist suggests that a participant will have certain experiences or perform certain behaviors.
- The *Stanford hypnotic susceptibility test* measures how suggestible a person may be to hypnosis, and indicates that about half the population is moderately or very hypnotizable.
- Hypnosis can be used to reduce the experience of pain, either acute pain during surgery or chronic pain conditions, apparently by reducing the activity of brain regions associating negative emotions with pain.
- Hypnosis can sometimes help people stick to a diet plan, but is not very effective treatment in addressing addictions.
- There is no evidence that hypnosis reliably improves recall and ample evidence that hypnosis may implant false memories.
- Theories put forward to explain hypnosis fall into two categories: those that say hypnosis is a special *trance* state of some sort, and those that characterize hypnosis as an elaborate, cooperative type of *social role-playing*. Close examination of these two types of theory suggest they are entirely compatible.
- *Meditation* resembles hypnosis in that the person relaxes the body and concentrates attention.
- A person practicing meditation directs his or her attention to some simple object or process in order to empty the mind.
- People in meditation show many physiological changes, including reduced heart rate and breathing rate, as well as increased alpha rhythms in the EEG, indicating relaxation.
- Meditation is beneficial to your health, but it is not clear whether the mental processes of meditation itself or the resulting body relaxation provide that benefit.

REVIEW QUESTIONS

1. Describe how one person might hypnotize another.
2. What are the two major theories to describe what happens in hypnosis?
3. What, if any, benefits have been proven to result from hypnosis?
4. What is meditation, and how might it benefit your health?

Food for Thought

Given what you've learned here about hypnosis, would you be willing to try using hypnosis to get by with fewer drugs during surgery? Would you advise a friend who was undergoing surgery, or was about to give birth to a baby, to try using hypnosis to control pain?

7.4 Psychoactive Drugs

Psychoactive drugs are drugs whose primary effect is altering mental function, affecting consciousness. Humans have long sought out psychoactive drugs: Stone Age peoples cultivated poppies for opium, and virtually every human society known has produced and consumed alcoholic beverages. While we may characterize drug use as "natural" given that our species has been at it for so long, misuse of drugs has had a devastating effect on the lives of millions of people today.

In this section we'll learn how psychoactive drugs reach and then affect our mind. We'll talk about some of the myriad psychoactive drugs and how they are classified based on the general effects they have on the mind. Then we'll take up the serious problem of drug abuse, trying to understand both why it happens and which strategies may help people who are caught in the vise of addiction. The psychoactive drugs that are used to treat mental disorders like depression and schizophrenia will be discussed in Chapter 16.

Things to Learn

- Mechanisms of drug action in the brain
- Classification of psychoactive drugs by effects on mental function
- Brain mechanisms underlying the "rush" of illicit drugs
- Social consequences of legal war on drugs
- Potential risk of marijuana use for teenagers

Psychoactive drugs affect the mind by acting on neurotransmitter systems

For a drug to be psychoactive, to affect mental function, it must contain molecules that affect chemical signaling at synapses in the brain. Normally, that chemical signaling consists of one neuron releasing neurotransmitter molecules into a synapse to affect specialized receptors on a target neuron. The three-dimensional shape of a neurotransmitter molecule fits into the receptor, thus changing the receptor's shape, which in turn makes the target neuron either more or less likely to fire, depending on what kind of channel is opened (**Figure 7.25A**).

There are three basic ways in which psychoactive drugs interfere with neurotransmitter signaling. Psychoactive drugs are classified as agonists, antagonists, or neuromodulators depending upon how they affect the target neuron.

An **agonist** is a drug that attaches to and stimulates neuron receptors in much the same way as the body's neurotransmitters (**Figure 7.25B**). The shape of the agonist drug molecule is similar enough to that of a neurotransmitter to bind to receptors on the target neuron. Binding can make these neurons more or less likely to fire. Basically, the agonist drug molecules provide target neurons with signals that ordinarily would come from another neuron. The target neuron is unable to distinguish between the drug molecule and a genuine neurotransmitter, and it responds as though the other neuron had fired.

An **antagonist**, on the other hand, is a drug that affects neuronal signaling by *preventing* a neurotransmitter from binding to its receptor. The shape of the drug molecule may be sufficiently like that of the neurotransmitter to bind to the receptor, but different enough that the receptor doesn't respond (**Figure 7.25C**). You might think that an antagonist would have no effect on the brain, since the receptor does not respond, but by occupying the receptor, the antagonist molecule prevents neurotransmitter from acting on the target neuron.

A **neuromodulator** is a drug that affects neurotransmitter signaling without displacing the normal neurotransmitter. Some neuromodulators bind to a different part of the receptor and change how the receptor responds when a transmitter binds to it (**Figure 7.25D**). For example, a neuromodulator may cause the receptor to make a larger or smaller response to the neurotransmitter.

agonist A drug that activates a receptor in the same way as the normal neurotransmitter.

antagonist A drug molecule that interferes with neuronal signaling by preventing a neurotransmitter from binding to its receptor.

neuromodulator A drug molecule that affects neurotransmitter–receptor signaling without displacing the normal neurotransmitter.

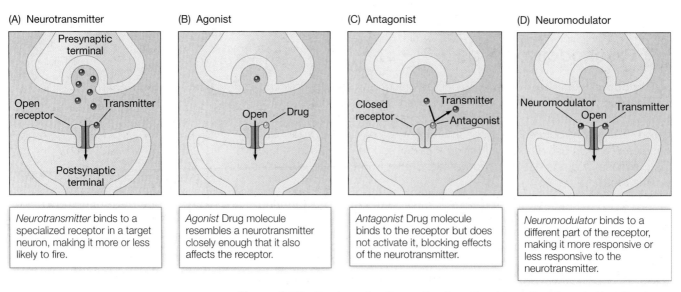

(A) Neurotransmitter

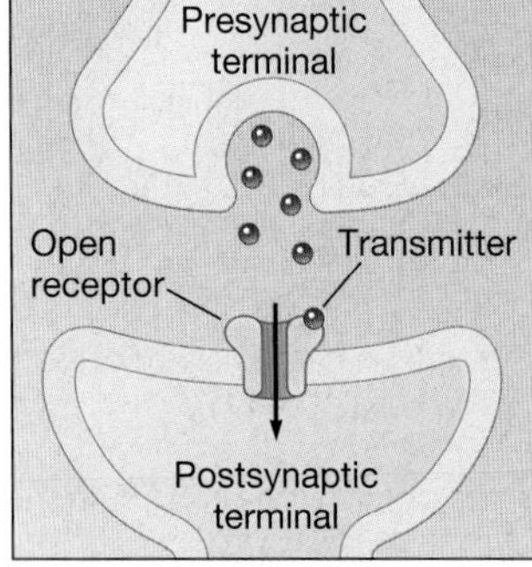

Neurotransmitter binds to a specialized receptor in a target neuron, making it more or less likely to fire.

(B) Agonist

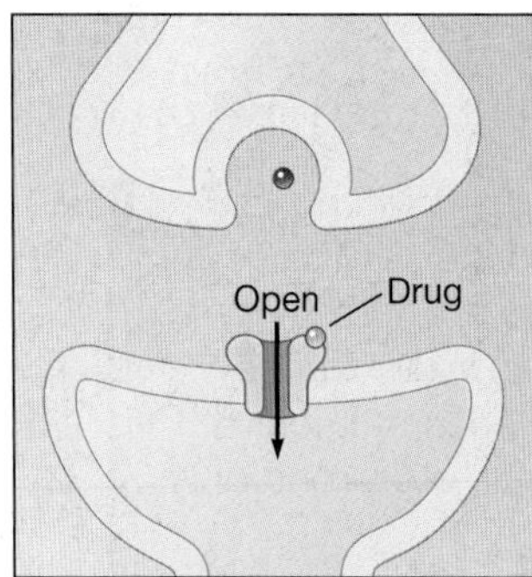

Agonist Drug molecule resembles a neurotransmitter closely enough that it also affects the receptor.

(C) Antagonist

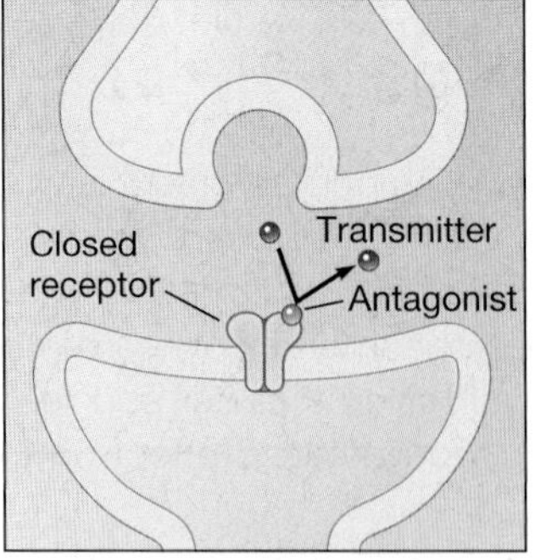

Antagonist Drug molecule binds to the receptor but does not activate it, blocking effects of the neurotransmitter.

(D) Neuromodulator

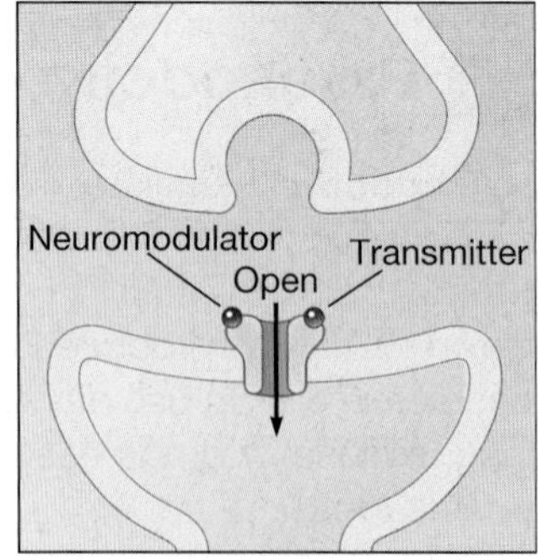

Neuromodulator binds to a different part of the receptor, making it more responsive or less responsive to the neurotransmitter.

Figure 7.25 Psychoactive Drugs Psychoactive drugs affect the mind by affecting neurotransmitter systems that normally communicate information within the brain.

The exact effect of a psychoactive drug on mental functioning depends not only on which of these various mechanisms of action it has, but also which type of receptor is affected. We'll see that drugs that boost the signaling at receptors for the neurotransmitter GABA tend to have a calming effect, while those that boost the signaling at receptors for catecholamine neurotransmitters (epinephrine, norepinephrine, and dopamine) tend to have an activating effect. Marijuana is an agonist at one type of receptor, while heroin acts as an agonist on another type of receptor. Alcohol is a neuromodulator, increasing the responsiveness of receptors to one neurotransmitter (GABA), while amphetamines act as a neuromodulator causing the release of catecholamines (see Figure 7.25D).

Drugs can be classified by their general effects on mental activity

The array of psychoactive drugs is large and growing. The easiest way to learn about the most common psychoactive drugs is to classify them by the general effect they have on mental functioning. First we'll consider drugs like alcohol that have a calming effect, then drugs like amphetamines that have an activating effect. Then we'll consider drugs like heroin that cause a brief euphoria, and conclude with drugs like LSD that cause sensory distortions.

DEPRESSANTS Drugs that tend to slow down mental processes and behavior are called **depressants**. Depressants also tend to reduce how frequently neurons produce action potentials. Often the inhibition of neuronal activity can result in inhibited behavior. We have all seen how even a small dose of depressant, such as alcohol, may make people behave in a more animated, less restricted fashion. This behavior is usually understood as the drug depressing those parts of the brain that normally inhibit our behavior. With higher doses, the depressant nature of the drugs is more apparent as the person eventually becomes quieter and eventually loses consciousness.

The extent of a depressant's effect depends on the dose: low doses make people more sedate, moderate doses make them less anxious, high doses induce sleepiness. Doses that are even higher will eventually depress brainstem centers controlling breathing, so the person stops breathing and dies. This fatal potential of depressants makes them very dangerous drugs.

Perhaps the most ancient psychoactive drug is alcohol, which is described in humankind's earliest known writings available to us today. **Alcohol** is a small, simple molecule that is very easy to produce because microorganisms called yeast will eventually fall from the air onto moist vegetable matter and start turning sugars into alcohol. For this reason, almost every society seems to have found some way to make wine, beer, or similar alcoholic beverages.

Barbiturates ("downers"), on the other hand, are human made drugs that were originally used to help people fall asleep. Barbiturates are rarely prescribed as sleep aids anymore because of the danger of overdosing. Barbiturates are useful because they can depress mental activity enough to result in **anesthesia**, a drug-induced loss of consciousness. Carefully controlled doses of barbiturate can maintain anesthesia long enough to complete even very complicated surgeries.

A third example of depressants are the **tranquilizers**, drugs that typically make people feel less anxious. Most tranquilizers belong to a class of molecules called benzodiazepines, including those with trade names such as Xanax, Librium, Valium, and Ativan.

Almost all depressants have their effect through receptors for the neurotransmitter GABA. As we mentioned in Section 3.2, most GABA receptors, when activated by the neurotransmitter, inhibit the target neuron. Thus the more GABA stimulation in the brain, the less electrical activity will occur. De-

depressant A drug that tends to slow down mental processes and behavior.

alcohol The most common depressant, a neuromodulator that increases the responsiveness of GABA receptors.

barbiturates A class of depressant drugs.

anesthesia A drug-induced loss of consciousness.

tranquilizer A depressant that typically makes people feel less anxious.

stimulants Drugs that tend to increase neural activity and also speed up cognition and behavior.

nicotine A stimulant found in tobacco that acts as an agonist at many acetylcholine receptors.

pressants act as neuromodulators that bind to GABA receptors and make them much more responsive to the GABA when it arrives (see Figure 7.25D). If you think of GABA receptors as akin to the brakes of a car, decreasing neural activity, then you can see how depressants boost the effectiveness of the neurotransmitter by increasing its braking action, which slows neural activity and hence mental function and behavior.

Tragically, every fall as a new crop of students enters colleges, where they typically find it easier to obtain and drink alcohol, young people die from alcohol poisoning. Having drunk a little alcohol, losing their inhibitions, they may begin to drink faster and faster, in other words, *bingeing*. Or they may play a drinking game where they take a drink over and over, or they may decide to have 21 shots on their 21st birthday with the encouragement of so-called friends. When the person passes out, the friends may leave them to "sleep it off." But as more alcohol leaves the digestive system, brainstem breathing centers stop working and the person suffocates. Sometimes the brainstem, in a last heroic attempt to stay alive, causes the person to throw up, but he or she is too intoxicated to get the fluid out of the way and chokes on the vomit.

Alcohol kills even more people when they get behind the wheel of a car. Driving under the influence of any depressant is dangerous because these drugs slow down reaction time and impair judgment (Hanchar et al., 2005). In one year alone an estimated 1,400 college students died from alcohol-related unintentional injuries, including motor vehicle crashes, and *half a million* students received alcohol-related injuries (Hingson et al., 2002). The Centers for Disease Control estimate that more than 88,000 Americans die of alcohol-attributable causes each year (Gonzales et al., 2014).

Taken in moderation, alcohol is harmless or even beneficial to the health of an adult. For example, a drink per day is associated with reduced risk of cardiovascular and Alzheimer's diseases, and with improved control of blood sugar levels (Leroi et al., 2002; Mukamal et al., 2003). Excessive alcohol consumption, however, is very damaging and linked to more than 60 disease processes. Chronic alcohol use damages the brain, especially the frontal cortex (Kril et al., 1997). Some of the anatomical changes associated with chronic alcoholism may be reversible with abstinence. MRI studies show an increase in the volume of cortical gray matter in alcoholics within weeks of giving up alcohol (**Figure 7.26**) (Pfefferbaum et al., 1995).

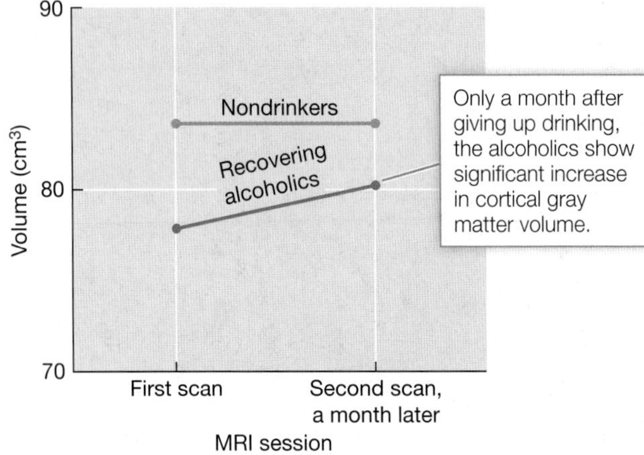

Figure 7.26 Chronic Alcohol Use Shrinks Anterior Cortex (After Pfefferbaum et al., 1995.)

STIMULANTS Drugs that tend to increase neural activity and also speed up cognition and behavior are called **stimulants**. Paradoxically, stimulants such as methylphenidate (Ritalin) have a calming effect in humans with attention deficit hyperactivity disorder (ADHD), perhaps because they boost neurotransmitters in brain regions important for directing attention (Berridge & Arnsten, 2013).

Nicotine, a stimulant found in tobacco, acts as an agonist at many acetylcholine receptors. Tobacco in the form of cigarette smoke reaches the large surface area of the lungs, causing nicotine to enter the blood and brain very rapidly. The nicotine increases heart rate, blood pressure, secretion of stomach acid, and intestinal activity. In the short run, these effects make tobacco use pleasurable. But these neural effects on body function, quite apart from the effects of tobacco tar on the lungs, make prolonged tobacco use very unhealthful. Unfortunately, nicotine is also very addictive. We will discuss the harmful effects of tobacco in detail in Section 13.2.

Perhaps the most widely used pick-me-up is **caffeine**, a stimulant found in many beverages, including coffee, tea, and many sodas. The United States alone consumes nearly 200 *billion* cups of coffee each year (http://www.ico.org/countries/usa.pdf). Caffeine blocks one of the body's natural neuromodulators, resulting in greater release of catecholamine neurotransmitter, causing arousal. As these catecholamine neurotransmitters tend to have an excitatory effect on target neurons, caffeine boosts neural activity, producing heightened alertness and even euphoria, promoting sustained effort without rest or sleep. Many studies have asked whether people who regularly drink a moderate amount of caffeine (one to two cups per day) are more likely to have various health problems than nondrinkers, and the answer is often no (O'Keefe et al., 2013). So this is one drug that, used in moderation, seems to be fairly safe.

Contrast that with the **amphetamines**, much more powerful stimulants that, like caffeine, increase the release of catecholamine neurotransmitters, although by a different mechanism. A small variant in the structure of the amphetamine molecule produces the even more potent stimulant methamphetamine (*meth* or *speed*).

Amphetamines illustrate a common phenomenon in drug use: **tolerance**, when a person must take a higher and higher dose of a drug to get the same effect. Tolerance to the effects of amphetamine develops rapidly, so chronic users have to take larger and larger doses, leading to sleeplessness, severe weight loss, and general deterioration of mental and physical condition. Prolonged use of amphetamine may lead to symptoms that closely resemble those of paranoid schizophrenia: compulsive, agitated behavior and irrational suspiciousness. In fact, some amphetamine users have been misdiagnosed as having schizophrenia. Worst of all, people who chronically abuse amphetamines display symptoms of brain damage long after they quit using the drug (Ernst et al., 2000).

Cocaine is a stimulant extracted from the leaves of the coca plant. For hundreds of years, people in Bolivia, Colombia, and Peru have used the leaves of the coca shrub—either chewed or brewed as a tea—to increase endurance, alleviate hunger, and promote a sense of well-being. This use of coca leaves does not seem to cause problems. But the more powerful cocaine is a very addictive stimulant that has damaged millions of lives. First isolated in 1859, cocaine was added to beverages (such as the original formula for *Coca*-Cola) and tonics for its stimulant qualities. Later it was used as a local anesthetic and an antidepressant. Today many users snort cocaine powder, which rapidly enters the bloodstream via the nasal membranes. *Crack* is a smokable form of cocaine that enters the blood and the brain even more rapidly, making it even more addictive than cocaine powder.

Cocaine acts by slowing the removal of catecholamines from synapses, resulting in greater catecholamine receptor stimulation. Cocaine may have neurotoxic effects, and an overdose can provoke marked changes in cerebral blood flow, including strokes (Holman et al., 1993), as well as reduction in cortical gray matter (Franklin et al., 2002). Cessation of cocaine use often produces very uncomfortable symptoms: initial agitation and powerful drug cravings, followed by depression and an inability to enjoy anything else in life. We'll discuss this and other aspects of addiction shortly.

caffeine A stimulant found in many beverages, including coffee, tea, and many sodas.

amphetamines Powerful stimulants that increase the release of catecholamine neurotransmitters.

tolerance The phenomena in which a person must take a higher and higher dose of a drug to get the same effect.

cocaine A stimulant extracted from the leaves of the coca plant.

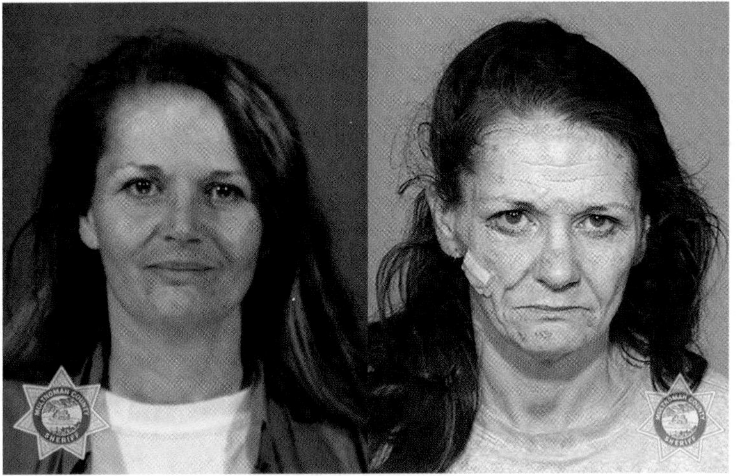

Effects of Prolonged Meth Use Chronic abuse of amphetamine and methamphetamine exacts a terrible toll on the body. Shockingly, these two photos were taken just 2 1/2 years apart. (Courtesy of Multnomah County Sheriff's Office, Oregon.)

opium An extract of the seedpod of the poppy flower; it has painkilling properties.

morphine The major active substance in opium, noted for its painkilling properties.

analgesic A substance that acts as a painkiller.

heroin A chemically altered form of morphine that is even more powerful and addictive.

endogenous opiates A class of neurotransmitters found in the brain, including endorphins.

opioid receptors A receptor that responds to endogenous and/or exogenous opioids.

hallucinogens Drugs that alter sensory perceptions in dramatic ways and produce peculiar experiences.

lysergic acid diethylamide (LSD) Also called *acid*. A hallucinogen that tends to alter or distort visual experiences.

mescaline Also called *peyote*. A hallucinogenic drug that affects visual experience by way of neural systems that use norepinephrine as a neurotransmitter.

psilocybin Also called *magic mushrooms*. A hallucinogenic drug that affects visual experience.

OPIATES **Opium**, extracted from poppy flower seedpods, has been used by humans since at least the Stone Age. **Morphine**, the major active substance in opium, is a very effective **analgesic** (painkiller) that has brought relief from severe pain to many millions of people. Unfortunately, morphine also has a strong potential for addiction, as does **heroin**, a chemically altered form of morphine that is even more powerful and even more addictive.

Heroin and morphine, called *opiates*, resemble a class of neurotransmitters found in the brain called **endogenous opiates** (here, *endogenous* means that it is normally found in the body; examples are endorphins and enkephalins). The opiate drugs such as morphine bind to those specific receptors—**opioid receptors**. Opioid receptors are concentrated in certain regions of the brain. Injection of morphine directly into parts of the brainstem produces strong analgesia, indicating that this is a region where morphine acts to reduce pain perception. The euphoria from opiates is due to stimulation of opioid receptors in the forebrain, as we'll discuss at the end of this section.

HALLUCINOGENS Drugs classified as **hallucinogens** alter sensory perceptions in dramatic ways and produce peculiar experiences. But the term *hallucinogen* is a misnomer. A *hallucination* is a novel perception that takes place in the absence of sensory stimulation (hearing voices or seeing something that isn't there), but the drugs in this category tend to alter or distort *existing* perceptions.

The effects of **lysergic acid diethylamide** (**LSD**, or *acid*) and related substances like **mescaline** (*peyote*) and **psilocybin** (*magic mushrooms*) are predominantly visual. Users often see fantastic images with intense colors, and they are often aware that these strangely altered perceptions are not real events. **Table 7.3** compares the different classes of psychoactive drugs.

Hallucinogens are diverse in their neural actions. For example, the Mexican herb *salvia* is rare among hallucinogens because it acts on an opioid receptor. Other hallucinogens, such as muscarine, found in some mushrooms, affect the acetylcholine system. Mescaline affects neural systems that use norepinephrine as a neurotransmitter. Many hallucinogens, including LSD, mescaline, psilocybin, and others, act as agonists at receptors for the neurotransmitter serotonin.

TABLE 7.3 Psychoactive Drugs

Drug type	Mechanism	Effects on behavior
DEPRESSANTS		
Alcohol, barbiturates, tranquilizers	Neuromodulators boosting response of GABA receptors	Generally calming
STIMULANTS		
Nicotine, caffeine, Ritalin, amphetamines, cocaine	Nicotine is an agonist at acetylcholine receptors. The others act as neuromodulators triggering release of catecholamines (epinephrine, norepinephrine, dopamine).	Excitatory and pleasurable
OPIATES		
Opium, morphine, heroin	Agonist at opioid receptors	Pleasurable and painkilling
HALLUCINOGENS		
Marijuana, LSD, mescaline, PCP, MDMA	Various (marijuana acts upon endogenous cannabinoid receptors; LSD is an agonist at serotonin receptors; PCP is a neuromodulator inhibiting glutamate receptors).	Sensory distortions

Following its discovery, LSD was intensively studied as a possible psychiatric treatment. Starting in the 1950s, research to see if LSD could produce psychosis did not bear fruit. But there has been a resurgence of interest in whether hallucinogens may relieve various psychiatric disorders, including depression and obsessive-compulsive disorder (Moreno et al., 2006). Former users of LSD sometimes report experiencing **flashbacks**—that is, experiences as if they had taken a dose of the drug, even though they are drug-free. These episodes can follow even brief use of LSD, but it is not yet clear whether they reflect permanent neural changes or a special form of memory.

Phencyclidine (commonly known as **PCP** or *angel dust*) was developed in 1956 as a potent analgesic and anesthetic agent. It is classified as a **dissociative drug** because it produces feelings of depersonalization and detachment from reality. It was soon dropped from use in anesthesia because it also caused agitation, excitement, delirium, hostility, and disorganization of perceptions. PCP continues to be used as a street drug, principally because of its hallucinogenic actions. Even at relatively low doses, PCP produces numerous undesirable effects, including combativeness and catatonia (stupor and immobility). Higher doses or repeated use can lead to long-lasting profound confusion, or convulsions and coma. PCP is a neuromodulator that reduces the responsiveness of glutamate receptors, so there is less excitation of some synapses.

Ecstasy is the street name for the hallucinogenic amphetamine derivative **MDMA** (3,4-methylenedioxymethamphetamine). Major actions of MDMA in the brain include the increased release of serotonin and changes in the levels of dopamine and certain hormones, such as prolactin. Exactly how these activities produce the subjective effects of MDMA—positive emotions, empathy, euphoria, a sense of well-being, and colorful visual phenomena—remains to be established. In lab animals, chronic use of Ecstasy produces persistent changes in the distribution of the neurotransmitter serotonin in the brain (Fischer et al., 1995; Monks et al., 2004), as **Figure 7.27** shows, which may increase the risk of prolonged depression.

flashback The experience, long after taking LSD, that a dose of the drug has just been taken, even though the person is drug-free.

phencyclidine (PCP) Also called *angel dust*. A drug developed as a potent analgesic and anesthetic agent.

dissociative drug A drug that produces feelings of depersonalization and detachment from reality.

ecstasy (MDMA) A hallucinogenic amphetamine.

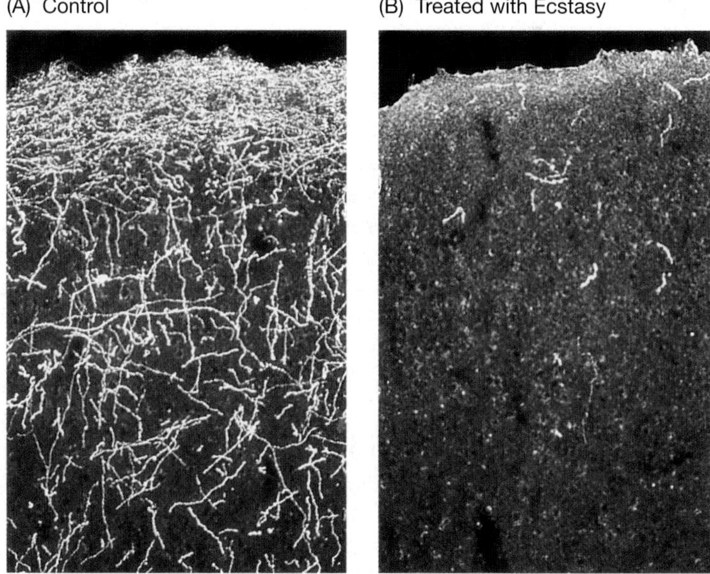

Figure 7.27 Long-Term Effects of a Single Dose of Ecstasy on the Monkey Brain
Serotonin axons in the cortex of (A) a control squirrel monkey and (B) a squirrel monkey that was treated with a single dose of MDMA (Ecstasy) 18 months earlier. (From Fischer et al., 1995; photos courtesy of George Ricaurte.)

Psychology in Everyday Life

BOX 7.2

Has the Legal Model of Drug Control Been Effective?

Does it strike you as illogical that pharmaceutical companies are spending money and time developing pills to deliver the active ingredients from marijuana to the brain, when smoking the plant delivers those same ingredients and has already proven effective (Joy et al., 1999)? Worse yet, the same federal government that will authorize use of the pills puts people in jail for smoking the plant.

This paradox results from the firmly entrenched model of drug use as a *legal problem* rather than a *medical problem* or a *behavioral disorder*. When statistics showed a growing use of drugs in the late 1960s, New York governor Nelson Rockefeller, who was trying to get the Republican nomination for president, instituted harsh mandatory minimum sentences for drug crimes. A person found with 4 ounces of heroin would get at least 15 years to *life* in prison, about the same punishment as for second-degree murder (Gray, 2009). Other states followed suit, and by 1971 President Nixon declared a "War on Drugs" (see figure).

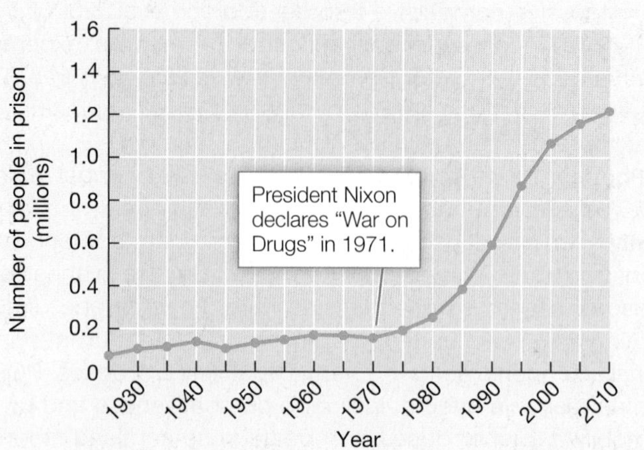

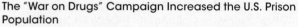

The "War on Drugs" Campaign Increased the U.S. Prison Population

The primary result of the so-called Rockefeller drug laws has been a sharp increase in the number of Americans in prison. While 11% of the prisoners in 1973 were drug offenders, by 1994 they made up

marijuana Drug obtained from the *Cannabis sativa* plant, generally ingested via smoking.

delta-9-tetrahydrocannabinol (THC) The major active ingredient in marijuana.

cannabinoids Naturally occurring neurotransmitters that normally stimulate the receptors that respond to THC in marijuana.

endocannabinoids Neurotransmitters that normally act on the receptors that are activated by marijuana and related drugs.

Marijuana and related preparations, such as hashish, obtained from the *Cannabis sativa* plant, have been used for over 4,000 years (Russo et al., 2008). Today they are the most widely used of all illicit drugs. Typically ingested via smoking, marijuana contains dozens of active ingredients. Chief among them is the compound **delta-9-tetrahydrocannabinol** (**THC**) (Gaoni & Mechoulam, 1964). The subjective experience of marijuana use is quite variable among individuals: relaxation and mood alteration are the most frequent effects, but stimulation, hallucination, and paranoia also occur in some cases.

Sustained use of marijuana can cause addiction (Maldonado & Rodríguez de Fonseca, 2002), and frequent smoking of marijuana, like that of tobacco, can contribute to respiratory diseases. As we'll discuss in The Cutting Edge at the end of this chapter, there is growing evidence that adolescents who smoke marijuana increase their risk for developing schizophrenia. As was the case with opiates, researchers found that the brain contains **cannabinoids** receptors that mediate the effects of THC. Cannabinoid receptors are spread widely throughout the brain (Devane et al., 1988) but not the brainstem. The discovery of cannabinoid receptors touched off an intensive search for an endogenous ligand, and several such compounds—termed **endocannabinoids**—were identified (Devane et al., 1992; Marsicano et al., 2003).

The study of endocannabinoids will aid the search for drugs that share the beneficial effects of marijuana: relieving pain, lowering blood pressure, combating nausea, lowering eye pressure in glaucoma, and so on. While treatment with "medical marijuana" remains illegal in most jurisdictions (although that is changing rapidly), synthetic cannabinoids patented by drug companies may eventually

35% of prisoners. Of those, only about one in six had any history of violence (Gray, 2009). The United States now has a greater proportion of citizens in prison than any other country at any point in history. Number two is China, which has four times as many citizens but nearly a million fewer prisoners (Pew Center on the States, 2008). This swelling of prison ranks with drug users happened during a decades-long *decline* in violent crimes—and remember, most people in prison for drugs have never been violent.

What the laws did *not* do is eliminate drug abuse in the United States. Nearly 24 million people in this country alone report having used illicit drugs in the previous month (Substance Abuse and Mental Health Services Administration, 2013). In fact, methamphetamine abuse seems to be skyrocketing, despite severe penalties (Maxwell & Brecht, 2011). These laws were doubly unsuccessful. Despite instituting the harshest antidrug laws the nation had ever seen, so he could look tough on crime, Governor Rockefeller did not gain the nomination for president.

Not only does spending time in prison wreak havoc on the drug user's life, it's also expensive for taxpayers, averaging over $31,000 per prisoner yearly (Henrichson & Delaney, 2012). As such expenses eat up government revenues, funds for counseling and support to help people refrain from drugs have dried up. For these and other reasons, many leaders are calling for a reconsideration of the "legal model" for treating drug abusers. For example, the district attorney in Brooklyn, NY, finds that people who are convicted of drug use and enter the Drug Treatment Alternative-to-Prison Program, which costs half as much as prison, are 87% less likely to return to prison within 2 years than are people in a comparison group (Zarkin et al., 2006).

People with addictions have a real problem, since we'll see that addiction is the result of dramatic events taking place in the brain. Perhaps the time has come for society to address addiction as a medical problem that requires treatment, rather than as a legal problem that requires imprisonment.

be legally prescribed to patients with the same medical conditions medical marijuana is commonly used to treat. In a sense, marijuana use is illegal therapy in these cases because no corporation can profit from it. You can't file a patent for a plant that's already been in use for millennia. The issues concerning illegal drug use are discussed further in **Box 7.2**.

Addiction involves physical and psychological dependence

Someone who keeps using a drug, even though it causes problems, suffers from **addiction**. In a clinical setting, the official term is **substance use disorder**, the strong desire to self-administer a drug of abuse. To be diagnosed as having this disorder, a person must meet at least 2 of 11 criteria relating to patterns of consumption, craving, expenditure of time and energy in serving the addiction, and impact on the other aspects of the person's life. The disorder can range from mild to moderate to severe, depending on how many of the criteria the person meets (Maccoun, 2013; see Table 16.2).

One aspect of drug use that enforces addiction is **withdrawal symptoms**, very unpleasant physical and mental sensations that arise when a person stops using a drug. In general, a person suffering withdrawal symptoms has experiences that are the opposite of those experienced with the drug. A drug like heroin reduces pain, slows down gastrointestinal activity (resulting in constipation), and brings euphoria. Quitting its use brings the opposite: high sensitivity to pain, cramps as the intestines become overactive, and intensely unpleasant feelings, called *dysphoria* (sadness, anxiety, and restlessness). The person aches and sweats, and experiences nausea, goose bumps, and diarrhea,

addiction The strong desire to self-administer a drug, even when it causes problems.

substance use disorder The official term for addiction, defined by meeting several criteria.

withdrawal symptoms The unpleasant sensations that occur when a person stops using a drug.

brain self-stimulation The repeated pressing of a bar to provide a small current of electricity to an area of the brain, producing a pleasurable sensation.

reward pathway A pathway from the midbrain to the frontal cortex that produces pleasurable sensations when stimulated electrically.

nucleus accumbens A region at the base of the forebrain that is part of the reward pathway.

among other symptoms. It usually takes a week or longer for withdrawal symptoms to disappear, but they are dispelled quickly by a dose of the drug that caused the problem in the first place.

Because withdrawal symptoms are so striking, early investigators proposed defining addiction by the development of withdrawal symptoms (Edwards & Gross, 1976). Addicts keep taking the drug to avoid withdrawal symptoms. However, there are some drugs upon which people can become dependent, such as cocaine, that have relatively few physical withdrawal symptoms (Wise, 1996). Sometimes people make a distinction between *psychological* addiction and *physical* addiction, but such a distinction seems irrelevant because either form of addiction can have disastrous, even fatal, consequences. Some scientists feel the distinction between psychological and physical addiction is artificial and unhelpful because it assumes that the symptoms that outsiders cannot see, such as dysphoria, are fundamentally different from the symptoms they can see, such as shivering and a runny nose (Everitt, 2014). Yet the brain is controlling all these symptoms, and the ones that can't be seen may be even more unpleasant than those that can be seen. Indeed, one of our principles is that psychological processes all have a physical basis in the brain, and are just as real as the muscular contractions that produce shivering or nausea.

To understand why drug addiction is much more than the avoidance of withdrawal symptoms, let's go back to a strange experiment that startled the world in the 1950s. Scientists surgically implanted small wires into the brain of a rat so that when it pressed a bar in the cage, a small current of electricity was delivered to the rat's brain. If the electrode was in a certain part of the brain, a remarkable thing happened—the rat quickly learned to press the bar, stimulating its brain again and again (Olds & Milner, 1954). The rat couldn't seem to get enough juice to its brain. Clearly this **brain self-stimulation** was intensely pleasurable, and it only happened when the stimulation was provided to certain parts of the brain. As scientists mapped out those brain regions, a pattern emerged. Electrical stimulation was rewarding as long as the electrode stimulated a particular pathway in the brain, now called the **reward pathway**, from the midbrain to frontal cortex. Stimulation of those same sites is also pleasurable in humans, who sometimes report it feels akin to sexual excitation (Heath, 1972).

The neurons in the midbrain that send their axons to make up this pathway to the frontal cortex use the neurotransmitter dopamine. It is the release of this dopamine in the frontal lobe that produces intensely pleasurable feelings. That effect of dopamine is especially effective if it is released in a region called the **nucleus accumbens** (**Figure 7.28**). In the decades since this discovery, researchers have found that a remarkably diverse range of behaviors cause dopamine release into the nucleus accumbens, and the one thing those behaviors have in common is that we derive pleasure from them: eating, sex, and drug use are all accompanied by release of dopamine in the nucleus accumbens. It's beginning to look as though this system provides a core "pleasure center," the source of all of our feelings of reward (see Figure 12.4). Natural selection has produced a system that rewards us with a little shot of dopamine when we do things that are adaptive, like eating a rich meal or having sex.

Unfortunately, many drugs tap into this system to provide us with a level of dopamine release that natural selection never arranged. When cocaine or heroin enters the brain, many people experience a pleasure, a "rush," more intense than any other they have known. This, then, is the beginning of addiction, when someone learns how to feel a level of pleasure that cannot be had any other way. But with repeated drug use, the pleasure a given dose used to offer no longer does. As unnaturally high levels of dopamine are released in the nucleus accumbens, the neurons there begin to reduce the number of dopamine receptors they pro-

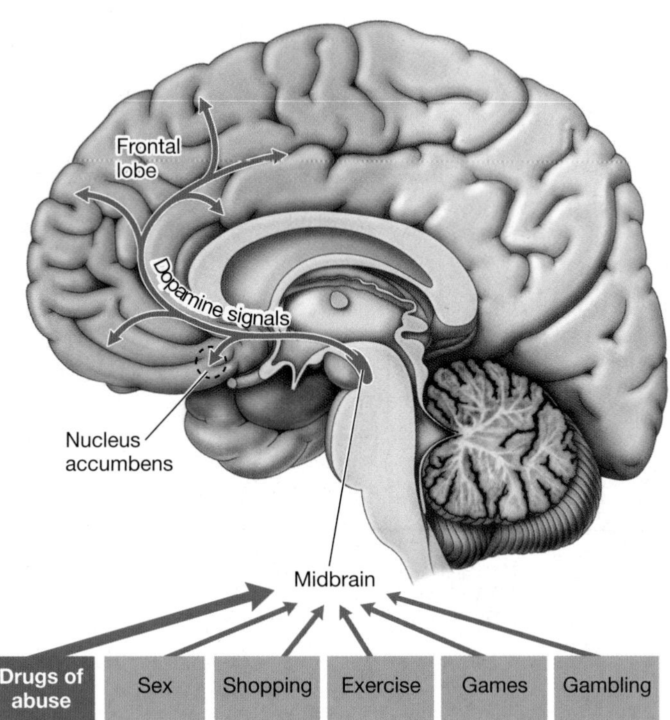

Figure 7.28 **Brain Self-Stimulation** A variety of different behaviors, including sexual behavior, gambling, and video game playing, normally activate the dopaminergic pathway that produces the experience of pleasure. Drugs of abuse exert a particularly strong influence on this system and may eclipse other sources of pleasure.

vide. So now the same amount of dopamine provides less pleasure than it did before. Drug addiction spirals out of control because of *tolerance*: it takes a greater and greater dose to get the same "high," the same amount of dopamine stimulation in the nucleus accumbens.

For those other pleasures in life, like eating, having sex, and exercising, the situation has now become grim. The brain systems that provide dopamine to the nucleus accumbens during those natural activities continue to release the same amount as before, but the target neurons in the nucleus accumbens are less responsive because they have reduced their dopamine receptors. As the pleasure from other activities fades, the drug user has only one way to feel better: more drug.

This process of addiction is studied in animals in experiments like the one in which the rat self-stimulated its brain by pressing a bar. Only now, when the rat presses the bar, a drug is delivered into the blood stream (**Figure 7.29A**). Like humans, rats must find cocaine pleasurable, because they avidly press a bar to get more and more cocaine. But in a sense, this rat is simply using a roundabout way to do what the rat in brain self-stimulation does: provide dopamine to the nucleus accumbens. When scientists measure brain dopamine as the rat delivers more and more cocaine, they can watch dopamine levels rise in the nucleus accumbens (**Figure 7.29B**).

So you can see that many psychoactive drugs conceal a horrible trap. You experience great pleasure from the drug, which leads you to use it more and more, but you no longer find any other activities as pleasurable as they were before. As you neglect other activities (like meals, personal hygiene, a job) and other people (like friends, a mate), you experience the consequences. Your health declines, you lose your job, and lose all but the most steadfast members of your social network. In those circumstances, the drug can seem like your only option to avoid misery, and yet all it really offers is more misery ahead.

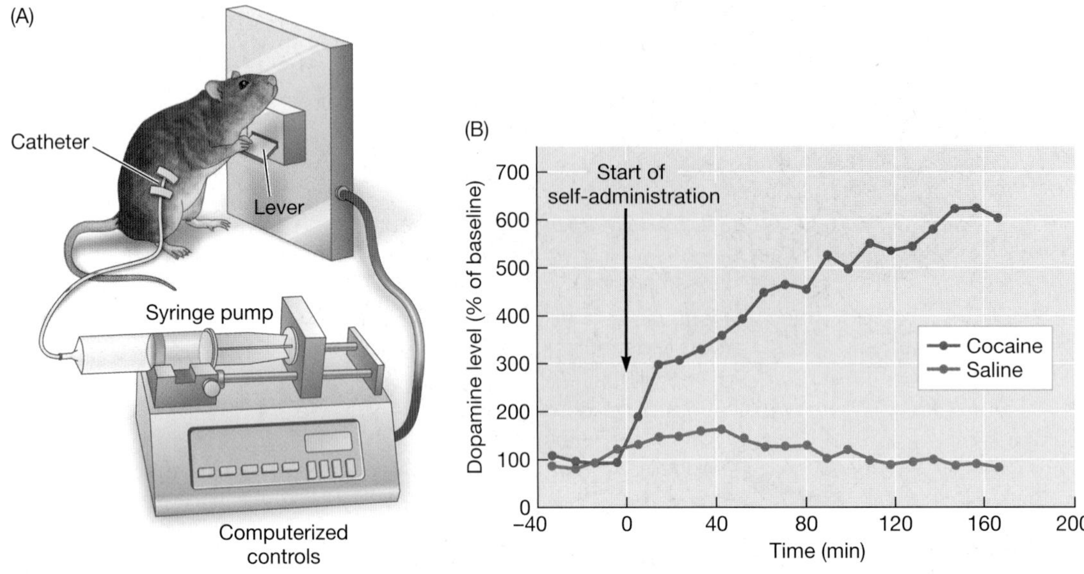

Figure 7.29 A Rat Will Self-Administer Drugs like Cocaine (A) The number of lever presses that the animal will perform to receive a drug is a measure of the rewarding properties and addictive potential of that drug. (B) Dopamine levels in the nucleus accumbens rise sharply in rats during self-administration of cocaine. (After Pettit & Justice, 1991.)

The Cutting Edge

Marijuana Is Risky for Teenagers

As more jurisdictions legalize medicinal or recreational use of marijuana, there is concern that use of the drug is growing among teenagers (Johnston et al., 2014), who may be particularly vulnerable. Adolescents who use marijuana are more likely to develop severe mental disorders by adulthood (Murray et al., 2007). A study found that men in the Swedish army who had smoked marijuana at least once as teenagers were twice as likely to develop schizophrenia as those who never did. Heavy smokers were six times more likely to develop schizophrenia (Zammit et al., 2010).

However, it is not clear whether the drug *causes* psychosis or whether adolescents who are prepsychotic are more likely to turn to marijuana (Proal et al., 2014). In a longitudinal study, only those adolescents carrying a particular gene were more likely to become schizophrenic after using marijuana, suggesting that some people are genetically vulnerable to this devastating effect of the drug (Caspi et al., 2005). People who smoked pot as teenagers display memory deficits and structural brain abnormalities that have also been associated with schizophrenia (Lisdahl et al., 2013; Smith et al., 2014). Still, were the brain differences there before these people smoked marijuana, or were they caused by the drug? There is no definitive answer, but one study noted that nearly all the people with schizophrenia who had smoked marijuana were using the drug heavily *before* they developed the disorder (Smith et al., 2014).

But really, isn't this a no-brainer for adolescents? If there's a risk that smoking pot as a teenager will lead to schizophrenia, do you really want to test that hypothesis with your own health? The drug will still be available for you to try later in life. As the title of one study put it, "Dare to delay" (Lisdahl et al., 2013).

7.4 SUMMARY

- *Psychoactive drugs* affect mental activity by affecting neurotransmitter communication in the brain.
- Some drugs are *agonists* that act like a neurotransmitter on the receptor. Other drugs are *antagonists* that interfere with neurotransmitter reaching the receptor. Yet other drugs are *neuromodulators* that either boost or inhibit neurotransmitter signaling.
- *Depressants* (*alcohol*, *barbiturates*, *tranquilizers*) inhibit neural activity, mental activity, and behavior, typically acting as neuromodulators to boost GABA receptor responsiveness.
- *Stimulants* (*caffeine*, *nicotine*, *amphetamines*) increase neural activity, mental activity, and behavior. Most stimulants act as neuromodulators to boost catecholamine signaling.
- Opiates (*opium*, *morphine*, *heroin*) produce euphoria and analgesia by acting as agonists at endogenous *opioid receptors*.
- *Hallucinogens* (*LSD*, *PCP*, *MDMA*) have a wide variety of neural mechanisms, but all distort sensory perceptions.
- *Addiction*, or *substance use disorder*, is repeated drug use despite problems caused by the drug.
- *Withdrawal symptoms*, unpleasant physical effects of ceasing drug use, tend to reinforce addiction because only continued drug use can stop withdrawal symptoms.
- Some drugs, such as *cocaine*, are very addictive even though there are no physical withdrawal symptoms.
- Addictive drugs activate the *reward pathway* that releases dopamine in the *nucleus accumbens*.
- Repeated drug use reduces dopamine receptors in the nucleus accumbens, requiring the user to resort to larger doses of drug to get the same high, but also reducing the ability of other behaviors, such as eating and being with other people, to provide pleasure.
- Marijuana use during adolescence may increase the chance of developing schizophrenia by adulthood.

REVIEW QUESTIONS

1. What are the main mechanisms by which psychoactive drugs can affect neurotransmitter receptors?
2. Describe the major classes of psychoactive drugs and give at least one specific example of each.
3. What is the difference between psychological addiction and physical addiction?
4. What is our current understanding of how psychoactive drugs trigger pleasurable sensations and why they can lead to drug dependence?

Food for Thought

Imagine a specially modified motorcycle helmet that you could put on and, by simply pushing a button on top, it would deliver a jolt of electricity to your brain that would cause a flood of dopamine to be released in your nucleus accumbens. If you could buy such a helmet for $100, would you?

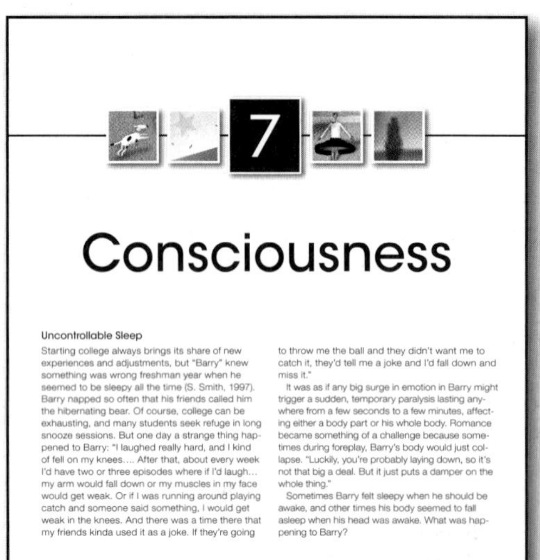

7

Consciousness

Uncontrollable Sleep

Starting college always brings its share of new experiences and adjustments, but "Barry" knew something was wrong freshman year when he seemed to be sleepy all the time (S. Smith, 1997). Barry napped so often that his friends called him the hibernating bear. Of course, college can be exhausting, and many students seek refuge in long snooze sessions. But one day a strange thing happened to Barry: "I laughed really hard, and I kind of fell on my knees.... After that, about every week I'd have two or three episodes where if I'd laugh... my arm would fall down or my muscles in my face would get weak. Or if I was running around playing catch and someone said something, I would get weak in the knees. And there was a time there that my friends kinda used it as a joke. If they're going to throw me the ball and they didn't want me to catch it, they'd tell me a joke and I'd fall down and miss it."

It was as if any big surge in emotion in Barry might trigger a sudden, temporary paralysis lasting anywhere from a few seconds to a few minutes, affecting either a body part or his whole body. Romance became something of a challenge because sometimes during foreplay, Barry's body would just collapse. "Luckily, you're probably laying down, so it's not that big a deal. But it just puts a damper on the whole thing."

Sometimes Barry felt sleepy when he should be awake, and other times his body seemed to fall asleep when his head was awake. What was happening to Barry?

Think Like a Psychologist:

Principles in Action

Whenever we encounter any interesting behavior we should consider the four principles. Here are some ways that the four principles relate to our opening story about Barry.

MACHINE

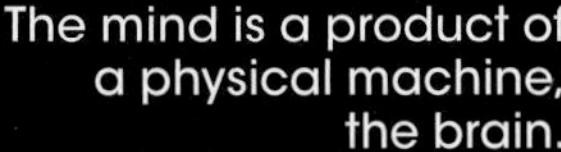

The mind is a product of a physical machine, the brain.

The absence of the neurotransmitter hypocretin, or of the receptors to respond to it, causes narcolepsy such as Barry experiences. This means he sometimes instantly falls asleep in the middle of the day, and sometimes falls limply to the floor while still wide awake.

UNCONSCIOUS

We are consciously aware of only a small part of our mental activity.

When Barry laughs or gets excited, parts of his brain that he has no control over, including sleep centers in the pons, rapidly paralyze him, in a state called cataplexy.

SOCIAL

We constantly modify our behavior, beliefs, and attitudes according to what we perceive about the people around us.

While Barry's cataplexy was amusing for his college friends for a while, it was a barrier to romance. As a physician today, Barry must keep his narcolepsy under control through medication for the safety and welfare of his patients.

EXPERIENCE

Our experiences physically alter the structure and function of the brain.

Barry's experience with narcolepsy, and his need to use stimulants to keep it under control, led him to conduct research in sleep and made him a sympathetic physician to patients with sleep disorders.

KEY TERMS

activation synthesis, 267
addiction, 299
agonist, 292
alcohol, 293
alpha rhythm, 264
amphetamines, 295
analgesic, 296
anesthesia, 293
antagonist, 292
barbiturates, 293
basal forebrain, 270
biological clock, 261
brain self-stimulation, 300
caffeine, 295
cannabinoids, 298
circadian rhythm, 261
cocaine, 295
confabulation, 255
consciousness, 248
corpus callosum, 253
delta-9-tetrahydrocannabinol (THC), 298
delta waves, 264
depressant, 293
desynchronized EEG, 264
dissociative drug, 297
easy problem of consciousness, 249
ecstasy (MDMA), 297
electroencephalogram (EEG), 264
endocannabinoid, 298
endogenous opiates, 296
fatal familial insomnia (FFI), 276
flashback, 297
free will, 256
hallucinogens, 296
hard problem of consciousness, 250
heroin, 296
hypnosis, 282
hypocretin, 271
insomnia, 277
internal dialogue, 252
jet lag, 263
K complexes, 264
latent content, 267
lysergic acid diethylamide (LSD), 296
manifest content, 267
marijuana, 298
meditation, 290
mescaline, 296
morphine, 296
narcolepsy, 271
neuromodulator, 292
nicotine, 294
non-REM (NREM) sleep, 266
nucleus accumbens, 300
opioid receptors, 296
opium, 296
phencyclidine (PCP), 297
psilocybin, 296
psychoactive drugs, 290
qualia, 250
rapid-eye-movement (REM) sleep, 265
REM behavior disorder (RBD), 268
reticular formation, 270
reward pathway, 300
sleep apnea, 278
sleep debt, 274
sleep paralysis, 272
sleep spindles, 264
sleep state misperception, 277
slow-wave sleep (SWS), 265
social theory of hypnosis, 288
split brain, 253
stage 1 sleep, 264
stage 2 sleep, 264
stage 3 sleep, 264
Stanford hypnotic susceptibility test, 283
stimulants, 294
subcoeruleus, 268
substance use disorder, 299
sudden infant death syndrome (SIDS), 278
suprachiasmatic nucleus (SCN), 262
tolerance, 295
trance theory of hypnosis, 288
tranquilizer, 293
withdrawal symptoms, 299

QUIZ YOURSELF

1. The question of how brain processes result in the subjective experience of a perception is known as
   a. the dilemma of qualia.
   b. the hard problem of consciousness
   c. the mind–body problem.
   d. the easy problem of consciousness.
   e. synchrony of brain regions.
2. Which theory suggests that a hypnotized participant is simply trying to accommodate another person, the hypnotist, so they can together accomplish a mutual goal?
   a. Social theory
   b. Trance theory
   c. Division of consciousness theory
   d. Conditioned inhibition theory
3. A psychoactive drug that affects target neurons in the same way as the body's neurotransmitter is ________.
   a. a pseudoreceptor
   b. a neuromodulator
   c. an antagonist
   d. an agonist
4. Filling in a gap in memory or understanding with a fabrication a person believes is true, such as is done by a split-brain patient when asked to explain a response to stimuli exposed only to the right hemisphere, is called ________.
5. The active–rest cycle of about one day that is controlled by an animal's biological clock is known as its ________ of activity.
6. A person who suffers from ________ may stop breathing during sleep and often has loud, interrupted snoring.
7. The practice of relaxing the body and focusing attention on a single, simple object or process to try to empty the mind of content is ________.
8. ________ is the phenomenon in which a person must take a higher and higher dose of the drug to get the same effect.
9. Drugs of abuse produce pleasure by triggering the release of ________ in the ________.

1. b; 2. a; 3. d; 4. confabulation; 5. circadian rhythm; 6. sleep apnea; 7. meditation; 8. Tolerance; 9. dopamine; nucleus accumbens

CUTLER

Learning

Afraid of Santa Claus

In 1919, John B. Watson, a brilliant, energetic psychologist at Johns Hopkins University, believed that most babies at birth have very few emotional reactions to the things around them. Yet adults have many, sometimes complex, emotional reactions to all sorts of things. Watson theorized that there must be some process by which we *learn* to have emotional reactions to various new places and objects we encounter in life.

To test his idea, Watson tried to teach an infant to be afraid of something harmless. A young woman worked at the Hopkins hospital as a wet nurse, which means she provided her breast milk to infants and children who were separated from their mothers. She had a 9-month-old son of her own, and Watson chose this boy, whom he dubbed "Albert B.," for study. When "Little Albert," as he came to be known, was exposed for the first time to a white rat, a dog, a rabbit, a monkey, masks, and burning newspapers, he showed no fearful response.

Could Albert be taught to be afraid of harmless objects? Later Watson brought the baby back to the lab and exposed him to a rat. Albert eagerly reached out to touch the rat, but as soon as he did, Watson made an awful banging noise slamming a hammer into a large steel bar, and Albert began to cry. A week later, Albert was again exposed to the frightful sound when he touched the rat. As the pairing of the rat with the sound continued, eventually Albert would cry and try to avoid the rat, even in the absence of the loud noise. Not only that, Albert was now afraid of other furry objects, such as the rabbit, the dog, and even the white fluffy beard of a Santa Claus mask.

A month later, Albert was still afraid of the rat, a fur coat, and the Santa Claus mask. Would these experiences make Little Albert afraid of furry objects for the rest of his life? Watson never knew, because Albert and his mother moved away from the hospital.

Watson's experiment, parts of which he filmed to teach people about the importance of learning, would be regarded as unethical today. Watson claimed that if he'd had more time he would have taught Albert to stop being afraid of rats. But there's no record to tell whether Albert ever unlearned his fears. Watson predicted that Albert's fears were "likely to persist indefinitely, unless an accidental method for removing them is hit upon" (Watson & Rayner, 1920). Publicly criticized for conducting these studies, Watson burned all his notes and papers before he died. In fact, all trace of Little Albert disappeared from the field until nearly 90 years later, as we will see at the end of this chapter.

(A)

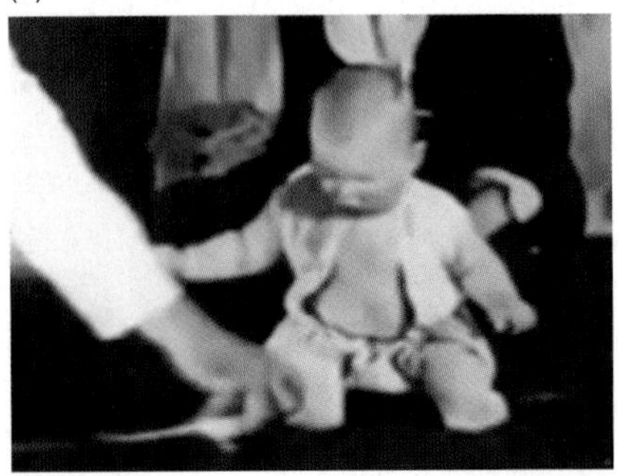

(B)

Figure 8.1 The Conditioning of Little Albert (A) The infant known as Little Albert showed no fear of a white rat or any other furry objects when John B. Watson and his research assistant Rosalie Rayner first presented them to the boy. (B) But after the researchers frightened the child with a loud noise several times in the presence of the rat, Albert learned to be afraid of the rat and of other furry objects, like a Santa Claus mask, as well.

Chapter Preview

In this chapter you will learn about learning! We will define **learning** as the acquisition of knowledge, skill, attitudes, or understanding as a result of experience. Usually we gauge whether people gained that new knowledge, skill, attitude, or understanding by observing their future behavior. For example, did Little Albert's experience with a furry white rat affect his future behavior or attitudes? Did he avoid animals? Was he afraid of white fur? If so, that would be evidence that he had indeed learned something in Watson's laboratory. Generally we are interested in *learning that results in a relatively long-lasting change in behavior.* In Little Albert's case, the acquired behavior was not entirely rational (furry white things are not always accompanied by unpleasant events) but nevertheless indicated that he had learned something. Indeed, we have all learned "facts" that turned out to be untrue (such as the psychological myths we discussed in Section 1.3). In the next chapter we will study memory, the ability to hold on to what we've learned, and there we will discuss what it means to forget something.

We'll begin this chapter by examining the type of learning that Little Albert displayed, in which he was *conditioned* to associate a white rat with a loud, upsetting noise (**Figure 8.1**). An understanding of conditioned learning is especially useful because it can usually help us predict the future. We'll see that it is sometimes difficult to unlearn fears such as those Little Albert acquired in Watson's lab. In Section 8.2 we'll discuss how we learn to behave a certain way to gain a reward or avoid a punishment, a type of learning that is well understood thanks to systematic experimentation by many psychologists. Although in these experiments it was often rats that were doing the learning, you'll see that the principles uncovered turn out to apply to humans as well—and, as far as we know, to all other animals. Finally, we'll discuss how we can learn about the world by observing the behavior of others. Once thought to be a unique ability of humans, it turns out many animals can learn by observing.

8.1 Predicting the Future

Things to Learn

- Three types of simple learning
- Classical conditioning
- Second order conditioning
- Taste aversion
- Fear conditioning

The one universal characteristic of all animals that have been studied so far is that they learn. Not just dogs and horses, but fruit flies, sea slugs, and microscopic worms all learn. What learning does for all animals is help them predict the future. When is it safe to go out, where will I find my mate, whom am I likely to encounter in that valley over there, if I climb that tree will I find something to eat? Learning about events in the world around us helps us predict the answers to these and many other questions. It can also help us solve problems that we encounter in the future. Because learning may have a tremendous influence on how successfully an individual will reproduce, natural selection favors the evolution of learning. Put another way, it seems a safe bet that the common ancestor of all animals was capable of learning, and we'll see that some aspects of learning are much the same in descendants as diverse as slugs and people.

Recall from Section 6.1 that any physical event that affects a sensory cell so that an individual can detect the event is called a **stimulus**. The simplest forms of learning involve just a single stimulus, so we'll begin this section with such cases, centering on how a subject learns to ignore a stimulus that is of no importance. Then we will study a slightly more complex type of learning, called *classical conditioning*, that involves two different stimuli, and the subject learns that one of those stimuli is often followed by the other. (Example: Little Albert learned that the approach of a white rat was followed by an upsetting noise.) We

learning The acquisition of knowledge, skill, attitudes, or understanding as a result of experience.

stimulus In the context of learning, a sensory event that an individual can detect.

will review Pavlov's famous studies of this type of learning in dogs, and will consider the revelation that certain types of conditioning are so vital to survival that natural selection has primed us to learn them after just one experience.

habituation A simple type of learning in which repeated presentation of a stimulus elicits a weaker and weaker response.

The simplest learning tasks involve only one cue

If, like me, you fantasize about being able to predict the future, you probably imagine predicting important future events: natural disasters or accidents, or the outcomes of Super Bowl games or national elections. There's no value in foretelling *unimportant* events. That's why natural selection has provided every animal with the ability to learn to ignore unimportant events. This simple type of learning is **habituation**, when the repeated presentation of a stimulus elicits less and less of a response. Note that two conditions must be met for the reduced responsiveness to be considered true habituation. First, the subject must still be *able to respond*—a reduced response caused by muscle exhaustion is not habituation. Second, the subject's sensory system must still be *able to detect* the stimulus. Recall from Section 6.1 that sensory systems sometimes stop responding to a stimulus in a phenomenon called *sensory adaptation,* especially when the stimulus is unchanging. Sensory adaptation is not considered learning. But if the subject is still able to *detect* the stimulus, and is still able to *respond* to the stimulus, then the reduced responsiveness must be learned, and that's what we call habituation.

Surely you've noticed times when you've habituated to some stimulus. Perhaps you've sat reading in a café where a chime sounds or a bell rings each time someone walks through the door (**Figure 8.2A**). At first, the unexpected sound of the bell may startle you. But with each new sounding of the bell, you respond less and less until eventually you don't respond to the bell at all. You can still hear the bell (there's been no sensory adaptation to that sound), and your muscles can still move, but you've learned that the bell is unimportant.

(A)

Bell above door

You look up the first time the bell rings.

After repeated bell rings, you no longer notice. You are habituated to that sound.

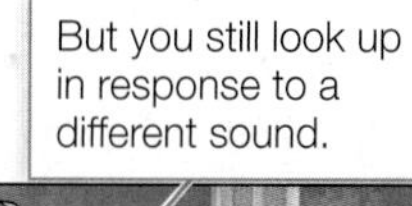
But you still look up in response to a different sound.

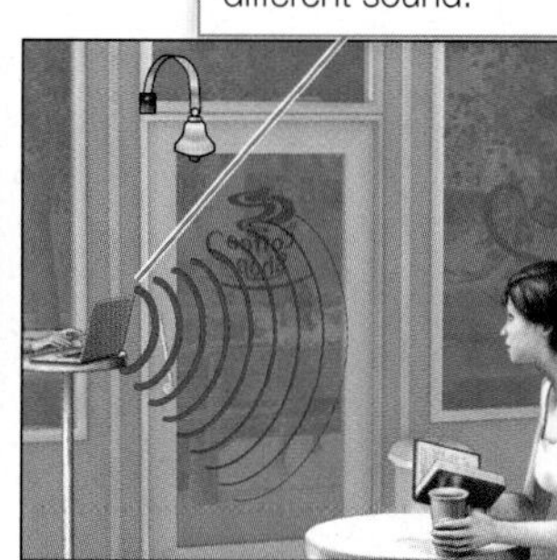

(B)

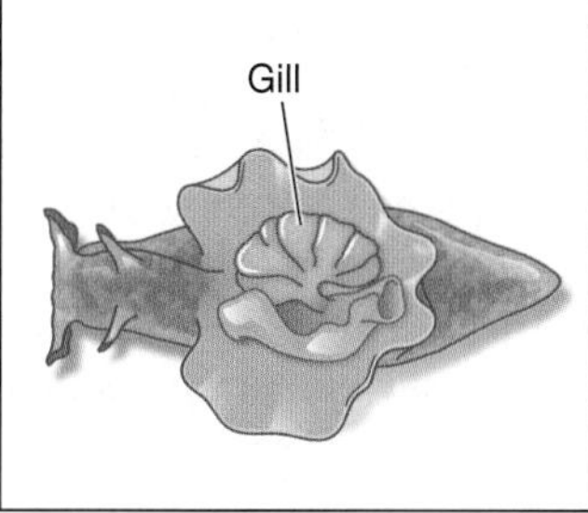
Gill

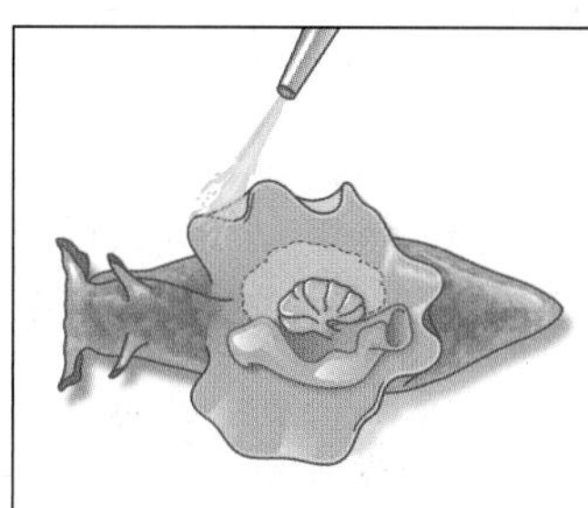
The sea slug withdraws its gill in response to a squirt of water.

After repeated squirts, the animal stops withdrawing its gill. It has habituated to that stimulus.

But the slug still withdraws its gill in response to a squirt of water elsewhere.

Figure 8.2 Habituation in Humans and Slugs This simple type of learning involving only one stimulus has been seen in all animals that have been studied so far.

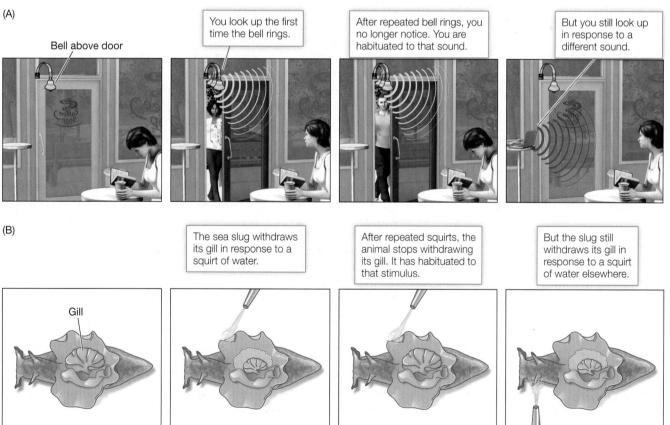

I once lived in an apartment that was near a mass transit train track. At first I really noticed the noise every time a train went by, but after a few days I stopped noticing the sound at all. It's not that I couldn't *hear* the sound—if someone else pointed out the noise, I could still hear it just fine. But I no longer reacted to the sound, which was good because the rent on that apartment was a bargain, precisely because most people didn't want to hear that train every day. Thanks to habituation, I got the bargain but rarely heard the train.

We recognize habituation as a simple form of learning because even the simplest animals habituate (Wood, 1988). For example, scientists found that if they squirted a gentle stream of water at the body of a sea slug called *Aplysia*, the animal would withdraw its gill. Presumably the animal was alarmed by the squirt of water and was trying to protect its delicate gill. However, if the scientists squirted the same part of the slug's body repeatedly, the animal eventually stopped withdrawing its gill (**Figure 8.2B**). This appears to be an example of habituation, when the repeated presentation of a stimulus (in this case a squirt of water to the body) elicits less and less of a response (in this case, gill withdrawal).

In true habituation, an animal's sensory system does not lose the ability to detect the stimulus; it has learned to ignore the stimulus. One way to test whether the animal's sensory system can still detect the squirt of water would be to find the touch receptors stimulated by the squirt and confirm that they are still responding. We can show that the animal can still withdraw its gill by squirting a *new* part of the body (see Figure 8.2B). The gill withdraws promptly, proving there is nothing wrong with the muscles involved. The stimulus is still being detected and the animal is still capable of showing a response, but it has learned not to respond. It has *habituated* to that particular touch, just as you habituate to the sound of a bell in a coffee shop.

As pointed out earlier, habituation is a form of learning while sensory adaptation simply reflects the way sensory receptor cells are built. But the two processes seem to serve the same purpose. Both habituation and adaptation help us ignore repetitive or constant stimuli that tend to be unimportant for survival. Sensory adaptation filters out constant stimuli, like the pressing of our clothes on our skin or the constant hum of a desktop computer. For repeated stimuli that are spread apart, like that bell ringing in the coffee shop, too much time elapses between stimuli for sensory adaptation to set in. In such cases, parts of the nervous system receiving the sensory information must filter out the unimportant, repeating stimulus, and that is what habituation does for us.

REVERSING HABITUATION If someone sets off a loud firecracker just outside the coffee house, you will be startled. Eventually you'll see that there's no danger and settle back to your book. But the next time someone enters, ringing that bell, you may look up (**Figure 8.3A**). The sudden return of a response that had formerly been habituated is called **dishabituation**. We can demonstrate dishabituation in *Aplysia* by applying an electrical shock to the animal's tail. Now that squirt of water will again elicit a full-blown gill withdrawal that had formerly been habituated (**Figure 8.3B**).

Another simple form of learning is called **sensitization**, when a very strong stimulus, typically an obnoxious, unpleasant one, causes an *enhanced* response to a variety of other stimuli. For several hours after the electrical shock, not only does the *Aplysia* respond to that squirt of water it had formerly habituated to, but now a squirt of water *anywhere* on the body elicits an exaggerated, more extensive retraction of the gill (see Figure 8.3B). The animal is sensitized. Likewise, after that nasty scare from the firecracker, you may be sensitized too, overresponding to any sudden stimulus.

dishabituation The sudden return of a response that had formerly been habituated.

sensitization A simple form of learning in which a strong, aversive stimulus causes a subject to show an exaggerated response to other stimuli.

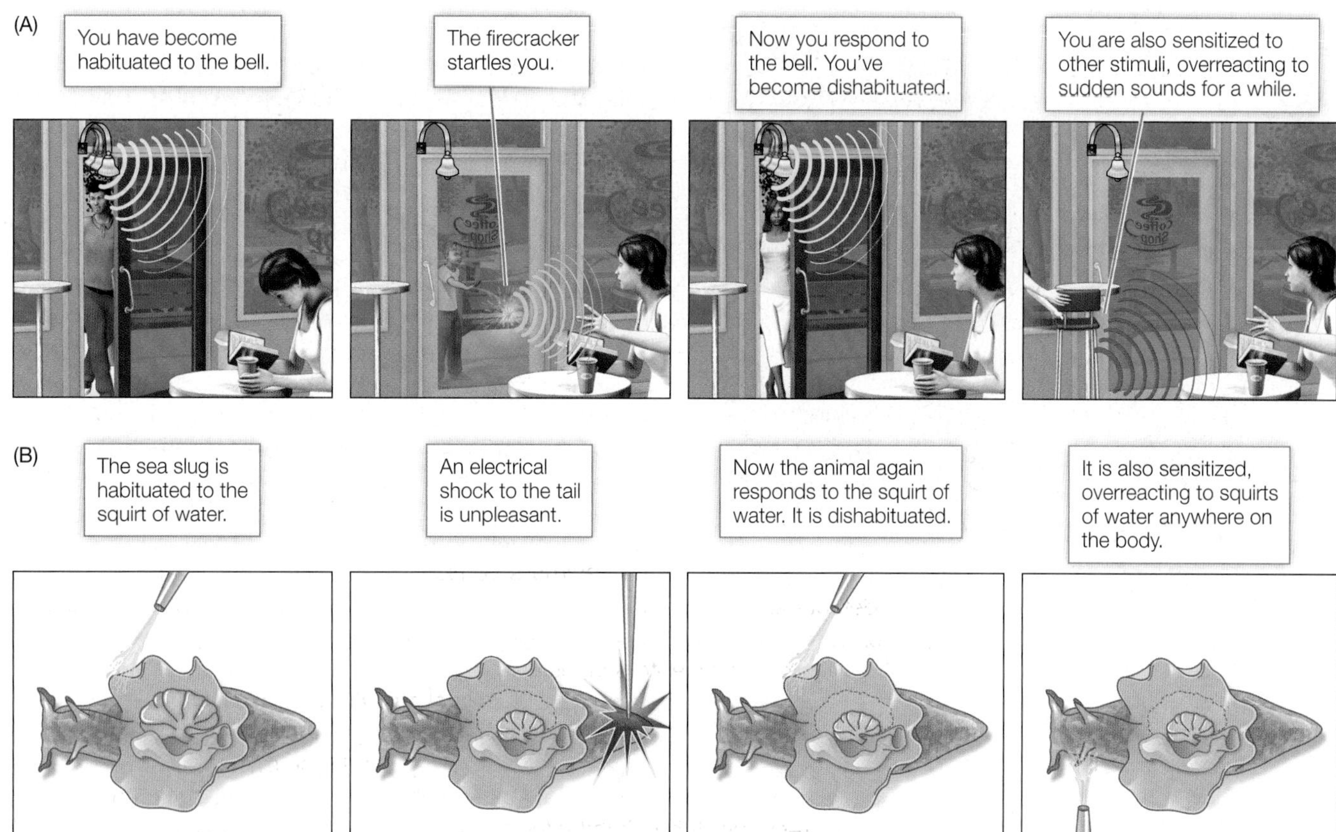

Figure 8.3 Dishabituation and Sensitization in Humans and Slugs

One of the reasons we consider these three forms of learning—habituation, dishabituation, and sensitization—to be simple is that in each case we are measuring a single response to a single stimulus. Even in the case of sensitization, where an obnoxious stimulus makes us overreact for a while, there's no relationship between the obnoxious stimulus and the later stimuli to which we overreact. We tend to overreact to *any* stimulus for a while. So these simple forms of learning are called **non-associative learning**, where there is no particular predictive relationship between any two stimuli.

The more complex forms of learning that we'll consider next are situations where two *different* events repeatedly occur at about the same time. This is **associative learning**, when we learn that there is a special relationship between two sets of stimuli, or between a particular stimulus and a behavior. The two stimuli are *associated* with one another, or a particular stimulus is *associated* with a particular behavior, so that the occurrence of one helps predict the arrival of the other. The two best-studied forms of associative learning are classical conditioning, which we will cover in the rest of this section, and operant conditioning, which we'll cover in Section 8.2.

non-associative learning Simple forms of learning involving changes in the response to a single stimulus.

associative learning A type of learning in which a relationship is formed between two stimuli or between a stimulus and a behavior.

Classical conditioning teaches us to anticipate the future

You may have heard of the pioneering work of Russian physiologist Ivan Pavlov in classical conditioning. Indeed, his name is so firmly attached to this type of learning that it is sometimes called *Pavlovian conditioning*. It will be much easier to understand the formal definition of classical conditioning if we

Figure 8.4 Russian Physiologist Ivan Pavlov (1849–1936) Here Pavlov (right, white beard) poses in the laboratory with his assistants and a canine subject in 1926.

first describe the process. While studying digestion, Pavlov noted that when he placed some meat powder in a dog's mouth, the animal would salivate (**Figure 8.4**). This was a reflexive, unlearned response to food. Other stimuli, such as the sound of a bell, had no effect on salivation. In his most famous experiments, Pavlov would ring a bell and almost immediately afterward place meat powder in the dog's mouth, triggering salivation ("Pavloff," 1923; Thomas, 1994). After repeatedly being exposed to this pairing of stimuli—the sound of the bell followed by meat powder—the dog learned to associate the two stimuli. Pavlov could tell the dog had formed this mental association because eventually the dog salivated in response to the bell alone, even if no meat powder was provided. In the terminology of the field, the dog was *conditioned* to respond to that initially neutral stimulus, the bell, by salivating (**Figure 8.5**). So now you should find it easier to understand a formal definition of **classical conditioning**: a basic form of learning in which a neutral stimulus (here, the bell) is repeatedly followed by another stimulus (in this case, meat powder), which normally elicits a response (salivation), until the formerly neutral stimulus (bell) now elicits that response. Phew.

classical conditioning Also called *Pavlovian conditioning.* A basic form of learning in which a neutral stimulus is repeatedly followed by another stimulus that normally elicits a response, until the formerly neutral stimulus now elicits that response.

unconditioned stimulus (US) A stimulus that naturally evokes a specific response.

unconditioned response (UR) The specific response that is naturally evoked by that US.

Specialized terminology is used in classical conditioning research. First let's consider the stimulus that elicits a response without any training at all. In Pavlov's experiment, the presence of meat powder in the dog's mouth reflexively elicits salivation. The dog didn't *learn* to salivate in response to tasty food in its mouth, that's just how dogs are made (me too). Specific terms are used to describe a stimulus–response pairing to emphasize when it is *not* the result of learning or conditioning. A stimulus that naturally (that is, reflexively) evokes a specific response is called an **unconditioned stimulus** (**US**), and the specific response that the US evokes is called the **unconditioned response** (**UR**). In contrast, the previously neutral stimulus (the bell) that, after repeated pairing with the US, eventually triggers the response is called the **conditioned stimulus** (**CS**). The response in question, salivation, is considered a UR as

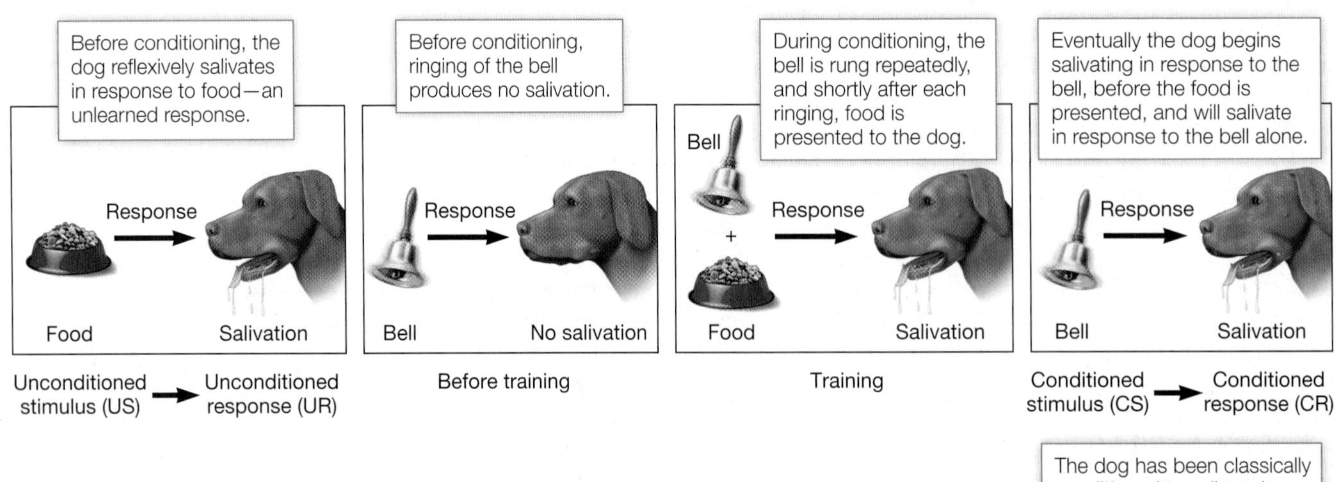
Before conditioning, the dog reflexively salivates in response to food—an unlearned response.
Response
Food
Salivation
Unconditioned stimulus (US)
Unconditioned response (UR)
Before conditioning, ringing of the bell produces no salivation.
Response
Bell
No salivation
Before training
During conditioning, the bell is rung repeatedly, and shortly after each ringing, food is presented to the dog.
Bell
+
Response
Food
Salivation
Training
Eventually the dog begins salivating in response to the bell, before the food is presented, and will salivate in response to the bell alone.
Response
Bell
Salivation
Conditioned stimulus (CS)
Conditioned response (CR)
The dog has been classically conditioned to salivate in response to the bell.

Figure 8.5 Classical, or Pavlovian, Conditioning

long as it is in response to the US (meat powder). But when the dog eventually becomes conditioned to salivate in response to the bell alone, without the meat powder (see Figure 8.5), the *learned* response is called the **conditioned response** (**CR**).

Let's consider another example of classical conditioning to help you incorporate this terminology. If I blow a puff of air at your eye, you'll blink. Your blink is an unlearned, reflexive behavior that would protect the eye from any dust or debris in the air. The puff of air is a US and your blink is a UR. Gently ringing a bell would not cause you to blink. But if I repeatedly ring the bell and, half a second later, send a puff of air to your eye each time, eventually you will be *conditioned* to blink your eye when I ring the bell, even without the puff of air. You will have associated the air puff (the US) with the bell (the CS) and, quite sensibly, you will blink (the CR) in anticipation of a puff of air (that may never arrive). In this sense you will have learned to foretell the future: "Every time that bell rings, a gust of air hits my eye soon after." This is an excellent lesson to have learned because, outside the laboratory, it's a good idea to close your eye if a gust of wind is coming. Although I've described this lesson as if the participant were thinking about what's going on, in fact most people in such experiments find that they don't have to think about what to do. Their eye blinks so quickly after the bell rings that they don't have time to consciously think about what to do. It feels as though the eye is blinking automatically, on its own.

Whether it's a dog learning to salivate in response to a bell or a person blinking in response to a tone, the gradual appearance of the CR in response to the CS is called **acquisition**. It's as though you have "acquired" the eye-blink response to the bell, or have acquired an *association* between the CS and the US ("when that CS happens, the US often follows").

Classical conditioning can be powerful in that almost any stimulus can be paired with the US, so a dog can learn to salivate, or a person can learn to blink, in response to a bell, a buzzer, or a picture of a circle. Likewise, a neutral stimulus can be used through conditioning to elicit any response that we can reliably elicit with a US. It's also easy to see why classical conditioning is adaptive. By learning that one particular stimulus is often followed by another, we learn to anticipate what will happen next. If food is coming, we should get ready to digest it. If a gust of air is coming, we should protect our eyes.

The studies we've examined thus far suggest that classical conditioning is adaptive because it helps us predict the future, but is that really what it's for? To test that idea, Robert Rescorla taught one group of rats that a tone would soon be followed by an electrical shock to the floor of their cage. Rats freeze in response to such shocks, apparently to stand the shock better. By the way, the shock is irritating but not awful (at least when I've put my hand on such grids), doing no tissue damage (to rats or to me). Soon the rats would freeze in response to the tone alone. If classical conditioning really has evolved to help us predict the future, then if we rearrange things so that hearing the tone has no predictive value, then the rats shouldn't learn to freeze in response to that sound. Rescorla (1968) demonstrated this by exposing another group of rats to the same number of tone presentations, and the tone was always followed by foot shock, but these animals were exposed to foot shocks at *other* times too. In fact, a foot shock was just as likely to happen whether the tone was sounding or not. So in this case the tone was not useful for predicting whether a shock was coming. The rats did not learn to freeze in response to the tone alone, confirming the idea that rats are built to learn to associate a neutral stimulus with the US *if and only if* that neutral stimulus really does help them predict the future.

conditioned stimulus (CS) The previously neutral stimulus that, after repeated pairing with the US, eventually triggers the response.

conditioned response (CR) The learned response to a previously neutral stimulus that was repeatedly paired with an US.

acquisition In the context of classical conditioning, the gradual appearance of the CR in response to the CS alone.

Figure 8.6 Classical Conditioning in the Service of Commerce Advertisers hope to tap into our positive feelings about one stimulus and associate those good feelings with their product. If the strategy works, and we come to have warm feelings about the products, then we are displaying second-order conditioning.

Subjects in classical conditioning learn about more than just the conditioned stimulus

One interesting aspect of experiments in learning is that sometimes the subject learns more than what the experimenter intended. Indeed, Pavlov's work on classical conditioning began when he was studying digestion and noticed that dogs began salivating when workers wearing white lab coats entered the room. These workers brought the food, and the dogs had become conditioned to respond to white lab coats. The dogs had learned that white lab coats predicted the coming of food, and Pavlov's observation of their anticipation launched his studies of conditioning.

Pavlov soon realized that once the dogs had become conditioned to salivate in response to one formerly neutral stimulus, like the ticking of a metronome, he could use that CS to condition *another* stimulus, for example the presentation of a large black square of cardboard. If a dog was repeatedly shown the black square, followed shortly after by the ticking sound, the dog soon began to salivate when shown the square. This is an example of **second-order conditioning** (or *secondary conditioning*), when a previously learned CS, which elicits a CR, repeatedly follows another neutral stimulus so that that second neutral stimulus also comes to elicit a CR.

Advertisers try to make use of second-order conditioning to get us to buy things. This is why advertisements almost always have very attractive people using the product. By associating their product with images of people or situations we like, advertisers hope we begin to feel warm and fuzzy about their product (**Figure 8.6**). If you want men to buy your beer, show them lots of beautiful bikini-clad women (US) in the background while the beer label (CS) is in the foreground. Those men weren't born liking girls in bikinis; they had learned to associate them with pleasant activities while growing up. The hope is that the men will develop a second-order CR of arousal to that bottle and so want to buy one. If you want Americans to buy your soda, show them images of your Coca-Cola bottles in the hands of a gentle, lovable Santa Claus (Santa might not have been an effective US for Little Albert).

Pavlov also studied another instance of a subject in a classical conditioning situation learning about more than the CS. A dog repeatedly exposed to a particular sound, say a tuning fork that played middle C, followed by the meat powder would soon become conditioned to salivate in response to that sound. But in fact, tones with a slightly lower or higher pitch than middle C would also elicit salivation. This is an instance of **stimulus generalization** (or simply *generalization*), when the subject displays a CR to stimuli that are similar to, but not exactly identical to, the CS used in training (Honig & Urcuioli, 1981). The more similar the stimulus is to the original training CS, the stronger the CR elicited (**Figure 8.7**). Little Albert was showing stimulus generalization when he was afraid of any fuzzy thing, not just the rat.

If we repeatedly present tones of different pitch, and only pair the meat powder to middle C, then eventually the dog will learn to salivate only in response to that pitch and not the others. We say the dog is displaying *stimulus discrimination*, associating the sound from only one specific tuning fork, not all of them. In fact, by testing whether the dog can learn to discriminate middle C from similar pitches, we can tell what pitches the dog can, or cannot, discriminate.

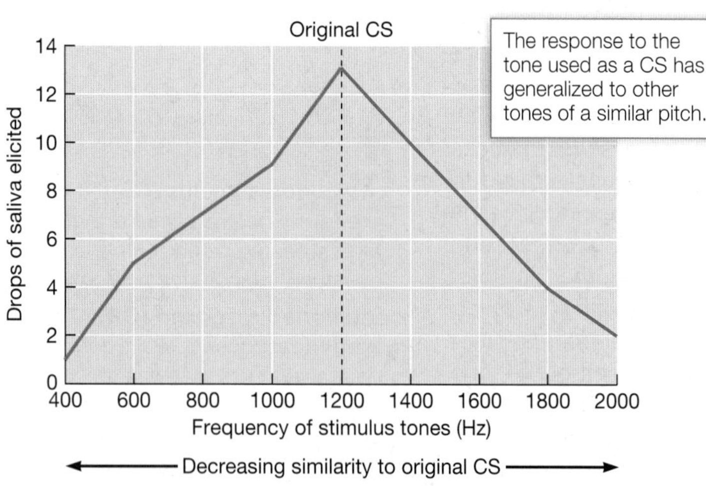

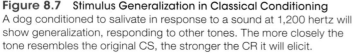

Figure 8.7 Stimulus Generalization in Classical Conditioning A dog conditioned to salivate in response to a sound at 1,200 hertz will show generalization, responding to other tones. The more closely the tone resembles the original CS, the stronger the CR it will elicit.

Our everyday behavior reflects what we've learned by classical conditioning

We've all experienced instances of classical conditioning in everyday life. In my household, our dog Dipsy became conditioned to the sounds of someone going to the silverware drawer to get a fork to scoop out canned dog food. Pet owners with electric can openers often find that their animals dash to the kitchen whenever the opener makes noise, thus exhibiting acquisition (**Figure 8.8A**). It might be funny at first to produce whichever noise your pet associates with feeding, to watch the animal's response and then not feed it, but eventually the pet will catch on. The animal will respond more and more slowly until it stops responding at all to that sound, at least for a while. This is an example of **extinction**, when repeated presentation of the CS (sound) without the US (food) results in a weaker and weaker CR (**Figure 8.8B**). When the CR has disappeared altogether, we say it has been extinguished.

Does extinction make an animal completely forget an association of the CS with the US? To find out if an animal still recalls a prior association, we can present a few more pairings of the US followed by the CS. As seen in **Figure 8.8C** the CR not only returns with reintroduction of the prior association, but appears much more quickly than when the conditioning procedure first began. Can we see a second round of extinction if we again repeatedly offer the CS without the US (**Figure 8.8D**)? Just as the animal usually acquires the association between the US and the CS more quickly when they are paired in a second session, the animal's CR similarly is extinguished more rapidly during the second session when the CS is presented alone.

There's another demonstration that the learned association between the US and the CS is not gone completely after extinction. If we give the animal a "rest," where there are no presentations of either the US or the CS, and then present the CS (bell) alone, the animal may show a vigorous CR (salivation). This is an example of **spontaneous recovery**, when the previously extinguished CR in response to the CS returns after a period of rest (**Figure 8.8E**). Of course, if we present the CS alone over and over, the animal's response will quickly be extinguished again.

second-order conditioning Also called *secondary conditioning*. Learning in which a previously learned CS, which elicits a CR, repeatedly follows another neutral stimulus so that that second neutral stimulus also comes to elicit a CR.

stimulus generalization When the subject displays a CR to stimuli that are similar to, but not exactly identical to, the CS used in training.

extinction In classical conditioning, the loss of the conditioned response, caused by repeated presentation of the CS without the US.

spontaneous recovery The return of a previously extinguished CR in response to the CS after a period of rest.

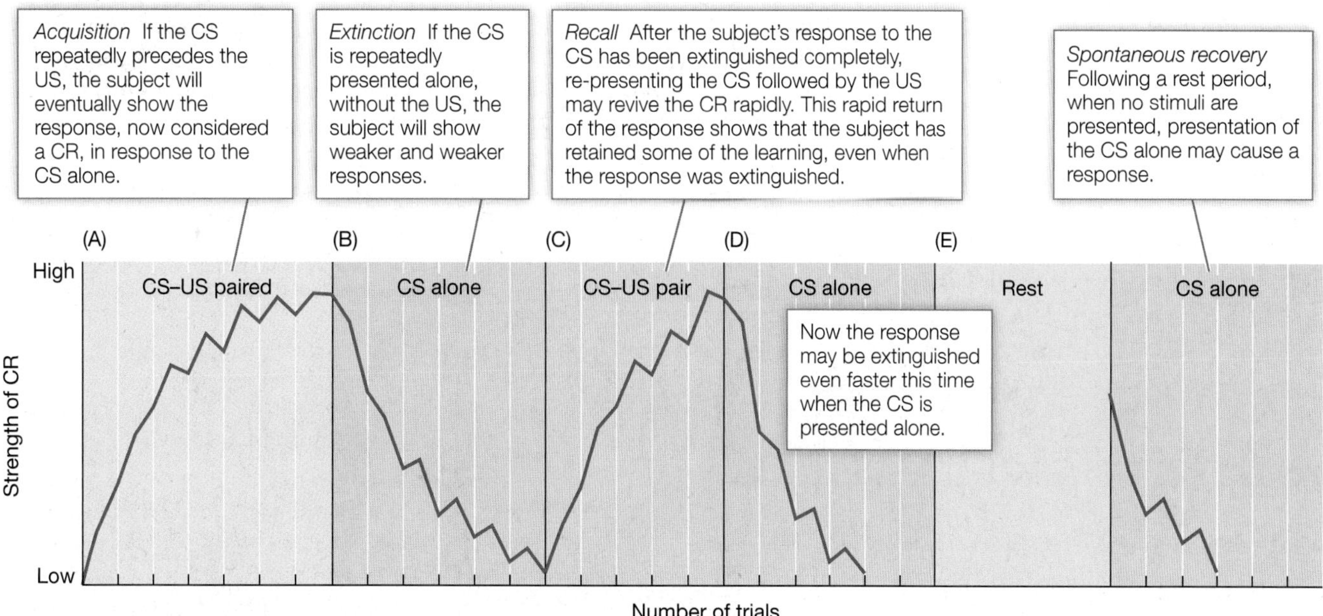

Figure 8.8 Acquisition, Extinction, and Spontaneous Recovery in Classical Conditioning

John Garcia (1917–2012)

Taste aversion proved the relevance of evolution to conditioning

By the mid-twentieth century, experimenters began a quest to try to find the most fundamental laws of learning, expecting that principles discovered from animal learning could be used to help humans learn. In general, this expectation would be well confirmed. For classical conditioning, one principle seemed obvious: animals could learn to associate any UR with any type of stimulus—a light, a tone, a touch on the back. No matter which stimulus was chosen for the CS, repeated pairing of that stimulus with the US would eventually cause the stimulus to elicit the response (a UR). How quickly the animal learned to associate that response with the stimulus seemed to be merely a question of how closely the US preceded the CS, and how often that pairing happened. There was great appeal to this notion that animals are learning "generalists," prepared by natural selection to be able to associate any two stimuli they might encounter in the world.

But this principle that animals could learn to produce any UR in response to any stimulus, that "all stimuli are created equal," was soon overturned by a newcomer to the field. John Garcia began life far away from academia, working his parent's farm until he was 20, then becoming a truck mechanic, a ship fitter, and an Army Air Corps intelligence specialist before attending college.

Perhaps because of his varied life experience, Garcia felt that some associations might be easier to learn than others. Some observations when studying the effect of X-rays on rats led him to think that animals might more readily associate nausea with tastes than with other stimuli. He set out to test this idea, as we'll see next in **Figure 8.9**.

☑ Researchers at Work

Some associations are made more readily than others

Figure 8.9 Taste Aversion (After Garcia & Koelling, 1966.)

■ **Question:** Are all stimuli really equal in their ability to invoke an unconditioned response?

■ **Hypothesis:** It may be adaptive to readily associate illness with taste (e.g., poisonous berries).

■ **Test:** Establish what dose of radiation would induce nausea in rats. Then study two groups of rats given an US of sweetened water followed by either (1) a buzzer, a flash of light, and a shock, or (2) a buzzer, a flash of light, and enough radiation to induce nausea.

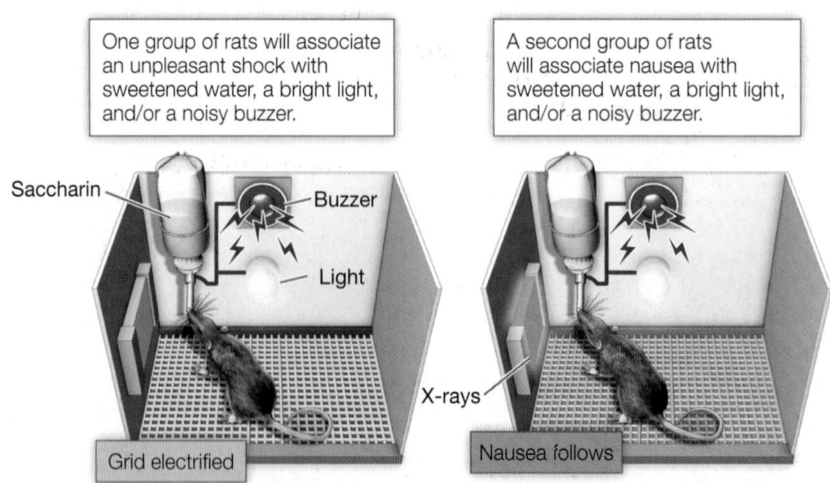

One group of rats will associate an unpleasant shock with sweetened water, a bright light, and/or a noisy buzzer.
A second group of rats will associate nausea with sweetened water, a bright light, and/or a noisy buzzer.
Saccharin
Buzzer
Light
X-rays
Grid electrified
Nausea follows

Follow up: After conditioning both groups, give rats a choice of sweet water alone, or plain water with the light and buzzer.

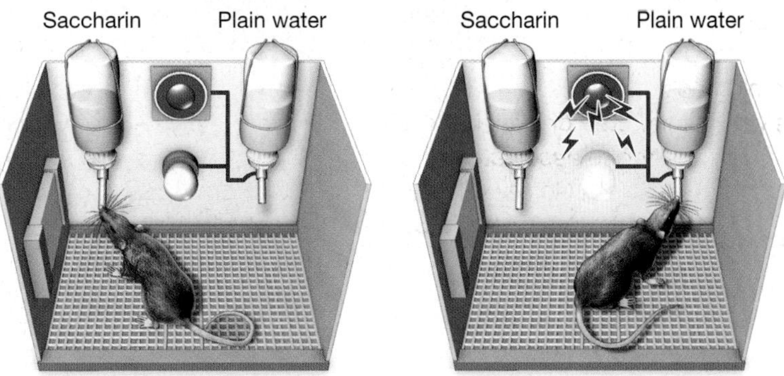

■ **Results:** Rats that had been shocked associated the shock with the noise and light, not with the sweet water, and continued to drink sweet water. Rats that had been sickened associated the nausea with the sweet water, and subsequently drank less sweet water than rats in the no-radiation group.

■ **Conclusion:** The particular stimulus used in classical conditioning does matter. Natural selection has favored the tendency to readily associate nausea with something we previously ate or drank. This may help us avoid ingesting poisons or toxins that make us ill.

conditioned taste aversion Also called *taste aversion* and *Garcia effect*. The acquired repulsion to a taste or flavor that was previously followed by nausea.

Later experiments revealed that rats associated a new taste with nausea so readily that a *single* pairing, the taste followed by nausea, was enough to cause them to avoid that taste in the future (**Figure 8.10**). Today this readily acquired aversion to a taste that has been followed by nausea is known as **conditioned taste aversion** (or simply, *taste aversion*, also sometimes called the *Garcia effect*). Despite the name, in fact it is the *flavor* of the food, that combination of odor and taste (see Section 6.5), the rats find aversive.

Conditioned taste aversion disproved three different ideas, widely held at the time, about classical conditioning:

1. that *all* stimuli could be associated equally well with a UR—Garcia's rats much more readily associated nausea with taste than with sound or lights;
2. that *repeated* pairings are needed to acquire an association—rats could learn to avoid a new taste after just *one* pairing with nausea; and
3. that the US must be presented *soon* after the CS, usually in a matter of seconds, for the animal to acquire the association—rats would associate taste with nausea that might arrive an *hour* later.

Garcia argued that natural selection works against those rules in the case of taste aversion. First, the predisposition to associate taste with illness is a survival strategy: nausea serves to signal a food as poisonous and supersedes sights and sounds as indicators of a poisonous food. If animals become ill, even once, after eating a new food, they avoid that food in the future. Indeed, rats outside the laboratory display *neophobia* (fear of new things) toward any new food item, eating just a little the first time they encounter it. Second, it is very adaptive for animals to show this aversion to the new food after just one trial—a second trial could be fatal. Finally, the ability of animals to associate a taste with nausea, even when nausea occurs an hour after the taste, makes perfect sense because sometimes poisonous food evokes symptoms hours after it's been eaten.

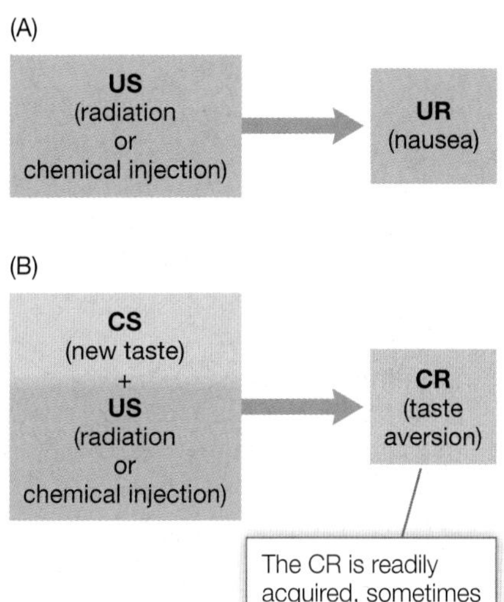

Figure 8.10 The Study of Taste Aversion (A) In experiments testing taste aversion, Garcia and colleagues used an unconditioned stimulus (US), such as radiation or chemical injections, to elicit the unconditioned response (UR) of nausea. (B) If a new taste was used as a conditioned stimulus (CS), presented just before the US, animals quickly learned to avoid that taste. Their avoidance of the taste (taste aversion) was a conditioned response (CR), which could be displayed after only one pairing of the taste with nausea and was very resistant to extinction.

Figure 8.11 Taste Aversion at Work A blue jay that eats a monarch butterfly soon becomes ill and will thereafter avoid eating other such butterflies.

Conditioned taste aversion was soon proven to be at work in the natural world. For example, a blue jay will readily snap up a tasty-looking monarch butterfly the first time it sees one. Score one for the blue jay. But toxins in the monarch's body will soon make the jay nauseated (**Figure 8.11**). From that point on, the blue jay will avoid eating any other monarch butterflies it might encounter. Presumably, the butterflies have evolved the ability to retain toxins in their bodies because the toxins make predators like the blue jay sick, and so less likely to eat such butterflies in the future. Along with the retained toxins, the butterflies have also evolved bright coloration to make them easy to recognize, so jays avoid them.

Many people have personally experienced conditioned taste aversion. In my family, the famous example is a party we hosted that was catered by a sushi restaurant. Later that night and the next day several partiers, including my youngest son, became ill with nausea and vomiting. It turned out that the sushi was *not* the cause of the illness. How do I know? Two days later my older son and his fiancée dropped in, and two days after that, they exhibited the same symptoms. So apparently we did not have food poisoning, but some virus that spread from person to person. Nevertheless, my youngest son, who loved sushi until that party, hasn't eaten a bite of it since. The strength of conditioned taste aversion has been tapped to solve several important problems (**Box 8.1**).

Conditioned taste aversion experiments represent one of the earliest demonstrations that natural selection shapes how well animals can learn various tasks. Later research revealed other types of adaptive learning in animals. For example, **imprinting** is the tendency of newly hatched birds to recognize and bond with the first moving object they see, and to follow it (Spalding, 1872). If that object is a man, they will follow him (**Figure 8.12**). Normally, of course, that first moving object is the mother, and so it is very adaptive for newly hatched chicks to learn

imprinting The behavior by which birds are predisposed to follow any moving object that they see shortly after hatching.

Figure 8.12 Follow Your Mother? Here Konrad Lorenz is being followed by goslings that had imprinted on him. John Garcia wrote about having chicks imprint on him as a farm boy (see Ellins, 2006).

Psychology in Everyday Life

BOX 8.1

Taste Aversion Saves Lives

Most people who experience conditioned taste aversion, getting sick after eating some distinctive food, report their aversion as a very strong, almost reflexive response. Even if intellectually they are convinced that the food was not the cause of the problem, they find that the very *idea* of that taste can make them feel nauseated. That strong, reflexive nature of conditioned taste aversion is another testament to its obvious adaptive significance, as is the evidence that this learning takes place in the evolutionarily older brainstem (Grill, 1985) rather than in the cortex.

In fact, the power of conditioned taste aversion has been proven in the wild. In a series of experiments, scientists laced sheep meat with chemicals and left it out for wild coyotes to consume. As predicted, the coyotes got ill after eating the tainted meat, and coyote predation on sheep flocks plummeted (Gustavson et al., 1982). Many scientists have advocated using conditioned taste aversion to control coyote populations that encroach on farmers, but usually poisons and kill traps are preferred. Similar experiments with captive coyotes and wolves have also been effective (see figure). One coyote that had been subjected to conditioned taste aversion to sheep meat actually ran away from a tiny lamb! Conditioned taste aversion has been used to protect the nesting grounds of endangered sandhill cranes. Scientists produced eggs that resembled the sandhill crane eggs and placed them in the nesting grounds after lacing them with drugs that produce nausea in the coyotes, raccoons, and crows that normally prey on the eggs (Nicolaus, 1987). Sure enough, far fewer of the genuine sandhill crane eggs were eaten by predators. In fact, those crows that had gotten ill eating the eggs would drive off other crows from the crane nests, apparently trying to spare their fellows from illness!

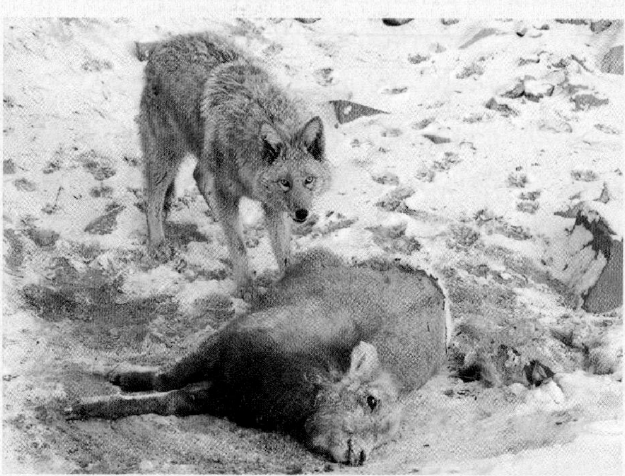

Coyote Versus Sheep Predators can be taught to dislike the taste of sheep.

Sometimes conditioned taste aversion is a bad thing. For example, most chemotherapy treatments for cancer induce severe nausea. That means people receiving chemotherapy may associate that nausea with whatever foods they had eaten beforehand. They may now be nauseated by those flavors. In addition to potentially depriving people of a food they had enjoyed before, the repeated process leaves people with fewer food options, so they lose weight just when their body needs nourishment to build up their defenses. Broberg and Bernstein (1987) exploited conditioned taste aversion by providing clients with a unique "scapegoat" taste (coconut- or root beer–flavored candy) just before chemotherapy. The idea was for the clients to attribute the nausea to the candy, not to the healthful normal foods they had eaten beforehand. Clients really came to hate that scapegoat taste, but they seemed to avoid associating *other* flavors with the nausea, and so were able to eat more between chemotherapy sessions (Mattos, 1994).

to recognize and follow her. We discussed this phenomenon in Section 5.2. The observation that some behaviors are more easily learned by one species than another is sometimes described as **biological constraints on learning** (or *biological preparedness to learn*). In Section 10.1, we'll see that many researchers believe humans are biologically prepared to learn a language readily as infants.

biological constraints on learning Also called *biological preparedness to learn.* The observation that some behaviors are more easily learned by one species than another.

Fear conditioning is a type of classical conditioning using a painful unconditioned stimulus

While animals appear to attribute nausea and illness to the taste of food rather than to sights or sounds, just about any stimulus can become associated with pain. Pavlov found that if a stimulus was followed by electrical shock, the animals that were previously indifferent to that stimulus would now show signs of fearfulness. Today most such experiments are done with rats, where the electri-

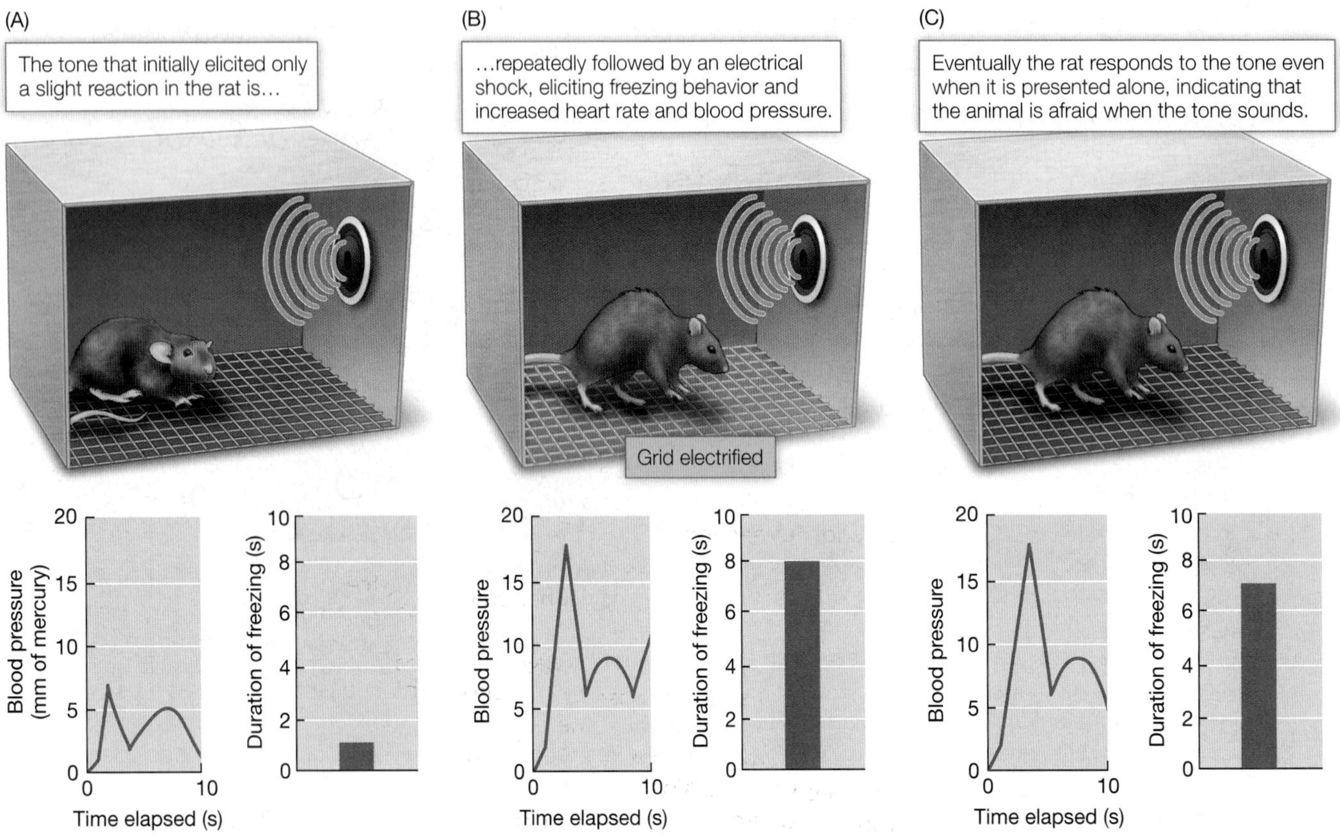
(A)
The tone that initially elicited only a slight reaction in the rat is...
(B)
...repeatedly followed by an electrical shock, eliciting freezing behavior and increased heart rate and blood pressure.
(C)
Eventually the rat responds to the tone even when it is presented alone, indicating that the animal is afraid when the tone sounds.
Grid electrified
Blood pressure (mm of mercury)
Duration of freezing (s)
Time elapsed (s)
Blood pressure
Duration of freezing (s)
Time elapsed (s)
Blood pressure
Duration of freezing (s)
Time elapsed (s)

Figure 8.13 Fear Conditioning

cal shock is delivered to the floor of the cage. Rats "tense up" when the shock is applied, which may help reduce the discomfort or may simply be a natural reaction to sudden pain. In the wild, animals often freeze when they detect a predator, which may keep the predator from noticing them.

A type of classical conditioning called **fear conditioning** involves pairing a previously neutral stimulus with a painful stimulus until the subject shows fearful responses to the first stimulus. In the typical experiment, a sound that elicited only a slight reaction from the rat originally (**Figure 8.13A**) is repeatedly presented just before electrical shock (**Figure 8.13B**). Eventually the animal learns to associate the sound with the shock, as we can tell when the animal freezes even if the sound is presented by itself. What's more, now the rat's blood pressure and heart rate both rise rapidly when the sound is presented (**Figure 8.13C**). In this case, the sound is the CS that is repeatedly paired with the US (shock) that normally elicits a UR (freezing, increased blood pressure and heart rate), until eventually the CS elicits the same responses as a CR. The observation that rats will freeze in response to a sound only if the sound accurately foretells a coming shock is an example of fear conditioning. In Section 13.1 we'll discuss how fear conditioning in animals results from changes in a brain region called the *amygdala*, and that people with damage to the amygdala don't seem to be afraid of anything. We'll also discuss posttraumatic stress disorder, which can be understood as the result of fear conditioning (see Box 13.2).

fear conditioning A type of classical conditioning, in which a previously neutral stimulus is repeatedly paired with a painful stimulus until the subject shows fearful responses to the first stimulus.

Fear conditioning is the type of classical conditioning that was administered to Little Albert, whom we met at the start of the chapter. The US was a sudden, intense noise and the CS was a furry rat, which Albert came to fear. Albert also showed stimulus generalization, which we discussed earlier, because he was afraid not just of a furry rat, but of any of a number of furry animals and objects. John Watson suggested that experiences such as Albert's could lead to a **phobia**, an irrational fear of particular objects or situations. We'll talk about phobia in further detail in Chapter 16, but note for now that a fear of truly dangerous objects, like a loaded gun, a sudden drop on a cliff, or a wild animal, is by definition *not* a phobia. Many people report having phobias of one sort or another, and the experience is one of feeling afraid despite knowing, intellectually, that the fear is an overreaction or even irrational. Some people can even remember an unpleasant experience where the object of the phobia played a part.

In laboratory experiments, an animal's fearful reaction to a previously neutral stimulus can be unlearned. The way to do that is to repeatedly present the previously neutral stimulus *without* shock. This is another example of extinction, presenting the CS without the US until the animal unlearns the association between the two. Eventually, the animal learns that the previously neutral stimulus no longer predicts shock, and the animal's fearful reaction to the stimulus abates. As in any other classical conditioning, if we wait a while and present the sound alone, the animal may show a reaction at first, an example of spontaneous recovery. Likewise, re-pairing the CS with the US, even just once, may quickly reinstate the animal's full response to the CS alone, until extinction sets in again.

There is another aspect of Little Albert's case to consider. In Albert's case, the previously neutral, now aversive stimuli were brought up close to him, and Albert showed a very natural response of *trying to get away from* the objects. Presumably Albert felt better, more secure, when he could get away from the furry objects. So in those last sessions intended to gauge Albert's fear, the baby was learning something new—how to move away from the feared objects so they no longer touched him, which made him feel better. In the next section we will concentrate on this other type of learning that Albert was showing, when actively doing something brings you something you want.

Frightening Hockey Mask? The *Friday the 13th* movies have paired the image of a hockey mask with many frightening scenes, so that now the mask itself may be unsettling.

phobia A marked, long-lasting fear of an object or situation that is out of proportion to the real danger.

8.1 SUMMARY

- The simplest forms of *learning*, such as *habituation*—the decreased response to a repeated *stimulus*—involve a single stimulus and are displayed by all animals. In true habituation, the subject is still capable of the response, and the sensory system has not adapted to the stimulus.
- *Sensitization* takes place when a strong, aversive stimulus causes a subject to show an exaggerated response to other stimuli. Such a stimulus can also cause a previously habituated response to return suddenly, a phenomenon known as *dishabituation*.
- The simpler forms of learning, which involve a single stimulus, are known as *non-associative learning*.
- Examples of *associative learning* include *classical conditioning*, the learning process by which repeated pairing of a neutral stimulus just before presentation of an *unconditioned stimulus* (US)—a stimulus that reflexively elicits a particular behavior—eventually causes the subject to show that same behavior in response to the previously neutral stimulus.
- In classical conditioning, the natural, often reflexive, response to a US is called the *unconditioned response* (*UR*), and a previously neutral stimulus that now evokes the response is called the *conditioned stimulus* (*CS*). Eventually the CS alone will elicit the response, which is then called a *conditioned response* (*CR*).
- The process of learning a classical conditioning task is called *acquisition*, while the loss of the conditioned response, caused by repeated presentation of the CS without the US, is *extinction*.

- *Second-order conditioning* takes place when a previously learned CS, which elicits a CR, repeatedly follows another neutral stimulus so that the second neutral stimulus also comes to elicit a CR.
- Subjects usually show *stimulus generalization*, displaying at least a partial response to stimuli that are similar to the CS.
- *Conditioned taste aversion* is the acquired aversion to a taste or flavor that has been followed by nausea. This is an example of a *biological constraint on learning*, as animals will much more readily associate nausea with a flavor than with a sound or a sight. Another example of a biological constraint on learning is *imprinting*, the behavior by which birds are predisposed to follow any moving object that they see shortly after hatching.
- Repeated pairing of a neutral stimulus followed by an aversive stimulus, such as loud sound or pain, induces *fear conditioning* such that the subject now shows aversive responses to the previously neutral stimulus.

REVIEW QUESTIONS

1. Describe the simplest types of learning and explain why they are adaptive.
2. Describe an example of classical conditioning as it might be done in a lab, being sure to include the specific terms for the various stimuli and responses. Now describe an instance of classical conditioning in everyday life, applying those same terms for the stimuli and responses.
3. What is conditioned taste aversion, and how does it seem to violate some rules of classical conditioning?

Food for Thought

Why do you think ranchers and farmers are reluctant to rely on conditioned taste aversion to control animals that prey on livestock?

8.2 Reinforcing Behavior

Things to Learn

- Law of effect
- Operant conditioning and shaping
- Superstitions in pigeons and people
- Reinforcement and punishment
- Active and passive avoidance
- Reinforcement schedules

The learning we've considered so far is relatively simple: learning from a single stimulus, as in habituation, or learning that there is a predictable relationship between two stimuli, as in classical conditioning. It's easy to see these as rather passive forms of learning, imagining that the subject is simply sitting there idle, waiting for stimuli to come along and then either reacting or not. But organisms in real life are not passive. They move about, using their senses to explore the environment to find food, shelter, and companionship, while trying to avoid harsh weather, predators, or those people trying to get you to buy something you don't want. In these real-life conditions, we and other animals are constantly learning which of our actions bring the outcomes we want, and which actions avoid the outcomes we don't want.

Probably humans have always known that we and other animals learn in this way, but it wasn't until the twentieth century that people began studying such learning in a truly systematic, scientific fashion. Using animal models, scientists uncovered fascinating details about how this learning takes place, and about which factors promote or impede it. Amazingly, almost everything discovered about this type of learning in animals, down to the details of the best way to reward behaviors, turned out to apply to our own species as well.

In this section you'll learn about an important field of psychological research that proved to be immediately relevant to human behavior. As you read, you may want to think about how to use these principles to improve your own life, to learn faster how to achieve the life outcomes you want and avoid the outcomes you don't.

Live and learn: Thorndike's law of effect

Edward L. Thorndike (1874–1949) had a lifelong interest in how we learn. The young Edward distinguished himself as a brilliant student, but became skeptical of the idea that we can learn very much by sitting in a classroom listening to someone lecture to us. He was also strongly influenced by Darwin's theory of evolution, so when he had difficulty getting human subjects for his graduate studies, he began studying learning in non-human animals.

Thorndike studied cats and dogs in famous experiments where a hungry animal was placed inside a **puzzle box**, basically a cage equipped with levers and latches so the animal could open a door to escape. To encourage the animal to escape, Thorndike placed attractive food just outside the box (**Figure 8.14**). He would then carefully measure how long it took the cat or dog to get out of the puzzle box. Thorndike assumed the animals would not be able to simply look at the levers, pulleys, and chains and reason how to open the door. And indeed, the first time an animal was placed in a particular puzzle box, it became very active but its behavior seemed random, not directed at any particular part of the box. Therefore it might take the animal quite a while to escape the first time.

But after escaping from the box the first time, what about the next times? If the animal had actually figured out how that puzzle box worked, then we would expect it to go straight to the correct latch and quickly solve the puzzle. We would know when the animal had finally made this insight because it would solve the box quickly on that trial and every trial thereafter. While it is true that an animal generally got out of the box faster with each subsequent trial, Thorndike noted that the process seemed very gradual and rather hit-or-miss. In other words, there was no evidence that the animal ever gained an "insight" into the puzzle box. It might open the door quickly in one trial and take longer in the next one (**Figure 8.15A**).

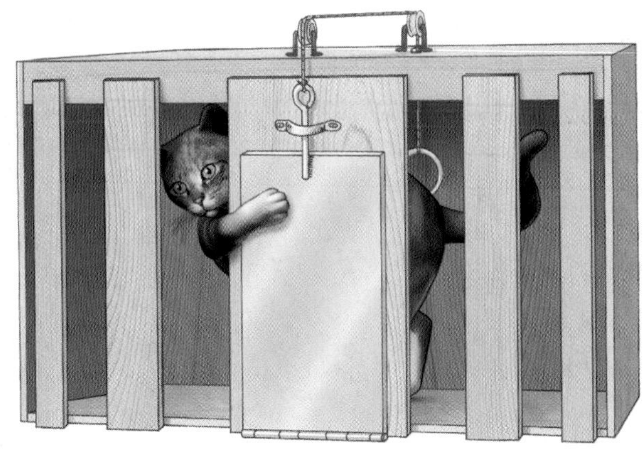

Figure 8.14 Puzzle Boxes Animals had to figure out how to open the box to get to the food. (After Thorndike, 1911.)

puzzle box A cage equipped with levers and latches so that an animal must open a door to escape.

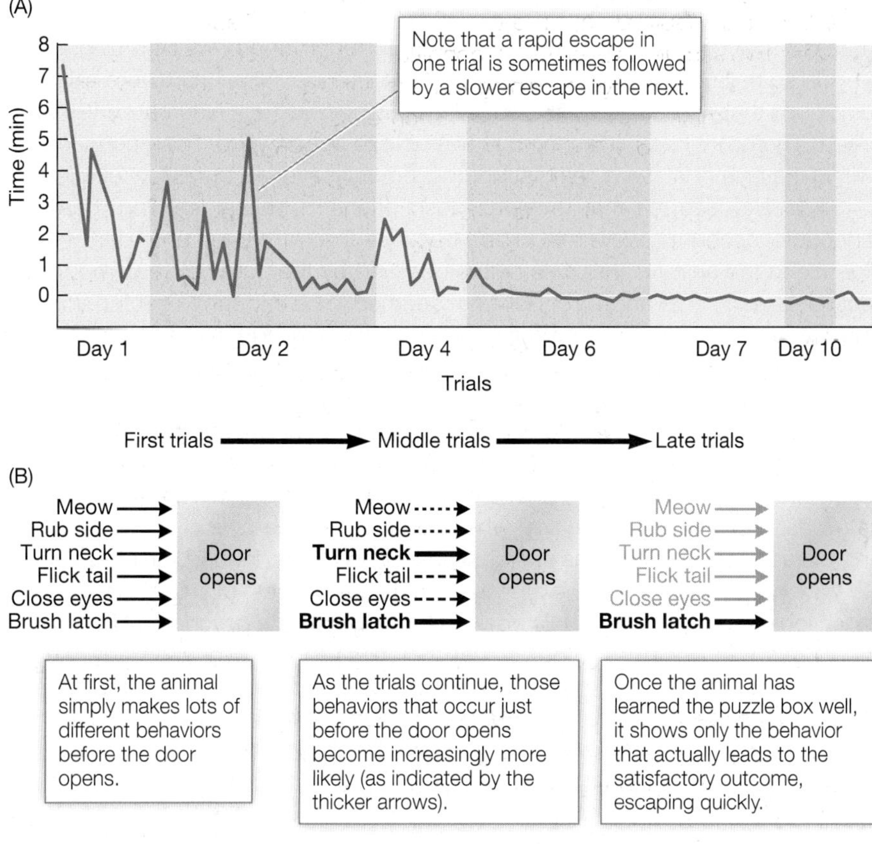

Figure 8.15 Trial and Error in Solving the Puzzle Box (A) Escape times for cat number 10 in one particular puzzle box. (B) A model of Thorndike's law of effect.

Thorndike concluded that animals solved the puzzle boxes by *trial and error*, moving about more or less at random until the door popped open. That meant the learning process, rather than being sudden and insightful, was gradual, incremental. With each trial, the animal seemed to learn just a little bit more.

What, exactly, was the animal learning? In Thorndike's view, the animal was learning to connect a particular *response* with the pleasant *outcome* of the door opening. Because the animal's behavior was unguided and random (nearly frantic sometimes), the first few times it managed to open the door, many different responses preceded that outcome (**Figure 8.15B**). Only one of those responses, brushing against a latch in this case, caused the door to open, but the cat had no way of knowing that. However, with repeated trials, only that behavior of brushing against the latch *always* preceded the door opening, so the animal was exposed to the repeated pairing of response (brushing against the latch) and satisfactory outcome (door opening). With each pairing of the response with the outcome, the connection between the two was strengthened until the animal learned which response opened the door to provide food (see Figure 8.15B).

To explain this type of learning, Thorndike proposed the **law of effect**: of the various responses a subject makes in a particular situation, those responses that are quickly followed by a satisfactory outcome are more likely to recur the next time the subject is in that situation. The law also predicts that any response quickly followed by an *unpleasant* outcome will be *less* likely to recur in the future. Thorndike conceived the process as one in which mental connections are strengthened for responses that produce good outcomes (see Figure 8.15B) and weakened for responses that produce bad outcomes, so his view was sometimes referred to as *connectionism*. Learning "stamps in" the connections, while forgetting causes connections to fade.

Although Thorndike thought of learning as a strengthening of some connections within the brain, he felt we can productively study learning by observing behavior without concerning ourselves with questions about how the brain actually makes those connections. He was content to regard the brain as a single unit. This is sometimes called a *black box perspective*, as if the brain were simply a black box that we can study without ever opening it up (Von Neumann, 1951). Indeed, Thorndike had no technology available to actually find those connections within the brain that were being strengthened or weakened by his law of effect.

Thorndike also felt that previous descriptions of animal learning, basically anecdotal accounts, were misguided because they attributed an order of intelligence to the animals that was neither justified by the data nor required for an animal to learn. Trial-and-error behavior seemed to be enough to get the animals out of the box. Thorndike's perspectives, regarding the brain as a black box and rejecting the idea that animals rely on reasoning and insight, would continue to shape studies of learning.

The perspective that psychologists should only study externally visible behavior rather than make inferences about internal processes was called **behaviorism** by John B. Watson, whom we met at the start of the chapter. For Watson, behaviorism was the future of psychology, which would reveal the laws of learning, including the acquisition of phobias such as the one he tried to induce in Little Albert.

Watson (1913) rejected the study of mental processes, events such as introspection or consciousness. His position would dominate psychology for several generations. It became taboo for psychologists to even mention any mental process that might be going on inside that "black box" between the rat's ears. The extreme version of this perspective, sometimes called *radical behaviorism*, might consider a child to be a "blank slate," which in Latin is a *tabula rasa* (see Section 1.1). On this idea Watson declared,

law of effect The notion, proposed by Thorndike, that any behavior that results in a satisfactory outcome is more likely to recur in the future.

behaviorism The perspective that psychologists should study only observable behavior and not subjective mental events.

Give me a dozen healthy infants, well-formed, and my own specified world to bring them up in and I'll guarantee to take any one at random and train him to become any type of specialist I might select—doctor, lawyer, artist, merchant-chief and, yes, even beggar-man and thief, regardless of his talents, penchants, tendencies, abilities, vocations, and race of his ancestors.

(*Watson, 1924, p. 82.*)

By this time, Watson himself was no longer doing *any* experiments, with infants or anyone else. Fired for having an affair with the graduate student who helped him conduct the Little Albert study, Watson went into advertising (where he made much more money than as a professor).

As vocal and articulate as Watson was, behaviorism's dominance in psychology for 50 years was primarily due to another scientist, whom we'll consider next.

Everyone likes to be rewarded

B. F. Skinner wanted to be a novelist but soon gave that up to get a doctorate in psychology instead. As a graduate student, Skinner funneled his creativity into building devices to study learning in animals. Rather than build ever-more elaborate puzzle boxes like Thorndike did, Skinner sought to *standardize* testing so that he could systematically vary conditions to see how they affected learning. To do this Skinner built boxes that could easily accommodate an animal subject, usually a rat or a pigeon, offering the animal a chance to learn a simple task, such as pressing down on a bar to cause a small pellet of food to fall into a nearby hopper (**Figure 8.16**). Skinner found that rats would quickly learn to press the bar to get the food.

This type of learning was in some ways the reverse of Pavlov's classical conditioning, where a particular stimulus (meat powder or an air puff) elicited the animal's behavior (salivation or eye blinks). In Skinner's chambers, the animal's behavior (a bar press) elicited the stimulus (food). To distinguish it from classical conditioning, Skinner termed such learning, where the subject's behavior *operated* on the environment, controlling what would happen next, **operant conditioning**. Therefore Skinner named his chambers **operant conditioning chambers**, but most people refer to them informally as *Skinner boxes*. Operant conditioning is sometimes called *instrumental learning* because the subject's behavior is instrumental to what happens next. In both operant conditioning and classical conditioning, there is an association between a stimulus and the animal's behavior. In classical conditioning the stimulus comes to elicit a behavior, while in operant conditioning a behavior comes to elicit a stimulus. Because in both cases a stimulus and response become *associated* together, both instrumental learning and classical conditioning are sometimes referred to as *associative learning*, when a particular stimulus and a particular response come to be associated together. We may say that the subject learns to associate a particular stimulus with a particular response.

A rat in a Skinner box learns to associate bar pressing with the delivery of food. The delivery of food makes the animal more likely to press the bar in the future, *reinforcing* that particular behavior. So Skinner called the food a **reinforcer**, a stimulus that appears in response to behavior

operant conditioning Also called *instrumental learning*. A form of associative learning in which the likelihood that an act will be performed depends on the consequences that follow it.

operant conditioning chambers Also called *Skinner boxes*. Cages in which animals can learn to do a simple task, such as press a bar, to obtain a reward.

reinforcer A stimulus that appears in response to behavior and increases the probability of that behavior recurring.

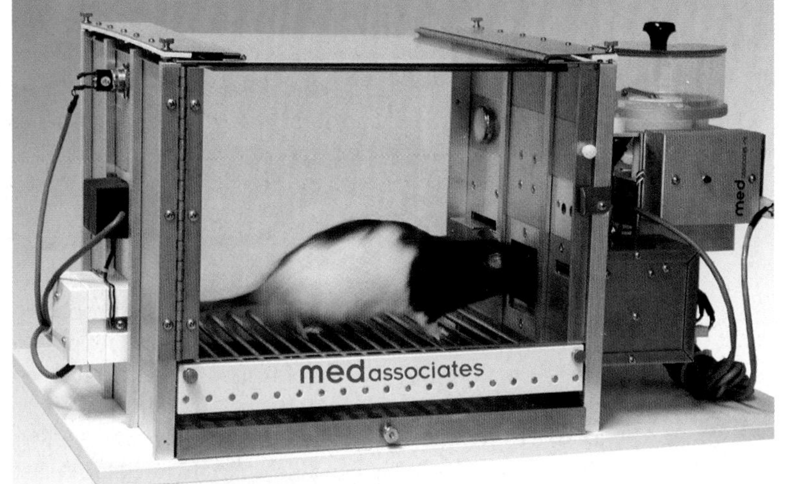

Figure 8.16 Learning to Press a Lever While B. F. Skinner preferred to call this an operant conditioning chamber, or lever box, it came to be known as a "Skinner box."

Skeptic at Large

BOX 8.2

Operant Conditioning for Fun and Profit

Would you be willing to bet a dollar that you could beat someone at tic-tac-toe? Even if your opponent got to choose the first square? If you know much about playing tic-tac-toe, you'll say no, because if your opponent knows the game well, he or she can *always* draw a tie.

But would you be more interested if your opponent was a chicken? In various parts of the country, you can put coins in a slot for the chance to beat a live chicken at tic-tac-toe (see figure). You choose your move and then the hen pecks at a screen to choose her move. At one Las Vegas casino, people could play for free with a $10,000 payoff promised, but they were limited in how many times they were allowed to play each day (Padgett, 2002). The casino presumably offered the free play in hopes of luring customers to spend money in other gambling opportunities. Strangely, it's not clear that any humans ever beat the various hens that took turns playing.

Who's the Better Player? There are two examples of operant conditioning in this photo. The hen plays the game to get food. The human plays in hopes of getting money. One of them is making a smarter move than the other.

How do the hens learn to play? First, it's clear that these animals have been taught through operant conditioning to peck at the screen: after each game is either tied or won by the hen, food drops into a hopper (yes, the birds work for chicken feed). Indeed, as soon as the human opponent makes his or her move, the hen quickly pecks at the screen. At first glance, the phenomenal success of the hens at tying or beating humans in a game of strategy seems to be a tremendous testimonial to the power of operant conditioning. The hens seem to have learned to peck exactly the right square in each of hundreds of different situations, in response to the humans' moves.

But are the birds really playing tic-tac-toe, really choosing which square to occupy next? Notice that there is a metal plate (labeled "Think'in Booth") in front of the hen's screen, so we can't really see the screen. The trainer says the screen helps the chickens focus on the task, but for all we know, the hens can peck anywhere on the screen to trigger the next move and a computer program may decide which square to fill in. I first saw one of these hen-playing tic-tac-toe booths as a teenager visiting Hot Springs, Arkansas. It was before the advent of personal computers, and the various moves were displayed by bulbs lighting up on the board. But even then it was fairly simple to wire a board to "choose" the correct next move (especially because the hens always got the first move and it was always the same square). Perhaps the hens really do learn to make different moves depending on the state of the game in play, but I'll not believe it until I can actually see the bird choose one square over another. In the meantime, it is impressive that the hens learn to peck the screen eagerly when it's their turn. It's even more impressive that people will line up and *pay* up in the hopes of besting a chicken.

and increases the probability of that behavior recurring. Food is not the only reinforcer, of course. Animals will learn to press a bar to receive water, or access to a sexual partner, or even to receive an injection of a drug like cocaine. These sorts of reinforcers probably cause dopamine to be released in the reward pathway of the brain (Olds & Milner, 1954) that we discussed in Section 7.4, and will take up in more detail in Section 12.4. Although the most commonly tested behavior was pressing a bar, animals could learn to do almost anything in order to receive a reinforcer. **Box 8.2** presents an interesting application of this concept.

Skinner boxes taught us a tremendous amount about learning, in part because the standardized situation allowed for a very systematic approach. For

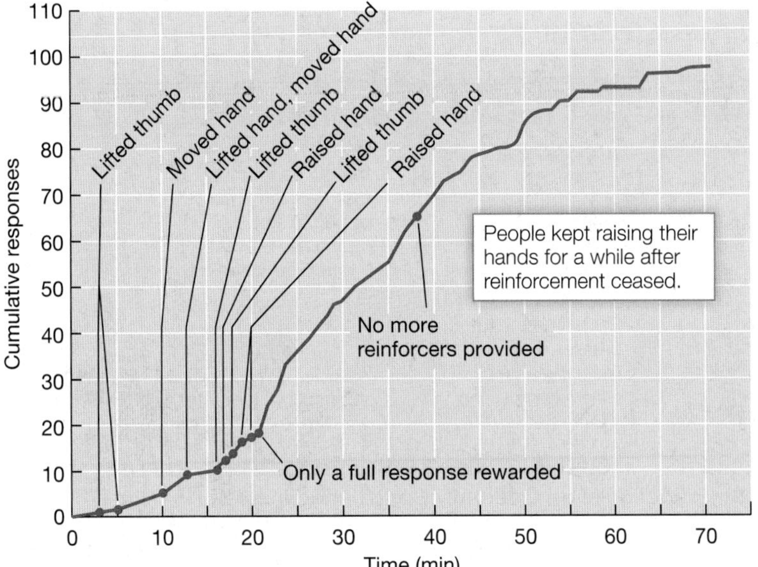

Figure 8.17 Shaping Human Behavior
Subjects were not told what they should do. But they were told when they had earned "points" with their behavior. In this case the experimenter wanted them to raise their hand, so at first participants were given rewards for raising a thumb, then for moving their hand, until they could only earn points when they raised their hand. Only about half the participants could describe what they were doing to earn points. (After Verplanck, 1956.)

example, rats left unattended in the chamber would eventually learn to press the lever to get food, but the experimenter could help them catch on sooner through **shaping**, initially providing reinforcers whenever the subject came close to making the desired response. For example, at first the experimenter might cause some food to drop into the hopper whenever the animal approached the bar. Then the experimenter might cause food to appear only when the animal touched the bar, which would soon lead to the animal pressing down on the bar, causing the food to appear automatically. Skinner invented a device to record the animal's behavior as a *cumulative response*, where time runs along the *x*-axis and the line goes up each time the subject performs the response, such as pressing a bar.

shaping The process by which a subject is readily provided with a reinforcer whenever the subject comes close to showing the desired behavior, and then is required to come closer and closer to that desired behavior before receiving the reinforcer.

The behavior of people can be shaped too. In one classic experiment, people were told they would get a "point" whenever they did some particular behavior, but weren't told what that behavior was. In the case of **Figure 8.17**, the behavior was raising the hand (Verplanck, 1956). At first the participants gained points for lifting a thumb, then for moving the hand, until finally only by raising a hand could they gain points. Although participants clearly increased their display of the reinforced behavior, only about half of them could identify what they were doing to gain points.

The effectiveness of shaping, which might have been considered simply a way of speeding up experiments, in fact offered an important lesson. By rewarding participants in stages, encouraging the *beginning* of the desired behavior and requiring participants to come closer and closer to the final product, it is possible not only to speed up learning, but also to teach highly complex behaviors. You can even teach animal subjects a *chain* of responses, learning first to climb a ladder, then ring a bell, then push a ball.

This notion of shaping behavior gradually was widely adapted by educators around the world. If you ever have the chance to teach a youngster to tie her shoes, try shaping, and chaining behaviors, starting at the end of the process. First make the loops for her and teach her how to pull that final loop through. Then teach her how to make the loops, then how to set up the loops, and so on. You don't need tiny food pellets for a reinforcer. Your praise at each step will be enough.

Recall that in classical conditioning, if you stop pairing the stimuli together, repeatedly ringing the bell without providing the meat powder, the subject even-

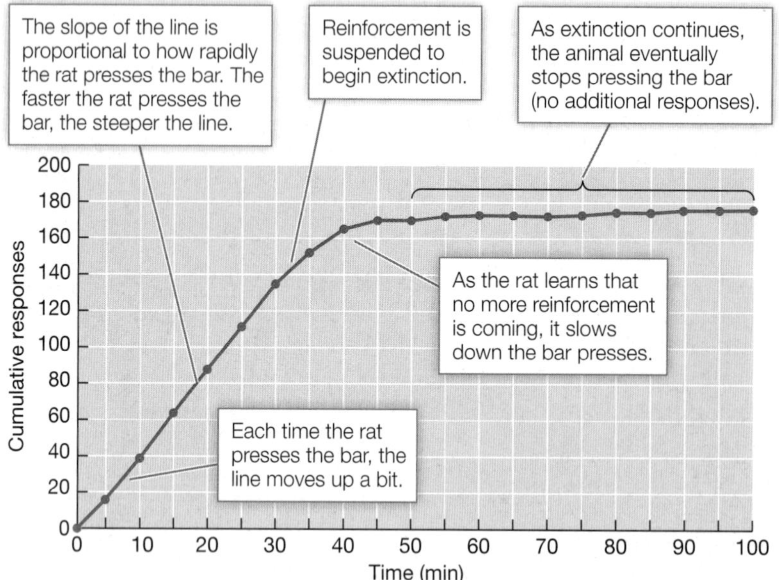
The slope of the line is proportional to how rapidly the rat presses the bar. The faster the rat presses the bar, the steeper the line.
Reinforcement is suspended to begin extinction.
As extinction continues, the animal eventually stops pressing the bar (no additional responses).
As the rat learns that no more reinforcement is coming, it slows down the bar presses.
Each time the rat presses the bar, the line moves up a bit.
Cumulative responses
0
20
40
60
80
100
120
140
160
180
200
0
10
20
30
40
50
60
70
80
90
100
Time (min)

Figure 8.18 Extinction of an Operantly Conditioned Behavior in a Rat

superstition The false belief that a particular behavior will bring about a stimulus or event.

positive reinforcement The addition of a stimulus following a behavior, increasing the likelihood of that behavior.

tually stops showing a conditioned response (extinction). In operant conditioning, extinction is the gradual disappearance of the operantly conditioned response when reinforcement is no longer provided. If we stop providing the food pellets, the rat will soon stop pressing the bar (**Figure 8.18**). As in classical conditioning, extinction in operant conditioning can be reversed if we again provide reinforcements for the behavior.

Another insight about human learning came to Skinner when he had the operant chambers provide food to pigeons *at random*, with no reference whatsoever to the bird's behavior. He noticed that some birds acted as though their behavior mattered. One bird might repeatedly stick its head in a corner while another might turn around counterclockwise in the chamber. Skinner inferred that each bird initially had been doing a particular behavior when the food first appeared. Some of them then seemed to think their behavior was *causing* the food to appear, so they kept displaying that behavior. For Skinner, the animals were displaying **superstition**, the false belief that a particular behavior will bring about a stimulus or event. Each pigeon performed a ritual, thinking it was causing the reinforcer to appear. Baseball players are famous for displaying many superstitious behaviors, where both hitters and pitchers (**Figure 8.19**) may go through elaborate rituals before every pitch.

Figure 8.19 **A Superstitious Athlete** Nicknamed "The Bird" for his resemblance to the popular Sesame Street character, Mark Fidrych became famous for his antics on the mound, fidgeting, talking to the ball, and carefully arranging the dirt. He had a terrific rookie season in 1976—19 wins. By 1981, however, after five abbreviated seasons, Fidrych was out of the majors.

So far I've talked about reinforcers that are pleasant, like food, water, or a strikeout. But technically, a reinforcer is a stimulus that, upon following a behavior, makes the individual more likely to do that behavior again. That means that reinforcers can be either pleasant or unpleasant, as we'll see next.

Reinforcement and punishment can be positive or negative

Four different kinds of stimuli can change the probability that a behavior will recur (Skinner, 1969). *Reinforcements* are stimuli that make a behavior *more* likely to recur, while *punishments* make the behavior *less* likely to recur. There are two kinds of reinforcements and two kinds of punishment. **Positive reinforcement** is when a favorable stimulus, such as a tasty bit of food, is *added* following a particular behavior, thus increasing the probability of that behavior. **Negative reinforcement** happens when a behavior is followed by the *removal* of an aversive stimulus, such as being cooped up in a cage in one of Thorndike's puzzle boxes (where animals also had a positive reinforcement of gaining food once they got out), or to get away from foot shock or a loud noise. Often, as in these cases, the negative reinforcement can be thought of as an escape, as we'll discuss shortly. Notice that both positive and negative reinforcements can be thought of as a reward: either gaining something desired or losing something despised. Also, they are "reinforcements" because when they follow a behavior, they "reinforce" it, making it more likely to appear again. In this terminology, the words "positive" and "negative" simply indicate whether something is being provided to or taken away from the subject.

There are also two kinds of punishments, stimuli that make the behavior *less* likely to recur. **Positive punishment** following a response makes the behavior less likely to happen in the future, and is usually an aversive stimulus, like spanking. It's certainly not "positive" in the sense of being enjoyed. It is positive in the sense that the stimulus was not present before the response was made, but is *added* to the scene once the response occurs. In contrast, **negative punishment** is more like a penalty, when a stimulus is *removed* after a particular response. For example, depriving a teenager of freedom (grounding) in response to "bad behavior" is a negative punishment.

Stimulus type	Increase the behavior	Decrease the behavior
	Reinforcements following a behavior make it more likely to appear again.	Punishments following a behavior make it less like to appear again.
Pleasant	*Positive reinforcement*: Add reward. Reward the child's good behavior with smiles and a compliment.	*Negative punishment*: Remove reward. When the child misbehaves, take away her favorite toy.
Unpleasant (aversive)	*Negative reinforcement*: Remove aversive stimulus. When the child behaves well, end a "time-out."	*Positive punishment*: Add aversive stimulus. When the child misbehaves, enforce a "time-out."

Figure 8.20 Overview of Different Types of Reinforcements and Punishments

negative reinforcement The removal of a stimulus following a behavior, increasing the likelihood of that behavior.

positive punishment The addition of a stimulus following a response, decreasing the likelihood of that behavior.

negative punishment The removal of a stimulus following a response, decreasing the likelihood of that behavior.

It is not always easy to decide which of these four categories a real-life stimulus fits into—sometimes the lines are blurred. For example, a father grocery shopping with a young daughter in the seat of the cart goes to the first available checkout counter, which has an array of yummy looking candy on display. Suppose the child starts crying for candy that the father doesn't want to buy—how might he change the child's behavior? When she pauses in her crying, he might smile at her and praise her for not crying, being such a good girl. This would be a case of positive (Dad added smiling and praise) reinforcement (she continues to sit quietly). Or, when she starts crying, he might take away a toy she's carrying and tell her she can't have it until she stops. That would be a punishment (she stops crying) and it's negative because he removed the toy. Alternatively, when she starts crying he could give her a time-out, which is a positive (adding a timeout) punishment (her crying is reduced). Then once she becomes quiet, he could lift the time-out, which is a reinforcement (she continues being quiet) that is negative (he removed the aversive time-out). Notice that in the case of the timeout, whether that is punishment or reinforcement depends on which of the child's behaviors you're considering (being quiet or crying) and which stimulus you're considering (adding the time-out or lifting the time-out). It is always important to be clear about which particular behavior you are considering when classifying stimuli as reinforcement or punishment, and which stimulus you're considering when classifying it as positive or negative. **Figure 8.20** offers an overview of the different types of reinforcements and punishments.

Punishment can be counterproductive

The 1960s and 1970s were marked by a debate on whether it is ever appropriate or effective to use punishment in child rearing. Researchers pointed out a number of "side effects" to punishment—including fear. Making the child afraid of the parent may cause more problems in the future. Because certain types of punishment—such as spanking—constitute aggressive behaviors, might the parent be teaching the child a bad behavior (aggression) while trying to discourage another? Moreover, if the parent spanking a child is angry, the punishment may go too far. Also, if punishment is used inconsistently, the child may not be able to predict when it might come and in that case he may simply "give up" rather than try to figure out how to behave. And in some instances punishment simply ends up teaching the child certain behaviors are to be avoided only when parents are around! By the end of the debate, most experts agreed that reinforcement with rewards was usually better than punishment.

However, some analyses of the effects of punishment in children were not very well controlled. It's true that children who are spanked a lot have more behavioral problems as they grow older than children who are not spanked much (Gershoff, 2002; MacKenzie et al., 2013). But what if those two groups of children were already different from one another in the first place? In other words, maybe children with certain dispositions or disorders are more likely than other children to elicit punishments from their guardians. As one journalist put it, "the debate over spanking is short on science, high on emotion" (Sanders, 2014). There's simply no ethical way to rigorously test whether spanking does more harm than good. Some psychologists have suggested that if you start with a comparable group of children, say those who already display antisocial behaviors, then those who are occasionally swatted for inappropriate behavior may actually benefit compared with those who are not swatted (Larzelere & Kuhn, 2005). Of course, there are other ways of punishing without spanking, such as the time-out example we discussed above.

Psychologists argue that punishment should be used sparingly, and only in combination with lots of positive reinforcements, including praise. After all, discouraging bad behavior won't help teach the child what good behaviors are. For those cases where punishment is used, there are several guidelines to make sure it is effective. First, it needs to be swift, coming soon after the offense, so the child clearly understands what behavior precipitated the swat or time-out. For the same reason, it is important to explain to the child what behavior triggered the punishment and why it was inappropriate. This may also avoid having the child become afraid of the parent. Finally, punishments must be used consistently to be effective.

Active avoidance is especially resistant to extinction

One particular type of negative reinforcement (increasing a behavior by removing an aversive stimulus) is **escape conditioning** (or "escape learning"). In this case, an animal is subjected to an unpleasant stimulus, say a loud noise or an electrical shock, and must learn to do something to stop that stimulus. Pavlov studied such behavior in dogs put in a chamber divided into two parts by a small barrier. If the dog was given a mild electrical shock, it could escape that shock by hopping over the barrier to the other side. Later, when shock was applied to that side, the dog could again escape by jumping over the barrier. Soon the dogs learned to hop back and forth over that barrier as soon as the shock began. Although Pavlov is famous for classical conditioning, note that this is an *operant* conditioning task: the dog is operating on the environment by jumping over that barrier.

If Pavlov gave the dogs a warning before the shock, such as sounding a tone, they could jump over the barrier to avoid the shock entirely. Soon, whenever the tone sounded, the dogs would readily hop over the barrier to avoid the shock. This response became known as **active avoidance**, when the subject must display a particular behavior to avoid an unpleasant stimulus (**Figure 8.21A**). Note that here the shock is an example of negative reinforcement (the hopping behavior increases because the aversive stimulus is removed). This is perhaps the simplest form of active avoidance, to run away. In nature, we reflexively pull our hand away from hot objects, and it makes sense to move away from anything that's hurting us.

Once a dog had learned this task, Pavlov found it very difficult to get the animal to *unlearn* it. In other words, it was hard to extinguish the dog's response. Because the dog faithfully jumped over the barrier every time the tone sounded,

escape conditioning A form of negative reinforcement in which the subject learns to perform a response to remove an aversive stimulus.

active avoidance A response a subject has learned to avoid an aversive stimulus.

it had no way of knowing that the shock was never applied. As far as the dog knew, the reason the shock never came was because it had hopped over the barrier. Eventually Pavlov found that the only way to extinguish the active avoidance, to teach the animal that the tone no longer predicted an oncoming shock, was to close the space between the two compartments, making it impossible for the dog to get to the other side (**Figure 8.21B**). After the dog had been exposed to the tone many times in this condition without shock, Pavlov would gradually lower the barrier. Now the dog could get over, but it was difficult so sometimes it failed to jump over (and, of course, no shock came). Eventually the dog had easy access to both sides and would no longer jump over when the tone sounded.

Irrational fears, or phobias, have been connected to the difficulty we have in extinguishing active avoidance. John Watson suggested that Little Albert's fear of furry objects was likely to persist unless it was extinguished by "accident," such as the boy being forced to be near furry objects without anything bad happening. The films of Little Albert make it clear that after the classical conditioning made him associate furry objects with loud noises, he actively moved to get away from the rat and other furry objects. If as he grew up, Albert always avoided furry things, he couldn't learn they might be harmless.

As we mentioned in Section 1.2, Mary Cover Jones (1924) brought a feared object (a rabbit) closer and closer to eliminate a phobia in a boy (not Little Albert). In Section 16.2, we'll describe this approach, known as systematic desensitization.

Animals can also learn **passive avoidance**, when subjects must *refrain* from showing a particular behavior to avoid unpleasant stimuli. In the simplest case, the animal must learn to do nothing, just stay still when the stimulus arrives, to avoid shock. In Section 16.2 we'll talk about people with extreme social phobia, who are afraid people will belittle them and hurt their feelings. By staying in their homes, an instance of passive avoidance, they never learn that some social encounters can be pleasant and rewarding.

(A)

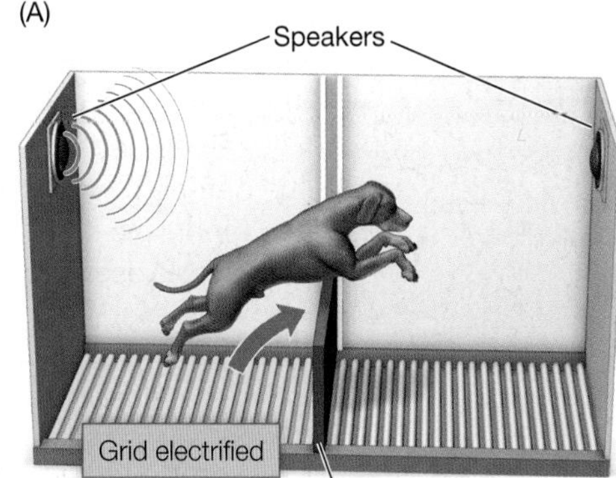

When the tone sounds, the dog can avoid being shocked by hopping over the barrier.

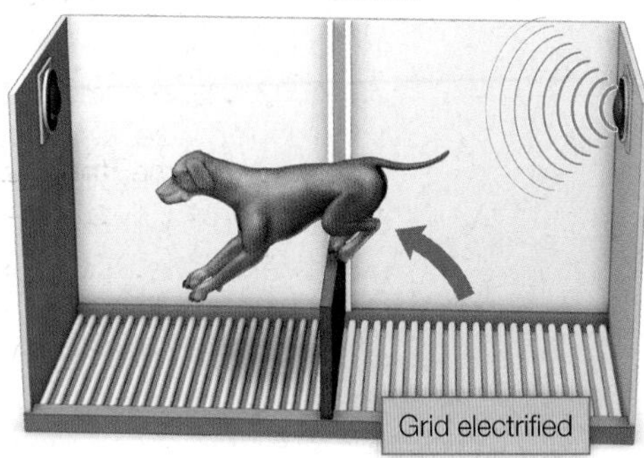

Now the dog must hop back over the barrier to avoid the shock signaled by the tone. Soon the dog hops over the barrier every time the tone sounds, so it *never learns whether the shock still arrives.*

(B)

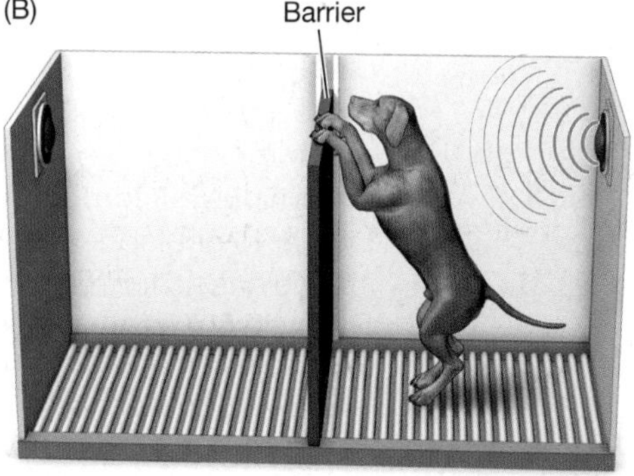

Only by being restrained, forced to stay in place when the tone sounds, can the dog learn to extinguish the active avoidance behavior.

Figure 8.21 Active Avoidance Behaviors Are Difficult to Extinguish (A) Acquisition of active avoidance. (B) Enforced extinction of active avoidance.

Perhaps the most disturbing form of learning with aversive stimuli is **learned helplessness**, when a subject learns that there is *no response* that can prevent an aversive stimulus. In the first studies of learned helplessness, dogs were put in harnesses and either released a while later or given an electrical shock (Seligman & Maier, 1967). The electrical shock was delivered to pairs of dogs, each given the same shock, but one of those two dogs could turn off the shock by pressing a button. The other dog in the pair had no control over the shock—it would end when the other dog pushed that button. Although the two dogs in a pair received exactly the same number and duration of shocks, they were affected differently by the experience. When placed in an active avoidance chamber, where jumping over a barrier would turn off

passive avoidance A response a subject has learned to refrain from displaying, to avoid an aversive stimulus.

learned helplessness A type of learning in which the subject learns that an aversive stimulus cannot be avoided.

the shock, the dogs that had been able to push a button previously to stop the shock quickly learned to jump over the barrier and stop the shock. But the other dogs, which had never been given the opportunity to stop the shock before, now tended to lie down in the chamber and whine rather than jump over the barrier. It was as though these dogs had learned to be helpless, and suffered for it.

Learned helplessness has been suggested as a model of humans who are clinically depressed, which is not so much typified by sadness as by a disinterest in being active and a lack of belief that taking action will improve things. It is interesting that not all dogs seemed susceptible to learned helplessness—they would readily learn to jump over the barrier in the active avoidance component of the study. When we discuss depression further in Section 16.3, we'll see that some people seem more susceptible than others to depression, and that heredity accounts for at least some of that variation.

Today it is difficult to appreciate what a powerful effect studies of operant conditioning had on American psychology. Perhaps the biggest payoff from studying instrumental learning in Skinner's operant conditioning chambers came when psychologists began varying when and how often they provided a reinforcer, as we'll see next.

The pace of rewards affects how quickly and well we learn

The standardization of learning in operant conditioning chambers allowed Skinner to systematically vary conditions to promote optimal performance. Of the many aspects of operant conditioning that Skinner studied, perhaps the most fruitful was varying how often the subject is given reinforcement. The rules determining the frequency with which an operant conditioning subject is reinforced came to be known as the **reinforcement schedule**. If the goal is to have the rat press the bar as much as possible, then you might expect that the best way to maximize that behavior would be to reward each and every response, which is a **continuous reinforcement schedule**. But if the subject is a hungry rat pressing the bar to get food, and it gets food for every bar press, then it soon becomes full and has no further reason to press the bar. To get more bar presses from the animal, you can put it on a **partial reinforcement schedule** (or *intermittent reinforcement schedule*), where only *some* of the responses are reinforced. What is striking about the comparison of these different reinforcement schedules is that they tended to have the same effects no matter what organism was studied—rats, pigeons, or people.

The simplest partial reinforcement schedule is to require the subject to press the bar a certain number of times, say ten times, for each reward. Because the number of bar presses required to get a reward is "fixed," and because there's a certain "ratio" of responses for each reward, this is known as a **fixed ratio** (**FR**) schedule, where a reinforcement is delivered after every nth response.

Subjects on a fixed ratio schedule (**Table 8.1**) how a very common pattern of performance. They press the bar fine until the reward arrives, but after that they stop pressing for a while. This makes sense if you put yourself in the place of the rat. You just pressed that bar ten times to get some food and now you'll have to press it ten times more for the next morsel. So the cumulative response shows "plateaus," as the subjects slack off for a bit after each reinforcement. This is sometimes called the *post-reinforcement pause.*

Animals will perform more consistently if, instead of rewarding every tenth response, we *vary* how many responses are required to trigger a reinforcement, which is known as a **variable ratio** (**VR**) schedule (see Table 8.1). Now after each reinforcement, subjects have no way to know whether it will take 10 more, 20 more, or only 5 more presses to get the next reward. Thus the cumulative response record of subjects on a VR schedule no longer shows the pause in re-

reinforcement schedule The rules determining the frequency with which an operant conditioning subject is reinforced.

continuous reinforcement schedule The rewarding of a behavior every time it is displayed.

partial reinforcement schedule Also called *intermittent reinforcement schedule*. The rewarding of a behavior only some of the time it is displayed.

fixed ratio (FR) A schedule in which every nth response is rewarded.

variable ratio (VR) A schedule in which the number of responses required to obtain a reward changes.

■ **TABLE 8.1 Operant Conditioning Partial Reinforcement Schedules**

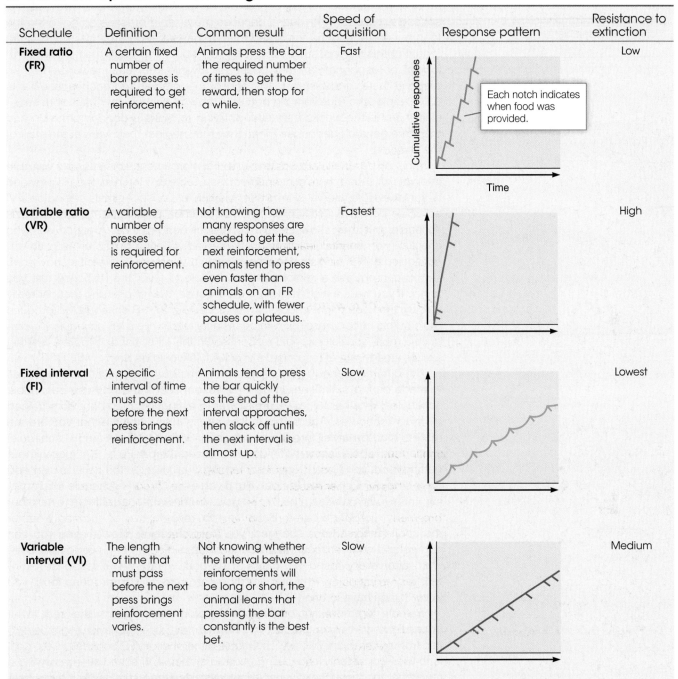

Schedule	Definition	Common result	Speed of acquisition	Response pattern	Resistance to extinction
Fixed ratio (FR)	A certain fixed number of bar presses is required to get reinforcement.	Animals press the bar the required number of times to get the reward, then stop for a while.	Fast	Cumulative responses; Time; Each notch indicates when food was provided.	Low
Variable ratio (VR)	A variable number of presses is required for reinforcement.	Not knowing how many responses are needed to get the next reinforcement, animals tend to press even faster than animals on an FR schedule, with fewer pauses or plateaus.	Fastest		High
Fixed interval (FI)	A specific interval of time must pass before the next press brings reinforcement.	Animals tend to press the bar quickly as the end of the interval approaches, then slack off until the next interval is almost up.	Slow		Lowest
Variable interval (VI)	The length of time that must pass before the next press brings reinforcement varies.	Not knowing whether the interval between reinforcements will be long or short, the animal learns that pressing the bar constantly is the best bet.	Slow		Medium

sponse seen with FR schedules. Not only do animals tend to press the bar more times and at a faster rate, but the VR schedule gets this increased performance with fewer reinforcements than an FR schedule. Slot machines offer a VR schedule, resulting in people persistently shoving in coins and pulling the handle hoping for a jackpot.

Instead of varying how *many* responses subjects must make to get a reward, we can vary how much *time has passed* before they get another reinforcement. If the response is only rewarded every 5 minutes, this is an example of a **fixed interval** (**FI**) schedule, where a reinforcement is provided for

fixed interval (FI) A schedule in which a reinforcement is provided for the first response after a fixed length of time since the last reinforcement.

variable interval (VI) A schedule in which reinforcement for the response is provided at some variable interval of time after the last response.

the first response after a fixed length of time since the last reinforcement. A rat on an FI schedule will not press the bar as rapidly as rats on an FR or VR schedule, which makes sense because more rapid presses do not bring the food faster—only once the timed interval has lapsed can a bar press bring food. For this reason, subjects on an FI schedule show a characteristic "scalloping" of responses, as they pause for a while after each reward and then respond faster and faster as the end of the interval approaches (see Table 8.1). People who receive a big bonus at the end of each year may work especially hard in the weeks beforehand, trying to make a good impression and therefore get a bigger bonus. Then they may neglect their work at the start of the new year.

You may be able to anticipate the next reinforcement schedule. In a **variable interval** (**VI**) schedule of reinforcement (see Table 8.1) the response is provided at some *variable* interval of time after the last response. Animals trained on a VI schedule do not typically press the bar as often as animals on an FR or VR schedule, but they show steady, consistent performance. A supervisor who checks in on employees at irregular intervals, offering praise or even an unscheduled bonus from time to time, is using a VI schedule to elicit steady work.

You can choose a reinforcement schedule to favor the response rate you prefer. If you want a high frequency of response, the rat pressing that bar really quickly, then you might choose a ratio schedule. An FR schedule will produce rapid bursts of bar pressing, with occasional lulls, while a VR schedule will produce a more consistent, rapid response. On the other hand, if you are seeking a slow, steady rate of response, a VI schedule would be best.

The different schedules also differ in terms of how quickly the responses will fade during extinction. In general, responses trained by use of variable schedules, whether VR or VI, are slower to extinguish than behaviors trained by fixed schedules. Again, this makes sense if you imagine that you are the rat. If a food pellet fell into the hopper after 10 bar presses (an FR schedule) all morning, and this afternoon you've pressed the bar 20 or 30 times without getting food, you already know something is up. Maybe the party is over and there's no point pressing the bar. But if you were on a VR schedule this morning, then you've pressed the bar 30 times before without getting a reward but eventually more food came. Because you have no way of knowing whether the contingencies have changed, you keep pressing. Now maybe you can understand another reason why continuous reinforcement, providing the reward after every response, may not be best. That sort of response extinguishes very quickly—the first time the bar press fails to produce food, you know things have changed.

Parents commonly reinforce a child's appropriate behavior with a treat. What schedule works best in this context? While more "good" behavior might be elicited from fewer treats with a VR schedule rather than an FR schedule, if the goal is to elicit consistent, long-lasting behaviors, then a VI schedule—bestowing a reward for the response at variable intervals since the last reward—may be best in the long run. This consideration is especially relevant to the classroom. A teacher rewarding young students who read with praise cannot constantly attend every child in the classroom to maintain an FR schedule. But the teacher can make a point of praising each student's behavior after variable intervals for any particular student.

The workplace is perhaps the most common context in which we see schedules of reinforcement routinely applied. Most people do their work for the pay. That's what makes it "work" rather than "play." So if you are a manager trying to get the most effort out of your workers while paying them the least amount of money, you should be very interested in the different outcomes from different

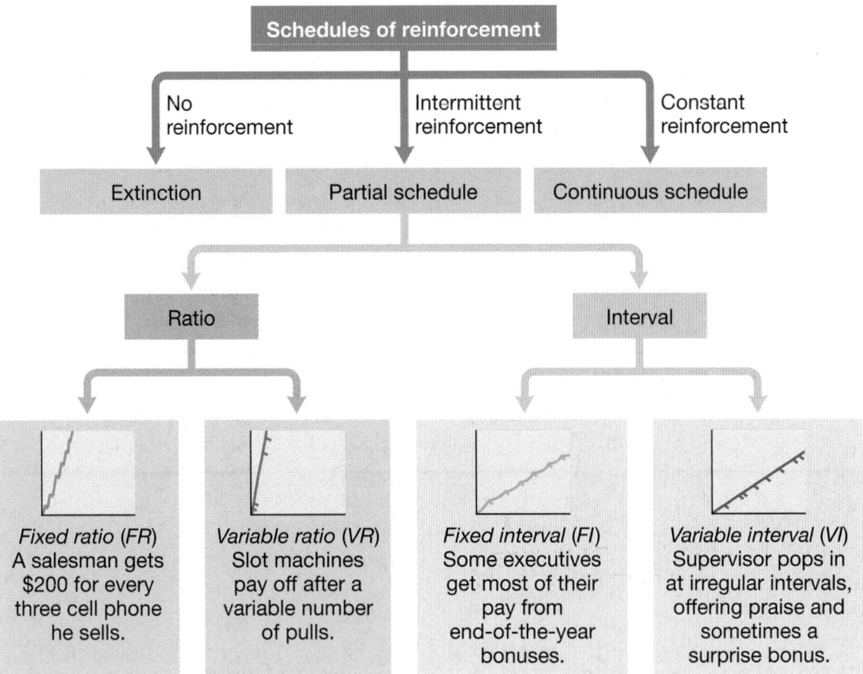

Figure 8.22 Overview of Different Types of Reinforcement Schedules

schedules of reinforcement. Paying a worker for every fifth widget he completes is an FR schedule. You would expect faster and more consistent production of widgets if you could pay the worker only after some variable number of completions, a VR schedule, but most people won't accept such work (and fair labor laws may forbid it). However, you can legally pay the worker an occasional bonus for completing a widget, and can vary whether it's the 5th, 10th or 22nd widget made since the last bonus. An FI schedule, paying the worker for a completed widget only on Friday, would give the worker no incentive to work the other days of the week, so not many widgets would get made. **Figure 8.22** presents an overview of different reinforcement schedules.

Another concept related to operant conditioning that is easily understood in the context of the workplace is the difference between a *primary* and a *secondary* reinforcer. A **primary reinforcer** is typically something that fills a biological need (like food, water, or sex), or in the case of punishments, something the subject already finds unpleasant that can be used to increase or decrease particular behaviors. All species "work" to survive and reproduce; primary reinforcers thus have an evolutionary basis. Money is not a primary reinforcer, however, because money itself does not reduce our hunger or thirst. Rather, money allows us to buy the food or water; we say money is a **secondary reinforcer**, something the subject comes to associate with one or more primary reinforcers, and which can therefore be used to increase or decrease particular behaviors. In animal experiments, the bar a rat has learned to press for food is a secondary reinforcer. The rat can be taught to do some other task in order to get access to that bar.

We don't know how animals feel about secondary reinforcers, but for most humans money elicits very positive reactions. People become ecstatic given a windfall of money, knowing that money provides access to many important things in life, including food, water, shelter, and transportation.

primary reinforcer A stimulus that fills a biological need or that the subject already finds unpleasant.

secondary reinforcer A stimulus the subject comes to associate with one or more primary reinforcers.

8.2 SUMMARY

- Thorndike's *law of effect*, formulated by studying animals escaping from *puzzle boxes*, states that any behavior that results in a satisfactory outcome is more likely to recur in the future.
- *Behaviorism* asserts that the proper study of psychology should be limited only to behaviors that can be reliably measured, ignoring internal mental states that are not observable to an outsider.
- B. F. Skinner made *operant conditioning chambers* where animals could learn to do a simple task, such as press a lever, to get a small piece of food. In such *operant conditioning* procedures, the food served as a *reinforcer*, an event that, when following a behavior, makes that behavior more likely to happen again. The operantly conditioned behavior will gradually be *extinguished* if the reinforcer is withheld.
- *Shaping* is the process by which a subject is at first readily provided with a reinforcer whenever the subject comes close to showing the desired behavior, then is required to come closer and closer to that desired behavior before receiving the reinforcer.
- Reinforcements are stimuli that, when following a behavior, make it more likely to recur. *Positive reinforcement* is the addition of a pleasant outcome, such as a tasty bit of food, while *negative reinforcement* is the removal of an unpleasant outcome, such as being stuck in a cage. Punishments are stimuli that, when following a behavior, make it less like to recur. *Positive punishment* is the addition of a stimulus (like a shock), while *negative punishment* is the removal of a pleasant stimulus (like a chance to go out on a Saturday night).
- In *escape conditioning* the subject learns to perform a behavior to remove an aversive stimulus. In *active avoidance,* the subject must perform the behavior to avoid an aversive stimulus. Such behavior is very difficult to extinguish.
- *Learned helplessness* occurs when subjects no longer try to avoid the unpleasant stimulus, presumably because they believe that is impossible.
- Various *reinforcement schedules*—the rules that determine how often a reinforcer is provided—result in different rates of learning. A *continuous reinforcement schedule*, where a reinforcer follows the behavior every time, may lose effectiveness, as for example when a hungry rat has gotten enough food to feel full.
- *Partial reinforcement schedules* provide the reinforcer intermittently. A *fixed ratio* (*FR*) schedule rewards the subject after the behavior has been displayed a certain number of times. A *variable ratio* (*VR*) schedule provides a reinforcer after some variable number of times the behavior occurs, and tends to result in more rapid display of the behavior than an FR schedule.
- A *fixed interval* (*FI*) schedule reinforces the particular behavior only after a certain amount of time has passed since the last reinforcement. In a *variable interval* (*VI*) schedule, the interval between delivery of the reinforcer varies.

REVIEW QUESTIONS

1. What is Thorndike's law of effect, and how does it explain the behavior of animals in a puzzle box?
2. Describe an example of operant conditioning in a Skinner box and in real life. How do different reinforcement schedules affect behavior in both instances?
3. What is active avoidance learning, why is it slow to be extinguished, and how might it be related to human behavior?

Food for Thought

Do you think John B. Watson was correct in his bold declaration that he could mold any healthy infant to fulfill any human occupation as an adult?

8.3 Observational Learning

The triumph of behaviorism in twentieth-century psychology was so complete that many courses in "Learning Psychology" covered only classical and operant conditioning, as though these represented the entirety of learning. But recall for a moment what you know of recorded history, the changes in the world from the Egyptian pharaohs through the industrial revolution to probes sent to study Mars. Surely those tremendous technological and cultural changes must have required someone learning something that was never known before. Do you think it likely that classical conditioning and operant conditioning accounted for it all? It seems pretty clear that people can learn from events in their environment and from other people, and can use reason and science to learn more. But those learning processes were largely ignored by behaviorism because studying them requires speculating about internal, mental processes rather than externally visible behavior.

Things to Learn

- Cognitive maps in rats and humans
- Latent learning
- Observational learning
- Social learning
- Examples of insight

By the mid-twentieth century, many investigators suggested that even rats are learning more about the world than simply which stimulus tends to precede another (as in classical conditioning), or which behaviors lead to rewards or punishments (as in operant conditioning). In this section we'll first discuss how rats running in a maze are learning a lot more than simply which turns lead to a reward. Then we'll describe instances in nature where animals can learn by observing one another. That will lead us to talk about how much people, especially children, learn by observing others. Finally, we'll describe insight, instances where those internal mental processes, which extreme behaviorism rejected as irrelevant, can prove crucial to solving a problem.

cognitive map An internal representation of the layout of an area.

Does a rat in a maze become lost in thought?

A behaviorist could understand a hungry rat solving a maze for food as simply operant conditioning. On the first trial, the rat wanders about the maze aimlessly, but upon turning that last corner of the maze, it is reinforced by food. So the animal is more likely to make that last turn in the future. In fact, that last turn may serve as a secondary reinforcer, rewarding the rat's turn just *before* that last turn. As it runs the maze over and over, the rat learns the fastest route, the story goes, because each turn is reinforced by the next turn, bringing the rat closer to the positive reinforcement. For the rat, solving the maze could simply be a long string of operant tasks—first turn left, then right, right again, then left, left again, and finally turn right to find the reward.

Edward Tolman (1886–1959) felt that this explanation was inadequate, and instead suggested that when rats wander around a maze, they build up ideas about the layout of the maze, a **cognitive map** (Tolman, 1948). A famous experiment (Tolman & Honzik, 1930a) supported this idea. In this experiment, rats learned to run a very strange-looking maze, shown in **Figure 8.23**. The maze consisted

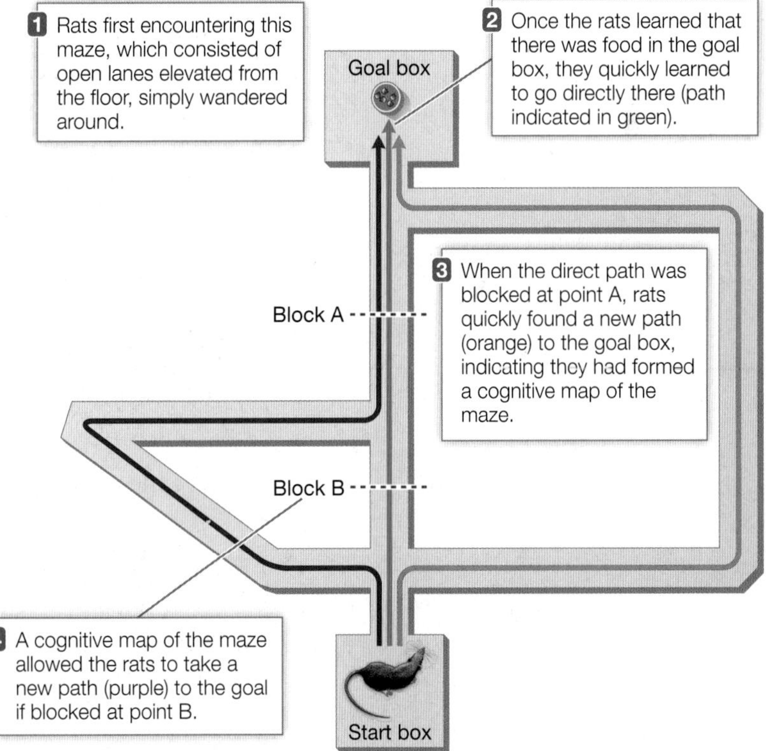

Figure 8.23 **Rats Can Form a Cognitive Map** (After Tolman & Honzik, 1930a.)

of elevated strips, without any walls, so rats leaving the start box could see the entire maze, including the goal box. As in any maze, the rats wandered around the entire maze at first, but once they learned there was food in the goal box, they soon went directly toward it. When the experimenters now placed barriers in the maze, the rats quickly chose an alternate pathway, which meant a very different series of turns, to reach the food. In fact, *which* alternate pathway they chose depended on *where* in the maze the blockade was placed (remember, the entire maze was visible). Like human drivers hearing a radio report of stopped traffic ahead, the rats chose the most efficient available pathway to the food.

At the height of behaviorism's dominance in American psychology, Tolman's suggestion that rats have a cognitive map, referring to mental processes going on in the brain, was provocative. Not only was he talking about mental processes rather than observable behavior, he was talking about mental processes in rats! One critic supposedly complained that Tolman had left the rat "lost in thought" in the middle of the maze. But time has been kind to Tolman's conclusions about cognitive maps. Many neuroscience experiments have established that neurons in one part of a rat's brain, the *hippocampus* and nearby cortex, fire only when the rat is in a particular part of a maze, regardless of whether there's any food reward (O'Keefe & Dostrovsky, 1971; Moser & Moser, 2014). In humans too, neurons in the hippocampus fire when the person is in a particular location (O'Keefe et al., 1998). Investigators who uncovered these neurons were awarded a Nobel Prize in Physiology and Medicine in 2014. In other words, one part of the brain seems to keep careful track of where we are in space, which is certainly consistent with a function as a cognitive map. From an evolutionary perspective, it seems that all animals, especially those such as rats that make their living by exploring to find food, need to keep track of where they are. So natural selection has surely favored the development of cognitive maps as important adaptations for survival.

The behaviorist perspective also emphasized the importance of reinforcement for learning—without reinforcement or punishment, no learning should take place. Tolman, on the other hand, considered whether a rat could learn something about a maze even in the absence of reinforcement. After all, he observed rats readily exploring a maze when they had no idea of whether a food reward might be present. If reinforcement is crucial for learning anything about the maze, does the rat learn *nothing* as it wanders about? Tolman and Honzik (1930b) tested the idea, as we'll see next in **Figure 8.24**.

Researchers at Work

Latent learning

Figure 8.24 Latent Learning in a Maze (After Tolman & Honzik, 1930b.)

■ **Question:** Can rats learn only in response to a reinforcement such as food?

■ **Hypothesis:** Rats wandering around a maze will learn about that maze even if they are not provided with a reinforcer such as food.

■ **Test:** Place rats in a complex maze with several one-way doors so that eventually a rat wandering around will reach the goal box. When they do, return them to their home cage. Repeat this daily for several days.

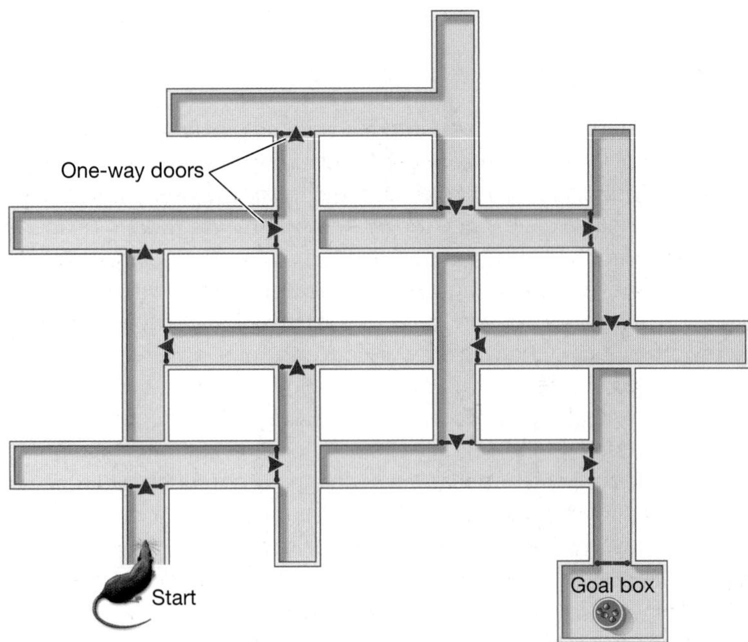

Assign rats to one of three groups. For one group, provide food in the goal box every day. For another group, provide no food in the goal box until the 11th day. For the third group, never put food in the goal box. Measure how many errors the rats make en route to the goal box across trials.

■ **Results:** Rats receiving food in the goal box from the beginning (red) quickly learned to go there with few errors. Rats provided no food until the 11th day (blue) made many errors up to that point. However, on the 12th day, after having found food in the goal box the day before, these rats made even fewer errors than the rats provided food all along. As expected, rats that were never given food in the goal box (orange) continued to make errors.

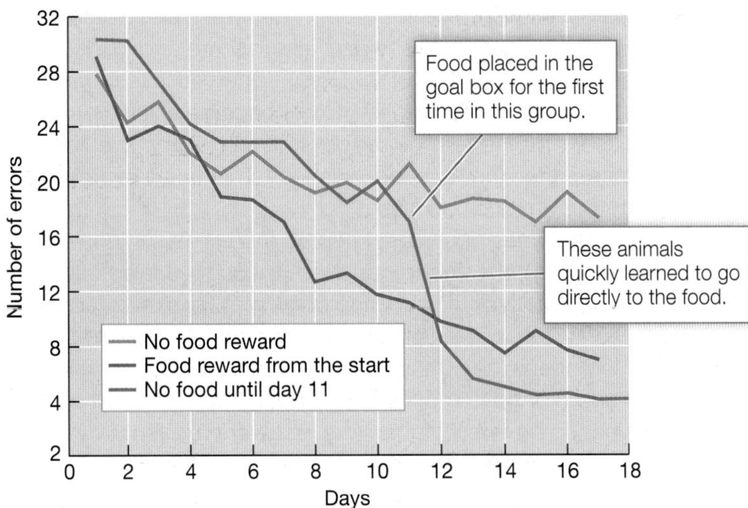

■ **Conclusion:** The rats provided no food for the first 11 days must have nevertheless learned about the maze, because on the 12th day they made fewer errors than rats given food all along. Animals can, in fact, learn about a maze even in the absence of any apparent reinforcement.

latent learning Learning that occurs without being immediately apparent and often without reinforcement.

observational learning Learning that occurs when one individual imitates the behavior of another individual.

The Tolman–Honzik experiment offers an example of **latent learning**, when a subject has in fact learned something without showing it right away. Typically, the experimenter must do something to get the subject to show that learning has in fact taken place. In this case, once the rat knew there was food to be found in the goal box, it showed that it had learned about the maze by going straight there.

For Tolman, the latent learning experiments also indicated that learning could take place *without reinforcement*. While the rats were strolling through the maze, with no reward awaiting them, they were nevertheless learning about the maze. Now you might object that to a rat living in a cage, exploring a maze is itself reinforcing, and surely that is true. But note that this assertion already attributes more cognitive ability to the rat than simply chaining together responses to get food. To say that rats find exploring *per se* to be rewarding is not much different from saying that rats display curiosity. And whether you are a rat or a person, isn't the whole point of satisfying your curiosity to learn something that you don't already know? So while the latent learning experiments do not disprove the importance of *reinforcement* in learning, they do establish that subjects, even rats, are actively learning about their environment, whether we are trying to teach them something or not. It appears that natural selection has produced rats that are built to learn about their environment, even when nothing seems to be at stake, and likely all animals are built that way.

"You can observe a lot by watching"

This aphorism from the great baseball player Yogi Berra, like many of his best quotes, works so well because, beneath the double-talk, we recognize an important truth: that you can *learn* a lot by watching. (Another example from Yogi Berra: "Always go to other people's funerals, otherwise they won't go to yours.") Of course you can learn a lot by observing inanimate objects, but in psychology **observational learning** refers to things one individual learns by observing another individual.

My household got a kick out of the observational learning displayed by our dog, Dipsy. Dipsy never showed any interest when we loaded the dishwasher until my in-laws visited with their dog, Tulip. Tulip wasn't just interested in the process of loading the dishwasher; she got right in there and busily licked off every soiled plate as soon as it was put in. Dipsy observed this behavior and clearly learned from it, because once Tulip left, Dipsy became an avid participant in loading our dishwasher for the rest of her days. (Don't worry, she had no interest in licking the dishes after they'd been washed.) This is an example of *modeling*, when one individual imitates another.

Modeling behavior has been documented many times in non-human animals. One famous example was among Japanese macaques, also called "snow monkeys." Researchers studying a wild troop of the monkeys on a Japanese island left yams on a beach where a river emptied into the ocean. They hoped to tempt the monkeys into the open where they could be observed. One day a female monkey took her yam and dipped it into the river, apparently to wash the sand off. Other monkeys seemed to be watching her (the researchers eventually named her Imo, which means "yam"). At first only Imo's siblings and mother imitated her, but gradually other monkeys took up the practice until the whole troop was doing it. *Then* Imo began dipping her yam into *sea*water, presumably because she liked the seasoning from the salt. Again the other monkeys observed Imo's behavior, and soon they found that they preferred dipping yams into seawater too (Kawai, 1965). This behavior has been passed on for several generations now (**Figure 8.25A**).

In England, learning spread in a similar way when birds known as blue tits, related to the chickadees of North America, learned to open the tinfoil tops of milk bottles to steal cream (**Figure 8.25B**). As the bottles had been in use for quite some time before this began, and the number of birds stealing cream increased rapidly, an individual bird must have learned the trick first, and others

(A)

(B)

Figure 8.25 Observational Learning (A) The snow monkey Imo learned to wash yams in seawater to get rid of sand and add some salt, and now all the monkeys in her troop do the same. (B) This blue tit is stealing cream from the top of a milk bottle by piercing the foil lid.

must have imitated it. Recently another new behavior rapidly spread among the closely related great tits of Hungary: when food becomes very scarce in winter, they've started flying into caves to kill and eat hibernating bats! Again, this behavioral innovation seems to be passing down from generation to generation (Estók et al., 2010).

But the most famous example of observational learning in birds is singing. In many bird species, males sing to attract a mate. The males of different species sing very different songs. Although the songs of males from a single species are similar to one another, there are noticeable individual differences in the songs produced by different males. What's more, if you study the songs of, say, white-crowned sparrows in different regions, you find there are "dialects": males in San Francisco sing slightly different songs than the white-crowned sparrows north or east of there (Marler & Slabbekoorn, 2004) (**Figure 8.26**). These individual differences come about because males learn their song by listening to their father's singing. If you take nestling white-crowned sparrows from San Francisco and

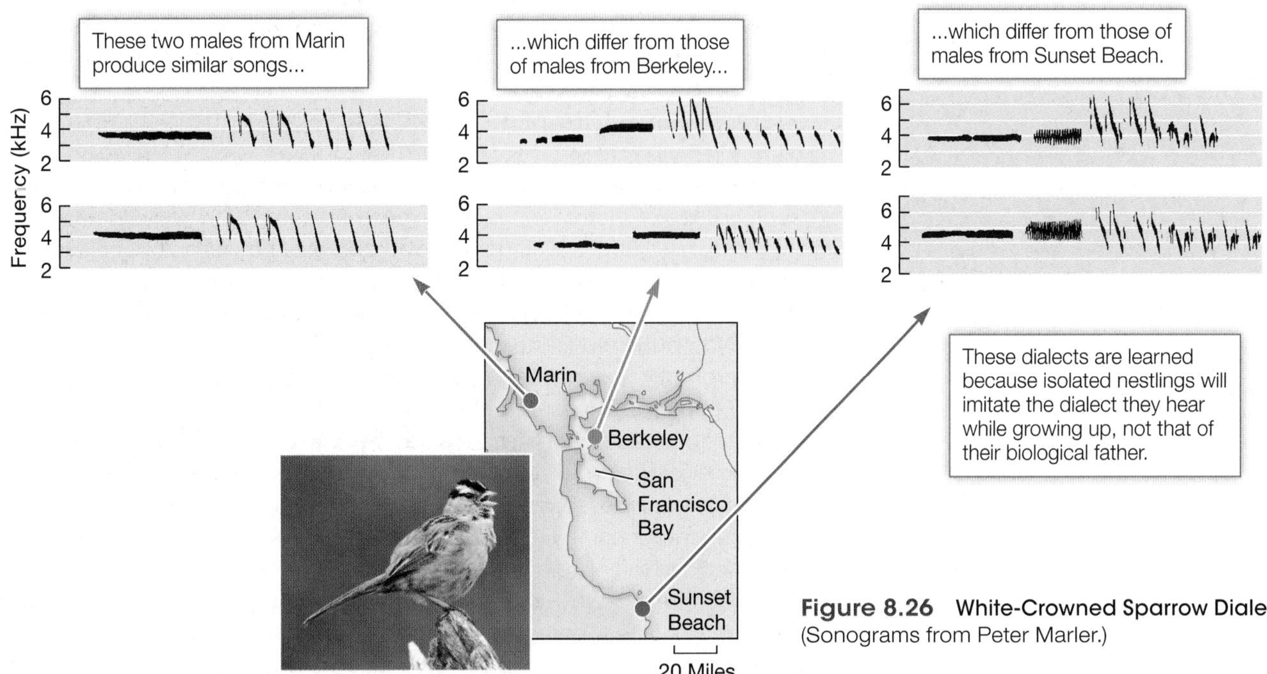
These two males from Marin produce similar songs...
...which differ from those of males from Berkeley...
...which differ from those of males from Sunset Beach.
Frequency (kHz)
6
4
2
These dialects are learned because isolated nestlings will imitate the dialect they hear while growing up, not that of their biological father.
Marin
Berkeley
San Francisco Bay
Sunset Beach
20 Miles

Figure 8.26 White-Crowned Sparrow Dialects (Sonograms from Peter Marler.)

social learning Changes in behavior brought about by interacting with other individuals.

Bobo doll studies A set of social modeling experiments conducted by Albert Bandura.

place them into a nest of sparrows from across the bay in Berkeley, the males will learn the song of their *foster* father and grow up singing the Berkeley dialect rather than the San Francisco dialect that their *biological* father sings.

In Section 10.1 we'll discuss how babies also learn to speak the language and dialect that they hear while growing up, which is another example of observational learning. We'll also discuss birdsong learning again and ask whether it represents a model of how we learn language. But our next topic in observational learning concerns social behaviors.

Social learning profoundly shapes human behavior

We all know the sorts of things children do when they play, but you may be surprised to learn that the young of many species of animals also play. For example, one category of child play is *rough-and-tumble play*: loud, boisterous play that involves running, chasing, wrestling, or even open-handed slapping that is generally accompanied by smiling or other facial indications of positive emotions. Except for the smiling expression, young monkeys and rats show these same behaviors. What's more, males are more likely than females to engage in rough-and-tumble play in all three species. Interestingly, adding just a few males into a group of young female monkeys will elicit more rough-and-tumble play from those females. In monkeys and rats there is evidence that play behavior, including rough-and-tumble play, has an influence on shaping adult behavior. For example, male rats raised without the opportunity to play show reduced sexual arousal as adults (Cooke et al., 2000). In monkeys, animals raised without the opportunity to play with others grow up to be inept in almost every social sphere, not only unable to mate properly but unable to get along with other monkeys, and unable to care for their young (Harlow & Suomi, 1971). We can't ethically do experiments to prevent children from playing, but in a few tragic cases authorities have found children raised with little or no interaction with other people. Those children are profoundly dysfunctional, unable to talk or take care of themselves. We discussed one such heartbreaking case in detail in Chapter 5.

Humans probably spend more time in play than any other species, and a great deal of that play behavior is social, whether it's rough-and-tumble play, games, imaginary tea parties, or "playing house." Even a child playing alone is often pretending to be interacting with someone else—picture a lone child playing with a doll or action figure. Play teaches us how to interact with other people, and it's just one aspect of the overall process of **social learning**, changes in behavior brought about by interacting with other individuals. For psychologist Albert Bandura, a crucial aspect of social learning is that the individual observes and imitates the behavior of others, and Bandura explored this process with the help of a toy.

THE BOBO DOLL STUDIES One of Bandura's explorations of social learning became one of the most famous experiments in psychology, the **Bobo doll studies**. You may never have seen a Bobo doll, as it has fallen out of favor these days, but it used to be quite common. It was an inflatable doll, about 5 feet tall, printed with an image of Bobo the clown and having a heavily weighted, round bottom. If you punched Bobo's head, it would bounce away from your punch but then promptly swing back into place again. Bandura and his colleagues (1961) brought 3- to 6-year-old children, one at a time, into a room and introduced them to an adult who served as a "model." In the control case, the model sat in a corner of the room playing with Tinkertoys and ignored the Bobo doll for 10 minutes. In other cases, the adult model started off playing with the Tinkertoys but then began punching Bobo. Then the adult laid Bobo on its side, sat on it, and punched it in the nose again and again. Next the adult hit Bobo on the head with a mallet, threw Bobo in the air, and began kicking it. Poor Bobo suffered this sequence three times, sometimes with the adult saying aggressive things like "Sock him in the nose." After 10 minutes with the adult model, the child was re-

Figure 8.27 Bandura's Four Factors Necessary for Modeling Behavior

trieved by the experimenter and taken to another room with many toys, including a Bobo doll. As you have probably guessed, children exposed to an aggressive model were much more likely to play aggressively with Bobo, sometimes even reproducing the sequence of aggressive acts and language. On average, boys were more aggressive than girls, especially if the model was a man.

Bandura (1986) systematically varied the conditions of these experiments, finding that children's behavior was affected just as much whether they saw the adult abuse Bobo on TV or in person. Generally, the children were more likely to imitate the model if the model possessed characteristics the children admired. Bandura's analysis of these varied experiments suggested that a person emulates modeled behavior when four criteria are met (**Figure 8.27**):

1. The person must be paying *attention* to the model's behavior.
2. The person must *retain* the information gained about the observed behavior.
3. The person must *reproduce* the behavior, and may get progressively better at imitating the behavior with practice.
4. The person must be *motivated* to reproduce the model's behavior.

Several aspects of Bandura's conclusions were out of step with the behaviorist views of the time. For one thing, the first two steps are purely mental events that cannot be directly observed: paying attention and retaining memories. For another, these experiments were conducted with an effort never to instruct the child how to behave, and not to provide any reinforcement to the child. Yet the children learned from the model, as their imitative behavior made clear, without any apparent reinforcement. That result suggests that behaviors can be learned without any of the external reinforcers that are emphasized in behaviorism.

But Bandura certainly was not disputing the importance of reinforcers, since the fourth stage, the person's motivation to reproduce the behavior, could be greatly influenced by whether he was rewarded or punished for the behavior. In fact, how faithfully the children imitated the aggressive behavior could be influenced by whether they observed the *model* being rewarded or punished. Girls seemed more sensitive than boys to this effect, as they were very unlikely to imitate the behavior if the model was punished for it. *Social monitoring*, or *social referencing*, refers to when an individual observes the consequences of someone else's behavior to guide their own behavior. You can observe social monitoring when young children are brought by a parent into a new situation: as the child wanders about, she will often look at her parent's face, looking for signs of approval or concern. If the parent looks calm and happy, then things are probably OK. But the child may run back to the parent if the parent looks alarmed or frightened.

insight A sudden understanding of a problem that leads to a solution.

In that film from long ago, Little Albert often looks up at the faces of the adults around him. Albert looks up at Watson's face after being exposed to the rabbit as if looking for Watson's reaction to the rabbit (Digdon et al., 2014). Was social monitoring playing a role in Albert's reactions? Did Watson make a "fear face" to cue Albert that he should be afraid? In any case, would social monitoring not have served to help the baby? Might Little Albert have had an opportunity to observe his mother and others calmly and happily handling fluffy things? Because Watson and other researchers lost track of Little Albert, we unfortunately do not know whether he was ever able to unlearn the irrational fears of white fluffy things that were induced by Watson's unethical experiment.

Sometimes insight plays a role in learning

There are several famous examples of **insight**, a sudden understanding of a problem that leads to a solution without having to resort to trial and error. When Archimedes (287–212 BCE) of ancient Greece noticed that easing himself into a bathtub displaced water, he suddenly understood how he could measure the volume of any object—the greater the volume, the more water it would displace. Supposedly he said "Eureka" (meaning "I've got it"), so such instances are sometimes called "Eureka moments" or "Aha! moments." We discussed one example of insight in Section 3.1 when we talked about Otto Loewi's sudden realization (which came to him in a dream) about how to test whether neurotransmitters are released from nerves.

German psychologist Wolfgang Köhler (1887–1967) studied insight in chimpanzees living in a large outdoor pen, where he gave them a variety of toys to play with (Köhler regarded the pen as a "playground"). He gave the chimps problems to solve, typically how to get access to bananas that were suspended far overhead. In some of the films Köhler (1925) made, a chimp can be seen leaping at the bananas fruitlessly (pun intended) and then walking away in disgust or frustration. Then the chimp can be seen looking at the bananas, looking at the various toys lying about, and then looking back at the bananas. Suddenly he begins gathering objects. He might drag a crate under the fruit, then climb on top with a stick to knock down the bananas (**Figure 8.28**). In many ways, these tests are like Thorndike's puzzle boxes for cats and dogs, but while Thorndike's animals seemed to solve the puzzle by trial and error, Köhler's chimps did not thrash around randomly until the solution came. Rather, they seemed to be

Figure 8.28 Insightful Problem Solving in Chimpanzees Chimps found creative ways to reach bananas.

Figure 8.29 The Candle Problem

thinking about the problem, looking at the objects around them, and then suddenly would see a solution. If trial and error was involved, many of the trials seemed to be going on inside the chimp's brain.

Psychologists have also studied insight in human problem solving. A famous example, called the *candle problem*, is to ask someone to find a way to mount a lighted candle on a bulletin board, then hand him a candle, a box of tacks, and a book of matches (Duncker, 1945). Most people are stumped by this task, at least for a while. To solve it requires the insight that the *box* that the tacks come in can be used for a different purpose (**Figure 8.29**). The solution is elusive because it requires thinking about the box in a different fashion—it's not just a container for objects, it's also a resource that can be used to make a platform. This ability to imagine a new use for an object is often crucial for insightful learning, and is a pretty good definition of what we mean when we say someone is creative. Maybe this is why we seem to benefit from a change of scenery once in a while. It gives us a chance to see familiar objects in a new light. Of course, insight is not the only way to solve problems. We'll discuss more systematic approaches to problem solving in Section 10.3.

What Ever Happened to Little Albert?

Eighty-nine years after Watson's publication about Little Albert, researchers may have found out what happened to Little Albert. The U.S. Census Bureau counted residents around Johns Hopkins on January 2, 1920, just between the initial screening test of Albert at 9 months of age and the learning sessions at 11 months of age. The census recorded three women living in the hospital who were described as foster mothers. One of them, Arvilla Merritte, had a son, Douglas, who had been born at the hospital. A host of circumstantial evidence suggested that Douglas was Little Albert (Beck et al., 2009). Did Douglas have a fear of furry objects the rest of his life?

His story proved much sadder than that. The unmarried Arvilla had to leave her parents' home because she was pregnant. So when she came to Johns Hopkins hospital to have Douglas, she was on her own. The work Arvilla gained at the hospital, offering some of her milk for other babies, was her only income until Watson offered her a dollar for each of Douglas's "visits" to the lab (Beck et al., 2009). Douglas Merritte's medical records revealed that he had been diagnosed with hydrocephalus (Fridlund et al., 2012), a condition in which improper fluid circulation causes swelling of the brain that can cause mental disability. If Douglas was Little Albert, then Watson's reputation is further tarnished, as it seems likely he knew the boy was neurologically impaired, but reported that the baby was "healthy" and "normal". Douglas continued to have health problems and died at age 6, apparently as a consequence of the hydrocephalus. Arvilla, who eventually married and raised a family, lived 66 years after Douglas's death, yet her other two children never knew they'd had an older brother until they found Douglas's baby photo among Arvilla's belongings after she died. So, if Douglas was "Little Albert," he did not grow up to be a man with an irrational fear of Santa Claus, because he never grew up. We don't know if Douglas as a boy was afraid of furry things, because his mother never talked about her poor, lost child.

But, shortly after these discoveries, another team of researchers tracked down another of the women working as a wet nurse at Hopkins (Powell et al., 2014). Like Arvilla, this woman was an unwed mother whose son, William Barger, was called by his middle name, Albert! William Albert Barger died at age 87, before researchers tracked him down. So they couldn't ask if he was afraid of furry objects. But his surviving relatives report that they used to tease Uncle Albert because he *really* disliked dogs, and never had any pets (Bartlett, 2014). Recall that after conditioning Little Albert was afraid of the dog. If Albert Barger was "Little Albert," then we'll have to wonder forever whether Watson had indeed managed to instill a phobia to last a lifetime.

The Cutting Edge

What Makes You So Smart?

Why are humans so good at learning? One obvious explanation is that we have rather large brains compared with other species (although whales and dolphins have even larger brains). The fossil record makes it clear that this marked growth in brain size evolved rapidly, presumably because learning was adaptive for our ancestors. But size isn't everything. Maybe in addition to large brains we also evolved neurons that are especially good at learning.

That's probably true, but a recent experiment indicates that it's not just our neurons that are adapted for learning. The other type of cells in the brain, glial cells, also appear to be well adapted for learning. Scientists trying to find treatments for diseases of glial cells transplanted human glial cells called astrocytes into the brains of mice (**Figure 8.30**). These transplanted human astrocytes were much larger than the mouse's own astrocytes but the transplantation was successful. The surprise was that the human astrocytes made the mice smarter! Mice provided with human astrocytes were faster

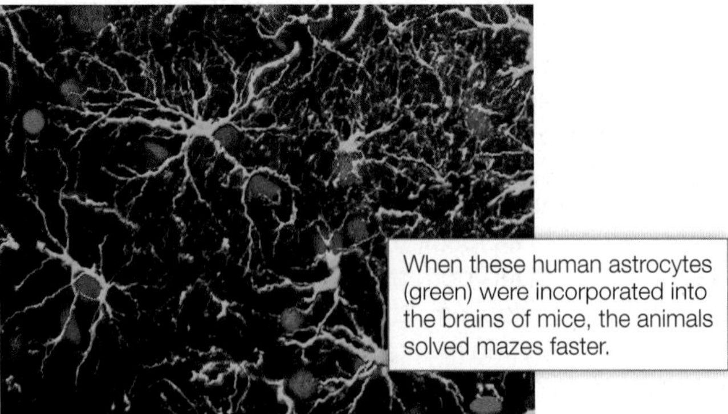

When these human astrocytes (green) were incorporated into the brains of mice, the animals solved mazes faster.

Figure 8.30 Glial Cells Play a Role in Learning

at solving mazes, better at remembering the location of objects, and more responsive to aversive conditioning than other mice (Han et al., 2013). Transplanting astrocytes from other mice didn't make the experimental mice any smarter, so it wasn't that any old transplants, or just having additional astrocytes, boosted learning. So our astrocytes seem to be especially good at facilitating learning in the brain. No one knows (yet) how astrocytes boost learning, but it's interesting to wonder whether any individual differences in human learning ability are due to differences in astrocytes. If so, then might we someday boost a person's learning power by transplanting "super smart" astrocytes into his or her brain?

8.3 SUMMARY

- Edward Tolman demonstrated that rats show *latent learning* and that they can make a *cognitive map* of a maze, even if not motivated by a food reward.
- Many animals have shown examples of *observational learning*, where one animal shows a novel behavior and other animals model that behavior.
- The young males in many species of birds listen to the songs of the adult male that feeds them, and later produce their own song that closely resembles that song. Over time, the songs from males of a particular species may vary from one location to another, as examples of dialects.
- *Social learning* embraces instances where individuals, especially youngsters, learn to model the behavior of others. In Bandura's famous *Bobo doll studies*, children who observed an adult hitting a toy were much more likely to show similar aggressive behavior themselves when offered access to the Bobo doll.
- *Insight* is a sudden understanding of a problem that leads to a solution. There are many examples of insight in human history, but chimpanzees faced with problems have also shown instances of insight, as in how to arrange object to get access to bananas.

REVIEW QUESTIONS

1. What is latent learning, and how can you demonstrate that rats wandering about a maze without reward are nevertheless learning something?
2. Describe examples of observational learning in animals.
3. What were the results of the Bobo doll studies, and what four-part model did Bandura propose to understand those results?

Food for Thought

To what extent do you think observational learning, or modeling, affects the behavior of people who play video games?

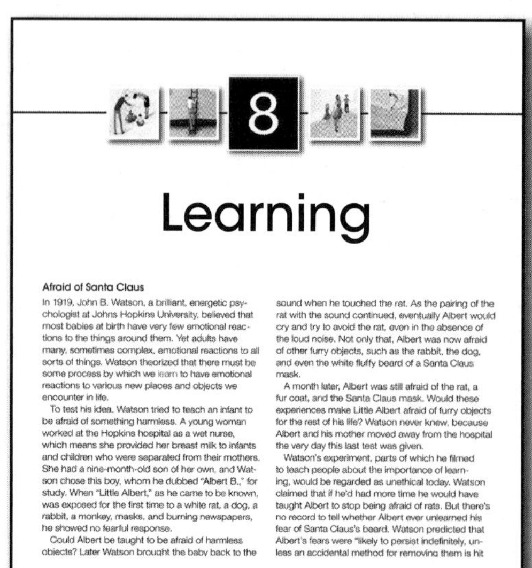
8

Learning

Afraid of Santa Claus

In 1919, John B. Watson, a brilliant, energetic psychologist at Johns Hopkins University, believed that most babies at birth have very few emotional reactions to the things around them. Yet adults have many, sometimes complex, emotional reactions to all sorts of things. Watson theorized that there must be some process by which we learn to have emotional reactions to various new places and objects we encounter in life.

To test his idea, Watson tried to teach an infant to be afraid of something harmless. A young woman worked at the Hopkins hospital as a wet nurse, which means she provided her breast milk to infants and children who were separated from their mothers. She had a nine-month-old son of her own, and Watson chose this boy, whom he dubbed "Albert B.," for study. When "Little Albert," as he came to be known, was exposed for the first time to a white rat, a dog, a rabbit, a monkey, masks, and burning newspapers, he showed no fearful response.

Could Albert be taught to be afraid of harmless objects? Later Watson brought the baby back to the sound when he touched the rat. As the pairing of the rat with the sound continued, eventually Albert would cry and try to avoid the rat, even in the absence of the loud noise. Not only that, Albert was now afraid of other furry objects, such as the rabbit, the dog, and even the white fluffy beard of a Santa Claus mask.

A month later, Albert was still afraid of the rat, a fur coat, and the Santa Claus mask. Would these experiences make Little Albert afraid of furry objects for the rest of his life? Watson never knew, because Albert and his mother moved away from the hospital the very day this last test was given.

Watson's experiment, parts of which he filmed to teach people about the importance of learning, would be regarded as unethical today. Watson claimed that if he'd had more time he would have taught Albert to stop being afraid of rats. But there's no record to tell whether Albert ever unlearned his fear of Santa Claus's beard. Watson predicted that Albert's fears were "likely to persist indefinitely, unless an accidental method for removing them is hit

Think Like a Psychologist:

Principles in Action

Whenever we encounter any interesting behavior we should consider the four principles. Here are some ways that the four principles relate to our opening story about Little Albert.

MACHINE

The mind is a product of a physical machine, the brain.

In animals, fear conditioning such as Little Albert experienced is the result of changes in a brain region called the amygdala. People with damage to the amygdala don't seem to be afraid of anything, so it would be impossible to induce fear conditioning in them.

UNCONSCIOUS

We are consciously aware of only a small part of our mental activity.

People subjected to classical conditioning report that they do not consciously produce the conditioned response; it seems to happen on its own, in a reflexive fashion. Little Albert's fearful responses certainly appear reflexive. If Albert Barger was indeed Little Albert, and if his dislike of dogs was a result of Watson's manipulations, he was unaware of the connection.

SOCIAL

We constantly modify our behavior, beliefs, and attitudes according to what we perceive about the people around us.

Whichever child was the true Little Albert, he was available for Watson's study because his mother, pregnant out of wedlock, had few options to support them. This was the result of social attitudes at the time, which heaped shame on unwed mothers. Was Watson more willing to conduct his experiment on a child in such circumstances than a child of middle-class parents?

EXPERIENCE

Our experiences physically alter the structure and function of the brain.

Whatever Little Albert's true name, he became terrified of many furry objects as a result of experiencing the pairing of such stimuli with loud, startling sounds. Indeed, all instances of learning result from experience. It is possible that Albert Barger's lifelong dislike of dogs was a result of his experiences as an infant.

KEY TERMS

acquisition, 313
active avoidance, 330
associative learning, 311
behaviorism, 324
biological constraints on learning, 319
Bobo doll studies, 342
classical conditioning, 312
cognitive map, 337
conditioned response (CR), 313
conditioned stimulus (CS), 313
conditioned taste aversion, 317
continuous reinforcement schedule, 332
dishabituation, 310
escape conditioning, 330
extinction, 315
fear conditioning, 320
fixed interval (FI), 333
fixed ratio (FR), 332
habituation, 309
imprinting, 318
insight, 344
latent learning, 340
law of effect, 324
learned helplessness, 331
learning, 308
negative punishment, 329
negative reinforcement, 329
non-associative learning, 311
observational learning, 340
operant conditioning, 325
operant conditioning chambers, 325
partial reinforcement schedule, 332
passive avoidance, 331
phobia, 321
positive punishment, 329
positive reinforcement, 328
primary reinforcer, 335
puzzle box, 323
reinforcement schedule, 332
reinforcer, 325
secondary reinforcer, 335
second-order conditioning, 315
sensitization, 310
shaping, 327
social learning, 342
spontaneous recovery, 315
stimulus generalization, 315
stimulus, 308
superstition, 328
unconditioned response (UR), 312
unconditioned stimulus (US), 312
variable interval (VI), 334
variable ratio (VR), 332

QUIZ YOURSELF

1. New residents in a neighborhood that is under the flight path for an airport are often disturbed by the airplane noise. After a few days, they scarcely notice it. This decrease in response is known as
   a. habituation.
   b. sensitization.
   c. adaptation.
   d. extinction.
2. Slot machines give jackpots in an unpredictable manner. The type of reinforcement schedule used in these machines, which produces the most responses at a fast rate, is
   a. fixed ratio.
   b. variable ratio.
   c. fixed interval.
   d. variable interval.
3. Which of the following is *not* a simple form of learning or a single response to a single stimulus?
   a. Habituation
   b. Dishabituation
   c. Classical conditioning
   d. Sensitization
4. A small child sees an older sibling working on homework. Their father stops by to give the older child a word of encouragement. Soon the younger child is sitting surrounded by books, papers, and crayons, looking quite studious. What type of learning is the younger child displaying?
   a. Operant conditioning
   b. Secondary reinforcement
   c. Imprinting
   d. Social learning
5. White-crowned sparrows learn their dialect of song through
   a. operant conditioning.
   b. secondary reinforcement.
   c. imprinting.
   d. social learning.
6. The tendency of newly hatched birds to follow the first moving object they see resulted in Konrad Lorenz becoming the leader of a group of goslings. This tendency is called ________.
7. In Pavlov's experiments with dogs, the sound of the bell became the ________ and the salivation in response to that sound became the ________.
8. Dogs that had been repeatedly shocked and had no control over the shock behaved differently than dogs that could turn off the shock when placed in an active avoidance chamber. The dogs that had been able to control the shock learned to jump over the barrier, but the dogs that had had no control over the shock tended to lie down and whine. This behavior is known as ________ ________.
9. The sudden understanding of a problem without having to resort to trial-and-error is known as ________.
10. Madison loves to play ice hockey. When she commits a foul, she is sent to the penalty box for a period of time. This time spent away from something she enjoys falls into the category of the removal of a pleasant stimulus or a ________.

1. a; 2. b; 3. c; 4. d; 5. d; 6. imprinting; 7. conditioned stimulus; conditioned response; 8. learned helplessness; 9. insight; 10. negative punishment

Memory

Trapped in the Eternal Now

For over 50 years, Henry Molaison was known to the world as "patient H.M.," probably the most famous research participant in the history of psychology. Henry suffered seizures during adolescence, and by his late twenties, Henry's epilepsy was out of control. In 1953, because tests showed that Henry's seizures began in both hemispheres, a neurosurgeon removed most of Henry's anterior temporal lobes.

After Henry recovered from the operation, his seizures were milder, and they could be controlled by medication. But this relief came at a terrible, unforeseen cost: Henry had lost the ability to form new memories (Scoville & Milner, 1957). For more than 50 years after the surgery, until his death in 2008, Henry could retain any new fact only briefly. As soon as he was distracted, the newly acquired information vanished from his memory. Long after the surgery, he didn't know his age or the current date, and he didn't know that his parents (with whom he lived well into adulthood) had died years previously. His IQ remained a little above average (Corkin et al., 1997); despite problems with acquiring new information, he could perform well on IQ tests because they do not require remembering new facts for more than a few minutes. The knowledge Henry had gained before the surgery was intact, allowing him to solve crossword puzzles, which he loved. But Henry knew something was wrong with him, because he had no memories from the years since his surgery, or even memories from earlier the same day.

> *Every day is alone in itself, whatever enjoyment I've had, and whatever sorrow I've had.... Right now, I'm wondering, have I done or said anything amiss? You see, at this moment everything looks clear to me, but what happened just before? That's what worries me. It's like waking from a dream. I just don't remember. (Milner, 1970, p. 37.)*

Henry's inability to form new memories meant that he couldn't construct a lasting relationship with anybody he met after his surgery. No matter what experiences he might share with someone he met, Henry would have to start the acquaintance anew the following day. What happened?

Chapter Preview

memory The ability to store and retrieve information we have learned.

sensory buffer Also called *sensory memory*. A very brief type of memory for sensory information.

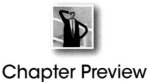

All the distinctively human aspects of our behavior are learned: the languages we speak, how we dress, our skills, our motivations. So much of our own individuality depends on *learning*, the process of acquiring new information, which we studied in the previous chapter. But to make full use of our tremendous learning capacity, we must retain that information so we can use it, and perhaps build upon it by learning more and more each day, as when we learned language. The ability to store and retrieve the information we have learned is **memory**.

We'll begin this chapter by discussing the formation of memory, a process that occurs in distinct stages. Each stage, from encoding to more-or-less permanent storage, is susceptible to different influences. Then we'll discuss the process of forgetting, the vulnerability of memory to fade. Finally, we'll learn that there are distinct classes of memories in that more-or-less permanent storage, as revealed by cases of people like Henry who, due to injury or disease, have an unusually difficult time holding onto particular sorts of memories. Disturbing as they are, these cases have revealed which parts of the brain are required to make new memories. We'll wrap up by discussing what we know about the physical basis of memory storage in the brain.

9.1 The Stages of Memory Formation

Things to Learn

- Stages of memory formation
- Fading of the sensory buffer
- Rapid loss of short-term memory
- Model of long-term memory storage and retrieval
- Value of encoding and chunking
- Vast store of long-term memory

Memories are not formed instantly. When our sensory systems first detect any stimulus, a *process* begins that will determine whether we will remember that event, whatever it was. In fact, most of the events occurring around us are never even noticed because we are not paying attention to them. In the next chapter we'll discuss attention—concentrating the mind on a particular object or event—in greater detail. In this chapter, while discussing memory, we'll restrict ourselves to events to which we were paying attention, events that at least had a chance of being remembered.

Most of the events we attend to are forgotten later, but some stimuli communicate events that are important, so we remember them. Even these memories vary in persistence, some forgotten in a moment, others kept for life. The observation that different memories last for different durations was a hint to researchers that there are distinct stages of memory formation, and that a memory can be kept, lost, or misplaced at each stage.

Something we have learned gets transferred to memory in three stages. The first stage, *sensory memory,* is brief: information about raw stimuli is retained only for a few seconds. The second stage is *short-term memory*, which can hold the information for only a few minutes while we are using it. The third stage is *long-term memory* for those relatively few items that move from short-term memory into more permanent, perhaps lifelong, storage. We'll see that an important factor for getting information into long-term memory is to lend meaning to the material, which helps us remember it. We can exploit this process when we want to memorize material.

We retain raw sensory information for only a few seconds

The first stage of memory formation begins with sensation, when we detect a particular stimulus that has reached us. That sensory information is kept for only a short while, in what is called the **sensory buffer** (or *sensory memory*), which absorbs a fleeting impression from a sensation. These brief sensory memories have been attributed to residual neural activity, as if the information about the

Skeptic at Large

BOX 9.1

Does Anyone Have Photographic Memory?

If a person had iconic memory that did not fade with time, he or she would have what is sometimes called **photographic memory** (also called *eidetic memory*), the ability to recall entire images with extreme detail. Such a person, for example, could look at a page of text and, even without taking the time to read it, recall the scene well enough to report every word, line by line, days later. While many people claim to have such ability, it's not at all clear whether *anyone* has *ever* had this ability. For example, in 1970 a study participant called Elizabeth claimed such ability. She looked at a random pattern of 10,000 dots (see figure) with her right eye one day, then another dot pattern with her left eye the next day, and supposedly remembered the first pattern well enough to mentally fuse the two images to reveal a three-dimensional object portrayed there (Stromeyer & Psotka, 1970). But the senior researcher later married Elizabeth, which raises the concern that he may not have been wholly objective in testing her claims, and she has declined to be tested ever again. Since no other such person has been found who could do this in the 40 years since, despite several efforts to find one (Merritt, 1979), we have to doubt whether it is really possible. Later we'll learn about people with truly prodigious memories, but they don't seem to be storing "photographs" of what they remember, either. So it would seem that iconic memory is very brief for everyone.

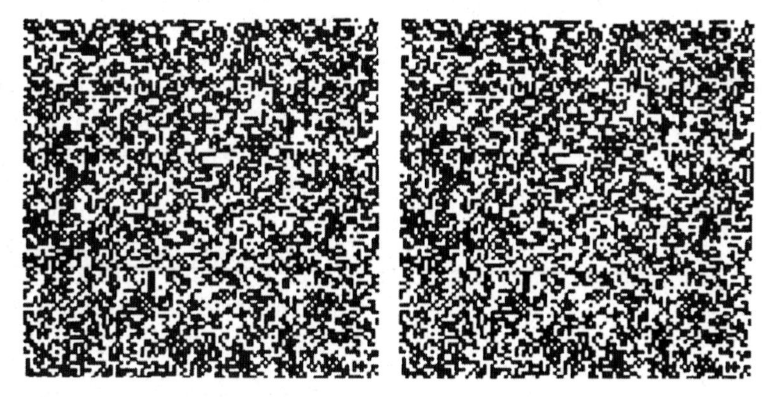

Does Anyone Have a Truly "Photographic Memory"? If so, it would be like having an iconic memory that does not fade. Each of these images alone is basically a random scattering of dots, but when participants stare at both images at once and fuse them, they should see a three-dimensional object (a square tilted slightly). A woman claiming to have performed this task when seeing the two pictures a day apart has declined to repeat the feat. (From Stromeyer & Psotka, 1970.)

photographic memory Also called *eidetic memory*. The supposed ability to recall entire images with extreme detail.

stimulus is still echoing around in the sensory organ. Indeed, sensory memory for auditory stimuli is sometimes called *echoic memory.* And visual memory is sometimes called iconic memory (from the Greek *eikon, "image").* These memories soon vanish. Such brief sensory memories are also sometimes called *sensory registers*, as if the sensory information is being held somewhere in the brain before it is sent on or disregarded (Atkinson & Shiffrin, 1968). You may have heard that some people can remember in detail any scene they see, displaying "photographic memory"; we'll talk more about this myth in **Box 9.1**. While we don't know for certain *where* this sensory information is being held, we know that it is only there very *briefly*, so briefly that if the person doesn't report the information right away, it will disappear within seconds, never to be reported.

When I say that the person will never be able to report the information that he had a few seconds ago, you might wonder how that's possible. If the person is unable to report the information to me, how can I tell he ever had it? The answer lies in a wonderfully ingenious set of experiments by George Sperling that we describe next.

George Sperling (1960) reasoned that our visual system can take in a scene with so much information so quickly that we could not possibly remember it all. To test this idea, he had participants look at a screen where a random set of letters was shown very briefly. He found that if 12 letters were shown, the participants might be able to report 4 of them, but not all of them. Does that mean they never got the information about the other 8 letters? No, as Sperling showed when he changed the task just a little bit. Now he told the participants that, after each set of letters was presented, he would ask them to report the letters in just one row. But in the time it would take to say "top row" or "bottom row," the information might already be gone. So Sperling cleverly found a way to very quickly tell the participants which row to report, before the information could fade, as we'll see in **Figure 9.1**.

☑ Researchers at Work

How to retrieve fading images

Figure 9.1 Iconic Memories Fade Away (After Sperling, 1960.)

■ **Question:** Can our sensory buffer take in more information from a brief visual scene than we can normally report?

■ **Hypothesis:** Our sensory buffer takes in all 12 letters, but that memory fades so fast that by the time we've reported a few, the rest have faded away. If so, then if we ask participants to report on just a *portion* of the vanished scene, before the sensory buffer fades, they should be able to accurately describe most or all of that portion.

■ **Test:** As before, show participants 12 letters in three rows. *After the scene is over*, sound a tone of either low, medium, or high pitch, signaling participants to report the bottom, middle, or top row of letters.

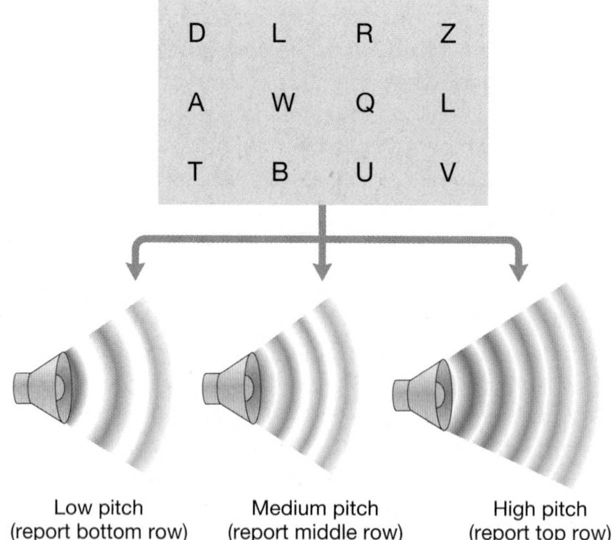

■ **Results:** In this version of the task, participants could recall most of the letters from *whichever row they were told to report*. Because the tone sounded *after* the screen went blank, participants could not have deliberately studied only the one row while it was in view. Sperling varied how long he waited after the visual scene ended before sounding the tone.

Participants did best when the tone sounded immediately after the visual scene ended. Accuracy fell rapidly after that.

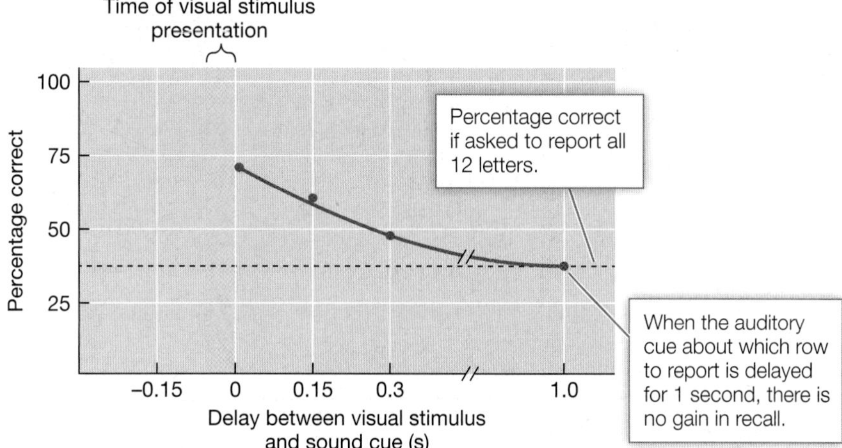
Time of visual stimulus presentation
100
75
50
25
Percentage correct
Percentage correct if asked to report all 12 letters.
When the auditory cue about which row to report is delayed for 1 second, there is no gain in recall.
−0.15
0
0.15
0.3
1.0
Delay between visual stimulus and sound cue (s)

■ **Conclusion:** Participants were able to absorb information about all 12 letters in the short stimulus period. They could accurately report most letters from any given row if quickly cued from that row. But this store of information about all the letters quickly faded. If they had to wait 300 milliseconds, or 0.3 seconds, before being told which row to report, *half* of the information had already faded away. If a full second elapsed before the cue, their accuracy was no better than if there were no cue at all.

Scientists studying echoic memory—the sensory buffer for sounds—find that, as with visual information, auditory information fades drastically in just 1 second. The very transient nature of the sensory buffer suggests that it exists in the brain in the form of neuronal activity, the *firing* of neurons, rather than as any change in the *structure* of the brain. What's fascinating is that, during that short time the information persists in the sensory buffer, we can access it, for example when told which line of letters to report. Once we've mentally retrieved those letters, we can hold onto the information about them for the several seconds it takes to report them. At that point, we have moved them from the transient world of the sensory buffer into the next stage of memory formation, short-term memory, which we'll discuss next.

Short-term memory is brief, but can be extended if we work with the information

We all have had the experience of receiving some new information and just a few seconds later finding that it has slipped away. Once, the most common example in everyday life was when trying to remember someone's seven-digit telephone number between looking it up in the phone book and dialing the number (these days most phones remember the numbers for us). This type of memory, somewhat longer than iconic memories but not lasting more than a few minutes, is **short-term memory** (**STM**). (This is quite different from what people might call short-term memory in everyday life, such as remembering what you had for dinner last night.)

How long is information kept in STM exactly? That depends. How long we retain newly acquired information in STM depends on whether we are *using* the information. Once information has entered STM, we can hold on to it by **rehearsal**, the conscious repetition of information. You've probably noticed that if you are trying to remember a newly encountered phone number, you keep it in mind through rehearsal, reciting the number over and over, either internally or

short-term memory (STM) A type of memory of limited capacity and duration of only seconds.

rehearsal The conscious repetition of information.

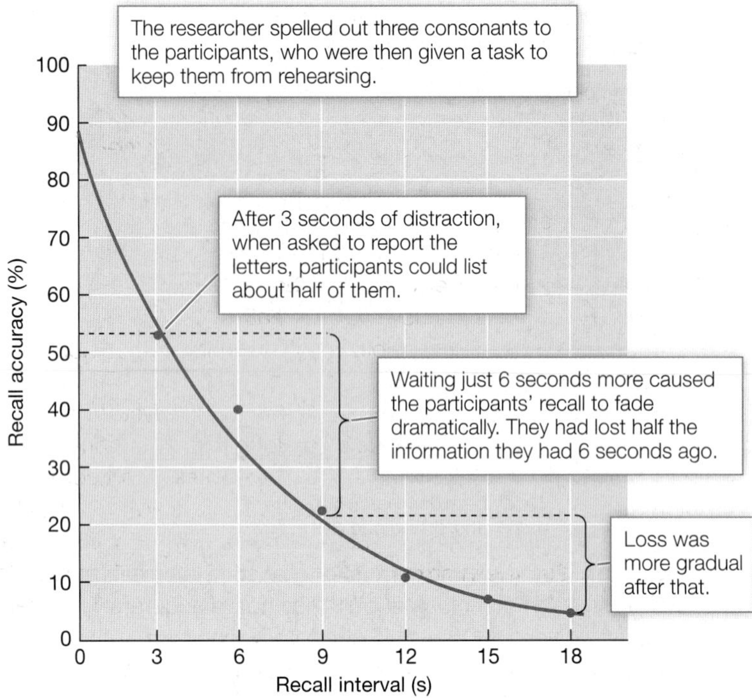

The researcher spelled out three consonants to the participants, who were then given a task to keep them from rehearsing.
After 3 seconds of distraction, when asked to report the letters, participants could list about half of them.
Waiting just 6 seconds more caused the participants' recall to fade dramatically. They had lost half the information they had 6 seconds ago.
Loss was more gradual after that.
Recall accuracy (%)
100
90
80
70
60
50
40
30
20
10
0
0
3
6
9
12
15
18
Recall interval (s)

Figure 9.2 **Without Rehearsal, Short-Term Memory Fades Exponentially** (After Peterson & Peterson, 1959.)

working memory A system that keeps memories available for ready access during performance of a task.

out loud, until you make the phone call. *Without* the aid of rehearsal, STMs last only about 20 seconds (**Figure 9.2**; Brown, 1958; Peterson & Peterson, 1959). *With* rehearsal you may be able to retain a STM until you turn to a new task a few minutes later, but when the STM is gone, it's gone for good.

One way to rehearse material to extend its "shelf life" in STM is by making *use* of the information. For example, if I ask you to multiply two numbers, 14 and 27, in your head, you must keep those numbers in STM as you do so. Try it now. Notice that at each stage of the mental arithmetic, after multiplying two digits and adding up totals, etc., you must remind yourself of what those original two numbers were. By working with those numbers, you rehearse them, keeping them in STM.

Because use, or rehearsal, is critical for keeping short-term memories alive, many researchers now refer to STM as **working memory**, in recognition of the way we use it—this is where we hold information while we are working with it to solve a problem, or are otherwise actively manipulating the information.

One influential model of working memory (Baddeley, 2003) subdivides it into three complementary components:

1. A *phonological loop* contains auditory information (such as speech). This is what you use to rehearse that phone number. It's called a "loop" because we tend to repeat the information over and over.
2. A so-called *visuospatial sketchpad* can hold visual impressions of stimuli. You use this to remember how objects were laid out on a table (as in the game *Memory*). It lasts longer than iconic memory but will soon fade if we stop using it.
3. An *episodic buffer* can contain more integrated information, spanning across sensory modalities, sort of like movie clips with both picture and sound.

Attention is an inescapable aspect of working memory—we hold bits of information in mind by attending to those bits, rather than others. Which factors influence how we direct our attention when using working memory is an active topic of research (Cowan et al., 2012; Oberauer & Hein, 2012; Shipstead et al., 2012).

Once we stop working or rehearsing with the information in STM, it will either fade away or be retained. If it has been retained for more than a few minutes, we say it has entered the next stage, long-term memory, which we'll discuss next.

Long-term memories also fade unless they are used

Memories that last for more than a few minutes, even if we aren't rehearsing them or using them, are called **long-term memories** (**LTMs**). Some LTMs last for years—the address of your childhood home, your first love—but those are the minority, and usually they are retained because they are personally very important to you or because you use the information regularly. A lot of everyday information enters our LTM, accessible to us for minutes or hours, and then fades away again.

In the late 1800s, Hermann Ebbinghaus (1885/1913) systematically studied how quickly relatively unimportant, everyday long-term memories fade away. His experiments focused on recall of **nonsense syllables**, short combinations of letters that are intended to be meaningless (such as CAJ, WID, GEK, NIQ, ZOF) that a participant would be unlikely to associate with a word or event that might prompt recall. Because the information was basically irrelevant to real life, there would be no reason to make use of it in the course of a day. The participant would have to rely solely on rehearsal to get the information into LTM. Ebbinghaus carefully tracked both the rehearsal and the fading of this purely arbitrary information, employing himself as the participant. He memorized hundreds of lists of different nonsense syllables—and tested his memory repeatedly. He kept meticulous records of how long it took to memorize lists and how many mistakes he made in recollecting the nonsense syllables.

Ebbinghaus carefully documented the benefit of rehearsal, repeating material, either mentally or aloud, to improve memory. For example, upon correctly repeating a list of syllables for the first time, he experimented with the value of reciting the list a few more times instead of going on to another task. As you probably expect, he found that those extra recitations, sometimes referred to as *overlearning*, enabled him to remember more of the syllables when tested later on.

Perhaps the most important lesson from Ebbinghaus's work concerns *forgetting*, the inability to recall a memory. For example, he might learn a list of syllables one morning, and when he tested himself a few hours later, he would not remember them all. But were those missing syllables *completely* forgotten? Maybe not: Ebbinghaus found that he could *relearn* that same list in less time than it had taken before, indicating that he had retained some memory for those syllables, even though he had not recalled them at first. He surmised that the remaining trace of memory for those syllables made it easier to relearn them. In this way, Ebbinghaus was one of the first researchers to formally recognize that what we normally think of as "forgetting" is actually a failure to *retrieve* information (an important point we'll consider further in Section 9.2). He then began to consider how it might be possible to develop a test to find some remnant of the forgotten information in the participant's mind. Ebbinghaus measured traces of memory very sensitively by asking *how much faster* he could rememorize the list at a later time. As expected, he found that the more time that had passed since he first learned the list, the longer it would take him to relearn it. The newsworthy aspect of his findings was that the loss of memory retention with time followed a very mathematical relationship (**Figure 9.3**). As time passed, memory was lost exponentially, meaning that the loss was rapid at first but then slowed down. So the most memory is lost in the first few hours, and then loss becomes more gradual. Ebbinghaus found he could still detect some memory a whole month later for absolutely useless information, because he relearned the same list about 20% faster than the first time.

long-term memory (LTM) The nearly limitless store of memories that last more than a few minutes.

nonsense syllables Short combinations of letters intended to be meaningless.

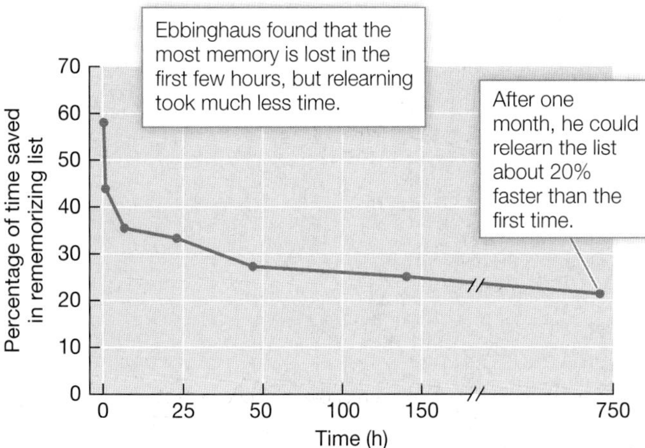

Figure 9.3 Memory Fades with Time Ebbinghaus measured how much information was retained by how quickly he could relearn the list of nonsense syllables to perfection after various lengths of time. For example, at the first time point (20 minutes) he rememorized the list in 60% less time than it took at first. This exponential loss of memory suggested a physical process that Ebbinghaus tried to model with mathematical formulas. (After Ebbinghaus, 1885/1913.)

Ebbinghaus believed the exponential loss of memory with time suggested an ongoing physical process that could be predicted mathematically. The similarity of the shapes of the three curves in Figures 9.1, 9.2, and 9.3 supports his notion. Compare the Ebbinghaus graph in Figure 9.3 with the graph in Figure 9.1 about iconic memory and the graph in Figure 9.2 about STM without rehearsal; in all three curves there's exponential loss of information—quick at first and more gradual thereafter. The shapes of the three curves are about the same. The only difference is in the timescale on the *x*-axis: iconic memories fade in less than a second, STMs in a less than a minute, and LTMs over the course of hours. Note that this rapid fading of LTM is for "pure" memories such as Ebbinghaus used—information that was useless, so it was not rehearsed as he went about his everyday life. Important, *useful* information may be retained in LTM for life, but that's because by definition "useful" information is accessed over and over.

Having learned that both STMs and LTMs fade exponentially, you may wonder whether there is only one memory system, with the duration of a memory simply part of a continuum from seconds to years. But many observations make it clear that STM and LTM are indeed separate from one another and must rely on different processes in the brain, as we'll discuss next.

Short-term memory and long-term memory rely on different processes

One of the most dramatic demonstrations that STM and LTM are separate systems was provided by Henry, whom we met at the start of the chapter. We know Henry had ample STM, because he could repeat a list of numbers, or add them in his head about as well as the average person, and he could hold a rational conversation with you while discussing some topic. Yet he never transferred STMs of what he learned in that conversation into LTM. Five minutes later he wouldn't remember ever having met you, and he wouldn't recall anything you told him about what's happening in the world. He lacked the ability to move memories from STM to LTM. His LTM from before the surgery seemed to be intact, but he could no longer add to that store.

There are drugs, such as Valium, that don't affect LTM but may cause people to forget what happened when they were under the drug's influence, as if the drug prevented transfer from STM to LTM. Using animal models, scientists have found that different classes of drugs affect different stages in the memory process. For example, some drugs can keep an animal from remembering something it had learned, but only if the drug is given during the STM stage after learning. Giving the drug later has no effect, indicating that memory that has entered LTM is now immune to the drug's effects (Löw et al., 2000; Reder et al., 2007). These and similar observations support the theory that memory involves at least three stages of formation, from sensory buffer through STM to LTM (**Figure 9.4**).

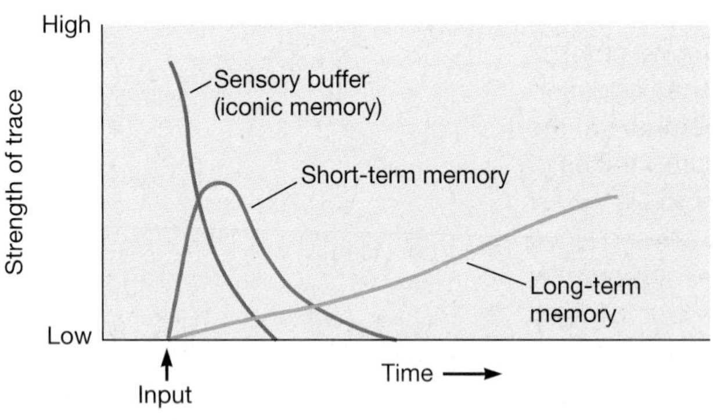

Figure 9.4 Stages of Memory Formation For information to enter our permanent memory, it must first enter into iconic memory, which lasts for less than a second, then into STM, which lasts for several seconds, and then into LTM, which can last a lifetime.

Another classic demonstration that STM and LTM are separate processes involves learning lists of words or numbers. If you hear a list of ten words and then try to repeat them back after a 30-second delay, you will probably do es-

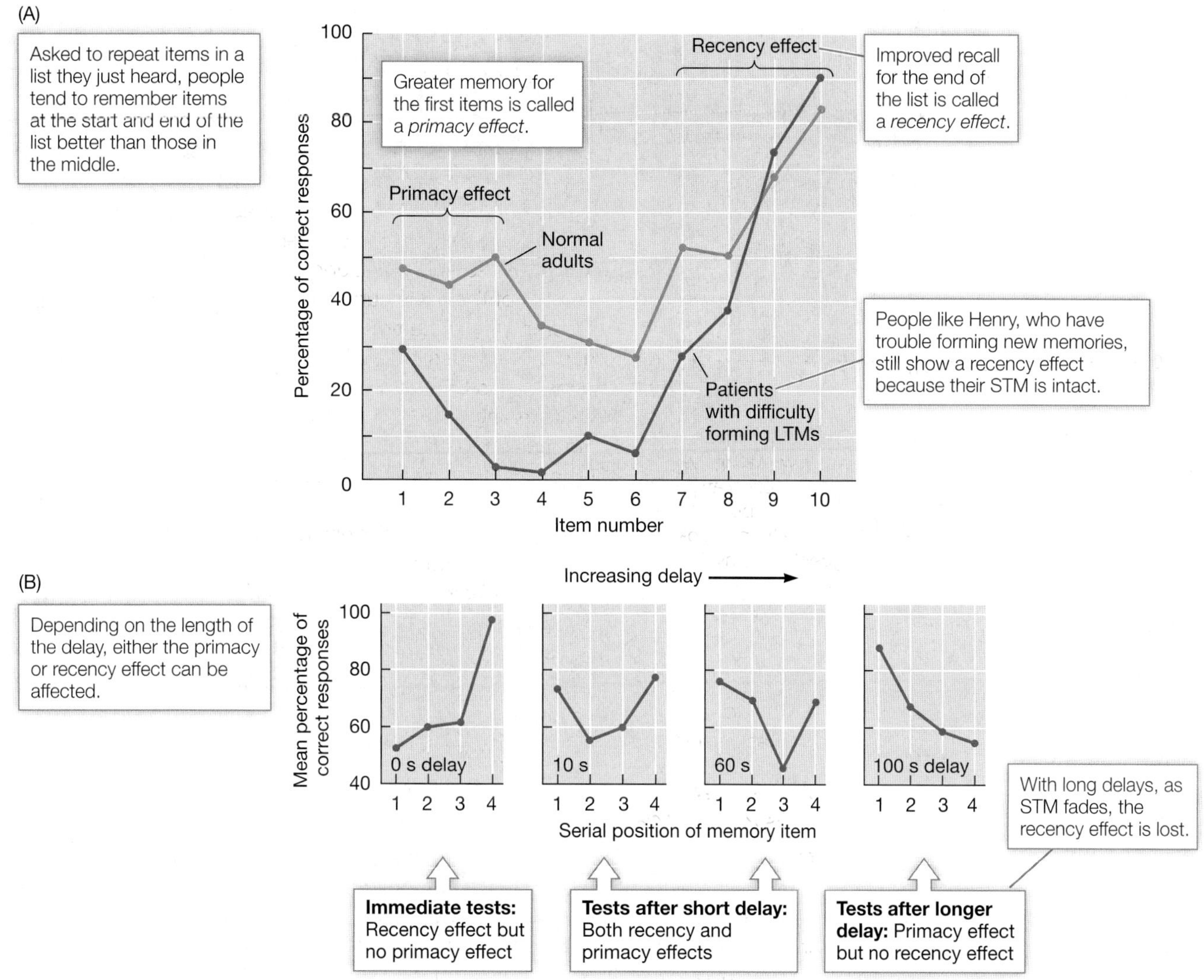
(A)
Asked to repeat items in a list they just heard, people tend to remember items at the start and end of the list better than those in the middle.
Greater memory for the first items is called a *primacy effect*.
Recency effect
Improved recall for the end of the list is called a *recency effect*.
Primacy effect
Normal adults
People like Henry, who have trouble forming new memories, still show a recency effect because their STM is intact.
Patients with difficulty forming LTMs
Percentage of correct responses
Item number
(B)
Depending on the length of the delay, either the primacy or recency effect can be affected.
Increasing delay
Mean percentage of correct responses
0 s delay
10 s
60 s
100 s delay
Serial position of memory item
With long delays, as STM fades, the recency effect is lost.
Immediate tests: Recency effect but no primacy effect
Tests after short delay: Both recency and primacy effects
Tests after longer delay: Primacy effect but no recency effect

Figure 9.5 Serial Position Curves (A after Baddeley & Warrington, 1970; B after Wright et al., 1985.)

pecially well with words from the start and end of the list, but you aren't likely to remember items from the middle of the list very well. **Figure 9.5A** shows the typical results from such an experiment: a U-shaped **serial position curve**, where recollection is best at the start and end of the series of items. Your improved ability to remember the earliest few words is called a **primacy effect**, because those words were first ("primary"). Your improved ability to recall the last few words is called a **recency effect**, because when we ask you to repeat the list, those last words are the ones you heard most recently. Several observations indicate that the recency effect is due to STM and the primacy effect to LTM.

One simple manipulation of this kind of test shows that the primacy and recency effects must rely on different processes. For example, if we omit the delay and ask you to repeat the list immediately, you will remember the end of the list but not the beginning (**Figure 9.5B, left**). You show a recency effect, as you would expect if recency reflects STM. STM fades quickly, and you heard the words at the end most recently. But you do not show a primacy effect if there's no delay. At first, that sounds counterintuitive—do you really remember items at the start of the list better if we *delay* asking you to report them? But it does make sense if you consider what happens when we delay. You *rehearse* the list, starting with the items at the beginning of the list, putting them into LTM. When we take away your chance to rehearse by asking you to repeat the list immediately, that information never enters LTM and so rapidly fades away. Only STM for the end of the list remains.

serial position curve A U-shaped curve showing the likelihood of remembering an item in a list based on its position in that list.

primacy effect The improved recall of items from the beginning of the list in a recall task.

recency effect The improved recall of the items at the end of the list in a recall task.

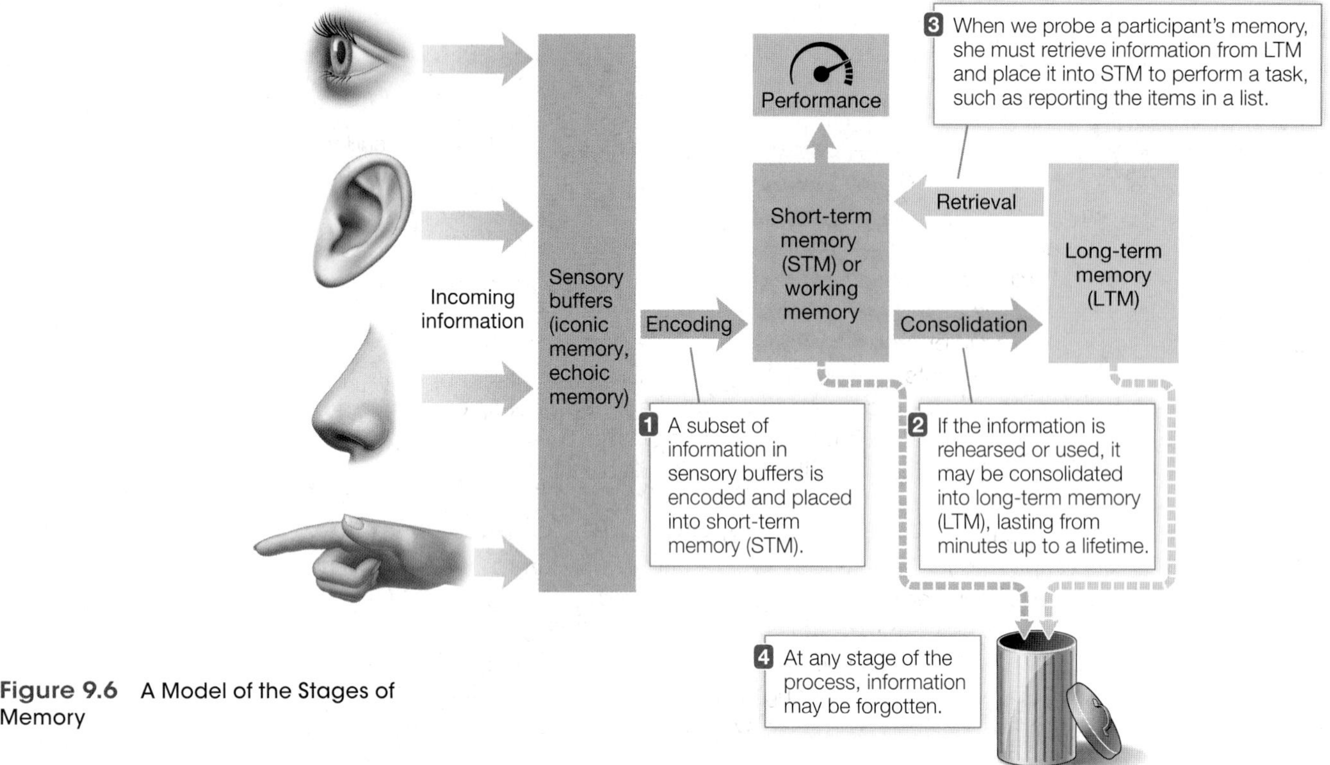

Incoming information
Sensory buffers (iconic memory, echoic memory)
Encoding
Performance
Short-term memory (STM) or working memory
Retrieval
Consolidation
Long-term memory (LTM)
3 When we probe a participant's memory, she must retrieve information from LTM and place it into STM to perform a task, such as reporting the items in a list.
1 A subset of information in sensory buffers is encoded and placed into short-term memory (STM).
2 If the information is rehearsed or used, it may be consolidated into long-term memory (LTM), lasting from minutes up to a lifetime.
4 At any stage of the process, information may be forgotten.

Figure 9.6 A Model of the Stages of Memory

On the other hand, if we extend for a few minutes the time between presenting you with the list and asking you to repeat it, your better recall of the end of the list—the recency effect—will fade (**Figure 9.5B, right**). The recency effect disappears because now it hasn't been all that recently that you heard those words at the end. Because the recency effect is short-lived, it is thought to reflect STM/working memory. The primacy effect, however, lasts longer and is attributed to LTM.

People like Henry, who have difficulty moving information into LTM, nevertheless show the recency effect (see Figure 9.5A). This result again indicates that the recency effect is due to STM, because that is intact in such patients. But as predicted, they show less of a primacy effect than control participants (see Figure 9.5A), as you'd expect if the primacy effect reflects LTM. In experimental animals, lesioning some brain regions can disrupt STM but not LTM, confirming the distinction between them (Kesner & Novak, 1982).

Figure 9.6 offers a summary of how three stages of memory formation—sensory buffer, STM, and LTM—fit into a current model of memory. Information enters sensory buffers, where it is either lost or placed into STM. Some of those STMs are then transferred to LTM. In the future that information can be brought back from LTM to be used in STM/working memory as we perform some task (Atkinson & Shiffrin, 1971). In the following sections we'll consider those three processes of information transfer:

1. *Encoding* The transfer of information from sensory systems to STM
2. *Consolidation* The transfer of information from STM to LTM
3. *Memory retrieval* The transfer of information out of LTM for use in STM

We have to encode information in order to store and retrieve it

To report a memory, we usually rely on language. For example, in the case of Sperling's experiment testing iconic memory (see Figure 9.1), participants had to say what letters they had seen. At some point then, they had to take the iconic memory of the shapes of those letters on the screen and "translate" them, working out which letters of the alphabet had been displayed. This process of taking raw sensory information and converting it into a form that we can understand and report is called **encoding**. Because we learn to read at a relatively young age, we are able to encode letters very rapidly and without effort. Reading words takes a little more time than reading individual letters, but also happens rapidly. Even when you are trying to remember nonverbal information, such as the details of some briefly glimpsed scene, you have to encode the information to make sense of it. Encoding is an automatic and inevitable aspect of any perception, so it is always involved in organizing information. For example, first you would need to know what the objects were in the scene to make any sense of how they were arranged with regard to one another. Was it a group of people around a table, a wall of shelves filled with books, or a horse grazing under a tree? After you've encoded this information, it either is discarded or enters STM, and perhaps goes on to LTM.

encoding The process of taking raw sensory information and converting it into a form that we can understand and report.

chunking An encoding strategy that reduces the total number of items to be remembered by combining them into meaningful units.

Encoded information is easier to remember because it is more efficiently packaged, making use of what you already know. The glimpsed scene of a horse grazing under a tree is easily remembered if you already know what horses and trees look like. Similarly, reading tasks present little difficulty if you already know what an *E* looks like; you only need to remember *E* to remember how the four lines making up that letter were arranged. For an extreme contrast, imagine trying to remember the positions of the many lines below:

電気

If, unlike me, you know how to read Japanese, you may instantly recognize that these characters mean "electricity." If you saw those characters for 1 second, and *encoded* them properly, then you would only need to remember that single concept "electricity" to tap into your preexisting knowledge of Japanese to reproduce those 20 or so lines. In contrast, because I could not encode all those lines into a single concept, I would have to remember the length and position of each line separately to reproduce them accurately. After seeing them for 1 second? Fat chance! The ability to code all those lines into a single "bit" of information is an example of encoding. Likewise, remembering a single English word makes it easy to recall the sequence of letters that spell that word (assuming you already knew how to spell it). You don't clutter up the STM with what the individual letters looked like in terms of shape or font.

There are several ways in which you can exploit encoding to help remember. One strategy is called **chunking**, when you break down a long list of items into several "chunks" to ease memorization. For example, you might have real difficulty memorizing this list of letters in order:

ALOLLSUFBIHULUZ

But if you break the string into chunks, it might be easy to remember them:

ALOLLSUFBIHULUZ

Why does chunking help? First, you are again taking advantage of the efficiency of tapping knowledge you already possess (A starts the alphabet, Z ends it, LOL means "laugh out loud," LSU is a big football school, etc.).

But in addition to that, *chunking reduces the absolute number of items to be memorized* from 15 to 6. This is important because people have theorized that STM can only hold about five to nine items at one time. In a very influential publication, George A. Miller (1956) proposed that there is something "magical" about the number 7, plus or minus 2. In his theorizing, Miller was thinking of STM as "working memory"—a store of information that is temporarily useful for some task. An obvious example is a local phone number, which consists of seven

Figure 9.7 Organizing Memory (A) Bower and colleagues (1969) found that people asked to remember a list of over 100 words like these presented at random could report about 20 or so. (B) But when the same list was presented to other participants in a hierarchically organized fashion, people could recall about three times as many of the words.

(A)

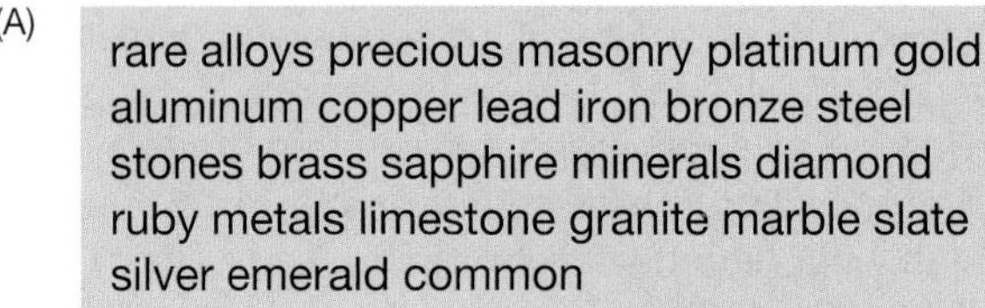

rare alloys precious masonry platinum gold aluminum copper lead iron bronze steel stones brass sapphire minerals diamond ruby metals limestone granite marble slate silver emerald common

(B)

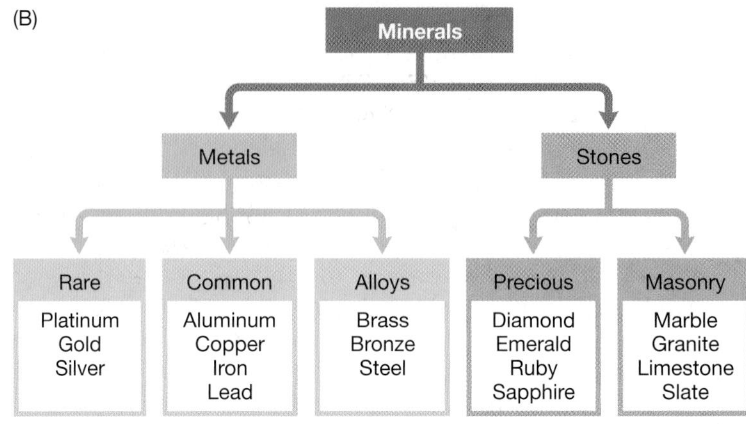

hierarchies Organizational structures where items have some relationship to one another.

numbers. Miller noted that most people can hear a list of seven items (digits, words, letters, etc.) and then repeat it pretty faithfully, but fewer people can repeat ten or more items without mistakes. From this perspective, breaking down any long list into seven or so chunks means they will fit within the working memory capacity of most people.

Another encoding strategy to promote memorization is the use of **hierarchies**, organizational structures where items have some relationship to one another. Again, this only works if you have prior knowledge that can be used to reduce the number of things you have to remember. In one classic example, people were asked to remember long lists of words. For some participants, the words were presented at random, but for other participants, the words were organized hierarchically (**Figure 9.7**). Participants who saw the words arranged hierarchically remembered about three times as many words as the participants given the list in random order (Bower et al., 1969).

In terms of remembering, knowledge about hierarchies is only helpful in a limited number of situations, where the important things to remember happen to have a hierarchical relationship to one another. In laboratory studies of "pure" memory, where participants are given information that is purposely arbitrary and meaningless as a control for rehearsal or usage, the items of information are not likely to have any hierarchical relationship to one another. But when you need to memorize new material in *real life*, even if the items don't have a strictly hierarchical relationship to one another, they are probably related to one another in *some* fashion. Whatever that new material is—the steps in refinishing a wood cabinet, the system of federal government in the United States, or the stages of memory formation—the components relate to one another in some way. If you can understand how the components relate to one another, it will help you remember the material. For example, seeing the relationship between the words in Figure 9.7B helps you recall those words in a particular sequence. In other words, you'll remember the information better if you try to *understand* it, rather than just memorize it by rote. In fact, one reasonable definition of what we mean when we say "understanding" is a more efficient encoding of a collection of information, making it easier to remember. As we'll discuss in more detail later in this chapter, organizing the material based on understanding also makes it easier to *retrieve* that information in the future.

Of course, sometimes in real life we do need to remember relatively arbitrary lists, like the digits in a telephone number, or which playing cards have been discarded in a poker game. Who among us doesn't struggle to remember all those different alphanumeric passwords for our online accounts? It often seems there is no meaningful way to organize the items in such lists. We'll consider some strategies to help memorize lists of unrelated items in Section 9.2. For now, let's consider how a small fraction of information in STM is consolidated into LTM, and processes that can affect that transfer.

consolidation The process of transferring information from STM into LTM.

Some short-term memories are consolidated into the vast store of long-term memory

As Sperling and others have shown, our senses can take in a lot more information than our STM can accommodate. Likewise, only a minority of information in STM is ever transferred to LTM. Because a lot of information is lost at each stage, only a tiny fraction of the information we take in is ever laid down in LTM. The process of transferring information from STM into LTM is called **consolidation**. Henry, whom we met at the start of the chapter, could not consolidate information from STM into LTM.

We've already seen that LTM is very different from STM in terms of duration, since STM lasts only a few seconds and LTM may be lifelong. But the *capacity* of LTM is also very different from that of STM. While most people can only store seven plus or minus two bits of information in STM, it seems that almost everyone stores truly massive amounts of information in LTM. In one classic experiment, participants viewed long sequences of color photos of various scenes. Then several days later the participants were shown pairs of images—in each case a new image plus one from the previous session—and asked to identify the images seen previously. Astonishingly, participants performed with a high degree of accuracy for series of up to 10,000 different photos! This prompted the researcher to conclude that, for all practical purposes, "there is no upper bound to memory capacity" (Standing, 1973). Similarly impressive feats of memory in other animals, such as pigeons that could learn to recognize over 300 different photographs in one session (Vaughan & Green, 1984), illustrate that this great capacity for information storage is a general property of brains across the animal kingdom.

The capacity of LTM is often said to be "immeasurably large" because we really don't know how to even count up all the things that an average person remembers. Language alone consists of many thousands of bits of information, including the meaning of over 10,000 words, the rules for assembling them into grammatically correct sentences, how they are spelled, etc. Then there's all the information you need to draw upon to ride a bicycle, play a video game, drive a car. The main problem in trying to determine the limits of LTM is trying to define and catalog how much knowledge any person has in LTM—what scientist is going to devote his or her life to making a catalog of what some other person knows? Even worse, if we want to know if someone has ever reached the *limit* of LTM, filling it completely, we'd have to catalog their entire LTM twice (!) to see if newly acquired information had squeezed out old information. Even then, although the person seemed to have forgotten something today, they might remember it tomorrow. So we will never really know the maximum capacity of LTM. We just know it's really, really large. That view is reinforced by the cases of a few very rare people who seem to recall enormous amounts of detail (**Box 9.2**).

Just as it is impractical to ever really test the limits of LTM capacity, we can never really be sure that any information that has entered LTM is lost entirely. Why? Because sometimes information we have forgotten at one time suddenly pops into our head at a later time. No matter what tiny, unimportant detail we're trying to recall, no matter how impossible conjuring up that information seems right now, it's always possible that we'll remember it later. If we do, then the in-

Psychology in Everyday Life

BOX 9.2

A Few People Have Prodigious Memories

You might think it would be wonderful to effortlessly recall almost everything from your past, but studies of real-life cases reveal that perfect recall—for example, being able to remember in detail what you did on a specific date for each of the last 10 years—can be a great burden (Luria, 1987; Parker et al., 2006). These cases remind us that the brain's memory systems—even the more fallible versions found in most of us—have the capability to retain vast amounts of information.

For a more concrete sense of how vast LTM can be, consider the case of Kim Peek, the model for the fictional film *Rain Man.* Kim was a **savant** (from the French for "knowing"), a person with an unusually well developed ability or skill (see Section 11.2). One of Kim's savant abilities was memory. Born with several brain deformities, including a misshapen cerebellum and an absence of the corpus callosum (Treffert & Christensen, 2005), Kim couldn't walk until age 4, but he was reading by age 3, and apparently never forgot what he read. Kim eventually memorized about 9,000 books (see figure), mostly nonfiction, each taking about an hour to read. (He was reading, not using a "photographic memory" as discussed in Box 9.1.) For example, he read the novel *The Hunt for Red October* in 75 minutes and when asked, 4 months later, to name a minor character, he not only knew the name but cited the page number where the character appeared and quoted several passages from the page verbatim! Sadly, Kim died of a heart attack at age 58 in 2009.

Kim Peek memorized an estimated 9,000 books, revealing the vast capacity of his long-term memory.
9,000 books
1,250 feet
Empire State Building

An earlier famous savant came to light one day in the 1920s, when a Russian reporter, Solomon Shereshevsky (1886–1958), was scolded for never writing down his editor's instructions. Solomon quickly recited the editor's long list of addresses and instructions to him and all the other reporters word for word. Although nearly 30 at the time, Solomon was surprised when the editor told him that other people sometimes forget things! Psychologist Alexander Luria (1987) began studying Solomon, finding he could remember long lists of numbers or words (even from languages Solomon did not understand) that were read aloud to him. Solomon never seemed to rehearse the material, but just seemed to listen attentively and then repeat the list, either forward or backward, when asked. How long a list could Solomon remember? Luria was never able to find out, because Solomon remembered every list Luria ever gave him, no matter how long it was. Remarkably, Solomon could repeat those lists 2, 8, and even *16* years later, although he was never warned that he would be tested again. The only difficulty of testing after so many years was specifying for Solomon which list he was being asked about ("Yes, yes...we were in my apartment...you were sitting at the table...wearing a gray suit").

Continued

Psychology in Everyday Life *Continued*

Despite this prodigious memory, Solomon had trouble recognizing people's faces ("they're very changeable"). This difficulty probably contributed to his lackluster career as a reporter, and Solomon eventually became a *mnemonist*, a professional memorizer (Luria's book about Solomon is titled *The Mind of a Mnemonist*). For decades, Solomon gave three or four performances a day where audience members would give him lists of hundreds or even thousands of words or numbers, written on a big blackboard, and then Solomon would face the audience, close his eyes, and repeat the list with the audience checking his performance. Solomon also experienced synesthesia, where any stimulus in one modality would evoke sensation in other modalities, which seemed to help his recall abilities. For example, each digit conjured up the image of a type of person, so in seeing "87" he thought of "a fat woman and a man twirling his moustache." Later in the chapter you'll read about a woman in her forties who seems to remember everything that has happened to her, on every day of her life, since she was 14.

While it seems obvious that these special people must have had special brains, it seems very unlikely that they used an entirely different process for storing information in LTM. It seems more likely that what made them special was how that information, once stored, seemed to be permanently available to them. Perhaps such people are unusual because natural selection favors the tendency to forget unimportant information. However unusual Kim and Solomon might have been, their brains were no larger than normal, demonstrating that an ordinary-sized human brain has the capacity to store unbelievably large amounts of information.

savant syndrome A very rare condition in which a mentally disabled person also exhibits exceptional ability in some limited field, such as memory, mathematics, or music.

formation was still in LTM all that time, and our problem was in accessing the information. That brings us to the question of why we forget, and whether forgetting represents a genuine loss of information or a problem in recovering information, which we'll discuss in the next section. We'll see lots of evidence that most forgetting is a problem in retrieval rather than total loss of the memory.

9.1 SUMMARY

- There are at least three stages of memory, including a *sensory buffer* that stores information for a second or so, short-term memory, and long-term memory.
- If the sensory information is *encoded* so that we can make sense of it, it may be transferred to *short-term memory* (*STM*), which is also called *working memory* because we can consciously use that information.
- Without rehearsal, we retain information in STM for only a few seconds, but with the conscious repetition of *rehearsal*, the information can be retained for several minutes and may be *consolidated* into *long-term memory* (*LTM*).
- Ebbinghaus memorized *nonsense syllables* to study the phenomenon that information in LTM fades exponentially, meaning the greatest proportion of loss happens first.
- After hearing or reading a list of items, people usually display a *serial position curve* in their recall of the items, remembering the beginning and end of the list better than the middle.
- The improved recall of the beginning of the list is called a *primacy effect*, and is thought to reflect greater consolidation into LTM, while improved recall for the end of the list is called the *recency effect*, and is thought to reflect the more recent presentation of the items and therefore reduced fading from STM.
- To store information in LTM efficiently, it must go through consolidation, which we can improve by *chunking* the information or organizing it in a *hierarchical* fashion.

- For most people, STM can faithfully retain only seven or so items at any one time, so encoding strategies allow us to fold more information into those seven or so "slots" in STM.
- In contrast, the capacity of LTM is so enormous that no one has been able to determine its limits.

REVIEW QUESTIONS

1. What are the stages of memory formation, and approximately how long is information retained at each stage?
2. What are the two aspects of recall that result in the serial position curve of recall for a list of items? How does manipulating the time between presentation of the list and recall affect performance?
3. Why did scientists studying memory use nonsense syllables for memorization tasks?

Food for Thought

Why do you think Solomon Shereshevsky, with his apparently limitless access to LTM, had a hard time recognizing faces?

9.2 The Vulnerability of Memory

Things to Learn

- Factors that interfere with memory formation
- Difficulty of retrieval and value of cues
- Memory distortion
- Seven sins of memory
- Tactics to improve memory

Some information that enters LTM lasts for decades, but most of us forget a lot of what we've known. There are basically two processes to explain why we forget, and probably both are at work: memories are either gone or misplaced. The first possibility, that the memory is entirely gone, requires that memories **fade**, gradually disappearing as a result of a physical loss of that memory from the brain. If the physical basis of the memory is truly gone, then the memory would be lost for good. If you go back to Figure 9.6, this loss of memory from LTM is represented by the green arrow leading from LTM to the trash can.

The second possibility is that the memory is still present but is misplaced, so that forgetting is a problem in **retrieval**, the act or process of accessing information from LTM (see Figure 9.6). Recall from the last section that we can never be sure a participant who fails to recall something today won't suddenly remember it tomorrow. So all a psychologist can be sure of is that the participant wasn't able to access that information when asked. Because we can never be sure information has really disappeared entirely from LTM, we need a definition of forgetting that encompasses both fading of memory and the failure to retrieve memory.

In this section we define **forgetting** as *the inability* to *retrieve information from LTM*, either because the information is gone entirely (which is difficult to prove) or because the participant cannot retrieve the information that is still there. The discomfort felt by those rare people with exceptional recall, such as those discussed in Box 9.2, suggests that forgetting is a normal, useful aspect of memory, helping filter out unimportant information, perhaps in order to free up needed cognitive resources (Kuhl et al., 2007). Indeed, we'll see soon that sometimes one set of information in LTM can interfere with our ability to retrieve another set of information.

Also note that when scientists talk about forgetting, they are only talking about that minority of information that moves from STM to LTM. In everyday life, sometimes people say they "forgot" something when *they never really got the information from STM to LTM in the first place.* A common example in college is when a student reads a chapter and then draws a blank when tested on some information from the chapter. Perhaps the student really forgot the information, but if he was reading the chapter without paying close attention and trying to *understand* it, then it may never have moved from STM (when the student read the words silently to himself) into LTM (i.e., the student never consolidated what the words *meant* and related them to the material before and after that in the chapter). This might be more a failure to properly *consolidate* the information into LTM than a failure of retrieval. In contrast, this section is concerned exclusively with inability to retrieve information that actually entered LTM.

fade The gradual disappearance of a memory based on its physical loss from the brain.

retrieval The act or process of accessing information from LTM.

forgetting The inability to retrieve information from LTM.

We'll begin by reviewing some factors that are known to make memory retrieval difficult, as well as factors that aid retrieval. Next we'll return briefly to a subject from Section 7.3, instances when a person's flawed memory can have tragic consequences. Then we'll close with a discussion of tips about how to improve your ability to retrieve information from memory.

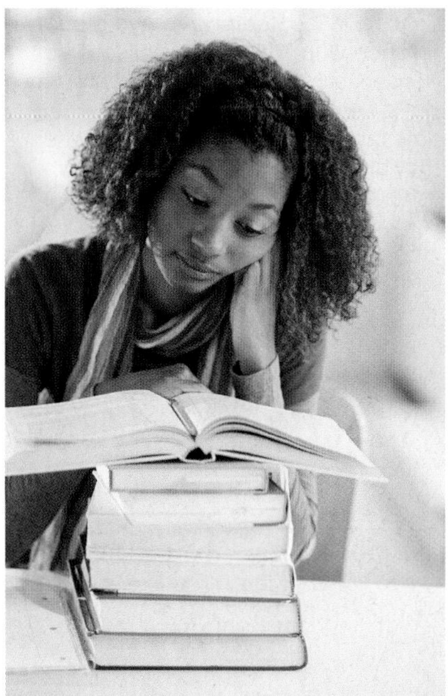

Ineffective Reading Sometimes our eyes are scanning the words but we're not really paying attention.

Sometimes one memory can interfere with another

It is relatively easy for psychologists to demonstrate how one memory can sometimes interfere with another, and most of us have noticed such interference in everyday life. In fact, study of memory interference began in the 1800s when a scientist (Hugo Munsterberg), who had kept his pocket watch in one pocket for many years, had to move it to another pocket. He noticed that he kept reaching into the old pocket when he wanted to know the time. This is an instance of **proactive interference**, when an existing memory interferes with formation of a new memory. The "pro" in the term "proactive" refers to the fact that the first memory is acting *forward* in time, interfering with the future, specifically the attempt to form a new memory. For example, say you have an old friend named Julia, who prefers being called Julie. If you meet another woman with that name, who hates the nickname, you may have a hard time remembering to call her Julia rather than Julie. Your previous memory of the old friend makes it hard for you to remember your new friend's preferred name. This may be especially true if the two friends resemble each other. Likewise, in the laboratory, *the more similar two stimuli are, the more the memories of those stimuli can interfere with one another.*

The other type of memory interference is **retroactive interference**, when forming a new memory makes it harder to retrieve an old memory. The "retro" in the term "retroactive" refers to the idea that this new memory is working *backward* in time, interfering with a previous memory. A common example of retroactive interference these days is when we register for some Web service and are required to generate a new password. If we log onto that service a lot, really sealing in that new password, we may have difficulty remembering an old password when logging onto a less-used website. The new password has made it hard to recall the old one.

Another common example of both proactive and retroactive interference may happen in learning languages. A person who has taken French in the past may find that the rules of pronunciation for that language interfere when learning Spanish—a case of proactive interference—the old memory reaches forward in time to interfere with new memories. If the person studies Spanish for several years and then visits France, he may find that his newly acquired memories for Spanish pronunciation retroactively interfere with his old memory for French pronunciation (**Figure 9.8**).

proactive interference The type of interference when an existing memory interferes with formation of a new memory.

retroactive interference The type of interference when forming a new memory interferes with retrieval of an old memory.

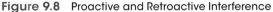

If interference is an important cause of forgetting, then if we could just turn off a person's brain after she had memorized something, and then turn it back on a few days later, her recollection for the material she learned just before losing consciousness should be pretty good. Of course, we don't know how to "turn off" a brain for a few days and successfully have it work again, and it's hard to know if that will ever be possible, even in the far future. But way back in 1924, some psychologists came up with an approximation of this experiment (Jenkins & Dallenbach, 1924). They had participants learn lists of nonsense words, and as expected, they saw an exponential decline in recollection of the lists with time. But they found that if participants memorized the lists just before going to *sleep*, a time during which they were presumably being exposed to little new interfering information, they

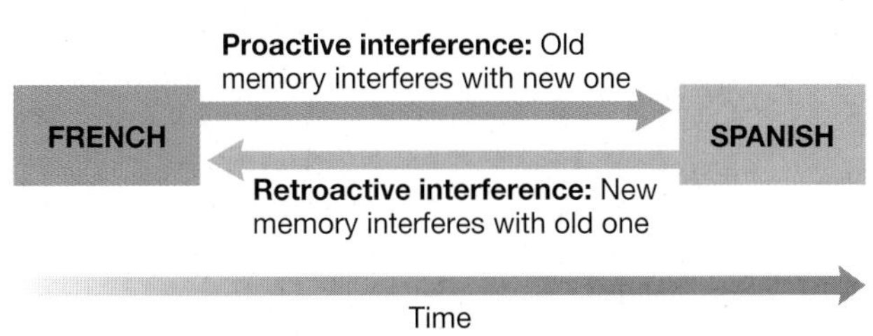
Proactive interference: Old memory interferes with new one
FRENCH
SPANISH
Retroactive interference: New memory interferes with old one
Time

Figure 9.8 Proactive and Retroactive Interference

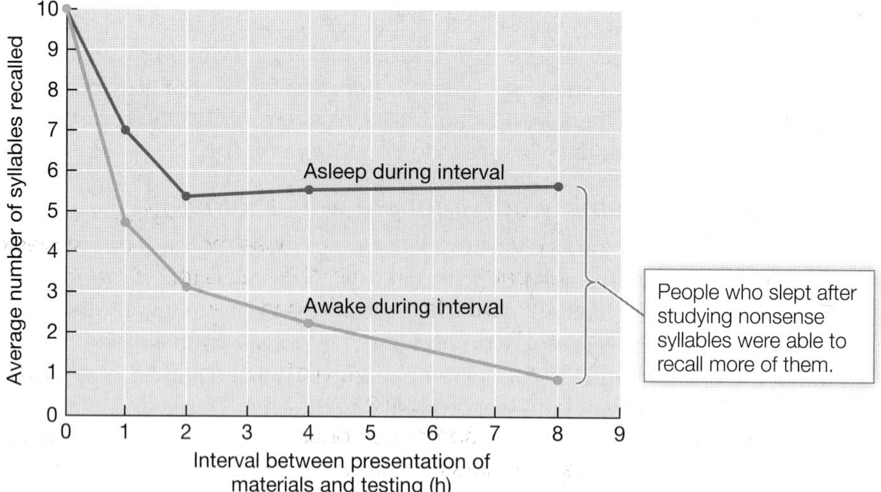

Figure 9.9 Sleeping to Avoid Interference with Memory Recollection of nonsense syllables decreases with time, but if participants sleep between the time they memorize the lists and when they are tested, they remember more. (After Jenkins & Dallenbach, 1924.)

remembered more of the words (**Figure 9.9**). The idea is that the participants who were sleeping were experiencing less retroactive interference than the participants who stayed awake. This suggests that, rather than staying up all night cramming information before a test, you might be better off learning some core of the material and then going to sleep so you can consolidate that information without interference.

In a funny way, proactive and retroactive interference may illustrate why, in the long run, it is good that we forget things. If we really remembered *everything*, as a few rare people seem to do, then there would be more similar memories that could interfere with our attempt to retrieve a particular one. Indeed, those special people we mentioned in Box 9.2 often needed help pinpointing which memory they were being asked for. And they seemed to have difficulty getting by in everyday life, including difficulties maintaining relationships with other people. Thus it is probably no accident that our brains are normally built to let information fade if we aren't making use of it. Whether the memory ever disappears entirely or not, the more it fades, the less likely it will interfere with our attempts to retrieve other memories.

Proactive and retroactive interference also reinforce the notion that forgetting is probably more a problem of *retrieval* of the memory than of the *loss* of the memory, for several reasons. First, given the huge capacity of LTM, it's not likely that you've filled your LTM so much that adding one more bit shoves out some old bit of memory. Indeed, the fact that memories that are more *similar* to each other produce more interference shows that the problem is not that *any old* memory was hard to recall, but specifically a memory that resembles the interfering memory. That fact seems more compatible with the idea that we use a similar method to retrieve either the desired or the interfering memory, so we sometimes "pull up" the wrong one. For an analogy, if my wife asks me to retrieve her green blouse, I'm more likely to grab the wrong one if there are four different green blouses, as opposed to only one. The similar blouses interfere with my ability to retrieve the desired one because I'm using this characteristic they have in common to find the one she wants. For that matter, our everyday experience tells us that a memory that has been interfered with usually isn't *lost*—each time that nineteenth-century scientist found his old watch pocket empty, he quickly remembered the new location of his watch, and you will remember your friend's married name eventually.

Let's explore further this question of whether memories are lost or simply misplaced.

Several psychological phenomena indicate that forgetting is probably due to a failure in retrieval

Once information has entered LTM, it is potentially permanent (or at least life-long), but if LTM is any memory that lasts more than a few minutes, then obviously we forget most of what's put into LTM. Don't believe me? OK, what did you eat yesterday? You remember it pretty well, right? Therefore that's in LTM. But so is what you ate last week—if I had asked you back then what you ate yesterday, you would have told me. Do you remember all those meals from last week now? Probably not. Except for particularly memorable meals (that Thanksgiving when Uncle Joe started singing over dessert), you can no longer retrieve information that had once been in LTM for a day or two after each meal. This is true for *thousands* of meals that you've had so far. And of course what we eat is just a tiny (albeit wonderful) part of our everyday life.

While we may have actually lost *some* memories (e.g., the dinner you had 2 years and 12 days ago), there are lots of reasons to think that at least traces of the information we have "forgotten" are actually still in our head somewhere. If that is so, then most forgetting must be a problem in retrieval.

For example, a month after Ebbinghaus had memorized a list of nonsense syllables, he would remember very few of the items. Were they *entirely* gone from his LTM? Probably not, because he could relearn that list in about 80% of the time it took him originally. If the information had been lost entirely, then it should have taken him just as long to relearn it as it had taken to learn it in the first place. If you think of LTM as a computer hard drive with millions of separate files of information, then the challenge isn't how to cram more information in there, or how to have the information persist over time once it's there, but rather how to retrieve the *particular* piece of information you are after.

A common way to show that someone has not forgotten something entirely is to offer a cue, some bit of information related to the forgotten information. Improved recollection resulting from a cue, hint, or guide to the answer is called **cued recall**. In contrast, in **free recall** a person must retrieve the information without any hints or guides. For example, if I give you a list of 20 words and you try to memorize them, and later I simply ask you to repeat the list, I would be testing your free recall. But if I were to give you a list providing the first two letters of each word, with blanks to indicate the remaining letters, I would be testing cued recall, and you would remember more of the words, perhaps all of them.

Closely related to the improvement in memory through cued recall is **priming**: exposure to a stimulus that influences response to a later stimulus. For example, if I show you a list that includes the word "stamp" and later ask you to complete some word stems, including STA--, you will be much more likely to think of the word "stamp." A person exposed beforehand to a list with the word "stand" will be more likely to think of that word in response to that same stimulus. In memory research, priming can be regarded as a particular type of cue to aid recall. Another example of priming would be if you were exposed to the word "dog" and then were asked to fill in WO--; in this case you'd be more likely to complete the word as "woof" or "wolf" rather than, say, "word" or "worm."

Priming effects suggest a theory of memory called **spreading activation**, the idea that words and objects that are related to one another are somehow connected in our memory, so that recalling one word is likely to lead us to recall another, related word. Once the word "dog" activated that part of your memory, the related word "wolf" would be more likely to be activated next. The term "spreading activation" is not meant to suggest that different memories are stored in adjacent parts of the brain, as though exciting a brain region containing one memory would spread to neighboring regions containing related memories. In fact, it seems clear that individual memories are not actually stored in some one

cued recall The memory testing condition in which a participant is provided some hints about the information requested.

free recall The memory testing condition in which the person must retrieve the information without any hints or guides.

priming The ability of information presented at one time to affect a person's response at a later time.

spreading activation The idea that memories are somehow linked to one another based on characteristics they share, so that recalling one word is likely to lead us to recall another, related word.

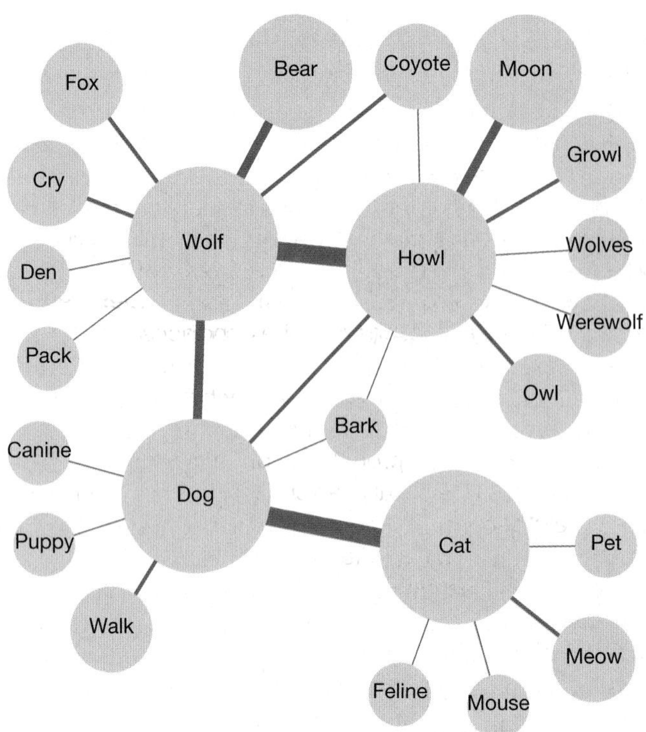

Figure 9.10 Semantic Networks Another way to organize a list of words exploits semantics, the meaning of words. The thickness of lines indicate how strong a relationship may be between two words in your semantic web.

semantic webs Large networks of words with meanings that have different degrees of connection to one another.

particular location in the brain, a topic we'll discuss later in this chapter. Still, it is clear that our memory really does work this way, as if by spreading activation. We all have the experience of how recollecting one memory brings another, related memory to mind.

Most memories are connected to more than one additional memory. If we take the example of our knowledge about words, we can think of entire networks of words, like "dog" and "wolf," which are related to each other to various degrees. The networks of this type that are most studied are those where the degree of relationships between words is determined by their meaning. As *semantics* is the study of meaning, such networks are called **semantic webs**, large networks of words with meanings that have different degrees of connection to one another (**Figure 9.10**). Because words are incorporated in many of our memories (as in memorized lists of words, for example), thinking of one word related to the memory in the semantic web may help retrieve another.

The powerful ability of cuing, priming, or semantic webs to help us remember something that otherwise seemed forgotten reinforces that unavoidable problem in studying memory we discussed earlier. Surely *some* memories fade away entirely, but how would we know? If we use free recall and the person doesn't remember, then OK, maybe that memory is completely gone. But if we now provide a cue and the person remembers, well, that shows the memory wasn't *completely* gone after all. The participant simply couldn't retrieve the memory in free recall. On the other hand, if the participant doesn't remember the information with cued recall, does that prove the memory is gone? What if we give two, three, or even a dozen cues and the person still doesn't remember? Maybe the memory is completely gone, but for all we know, *one more cue* might cause the participant to remember. In other words, *we can never be sure that any memory is completely gone*. Logically, all we can say is that the participant could not recall the information under the conditions in which we tested. As there are an infinite number of conditions in which we could test, and we cannot possibly try them all, we have to admit that there may be a set of conditions in which the participant would recall the information, indicating that it was buried somewhere inside the person's head all along.

Whenever we learn anything, we do so in some context: we have a particular mood, are in a certain setting, with various stimuli around us. As we learn the new material, we are also taking in information about our surroundings. When the time comes to retrieve that information, sometimes we benefit if those surrounding characteristics are also present. **Context-dependent retrieval** is the ability to retrieve additional information when the conditions in which the original learning took place are duplicated. This may be why some students prefer to take examinations for a class in the same room where lectures are delivered (some even want to sit in the same seat in that room).

Those students' concerns are probably a bit overblown, because it's not clear that context-dependent retrieval is a very strong effect in everyday life. To the extent that context-dependent retrieval does aid recall, it is probably best considered an example of a cuing effect—by recreating the environment or mental state of the original learning, we have provided a few more cues that were part of the consolidation process or in some other way exploited spreading activation. Unfortunately, cuing can sometimes cause us to *mis*remember, as we'll discuss next.

Context-Dependent Retrieval Does taking a test in the classroom where you heard the lectures help you retrieve information?

Memory is susceptible to distortion

Interestingly, research indicates that the **memory trace**, the physical record of a memory made in the brain by a learning experience, doesn't simply deteriorate from disuse and the passage of time. Instead, there is good evidence that memories tend to suffer interference from events before or after they were formed. In fact, each time a memory trace is activated during recall, it is subject to changes and fluctuations, so that with successive activations the memory may deviate more and more from its original form. For example, new information that is provided at the time of recall can add new aspects to the memory trace, so a later evocation of the memory is likely to reactivate the newer, *inaccurate* traces along with the older ones, and so produce distorted memories (Estes, 1997; Nader & Hardt, 2009).

Memory distortion offers one explanation of why people sometimes honestly remember events that never happened. False memories can be created by asking leading questions—"Did you see the broken headlight?" rather than "Was the headlight broken?"—or by providing misinformation via trusted channels (Loftus, 2003). This is known as the **misinformation effect**, the susceptibility of our memory to incorporate false details that fit in. In a famous experimental example, psychologists gathered information about a past event from the family members of participants, and then purposely injected some false details. After providing the written description of the event to the participants and probing them to remember other details, researchers found it relatively easy to plant a false memory of meeting Bugs Bunny at a Disney resort (Braun et al., 2002), which could not possibly have happened (because Bugs is a Warner Bros. character, who would never show up at a Disney resort). For the participants, recollecting that early event somehow made it open to distortion, so now they remembered something that never happened.

This possibility of planting false memories clouds the issue of "recovered memories" of childhood sexual or physical abuse. Controversial therapeutic methods such as hypnosis (see Chapter 7) or guided imagery (in which the patient is encouraged to imagine "hypothetical" abuse scenarios) can inadvertently plant false memories. The hypnosis or the encouragement to imagine what happened may give the person permission to "try on" new details of

context-dependent retrieval The improved ability to retrieve information when the conditions of the original learning are reproduced.

memory trace The physical record of a memory made in the brain by a learning experience.

misinformation effect The susceptibility of our memory to incorporate false details that fit in.

Figure 9.11 Flashbulb Memories Many people have vivid, detailed memories of where they were when they learned of the September 11, 2001, terrorist attack on the World Trade Center towers. But are those memories accurate?

their memories of an event, sometimes with tragic consequences. Chapter 7 discusses several cases in which dubiously "recovered memories" of sexual abuse, and even murder, have sent innocent men to prison and destroyed families. Some people may be more susceptible to the misinformation effect than others. People who had "recovered" memories of childhood sexual abuse, when brought to the laboratory and asked to remember lists of words, were more easily manipulated into falsely remembering a word than were control participants or people who had always remembered their childhood abuse (McNally, 2003).

Often recollected memories may become distorted with time, as is demonstrated with the phenomenon of **flashbulb memories**, especially vivid, detailed memories of an especially emotional or momentous occasion. The name derives from the idea of a camera flash that lights up a dark scene, suddenly showing vivid details that are instantly recorded. Likewise, our sense of the memory is as if it were brilliantly and clearly experienced, burned permanently into memory. For my generation, it was the day President John F. Kennedy was assassinated in 1963. I remember being in fourth grade, taking a test where we'd just been asked to spell "clock," when my third-grade teacher, Mrs. Mackey, came into the classroom to announce "President Kennedy's been shot!" For younger people, it might be when they learned of the September 11 terrorist attacks in 2001 (**Figure 9.11**) or the 2012 Newtown shootings. The occasion need not be a historic event; it might be a personally shocking or momentous event in your own life. For personally traumatic events, stressful memories may intrude into everyday life afterward, and it may be possible someday for people to choose a treatment that helps them forget the traumatic memories, as we'll see at the end of this chapter.

Because we tend to recall and recount flashbulb memories often, they may benefit from rehearsal more than do mundane, ordinary memories. But this frequent rehearsal may make them subject to distortion as well. It seems that while most people report very vivid, detailed memories, and are very confident that the details are reliable, there are reasons to think that these flashbulb memories are no more accurate than other memories. For example, one psychologist vividly remembered listening to a baseball game on the radio on the day of the Japanese attack on Pearl Harbor. He recounted the memory often for over 50 years before he realized there couldn't have been a baseball game broadcasted in December (Neisser & Hyman, 2000).

The best studies don't rely on such anecdotes but instead probe the same people's memories both shortly after the dramatic event and then again at a later time. For example, American college students were asked to remember where they were when the O. J. Simpson verdict was announced 15 months before (Schmolck et al., 2000). As is usual with flashbulb memories, the students reported vivid, very detailed memories, confident of their accuracy. When the same students were polled again 17 months later, they again reported vivid, detailed memories, but *in many cases the details were different.* Sometimes they were very different. One student first reported having watched the news on TV in a college lounge with friends, but later reported having been home with his sister and father! Obviously both memories cannot be correct. So unfortunately, self-reports of flashbulb memories, like other memories, are unreliable (Talarico & Rubin, 2003). This unreliability of flashbulb memories serves as an important reminder that our memories can be faulty *even when we feel strongly that they are accurate.*

We've seen repeatedly that our memory is susceptible to distortion. In this classic study, shown in **Figure 9.12**, experimenters were able to affect participants' recollection of simple drawings with just a few words (Carmichael et al., 1932).

flashbulb memories Vivid, detailed memories of a momentous event.

Researchers at Work

Language can impart a bias in visual memory

Figure 9.12 Slanting Visual Memory (After Carmichael et al., 1932.)

Question: How reliable is our visual memory?

Hypothesis: Suggesting that a simple drawing resembles a particular object will affect participants' memory of the drawing.

Test: Experimenters showed participants a series of sketches, suggesting that each resembled a particular object. In fact, each sketch was deliberately designed so that it could resemble two different objects. The experimenter would suggest that a given sketch looked like one object to one participant, and like the other object to another participant.

Results: When participants were asked to reproduce the drawings as faithfully as they could from memory, they often changed details of the drawing to more closely resemble whatever object had been suggested originally. For example, participants who were told a drawing resembled eyeglasses would make a different drawing than participants who were told the same sketch was of dumbbells. If the X shape was said to resemble an hourglass, the participant remembered different details than a participant who was told the X looked like a table.

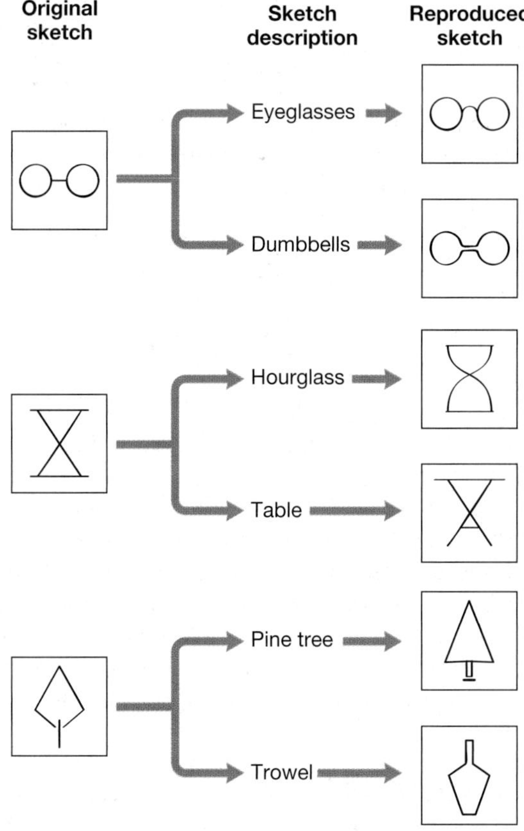

Conclusion: A few words expressed upon showing the sketches distorted the participants' memory in a predictable fashion. People need ways of encoding information and will allow suggestions to color the way they remember details of a drawing. Unfortunately, that method of encoding could distort their memory.

Psychology in Everyday Life

BOX 9.3

The Seven Sins of Memory

In his book *The Seven Sins of Memory: How the Mind Forgets and Remembers*, psychologist Daniel Schacter (2001) summarizes decades of research from many labs, including his own, about the difficulties in retrieving memories accurately. Playfully relating these difficulties to sins, he divides them into "sins of omission" when we forget, and "sins of commission" when recollections are distorted or unwanted. To help you remember them, I've arranged the seven sins in a table so you can use a mnemonic device to help recall them: BAT BLiMP (the vehicle that Batman and Robin use to chase slow-moving criminals by air). Note that BAT encodes the sins of omission, while BLiMP encodes the sins of commission.

Seven Sins of Memory

Sin	Description	Example
Sins of omission		
Blocking	Inability to retrieve the fact that you know you know, but the memory seems blocked	"Oh, that great young actor who played the Joker and then passed away; I know his name..."
Absentmindedness	Lapses of attention or forgetting to do things	"Where did we park the Batmobile?"
Transience	Fading of memories	No longer remembering the capitals of the 50 United States
Sins of commission		
Bias	Distorting old memories to fit current beliefs or knowledge	Remembering only the negative traits of an ex-boyfriend
Leading question	Retrieved memories are vulnerable to suggestibility, as when incorporating misinformation presented in a leading question	"Did you see the broken mirror?"
Misattribution	Attributing a remembered detail to the wrong source	Thinking a bank robbery you saw in a movie had been described in a news report
Persistence	When unpleasant memories linger and intrude into our thoughts	Posttraumatic stress disorder (PTSD; see Box 13.2)

I hope by now I've convinced you that human memory isn't nearly as reliable as we'd like to think it is. **Box 9.3** presents the "seven sins of memory," summarizing the factors that make accurate retrieval of memory a challenge. Because memories can be changeable, and are amenable to updating, how might we avoid contaminating our memory? In the courts, where people's liberty and life are at stake, investigators are cautioned to avoid inserting suggestions that could distort a witness's memory. What might we do in everyday life to preserve memories accurately?

How can you improve your memory?

It should not be surprising that one of the best ways to improve memory (and consequently, learning) is repeated retrieval (and thus repeated consolidation) of the stored information (Karpicke & Roediger, 2008). For your next exam, try making up some practice tests for yourself, or have a friend quiz you, instead of simply "cramming." Keep in mind the potential for changing retrieved memories makes them susceptible to distortion. To ensure accurate recall, you want to be sure to really test yourself, including feedback to make sure you're committing the correct items to memory.

As we mentioned earlier, recall is enhanced when new material that we must learn and remember consists of *related* information: how to wallpaper a room, how to drive a car with a manual transmission, or even the stages of memory formation. Making an effort to see how various bits of information fit together is an important way of *understanding* the information, making it more efficient to store. It also makes it easier to retrieve the information, because once you recall one fact ("iconic memory is really brief"), it leads to another ("information moves from iconic memory to STM") because you activate connections in your semantic web.

The boost in recollection provided by understanding the material and exploiting semantic webs is one reason why many laboratory studies of memory purposely use nonsense information, trying to get at memory in its "pure" form, free from outside influences. But sometimes real life resembles science, in that we sometimes need to remember information that is basically arbitrary. Recollecting passwords for Web services is a common example of very recent origin, but if you think about it, learning to read required you to memorize the names for 26 different shapes, each of which is arbitrary, associated with different speech sounds. Even before you learned written language, learning spoken language also required memorizing arbitrary names for object and actions. There is little relationship between the characteristics of an object and our word for that object, as the many differences between various languages make clear. In each of these cases, memorization of arbitrary "facts" is required in order to communicate symbolically. Perhaps nowhere is the need for memorization of symbolic information more common than in school, where students need to remember information that, to them at least, may seem like nothing more than a long list of arbitrary facts.

When we need to memorize a list of words, or facts, or the correct spelling of a term, **mnemonic devices** can be very useful. One of these is *chunking*, mentioned earlier. Breaking down material into a smaller number of "chunks" reduces the total number of items to be memorized, to aid recall. Perhaps the most common mnemonic device for recalling a list of items in a particular order is to associate a word or phrase with each item, where the first letter in the word or phrase indicates the first letter of the item to be remembered. Students in the United States are taught to remember the order of the colors in a rainbow (which corresponds to the order of their wavelengths: red-orange-yellow-green-blue-indigo-violet) by association with an amusing name: Roy G. Biv. An interesting mnemonic for remembering the digits in the number pi is conveyed in **Figure 9.13**.

mnemonic devices Methods of helping to memorize information.

One
A Poem

A Raven
Midnights so dreary, tired and weary,
Silently pondering volumes extolling all by-now obsolete lore.
During my rather long nap—the weirdest tap!
An ominous vibrating sound disturbing my chamber's antedoor.
"This," I whispered quietly, "I ignore."

3
1 4

1 5
9 2 6, 5 3 5,
8 9 7 9 3 2-3 8 4.
6 2 6 4 3 — 3 8 3!
2 7 9 5 0 2 8 8.
4, 1 9 7 1 6.

Figure 9.13 A Mnemonic for the Digits in Pi The poem *Cadaeic Cadenza* by mathematician Mike Keith, based on Edgar Allan Poe's poem *The Raven*, encodes the digits in the number pi. The number of letters in each word encodes the digit. Words with ten letters represent 0, while words with more than ten letters represent two digits (e.g., 12). The title and first stanza, consisting of 42 words, encodes the first 42 digits (3.141 592653589793238462643383279502884197 16), but the entire poem encodes nearly 4,000 digits and can be seen at http://cadaeic.net/cadenza.htm. Or check out Keith's book *Not a Wake*, encoding 10,000 digits. (From Keith, 2010.)

method of loci A mnemonic device where each item of a list is imagined in a separate location in a familiar place.

tip-of-the-tongue phenomenon When we feel that we can almost say aloud the word we are trying to remember.

Another mnemonic device is to simply put the information in a pleasing-sounding verse, such as "thirty days hath September, April, June, and November." Businesses and other organizations often offer a mnemonic to help you remember their telephone number, exploiting the letters that are found on the digits 2 through 9 on phones. It's easier to remember 1-800-RED-CROSS than the numbers 1-800-733-2767 (note that the final "S" doesn't matter for *dialing* the number, but makes it a lot easier to *remember*).

Described in ancient writings, a mnemonic device sometimes called the **method of loci** draws upon our knowledge of the rooms in a house, or the shops on a street, and has us imagine each of the items in some list to be memorized as occurring in a separate location (a *locus*) in that house or on that street. For example, if you need to remember a list of words—duck, sofa, George, red, root beer, celery, etc.—you can imagine each item in order as you walk into your house and take a circuitous route to your bedroom. Imagine a *duck* in the front yard, someone's put the *sofa* on the porch, *George* Washington is hanging from the coat rack, there's a bucket of *red* paint open in the front room, someone's spilled *root beer* in the hallway, etc. In general, the more vivid and bizarre the imagined scene is at each locus, the easier it is to recall the item there. With practice, people who apparently have ordinary memories have used this method of loci to memorize long lists of numbers (such as the digits in pi: 3.14159265358979…) in a short time.

A variant of the method of loci inserts each item into a particular place in a long, typically bizarre story, rather than a place in a particular route. For example, *Yo, Millard Fillmore* (Cleveland & Alvarez, 2011) is a book that offers an absurd story to memorize the order of the U.S. presidents. To memorize Washington-Adams-Jefferson-Madison-Monroe-Adams, picture a washing machine (Washington) full of atoms (Adams), which the chef's son (Jefferson) fries on a grill heated by a mad sun (Madison), which escapes to swallow a river, including a boat with a stack of money rowing (Monroe) away until it hits a dam (Adams). Recalling each event in the absurd story offers a sequence of cues to retrieve each president's name.

Freud recounted a little trick that often helps when we're trying to remember something that we *almost* remember. Usually termed the **tip-of-the-tongue phenomenon**, it happens when we feel that we can almost say aloud the word we're looking for, as if it were literally just out of reach of our tongue. When having a hard time calling to mind the name of a person, place, or object, Freud suggested, simply say random names out loud. For example, if you can't remember that person's name, just say names at random. He noted that most of the supposedly random names will in fact begin with the same letter as the name you're trying to remember (Freud, 1901). Sometimes this hint about how the name begins can help retrieve the whole name. In other cases, the "random" names or words will bear some other relationship to the name or word we're groping for, such as rhyming, or being historically related.

Being Freud, he offered elaborate, untestable explanations of why one part of your mind was actively trying to block your recollection, but a simpler explanation is that remembering is sometimes difficult because we store so much information in our heads. In that case, the reason the "random" names begin with the same letter, or the random words have some relationship to the missing word, is because you've activated some web of memories that are related to one another. As with other spreading activation phenomena, activation of the related information makes it more likely that the desired information will be activated and retrieved. To give Freud his due, he was of course correct in concluding that the random words bear a relationship to the sought word because some part of our mind, which we are not aware of, holds the answer even as we grope for it. Again we see that "forgotten" information may not be entirely gone from memory, just difficult to retrieve. This is also yet another demonstration of one of our four basic principles—namely, that we are often unaware of what our brain is doing.

While we all have difficulty retrieving memories once in a while, in the next section we'll learn about people with dramatic difficulty making or retrieving memories, who have taught us that there are different forms of memory.

9.2 SUMMARY

- While information may actually disappear from long-term memory (LTM), most *forgetting* is probably due to difficulty in *retrieval* of information from LTM.
- This would explain why *cued recall*, when a participant is provided some hints about the desired information, is usually much better than *free recall*, when the participant must retrieve the items without any cues.
- *Proactive interference* occurs when previous memories make it difficult for us to memorize new material, while *retroactive interference* is when learning new information makes it hard to recall old memories. In either situation, there is greater interference for items that are similar to each other.
- Sleep may improve consolidation by allowing us to avoid stimulation that may cause retroactive interference with memory.
- *Priming*, the ability of information presented at one time to affect a person's response at a later time, demonstrates that the participant retained some of that information, even if he could not consciously retrieve it.
- The concept of *spreading activation* suggests that recall can be prompted by associations between different memories—that memories can be linked to one another by shared characteristics. The meanings of words, for example, can be linked in a *semantic web*, so retrieving one item from LTM can increase the chances of retrieving others linked to it.
- The improved ability to retrieve information when the conditions of the original learning are reproduced, called *context-dependent retrieval*, demonstrates that forgotten information in fact remains in LTM.
- Retrieved memories are susceptible to distortion, as researchers demonstrate by injecting new, inaccurate information. The *misinformation effect* arises when the physical record of a memory, the *memory trace*, is altered and then reconsolidated in distorted form. *Flashbulb memories*, the vivid, detailed memories we have of particularly momentous events, can become distorted as we recount them to others.
- When memorizing a list, making sure the information is accurate and overlearning it helps cement the information in LTM.
- A variety of *mnemonic devices* can improve our retrieval of information from LTM.

REVIEW QUESTIONS

1. What phenomena indicate that most forgetting is due to a problem in retrieval of information rather than wholesale loss of information from LTM?
2. What are the two types of interference that impede our ability to retrieve information from LTM? Can you think of examples from your own experience?
3. What are some ways you can improve your recall of information in school?

Food for Thought

Why are flashbulb memories so vivid, and why do we feel so confident they are accurate?

9.3 Different Forms of Long-Term Memory

Things to Learn

- Two main types of amnesia
- Declarative versus non-declarative memories
- Korsakoff's syndrome and confabulation
- Autobiographical memories
- The physical basis of memory
- Hebbian synapses and long-term potentiation
- Non-matching to sample and importance of the medial temporal lobe

Clinical conditions that impair memory are really frightening, but we can discover a lot about memory by examining how it fails. Clinical case studies show that memory can fail in several very different ways, indicating that there are different forms of memory, and that multiple brain regions are involved. The clinical research has guided research with animal models and brain imaging. Together, these diverse approaches provide a comprehensive picture of the processes of learning and memory.

Many kinds of brain damage, caused by disease or accident, impair memory. These are not cases where information failed to be consolidated from short-term memory (STM) to long-term memory (LTM), but cases where information that had been in LTM was dramatically lost. These cases of memory impairment have revealed that several distinctly different classes of memory are kept in LTM.

There are different types of amnesia

Amnesia (Greek for "forgetfulness") is a severe impairment of memory. Loss of *old* memories formed prior to a trauma is called **retrograde amnesia** (from the Latin *retro*, "backward," and *gradi*, "to go") and is not uncommon after surgery or trauma. For example, the chauffeur driving in the accident that killed Princess Diana says he cannot remember what happened in the final few minutes before the crash. He has retrograde amnesia for that brief period before the trauma. Later we'll see that this is probably because the damage to his brain caused him to lose track of the events before he could record them permanently into memory.

Most of Henry Molaison's old memories—of the many years growing up with his parents before his surgery—remained intact. What made Henry (**Figure 9.14**), until his death known as **patient H.M.**, so striking was his more unusual symptom of being unable to retain *new* material for more than a brief period. The inability to form *new* memories after an event is called **anterograde amnesia** (from the Latin *antero,* "forward"). **Figure 9.15** offers a schematic to help you distinguish between retrograde and anterograde amnesia.

Over the very short term, Henry's memory was normal. When given a series of six or seven digits, Henry could immediately repeat the list back without error, which is why he continued to score normally on IQ tests. In other words, his STM was fine. But if Henry were given a list of words to study and then tested on them after intervening tasks, he could not repeat the list or even recall that there *was* a list. Henry's case provided clear evidence that STM of the sort we use to carry on a conversation differs from LTM needed to learn new facts, including facts about someone you've met and are getting to know. Likewise, Princess Diana's

amnesia A severe impairment of memory.

retrograde amnesia Amnesia for events occurring prior to an event, typically a trauma.

patient H.M. Henry Molaison, a patient who, because of bilateral medial temporal lobe damage, could not form new explicit memories.

anterograde amnesia Amnesia for events occurring after an event, such as a trauma.

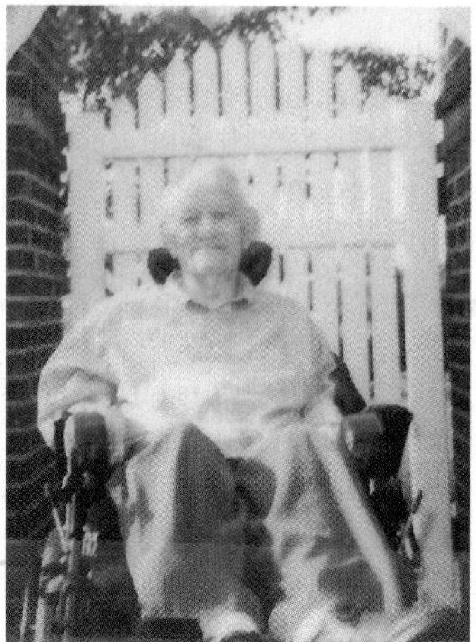

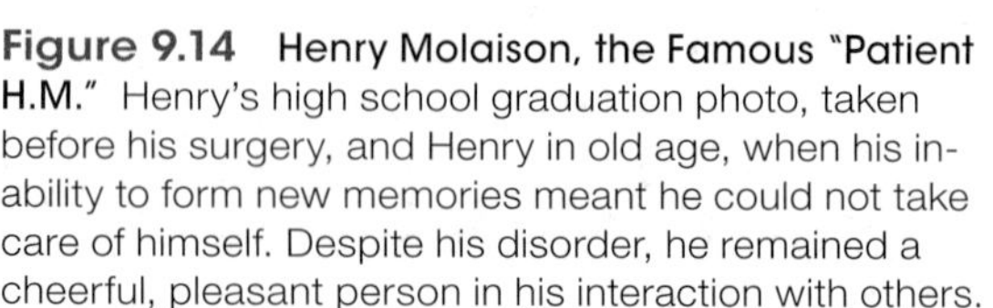

Figure 9.14 Henry Molaison, the Famous "Patient H.M." Henry's high school graduation photo, taken before his surgery, and Henry in old age, when his inability to form new memories meant he could not take care of himself. Despite his disorder, he remained a cheerful, pleasant person in his interaction with others.

Retrograde amnesia | Anterograde amnesia

Past | Preserved memories | Lost memories | New information | Future

Brain injury

Figure 9.15 Anterograde and Retrograde Amnesia

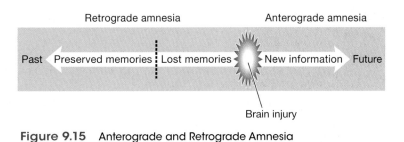

chauffeur probably had STM of events that happened up to the crash, but the trauma to his brain prevented him from moving them into LTM. In Henry's case, the inability to transfer memories from STM to LTM lasted the rest of his life.

The hippocampus is required to put some memories into LTM elsewhere in the brain

Henry's surgeon removed quite a bit of both temporal lobes of the cortex, including several structures beneath the surface. Comparison with other brain injury cases indicated that Henry's amnesia was due to the loss of the **medial temporal lobe**, which includes the **hippocampus** (**Figure 9.16A**) and neighboring cortical regions. The surgeons were surprised by Henry's outcome, because this region had been removed in other patients from either the left or right hemisphere without any amnesia afterward. But Henry's was the first case when the medial temporal lobe was removed from *both* sides (**Figure 9.16B**), and that seemed to account for his different, tragic outcome.

At first, doctors speculated that Henry's problem might be restricted to verbal function. But it turned out Henry and similar patients have difficulty reproducing

medial temporal lobe The innermost portion of the temporal lobe, which includes the hippocampus and neighboring cortex.

hippocampus Part of the limbic system that is crucial in the formation of permanent memories.

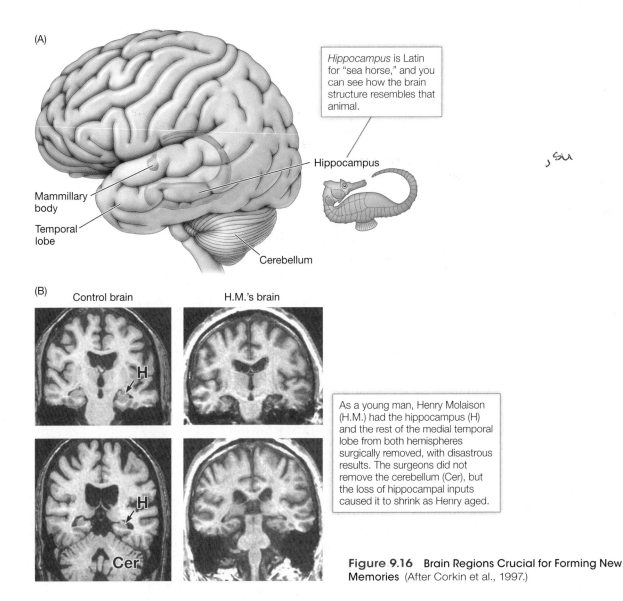

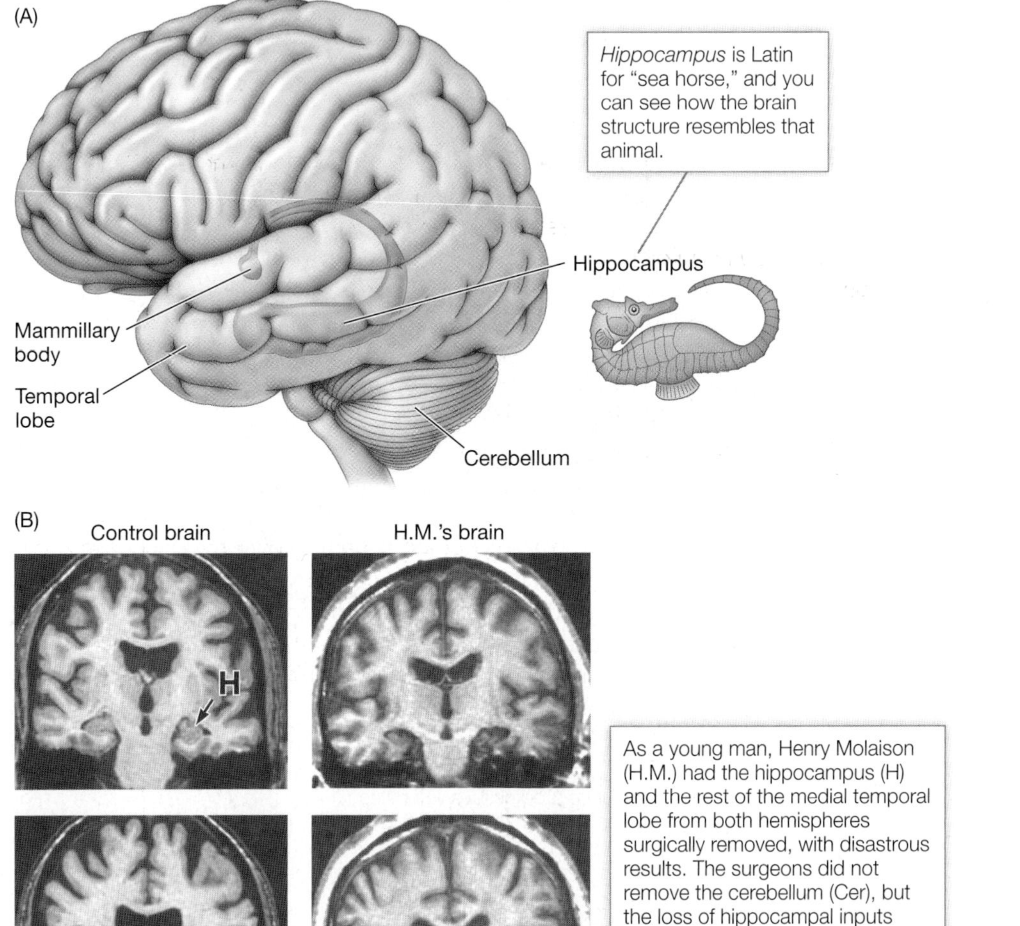

Hippocampus is Latin for "sea horse," and you can see how the brain structure resembles that animal.

Mammillary body

Cerebellum

Control brain
H.M.'s brain

Cer
As a young man, Henry Molaison (H.M.) had the hippocampus (H) and the rest of the medial temporal lobe from both hemispheres surgically removed, with disastrous results. The surgeons did not remove the cerebellum (Cer), but the loss of hippocampal inputs caused it to shrink as Henry aged.

Figure 9.16 Brain Regions Crucial for Forming New Memories (After Corkin et al., 1997.)

If you practice reading text that is mirror-reversed, you will become better and better at deciphering the text quickly. This is an example of learning a perceptual skill, and does not require an intact hippocampus.

Patients like Henry can learn to read mirror-reversed text quite well, even though they don't remember practicing it. This ability shows that their problem is not in learning verbal material, but in forming new declarative memories.

Figure 9.17 Reading Mirror-Reversed Text

or recognizing *pictures* and spatial designs, even when not asked to recall them in verbal terms. Also, although such patients have difficulty learning new verbal material, they can learn some kinds of information *about* verbal material (Cohen & Squire, 1980). For example, several kinds of amnesic patients can learn the *skill* of mirror reading very well, which is a verbal task (**Figure 9.17**) Yet these patients, like Henry, are unable to learn the meaning of specific new words. It turns out the deficit Henry had was one in retrieving a particular form of LTM, as we'll see in **Figure 9.18**.

☑ Researchers at Work

Henry was able to form new memories for some tasks

Figure 9.18 Henry's Performance on a Mirror-Tracing Task (After Milner, 1965.)

■ **Question:** Was Henry able to learn anything new?

■ **Hypothesis:** Henry's deficit after the surgery made it impossible for him to form new memories of any sort.

■ **Test:** Psychologist Brenda Milner (1965) gave Henry a mirror-tracing task and asked him to do it ten times for several successive days.

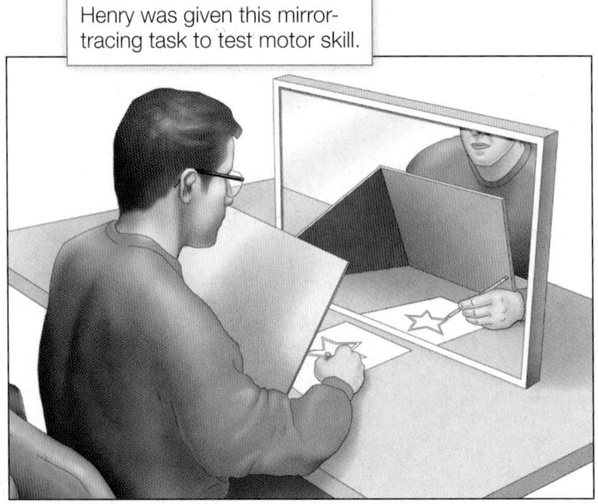

Henry was given this mirror-tracing task to test motor skill.

■ **Results:** In fact, Henry improved considerably over the course of ten trials the first day (Milner, 1965). The next day when the test was presented again, Henry did not remember having ever done it before. Yet his performance was better than at the start of the first day. Over three successive days, Henry never recognized the task, but his performance improved steadily.

Although Henry never recognized the task, his performance progressively improved over successive days, demonstrating a type of long-term memory.

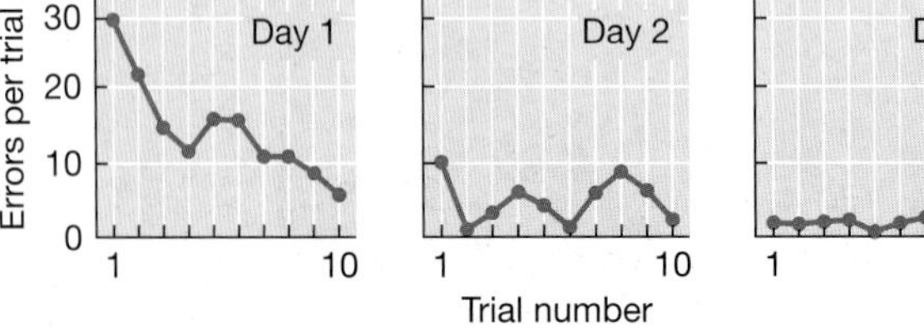

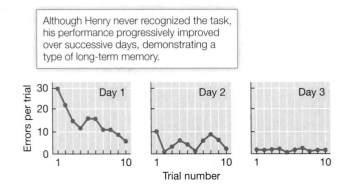

■ **Conclusion:** Even though Henry did not recognize having done the task before, his improved performance from one day to the next demonstrated a kind of memory in the form of motor skill. The fact that Henry could learn a new skill, without ever being aware that he had done it before, suggested that his deficit was restricted to a particular kind of memory.

Thus the important distinction illustrated by Henry's amnesia is probably not between motor and verbal performances but between two kinds of memory:

1. **Declarative memory** is what we usually think of as memory: facts and information acquired through learning that we can "declare" to others (Squire, 2009). It is memory we are explicitly aware of accessing, so it is sometimes referred to as *explicit memory*. This is the type of memory so profoundly impaired by Henry's surgery. Tests of declarative memory take the form of requests for specific information that has been learned previously, such as a story or word list.
2. **Nondeclarative memory**, or *implicit memory,* is a type of memory in which previous experience aids in the performance of a task. Nondeclarative memory is demonstrated by *performance* rather than by *conscious recollection*. *Procedural memory*—memory associated with perceptual or motor procedures—is an example: we remember how to ride a bike without thinking about it consciously. Other examples of nondeclarative memory include memory for the mirror-tracing task and for the skill of mirror reading, as we just described. This memory is "implicit" in the sense that our performance, at mirror drawing or riding a bicycle, shows that we have the memory needed, even if we cannot explicitly describe how we manage to perform the task.

To put the distinction between the two types of memory another way, declarative memory deals with *what*, and nondeclarative memory deals with *how*, as summarized in **Figure 9.19**.

Because Henry could make new implicit memories, but not new explicit memories, formation of these two types of memory must use different parts of the brain. There is another important lesson from Henry's tragic case. He remembered the events of his life before surgery, and retained the skills and knowledge he acquired while growing up, yet his hippocampus and the rest of the medial temporal lobe was missing in both temporal lobes. Therefore the medial temporal lobe could not have been the place where Henry's presurgery memories, either explicit or implicit, were stored. They must have been stored somewhere else in the brain, and we'll later describe evidence that the "somewhere else" is in the cortex. Rather than being a *repository* for memories, the medial temporal lobe is vital for *forming* declarative memories and depositing them *elsewhere* in the brain. We'll see next that the medial temporal lobe is just one part of a brain circuit for laying down declarative memories elsewhere in the brain.

declarative memory Also called *explicit memory*. Facts or information acquired through learning that can be stated or described.

nondeclarative memory Also called *implicit memory*. Memory about perceptual or motor procedures that is demonstrated by performance.

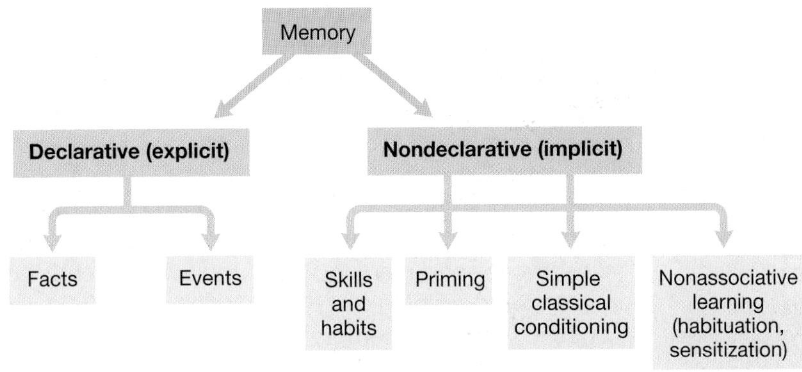

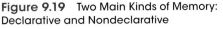

Figure 9.19 Two Main Kinds of Memory: Declarative and Nondeclarative

Korsakoff's syndrome A memory disorder, characterized by retrograde amnesia, anterograde amnesia, and confabulation, that is generally caused by thiamine deficiency.

confabulate To fill a gap in memory with a falsification; as seen in Korsakoff's syndrome.

mammillary bodies A pair of structures in the brainstem that receive inputs from the hippocampus; they are damaged in Korsakoff's patients.

patient K.C. A patient who, because of damage to his cortex, lost all memory for personal information but retained his memory for general knowledge.

episodic memory Detailed autobiographical declarative memory.

semantic memory Generalized declarative memory.

People with Korsakoff's syndrome, like H.M., have trouble forming new declarative memories

In 1887, Russian neurologist S. S. Korsakoff reported a syndrome of severely impaired memory, which was subsequently named after him. People with **Korsakoff's syndrome** display both retrograde amnesia, typically extending back several years, and anterograde amnesia such as Henry's. Like Henry, these patients are often unable to make new declarative memories. Shown an object or task at one point, they show no recognition of it just a few minutes later. Unlike Henry, people with Korsakoff's syndrome frequently deny that anything is wrong with them. Although clearly disoriented about time and place, they may **confabulate**—that is, fill a gap in memory with a falsification that they seem to accept as true.

The main cause of Korsakoff's syndrome is lack of the vitamin thiamine (vitamin B1). Alcoholics who obtain most of their calories from alcohol and neglect their diet often exhibit this deficiency. Treating them with thiamine can prevent further deterioration of memory functions, but it will not reverse the damage. Efforts to require manufacturers to add thiamine to alcoholic drinks, which would virtually eliminate any further cases of Korsakoff's syndrome, failed in the United States because political groups insisted that such measures might encourage drinking (Centerwall & Criqui, 1978; Price et al., 1987).

Although Henry's amnesia was similar to that of people with Korsakoff's syndrome, the areas of brain damage are different. Korsakoff's patients have normal-sized temporal lobe structures, including the hippocampus (Mair et al., 1979), but have shrunken, diseased **mammillary bodies** (named for their resemblance to breasts, which are also called mammaries) and damage to sites in the brainstem (**Figure 9.20**). It turns out that the mammillary bodies normally receive input from the hippocampus. In fact, if you reexamine Figure 9.16, you'll see that the "tail" of the hippocampus, which extends from the temporal lobe to the brainstem, ends at the mammillary bodies. The pattern of damage in these and related amnesia syndromes suggests that the mammillary bodies may serve as a narrow funnel through which connections from the hippocampus gain access to the cortex (Mair et al., 1979). It may be that damage to the basal frontal lobes, also found in patients suffering from Korsakoff's syndrome, causes the denial and confabulation that differentiates these patients from other patients who have amnesia, such as Henry.

Studies of clinical cases of amnesiacs, including Henry and people with Korsakoff's syndrome, indicate that a circuit, from the hippocampus in the temporal lobe to the mammillary bodies in the brainstem, is vital for our ability to form lasting declarative memories. Yet another clinical case made it clear that there are two different subtypes of declarative memories, as we'll discuss next.

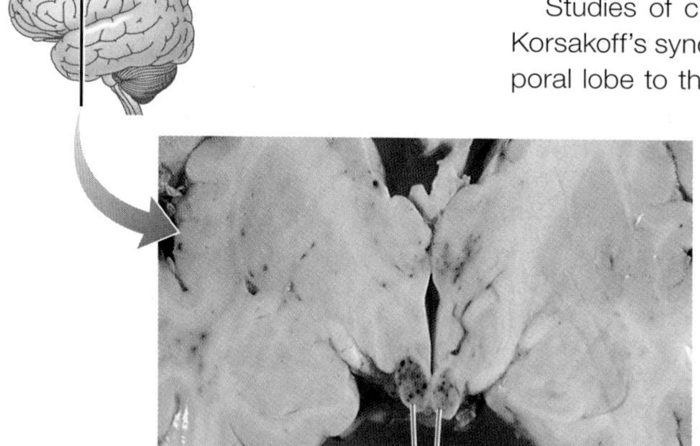

These oval-shaped mammillary bodies are darkened as a result of bleeding and cell death.

Figure 9.20 Site of Brain Damage in Patients with Korsakoff's Syndrome (Image courtesy of D. P. Agamanolis.)

Brain damage can destroy autobiographical memories while sparing general memories

Another striking case study illustrates that there are two different *subtypes* of declarative memory. **Patient K.C.** sustained brain damage in a motorcycle accident at age 30. K.C. can no longer retrieve any *personal* memory of his past, although his general knowledge remains good. He converses easily and plays a good game of chess, but he cannot remember where he learned to play chess or from whom. Detailed autobiographical declarative memory of this sort is known as **episodic memory**: you show episodic memory when you recall a specific *episode* in your life or relate an event to a particular time and place. In contrast, **semantic memory** is generalized declarative memory, such as knowing the *meaning* of a word without knowing where or when you learned that word (Tulving, 1972). You can think of semantic memory as a huge store of knowledge that we all carry with us. So if you remember the capital of France, but don't remember when you first learned it, that's semantic memory. In contrast, if you remember your first day of school, that is episodic memory.

Brain scans of K.C. reveal extensive damage to many different parts of his cortex, and severe shrinkage of the hippocampus (Rosenbaum et al., 2005). As with H.M., the bilateral damage to the hippocampus and neighboring cortex probably accounts for K.C.'s anterograde declarative amnesia, but the hippocampal damage doesn't really account for the nearly complete, selective loss of his entire autobiographical memory (i.e., retrograde episodic amnesia), because other patients with damage restricted to the medial temporal lobe are able to recall past events in their lives. K.C.'s inability to recall any autobiographical details of his life, not even personal memories from many years before his accident, seems to be caused by damage to his cortex (Tulving, 1989).

We noted earlier that Henry's intact memory for events before surgery, which included both semantic and episodic memories of his past, makes it clear that the medial temporal lobe, including the hippocampus, is *not* the place where such memories are *stored* for the long term. We also stated that while the hippocampus is needed to form new long-term memories, the memories are stored elsewhere. K.C.'s case suggests that the "somewhere else" for memory storage is the cortex. As was the case with Henry, amnesia has essentially stripped K.C. of the opportunity to have a full life, because he can't really have a continuing relationship with other people, either coworkers or a romantic partner.

Another indication that episodic memory is separate from semantic memory comes from cases of people who don't forget. Earlier we described two such people, Kim Peek and Solomon Shereshevsky, who could remember incredibly long lists of items (see Box 9.2), which would qualify as *semantic* memory—the knowledge may have been of a list of words or numbers that were meaningless, but it was still knowledge that they could declare. They may also have had strong episodic memories, remembering when they were presented each list ("you were wearing a gray suit"). But there are other people who are no better than average people at semantic memory, yet claim to have amazingly powerful *episodic* memory—to remember everything that has ever happened to them (Marcus, 2009). For example, Jill Price, who is now in her forties, reports remembering every event of every day of her life since she was about 14 (Price & Davis, 2008). Given a list of dates during that time period, she can report what was in the news that day, or given a list of historic events, she can provide the exact dates (in one case, the scientists thought she was wrong, but it turned out their reference book had the wrong date!). Jill finds her extraordinary memory a mixed blessing because she remembers every unpleasant thing anyone has ever said to her, and she also experiences these memories as popping up on their own, with full emotional impact. The cases of Jill and a very few other people with extraordinary recall for *only* autobiographical memories also indicate that episodic memory is distinct from semantic memory.

Finally, brain imaging studies have compared the parts of the brain that are active when a person is engaged in retrieving semantic memories with the parts that are active in episodic memories. While there are regions of overlap, there are several differences in the regions being activated (Lepage et al., 2000), further indicating that episodic and semantic memories rely on distinctive brain processes.

By the way, despite what you might think from popular entertainment, it is rare for retrograde amnesia to extend back to more than a few days before the traumatic event. So you should regard retrograde amnesia covering years, like that of the X-Man Wolverine and the superspy Jason Bourne, as highly fanciful inventions of the movies (**Box 9.4**).

BOX 9.4

Amnesia in Real Life Is Not Like It Is in the Movies

Many books, movies, and television shows have plots that revolve around a person who suddenly has dramatic amnesia, usually after a trauma. While they still know how to talk and do everyday things, these people don't remember their name, their friends or relatives, or anything about their past experiences. In other words, their autobiographical memory is gone. Does that sort of thing ever happen in real life?

The question is difficult to answer, in part because in real life it is always possible that the person is faking amnesia. There have been several widely reported cases of people claiming to have such amnesia who turned out to have good reason to lay low. The first well-documented case was a man who spent most of 1926 living comfortably in an asylum in Turin, Italy, claiming to not know who he was. Eventually a woman came forward and said he was her husband, a professor who'd gone missing 10 years earlier. Then an anonymous note said the man was Mario Bruneri, who was wanted by the police for fraud. It was front-page news as the courts tried to figure out whether the man was the professor who should go home to his wife and pension, or the crook who should go to prison. Neurologist Alfredo Coppola used tests to convince himself (and the court) that the man was indeed Bruneri, who was malingering—pretending to be sick—to avoid jail (Zago et al., 2004). As in most cases of *malingering amnesia*, Bruneri exaggerated his symptoms beyond those seen in real amnesia. Given a serial position test, he showed much less of a primacy effect; in other words, he remembered far fewer of the first items than real amnesiacs would (see Figure 9.5). Also, he claimed not to remember the colors of the flags of Italy or France! That would be a complete loss of *declarative* memory, as opposed to *autobiographical* memory, which no true amnesiac has ever reported. In a more recent case, a nurse who used a metal table leg to strike and kill an elderly patient claimed to have no memory of the events just before the killing. She was found not to be criminally responsible for her acts. Another woman, Colleen Ann Harris (see figure), avoided prison time by claiming she didn't remember killing her second husband. She later killed her third husband, like the second, by shooting him with a shotgun. Even if the person claiming to have amnesia is not trying to avoid criminal charges (Bourget & Whitehurst, 2007), it is possible that he or she enjoys the solicitous attention of medical staff and family. Or perhaps there's the attraction of getting to be somebody else.

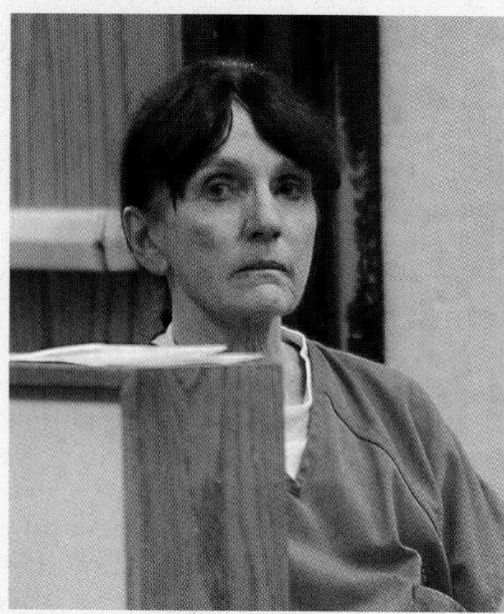

Convenient Amnesia Colleen Ann Harris, during her trial for the murder of her third husband in 2013. She murdered her second husband in 1985 but evaded prison by claiming "amnesia."

Genuine cases of retrograde amnesia typically occur after a physical trauma such as an accident or surgery, but the memory loss is usually restricted to a period of hours or weeks before the event. In one highly unusual case, a woman with a rare disorder that put her in a coma for days lost memories of the entire year before, but she still knew who she was and knew her family (Kruglinski, 2006). It is very rare that retrograde amnesia extends back more than a year, and even less likely that it extends back to a lifetime. One man (George V. Sims) who was presumed dead from the September 11, 2001, terrorist attack was found a year later in a hospital with no memory of his past. He could not recognize his family, but he was also diagnosed with schizophrenia, so his seems to be an extreme case.

In more typical cases of amnesia, the person recovers at least bits and pieces of the missing memories over time, especially of the earliest events that were lost. (Bruneri appeared to recover bits of his memory as a professor, but they turned out to be bits of information his "wife" had provided him.) Of course, it is difficult to be sure that a patient is faking any behavioral symptoms, especially for such an essentially private experience as amnesia, so we can't really be sure just how complete amnesia might be. A similar difficulty clouds reports of "split personality," when a person at one time claims to be a different person, with different memories, than he or she was before. This rare condition, known today as *dissociative identity disorder*, will be a topic in Box 16.1.

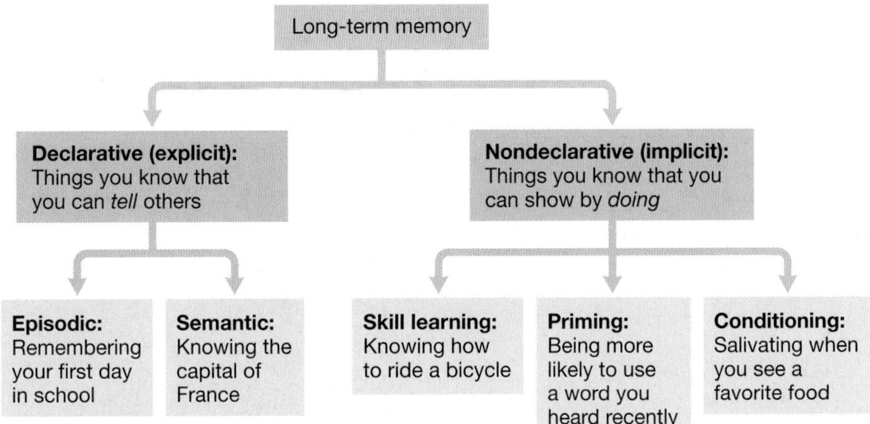

Figure 9.21 Subtypes of Declarative and Nondeclarative Memory

Different forms of nondeclarative memory serve varying functions

We have now seen that there are two different subtypes of declarative (explicit) memory: semantic memory and episodic memory. There are several different subtypes of nondeclarative (implicit) memory too.

Recall that nondeclarative memories are also usually displayed by the way a person can successfully perform a procedure, such as solving a puzzle. For example, in **skill learning**, participants perform a challenging task on repeated trials in one or more sessions. The mirror-tracing task performed by Henry (see Figure 9.18) is an example of a *motor* skill, as is riding a bicycle. Knowing how to read mirror-reversed text readily, also mentioned earlier, is a type of *perceptual* skill memory.

Earlier we discussed *priming*, when being exposed to a word at one time makes you more likely to think of that word in the future. Henry, who could not recall being shown the list of words, nevertheless showed an effect of priming. Control participants, with ordinary memory systems, are often unaware of the priming effect—they may not recall having seen the priming word on the list (Tulving et al., 1982). Thus priming is another subtype of nondeclarative memory.

Conditioning involves learning simple associations between stimuli, such as the classical conditioning we discussed in Section 8.1. Our taxonomy of memory is updated in **Figure 9.21**, adding the subtypes of declarative and nondeclarative memory, along with some examples.

skill learning Learning to perform a challenging task.

conditioning Learning simple associations between stimuli.

engram The physical encoding of a memory in the brain.

What is the physical basis of memory?

At least as long ago as the 1800s, scientists tried to understand how memories are stored in the brain (James, 1890). Most of these scientists accepted the idea that there must be a physical basis for memory storage, even if they had no idea how it was done. The term "memory trace," used to describe the physical record of a memory laid down in the brain, emphasizes the notion that the memory is part of a circuit, since the term "trace" suggests lines (as in tracing a drawing). Another commonly used term for the physical record of a memory is **engram**, which suggests a more discrete storage, as if each memory is in a separate compartment somewhere in the brain. Both concepts require that a learning experience *physically alters the brain*, which is one of our four principles of psychology. For many people, this idea that experience could physically alter the brain, that the brain is *plastic*, able to change its shape, was difficult to accept.

Figure 9.22 Synaptic Changes That May Store Memories

After training, each action potential in the relevant neural circuit causes increased response in the postsynaptic neuron.
(A)
Before training
After training
Several different changes can result in a more effective synapse.
Axon terminal
Dendritic spine
or
or
Postsynaptic receptive area
More transmitter is released from the axon terminal.
Postsynaptic membrane becomes larger and/or more sensitive to transmitter.
Synapse enlarges both pre- and postsynaptically.
(B)
A neural circuit that is used more often increases the number of synaptic contacts.
New synapses formed

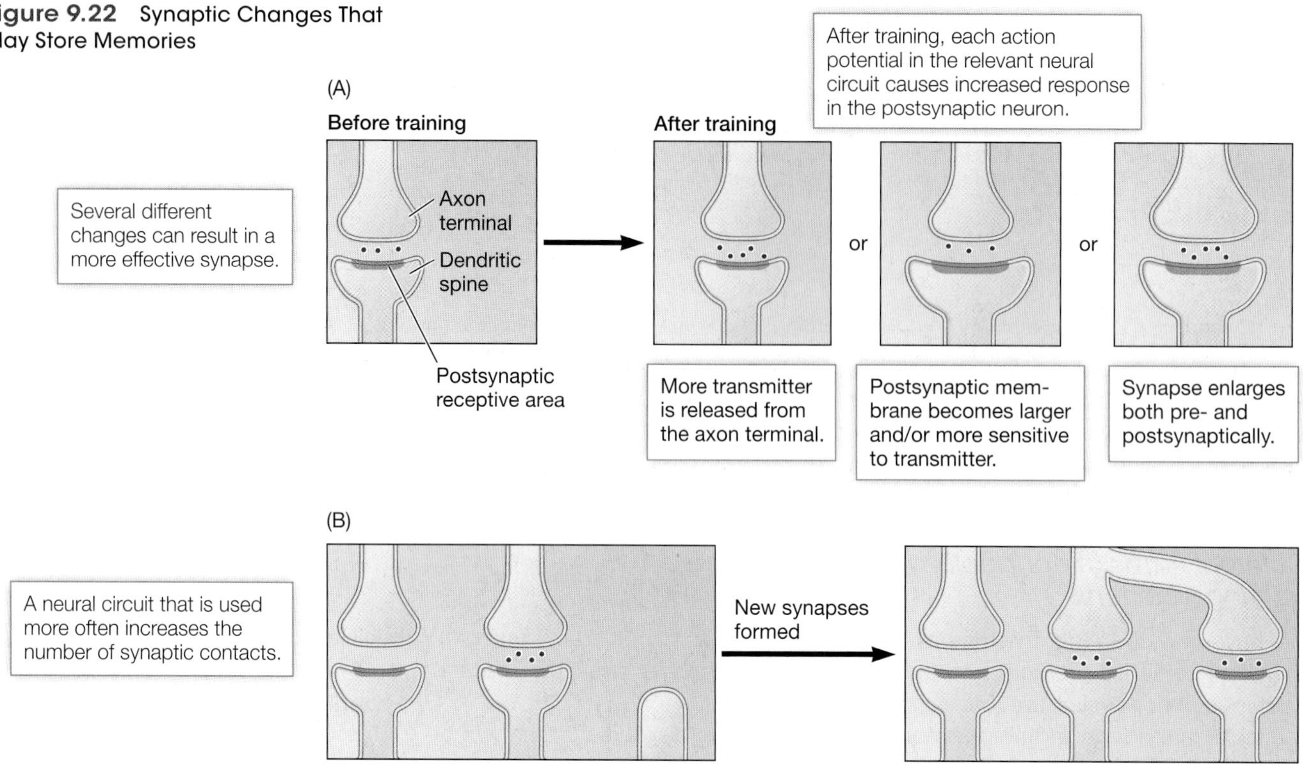

But this remarkable plasticity of the brain is not all that difficult to demonstrate. Experiments have shown, for example, pronounced biochemical and anatomical changes in the brains of rats that have been placed in a complex environment with many opportunities for new learning (Rosenzweig et al., 1961). In standard studies of environmental enrichment, rats are randomly assigned to different housing conditions—either impoverished condition (IC), with animals housed singly in standard lab cages, or enriched condition (EC), with animals housed in large social groups in special cages containing various toys (see Figure 4.10B). Enriched condition provides enhanced opportunities for learning perceptual and motor skills, social learning, and so on. In dozens of studies over several decades, a variety of plastic changes in the brain have been linked to environmental enrichment. For example, compared with IC animals, EC animals have a heavier, thicker cortex (Diamond, 1967; Rosenzweig et al., 1962), more dendritic branches in the cortex, and many more synapses on those branches (Greenough & Volkmar, 1973; Greenough, 1976). They also have larger synapses in the cortex (Diamond et al., 1975).

It's not just rats that benefit from environmental enrichment. Similar effects on brain processes and behavior are seen in fish, birds, mice, cats, and monkeys (Renner & Rosenzweig, 1987; Rampon & Tsien, 2000; van Praag et al., 2000; Will et al., 2004). And the evidence indicates that the human brain is no exception. For example, the hand area of the motor cortex becomes larger in people who play musical instruments professionally, presumably because of their extensive practice. In another example, 100 children assigned to a 2-year enriched nursery school program showed improvements in tests of orienting and arousal when reassessed at age 11 (Raine et al., 2001).

There are many different ways in which experience could alter synapses in the brain to leave a memory trace (**Figure 9.22**). Also, periods of intense learning are sometimes accompanied by the formation of new neurons in the brain, even in adult humans (Tavosanis, 2012).

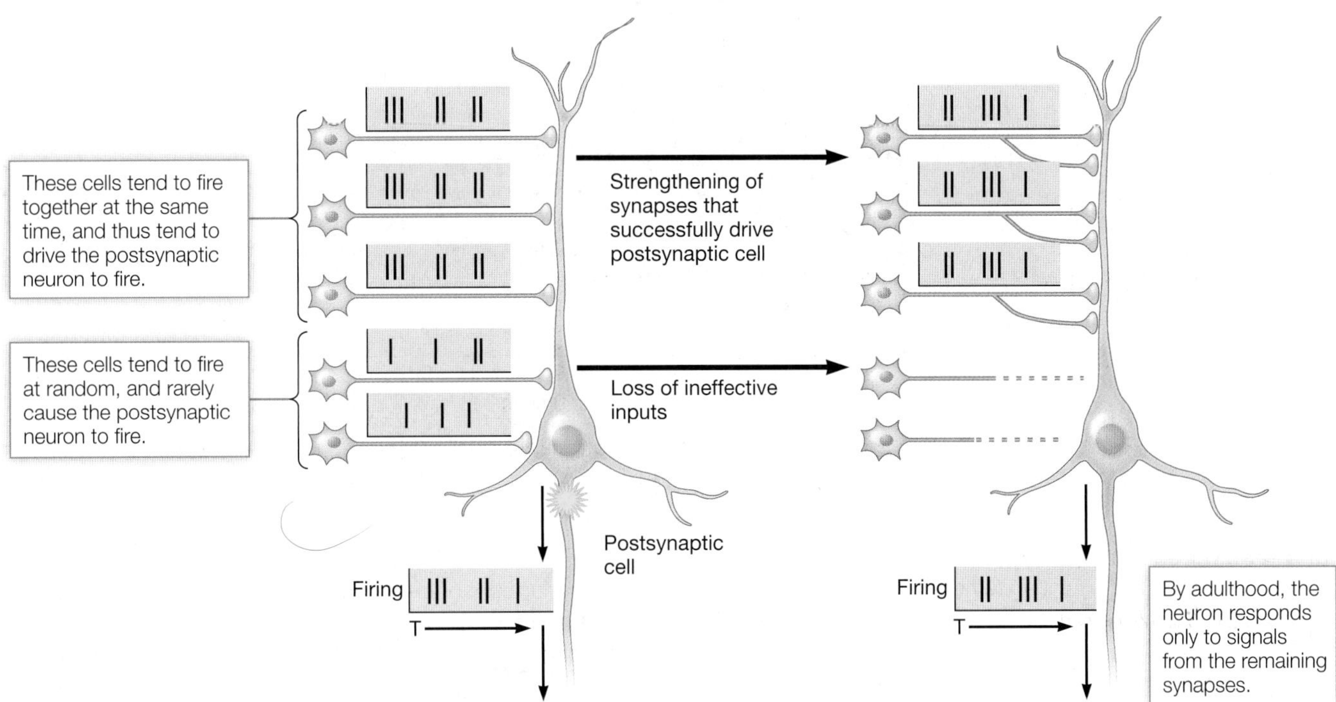

These cells tend to fire together at the same time, and thus tend to drive the postsynaptic neuron to fire.
These cells tend to fire at random, and rarely cause the postsynaptic neuron to fire.
Strengthening of synapses that successfully drive postsynaptic cell
Loss of ineffective inputs
Postsynaptic cell
Firing
T
By adulthood, the neuron responds only to signals from the remaining synapses.

Figure 9.23 In Hebbian Synapses, the Neurons That Fire Together, Wire Together

The best-studied model system for understanding how learning could physically alter the brain and lay down a memory trace is one found in the very region that was removed from Henry's brain, the hippocampus, as we'll discuss next.

Hebbian synapse A synapse that becomes stronger if it often causes the postsynaptic neuron to fire, and gets weaker if it rarely causes the postsynaptic cell to fire.

Long-term potentiation (LTP) may provide a physical basis for memory

In 1949, Canadian psychologist Donald Hebb published a book, *The Organization of Behavior*, that illustrated how a relatively simple form of synaptic plasticity could explain many different behaviors, including classical conditioning. Hebb's book was very persuasive because the synaptic plasticity was easy to understand. Named in his honor, a **Hebbian synapse** is one that becomes stronger if it often causes the postsynaptic neuron to fire, and gets weaker if it rarely causes the postsynaptic cell to fire. Hebb didn't identify any particular mechanism for a synapse growing stronger or weaker, but most researchers assumed that what changed was the amount of neurotransmitter (see Figure 9.22A). Eventually changes in neurotransmitter release was confirmed, but there were also many cases where the number of synapses between two neurons would also increase if the presynaptic neuron frequently caused the postsynaptic neuron to fire (**Figure 9.23**). The rule governing Hebbian synapses was later simplified to "the neurons that fire together, wire together."

While Hebb's idea about how synapses might change was a very attractive theory, it took quite a while to demonstrate that Hebbian synapses actually exist in real brains. Once researchers learned of the profound memory problems caused by loss of the hippocampus in Henry, many began looking in the hippocampus for neural plasticity that might represent the memory trace. Thus there was a lot of excitement when scientists found Hebbian synapses in the hippocampus (Bliss & Lømo, 1973). In these experiments, a stimulating electrode was placed in the rat hippocampus to stimulate a group of presynaptic neurons, while a recording electrode measured the response of the postsynap-

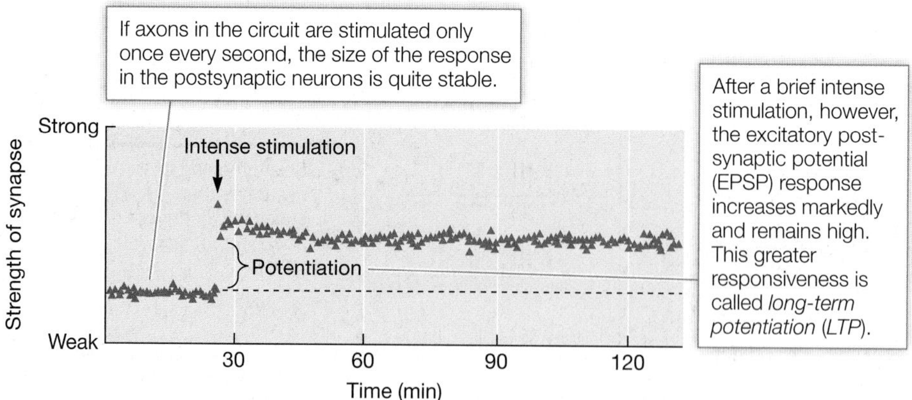

If axons in the circuit are stimulated only once every second, the size of the response in the postsynaptic neurons is quite stable.
After a brief intense stimulation, however, the excitatory post-synaptic potential (EPSP) response increases markedly and remains high. This greater responsiveness is called *long-term potentiation* (*LTP*).
Strong
Weak
Strength of synapse
Intense stimulation
Potentiation
30
60
90
120
Time (min)

Figure 9.24 Long-Term Potentiation (LTP) Occurs in the Hippocampus

long-term potentiation (LTP) The stable and long-lasting enhancement of synaptic transmission.

tic neurons. Normal activation of the presynaptic neurons caused a stable and predictable excitatory postsynaptic potential (see Section 3.2), as expected. Then the researchers applied a brief high-frequency burst of electrical stimulation to the presynaptic neurons, causing them to fire rapidly (hundreds of times per second). This abnormally high rate of firing of the presynaptic neurons caused them to stimulate the postsynaptic neurons so much that they too fired a lot. If the synapses between the presynaptic and postsynaptic neurons were acting like Hebbian synapses, then the repeated stimulation of postsynaptic neurons should have caused the synapses to grow stronger, which is just what happened. Now the postsynaptic neurons exposed to normal levels of presynaptic activity made a much larger response. In other words, the synapses appeared to have become stronger (**Figure 9.24**). This stable and long-lasting enhancement of synaptic transmission was named **long-term potentiation** (**LTP**) ("potentiation" means a strengthening).

The discovery of LTP in the hippocampus of rodents encouraged scientists to think that the hippocampus, which seems to be a brain structure crucial for consolidating information in LTM in humans, might serve the same function in laboratory animals. But to the puzzlement of researchers, it soon became evident that experiments involving lesions of the hippocampus on both sides of the brain in laboratory animals seemed not to produce widespread memory deficits (Isaacson, 1972). What might account for this discrepancy between humans and lab animals? Recall that Henry was able to learn some tasks, such as the mirror-tracing task, even though he never recognized that he had done it before. His improved tracings showed evidence of memory, in the form of motor skill. If an animal subject with comparable brain damage showed similar improvement on a task, we would probably conclude that the animal had normal memory, because we cannot ask animal subjects to tell us if they *recognize* the test. Also remember that Henry could learn new tasks using words, such as mirror reading. So an animal's inability to speak is probably not what accounts for its apparent immunity to brain surgery like Henry's. Rather, the culprit is the difficulty of measuring *declarative* memory, rather than nondeclarative memory, in animals.

It is relatively easy to teach an animal to perform a certain behavior to get food, and when the animal learns to quickly do that behavior, you know it has learned what to *do* to get food. But that is an example of an implicit, procedural memory, not an explicit, declarative memory. In that way, the behavior that gains access to food is no different from Henry's performance on the mirror-tracing task (for Henry, the reward was solving puzzles, which he liked

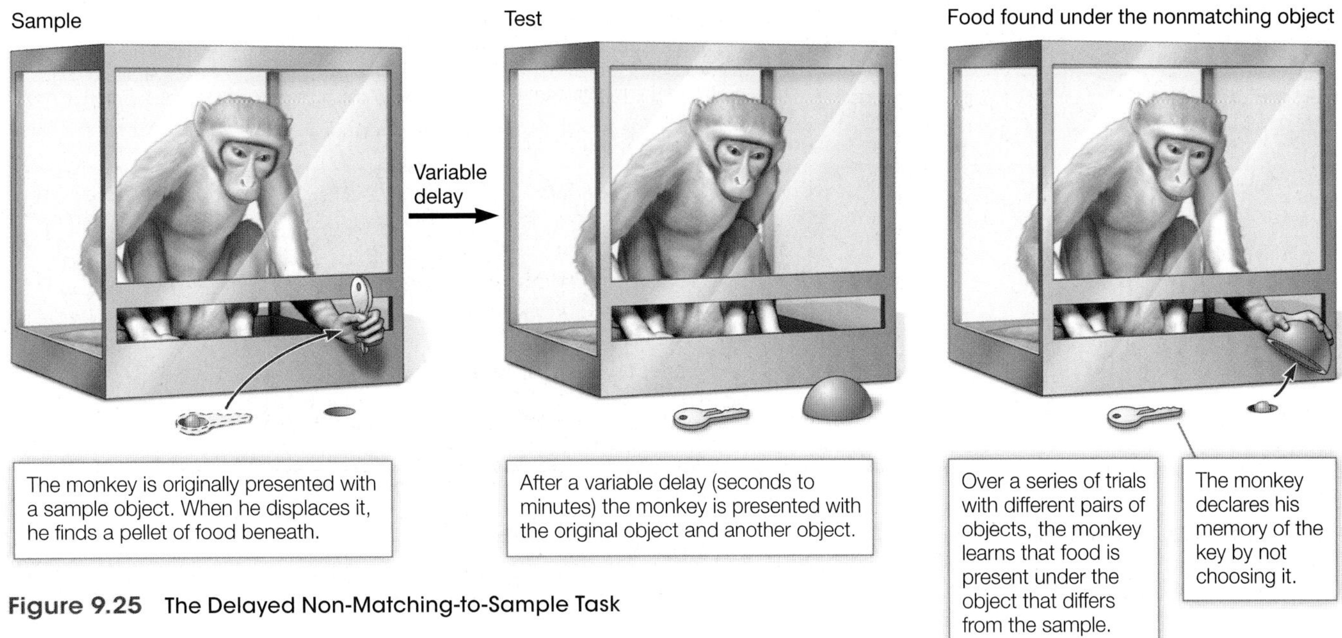

Sample
Test
Food found under the nonmatching object
Variable delay
The monkey is originally presented with a sample object. When he displaces it, he finds a pellet of food beneath.
After a variable delay (seconds to minutes) the monkey is presented with the original object and another object.
Over a series of trials with different pairs of objects, the monkey learns that food is present under the object that differs from the sample.
The monkey declares his memory of the key by not choosing it.

Figure 9.25 The Delayed Non-Matching-to-Sample Task

to do). So what was needed was a way to get an animal to "declare" through its behavior that it knows something about an object without having to do anything with that object. So scientists developed the **non-matching-to-sample test**, where the subject demonstrates recognition of an object by *not* touching it. Specifically, a monkey might be shown an object, such as a house key. When he picks it up, he finds a small food reward underneath. Then, after a length of time, you present the first object (the key) and a new object. In order to get a food reward, the monkey must pick up the new object, not the old one (**Figure 9.25**). By picking up the new object, the monkey has "declared" that he recognizes the old one by *not* picking it. Note that if the food were under the *familiar* object, then the monkey could simply follow a rule, "pick up familiar objects," which would be a procedural task. The animal might not remember the object but simply feel that it is familiar. But by picking up the other object, the animal must remember the old object.

non-matching-to-sample test A task where the subject demonstrates recognition of an object by not touching it; used to demonstrate declarative memory.

Researchers found that removing the hippocampus alone from animals had little effect on the non-matching-to-sample test (Mumby et al., 2002; Murray & Wise, 2012; Saksida et al., 2006). But, removal of the entire medial temporal lobe, much as had been done in Henry's case, resulted in animals that, like Henry, could not declare their recognition of the old object (**Figure 9.26**). The test required them to declare whether they had ever seen this object before, and their behavior, their inability to choose the new object, was equivalent to Henry saying "I've never seen that before." Thus the work with animals confirmed that the importance of the medial temporal lobe, which includes the hippocampus and associated cortex, for consolidating new long-term memories was not some peculiar property of Henry's brain alone. Rather, it looks like other mammals also depend on the medial temporal lobe, including the hippocampus, to transfer information from STM to LTM, presumably because the common ancestor to all the mammals relied on the hippocampus for this vital function hundreds of millions of years ago.

Henry died in 2008, at the age of 82. With his death the world at large learned for the first time that patient H.M., who had taught us so much about memory, was named Henry Molaison, as revealed in his obituary in *The New York Times*,

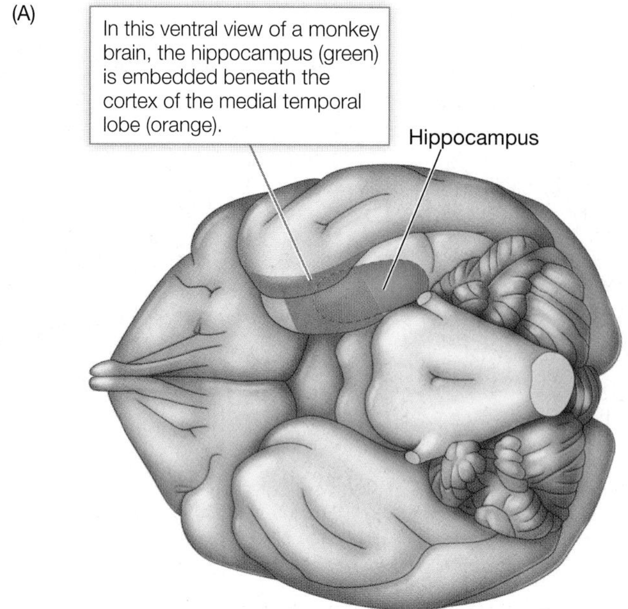
(A)
In this ventral view of a monkey brain, the hippocampus (green) is embedded beneath the cortex of the medial temporal lobe (orange).
Hippocampus

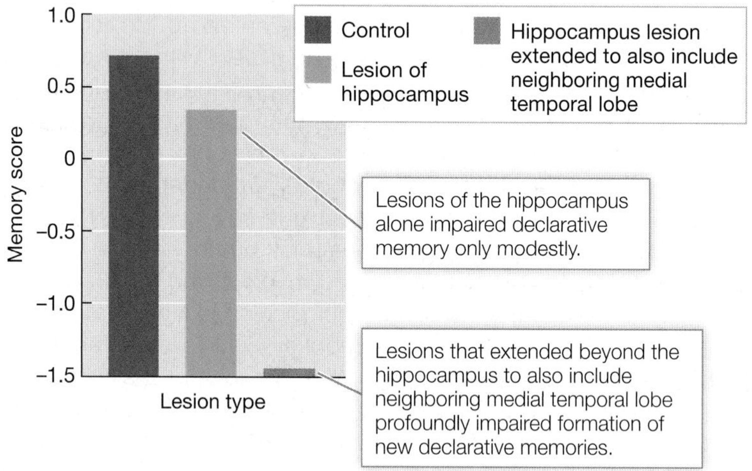
(B) Scores of groups with different lesions
1.0
0.5
0
-0.5
-1.0
-1.5
Memory score
Lesion type
Control
Lesion of hippocampus
Hippocampus lesion extended to also include neighboring medial temporal lobe
Lesions of the hippocampus alone impaired declarative memory only modestly.
Lesions that extended beyond the hippocampus to also include neighboring medial temporal lobe profoundly impaired formation of new declarative memories.

Figure 9.26 Memory Performance after Medial Temporal Lobe Lesions (After Squire & Zola-Morgan, 1991.)

which called him "an unforgettable amnesiac." Before his death, Henry and his court-appointed guardian agreed that when he died his brain could be examined by scientists. In 2009, webcasting technology made it possible fowr thousands of people to watch live as Henry's brain was carefully sectioned into thousands of slices to determine exactly what was damaged by that surgery 55 years before. Photomicrographs of every section are available to all researchers.

To the end, although he could remember so little of his entire adult life, Henry was courteous and concerned about other people. He remembered the surgeon he had met several times before his operation: "He did medical research on people.... What he learned about me helped others too, and I'm glad about that" (Corkin, 2002, p. 158). Henry never knew how famous he was, or how much his dreadful condition taught us about learning and memory while simultaneously robbing him of a normal human life. Yet despite being deprived of one of the most important characteristics of a human being, he held fast to his humanity.

The Cutting Edge

Are There Some Things We Should Forget?

When Kathleen was knocked down by a bike messenger, and was lying in the middle of a busy Boston street, several thoughts ran through her head. "Oh, why did I wear a skirt today? Are these people all looking at my underpants?" And of course she worried that a car might run over her. But she also remembered an earlier, even more traumatic experience when an armed stranger forced his way into her car and tried to rape her. It had taken her months to stop having awful memories of that carjacking. Now she worried that this accident would rekindle haunting memories of the earlier assault (Henig, 2004). Would she have to "forget" those horrible images all over again?

At the emergency room, Kathleen was offered a chance to participate in a study where she would take a pill that might make her memory of the bike accident feel less traumatic. She enrolled in the study, but she felt sure that her blue pills were placebos because she felt no effect. In fact, she was taking a drug called propranolol. Months later, listening to tapes of their own recountings of the traumatic events they'd suffered, Kathleen and the other participants given the drug showed fewer physiological signs of stress (increased heart rate, muscle tension, sweating) than did participants who got the placebo (Pitman et al., 2002). Interestingly, when asked whether painful memories of the trauma were affecting their everyday life, the two groups of participants seemed identical (Henig, 2004). Later studies confirmed that the drug erases the fear associated with the memory, not the memory itself (Kindt et al., 2009). Still, researchers think it may be possible one day to take a pill that may cause traumatic memories to fade entirely (Adler, 2012). Such a pill would be a great benefit to people like Kathleen.

In Greek mythology, the spirits of people who died traveled to Hades, where they were required to drink from a river called Lethe. One drink from this "River of Oblivion" would cause them to forget everything about their lives on Earth. Characters in the movie *Eternal Sunshine of the Spotless Mind* are given a similar opportunity to forget selected memories entirely. It may seem silly to erase memories of an ex-boyfriend, but a person who survived the September 11 attacks or prolonged torture is most likely tormented by vivid, horrible memories, as we'll discuss in detail in Box 13.2. Surely such a person would be happier in the aftermath if it were possible to forget those memories.

If you were given the opportunity to forget selected memories entirely, would you take that option?

9.3 SUMMARY

- *Amnesia* is a severe impairment of memory, either of events that happened before (*retrograde amnesia*) or events that happened after (*anterograde amnesia*) an event.
- It is quite common for a traumatic event, including brain injury, to cause retrograde amnesia that extends back hours or even days before the event, but retrograde amnesia for a whole lifetime probably occurs only in fiction.
- After his surgery, Henry Molaison (*patient H.M.*) had a normal STM capacity but could no longer consolidate new information from STM into LTM. His disability confirms the independence of STM and LTM and indicates that the medial temporal lobe, including the hippocampus, is required to consolidate information into LTM somewhere else in the brain, probably the cortex.
- Henry's disability applied only to *declarative*, or *explicit*, *memory*, facts and information we can explicitly declare to others. He could still form new *nondeclarative*, or *implicit*, *memories*, information he could demonstrate implicitly, such as *skill learning* like mirror tracing, priming, or classical *conditioning*.
- People with *Korsakoff's syndrome*, usually caused by severe malnutrition due to alcoholism, also have difficulty forming new declarative memories. In these patients, the *mammillary bodies* are damaged, and since the hippocampus sends axons there, they may be part of a pathway needed to consolidate new memories into LTM.
- Unlike Henry, people with Korsakoff's syndrome often *confabulate*, filling in memory gaps with false information they seem to believe.
- There are two kinds of declarative memory, *semantic memory* for facts and *episodic* (or autobiographical) *memory* for particular events in life. A few people with diffuse damage to their cortex seem to be unable to form new episodic memories but can still gain new semantic memory.
- We still don't know how the memory trace (or *engram*), the physical encoding of information in the brain, works, but Donald Hebb theorized that successful synapses—those that often cause the postsynaptic neuron to fire—may become stronger while unsuccessful synapses become weaker.
- An example of *Hebbian synapses* is seen in *long-term potentiation* (*LTP*), where causing a barrage of action potentials in one part of the hippocampus can cause a long-lasting increase in the strength of their synapses on another part of the hippocampus. Thus LTP may be important for the hippocampus to consolidate memories in the cortex.
- Animals cannot use speech to declare what they know, but *nonmatching-to-sample tests*, in which animals declare that they recognize an object by not choosing it, reveal that animals also have a deficit in forming new declarative memories after removal of the hippocampus and the rest of the medial temporal lobe.

REVIEW QUESTIONS

1. Name the two different subtypes of amnesia, and give an example of each.
2. What are the different subtypes of memory, and what is the evidence that they are at least partially independent of one another?
3. What is a Hebbian synapse, and how does LTP seem to represent this phenomenon?

Food for Thought

If you could drink a potion that allowed you to forget entirely just one episode in your life, say a particularly bad day, would you take it? Is the ideal human life one in which we have no bad memories?

Memory

Trapped in the Eternal Now

For over 50 years, Henry Molaison was known to the world as "patient H.M.," probably the most famous research participant in the history of psychology. Henry suffered seizures during adolescence, and by his late twenties, Henry's epilepsy was out of control. In 1953, because tests showed that Henry's seizures began in both hemispheres, a neurosurgeon removed most of Henry's anterior temporal lobes.

After Henry recovered from the operation, his seizures were milder, and they could be controlled by medication. But this relief came at a terrible, unforeseen cost: Henry had lost the ability to form new memories (Scoville & Milner, 1957). For more than 50 years after the surgery, until his death in 2008, Henry could retain any new fact only briefly. As soon as he was distracted, the newly acquired information vanished from his memory. Long after the surgery, he didn't know his age or the current date, and he didn't know that his parents (with whom he lived well into adulthood) had died years previously. His IQ remained a little above average (Corkin et al., 1997); despite problems with acquiring new information, he could perform well on IQ tests because they do not require remembering new facts for more than a few minutes. The knowledge Henry had gained before the surgery was intact, allowing him to solve crossword puzzles, which he loved. But Henry knew something was wrong with him, because he had no memories from the years since his surgery, or even memories from earlier the same day.

> *Every day is alone in itself, whatever enjoyment I've had, and whatever sorrow I've had.... Right now, I'm wondering, have I done or said anything amiss? You see, at this moment everything looks clear to me, but what happened just before? That's what worries me. It's like waking from a dream. I just don't remember. (Milner, 1970, p. 37.)*

Henry's inability to form new memories meant that he couldn't construct a lasting relationship with anybody he met after his surgery. No matter what experiences he might share with someone he met, Henry would have to start the acquaintance anew the following day. What happened?

Think Like a Psychologist:

Principles in Action

Whenever we encounter any interesting behavior we should consider the four principles. Here are some ways that the four principles relate to our opening story about Henry.

MACHINE

The mind is a product of a physical machine, the brain.

The loss of the medial temporal lobe, including the hippocampus, left Henry unable to transfer short-term memory into long-term declarative memory.

UNCONSCIOUS

We are consciously aware of only a small part of our mental activity.

Upon meeting a stranger, Henry could carry on a pleasant, intelligent conversation. But if the person left the room for a few minutes, Henry reported no awareness of having ever met before. His disability robbed Henry of conscious awareness of his own past.

SOCIAL

We constantly modify our behavior, beliefs, and attitudes according to what we perceive about the people around us.

Henry's deficit in forming new declarative memories meant, among other things, that he could not form any new social relationships nor build on any relationships he had before. This inability to conduct a social life prevented him from ever being able to live independently.

EXPERIENCE

Our experiences physically alter the structure and function of the brain.

Despite his disability, Henry benefitted from repeated trials on the mirror-tracing task. Even though he was unaware of his previous trials, they still improved his performance.

KEY TERMS

amnesia, 378
anterograde amnesia, 378
chunking, 361
conditioning, 385
confabulate, 382
consolidation, 363
context-dependent retrieval, 371
cued recall, 369
declarative memory, 381
encoding, 361
engram, 385
episodic memory, 382
fade, 366
flashbulb memories, 372
forgetting, 366
free recall, 369
Hebbian synapse, 387
hierarchies, 362
hippocampus, 379
Korsakoff's syndrome, 382
long-term memory (LTM), 357
long-term potentiation (LTP), 388
mammillary bodies, 382
medial temporal lobe, 379
memory, 352
memory trace, 371
method of loci, 376
misinformation effect, 371
mnemonic devices, 375
nondeclarative memory, 381
non-matching-to-sample test, 389
nonsense syllables, 357
patient H.M., 378
patient K.C., 382
photographic memory, 353
primacy effect, 359
priming, 369
proactive interference, 367
recency effect, 359
rehearsal, 355
retrieval, 366
retroactive interference, 367
retrograde amnesia, 378
savant, 365
semantic memory, 382
semantic webs, 370
sensory buffer, 352
serial position curve, 359
short-term memory (STM), 355
skill learning, 385
spreading activation, 369
tip-of-the-tongue phenomenon, 376
working memory, 356

QUIZ YOURSELF

1. In Sperling's iconic memory studies, if participants were able to report three out of four of the letters in the bottom row that he indicated by sounding the low tone, they could be assumed to have "taken in" how many letters total before the tone?
   a. 3
   b. 6
   c. 9
   d. 12
2. For information to enter permanent memory, it must first enter into _______ which lasts less than a ______, then into ________ which lasts several ________, and then into ________ which can last a lifetime.
3. When you hear a list of ten words and then repeat them back after a 30-second delay, you are more likely to remember the first few words and last few words. You can make a graph of the likelihood of a correct response based on the position of the word in the list. This is called a ________; the greater memory of the earliest items is the ________ effect and the greater memory for the last few items is the ________ effect.
4. The process of taking raw sensory information and converting it into a form we can understand is
   a. priming.
   b. encoding.
   c. fading.
   d. learning.
5. The process of transferring information from STM into LTM is
   a. consolidation.
   b. rehearsal.
   c. confabulation.
   d. retrieval.
6. You are shown a series of pictures, including one of a loaf of bread. You are then asked to complete some words, given the first two letters. When you are given BR _ _ _ , you now are more likely to write BREAD than BRICK or BRIDE. This is known as the ________ effect.
   a. misinformation
   b. primacy
   c. priming
   d. spreading activation
7. We can test declarative memory in monkeys by giving them a ________ test.

1. c; 2. sensory buffer (sensory memory); second; STM; seconds; LTM; 3. serial position curve; primacy; recency; 4. b; 5. a; 6. c; 7. non-matching-to-sample

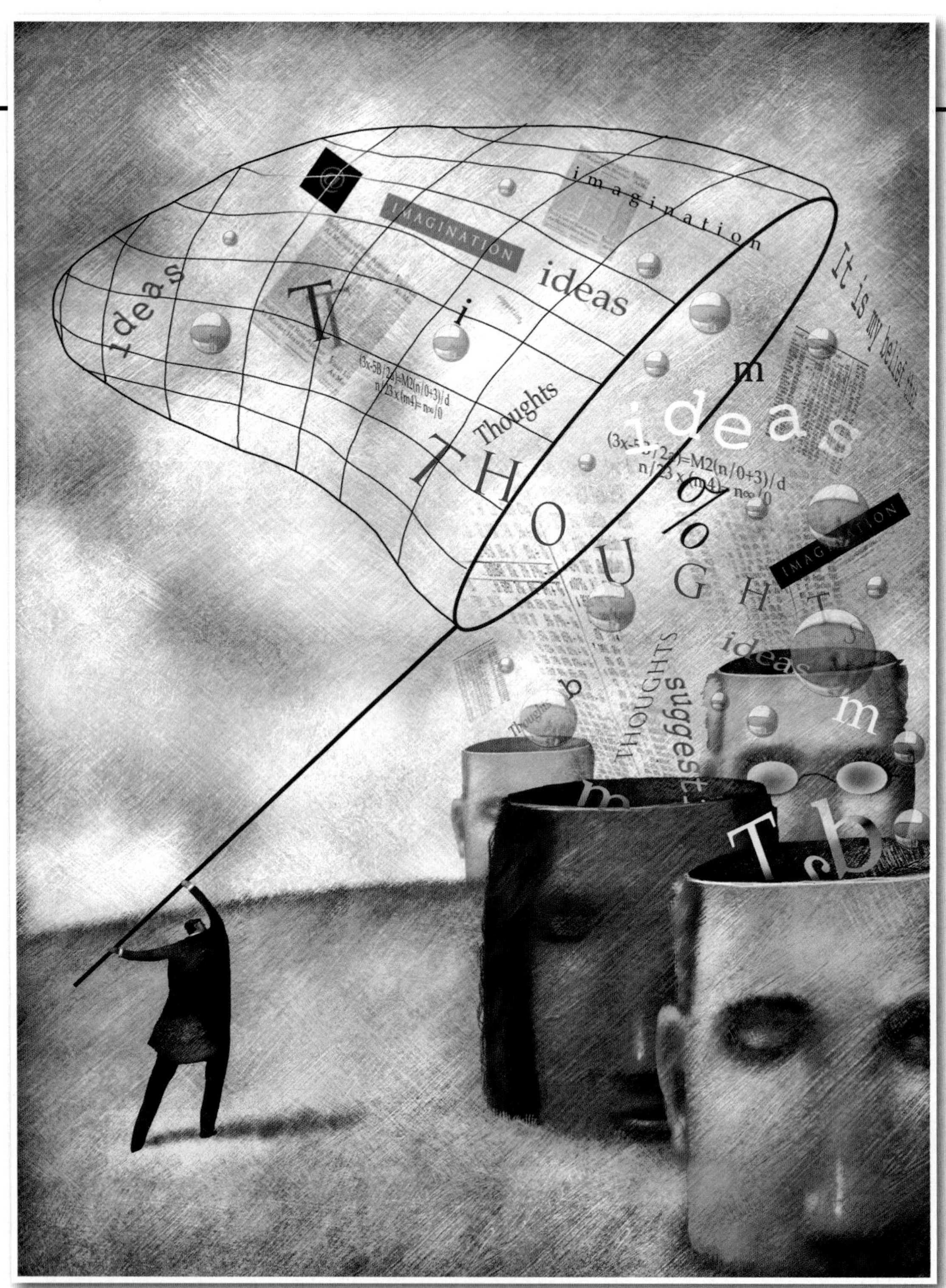

imagination
IMAGINATION
ideas
ideas
Thoughts
(3x-5B/2a)=M2(n/0+3)/d
n/23 x (m4)= n∞/0
It is my belief that
ideas
THOUGHT
IMAGINATION
ideas
THOUGHTS
suggest

10 Language and Cognition

Unheeded Warnings

Several months before the 9/11 attacks on the World Trade Center, the Central Intelligence Agency received information that Al-Qaeda leader Osama bin Ladin was planning a major attack on the United States. Alarmed by the many different sources that indicated an imminent attack, the director of the CIA requested an emergency meeting with the secretary of state on July 10, 2001, to discuss the threat. Less than a month later, President George W. Bush's daily briefing included a report headlined "Bin Laden Determined to Strike in U.S.," warning that bin Ladin was threatening to "follow the example of World Trade Center bomber Ramzi Yousef and 'bring the fighting to America'" in retaliation for U.S. attacks on Al-Qaeda bases in Afghanistan. The memo relayed the claim of one source "that Bin Ladin wanted to hijack a U.S. aircraft." Apparently no additional security steps were initiated in response to these warnings. Indeed, the next month, when bin Ladin's followers flew two hijacked airplanes into the World Trade Center towers, neither the secretary of state nor the president recalled having received any warnings of the attack. When the public learned in 2006 that warnings had in fact been issued, the administration was widely criticized for having failed to act to avert the attack (National Commission on Terrorist Attacks upon the United States, 2011).

But were the criticisms fair? Those warnings about bin Ladin represented a tiny minority of the flood of information that enters the White House daily. Should the administration have known what was coming? The larger question is, Just how good are we at sifting through information, recognizing the important nuggets of information, and making judgments about what is or is not likely in the future? As we'll learn in this chapter, we humans are not very good at a task such as this, and in fact, we are prone to make errors of several types, including when we look back at our own past decisions.

Chapter Preview

Language allows us to communicate a tremendous amount of information, including such theoretical and complex concepts as "threat," "retaliation," and "hijack." In the first section of this chapter you'll learn that the human brain is so finely adapted to learn language that babies pick it up effortlessly, and that parts of the brain are specialized to understand or produce language. The marvel of how our minds readily categorize and process information is covered in Section 10.2. You'll learn about the concept of attention, which is vital to information processing. We will discuss how attention is a limited resource, so directing it to one activity can make us blind to other events. In the final section we'll consider the process of how we make judgments and use them to make decisions. We'll see that we are not very good at making certain kinds of decisions and are susceptible to several kinds of bias in our judgments.

10.1 Language

Things to Learn

- Components of language
- Evolutionary beginnings of language
- Teaching language to animals
- Human language acquisition
- Language function is in the left cortex
- Language influences on thinking

One of the most amazing things about human speech is something most people take for granted: virtually every baby learns a language with *no formal teaching whatsoever*. Just by being around people who talk, babies learn the language (or *languages*) spoken around them. If you've ever tried to learn a new language as an adult, you will appreciate how remarkable it is that babies master not only words but syntax within a relatively short period of time. In this section we'll review evidence that the human brain is especially good at acquiring languages before we reach the age of 12 or so, but not thereafter (maddeningly, the precise age when many school systems begin teaching a second language!). We'll consider the special skill of reading and the fascinating question of why some children who are clearly very intelligent nevertheless have a hard time learning to read. We'll conclude this section by discussing evidence indicating that the language we learn, and the culture we learn it in, has an impact on the way we think.

What are the components of human language?

There are an estimated 7,000 languages in the world today, about 1,000 of which have been studied by **linguists** (Wuethrich, 2000), scientists who study language. Their analyses reveal that all these languages share similar basic characteristics. For example, all spoken languages are composed of a set of sounds and symbols that have distinct meanings. Those sounds and symbols are arranged according to rules that are characteristic of the particular language. Each language has basic speech *sounds*, or **phonemes**. English consists of about 50 different phonemes (exactly how many depends on the dialect of English), which include both vowels and consonants. Some languages have over 100 phonemes, others have as few as 11 (Crystal, 2010), but because there are estimated to be over 800 phonemes used in one language or another (Gibbs, 2002), it is rare for any two languages to use the exact same subset of phonemes. If you've tried to learn another language, such as French or Chinese, you've faced the challenge of making a sound that you had never tried to make before, as you try to reproduce a new phoneme.

In each language, phonemes are assembled into simple units of *meaning* called **morphemes**, and these morphemes are assembled into *words*. The word *unfathomable*, for example, consists of the morphemes *un*, *fathom*, and *able*

linguists Scientists who study language.

phonemes The basic speech sounds that make up languages.

morphemes The basic units of meaning in a language. They are composed of phonemes.

semantics The study of the meanings of words.

syntax The rules for constructing phrases and sentences in a language.

generative Term used to describe the capacity of a language to produce an infinite number of sentences.

surface structure The particular string of words that are put together in a sentence.

deep structure The particular meaning beneath the surface structure of a sentence.

(**Figure 10.1**). Words have meaning, and the study of those meanings is the field of **semantics**. Words, in turn, are assembled into meaningful strings, which may be complete sentences or just phrases. For each language, there are rules for constructing phrases and sentences, and those rules are the language's **syntax**. You might think of the rules for constructing sentences and phrases as *grammar*, but grammar typically refers to a set of rules about how you *ought* to structure your sentences. Syntax is concerned with how native speakers *actually* assemble sentences to communicate with one another. Anyone who knows the phonemes (sounds) and syntax (rules) of a particular language can speak sentences that convey information to others who have similar knowledge of the language. A speaker who also knows the symbols used to depict the phonemes, in our case the alphabet, can write sentences that convey information.

One powerful characteristic of all languages is that their words can be rearranged to produce many different sentences, with vastly different meanings. The number of English words is estimated at 1 million and growing (Michel et al., 2011), but probably no one could define them all without consulting a dictionary (**Figure 10.2**). The average American high school graduate is thought to know 50,000 to 60,000 words (Pinker, 1994). Knowing that many words means that, in practical terms, there are an infinite number of different sentences a speaker might construct. Because language has this vast capacity to produce so many different sentences, it is said to be **generative** (while not used often, this English word means "capable of producing lots of offspring"). I love listening to young children speak, because in their beginning efforts they often put words together in a way that sounds utterly fresh. "The ladybugs are having a race on the window!" I doubt I'd ever heard anyone say that before. This ability of even beginning speakers to produce new sentences illustrates both the *generative* capacity of language and the fact that a speaker is trying to represent a particular meaning, even if he or she doesn't yet have the vocabulary or the proper syntax to express it very clearly.

The meaning, or semantic content, of language brings up a distinction about how we use language. The famous linguist Noam Chomsky (1957) proposed that every sentence has two layers of representation. The **surface structure** is the particular string of words that are put together in a sentence. The **deep structure** is the particular meaning (semantic relations) beneath the surface structure. If two girls are skipping rope on the sidewalk, there are many different sentences we could put together to describe that. Each sentence would have a distinct surface structure, but they would all share the same deep structure—the underlying meaning. Linguists have noted this distinction between surface structure and deep structure to suggest that all human languages may share a common

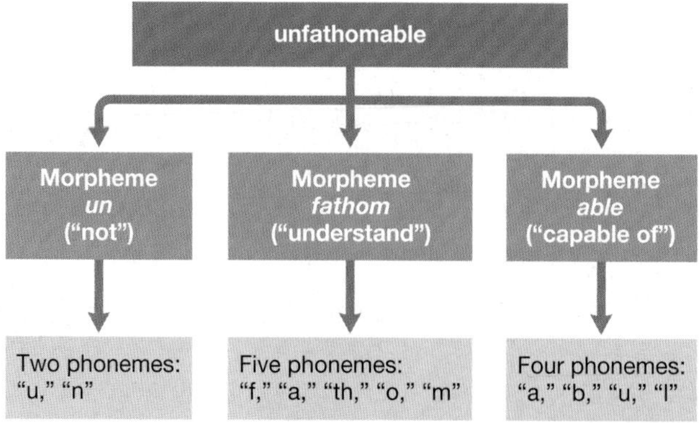

Figure 10.1 Phonemes Make Morphemes That Make Words Words are strung together according to the rules of a language, the syntax, to communicate meaning to others. (Note: Linguists use a very specific notation to identify phonemes, which we are not using here.)

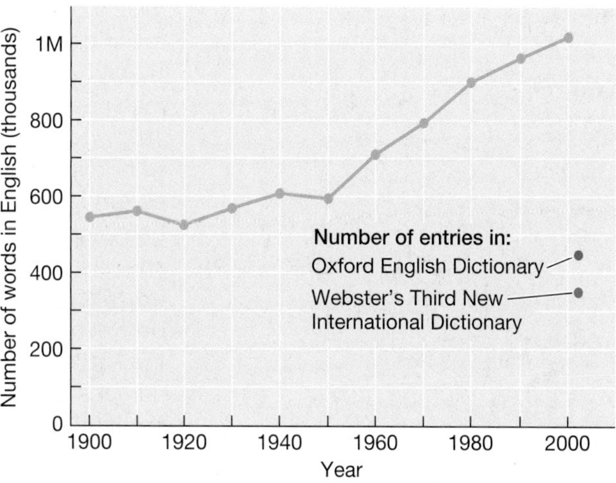

Figure 10.2 Number of English Words Note the rapid addition of words since 1950. The figures for the dictionaries for 2001 are for the number of entries, but many entries include variations of words (for example, the entry "blend" covers "blending," "blends," and "blender"). (After Michel et al., 2011.)

Born to Talk Noam Chomsky believes the human brain has evolved to acquire language.

deep structure. That issue is well beyond our scope, but the distinction between surface structure and deep structure also emphasizes how human language is filled with meaning. When we speak, we are symbolically representing how the world is, was, or should be.

I've emphasized the *generative* capacity of language and the *semantic* content of language because these issues will arise when we ask whether other animals can also use language, as we'll do next.

Animal communication reveals the evolutionary roots of language

Do animals use language? You might think that is a straightforward question, but in fact there is no easy answer. For example, scholars have suggested that speech and language originally developed from gestures of the face and hands (Corballis, 2002; Hewes, 1973). Even today, hand movements facilitate speech: people who are prevented from gesturing make more slips and have more pauses in their speech (Krauss, 1998). Furthermore, people who have been blind from birth, and so have never seen the hand gestures of others, make hand gestures while they speak (Iverson & Goldin-Meadow, 1998). Deaf children raised without access to an established sign language may invent one of their own, complete with structural features that characterize other spoken and sign languages (Goldin-Meadow, 2006). These observations suggest that gestures represent at least the beginnings of language. Lots of other species use gestures to communicate: many birds display elaborate courtship behaviors to attract a mate, chimpanzees shake their arms to signal threat, and dogs and wolves freeze and stare to alert other members of the pack (or the dog's owner) to the location of a potential prey. The gestures that other species use to communicate may well reflect the earliest beginnings of human language.

Plenty of non-human animals vocalize as well as gesture—producing chirps, barks, meows, and songs, among other sounds. Whales sing and may imitate songs that they hear from distant oceans (Noad et al., 2000), and some seal mothers recognize their pups' vocalizations even after 4 years of separation (Insley, 2000). In fact, many species—from elephants to bats to birds to dolphins—are capable of vocal learning and use their vocalizations to help form social bonds and identify one another (Poole et al., 2005; Tyack, 2003). Rats and mice produce complex ultrasonic vocalizations, which we cannot hear, that may communicate emotional information (Panksepp, 2005).

Although no one would suggest that it is an evolutionary precursor to human speech, birdsong offers intriguing analogies to human language (Marler, 1970). Many birds, such as chickens and doves, produce only simple calls with limited communicative functions, but songbirds like canaries, zebra finches, and sparrows produce complex vocalizations that are crucial for social behaviors and reproductive success. In these songbirds, only males of the species sing, and the song is learned—in much the same way that humans learn language (DeVoogd, 1994; see Figure 8.26). Another striking similarity between birdsong and human language involves the different contributions of the left and right cerebral hemispheres. We'll see later in this chapter that in humans the left hemisphere plays a crucial role in language—left-hemisphere damage is far more likely to disrupt language than right-hemisphere damage—and the same is true in some songbirds: only left-hemisphere lesions of the brain impair singing (Nottebohm, 1980).

One might dismiss the fact that birds control song with their left hemisphere while we control language with our left hemisphere as mere coincidence. But is it? Take into consideration that if the hemisphere that evolved to control an activity (such as language) were determined by chance, there would be a 50% chance that it would be the same in two species. On the other hand, several observations provide evidence that the left hemisphere may play a special role in ape communication, just as it does in people (Meguerditchian & Vauclair, 2006; Taglialatela et al., 2006). Several brain regions related to language are larger in the left hemisphere than in the right in humans, and those same regions are also larger in the left hemisphere in apes. Furthermore, apes tend to favor gesturing with the right hand, which is controlled by the left side of the brain. Was the left hemisphere specialized to control communication in the common ancestor of other apes and humans, or even in the common ancestor of birds and humans?

Acquiring Song Male zebra finches learn their song from their father.

Genetic studies support the idea that brain systems controlling language evolved from communication systems like those found in other animals. Analysis of a British family with a rare heritable language disorder led to the identification of a gene that appears to be important for human language. Children with a specific mutation of this gene, *FOXP2*, take a long time to learn to speak (Lai et al., 2001), and they display long-lasting difficulties with some specific language tasks, such as learning verb tenses (Nudel & Newbury, 2013). The pattern of brain activation in these individuals during performance of a language task is different from that seen in typical speakers—they show underactivation of Broca's area (**Figure 10.3**), a brain region important in language, which we will discuss later (Liégeois et al., 2003). The *FOXP2* gene in the other great apes is different from that of humans (Enard et al., 2002), suggesting that this gene has been evolving rapidly in humans, presumably because language is so adaptive in our species that, once begun, it became ever more elaborate in a short time (in evolutionary terms, within the past 1 million years).

Yet the basic function of *FOXP2* may have always been to support communication, because this same gene is also important for communication in other species. The ultrasonic vocalizations in rats and mice that we mentioned earlier are disrupted by mutations in the *FOXP2* gene (French & Fisher, 2014; Shu et al., 2005). What's more, when researchers selectively silenced *FOXP2* expression in the songbird brain, adolescent males failed to properly learn their song (Haesler et al., 2007). Because this same gene normally contributes to brain communication systems in both humans and other animals, it seems likely that human language evolved from a preexisting brain system that was already involved in communication. In that case, these animal communication systems really do represent the evolutionary beginnings of human language.

In natural settings, monkeys combine certain vocalizations into more complex calls, suggesting the *rudiments* of both syntax and semantic meaning (Arnold & Zuberbühler, 2006; Ouattara et al., 2009), but nothing like that seen in every human language. Even if we regard these monkey vocalizations as morphemes—combinations of sounds that convey particular meanings, like "hawk"

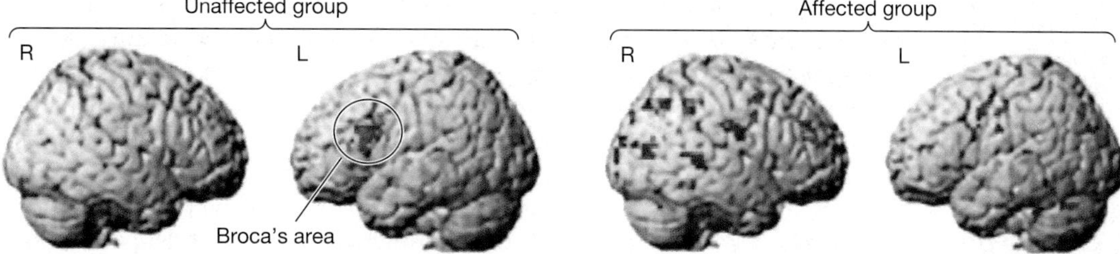

Figure 10.3 An Inherited Language Disorder Family members of the British family affected by the *FOXP2* gene show underactivation of Broca's area when carrying out a language task. Instead, the affected individuals seem to activate a scattering of brain regions, mostly in the right hemisphere. (After Fisher & Marcus, 2005.)

versus "snake"—there are too few to be considered a full-blown language. Nor is there evidence that animal vocalizations follow particular rules about how to string more than two sounds together to convey a particular meaning. In other words, we've yet to discern genuine syntax in any animal communication system in the wild. But if no other species *in nature* uses a full-blown language, do any species have enough rudiments of brain communication systems that they could be *taught* a language?

Can other animals acquire language with training?

People have long tried to communicate with animals, sometimes quite successfully: anyone who has watched a service dog at work, responding to commands from its owner, has to acknowledge that the human is transmitting lots of information to a highly intelligent companion. Instilling *language* in a non-human is a different matter, however. Every day, you utter sentences that you have never said before, yet the meaning is clear to both you and your listener because you both understand the speech sounds and syntax involved. Animals generally are incapable of similar feats, instead requiring extensive training with each specific utterance (e.g., each voice command to the sheepdog) in order for communication to occur at all. In other words, most animals appear to lack an understanding of the meaning of individual words (semantics) or the rules about putting words together to convey a particular message (syntax)—although, in fairness, we are asking them to learn *our* semantics and syntax when we know very little about theirs.

One strategy for teaching language to an animal is to choose a species as much like ourselves as possible, in other words, one of the other great apes. Because the vocal tracts of the other apes are very different from those of humans, scientists have given up attempting to train these animals to produce human speech. But can non-human primates be taught other forms of communication that have features similar to those of human language, including the ability to represent objects with symbols and to manipulate those symbols according to rules of order?

Our nearest primate relatives, chimpanzees, are capable of learning many of the hand gestures of American Sign Language (ASL), the standardized sign language used by some deaf people in North America. Chimps trained in ASL have been reported to use signs spontaneously, and in novel sequences (Gardner & Gardner, 1969, 1984). Gorillas apparently also can learn hundreds of ASL signs (Patterson & Linden, 1981) (**Figure 10.4A**). An alternative language system involves the use of assorted colored chips (symbols) that can be arranged on a magnetic board. After extensive training with this system, chimps reportedly organize the chips in ways that seem to reflect an acquired ability to form short sentences and to note various logical classifications (Premack, 1971). A third language system uses computerized keys to represent concepts; again, apes show some ability to acquire words in this language, which they appear to string together into novel, meaningful chains (Lyn et al., 2011; Rumbaugh, 1977).

Communication between Species
Service dogs learn to communicate with their human comrades.

The idea that apes can acquire and use rudiments of language remains controversial. According to many linguists, syntax is the essence of language, so investigators look for the ability of chimps to generate meaningful and novel sequences of signs that follow syntactical rules. The work of Gardner and Gardner (1969, 1984), Premack (1971), and others suggested that chimps do make distinctive series of signs, including categories and negatives, just as though they were using words in a sentence. However, other researchers argued that these sequences may simply be subtle forms of imitation (Terrace, 1979), perhaps unconsciously cued by the experimenter who is providing the training. Native ASL users dispute the linguistic validity of the signs generated by apes; and Pinker (1994) insists, "Even putting aside vocabulary, phonology, morphology, and syntax, what impresses one the most about chimpanzee signing is that

(A)

(B)

Figure 10.4 Communicating with Animals (A) Koko the gorilla, shown here with trainer Dr. Penny Patterson, communicates using American Sign Language. (B) Chimpanzees can learn to use arbitrary signs and symbols on a keyboard to communicate.

fundamentally, deep down, chimps just don't get it" (p. 349). Indeed, it's hard to imagine how we could even tell if an animal understood words for complex concepts like *retaliation* or *terrorism*.

Nevertheless, considering that apes can comprehend spoken words, produce novel combinations of words, and respond appropriately to sentences arranged according to a syntactic rule, it seems likely that the linguistic capacity of apes was underestimated historically (Savage-Rumbaugh, 1993). For example, a bonobo (pygmy chimpanzee) named Kanzi, the focus of a long-term research program (Savage-Rumbaugh & Lewin, 1994), reportedly learned numerous symbols and ways to assemble them in novel combinations, entirely through observational learning rather than the usual intensive training (**Figure 10.4B**). Kanzi's ability to produce novel strings of words suggests that his is a generative language, like human language. So although the debate is far from settled, the linguistic accomplishments of primates have forced investigators to sharpen their criteria of what constitutes language.

Another strategy for teaching language to animals is to choose a species that may not be closely related to us but is adapted for flexible, oral communication, namely a parrot. When Irene Pepperberg purchased a year-old African gray parrot and named him *Alex*, she soon became intrigued by how quickly Alex, like other parrots, would learn new phrases. She devised a new training system that exploited the highly social nature of parrots, working with another person, encouraging Alex to imitate the humans' use of language. Alex's job was to outcompete his rival (the other human) for treats, and for Pepperberg's approval and praise. Eventually Alex learned about 150 words. He could name the color, shape, and type of material that made up an object, even one he'd never seen before. He could sort objects by shape or color (**Figure 10.5**) and could count small numbers of objects (Péron et al., 2014). Most important, Alex could perform these feats even for a stranger, with Pepperberg out of the room. This meant that Alex was not like "Clever Hans," the horse we learned about in Section 2.1, who relied on his trainer's (unconscious) cues to stamp his hoof the correct number of times. Alex appeared to produce new

Figure 10.5 "You Be Good, See You Tomorrow" The African gray parrot Alex (1976–2007) spoke with his owner, Dr. Irene Pepperberg, and appeared to create new, meaningful sentences from a vocabulary of about 150 English words.

sentences and even new words. Shown a dried banana chip, he called it a "banacker," which sounds suspiciously like a blending of two words he already knew: "banana" and "cracker." As Pepperberg put him in his cage one night, Alex said his typical bedtime phrases to her: "You be good, see you tomorrow. I love you." The next morning he was dead, apparently of natural causes, at age 31. Despite Alex's accomplishments, one researcher still denied that Alex was using language. As quoted in *The New York Times* obituary for Alex, David Premack dismissed the parrot's ability as unlike human language because "there's no evidence of recursive logic, and without that you can't work with digital numbers or more complex human grammar" (Carey, 2007).

Personally, it seems to me that every time an animal manages to accomplish some aspect of language that was previously thought to be uniquely human, the bar for what constitutes true language gets raised. First we were told that animals didn't understand the symbolic aspect of language—that a particular set of sounds means "water." Then when animals learned to use keyboards with arbitrary symbols, or ASL gestures to represent objects, we were told they could not produce new sentences. Then when animals were demonstrated to have generated new sentences that seemed to make sense, the objection was that they don't understand syntax—they don't follow strict rules about the order of words used in a sentence. For goodness sakes, Alex's ability was dismissed because he couldn't work with "digital numbers" or do "recursive logic" (can you?)! It's hard not to suspect that some researchers feel threatened by the idea that humans are not unique in our abilities, or are eager to downplay the abilities of individuals that are just "animals."

The question of whether other animals can really learn language is not likely to be settled anytime soon. Although we have yet to experience the miracle of being able to carry on a conversation with another species, learning a language while growing up is miraculous in itself.

We start life ready to decode any language we happen to hear

A child's brain is an incredible linguistic machine, rapidly acquiring the phonemes, vocabulary, and syntax of the local language. Language is learned without any formal instruction; the baby simply has to hear the language spoken in order to learn it. Of course, the baby is not at all passive in this process. One of the reasons babies learn language so rapidly is because they are intensely interested in hearing speech and in watching a talking face. We'll see shortly that even newborns are willing to work in order to hear someone talk. As they avidly attend to language and soak it up, children pass through behavioral milestones of language development (**Table 10.1**). While the time line of when an individual child reaches a particular milestone varies considerably, the *sequence* is almost always the same. That finding indicates that each stage of language acquisition lays the groundwork to tackle the next stage.

Of course a child does not begin speaking in fully formed, grammatically correct sentences. A newborn will fuss, cry, and laugh, but by 6 months or so most babies **babble**, making meaningless sounds that are strung together such that they resemble speech. The first stages of babbling tend to be repetitive—"ba-ba-ba-ba-ba-ba-ba"—while later the babbling sounds are more variable. One of my favorite stages in the development of my own children was that point when they would wake up alone in their crib and begin babbling in that variable way. I would hear all the inflections and tones of human speech, but the words were pure nonsense. I could almost imagine the child was speaking some exotic foreign language.

babble The meaningless sounds strung together to resemble speech made by infants, typically before the age of 6 months.

telegraphic speech Communication form in young children, in which a few words are used to express an idea.

As the child learns to articulate specific words, she will use **telegraphic speech**, providing only a few words, or even a single word, to communicate.

■ **TABLE 10.1 Typical Stages of Childhood Language Development**

Age	Receptive language	Expressive language
Birth–5 months	Reacts to loud sounds Turns head toward sounds Watches faces that speak	Vocalizes pleasure and displeasure (laugh, cry, giggle) Makes noises when talked to
6–11 months	Understands "no-no" Tries to repeat sounds	Babbles ("ba-ba-ba, da-da-da") Gestures
12–17 months	Attends to book about 2 minutes Follows simple gestures Tries to imitate simple words	Points to objects, people Says 2–3 words to label object
18–23 months	Enjoys being read to Follows simple commands Points to body parts Understands simple verbs	Says 8–10 words (maybe with unclear pronunciation) Asks for foods by name Starts combining words ("more milk")
2–3 years	Understands about 50 words Understands pronouns Knows spatial concepts ("in," "out")	Says about 40 words Uses pronouns such as "you," "I" Uses 2- to 3-word phrases
3–4 years	Understands colors Understands groupings of objects (foods, clothes, toys, etc.)	Is mostly understandable by strangers Expresses ideas, feelings
4–5 years	Understands complex questions Understands "behind," "next to"	Says about 200–300 words Uses some irregular verb past tenses ("ran," "fell") Engages in conversation
5 years	Understands > 2,000 words Understands sentences > 8 words long Can follow series of three directions Understands time sequences (what happened first, second, last)	Uses complex and compound sentences

Sources: American Speech-Language-Hearing Association, n.d.; National Institutes of Health, 2014; PRO-ED Inc., 1999.

"Need cookie!" rather than "I want a cookie" or, better yet, "May I have a cookie, please?" Typically, adults will repeat the child's communication, filling in the missing words, so that by 3 years of age or so, most children speak in complete sentences. What's more, the child's pronunciation of words is likely to be imperfect at first. This means that in the early stages, the child's family and caregivers, who have learned to understand the child, may be the only ones who effectively get the message. As the child's language skills improve, she will also be understood by strangers. Another landmark for children in modern times is being able to understand speech, and produce comprehensible speech, over the telephone, without any visual cues to aid communication.

Psychologists use behavior to test babies' language ability

One of the first things babies must learn is how to tell different phonemes apart when they hear them. This is a more difficult task than you might think, because some of the sounds that, to our adult ears, sound very distinct are in fact physically very similar. For example, the syllables *ba* and *pa* are a lot alike, and differ only in terms of how soon we vocalize (make a "hum" in the back of our throat) after we pop our lips apart. Yet 4-month-old children can tell them apart. How do we know?

In a pioneering study, Peter Eimas and colleagues (1971) presented babies of different ages with different sounds. The babies were too little to talk, but

habituate To stop attending to a stimulus because it is no longer novel.

the researchers found a way to know whether the babies could distinguish between, for example, *ba* and *pa*. Babies were rewarded for sucking on an artificial nipple by being presented with brief speech sounds. They must have found this rewarding, because they would suck more eagerly when given that reward. This finding alone tells us something important about babies—they are eager to hear language, as we noted earlier. Most important, if we present the *same* word over and over, the babies eventually grow tired of hearing it. We say that they have **habituated** to the sound—they can still hear it, but they stop attending to it. In a variation of the habituation technique we discussed in Chapter 5 (see Figure 5.13), this tendency to habituate to sounds can be used to determine if the babies can tell *ba* from *pa*. If they've been hearing nothing but "ba" for a while, they slow down their sucking as they habituate. If we now present "pa," then the babies should regain interest and increase their sucking, but *only if they notice the difference in the phoneme.* Psychologists have exploited this logic to determine what babies can and cannot perceive in spoken language, as we'll see next (**Figure 10.6**).

Researchers at Work

"Reading babies' minds"

Figure 10.6 Babies Will Work to Hear New Speech Sounds (After Eimas et al., 1971.)

■ **Question:** Can babies distinguish between similar phonemes?

■ **Hypothesis:** Babies who have habituated to one phoneme will notice the difference in the other, slightly different phoneme.

■ **Test:** Have babies suck on a pacifier for a chance to hear sounds. If they are given the same sound repeatedly, they will habituate and suck less. If they are given a new sound, they will renew their sucking *if they can actually tell that the phoneme is new*.

■ **Results:** The babies increased sucking when presented with a new, different phoneme.

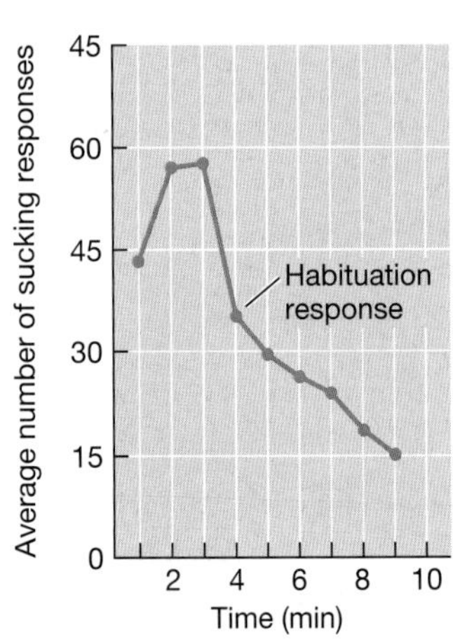

Two very similar phonemes

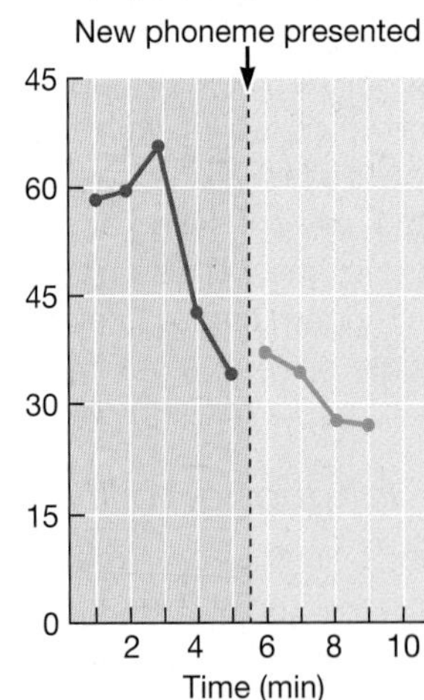

Two distinct phonemes

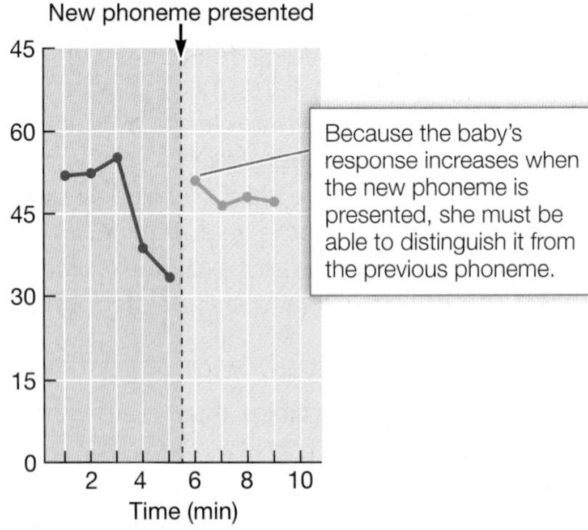

■ **Conclusion:** Even young babies can distinguish different phonemes. Later research would use similar methods to show that young babies can distinguish all the phonemes that have been found in *any* language.

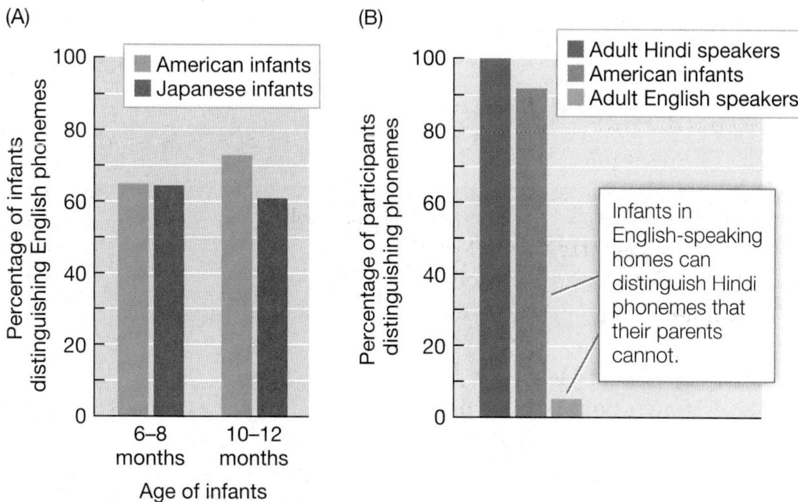

Figure 10.7 Sharpening Phoneme Detection Infants slowly lose the ability to distinguish phonemes if they are not exposed to them. (A) At 6–8 months of age, American and Japanese infants are equally good at distinguishing the sound of *r* versus *l*. A few months later, American babies become better at distinguishing the two sounds, but Japanese infants, having no exposure to English, begin to lose the capacity to tell the two phonemes apart. (B) American babies can distinguish phonemes in Hindi that English-speaking adults cannot. (A after Kuhl et al., 2006; B after Werker et al., 1981.)

Adult monkeys can also discriminate between phonemes (Ramus et al., 2000), so this ability may reflect a basic property of the primate auditory system. But there's more to the story about babies. By attending to the phonemes in the language spoken around them, human babies, who begin life babbling nearly *all* the phonemes known in all human languages, soon come to use only the subset of phonemes in use around them. Not only that, but human babies also get better and better at distinguishing the phonemes they're exposed to. As they get more and more exposure to the phonemes in use around them, they slowly lose the ability to distinguish other phonemes. For example, Japanese newborns can distinguish between the sounds for *r* versus *l*, but if they hear only Japanese while growing up, they will find it hard to tell those sounds apart as adults (**Figure 10.7A**; Kuhl et al., 2006). As another example, native English-speaking adults have a very difficult time distinguishing some of the phonemes in Hindi, one of the official languages of India. Yet 6- to 8-month-old babies from English-speaking households can detect those different Hindi phonemes (**Figure 10.7B**; Werker et al., 1981). Babies begin this process of losing the ability to distinguish phonemes they have not been exposed to at about the age they themselves start making halting language-like sounds, at 6 to 8 months of age.

The baby's developing language abilities are especially shaped by **motherese**, the singsong, high-pitched speech with slow, exaggerated pronunciation that parents use with their babies (Falk, 2004) in all cultures (Boysson-Bardies, 2001). Babies will work especially hard to hear this sort of speech. The lilting qualities of motherese convey emotional tone and reward, helping the baby attend to speech and use developing memory skills to attach meaning to previously arbitrary speech sounds.

The fact that babies go through this process of attending to speech and sharpening their ability to distinguish the phonemes they hear, and losing the ability to distinguish other phonemes, suggests that our brain is specialized to learn language. Certainly many linguists believe this, and to the extent that there

motherese The singsong, high-pitched speech with slow, exaggerated pronunciation that parents use with babies.

Psychology in Everyday Life

BOX 10.1

Williams Syndrome Offers Clues about Language

Williams syndrome, which occurs in approximately 1 out of 20,000 births (Bower, 2000), illustrates a fascinating disconnect between what we normally regard as intelligence and language. Individuals with Williams syndrome speak freely and fluently with a large vocabulary, yet they may be unable to draw simple images, arrange colored blocks to match an example, or tie shoelaces. The individuals are very sociable, ready to strike up conversation and smile. They may also display strong musical talent, either singing (see figure) or playing an instrument.

The Appearance of Williams Syndrome Children with Williams syndrome are often very fluent in languages and very expressive in music.

The syndrome results from the deletion of about 28 genes from one of the two copies of chromosome 7 (de Luis et al., 2000). No one understands why the remaining copies of these genes, on the other chromosome 7, do not compensate for the lost copies. The absence of one copy of the gene called *elastin* (which encodes a protein important for connective tissue in skin and ligaments) leads to pixielike facial features in people who have Williams syndrome. Several of the other missing genes are thought to lead to changes in brain development and to the behavioral features of the syndrome. Because speech development in Williams syndrome is spared in a brain that finds many other tasks difficult, the human brain may indeed be specialized to pick up languages in a way that's distinct from solving other tasks.

The psychological development of such individuals is complicated. As infants they may display a greater understanding of numbers than other infants, but as adults they may show a poor grasp of numbers. Conversely, their language performance is poor in infancy but greatly improved by adulthood (Paterson et al., 1999). These findings suggest that the developmental process is distinctively altered in Williams syndrome, which adds to the mystery of why these children seem to catch up in language but not other skills. Intriguingly, possession of *extra* copies of the identified genes on chromosome 7—rather than deletions of these genes—produces a syndrome that is, in many ways, the converse of Williams syndrome: very poor expressive language accompanied by normal spatial abilities (Somerville et al., 2005). These cases also suggest that the learning of language is distinct from other forms of intelligence, perhaps because humans evolved a specialized capacity to acquire language.

Williams syndrome A genetic disorder characterized by normal verbal abilities but severe deficits in spatial reasoning.

is any disagreement, it lies in different ideas about what it means to say the brain is "specialized." One reason to think that parts of the human brain are especially adapted to learn language, as opposed to being generalized to solve any problem, is the observation that some people have especially fluent speech but have great difficulty with non-speech tasks, discussed in **Box 10.1**.

While it is true that babies are remarkably good at picking up language, they need that exposure to language early in life in order to become proficient in language, as we'll discuss next.

There are sensitive periods for learning a language

There are many indications that humans go through a **sensitive period** for language, a time during development when we must be exposed to language in order to master it. In rare, tragic cases of children rescued from long-term isolation, little or no language develops, pointing to the importance of early experience. In Chapter 5 we learned about Genie, the girl who was raised in isolation, hardly ever being spoken to, until she was 13. Similarly, when hearing was restored to an adult woman who had been deaf most of her life, she did not learn to speak (Curtiss, 1989), presumably because the sensitive period for language acquisition had ended many years earlier. Indeed, deaf children who are exposed to American Sign Language early in life are more fluent than those who learn it at a later age (Newman et al., 2002). The sensitive period for learning languages may begin before birth, because newborns whose mothers spoke only one language during pregnancy prefer to hear that language over others. If their mother spoke two languages, the newborns have an equal preference for either one over any other language (Byers-Heinlein et al., 2010).

Bilingual Baby Growing up with parents who speak two different languages, this baby may reach certain language landmarks a bit later than other children, but will enjoy several lifetime benefits of bilingualism.

Genie eventually learned a few hundred words, but she never put together more than two or three words. Genie's failure to learn even the rudiments of grammar suggests that the sensitive period is especially crucial for learning syntax. By 7 months of age, infants pay more attention to sentences with unfamiliar structure than to sentences with familiar structure (Marcus et al., 1999), indicating that they have already acquired a sense of the syntax in use around them and are actively looking out for exceptions.

The ability of young people to readily learn more than one language is another indication that humans go through a sensitive period for languages. **Bilingualism** is the ability to fluently use more than one language. (If a person knows three or more languages, we can say she is *multilingual*, but such individuals, while not exactly rare, have not been studied extensively by psychologists.) The bilinguals who are most fluent, especially in two languages that are very different from one another, are those who were exposed to both languages as children. We've already seen one obvious advantage of being exposed to two languages as an infant—the child retains the ability to distinguish the phonemes of both languages.

Interestingly, infants exposed to more than one language may be a tiny bit slower at reaching some developmental milestones for language (Holowka et al., 2002), but afterward the bilingual child grows up to enjoy several advantages (in addition to being able to communicate with more people). People who, as infants, were exposed to two languages are better able to ignore distractions in complex cognitive tasks (Bialystok & Martin, 2004) and are better readers (Bialystok et al., 2005) than people who are monolingual. Not only that, bilingual people are less likely to develop Alzheimer's disease, and if they do, they develop it at a later age than people who speak only one language (Craik et al., 2010). How much later? On average, a bit more than 4 years. Considering how valuable 4 more years of productive life would be, that's a tremendous benefit of bilingualism.

sensitive period A time during development when exposure to a stimulus has the greatest effect on a particular behavior.

bilingualism The ability to fluently use more than one language.

The notion of a sensitive period for language acquisition is also supported by the difficulty that postadolescents experience in learning a second language. This contrasts with the relative ease with which children pick up second languages. That doesn't mean that adults cannot learn languages; clearly they can. But in terms of speaking a second language without a foreign accent, or really becoming proficient in the grammar of the second language, people taking up a second language as teenagers or adults don't do as well (**Figure 10.8**). Brain imaging studies indicate that people who learn a second lan-

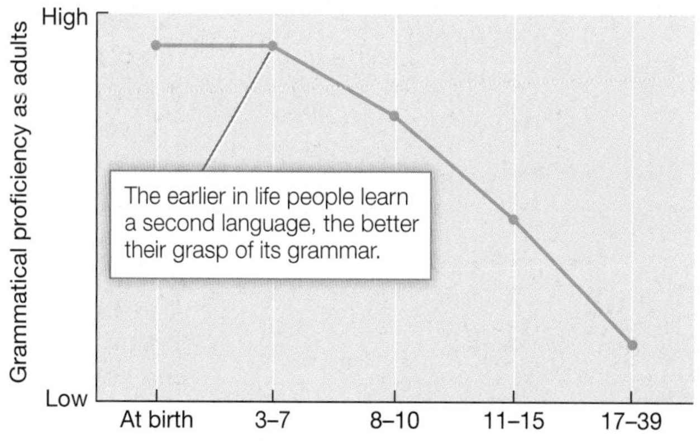

Figure 10.8 The Critical Period for Acquiring Fluency in a Second Language (After Johnson & Newport, 1989.)

guage early in life activate the same brain region when using either language. But people learning a second language after age 11 seem to use different brain regions for each language (Kim et al., 1997). It's as if people who learn the second language while young are more efficient—they don't activate as large an area of the brain to use the second language as people who learn it after adolescence. Thus it appears that early in life the brain is prepared to learn one or more languages and to build up an efficient brain network to support that ability. Learning the language later seems to entail somewhat different brain systems, which lack the proficiency of a native speaker.

Unlike in prehistoric times, in modern societies each person not only learns to speak and understand other speakers, but also learns to *read* that language. If you think about it, these are very different skills, and some people who have no problem learning to speak may have a hard time learning to read, as we'll see next.

Some people have a harder time learning to read

Children who have a particularly hard time learning to read are said to have developmental reading disorder, or **dyslexia**. By definition, people with dyslexia have adequate vision, and no matter what you've heard, they do not see letters "backward." Likewise, dyslexia is not associated with mental impairment—most people with dyslexia overcome the disorder and lead successful and productive careers, and many have above-average intelligence (Morris, 2002). Rather, people with dyslexia have difficulty learning to recognize written words, rhyming words, and determining the meaning of a simple sentence. They may also have difficulty remembering a sequence of instructions. Dyslexia is more common in boys than in girls and is estimated to affect about 5% of the population. Providing additional training to children with dyslexia, emphasizing the correspondence between letters and sounds ("phonics") and relating them to reading and spelling, can improve their reading ability. While this additional training is sufficient to raise the reading ability of some children with dyslexia to normal, in other cases people may read slowly even in adulthood.

There is considerable evidence that at least some cases of dyslexia result from abnormal migration of neurons during prenatal development. Postmortem examination of the brains of dyslexic people revealed a greater number of little nests of extra cells, called *ectopias*, in the cortex (Galaburda, 1994), suggesting that some migrating cells did not reach their appropriate destination. People showing MRI evidence of these abnormalities tend to have reading disorders (Chang et al., 2005). Several genes have been associated with dyslexia, and two of them are known to be crucial for normal cell migration in the developing brain (Hannula-Jouppi et al., 2005; Meng et al., 2005; Taipale et al., 2003). A third gene, identified because it was associated with dyslexia in humans, was manipulated in rats and resulted in ectopias in the cortex similar to those reported in people with dyslexia (Harold et al., 2006; Peschansky et al., 2010). Why this abnormal migration of neurons in development would lead to dyslexia remains unknown.

We'll see shortly that in most people the left hemisphere of the cerebral cortex controls language. Compared with control participants, people with dyslexia show diminished activation of several regions in the left cerebral hemisphere that are known to be involved in reading (Hoeft et al., 2006; Pugh et al., 2000; Shaywitz et al., 2003). While there are structural and functional differences in the brains of some people with dyslexia compared with control readers, please let me assure you that dyslexia is treatable. As I have repeatedly reminded you through this book, the mind is a process going on in a machine called the brain, and experience can physically alter that machine to change behavior. For example, the remedial training of people with dyslexia causes changes in the activation of left-hemisphere systems that are used for reading (**Figure 10.9**) (Finn et al., 2013; Simos et al., 2002; Temple et al., 2003). And even in those cases

dyslexia Difficulty learning to read.

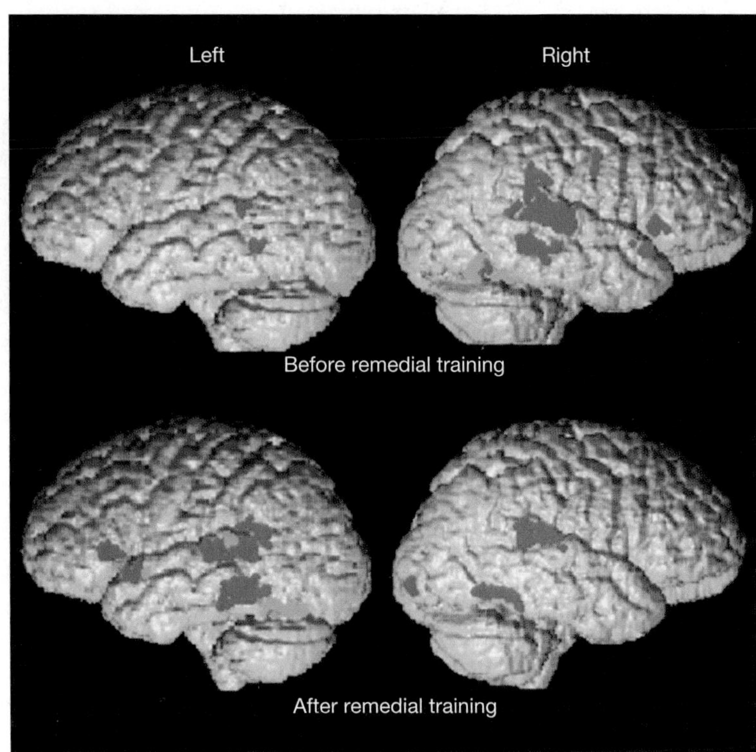

Figure 10.9 The Benefits of Training This individual with dyslexia did not show specific activation of speech centers in the left hemisphere when reading (upper). But after a comprehensive training program, those brain regions became active during reading (lower), as is typical of other readers. (After Simos et al., 2002.) Notice that there is less activation in the right hemsiphere after training, which may reflect a reduction in mental processes that distract from reading.

where early intervention does not allow the person with dyslexia to read as quickly as other people, don't make the mistake of thinking he or she is unintelligent. Several people with dyslexia have had extremely successful, high-profile careers that have made them billionaires.

For most people, the left hemisphere of the brain controls language

aphasia An impairment of language after acquisition, often the result of a brain injury or disease.

Tan A man who had lost the ability to utter more than the single syllable "tan," but seemed to understand language, as reported by Broca.

We've seen how vital language is and how readily we acquire it as children. Unfortunately, brain injury or disease can sometimes impair language after it has been acquired, a condition known as **aphasia**. The most common cause of aphasia is stroke, the loss of blood flow to a portion of the brain that causes cells there to die.

In turns out that only damage to particular parts of the brain are likely to cause aphasia. Egyptian medical records over 3,000 years old describe people who lost the ability to speak after blows to the side of the head (Finger, 1994). Later anecdotes suggest a folk awareness that brain injuries—especially on the left—could impair language. But it wasn't until 1861 that systematic study of the organization of the brain's language systems began, when French neurologist Paul Broca (1824–1880) examined a man who had lost the ability to utter much more than the single syllable "tan." The man had been this way since he'd been admitted to the hospital as a young adult, so everyone in the hospital called him **Tan**. Tan seemed to understand everything Broca said to him, and could

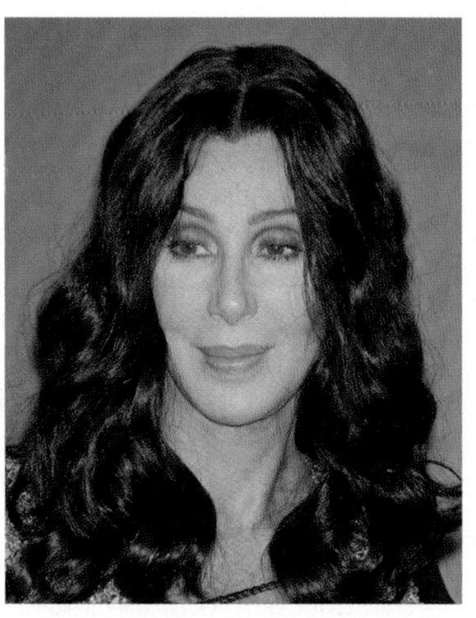

People with Dyslexia Many highly accomplished people report having dyslexia.

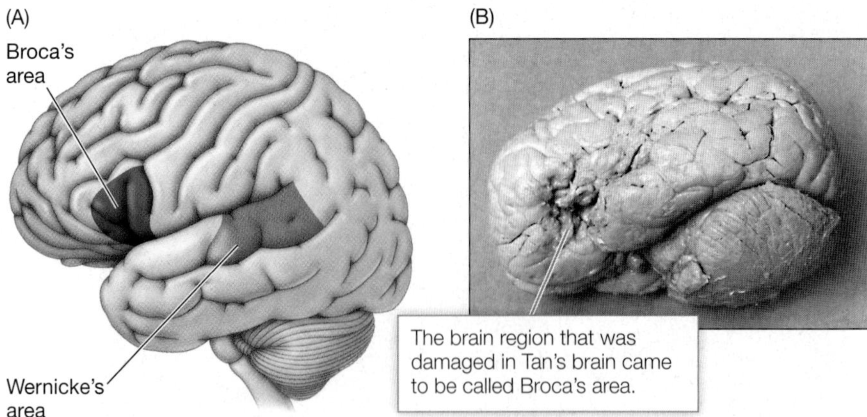
(A)
Broca's area
Wernicke's area
(B)
The brain region that was damaged in Tan's brain came to be called Broca's area.

Figure 10.10 The Brain of Tan (A) Injury to the anterior frontal region called Broca's area interferes with speech production; injury to an area of cortex called Wernicke's area interferes with language comprehension. In most individuals, these language-related systems are found only in the left hemisphere. (B) Photo of the preserved brain of M. Leborgne, known as "Tan" because he could only utter the syllable "tan" after his brain injury. The damage in what is now known as Broca's area is clearly evident in the photo. (B From Dronkers et al., 2007.)

Broca's area The bottom of the left frontal lobe, where Broca found damage producing nonfluent aphasia.

Broca's aphasia Also called *nonfluent aphasia*. An impairment in speech production, but not in comprehension.

Wernicke's aphasia Also called *fluent aphasia*. An impairment in understanding what is heard or read accompanied by fluent speech, which may be garbled.

Wernicke's area The area at the top of the temporal lobe that is damaged in fluent aphasia.

Wada test A test in which a short-lasting anesthetic is delivered into one brain hemisphere or the other to determine which hemisphere principally mediates language.

signal with his hand, for example, how many years he'd been in the hospital (30!). When Tan died, Broca examined his brain and found damage at the bottom of the left frontal lobe—a region now known as **Broca's area** (**Figure 10.10**). When only this region is damaged, a person will have extreme difficulty speaking—a condition known as **Broca's aphasia** or *nonfluent aphasia*. Damage to the same region in the right hemisphere usually has no discernible effect on language. Patients with nonfluent aphasia have considerable difficulty producing speech, talking only in a labored and hesitant manner. The ability to utter automatic speech, however, is often preserved. Such speech includes greetings ("Hello"); short, common expressions ("Oh, my God!"); and swear words. Despite the difficulty these patients have expressing themselves, their *comprehension* of language remains relatively good.

In contrast to people with nonfluent aphasia, people with *fluent aphasia* produce plenty of verbal output, but their utterances, although speechlike, may be somewhat garbled. These people tend to make sound substitutions (e.g., "girl" becomes "curl") and word substitutions (e.g., "bread" becomes "cake"), or make up new words. Some fluent aphasias are marked by difficulty in *naming* persons or objects. But people with fluent aphasia, also known as **Wernicke's aphasia** after the German neurologist who first described it, have difficulty *understanding* what they hear or read. Naturally, communication with people who have fluent aphasia is difficult, but is helped by the patient's intact understanding of gestures and facial expressions. Fluent aphasia is caused by damage to a different part of the left hemisphere, specifically the top of the temporal lobe (Damasio, 1995), which is known as **Wernicke's area** (see Figure 10.10A). Almost all patients with aphasia show at least some impairment in writing and reading. Interestingly, patients who recover from aphasia often pass through a stage of telegraphic speech, much like that of toddlers that we discussed earlier.

The fact that some 90% of people with aphasia have damage to the left hemisphere is strong evidence that the left side of the brain is crucial for language. This critical role of the left hemisphere is confirmed by the **Wada test**, when a

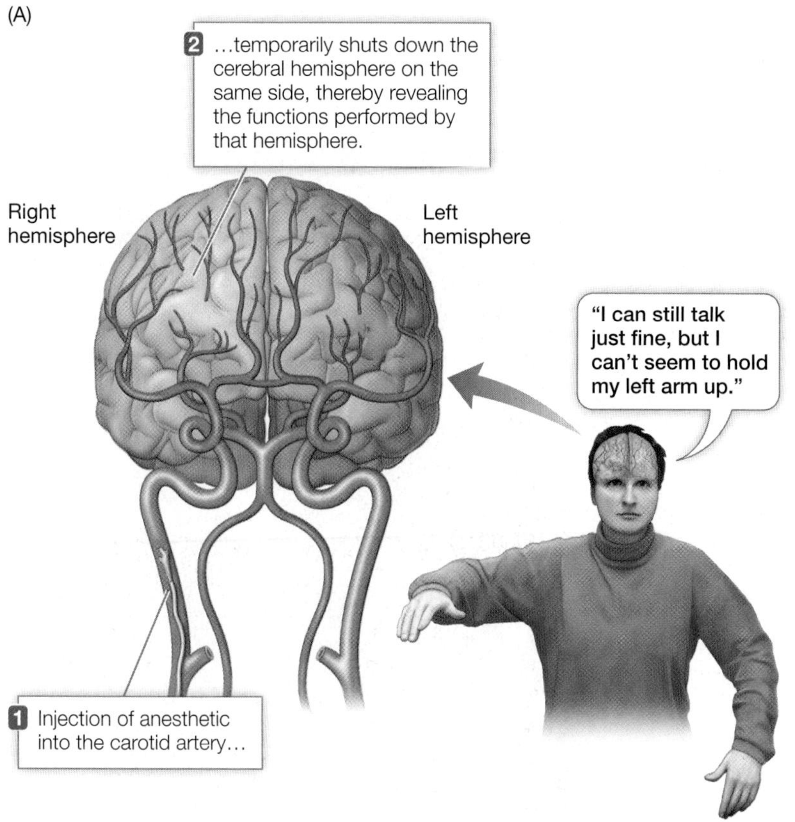
(A)
2 ...temporarily shuts down the cerebral hemisphere on the same side, thereby revealing the functions performed by that hemisphere.
Right hemisphere
Left hemisphere
"I can still talk just fine, but I can't seem to hold my left arm up."
1 Injection of anesthetic into the carotid artery...

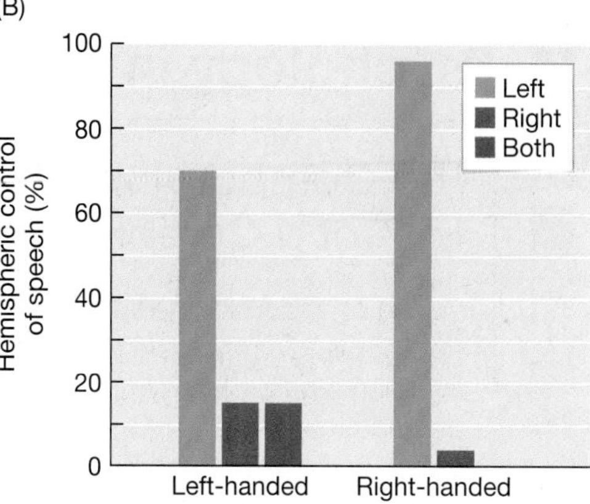
(B)
Hemispheric control of speech (%)
100
80
60
40
20
0
Left
Right
Both
Left-handed
Right-handed

Figure 10.11 Wada Test for Language Capacity (A) By injecting a fast-acting anesthetic into the blood supply of one cerebral hemisphere or the other, Rasmussen and Milner (1975) could ask which hemisphere must be "asleep" in order to impair speech. (B) While the majority of left-handers use their left hemisphere to control speech, they are more likely to have speech controlled by the right hemisphere than are right-handers. Interestingly, in some left-handed people, interfering with either hemisphere will affect speech. Today, similar results can be obtained through less invasive methods of inhibiting one hemisphere or the other. (After Epstein et al., 2000.)

fast-acting anesthetic is injected into blood vessels feeding one hemisphere or the other in healthy volunteers (Wada & Rasmussen, 1960). Anesthetizing the left hemisphere almost always disrupts speech, while anesthetizing the right hemisphere rarely affects speech (**Figure 10.11**). Despite a common psychology myth, the vast majority of left-handed people also have speech organized in their left hemisphere (Rasmussen & Milner, 1975). What we can say is that those rare cases where language seems to be organized in the right hemisphere are more common among left-handed people than among right-handed people. Interestingly, we know that if the left hemisphere is damaged *early in life*, the right hemisphere is able to take over language functions. In fact, some children have had their entire left cortex surgically removed and eventually recovered normal language, as discussed in **Box 10.2**. In contrast, even relatively small areas of damage to the mature brain, such as a stroke in Broca's area, can result in permanent loss of speech. That difference in recovery between adults and children is a dramatic illustration of how much more plastic the young brain is than the mature brain. That greater plasticity of the young brain probably explains why children can master second languages so much faster than adults.

Aphasia seems to confer one advantage: an experiment confirmed that patients who suffer from aphasia are better than controls at detecting when someone is lying (Etcoff et al., 2000). This sensitivity to lying may result from a lack of distraction by the words being spoken. If you can't understand the slick story or seductive words, then they can't take you in. But another reason why people with aphasia might be better at detecting liars is that aphasics tend to be good at interpreting other people's emotions based on their facial expressions. As we will discuss in Section 13.1, there is evidence indicating that the right side of the brain is important for processing information about faces. That brings us to the final topic of this section, which is the question of what functions are carried out by the right side of the brain.

Psychology in Everyday Life

BOX 10.2

The Comparatively Minor Effects of Childhood Loss of a Cerebral Hemisphere

During early development the brain is a vulnerable organ. Sometimes a prolonged, difficult birth involving a period of oxygen loss can cause brain damage to a single cerebral hemisphere. A child in whom one cerebral hemisphere is damaged may experience frequent seizures. These seizures can be hard to control with medication, and they may occur so often that they endanger the child's life.

One way to reduce seizures is to surgically remove the malfunctioning hemisphere, a procedure called *hemispherectomy*. Although at first some severe effects of the surgery in children are evident, over a long period of time behavior is almost completely restored. This result was strikingly illustrated in a case presented by Smith and Sugar (1975). The boy they described showed paralysis on his right side as an infant, and by 5 years of age he was experiencing 10 to 12 seizures a day. Although the boy's verbal comprehension was normal, his speech was hard to understand. To treat the problem, doctors removed all the cerebral cortex of the boy's left hemisphere. At first his language capacity worsened, but then it improved rapidly.

Long-term follow-up studies extended to age 26, when the young man was about to complete college. Tests revealed an above-normal IQ and superior language abilities; thus the early loss of most of the left hemisphere had not precluded language development. This patient also had remarkable development of nonverbal functions, including visuospatial tasks and manual tasks.

In another case, the left cerebral hemisphere was removed from a 3-year-old girl (see figure). Four years later she was bilingual in Dutch and Turkish (two very different languages) and leading a normal life. Periodic reviews of the literature confirm that hemispherectomy in children usually relieves epilepsy symptoms and that the children actually gain in cognitive skills afterward (Thomas et al., 2010), despite the drastic nature of the surgery. These results also demonstrate how much more plastic the young brain is compared with the adult brain.

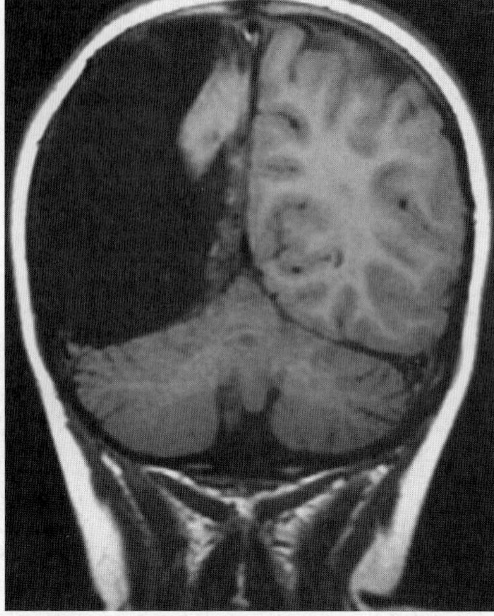

Dramatic Surgery, Dramatic Results An image from a girl who had her left cerebral hemisphere removed when she was 3 years old. Despite the drastic nature of the surgery, 4 years later she was bilingual in Dutch and Turkish and leading a normal life. (From Borgstein & Grootendorst, 2002.)

What is the right cerebral hemisphere for?

By the early twentieth century it was firmly established that the cerebral hemispheres are not equivalent in mediating language functions (Finger, 1994). The left hemisphere seems to make a greater contribution to this function and is commonly described as the dominant hemisphere because language is so crucial to much of our behavior. However, the right hemisphere does not just idly sit within the skull, awaiting an occasional call to duty. In fact, most researchers have abandoned the notion of hemispheric *dominance* in favor of models of hemispheric *specialization*, or **lateralization**. It appears that some functional systems are associated with one side of the brain or the other—that is, that functions become lateralized—and that each hemisphere is specialized for particular ways of working.

lateralization The tendency for the right and left cerebral hemispheres to differ in their specializations.

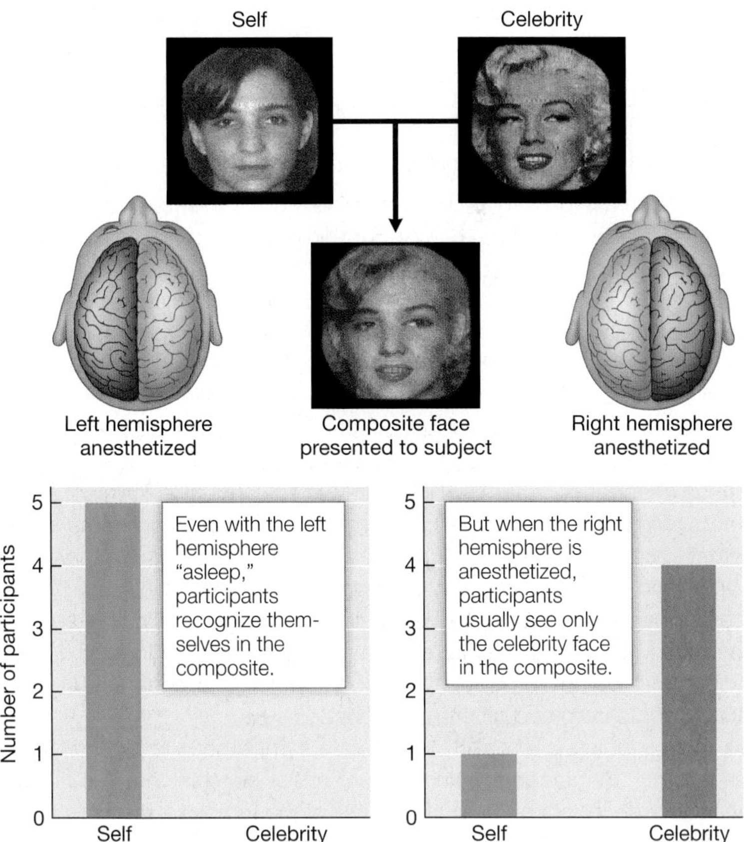

Figure 10.12 Use of the Right Hemisphere for Facial Recognition Anesthetizing the left hemisphere in a Wada test does not interfere with a participant's ability to recognize her own face in a picture that is a composite of her face and the face of a celebrity. But when the right hemisphere is anesthetized, the participant interprets the composite face as that of the celebrity. (From Keenan et al., 2001; courtesy of Julian Keenan.)

We've seen that damage to the left side of the brain usually impairs language. In contrast, damage to the right hemisphere usually spares language, but seems to affect the perception of music (Gazzaniga & Hillyard, 1971; Samson & Zatorre, 1994; Zatorre et al., 1994). So the right hemisphere may be responsible for our understanding and appreciation of music. There's also evidence that the right hemisphere seems to be better than the left at recognizing faces. Researchers used the Wada test to anesthetize either one hemisphere or the other, then asked participants whether they could recognize their own face in composite faces. They could recognize their own face when the left hemisphere was anesthetized. But if the right hemisphere was anesthetized, participants found it more difficult to distinguish their own face from that of a celebrity (**Figure 10.12**; Keenan et al., 2001). So the right hemisphere is more important than the left in distinguishing faces. In Section 13.1 we'll see that the left half of our face tends to be more expressive of emotions than the right. These observations suggest that the right side of the brain is specialized both to express our own emotions and to detect the emotions of others.

Dramatic as such results are, we should not overinterpret them. Information is rapidly shared between the two hemispheres through the corpus callosum. So the notion, now common among the public, that the two hemispheres are so different that they need separate instruction, is just silly. Likewise, the idea that people can have "left-brain" or "right-brain" personalities has no scientific foun-

linguistic relativism The hypothesis that the language we speak influences the way we think.

dation (Nielson et al., 2013). Normally, our two hemispheres work together seamlessly. It is only when the two have been surgically isolated from one another, as in split-brain patients (see Section 7.1), or when one hemisphere has been damaged, as in stroke victims, that we can discern dramatic lateralization of brain function.

Language and culture can influence our thought processes

Language is such a large part of our mental life that some researchers have speculated that language may severely limit our thinking, a hypothesis called *linguistic determinism*. In its strict form, linguistic determinism would suggest that people speaking very different languages would regard the world differently and that this would severely constrain how each could think. Today few linguists accept this extreme position, and it has been largely replaced by the hypothesis of **linguistic relativism**, that the language we speak *influences* (rather than determines) the way we think. Note that if language affects the thinking of the people who speak it, then it would also affect the culture those people create. This must be a two-way street, since changes in culture will inevitably affect language. Think of all the new words and phrases that have entered English due to developments in technology (*netizen, meme, spam, bitcoin*), entertainment *(podcast, bromance, chick-flick, YOLO)*, and politics *(flame war, locavore, carbon footprint, fiscal cliff*). In fact, because language and culture evolve together, it would be difficult to separate the influence of language versus culture on a person's thinking. Indeed, in practice, researchers who compare people who speak different languages are inevitably comparing people from two different cultures as well.

While most linguists and psychologists are sympathetic to the concept of linguistic relativism, that language and culture affect our thinking, it is not an easy hypothesis to test. It doesn't help that some of the famous examples turn out to be false. For example, early in the twentieth century an anthropologist reported that the Aleut language of people native to the northern polar regions has four different terms for snow (Boas, 1911). Later writers picked up on this idea, each copying and exaggerating from the ones before; eventually you could read in *The New York Times* that Aleuts have *100* different terms for snow (Martin, 1986). In fact, it's not clear that the Aleut language has any more terms for snow than English (*snow, frost, hardpack, flurry, dusting, hail, sleet, slush, freezing rain, snowflake, snowstorm, blizzard*), so don't fall for this myth (Pullum, 1991).

Another issue in linguistic relativism that you may have heard about concerns whether language affects our perception of colors. Not all languages provide the same number of words to describe different colors. For example, some languages do not offer different words for blue and green. This difference among languages has led researchers to speculate whether people exposed to different terms would differ in their ability to distinguish, classify, or remember colors (Berlin & Kay, 1969). This has been a long debate, and it is still unresolved. For one thing, it is increasingly difficult to find people who have not been exposed to modern Western culture through television, movies, and advertisements. Even when Eleanor Rosch worked with the Dani people of New Guinea, who have only two words for colors (basically, "light" and "dark"), she found they nevertheless can categorize colors for which they have no words (Rosch, 1975a). In fact, even people without any language at all can distinguish basic colors. Studies of infants, using a habituation approach like that which we described for studying phoneme perception (see Figure 10.6), show that they can detect the same main hues (e.g., red, orange, yellow, green, blue, violet) as adults (Bornstein et al., 1976).

Russian has two different words for blues, one for light blue (*goluboy*) and a very different word for dark blue (*siniy*). Given a task where they had to quickly discriminate various shades of blue, native Russian speakers were faster at discriminating shades that straddled the line between goluboy and siniy (**Figure 10.13**). The advantage of Russian speakers was greatest for really difficult discriminations, when the two colors were close together (Winawer et al., 2007).

(A)

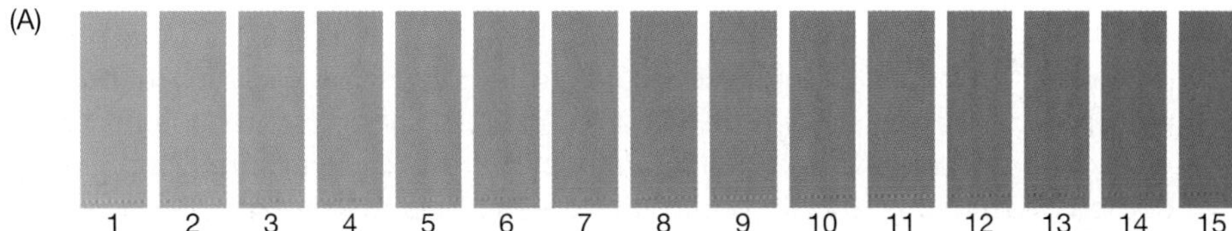

(B)

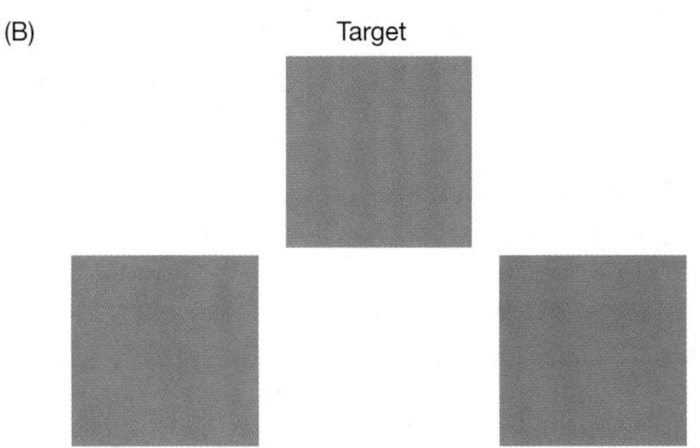

Figure 10.13 Does Language Affect Color Perception? (A) All of these stimuli can be referred to by the English label *blue*. Russian speakers, however, divide the set up into *goluboy* (light blue) and *siniy* (dark blue), with the boundary between them typically occurring between stimuli 8 and 9. (B) To respond correctly, subjects had to press a button on the left to indicate that the lower left square matched the top square in color. Russian speakers performed this task more accurately and more rapidly when the shades were close to the border of light blue (goluboy) and dark blue (siniy). (After Winawer et al., 2007.)

Thus it appears that differences in the ways languages label colors do not affect our ability to perceive colors or discriminate them, but may affect how *quickly* we can search, discriminate, or remember them.

Perhaps the perception of colors is not the best test case for the idea of linguistic relativism, given the biological basis of color perception, which depends upon three types of color-sensitive cones in the eye (see Chapter 6). So let's consider some other examples in which differences in linguistic expression appear to affect thinking. There are, for example, differences in the way people think about numbers that reflect the language used to denote numbers. Consider languages where the terms for numbers reflect the base ten system. In English we have distinct words for 11, 12, 13, and so on until we finally reach 20. Our words for numbers after that—*twenty-one, fifty-four, sixty-eight*—make it clear that the first word represents the "tens" place and the second word represents the "ones" place. In contrast, the Korean term for 11 means basically "ten-one," and so on. This may be why Korean-speaking children have an easier time understanding the concept of place value than English-speaking children (Miura et al., 1993).

Anthropologists have long known of several languages that have no higher numbering system at all, so-called "one, two, many" languages because a single word is used for anything above two. There is even a controversial claim that an Amazonian group, the Piraha, has no words even for "one" or "two." Instead, they have words for "a small size or amount," "a somewhat larger size or amount," and "a bunch" (Everett & Madora, 2012). Extremely adept at gathering nuts, fruit, and small game from the jungle, the Piraha have few tools and never store food in bulk, so perhaps their way of life doesn't require knowing the exact numbers of anything. Still, researchers can design tasks where this indifference to quantity affects the performance of Piraha. When shown a row of objects, like sticks, they can easily duplicate any number by lining up matching sticks. But when shown a row of objects, which are then covered, they make many mistakes in reproducing any number greater than two or three (Frank et al., 2008; Gordon, 2004). Again, culture doesn't seem to affect basic *perception* of number of objects, but affects *efficient encoding* of information about numbers. Because we have a word for "seven," we only have to remember that single piece of information to report how many sticks had been in that row.

How Many Were There? For the Piraha people, it is difficult to correctly reproduce the number of objects they had previously seen, such as 10 batteries or 9 balloons. (Courtesy of Ted Gibson.)

Another example of linguistic relativism involves how we think about the placement of objects around us. In some Australian aboriginal languages, there are no words for "left" and "right." Rather, in that culture all directions rely on compass directions—north, south, east, west. This means that the people in that culture always know which direction north is, whether they are inside or outside. In contrast, most people in our culture can't point accurately to north even when outside, much less indoors (Boroditsky, 2011). Clearly this difference in language affects how we speak of things ("My father is the one standing there on the east side of the canoe"), but does it affect the way we think? Apparently so, because people who speak languages relying on absolute compass directions are much better at keeping track of where they are, even inside unfamiliar buildings, than are people who speak other languages, like English (Levinson & Haviland, 1994). Asked to arrange a series of pictures depicting a man growing old, English speakers arrange them with the earliest picture on the left, the latest on the right. But people who speak languages relying on absolute direction arrange the pictures from east to west, no matter which direction they are facing. That means that sometimes they arrange the pictures from top to bottom, or from right to left, depending on which compass direction they are facing at the table (Boroditsky & Gaby, 2010). In such cultures, sequences always begin in the east, where the sun rises, and end in the west, where the sun sets.

Thus it seems clear that language influences, but does not *determine*, our way of looking at the world and our way of thinking. In this way, having a language that includes words for different colors, or for numbers, or for directions, means we can more efficiently encode information in tasks involving those characteristics. Efficient encoding reduces how much of our limited cognitive resources are needed to perform the task accurately and quickly. Note that all the experiments to detect linguistic influences on thought have relied on asking people to perform a particular task—distinguish colors, recall the number of objects, point to north, place pictures in chronological order—or on observing their behavior in a particular context. The strategy of observing a person's behavior in order to make inferences about how she is thinking is the hallmark of *cognitive psychology*, which we will take up in the next section of this chapter.

10.1 SUMMARY

- Human language is composed of combinations of sounds, called *phonemes*, that carry meaning (*morphemes*), which can be used to construct words. Words have meanings and can be combined, following the rules of *syntax*, into an infinite number of unique sentences. In addition to the particular words chosen for a sentence (the *surface structure*), a sentence also has a *deep structure* conveying *semantic* content.
- While non-human animals communicate, and the same gene (*FOXP2*) is crucial for both human language and animal communication, it is unclear whether other animals can learn human language.
- Infants readily learn languages as they retain the ability to discriminate the phonemes spoken around them and lose the ability to detect other phonemes during a *sensitive period*. Hence it is much easier to become *bilingual* if one is exposed to both languages early in life.
- *Dyslexia* is a difficulty in learning to read that is not associated with mental impairment.
- Stroke is much more likely to affect language when it occurs in the left hemisphere than in the right. Damage to *Broca's area* in the left frontal lobe causes *Broca's aphasia*, or nonfluent aphasia, but

spares language comprehension. Conversely, damage to *Wernicke's area* in the left temporal lobe interferes with comprehension of speech and causes *Wernicke's aphasia*, or fluent aphasia.
- The *Wada test* confirms that the left hemisphere mediates language in most people, including the majority of left-handed people.
- The ability of a particular language to influence our thinking, such as whether our language uses compass points versus left–right terms, or uses particular words to classify colors or numbers, is called *linguistic relativism*.

REVIEW QUESTIONS

1. What evidence indicates that animals are capable of understanding human words? Is there evidence that animals can come to understand syntax?
2. What are some of the important stages in learning a first language?
3. What are the different types of aphasia, and what do they tell us about brain organization of language?
4. Describe some examples of studies indicating effects of linguistic relativism.

Food for Thought

If we encountered a civilization from another planet that spoke a language entirely different from any human language, what approach would you recommend to teach humans the alien language?

10.2 Deconstructing Mental Processes

Things to Learn

- Importance of categorization
- Reaction times
- Mental processes take time
- Stages in acquiring a skill
- Ways to study attention
- Failures caused by limited attention

In this section we will discuss **cognitive psychology**, the study of internal mental processes, specifically how we acquire and process information to gain knowledge. If we unpack that definition, we see that cognitive psychology covers a lot of ground. For example, *acquiring information* includes sensation and perception. *Processing information* includes thinking, judging, imagining, and planning. *Gaining knowledge* includes learning and memory. That is why, in many ways, cognitive psychology represents the core of modern-day psychology. In addition to psychologists, many philosophers, neuroscientists, computer scientists, and linguists are also interested in these topics, and together they are sometimes described as *cognitive scientists*. What typifies a cognitive scientist is the mindset that *by carefully measuring a person's behavior, we can make inferences about the mental processes at work.*

We'll see many examples of this approach. For example, a cognitive psychologist will give a participant some task and carefully measure how quickly he accomplishes it. Then the scientist may systematically vary the conditions of the task and use the person's speed to infer what makes the task easier or harder. In this way the scientist may build up a model of the various mental steps a person must go through to solve the task. To test that model, the cognitive psychologist will make predictions about which conditions should interfere with various stages of the mental processing, and then test to see whether the participant's performance is affected as predicted.

Before talking about the timing of mental processes, we must first get a handle on what we mean by *ideas* or *concepts*, the building blocks of thinking. We'll see that concepts are inevitably wrapped up in *categories* and *hierarchies*. That will lead to the topic of mental images, and a famous demonstration that mental processes take time. This serves as yet another reminder that the mind is a process at work in a machine, and as with any machine, it takes time to work. We'll consider the stages by which we first learn and then master a skill or set of knowledge. Finally, we'll consider one of the most fascinating aspects of mental life—attention. Thought to be almost impossible to study just a few decades ago, attention is now one of the most active areas of cognitive psychology, which has taught us how surprisingly limited our attention really is.

cognitive psychology The study of internal mental processes, specifically how we acquire and process information and gain knowledge.

There are two kinds of people, and both of them categorize

Cognitive psychologists are keenly interested in information processing, which most people call "thinking." There are many aspects of thinking that most of us take for granted, so much so that we may never realize how remarkable the process really is. First of all, there is the matter of the recognition of things that are the subjects of our thoughts. For example, ancient philosophers grappled with the question of how someone could be shown a horse unlike any horse that had ever been seen—purple with one leg missing, ears like a cocker spaniel, belching out smoke—yet instantly recognize it as a horse. As another example, what makes a table a table? Most have four legs, but not all do—some have three, some have one, and lap tables have no legs at all. Some tables are short, some are tall, and they can be any color and made out of any solid material. Thus we have an *idea* of what constitutes a table, even though an infinite number of objects fit that idea. Psychologists regard this as an example of a **concept**, an abstract idea or mental representation of an object or event. Typically we will have a word for any particular concept, but the concept is the *mental representation* of the object or event, not the *word* for that object or event.

We say that no two snowflakes are entirely alike, that you cannot step into the same river twice, that every person is unique, and so on. This is of course literally true, but there is a certain "family resemblance" between some objects. While each breed of dog looks different from the others, all dog breeds share certain characteristics (four legs, elongated jaw, hairless nose, long tongue, and so on). While each breed is different, and each individual within a breed in some ways like no other individual, we nevertheless have no problem identifying them all as dogs. As with dogs, most other objects tend to share some characteristics with at least some other objects. Indeed, the world would be a very confusing place if we perceived every object or event as unique, unlike any other object or event. How would we come up with enough names to label objects, and who could remember them all?

The human mind avoids having to have words for every variant of every object or concept by recognizing characteristics that are shared by certain objects or events. That is, the mind relies on **categorization**, the process of recognizing the similarities and differences between concepts (which, remember, are mental representations of objects or events). Objects may be categorized by physical characteristics, or by purpose, or by any other aspect that seems important to us at the time. Our minds categorize objects and events so readily that we don't even notice. But if you examine the process more closely, categorization is not as simple as it seems.

As I noted above, a horse can have many unique characteristics and we will still categorize it as a horse. No single characteristic is sufficient to ensure that an object will fit the category "horse." Conversely, we can modify any single characteristic of an individual horse and we still regard it as a horse. How then are we able, in almost an instant, to categorize any object as "horse" or "not horse"? Psychologists theorize that for each concept we have in mind a **prototype**, a "best example" of a concept that fits a particular category. The prototype is a model of a concept that typifies members of a category. In categorizing any particular object or event, we look to see how well it fits or does not fit the prototype for a category. If this particular object or event shares enough characteristics with the prototype, then we perceive it as belonging to that category.

concept An abstract idea or mental representation of an object or event.

categorization The process of recognizing the similarities and differences between concepts.

prototype The best example of a concept that fits a particular category.

Prototypes greatly simplify the work of thinking. There are thousands of different-looking dogs, yet we can think about any of them, or all of them, as fitting the category "dog" (**Figure 10.14**). There is no absolute authority to describe for us what the prototype is for any category. But we can get an inkling of what the prototype is, for example, for the concept "furniture" by having people rank objects based on whether they are good examples of furniture. American college students felt that a chair and sofa are very good examples of furniture, that a

Figure 10.14 Objects Fitting the Category of "Dog" Dogs come in a bewildering variety of shapes and sizes, yet all are quickly recognized as dogs. We could get a sense for what the prototypical dog looks like by having people rate which of these is the best example of a dog, or by asking them to classify these and other pictures quickly as "dog" or "not dog." We can infer that the pictures that are most quickly recognized as dogs are closest to the prototype of a dog. Note that people from different cultures may have different ideas about which breed is the best example of a dog.

desk and bed are almost as good examples, and that a wastebasket and stove are poor examples (Rosch, 1975b). So chair and sofa more closely fit the prototype of "furniture" than do wastebasket and stove. One way psychologists investigate our sense for a prototype is to observe how quickly people can indicate whether a particular object fits a category. The more quickly people identify an object as fitting the category, the more likely it is to resemble the prototype. We can then systematically vary the objects to see which characteristics best fit the prototype. Note that any particular prototype is inevitably limited to the particular people we are probing. Russian retirees in the year 2075 may have different ideas about what constitutes furniture than American college students did in 1975. In other words, prototypes can differ across cultures and change with time. Yet if two groups were given millions of objects to categorize, they would usually agree on whether a particular object was furniture.

Mental processes take time

We've noted that mental processes, like all processes, take time. You have probably heard of a test the psychoanalyst C. G. Jung created, called *word association*, where the therapist says a word and the patient is to reply with whatever word pops into her head first (Jung, 1906/1919). As portrayed on TV and in movies, the point of the test is for the therapist to note which word the patient comes up with, and make inferences about her conscious and unconscious thinking. But in fact, for Jung an equally important measure was the **reaction time**, the time it takes for a person to start or complete a response, in this case to offer a word in response to his. Jung felt that if the patient took a long time to answer, the stimulus word had triggered many emotionally charged images, and that the patient needed time to suppress (consciously or unconsciously) those images before responding. So Jung always noted the reaction time, as well as the word elicited in response to his word.

Ironically, while most of Jung's ideas about mental disorders have been dismissed, reaction time is perhaps the most common variable measured by psychologists, especially cognitive psychologists. Furthermore, the rationale for measuring reaction times in modern psychology is basically the same as it was for Jung, namely as an indication of how much mental processing is required for the participant to respond. Let's say we ask a person to watch a light and, as soon as it comes on, push a button. We measure how much time elapses between when the light comes on and when the button gets pushed. The participant pushes faster on some trials than others, so we take several trials and measure the average reaction time, called *simple reaction time*. The time that

reaction time The amount of time it takes a subject to initiate some action after a predetermined signal.

elapses between when the light comes on and when the participant pushes the button includes whatever sequence of steps the mind went through. In this case, the person needed only to see if the light was on.

Even in this simple reaction time task, the person must accomplish several tasks. First, he must attend to the light, then he must detect when it comes on, then move his hand to push the button. Of course, some time is needed for the stimulus, the light, to reach the eye and for that information to move from the eye to the brain. Also, once the participant decides to push the button, it takes some time for that command to reach his muscles and a bit more time for his finger to push the button. We can presume that the time needed for each of these processes is about the same, no matter what task we give the person. But as we make the task more difficult, the participant must process more information to decide whether to push the button. That additional processing time gets added, sandwiched between the arrival of the stimulus to the participant's brain and the decision to move his finger. The reaction time is longer.

Although he didn't use Jung's term *reaction time*, Dutch physician Franciscus Donders used this measure to make such inferences about time needed for mental processing back in the 1860s (Donders, 1869). After measuring a participant's simple reaction time, Donders made the task more difficult by asking the person to watch two lights and press the button when the red one was lit, but not the blue one. Donders found that the average reaction time was a bit longer than in the simple reaction time task. This slower reaction time represented the additional time the person needed to process the information (red light was on, blue one was not). Donders then made the task slightly more difficult yet: he offered two lights and asked the participant to press the button only if the one on the left was brighter than the one on the right. The closer the two lights were in brightness, the more time the person needed to decide whether the left one was brighter, and therefore the longer his reaction time.

In a more modern test of reaction times, participants are shown a pair of letters and asked to push a button if they are identical. This takes a bit longer than a simple reaction time test (just hitting the button when any letter appears), but not much longer. Next, participants are presented with two letters that can be either uppercase or lowercase, in any font, so that two *D*s might look very different (d versus 𝒟, say). We can predict that this task is more difficult because the person will need to decode each letter, rather than simply see whether they are identical. Indeed, reaction times are a bit longer, confirming our prediction. Next we can ask the participant to push the button only if the two letters are the same type of letter—vowel versus consonant—and that makes the reaction time longer yet (Posner, 1978, 2005).

It's remarkable how reliably reaction time reflects mental processing time. In another example, people are asked whether a digit displayed on a screen is greater or less than five (**Figure 10.15**). On average, people do this task faster when shown Arabic digits (3, 7, 8) than when the number is spelled out (three, seven, eight). Presumably this is because it takes more time to decode the letters to get to the word. People also respond faster when the digits are farther from five (2, 8) than when they are close to five (4, 6), and they respond faster when using their right hand rather than their left hand to push the button (Dehaene, 1996).

As people grow older, even simple reaction times get longer. We don't know for certain why this happens, but it seems a pretty safe bet that it reflects a slowing down of mental processes in the aged. In Section 11.2 we'll see that this slowing down of mental processes affects performance on some aspects of IQ tests. While the longer reaction times of the elderly don't tell us *why* their mental processes have slowed—is it loss of neurons, loss of synapses, reduced myelin

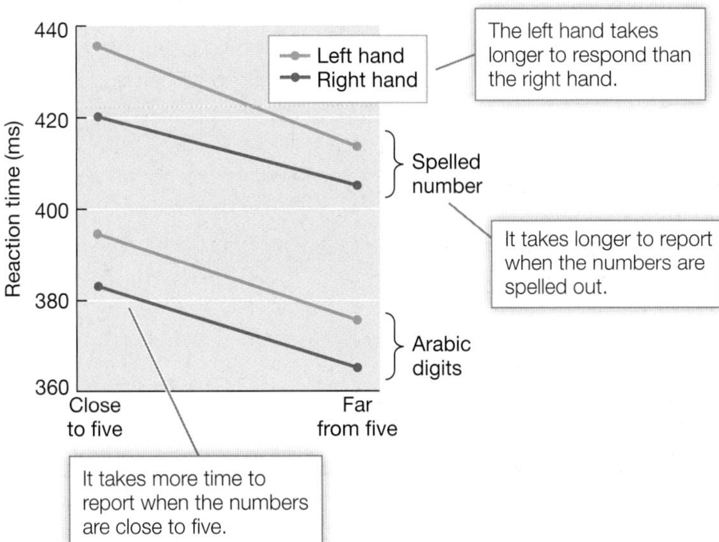

Figure 10.15 Reaction Times Reveal Mental Processing Time When asked whether a displayed number is greater or less than five, we react faster when the number is far from five (right side of graph) than close to five (left side of graph). We also react faster when shown arabic numbers (lower lines) than spelled-out words (upper lines). Finally, most people react faster if they use their right hand to push a button (red lines) than their left hand (blue lines). (After Dehaene, 1996.)

(Watanabe et al., 2013), and therefore slower action potential conduction?—it is impressive that such a simple measure can detect the changes with age.

Perhaps the most famous use of reaction time in modern psychology has been in experiments involving mental imagery, which we'll take up next.

We reproduce images and manipulate them in our mind

Stop a moment and imagine the front of the house or apartment building you grew up in. If you close your eyes, you can probably reproduce where the windows are, the door, the street, and other details. For a really familiar object like this, most people have the experience that they "can almost see it." This is an example of **mental imagery**, the ability to visualize images or events in our mind. Our experience of mental imagery, in this case of an object that's no longer visible, nevertheless resembles the perception we have when looking at that object itself. We can even manipulate the object in our "mind's eye." Imagine if that building were lifted in the air, rotated 180 degrees clockwise, then 90 degrees counterclockwise, and then placed back on the ground. Which way would the door face now? What was your experience as your mind rotated that mental image? If you were Superman and could actually pick up the building and move it, that would take a certain amount of time to rotate it first clockwise and then counterclockwise. In **Figure 10.16** we consider to what extent mental rotations take time.

mental imagery The ability to visualize images or events in our mind.

☑ Researchers at Work

We need time to move mental images

Figure 10.16 Same or Different? (After Shepard & Metzler, 1971).

■ **Question:** Does the time needed to move mental images around in our mind reflect the amount of "movement"?

Continued

Researchers at Work *Continued*

■ **Hypothesis:** Participants need more time to move mental images over greater virtual distances.

■ **Test:** In one of the most famous experiments in psychology, participants were asked to examine pairs of drawings of three-dimensional objects, as shown here.

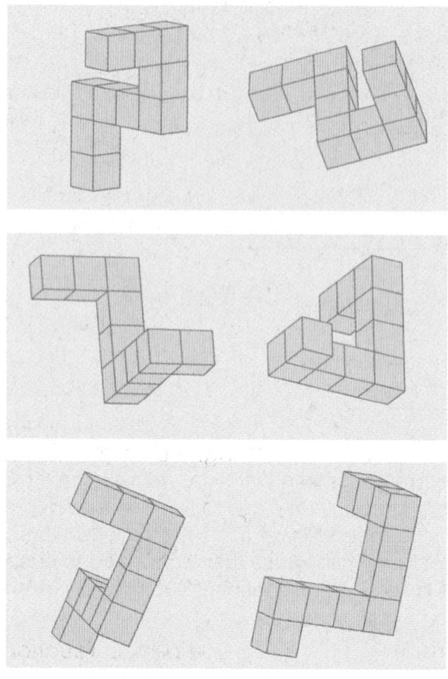

The participants' task was to say whether the objects in each pair were identical or different. In some cases, the two objects were the same and differed only in how the two-dimensional depiction was rotated (top). In other cases, the objects were the same but would have to be rotated in three dimensions, into the "depth" of the page, to be aligned (middle). In other cases, the objects were not actually the same (bottom). The experimenters had hundreds of these pairs. Among those that depicted objects that were the same, they differed in one important respect: how much one object would have to be rotated to be aligned with the other.

■ **Results:** The more degrees of rotation that were required to line up the two images, the more time participants needed to complete the task. Each additional 20 degrees of rotation reliably increased the average time needed to judge whether the objects were the same.

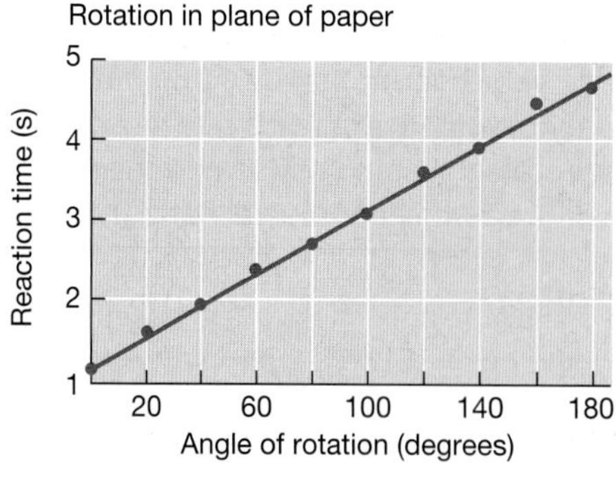

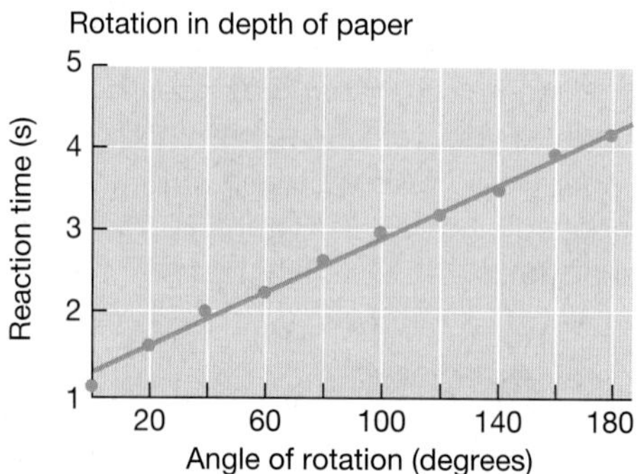

■ **Conclusion:** When we rotate mental images in our mind, we do so in "real time," so we need more time to imagine longer rotations than short rotations.

An ongoing debate among cognitive psychologists is whether, when we experience these mental images, the same parts of the brain are being activated as when we actually see the original object (Kosslyn et al., 2006). The details of that debate, and the implications for how our minds manipulate imagery, are beyond what we have time to explore here, but we do know that visual cortex is active when people are engaging in mental imagery. For example, when people are mentally imagining a large object, more visual cortex is active, just like when they are actually seeing a large object (Kosslyn et al., 1995). But how faithfully and completely does brain activity when *imagining* an object reproduce brain activity when actually *seeing* it? At present, that question cannot be settled because we simply are not able to monitor brain activity with enough sensitivity to know.

Of course, we don't just imagine sights. When people are imagining a smell, they activate the same parts of the brain that are activated by genuine smelling (Bensafi et al., 2003). But the same limitations for the study of mental imagery apply to mental "odors." We can't yet tell any difference in brain activity when a person is smelling peppermint versus rosemary, so there's no way to know whether a person imagining a particular smell is activating the exact same brain regions as when they perceive the actual odor. In fact, if *exactly* the same brain regions were active when we imagined an object as when we see (or smell) that object, then presumably we would be unable to distinguish our imagined perceptions from those imposed by reality. Since our *experience* of imagined versus genuine stimuli is different, something about our brain activity during these occasions must also be different. No one knows what that difference in brain activity is.

In addition to carefully timing a participant's reaction time in cognitive tasks, cognitive psychologists have examined how quickly people can perform skilled behaviors. Here again, carefully measuring people's behavior offers insight into how the mind works.

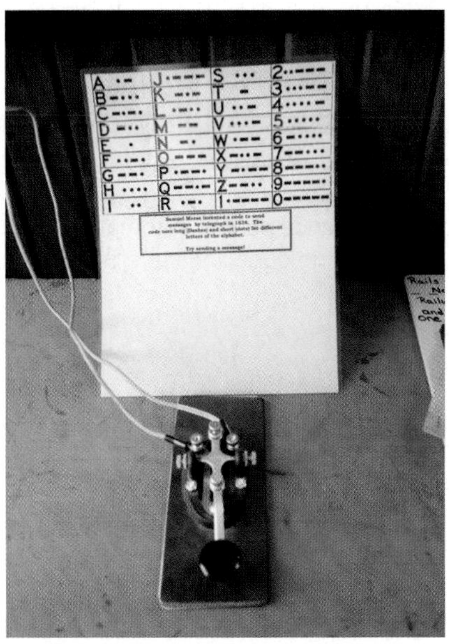

Morse Code Machine Before the widespread use of telephones, people who could accurately use a telegraph key to transmit and receive information were prized for that skill.

There are at least three stages in acquiring a skill

Every day, psychologists bring people into the laboratory, and give them some task that has been carefully designed to test a specific hypothesis about behavior. Often these tasks involve doing something that the participants (or anybody else) would not normally do. But psychologists have also studied performance at real-life skills. In this context let us define **skill** as a maximum of performance with a minimum of effort (Guthrie, 1952).

One early and very influential study of skill looked at the ability of people who worked as telegraph operators, transmitting and receiving messages in Morse code (Bryan & Harter, 1899). Individual operators' skills seemed to reach more than one plateau of performance as their practice continued. Having reached a certain skill level, they stayed at about the same performance level for a long time. Then they would quickly get significantly better and stay at a new, higher plateau for a while. What was happening?

Years later, Fitts and Posner (1967) took up the question of why skill tends to improve in stages in a study of touch-typing. It was easy to find lots of people who had been practicing this skill, and to compare what they were doing. Also, the psychologists could find people who did not yet know how to type, and study their behavior as they acquired this skill in the lab.

Summarizing years of work, Fitts and Posner proposed that there are three phases in learning a skill like touch-typing:

1. At the **cognitive phase**, typical of a beginner, the person is consciously aware of what he is doing, frequently checking himself (either mentally or by consulting a chart). Performance is slow, with frequent errors, and the person's movements are stiff. It's called the cognitive stage because the person is *thinking about* what finger he needs to use for each letter, and that process is effortful.

skill The ability to perform very well with a minimum of effort.

cognitive phase The earliest stage of skill acquisition, during which there is conscious awareness of efforts.

associative phase The second stage of skill acquisition, in which performance is faster with fewer errors.

autonomous phase The third stage of skill acquisition, during which performance seems automatic and requires no conscious attention.

2. In the **associative phase**, performance is faster with fewer errors than in the cognitive phase, and movements are smoother. The person's conscious experience is that he no longer needs to think about which finger to use for which letter; he seems to know which finger is associated with which letter (hence the name of the phase). At this stage, the person still has to concentrate on the task. If he is distracted by some other task, performance will decline significantly.
3. In the **autonomous phase**, the hands seem to automatically know what to do without the person having to pay much attention. In other words, the task now seems automatic (which is what *autonomous* means here). Finger movements are smooth, rapid, and efficient, even though the person isn't really paying attention to how they move. If asked, the person may not be able to describe how he is doing what he does—it's just something he does.

We can give a person who has reached the autonomous phase some additional task, taking up some of his attention, yet his performance won't be affected very much. In real life, such a typist can focus on the *content* of what he is typing, and the actual act of typing seems to take care of itself. In contrast, distracting someone in the earliest cognitive phase is likely to stop him entirely, as if he has absolutely no attention to spare.

Performance in other, more interesting domains has been observed to progress through these same three phases. For example, music, chess, and athletic performances also seem to follow this pattern of transition from cognitive to associative to autonomous phase. What's more, in these fields there are people who passionately pursue excellence long past the limitations of a laboratory study (where experimenters can afford to pay someone to acquire a skill only for so long). Performance in these real-world fields suggests that there are further stages past autonomous, in which true expertise develops.

I wish it weren't so, but apparently the only way to reach really outstanding performance in these activities is to invest your time. The outstanding tennis players Serena and Venus Williams began learning their sport at 4 years of

Outstanding in Their Fields Counter-clockwise from the top: Shown here at age 13, Bobby Fischer became a phenomenal chess player without having put in 10,000 hours of intensive practice, but he had easily spent that much time playing chess by the time he won the world championship. Yo-Yo Ma began playing the cello when he was 4, after having played the violin for a while. Serena Williams took up tennis at age 4.

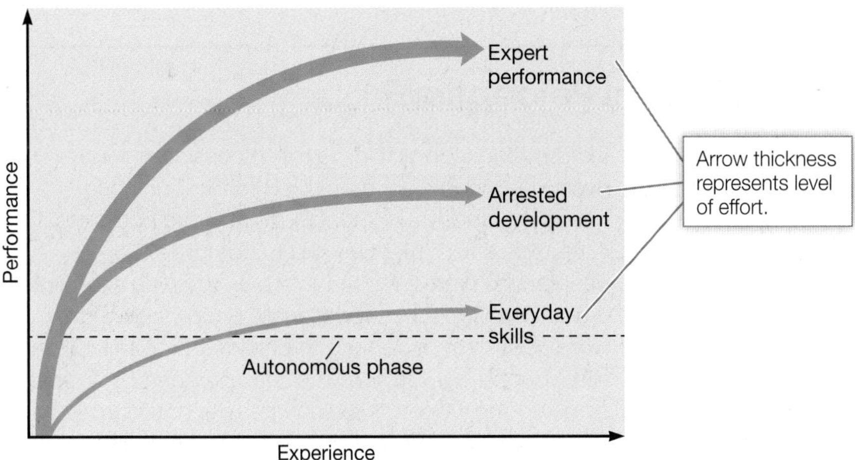

Figure 10.17 Skill Learning and Expert Performance If you want to type well enough to get by, then you are satisfied with reaching a level where you can perform the task reasonably well in an autonomous fashion. To be an expert, you have to keep pushing, which requires more effort as you grapple with harder and harder tasks. (After Ericsson, 1998.)

age. Researchers have estimated the many hours put in by those who became merely excellent and those who became truly outstanding. There seems to be a growing consensus that really outstanding performance, the kind you see in professional athletes and musicians, requires about 10,000 hours of high-quality practice (Ericsson, 1998, 2000). Likewise, the chess players who gain national and international standing are those who have played chess, against increasingly challenging opponents, for about 10,000 hours (Levitin, 2006). This is a lot of practice: about 20 hours per week for 10 years!

What's interesting about this research is that these three areas of achievement—athletics, music, and chess—are those where we tend to think that people are either born gifted—or not. But however "gifted" a person may seem, no matter what his inheritance, no one can become a professional athlete, or musician, or chess player without putting in the hours (Macnamara et al., 2014).

Nor will just any old kind of practice do the job. Achieving excellence depends upon getting rapid, high-quality *feedback*. Furthermore, experts in all fields have an explicit concern for *technique*, trying to find the most efficient way to accomplish each step of the process, whether it's how to handle the bow of a violin for a partita, or the baseball bat when expecting an inside pitch. Finally, practice produces the best results if the person continually pushes herself to more and more *challenging* tasks. If a person stops facing greater challenges, her performance will plateau to match the challenges she's taken on, not progressing further to become truly outstanding (**Figure 10.17**).

If to become truly outstanding at any activity you have to put in 10,000 hours of challenging practice, then you'd better really love that activity. Otherwise, how are you ever going to be able to put in the time you need? Since most of us prefer doing activities that come easily to us, it's hard to eliminate the possibility that people who become truly outstanding athletes, musicians, or chess players may have been those who were particularly well suited to do well in that domain from the start. Also, it is clear that some people need less practice than others to reach a particular level of skill (Macnamara et al., 2014).

Early experience seems to be especially helpful to achieve expert status. One study of professional soccer players in Europe found that there was a clear correlation between the month of birth and skill—those born early in the year, January through March, were more skilled than those born late in the year. Was this an effect of players' horoscope signs? Not likely. It turns out that the youth leagues that produce these players have a birthday cutoff date of December 31. So each year as the first teams of the youngest kids are formed, those born in January are older, and therefore bigger and more skilled, than those born in

Skeptic at Large

BOX 10.3

Is There Such a Thing as Subliminal Perception?

It's discouraging, sometimes, to see how an intriguing tale persists, no matter how many times it has been debunked. In 1957, when a market researcher claimed to have increased theater sales of Coke and popcorn by flashing slogans ("drink Coke" "eat popcorn") on the screen so briefly that the audience wasn't even aware of them, Americans were horrified to think they might be manipulated so easily. Newspapers and magazines sounded the alarm, and Congress passed laws forbidding the practice, but for some reason, psychologists could not reproduce such effects in the laboratory. Five years later the market researcher admitted he had made up his claims (Pratkanis, 1992), but no one seemed to notice, since the story continues to circulate. Have you heard it?

Is there any such thing as **subliminal perception**, when a participant shows evidence of having perceived a stimulus without being consciously aware of it? The term suggests that while perception of some stimuli is *supra*liminal, "above threshold" for conscious perception, others are below the threshold for conscious perception. In the laboratory, if people are shown an image briefly enough, say for a 20th of a second (50 milliseconds), they will not be consciously aware of seeing it. But there are various ways of showing that they must have had some perception of the image. For example, if shown a series of words in this fashion, each too quickly to reach conscious awareness, participants are more likely to think of those words in a subsequent test, such as word completion. If the task is to think of a word to complete GU____, people who were exposed to the word *guide* are more likely to provide that answer, while people shown the word *guess* are more likely to provide that word. Likewise, people can be shown letters, numbers, or words so briefly they report they saw nothing, but if forced to guess what they saw, they are more likely to guess correctly than would be expected by chance alone. In Section 1.3, we saw evidence that subliminal perception of a white or African American face affected visual recognition of crime-related objects.

People who are surgically anesthetized almost always report remembering nothing while they were under. However, if during surgery they wear earphones that repeat certain words, like *proud*, the patients are more likely to complete the prompt PR___ with *proud* than would be expected by chance alone (Merikle & Daneman, 1996). It's spooky to contemplate, but anesthetized people do seem to be taking in some information during their surgery.

Still, it's important to recognize how subtle the effects of subliminal perception are, and how hard psychologists have to work to detect any effect at all. For example, in one classic study (Marcel, 1983),

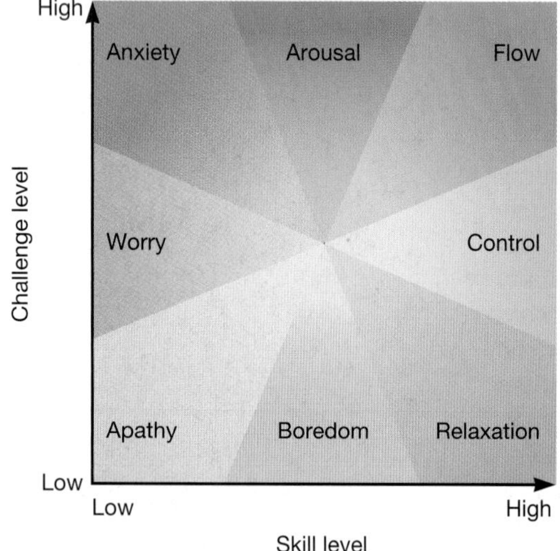

Figure 10.18 Flow According to Csíkszentmihályi, flow, or feeling "in the zone," happens when a person has very high skills and is taking on challenges that are equivalent to that skill. If the challenges are too high for a person's skill level, he will likely feel anxious. (After Csíkszentmihályi, 1998.)

December (Ericsson, 2000). That means they are more likely to be picked by the best coaches and more likely to get that coach's attention for extra practice and extra experience playing in games. That extra time in practice and on the field may be enough to get these young players to the 10,000-hour mark by the time they're grown.

Closely related to the production of experts is the concept of experiencing **flow**, when we are wholly involved in some activity, just for its own sake, and time seems to fly by and we seem to know what to do without having to consciously think about it (Csíkszentmihályi, 1998). Musicians and athletes may call it being "in the groove" or "in the zone," while computer programmers may call it "hack mode." The peak experience of flow seems to occur when a highly skilled performer is tackling highly challenging tasks (**Figure 10.18**). In some ways, this sounds almost like an extension of the autonomous phase, where no conscious thinking is required for outstanding performance. Indeed, some people who have reached this level report that *thinking* about the process may *impair* performance. Yogi Berra, an outstanding hitter and coach, once commented, "How can I hit and think at the same time?"

If there are few scientific studies of flow itself, there has been a tremendous growth in the study of an aspect of experience that seems altered during flow—attention. At that level of performance in participants were exposed to very brief presentations of particular words and then asked to look at a list of words and indicate as quickly as possible whether each one was a genuine word (*lawyer*) or a nonsense word (*rleyaw*). If the word had been presented subliminally, the people were slightly faster at recognizing it in the subsequent list. But even if they had been subliminally presented with the word 20 times, they were only about 15% faster at recognizing it (see figure).

Thus while there is ample evidence of subliminal *perception*, there is no evidence of subliminal *persuasion*—that such messages actually affect people's behavior, including what brand of products they buy. Smith and Rogers (1994) found that in television commercials, the *supra*liminal messages—those that people could report seeing—were ten times more effective than subliminal messages at eliciting positive responses from the participants. For advertisers, a technique that is far more effective than subliminal perception is *product placement* (or "embedded marketing"): putting an example of the product into a film or television show. Many industries, including makers of soft drinks and automobiles, have invested heavily in product placement. Perhaps the tobacco industry has spent the most money on product placement, paying $100,000 to have a character smoking their brand of cigarette on screen in a movie (Mekemson & Glantz, 2002). Clearly the tobacco industry believes that portraying cigarette smoking as glamorous will help recruit new addicts to their products.

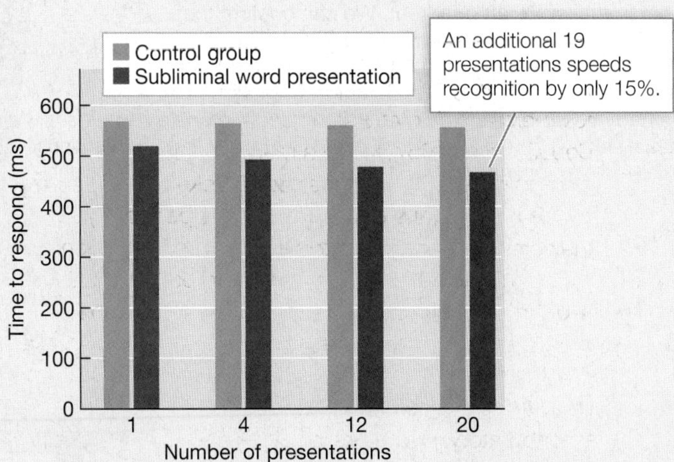

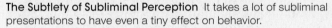

The Subtlety of Subliminal Perception It takes a lot of subliminal presentations to have even a tiny effect on behavior.

But the whole point is there is nothing *subliminal* about the presentation.

Likewise, audio recordings with subliminal messages that claim to help people lose weight or stop smoking have no effect when tested (Pratkanis et al., 1994).

subliminal perception When a participant shows evidence of having perceived a stimulus without being consciously aware of it.

athletics, music, or any other endeavor, we may perceive information that we are not consciously aware of. The fact that we can take in information without being aware of it is the subject of a persistent myth we discuss in **Box 10.3**.

Attention is the spotlight of the mind

> *Everyone knows what attention is. It is the taking possession by the mind, in clear and vivid form, of one out of what seem several simultaneously possible objects or trains of thought.*
>
> —*William James (1890)*

Because we all have experience with directing our **attention**, we can readily define it as the process of selectively concentrating the mind on one particular object or process while ignoring others. That business of ignoring other things while attending to something seems to be an inescapable aspect of attention, which again we have all experienced. We seem to have only so much attention available, so attending to one thing inevitably makes us less attentive to others. Thus the difficulty with studying attention is not to define it, but to figure out *how to study it*.

Cognitive scientists of the 1950s developed ways to tell whether a participant was paying attention to something. For example, a person can be asked to stare at a red dot on a screen, and a camera can be used to track his eyes to be sure he's looking at the red dot. Then images can be flashed on the screen, such as

flow The experience of being wholly involved in some activity, just for its own sake, and time flies by and you seem to know what to do without conscious effort.

attention A concentration of the mind on a particular object or process.

Figure 10.19 The Attentional Spotlight A participant staring at the red dot in the center of the screen can be warned that a signal, say the letter *V*, may appear in the lower left quadrant. We can confirm that he does not move his eye from the red dot. Yet by directing his attention to that area, like an attentional spotlight, he is more likely to detect the signal than if he had no warning and needed to attend to the entire visual field.

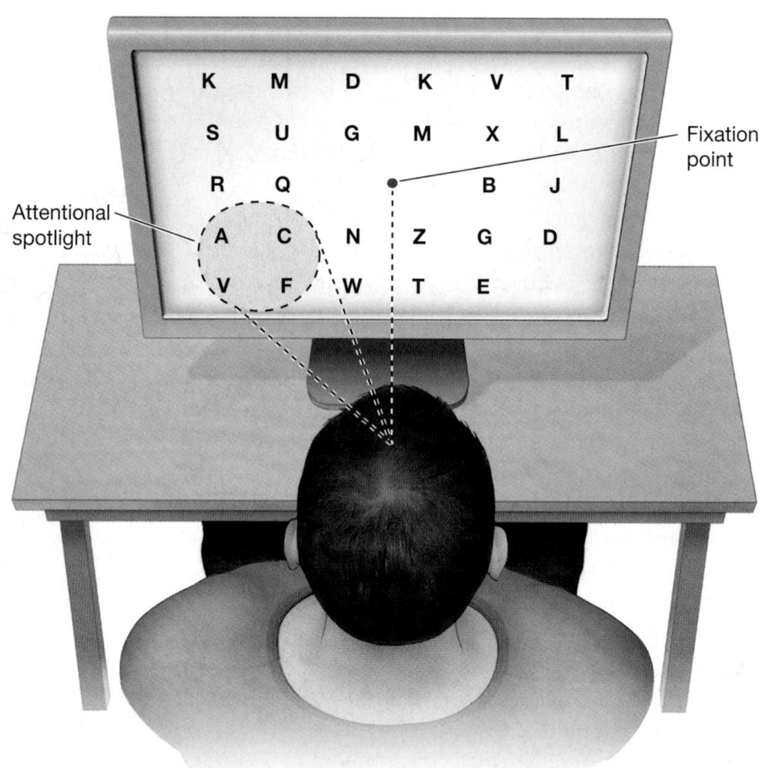

attentional spotlight The ability to direct our attention to one part of our visual field.

cocktail party effect A phenomenon in hearing when a person selectively attends to a particular conversation out of many.

letters of the alphabet, and the person can be asked whether he saw a particular target, say the letter *V*. In such experiments, if participants are told where the target is going to appear, such as in the lower left quadrant of the screen, they are better at detecting it (**Figure 10.19**). Importantly, the camera tells researchers that people are *not* shifting their gaze to that quadrant—that they're still gazing at the dot. Yet their *attention* can be directed to the lower left, and when they do this, they're much more likely to detect targets that appear there, as opposed to in another quadrant of the screen. These studies indicate that we have an **attentional spotlight**, an ability to direct our attention to one part of our visual field. It's as though our attention is a spotlight that we can shine onto different parts of the visual field, so that we can "see" things better there. Of course we're not really *seeing* better, we're *attending* better to that region. In real life, we say someone is looking "out of the corner of his eye." Imagine a teacher gazing at the student up at the blackboard, but really attending to the class clown in the front row. ("How did she see me pass that note?")

The idea of an attentional spotlight in vision is closely related to a well-known phenomenon in hearing, the **cocktail party effect**, when a person selectively attends to a particular conversation out of the many conversations taking place. You've probably experienced this as you carry on a conversation despite the loud din around you. You might not even be aware of how loud the party is. This phenomenon can be studied in the laboratory by having people listen to many sounds and asking them to listen for a particular target word in one conversation versus another, or in a woman's speech rather than a man's. In real life, you can exploit the cocktail party effect when the conversation you're having gets boring.

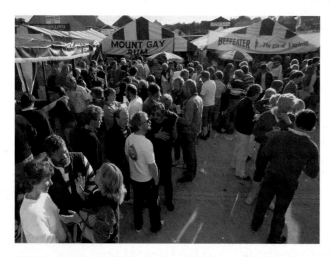

The Cocktail Party Effect Because of all the noise at events like this, it would be very hard to carry on a conversation without the cocktail party effect: the ability to attend to just one aspect of the sound around us, filtering out the rest.

Figure 10.20 **Gorillas in the Midst** Who could miss the gorilla here? Most people do if they are concentrating on another task, such as counting the number of times people in white shirts touch the ball. (From Simons & Chabris, 1999.)

You might start attending to a nearby conversation that sounds more interesting. Hmmm, I wondered why your eyes glazed over when I was saying such interesting things about attentional spotlights.

An important take-home message from these and similar experiments about attention is that *there is a limited amount* of it. One modern example of this, which has become rather famous, is to ask people to watch a short video of a group of students passing two basketballs back and forth in a school hallway. If you ask people only to watch the video (without any other instruction), everyone notices a person in a gorilla costume slowly walk into the picture, stop to beat its chest, and slowly walk out of the picture (**Figure 10.20**). Who could miss it, right? But if the first time you show the video you ask people to focus their attention on some task, like counting how often the people in white shirts touch the basketball, about half the participants never even notice the gorilla (Simons & Chabris, 1999)! This is a striking effect to experience. Usually when I do this demonstration (at least, until it became so famous), very few people notice the gorilla while doing the task. When I ask them about the gorilla, they don't know what I'm talking about. But when I ask them to watch the clip again without attending to the basketball, they typically laugh at how obvious it is. Some people even wonder if I'm tricking them, showing a new video instead of the original. (Happily, there are always some audience members who noticed the gorilla the first time, so they can reassure the skeptics.) This phenomenon is referred to as **inattentional blindness**, when we appear to be "blind" to things that we are not attending to.

Inattentional blindness experiments dramatically demonstrate how much attention matters. If you're attending to the basketball, you may miss the gorilla. Interestingly, most people believe that they could not miss the gorilla, but we know that many of those people are wrong, since about half of all participants miss it. So the other great lesson of the gorilla video clip is that *we don't have as much attention available to us as we think we do*. This is, of course, another example of how we are not consciously aware of a lot of our mental processing.

For your own safety I feel compelled to point out that texting or talking on the phone (even if your hands are free) while driving inevitably draws your attention away from the road. It's amusing if you fail to notice a gorilla in a film clip, but failing to notice a truck bearing down on you—not so much.

inattentional blindness The phenomenon of appearing to be blind to things that we aren't attending to.

Our limited attention surely contributed to the failure of the White House to act on the warnings about the 9/11 attacks, as described in the opening of the

change blindness The failure to detect a change in a visual scene.

chapter. If the memo is seen alone, the clues warning about the attack seem obvious, but in the context of many other memos, briefings, and events, there was nothing to draw attention to those clues. If people in the administration are busy with everyday chores—the equivalent of counting basketballs—they might not notice the gorilla shambling by. The limitations of our attention also affect our ability to notice change, as we'll discuss next.

Even a brief break in our attention can make us "blind"

We won't talk much about factors that grab our attention. For the cocktail party phenomenon, you may have noticed that, no matter how fascinating you find your conversation with me, if someone nearby mentions your name, you're likely to hear it and that will grab your attention to that conversation. Similarly, people looking steadily at a screen are very likely to notice if some part of the scene suddenly changes. Indeed, our visual system has evolved to be very sensitive to any change in visual stimuli. But if our vision is interrupted, even very briefly, we can be remarkably unaware of any changes.

Change blindness refers to the failure of people to detect a change in a visual scene (Simons & Rensink, 2005). Change blindness can be readily studied in the lab. If the screen flickers, even if it's just for a tenth of second, people may not notice changes on the screen (Pashler, 1988). You may have a hard time gauging whether that's a surprising outcome, so let's consider a more common demonstration of change blindness. People recruited for a study were directed to a room and up to a counter. There an experimenter on the other side of the counter gave them a form to sign. Then the experimenter took the form, bent down behind the counter, out of the participant's sight, and a new experimenter rose up to hand them back the form and direct them down the hall. About *75% of the participants did not notice the switch*, even though the person who directed them down the hall had different hair, a different-colored shirt, and a different face than the one who had asked them to sign the form (Simons & Chabris, 1999). The participants were blind to this big change.

Change blindness has been demonstrated even more dramatically by choosing unsuspecting participants from the public. One researcher, posing as someone new to a public area trying to use a map, stops someone to ask for directions. As the unsuspecting "participant" tries to show where they are on the map and how to get to the requested destination, a group of people carrying a picture passes between the researcher and participant. While the picture is blocking the participant's view, one of the people carrying the picture switches places with the "lost" researcher (**Figure 10.21**). Does the participant notice that a different person is now holding the map and asking for directions? About half the participants do not seem to notice (Simons & Levin, 1998). They simply resume the conversation, pointing to the map and offering directions. When interviewed afterward, they are completely unaware that a switch was made. When British magician Derren

Figure 10.21 Change Blindness We have a hard time noticing change if our attention is broken. The bearded gentleman giving directions to the researcher (A), is briefly interrupted by people carrying a picture (B), then doesn't notice that he is now talking to a different person. (From Simons & Levin, 1998.)

(A)

(B)

(C)

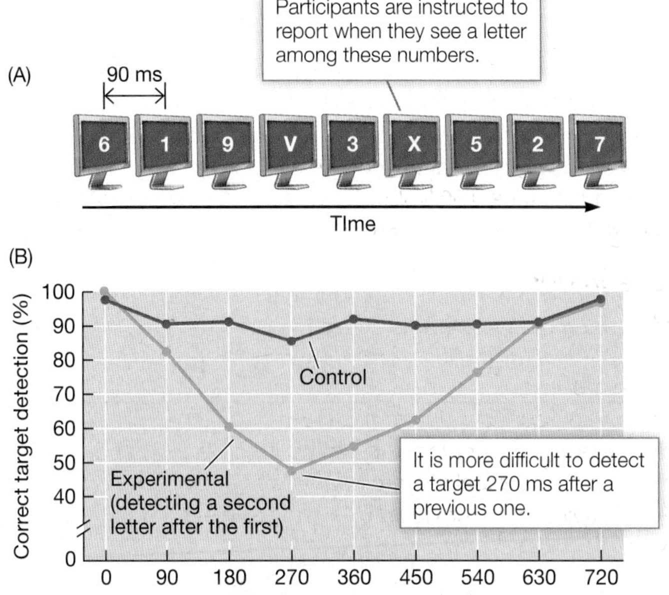

Figure 10.22 **Attentional Blink** (A) When participants watching a stream of characters appearing on screen are asked to detect two targets, say letters amid a string of numerals, they can readily do so, even if the characters are flashing by once every 90 ms. Experimenters can vary how soon the second target appears by changing its position in the line of characters. (B) If the second target appears 180–450 ms later than the first target, participants will miss it about half the time. It is as if their attention has "blinked" shortly after detecting the first target. (After Raymond et al., 1992.)

Brown recreated this experiment on the streets of London and New York, most people failed to notice when the swapped person wore different clothes, or if one person had a shaved head and the other had a full set of hair. They even failed to notice when the swap involved confederates of a different race and sex!

attentional blink A brief lapse of attention that occurs shortly after a person detects a target.

Closely related to change blindness is a phenomenon known as **attentional blink**, a brief lapse of attention that occurs shortly after we've detected a target. In these studies, experimenters ask participants to watch a screen and to look for two different targets out of a stream of characters. For example, people might be asked to look for two letters interspersed between a series of numerals (**Figure 10.22A**). The characters are presented fairly quickly, say ten per second, but that's slow enough that most participants almost always detect the first target. In fact, if the second target appears right after the first target, say within 90 milliseconds (ms), the participants detect them both. What's interesting is that if the second target is displayed a bit later, say 200 ms later, people fail to detect it about half the time (**Figure 10.22B**; Raymond et al., 1992). It's as if their attention is turned off for 200 to 500 ms after detecting the first target—that's the attentional blink.

It is not at all clear why the attentional blink happens. It isn't that the targets appear too quickly, because we can detect a second target that appears 90 ms later *better* than one that appears 270 ms later (see Figure 10.22B). Rather, having detected the first target, our attention remains focused for a short while longer and then fades out for a bit. It's almost as if our attention is like a digital camera that, on taking a first picture, can capture anything that appeared during that time, but cannot take another picture until the first one has been completed.

One could argue that the attentional blink is an artifact of laboratory studies, unrelated to real life. Indeed, although we often must pay attention to a fast-moving scene to detect important signals, maybe they're not that important if we need half a second after detecting one important event before we can detect another. But an important lesson of the attentional blink is that we have absolutely *no conscious awareness* that we have "gone blank" for nearly half a second. Our experience is that we are paying continuous attention, not that we are paying attention at one time and then taking half a second off.

Needless to say, experiments such as these showing how limited our attention is, and how readily it can be disrupted, suggest that we humans, despite our best efforts, are not necessarily accurate observers. In our personal lives, we would all do well to remember how fallible our attention is—for example, when our cell phone rings while we're driving. These results also have relevance to the criminal justice system. If having a person out of our view for the 2 seconds it takes for a door to be carried past renders us unaware that a white man has been replaced by an Asian woman, then how reliable are eyewitness reports, really? Yet in most judicial systems, including in the United States, judges and juries weigh eyewitness reports much more heavily that physical evidence, such as fingerprints and DNA. This is just one example of how humans, when making judgments, may be mistaken. In the next section we'll take up judgment and decision making, including the many errors of judgment we are all prone to make.

10.2 SUMMARY

- A *concept* is an abstract mental representation of an object or event that is separate from the word for that object or event. Human minds actively *categorize*, recognizing similarities and differences, so that we build up a *prototype* (such as for "dog" or "horse"), the best example of a concept that fits a particular category.
- Mental processes take time, so by measuring the time taken to complete a task, such as with *reaction time*, we can make inferences about the steps in mental processing. For example, we seem to use *mental imagery* to rotate objects at a particular speed "in our heads."
- We gain *skills* in phases, first in a *cognitive phase* when we are consciously aware of our efforts, then in an *associative phase*, when performance is faster with fewer errors. In the *autonomous phase*, we seem to complete the task automatically. There's evidence that truly outstanding performance requires 10,000 hours of practice with high-quality feedback.
- We have only limited amounts of *attention*, a concentration of the mind on a particular object or process. We can direct our visual attention to somewhere other than the center of our gaze, and we can listen to particular conversations in a crowd (*cocktail party effect*).
- Unless we are paying attention, we take in little information (*inattentional blindness*). We may fail to detect large changes in a scene (*change blindness*), and we are subject to an *attentional blink*, a brief period after we've spotted a target when we are unlikely to detect another.

REVIEW QUESTIONS

1. How do we use categorization to build up prototypes about objects and processes in the world?
2. How did Donders add to the complexity of tasks to show that steps in mental processing take time?
3. What relationship did Shepard and Metzler find between the degree of rotation between two objects in certain tasks and time needed to respond?
4. What are the stages in acquiring a skill?
5. Give examples of findings illustrating change blindness and the attentional blink.

Food for Thought

We have only a limited amount of attention, and we are remarkably unaware of objects and events that we are not attending to. Yet in our everyday experience we are unaware of these large gaps in our perception. Why do you think we are unaware of these gaps? Is this ignorance evolutionarily advantageous?

10.3 Decision Making and Problem Solving

Things to Learn

- Common biases that affect our judgment
- Anchoring effect
- Hindsight bias
- Belief persistence
- Loss aversion and the framing effect
- Strategies for problem solving

In psychology, **decision making** is the cognitive process of assessing information to select a course of action among several alternatives. We all have to make decisions, and psychologists have long been interested in this process. In the most basic sense, we decide what to do, so any study of behavior must come to grips with why an individual does one thing versus another. But cognitive psychologists are particularly interested in situations where a person must weigh several different sources of information to make a decision. Thus one aspect of decision making is **judgment**, the cognitive process of forming an opinion or making an evaluation by comparing possible actions. In the laboratory it is relatively easy to vary the information at hand and monitor how that affects people's judgment and therefore their final decision. The idea is to get insight into how we weigh different pieces of information in order to make a decision. We'll see that our judgment is imperfect, and several factors make judgment difficult and can therefore lead to irrational decision making. For example, we have difficulty understanding the probability of successive events and understanding proportions. Even more troublesome are some persistent biases we have in our judgment, which make us particularly susceptible to making poor decisions. Sometimes we are too readily swayed by our initial judgment, and sometimes we are even swayed by information that we know is entirely unrelated to the decision at hand. We'll also see that if a question is posed in one way, we tend to make risky decisions, but having that same situation described in another way leads us to avoid risk.

decision making The cognitive process of assessing information to select a course of action among several alternatives.

judgment The cognitive process of forming an opinion or making an evaluation by comparing possible actions.

We'll conclude the chapter with problem solving, which is closely related to decision making. After all, most problem solving requires us to decide which course of action will lead to a solution. There are several strategies to help us solve problems, and naturally, psychologists have identified other factors that often keep us from finding a solution.

Every judgment is subject to error and bias

Perhaps the simplest approach to monitoring judgment is to rely on reaction times, asking how quickly people can tell, for example, which of two lines is longer. If the difference in length is small, people need more time to judge which line is longer (**Figure 10.23**).

As we discussed in Chapter 6 (see Figure 6.7), in even the simplest judgments, such as whether a phone is ringing, we can make two different types of mistakes: (1) a miss or (2) a false alarm. A *miss* occurs when we fail to detect a signal that was there. A *false alarm* occurs when we mistakenly report a signal that wasn't really there. If we are screening X-rays for breast cancer, failing to see a tumor that is present would be a miss, while reporting that a tumor is present when there isn't would be a false alarm.

In addition to the possible errors inherent in any difficult judgment, humans are remarkably susceptible to bias, as discussed in Chapter 2. Psychology experiments must be carefully designed to avoid planting bias in participants. The only way to be sure that some piece of information will not bias a person's decision is to keep the information from the participant. The inherent bias in human judgment, no matter how hard we try to be objective, has been demonstrated clearly and often. For example, high school teachers rated the very same essay a full letter grade higher, on average, if it was written in excellent penmanship (Sloan & McGinnis, 1982). In another study, educators graded essays written by sixth graders as better when they believed they were written by boys than when they thought they had been written by girls (King, 1998). It may be for this reason that most law schools use "blind grading," where the evaluator does not know the name, gender, or anything else about the student who wrote the paper (Archer & McCarthy, 1988). Of course, the author's personal characteristics are not the only possible bias for a grader. In one bold demonstration, some high school students taking the essay portion of the SAT exam deliberately wrote nonsense and yet got a score of 5

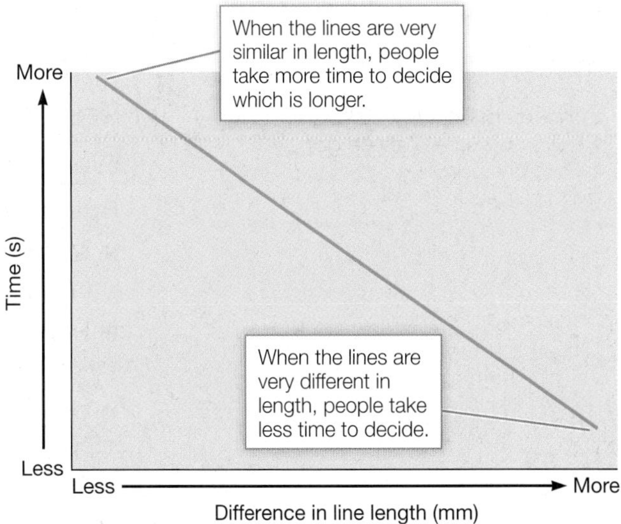
When the lines are very similar in length, people take more time to decide which is longer.
More
Time (s)
Less
When the lines are very different in length, people take less time to decide.
Less
More
Difference in line length (mm)

Figure 10.23 Harder Decisions Take Longer to Make (After Johnson, 1939.)

(out of 6), probably because they used high-falutin' words like *plethora* and *myriad* (Jaschik, 2007). Presumably the use of such words impressed the readers, even if the essay was incoherent. Apparently "wordiness" can also bias judgment about the quality of SAT essays, since just counting the number of words in an SAT essay provided the same grade as the official readers about 90% of the time (Winerip, 2005). Too bad if your handwriting is poor and slow.

Bias in judgment is not confined to academia. One analysis came to a startling explanation of the home-field advantage in sports, the fact that teams are more likely to win while playing at home than away. It turns out that the cheers and jeers of the crowd really matter, but not to the *players*. For example, basketball free-throw percentages are the same at away and home games. Rather, the crowd influences the *officials* enforcing the rules. A baseball umpire is less likely to signal a called strike (ruling the ball is in the strike zone when the batter does not swing) for the home team, especially in crucial situations. Visiting basketball players are more likely to be called for traveling, and visiting soccer players receive more penalty calls and fewer injury time-outs, than home players (Moskowitz & Wertheim, 2011). No one is suggesting that the officials in these sports *deliberately* favor the home team; I'm sure they are unaware of their bias. But everyone wants to be liked, even umpires. That means that in close-call situations, they are slightly more likely to please the home crowd (and slightly less likely to make them angry). Officials are like all other humans. No matter how hard we try to make unbiased judgments, we are going to be swayed by our surroundings and any information we have available to us.

Another sphere in which the bias of even supposedly objective experts has been revealed is music. For centuries, experts extolled the outstanding sounds of violins and cellos handcrafted by seventeenth- and eighteenth-century Italian masters like Stradivarius and Guarneri. "Everyone knows" that these instruments have a richer sound than modern instruments, and many people have tried to figure out what secrets the old masters used to produce them. Yet when world-class experts were asked to judge the quality of instruments by playing and listening to them while blindfolded (so they couldn't tell whether the instruments were old or new), they found the quality of sound from the newly made and the old violins to be equivalent (Fritz et al., 2012). Only by keeping judges "blind" to information can we be certain it will not bias their judgment. We discussed this issue extensively in Chapter 2, when we talked about the importance of "blind" auditions for musicians.

Perhaps it is even more disturbing to realize that our judgment can be biased by information that we know has absolutely no relevance to the task, as we'll see next (**Figure 10.24**).

☑ Researchers at Work

Even random information can induce bias

Figure 10.24 The Anchoring Effect (After Tversky & Kahneman, 1974.)

■ **Question:** Can our judgment be influenced by information that we know is irrelevant?

■ **Hypothesis:** Just exposing people to a number will not influence their estimates.

■ **Test:** Participants were asked to spin a fortune wheel to get a supposedly random number (in fact, the wheel was rigged to stop on either 10 or 65). Then they were asked if the percentage of countries in the U. N. that are from Africa is less or more than that number. After making this judgment, participants were asked to estimate the percentage of African nations in the U. N.

■ **Results:** People who had spun to 65 were more likely to overestimate the percentage of nations than were people who had spun to 10. Participants appeared unaware of how exposure to a random number affected their subsequent estimate.

■ **Conclusion:** Exposure to a number biased participants' estimates even though they believed that the number coming up on the wheel was random. It was as if the mere *exposure* to that random number served as an "anchor" for a participant's mind, and subsequent estimates began with numbers close to that one. For that reason, our tendency when making decisions to rely too heavily on an initial piece of information—even random information—is known as the **anchoring effect**.

Psychologists find that the anchoring effect is especially powerful in our judgment in the marketplace. For example, people were given a lot of information about various real estate properties for sale, including the current asking price, and then were asked to evaluate how much each property was worth. But they weren't told the genuine asking price; the researchers deliberately misled participants about the asking price. As you might guess, on average, the higher the purported asking price, the higher the value that people assigned to the property. Exposure to that asking price served as an "anchor" around which the participants placed their estimates. Remarkably, this trend was seen even when the *participants were real estate experts* (Northcraft & Neale, 1987). Retailers appear to be well aware of the effect of anchors when they list "regular" and "sale" prices for items. Gee, if the usual price is $100, then this is a real bargain at $60. Similarly, people who are first shown a huge, expensive TV end up buying a more expensive model, on average, than people who are first shown an inexpensive TV (Donoho, 2003). The anchoring effect doesn't just affect how valuable we think an item is; it also affects how *many* items we think we need. When grocery stores have prominent signs saying things like "5 for $2," people tend to buy more of the items than when only the individual price (40 cents) is displayed (Wansink et al., 1998).

anchoring effect The tendency to rely too heavily on an initial piece of information when making a judgement.

Some decisions are especially difficult, including situations where we have to estimate the probability of one outcome that depends on another, as we'll discuss next.

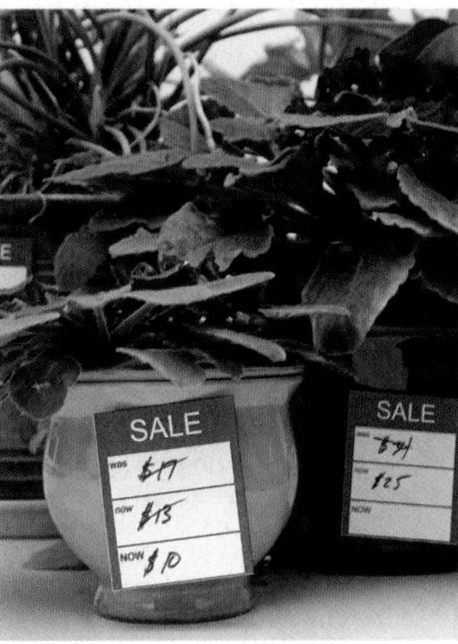

Plants for Sale Thinking an item used to be more expensive makes it appear a bargain.

We are all prone to particular errors of judgment

Difficult as decision making is, perhaps it's not surprising that no one does it perfectly, by which I mean always making the correct choice, achieving the best possible outcome. In real-life situations there are times when it's not at all clear what the best outcome is. In the laboratory, however, scientists prefer to study

(A) Contestant chooses **Door 1**; Monty opens Door 2
Switching loses

(B) Contestant chooses **Door 2**; Monty opens Door 3
Switching wins

(C) Contestant chooses **Door 3**; Monty opens Door 2
Switching wins

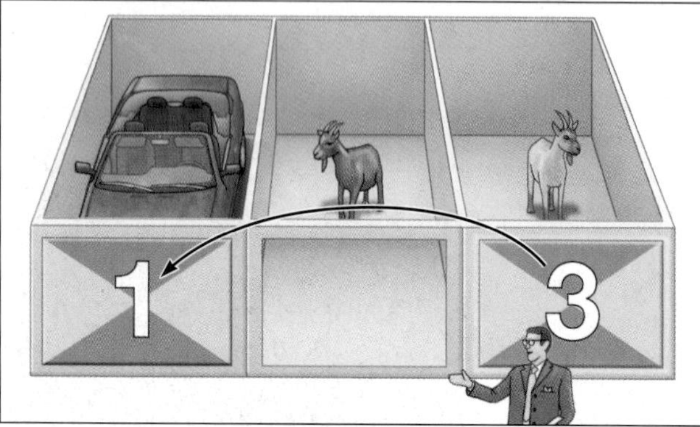

Figure 10.25 A Look behind the Scenes of the Monty Hall Problem "Monty" knows what's behind each door. (A) If your initial choice was right, which will happen one-third of the time, then switching doors when Monty opens the other door will cause you to lose. (B,C) But more often (two-thirds of the time), you will choose the wrong door initially. Then switching will cause you to win. So if you *always* switch, you will lose only when your initial choice was correct, which is one time out of three, or 33.3% of the time. The other 66.7% of the time switching wins. If you *never* switch, you win only 33.3% of the time—that one time out of three when your initial choice was correct.

decision making in situations where everyone would agree on what is correct—for example, where people are trying to maximize how much money they receive, or minimize how much money they might lose. These studies have shown that, in certain situations, the average person will make the wrong decision, reducing his payoff. This is not because the person is being tricked—but rather that despite being clearly informed of the parameters, the person makes the wrong decision anyway.

One example is the **Monty Hall problem**, when someone fails to properly estimate the probability of a particular outcome after being given additional information. The problem is named after the original host of the TV game show *Let's Make a Deal*, where the host, Monty Hall, often presented contestants with the following situation: The contestant is shown three doors and told that a fabulous prize, say a new car, is behind one door, but behind each of the other two doors is a worthless gag prize, say a goat (Selvin, 1975). Let's say you are the contestant, and you choose door number 1. Then Monty, who knows exactly what's behind each door, does something a little devious. He says, "OK, you chose door number 1. You know what, I'm going to open another door, door number 2, and show you the goat behind it. Now, do you want to stick with your first choice, door number 1, or switch to door number 3?"

What would you do?

Most people recognize that initially you have a one out of three chance of being right, that the car is behind door number 1. From that perspective, knowing that a goat is behind door number 2 should not change the odds that your initial choice was right. And indeed it doesn't. Nevertheless, you're *twice* as likely to win if you switch doors (**Figure 10.25**). This outcome is so counterintuitive that it is sometimes called paradoxical. A newspaper columnist who said your odds were better by switching got over 10,000 letters, some from mathematics teachers, insisting she was wrong. But she was right.

Why is it better to switch? Most important, *Monty knows where the car is, and he always reveals a goat.* That means that if you initially chose the wrong door, then Monty *has* to show you where the other goat is. Or think of it this way. If there are 1,000 doors, and you choose door number 326, your chances of winning are 1 in a 1,000, right? But what if Monty now opens up 998 other doors, leaving only your door and one other: number 658. Since he *had* to leave the door concealing the car closed, then it's a pretty good bet that the car is behind that door he left closed; otherwise he might have opened it. In that case, your chances of winning are *much better* if you switch. Your odds of winning with the initial choice were tiny: 1 out of 1,000. By switching, your odds of *losing* are tiny: that 1 time out of 1,000 when you happened to guess the right door at the start.

Assuming that you are learning about the Monty Hall problem for the first time here, does the advantage of switching doors seem so obvious that you are sure you would have taken up Monty on his offer to switch? You may be suffering from hindsight bias, which we'll discuss next.

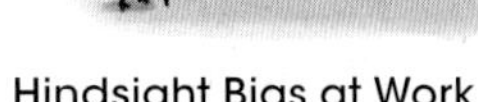

Hindsight Bias at Work

Our hindsight seems so good because our memory is so easily distorted

We say that hindsight is 20/20, meaning that after we know what happened, it's easy to come up with an explanation of why it happened, even if we did not predict it. Another reason why hindsight is so good is that *we may misremember our past judgment to fit our current views*. This is **hindsight bias**, the tendency to misremember our previous views to fit our current knowledge or beliefs. In practice, this means we regard past events as being more predictable than they really were. People may wrongly believe that they *knew* the event was going to happen. "I knew it all along!" In one study, people were asked to rate the probability of a political outcome beforehand. When surveyed again after that outcome had actually happened, about 75% of them remembered giving a higher probability than they actually had (Fischhoff & Beyth, 1975). What is worrisome about hindsight bias is that it is so rewarding to our self-image. If people believe their predictions were correct, when in fact they were not, then they may have an exaggerated trust in their judgment.

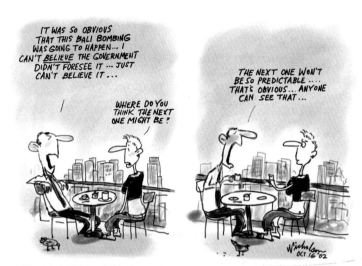

By the way, hindsight bias is also a common problem for students in an introductory psychology class who claim, "It's all stuff everybody knows." Yet the students may find the tests challenging, suggesting that the material is not quite as obvious as they had thought (see Section 1.3). But don't feel bad; we are all victims of hindsight bias. In one classic example, Paul Lazarsfeld (1949), in reviewing a major study of American soldiers during World War II, offered a list of findings and the obvious explanation for each, some of which I paraphrase below:

- Better-educated men were more traumatized by wartime events because less-educated men had been street-toughened.
- Soldiers from rural areas were in better spirits than men from city backgrounds because they were more used to hardships.
- Men from the South tolerated the South Pacific climate better than northern men because they were more accustomed to hot weather.
- Southern African Americans preferred white officers from the South over those from the North because the Southern officers knew how to get along with African Americans.
- Men were more eager to return to the States before the enemy surrendered than afterward because naturally they wanted to avoid injury or death.

For each of those statements, the explanation, that string of words following *because*, sounds perfectly reasonable, even obvious. Yet each of the five statements is the *exact opposite* of what the study found, so the "obvious" explanations cannot be true. The less-educated men were *more* traumatized, men from rural areas were *less* cheerful, men from the *North* tolerated tropical weather better, Southern African American privates preferred officers from the *North*, and men were more eager to return home *after* the enemy surrendered.

More recently, when a book claimed that women had been found to talk more than men, uttering 20,000 words per day versus 7,000 (Brizendine, 2006), it was widely reported on television and radio, in newspapers and magazines.

Monty Hall problem An example of an error in decision making in which someone fails to properly estimate the probability of an outcome after being given additional information.

hindsight bias The tendency to misremember our previous views to fit our current knowledge or beliefs.

Many of the reports made the point that this was hardly news—"Here's a news flash. Women talk more than men. Duh." But it later turned out that the book's author was citing a self-help guru who had simply "guestimated" those numbers. When scientists directly *tested* the idea, by outfitting hundreds of U.S. college students with devices that recorded their daily utterances, they found no sex difference at all in the number of words said. Both sexes uttered about 16,000 words per day. In fact, the top three talkers in the study were all men (Mehl et al., 2007)! We'll see more examples of people misremembering their previous beliefs in The Cutting Edge at the end of this chapter.

Let's return to those warnings about terrorist attacks that began this chapter. In hindsight, the warnings may seem crystal clear to you in light of the attack that followed. But had you been the person reading that memo, in a world in which the 9/11 attacks had not yet happened, you might have dismissed them as too vague or unlikely to act on.

Closely related to hindsight bias is **confirmation bias**, the tendency for people to detect and remember information that confirms their preconceptions. For instance, people who disapproved of President Bush before the 9/11 attacks felt their judgment was confirmed when they learned of the prior warnings, and criticized Bush for not acting. For people who had long approved of Bush, such criticism for not acting on what were, in their eyes, only vague warnings confirmed their belief that he was often treated unfairly. It's important to realize that the person succumbing to confirmation bias is unaware that he is recalling examples that confirm his preconceptions and ignoring or forgetting exceptions. For example, many emergency room physicians and nurses are convinced that their facility is especially busy around a full moon (Vance, 1995), but statistics show there is no difference in emergency room activity (or in traffic accidents, stabbings, gunshot wounds, psychiatric admissions, etc.) around the full moon in the United States (Kelly et al., 1996; McLay et al., 2006), Canada (Belleville et al., 2013), or Iran (Zargar et al., 2004) (**Figure 10.26**). Why do the professionals working in the emergency room think there's a peak in admissions around the full moon? Probably because when an especially hectic shift falls within a day or two of a full moon, they note and remember that evening. No one remembers a full moon when nothing much happens. Likewise, there is no peak in suicides or calls to crisis centers around the full moon (Gutiérrez-García & Tusell, 1997) or around the Christmas holidays. In fact, suicides peak in the spring, as we'll discuss in Chapter 16 (see Box 16.1). Yet whenever an instance of suicide occurs around the holidays, our confirmation bias attributes it to the holiday, "explaining" the suicide and thereby confirming our bias.

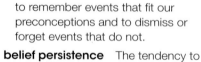

confirmation bias A tendency to remember events that fit our preconceptions and to dismiss or forget events that do not.

belief persistence The tendency to hold on to a belief, even in the face of contradictory evidence.

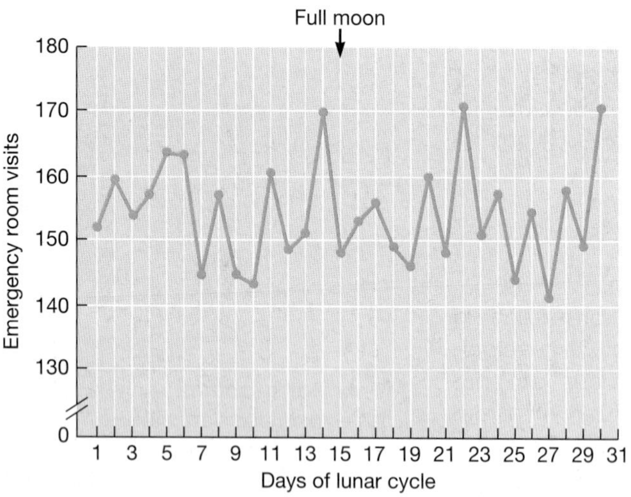

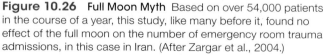

Figure 10.26 Full Moon Myth Based on over 54,000 patients in the course of a year, this study, like many before it, found no effect of the full moon on the number of emergency room trauma admissions, in this case in Iran. (After Zargar et al., 2004.)

Together, hindsight bias and confirmation bias feed **belief persistence**, the tendency to hold on to a belief, even in the face of contradictory evidence. It seems to me that the explosion of political television shows and Internet sites has fueled belief persistence and polarized American politics more than ever before. It's not just that there are so many options for political commentary, but that so many of those options consistently present only one type of view. That means we can find an outlet that supports whatever view we already have. One study found that people who already supported presidential candidate Barack Obama tended to buy books that favored him, while people opposed to Obama purchased books that were critical (Krebs, 2000). A laboratory study found that people spend more time reading political essays that agree with their own views (Knobloch-Westerwick & Meng, 2009). Confirmation bias to maintain belief persistence is so powerful that the very same TV show can support widely divergent views. One study found that conservatives and liberals who watch *The Colbert Report* find it equally funny. But while liberals see the show as satire, showing the absurdity of conservative views, the conservatives regard Colbert quite differently. They think he is only pretending to be joking, and that he genuinely means what he says (LaMarre et al., 2009).

framing effect A cognitive bias that occurs when the way information is presented makes a significant difference in what people will decide.

We hate loss more than we love gain

Sometimes we can affect the sorts of decisions people will make simply by changing how we present the problem. This is sometimes called the **framing effect**, when the way information is presented makes a significant difference in what people will decide. In a famous example, two groups of people were asked to pretend they worked for the Centers for Disease Control and Prevention (CDC) and to make a choice between two programs to combat the "Mojave flu" that had reached a town of 600 people (Tversky & Kahneman, 1981) (**Figure 10.27**). All 600 people in the town were expected to die if you did nothing. The program options were framed as follows:

For Group 1:

- Program A: 200 people in the town will be saved.
- Program B: There is a 33% probability that 600 people will be saved, and a 67% probability that no people will be saved.

For Group 2:

- Program C: 400 people in the town will die.
- Program D: There is a 33% probability that nobody will die, and a 67% probability that 600 people will die.

Which program would you choose? Seventy percent of participants in Group 1 preferred Program A. But in Group 2, over 80% of participants chose Program D, even though it was *exactly equivalent to Program B, which participants in Group 1 did not prefer.* Just by being framed differently, this option went from appearing lousy to appearing preferable. What's different about the framing? The first pair of choices is framed in terms of positive results—saving people. The second pair of choices is framed in terms of negative results—people dying. One theory is that we are so reluctant to lose, that when the question is framed around deaths, we are willing to take a risk to avoid any deaths. But when the question is framed around survivors, we aren't willing to take a risk to save more.

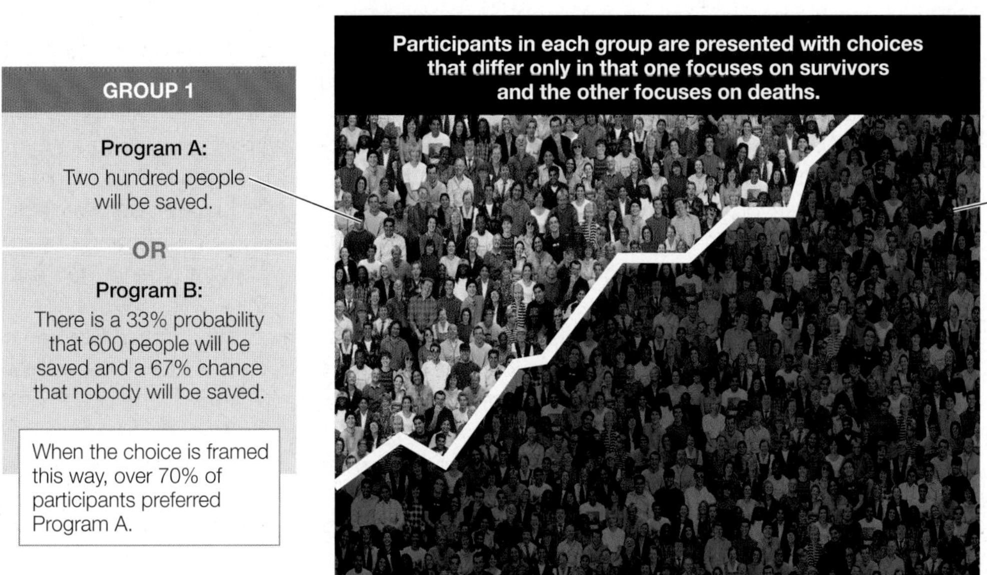

GROUP 1
Program A:
Two hundred people will be saved.
OR
Program B:
There is a 33% probability that 600 people will be saved and a 67% chance that nobody will be saved.
When the choice is framed this way, over 70% of participants preferred Program A.
Participants in each group are presented with choices that differ only in that one focuses on survivors and the other focuses on deaths.
GROUP 2
Program C:
Four hundred people will die.
OR
Program D:
There is a 33% probability that nobody will die, and a 67% chance that 600 people will die.
When the choice is framed this way, nearly 80% of participants chose Program D, even though it is exactly equivalent to Program B, which most people rejected.

Figure 10.27 The Framing Effect on Decision Making In this study, two groups of people were asked to choose between two alternative programs to combat the "Mojave flu." (After Tversky & Kahneman, 1981.)

Gambler's Fallacy If the ball fell in red slots twice in a row, is it more likely to fall in a black slot next?

The framing effect also influences how people make financial decisions, where once again we dislike losses more than we like gain. This basic finding contradicts many economists' assumption that people make rational decisions about money, specifically that they make choices to maximize gain and minimize loss. Money is money; a rational person would be just as concerned about how much money he gains as how much money he loses. But the following example shows that people do not always "do the math." When asked whether they would prefer:

A: a sure gain of $240
or
B: a 25% chance to gain $1,000 and a 75% chance to gain nothing,

most people choose A, the sure thing. Yet when asked to choose between the following:

C: a sure loss of $750
or
D: a 75% chance to lose $1,000 and a 25% chance of losing nothing,

most people choose option D even though it is *exactly equivalent to B*, which most people rejected. Why?

It appears that people really hate to lose money. They hate losing money far more than they enjoy gaining money. In other words, humans tend to be **loss-averse**: we don't like to risk losing, whether it's losing money or losing other people's lives. In general, a choice presented within a positive frame (lives saved, money gained) is more likely to be taken than one presented within a negative frame (deaths, money lost) because we are loss-averse. Thus gambling enterprises, like casinos and lotteries, emphasize the large winnings that *may* result (for a very few people), not the slow, certain loss of money that the vast majority of players experience.

The gambling industry cruelly takes advantage of people's tendency to be loss-averse. People really hate to write off their losses. In fact, the more money a gambler has lost, the more eager he is to regain his money by playing some more. Every gambling establishment is, unfortunately, carefully constructed to stack the odds against the gambler's winning, and those odds are the same no matter how much money the gambler has lost already. A kind of myth gamblers live by, called the **gambler's fallacy**, is the belief that the outcome of random events up to a given point will affect the probability of future random events. Examples of the gambler's fallacy are thinking that if a coin has come up heads three times in a row, it is more likely to come up tails on the next flip, and that having received bad cards in the last four poker hands, you're likely to draw a good hand in the next. Don't get caught thinking, If I've lost this much, surely I'll start winning soon!

Daniel Kahneman (2011) has speculated that loss-aversion may have an evolutionary origin—in prehistoric times, losing resources, like a store of food, could cost you your life. Likewise, if you love gaining too much, you might behave recklessly to get some piece of food, and that can kill you too. So our minds seem to favor fundamentally conservative thinking—hold on to what you've got, and don't risk too much to get more.

loss averse Characteristic of being very reluctant to do anything that might lead to loss.

gambler's fallacy The belief that the outcome of random events up to this point will affect the probability of future random events.

The framing effect can affect our memory as well as our judgment. Students were shown film clips of traffic accidents and then asked a question: "About how fast were the cars going when they ________ into each other?" The blank was filled in with different words for different groups of participants. Some were asked how fast the cars were going when they *smashed* into each other, while for other students the word used was *collided* or *hit* or *contacted*. The more active the verb used, the higher the students' estimate of the speed (Loftus &

Palmer, 1974). Even more impressive is what happened when the students were contacted a week later and asked whether they saw any broken glass in the film. In fact, there was no broken glass, but students who had heard the verb *smashed* were twice as likely to remember seeing broken glass as students who had heard the verb *hit*. That seemingly small difference, the choice of which verb was used when framing the original question, shaped the participants' judgment and affected their memory of the film.

Tower of Hanoi A problem in which you transfer a series of different-sized disks from one spindle to another following a specific set of rules.

initial state The situation at the beginning of a problem.

goal state The desired outcome of a problem.

constraints Rules that govern how you can get from the initial state to the goal state in a problem.

algorithm A specific set of steps that will always solve a particular problem.

Problem solving involves algorithms, heuristics, and representations

Most cognitive psychologists who study problem solving favor problems that can be solved only by a thoughtful, systematic approach, because it's easier to manipulate such problems to see how they affect people's thinking.

A famous example is the **Tower of Hanoi**, where you try to transfer a series of different-sized disks from one spindle to another following a specific set of rules (**Figure 10.28**). The Tower of Hanoi shares several characteristics of all problem solving:

- An **initial state** (here, all the disks stacked on one spindle)
- A **goal state** (all the disks stacked on the final spindle)
- **Constraints**, or rules, about how you can get from the initial state to the goal state

The first time you encounter the Tower of Hanoi problem, it looks impossible. The important insight is that you must sometimes work "backward," temporarily returning a disk to the original spindle (see Figure 10.28). Once you understand this can happen, it is possible to transfer any number of disks from one spindle to another following these rules. This solution is an example of an **algorithm**, a specific set of steps that can be followed that will always solve a particular problem. In the kitchen, correctly following the algorithm (that is, the "recipe") for a cake will always produce a cake. In math, correctly following the steps in long division will always give you an answer. Google uses a closely guarded algorithm to determine which websites are more likely to provide what you want from a search. The algorithm for the Tower of Hanoi problem is easier to discover on your own or to watch than to describe with words. The algorithm can be described by mathematicians, who find that the number of moves required to solve the puzzle is $2^n - 1$, where n is the number of disks. This means that 8 disks would require $2^8 - 1 = 255$ moves, while 16 disks would require 65,535 moves. Someone who started a 64-disk version at the start of the universe, moving 1 disk per second and using that same algorithm, would be 3% done by now. It would be awfully tempting to just pick up the whole stack and move it.

Some algorithms may be quite elaborate, requiring many steps and careful monitoring of the outcome, which is perfect for computers because they can complete many steps every second and can securely store information at each point. But for humans such an algorithm may be too complex to remember or to reliably follow. What's more, outside of computer programs crunching numbers,

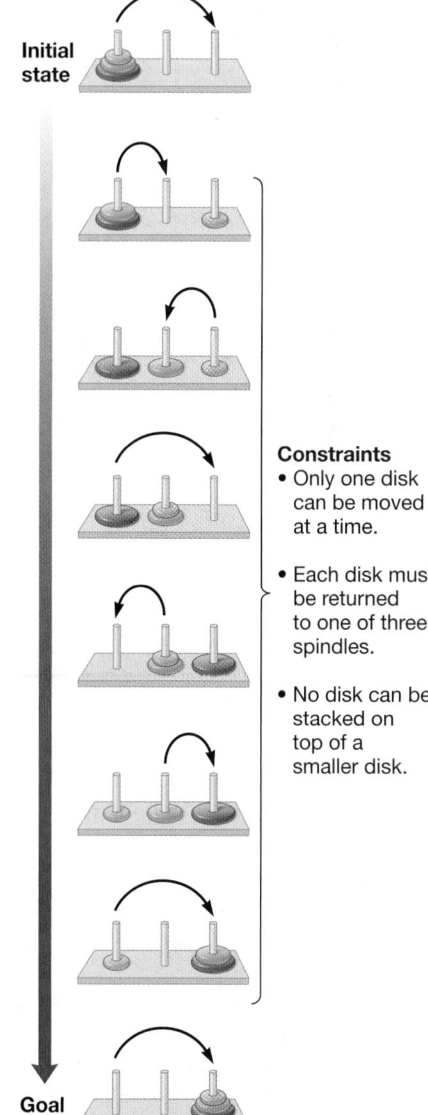

Initial state
Constraints
• Only one disk can be moved at a time.
• Each disk must be returned to one of three spindles.
• No disk can be stacked on top of a smaller disk.
Goal

Figure 10.28 **The Tower of Hanoi** The task is to transfer all the disks from the first spindle to the third spindle, moving one disk at a time and never stacking a larger disk on top of a smaller one. The puzzle can be solved by sometimes going backward—returning a disk to the original spindle in order to maneuver. The same algorithm will work to transfer any number of disks from one spindle to another. However, the number of moves required to transfer the disks grows exponentially with an increasing number of disks.

in many everyday situations we don't know enough to be sure that an algorithm will actually accomplish a task. In such cases we may rely on a **heuristic**, a relatively easy-to-follow set of rules that often, but not always, solves the problem. We more commonly refer to a heuristic as "an educated guess," or a "rule of thumb," a phrase that stems from carpenters' use of the width of their thumb as an approximation for 1 inch.

Strategies may help or impede problem solving

One heuristic on which we often rely is the **availability heuristic**, with which we judge the frequency or likelihood of an event based on how readily an example can be brought to mind (Tversky & Kahneman, 1974). Basically, this means that if you can think of it, it must be common or important. In many cases, the availability heuristic works. If you don't recall ever having seen a white squirrel, they're probably pretty rare. If you can think of lots of people you know named David but no one named Igor, then David is probably the more common name in the country where you live.

The availability heuristic can sometimes mislead us and lead to bias. Consider the impact of vivid stories of shark attacks that keep people from enjoying the ocean. Many people mistakenly assume you are more likely to be killed by a shark than by falling airplane debris, but in fact Americans are 30 times more likely to die of fallen airplane debris than shark attack (Plous, 1993). We overestimate the probability of shark attack because the idea is so disturbing, and because it has been repeatedly made *available* to our thinking. (Apparently more people have seen the movie *Jaws* than the movie *Donnie Darko*.) Likewise, lurid stories about gruesome crimes and accidents are, by their very nature, memorable. If you ask people whether more Americans die from (A) murder and car accidents or (B) diabetes and stomach cancer, most guess A. However, twice as many Americans die of diabetes and stomach cancer as die from car accidents and murder. Perhaps it is because crime comes so readily to mind that most Americans believe crime is on the rise when in fact crime rates in the United States, for both violent crimes and property crimes, have declined every year for the past 20 years (Federal Bureau of Investigation, 2009). In other words, our use of the availability heuristic, fed by media with a financial incentive to get our attention, may cause us to overestimate crime rates. Likewise, gruesome photographs of airplane crashes may be on the minds of people buying life insurance before stepping on a plane.

For some problems, especially those for which there is only one successful outcome, the strategy of **working backward**, starting with the desired end result and reversing the steps needed to get there, can be helpful. An everyday example would be when you want to drive to some destination that you know is on a one-way street. Knowing which direction you must be driving on the street to get to that address, you may then work out what route you need to take to be going the proper direction on that street. An entire class of traditional math problems is usually easier to solve by working backward. For example, Jenny had three times more Mardi Gras necklaces than Mary. Then Jenny threw four into the crowd, so she has five left. How many necklaces does Mary have? Starting at the end, with Jenny's five remaining necklaces, then she must have had 5 + 4 = 9 before. If that's three times what Mary has, then Mary must have three necklaces. Similarly, when teaching a child how to complete a complicated set of instructions, like tying shoelaces, it might help to work backward, doing the first few steps for them so they can practice that final step of tying the loops together. Then you can teach them the steps before that, and so on, a case of identifying subgoals.

heuristic A relatively easy-to-follow set of rules that often, but not always, solves the problem.

availability heuristic The tendency to rely on how readily an event comes to mind in judging its likelihood in the future.

working backward The problem-solving strategy of starting with the desired end result and reversing the steps needed to get there.

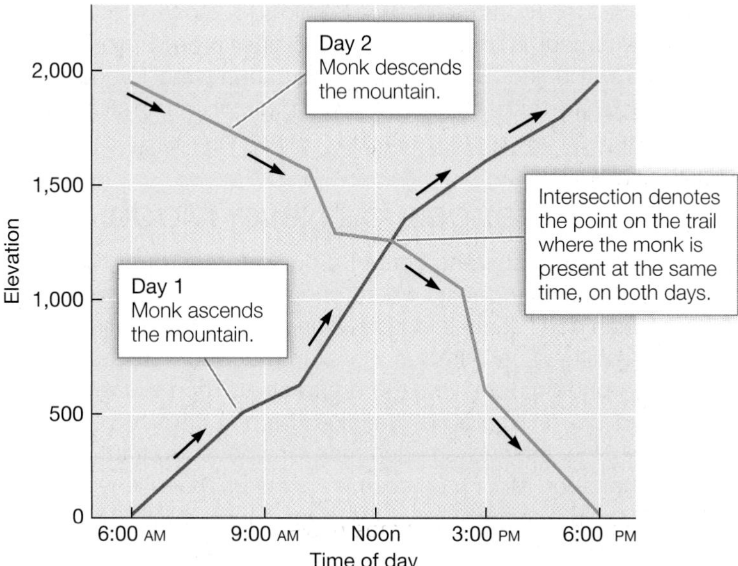

Figure 10.29 The Mountain-Climbing Monk Seen graphically, it is obvious that there must be some point along the mountain trail where the monk is present at exactly the same time on both days. Another way to see that this must be true is to imagine two monks, one walking from base to peak, the other from peak to base. At some point in the path, they will be present at the same time, no matter how randomly they stop or vary their speed.

Sometimes the easiest way to solve a problem is to find a good way to represent it. We saw an example of that strategy in the Monty Hall problem, where representing the three possible outcomes visually, as in Figure 10.25, lets you see why your odds are better if you swap doors. Another famous example of a problem that seems especially thorny until you find a way to represent it is the mountain-climbing monk. In this problem, a monk leaves at sunrise one morning to walk a narrow, winding trail to the top of a mountain, arriving just at sunset. He spends the night in the temple on the mountaintop, leaving at the next sunrise to take the same trail down again, arriving at sunset. Both climbing and descending, he makes frequent, random stops and moves at a randomly variable speed. The question: Is there any point along the trail where the monk is present at the exact same time of day on both days? It's not easy to be sure of the answer unless you graphically represent the problem as in **Figure 10.29**. Then you see that, no matter how many random stops or changes in speed the monk makes, there must be some spot along the path where he is present at the exact same time both days.

insight The sudden understanding of a problem that leads to solution without resorting to trial and error.

In Section 8.3 we discussed **insight**, the sudden understanding of a problem that leads to solution without having to resort to trial and error. There's also an insightful way to solve the mountain-climbing monk problem. Imagine there are *two* monks, one walking from the top down, the other from the base up on the *same* day. The two monks would *have* to meet along the narrow path at some time during the day.

Of course, this insightful way to solve the monk problem is also brought about by representing the situation in such a way that the solution, which may have seemed elusive before, now seems obvious. Perhaps in terms of problem solving in everyday life, this is the most important advice we can follow: try to find as many different ways as possible to look at the problem, because there may be a perspective from which the solution is obvious. Talk to people you trust and

choice blindness The tendency of people not to notice when they have made a choice between two things and are subsequently told they had made the opposite choice.

get their perspective. Indeed, as we'll see in Section 16.2, one important aspect of psychological treatment is for the therapist to offer a new, problem-solving perspective on life's troubles. Sometimes an individual who is not personally involved in the difficulty, whether it's tense social interactions, irrational fears, or unexplained moods, can see more clearly how to resolve them.

The Cutting Edge

Defending Preferences You Never Made

Another set of findings that casts doubt on our judgment and self-awareness concerns **choice blindness**, where people make a choice between two stimuli and then don't seem to notice when researchers assert that they had actually chosen the *other* stimulus. For example, men were asked which of two women in photographs was more attractive. Then the researchers secretly switched the photographs, handing the non-chosen photograph back to the men. Now they asked each man why he found that face more attractive than the other. Most men seemed unaware that this was *not* the photograph they had chosen (hence the term *choice blindness*). What's more, having accepted that this was the face they'd chosen, the men gave persuasive reasons why they preferred that one (Johansson et al., 2005). This is reminiscent of hindsight bias, because the men defended a choice they *thought* they made earlier.

The same researchers later asked grocery shoppers which of two different types of jam they preferred (**Figure 10.30**). Then they gave each shopper another sample of the jam, using trickery so that the shoppers *thought* this was the jam they had preferred, when in fact it was the other jam. Again, most people seemed blind to their own choice, accepting this non-preferred taste as the one they had chosen. And again they gave plausible reasons why they liked that taste more (Hall et al., 2010). You might think maybe there's not much difference between jams anyway. But in some cases, the jams were really different—like cinnamon-apple versus bitter grapefruit.

Political views appear to be subject to choice blindness too. Swedish voters were asked to agree or disagree with political statements like "Gasoline taxes should be increased" or "The legal age for criminal responsibility should be lowered." After an interruption, researchers used sleight of hand to make it look like the participant had made the *opposite* choice. Once again, most people displayed choice blindness—they didn't seem to

Figure 10.30 **Choice Blindness** "I chose this bitter grapefruit jam because it has a bright taste." But in fact, the shopper had said she preferred the cinnamon-apple.

notice that this was not the choice they'd made (Hall et al., 2013). And once again they offered compelling reasons why they had taken this position (when in fact they had not). On the one hand, this finding suggests that people are open to changing their minds, since voters could argue convincingly in favor of opinions that were the opposite of their own. But from another point of view, how can our political views reflect our careful consideration of all the available evidence if we don't even notice when we've swapped sides?

10.3 SUMMARY

- The only certain method of preventing particular pieces of information from adding bias to human *judgment* is to withhold that information, as when experts "blindly" assess the qualities of a violin or the value of real estate. Even irrelevant information can bias judgment, as the *anchoring effect* shows—initial exposure to a number chosen at random will nevertheless affect subsequent judgments about quantity or value.
- Humans are particularly poor at revising judgments about the probability of an outcome in the face of new information, as the *Monty Hall problem* demonstrates. *Hindsight bias* is the tendency to misremember the views we had before an event was revealed. *Confirmation bias*, the tendency to detect and remember information that confirms our preconceptions while ignoring or forgetting contradictory information, leads to *belief persistence*. In *choice blindness*, people can defend a preference that is the opposite of what they had declared earlier.
- Because humans tend to be *loss-averse*, our judgment is easily affected by *framing effects*—we may come to opposite decisions about the very same alternatives based on how they are presented. When alternative outcomes are presented as negative events, we are risk-averse, but when the alternatives are presented as positive events, we are more likely to take risks. Our reluctance to write off losses, plus the *gambler's fallacy* regarding random events, can lead people to economic ruin.
- Some problems can be solved by *algorithms*, specific steps that lead to a solution. The algorithm for the *Tower of Hanoi* problem, for example, can be described in terms of an *initial state* and a *goal state* and *constraints* or rules about how to get from one to the other.
- A *heuristic* is a relatively easy set of rules that can often be helpful in problem solving. The *availability heuristic*, for example, suggests that the frequency of an event can be predicted by how readily we can think of an example. The availability heuristic, however, can bias judgment because some especially vivid events may come readily to mind, even if they are in fact very rare.
- Some problems are better solved by *working backward*, starting with the goal state and working out the steps that must precede that. In other cases, as is illustrated by the puzzle of the mountain-climbing monk, a solution may become more obvious if the problem is laid out in a different way, which may lead to an *insight*.

REVIEW QUESTIONS

1. Give an example of how the anchoring effect can bias judgment.
2. Suggest a way hindsight bias and confirmation bias could lead to belief persistence.
3. What are some examples of how humans tend to be loss-averse?
4. What are the various approaches that can help in solving problems?

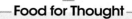

Food for Thought

Americans appear to be as fearful of violent crime (murder and rape) as ever, despite a yearly decline in crime rates. What is the role of the major media in this disconnect between the frequency of crime and the perception of crime risk? How might biases in human judgment keep Americans fearful?

10

Language and Cognition

Unheeded Warnings

Several months before the 9/11 attacks on the World Trade Center, the Central Intelligence Agency received information that Al-Qaeda leader Osama bin Ladin was planning a major attack on the United States. Alarmed by the many different sources that indicated an imminent attack, the director of the CIA requested an emergency meeting with the secretary of state on July 10, 2001 to discuss the threat. Less than a month later, President George W. Bush's daily briefing included a report headlined "Bin Laden Determined To Strike in U.S.," warning that bin Ladin was threatening to "follow the example of World Trade Center bomber Ramzi Yousef and 'bring the fighting to America'" in retaliation for U.S. attacks on Al-Qaeda bases in Afghanistan. The memo relayed the claim of one source "that Bin Ladin wanted to hijack a U.S. aircraft." Apparently no additional security steps were initiated in response to these warnings. Indeed, the next month, when bin Ladin's followers flew two hijacked airplanes into the World Trade Center towers, neither the secretary of state nor the president recalled having received any warnings of the attack. When the public learned in 2006 that warnings had in fact been issued, the administration was widely criticized for having failed to act to avert the attack.

But were the criticisms fair? Those warnings about bin Ladin represented a tiny minority of the flood of information that enters the White House daily. Should the administration have known what was coming? The larger question is, just how good are we at sifting through information, recognizing the important nuggets of information, and making judgments about what is or is not likely in the future? As we'll learn in this chapter, we humans are not very good at a task such as this, and in fact, we are prone to make errors of several types, including when we look back at our own past decisions.

Think Like a Psychologist:

Principles in Action

Whenever we encounter any interesting behavior we should consider the four principles. Here are some ways that the four principles relate to our opening story about 9/11.

MACHINE

The mind is a product of a physical machine, the brain.

Like any other machine, there are physical limitations to what the brain can accomplish, so attention is always limited. In the case of the memo before the 9/11 attacks, there was nothing to draw attention to this particular piece of intelligence, and so it was forgotten.

UNCONSCIOUS

We are consciously aware of only a small part of our mental activity.

Afterward, White House staff had no recollection of the memo. Critics of the White House had no awareness of how hindsight bias made the memo appear more prominent and specific than it really was.

SOCIAL

We constantly modify our behavior, beliefs, and attitudes according to what we perceive about the people around us.

Because of confirmation bias, people who disapproved of President Bush before the 9/11 attacks felt the memo confirmed their judgment, while those who approved of Bush believed the critics were, once again, treating him unfairly.

EXPERIENCE

Our experiences physically alter the structure and function of the brain.

When the memo was first circulated, everyone reading it had grown up in a United States that had been relatively immune to terrorist attacks that were common in other parts of the world. Their experience to that point meant that the abstract warnings in the memo failed to get their attention.

KEY TERMS

algorithm, 443
anchoring effect, 437
aphasia, 411
associative phase, 426
attention, 429
attentional blink, 433
attentional spotlight, 430
autonomous phase, 426
availability heuristic, 444
babble, 404
belief persistence, 440
bilingualism, 409
Broca's aphasia, 412
Broca's area, 412
categorization, 420
change blindness, 432
choice blindness, 446
cocktail party effect, 430
cognitive phase, 425
cognitive psychology, 419
concept, 420
confirmation bias, 440
constraints, 443
decision making, 435
deep structure, 398
dyslexia, 410
flow, 429
framing effect, 441
gambler's fallacy, 442
generative, 398
goal state, 443
habituate, 406
heuristic, 444
hindsight bias, 439
inattentional blindness, 431
initial state, 443
insight, 445
judgment, 435
lateralization, 414
linguistic relativism, 416
linguists, 398
loss-averse, 442
mental imagery, 423
Monty Hall problem, 439
morphemes, 398
motherese, 407
phonemes, 398
prototype, 420
reaction time, 421
semantics, 398
sensitive period, 409
skill, 425
subliminal perception, 429
surface structure, 398
syntax, 398
Tan, 411
telegraphic speech, 404
Tower of Hanoi, 443
Wada test, 412
Wernicke's aphasia, 412
Wernicke's area, 412
Williams syndrome, 408
working backward, 444

QUIZ YOURSELF

1. At what age do humans begin to lose the ability to distinguish between phonemes to which they haven't been exposed?
   a. At about 6–8 months of age
   b. At about 6 years of age
   c. At puberty
   d. They never lose this ability
2. Which of the following is not a characteristic of the practice sessions of people who become truly outstanding musicians, athletes, and chess players?
   a. Constantly increasing challenges
   b. Significant material rewards
   c. Concern for technique
   d. Rapid, high quality feedback
3. The best example of an abstract idea or mental representation of an object or event that fits in a particular collection is called a
   a. prototype.
   b. concept.
   c. category.
   d. heuristic.
4. Which of the following statements is true in the Monty Hall problem?
   a. It makes no difference if you stay or switch, since your chance of being correct is the same in either case.
   b. You should stay with your original choice because your first choice is generally correct.
   c. It is an example of choice blindness that makes you chose the correct door.
   d. You should switch because you are twice as likely to win if you do.
5. If the way information is presented makes a significant difference in people's decisions, it is termed the
   a. hindsight bias.
   b. anchoring effect.
   c. framing effect.
   d. confirmation bias.
6. In each language, there is a set of speech sounds or ________. These are assembled into simple units of meaning called ________. One or more of these simple units make up a word.
7. If brain injury or disease causes an impairment of language after it was acquired, it is a condition known as ________. The most common cause of this condition is ________.
8. The hypothesis that the language we speak influences the way we think is ________.
9. ________ is the study of internal mental processes, specifically how we acquire and process information to gain knowledge.
10. The two different types of mistakes we can make in judgments are ________ and ________.

1. a; 2. b; 3. a; 4. d; 5. c; 6. phonemes, morphemes; 7. aphasia, stroke; 8. linguistic relativism; 9. Cognitive psychology; 10. miss, false alarm

CAPSTONES
Undergraduate Research
Lose a turn
Option B
Option A
WRITING
OPPORTUNITIES
Global Studies
Service Learning
ASSESSMENT
Collaborative Projects
Inquiry
First-Year Programs
High School
High School
High School
CRITICAL THINKING
Math & Science
HIGH SCHOOL GRADUATION
COLLEGE ORIENTATION

11 Intelligence

The Admirable Crichton

When the play *Peter Pan* first opened in London in 1904, audiences were still packing the theater to see playwright J. M. Barrie's hit from two years before, *The Admirable Crichton*. Crichton, butler to the English Lord Loam, sees to the needs of his social superiors with total submission. In return for a paltry salary and a place to live, Crichton works long hours so that the aristocratic family can eat fabulous meals and while away their hours in frivolous conversation and trivial pursuits. The butler believes that the British class system of the day, where most people toil away in poverty so that a select few can lead rich lives of leisure, is a "natural outcome of a civilized society" (Barrie, 1902).

Then Crichton is required to accompany his employers on a sea voyage and they are all shipwrecked on a tropical isle. Unlike the castaways on TV's *Lost*, these refugees face dire problems, such as finding shelter and getting enough food to survive. Crichton is the only person among them who has enough practical skills to be of any use. Soon he becomes the leader, organizing and teaching the others what they must do. For one thing, everyone needs to work, a great shock to the aristocrats, who threaten to go off and leave him alone. But only Crichton has enough knowledge and skill to produce a pot of soup. The lord's family, drawn irresistibly to the aroma, comes crawling back to beg for a portion.

After a few years of Crichton's leadership, the island is civilized through a program of farming and building where everyone works hard except the former butler. Crichton, now the highly respected "Governor," continues making decisions and giving orders but spends much of his time in leisure pursuits. Lord Loam's daughter, Lady Mary, falls deeply in love with Crichton. They are on the verge of marriage—when a ship rescues them all.

Such a marriage is unthinkable back in England, where Crichton is again the humble, toiling butler and the aristocrats resume their carefree days. Barrie considered a different ending, where Lady Mary and Crichton marry after the rescue, but he decided that audiences of the day "wouldn't stand it."

Chapter Preview

intelligence The ability to acquire, retain, and apply knowledge.

The Admiral Crichton is a comedy, but it raises intriguing questions about intelligence. In aristocratic England, people with nothing to do but talk needed to be witty if they were to be admired, and practical skills like farming or fighting were useless. On the island, verbal skills counted for nothing, and practical skills were not just admirable but critical for survival. The play illustrates that what counts for outstanding intelligence in one context may be useless in another.

In this chapter on intelligence we must wrestle with the very definition of the term. So for now, let us define **intelligence** as the ability to acquire, retain, and apply knowledge, with the understanding that there are many different spheres of knowledge. But do keep in mind that there is no universally accepted definition of intelligence (Jensen, 1999). Indeed, when 24 different scientists who study intelligence were asked to define the word *intelligence*, all definitions varied (Neisser et al., 1996).

Efforts to develop intelligence tests began in the early twentieth century, primarily to help people decide which classrooms to assign children to and which jobs to assign to adults. How to determine whether such tests actually measure intelligence as advertised is one of the questions we pursue in this chapter. We'll ponder, too, whether there is more than one kind of intelligence, and whether intelligence is fixed at birth or subject to improvement.

The chapter's final section will take up the question of genetic influences on intelligence (which are clearly present) and the controversial question of whether genetic influences on intelligence are responsible for racial differences in average scores on intelligence tests. We'll find that intelligence is not fixed at birth and that many environmental factors influence intelligence scores.

11.1 History and Development of Intelligence Tests

Things to Learn

- History of intelligence tests
- Meaning of intelligence quotient (IQ)
- Percentile scores
- Three kinds of reliability in tests
- Three kinds of validity of IQ tests
- "Predictions" from IQ scores

The first intelligence tests were designed over a hundred years ago, and were intended to decide which children should be sent to the most challenging and least challenging schools. The children's financial status was intended to be irrelevant, but those early tests almost certainly ended up sorting children by social class and family income. In general, children from poor families were assigned to the poor schools.

Soon similar tests were adopted to sort large numbers of men, specifically new soldiers, into those who should lead and those who should follow. Again, verbal abilities, which tended to be greater in men from affluent families, were used to select leaders. As newer intelligence tests evolved, psychologists developed new statistical tools. From the very beginning, the psychologists were concerned about the quality of intelligence tests, which will bring us to the questions of the *reliability* and *validity* of such tests. We'll close this section by asking how well intelligence tests predict a person's future accomplishments.

Intelligence tests were first created to make a more ordered society

The Englishman Sir Francis Galton (1822–1911), a distant cousin of Charles Darwin, coined the phrase "nature versus nurture" to convey the question of whether it is genes or upbringing that has the most effect on our minds. Galton was convinced that intelligence was heritable (see Chapter 4; we'll also discuss heritability in more detail later in this chapter). He thought governments should offer financial incentives to get intelligent people to marry one another and have children (Galton, 1869). But Galton never came up with a way to objectively measure intelligence.

In 1904 the French government asked psychologist Alfred Binet (1857–1911) to find a way to determine which schoolchildren were mentally disabled, in order to send them to alternative schools to provide them with additional help that they might need (**Figure 11.1**). Binet recruited Theodore Simon to help him develop the **Binet-Simon scale**, an intelligence test consisting of 30 different tasks of increasing difficulty (Binet, 1905/1916). These tasks varied from easy ones like shaking hands, to repeating a series of three numbers, to reproducing a drawing from memory. More difficult tasks asked the child to define abstract terms; for example, "What is the difference between esteem and affection?" The idea was that as children grow older, they should be able to perform more of the tasks until, like any reasonably intelligent adult, they can complete them all (**Figure 11.2**). Binet readily acknowledged the limitations of the scale. It was only intended as a rough indication of which children might be mentally disabled, rather than as a way to draw distinctions among mentally normal children. In fact, Binet was skeptical of Galton's belief in hereditary influences on intelligence. He emphasized instead that education can greatly improve mental ability (Binet, 1909/1984).

Figure 11.1 Alfred Binet Testing a Student The first intelligence tests were used to determine which French schoolchildren would need additional help to get a good education.

The Binet–Simon scale was meant to reveal whether a child's **mental age**, the intellectual abilities commonly found in children of a particular age, matched his or her actual (*chronological*) age. In other words, can this 8-year-old boy perform all the tasks that most other 8-year-olds can do, but not the tasks that most 9-year-olds can do? If so, then his mental age is 8, matching his chronological age. If he can also do harder tasks, such as those that most 10-year-olds can do, then his mental age is greater than his actual age. If he can only do those tasks that 6-year-olds can do, but not the ones that 7- or 8-year-olds can do, then his mental development has fallen behind his chronological age.

In 1916, American psychologist Lewis Terman of Stanford University translated and revised the Binet–Simon scale for American children to produce what became known as the **Stanford-Binet test**. Soon after, when the United

Binet-Simon scale An intelligence test developed by Binet and Simon for children that consists of 30 different tasks of increasing difficulty.

mental age The intellectual abilities commonly found in children of a particular age.

Stanford-Binet test An intelligence test for American children developed by Terman of Stanford University, based on the Binet–Simon scale.

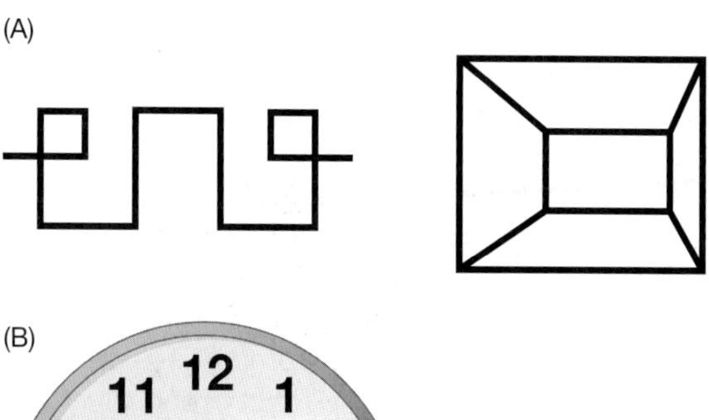

Figure 11.2 Sample Items from the Binet-Simon Scale (A) Task #18 in the scale of 30 increasingly difficult tasks involved drawing a design from memory. The child would be shown a figure, such as the two shown, for exactly 10 seconds, and then asked to reproduce it as closely as possible from memory. (B) Task #28 entailed imagining the reversal of the hands of a clock. First the child would be asked to imagine where the hands of a clock were at 11:15. Then the child would be asked what time it would be if the long and short hands were reversed. This was a task that any adult could readily do in Binet's day, but is that still true today? (After Binet, 1905/1916.)

Figure 11.3 Sorting Soldiers The first widely used intelligence tests for adults were developed by American psychologists to determine which of millions of draftees should be officers, based on their performance on the written Army Alpha test.

Army Alpha A written group test of intelligence used to place recruits in World War I.

Army Beta An orally administered intelligence test used to place recruits in World War I.

intelligence quotient (IQ) Originally, the ratio of a child's mental age divided by his or her chronological age and then multiplied by 100. Today, a measure of a person's performance relative to a comparison group of people on intelligence tests.

Wechsler Intelligence Scale for Children (WISC) An intelligence test designed for children 6 to under 16 years of age.

Wechsler Adult Intelligence Scale (WAIS) An intelligence test designed for adults, 16 to 89 years of age.

States entered World War I, the U.S. Army asked psychologists for help in sorting the huge numbers of draftees. In response, Terman and other psychologists developed two intelligence tests. The **Army Alpha** was a written test designed to quickly decide which men should be officers versus ordinary soldiers (**Figure 11.3**). The **Army Beta** was an oral test for men who were illiterate, designed to determine whether a man was intelligent enough to serve even as an ordinary soldier. The psychologists felt that about 3% of drafted men were too mentally deficient to serve, but the Army needed soldiers. In the end, only about 0.5% of the men were excused from service because they were thought to be too unintelligent (Yerkes, 1919). Within a few years, nearly 2 million American men took one of the two tests.

Once the war was over, intelligence testing of adults faded in importance, but the demand for tests to help classify children for schools was greater than ever. Educators turned to a test comparing mental and chronological age, providing a score known as the **intelligence quotient** (**IQ**), originally defined as the ratio of a child's mental age divided by his or her chronological age and then multiplied by 100 (Stern, 1912/1914):

$$\text{IQ} = (\text{Mental age}/\text{chronological age}) \times 100$$

The last step, involving multiplying by 100, was done just to avoid having to use decimals. So a 10-year-old child who knows only what most 10-year-olds do would have an IQ of:

$$(10 \div 10) \times 100 = 1 \times 100 = 100$$

See **Table 11.1** for more examples of IQ calculations. Notice that, by definition, the average IQ of a large group of randomly selected children should be 100.

The Stanford–Binet test has been revised several times and is still in use today. But today the most widely used intelligence test for children is the **Wechsler Intelligence Scale for Children** (**WISC**), designed for children 6 to under 16 years of age. It provides an IQ score and four subscores: verbal comprehension, perceptual reasoning, working memory, and processing speed. The **Wechsler Adult Intelligence Scale** (**WAIS**) is a similar test designed for adults, 16 to 89 years of age. Like the Stanford–Binet, both the WISC and WAIS have been revised several times. Each consists of many individual tasks of two basic types: *verbal tasks* (relying on written or spoken language) and nonverbal *performance tasks*, such as using blocks to form a shape (or the famous test sorting differently shaped blocks into holes that match).

TABLE 11.1 The Original Notion of Intelligence Quotient (IQ)

Mental age	Chronological age	IQ
8	10	80
10	10	100
12	14	86
16	10	160

Note: Originally, IQ = (Mental age/chronological age) × 100.

How are intelligence tests administered?

The Stanford–Binet, WISC, and WAIS are all individually administered tests, meaning that participants are tested one at a time with one examiner. The examiner asks the person questions, shows her pictures to copy, gives her blocks to assemble into particular shapes, and so on (**Figure 11.4**). The entire test takes about an hour and a half to administer, so it is costly to pay a lot of examiners to give the test to a large number of people.

Because many examiners are required in the administration of IQ tests, it is important that tests be standardized. **Standardization** is a process whereby every examiner follows a specific list of instructions on how to administer the test, including the exact words to use to ask questions, and how to hold testing materials such as pictures. The idea is to control as much as possible all the conditions of the test so that the score reflects only the *test-taker's* ability, not accidents of how the examiner happened to phrase a question or display a picture. Standardization is critical if people taking the same test given by many different examiners are to be legitimately compared with one another.

Intelligence tests have also been **normalized** (or *norm-referenced*), meaning that we have a good idea of how participants perform, on average, and how much variability there is in scores. It is possible to get a good sense of "norms" only when a test has been administered to many participants. Intelligence tests for children have been normalized for all ages so that we know how children age 6 or 7, or any age up to 16, do on the WISC. Likewise, the WAIS has been normalized for adults.

Figure 11.4 Materials for Individually Administered IQ Tests IQ tests are divided into verbal tasks and performance tasks, such as reproducing patterns of blocks.

Modern-day IQ scores compare individuals of the same age group

Modern-day intelligence tests measure IQ scores differently than the original Stanford–Binet test. Today IQ scores do not compare mental age to chronological age. Assessing intelligence in terms of mental age versus chronological age may make sense when applied to children but doesn't work well in assessing adults. While children encounter certain developmental milestones as they grow older, learning certain series of facts and skills as they grow up, once adulthood is reached, it's no longer obvious what tasks "should" be learned, or in what order. At what age should someone learn to change a flat tire on a car, file a tax return, or change a baby's diaper efficiently? In other words, in comparing adults, their precise age is not necessarily relevant to how much they know, what they can do, how well they read, or how quickly they can solve life's various problems. For adults, it makes more sense to ask how intelligent an adult is in comparison with other adults, whatever their ages.

David Wechsler (1896–1981) proposed a new way of comparing individuals' intelligence that continues to be used in today's intelligence tests for both adults and children. Instead of asking if a 10-year-old knows what a 12-year-old "should" know, why not ask how much a 10-year-old knows compared with other 10-year-olds? If a 10-year-old knows more than what 90% of other 10-year-olds know, that 10-year-old must be smart, right?

There are two big advantages to gauging intelligence relative to that of age-matched peers. First, we no longer have to decide what a child of a particular age "should" know—always a difficult decision to make. The only objective way to determine what a child of a given age should know would be to test many children at each age and see what most of them do and don't know. And you might not be able to rely on that "standard" for long because what children might be expected to know at a given age could change as the world changes. For example, Binet's test measured children's ability to tell time on a clock face (see Figure 11.2B), a task that even some young adults, raised in a world of digital clocks, may find difficult today. The second advantage of measuring intelligence by comparing people of the same age is that

standardized A test administered according to a set of instructions intended to control the conditions of the test.

normalized Also called *norm-referenced*. A test that has been administered to many people so that the performance average and variability are established.

we can use that same approach with adults. A really smart adult, age 19 or 91, should know more than most other adults of any age.

Wechsler's approach to measuring IQ involved testing lots of children of all ages, and lots of adults, to determine how well the average person at each age performs on each question. While such tests could be used to judge whether a person is below average, average, or above average in intelligence, a good test needs to be more precise. What we want to know is *how much* above average, or below average, a person's intelligence is. One way to be more precise is to ask what percentage of people is more or less intelligent than this particular person. Is she more intelligent than 90% of the population? Than 80%? Than 50%? Conversely, if her intelligence ranks above only 10% of the comparison group, that would suggest she is not very intelligent.

The **percentile** is the percentage of the comparable population that scores *below* a given score. A score in the 99th percentile exceeds that of 99% of the population, while a score in the 1st percentile is at the bottom (99% of the population got a higher score). Notice that by this definition, there can be no score in the 100th percentile—you can't have a score higher than 100% of the people, because you are one of those people, and your score is not *greater* than your score! Sometimes the scores are written as "%-ile," as in the 30th %-ile, or 80th %-ile.

Percentiles are only useful if you are comparing, say, a 10-year-old's score with that of all other 10-year-olds, or an adult's score with that of other adults. In other words, to understand the percentile score, you need to know *with what population the score is being compared.* If you took a college entrance exam such as the SAT (Scholastic Achievement Test) or ACT (American College Testing), you received a percentile score comparing you with other high school students taking that exam ("college-bound high school seniors"). **Table 11.2** provides sample scores from the 2013 SAT exams. The average student would score in the 50th percentile—better than half the students, but not as well as the other half—which would be a score of about 500 in Critical Reading, about 520 in Mathematics, and about 490 in Writing. Note that the average score (the *mean*; see Section 2.2) is pretty close to the 50th percentile scores.

Today all IQ scores provide this sort of information, indicating how the person's score compares with that of other people in the appropriate comparison group. More than that, the modern system of calculating IQ scores makes it easy to have a quick sense of about where any given score will fall within that group. To understand this aspect of modern intelligence tests, we need to think about how things vary in nature.

percentiles A way of comparing scores on a test using the percentage of the comparable population that scores below a given score.

TABLE 11.2 College Entrance Exams: An Alternative Way to Gauge Intelligence

	Percentile		
Score	Critical reading	Mathematics	Writing
800	99	99	99
700	95	93	96
600	80	75	82
520	57	52	61
500	51	45	55
490	48	42	51
Mean	491	514	488

Source: © 2013 The College Board.

Intelligence test scores are normally distributed

Following the convention of the Stanford–Binet, where the average IQ score should be 100, Wechsler constructed his tests so that the mathematical average, technically known as the mean, would always be a score of 100. In this way, a child with an IQ of 100 would have the "average" score, and of course that's equivalent to the original Stanford–Binet concept of having a mental age that is equivalent to the chronological age.

But Wechsler also had the insight, inspired by innovations in statistical theory, to calculate the scores of IQ tests in a way to make judging percentiles relatively easy. Recall that you *normalize* a test by giving it to thousands of people to determine the mean score and how much each score varies from that mean. It turns out that in many types of quantitative measurement, from test scores to measurements of natural phenomena, scores tend to vary around the mean in a particular, symmetric pattern known as a *normal distribution*. To demonstrate why things in nature tend to vary in this particular way, Francis Galton invented a machine, commonly called a *bean machine*. Today it consists of lots of tiny balls (rather than beans as Galton used) that drop down a funnel centered over a series of pins (**Figure 11.5A**). As each ball hits a pin, it has a 50-50 chance of bouncing to the right or left. Similarly, it bounces to either the left or right as it encounters the next pin, and the next pin, until it falls into one of the slots at the bottom. If there are several layers of pins, say 10 or 12, then it is rare for a ball to bounce to the left of *every* pin, to end up in the far left slot. Likewise, few balls bounce to the right of every pin to end up on the far right. Most balls bounce to the right sometimes and to the left other times, so many of the balls end up in the slots that are clustered directly beneath the end of the funnel. Galton noted that the distribution of the balls at the bottom of the machine always took the form of a *bell-shaped curve* (**Figure 11.5B**).

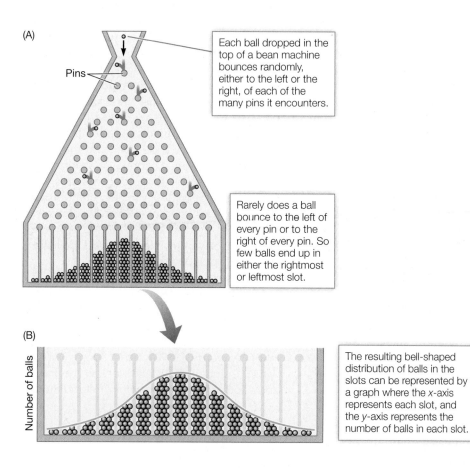

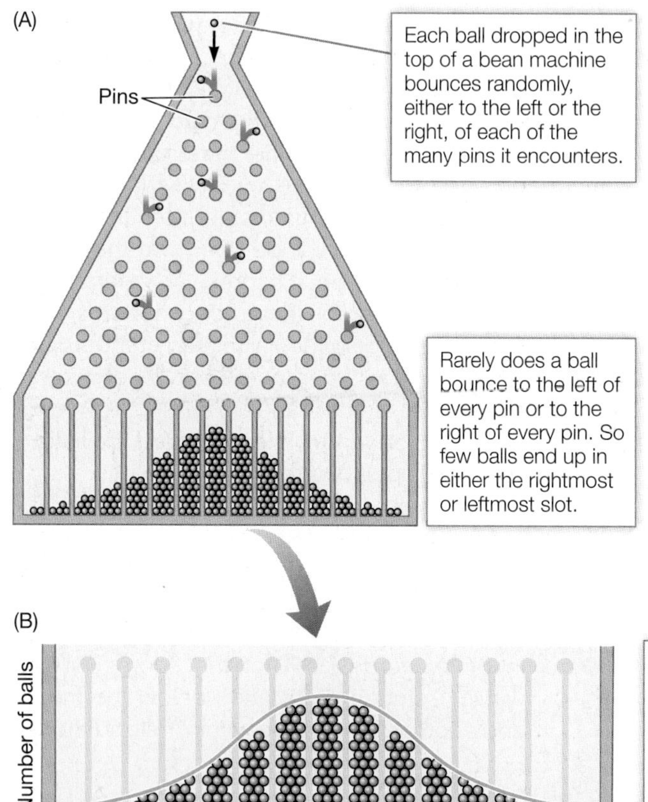

(A)
Pins
Each ball dropped in the top of a bean machine bounces randomly, either to the left or the right, of each of the many pins it encounters.
Rarely does a ball bounce to the left of every pin or to the right of every pin. So few balls end up in either the rightmost or leftmost slot.
(B)
Number of balls
The resulting bell-shaped distribution of balls in the slots can be represented by a graph where the x-axis represents each slot, and the y-axis represents the number of balls in each slot.

Figure 11.5 Galton's Bean Machine Demonstrated the Origins of the Normal Distribution

frequency distributions Graphs in which a score is noted on the *x*-axis while the number of people who have each score is noted on the *y*-axis.

normal distribution A bell-shaped curve describing the distribution of scores around a mean.

standard deviation The average amount that each individual score falls above or below the mean, used to express variance.

A graph of the bell-shaped curve can be drawn by plotting the slot number (slot 1, slot 2, etc.) along the *x*-axis (the horizontal axis), and the number of balls that fall into each slot on the *y*-axis (the vertical axis). As we discussed in Chapter 2, psychologists often plot the test scores of large numbers of people in a similar way, as a **frequency distribution**, where the range of scores is plotted on the *x*-axis and the number of people who got each score is plotted on the *y*-axis (see Figure 2.14).

As a thought experiment, imagine what would happen if you had millions of tiny balls, millions of pins, and millions of slots at the bottom. Mathematicians can readily predict the probability of a ball falling into each slot if such a "super keen bean machine" were made. When they do, the shape of the predicted curve is the famous **normal distribution**, a family of bell-shaped curves describing the distribution of variables, like IQ scores, around a single mean or average.

IQ scores are no exception—they, too, vary to form a normal distribution. That makes a lot of sense when it comes to something as complex as intelligence, measured by how much you know, how well you figure out various puzzles, and so on. Think of all the processes that influence performance on such tests. Does your parents' dinner conversation sometimes include the word that appeared on the test? Did you once play with a puzzle like the one in the test? The answers will be different for each person, representing another source of variability (or if you like, another layer of pins for the ball to bounce to the left or right of). In the final section of this chapter we'll review evidence that IQ test performance is influenced by genes, probably more than 180 of them, so genes provide yet another source of variation (Lango et al., 2010). The odds that someone would inherit the best version of all those genes are as likely as a ball hitting 180 pins and always bouncing to the left. All these sources of variation cause IQ performance to fit a normal distribution.

An important mathematical property of any normal distribution is that we can predict the percentage of scores that will be clustered around the mean. To do this, we need to revisit another mathematical concept from Section 2.2 called the **standard deviation**, which is the average distance, or "deviation," of each score from the mean. The standard deviation is calculated by measuring how far above or below each score is from the mean, adding up those distances, and dividing by the number of scores (readily calculated by computers these days). A key idea is that the more variability there is in a distribution, the farther individual scores will deviate from the mean. In other words, when scores vary over a large range, the average deviation of scores from the mean, and so the calculated standard deviation, will be larger than it would be if scores varied over a small range.

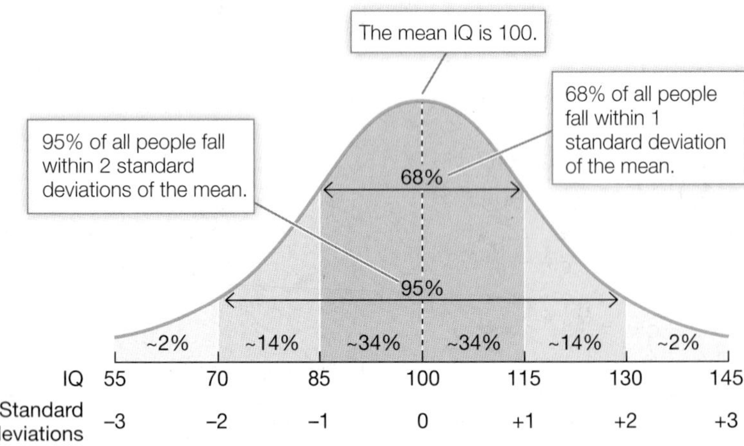

Figure 11.6 The Standard Distribution of IQ Scores

Once you know the standard deviation, you can apply certain useful mathematical properties of all normal distributions. For instance, no matter what the mean or standard deviation of a normal distribution happens to be, 68% of the population will fall within 1 standard deviation of the mean (**Figure 11.6**). In other words, 34% of the scores will be within 1 standard deviation below the mean, and another 34% will be within 1 standard deviation above the mean. Furthermore, 95% of the scores will fall within 2 standard deviations of the mean. Finally, 99% of the scores will be within 3 standard deviations of the mean. You can be sure that very few scores will be farther than 3 standard deviations away from the mean.

Since IQ scores are normally distributed, then 68% of scores are within 1 standard deviation of the mean, 95% within 2 standard deviations, and 99% within 3 standard deviations. So if you know the mean IQ score (100) and the standard deviation, then you can predict just how rare any score will be. A score that is 4 standard deviations above the mean would be extraordinary. Conversely, a score that is 1/2 a standard deviation below the mean would be quite common. In fact, if you think of the 68% of the people clustered around the mean as "average," then any score within 1 standard deviation of the mean would be average.

As noted earlier, by convention the mean score on IQ tests is always set at 100 points. Similarly, by convention all IQ tests are mathematically manipulated to have standard deviations of 15 points. So 68% of IQ scores fall within 15 points of 100, meaning scores between 85 (100 – 15) and 115 (100 + 15). The vast majority (95%) of scores fall within 2 standard deviations (30 points) of 100, ranging from 70 to 130. Notice that with this system we can be quite specific, calculating the percentile rank for any score. An IQ of 100 is the 50th percentile, a score of 115 is the 84th percentile (34% above a score of 100), and 130 is the 98th percentile. An IQ of 85 is the 16th percentile, while 70 is the 2nd percentile. An IQ score of 145, in either a child or an adult, is quite rare, happening about once out of 1,000 people.

Closely related to IQ tests are **achievement tests**, multiple-choice exams given to groups of students to assess readiness for college study. The SAT and ACT are examples. Like modern IQ tests, achievement tests report participants' percentile rankings in various subjects. Participants' percentile rankings on achievement tests are very similar to their percentile rankings on IQ verbal tests, so the two types of test are roughly equivalent.

There is no doubt that modern IQ tests and achievement tests accurately report how one person's performance on the test compares with other people's performance. But that's only important if IQ tests really do measure intelligence. Do they?

A reliable psychological test provides consistent results

For any psychological test, including intelligence tests, we must always consider two issues, *reliability* and *validity*. We introduced these concepts in Section 2.2, and will revisit them in more detail here and in several other chapters. We'll see that establishing the reliability of IQ tests is relatively easy. Indeed, all the major IQ tests (which do not include those supposed IQ tests you find on the Web) have been established to be very reliable.

For a psychologist, a **reliable** test is one that gives consistent results. Please note that just because a test is reliable doesn't mean it is *useful*. As one wit noted, a stopped watch is extremely reliable because it always shows the exact same time, but it isn't useful. On the other hand, if the tests are not reliable, then they probably aren't measuring anything that's real. So we must establish whether intelligence tests are reliable before we can even bother with the question of whether they are useful.

There are several ways to assess the reliability of a test. For example, if the test is supposed to be measuring an enduring psychological trait, like intelligence, then it should display **test-retest reliability**, meaning that someone taking the test on two different occasions (without too much time passing) should

achievement tests Multiple-choice exams given to groups of students to assess readiness for college study.

reliability The degree to which a measurement tool produces consistent, repeatable results.

test-retest reliability The quality of giving similar results when a test is administered more than once to the same person.

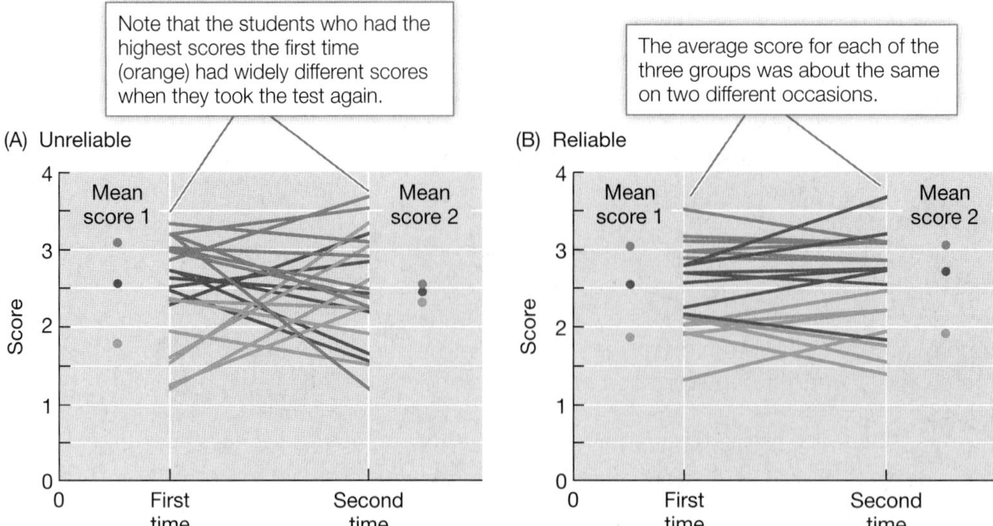

Figure 11.7 Unreliable and Reliable Tests of a Psychological Trait (A) If a test is unreliable, then the scores that three different groups of participants get on one occasion will differ on another occasion. Here, the groups of people getting the highest scores (orange), the lowest scores (green), and the middle scores (purple) the first time they took the test all average about the same score when they take the test again—that test is unreliable. (B) If the test is reliable, then the rank order of the three different groups will be about the same on the two occasions, as here.

get about the same score (**Figure 11.7**). If a bathroom scale gives you a different answer every time you put the same 20-pound bag of sugar on it, that scale has low test–retest reliability.

Test–retest reliability is especially important for individually administered tests, such as the Stanford–Binet and WISC. Each person should get about the same score no matter which examiner administers the test. As we mentioned earlier, this is why those tests offer very specific instructions for how they should be administered, trying to standardize the presentation.

This issue of different examiners administering the same test brings us to a second aspect of reliability. **Scoring reliability** is the extent to which two different scorers report the same score for the participant (**Figure 11.8A**). This is important for individually administered tests because the examiner is also the *observer* or *rater* who scores how well the participant performed. For this reason, scoring reliability is sometimes called *inter-observer reliability* or *inter-rater reliability*. If the people administering the test are properly trained and do their job well, scoring reliability should be high. For many modern intelligence tests, such as the college entrance exams, scoring reliability is quite high because participants read the test by themselves and report their answers by filling in circles on computer-scored forms.

Constructing reliable tests depends in part upon ensuring that all items on the test are appropriate for the group being tested. **Split-half reliability** is the extent to which different parts of the exam produce similar scores (**Figure 11.8B**). The easy way to evaluate this is to simply compare performance on the first and second halves of the test, as the phrase implies. If there are 100 questions, you can compare the performance on items 1 through 50 to performance on items 51 through 100. If many people have taken the test, then you already know how difficult each item is, and you can deliberately balance the two halves of the test to make them equally difficult. In fact, you can divide up the test questions into every possible set of two halves. If you're careful to keep the two halves balanced in terms of difficulty, and if split-half reliability is high, then performance should always be about the same for both halves.

scoring reliability The extent to which two different scorers report the same score for the subject.

split-half reliability The extent to which different parts of the exam produce a similar score.

cross-test reliability The extent to which two different tests thought to measure the same trait agree.

validity The extent to which a test actually measures the trait it is intended to measure.

That outcome is sometimes called *internal consistency reliability* because it indicates a consistency across the questions found inside the same exam. All the major intelligence tests have excellent internal consistency. In fact, the tests are crafted, the items carefully selected and adjusted, to maximize internal consistency.

If intelligence really is a stable characteristic that differs across people, then there should be a nearly infinite number of ways one might be able to measure it. Indeed, we've seen that two different tests, the Stanford–Binet and the WISC, both claim to measure intelligence. If each test is reliable, then they should have high **cross-test reliability**, the extent to which two different tests, both intended to measure the same trait, agree (**Figure 11.8C**). If cross-test reliability is low, meaning results from the two tests do not often agree, then either the two tests do not measure the same trait, or at least one of the tests must be unreliable in measuring that trait. In fact, cross-test reliability between the Stanford–Binet and the WISC is high. What's more, both tests show good cross-test reliability with many other tests intended to reflect intelligence, such as the college entrance exams.

The fact that all of these tests are very reliable indicates that they must be measuring *something* that differs across people and is relatively stable in each person. But a critic might not be very impressed with this reliability. After all, the Stanford–Binet and the WISC tests are very similar in many ways, just as the two college entrance exams, the SAT and the ACT, are very similar to one another. So perhaps it's no surprise that they are reliable. The issue of whether IQ tests actually measure *intelligence* lies at the heart of the question of the *validity* of these tests, which we'll take up next.

Establishing test validity is more difficult

As we have just seen, modern-day intelligence tests have been carefully constructed so that they are very reliable. The other, more problematic criterion for judging an intelligence test is **validity**, the extent to which a test actually measures the trait it is intended to measure. In psychology, this is sometimes referred to as *construct validity*, because it is the extent to which a test actually measures some psychological *construct*, like intelligence.

The fact that IQ tests are quite reliable is good, because it makes it possible that they might also be valid. So are IQ tests a valid measure of intelligence? There seems to be no way to prove beyond any doubt that IQ tests measure intelligence. For one thing, as we've already said, many psychologists studying intelligence may disagree on a definition of the term. If we can't agree on what intelligence really is, then there's always room to argue about whether an IQ test measures it.

(A) **Scoring reliability**

Day 1: Examiner A administers the test

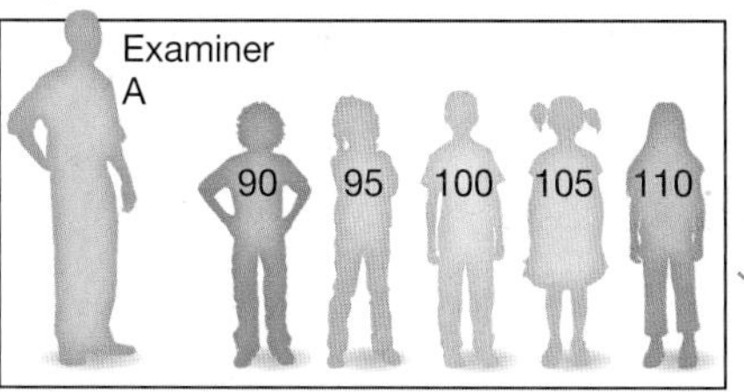

Day 2: Examiner B administers the test

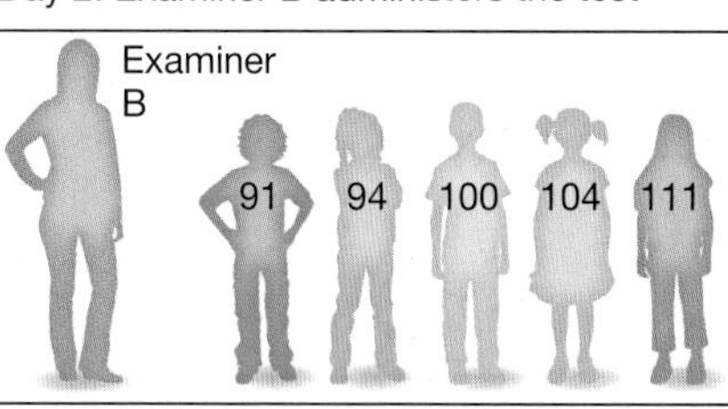

(B) **Split-half reliability**

Day 1: Performance on half the test items

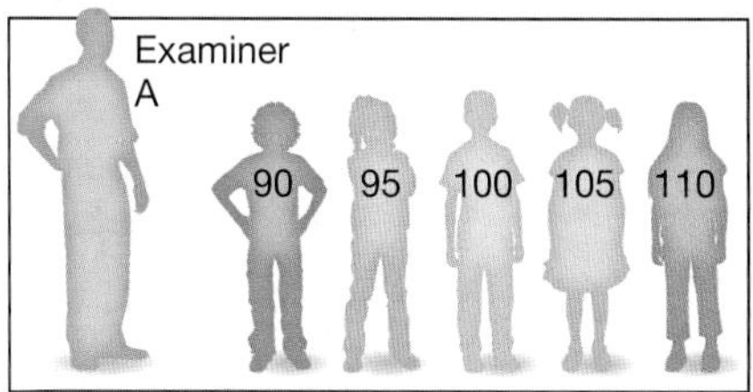

Day 2: Performance on remaining test items

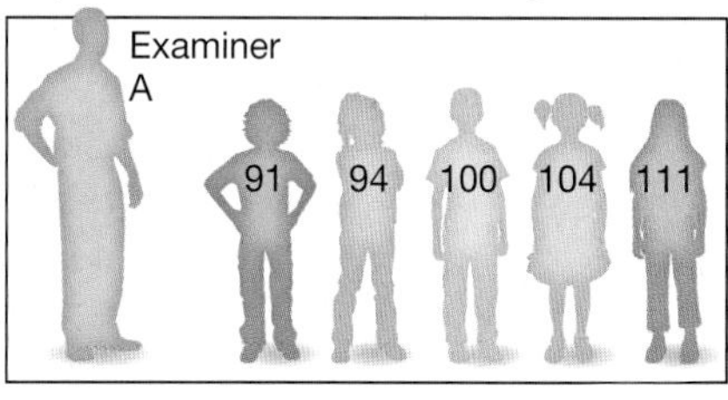

(C) **Cross-test reliability**

Day 1: Stanford–Binet test

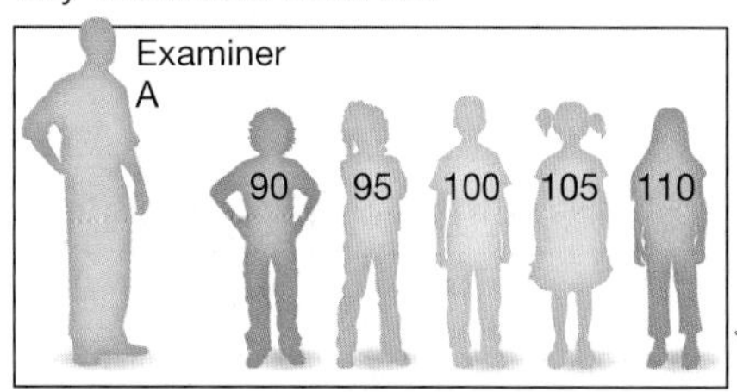

Day 2: WISC test

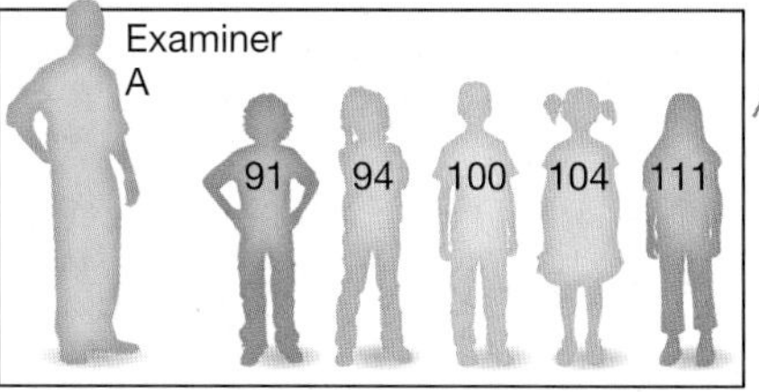

Figure 11.8 Different Ways to Determine the Reliability of Psychological Tests

convergent validity The extent to which several different tests intended to measure the same psychological trait give comparable results.

content validity The ability of a test to measure all the various facets of the psychological trait in question.

criterion-related validity The extent to which the scores on a psychological test predict someone's real-life performance, based on some standard.

Maybe an IQ test truly measures what *you* call intelligence, but it might not be measuring what *I* call intelligence. Nevertheless, we'll see that IQ tests do measure *something,* some genuine human characteristic, which varies across individuals and makes a difference in their lives.

You may have heard the term *face validity*, which means that a test looks valid "on the face of it." For a scientist, face validity isn't useful because it depends on who, exactly, is looking at the test. In other words, face validity is a purely subjective, unscientific criterion. Instead, to assess a test, psychologists consider several different aspects of validity that can be objectively measured. The three most important aspects of validity are *convergent validity*, *content validity*, and *criterion-related validity*, which we'll discuss in turn. You can consider these to be subcategories of overall validity.

Convergent validity is the extent to which several different tests intended to measure the same psychological trait, like intelligence, give comparable results. In other words, the different tests seem to be *converging* on the same score. In fact, different IQ tests agree pretty well. Notice that this is also a characteristic of reliability, specifically *cross-test reliability* that we discussed above, where different tests, like the Stanford–Binet and the WISC, report similar IQ scores for children. Indeed, that's all convergent validity indicates—that the two tests are measuring the same thing—but it doesn't really tell you *what that thing is*, whether it truly is intelligence. It might be intelligence, or some other trait.

Content validity is the ability of a test to measure all the various facets of the psychological trait in question. For intelligence testing, the question is the extent to which the test really covers the whole range of abilities that we consider intelligence. As you might have guessed, this also depends heavily on how we define intelligence. So to the extent that researchers disagree about what intelligence really is, it is difficult to agree on whether any particular test measures all aspects of intelligence. We'll see in the next section that many researchers think there are aspects of intelligence, abilities that are important in real life, that are not even considered in standard IQ tests.

Criterion-related validity is the extent to which the scores on a psychological test predict someone's real-life performance, based on some *criterion*, hence the name. Because this is a question of whether the test measures something that makes a real, concrete difference in life, it is sometimes called *concrete validity*. **Table 11.3** compares these different kinds of test validity. Criterion-related validity still depends on your definition of intelligence, but once you settle on the criterion to evaluate performance, this aspect of validity can be addressed readily with data. For example, if you think intelligent people should get good

TABLE 11.3 Three Different Aspects of Test Validity

Type of validity	Standards	Example
Convergent validity	Do different tests converge, offering similar results?	Stanford–Binet and WISC provide similar IQ scores, which indicates that the two tests measure the same thing.
Content validity	Does the test cover all aspects of the trait, or just a few aspects of the trait?	This depends on the definition of intelligence. There is wide disagreement about whether IQ tests really test all aspects of "intelligence."
Criterion-related validity (concrete validity)	Does the test offer any statistical predictions about real-life performance to reach some criterion?	*Across groups of subjects*, IQ tests correlate with performance in school and the workplace, and in many areas of life. However, the predictions do not always apply to *individuals*.

grades in school, then you can see whether people with higher IQ scores have better grade point averages than people with low IQ scores. If you think the ability to earn money is a better criterion for intelligence, then you can compare the incomes of people with different IQ scores. If intelligence is the ability to make a delicious, nutritious soup when shipwrecked on an island, then the admirable Crichton was brilliant. The question becomes whether knowing people's IQ scores lets you predict how well they meet a particular criterion. In fact, IQ scores have considerable criterion-related validity. As we'll see next, IQ scores do, in fact, offer some predictions about how well people will do, on average, in many aspects of real life.

Dumb and Dumber It seems unlikely that either Lloyd or Harry would get a very high score on any standard IQ test.

What do IQ scores "predict"?

First, what does it mean to say, for example, that IQ scores in childhood "predict" various outcomes in life? It does not mean they predict what will happen to any *particular individual*. For example, there's no high IQ score (130, for example) that guarantees an individual a healthy, happy life and a great career. Nor is any IQ score so low, say 70, that it guarantees an unhealthy or unhappy life. Likewise, knowing that two people have IQs that are 10 points apart, say 95 versus 105, does not let us predict with any confidence which one will attend school longer, earn more money, or live longer.

Rather, the studies show that when we consider the IQ scores of *many people*, there are *statistical trends* that hold up across the group. What we can say is that a group of people with an IQ of 105 will, on average, earn better grades in school, earn more money as adults, and live longer than a group of people with an IQ of 95. In short, there is a *correlation* between IQ scores and these other various outcomes, meaning that they tend to vary together. (Recall that we discussed correlation in Section 2.1 in some detail.) As always, *correlation does not prove causation*, and we'll discuss other possibilities as well.

For now, keep in mind that these correlations are not strong enough to let us predict with confidence which particular individual will live longer or have a better job. For example, in 1916 hundreds of California children were tested to find the very smartest, and two boys who did not "make the cut" went on to win Nobel Prizes in physics (Shurkin, 2006). (Ironically, one of them, William Shockley, would go on to argue that IQ tests are extremely valid measures of intelligence. The other boy was physicist Luis Alvarez.)

Taken together, these data strongly support the idea that IQ tests measure some psychological trait that actually matters to everyday life, particularly in our culture of grades, careers, and life satisfaction (Hunt, 2010; Mackintosh, 2011). Let's look at the following various criteria to test the validity of IQ scores as measures of intelligence.

BRAIN CORRELATES There is a long history of trying to relate intelligence to brain size, but the early efforts were deeply flawed by distortions promoting the racial prejudices of the times (Gould, 1981). The development of IQ tests and noninvasive brain imaging created more objective studies that indicate modest but reliable positive correlations between IQ scores and overall size of the cortex (Andreasen et al., 1993; Karama et al., 2009), especially frontal cortex (Colom et al., 2013). Correlations have also been seen between performance on cognitive tasks and neural activity (Neubauer & Fink, 2009) and brain connectivity (Chiang et al., 2009). These correlations indicate that IQ tests indeed measure something about the brain, and it seems reasonable to presume that brain size would be related to intelligence. On the other hand, these reports indicate that brain function and structure account for only about 10–16% of all the variability in IQ scores, so there is plenty of room for other factors to influence IQ, as we'll discuss below.

HEALTH AND LONGEVITY There is strong evidence that people with high IQ scores are more likely to have longer and healthier lives, which is rather startling (Deary, 2008). In one study, 11-year-old children who scored high on an IQ test given in 1932 were more likely to be alive 65 years later than were lower-scoring children (Whalley & Deary, 2001). In another study, children displaying a high IQ in the 1950s tended to be hospitalized for accidents less often over the next 50 years (Lawlor et al., 2006). At the very least, these results suggest that IQ scores measure something that is real, whether or not that something is intelligence.

These data can be interpreted in several different ways. Maybe people with a high IQ really are smarter about avoiding injuries and staying healthy. Or perhaps people inherit genes that make them healthier, and that leads them to develop a higher IQ as they grow up, and also have fewer hospitalizations and longer lives. Or perhaps children growing up in impoverished conditions are exposed to influences, such as poor nutrition, that impair both their intelligence and their long-term health. Both of the studies cited in the previous paragraph tried to control for socioeconomic status, and they reported that high IQ scores still predicted a longer and healthier life, even when comparing people from similar economic backgrounds.

But if there were something in the environment that was unrelated to economic conditions, such as a hidden toxin or disease, that affected both IQ and health, it might be difficult to detect. Several toxins are known to reduce childhood IQ. They include lead (Bellinger et al., 1992; Chen, et al., 2005; Grandjean & Landrigan, 2006), a heavy metal that was once widely used in paint. Lead-based paint was taken off the market and has been replaced in most homes but is still sometimes found in older city buildings and older, low-income homes. Children can absorb lead by eating paint chips or touching walls with lead-based paint, or even breathing the air near such walls. As shown in **Figure 11.9**, there are strong correlations between levels of lead found in the blood of children and their IQ scores. Note that none of the children with a blood lead level above a certain level—15 μg/dL—had an IQ of 100 or more. What's more, adults who were exposed to lead as children have smaller brains than control participants (Cecil et al., 2008). There is no known

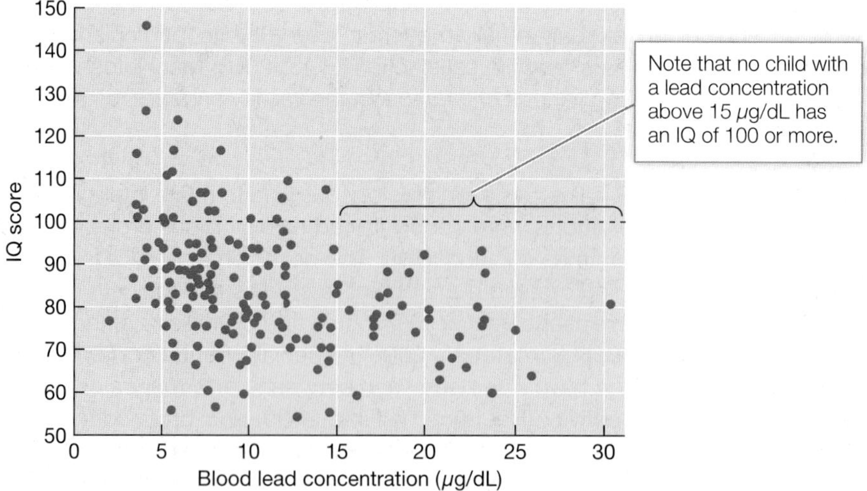

Figure 11.9 Circulating Levels of Lead and IQ In this study of 6-year-olds, there is a clear relationship between concentrations of the toxic metal lead and IQ. (After Jusko et al., 2008.)

level of lead poisoning that is too small to affect IQ (Salkever, 2014; Schwartz, 1994; World Health Organization, 2010a).

Malnutrition can also reduce IQ. For example, children born in areas of China with low iodine (and no iodized salt) have IQs 1 standard deviation lower than those born in regions with iodine (Qian et al., 2005). (Iodine is a crucial component of thyroid hormone, which boosts brain development.) While these studies, too, indicate that IQ scores measure something real (otherwise how could toxins or nutritional deficiency affect it?), it means we have to be cautious in interpreting the better health of people with high IQs. In other words, there may be toxins, dietary deficiencies, or diseases that affect both IQ and health, which we haven't discovered yet. Lead is more common in lower-income homes, but note that if some other, unidentified toxin is distributed *randomly* across people's homes, that would cause health and IQ to be correlated.

In the last section of this chapter we'll review the solid evidence that IQ scores are influenced by genes and environment. That finding suggests another explanation for the correlation between IQ scores and health. Perhaps genes that promote the development of a body that will enjoy good health also promote development of brains that will work well. This idea is supported by findings that people with lower IQ scores, averaging below 70, often report significantly more health problems than people with higher IQ scores (Batty et al., 2008; Keogh et al., 2004). Conversely, maybe growing up with a healthy body, as judged by the fact that it has fewer health problems, allows a child to more freely interact with the world. That, in turn, might maximize the child's intellectual stimulation and therefore IQ score.

But note that this same reasoning about the effect of genes on IQ would also apply to the effects of the environment on IQ. Maybe growing up in a secure, healthy environment also allows a child to maximize IQ.

SCHOOL PERFORMANCE What else do IQ scores predict? Perhaps the most consistent finding is that people with high IQ scores tend to do well in school. The correlation between IQ scores and grades has been seen so often (Brody, 1997) that few researchers even look for it any more. In some ways, this correlation is not surprising. After all, the tests were designed to predict academic performance and have been revised several times by retaining those test items that, in the past, best correlated with performance in school.

Still, at least some researchers have suggested that one reason IQ scores tend to correlate with school performance may be a matter of a self-fulfilling prophecy. If IQ scores are used to decide which children will get which educational resources, like better schools, better teachers, a more advanced curriculum, then children scoring well on the IQ test may get better grades because they are put into a better educational setting (Byington & Felps, 2010). And getting better schools might lead to better jobs, an issue we'll take up shortly.

The possibility that just reporting a high score on an IQ test, whether it is real or a falsely reported score, may *cause* a person to get better grades and jobs is also difficult to eliminate entirely. We'll have to remember this possibility as we discuss the next factor that correlates with IQ scores: occupation and personal income.

OCCUPATION AND PERSONAL INCOME People with a very low IQ are unlikely to go to college, and far less likely to graduate from college, attend medical school, and become physicians. In other words, some careers require a certain level of intelligence. IQ scores, even if they are imperfect measures of intelligence (however you define it), can be a useful indicator of suitable education and career choices (**Figure 11.10**).

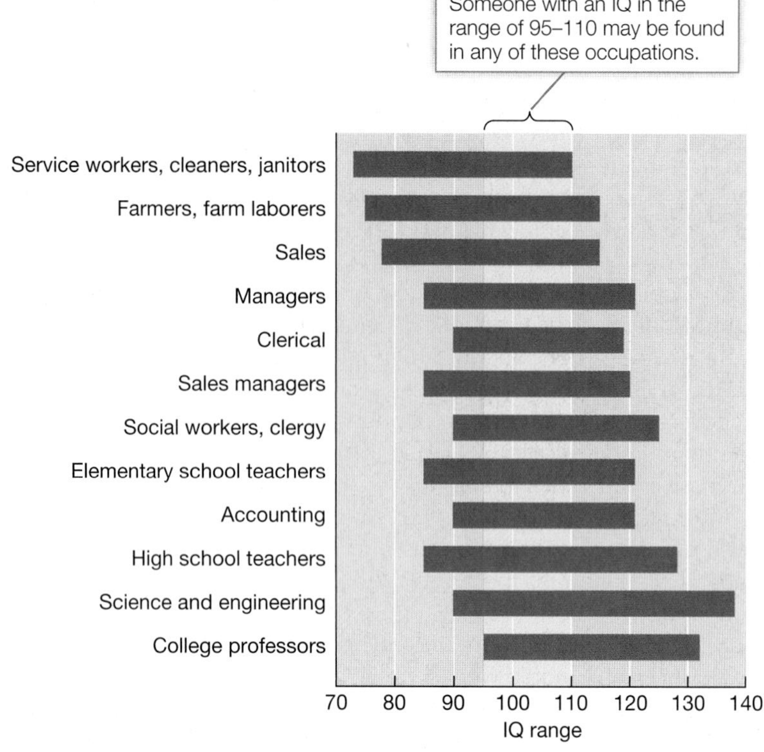

Figure 11.10 Occupation and IQ IQ scores correlate overall with occupations, but a wide range of IQs are seen in each. Interestingly, the very widest range of IQs are in science and engineering jobs. (After Hauser, 2002.)

But even when we set aside individuals with low IQ scores, a relationship between IQ score and job placement is still seen (Neisser et al., 1996; Schmidt & Hunter, 1998; Watkins et al., 2007). Given a relationship between IQ and job placement, it's not surprising that IQ also correlates with economic income (**Figure 11.11A**). Of course, educational level affects income, but even among college graduates, people with a higher IQ also tend to have a higher income (**Figure 11.11B**). In fact, even within a profession, such as lawyer or doctor, IQ correlates with annual income (Schmidt & Hunter, 1998). In one study, each additional IQ point brought in, on average, an additional $202 per year (Zagorsky, 2007). Interestingly, this same researcher found that while there is some

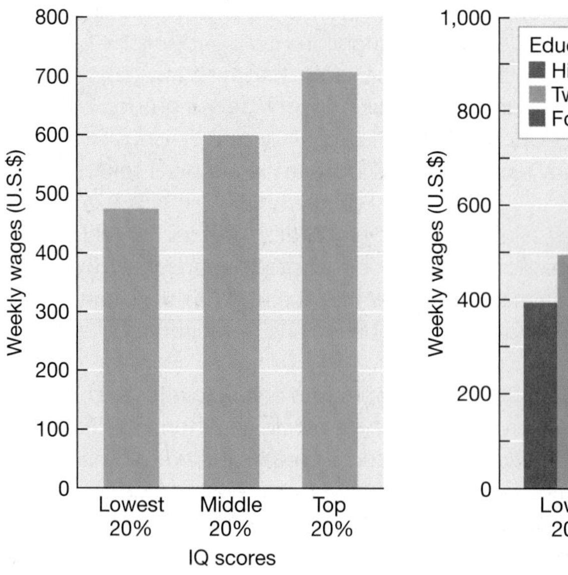

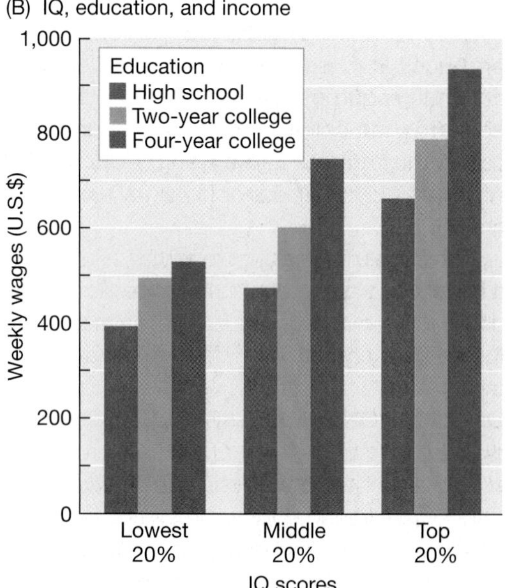

Figure 11.11 Both IQ Scores and Education Matter in the Marketplace (A) When a large number of individuals were classified in terms of whether they were in the lowest, middle, or top 20% for IQ scores, it was evident that higher IQ scores correlate with higher income, on average. (B) But education matters, too. Within each group of people classified by IQ score, those with more education earned more money. (After Ceci & Williams, 1997.)

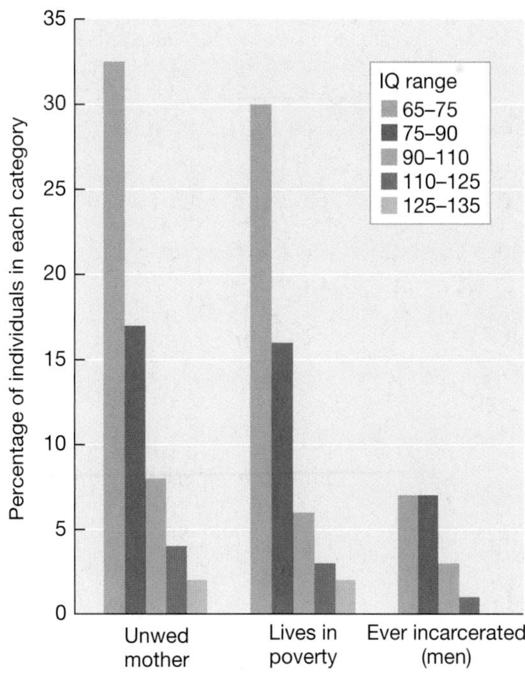

Figure 11.12 Criteria-Related Validity of IQ Scores On a wide range of real-life criteria, including living conditions, parenthood, and incarceration, IQ scores offer some predictive power across groups. Of course, this does not mean that every person with an IQ of 120 will make more money, and spend less time in prison, than someone with an IQ of 100. (After Gottfredson, 1997.)

minimum IQ required to make a lot of money, after that point additional IQ does not correlate with additional income. The author points out that many careers that are attractive to people with high IQs, like being college professors, are not necessarily well paid. As another researcher put it, "It is important to have enough of it [IQ], but having lots and lots does not buy you that much" (Hunt, 1995, p. 362). Many other real-life criteria correlate with IQ scores (**Figure 11.12**), and it is difficult to know how much these other effects reflect differences in earnings.

FAMILY LIFE From the point of view of natural selection, intelligence might be measured by how many offspring one leaves behind, and perhaps that was true for our prehistoric ancestors. But one thing high IQ scores do not predict, in Western cultures at least, is reproductive success. People with higher IQs do not tend to produce more children than people with lower IQs. In fact, the trend is rather the opposite, since people with high IQs tend to get more education, and highly educated people tend to have fewer children than people with less education (Kristensen & Bjerkedal, 2007).

HAPPINESS People who are mentally impaired, and therefore have a low IQ, are not as satisfied with their lives as people with higher IQs. In one study, people with an IQ of 85 or less reported lower levels of psychological well-being than their siblings with higher IQs (Seltzer et al., 2005). Even among people with low IQs, there is still a correlation between IQ and life satisfaction (Keogh et al., 2004), but IQ also correlates with overall physical health among these mentally disabled people. The poor health of people with low IQs is probably due to developmental disorders that affected many parts of the body, including the brain. For this reason, it is hard to know whether people with low IQs are less happy because of their low IQ, or because of health problems that tend to accompany low IQ.

Setting aside people with very low IQ scores, there is little evidence that IQ correlates with happiness, or life satisfaction (Veenhoven, 2010). Happiness is elusive despite the correlation of IQ with things that you might expect to bring happiness, such as good health, educational achievement, career performance, and personal income. Given those correlations, you would think life satisfaction would increase with IQ scores, and the fact that it does not poses something of a puzzle. One possibility is that the positive aspects of intelligence may be offset by some negative aspects. Does a higher IQ make a person more sensitive to the bumps and letdowns of life? Do people with high IQ scores expect to do better in life and so feel disappointment when they fail? Whatever the explanation, the lack of correlation between IQ and life happiness is a reminder that intelligence alone is not enough to live a happy and fulfilled life.

In the next section we'll discuss the idea that there are more kinds of intelligence than those measured by traditional IQ tests. As we review these other "intelligences," think about whether some of them might be as important as, or more important than, the abilities measured by IQ tests.

11.1 SUMMARY

- While there is no universally accepted definition of human *intelligence*, we can define it as the ability to acquire, retain, and apply knowledge in many different spheres of life.
- The first intelligence test were the *Binet–Simon scale* developed in 1904 to identify French schoolchildren who might need special assistance in their education.
- The first intelligence tests for adults were the U.S. Army's *Army Alpha* test, to screen draftees for potential officers, and the *Army Beta* test, designed for illiterate men, to determine if a man was too unintelligent to serve.
- The *Stanford–Binet* test provided an *intelligence quotient* (*IQ*) by dividing a child's *mental age* by his or her chronological age and multiplying by 100. Hence the average IQ, when mental age and chronological age are equal, is 100.
- The most common IQ tests today are the *Wechsler Intelligence Scale for Children* (*WISC*) and the *Wechsler Adult Intelligence Scale* (*WAIS*). Like the Stanford–Binet, these are individually administered tests that have been *standardized* to make the examination as similar as possible for all participants.
- The WISC and WAIS are *normalized* to reflect the average performance and a normal range of variability. Normalized IQ scores indicate a participant's performance relative to that of other people of the same age.
- The average IQ score today is still 100, with a *standard deviation* of 15 points.
- Measurements and scores that fall into a bell-shaped *normal distribution* can be described based on their *percentile* rankings.
- IQ tests and the closely related *achievement tests* are very *reliable*; in other words, they give consistent results, whether people are tested on two different occasions (*test–retest reliability*), tested by two different examiners (*scoring reliability*), or given two different versions of the test (*cross-test reliability*).
- A test on which scores are consistent across the first and second halves is said to have *split-half reliability*.
- A good psychological test must have *validity*, meaning it actually measures what it is intended to measure. While the different IQ tests display *convergent validity*, meaning they all give roughly the same evaluation of subjects, it is more difficult to assess their *content validity*, the extent to which they assess all the various facets of intelligence. This difficulty primarily stems from disagreement about what intelligence truly is.
- IQ tests display good *criterion-related validity*, meaning they offer a statistical prediction of people's performance on several criteria that we would expect to reflect intelligence. For example, IQ scores are correlated with performance in school and in the workplace.
- IQ scores also correlate with health and longevity, which suggests that environmental and genetic factors that impair body function may also impair intelligence. People with very low IQs often have more serious health issues than their siblings with normal IQs.
- Discounting people with very low IQs, there is little correlation between IQ and overall happiness.
- All "predictions" based on IQ scores apply only to large groups of subjects. It is not possible to accurately predict how any one individual will fare in school, the workplace, or life.

REVIEW QUESTIONS

1. Contrast the original meaning of intelligence quotient with the way modern IQ tests assess performance.
2. How are modern IQ test scores distributed, and how does that distribution make it easy to use IQ scores to gauge a person's percentile ranking?
3. What do psychologists mean by the reliability of a test, and what are the different means of assessing reliability?
4. What does validity mean for a psychologist? Considering each of the three different types of validity of psychological tests, how valid are IQ tests?
5. What are some aspects of life that correlate with IQ? Which of these aspects reflect something that you would consider intelligence?

Food for Thought

Have you heard the myth that incredibly intelligent people are physically frail? In fact, people with high IQs are often quite healthy. What factors may explain why people with high IQs tend to live longer, healthier lives? Since IQ correlates with health and longevity, why does it not correlate very well with happiness?

11.2 The Many Facets of Intelligence

Things to Learn

- Generalized intelligence (*g* factor)
- Fluid versus crystallized intelligence
- Sternberg's three intelligences
- Gardner's multiple intelligences
- Developmental intellectual disabilities
- Savant syndrome
- Flynn effect
- Aging intelligence

We've established that the IQ tests developed over the twentieth century are reliable. These tests are also valid to the extent that there is generally good agreement among the various tests, and the scores have some predictive value for how children will do in school and in the workplace, and how long they will live. Yet we are still left with a central question: Do IQ tests actually measure *intelligence*?

Is that all intelligence is—the ability to get good grades in school and to get a good job afterward? If so, then we can stop giving IQ tests and just use grade point averages to determine intelligence in children, and income tax records to determine intelligence in adults. But many people do not think those are the only measures of human intelligence. By the mid-twentieth century, more and more psychologists began suggesting that human intelligence is a much broader characteristic than what's measured on IQ tests.

Most psychologists today will say there is more than one kind of intelligence. Consider, for example, people who are extremely gifted in some mental tasks, but quite ordinary, or even disabled, at others. Consider also that intelligence changes as we age, so we get better at some tasks (and, sad to say, worse at others).

Is there any such thing as general intelligence?

Francis Galton favored the idea that there is some overall, general ability called intelligence, such that people who are good at one mental task are likely to be good at all of them. As IQ tests developed in the twentieth century, British psychologist Charles Spearman (1904; 1927) used newly developed statistical tools to confirm that people who scored well on one part of a test tended to score well on the other parts of the test too. For example, you might think there are some people who are very verbal and other people who are really good at math. But Spearman found people who did well in verbal tasks tended to do well at math too. They also tended to be better than average on memory tasks and at abstract reasoning. Spearman proposed that there is a **generalized intelligence** (or ***g* factor** or simply ***g***) that reflects an overall mental ability and affects many different kinds of behavior, and therefore will be reflected in tests of many different kinds of ability.

Spearman suggested that *g* represents pure mental *ability*, not what a person happens to know from experience at school or at home. While parts of every IQ test include some items that require specific knowledge (like the meaning of the

generalized intelligence (*g* factor, *g*) A general ability that reflects an overall mental ability.

word "esteem"), Spearman felt that statistical analysis could filter out those bits of random "noise" to reveal the underlying *g*. For all practical purposes, IQ scores reflect what Spearman considered to be *g*.

From the beginning, the idea of a *g* factor was controversial, and there's little sign that the debate is settled (Mackintosh, 2011). One issue was the assumption that genes must to some degree affect generalized intelligence. If *g* is an inherited trait measured by IQ tests, should we use IQ tests to decide who gets to go to particular schools, apply for particular jobs, or even marry particular people? Is the use of IQ tests to screen candidates for schools and jobs consistent with the notion that everyone should have equal opportunity to achieve the most they can in school and the marketplace? Some researchers have argued that IQ tests can be abused to effectively prevent people from reaching their full potential in life. Concerns have been raised also as to whether, fairly or unfairly, IQ tests may lead people to believe that some races of people inherit less *g* than others. We'll talk about these important, potentially explosive, issues in detail in the last section of this chapter. We'll see that there's room for disagreement on the questions of why people of some races tend to score higher on IQ tests than others. Virtually all psychologists agree that IQ scores and *g* are affected by environmental factors, especially early in life.

Related to the concept of the *g* factor is the idea that *g* is itself made up of two different spheres of intelligence, which Raymond Cattell (1987) named *fluid* and *crystallized* intelligence. **Fluid intelligence** (or g_F) is the ability to think and reason abstractly and to solve problems that are presented for the first time, independent of what you know already. It is "fluid" in the sense that it can be brought to bear on any problem. For that reason, Cattell suggested that we could measure fluid intelligence in a culture-free fashion, asking people to reason abstractly about problems no human, from any culture, had ever seen before. Some examples of tests intended to be appropriate for people from any culture, including the *Raven's progressive matrices*, are shown in **Figure 11.13**.

In contrast, **crystallized intelligence** (or g_C) is the *knowledge*, the store of facts that a person has learned, and the ability to use it appropriately. A child who has learned the multiplication tables has added to her crystallized intelligence, but her fluid intelligence, her ability to solve math problems generally, is unaffected. Because crystallized intelligence includes many such facts that each particular culture teaches us, it would be difficult to measure without referring to culturally specific concepts like the square footage of rooms, the composition of orchestras, types of power tools, and so on. A person with a lot of crystallized intelligence would do well in trivia contests or solving crossword puzzles.

Cattell thought that both fluid and crystallized intelligence change as we develop. Fluid intelligence seems to peak in young adulthood and then begins to decline at middle age (Ryan et al., 2000). In contrast, we can continue to learn and build up greater crystallized intelligence throughout life (Horn & Cattell, 1967), as we discussed in Chapter 5 (see Figure 5.33) and return to later in this chapter. In that sense, fluid and crystallized intelligence are at least somewhat independent of each other, since only one can grow throughout life. But limited fluid intelligence would make it difficult to add to the store of crystallized intelligence.

As daily interactions with computers have become more commonplace in developed nations, some psychologists have drawn an analogy between computers and human intelligence. Fluid intelligence can be likened to *processing speed*, how quickly one can solve problems, while crystallized intelligence might represent *information that is stored* on the hard drive, available when needed. Two computers might differ in terms of how quickly they can run a particular program if one is able to perform individual calculations faster than the other. All

fluid intelligence (g_F) The capacity to reason logically and solve new problems, independent of what you know already.

crystallized intelligence (g_C) The knowledge a person has acquired and the ability to use it appropriately.

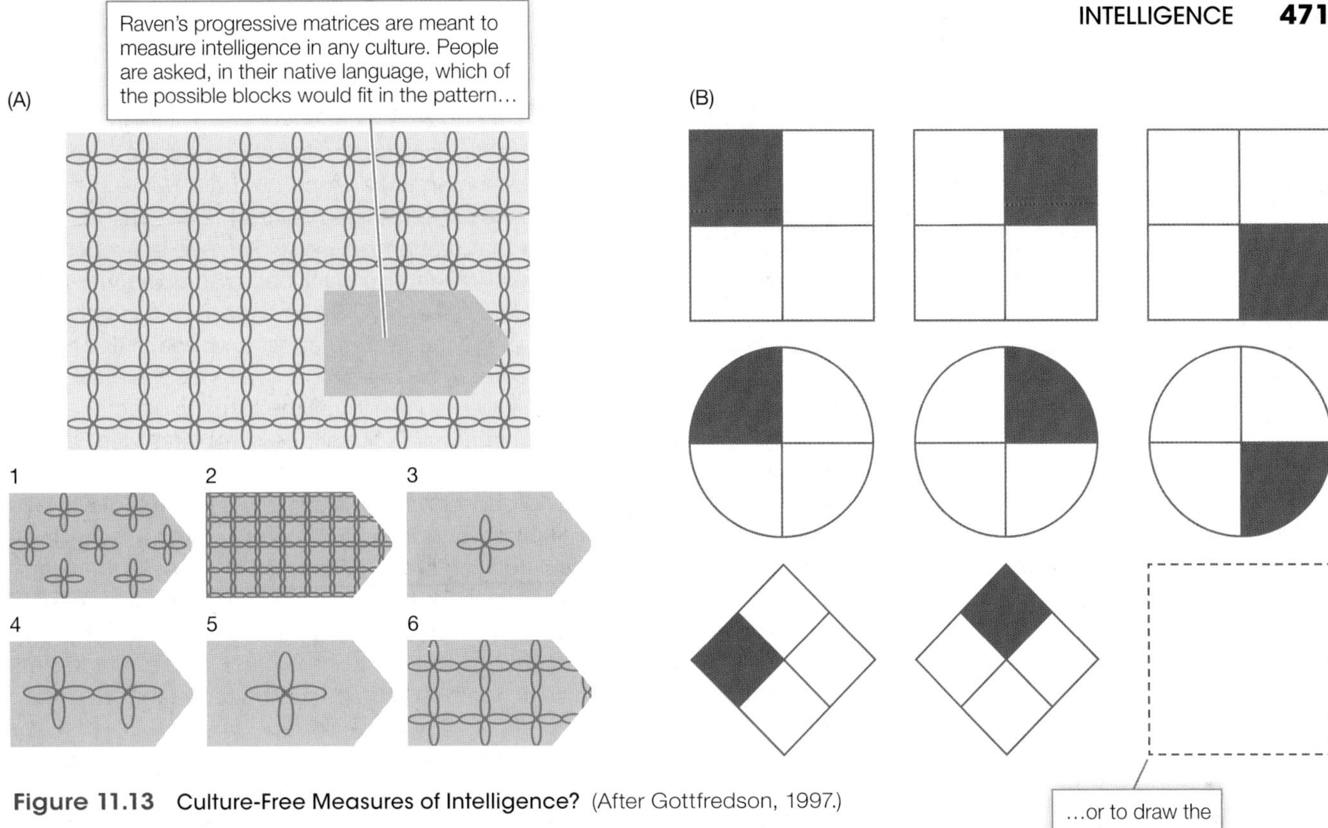
Raven's progressive matrices are meant to measure intelligence in any culture. People are asked, in their native language, which of the possible blocks would fit in the pattern...
(A)
1
2
3
4
5
6
(B)
...or to draw the next square.

Figure 11.13 Culture-Free Measures of Intelligence? (After Gottfredson, 1997.)

other things being equal, a computer that performs 2 million calculations per second will complete the task faster than one performing only (!) 1 million calculations per second. Perhaps some human brains are similarly able to process information faster than others, allowing them to solve problems faster. This faster speed might also allow them to reach solutions that would be out of the reach of people who process the information more slowly. This proposition is intriguing because psychologists can objectively measure how quickly people process information. Indeed, that is the basis of many psychological studies, where the time it takes to perform a task offers a clue to the mental steps behind the performance.

reaction time The amount of time it takes a subject to initiate some action after a predetermined signal.

In fact there is a correlation between IQ scores and **reaction time**, the amount of time it takes a person to initiate some action after a predetermined signal. A simple example is for a participant to hit a button as soon as possible after a light comes on. A slightly more complex version would be for the participant to hit one button in response to one signal, say a light, and another button in response to a different signal, a buzzer perhaps. In general, people with higher IQs tend to hit the button sooner, displaying shorter reaction times.

One study finding a correlation between IQ and reaction times went a step further to ask which of these measures was a better predictor of health and longevity. Studying a group of middle-aged people, the researchers replicated the finding that IQ correlated with longevity—those with a higher IQ were more likely to be alive 14 years later. However, reaction time was an even better predictor of longevity than IQ (Deary & Der, 2005). As with all correlations, there are several ways to interpret this finding. Maybe reaction times and IQ scores represent two different ways to measure the same thing—a well-functioning brain. That in turn might help a person make better health decisions and avoid accidents, leading to longer life. But maybe a fast reaction time in middle age has more to do with how well your body is functioning than with your IQ. In that case, a slow reaction time in middle age may be caused by underlying health problems that haven't come to the surface yet.

Last One in Is a... This diver may have been distracted just before the starter pistol sounded, but on average, there is a correlation between faster reaction times, higher IQ, and longer life spans.

Newer models emphasize "intelligences"

Many psychologists have rebelled against the notion that traditional IQ tests measure all important aspects of human intelligence. Without denying that IQ tests measure one important aspect of intelligence, they ask whether there are other aspects of intelligence that matter too. After all, until very recently in our evolutionary history, there was no adaptive significance to doing well in the classroom, because classrooms did not exist. Prior to civilization, every human group spent a part of each day gathering food to survive, so the ability to find edible roots, or throw a spear accurately at an edible animal, was probably more important than solving algebra problems. And for all the talk of a *g* factor applying to many different types of problems, virtually all those problems were paper-and-pencil tests of the sort that can be completed in a classroom.

Several psychologists have proposed alternative models of **multiple intelligences**, expanding the definition beyond the abilities gauged by IQ tests. They tend to disagree about exactly how many different "intelligences" there are. Robert J. Sternberg (1988) proposes that there are three different components to intelligence (**Figure 11.14**). He considers the intelligence measured by traditional IQ tests to be *analytical intelligence*, or "book smarts," the ability to deal with abstract information, as in academic problem-solving tasks, found in most IQ tests.

The other two types of intelligence that Sternberg proposes both draw on existing knowledge and skill, which are also important to human life. One is *practical intelligence*, or "street smarts," the ability to adapt to everyday life, doing what needs to be done in a specific setting. This is the ability to realistically apply theoretical ideas. The other is *creative intelligence*, the ability to deal with new and unusual situations, and to have "insight," proposing solutions that might not occur to other people. The admirable Crichton was not very skilled with verbal repartee, and so he might have scored poorly on a traditional IQ test of analytical intelligence. However, on the island Crichton had the practical and creative intelligence to survive, and even thrive.

Sternberg developed a *Triarchic Abilities Test* to measure all three of the components of intelligence, but it has not been widely adopted. Despite the difficulty in measuring them, there seems little doubt that both practical intelligence and creative intelligence are important aspects of human accomplishment. Think how impoverished our lives would be if no one had ever built the many devices we use, or if no one had ever composed music or written a novel.

multiple intelligences Models of intelligence that extend beyond the aspects measured by traditional intelligence tests.

Howard Gardner (1993, 1999) suggests there are more than three kinds of intelligence, and acknowledges the difficulty of knowing just how many there are. For now, he suggests that all humans possess eight intelligences, which are what make us human. Most important, Gardner proposes that people differ in how gifted they are in each of the eight intelligences (**Figure 11.15**). These include several abilities that are measured primarily by traditional IQ tests and that make up most of what psychologists regard as the *g* factor. They include *linguistic intelligence*, facility with spoken and written words; *logical-mathematical intelligence*, which includes logic, reasoning, and facility with numbers; and *spatial intelligence*, the ability to visualize with the mind's eye, which is required for solving some of the "performance" items in traditional IQ tests. These three intelligences are the abilities that Sternberg collectively calls analytical intelligence.

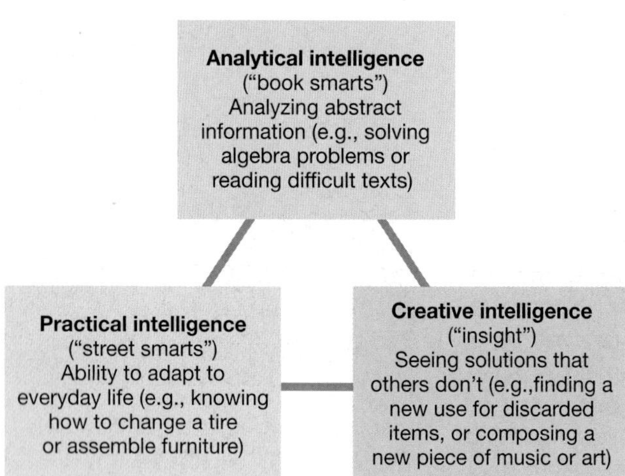

Figure 11.14 Sternberg's Three Types of Intelligence

But Gardner suggests that *musical intelligence*, the ability to produce and appreciate music, and *bodily kinesthetic intelligence*, the ability to control one's body motions and han-

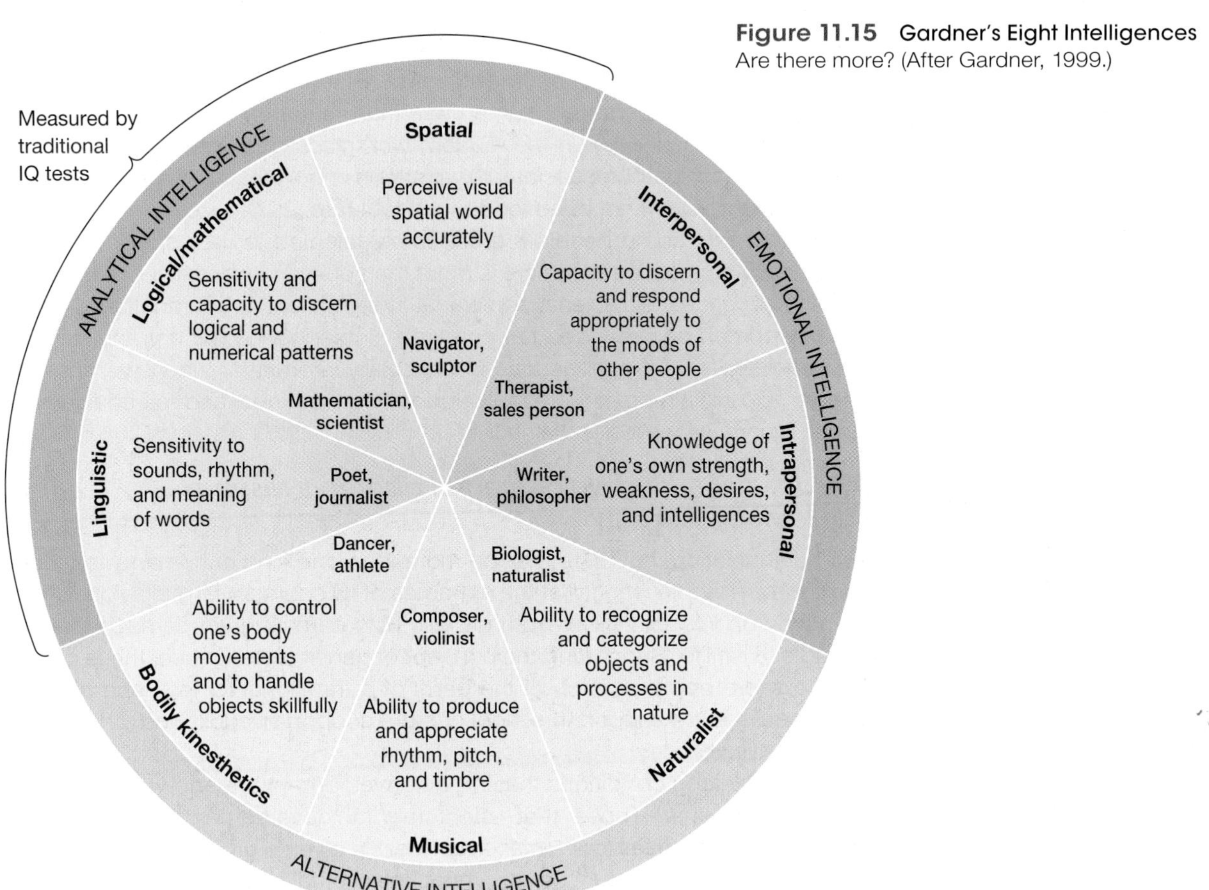

Figure 11.15 Gardner's Eight Intelligences
Are there more? (After Gardner, 1999.)

dle objects skillfully, are also important human abilities that are neglected by traditional IQ tests. Similarly, an ability to understand what's going on in nature, a *naturalist intelligence*, might be another alternative intelligence that was once crucial for humans.

Noting that humans must deal with many complex social interactions, Gardner suggests that two more abilities are crucial for human success. *Interpersonal intelligence* is the ability to interact with other people. High interpersonal intelligence is usually seen in outgoing people (in Section 14.2 we'll call such people *extraverts*), who are talented in sales, teaching, and social work. Interpersonal intelligence helps a person get along in a group, understanding the emotions of others and getting their cooperation. *Intrapersonal intelligence* is the ability to be introspective, sensitive to what the individual himself is feeling. Intrapersonal intelligence is important in social life, since it helps us predict how we will feel if social events unfold in one way versus another, and thus is helpful in choosing how to behave. Together, interpersonal and intrapersonal intelligence might be considered *emotional intelligence*. We mentioned earlier that if we leave out mentally disabled people, there is no correlation between traditional IQ and life happiness. Perhaps interpersonal and intrapersonal intelligences are more important for a happy life than the types of intelligence measured by IQ tests (Kaufman & Kaufman, 2001; Mayer et al., 2008).

Yet the idea of multiple intelligences has been criticized (Schaler, 2006), in part because it is difficult to know how many there really are. Are there three intelligences? 7, 8, 20? Unless there are objective criteria to help us decide between an "intelligence" and a "skill" or "talent" or "ability," it's hard to know where to stop. To prize linguistic skill over bodily kinesthetic skill, by calling the first one "intelligence" and the second a mere "ability" is something of a value judgment. Why is one a more important human trait than the other? Because one trait is more helpful in school, or in the modern workplace? As Sternberg (2005) has said, "In a hunter-gatherer society, IQ will still be important, but if a hunter cannot shoot straight, IQ will not bring food to the table" (p. 297).

The fact that some people are extremely talented in very specific ways is consistent with the idea that there is more than one kind of intelligence, and that these intelligences are at least somewhat independent of one another. In other words, you can be really good at one type of intelligence but not another. The idea of independent intelligences is especially prominent when we consider people who are almost unbelievably good at some things, and rather incompetent at others, as we'll discuss shortly.

A wide variety of developmental disorders result in intellectual disability

Another indication that there may be more than one kind of human intelligence comes from people who fall at the extremes of IQ scores. Many individuals who do poorly on IQ tests suffer from genetic disorders or brain damage that occurred early in life. Supporting the concept of general intelligence, these people tend to score poorly in each of the parts of a traditional IQ test, and many of them require extra support in school or extra support in adulthood to take care of themselves.

Severe, lifelong conditions that impair development are known as developmental disabilities. Those that affect mental development are known as **intellectual disabilities** (or *mental disabilities*), a diverse group of lifelong conditions that impair intellectual development. Intellectual disability was formerly referred to as "mental retardation," which emphasized that these children progress more slowly than other children. Many families with mentally disabled children feel that the old term is stigmatizing, so it is falling out of use (Schalock et al., 2009). In 2007, the American Association on Mental Retardation changed its name to the American Association on Intellectual and Developmental Disabilities to avoid the older term (www.aaidd.org). Earlier in the twentieth century, more elaborate classification schemes used even more offensive terms like *imbecile* and *moron*, based on arbitrary IQ thresholds. Today, classification of mental disability focuses on the level of function (**Table 11.4**) rather than on disparaging names. Alternatively, people with intellectual disability may be classified based on how much support and supervision they require.

intellectual disabilities Also called *mental disabilities*. A diverse group of lifelong conditions that impair intellectual development.

TABLE 11.4 One Classification of Intellectual Disability

Degree of intellectual disability	Approximate IQ range	Ability
Mild	50–69	Can acquire academic skills to about 6th-grade level, become fairly self-sufficient, and may live independently, with community/social support. This category accounts for about 85% of people with intellectual disability.
Moderate	35–49	Can carry out work and self-care with some supervision. (About 10% of cases)
Severe	20–34	May master basic self-care, some communication skills, and may be able to live in family or group home. (About 3–4% of cases)
Profound	< 20	May develop basic self-care skills, require high level of structure and supervision. (About 1–2% of cases)

Source: World Health Organization, 2010b.

(A)

(B)

Figure 11.16 Two of the Most Commonly Known Genetic Causes of Mental Disability (A) Fragile X syndrome is caused by dysfunction of a gene on the X chromosome. It is more common in males than in females and causes an elongation of the face and ears, which becomes more prominent with growth, as well as mental disability. (B) Down syndrome, caused by having a third copy of chromosome number 21, results in a characteristic facial pattern and a range of mental disabilities from mild to severe.

By convention, children with an IQ of less than 70, which represents a score 2 standard deviations below the mean, are considered mentally disabled. While this would represent about 2.5% of the U.S. population, only about 1% of the population actually requires additional services because of mental disability, which indicates that many of these people learn to take care of themselves without government assistance.

In nearly half the cases of mental disability, the cause is unknown (Schalock et al., 2009), but many instances are due either to genetic defects or to a difficult delivery that caused brain damage at birth. Many of the genetic causes of mental disability also affect other parts of the body. For example, **fragile X syndrome**, so called because it is due to a dysfunctional gene on the X chromosome, results in an elongated face and prominent ears, as well as extreme shyness (Holsen et al., 2008) and mental disability (**Figure 11.16A**). **Down syndrome** is caused by having a third copy of chromosome 21, resulting in a characteristic facial pattern, short stature, and mild to severe mental disability (**Figure 11.16B**). There are a few other syndromes like Down syndrome, in which children inherit an atypical number of chromosomes, and all of them affect various parts of the body and are accompanied by some degree of mental disability.

In the next section we will discuss another genetic disorder, phenylketonuria (also discussed in Chapter 4; see Figure 4.12), which was once a leading cause of mental disability. Today babies in developed countries are screened for the genetic trait so that those with phenylketonuria can be put on a special diet that prevents them from suffering the same degree of mental disability.

While genetic causes of intellectual disability are difficult to prevent, another cause is completely preventable. **Fetal alcohol syndrome** is a birth defect caused by a mother who drinks alcohol while pregnant, which affects her child's developing brain, resulting in mild to severe mental disability. Children with this syndrome often have a characteristic facial appearance, including absence of the typical folds between the nose and upper lip, and close-set eyes (see Figure 5.4). In severe cases, the brain is so affected that the nerves connecting the left and right halves of the cortex are missing. Earlier in this chapter we saw that children exposed to lead also suffer mental impairment, and just as there is no known level of lead exposure that is too low to affect IQ, the Centers for Disease Control assert that "there is no known safe amount of alcohol use during pregnancy" (Centers for Disease Control and Prevention, 2014). Down syndrome, fragile X syndrome, and fetal alcohol syndrome are the most common identified causes of mental disability, accounting for nearly a third of all cases.

Another syndrome that can result in a low IQ score is **autism**, a disorder of impaired social interaction and communication, sometimes accompanied by repetitive behaviors. In severe cases, children with autism may not speak at all, and may not be able to complete any of the various tasks on a traditional intel-

fragile X syndrome An intellectual disability due to a dysfunctional gene on the X chromosome, resulting in an elongated face and prominent ears, as well as extreme shyness.

Down syndrome A condition caused by a third copy of chromosome 21, resulting in a characteristic facial pattern, short stature, and mild to severe intellectual disability.

fetal alcohol syndrome (FAS) A condition in which children exposed to alcohol from their mother's drinking are born with distinct facial features and varying degrees of mental impairment.

autism A spectrum of disorders characterized by impaired social interactions, problems communicating, and severely restricted behavior and interests.

autism spectrum disorder (ASD) A disorder characterized by deficits in social communication and interaction accompanied by restricted, repetitive behaviors and interests, which can range from mild to severe.

savant syndrome A very rare condition in which a mentally disabled person also exhibits exceptional ability in some limited field, such as memory, mathematics, or music.

ligence test, so they have very low IQ scores. Yet the severity of autism varies widely. These days it is referred to as **autism spectrum disorder** (see Section 16.1), to acknowledge that some people with autistic characteristics may be quite gifted verbally. (In my experience, many college professors, myself included, show at least some autistic qualities.) Intriguingly, some people with autism that is severe enough to make it difficult for them to learn to care for themselves are remarkably gifted in certain areas, as we'll discuss next.

A few people are remarkably gifted at specific mental abilities

You have probably heard of the rare individual who has extraordinary ability in a field, such as verbal or visual memory, or extreme musical or mathematical talent—abilities that far exceed what most other people can do. In many cases, however, the person's talent is limited; in many other respects the person may be intellectually disabled. Such a person was once termed an "idiot savant" to convey the paradoxical pairing of a mental disability with a remarkable gift (a "savant" is a knowing or wise person). The insulting term *idiot* is inappropriate, because as we will see, some of these individuals are clearly very intelligent in many ways. Today these individuals are said to have **savant syndrome**, a very rare condition in which a mentally disabled person also exhibits exceptional ability in some limited field, such as memory, mathematics, or music. Most people with autism do not have any savant gifts, but about half of the individuals with savant syndrome also display autism. People with savant syndrome may speak very little, have difficulty recognizing other people's emotions, or have difficulty maintaining social relationships. As noted above, autism is regarded as part of a spectrum of severity, and we'll see that while some people with savant syndrome have an extremely limited ability to speak or converse, others are quite articulate. Autism is more common in males than in females, and likewise most people with savant syndrome are male.

Why are are people with savant syndrome able to perform seemingly impossible feats in music, mathematics (Rush, 1789), and art? We don't know. Nevertheless, they represent an "existence proof"—because they are exceedingly gifted in some areas and impaired in others, clearly there are different brain mechanisms underlying these different abilities. This circumstance stands in contrast to any simple notion that intelligence, or *g* factor, encompasses all aspects of human intelligence.

The alternative is to dismiss these special abilities—to remember every word of a book after a single reading, or perfectly reproduce a piano sonata after a single hearing, to quickly multiply two six-digit numbers together, or learn a new language in a week—as irrelevant to true human intelligence. But that would make the definition of *g* factor circular: it encompasses all areas of human intelligence except for those areas it does not include! The existence of these savants certainly seems to bolster the notion that there is more than one type of intelligence, beyond that measured by traditional IQ tests.

MEMORY SAVANTS In Chapter 9 we met the late Kim Peek, who loved to read and seemed to remember everything he read, even the entries in a telephone directory (see Box 9.2). You may recall that in one test of his memory, he was given a novel to read, which took him only 75 minutes. Four months later, when asked about a minor character in the novel, Kim not only knew the name but cited the page number where the character appeared and quoted several passages on that page verbatim. Kim's father had to stop taking him to performances because if, for example, actors in a Shakespeare play messed up the lines, Kim would stand up to object. This anecdote not only shows how astute his memory was, but also reveals Kim's difficulty learning social rules.

ARTISTIC SAVANTS Some savants show a remarkable visual memory, something like "photographic memory" that seems well beyond most of us, and some can draw faithful reproductions of what they've seen. For example, British savant Stephen Wiltshire was diagnosed as autistic at age 3 because he did not interact with other people and did not speak. However, he loved to draw, so teachers encouraged him to talk by withdrawing art supplies until he spoke. His first word? "Paper." He learned to talk by age 9, but still preferred drawing and became obsessed with architecture. Now grown, Stephen can faithfully draw from memory any building he sees (**Figure 11.17A**). For a BBC television program, Stephen was flown by helicopter over London and then asked to draw what he had seen. In 3 hours, he produced a detailed, perfectly scaled aerial view of a 4-square-mile area, including over 200 structures. He now earns a living selling his artwork (www.stephenwiltshire.co.uk). Apparently he is unable to carry on much of a conversation (Sacks, 1996).

MUSICAL SAVANTS Thomas Wiggins was born into slavery in Georgia in 1849 (**Figure 11.17B**). Blind from birth, he loved imitating the sounds around him and was exposed to the piano in his owner's house. By age 4 he could perfectly reproduce on the piano any pieces played by others. Thomas spent his life doing public concerts, billed as "Blind Tom." Initially greeted with skepticism, his appearances included challenges, where anyone from the audience could bring up piano music and play it, then Tom would sit down and reproduce the piece, apparently perfectly. He gathered many admirers, including writers Mark Twain and Willa Cather. Tom eventually boasted a repertoire of over 7,000 pieces, all from memory. He also composed pieces, transcribed by others, that were popular in their day. A modern day musical savant, who was also born blind, is Leslie Lemke (Treffert, 2013). You can find videos of his piano performances on YouTube.

MATHEMATICAL SAVANTS A mathematical savant, Daniel Tammet (**Figure 11.17C**) breaks the rules of savant syndrome in some ways, because he is very articulate and has several close relationships, including with his eight siblings. On the other hand, he cannot drive a car, has difficulty telling his left from his right, and finds trips to the beach uncomfortable because he feels compelled to count the number of pebbles, which even he admits are too numerous to count. Daniel can recall the mathematical constant pi to more than 20,000 decimal places (3.1415...), can instantly multiply three-digit numbers, and speaks ten languages.

Savant Daniel Tammet's articulate nature offers a rare insight, as he can tell us what goes through his mind when he is performing mathematical feats. Daniel has *synesthesia*, a vivid experience of seeing a color or shape in response to letters and numbers. For him, each of the thousands of digits of pi has a unique color and shape, which together form a picture in his mind (**Figure 11.18**). As Daniel has no problem remembering all the details of such a picture, he can recall the picture to conjure up the digits. Likewise, when doing mathematical calculations, he "sees" the digits interacting visually, quickly providing him with the answer.

Another point that is often emphasized by people who think there is a general intelligence is the idea that intelligence is relatively unchanged across life. Yet there is evidence that our intelligence can change as we age, as we'll discuss next.

(A)

(B)

(C)

Figure 11.17 People with Savant Syndrome (A) Stephen Wiltshire. (B) Thomas Wiggins. (C) Daniel Tammet. Each of these individuals is known for being remarkably talented in one or a few areas of intelligence, but in other areas for having either ordinary intelligence or even being disabled.

Figure 11.18 The First 20 Digits of Pi as Visualized by Daniel Tammet Daniel Tammet has memorized over 20,000 digits of pi, which in his mind form a much larger image than this.

Intelligence, and intelligence scores, can change over the life span

One important indication that IQ scores are susceptible to environmental influence is the **Flynn effect**, the substantial increase in average scores on IQ tests that has taken place since the first IQ tests were developed. It is named after psychologist James R. Flynn, who documented this effect in many populations around the world (Flynn, 1987). (No, he did not name the effect after himself—other psychologists did that.) Because of the Flynn effect, the standardization for each revision of IQ tests has had to be altered so that test-takers must perform better and better just to reach the average score of 100. In other words, performance on the Stanford–Binet that might have resulted in an IQ score of 100 in 1932 would only net a score of about 80 in the 1991 version (Neisser, 1997). It is as if the world population has gained an average of 20 IQ points in less than a century, averaging out to about 6 IQ points per decade (**Figure 11.19**). That change is far too rapid to be explained by any change in genes in the course of evolution, so many people have tried to find some other explanation for the Flynn effect.

Flynn effect The substantial increase in average scores on IQ tests that has taken place since they were developed.

Most psychologists agree that IQ tests measure at least some important aspects of intelligence, so the Flynn effect is intriguing. For example, in one study of two large samples of Spanish children, tested 30 years apart, the average IQ score increased nearly 10 points, primarily because *there were fewer children receiving low scores* (Colom et al., 2005). In other words, it's not that significantly more children were getting top IQ scores, but that fewer children were getting low IQ scores. That result suggests that the increased *average* IQ in the more modern group happened because some children knew more than they would have if they'd been born 30 years earlier. The

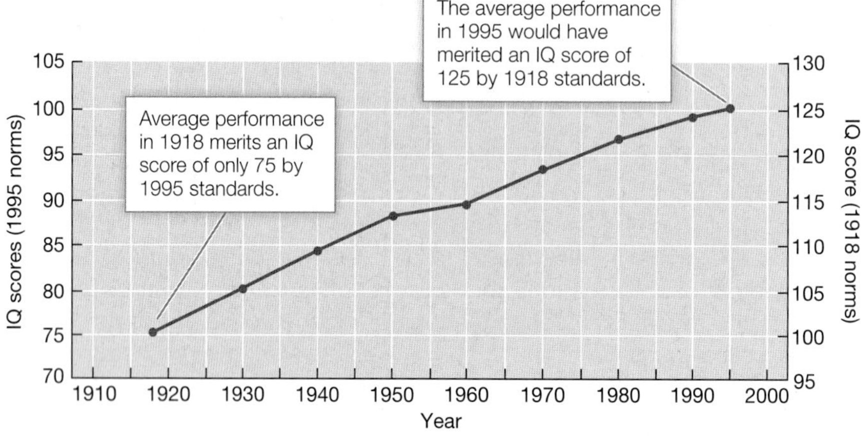

Figure 11.19 The Flynn Effect Comparing young men tested for military service in different eras, average performances on Raven's progressive matrices steadily grew from 1918 to 1995. (After Flynn, 1998.)

researchers suggested that improved nutrition might be responsible, as the earlier-born children might have received inadequate food to develop their full intellectual potential. Indeed, there is ample evidence that, at least in developed countries, nutrition and medical care have improved over the past century or so, and they probably account for the increase in average height. Not only have people gotten taller over the past century, but brain size has gotten larger too (Jantz, 2001). Thus, improved medicine and nutrition probably account for some of the Flynn effect.

But most experts think that the increase in average IQ is due to more than improved nutrition. While acknowledging that such factors may contribute, Flynn (2009) himself believes that the worldwide increase in IQ is due to greater intellectual stimulation. For example, modern occupations are more intellectually demanding than the subsistence farming that was common, even in industrialized societies, when the first IQ test was made. Asked what a dog and rabbit have in common, a farmer might have said something *concrete*, like dogs catch rabbits to provide the family with food. A city dweller is more likely to say they are both warm-blooded, or are both mammals. That sort of *abstract* reasoning is precisely what IQ tests of *g* strive to measure. Also, the development of widespread, cheap media, first radio, then television, and now smart phones and the World Wide Web, has opened up a world of information, including abstract discussions of issues and concepts (like "the economy," "intelligent design," or "random sample") that most people had never heard in the past. To use our earlier terminology, most of the Flynn effect is due to increases in fluid intelligence, dealing with abstract reasoning, rather than crystallized intelligence.

Does IQ decline with age?

Before psychologists understood the importance of improved IQ scores across generations, it appeared that intelligence declined sharply as we aged. But these data were deceiving—the 20-year-olds had grown up in more modern times than the 60-year-olds. That meant that the 20-year-olds had benefitted from more education than the 60-year-olds. If you compare 20-year-olds drawn from different eras—people who were in their twenties in 1930 to people who were in their twenties in the 1950s or 1970s—the story is different. Using that approach, the peak in verbal skills in the United States was seen in the early 1950s (Schaie & Zanjani, 2006). Once psychologists controlled for educational experience and the restandardized scales, change in IQ with age appeared much more modest. Nevertheless, there does seem to be a decline in IQ scores after age 45 or so (**Figure 11.20**).

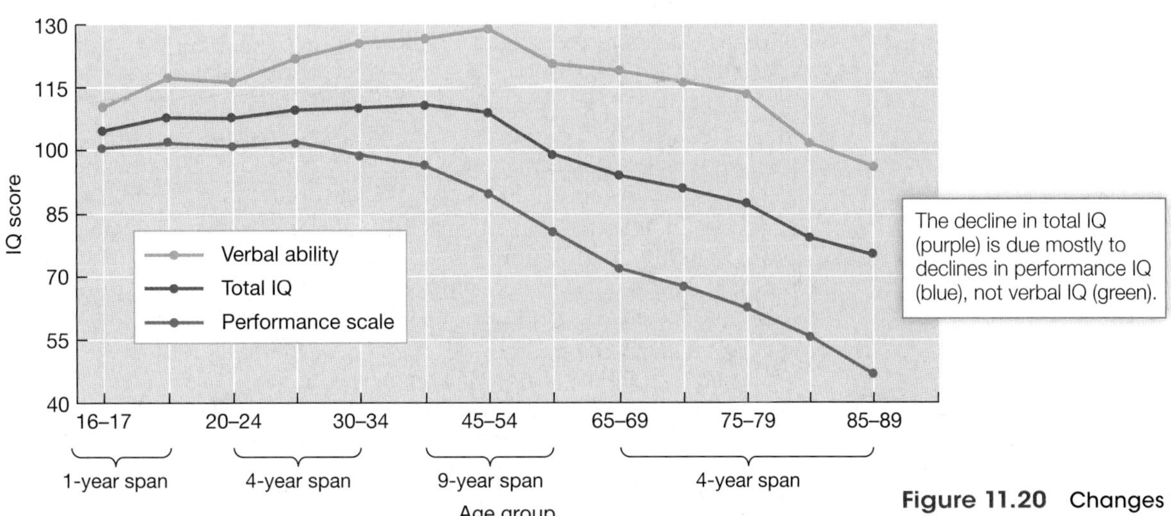

Figure 11.20 Changes in IQ with Age (After Kaufman, 2001.)

What's interesting about this decline is that it is not the same for all portions of the IQ test. In fact, verbal ability declines more slowly than the "performance" portion of the test that relies on timed tests (see Figure 11.20). In other words, crystallized intelligence, memory for hard-won knowledge about words and the like, declines more slowly than fluid intelligence, the ability to use reason to swiftly solve a newly encountered problem or situation. As we age, we continue to add to our store of knowledge, but we start to lose our edge for solving new problems rapidly (see Figure 5.33). To return to an earlier metaphor, it's as if we're retaining information in our hard drive but our processing speed is declining with age.

Because we continue to learn as we grow up and age, and because experience can affect IQ, it is clear that IQ is not fixed and unchangeable. Keep in mind that IQ can be changed, either impaired through toxins like lead or alcohol or through malnutrition, or boosted by exposure to more information, as we consider the overwhelming evidence that genes affect IQ in the next section. We'll see that although the genes we inherit clearly affect our IQ, that doesn't necessarily mean that all IQ differences are due to genes.

11.2 SUMMARY

- IQ tests measure the ability to solve problems using abstract reasoning. People who do well on one part of an IQ test tend to do well on the other parts of the test.
- Debate continues concerning whether IQ tests truly measure *generalized intelligence* (g *factor*), and whether there is such a thing as generalized intelligence.
- Psychologists distinguish between *fluid intelligence* (g_F), the ability to reason logically to solve new problems, and *crystallized intelligence* (g_C), specific knowledge that a person has acquired and the ability to apply that knowledge.
- Some researchers have suggested that fluid intelligence may represent some sort of "processing speed" that can be assessed by measuring *reaction time*, the amount of time it takes someone to detect a signal and make an appropriate response.
- Fluid intelligence, which is typically assessed by how quickly a person can solve a problem, peaks in young adulthood and then declines, but crystallized intelligence declines more slowly.
- Several psychologists have suggested that there are *multiple intelligences*, and that a person may be significantly more intelligent in one category than another. Robert Sternberg suggests there are three intelligences: analytical intelligence, practical intelligence, and creative intelligence.
- Howard Gardner proposes even more kinds of intelligence, including musical intelligence, bodily kinesthetic intelligence, interpersonal and intrapersonal intelligence, and naturalist intelligence.
- *Intellectual disabilities* (mental disabilities) are a diverse group of lifelong conditions that impair intellectual development. By convention they are considered to reflect an IQ of less than 70.
- Several genetic conditions, such as *fragile X syndrome*, *Down syndrome*, and phenylketonuria, impair intellectual development, as do several environmental conditions such as *fetal alcohol syndrome*, exposure to the environmental toxin lead, and iodine deficiency.
- *Autism* is a disorder characterized by severely impaired social interaction, which may include impaired verbal behavior and low IQ scores. A small minority of people with autism also display *savant syndrome*, having extraordinary ability in some limited field, such as memory, mathematics, or music, accompanied by mental disability in other areas of life.

- IQ tests must be periodically adjusted to keep the average score at 100 because of a steady increase in average test performance over time, a trend called the *Flynn effect*.
- We don't know what is causing the Flynn effect, but one factor could be technological progress, especially the widespread availability of media that exposes people to the type of abstract reasoning that is measured by IQ tests.

REVIEW QUESTIONS

1. What do psychologists mean by the *g* factor, and what are the two different aspects of the *g* factor?
2. Compare and contrast Sternberg's proposal of three kinds of intelligence with Gardner's proposal of eight or more different intelligences.
3. What is the Flynn effect and what explanations have been offered to account for it?

Food for Thought

Is it a coincidence that verbal ability of high school students, as measured by high school achievement tests, began to decline as television viewing became a more important part of American life?

11.3 The Controversy over Group Differences in IQ

Things to Learn

- Heritability of IQ test performance
- Gene-environment interactions
- Racial differences in average IQ
- Success of early interventions
- Stereotype threat in IQ testing

Whatever it is that IQ scores measure in modern humans, it probably mattered over the course of our evolution as well. For example, you could argue that having good health was even more important in the bad old days when what passed for medicine probably did more harm than good. In other words, millions of years before Alfred Binet was asked to select schoolchildren for special attention, natural selection must have been favoring genes that produce minds capable of a high IQ score.

We'll begin this section by reviewing the strong evidence that IQ scores are indeed heritable. In reviewing how heritability is estimated, we'll revisit the limitations of those estimates and their application that we discussed in Section 4.4. The short version is that heritability does not mean what most people think it means. For example, knowing that a trait like IQ is heritable tells us nothing about why any two people, or any two groups of people, differ in their IQ scores. There is no evidence that differences in the average IQ scores among groups of Americans of different races are related to the genes they carry. Also, just because a trait like IQ is heritable, that doesn't mean that the environment is unimportant. There's overwhelming evidence that quality education early in life can significantly and permanently raise IQ scores, and that children from lower-income families benefit the most from such education. By the end of the section we'll understand why there is no contradiction between the ideas that IQ performance is heritable and that early education can raise IQ to have a tremendous, positive influence in life.

How do we measure the heritability of IQ?

Heritability is a statistical estimate of the extent to which individual differences in genes contribute to individual differences in a trait, such as IQ performance, in a population. As discussed in Section 4.4, the heritability of a trait can be estimated by comparing individuals who are related and determining whether people who are more closely related are also more alike in terms of that trait. Perhaps the simplest approach is to compare **monozygotic (MZ) twins** (also called *identical twins*), who are genetically identical, with **dizygotic (DZ) twins** (also called *fraternal twins*), who are carried in the same womb at the same time but who share no more genes than any other pair of siblings. DZ twins share only half their genes, so any trait that is affected by genes should be more similar in MZ twins than in DZ twins.

heritability A statistical estimate of the extent to which individual differences in genes in a population contribute to individual differences in a trait.

monozygotic twins Also called *identical twins*. Twins derived from a single fertilized egg.

dizygotic twins Also called *fraternal twins* or *non-identical twins*. Twins derived from two separate eggs.

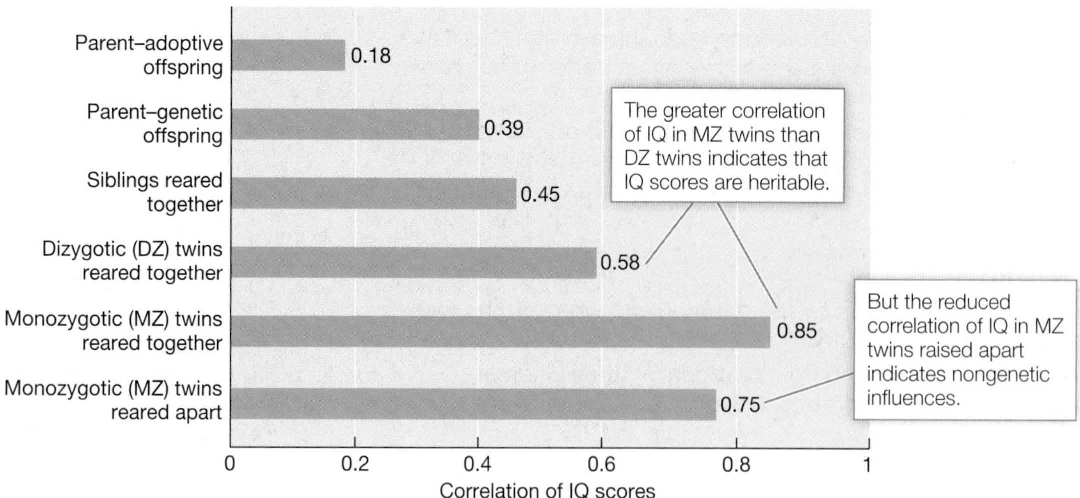

Figure 11.21 Comparing Relatives' IQ Scores to Estimate Heritability (After Bouchard & McGue, 1981.)

As correlations in **Figure 11.21** show, IQ scores are indeed more similar in MZ twins than in DZ twins. Recall that perfect correlation is scored at 1. The correlation of IQ scores in ordinary siblings is about 0.45, but the correlation in DZ twins is higher—0.58—meaning DZ twins are more alike in terms of IQ than are ordinary siblings. What causes that additional similarity? One factor is that DZ twins have more similar environments before birth, and more similar experiences growing up, than ordinary siblings. The IQ between MZ twins is even higher, at 0.85. We presume MZ twins are more alike in terms of IQ because they are even more closely related than are DZ twins.

One way to estimate heritability of IQ is to calculate how much more the MZ twins' correlation score differs from the DZ twins' correlation score, and assume that this additional similarity in MZ twins is due to an additional one half of genes shared. Subtracting the DZ correlation (0.58) from the MZ correlation (0.85) and multiplying the result by 2, we get 0.54:

$$0.85 - 0.58 = 0.27 \times 2 = 0.54$$

Although lots of different methods have been used, including comparing many different kinds of relatives and using much more sophisticated statistical tools, most estimates of the heritability of IQ come in pretty close to this estimate of 0.50.

What does it mean to say that the heritability of IQ is about 0.50? According to our definition of heritability, it means that about half (50%) of the variability in IQ scores in the population is due to variability in genes. And, if about half the variability in IQ scores is due to genes, the other half of the variability must be due to variability in other factors. These conclusions are consistent with knowing that many environmental factors, such as quality early education and lead exposure, can significantly affect IQ.

Just because IQ is heritable doesn't mean it can't be changed

Education will raise IQ, and deprivation will lower it, as we'll see. Twin data confirm that the environment affects IQ: the IQ scores of MZ twins raised together are more similar than those of MZ twins reared apart. Whether raised together or apart, they are genetically identical, so the additional similarity seen in MZ twins raised together must be due to shared experiences. Furthermore, we know for certain that many environmental factors, including toxins like lead, especially early in life, can permanently decrease IQ. Plus, the Flynn effect makes it clear that people raised in different generations differ in their performance on IQ tests. Even though the genes we inherited before birth are the only genes we will ever have, including the as-yet-unknown genes that influence IQ, our IQ is not determined by those genes alone.

You may have noticed that in this discussion we have been speaking of the heritability of *IQ performance*, not the heritability of *intelligence*. We can state with confidence that genes affect IQ scores and that the heritability of IQ is about 0.50. But whether IQ scores reflect intelligence depends, as ever, on how we define intelligence. We've already established that reasonable people disagree about what intelligence is (Jensen, 1999) and that there is more than one kind of intelligence.

It's important to distinguish between IQ scores and intelligence because there's plenty of reason to worry that IQ tests may be **culturally biased**, meaning that performance can be affected by the particular culture(s) to which the test-taker has been exposed. In the United States, the question is: To what extent are IQ tests easier for people who were raised in middle- or upper-income homes versus people who were raised in impoverished conditions? How poverty affects IQ test performance is the topic of **Box 11.1**.

Given irrefutable evidence that IQ performance is heritable, what outcomes, if any, can we predict from this information?

culturally biased Tests on which performance can be affected by the particular culture the test-taker has been exposed to.

Skeptic at Large

Class Bias Is Found in Most IQ Tests

There have been several attempts to construct culturally unbiased intelligence tests, which typically consist of tasks that don't rely on vocabulary or culturally specific objects. Instead, the tasks are based on fairly abstract reasoning and logic. In the figure here, the first two items, labeled "Matrix reasoning," differ from the other items because solving them doesn't require having any previous instruction in mathematics (which would definitely help performance on items 3–6) or a vocabulary that includes words such as *mercy* in item 8. To the extent that items 1 and 2 do not require knowledge of any particular language, they are indeed culturally neutral. All you need is an examiner who knows the local language to ask "Which of these items should go in the blank square?"

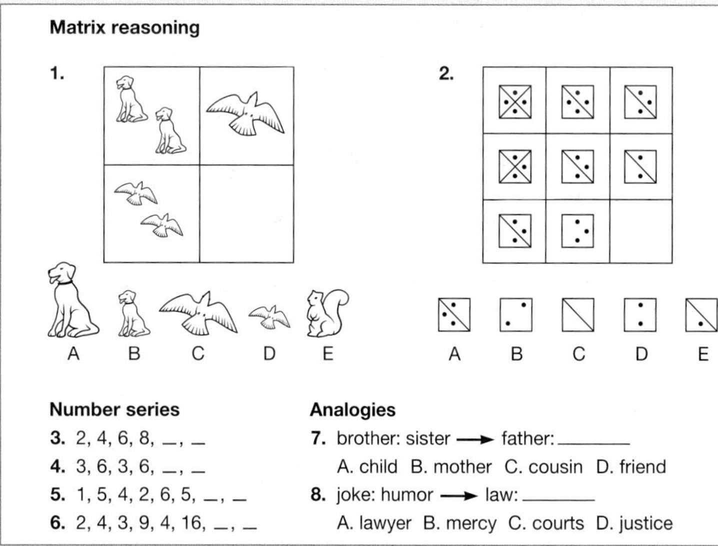

Matrix reasoning
1.
A B C D E
2.
A B C D E
Number series
3. 2, 4, 6, 8, _, _
4. 3, 6, 3, 6, _, _
5. 1, 5, 4, 2, 6, 5, _, _
6. 2, 4, 3, 9, 4, 16, _, _
Analogies
7. brother: sister → father: ____
A. child B. mother C. cousin D. friend
8. joke: humor → law: ____
A. lawyer B. mercy C. courts D. justice

Different Ways to Test Intelligence The first two items are intended to be culturally unbiased (Gottfredson, 1997). (Answers: 1. A; 2. D)

But even so-called culturally unbiased tests cannot compensate for all cultural differences. It is not clear, for example, that tests that focus on abstract reasoning are devoid of class bias. Consider that one of the facts of life in impoverished conditions is that you have to spend lots of time seeing to practical matters, such as where to get your next meal and how to stay warm. How much time do people struggling in such conditions have for tasks involving abstract problem solving compared to middle-income individuals with leisure time for less practical, more theoretical pursuits such as puzzles and video games? Can we rely on IQ tests that depend upon abstract reasoning as an indicator of intelligence if some environmental conditions encourage more abstract reasoning than others? It seems likely that children in the United States who live in impoverished conditions have fewer reasons,

Continued

BOX 11.1

and fewer opportunities, to engage in purely abstract reasoning.

Another question to consider: *Should* intelligence tests be culturally unbiased? Do we need to know how culture affects an individual's ability to perform in a given environment? Let's say that the WISC test asks a child to explain what the word *debilitating* means. An American child from an impoverished family is not as likely to have heard this word in conversation as a child from an affluent household is. (One study estimated that by the time children are 4 years old, those growing up with parents in professional occupations, such as teachers, lawyers, and doctors, have heard *32 million more words* than children raised in poor families [Risley & Hart, 1995].) Many critics of intelligence tests say that it's unfair to construct intelligence tests using terms impoverished children may have never heard but would readily have learned had they been raised in educated families. Others, however, assert that having an extensive vocabulary is part of what it means to be intelligent in our culture, and that the question of how a child acquires that vocabulary is irrelevant. The impoverished child could have gone to the library and checked out books, for free, that use the word *debilitating*. The argument is that experience can feed and boost intelligence, and that experience can be gained either by growing up around highly educated and conversant adults or by taking advantage of other opportunities, such as that offered by libraries.

Let's look at this question yet another way. A modern adult who is very intelligent in our culture may have no idea how to plant and harvest a field of wheat. Hundreds of years ago someone without that knowledge would have been thought as lacking intelligence. Neither judgment—intelligent today, stupid then—is wrong, but each applies only to a particular culture. As we saw at the start of the chapter, the butler Crichton, inept in witty conversations with his rich employers in England, was brilliant at staying alive on the island.

Good measures of intelligence in everyday life will have to gauge a person's understanding of the cultural environment, and IQ tests certainly do that. Perhaps one reason IQ scores correlate with so many measures of accomplishment—in terms of school, work, and lifetime earnings—is precisely because all those measures are boosted by a solid understanding of our culture, as manifested in our schools, workplaces, and the marketplace. If IQ scores didn't reflect our culture, they might not predict accomplishments in schools, workplaces, and the marketplace as well as they do.

We can go round and round in such discussions, but the bottom line is that it is probably impossible to construct a test that gauges "intelligence" in terms of how one behaves in our culture unless it is testing knowledge of that culture. So if poverty reduces IQ performance, as it clearly does, maybe that's because poverty reduces intelligence too. Indeed, one exhaustive survey found a strong correlation (0.76) between average IQ scores across many countries and national income in each country (Lynn & Vanhanen, 2002). This point will be important when we consider why some groups of people in the United States score better than others on IQ tests.

Heritability does not mean what most people think it does

As noted in Section 4.4, there are several common misunderstandings about heritability estimates. A key thing to remember is that heritability estimates concern *populations*, and thus tell us nothing about individuals. For example, if the heritability of IQ is estimated to be 50%, that does not mean that half your IQ score depends on your genes and the other half on the environment. Nor does it mean that half the people inherited their IQ while the other half learned what they needed for the test. Everyone inherits some genes that affect IQ, and everyone must learn about the world in order to answer any test item.

Also, we can't assume that just because a trait seems biological, then variation in that trait must be heritable. For example, the number of hands a person is born with is clearly a biological trait, requiring the action of many genes to build hands before birth. Yet most of the variation in the number of hands a baby is born with is caused by exposure to toxins that cause birth defects, not by the genes the baby inherited.

Recall from Section 4.2 that our genes do not change as we grow up and grow old, but *how those genes are used*—when and where they are called on—depends on *experience*. This is one reason why experience affects IQ, despite the influence of genes on IQ. Another way to think of it is that if genes account for 50% of the variability in IQ scores, then other factors, like experience, must

■ TABLE 11.5 What Heritability Does *not* Mean

Just because a trait, like IQ, is heritable, that does *not* mean	Because...
The trait is unaffected by the environment.	Many environmental factors can change IQ.
An individual's IQ cannot be changed by education.	Educational programs, especially early in life, can permanently raise IQ scores.
Culture doesn't matter	Impoverished children adopted by middle-class families enjoy a boost in IQ.
You can predict anything about why an *individual* has a particular IQ.	It could be due either to a fortunate set of genes or a favorable environment, or both.
The trait is a "more biological" trait than others.	Heritability of having two hands is close to 0, because loss of hands is usually caused by toxins causing birth defects in babies, or accidents affecting adults.
The average differences seen between two groups, such as between two races, are caused by differences in genes.	The difference in average IQ between African Americans and white Americans shrank steadily across the twentieth century.

account for the other 50%. Likewise, we saw that human IQ has also risen steadily across the twentieth century, and this rise cannot be due to changes in genes that were inherited, so it must be due to changes in how those genes are used. **Table 11.5** summarizes some of the things heritability does *not* mean.

To understand some other limitations of heritability estimates, let's talk about how the *interaction* of genes and the environment affects development of any trait, whether it's IQ performance, physical strength, or height. The interaction of genes and the environment is easier to understand if we consider a physical trait in a simple organism, so let's think about how tall plants might grow. (In fact, the concept of estimating heritability originated from the study of plants.)

Figure 11.22 shows seven strains of wild yarrow plants grown at different elevations. In the top graph the strains (A–G) are arranged according to how well they

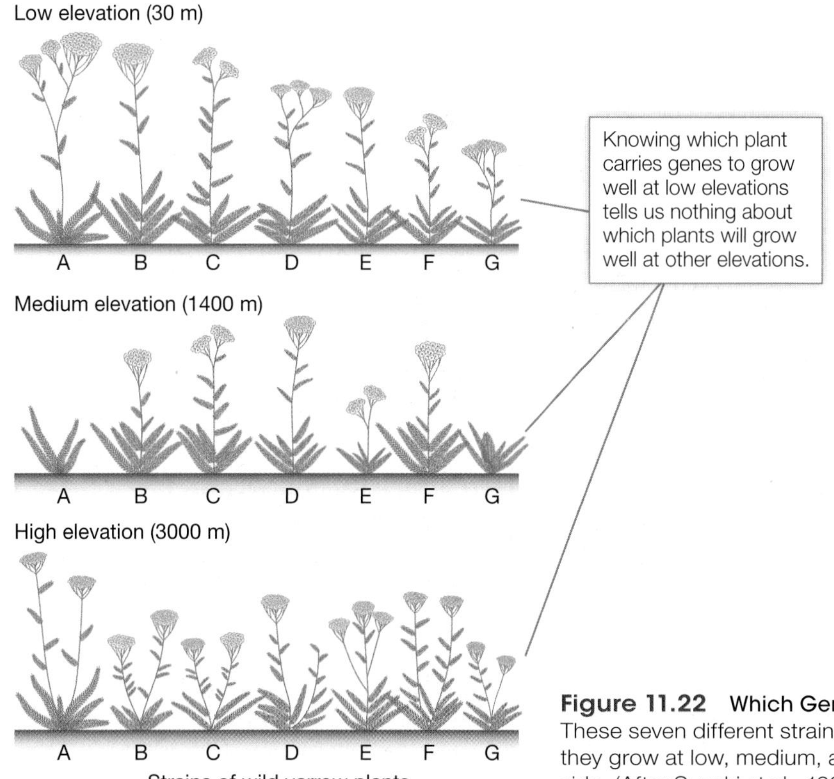

Figure 11.22 Which Genes Are Best Depends on Environment These seven different strains of wild yarrow plants differ in how well they grow at low, medium, and high elevations along a mountainside. (After Suzuki et al., 1981.)

grow at the low elevation, and the next two graphs show how well they grow at medium and high elevations. Note that the relative success of the different strains at the low elevation tells you *nothing* about how they will do at the medium and high elevations, where temperature, winds, and moisture may be different. This is an example of the interaction of genes and the environment, where genes are expressed differently, depending on environmental conditions (see Chapter 4).

An interesting example of a gene–environment interaction for IQ is the finding that infants who are breast-fed grow up to have higher IQs than those who are bottle-fed, a clear environmental influence on IQ. Interestingly, only infants carrying a particular version of one gene experience this boost in IQ from breast-feeding (Caspi et al., 2007). If the baby doesn't happen to carry that version of the gene, then breast-feeding won't make any difference to IQ.

We discussed an example of an interaction of genes and environment in Section 4.2, concerning rat strains that had been artificially selected to be either good at solving mazes ("maze bright") or poor at solving mazes ("maze dull"). It was clear that the two strains of rats carried different genes and that these different genes were responsible for their different maze-solving abilities. However, those genetic differences between the strains disappeared if the rats were raised in impoverished conditions (each rat living alone in a cage), as both strains were then equally poor at maze solving. Conversely, the difference between the strains in maze solving also disappeared if the rats were raised in enriched conditions, living in large cages with lots of toys and other rats to play with. Coming from an enriched environment, both strains performed well, and the difference between them disappeared (Cooper & Zubek, 1958; see Figure 4.10).

The interaction of genes and experience also explains a consistent finding in the IQ literature: Children from impoverished conditions who are adopted by middle-income families grow up to have a higher IQ, on average, than their biological parents. A similar set of genes produced a low IQ in biological parents reared in impoverished conditions and a higher IQ in the children raised in better conditions. A hypothetical example of this phenomenon is illustrated in **Figure 11.23**. While theoretical, this example illustrates *two results that have been seen repeatedly in real data sets*. The first is that people from middle-income families have higher IQs than those from impoverished families, and the second is that children adopted from impoverished families into middle-income conditions have higher IQs than their biological parents. On average, the children gain 12 to 18 IQ points when they're taken out of poverty—the more affluent the adoptive

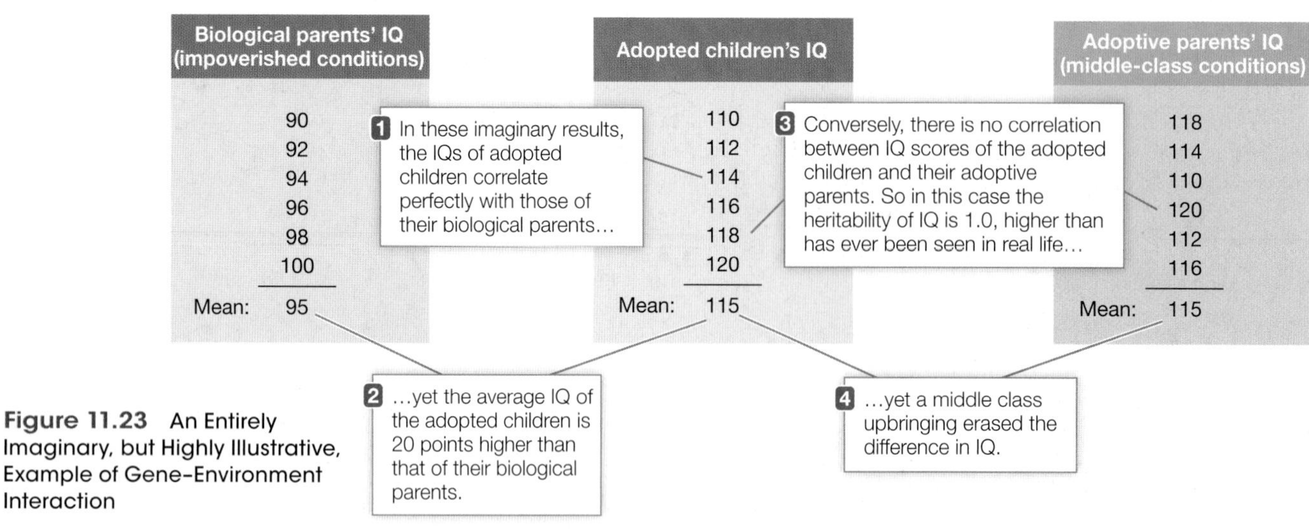

Figure 11.23 An Entirely Imaginary, but Highly Illustrative, Example of Gene-Environment Interaction

family, the greater the IQ gain (Duyme et al., 1999). In the figure, the estimate of heritability of IQ from comparing relatives is a whopping 100%—there's a perfect correlation in the IQs of biological parents and the offspring (notice that the rank order of the biological parents' IQs is perfectly matched by the rank order of the children's IQs). Learning from this result that IQ is heritable, you might be tempted to say that the lower IQ in the biological parents is due to differences in the genes they carry. Yet their biological children, carrying genes only from those impoverished parents, when adopted into middle-income conditions, have an average IQ that is equal to that of their adoptive parents.

Phenylketonuria (**PKU**), which we first discussed in Chapter 4, offers another example of how environment can override even a strong genetic influence. This genetic disorder can cause severe mental disability, including a very low IQ. Heritability of PKU is 100%. However, if the baby is reared in an environment with little or no phenylalanine in the diet, mental development is normal, including a normal IQ score (see Figure 4.12).

phenylketonuria (PKU) An inherited disorder of protein metabolism in which the absence of an enzyme leads to a toxic buildup of certain compounds, causing intellectual disability.

Whenever heritability estimates are given, it's important to know from what population the data were taken. An estimate of heritability based on comparison of relatives is limited to the range of environments those relatives experienced, and the range of genes those relatives possessed (Johnson et al., 2010). For example, if a heritability estimate were gathered from middle-income people in the United States, it may or may not apply to people living in the Kalahari desert in southern Africa. Later we'll consider estimates of IQ heritability in lower-income Americans that differ in interesting ways from those derived from middle-income families.

Understanding that heritability estimates tell us nothing about why the average IQ might differ between two groups of people carrying different genes and living in different environments is crucial for understanding the controversy over race and IQ, which we'll consider next.

Knowing a trait is heritable does not address the cause of average group differences

The solid findings that IQ performance is heritable, gathered throughout the twentieth century, became controversial when it was widely reported that Americans of different races and ethnic groups also differ, on average, in IQ scores. Jewish Americans have higher average IQ scores than Asian Americans, who have higher mean IQ scores than white Americans, who have higher mean IQ scores than Latino Americans and African Americans (Mackintosh, 2011). It is important to emphasize that these are *average* differences, with loads of overlap. Over 20% of African Americans have a higher IQ than the average white American, so you cannot accurately judge an individual's IQ by the color of his or her skin. Still, the average differences among races in IQ have been seen repeatedly.

Unfortunately, many people put these findings together to conclude mistakenly that the differences among the races in average IQ must be due to differences in genes among various races. Let me telegraph the punch line for the remainder of this chapter, which can be summarized in two points:

1. Knowing a trait is heritable tells us *nothing* about why the trait differs between two groups, even if those groups have different genes.
2. Many studies have repeatedly found that *environmental factors, including experience, have profound effects on IQ scores*.

In other words, we still do not know whether differences in genes are responsible for racial differences in IQ. What we do know, for certain, is that there are average differences in socioeconomic conditions among the races, and that socioeconomic conditions, especially early in life, affect IQ performance.

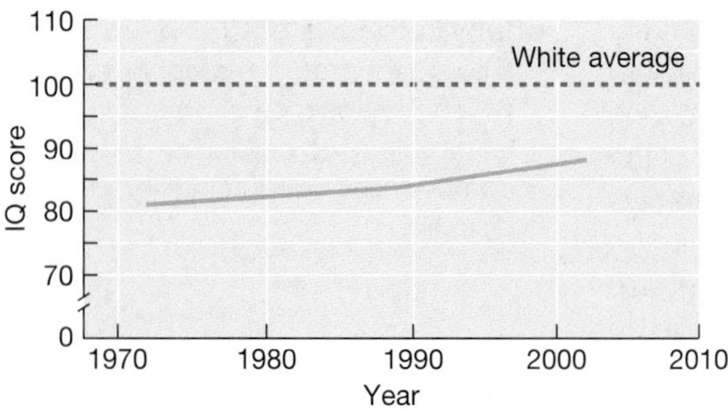

Figure 11.24 Shrinking Racial Differences in IQ Scores at the End of the Twentieth Century Wechsler Intelligence Scale for Children (WISC) IQ scores for African Americans across three decades. Note that this is in addition to a large shrinkage of the gap in the first half of the century. (After Dickens & Flynn, 2006.)

We noted earlier that knowing that a trait like IQ performance is heritable does not mean it is fixed, inevitable, or unaffected by the environment. If the heritability of IQ is 0.50, then clearly there are other factors affecting the trait, and so environmental factors could, in theory, account entirely for the racial differences. Only if the environmental factors were exactly the same for Americans of different races could we attribute the racial difference to genes, but we know conditions are not the same for different races.

In thinking about racial differences in IQ, consider another case of average differences between groups: sex differences in test performance. Until the 1980s, the superior male performance on standardized tests of mathematics, like the math portion of the SAT, was widely attributed to biological differences between the sexes (Benbow & Stanley, 1980). But that sex difference in math performance shrank continuously in the second half of the twentieth century until now there are reports that there no longer is a sex difference in America (Hyde et al., 2008) or worldwide (Else-Quest et al., 2010; Guiso et al., 2008). (See Figure 15.14 about sex differences in math scores across countries.) As far as we know, the biology of the sexes has not changed during those decades. The improved performance of females on those tests must have been due to environmental factors, such as greater encouragement to learn math and take math courses.

As with sex differences in math ability, we should be skeptical of the idea that the racial gap in IQ is due to genetic influences. The gap in average IQ between white Americans and African Americans shrank considerably in the course of the twentieth century (Murray, 2007), including in the last two decades (Dickens & Flynn, 2006), as average scores for African Americans rose (**Figure 11.24**). Since genetic makeup could not have changed in such a short period, what factor(s) might explain the improved scores? The most likely factor seems to be the improved economic and social conditions of African Americans in the twentieth century.

That the racial difference in IQ among Americans may be due to socioeconomic factors is strongly supported by an early study of German children who were fathered by American soldiers stationed in Germany. Reared in Germany, these children had similar IQ scores whether their father was white or black (Eyferth, 1961). The racial difference in IQ seen among the general American population was also present in soldiers of that era. If that difference in IQ was caused by white soldiers carrying more genes favoring high IQs, why didn't their children have higher IQs than children fathered by black soldiers?

Heritability estimates are higher in middle-class and affluent populations than in poor people

Additional evidence of a socioeconomic basis for the racial differences in average IQ comes, paradoxically enough, from studies estimating heritability of IQ. As mentioned earlier, almost all the heritability estimates for IQ come from middle-income American families, and heritability estimates from one population may not apply to another population. When psychologists studied IQ in impoverished families, they found that the heritability of IQ was almost 0 (Turkheimer et al., 2003). In other words, in poor families, the IQ scores of MZ twins are no more alike than those of DZ twins! We know the DZ twins have more genetic differences than MZ twins, so why aren't their IQs more variable than those of MZ twins? The most obvious possibility is that the differences in potential IQ that the DZ twins inherited were overwhelmed by the environment. Without access to economic and intellectual resources, each DZ sibling was unable to reach his or her full potential. In one study that looked at reading ability, which is an important component of IQ scores, the heritability of reading ability was high in people who had grown up with educated parents but was very low in people whose parents had been uneducated (Friend et al., 2008; Kremen et al., 2005). In other words, an economically or educationally impoverished environment is a limiting factor that does not allow us to see the contributions genes might have made. Most important, this limiting factor would cause the average IQ from impoverished families to be lower, because *those who had the genes to achieve a high IQ never got the chance to use them.*

So why are heritability estimates for IQ so high in middle-income and affluent families? Probably because children in those conditions have access to all the economic and intellectual resources they need to reach their full potential IQ. If everyone in the study population has access to educated parents in the home, good schools, and safe neighborhoods, then everyone can make maximum use of their genes to reach their full potential IQ. In that case, we'll see a big contribution of differences in genes to differences in IQ. Heritability estimates for IQ from those families will be high. And not coincidentally, the *average* IQ in that group will be boosted by those folks who received genes that could benefit from that good environment to develop a high IQ.

While the mean difference in IQ between African Americans and whites has grown smaller, it persists today, and experts continue to disagree on whether that gap is going to close entirely (Mackintosh, 2011; Nisbett, 2005; Rushton & Jensen, 2005). Researchers do, however, concur that early education can permanently improve IQ scores in any group, as we'll see next.

Experience Matters Several studies have confirmed that early intervention projects boost IQ and improve the lives of children in poverty.

Early intervention programs for children can raise IQ scores

One of the most important indications that the environment can raise IQ scores is the Flynn effect mentioned earlier—the persistent increase in average IQ scores for as long as there have been IQ tests. No matter which of several explanations for the Flynn effect you prefer—improved nutrition, improved medical care, increased intellectual stimulation—they are all environmental effects. If environmental changes can account for the average gain of 20 IQ points from 1932 to 1991, then environmental differences could also be responsible for the 12-point difference between races (see Figure 11.24). Furthermore, one of the most consistent findings in the field of intelligence testing is that quality educational programs, especially early in life, can lead to permanent increases in IQ (Campbell & Ramey, 1995).

One indication that education boosts IQ is the fact that American children perform better on IQ tests before summer vacation than they do after summer vacation (Hayes & Grether, 1969). The biggest "fading" of IQ over the summer is seen in children from impoverished families, presumably because their homes over the summer are less intellectually stimulating than the homes of middle-income students (Cooper et al., 1996).

The *Abecedarian Project* is one of several studies that have directly tackled the issue of the racial difference in IQ. The project identified 3-month-old babies from impoverished families, 90% of whom were African American, and randomly assigned them to one of two groups. The control group received no help, while the other group received intensive day care and education. By 3 years of age, the children receiving the preschool education had an average IQ 15 points higher than those in the control group (Ramey & Ramey, 1998). In another study (the *Milwaukee Project*), children entering first grade who had received intensive education since they were babies had an average IQ of 119, versus an average of 87 for the control group (Garber, 1988). Was this a lasting improvement? Apparently so, because once the children reached adolescence, there was still a 10-point difference in IQ between the two groups. In another case, intervention with Romanian orphans was reported to boost IQ 8 points (Almas et al., 2012).

Head Start programs, which begin with children older than those in the Abecedarian and Milwaukee Projects and offer less intensive education, would not be expected to be as effective. Nevertheless, many analyses have repeatedly shown that Head Start interventions increase IQ by the program's

Skeptic at Large

BOX 11.2

The Bogus Mozart Effect

Many music lovers have noted that the compositions of Wolfgang Amadeus Mozart (1756–1791, see figure) have an exquisite, orderly quality. Perhaps it was this orderly quality of Mozart's music that led physician Alfred Tomatis to suggest that listening to Mozart might benefit children with certain disorders, such as autism, who have difficulty communicating. In his book *Why Mozart?*, Tomatis (1991) claimed to have helped such children enormously by having them listen to, among other things, modified versions of Mozart compositions. Unfortunately, when other scientists tested his ideas, the therapy was not effective. Sometimes, the autistic children listening to the music did *worse* than the children receiving placebo treatment (Corbett et al., 2008).

Perhaps it was Tomatis's misguided reports that led Rauscher et al. (1993) to test whether having college students listen to Mozart could improve their performance on some specific tests of abstract spatial reasoning taken from the Stanford–Binet test. The authors reported in the prestigious journal *Nature* that subjects listening to Mozart had scores of 119 compared with 111 for those listening to a relaxation tape, and 110 for those listening to silence. It didn't take long for the mass media to distort the findings, declaring that "listening to Mozart actually makes you smarter." Within 5 years, a best-selling book was urging everyone to expose their children, even before birth, to Mozart's music to benefit IQ. The governor of Georgia seriously proposed providing every child in the state with a tape or CD of classical music to boost intelligence.

Unfortunately, the reality does not live up to the hype. Even the original authors of the *Nature* paper never claimed that listening to Mozart boosted overall intelligence—only that it improved performance on some specific items from an IQ test, and that even those improvements were considered temporary. Many scientists offered alternative explanations for even the modest effects that were seen originally. Perhaps it was not the organization of Mozart's composition that mattered, but the effects of the music on mood and arousal. It turned out that listening to a passage from a Stephen King novel could also improve scores on those items, but *only if the participant enjoyed the passage* (Steele et al., 1999).

A Tutor for IQ Tests? Wolfgang Amadeus Mozart was a great musical prodigy as a child.

A review found that many studies had been unable to replicate the original findings. In reports that did see an effect of music, almost any sort of music was effective, and even then the effect lasted no more than 20 minutes (Abbott, 2007).

Despite these findings, an entire mini-industry continues to tout the remarkable benefits of Mozart. A recent search for "Mozart effect" on Amazon.com brought up more than 900 books, DVDs, and CDs. Despite the aggressive marketing of the Mozart effect, there's no reason to think this music will actually make you, or your child, smarter (Waterhouse, 2006). So if you prefer listening to Beethoven, or Linkin Park, feel free—it won't hurt your IQ performance.

end (Caruso et al., 1982), typically 5 to 6 years of age. Critics note, however, that in several cases, improved IQ fades after children leave the Head Start program and enter public school (Currie & Thomas, 1995). Might this be because most of these impoverished children go on to attend impoverished schools (Lee & Loeb, 1995)? One study confirming that the boost in IQ from Head Start had faded by young adulthood nevertheless noted that the preschoolers who had participated in Head Start were, at 19 years of age, 20% more likely to have graduated from high school and 20% less likely to have been imprisoned (Cunha & Heckman, 2009).

You may have heard that babies exposed to classical music grow up to be smarter, but that is a myth, as we discuss in **Box 11.2**. Still, because other early environmental interventions really do raise IQ, it is possible that the average difference in IQ between Americans of different races could be entirely due to differences in the environment that children of different races experience. We've been talking mostly about average differences among the races in terms of economics, and there's no doubt that people living in poverty are more likely to be exposed to toxins (such as lead), are more likely to suffer malnutrition, and are less likely to have educated parents.

In addition, children in more impoverished conditions are more likely to live with only one parent. In fact, the rankings of different races in average IQ pretty much mirror the rankings in terms of single-parent families. In 2012, only 17% of Asian American children lived in single-parent households in the United States, versus 25% of white, 42% of Hispanic or Latino, and 67% of African American children (Annie E. Casey Foundation & KIDS COUNT Data Center, 2014). In other words, the race with the lowest percentage of kids in single-parent families has the highest average IQ. This may not be a coincidence. Presumably, children in single-parent households get less parental attention, including intellectual stimulation, than children living with both parents.

stereotype threat A phenomenon occurring when exposure to a derogatory stereotype about a particular group causes group members to perform worse.

Emotional state affects performance on intelligence tests

The very fact that racial differences in IQ are widely known, and that our society holds stereotypes suggesting that African Americans are less intelligent than other groups, is almost certainly perpetuating those racial differences. **Stereotype threat** is an emotional state experienced when exposure to a derogatory stereotype about a particular group (such as the stereotype that African Americans are unintelligent, or that females can't do math) causes its members to perform worse. The unflattering prediction about their performance becomes a self-fulfilling prophecy, seemingly confirming the stereotype (Walton & Spencer, 2009), as we'll see next (**Figure 11.25**).

☑ Researchers at Work

The test you are about to take...

Figure 11.25 Stereotype Threat Affects Test Performance
(After Steele & Aronson, 1995.)

■ **Question:** Do societal stereotypes about race differences in intelligence impair test performance of members of minorities?

■ **Hypothesis:** Reminders of racial stereotypes about intelligence will affect the performance of African Americans taking a test.

■ **Test:** Have groups of white and African American students take a test composed of questions typical of IQ tests. For one group, ask the students to report their race before taking the test. For the other group, do not ask them to report their race beforehand.

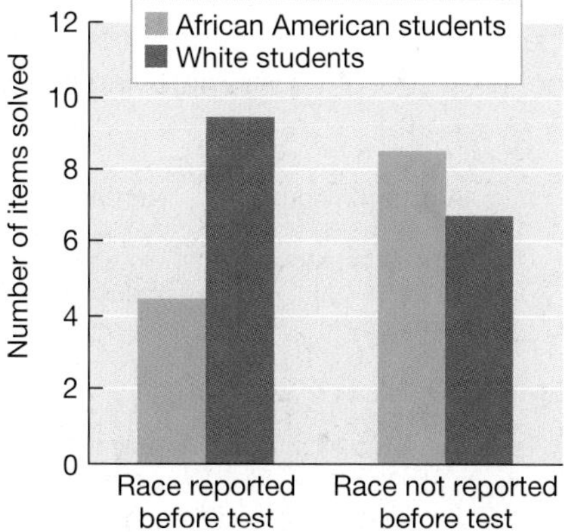

Continued

Researchers at Work *Continued*

■ **Results:** African American students who had to report their race before taking the test solved fewer problems than those who did not have to report their race. Reporting race did not significantly affect the performance of white students.

■ **Conclusion:** Even a reminder about race can affect IQ test performance of minority students, probably because it prompts thoughts of stereotypes about race and intelligence. Recollecting such stereotypes may discourage minority students from trying their best. The prevalence of stereotypes may very well contribute to group differences in IQ scores among races.

In a related experiment, African American students did better on IQ-type questions when they were told it was a test of "problem solving" than when they were told the test was of "intelligence" (Steele & Aronson, 1995). In another study, people took an academic test under two conditions (Blascovich et al., 2001). For one group, the researchers indicated at the start of the test that African Americans don't do as well as other groups on this test. This offered a stereotype threat to the African American test-takers. The other group was not told this but was otherwise treated the same. Under stereotype threat conditions, African Americans showed more physiological signs of stress (an increase in blood pressure) and performed worse on the test than when no stereotype threat was presented. Non-African American test-takers had the same blood pressure and performance under both conditions (**Figure 11.26**). So if African Americans have heard that they, as a race, do not do well on IQ tests, then exposure to that stereotype will hurt their performance on the test. Normally no one makes statements like this before students take an exam, but because our society has often portrayed the stereotype that African Americans are less intelligent than other races, every African American has always taken IQ tests under the burden of this stereotype threat.

In Section 15.1, we'll review evidence that the sex difference in math performance may be a reflection of stereotype threat (Dar-Nimrod & Heine, 2006; Spencer et al., 1999). A similar study did a simple manipulation aimed at racial stereotype threat—having students write a brief essay in class about their own adequacy. Having the students write such an essay before taking the test reduced the difference between African American and white students by 40% (Cohen et al., 2006). So we have to wonder whether the racial difference in IQ tests might disappear entirely if we could go back in time and erase the stereotype that some races are less intelligent than others. Since we have no such time machine, we will have to hope that, with time and social progress, the stereotypes will fade. If that happens, perhaps the racial differences in average IQ will disappear as well. If so, perhaps scientists who presently spend their time trying to prove that genetics does or does not account for racial differences in IQ might instead direct their effort toward improving intelligence in everyone.

	African Americans	Non-African Americans
No stereotype threat presented	No effect on blood pressure or performance	No effect on blood pressure or performance
Stereotype threat presented ("African Americans don't tend to do well at this test.")	Higher blood pressure; decreased performance	No effect on blood pressure or performance

Figure 11.26 Stereotype Threat
Telling students that African Americans don't do well on a test raises blood pressure and impairs performance only in black students.

The Cutting Edge

Can the *N*-Back Procedure Increase Fluid Intelligence?

A report that young adults could increase their fluid intelligence by practicing a difficult cognitive task on a computer (Jaeggi et al., 2008; Jaeggi et al., 2010) generated a lot of interest, not only among intelligence researchers but in the popular media as well (Hurley, 2012). For researchers, the report challenged a widely held view that fluid intelligence is a stable, lifelong trait. For the public, there was the possibility that playing a computer game would make them smarter (Madrigal, 2008).

The procedure is called the ***n*-back task**, and participants are given a sequence of items—say, hearing a long list of random letters read aloud—and must report whenever the current item is identical to the one "*n*" items before. The task is easy when $n = 1$; you simply indicate when the current letter is the same as the one just before. In other words, you heard a letter repeated. When $n = 2$ (2-back), you have to report when the current letter (*B*) was the same as the one two letters ago. To perform well at this version, you must keep a mental list of the order of letters so far (*Z*, *X*, *B*, *R*, *B*), which makes it noticeably more difficult. Harder yet is the $n = 3$ (3-back) version, when you have to indicate when the current letter is the same as the one presented three back. Nevertheless, with practice, participants get better and are eventually able to perform well in the 4-back and 5-back versions (Jaeggi et al., 2008). Participants are also given a test of fluid intelligence, such as the Raven's progressive matrices (see Figure 11.13), before and after training. Overall, the participants' fluid intelligence scores are higher after training than before. Also, the more days they spent training, the bigger their improvement (Jaeggi et al., 2008). A control group given other cognitive tasks showed no change in fluid intelligence.

What makes this a cutting edge topic is that, despite a replication from the original researchers (Jaeggi et al., 2010), several other groups have been unable to see any improvement in fluid intelligence after participants mastered the *n*-back task (Chooi & Thompson, 2012; Redick et al., 2013). So investigators are trying to sort out why they don't all get the same results. For now, then, it would be wise to suspend judgment about whether the *n*-back task, or any other training, really increases fluid intelligence. Of course, that hasn't prevented commercial groups from trying to sell us software to raise our IQ (**Figure 11.27**). You can try it for free at: http://www.soakyourhead.com/dual-n-back.aspx.

Dual N-Back Training - Proven to Raise IQ

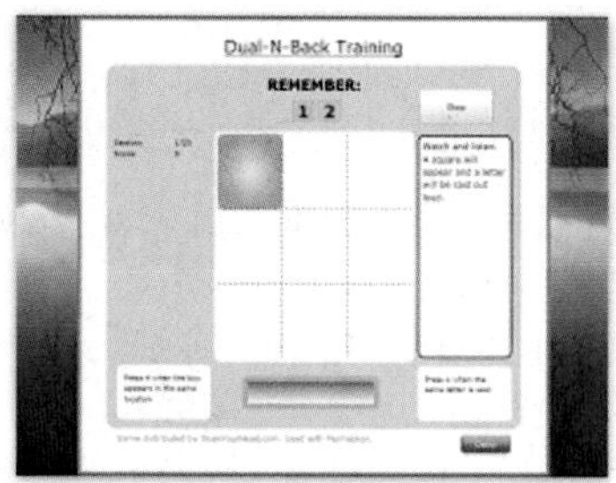

Play: Small | Medium | Large

Yes, you can get smarter! Dual n-back training has been shown to **increase a person's intelligence quotient (IQ)**.

It does this by increasing the number of items that can be held in working memory, the bottleneck of learning. In a famous study by Jaeggi, et al., participants who completed 20 minutes of dual n-back training each day raised their fluid intelligence and IQ scores.

Now you can do the same. To begin, click the Medium link at left to open the dual n-back game in a pop-up window.

Figure 11.27 Can *N*-Back Training Really Make You Smarter? Despite the claims of the app developers, the jury is still out on whether *n*-back training really raises IQ.

***n*-back task** A procedure where participants are given a sequence of items and must report whenever the current item is identical to the one "*n*" items before.

11.3 SUMMARY

- The more closely related people are, the more likely they are to have similar IQ scores, suggesting that genes influence IQ. For example, the correlation of IQ scores is greater among *monozygotic* (*MZ*) *twins*, who are genetically identical, than among *dizygotic* (*DZ*) *twins*, who share only half of their genes.
- The *heritability* of IQ is approximately 0.50, which means that about half of the variability in IQ scores in the population is due to variability in the genes.
- Several environmental factors, such as lead, fetal exposure to alcohol, and family size, can affect IQ.
- The interaction of genes and the environment can be seen in babies who inherit *phenylketonuria* (*PKU*); such babies can avoid becoming mentally disabled despite this genetic defect if they do not eat phenylalanine.
- Average IQ differences among races have been consistently seen but these are population-level differences; so you cannot accurately estimate an individual's IQ by knowing his or her race. The 0.50 heritability estimate for IQ means that those racial differences in IQ measurement may be due either to genetic differences or to environmental differences, or to both.
- Several observations suggest that the gap in average IQ score between African Americans and white Americans may be due to environmental differences. The gap became considerably smaller in the twentieth century, as social reforms provided black Americans with better education and less discrimination. Socioeconomic factors, such as living in poverty, have been associated with differences in IQ scores among races.
- Children adopted out of impoverished families tend to develop higher IQs than their biological parents, a reflection of a gene–environment interaction. Paradoxically, estimates of the heritability of IQ are nearly 0 among impoverished Americans, suggesting that impoverished conditions do not allow individuals to develop the full IQ that their genes would allow them if they were in middle-income conditions.
- Early intervention programs, such as Head Start, consistently raise the IQ of impoverished children. It is not known why in some cases improved IQ "fades" after a child enters public school; it could be due to the poor quality of some public schools in impoverished communities.
- The performance of African Americans on IQ tests is subject to *stereotype threat*, in which exposure to derogatory stereotypes about a particular group affects the performance of members of that group.

REVIEW QUESTIONS

1. How do we estimate the heritability of a trait like IQ performance, and what do those estimates tell us about the influence of the environment on IQ?
2. Discuss examples of the interaction of genes and the environment for both physical traits in plants and IQ scores in people.
3. What is phenylketonuria, and how does it illustrate gene–environment interaction with respect to IQ?
4. Review the evidence that the difference in average IQ between black Americans and white Americans may be due to differences in their environments.
5. What is stereotype threat, and how might it play a role in racial differences in average IQ?

Food for Thought

Construct a "thought experiment" in which you have the power to do whatever you want to manipulate genes and/or the environment, to test whether racial differences in average IQ are due to genes or the environment. Do you think such a test will actually be conducted any time soon?

Intelligence

The Admirable Crichton

When the play *Peter Pan* first opened in London in 1904, audiences were still packing the theater to see playwright J. M. Barrie's hit from two years before, *The Admirable Crichton*. Crichton, butler to the English Lord Loam, sees to the needs of his social superiors with total submission. In return for a paltry salary and a place to live, Crichton works long hours so that the aristocratic family can eat fabulous meals and while away their hours in frivolous conversation and trivial pursuits. The butler believes that the British class system of the day, where most people toil away in poverty so that a select few can lead rich lives of leisure, is a "natural outcome of a civilized society."

Then Crichton is required to accompany his employers on a sea voyage and they are all shipwrecked on a tropical isle. Unlike the castaways on TV's *Lost*, these refugees face dire problems, such as finding shelter and getting enough food to survive. Crichton is the only person among them who has enough practical skills to be of any use. Soon he becomes the leader, organizing and teaching the others what they must do. For one thing, everyone needs to work, a great shock to the aristocrats, who threaten to go off and leave him alone. But only Crichton has enough knowledge and skill to produce a pot of soup. The lord's family, drawn irresistibly to the aroma, comes crawling back to beg for a portion.

After a few years of Crichton's leadership, the island is civilized through a program of farming and building where everyone works hard except the former butler. Crichton, now the highly respected "Governor," continues making decisions and giving orders but spends much of his time in leisure pursuits. Lord Loam's daughter, Lady Mary, falls deeply in love with Crichton. They are on the verge of marriage—when a ship rescues them all.

Such a marriage is unthinkable back in England, where Crichton is again the humble, toiling butler and the aristocrats resume their carefree days. Barrie considered a different ending, where Lady Mary and Crichton marry after the rescue, but he decided that audiences of the day "wouldn't stand it."

Think Like a Psychologist:

Principles in Action

Whenever we encounter any interesting behavior we should consider the four principles. Here are some ways that the four principles relate to our opening story about Crichton.

MACHINE

The mind is a product of a physical machine, the brain.

There is no doubt that genes play a role in intelligence. For Edwardian England, it was obvious that the upper class members were more intelligent than the lower classes because of "breeding," the supposedly superior hereditary endowment of the noble class.

UNCONSCIOUS

We are consciously aware of only a small part of our mental activity.

Most of us are unaware of how our concept of intelligence is shaped by our culture. Lord Loam never considered practical knowledge of any value until his life depended on it. Our current ideas of intelligence are shaped by a society that values verbal ability and economic achievement.

SOCIAL

We constantly modify our behavior, beliefs, and attitudes according to what we perceive about the people around us.

In the Edwardian era, the definition of *intelligent* depended on your social stratum. In the upper classes, a sharp wit was considered intelligent, whereas in the service class, manual dexterity and problem-solving ability was considered intelligent. The definition of intelligence will always depend upon society's values.

EXPERIENCE

Our experiences physically alter the structure and function of the brain.

In fact, any differences in abilities between Crichton and his employers were unlikely to have anything to do with heredity. Rather, Crichton had a long history of experience in manual tasks and problem solving that Lord Loam and his family had never acquired.

KEY TERMS

achievement tests, 459
Army Alpha, 454
Army Beta, 454
autism, 475
autism spectrum disorder, 476
Binet–Simon scale, 453
content validity, 462
convergent validity, 462
criterion-related validity, 462
cross-test reliability, 460
crystallized intelligence (g_C), 470
culturally biased, 483
dizygotic (DZ) twins, 481
Down syndrome, 475
fetal alcohol syndrome, 475
fluid intelligence (g_F), 470
Flynn effect, 478
fragile X syndrome, 475
frequency distribution, 458
generalized intelligence (*g* factor, *g*), 469
heritability, 481
intellectual disabilities, 474
intelligence quotient (IQ), 454
intelligence, 452
mental age, 453
monozygotic (MZ) twins, 481
multiple intelligences, 472
***n*-back task**, 493
normal distribution, 458
normalized, 455
percentiles, 456
phenylketonuria (PKU), 487
reaction time, 471
reliability, 459
savant syndrome, 476
scoring reliability, 460
split-half reliability, 460
standard deviation, 458
standardized, 455
Stanford–Binet test, 453
stereotype threat, 491
test–retest reliability, 459
validity, 460
Wechsler Adult Intelligence Scale (WAIS), 454
Wechsler Intelligence Scale for Children (WISC), 454

QUIZ YOURSELF

1. ________ tests are tests where each examiner follows specific instructions on how to administer the test.
   a. Individualized
   b. Normalized
   c. Standardized
   d. Reliable
2. Today, the most commonly administered intelligence test for children is the
   a. Stanford–Binet.
   b. WAIS.
   c. Army Alpha.
   d. WISC.
3. Which of the following is *not* a genetic cause of intellectual disability?
   a. Fetal alcohol syndrome
   b. Down syndrome
   c. Phenylketonuria
   d. Fragile X syndrome
4. Which of the following is true of the heritable trait of IQ?
   a. An individual's IQ is strictly determined by genetics and is unaffected by the environment.
   b. On average, the IQs of identical twins are more highly correlated than those of fraternal twins.
   c. IQ tests have been carefully designed so that culture is not a factor in IQ score.
   d. While IQ scores can be raised by educational experience, there is no permanent change in IQ scores due to education.
5. Two tests of intelligence that give very similar results have both ________ reliabilty and ________ validity.
   a. test–retest; criterion
   b. scoring; criterion-related
   c. split-half; face
   d. cross-test; convergent
6. ________ validity is the ability of a test to measure all facets of the psychological trait in question. ________ validity is the extent to which scores on a psychological test predict someone's real-life performance. ________ validity is the extent to which several tests designed to measure the same psychological trait agree.
7. A plot showing the range of test scores for a large group of people on the *x*-axis and the number of people who got each test score on the *y*-axis is a ________. For IQ scores, the bell-shaped curve of this plot is a ________.
8. ________ reflects overall mental ability. It is composed of ________, which can be thought of as analogous to the processing speed of a computer; and ________, which can be thought of as the information on the hard drive of a computer.
9. The ________ effect is the substantial increase in average scores on IQ tests that has occurred since the development of IQ tests.
10. The phenomena of one group performing worse on a particular type of test when reminded of widespread beliefs about the lack of ability of that group to do well in that area is termed ________.

1. c; 2. d; 3. a; 4. b; 5. d; 6. Content; Criterion-related (or concrete); Convergent; 7. frequency distribution; normal distribution; 8. Generalized intelligence (or *g*-factor or *g*); fluid intelligence; crystallized intelligence; 9. Flynn; 10. stereotype threat

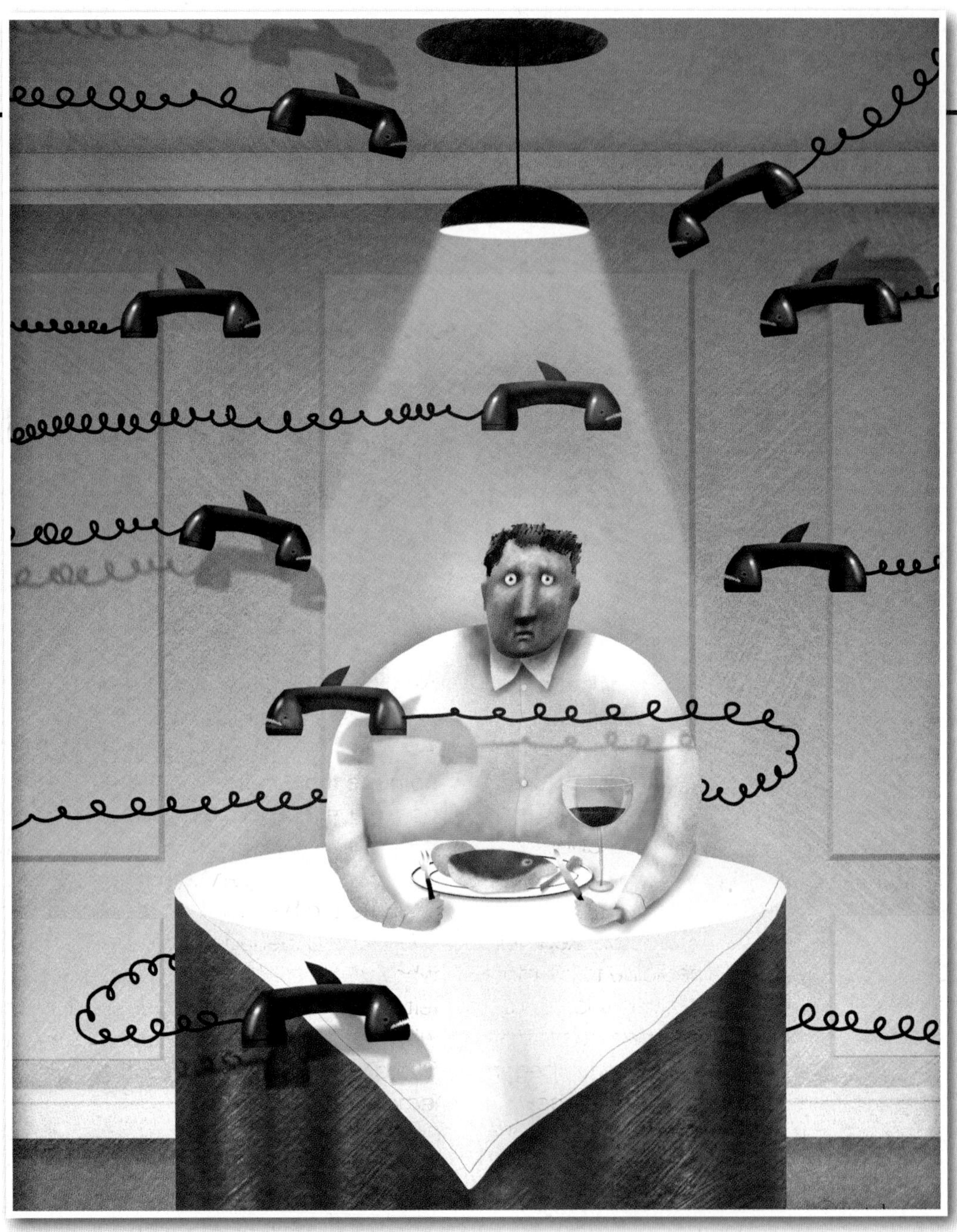

Motivation and the Regulation of Behavior

Brenda, the "Cave Woman"

Brenda never really felt like she was one of the girls. She had no interest in playing with dolls or wearing a dress. On the school playground, where she often had to stick up for her twin brother, Brian, the other children made fun of her, called her a "cave woman." No matter how much social pressure was applied, Brenda fantasized about growing up to be a man with a mustache, sports car, and a girlfriend. It didn't help that her parents and a team of doctors kept telling Brenda that she should take medicine to be more like a girl and needed surgery so her genitals would look more like those of other girls. Brenda adamantly refused to have surgery. When she reluctantly began taking the pills to please her parents, she felt the medicine just made her feel worse. Why couldn't she fit in?

Then one day, when Brenda was 14 and being driven home after another angry refusal to cooperate with doctors, her father parked the car in their driveway and quietly began telling her the truth. Brenda had been born a boy, and originally was named Bruce. But when Bruce and Brian were 7 months old they had been brought to the hospital to be circumcised, where a bumbling doctor had misused a surgical instrument, burning off Bruce's penis. With no hope that Bruce would ever have anything like a normal penis, the doctors had persuaded his parents to change his name to Brenda and to raise him as a girl. They did surgery to remove the testicles and try to make the baby's genitals look like those of a girl.

Of course teenaged Brenda was shocked, and the whole story sounded so unbelievable, but mostly she felt tremendous relief. "Suddenly it all made sense why I felt the way I did. I *wasn't* some sort of weirdo." She changed her name to David, stopped taking female hormones, and demanded to be given male hormones instead. David also insisted on having surgery to remove his breasts (created by those pills he had been taking) and to try to reconstruct a rudimentary penis. From that day on, David lived his life as a male. From the time he was an infant, David's family had treated him like a girl. Where did these urges to act like a boy come from, and why were they so persistent?

Chapter Preview

In this chapter we'll explore the topic of **motivation**, the internal and external forces that regulate our behavior, driving us to behave in certain ways, usually with a particular goal. Sometimes we have a pretty good understanding of why we want to do something: we want to eat if we haven't eaten lately, or drink if it's a hot day. But sometimes, like Brenda/David, we are unaware of *why* we want to do particular things. First, we'll talk about motivation generally, then hunger and body weight regulation. Then we'll discuss sexual motivation before the final section on social motivation.

12.1 Motivation

Things to Learn

- Drive reduction and optimal arousal
- Homeostasis and negative feedback
- Dopamine reward pathway
- Maslow's hierarchy of needs

Before discussing particular kinds of motivated behavior, we'll need a general understanding of the construct of motivation. A lot of motivated behaviors are important for maintaining the physiology of the body so that we remain in good health. We might say, then, that motivation serves to regulate our behavior in order to regulate physiological systems. We'll see in this section that all or most motivated behaviors can also be explained by other factors, including brain systems that supply us with pleasure.

What do we mean by motivation?

We've already given one definition of motivation, but many competing definitions have been proposed. This variety of definitions is a clue that there is something slippery about the concept of motivation. For one thing, motivation is not an object, something you can see or touch. We infer the presence of motivation based on an individual's behavior. If a person persistently tries to do something, overcoming obstacles along the way, we say she is deeply motivated. Sometimes we can tell that she has a particular goal in mind, such as eating a cupcake, drinking coffee, or swimming the English Channel. Often we can't really tell what the goal is, but if someone keeps going, even when it is difficult, she must be motivated and there surely is some goal, even if she isn't aware of what it is.

Factors that bear on motivation fall into two general classes: external and internal. **External** (or *extrinsic*) **motivating forces** (or factors) can be pleasant, such as incentives, rewards, and recognition, or unpleasant, such as punishments and disapproval. Many external motivational forces are obvious, such as the rules we are explicitly taught by our family and school, and the laws that are passed to govern behavior. Likewise, money serves as an obvious and important external factor motivating many behaviors. **Internal** (or *intrinsic*) **motivating forces**, on the other hand, are forces at work inside the body, where they are more difficult to study because they are normally hidden from view. Hormones and physiological conditions are internal motivating forces.

Most behavior is the result of both external and internal motivating forces. For example, why do people face the door in an elevator? Most people do that and expect you to do the same, so we consider other people's behavior as an external factor. But there's an internal factor at work too—most of us want to fit in, or at least don't want to stand out too much—and that must reflect something about our internal state.

External motivating forces are relatively easy for psychologists to study because we can directly manipulate them. For example, we can vary whether a CD cover is flashy or dull, and ask whether that affects how much people enjoy

motivation Forces that regulate behavior toward a goal.

external motivating forces Factors originating outside the body that regulate behavior.

internal motivating forces Factors originating inside the body that regulate behavior.

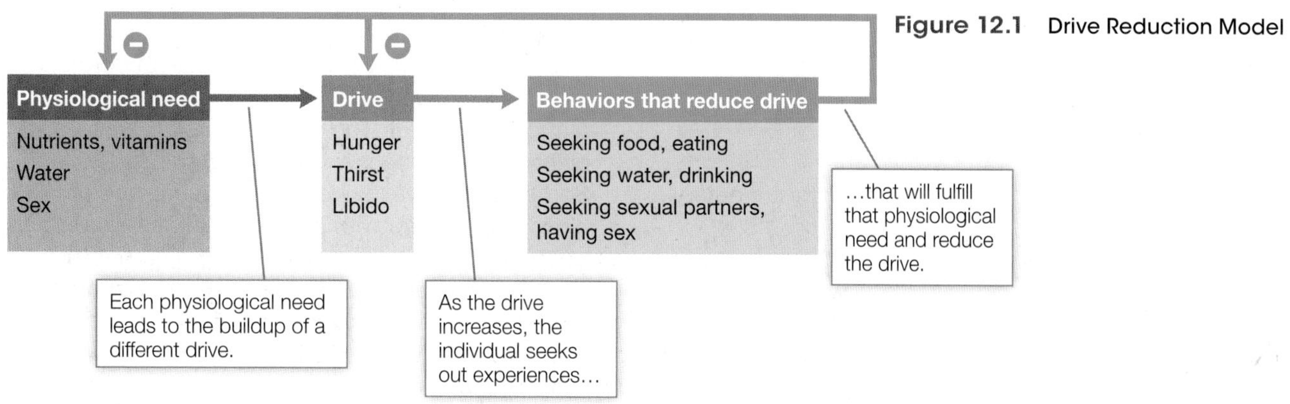

Figure 12.1 Drive Reduction Model

hearing the CD. Or we can see how much we have to pay subjects to complete a mind-numbingly dull survey. Such studies of external motivating forces are often examined in studies of learning, which we considered in more detail in Chapter 8.

Because we can't normally see or directly manipulate internal motivating forces, psychologists resort to theorizing about these internal forces. Two theories about internal motivating forces have been found especially useful: the drive reduction model and the optimal arousal model. The most famous of these, the **drive reduction model**, posits that an internal, physiological need generates a drive, and the individual seeks out behavior that will reduce that drive (Hull, 1943). In this model, the physiological need for food generates the drive for food, which we call "hunger," and the behavior of eating meets that need and reduces the drive (**Figure 12.1**). The drive reduction model suggests that we have many different drives going on inside us. The need for food creates the drive called hunger, the need for water creates the drive called thirst, the need to reproduce creates the sex drive (libido), and so on. In each case, the greater the need, the more drive and therefore the more motivated the individual will be to reduce that drive. Also, the greater our physiological need, let's say for food, the more we'll need to eat to reduce that built-up hunger.

Don't take the drive reduction model too literally. Analogies seldom fit all cases. After all, how many different drives are there? Six? A hundred? Does the analogy apply to the drive to care for children (if you think there is such a drive) or to have money? It isn't always easy to identify a physiological need behind a drive. Is there a physiological need to have sex? Certainly not in the sense that you need it to live in the same way you need food and water to live, yet clearly people have a sex drive. Similarly, it's difficult to conceive of our obvious drive to gain approval from other people as a physiological need like hunger. When we consider the internal mechanisms in the brain that control obvious physiological needs such as thirst and hunger, the drive reduction model is of little use in understanding the mechanisms involved. The drive reduction model is useful primarily in providing an analogy for why our motivation to display different behaviors may build up with time, and why, having engaged in the motivated behavior, we are less likely to do so again soon.

The **optimal arousal model** asserts that motivation arises from a need for a certain dose of arousal. The idea is that we perform our best when we are alert, but that too much arousal may distract us from the task at hand. This model suggests that there is an optimal level of arousal for optimal performance, the so-called *Yerkes–Dodson law*, and for that reason, we constantly seek that level of arousal (Yerkes & Dodson, 1908). For example, when taking a difficult test, you'll do poorly if you're really sleepy, but having too many cups of coffee might hurt your performance, too. You'll seek the right level of arousal for peak perfor-

drive reduction model The concept that internal motivation is the result of a physiological need that generates a drive, leading to behaviors that reduce that drive.

optimal arousal model The concept that individuals have an internal motivation to maintain the right amount of arousal.

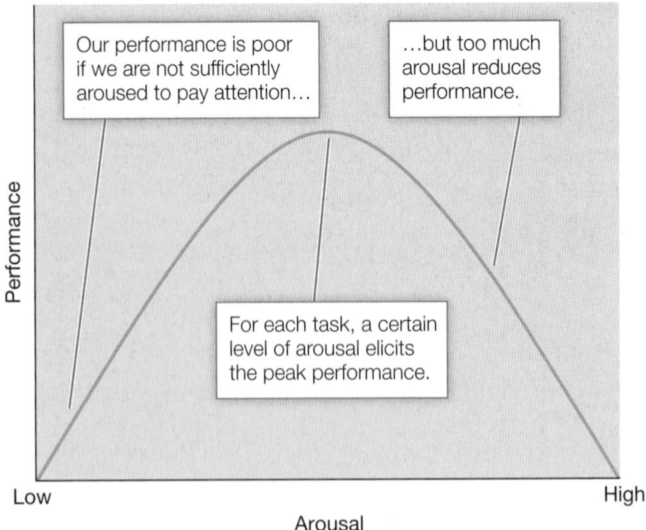

Our performance is poor if we are not sufficiently aroused to pay attention...
...but too much arousal reduces performance.
For each task, a certain level of arousal elicits the peak performance.
Performance
Low
High
Arousal

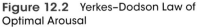

Figure 12.2 Yerkes–Dodson Law of Optimal Arousal

mance (**Figure 12.2**). There is no doubt that either too little or too much arousal can impair performance on most tasks, and for that reason alone the optimal arousal model is useful. The model also takes into account differences among individuals in their need for arousal. Some people love to ride roller coasters, and other people love to curl up with a good book, as we discuss in Section 14.2. The concept of a drive for an optimal level of arousal is useful in understanding why people are motivated to skydive or to quietly meditate. But the optimal arousal model doesn't explain why sometimes we feel like eating and other times we feel like seeing a movie, nor does it explain why sometimes we don't want any arousal at all and want to go to sleep. Presumably other forces, such as our interactions with other people, or exercise, influence what we find to be the optimal level of arousal.

Homeostasis is the regulation of internal states

Physiologists in the twentieth century discovered an important principle, namely that all the physiological processes in the body work best only within a narrow range of physical conditions. For example, if the body is too cold, everything slows down and eventually cells die. But if the body is too hot, the cells will also die. Therefore many processes at work in the body ensure a temperature that stays close to 37°C (98.6°F), the optimal temperature for most physiological processes. Likewise, the body carefully regulates how much water it retains, how much oxygen and sugar are present in the blood, and so on. These observations led to the concept of **homeostasis**, the process of keeping a constant, stable internal environment in the body (Cannon, 1932). Realizing the importance of this concept, physiologists began studying *how* the body keeps internal conditions constant.

Perhaps the example of homeostasis that is easiest to understand is body temperature, because in many ways the brain works like a thermostat that you probably have in your home. To work properly, the thermostat must have a thermometer of some sort that monitors temperature. When temperatures drop below the desired level, the thermostat turns on the furnace to heat the house (**Figure 12.3**). That prevents the house from getting too cold, but if left unchecked, the furnace would eventually make the house too hot. So once the house reaches the desired temperature, the thermostat detects that and stops running the furnace. We call that desired temperature the **set point**, the particular value of some measure to which a system keeps returning. For thermostats, the set point is the temperature the occupant chooses. The act of the heat from the furnace eventually turning off the call for heat is an example of **negative feedback**, when the result of a process turns off that process. *Negative feedback is found in all homeostatic systems.*

In our bodies, temperature regulation is controlled by the part of the brain called the **hypothalamus** (see Chapter 3). Functioning as the "thermostat," the hypothalamus carefully measures body temperature, and if it changes, the hypothalamus directs the body either to warm up (for example, by shivering) or to cool down (for example, by sweating), thereby restoring the body temperature to its set point (about 98.6°F), providing negative feedback to turn off the brain thermostat. We saw another example of negative feedback earlier (in the drive reduction model) when we said that behavior satisfying a physiological need (such as eating) reduces the drive for a behavior (such as hunger).

homeostasis The process of keeping a constant, stable internal environment in the body.

set point A particular value that a system keeps returning to.

negative feedback A signal to a system to decrease activity.

hypothalamus A part of the brainstem beneath the thalamus that regulates many physiological processes, including hunger, thirst, and temperature.

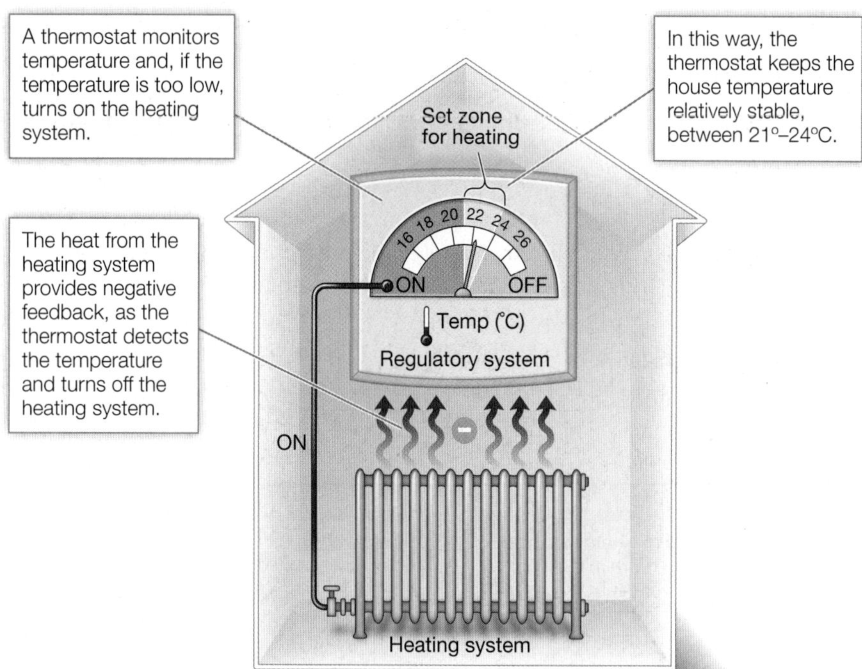

A thermostat monitors temperature and, if the temperature is too low, turns on the heating system.
In this way, the thermostat keeps the house temperature relatively stable, between 21°–24°C.
Set zone for heating
16 18 20 22 24 26
ON
OFF
Temp (°C)
Regulatory system
The heat from the heating system provides negative feedback, as the thermostat detects the temperature and turns off the heating system.
ON
Heating system

Figure 12.3 Negative Feedback Maintains Homeostasis

Homeostasis maintained through negative feedback typifies many aspects of motivated behavior. In some ways, the concept may seem trivial—eating makes you less hungry. But thinking in terms of homeostasis and negative feedback can sometimes help frame questions. For example, we can ask, what signals provide negative feedback to tell the brain when we've eaten enough food or drunk enough water? If, after a long period of not talking to anyone, we start a conversation with a friend, does that talking change some brain process? We need to ponder, however, whether the concept of homeostasis and negative feedback applies to *all* behavior that seems motivated. For example, does receiving approval from other people reduce our drive for approval, and for how long? Do we seek approval in order to keep something constant and stable inside our mind? Drive reduction, homeostasis, and negative feedback have proven to be valuable ideas for provoking our thinking and inspiring experiments, but each model has its limitations.

Motivation is commonly related to the realization that some experiences are pleasant and others unpleasant. If we were to believe that external motivating forces such as rewards and punishments are enough to account for all behavior, it would follow that we believe people like rewards and dislike punishments. But is "reward" always rewarding? We'll see that pleasure plays a role in many motivated behaviors, including some that are not good for us.

A pathway in the brain provides us with intense pleasure

The science-fiction novel *Ringworld* opens with a character who has a device that sends a mild electrical charge through a wire implanted into his brain. When electricity is flowing into the wire, he experiences the most wonderful ecstasy and smiles blissfully. This character is fictional, but the idea is quite sound. In the 1950s, researchers trying to understand how rats learn to press a lever for food discovered a brain pathway that may underlie all our pleasurable experience (Olds & Milner, 1954), as we'll see next (**Figure 12.4**).

☑ Researchers at Work

The quest for pleasure

Figure 12.4 The Dopamine Reward Pathway (After Olds & Milner, 1954.)

■ **Question:** What parts of the brain are active when an individual experiences pleasure?

■ **Hypothesis**: Electrically stimulating some parts of the brain will activate regions normally active during pleasure and will be experienced as pleasurable.

■ **Test:** Implant electrodes in various brain regions in rats, then give them access to a bar they can press to provide electrical stimulation of that region. If electrical stimulation of a region is experienced as pleasurable, the rats should learn to press the bar more often.

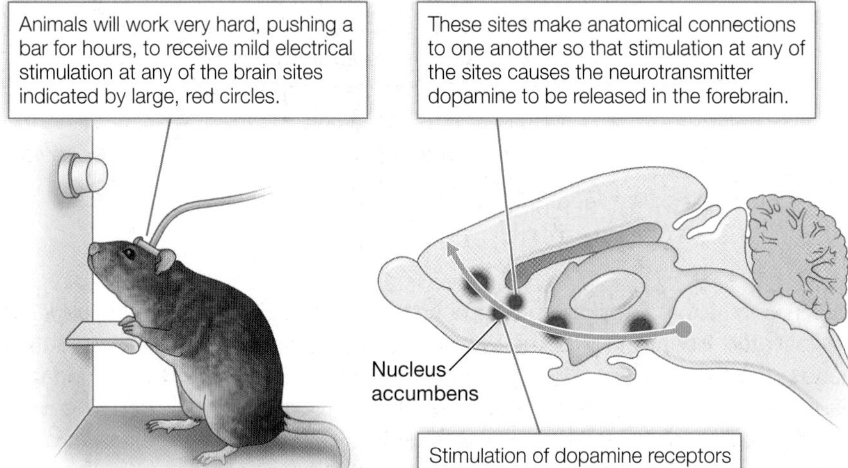

Animals will work very hard, pushing a bar for hours, to receive mild electrical stimulation at any of the brain sites indicated by large, red circles.
These sites make anatomical connections to one another so that stimulation at any of the sites causes the neurotransmitter dopamine to be released in the forebrain.
Nucleus accumbens
Stimulation of dopamine receptors in these regions provides an intensely pleasurable sensation.

■ **Results:** Electrodes implanted in most brain regions did not lead to active bar pressing, indicating that the rats did not find activity there pleasurable. However, rats learned to press the bar avidly to receive electrical stimulation at several other brain sites. Eventually investigators mapped out these regions and found most of them formed a pathway from the midbrain to frontal cortex.

■ **Conclusion:** This reward pathway may serve to regulate motivated behaviors, increasing the occurrence of behaviors that increase chances of survival and reproduction. Researchers hypothesized that this is a **reward pathway** in the brain: sites where excitation of neurons normally provides the individual with intense pleasure (Volkow et al., 2011). Scientists mapping out the pathway found that it releases the neurotransmitter **dopamine** in forebrain sites including the **nucleus accumbens**.

reward pathway A pathway from the midbrain to the frontal cortex that produces pleasurable sensations when stimulated electrically.

dopamine A neurotransmitter involved in movement and in signaling pleasure.

nucleus accumbens A region at the base of the forebrain that is part of the reward pathway.

One hypothesis is that whenever humans or other animals do something that gives pleasure, they are experiencing the release of dopamine in these forebrain regions that were mapped out in the research we described above. For example, engaging in sexual relations stimulates this system in rats. Likewise, when a thirsty animal drinks or a hungry animal eats, these behaviors activate the reward pathway, and the pleasure from this experience motivates the animal to repeat those behaviors the next time it is thirsty or hungry. From the perspective of drive reduction, you could think of the dopamine reward pathway as underlying all drives, providing a pleasurable feeling to reward the individual when a physiological need is being met. The drive to eat, for example, is reduced upon sensing fullness; that is, there comes a point when eating is no longer pleasurable. At that point each additional mouthful of food seems to cause less and less dopamine to be released in the forebrain (Wise, 2006), so the animal stops eating.

The reward pathway worked out in animals appears to be there in humans as well. Several experiments in which electrodes have been implanted in human brains, either to trace epileptic seizures (as in Deidre at the start of Chapter 3) or to treat movement disorders, have confirmed that electrical stimulation in the same pathway is very pleasurable. One woman described the sensation as intensely erotic, although it was never accompanied by an orgasm (Portenoy et al., 1986). It was so pleasant that she found herself stimulating the electrode so often that she developed a sore on the tip of the finger used to push the button! There is considerable evidence that drugs of abuse feel so good because they stimulate dopamine release in the reward pathway (Wise et al., 1992). Studies of addiction suggest that once the brain reward system has been overstimulated with drugs, it becomes harder and harder to derive pleasure from other, simpler activities such as eating or talking to a friend, as we noted in Section 7.4. In this chapter, we will see how our motivations to eat and engage in sexual behaviors may derive from this powerful brain reward system.

Motivational systems fulfill a hierarchy of needs

In discussing specific kinds of motivation, it is useful to consider American psychologist Abraham Maslow's hierarchy of human needs (Maslow, 1943). Maslow (1908–1970) observed that some needs are more basic to survival than others. Maslow developed a hierarchy of needs in the form of a pyramid, with more basic *physiological* needs (such as hunger) assigned to the bottom level (**Figure 12.5**). The next level of need is for *safety*, for example, the need to be taken care of as a child, to have resources such as a job, and a home as an adult. After these motives to simply stay alive and healthy come motives such as those for

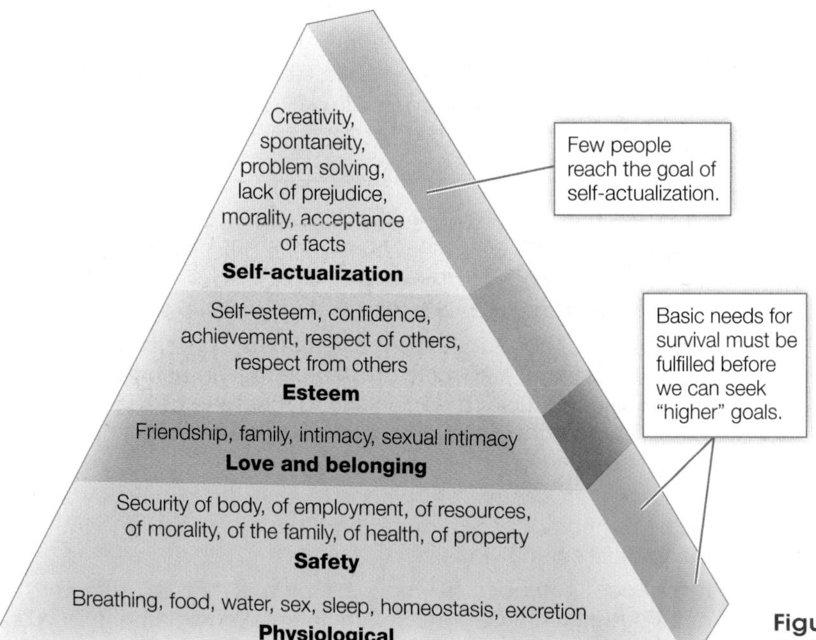

Figure 12.5 Maslow's Pyramid of Needs That Drive Human Motivation

self-actualization The top of Maslow's pyramid, the need to fulfill one's potential.

love and belonging, which are not needed for survival but appear to be crucial for happiness (see Chapter 5). One of the motives at this level is the desire for a warm and fulfilling sexual relationship. The next level of need, for *esteem* and self-confidence, also drives the motivation to belong and feel appreciated. At the top of Maslow's pyramid is the need for **self-actualization**, a term he coined for a person's need to fulfill his or her potential, to be the best person he or she can be. For example, some people may have the potential to be a great musician, and such people would feel the need to make music, while other people would feel the need to paint, or write, or teach.

The different needs are represented as a hierarchy for several reasons. First, Maslow thought that a person could not attend to the motives at one level of the hierarchy unless those below it were satisfied. You can't concentrate on developing sexual intimacy if you haven't had your physiological and safety needs met. Likewise, you're unlikely to become the artist you might be if you don't gain some measure of self-esteem and the respect of others. Also, as you go up the pyramid, you find fewer and fewer people who have those needs satisfied. Most people in the industrialized world have food and water, but many live in unsafe environments and cannot move to another environment. Even people who have their basic physiological needs met and are safe may have difficulty securing the warm, supportive family, friendships, and sexual relations they crave. Finally, Maslow believed that very few people achieved complete self-actualization. Partly this is because all the other needs must be met first, and partly this is because fulfilling your potential completely may not be entirely within your control. A measure of luck and chance encounters, offering crucial opportunities to learn and achieve, may be needed for complete self-actualization. The motives are also a pyramid in the sense that you can strive to get to the top, to become the best person you can be.

One might debate whether sex is a physiological need, whether there is a need for "security of morality," but there are no scientific tests to settle such disputes because the pyramid is not the result of scientific findings. Nevertheless, the ideas embedded in Maslow's pyramid ring true for many people and they help us organize our thoughts about motives.

In the rest of this chapter we will discuss three different types of motivation. We'll begin with the motivation to satisfy hunger, a basic physiological need at the base of the pyramid. Then we will consider the drive for sex and sexual intimacy. We'll wrap up with social motivations, the types of needs found near the top of Maslow's pyramid. Aggression can also be viewed as a motivated behavior, but we will deal with that topic in Section 15.3.

12.1 SUMMARY

- Behaviors can be motivated by *external motivating forces*, such as punishments and reward, or by *internal motivating forces*, which cannot normally be observed directly and so must be studied by making inferences from behavior.
- The *drive reduction model* suggests that any physiological need in the body activates a specific drive to engage in behaviors that meet that specific need (such as drinking to meet the need for water), and that having met the need, the drive will be reduced (until the physiological need arises again).
- The *optimal arousal model* asserts that we are constantly seeking just the right amount of arousal, and that this "right amount" differs among different individuals.
- The concept *homeostasis* suggests internal motivating factors arise from a need to maintain a constant internal environment. The brain senses deviations from healthy *set points* and is driven to correct

imbalances. If the body becomes short of water or nutrients, for example, the individual is driven to seek them. Getting water or food restores the set points, providing *negative feedback* to reduce the drive and maintain homeostasis.

- A *reward pathway* in the brain that releases the neurotransmitter *dopamine* is another internal force driving behavior. Dopamine provides the individual with pleasurable sensations whenever a need is being met.
- Maslow described a hierarchy of human needs, from the basic physiological needs for food and water, through the needs for safety, for love and belonging, for esteem, and for *self-actualization*.

REVIEW QUESTIONS

1. Describe the drive reduction model for understanding motivated behaviors.
2. How does negative feedback maintain set points, and how does that relate to the concept of homeostasis?
3. Describe the reward pathway in the brain and how it might relate to motivated behavior.
4. In what ways are the various levels of human needs either "higher" or "lower" in Maslow's pyramid?

Food for Thought

Maslow asserted that few humans ever reach the goal of full self-actualization. What do you see as the factors that would prevent most people from achieving this goal?

Can you identify what barriers, if any, might prevent you, personally, from achieving self-actualization?

12.2 Hunger

Things to Learn

- Body weight set points
- Dieting and basal metabolism
- Arcuate nucleus and hormonal signals
- Lifestyles to control weight
- Eating disorders

Perhaps no motivated behavior has been as well studied as eating, in part because it is readily studied in animals and in part because it's a basic need that must be met before we can pursue other needs. There are, as well, many studies of body weight because it can affect so many other aspects of health. An understanding of hunger—why people eat the way they do—and why the body gains or loses weight, could lead to new ways to help people maintain a healthful body weight.

In this section we'll see that, as in most bodily processes, the brain is very much involved in regulating how much we eat and how much we weigh. A lot of what goes on in the brain to maintain a particular body weight is outside our awareness or conscious control, which is one reason why it is difficult to lose weight. We'll consider methods that help people control weight—and many that don't. Finally, we'll discuss those life-threatening disorders in which people refuse to eat enough to maintain a healthy body weight.

Body weight is tightly regulated by the brain in animal models and humans

Excess body weight is bad for our health, increasing the risks for diabetes, heart disease, and strokes. Thus many scientists have studied how body weight is regulated in both humans and animals. Perhaps the single most important thing scientists have learned is that *body weight is closely regulated by the brain,* often outside our conscious awareness or control. This is most obvious in animal models, where scientists have found that many manipulations that you might expect to change an animal's body weight have no such effect. Only fairly drastic measures affect an animal's body weight, and then, as soon as the original conditions are restored, the animal's body quickly returns to its prior weight. Such experiments have led to the concept of a **body weight set point**: the idea that brain systems function to maintain body weight at a particular set point, just as house heating systems function to maintain temperatures at a set point.

body weight set point The body weight that is maintained by brain systems.

The most direct demonstrations that the brain maintains a body weight set point come from experiments in which damage to a particular brain region in rats causes a dramatic shift in that set point. For example, lesions of

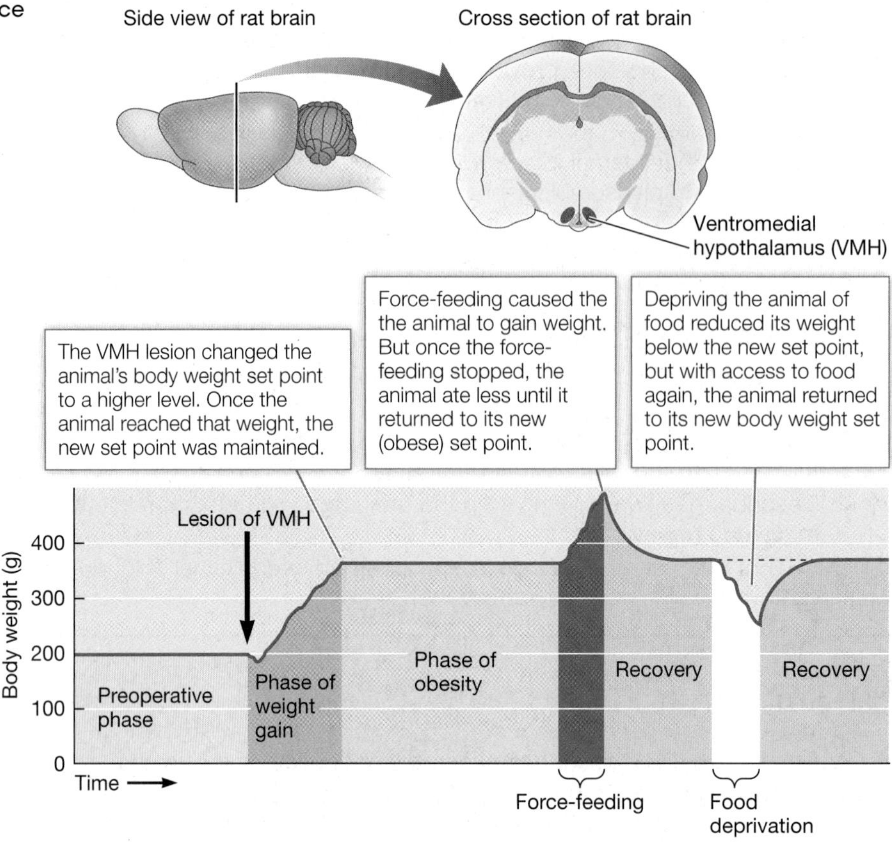
Side view of rat brain
Cross section of rat brain
Ventromedial hypothalamus (VMH)
The VMH lesion changed the animal's body weight set point to a higher level. Once the animal reached that weight, the new set point was maintained.
Force-feeding caused the the animal to gain weight. But once the force-feeding stopped, the animal ate less until it returned to its new (obese) set point.
Depriving the animal of food reduced its weight below the new set point, but with access to food again, the animal returned to its new body weight set point.
Lesion of VMH
Body weight (g)
400
300
200
100
0
Preoperative phase
Phase of weight gain
Phase of obesity
Recovery
Recovery
Time
Force-feeding
Food deprivation

Figure 12.6 Brain Lesions Can Induce Obesity (After Sclafani et al., 1976.)

the **ventromedial hypothalamus** (**VMH**) in rats cause the animals, which always have had constant access to unlimited food, to suddenly eat more and gain weight. The animals become **obese**—so overweight that they are unhealthy (**Figure 12.6**). Significantly, the animals were not observed to be eating as much as possible, but to be eating to reach a new (obese) set point. Upon reaching this new set point, the animals then ate more normally and their weight stabilized. Animals that had been force-fed (by putting a tube down their throats to deliver Calorie-rich liquid) to gain weight beyond the new set point, or that were deprived of food to make them lose weight, adjusted their eating afterward to return to their new (obese) set point. Humans who suffer a stroke in this region similarly begin regulating their body weight at a higher, obese set point (Erdheim, 1904).

Lesions in another brain region, the nearby **lateral hypothalamus** (**LH**), have the opposite effect. Animals with LH lesions eat so little that they eventually starve themselves to death. If starvation is prevented by force-feeding, the LH-lesioned rats eventually start eating again, but enough only to maintain their body weight at a new, lower set point (but not so low that they starve). As in the VMH studies, if LH-lesioned rats are deprived of food, or force-fed with rich, fattening food, their weight will change, but if allowed to choose how much to eat, the rats return to their (low) body weight set point (**Figure 12.7**).

For years scientists tried to explain the effects of lesioning the VMH and LH in terms of "brain centers" with particular functions. For example, if the VMH were a brain center for *satiety* (feeling satisfied or full), then maybe lesioning the center would keep the animals from ever feeling full. And if the LH were a hunger center, then maybe lesions there would keep the animals from ever feeling hungry. But these simple ideas did not explain why VMH- and LH-lesioned animals regulate their body weight around their new set points; apparently these animals exhibit hunger when they are below their new set point and satiety when forced above

ventromedial hypothalamus (VMH) A brain region related to the body weight set point. Damage to this region results in a new, higher set point.

obese Overweight such that it is unhealthy.

lateral hypothalamus (LH) A brain region related to the body weight set point. Damage to this region results in a new, lower set point.

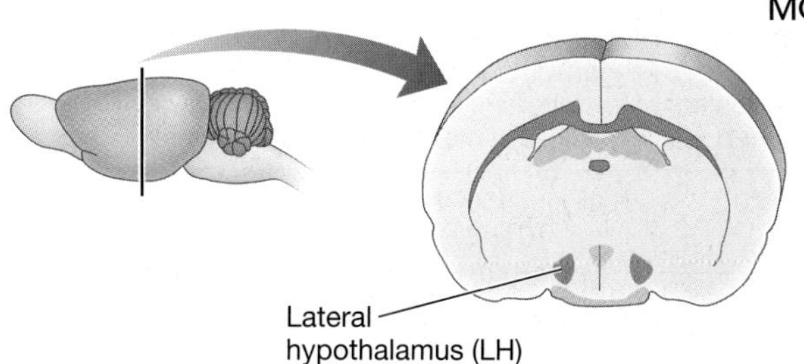

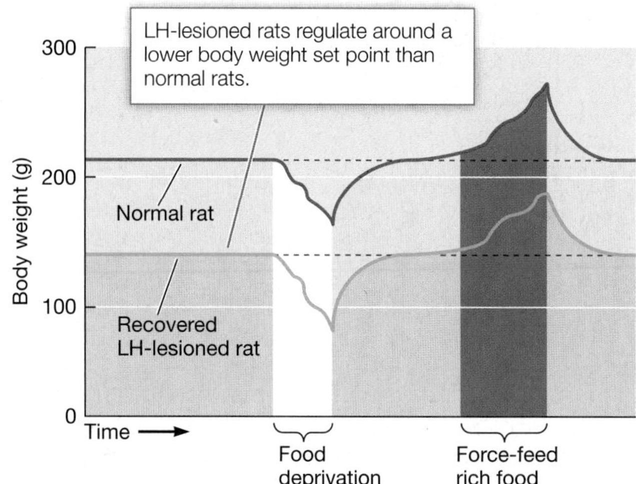

Figure 12.7 Brain Lesions Can Also Reduce the Body Weight Set Point (After Keesey & Boyle, 1973.)

it (see Figures 12.6 and 12.7). Brain-lesioning experiments dispel the notion that the brain has a "hunger center" and a "satiety center" (King, 2006), demonstrating instead that the *brain works hard to keep body weight in homeostasis*, just as it keeps body temperature and water balance in homeostasis.

Unfortunately, the brain may sometimes want us to weigh more than is good for us when food is plentiful. Why should this be so?

Research has shown that the brain regulates body weight around a set point to control how efficiently we use food for energy (Sclafani et al., 1976). Food is our energy source, and just as cars break down gasoline to produce energy, we break down food to produce energy. In both cases, the breakdown process produces heat. In the case of our bodies, that heat is needed to maintain our temperature at about 37°C, at which the body functions properly. One way the brain controls body temperature is by varying **basal metabolism** (also just called metabolism), the collective bodily processes that break down what we eat to provide energy for body warmth, growth, movement, and other activities. When our metabolic rate is high, we are breaking down lots of molecules to provide body heat, more heat than we really need, in fact. The body dissipates much of that heat into the air around us by sending warm blood to the skin surface. When our metabolic rate is low, we are using less energy to keep up our temperature, and the body conserves that heat carefully by, among other things, reducing how much warmth is sent to the skin surface to be lost.

What does basal metabolism have to do with body weight? When we eat less, the brain detects the reduced intake and reduces our metabolic rate so that less food is needed to keep up our body temperature. In other words, the body becomes more efficient, using less energy for overall metabolism, so that more energy is available to *maintain body weight*. That means our body weight won't change much even though we are eating less food. In times of famine, a lower metabolic rate is advantageous, but it is not when we wish to lose weight. In one early demonstration of this cruel fact of dieting, subjects went from eating 3,500 Calories per day to only 450 Calories per day—to a highly restricted diet

basal metabolism The bodily processes that break down food for energy.

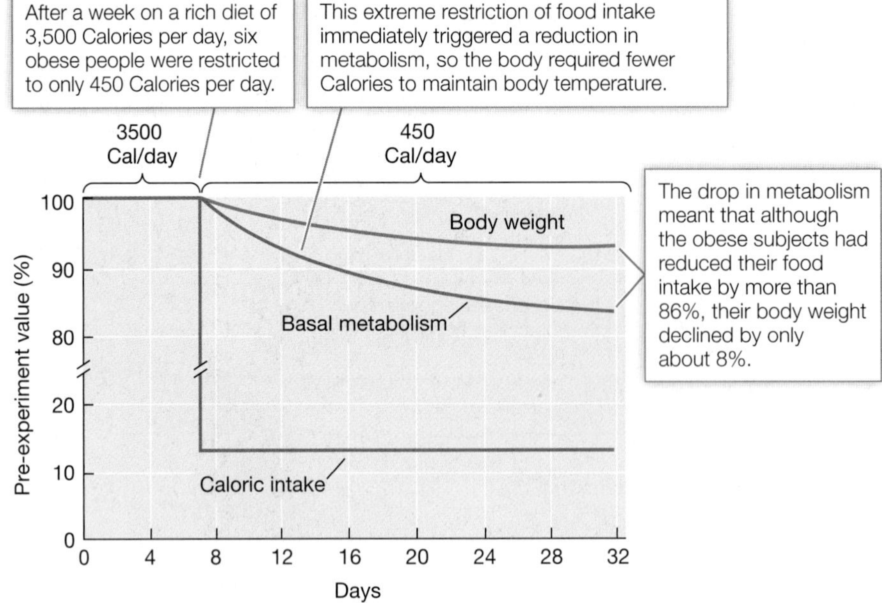
After a week on a rich diet of 3,500 Calories per day, six obese people were restricted to only 450 Calories per day.
This extreme restriction of food intake immediately triggered a reduction in metabolism, so the body required fewer Calories to maintain body temperature.
3500 Cal/day
450 Cal/day
The drop in metabolism meant that although the obese subjects had reduced their food intake by more than 86%, their body weight declined by only about 8%.
Body weight
Basal metabolism
Caloric intake
Pre-experiment value (%)
100
90
80
20
10
0
0
4
8
12
16
20
24
28
32
Days

Figure 12.8 The Cruel Facts of Dieting (After Bray, 1969.)

providing about 13% as much food as before. Once the subjects began dieting, their body metabolism declined nearly 20%. Because fewer Calories were used to maintain body temperature, a greater proportion of the Calories in the reduced diet were available to maintain body weight (**Figure 12.8**). The result? An 86% drop in eating brought only an 8% drop in body weight. How discouraging if we're trying to lose weight!

Of course, despite the drop in basal metabolism, reducing food intake will eventually result in weight loss. After all, the brain can only reduce basal metabolism so far. But only large changes in diet, which we can consciously control, will overcome those efforts of the brain that are outside our conscious control to maintain body weight. But don't be too discouraged. The body weight set point *can* be changed, and there are effective methods for losing weight.

The brain carefully regulates sugar and fat to avoid energy shortages

Natural selection favors close monitoring of body weight because managing energy stores is absolutely critical for survival. The most immediate source of energy in our bodies is a simple sugar called **glucose** or "blood sugar." In fact, glucose is the only energy source that brain cells can use, so we must always have a certain amount of glucose circulating in the blood or we'll lose consciousness and die. Most body cells also use glucose for immediate energy, but unlike the brain, these body cells cannot use the sugar unless insulin is present. *Insulin* is a hormone released from the pancreas to help glucose enter body cells so they can use the sugar for energy.

When we eat, three processes trigger the release of insulin so our body can make use of glucose right away: (1) The sight and smell of food, especially when we're hungry, is detected by the brain, which then sends commands to the pancreas for insulin release. (2) Food entering the stomach and gut causes these organs to release hormones that, among other things, trigger more insulin release. (3) A surge of glucose released from the food enters the blood, and that glucose also triggers more insulin release (**Figure 12.9A**).

Because running out of glucose would be fatal, we also have systems for storing glucose in the body to make sure we never run out. For shorter-term storage, glucose can be converted to *glycogen*, a more complicated molecule that is stored in the liver and in muscles. When eating a meal triggers insulin release, the insulin not only helps body cells use glucose immediately, but it also converts glucose into glycogen for short-term storage (**Figure 12.9B**). As the amount of glucose in the blood falls, the pancreas reduces insulin release. This

glucose A simple sugar used by brain and body cells for energy.

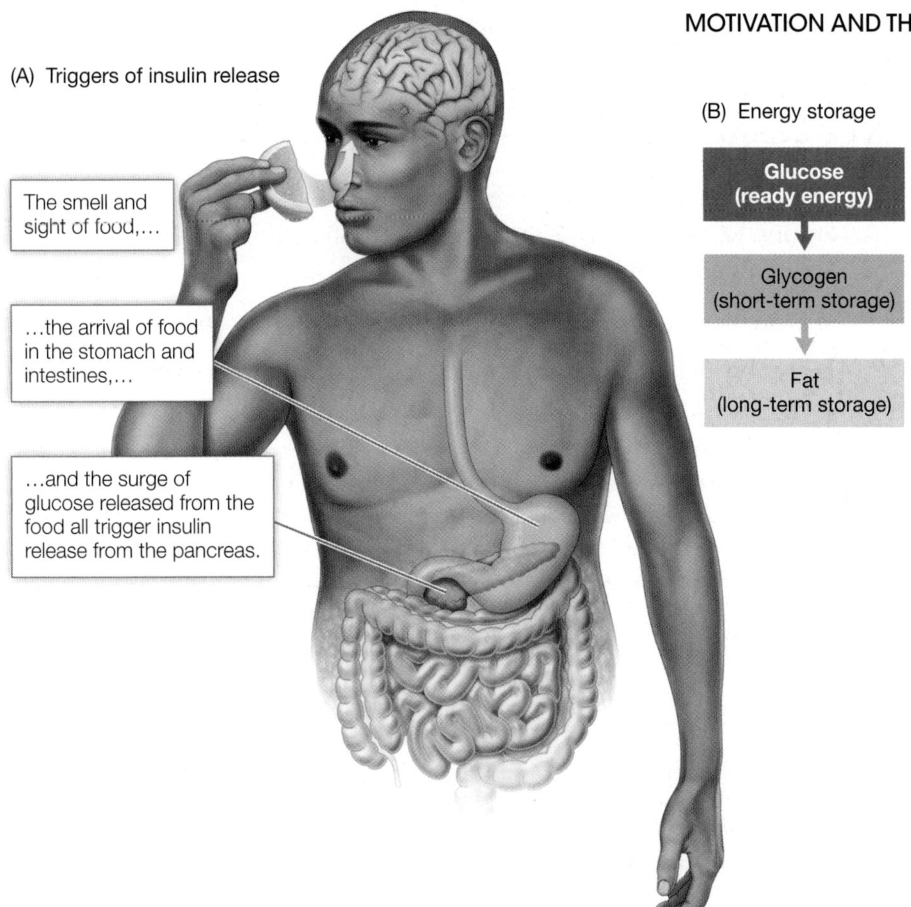
(A) Triggers of insulin release
The smell and sight of food,...
...the arrival of food in the stomach and intestines,...
...and the surge of glucose released from the food all trigger insulin release from the pancreas.
(B) Energy storage
Glucose (ready energy)
Glycogen (short-term storage)
Fat (long-term storage)

Figure 12.9 Production and Storage of Energy for the Body (A) Food triggers insulin release, providing glucose for the body. (B) Glucose provides immediate energy to the brain and body, but the body requires the hormone insulin to use it. Insulin also converts excess glucose into glycogen for short-term storage. Glycogen may eventually be converted to fat for long-term storage, or it can be converted back to glucose.

controlled release of insulin serves to keep circulating levels of glucose in homeostasis. When glucose levels continue to fall, a different pancreatic hormone converts glycogen back into glucose, also keeping circulating levels of glucose relatively steady. Too little glucose would leave the brain and body without energy, but too much circulating glucose is harmful too. Most organs deteriorate if they are exposed to high levels of glucose for too long.

In addition to short-term storage in glycogen, we also have an important long-term reservoir for glucose—fat. You can think of a molecule of **fat**, or **lipid**, as consisting of many glucose molecules linked together, providing long-term storage for glucose.

fat Also called *lipid*. Our long-term reservoir for glucose.

Now that you've seen how the brain tightly regulates body weight around a set point, and closely regulates how much glucose is present in the bloodstream, let's consider several factors that affect whether we feel hungry or full.

What are the factors that control appetite?

The great value of scientific thinking is that it sometimes rules out what appears to be a self-evident "truth." For example, you might think that thirst is triggered by a dry mouth. But this idea was disproved in the mid-twentieth century by scientists who surgically altered animals so that whatever they swallowed went through a tube and fell outside the body (Blass et al., 1976; Salisbury & Rowland, 1990). No matter how much water these animals "drank," or how wet their mouths became, they continued to be thirsty and continued to drink. Putting water into their stomachs, however, quenched their thirst; they stopped drinking. Similar experiments allowing surgically altered animals to eat likewise did not quench hunger; animals continued to "eat" unless food was put into their stomachs. These experiments show that neither hunger nor thirst depends on signals from the mouth. The drive to eat or drink comes from somewhere else inside us. One signal comes from the stomach itself, as we see next (**Figure 12.10**).

☑ Researchers at Work

Monitoring hunger pangs

Figure 12.10 Hunger Pangs Are the Result of Stomach Contractions (After Cannon & Washburn, 1912.)

■ **Question:** What bodily processes underlie our experience of hunger?

■ **Hypothesis:** Contractions of the stomach outside our control are experienced as hunger pangs, informing us about when we should eat.

■ **Test:** One investigator swallowed a balloon attached to a hollow tube (do not try this, as it is very dangerous!). By measuring the pressure inside the balloon, researchers could monitor stomach contractions. While one investigator recorded stomach contractions, the participant carrying the balloon reported any experience of hunger pangs.

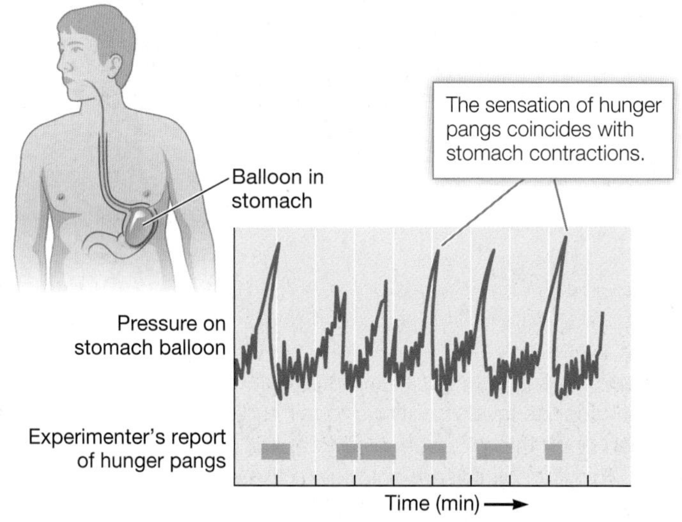

■ **Results:** The sensation of hunger pangs indeed coincided with literal contractions of the stomach.

■ **Conclusion:** What we experience as hunger pangs are indeed involuntary contractions of the stomach, and this is one cue about when we are hungry. However, people who have had their stomachs surgically removed still report feeling hungry and regulate their diet. Likewise, rats continue to regulate feeding and body weight after surgical removal of the stomach, so pangs cannot account entirely for the sensation of hunger.

---

hormones Chemicals released from one part of the body that enter the bloodstream and affect other parts of the body.

arcuate nucleus A hypothalamic region that receives hormonal signals about energy stores and stimulates other brain regions to trigger either hunger or satiety.

So while the stomach contributes to our sensation of hunger and fullness, it is not necessary for us to have these sensations. We'll see that in fact *many* signals report to the brain how much and what kind of food is eaten, as well as the state of energy reserves in the body. Once the brain integrates all these signals, the sensation of hunger is either relieved or continues. What are these additional internal signals that determine whether we feel hungry? Probably the most important of the many different signals at work are **hormones**, chemicals that are released from one part of the body that affect another part. In the case of hunger and satiety, hormonal signals from several different organs inform the brain about nutrient stores. These various hormones come together in the **arcuate nucleus**, a hypothalamic region that integrates information about energy stores and body weight and then activates other brain regions to trigger either hunger or satiety. If

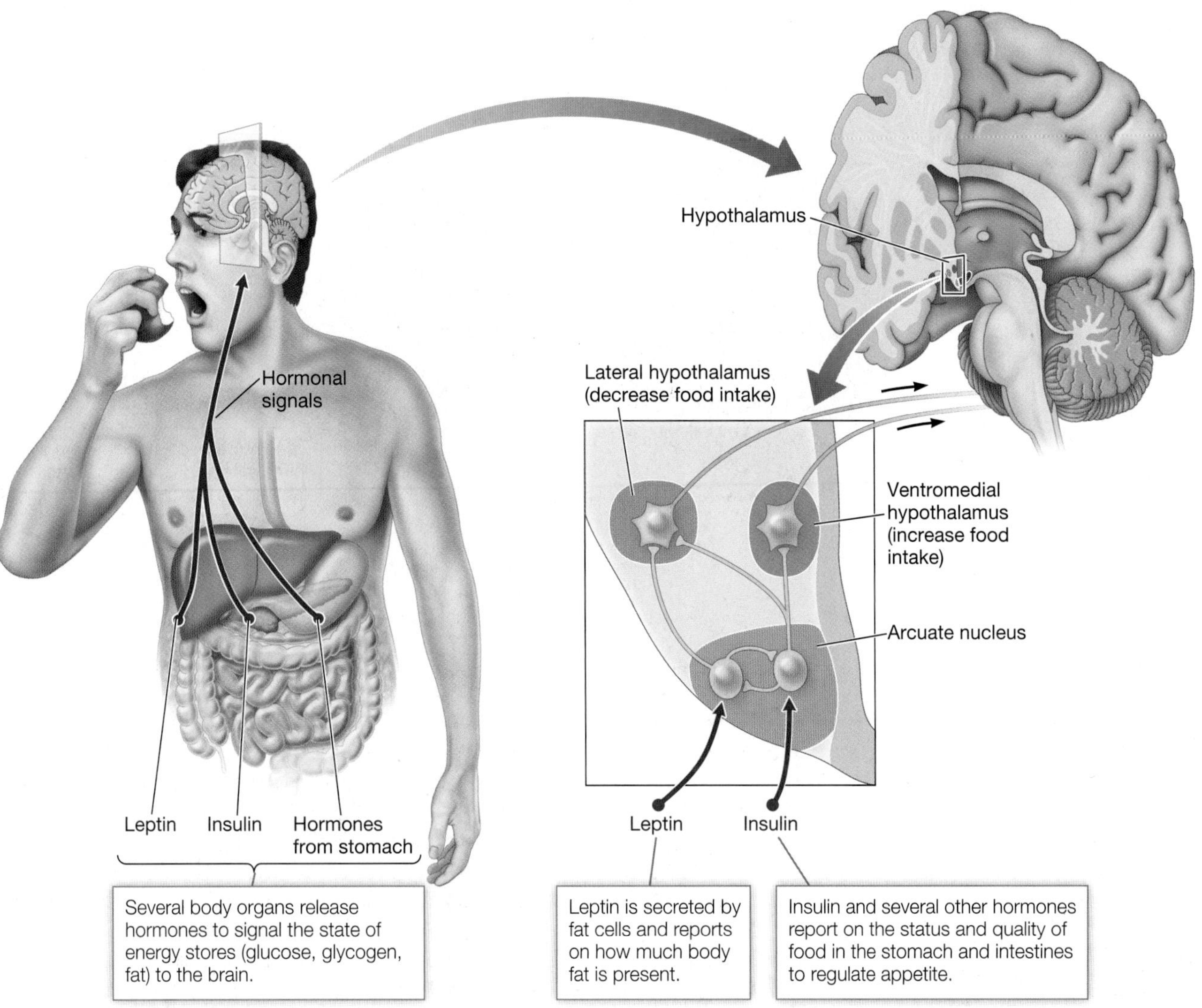

Hypothalamus
Hormonal signals
Lateral hypothalamus (decrease food intake)
Ventromedial hypothalamus (increase food intake)
Arcuate nucleus
Leptin
Insulin
Hormones from stomach
Leptin
Insulin
Several body organs release hormones to signal the state of energy stores (glucose, glycogen, fat) to the brain.
Leptin is secreted by fat cells and reports on how much body fat is present.
Insulin and several other hormones report on the status and quality of food in the stomach and intestines to regulate appetite.

Figure 12.11 Several Hormones Tell the Brain about Body Stores Hormones from the pancreas, stomach, intestines, and fat cells converge on the arcuate nucleus of the hypothalamus. Cells in the arcuate nucleus integrate all this information and then stimulate other brain regions, mainly in the hypothalamus, to trigger hunger or satiety. The LH and VMH are two of many brain regions involved in this process.

our brain calculates that we have enough energy stores to maintain body weight and internal processes for a while, then we experience satiety. If we need to take in more food to maintain energy stores and body weight, we experience hunger. Let's consider some of these hormonal signals that converge on the arcuate nucleus.

We already mentioned the rise in the pancreatic hormone insulin that is triggered by a meal. In addition to favoring the influx of glucose into body cells and the conversion of glucose to glycogen stores, insulin also reaches the arcuate nucleus. This signal tells the brain that we've eaten, but by itself insulin does not trigger the feeling of satiety. We know this because treating animals with insulin makes them *more* likely to eat.

Insulin is not the only hormone to act on the arcuate nucleus; two hormones from the stomach also signal this part of the brain: one that decreases appetite, and another that increases it. We don't yet know what determines whether the hormones will be released from the stomach, but we do know that individuals without a stomach, who lack these hormones, can still regulate body weight (**Figure 12.11**).

Perhaps the most famous hormone informing the brain about body stores is **leptin**, which is secreted by fat cells. Leptin acts like a reporting mechanism: the more fat present in the body, the more leptin is secreted into the bloodstream. Leptin is detected in the arcuate nucleus, constantly telling the brain how much

leptin A hormone secreted by fat cells that signals the arcuate nucleus about energy stores.

Figure 12.12 Inherited Obesity

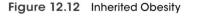

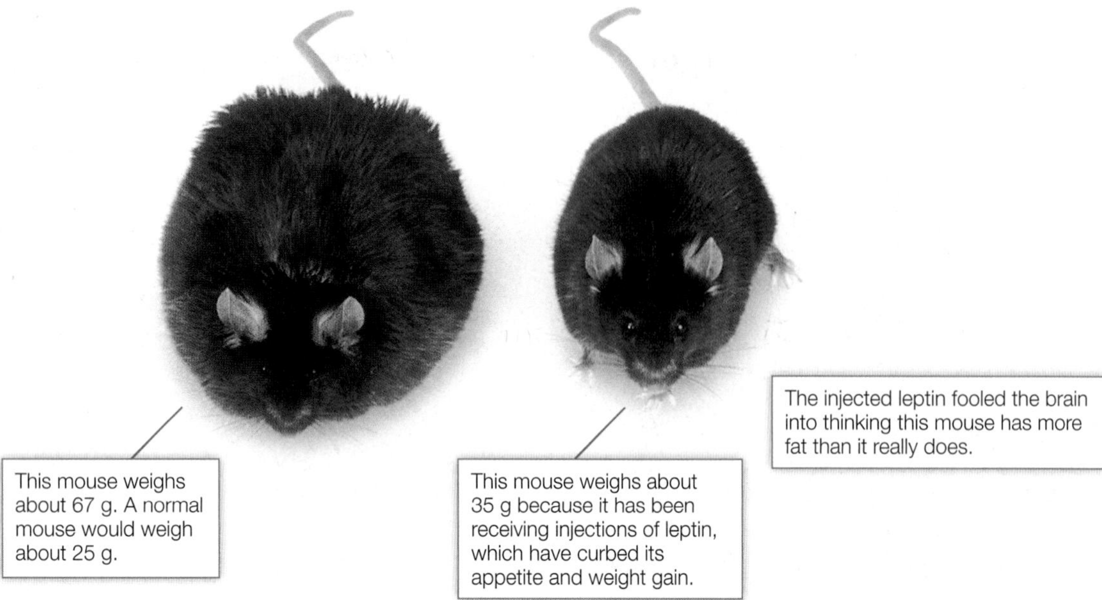

Both of these mice have two defective copies of the gene for leptin, so they are impaired at reporting the state of body fat stores to the brain.
The injected leptin fooled the brain into thinking this mouse has more fat than it really does.
This mouse weighs about 67 g. A normal mouse would weigh about 25 g.
This mouse weighs about 35 g because it has been receiving injections of leptin, which have curbed its appetite and weight gain.

body mass index (BMI) A gauge of body weight based on the ratio of weight to height.

long-term storage of glucose we have in fat. Mice with a genetic defect in the gene for leptin don't seem to get the signal that they have enough fat, so they overeat until they become remarkably obese (Zhang et al., 1994). These mice can be prevented from becoming obese by injecting them with leptin (**Figure 12.12**). For a while these findings about leptin raised the hope that leptin injections might do for obese people what they did for mice. Unfortunately, it turns out only a few people in the world are obese because they lack leptin (Montague et al., 1997). Virtually all other people who are obese have as much or more leptin than non-obese people. For this reason, leptin injections have very little effect on their appetite.

We've learned that no single hormone accounts entirely for hunger and satiety, that we may not hope to lose weight by controlling any one factor. This brings us to the question: Which methods actually work for controlling body weight?

There are some methods of weight loss that work for some people

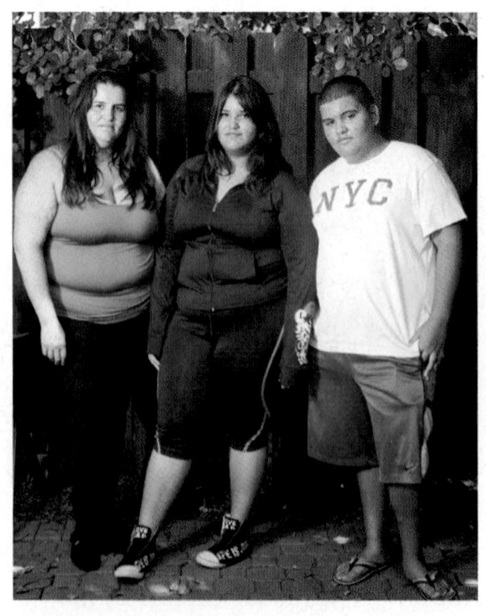

All in the Family There are genetic influences on body weight.

We know there is a genetic influence on obesity, because comparing relatives, even relatives living apart, shows that the more closely people are related to a person who is obese, the more likely they are to be obese themselves. But there are almost no cases where we know which genes are responsible for obesity. So genetic effects on body weight are probably the result of many genes acting in concert. For this reason, it is unlikely that we will be able to manipulate any single gene to prevent or reverse obesity.

It is evident that many environmental factors promote or discourage obesity. For example, obesity is increasing in many industrialized nations, and this is happening too quickly to be due to any change in genes in the population (**Figure 12.13**). Other factors, including the ready availability of tasty food with loads of Calories, must contribute to the increase in body weight.

The most prominent way of gauging body weight is the **body mass index (BMI)**, defined in **Table 12.1**. Based on BMI, nearly 70% of adults in the United States are overweight and nearly a third are obese (Flegal et al., 2002; see Figure 12.13). Let's consider some steps people can take to control their weight.

CHANGING LIFESTYLE For most people the word "diet" refers to a specific amount or type of food that is eaten for a short while to reduce body weight.

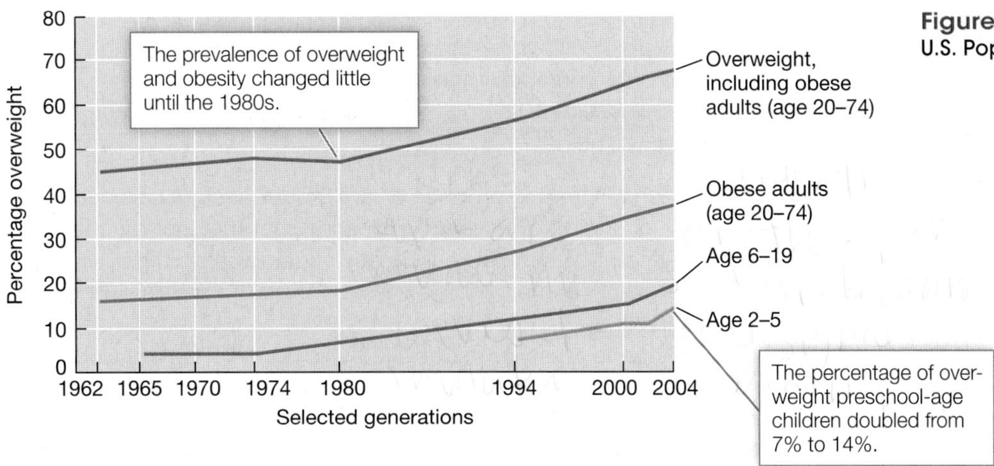

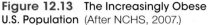

Figure 12.13 The Increasingly Obese U.S. Population (After NCHS, 2007.)

There are many competing claims for which type of diet works best. On Amazon.com, searching among books for the word "dieting" brings up more than 43,000 results, but in fact *no temporary change in eating habits results in a long-lasting reduction of body weight*. No matter which dieting method you use to lose weight, when you stop the diet, body weight returns to its set point. This "yo-yo" effect has been famously demonstrated by media star Oprah Winfrey, who has been admirably candid about her efforts to control her weight. She lost more than 65 pounds by eating no solid foods whatsoever for 4 months, but 2 hours after the show proclaiming this triumph, she went back to her old eating habits and began regaining weight.

Many *fad diets* claim you will quickly and easily lose weight by eating one type of food or avoiding another. But few of these many "miracle" diets make the same recommendation. There's the South Beach diet, the cabbage soup diet, the Scarsdale diet, the Hollywood diet, and the grapefruit diet, among many. How can all these diets be effective if they are so different from one another? In fact, *none of these fad diets results in lasting, significant weight loss*. One problem is that people go on these diets with the expectation that they will follow the diet just long enough to lose weight and then return to their normal eating habits. Even if people lose weight while on the diet, it quickly returns when they go off the diet, as Oprah found.

The other, more troubling problem with fad diets is that many of them may be dangerous to your health. For example, the Atkins diet, which emphasizes eating lots of protein (such as meat) and avoiding carbohydrates (such as pasta and potatoes), results in weight loss (Gardner et al., 2007) as long as you stay on the diet. But might life-long adherence to the Atkins diet impair your overall health in the long run? A radically high protein diet is hard on the kidneys and may increase blood cholesterol levels (Barnett et al., 2009; Siener, 2006).

The only changes in behavior that safely result in long-term loss of body weight are permanent changes in diet and exercise (Jakicic et al., 2008). In other words, a change in lifestyle—what you eat and do every day—is required to control body weight in the long run (Pettman et al., 2008). It's also clear what the changes in lifestyle should be—eat less and exercise more:

- Choose smaller portions of food.
- Avoid foods that are Calorie-dense, such as meats, fats, and sweets, and eat low-Calorie, high-nutrient foods such as vegetables, fruits, and grains.
- Eat breakfast. For reasons no one quite understands, eating a healthy breakfast every day helps reduce body weight. In one study, women on a rigidly controlled diet who ate breakfast lost more weight than those

TABLE 12.1 Body Mass Index (BMI)

BMI value	Body weight category
<15	Starvation
15–18.5	Underweight
18.5–25	Ideal weight
25–30	Overweight
30–40	Obese
>40	Morbidly obese

Note:

$$BMI = \frac{\text{weight (kg)}}{\text{height} \times \text{height (m} \times \text{m)}} \quad \textit{or}$$

$$BMI = 703 \frac{\text{weight (lb)}}{\text{height} \times \text{height (in.} \times \text{in.)}}$$

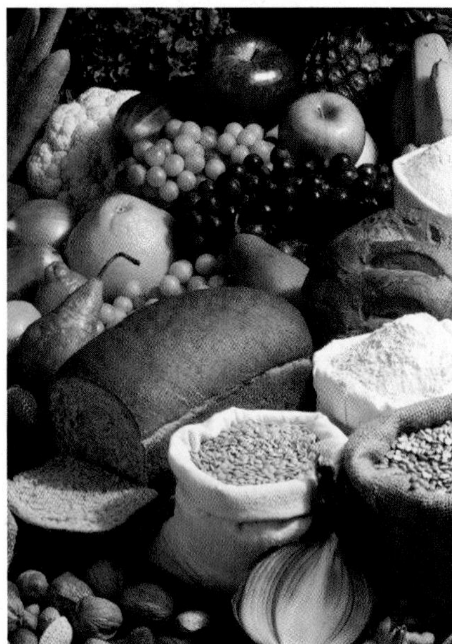

A Healthful Diet These foods illustrate writer Michael Pollan's (2008) haiku for a healthy diet, "Eat food. Not too much. Mostly plants."

who did not, *even though the women eating breakfast took in more total Calories* (Jakubowicz et al., 2008). This finding suggests that eating breakfast affects body metabolism to reduce weight.

- Be physically active every day. You don't have to be an athlete. Any activity, including walking, will help.

These lifestyle changes tend to produce a very gradual weight loss of around a pound per week, extending over years, indicating that they act by changing the body weight set point. When you eat mostly vegetables and fruit with little meat or fat, your set point seems to go down. When you are physically inactive, your set point goes up.

A wholesale change in lifestyle, especially avoiding Calorie-rich foods and becoming physically active, is difficult for some people to maintain. One study reported that about one out of every three American adults say they are trying to lose or control their weight. But of those, only about a third were applying the tried-and-true methods of reducing Calories and increasing activity (Kruger et al., 2004), probably because those steps can be so difficult. For one thing, the social context may interfere: if everyone else in your family eats one way, it's difficult for you to eat differently. For another, reducing portion size requires you to stop eating *before* you feel full. For this reason, many people hold out hope that a pill will be produced to control appetite, as we'll consider next.

APPETITE CONTROL Over the years, people have tried, through trial and error, to find medicines that reduce appetite without having harmful side effects, but this enterprise has been discouraging. Several modern medicines that were found to reduce appetite (aminorex, fen-phen, phenylpropanolamine) were later shown to have dangerous side effects, so governments have taken them off the market. Likewise, amphetamines ("uppers," "meth") increase activity and reduce appetite, but only as long as the person is taking the drug. Then, just as when you stop a fad diet, the weight comes right back on. Because long-term amphetamine use is dangerous and the drugs are widely abused, they are no longer used for controlling body weight. This discouraging history led scientists to try to find some way of manipulating the body's normal signals for hunger and satiety, reasoning that we may be able to stop hunger by short-circuiting the normal signal(s).

The hormones discussed above have all been targeted in an effort to control appetite. Hopes for a pill using leptin were dashed, but another approach being tested is a nasal spray to deliver a hormone that is normally produced by the intestines to stimulate the arcuate nucleus to reduce appetite (Sileno et al., 2006). It has long been known that marijuana use stimulates appetite (the "munchies") by simulating the effects of neurotransmitters called **endocannabinoids** (see Section 7.4). The drug rimonabant was developed to block endocannabinoid receptors and was found to suppress appetite (acting as an "anti-munchies" signal). Unfortunately there are indications that the drug may increase the risk for depression and suicide, presumably because it also acts as an "anti-happy" signal. (Are you willing to feel suicidally depressed in order to lose weight?) For this reason, use of rimonabant was suspended in Europe.

When it is all said and done, we do not have any safe, effective drug to suppress appetite. Until one is found, the best approach to controlling your weight is to change your lifestyle to eat less and exercise more. However, people whose weight is endangering their health sometimes consider drastic procedures, such as liposuction and gastric bypass surgery.

endocannabinoids
Neurotransmitters that normally act on the receptors that are activated by marijuana and related drugs.

ANTI-OBESITY SURGERY One surgical approach is to remove fat deposits from the body, usually by *liposuction*, whereby needles placed under the skin suck out as much as 10 pounds of fat (while the client is anesthetized). It is

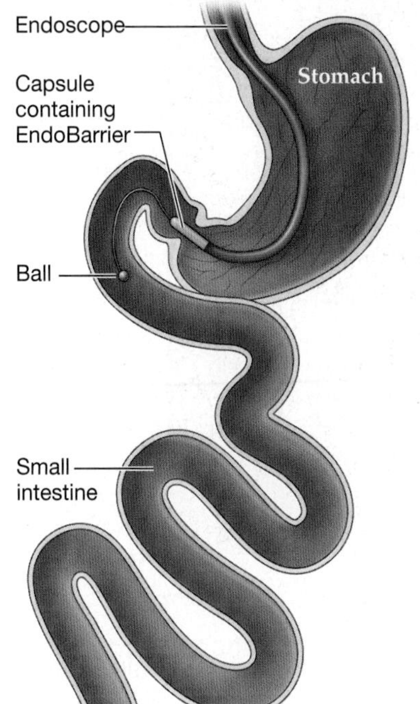

The EndoBarrier is inserted through the mouth via an endoscope and is guided into position by use of a ball and catheter.
Endoscope
Capsule containing EndoBarrier
Stomach
Ball
Small intestine

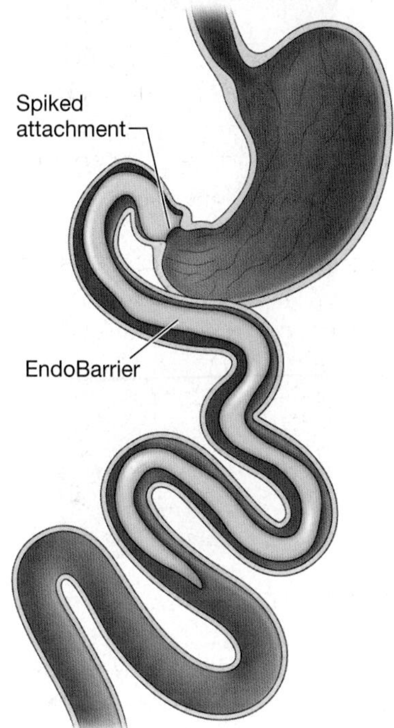

The sleeve lines the small intestine and is held in place with a spiked attachment. It interferes with the absorption of nutrients, promoting weight loss.
Spiked attachment
EndoBarrier

Figure 12.14 Fat-Busting Liner for the Intestine

difficult to find objective information about liposuction because so many commercial interests, including medical organizations, are financially dependent on finding customers for the procedure. Put simply, this method does not work for long-term weight loss (Rinomhota et al., 2008), which is why it is considered cosmetic surgery. People and animals (Dark et al., 1984; Zucker, 1988) who have liposuction will regain the fat unless they also alter their diet.

A much more extreme anti-obesity procedure is *bariatric surgery*, surgery on the stomach and/or intestines designed to reduce body weight (**Figure 12.14**). The most common form of bariatric surgery is to reduce the size of the stomach so that only small amounts of food can be eaten without discomfort. Another approach is to surgically bypass parts of the intestines so that food passes through more rapidly, with fewer Calories absorbed. While they are effective for long-term weight loss, both types of surgery are serious, with potentially fatal complications. About 2% of patients die within a month of surgery (Flum et al., 2005), so these surgeries are usually seen as a last resort. If obesity is likely to shorten a patient's life span appreciably, surgery with all its risks may be the better choice.

These desperate choices emphasize how useful it would be to find a safer, nonsurgical method of manipulating appetite to reduce body weight. Alternatively, if we could find a way to help people eat less and exercise more, no one would have to consider potentially fatal surgery. Paradoxically, there are some people who die because they refuse to eat enough, as we'll see next.

Eating disorders usually arise in adolescence and are more common in girls than boys

While many people struggle to avoid being overweight, some people have the opposite problem—they shun food so much that they lose too much weight. **Anorexia nervosa** is a condition in which people become obsessed with their

anorexia nervosa A condition involving obsession with body weight that leads to extreme weight loss.

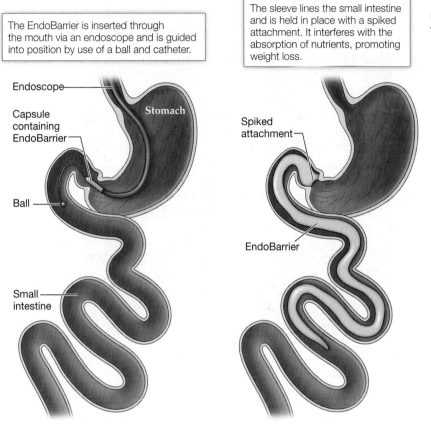

Figure 12.15 Changing Ideals of Female Beauty (A) Today actress Keira Knightley provides an extreme example of modern society's emphasis on thinness as beauty. (B) In contrast, when Peter Paul Rubens painted his ideal of feminine beauty about 1630, he emphasized a much more substantial body build.

family-based treatment For anorexia, a follow-up treatment to hospitalization that involves a family member in constant attendance who insists that the patient eat.

body weight and display behaviors, such as avoiding food, taking laxatives, overexercising, and drinking lots of water, that lead to extreme weight loss. This condition is much more common in adolescent girls and young women than in boys or men. It is a life-threatening condition, and approximately 10 million people suffer from anorexia in the United States (Klump et al., 2009). It is estimated that nearly 20% of these people will die from complications of anorexia, basically malnutrition.

Anorexia nervosa is very difficult to treat, in part because the victims have a distorted body image: although everyone else sees them as haggard and emaciated, they see themselves as fat. For this reason, they may sabotage any attempt to increase their body weight, hiding food rather than eating it, or vomiting in secret. This means that fulfilling the primary goal of immediate weight gain often requires hospitalization and close supervision. One follow-up approach, pioneered by Maudsley Hospital in London, is **family-based treatment**, an intensive "refeeding" whereby a parent or other close family member is with the patient 24/7 and keeps insisting that the patient eat (Le Grange, 2005; Lock et al., 2010). The person with anorexia may be terrified by the prospect of eating a piece of cake, tearfully complying only under intense social pressure. Not until victims have recovered some weight do they seem capable of rationally understanding that they are dangerously thin and need to eat to survive. We will review studies indicating a disordered cognition in people with anorexia in The Cutting Edge at the end of this chapter.

Afraid to Eat People suffering from anorexia may actually be afraid of food.

Because modern societies emphasize thinness as an ideal of feminine beauty (**Figure 12.15A**), some people suggest that anorexia is caused by social pressures for thinness. But historical analysis shows that anorexia was first described in the late 1600s, when feminine ideals did not emphasize thinness (**Figure 12.15B**). The condition was common enough in the late 1800s when the term *anorexia nervosa* was first used, even though the ideal woman's body was heavier back then (see Bliss & Branch, 1960). Societal pressures may have increased the number of girls suffering from anorexia nervosa, but some women suffered from the disorder long before such pressures arose. This historical persistence of anorexia suggests that it has a deeper, more biological basis.

Bulimia (or *bulimia nervosa*) is a related disorder where people of normal weight believe they are fatter than they really are and periodically gorge themselves, usually with "junk food," and then either vomit the food or take laxatives to avoid gaining weight. As with anorexia, bulimia is more common in females than males, and in adolescents and young adults than in adults. Not all people with bulimia become emaciated, but repeated vomiting or overuse of laxatives can still upset the composition of body fluids enough to be fatal. Both anorexia nervosa and bulimia can kill because in each case the patient's lack of nutrient reserves damages various organ systems or leaves the body ill-equipped to fight otherwise mild diseases.

bulimia A disorder in which people of normal weight see themselves as overweight and, following overeating, induce vomiting or take laxatives to avoid weight gain.

12.2 SUMMARY

- The brain carefully regulates energy stores to maintain a *body weight set point*. For example, when people reduce how much they eat, the brain may reduce *basal metabolism* to prevent weight loss.
- The brain carefully regulates the use of food, maintaining adequate levels of a simple sugar, *glucose*, so the brain and body can function.
- The pancreatic hormone insulin is required for body cells (but not brain cells) to use glucose, so the brain drives insulin release in anticipation of a meal. Insulin also directs excess glucose into short-term storage as glycogen in muscles and the liver.
- Another pancreatic hormone converts the glycogen back to glucose when needed. Built-up glycogen stores may be converted to long-term *lipid* (*fat*) stores around the body.
- Several *hormones* inform the brain about nutrient stores in the body. Hormones from the stomach and intestines, for example, report on the status and quality of food. *Leptin*, secreted by fat cells, reports on the status of body fat. The *arcuate nucleus* in the hypothalamus integrates all this information and then stimulates other brain regions to trigger hunger or satiety to regulate body weight around the set point.
- The only reliable way to achieve long-term weight loss is to make permanent changes in diet and/or activity, which seem to slowly change the body weight set point.
- As yet there are no effective drugs to reduce appetite appreciably without potentially damaging side effects.
- People with the eating disorders *anorexia nervosa* (avoiding food and becoming dangerously thin) and *bulimia* (periodic binging and purging) have the irrational belief that they are overweight. These disorders usually arise in adolescence or young adulthood and are much more common in females than males.
- While modern pressures for women to be thin may increase the incidence of eating disorders, historical analysis indicates that these disorders are not always a response to social pressures alone.

REVIEW QUESTIONS

1. Describe some of the evidence that the brain enforces a body weight set point, using data from both non-human animals and humans.
2. What hormones inform the brain about body weight, and which part of the brain receives and integrates that information?
3. What behaviors can lead to a long-term reduction in body weight, and how do they compare with fad diets?
4. Describe the major eating disorders and evaluate the evidence that they may result from societal pressures to be thin.

Food for Thought

In contrast to biases against people of various races, religions, and sexual orientations, bias against people who are obese is one of the last remaining prejudices in industrialized nations.
Given what you've learned about body weight regulation, do you expect this bias to remain?

12.3 Sexual Behavior

Things to Learn

- Hormonal influences on sexual behavior
- Stages of human sexual response
- Fetal sexual differentiation
- Testosterone organization of animal brain
- Prenatal influences on human sexual orientation

Sexual behavior is another motivated behavior that occupies much of our time and attention, but the study of sexual behavior presents several problems due to the intensely personal and emotionally charged nature of sexual behavior. Society has many written and unwritten laws about sexual behaviors, and people are reluctant to talk about sex even in private, let alone in an open public discussion or research enterprise. Yet despite the obstacles, researchers have learned quite a lot about sex. They have learned, for example, that in animals sexual behavior is closely regulated by hormones acting on the brain. Hormones play less of a role in human sexual behavior, but they still have some effects, primarily on **libido**, the desire to have sex, rather than on which sexual behaviors are displayed. We'll find that basic sexual response is similar in men and women, yet there are interesting differences as well, and we'll explore powerful cultural influences on sexual behavior.

Then we'll discuss the complex issue of *sexual orientation*—whether a person is attracted to opposite- or same-sex partners—and whether animal models of the development of sexual behavior apply to humans. One of society's laws, which is both written and unwritten, is that a person must be either male or female. We'll see, however, how some biological phenomena do not respect such laws, and how some people do not fit neatly into the "either male or female" distinction. The insistence that a child behave either entirely like a girl or entirely like a boy brought isolation and taunting to Brenda, whom we met at the beginning of the chapter. By the end of this section you'll have a better understanding of why Brenda could not fit in as a girl.

libido The motivation to have sex.

coitus Also called *copulation* or *intromission*. The sexual act; occurs when the male's penis enters the female's vagina.

ejaculation The forceful expulsion of semen from the penis.

semen A mixture of fluid, including sperm, that is released during ejaculation.

stereotyped In this context, the species-specific unvarying form of sexual behavior in non-human animals.

In non-human animals, sexual behaviors are stereotyped and closely regulated by hormones

There are several different words for the core of mating behavior in mammals, which occurs when the male's penis enters the female's vagina: **coitus**, **intromission**, or sexual intercourse. It may also be referred to as **copulation**, especially when referring to non-humans. Intromission usually leads to **ejaculation**, when the male's penis squirts a mixture of fluids called **semen** (which contains sperm) inside the vagina. If a sperm fertilizes an egg, and if the fertilized egg develops properly, then the female will be pregnant and later give birth to one or more new individuals. Humans engage in many sexual behaviors in addition to coitus, and in animals, at least, we can think of sexual behavior as all the behaviors leading up to and including copulation.

In non-human animals, sexual behavior tends to be much the same from one bout to another, or from one pair of animals to another. We say the behavior is **stereotyped**, having an unvarying form or pattern. For example, if we put a female rat into a male rat's cage, he will soon try to initiate sex by *mounting*, getting on top of the female to bring his penis near her vagina, in a stereotyped fashion. In fact, the male will almost always try mounting any rat placed in the cage with him, whether it's a male or a female. Most of the time, females ignore the male's mounting efforts, so nothing happens and he soon gives up. But at other times the female rodent may be receptive to the male's efforts. In this case, when the male mounts her she displays a stereotyped posture, called *lordosis*, in which she lifts her head and rump and pushes her tail to one side (**Figure 12.16**). The lordosis posture allows the male to insert his penis into the female's vagina.

Figure 12.16 Mating Postures in Rats The male mounts the female from behind, grasps her sides with his forepaws, and rhythmically shoves his pelvis against her rump. If the female is receptive, she displays the lordosis posture seen here, raising her head and rump and pushing her tail to one side, allowing the male's penis to enter her vagina.

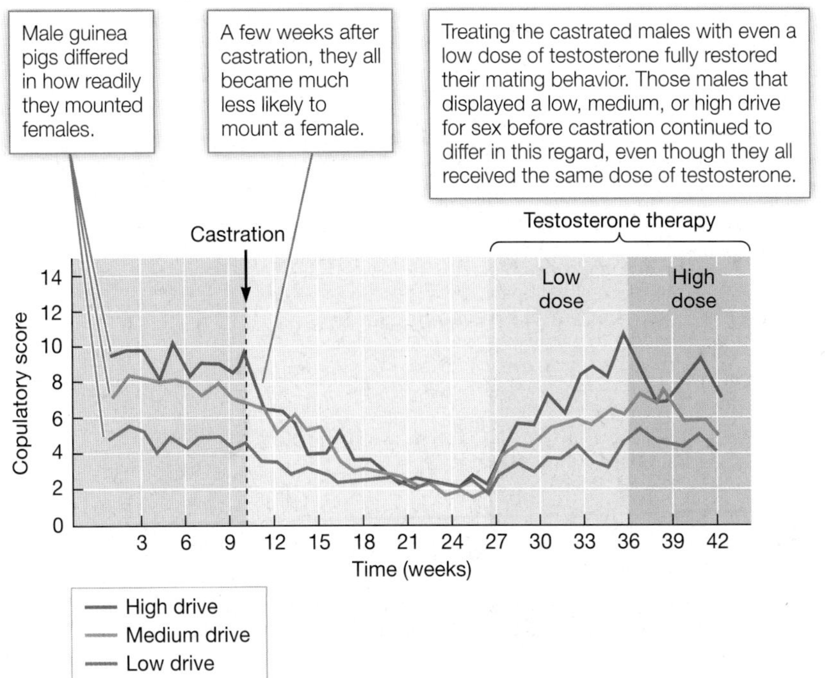
Male guinea pigs differed in how readily they mounted females.
A few weeks after castration, they all became much less likely to mount a female.
Treating the castrated males with even a low dose of testosterone fully restored their mating behavior. Those males that displayed a low, medium, or high drive for sex before castration continued to differ in this regard, even though they all received the same dose of testosterone.
Castration
Testosterone therapy
Low dose
High dose
Copulatory score
0
2
4
6
8
10
12
14
3 6 9 12 15 18 21 24 27 30 33 36 39 42
Time (weeks)
High drive
Medium drive
Low drive

Figure 12.17 Androgens Activate Mating Behavior in Male Rodents These experiments established that individual differences in sex drive among the male guinea pigs could not be accounted for by differences in levels of testosterone. (After Grunt & Young, 1953.)

Both the mounting behavior of males and the lordosis behavior of females are stereotyped. Both are also affected by hormones secreted by the **gonads**, the reproductive organs that make either sperm (in the case of **testes**; singular, *testis* or *testicle*) or eggs (in the case of **ovaries**; singular, *ovary*). The main hormones produced by the testes are the **androgens**, the most prominent of which is **testosterone**, which acts on many parts of the body and is crucially involved in the production of sperm. Ovaries produce two types of hormones: **estrogens** (such as **estradiol**) and **progesterone**. The ovarian hormones also act on many parts of the body and are crucial for the maturation and release of eggs. Both male and female gonads secrete all of these hormones; they differ only in the relative proportion of each. We can think of the gonadal hormones as coordinating agents, circulating throughout the body to have different effects in different regions. In general, androgens prepare the body for reproduction as a male, whereas estrogens and progesterone prepare the body for reproduction as a female. These same hormones also act on the brain to trigger reproductive behaviors.

Castration (removal of the testes, sometimes called "neutering") of male rodents causes them to stop mounting in just a few weeks due to lack of testosterone. If castrated males are injected with testosterone every day, they start mounting again within 1–2 weeks (**Figure 12.17**). Interestingly, even a very low dose of testosterone, lower than is normally seen in healthy males, will completely restore mating behavior.

In female rodents, ovarian hormones control whether they will be receptive to a male's mount. These hormones are produced as part of the cycle controlling *ovulation*, the release of eggs from the ovary so they can be fertilized. These hormones also act on the brain so that, around the time of ovulation, the female will be receptive to male mounting. Receiving sperm just as the eggs are released from the ovary maximizes a female's chances of getting pregnant. If a

gonads The reproductive organs that make either sperm (testes in males) or eggs (ovaries in females).

testes The male gonads, which produce sperm for reproduction.

ovaries The female gonads, which produce eggs for reproduction.

androgens The primary steroid hormones produced by the testes.

testosterone The most prominent androgen, crucial for the production of sperm.

estrogens One of two classes of ovarian hormones that are crucial for female reproduction.

estradiol The most common form of estrogen.

progesterone One of two classes of ovarian hormones that are crucial for female reproduction.

castration The removal of the testes.

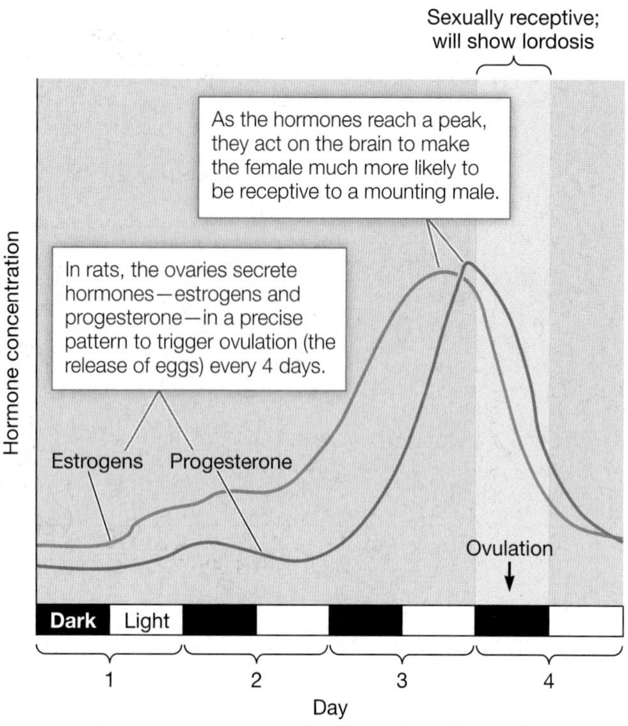

Figure 12.18 Sexual Receptivity in Female Rodents

activation In the context of sexual behaviors, the action of hormones in adulthood that make particular behaviors more likely to occur.

female rodent's ovaries are removed, she will never be receptive to a male again unless her ovarian hormones are replaced. In these ways, gonadal hormones are said to **activate** behavior in adult animals: when the hormones are present, the animal is more likely to display mating behaviors, and as the hormones decline, the behaviors decline as well (**Figure 12.18**). Androgens activate masculine behaviors in males, while estrogens and progesterone activate feminine behaviors in females.

Experimenters have pinpointed specific parts of the rodent brain where testosterone activates male mounting, and other brain sites where estrogens activate female lordosis. Most of these brain regions are found in various parts of the hypothalamus. Some parts of the hypothalamus regulate male mounting behavior, and other parts regulate lordosis. The important point to remember is that the same gonadal hormones that prepare the body for reproduction also act on parts of the brain, including the hypothalamus, to activate reproductive behaviors.

In humans, sexual behavior is neither as stereotyped nor as hormonally regulated as in animals

In contrast to rodents and other non-human animals, where mating positions are the same across all couples and on every occurrence, human sexual behavior is remarkably varied. The *Kama Sutra*, a text that was first compiled in India 2,000 years ago, lists at least 64 different sexual acts, including oral sex and many different sexual positions. Inexperienced male rats may sometimes mount a female in some way other than that displayed in Figure 12.16, but they soon learn the standard approach or they will not be able to mate. Humans, by contrast, seek more variety in sexual behavior. Other large-brained, intelligent species, such as chimpanzees and dolphins, also display a greater variety of sexual acts and positions than rodents. Does this preference for variety reflect a certain level of intelligence? Another difference is that most humans are concerned about pleas-

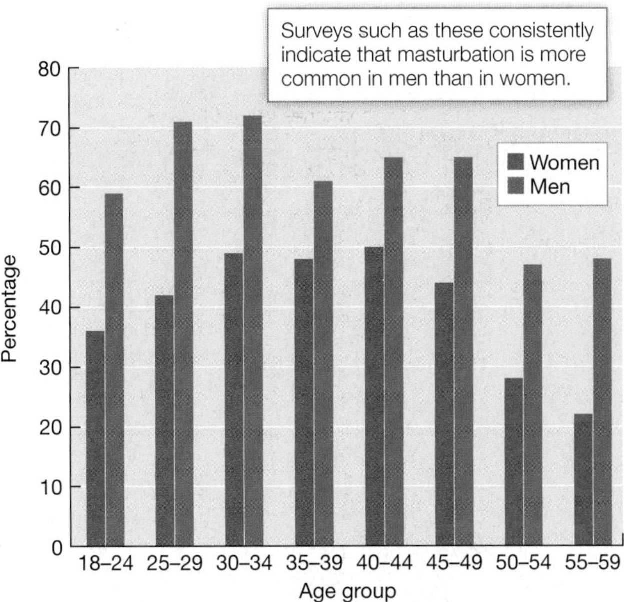

Figure 12.19 **Percentage of People Who Masturbate** (After Laumann et al., 1992.)

ing their partner during sex. It's not clear that either partner is seeking to please the other when other animals engage in sex. The goal of pleasing a partner also requires a certain degree of intelligence and of social sophistication.

Pioneering biologist Alfred Kinsey supervised a massive survey of sexual behavior by conducting intensive, one-on-one interviews with thousands of Americans in the mid-twentieth century. When his team published their results for men (Kinsey et al., 1948) and women (Kinsey et al., 1953) in best-selling books, Americans were shocked to learn about the variety of sexual behaviors being practiced. They learned that many women and almost all men masturbate, that college-educated people are more likely to engage in oral sex than people who have not gone to college, and that many people have had same-sex sexual experiences. This information about what men and women do when they are being sexual was an enormous departure from the past, when society forbade any public discussions about sex. Today we don't rely too heavily on certain Kinsey data, recognizing that his team did not get a random sample of subjects (the importance of random sampling is covered in Chapter 2). At the time, they felt that only a few people would be willing to answer so many questions about so many sexual behaviors, so they sought out groups that would be more open about such matters. They often interviewed friends and colleagues, for example, resulting in an overrepresentation of academics and college-educated people. More important, the face-to-face interview meant that only people who were very comfortable with sexuality were surveyed. Today, anonymous surveys still show that most people masturbate and that men are more likely to masturbate than women (**Figure 12.19**).

BASIC HUMAN SEXUAL RESPONSE Not until the end of the 1950s was there any organized effort to study what actually happens when men and women engage in coitus. Physician William Masters and psychologist Virginia Johnson applied medical devices to measure heart rate, blood pressure, respiration, and many other variables while couples were having sex in the laboratory. They studied factors that affect *erection*, the swelling of the penis with blood, which causes it to enlarge and become stiffer, as well as the factors that cause the vagina to secrete thin, slippery fluid that serves as a lubricant for intromission.

Masters of Sex William H. Masters and Virginia E. Johnson.

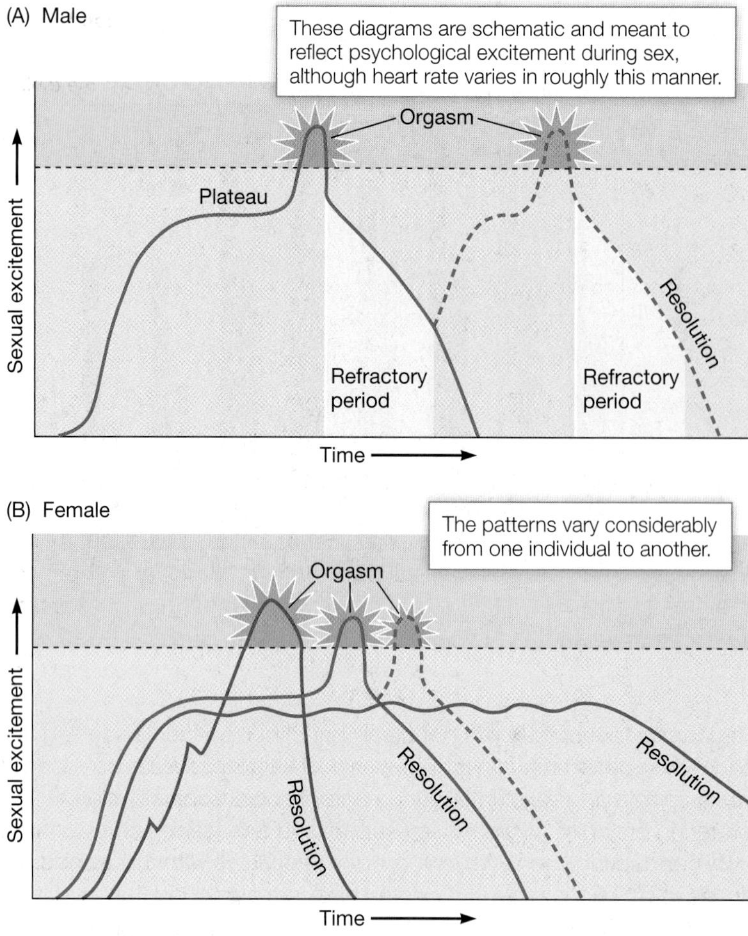
(A) Male
These diagrams are schematic and meant to reflect psychological excitement during sex, although heart rate varies in roughly this manner.
Orgasm
Plateau
Sexual excitement
Refractory period
Refractory period
Resolution
Time
(B) Female
The patterns vary considerably from one individual to another.
Orgasm
Sexual excitement
Resolution
Resolution
Resolution
Time

Figure 12.20 Human Sexual Response (A) In males, orgasm is followed by a refractory period where erection is not possible. Dotted lines indicate patterns that are sometimes seen. (B) Females show more individual differences in sexual response (indicated by the different-colored curves), as some may experience multiple orgasms while others may report having a fulfilling experience without orgasm. (After Masters & Johnson, 1966.)

Masters and Johnson found that the basic pattern of sexual arousal was similar in men and women and was characterized by four successive phases:

1. *Arousal* is a gradual increase in excitement, which is reflected in increased heart rate and respiration and the swelling or erection of the penis in men and the clitoris in women.
2. *Plateau* is the prolonged period of excitement.
3. *Orgasm* is the brief and intensely pleasurable sensation experienced by most men during ejaculation and by most women during coitus.
4. *Resolution* is the gradual decline in excitement following orgasm.

Despite the overall similarity of sexual response in men and women, there were differences too. For example, in most men, the penis loses its erection after orgasm. Masters and Johnson called this time the **refractory period**, when no amount of stimulation can produce an erection, so the man cannot have another orgasm right away (**Figure 12.20A**). Only after the refractory period has ended (which can vary from minutes to hours) can the man achieve another erection. On the other hand, women don't seem to have a refractory period, and many women can have multiple orgasms during a single bout of coitus, just as the Kinsey surveys had indicated. In this way women presented a more variable sexual response than men. Some women reliably achieved only one orgasm per bout, others reliably achieved several, and yet other women did not experience orgasm at all, remaining at the plateau phase until resolution (**Figure 12.20B**).

refractory period The time following a male orgasm, during which stimulation cannot produce an erection.

Masters and Johnson also confirmed the Kinsey findings that for most women the only reliable way to achieve orgasm is by stimulation of the clitoris. They found that the clitoris swells during sexual excitement much the way the penis does in men, and that this swelling can help provide more stimulation, leading to orgasm. Today this understanding that clitoral stimulation is important to achieve orgasm may seem obvious, but until the mid-twentieth century the "experts" considered the clitoris irrelevant to sexual satisfaction. (Most of these experts were men, such as Sigmund Freud.) Despite its lavish attention to pleasing female partners during sex, even the *Kama Sutra* gives no indication that the clitoris exists.

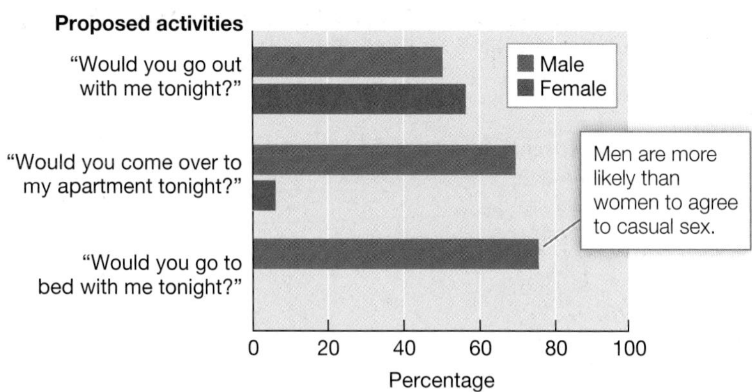
Proposed activities
"Would you go out with me tonight?"
"Would you come over to my apartment tonight?"
"Would you go to bed with me tonight?"
Male
Female
Men are more likely than women to agree to casual sex.
0
20
40
60
80
100
Percentage

Figure 12.21 A Sex Difference in Sexual Attitudes (After Clark & Hatfield, 1989.)

Another difference in sexual behavior between men and women, which has been documented in many different societies, is that men are generally more interested in having casual sex than are women. In one famous experiment, physically attractive men and women who were part of a research team went to coffee shops and bars around a university campus and started up a conversation with a stranger of the opposite sex. Eventually the researcher asked the stranger one of three questions: "Would you go out with me tonight?", "Would you come over to my apartment tonight?", or "Would you go to bed with me tonight?" About half the participants, both men and women, agreed to go out with the researcher when asked. But very few of the women who were asked to go to the researcher's apartment agreed, and none of them agreed to have sex with the researcher (Clark & Hatfield, 1989). Among male participants, most who were asked either to go to the apartment or go to bed with the researcher said yes (**Figure 12.21**).

HORMONES AND HUMAN LIBIDO Do hormones such as testosterone and estrogens activate sexual behavior in humans? Yes, but hormones have a much more subtle effect in humans than in other animals. For example, while rats stop mating altogether a few weeks after castration, men who have lost their testes, either to accident or to disease, may continue to have sex years later. However, men who have lost their testes are definitely less interested in sex. Double-blind, placebo-controlled studies demonstrate that treating these men with testosterone will restore their sexual interests (Davidson et al., 1979).

You may wonder if the reason some men are more interested in sex than others is because of differences in circulating testosterone. The answer is quite clearly no: men who seek lots of sex do not produce more testosterone than men who do not. So something other than testosterone is responsible for variations in libido among men, and social influences, including upbringing, opportunity, and chance, play a role. Recall that for animals, too, complete loss of testosterone abolishes male sexual behavior, but even very low doses of testosterone will restore it, as Figure 12.17 indicated. Also note from this figure how the same dose of testosterone given to many different castrated males restores the same level of sex drive they had before castration: low, medium, or high. So differences in circulating testosterone cannot account for differences in male sex drive in either animals or men.

In women, hormones influence libido in ways that are more subtle than in men. Some women report reduced interest in sex after **menopause**, when the menstrual cycle stops around 50 years of age. As the menstrual cycle stops, the ovarian hormones underlying the cycle decline as well. The decline in estrogens causes the vagina to produce less lubricant for easing intromission, and that can put a damper on sexual relations. Is that why the women

menopause The time a woman's menstrual periods stops, around age 50.

Figure 12.22 Testosterone Can Boost Libido in Women Too (After Sherwin & Gelfand, 1987.)

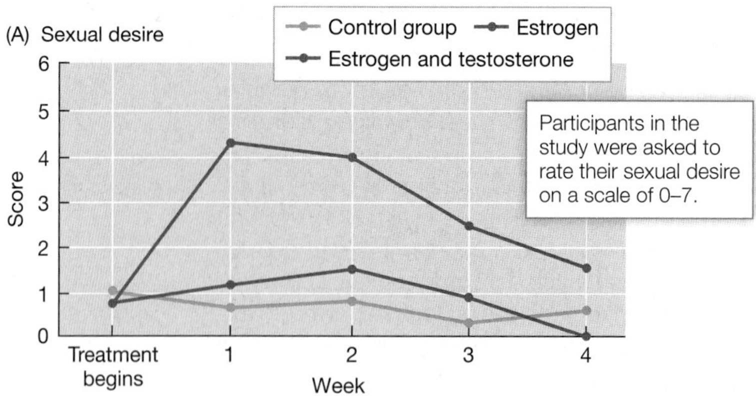
(A) Sexual desire
Control group
Estrogen
Estrogen and testosterone
Participants in the study were asked to rate their sexual desire on a scale of 0–7.
Score
Treatment begins
Week

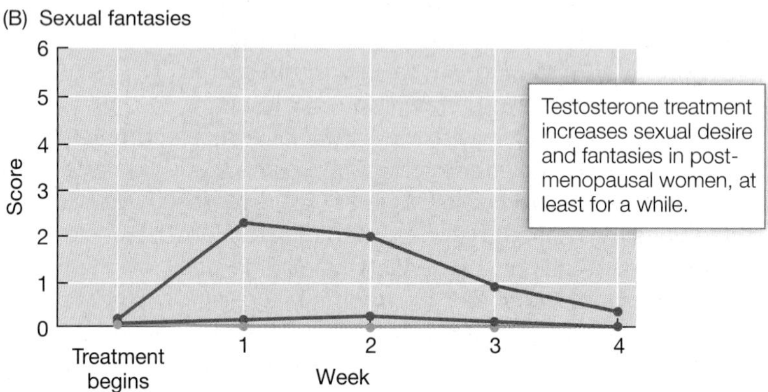
(B) Sexual fantasies
Testosterone treatment increases sexual desire and fantasies in post-menopausal women, at least for a while.
Score
Treatment begins
Week

become less interested in sex? Not entirely, because for one thing, external lubricants such as K-Y Jelly can compensate for the loss of natural lubricant. Also, estrogen treatment, either by application directly to the vagina or by taking pills, can restore natural lubrication but does nothing to restore libido. It turns out that the most effective medication for restoring libido in women at menopause is low doses of androgens such as testosterone (**Figure 12.22**). Normally all of the gonadal hormones are made by both testes and ovaries, but men make a lot more androgens than women do, and women make a lot more estrogens and progesterone than men do. At menopause, providing androgens, at very low levels, can restore libido (Sherwin, 2002), and this is presumably due to activation of sexual interest in the brain. Androgens alone have no effect on vaginal lubrication.

Although it is clear that testosterone can increase libido in both men and women, it's important to note that how a person acts to fulfill her or his libido is remarkably varied. A person's behavior also depends on the context, or circumstances, surrounding the behavior, including whether a sexual partner is available, the person's feelings at the time, and the cultural rules for sexual behavior. So while hormones may tend to activate particular patterns of behavior in other animals, in humans the social context has a tremendous influence on what, exactly, people do when they are motivated to have sex.

So far we've said nothing about choosing a partner for sex. When Brenda, whom we met at the beginning of the chapter, was young, she fantasized about growing up to have a mustache and a girlfriend. Even before she knew that she'd been born a boy, she felt the sort of attractions that many boys have: for girls. She felt this attraction despite having been raised as a girl and being told for as long as she could remember that she was a girl. What accounts for her resistance to all those social pressures to want a boyfriend? To understand Brenda's sexual preferences, we need to consider the hormonal influences before birth that shape the human body into that of a male or a female.

Prenatal hormones shape the sex of the body in humans and other mammals

You've probably learned that sex chromosomes determine whether a person will be male or female. We all inherit one X chromosome from our mother. Those of us who inherit an X chromosome from our father become females, and those who inherit a Y chromosome from our father become males. This simple rule applies to virtually all mammals. But did you know that the main job of the sex chromosomes is to determine what type of gonads we develop before birth?

Early in gestation every embryo has a pair of gonads that look unformed, resembling some mix of testes and ovaries, so they are called **indifferent gonads** ("indifferent" as in undetermined). If the embryo has inherited two X chromosomes, the indifferent gonads grow into ovaries. If the embryo inherited a Y chromosome, the gonads grow into testes. After that development takes place, the further development of sex differences in the body, a process called **sexual differentiation**, depends on hormones produced by the gonads. If testes form, they begin to secrete androgens, such as testosterone. Testosterone then directs the internal and external development of masculine structures, including a *penis* and *scrotum* (the fleshy sac holding the testes). In the absence of androgens, the fetus develops feminine structures, including a *clitoris*, *vagina*, and *labia* (fleshy folds around the vagina and clitoris) (**Figure 12.23**). The fetal ovary doesn't secrete much hormone, so it doesn't seem to play a role at this point. But in adolescence the secretion of estrogens from the ovaries will promote further changes, including development of breasts.

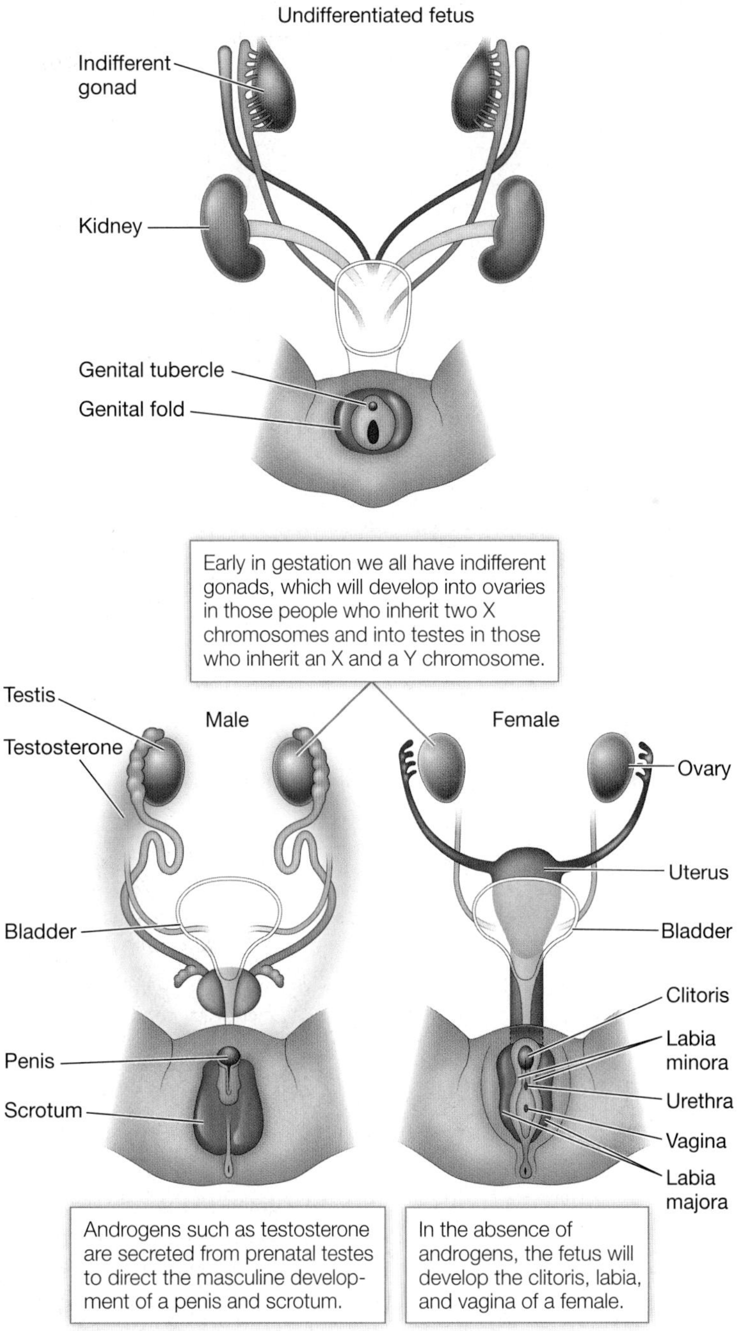

Undifferentiated fetus

Indifferent gonad

Kidney

Genital tubercle

Genital fold

Early in gestation we all have indifferent gonads, which will develop into ovaries in those people who inherit two X chromosomes and into testes in those who inherit an X and a Y chromosome.

Male

Female

Testis

Testosterone

Bladder

Penis

Scrotum

Ovary

Uterus

Bladder

Clitoris

Labia minora

Urethra

Vagina

Labia majora

Androgens such as testosterone are secreted from prenatal testes to direct the masculine development of a penis and scrotum.

In the absence of androgens, the fetus will develop the clitoris, labia, and vagina of a female.

Figure 12.23 Sexual Differentiation of the Genitals

The fetal development of either a masculine or feminine exterior is a watershed event. People who encounter the individual from birth onward behave somewhat differently depending on whether they perceive this person as boy or girl, man or woman (**Figure 12.24A**). Adults talk more to girls and are more active with boys. Now, you might think that adults are simply responding to differences in what girls and boys like to do, and that may be part of the story. But in a series of **Baby X studies**, researchers handed an infant to an adult and reported the sex, but sometimes the baby they *said* was a girl was actually a boy, or vice versa. These studies showed that what sex the adult *thinks* the baby is affects how the adult interacts with the baby. Adults spend more time looking a baby in the face and talking to it if they think it is a girl. They spend more time actively moving the baby up and down and encouraging physical activity if they think it is a boy (Block, 1983; Golombok & Fivush, 1994; Smith & Lloyd, 1978). People are also more likely to offer boy-typical toys (cars, construction kits, sports toys) to "boys" and girl-typical toys (dolls, tea sets) to "girls" (Seavey et al., 1975; Stern & Karraker, 1989). These interactions with adults surely leave their mark on the child's brain (and therefore the child's mind). Could it be that far more men than women choose careers in engineering because boys

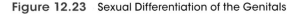

indifferent gonads The unformed gonads in a fetus, which resemble a mix of testes and ovaries.

sexual differentiation The process in fetal development, controlled by the hormones produced by the gonads, of forming either male or female structures.

Baby X studies Investigations of the behavior of adults with babies as a function of their belief about the sex of the baby.

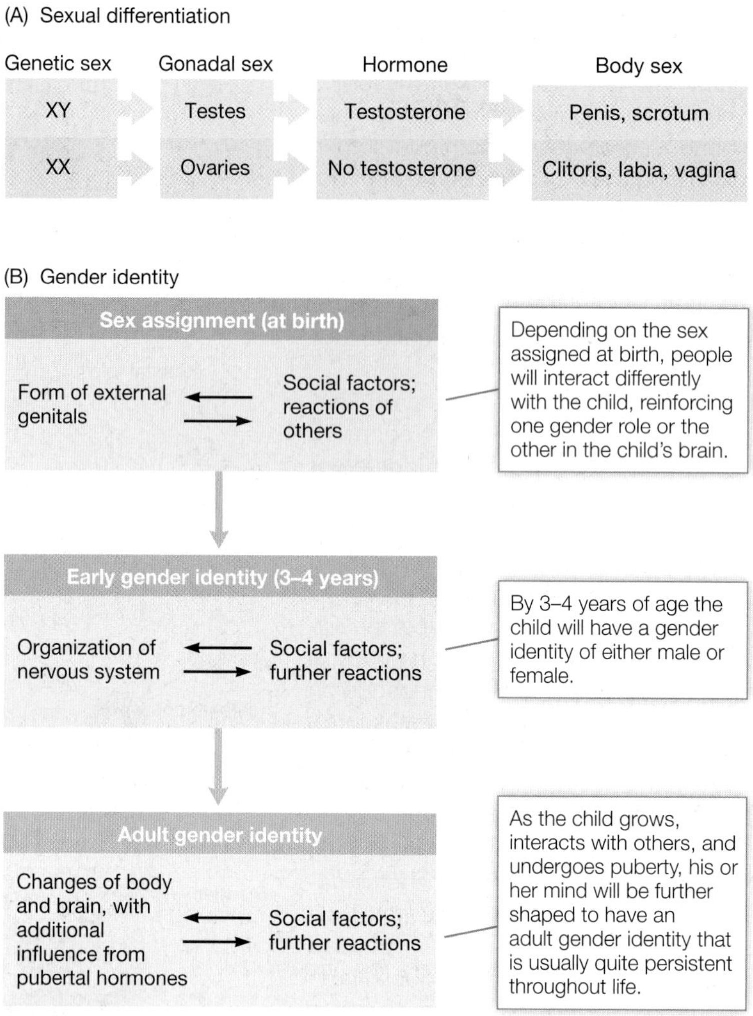

(A) Sexual differentiation

Genetic sex	Gonadal sex	Hormone	Body sex
XY	Testes	Testosterone	Penis, scrotum
XX	Ovaries	No testosterone	Clitoris, labia, vagina

(B) Gender identity

Sex assignment (at birth)

Form of external genitals ⇄ Social factors; reactions of others

Depending on the sex assigned at birth, people will interact differently with the child, reinforcing one gender role or the other in the child's brain.

Early gender identity (3–4 years)

Organization of nervous system ⇄ Social factors; further reactions

By 3–4 years of age the child will have a gender identity of either male or female.

Adult gender identity

Changes of body and brain, with additional influence from pubertal hormones ⇄ Social factors; further reactions

As the child grows, interacts with others, and undergoes puberty, his or her mind will be further shaped to have an adult gender identity that is usually quite persistent throughout life.

Figure 12.24 Sexual Differentiation and Gender Identity

have more experience than girls with toys that emphasize physical movement and construction (**Box 12.1**)?

As the child learns language, the rules for how boys and girls should act are explicitly explained and enforced. Most children, by the time they are 3 or 4 years old, have a firmly developed sense of whether they are male or female, which is called a **gender identity**. The terms "sex" and "gender" are often used interchangeably, and there are no universal rules for which term to use in which context. One widely promoted distinction is that "sex" refers to biological structures or processes, while "gender" refers to behavioral, cultural, or psychological traits typically associated with one sex or the other. In this book we use the term "gender identity" rather than "sex identity" because so much of what societies associate with the "proper" behaviors of boys and girls, and men and women, is culturally dependent. In some societies all boys are expected to learn to hunt. In other societies women are expected to show very little of themselves in public. So gender identity is definitely influenced by cultural expectations. As the child grows up, interacting with other people and learning more about cultural expectations, he or she develops an adult gender identity that has been shaped by all these influences (**Figure 12.24B**). In most cases, gender identity matches the sex that was assigned to the child at birth.

gender identity The sense, developed in childhood, of whether one is male or female.

Psychology in Everyday Life

BOX 12.1

Why Aren't There More Women Scientists and Engineers?

The vast majority of engineers and senior scientists in Western society are men. This imbalance (see figure) has been a contentious and lasting concern. Is the underrepresentation of women in these fields the result of society offering fewer opportunities for women than for men? Are men innately more capable in those fields?

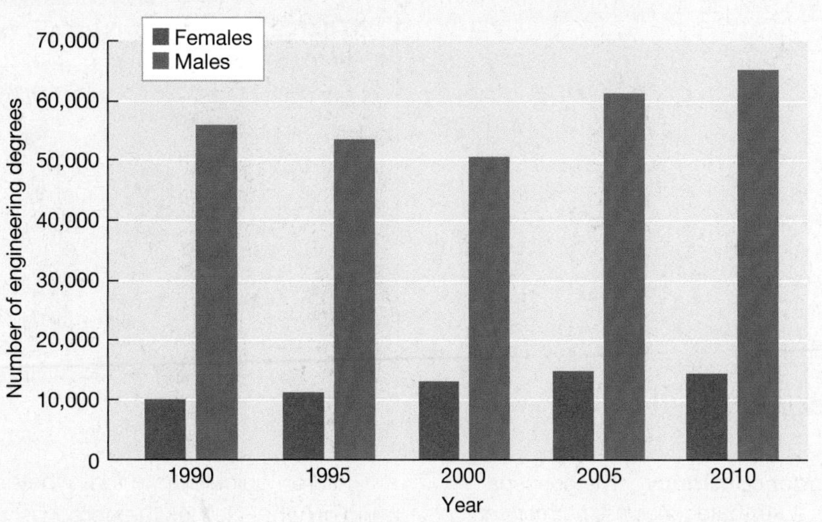

Engineering Imbalance This graph shows the number of bachelor's degrees awarded in engineering in the United States, by gender, from 1990 to 2010. (After National Science Foundation, 2013.)

It's easy to show that several external factors are playing a role in this imbalance. For example, until the 1970s women weren't even allowed to apply for admission to many of the most prestigious colleges. The time line is short enough that the significant increases in the number of women in science and engineering during the twentieth century cannot be due to any change in the biology of sex differences. Instead, societal factors must be involved.

On the other hand, because androgens such as testosterone work prenatally to masculinize the brains of other mammals, could they be acting on the human brain to make boys more suited than girls to scientific pursuits? This question is far from answered, but there are several findings indicating that if hormones are playing a role, they may be affecting boys' and girls' *motivation* for science and math rather than their *capability* in those fields. For example, in the United States boys score higher, on average, than girls on standardized math tests (although that difference has been shrinking; see Chapter 11 and Figure 15.16). Now, it is clear that someone needs a firm understanding of mathematics to succeed in engineering programs. However, if we take the average math scores of boys admitted to engineering schools, we can ask how many girls with that same level of math score choose to enter engineering programs.

The interesting result is that, even when we compare groups of boys and girls who are equally good at math, the boys are much more likely to apply to and enter engineering programs (Cech et al., 2011). In other words, even girls who are as good as boys at math are less interested in engineering as a career. Of course, there may be social pressures that keep girls who are talented at math out of engineering. Maybe the engineering programs are not "girl friendly," or maybe people disapprove of girls who become engineers. But it is also possible that girls are simply not as motivated to enter engineering and are more interested in other fields.

Indeed, the biggest sex differences in human behavior do not involve math abilities (in which males tend to do better) or verbal abilities (in which females tend to do better). The sex differences in career *interests* are much bigger than either of those. For example, girls and women are much more likely than boys and men to say they are interested in being a teacher, social worker, or manager. Males are much more likely than females to be interested in being an engineer, farmer, or mechanic (Lippa, 2010). So perhaps the greater number of men in science and engineering reflects that fewer females are motivated to pursue those careers. Or perhaps females perceive those careers (correctly or incorrectly) as inappropriate for women. Supporting that idea is the finding that female college students who are exposed to women role models in science and engineering are more likely to enter those fields (Stout et al., 2011).

Even if we could be sure the sex difference in these fields reflected a sex difference in motivation, we still would not know how boys and girls came to be different in their interests.

Figure 12.25 Gender Constancy

gender constancy The concept that sex categories are permanent and not affected by variations in appearance.

congenital adrenal hyperplasia (CAH) A condition caused by the secretion of excess testosterone by the adrenal glands before birth. At birth, the genitals may resemble those of a boy.

Children quickly learn that whether a person is male or female does not depend on what clothes the person is wearing or what activity the person happens to be doing at the time. Very young children may believe that anyone who puts on a dress or a long-haired wig somehow "becomes" a girl, but by the age of 3 or 4 most children develop the concept of **gender constancy**, the understanding that sex categories are permanent, reflecting some essence of a person rather than some transient quality (**Figure 12.25**).

Sometimes it is not clear whether a newborn is a boy or girl. Sometimes in a genetically female (XX) baby, the adrenal glands (located just above the kidneys; see Figure 13.18) grow too large and secrete more testosterone than is normal in a girl, a condition called **congenital adrenal hyperplasia** (**CAH**). ("Congenital" means present at birth, and "hyperplasia" means excess growth.) In extreme cases, a girl with CAH may be mistaken for a boy at birth because the testosterone has produced a penis and scrotum rather than a clitoris and labia, but in most cases the baby's genitals look like something in between those of other girls and boys (**Figure 12.26**). Most of these babies, as adults, will be able to reproduce as mothers and so they are typically raised as girls. In past years it

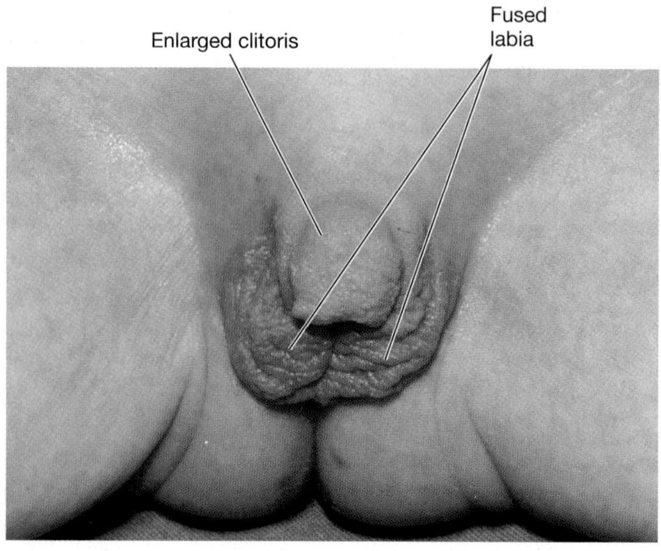

Figure 12.26 Sometimes the Boy/Girl Distinction Is Not So Clear The genitals of this baby look like something in between those of most boys and most girls. This child is a genetic female (XX) with congenital adrenal hyperplasia (CAH), caused by the adrenal glands producing excess testosterone before birth.

Figure 12.27 **Androgen-Insensitive Women** This photo shows a group of women with AIS and similar intersex conditions at a support group meeting.

was common practice for doctors to urge parents to have such children subjected to surgery right away so they would have genitals that look like those of all the other girls. But these surgeries carry some risk and do not always have a good outcome. Some women who had such surgeries as children are very dissatisfied and feel the surgery has made it more difficult for them to have an orgasm. So people are beginning to question the wisdom of subjecting children to what is essentially cosmetic surgery without their consent. The alternative is to allow the child to grow up intact and decide for herself whether and what type of surgery she might want.

androgen insensitivity syndrome (AIS) A condition in genetic males resulting from a mutation that makes the body insensitive to androgens. The genitals at birth resemble those of a girl.

In other cases, genetic males (XY) are born who, at birth, appear to be girls. This happens when a fetus with a Y chromosome has a genetic mutation that makes the body insensitive to testosterone and other androgens, a condition called **androgen insensitivity syndrome** (**AIS**). Such children grow testes, which secrete testosterone, but their bodies cannot respond to the hormone. As a result, the genitals develop as a clitoris, vagina, and labia. Thus the child is given a girl's name, raised as a girl, and at puberty develops breasts (because of estrogens from the testes and adrenal glands). However, she will not have a period because there are no ovaries to support the menstrual cycle. A medical exam will reveal that this apparent adolescent girl has high levels of testosterone in her blood, a Y chromosome, and a pair of testes in her abdomen. Women with AIS cannot reproduce, but otherwise they are like other women in their appearance (**Figure 12.27**), behavior, and gender identity.

Testicular steroids masculinize the developing brain of animals and perhaps of humans

In animal models, the same testicular hormones that masculinize the body also masculinize the brain. This effect was first demonstrated by looking at the behavior of guinea pigs (Phoenix et al., 1959), but it has since been demonstrated for many mammalian species and for many different behaviors. The experimenters knew that female guinea pigs are much more likely to display lordosis if they are treated with estrogens, and that male guinea pigs are much more likely to mount females if they are treated with testosterone. However, the hormones normally do not work the other way around. That is, males do not display lordosis when another male mounts them (**Figure 12.28A**), even if treated with

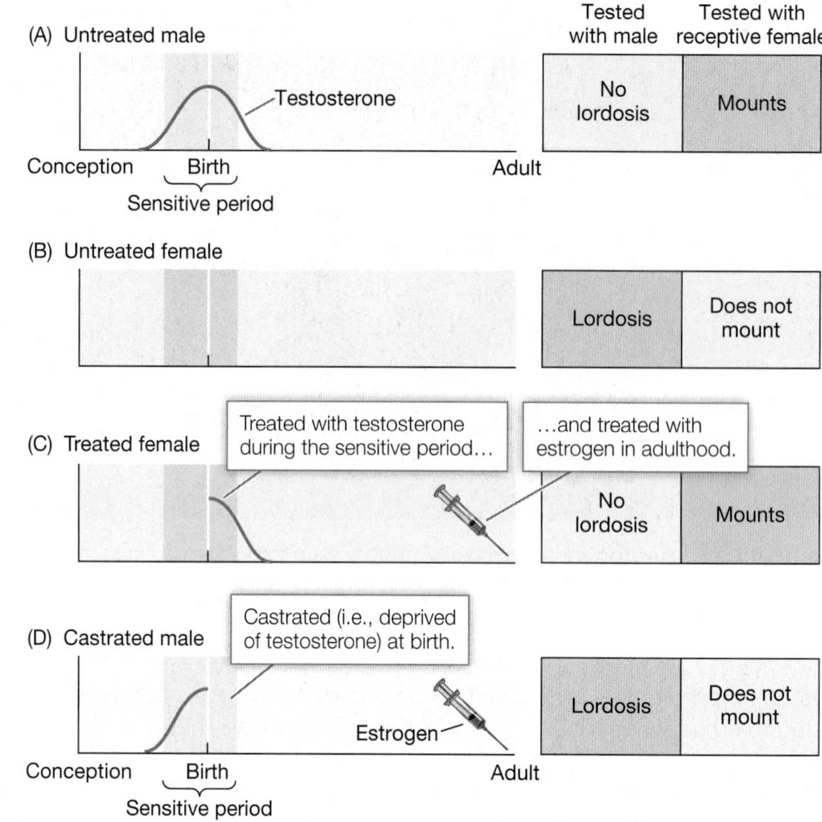

Figure 12.28 Exposure to Hormones Early in Life Organizes Later Sexual Behavior in Rats

the same estrogens that activate lordosis in females. Likewise, female guinea pigs normally do not mount other females very often (**Figure 12.28B**). But the researchers learned that a female rodent that is exposed to testosterone early in life (before birth in guinea pigs) will, as an adult, behave like a male. Specifically, she will not display lordosis in response to a mounting male, even if given the estrogens that activate lordosis in other females (**Figure 12.28C**). Instead, this female will be eager to mount other females. Conversely, male rodents deprived of testosterone around the time of birth, by surgical castration, will in adulthood behave like females: they will display lordosis when treated with estrogens and will display little or no mounting of females (**Figure 12.28D**).

These experiments quickly became famous because they suggested a simple yet powerful hypothesis to explain how males and females come to display different behaviors as adults. The **organizational hypothesis** posits that the same testicular hormones that masculinize the developing genitals also masculinize the developing brain, permanently masculinizing the animal's behavior in adulthood (Phoenix et al., 1959). From this perspective, the brain is simply one more organ that undergoes sexual differentiation. As is the case for the rest of the body, early exposure to androgens such as testosterone would favor masculine development, while in the absence of androgen the brain would develop in a feminine fashion. Also, just as the genitals had to be exposed to testosterone early in life to develop in a male fashion, the animal's brain had to be exposed to testosterone early in life to develop in a male fashion. So there is a **sensitive period**, a time when the brain can be affected by a particular influence, in this case testosterone.

organizational hypothesis The proposal that the brain is permanently masculinized by exposure to androgens during development.

sensitive period A time during which the brain can be affected by a particular influence; here, exposure to testosterone.

Eventually scientists began looking at the structure of the brain, especially in the hypothalamus, because this region was known to be important in regulating hormones and sexual behavior. As the organizational hypothesis had predicted,

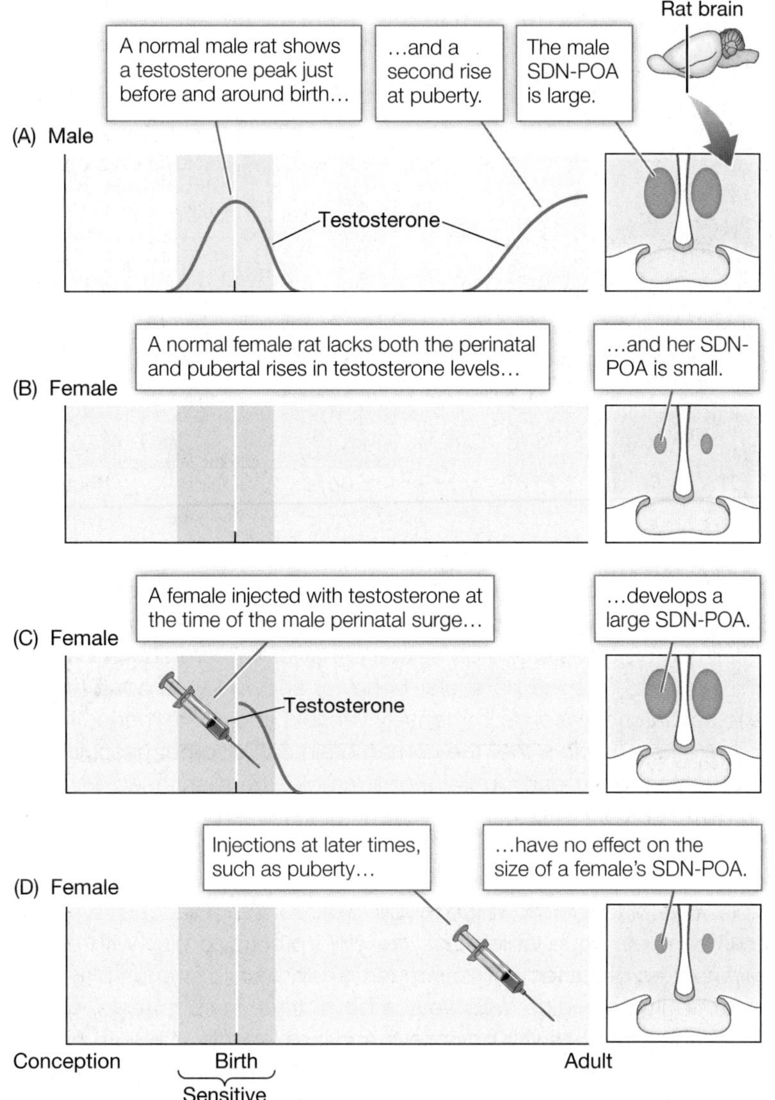

Figure 12.29 The Sexually Dimorphic Nucleus of the Preoptic Area (SDN-POA)

scientists found a nucleus in the hypothalamus, which they named the *sexually dimorphic nucleus of the preoptic area* (*SDN-POA*) and which is different in males and females (Gorski et al., 1980). The SDN-POA is five to six times larger in volume in male rats than in female rats (**Figure 12.29A**). The SDN-POA fits the organizational hypothesis beautifully. The nucleus is normally small in female rats (**Figure 12.29B**), but giving a female just a single injection of testosterone during the sensitive period (the first few days of life) causes her to develop a large, masculine SDN-POA for life (**Figure 12.29C**). The testosterone has to be given when the female is a pup. If it is given to an adult female, the SDN-POA remains feminine (**Figure 12.29D**). Conversely, removing androgens from a newborn male rat results in a small, feminine SDN-POA in adulthood.

Thus we have an excellent understanding of how sex differences in the brain and behavior of laboratory animals come about: they arise through the permanent organization of the brain by hormones early in life, and the transient activation of behaviors by hormones in adulthood. What remains unclear is to what extent these same mechanisms explain the development of sex differences in human behavior. For one thing, there are such wide differences across cultures

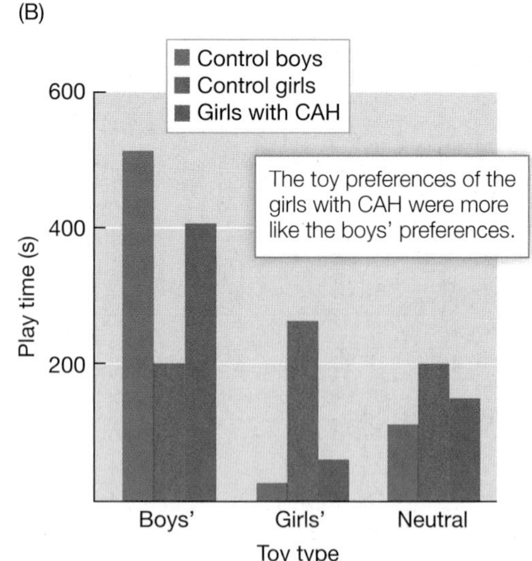

Figure 12.30 Do Fetal Hormones Masculinize the Human Brain? (B after Berenbaum & Snyder, 1995.)

in terms of what men and women typically do, that we know culture and social upbringing play major roles in guiding human behavior. And we've already seen that the influence of testosterone on sexual behavior is more subtle in humans than in animals, and that the particular behavior shown by an adult human in response to sexual motivation is immensely variable and context-specific.

Yet there are several hints that the human brain can also be masculinized by exposure to testosterone early in life. For example, we mentioned earlier girls with CAH, who are exposed to enough prenatal testosterone that their genitals are masculinized. There is evidence that the behavior of these girls may also have been masculinized by prenatal testosterone (Berenbaum & Hines, 1992). For example, if we place a child in the middle of a room with various toys (**Figure 12.30A**), we can videotape which toys the child prefers to play with and later have experimenters keep track of how much time the child spends playing with toys that are traditionally girls' toys versus boys' toys. In such tests, girls with CAH are more likely to play with boys' toys and less likely to play with girls' toys than are other girls (**Figure 12.30B**). Other studies have shown that girls with CAH are more likely than other girls to engage in the type of rough-and-tumble play that boys favor. Did the prenatal testosterone make the girls with CAH more interested in boys' toys and rough-and-tumble play, and did such play affect the growing brain? That's one possibility. In juvenile monkeys, again males prefer to play with cars and balls while females prefer playing with dolls and pots (Alexander & Hines, 2002). Those toy preferences seem more likely to arise from prenatal hormones than social influences.

It becomes even more difficult to say whether prenatal testosterone organizes sex differences in other human behaviors. So this remains an active area of research. Perhaps the most controversial question is whether the presence or absence of prenatal testosterone plays a role in the establishment of human sexual orientation, the question we consider next.

sexual orientation The direction of a person's sexual interest.

heterosexuality Sexual orientation with attraction directed toward members of the opposite sex.

homosexuality Sexual orientation with attraction directed toward members of the same sex.

bisexuality Sexual orientation with attraction directed toward both sexes.

Sexual orientation is a complex behavior that in humans appears to be affected by prenatal hormones

Sexual orientation is the direction of a person's sexual interest, either attraction to members of the opposite sex (**heterosexuality**), members of the same sex (**homosexuality**), or both sexes (**bisexuality**). Men who are homosexual are often described as being *gay*, while homosexual women may be referred to as *lesbians*, and heterosexual individuals may be called *straight*. Note that gender identity—whether people consider themselves to be male or female—is independent of sexual orientation.

Kinsey's surveys of the 1940s and 1950s suggested that up to 10% of Americans had a homosexual orientation, but we now know this to be an inflated figure, probably due to sampling bias (see Chapter 2) because only people comfortable talking about sex were surveyed. More reliable modern estimates indicate that slightly more than 2% of American men are attracted solely to other men (homosexual), with another 1% or so either mostly attracted to men or equally attracted to both sexes (bisexual). Interestingly, women are much less likely than men to be attracted solely to the same sex (**Figure 12.31**; Laumann et al., 1992). So one difference between men and women in terms of sexual orientation is that men are more likely than women to be either homosexual or heterosexual.

The strong societal pressures against homosexuality make it an interesting behavior to consider when we ask the extent to which nature or nurture underlies human behavior. American culture offers a pervasive view that people should fall in love with and marry someone of the opposite sex. This model is presented to children very early on—think of all those Disney movies with a heterosexual romance at the core. If sexual orientation were a product of culture and upbringing alone, then the existence of homosexuality would be puzzling. Although attitudes about homosexuality are changing, the stigma of being homosexual was still severe in the 1950s and 1960s: you could lose your job, lose your family, even go to jail for engaging in homosexual acts. And many homosexual individuals of that era accepted society's judgment that what they were doing was wrong, even evil, hating themselves for their feelings. It is difficult to see how, given the severe negative consequences, anyone would "choose" to be homosexual. Indeed, when most people report about their earliest "crush," it was on someone with the sex they are attracted to as adults. Heterosexual individuals tend to have their first crush on someone of the opposite sex, and homosexual individuals have their first crush on people of the same sex (Herdt & McClintock, 2000).

Even if we dismiss the notion that people "choose" their sexual orientation, there remains the mystery of how a homosexual orientation could arise in anyone immersed in our fiercely heterosexual culture. Could the organizational hypothesis about the development of sex differences in animal behavior be relevant to humans? Is our sexual orientation dependent on whether our brain was exposed to testosterone before birth? Or is our sexual orientation formed by the way we are raised?

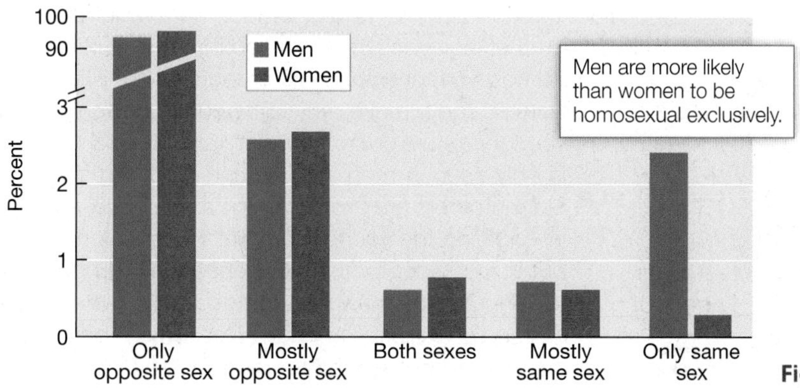

Figure 12.31 Sexual Orientation Data (After Laumann et al., 1992.)

Nature seems to have some influence on sexual orientation

Women with complete androgen insensitivity syndrome (AIS) are almost always attracted to men, and they usually marry men and often adopt children. In other words, they are heterosexual women, despite their Y chromosome and testes (Hines, 2011). But studying women with AIS doesn't really tell us whether hormones or social upbringing are responsible for sexual orientation. We can't know whether these individuals are attracted to men because their developing brains were insensitive to testosterone and so were not masculinized, or because they were raised as girls and taught to be attracted to men.

Studying women with congenital adrenal hyperplasia (CAH) is a little more informative. Most of these women are attracted to men, marry, and have children. So that would suggest that social upbringing steered them to be attracted to men, despite their prenatal exposure to testosterone. On the other hand, while most women with CAH are heterosexual, they are much more likely to be homosexual than are other women (Meyer-Bahlburg et al., 2006). Are they more likely to be homosexual because their brains were exposed to enough prenatal testosterone to masculinize them, making them attracted to women? Or is it because girls with CAH grow up aware of their sometimes ambiguous genitals, and maybe this awareness confuses them about their gender identity, blurring their ideas about which sex they should find attractive?

There is no definitive answer to the question of whether prenatal testosterone affects human sexual orientation. Ideally we would need to carefully measure prenatal levels of circulating testosterone in many fetuses and then find those babies 20-some years later to determine their sexual orientation. But that simply isn't possible at present. Still, there are several hints that testosterone has *some* effect on human sexual orientation. There are several aspects of the body that are affected by prenatal testosterone and can be measured in adulthood. For example, physiological responses of the ears, the pattern of eye blinks, and the length of bones in the fingers and limbs all seem to be affected in a subtle way by prenatal testosterone (Breedlove, 2010). These aspects have also been reported to be slightly more masculine in lesbian women than in heterosexual women (**Figure 12.32**). It is difficult to explain these data except to say that, on average, women who were exposed to greater prenatal testosterone are more likely to have a homosexual orientation when they grow up.

fraternal birth order effect The finding that the more older brothers a boy has, the more likely he is to grow up to be gay.

These markers of prenatal testosterone do not present as clear a picture in men, but there is another well-established influence on homosexuality in men that seems independent of social upbringing, called the **fraternal birth order effect**. If you gather large samples of men and classify them according to the number of older brothers they have, it turns out that men with older brothers are more likely to have a homosexual orientation (**Figure 12.33**). In fact, each additional older brother increases the likelihood that the man will have a homosexual orientation (Blanchard et al., 2006). Older sisters don't make any difference, and neither do younger sisters or brothers. This effect of older brothers is only seen in men, not women. You might think the older brothers are exerting a social influence, somehow intimidating the younger brother to be less masculine, but in fact older brothers influence the likelihood of the younger brother having a homosexual orientation *even if the two were raised apart*. Conversely, being raised around older stepbrothers makes no difference to a boy's orientation (Bogaert, 2006). The crucial variable seems to be how many sons the boy's mother carried before him. It is unclear how this happens, but the older

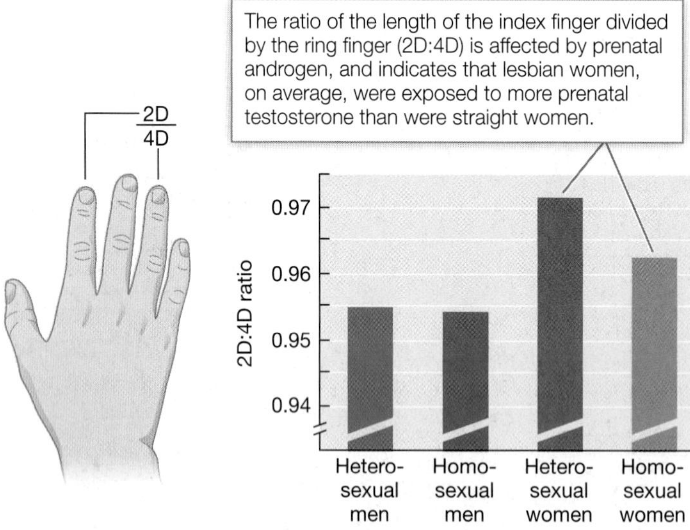
The ratio of the length of the index finger divided by the ring finger (2D:4D) is affected by prenatal androgen, and indicates that lesbian women, on average, were exposed to more prenatal testosterone than were straight women.
2D
4D
2D:4D ratio
0.97
0.96
0.95
0.94
Hetero-sexual men
Homo-sexual men
Hetero-sexual women
Homo-sexual women

Figure 12.32 Bodily Indicators of Prenatal Androgen (After Williams et al., 2000.)

brother effect on male sexual orientation appears to be unrelated to the social environment while growing up. Fascinatingly, the effect applies only to right-handed boys (see Figure 12.33). It appears that the older brother effect, whatever the mechanism, only works if the boy's brain is organized in a right-handed manner.

There is also a well-established difference between the brains of homosexual and heterosexual men. In the same region of the brain that contains the SDN-POA in rats, there is a nucleus called INAH-3 that is larger in men than in women. This nucleus is also larger in heterosexual men than in homosexual men (**Figure 12.34**), a finding that was first reported in 1991 (LeVay, 1991) and then confirmed by another lab that had been skeptical of the original report (Byne et al., 2001). Unfortunately, INAH-3 is too small to be measured except by sectioning the brain after death, so we don't know when the difference in heterosexual versus homosexual men's brains arises. Were some boys born with a small INAH-3, which caused them to develop a homosexual orientation, or did something else cause them to develop a homosexual orientation and that in turn caused INAH-3 to grow smaller? We don't know, but the same nucleus is also present in sheep, where it is also larger in males than females. Remarkably, the nucleus is also smaller in that minority of male sheep that prefer to mount other males rather than females (Roselli & Stormshak, 2009).

The parallel between brain anatomy and sexual orientation in humans and sheep, which differ so much in terms of social behavior, suggests that male homosexuality is not solely a result of social influences, but that biological factors matter too. In any case, the structural differences in the brains of homosexual and heterosexual men indicate that these men are not just superficially different from one another.

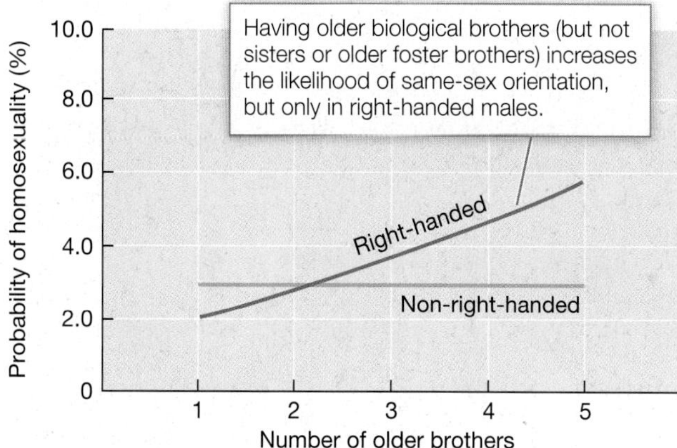

Figure 12.33 Fraternal Birth Order and Sexual Orientation (After Blanchard et al., 2006.)

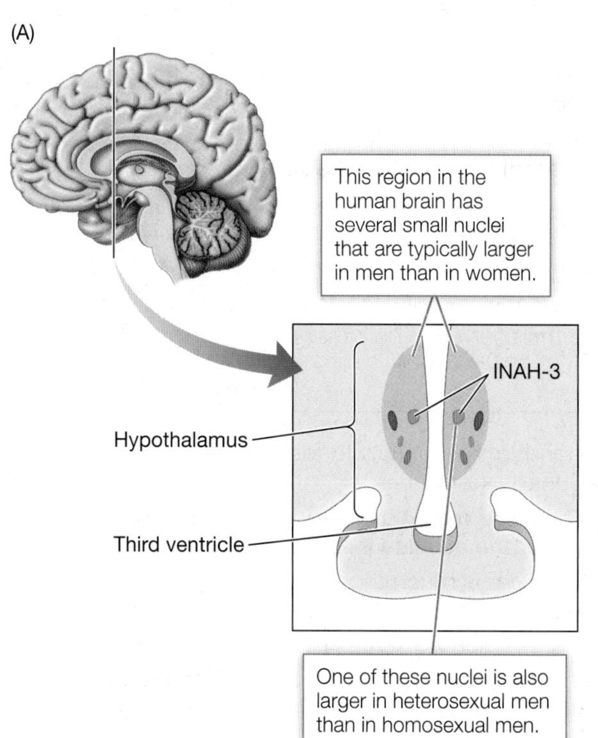

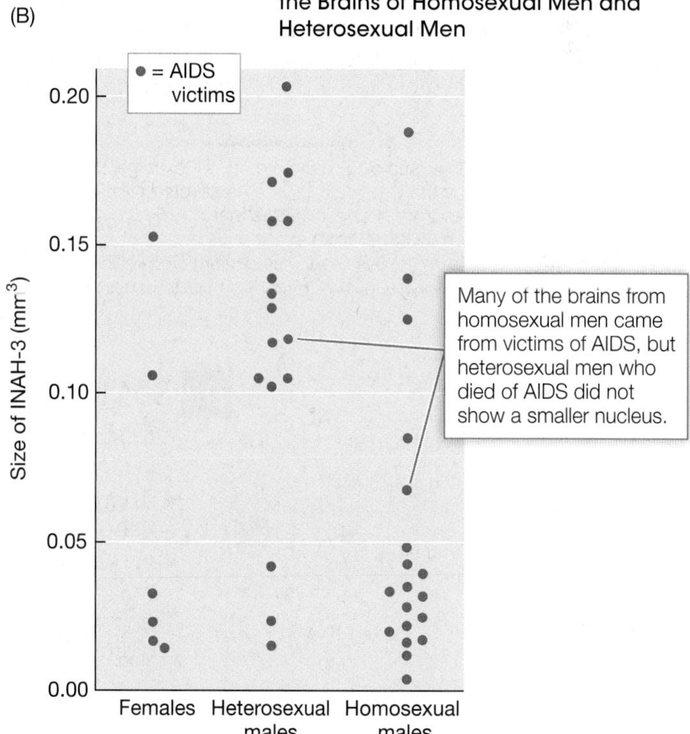

Figure 12.34 Differences between the Brains of Homosexual Men and Heterosexual Men

Figure 12.35 **Bruce Became Brenda Became David** David Reimer developed a male gender identity, despite being raised as a girl. Was that because his brain was exposed to testosterone before birth?

The poignant case of Brenda also brings home this idea that gender identity and sexual orientation are core characteristics of human existence. Despite being told by everyone that she was a girl, her inability to fit this role very likely was the result of exposure to male-typical levels of testosterone before birth. Once Brenda found out that she had been born a boy, she quickly embraced the gender identity that felt right, changing her name to David (Diamond & Sigmundson, 1997). David eventually fell in love with and married a woman with young children, eagerly adopting them to take on the role of father (Colapinto, 2000).

I wish I could say that this relatively happy scene was the end of the story, but David and his twin brother remained scarred by the years of never fitting in. A few years after David married, his story came out in a remarkable book, *As Nature Made Him* (Colapinto, 2000). The whole world learned David's real name and where he lived, and he ended up in the spotlight of television appearances all over the world (**Figure 12.35**). Eventually the spotlight moved on and, a few years later, David's twin brother died of an overdose of medication. Not long after that, David's share of royalties from the book, which had been invested with a "friend," evaporated. Then David and his wife of 14 years separated. Two days later, despondent and isolated, David killed himself at the age of 38. Even in death, he behaved like a male, shooting himself in the head, a suicide method rarely used by women.

There seems little doubt that most of the factors that brought David to his unhappy end originated in the attempt to convert a boy into a girl. David's miserable childhood of being taunted and never fitting in, which contributed to his brother's depression, left him with few friends. He felt inadequate to fulfill one life-long dream of being a man because, without testes, he could not father children of his own.

Could David have had a happy life if society's expectations about sex were different? Why did his parents feel compelled to choose what sex he should be after the accident? If his testes hadn't been removed, he could have fathered children of his own. The surgery was performed in the belief that every person must be either male or female—that a person cannot be both. Why can't a young child be raised "neutral," waiting to see which gender fits most comfortably? The case of David, and of other people born with genitals that are somewhere in between those of typical males and females, compels us to think about why so many members of our society will not tolerate people with ambiguous gender, who do not declare themselves to be either man or woman, boy or girl.

12.3 SUMMARY

- Sexual behavior in non-human animals tends to be *stereotyped*, and is closely linked to gonadal hormones.
- *Androgens* such as *testosterone* activate masculine behaviors, while *estrogens* and *progesterone* activate feminine behaviors.
- In humans, sexual behavior is much more varied than in other animals. Testosterone has a measurable effect on *libido* in both men and women, but the resulting sexual behavior depends on context, culture, and experience.

- *Sexual differentiation* in all mammals, including humans, is directed by prenatal hormones: testosterone directs the developing body to form male genitals; female genitals will form in the absence of prenatal testosterone.
- In humans, sexual differentiation is also affected by social influences, including cultural norms for how males and females should behave. Children soon learn that gender is a constant quality, and they form a *gender identity* for themselves.
- In animals, exposure to testosterone during a *sensitive period* masculinizes the brain, organizing it in a male fashion so that the animal is more likely to display masculine behaviors. Early testosterone masculinizes the sexually dimorphic nucleus of the preoptic area (SDN-POA) of the rat brain.
- Most humans have a *heterosexual* orientation, preferring opposite-sex partners, but the existence of a minority of those with a *homosexual* orientation challenges the idea that *sexual orientation* results from social influences.
- A wide range of data indicate that lesbians were on average exposed to more prenatal testosterone than were straight women, so prenatal androgens may organize the human brain to be attracted to women.
- For men, the evidence for the influence of testosterone on sexual orientation is less consistent, but a brain region similar to the SDN-POA, called INAH-3, is smaller in homosexual men than in heterosexual men. Clinical cases such as that of David recounted in this chapter also suggest that early exposure to testosterone organizes the human brain to be masculine in outlook and behavior.
- The *fraternal birth order effect*—that men with older brothers are more likely to have a homosexual orientation—does not seem to be related to social influences, suggesting that a mechanism at work before birth influences adult sexual orientation. There is little or no evidence that homosexual or heterosexual individuals "choose" their orientation.

REVIEW QUESTIONS

1. What is the role of gonadal steroids in the organization and activation of sexual behavior in non-human animals?
2. Describe the role of hormones in sexual differentiation of the mammalian body, and the two conditions that result in a body that is masculine in some characteristics and feminine in others.
3. How does exposure to testosterone affect the size of the SDN-POA in rats?
4. What is the evidence that prenatal exposure to testosterone affects sexual orientation in humans?
5. Describe the fraternal birth order effect on sexual orientation in men and weigh the evidence that it is due to social influences of brothers.

Food for Thought

Given what you've learned about the fraternal birth order effect, what would you expect to be the frequency of homosexuality in groups of people who encourage large families?

12.4 Social Motivation

Things to Learn

- Need for affiliation
- Industrial/organizational psychology
- Hawthorne effect

So far we've discussed motivation generally and applied those concepts to hunger and libido. It seems pretty obvious that individuals must be motivated to eat in order to survive. Likewise, natural selection would clearly favor individuals who are motivated to reproduce (every one of your millions of ancestors did so). These seem to be simple cases of biological necessity, but the last category of motivation we'll discuss, at the heart of Maslow's pyramid of needs, may not seem crucial for survival. Yet **social motivation**, the drive to interact with, please, and gain recognition from others, is no less important for some species,

social motivation The drive to interact, please, and gain recognition from others.

including humans. Only by banding together could our ancestors on the plains of Africa survive, and for this reason social motivation became an essential part of what makes us human. Little is known about the biological mechanisms underlying social motivation (although they must be there), but we can learn a lot about these important drives from behavior alone. First we'll consider the basic human need to belong to a group; then we'll discuss the factors that motivate people to seek achievement and to lead their comrades.

Everyone feels the need to belong

Most people have a **need for affiliation**, to establish and maintain relationships with other people (Baumeister & Leary, 1995), related to Maslow's term "belonging" in the middle of his needs pyramid (see Figure 12.5). One way to study this need is to give people pagers that go off at various intervals and ask them to record in a diary whether they are alone or with someone else when the pager buzzes. They also note whether they *want* to be with someone else or would rather be alone. Such studies indicate that some people seek to affiliate more than others (O'Connor & Rosenblood, 1996), which is reminiscent of our earlier discussion that people differ in how much arousal they prefer. In other words, people behave as though there is some optimal amount of affiliation that they prefer, suggesting that the need to affiliate is another variable, like body temperature or body weight, that humans keep in homeostasis. For example, people who said they felt like being alone at one time point (whether they were with someone or not) were more likely, when the pager went off again, to be alone. People who said they wanted company at one time point were more likely to be with someone the next time the pager buzzed. Thus each person strives to establish the amount of affiliation that is optimal for her or him.

Several characteristics distinguish people with a high versus low need to affiliate. It's not surprising that people with a high need to affiliate spend more time contacting people, engaging in conversations, phone calls, emails, and so on, because this is *true by definition* (the reason we know they have a high need for affiliation is because they behave this way).

need for affiliation The motivation to establish and maintain relationships.

More interestingly, people with a high need for affiliation are also more likely to be concerned about whether people accept them and like them. They are less likely to rock the boat to have their way when a group makes a decision, and less likely to be argumentative in conversation. They also feel more anxious when they're being evaluated by their peers (Koestner & McClelland, 1992). It's possible that this greater anxiety about how their peers will judge them may motivate them to be more affiliative. The more time you spend with people, especially if you're easygoing, the less likely they are to be critical of you. We'll talk again about individual differences in seeking social relations in Chapter 14.

Need for Affiliation Which activity appeals to you more?

Even for people with a fairly low need for affiliation, being excluded from a group is extremely painful (MacDonald & Leary, 2005). That's why giving a child a "time out" is such effective punishment. Among children and adolescents, physical aggression and bullying are much more common in males than females, but educators have noted that girls can also be very aggressive to other girls, causing psychological rather than physical pain, by excluding them (Simmons, 2002). In some ways this aggression is more insidious than physical aggression by boys because it is mostly unseen by teachers and adults (Leary et al., 2006). Even if other people notice that a group of girls is hurting another girl by excluding her, there is little benefit in forcing the victim and the other girls to interact. That only provides further opportunities for the aggressive girls to shut the victim out of conversations or to use other, more subtle means of verbal abuse. A better tactic is to provide the bullied girl with other social outlets. Having at least one friend makes the girl less vulnerable.

Many people have noted that times of stress seem to increase our need to affiliate ("tend and befriend"; Taylor et al., 2000). In one classic experiment, female college students selected to be in an experiment were told that they would experience either painful electrical shocks or merely tickling shocks. They then could choose to wait alone or wait with some other subjects. In fact, none of them were ever given shocks, but those who *thought* they were about to experience painful shocks, and therefore were presumably more afraid, were more likely to want to wait with other people rather than alone (Schachter, 1959). You may have seen such behavior yourself. After the terrorist attack on the World Trade Center in 2001, for example, many people left their offices to talk with other people, trading observations and reflections with others.

One of Maslow's needs in the category of "love and belonging" was for intimacy, and one characteristic of intimate relationships is that the people spend a lot of time together. But for a relationship to be intimate, there must be a measure of self-disclosure, revealing to the other person things about yourself that are not widely known. Researchers have done studies where they ask people to keep a log of every time they lie, mostly what we think of as "white lies," or in other ways "intentionally try to mislead someone" (DePaulo & Kashy, 1998). As **Figure 12.36** shows, in general we are more honest with people we feel close to. We are more honest with acquaintances than strangers, more honest with best friends than friends, and more honest with family than ordinary friends.

industrial and organizational psychology (I/O psychology) The study of factors affecting performance in the workplace.

need for achievement The motivation to take on challenging tasks that can be done successfully.

Two interesting cases appear to be exceptions to this rule. For example, people are less honest with romantic partners than with friends (DePaulo & Kashy, 1998). This may be an issue of "image management" while trying to win a mate, because people are more honest with a spouse than even a best friend, much less a romantic partner. For most people, especially in happy marriages, an important aspect of intimacy with a spouse is the feeling that you can really be yourself. We'll talk more about friendship and romance in Chapter 15. The other interesting exception is that Americans are less honest with their mother, on average, than with even ordinary friends. This could mean that people are not as close to Mom as they are to friends, but can you think of any alternative explanations?

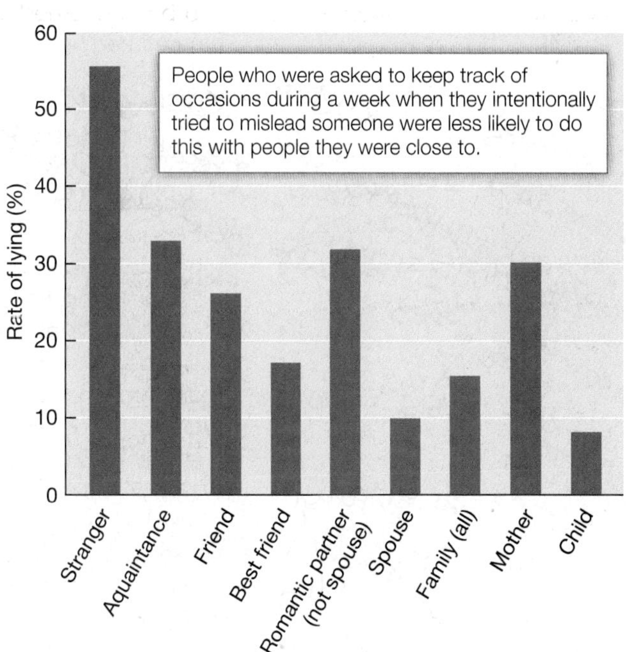

Figure 12.36 When We Feel Close to People, We Are More Honest (After DePaulo & Kashy, 1998.)

Industrial and organizational psychology is the study of the behavior and attitudes of people in workplaces and organizations

Researchers in the field of **industrial and organizational psychology**, also known as **I/O psychology**, sometimes study social motivations, including the need for affiliation, that can affect people's performance. I/O psychologists also study the **need for achievement** (or *achievement motive*), the extent to which a person wants to perform

need for power Also called the *power motive*. The motivation to be in charge.

well on challenging tasks (McClelland et al., 1953). In common language we talk about "overachievers," people who seem to pursue lofty accomplishments for their own sake. People with a high achievement motive avoid taking on easy tasks because succeeding wouldn't mean much, but they are careful to avoid taking on a challenge so great that they are likely to fail. In other words, people with a high need to achieve crave success and positive feedback. When brought into the lab and given a fairly arbitrary task (toss this ring to land on that peg), they will choose to stand far enough away from the target so that it is not too easy, but not so far away that they can't learn to succeed. People with a high need to achieve make good managers as long as they learn to set realistic goals for their workers.

The **need for power** (or *power motive*) is the extent to which a person likes to be in charge. People with a high power motive like to compete, and they like to win. They seek high-status positions but may have a hard time getting along with other people, including people they supervise.

The needs for affiliation, achievement, and power are examples of internal motivation, drives that come from inside the person rather than from the environment, as we noted at the start of the chapter. Recall that external motivation is the desire to perform a task in order to gain money or some other external reward. I/O psychologists study both types of motivation. For example, they might ask which rewards are best suited for someone with high versus low needs for affiliation or achievement. In considering external motivation, I/O psychologists try to determine what external incentives maximize productivity. Money is the most obvious external incentive that motivates people to work. In general, the more people are paid to do a task, the more conscientiously they will do it. But given the real-world limits on payrolls, it's worthwhile to think about how to arrange external incentives to maximize performance. Is it better to pay someone for each task they complete, or to pay them for each hour they work? The answer depends on the particular task and environment as well as the type of person you're considering.

For example, sometimes providing an external motivation may dampen internal motivation. In one classic study, college students were asked to play with some interesting puzzle blocks. The students readily played with the puzzles and then were given a break. But during the break the experimenter secretly measured how much time the students continued to play with the puzzles. After the break, half the students were told that now they would be paid a set amount of money for each puzzle they completed, while the other students were just asked to play with the puzzles. Not surprisingly, the students given an external motivation played more with the puzzles than those given no financial incentive to solve them. Then there was another break, and again the amount of free time the students spent with the puzzles was secretly monitored. Students who had been paid to play with the puzzles now paid less attention to them (Deci, 1971). Whatever internal motivation they had for the puzzles was diminished after they were paid to play with them.

One objective of I/O psychology is understanding how to enhance the productivity and satisfaction of people in the workplace. Some people trace the origins of I/O psychology to studies of factors influencing the productivity of workers at the Western Electric Company's Hawthorne facility outside Chicago in the 1930s (Mayo, 1933). Over the course of 5 years, psychologists manipulated physical aspects such as how bright the lights were and how work tables were arranged, as well as psychological variables such as how work breaks were spread out, group pressures, and managerial styles (Roethlisberger & Dickson, 1939). These studies yielded several interesting findings, including that it is not always easy to predict how changing conditions, even simple things such as lighting, will affect worker productivity. Some changes in lighting improve productivity and others don't. Likewise, some ways of increasing the pressure for workers to produce, such as eliminating certain breaks, improve the productivity of some workers and not others.

Early I/O studies forced researchers to rethink their hypotheses about what will or will not improve performance. Changes that they thought beforehand would make workers happier or more productive were not always proven to do so. I/O researchers emphasized the importance of first testing new ideas in well-controlled, small-scale pilot studies. The Hawthorne studies underscored the value workers place on having social life with coworkers. Friendships, attitudes, and relations affect how productive a workplace is. In general, the physical conditions of the workplace do not affect morale and productivity as much as the psychological conditions do. To reach the peak of productivity, people need to feel secure, need to feel like they belong in the group (satisfying the need for affiliation), and need to feel recognized and appreciated (satisfying the need for achievement). Notice that these needs fit right into the middle of Maslow's hierarchy of motivations: safety, love and belonging, and esteem (see Figure 12.5). The Hawthorne studies and their successors proved that the workplace is a social system and that steps to improve that social system will improve productivity at least as much as improvements in physical factors.

Ironically, these groundbreaking studies of a wide range of issues are most famous for another effect the scientists described. Put simply, the **Hawthorne effect** states that people behave differently when they know they are being monitored. For the most part, people are on their best behavior and are most productive when they know they are being watched. In that original study, productivity dropped once the scientists left the factory. In fact, there has been continued debate about whether the Hawthorne effect really happened. There may have been other reasons productivity fell when researchers left (Wickström & Bendix, 2000), and attempts to replicate the effect have failed (Izawa et al., 2011).

Providing workers with feedback that makes them feel secure, competent, and appreciated (those three middle levels of Maslow's hierarchy again) tends to maximize their productivity and at the same time maximize their job satisfaction. Most factory jobs do not provide workers with the opportunity to reach the peak of Maslow's hierarchy, self-actualization. Presumably people who do the same type of work every day must seek self-actualization outside their careers, in family and community. But in many lines of endeavor, including the arts, science, engineering, business, and education, institutions should also provide their members with the opportunity to be the best scientist, engineer, fashion designer, or educator they possibly can be to maximize career satisfaction.

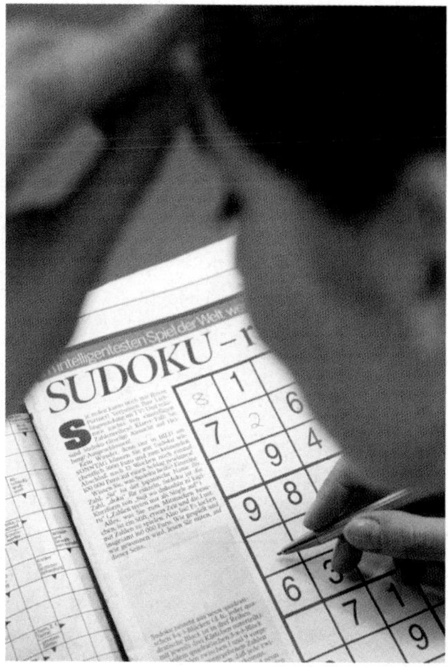

Pay to Play? Would you get less enjoyment out of doing puzzles in your spare time if you were paid to do them at work?

Hawthorne effect The phenomenon that people may behave differently when they know they are being studied.

The Cutting Edge

Distracted by Food

There's growing evidence that the brains of people with anorexia process information, especially information about food, differently from the brains of other people. For example, when women who have recovered from anorexia are unexpectedly given a small taste of sugar water, they show less of a response in reward-processing brain regions than control women do (Oberndorfer et al., 2013). This result suggests that the women recovered from anorexia do not find food as rewarding as other people. But we don't know whether their lack of appreciation for food caused the women to develop anorexia, or the development of anorexia interfered with their appreciation for food. This reduced response to food may be one reason why people recovering from anorexia have to continue making an effort to eat to avoid relapse.

However, there's reason to think that, despite their muted pleasure in response to food, people with anorexia are nevertheless very sensitive to food cues, but in a negative way. People suffering from anorexia often report being afraid of food, such as a slice of chocolate cake or a big, juicy hamburger (**Figure 12.37**). It's easy to see how this fear of food would get in the way of eating, but it may also make it harder for people with anorexia to think straight. When a group of women with anorexia were given a memory task that was difficult, they performed better than a group of control women. When the women were exposed to images very briefly, too briefly for them to report what they'd seen, an interesting difference arose. Exposure to a brief image of a food item, like a hamburger, did not affect the performance of the control women, but it interfered with the memory of women with anorexia, and they now performed no better than the control group (Brooks et al., 2012). These results suggest that people with anorexia may have a hard time thinking straight when confronted with food. This is one reason why family-based therapy relies on loved ones to urge the patient to eat, no matter how afraid they might be of that slice of pizza.

Figure 12.37 Fear of Feeding Even brief exposure to images such as this may interfere with the cognitive performance of people suffering from anorexia.

12.4 SUMMARY

- Humans are motivated to interact with other people. Among these *social motivations* is the *need for affiliation*, maintaining a relationship with other people, which is greater during times of stress or uncertainty.
- Everyone wants to be alone some of the time, but each person seeks an optimal amount of affiliation, so being excluded from other people can be extremely painful.
- In close relationships, we are more willing to reveal more of ourselves to achieve intimacy.
- Humans also have a *need for achievement*, which is greater in people who consistently take on challenging but feasible tasks.
- People also vary in their *need for power* (being in charge of situations or people).
- *Industrial and organizational (I/O) psychology* uses questionnaires to gauge people's needs for affiliation, achievement, and power. I/O psychologists study how these factors, as well as physical factors and social factors, affect morale and productivity in the workplace.
- People may behave differently when they know they are being studied, a phenomenon known as the *Hawthorne effect*.

REVIEW QUESTIONS

1. What are some of the basic social needs that people display?
2. Describe how the Hawthorne effect was first noted and how it might relate to modern-day institutions.

Food for Thought

Can you get an accurate view of what a person is like based on their profiles in social media such as Facebook?

What are the advantages and dangers of being completely honest on such sites?

Motivation and the Regulation of Behavior

Brenda, the "Cave Woman"

Brenda never really felt like she was one of the girls. She had no interest in playing with dolls or wearing a dress. On the school playground, where she often had to stick up for her twin brother, Brian, the other children made fun of her, called her a "cave woman." No matter how much social pressure was applied, Brenda fantasized about growing up to be a man with a mustache, sports car, and a girlfriend. It didn't help that her parents and a team of doctors kept telling Brenda that she should take medicine to be more like a girl and needed surgery so her genitals would look more like those of other girls. Brenda adamantly refused to have surgery. When she reluctantly began taking the pills to please her parents, she felt the medicine just made her feel worse. Why couldn't she fit in?

Then one day, when Brenda was 14 and being driven home after another angry refusal to cooperate old they had been brought to the hospital to be circumcised, where a bumbling doctor had misused a surgical instrument, burning off Bruce's penis. With no hope that Bruce would ever have anything like a normal penis, the doctors had persuaded his parents to change his name to Brenda and to raise him as a girl. They did surgery to remove the testicles and try to make the child's genitals look like those of a girl.

Of course teenaged Brenda was shocked, and the whole story sounded so unbelievable, but mostly she felt tremendous relief. "Suddenly it all made sense why I felt the way I did. I *wasn't* some sort of weirdo." She changed her name to David, stopped taking female hormones, and demanded to be given male hormones instead. David also insisted on having surgery to remove his breasts (created by those pills he had been taking) and to try to reconstruct a rudimentary penis. From that day on, David lived his life as a

Think Like a Psychologist:

Principles in Action

Whenever we encounter any interesting behavior we should consider the four principles. Here are some ways that the four principles relate to our opening story about Brenda who became David.

MACHINE

The mind is a product of a physical machine, the brain.

David's brain was exposed to normal male levels of testosterone before birth. In animals, fetal testosterone organizes the brain to take on a male-typical structure, facilitating masculine behavior in adulthood. Testosterone may have had that effect on David's brain as well.

UNCONSCIOUS

We are consciously aware of only a small part of our mental activity.

While being raised as a girl, Brenda had no awareness of why she had fantasies of growing up to have a girl friend and a sports car. She felt these desires without any idea where they came from.

SOCIAL

We constantly modify our behavior, beliefs, and attitudes according to what we perceive about the people around us.

Of course, the particulars about this fantasy, such as having a sports car, arose from twentieth-century culture. Likewise, the particulars of how men and women are supposed to behave, such as whether to have long or short hair, was communicated by the people around her.

EXPERIENCE

Our experiences physically alter the structure and function of the brain.

Brenda learned about these gender constancy ideas and gender roles while growing up and seeing them in action around her. Tragically, the conflict and stress he had experienced being raised as a girl may have made David more susceptible to depression and suicide.

KEY TERMS

activation, 522
androgen insensitivity syndrome (AIS), 531
androgens, 521
anorexia nervosa, 517
arcuate nucleus, 512
Baby X studies, 527
basal metabolism, 509
bisexuality, 534
body mass index (BMI), 514
body weight set point, 507
bulimia, 519
castration, 521
coitus, 520
congenital adrenal hyperplasia (CAH), 530
dopamine, 504
drive reduction model, 501
ejaculation, 520
endocannabinoids, 516
estradiol, 521
estrogens, 521
external motivating forces, 500
family-based treatment, 518
fat , 511
fraternal birth order effect, 536
gender constancy, 530
gender identity, 528
glucose, 510
gonads, 521
Hawthorne effect, 543
heterosexuality, 534
homeostasis, 502
homosexuality, 534
hormones, 512
hypothalamus, 502
indifferent gonads, 527
industrial and organizational psychology (I/O psychology), 541
internal motivating forces, 500
lateral hypothalamus (LH), 508
leptin, 513
libido, 520
menopause, 525
motivation, 500
need for achievement, 541
need for affiliation, 540
need for power, 542
negative feedback, 502
nucleus accumbens, 504
obese, 508
optimal arousal model, 501
organizational hypothesis, 532
ovaries, 521
progesterone, 521
refractory period, 524
reward pathway, 504
self-actualization, 506
semen, 520
sensitive period, 532
set point, 502
sexual differentiation, 527
sexual orientation, 534
social motivation, 539
stereotyped, 520
testes, 521
testosterone, 521
ventromedial hypothalamus (VMH), 508

QUIZ YOURSELF

1. Which of the following is not a recommended change in permanent behavior to control body weight?
   a. Be physically active every day.
   b. Avoid calorie-dense foods.
   c. Choose smaller portions of food.
   d. Skip breakfast.
2. The motivation to have sex is called
   a. libido.
   b. basal metabolism.
   c. need for affiliation.
   d. homeostasis.
3. The critical factor in the fraternal birth order effect on a boy is
   a. the number of older boys present in the boy's home when he is developing.
   b. the number of sons a mother has given birth to prior to carrying the boy.
   c. the number of older siblings the boy has.
   d. the lifetime total number of live births the mother of the boy has.
4. ________ is the process of maintaining a constant, stable internal environment.
5. In rats, lesions of the ________ raise the animal's body weight set point, while lesions of the ________ lower it.
6. ________ is a condition in which people become obsessed with their body weight to the point of losing too much weight. ________ is a condition in which people believe they are fatter than they are, and binge eat and then vomit or use laxatives to avoid gaining weight.
7. A very young child sees his father wearing a Scottish kilt and says his father has become a girl. This child has probably not yet developed an understanding of ________.
8. The main hormone produced by the testes is ________. The two types of hormones produced by the ovaries are ________ and ________.

1. d; 2. a; 3. b; 4. Homeostasis; 5. ventromedial hypothalamus; lateral hypothalamus; 6. Anorexia nervosa; Bulimia; 7. gender constancy; 8. testosterone; estrogens; progesterone

cutler

Emotions, Stress, and Health

The Stresses and Strains of Baboon Life

You might think the life of a baboon on the Serengeti plains of Africa would be sheer bliss. Baboons are highly social animals, meaning there are so many vigilant eyes that predators almost never manage to sneak up close, and if one does, it may regret it when an entire troop of adult baboons fights back. Food is relatively plentiful, so the baboons only need to work about 3 hours a day to get the calories they need. And yet, these baboons lead highly stressful lives. Why? Because as American researcher Robert Sapolsky (2008) puts it, if you only spend 3 hours a day working, then "you've got nine hours of free time every day to devote to making somebody else just *miserable*."

When Sapolsky first began studying a group of baboons that he named the Forest Troop, the animals' lives were dominated by the hyperaggressive interactions of the oldest, strongest, meanest males. These males were constantly picking fights with each other, occasionally resulting in injuries, even for the "winner." But it wasn't just the rowdy males that were affected. When one of those males was in a bad mood, for example after losing a fight with another male, he might attack females or even young baboons. The behavior of these aggressive males required all the baboons in the troop to be constantly vigilant, not for lions or food but for other baboons.

Physiological examination of the baboons confirmed what behavioral observations suggested: the entire troop was *stressed out*. Their blood had high levels of hormones that are released from the adrenal glands during times of stress. The blood samples also revealed that these baboons had fewer immune system cells with which to produce antibodies to ward off illness (Sapolsky, 2002).

That lowered immunity may have played a role in the disaster that shattered the troop after a hunting lodge on the edge of their territory began dumping leftover food in the open. Of course, only the meanest, most aggressive males were getting food from the dump, because they wouldn't let any of the other baboons get close. They might have lived this way forever, but when some tainted meat was left in the dump, several baboons became ill and suffered agonizing deaths (Angier, 2004). Those deaths altered the Forest Troop profoundly, as we'll see at the chapter's close.

Baboons Experience Stress Too
The baboons of the Forest Troop in Kenya went through a drastic social reorganization.

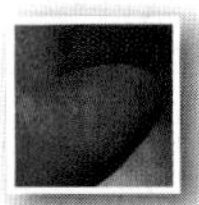

Chapter Preview

We'll begin this chapter by talking about emotions, those arousing, subjective experiences that add spice to our mental life. First we'll talk about the physiological reactions that accompany many emotions, especially unpleasant ones. Next we'll explore the ancient notion that we need to express negative emotions in order to get rid of them. In fact, scientific findings seem to contradict that idea. Those findings will bring us to the question of what makes us happy and how we can maximize our happiness. We'll conclude our discussion of emotion by reviewing brain circuits involved in emotions, especially the emotion of fear.

The second section of the chapter concerns stress, when we sometimes find ourselves experiencing more arousal and anxiety than is good for us. We will consider how we can cope with stress, and what we can do to maximize our mental health. We'll see that behaviors that are good for our physical health are also good for our mental health, and vice versa.

13.1 Emotions

Things to Learn

- Relationship between physiological reactions and emotion
- Number of different emotional facial expressions
- Cultural influences on recognizing emotions
- Facial feedback hypothesis
- Things that make us happy
- Brain circuit for fear
- Asymmetry of facial displays of emotion

What exactly is an emotion? The answer to this question is complicated because we associate this one word with several different things. Emotion is a private, subjective feeling that we may have without anyone else being aware of it. But the word "emotional" is also used to describe many behaviors that people show, such as fearful facial expressions, frantic arm movements, or loud yelling. Furthermore, when we are experiencing an emotion, our body often shows signs of physiological changes, such as a rapid heartbeat, shortness of breath, or tears. To encompass all three of these aspects, we will define **emotion** as a subjective mental state that is usually accompanied by distinctive behaviors as well as involuntary physiological changes. Typically we experience an emotion for only a brief time, but we'll see later in this chapter that the anxiety associated with prolonged stress can be very bad for our health.

We'll begin this section by discussing the major theories of how we experience emotions, including efforts to determine whether emotional experience causes physiological arousal or vice versa. Then we'll discuss the different types of emotions and how they relate to one another. We'll note the distinctive facial expressions associated with each emotion, and learn that people in very different cultures recognize most of these expressions. We'll see that the near-universal expression of emotion suggests that emotions have evolved because facial displays of emotional experience may help us get along with others. Then we'll discuss happiness, that emotion we all seek, and talk about what makes us happy and unhappy. Finally, we'll talk about the neuroscience of emotion, which has revealed brain circuits that are active during emotional experience, including a specialized brain circuit for fear.

What is the relationship between emotional experience and the body's physiological reactions?

Many emotions are accompanied by particular patterns of body reactions that are often outside our control. When we're afraid or angry, our heart races. When we are happy and calm, our heart rate is low and we may feel warm inside. When we are embarrassed, we may blush. These involuntary components of emotional response are controlled by the **autonomic nervous system**, which regulates many body processes that are not under our conscious control (hence the name "autonomic," meaning "independent").

emotion A subjective mental state that is usually accompanied by distinctive behaviors as well as involuntary physiological changes.

autonomic nervous system A part of the nervous system that is not under our conscious control, consisting of the sympathetic and parasympathetic nervous systems.

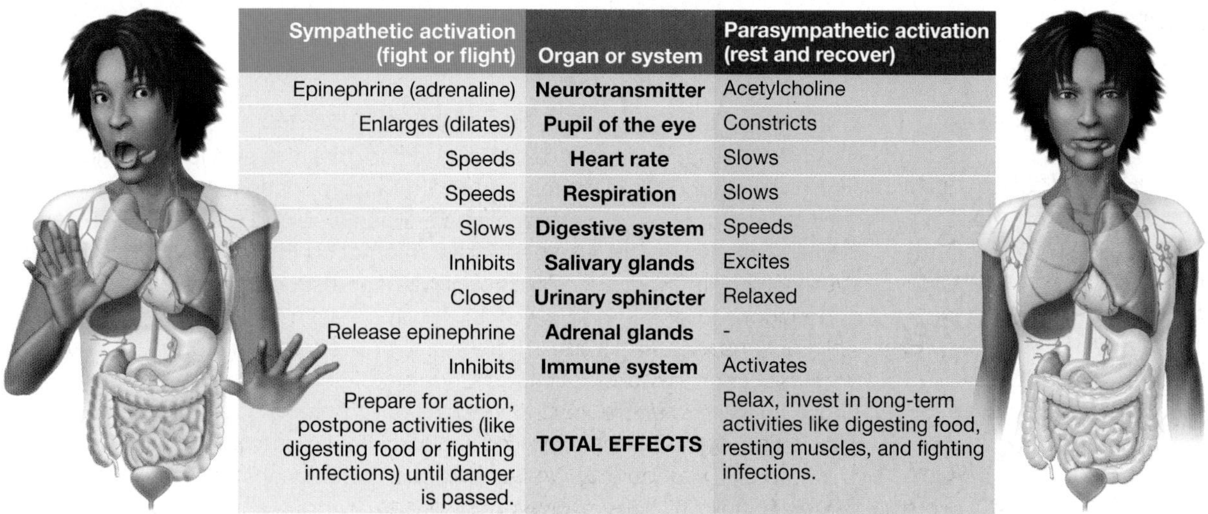

Sympathetic activation (fight or flight)	Organ or system	Parasympathetic activation (rest and recover)
Epinephrine (adrenaline)	**Neurotransmitter**	Acetylcholine
Enlarges (dilates)	**Pupil of the eye**	Constricts
Speeds	**Heart rate**	Slows
Speeds	**Respiration**	Slows
Slows	**Digestive system**	Speeds
Inhibits	**Salivary glands**	Excites
Closed	**Urinary sphincter**	Relaxed
Release epinephrine	**Adrenal glands**	-
Inhibits	**Immune system**	Activates
Prepare for action, postpone activities (like digesting food or fighting infections) until danger is passed.	**TOTAL EFFECTS**	Relax, invest in long-term activities like digesting food, resting muscles, and fighting infections.

Figure 13.1 The Autonomic Nervous System The sympathetic and parasympathetic divisions of the autonomic nervous system exert opposite effects on physiological systems. Further details of the autonomic nervous system are shown in Figure 13.18.

One part of the autonomic nervous system is the **sympathetic nervous system**, which generally activates the body for action, speeding up heart rate and breathing, opening the pupils, and shutting down the digestive system (if you are in danger, your body doesn't waste energy trying to digest your lunch, because that can wait). The sympathetic nervous system is sometimes called the "fight or flight" system because its activation can help us either do battle or run away. The other part of the autonomic nervous system is the **parasympathetic nervous system**, sometimes called the "rest and recover" system, which generally prepares the body to relax and recuperate—heart rate and breathing slow down, while the digestive system may be activated to break down food and provide nutrients for body growth and repair (**Figure 13.1**). Some emotions, such as fear and anger, are accompanied by sympathetic activation, while other emotions, such as happiness and affection, are accompanied by parasympathetic activation.

Because the subjective experience of a strong emotion and the physiological reactions of the body happen at pretty much the same time, it's not easy to determine whether one comes before the other. It has been traditionally held that physiological reactions *result* from our having an emotional response to something we perceive (e.g., a loved one's smile or a dangerous animal's threatening posture) and that an emotional reaction (e.g., happiness, fear, or anger) is quickly *followed* by body responses (**Figure 13.2A**).

sympathetic nervous system The part of the autonomic nervous system that activates the body for action (the "fight or flight" response).

parasympathetic nervous system The part of the autonomic nervous system that prepares the body to relax and recuperate.

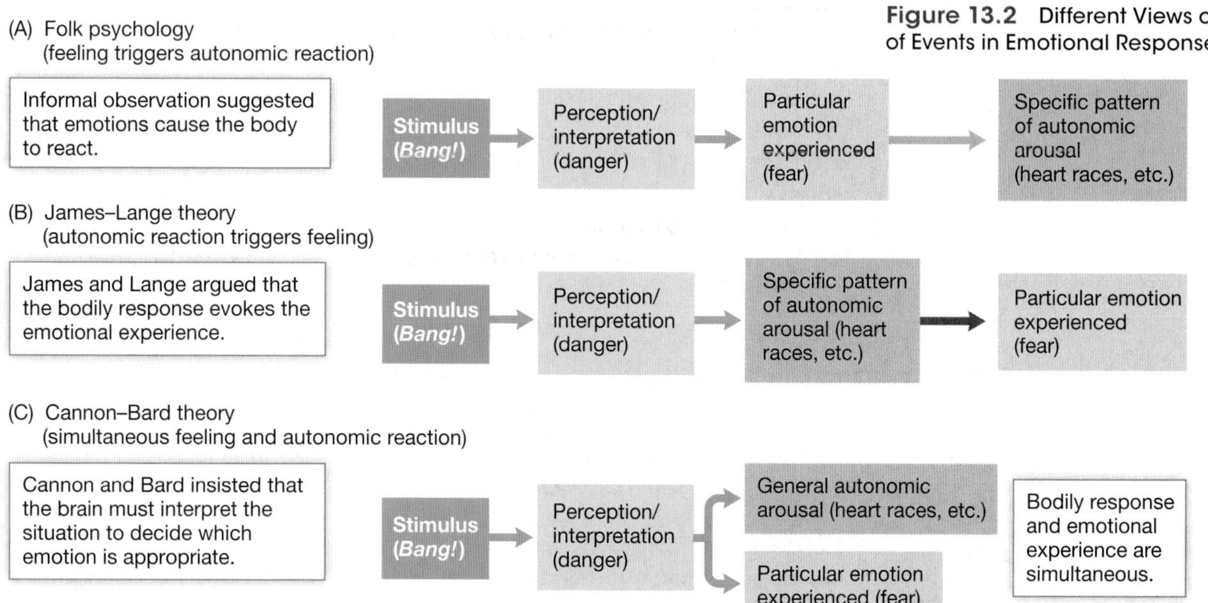

Figure 13.2 Different Views of the Chain of Events in Emotional Responses

James-Lange theory The theory that our experience of emotion is a response to the physiological changes that accompany it.

Cannon-Bard theory The theory that our experience of emotion is independent of the simultaneous physiological changes that accompany it.

In the late 1800s two researchers, William James (1842–1910) and Carl Lange (1834–1900), each independently suggested that the sequence might be the other way around. The **James-Lange theory** proposes that when we perceive something, the physiological reactions happen first, and then the mind, perceiving those body reactions, experiences an emotion that is appropriate for those physiological changes. For example, if we hear a sudden loud sound, we startle and our heart races—and then our mind, detecting the racing heart, experiences alarm (**Figure 13.2B**). There's probably something to this idea that our body reactions at least contribute to our experience of emotion. For example, people with spinal cord injuries that prevent them from sensing autonomic responses from the body seem to have less intense emotions (Hohmann, 1966). The James-Lange theory implies that each emotional state results from a distinctive pattern of body sensation, so we experience surprise, joy, or fear as a result of a particular pattern of autonomic activity.

In other words, the idea is that if my body is producing one particular pattern of autonomic responses, then I must be angry. My mind notices those responses, and then I experience anger. If my blood pressure were still high, but a bit lower than during anger and my breathing a bit faster than in anger, then I would be afraid. Unfortunately for the James-Lange theory, no one has ever been able to identify a particular pattern of autonomic response that is specific for each emotion (Levenson, 1992). Some emotions, such as anger, fear, and anxiety, produce more sympathetic responses, while other emotions, such as contentment, have more parasympathetic responses. But there doesn't seem to be any pattern that distinguishes fear from anger, or fear from anxiety, as the James-Lange theory would require.

Furthermore, autonomic responses appear to be too slow to be the only cue for our emotional experience. Walter Cannon (1871–1941) and Philip Bard (1898–1977), insisted that what we perceive starts two separate processes *simultaneously*, triggering a rapid emotional experience, followed within a second by the physiological response (**Figure 13.2C**). The **Cannon-Bard theory** asserts that our emotional experience can be independent of physiological responses. In other words, physiological reactions accompany, but are not solely responsible for, our emotional experience. In fact, a clever experiment made it clear that our *interpretation* of those physiological reactions, whether we experience them as anger or exhilaration, depends on our thought processes at the time.

Manipulating sympathetic arousal gives rise to the two-factor theory of emotional experience

In a classic study, Stanley Schachter and Jerome Singer (1962) deliberately activated the sympathetic nervous system of some students by injecting them with the drug epinephrine (also known as adrenaline) (**Figure 13.3**). This drug would increase heart rate and breathing within 3–5 minutes. All students were told they were being given a "vitamin," but only a few were told to expect increased heart rate and breathing (for this reason, such an experiment would probably not be allowed today). For the students who were not told to expect these effects, how would this unexplained sympathetic system activation affect their emotional experience?

☑ Researchers at Work

Arousing emotions

Figure 13.3 The Classic Schachter and Singer Experiment (After Schachter & Singer, 1962.)

■ **Question:** What is the relationship between autonomic system activation and emotional experience?

■ **Hypothesis:** Activation of the sympathetic nervous system will affect emotional experience.

■ **Test:** Inject participants with epinephrine to activate the sympathetic nervous system or, as a control, saline. Then bring them to a room with another "participant," who is really a *confederate*, a person who is helping the researchers by pretending to be just another participant. The confederate acts either angry (complains and curses about a questionnaire that has to be filled out) or playful (making cheerful small talk). The researchers secretly observe the participants and afterward have them fill out a survey about how they felt.

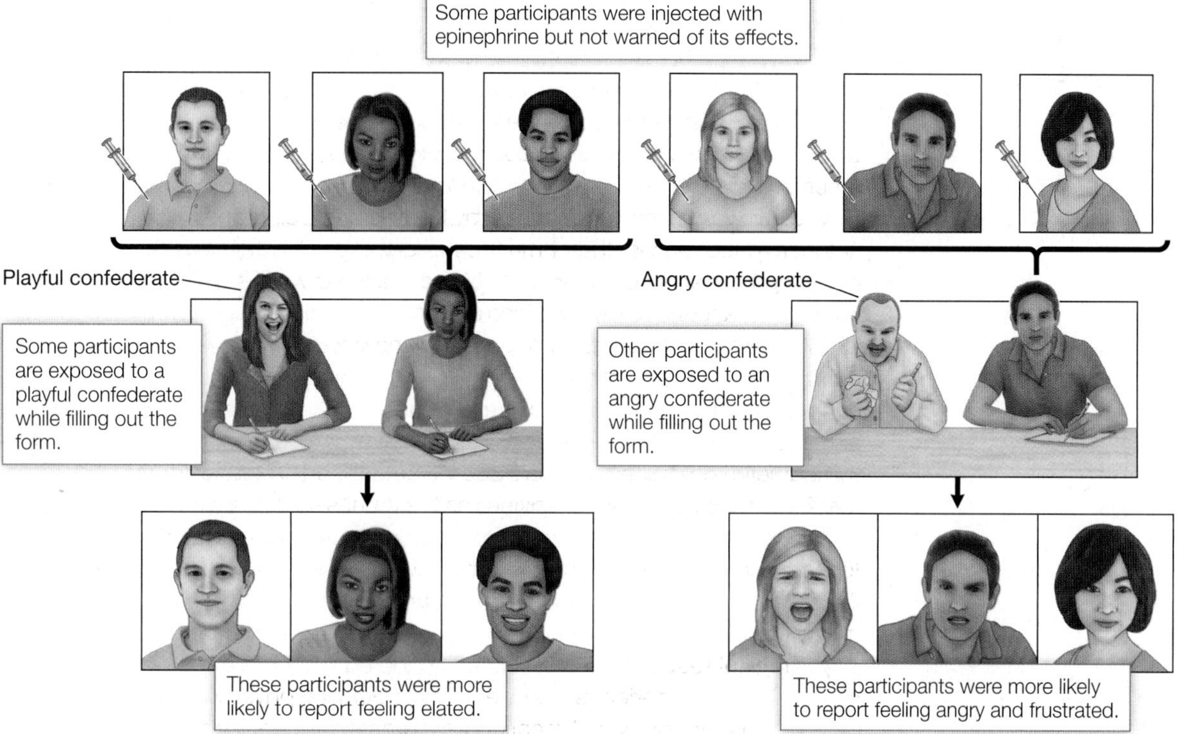
Some participants were injected with epinephrine but not warned of its effects.
Playful confederate
Some participants are exposed to a playful confederate while filling out the form.
Angry confederate
Other participants are exposed to an angry confederate while filling out the form.
These participants were more likely to report feeling elated.
These participants were more likely to report feeling angry and frustrated.

■ **Result:** The participants who were injected with epinephrine but not warned about the side effects displayed more emotion, and reported experiencing more emotion, than did participants injected with saline. As predicted by the James–Lange theory, arousal by epinephrine triggered an emotional experience—the greater the arousal, the stronger the emotion. But *which* emotions did the injected participants experience? The James–Lange theory would suggest that, given the same drug triggering the same autonomic reactions, all the epinephrine-injected participants should experience the same emotions. However, the uninformed participants given epinephrine were more likely to report *whichever emotion the confederate displayed*. In other words, participants waiting with an angry confederate were more likely to report negative emotions, while those waiting with a playful confederate were more likely to report positive emotions.

■ **Conclusion:** The epinephrine made uninformed participants more likely to feel either angry or playful, depending on the confederate's emotional display. Importantly, the epinephrine-injected participants who were told to expect the side effects of physiological arousal did not experience any particular emotion accompanying that arousal. In other words, the epinephrine made the participants more likely to experience the confederate's emotions only if they had no other explanation for their physiological arousal. Schachter and Singer concluded that the misinformed participants attributed their physiological arousal to their emotional experience: "My heart's really pounding—I'm so angry!" or "My heart's really pounding—I'm so elated."

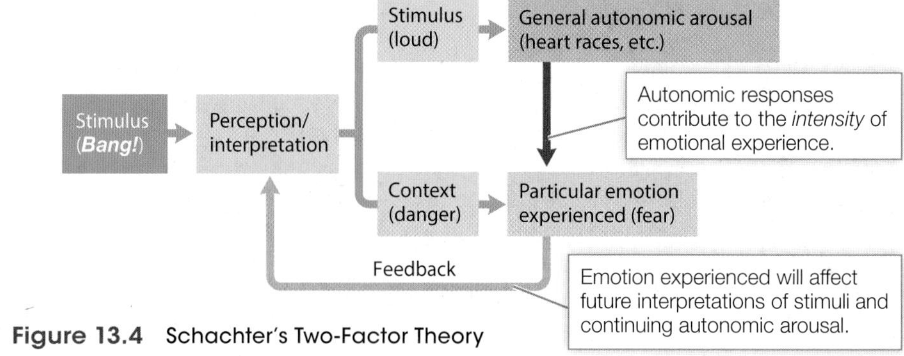

Figure 13.4 Schachter's Two-Factor Theory

two-factor theory of emotion A theory that physiological arousal determines the intensity of the emotion while cognitive interpretation determines the type of emotion experienced.

Such experiments led to the **two-factor theory of emotion**, which says that physiological arousal is the first factor, informing us about the intensity of our emotion, while a second factor, the *cognitive interpretation* of what is causing that arousal, determines which type of emotion we experience (**Figure 13.4**). In Schachter and Singer's experiment, the students' cognitive interpretation of which emotion they experienced was affected by their environment. It was as if the behavior of the confederates informed the test participants of which emotion they should feel. On the one hand, these results conform to the James–Lange theory that experiencing a particular pattern of physiological response causes us to experience emotion. After all, the uninformed subjects given the epinephrine did experience more emotion. But the *particular* emotion they experienced in response to that stimulus could be anger or happiness, depending on the participant's interpretation. Of course, there is something artificial about this experiment (which no ethical review board would allow to be conducted today), because the participants found themselves experiencing a physiological arousal from out of nowhere. Still, the fact that they could experience an unexplained physiological arousal as either a positive or negative emotion, depending on their environment, strongly suggests that emotional experience is "steered" by our intellect. In other words, there is a cognitive component to emotional experience. It's as if we are constantly trying to make sense of what we are feeling.

In addition, the two-factor model suggests that our emotional experience, which has been directed to one emotion or the other by cognitive processes, can influence our interpretation of future events (see Figure 13.4). That is, emotions can, at least for a time, be self-reinforcing—the student's *experience* of epinephrine's side effects as anger, triggered by the confederate's outrage, may have caused the student to perceive the questionnaire as infuriating, when otherwise he or she might have seen it as simply tedious. We'll return shortly to the question of whether expressing an emotion reinforces that emotion or drains it away. But first let's consider how many different emotions there really are.

A range of emotions are seen as variations on a theme: four pairs of opposing emotions.

Levels of intensity

High: Ecstasy, Vigilance, Adoration, Rage, Terror, Loathing, Amazement, Grief

Medium: Happiness, Expectation, Affection, Anger, Fear, Disgust, Surprise, Sadness

Low: Contentment, Alertness, Regard, Annoyance, Apprehension, Boredom, Distraction, Pensiveness

Eight basic human emotions vary in intensity from high to low.

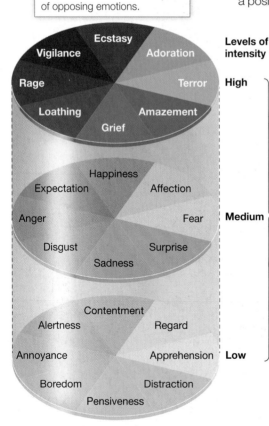

Figure 13.5 Eight Basic Emotions in Opposing Pairs (After Plutchik, 1994.)

How many different emotions are there?

Several researchers have tried to determine how many different emotions we experience. One avenue is to examine language, with the notion that we must have come up with a distinctive word for each distinctive feeling. Surely truly basic emotions, feelings that nearly all humans have experienced at one time or another, would have words to describe them in most languages. In one such classification scheme, eight basic human emotions are identified, consisting of four pairs of opposite emotions: happiness versus sadness, affection versus disgust, fear versus anger, and surprise versus expectation (**Figure 13.5**). The range of human emotional experience is accounted for by variations in the intensity of each basic emotion from high to low as Figure 13.5 shows. While many English words for emotional state lend themselves to this classification system, whether it embraces *all* of the human emotions is debatable. For example, where would embarrassment, resentment, and jealousy fit into this scheme?

Studying facial expressions offers another interesting strategy for determining how many basic emotions humans experience. Under the human face there are many muscles, some of which engage in physiologically important activities such as chewing and blinking the eyes. But other facial muscles are thin and sheetlike and attach to the skin. Their only purpose seems to be to change facial appearance (**Figure 13.6**). Charles Darwin noted that many other animals also seem to display emotions, and he pointed out how our closest relatives, monkeys and apes, also have very expressive faces (**Figure 13.7A**). Modern researchers have confirmed that other primates show facial expressions similar to ours. Grinning (revealing clenched teeth) signals that an individual is friendly and unthreatening (**Figure 13.7B**). On the other hand, an open mouth, with lips pulled back to reveal the teeth and gums, may signal that an individual is upset or feels threatened (**Figure 13.7C**).

The facial nerve innervates the superficial muscles that contribute to emotional expression.

Deep facial muscles, like those controlling the jaw, are innervated by the trigeminal nerve (not shown).

Figure 13.6 Superficial Facial Muscles and Their Neural Control

Facial expressions may have evolved to aid social communication. It's easier to get along with other adults if you can detect their moods and thus avoid conflicts that could prove dangerous. For this reason it's adaptive to learn how to read the faces, and thus the moods, of your companions. For the same reason, it's adaptive for you to signal your emotions to others. Natural selection favored the evolution of facial signals to communicate emotions. For example, most people assume that yawning serves some physiological function, but in fact its only known function is to communicate to others, as we discuss in **Box 13.1**.

For facial communication of emotion to be effective, it must signal emotions accurately. This brings us back to the question: How many distinctive emotions

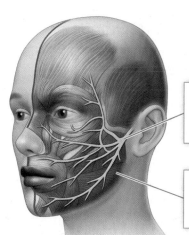

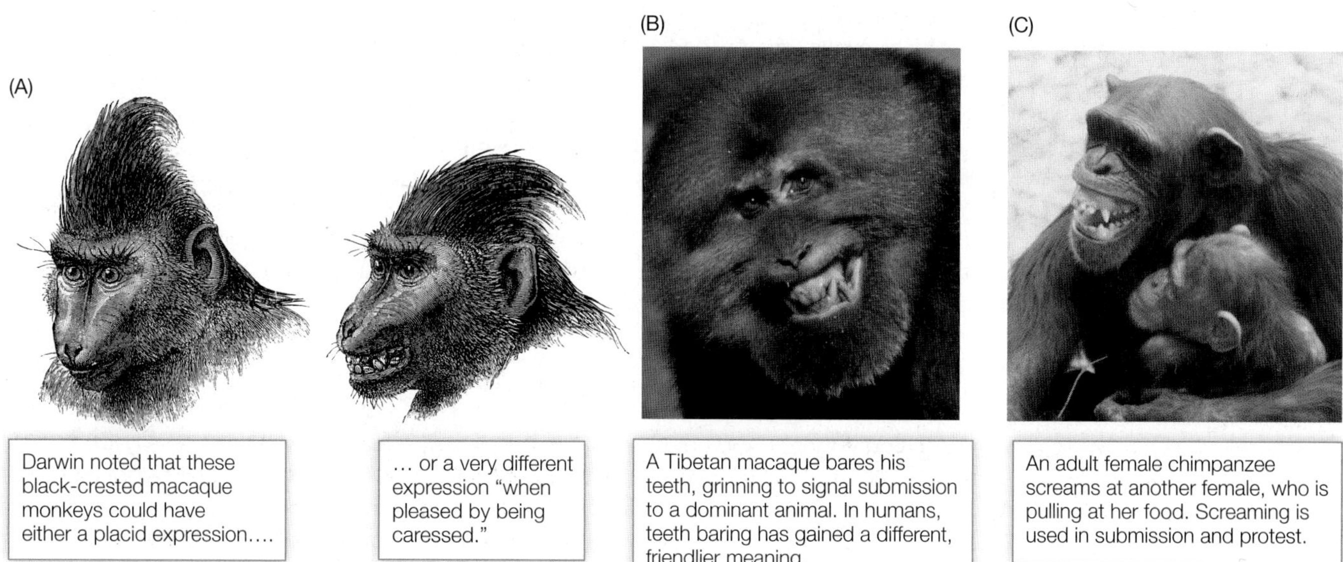

(A)
(B)
(C)
Darwin noted that these black-crested macaque monkeys could have either a placid expression....
... or a very different expression "when pleased by being caressed."
A Tibetan macaque bares his teeth, grinning to signal submission to a dominant animal. In humans, teeth baring has gained a different, friendlier meaning.
An adult female chimpanzee screams at another female, who is pulling at her food. Screaming is used in submission and protest.

Figure 13.7 Facial Expression of Emotions in Non-Human Primates
(Drawings from Darwin, 1872; photographs by Frans de Waal, from de Waal, 2003.)

Skeptic at Large

BOX 13.1

Why Do We Yawn?

Because we tend to yawn when we are sleepy, people have speculated that yawning is triggered by having low levels of oxygen, or high levels of carbon dioxide, in our blood circulation. But when researchers deliberately manipulated oxygen and carbon dioxide, there was no change in yawning (Provine et al., 1987), so those ideas were not supported by evidence. Nor is there any evidence that yawning boosts oxygen or reduces carbon dioxide in circulation. In fact, no one has found any physiological measure that helps us predict if a person will yawn.

If yawning serves no physiological purpose, what purpose does it serve? One possibility is social communication. Darwin noted that in some primates, males yawn much more than females do, and he hypothesized that males yawn to show off their big, dangerous canine teeth—that yawning may be a social signal of dominance. Supporting that view, raising testosterone levels in monkeys also increases yawning behavior (Graves & Wallen, 2006). But we humans don't have impressive canine teeth to show off, and men do not yawn more than women (Schino & Aureli, 1989), so for our species, yawning must communicate some other signal, presumably lack of alertness. Most people interpret a yawn as a signal of sleepiness.

How do we explain the contagious effect of yawning? Seeing someone yawn can make you yawn. In fact, if I ask you to think about what it feels like to yawn, you might give a yawn just in response to reading this. Believe it or not, I just yawned in response to writing that! Yawning is also contagious in other primates, including chimpanzees (Anderson et al., 2004), and dogs sometimes yawn in response to seeing a human yawn (Joly-Mascheroni et al., 2008). Children with autism spectrum disorder, who have difficulty reading emotional expression on other people's faces and show little empathy, are less susceptible to contagious yawning (see figure; Senju et al., 2007). These results all suggest that yawning serves a social, not a physiological, function.

If yawning is a social cue to let others know how we feel, then it could be regarded as yet another facial expression of our emotional state. Supporting this idea is the finding that a person's susceptibility to contagious yawning correlates with activity in the cortex around the amygdala (Schürmann et al., 2005), a brain hot spot for emotional functions. You've probably been in situations where you felt like yawning and didn't want people around you to know. It can be embarrassing. People may think you are bored, and worse yet, you may actually be bored!

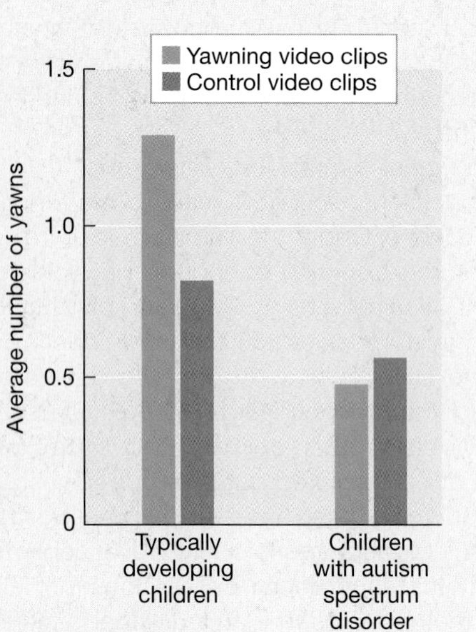

Cuing in on Yawning Children with autism spectrum disorder are less susceptible than typically developing children to contagious yawning in response to videos. (After Senju et al., 2007.)

But sometimes we yawn when we are shifting from sleepy to alert, as for example, when we yawn upon awakening. A classic study of paratroopers found they yawned more when they were about to jump out of a plane to do battle, when their alertness was increasing, not decreasing. Some people yawn just before having sex, and again, that can only be understood as signaling *increased* arousal (Provine, 2005). So next time you're embarrassed because you yawned, explain that sometimes yawning indicates an increase in interest and arousal. It *might* work...

are there? And can they all be signaled by facial expressions? As **Figure 13.8A** illustrates, most of us can recognize on the faces of others at least eight different emotions. We are so finely attuned to detect emotional faces that we can detect them in even the barest outlines, such as emoticons (**Figure 13.8B**).

The eight emotions recognized through facial expression shown in Figure 13.8 are not, however, exactly those illustrated in Figure 13.5. Anger, sadness,

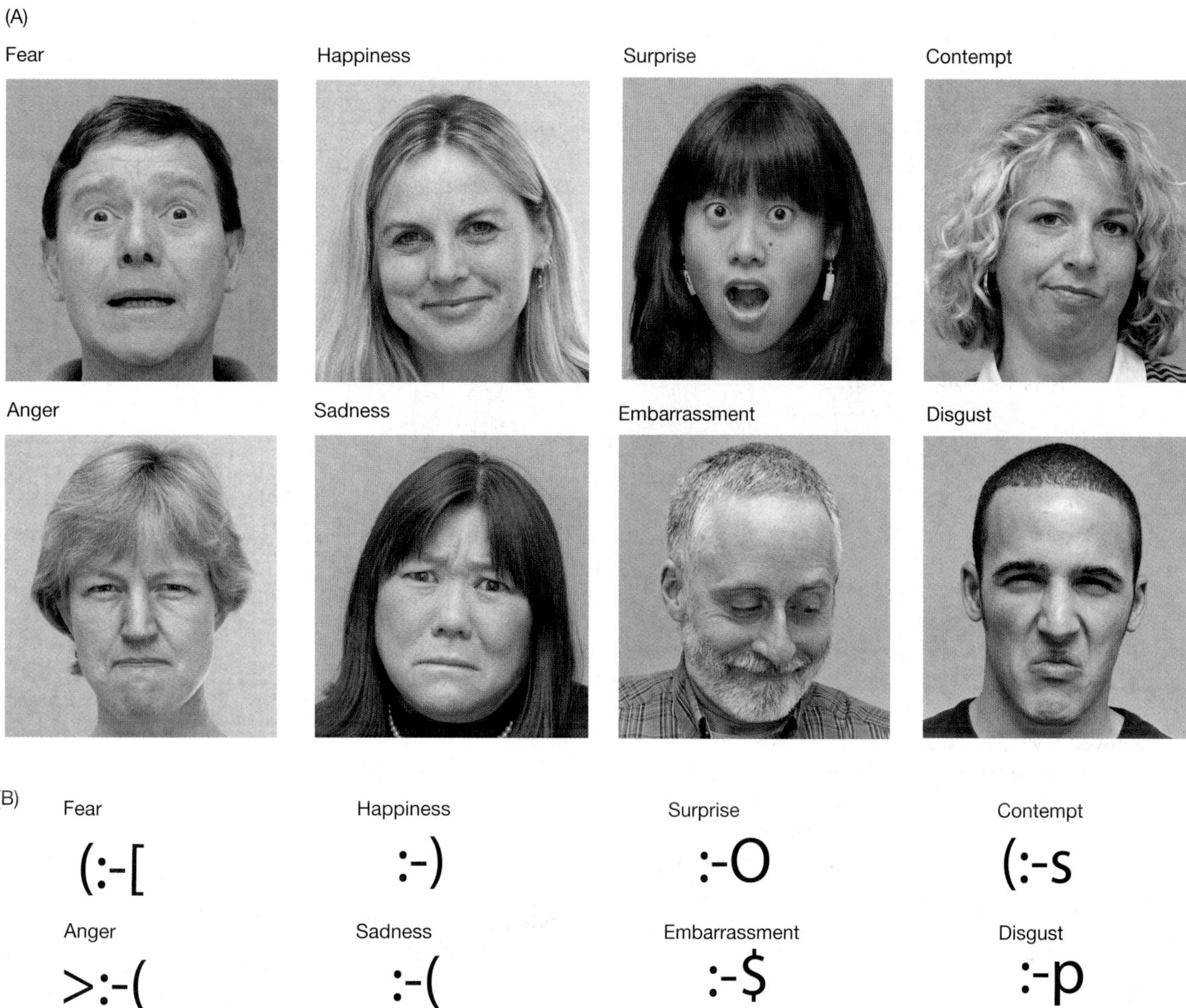

Figure 13.8 Emotional Faces (A) Each of these eight emotions is accompanied by a distinctive pattern of facial expression. (B) Our brains are so attuned to detecting emotions in faces that we readily interpret emoticons that provide only the barest outlines of facial features, as in these examples.

happiness, fear, disgust, and surprise appear in both figures, but expectation doesn't have a very distinct facial expression, and it's difficult to tell an affectionate face from a merely happy one. The facial expressions shown in Figure 13.8A for disgust and contempt are quite distinct (it has been suggested that signaling disgust might warn other individuals, including your relatives, that some food or water source is bad and therefore potentially harmful). Likewise, embarrassment is not depicted in the classification of emotions in Figure 13.5, but it has a distinctive facial pattern (eyes lowered and averted, a small smile) as well as the distinctive signal of blushing. Blushing suggests that signaling embarrassment may be particularly important in a socially complex species such as ours. We all make mistakes, and it may be adaptive to have a clear signal of when we recognize and acknowledge an embarrassing gaff. "Gee, I don't know why I did that. My bad. Don't be angry."

If facial expressions conveying emotions evolved in an ancestor to all humans, we would expect people from any culture to recognize them. These days it is difficult to find groups of people who have not been exposed to Western

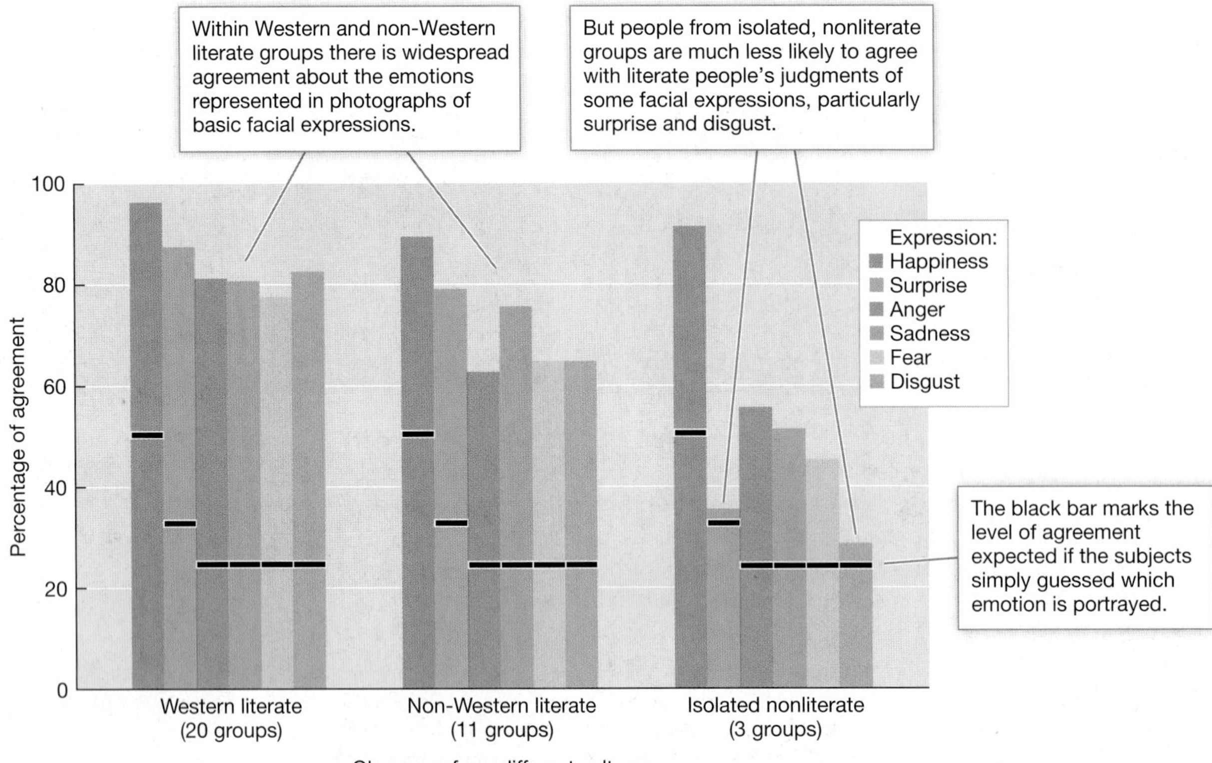
Within Western and non-Western literate groups there is widespread agreement about the emotions represented in photographs of basic facial expressions.
But people from isolated, nonliterate groups are much less likely to agree with literate people's judgments of some facial expressions, particularly surprise and disgust.
The black bar marks the level of agreement expected if the subjects simply guessed which emotion is portrayed.
Expression:
Happiness
Surprise
Anger
Sadness
Fear
Disgust
Percentage of agreement
100
80
60
40
20
0
Western literate (20 groups)
Non-Western literate (11 groups)
Isolated nonliterate (3 groups)
Observers from different cultures

Figure 13.9 Cultural Differences in Recognizing Facial Expressions (After Russell, 1994.)

cultural display rules How and when emotions are expressed in a particular culture.

culture via magazines, television, movies, and the Internet. Nevertheless, researchers have tried to determine whether people from other cultures recognize the same facial emotions that people from Western cultures do, by having them identify the emotional states of people in photographs (**Figure 13.9**). People from both Western and non-Western literate groups tend to agree on which emotions are displayed in the photos. People from isolated, nonliterate groups recognize many of the same emotions that people of literate cultures perceive, including happiness, anger, sadness, and fear. But people from the isolated nonliterate groups do not agree very well on what facial expressions communicate surprise and disgust.

The near-universal use of certain facial expressions to express specific emotions supports the idea that emotional expression was favored by natural selection. However, both nature and nurture influence our emotional makeup. The finding that not all cultures recognize the same facial expressions for every emotion suggests that social influences are at play as well. Cultural influences on emotional expression are common; for example, in France people sometimes turn down both corners of their mouth in a small grimace called a *moue*, a facial expression indicating distaste at someone's bad manners that is seldom seen in other cultures.

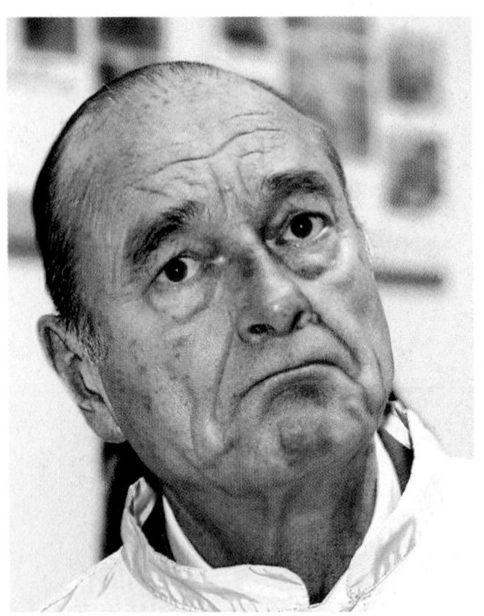

Culture-Specific Facial Expression The French are much more likely to display a little grimace called a *moue* than are Americans.

People sometimes exaggerate or inhibit facial expressions, depending on what signals they wish to convey, following the so-called **cultural display rules** of emotional expression—displays that vary with what a culture expects. These rules can change. As suggested by **Figure 13.10**, how we mediate the expression of our emotion will vary with the times and with the culture. For example, in 1968, one American politician's career was severely damaged when he cried in public (Broder, 1996), but today several male political figures cry in public quite often, presumably because they feel it aids their career.

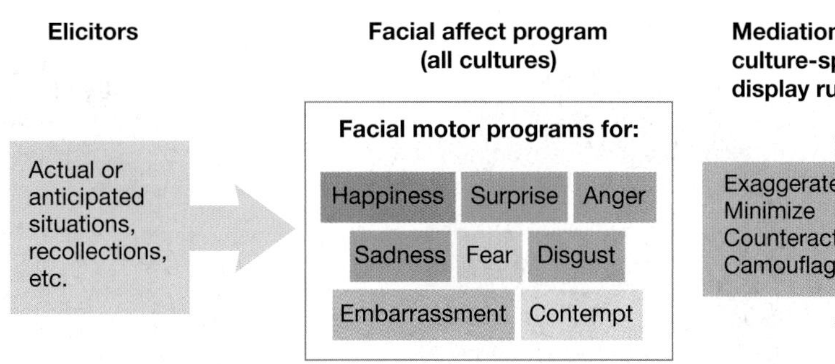

Each culture has rules about how we display our emotions. Politicians, under intensive scrutiny from many people, need to be particularly careful about how they display their emotions.

Figure 13.10 Cultural Display Rules for Emotions

The ancient theory of emotional catharsis is not supported by modern research

The great ancient Greek philosopher Aristotle (384–322 BCE) offered a theory of human emotion that applied to both the theater and everyday life. Aristotle thought that experiencing an emotion served to clean it from the mind, as if each emotion slowly accumulates in our mind until we manage to get rid of it by expressing it. Aristotle felt that theater was good for people, because by identifying with the characters in a tragedy, feeling their extreme emotions, people could get rid of unpleasant emotions such as sorrow and fear. They would then leave the theater feeling calm and relaxed, having gotten those other emotions out of their system. Aristotle described this process as **catharsis**, a cleansing or purging of the emotions. In his medical writings, Aristotle used the word catharsis to describe getting rid of body fluids by vomiting, sweating, or diarrhea (a strong laxative is a "cathartic"). Just as it was good to get rid of toxins, he thought it was good to get rid of emotional buildup by experiencing and expressing those emotions.

Aristotle's notions about emotional catharsis, based on nothing but his anecdotal observations and speculation, had an enormous influence on subsequent thinking about emotions. Sigmund Freud's elaborate theories that we experience a buildup of mental energies that must be released (see Chapter 14) were directly related to Aristotle's idea of catharsis, as Freud himself acknowledged. Freud's therapy involved helping patients remember past traumas they had repressed from memory, and experience the painful emotions surrounding that trauma. He thought expressing those painful emotions would weaken them, allowing the patient to lead a happier life. Today Freud's ideas about the causes and treatment of anxiety disorders and other mental disturbances have been rejected by almost all mainstream psychologists and psychiatrists. Yet Aristotelian ideas about emotional release are still prominent in many of our cultural ideas about emotions. We talk about people expressing frustration or anger by "venting" or "blowing off steam," as if they are getting rid of those emotions so they can feel better.

Modern scientists are skeptical of the therapeutic value of catharsis, the notion that expressing an emotion will help a person feel less of it. In fact, it has been repeatedly demonstrated that expressing an emotion can cause a person to feel that emotion *more* strongly. The **facial feedback hypothesis** suggests that the sensory feedback from our face when displaying an emotion makes us more likely to actually feel that emotion (Adelmann & Zajonc, 1989; Cappella, 1993; Davis et al., 2009; Soussignan, 2002). It is as if our mind determines how we feel, in part, based on what expression is on our face. For example, when scientists have people deliberately make a happy face, they find it makes the people feel happier afterward. In one study, people were asked to hold a pencil with their facial muscles, supposedly to help understand how people without hands can get by (Strack et al., 1988). One group of people was asked to use their upper lip to hold the pencil against the bottom of the nose. This activates the muscles that are normally used when

catharsis A cleansing or purging of emotions.

facial feedback hypothesis The hypothesis that sensory feedback from our face affects our emotional experience.

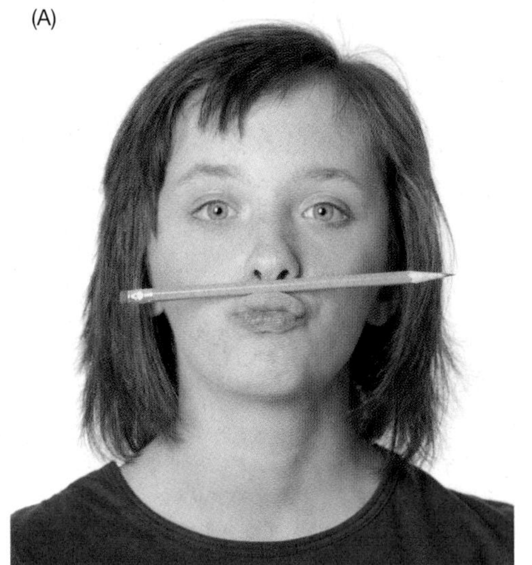

Figure 13.11 Facial Feedback Hypothesis Several studies indicate that when subjects are manipulated into mimicking facial expressions of sadness (A) or happiness (B), their emotional mood is affected. Several researchers have suggested that forcing yourself to put on a happy, cheerful expression may actually help you feel better.

frowning. Another group was asked to hold the pencil with their teeth, activating muscles that are normally used when smiling (**Figure 13.11**). A third group, as a control, was asked to hold the pencil with their nondominant hand. People in all three groups were given a distracting task while holding the pencil and then were asked to rate how funny they found a cartoon. People who had been using their smiling muscles found the cartoon more amusing than those in the control group did. People who had been using their frowning muscles found it less amusing than those in the control group did. In another study, adhesive bandages and rubber bands were used to either raise the cheeks, which made the people feel happier, or lower the cheeks, which made them feel sadder (Mori & Mori, 2009).

Does Botox Affect Emotional Experience? Several studies have suggested that people who receive Botox injections, which reduce wrinkles by paralyzing facial muscles, may have reduced emotional experience because of loss of facial feedback.

Facial feedback effects on emotion have been demonstrated in people who get injections of Botox in a procedure to smooth out wrinkles, making the face look younger (at least to some people). Botox, a toxin, incidentally also paralyzes facial muscles, limiting facial feedback. People who receive Botox injections still experience emotions, of course, but there's evidence that they do not experience them as fully as people who don't receive Botox injections (Davis et al., 2010), perhaps because they're lacking some of the facial feedback that normally accompanies emotions. In one study, people were asked to make an angry face before and after getting Botox injections. Brain scans revealed that brain activation while making the angry face was reduced after the frowning muscles had been paralyzed by Botox (Hennenlotter et al., 2009). These findings suggest that there's a self-reinforcing quality about emotions. If expressing an emotion causes you to feel it more fully, then presumably that will make you even more likely to show that emotion on your face, further amplifying the experience. This idea also supports the James–Lange theory that your experience of emotion reflects what you perceive to be going on in your body.

On a practical level, these findings suggest that you can improve your mood by deliberately acting happier than you feel: "Fake it until you feel it." It may seem false or hypocritical to act happier than you feel, but it's not as if the acting will hurt anyone—in fact, acting happier than you feel may benefit those around you by elevating their mood too (as in the Schachter and Singer experiment we discussed earlier). Furthermore, if you do end up feeling better, then this strategy would be more of a self-fulfilling prophecy than a matter of deceiving anyone. Of course you can take this advice too far. If there really is a problem in your life that needs to be addressed, then eventually you have to acknowledge the problem in order to do something about it. But as long as you are addressing the problem, dwelling on it and feeling unhappy about it probably will not help either solve the problem or improve your mood.

If feedback from facial expression augments our emotional experience, might sensory feedback from other parts of the body affect our emotional state as well? Does screaming and yelling in rage cause us to feel less angry, as Aristotelian catharsis would suggest, or does the sensory feedback from that outburst make us feel even angrier? William James, who thought emotional experience is determined by physiological processes, rejected Aristotle's theory. Indeed, James felt that expressing an emotion like anger would simply cause you to experience more of it. If you really wanted to stop feeling angry, James advised you to remain calm: "Refuse to express a passion, and it dies" (James, 1890, p. 463). In this line of thinking, a quarreling couple may be better off going to bed angry; by morning they may be calmer and better able to deal with the problem.

Modern research seems to back up James's position and refute the idea of catharsis. In one experiment, people read a passage extolling the virtues of catharsis—how expressing your anger helps you to calm down and get over it. However, when some of these people were then given a chance to hit a punching bag, they behaved more aggressively afterward than did people who were given another activity (Bushman et al., 1999). Researchers wondered whether the physical activity involved in punching influenced people to behave aggressively. To control for that possibility, a later study had *all* the people hit the punching bag; some were instructed to think about how it would get them into better shape, while others were shown a picture of a stranger who was described as dislikable, and encouraged to imagine hitting him while punching the bag. Afterward, everyone had a chance to act aggressively toward the man who had been pictured. The people who had imagined hitting him acted more aggressively than those who had punched the bag for fitness (Bushman, 2002). Thus, expressing anger seems to make people behave more aggressively, not less aggressively.

What about a particular modern activity in which people, especially children, are encouraged to behave in incredibly aggressive fashion—playing video games? If Aristotle were correct, we might expect such behavior to make people less aggressive afterward. However, playing aggressive video games, or watching aggressive acts on television, is associated with people who are more likely to behave aggressively, not less likely (Carnagey and Anderson, 2007) (see Box 15.2).

While Artistotle's belief in catharsis appears to be wrong, his ideas on how to be happy may have some merit. Artistotle believed that we achieve happiness by living a balanced life, and actively doing something well, as we'll see next.

Whistle While You Work Being deeply involved in an activity can help us feel happy.

The pursuit of happiness

The U.S. Declaration of Independence proclaims that we all have a right to "life, liberty and the pursuit of happiness." But what should we do if we want to build happy lives? We've already seen that just using the facial muscles that normally produce a smile can help us actually feel happier—we find cartoons funnier, for example. Does money bring happiness, the more money the merrier? What does make us happy? Let's review the evidence.

ACTIVITY Perhaps the most straightforward test of which activities make us happy comes from a survey of people who agreed to be paged over their iPhone at random times during the day. Whenever that prompt came, they were to report what they were doing and how happy they felt (Killingsworth & Gilbert, 2010). Supporting Aristotle's claim that happiness comes from being active, people felt most happy when they were busily engaged in some activity, and were least happy when they were doing nothing and just letting their minds wander. In other words, daydreaming tends to make us unhappy.

This finding comes as a surprise if you think people generally daydream about pleasant fantasies. In the study, most people's daydreams were indeed about pleasant topics, yet they were still less happy when daydreaming, on average, than when they were engaged in doing something, regardless of what that activity was. Which activities made people happiest? You can probably guess: "making love," exercising, and engaging in conversation all got high ratings. People were least happy when they reported resting, using a home computer, or being on the job.

Of course there may be a big difference between what makes us happy in the short term versus the long term: however unpleasant some people may find working in the short run, they might be even less happy in the long run if they stopped working altogether. In fact, working hard toward a goal, and making progress toward that goal, makes people happy and makes them less likely to have negative emotions afterward (Davidson & Irwin, 1999). Follow Aristotle's advice to find something you enjoy doing, and exert a lot of effort learning to be better and better at it. It's good to have goals. There are several different arenas in which you can work hard toward a goal. It may be personal improvement, as in physical fitness, healthy eating habits, or improving your mind.

MONEY For many people, getting money is an important goal, but does it make you happy? Finding fulfillment in working hard toward achieving goals in school or the workplace not only improves our mood, but also can be a good strategy for economic success. There's an old saying that you can't buy happiness, but in fact people living in poverty are much less happy than other people. For example, people who make more than $75,000 per year are more than twice as likely to say they are "very satisfied" with their lives than are people who make $25,000 or less per year (Kahneman & Deaton, 2010).

On the other hand, once people are past the level of poverty, there's a limit to how much additional money will help them to be happy. If we ask people how they felt over the past 24 hours, as a measure of day-to-day happiness, there is no additional benefit to having an income above about $75,000 (**Figure 13.12**). At the time of the study, about one-third of American households had incomes above that amount, so we may consider this amount of money "well-off," but not rich. Interestingly, if instead of asking how happy they were over the past few days, we ask people to look back and report how satisfied

Figure 13.12 Money Can Buy You Happiness, but Only up to a Point (After Kahneman & Deaton, 2010.)

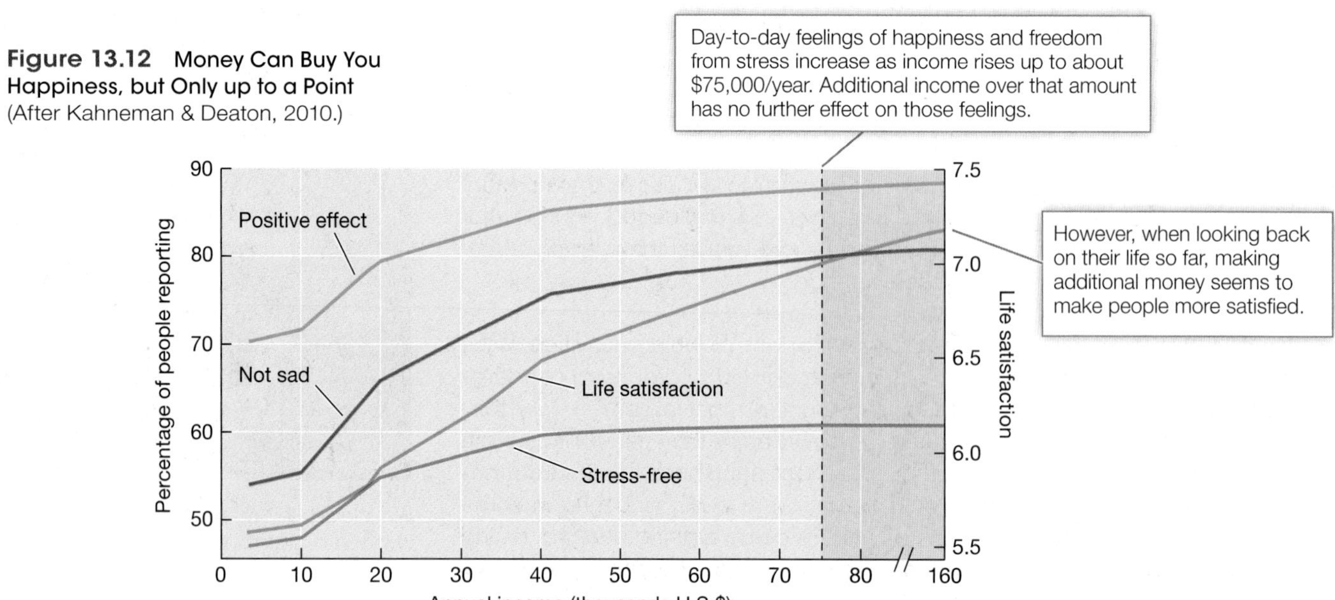
Day-to-day feelings of happiness and freedom from stress increase as income rises up to about $75,000/year. Additional income over that amount has no further effect on those feelings.
However, when looking back on their life so far, making additional money seems to make people more satisfied.
Positive effect
Not sad
Life satisfaction
Stress-free
Percentage of people reporting
90
80
70
60
50
Life satisfaction
7.5
7.0
6.5
6.0
5.5
0
10
20
30
40
50
60
70
80
160
Annual income (thousands U.S.$)

they are with their lives, then additional wealth does bring additional satisfaction. However, we have to suspect that when these folks are talking about how satisfied they are with their lives, how much money they have plays heavily in their thinking. They are probably not aware that the additional money did not, in fact, bring more day-to-day happiness or reduce day-to-day stress (Quoidbach et al., 2010).

Another example of money's limited ability to bring happiness is seen in people who win lotteries. While such people are initially much happier, within a few years, and often within a few months, they are no happier than they were before they won (Brickman et al., 1978). Similarly, when the average income in a nation increases, as happened in the United States in the decades after World War II, the average happiness that its citizens report does not change (Easterlin et al., 2010). In general, people tend to overestimate the emotional impact that changes such as winning the lottery, getting a better job, or acquiring some desired object will make on their lives (Wilson & Gilbert, 2005). In one study, people were asked before a presidential election to predict how happy or sad they would be, depending on whether their candidate won. When contacted afterward, those supporting the winner were not as happy as they had predicted, and those supporting the loser were not as sad as they had predicted (Wilson et al., 2003).

The Good Life? Months after winning the lottery, this couple separated. They moved out of their dream home, and both went back to work.

SOCIAL RELATIONSHIPS Having strong personal relationships has been proven to increase happiness. In one survey of college students, the happiest people were highly social, and reported stronger romantic and social relationships than other people. Not surprisingly, the happiest people also tended to be outgoing, but they did not seem to have benefitted from more "lucky breaks" in their lives, nor did they exercise more or participate in religious activities more than other people (Diener & Seligman, 2002). Sociability is not just good for college students. A broad-based survey of adults found that the more social activities people participated in, the happier they were (Robinson & Martin, 2008). In contrast, the more television people watched, the less happy they were. Do people who watch a lot of television have fewer or less satisfying social connections?

How important is the happiness derived from friendship? One review of more than 140 different studies, including hundreds of thousands of respondents, concluded that people with strong social relationships were significantly more likely to stay alive for the following year (Holt-Lunstad et al., 2010). In fact, having few social relationships affected survival nearly as much as cigarette smoking! In line with college students who are happier if they have a romantic relationship, married people are happier, on average, than single adults. Even people in relatively unhappy marriages are more likely to be happy than single people (Dush & Amato, 2005; Musick & Bumpass, 2012) (see Figure 15.20).

There is also evidence that happiness can spread through social networks—from friend to friend. People who are surrounded by happy people are more likely to be happy in the future (Fowler & Christakis, 2008). One researcher noted that "if your friend's friend's friend becomes happy, that has a bigger impact on you being happy than putting an extra $5,000 in your pocket" (Belluck, 2008)!

RELIGION There is a tendency for people who consider themselves to be religious to be more satisfied with life than other people. For example, in a large survey of Germans, those who attended church regularly reported being happier than did non-churchgoers (Headey et al., 2010). To the extent that there are conflicting reports in this area, they seem to be due to different definitions of "religious" (Hackney & Sanders, 2003). Religious activity is more likely to correlate with life satisfaction if the person strongly identifies with the religion, and correlates even more strongly in people who report being personally devoted. Religiosity may also help people undergoing stressful life events to avoid de-

amygdala A group of nuclei, one in each temporal lobe, that is key in producing and recognizing fear.

pression (Smith et al., 2003). These studies were done in countries such as the United States and Germany, where a majority of the people identify with a particular religion—Christianity. So it is possible that one benefit of religiosity in these cases derives from feeling solidarity with the majority of fellow citizens. By contrast, when similar studies were done in countries such as the Netherlands and Denmark, where fewer people report being religious, there was no correlation between happiness and religiosity (Snoep, 2008). Given the positive correlation between religious activity and happiness in places such as Germany and the United States, you might speculate that people in the less religious countries of Denmark and the Netherlands are unhappy. But in fact, those two countries are among the top five worldwide (155 nations were studied) in terms of how happy their citizens claim to be (Levy, 2010). The happiness of citizens in the United States was ranked 14th, and that of citizens in Germany was 33rd.

AGE As we noted in Chapter 5, happiness increases with age, even into old age, as people seem to be better able to adapt emotionally to circumstances and spend more time thinking about positive events and less time dwelling on negative events (Charles & Carstensen, 2010). The best predictor of whether older people are happy is how many strong personal relationships they have with other people. The take-home message is that the best move you can make for a lifetime of happiness is to start building a strong social network now.

A specialized brain circuit underlies the adaptive experience called fear

We like being happy, but we should also be grateful for an unpleasant emotion—fear. Fear prompts us to run away from danger, improving our chances of reproducing, so it's easy to see why natural selection favored the evolution of fear. When we are afraid, the sympathetic nervous system revs up the body for action, increasing heart rate, respiration, and blood pressure. Many other animals display those same reactions under conditions that provoke fear, such as exposure to a predator. The obvious benefits of fear and the similarity of fear-related behaviors across species may explain why we know much more about the neural circuitry of fear than of any other emotion (LeDoux, 1995). For example, it is easy to reliably elicit fear by using classical conditioning (see Figure 8.13), in which a person or animal is presented with a stimulus such as light or sound that is paired with a brief aversive stimulus such as a mild electrical shock. After several such pairings, the response to the sound or light itself is the typical fear portrait, including freezing and the physiological results of sympathetic activation.

Studies of such fear conditioning have provided a map of neural circuitry that includes the almond-shaped brain region called the **amygdala** (Greek *amygdale*, "almond") as a key structure producing fear. Buried within each temporal lobe, the amygdala is composed of about a dozen different nuclei, each with a distinctive set of connections. In the 1930s, researchers found that lesioning the amygdala on both sides of the brain in monkeys made them fearless—they no longer acted afraid of humans or attacked other monkeys (Klüver & Bucy, 1938). Lesioning only the central nucleus of the amygdala has the same effect in both monkeys and rats, preventing blood pressure increases and freezing behavior in response to a conditioned fear stimulus, such as a sound or light that signals an electrical shock to the feet.

Information about fear-provoking stimuli—for example, a scorpion with its tail poised to jab your toe—appears to reach the central amygdala by two different routes (**Figure 13.13**). A pathway of sensory information directly to the amygdala, called the "low road" for fear responses, bypasses conscious processing and allows for immediate reactions to fearful stimuli (LeDoux, 1996).

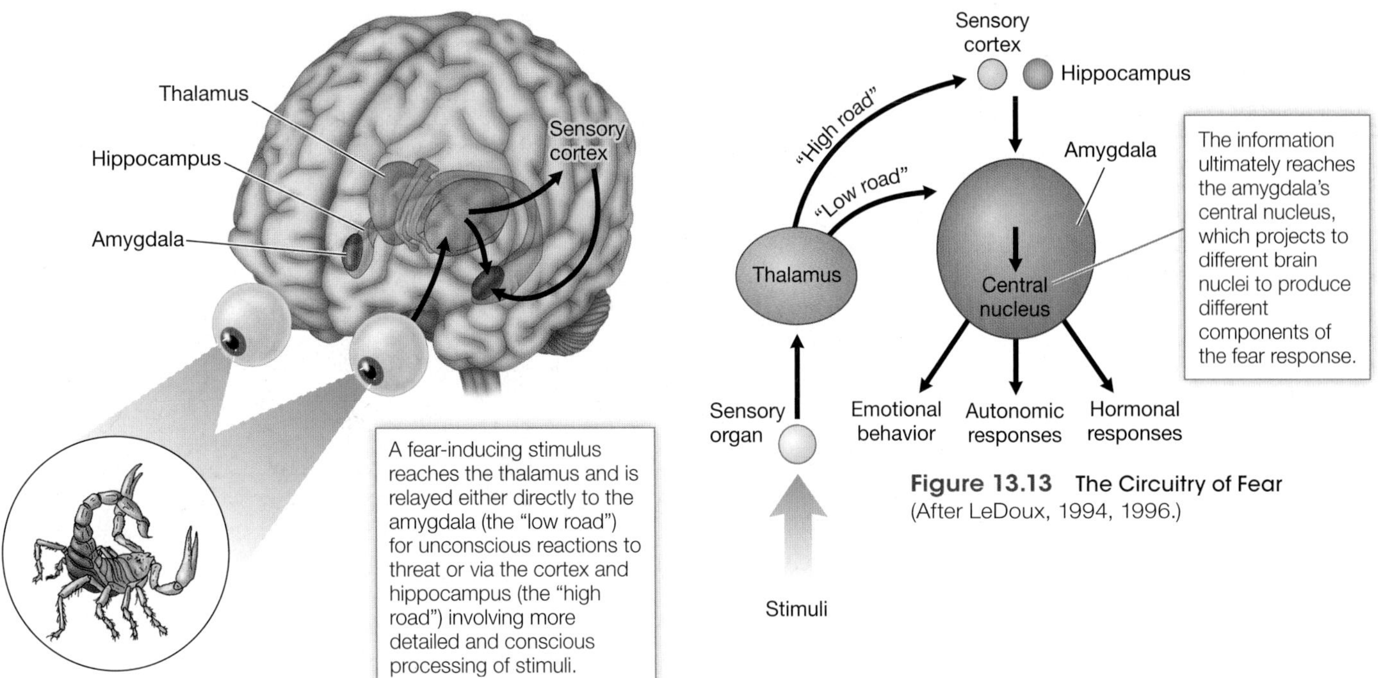
Thalamus
Hippocampus
Amygdala
Sensory cortex
A fear-inducing stimulus reaches the thalamus and is relayed either directly to the amygdala (the "low road") for unconscious reactions to threat or via the cortex and hippocampus (the "high road") involving more detailed and conscious processing of stimuli.
Sensory cortex
Hippocampus
"High road"
"Low road"
Amygdala
Thalamus
Central nucleus
The information ultimately reaches the amygdala's central nucleus, which projects to different brain nuclei to produce different components of the fear response.
Sensory organ
Emotional behavior
Autonomic responses
Hormonal responses
Stimuli

Figure 13.13 The Circuitry of Fear (After LeDoux, 1994, 1996.)

That path will get your sympathetic arousal going right away. An alternative "high road" pathway routes the incoming information through the sensory cortex, allowing for processing that, while slower, is conscious, more graded, and integrated with higher-level cognitive processes, such as memory. This pathway may remind you to draw your foot slowly away. The prefrontal cortex and anterior cingulate cortex (see Figure 13.15) use this pathway to offer an additional level of fear conditioning: *observational fear learning*, in which fear of potentially harmful stimuli is learned through watching the behavior of others (Olsson & Phelps, 2007). To extend our example of the scorpion, children might learn to fear scorpions by observing another person's reactions of fear and pain, without personally experiencing a scorpion attack themselves. Given the considerable adaptive benefits that observational fear learning confers, it's not surprising that it is seen in diverse species other than humans, including mice, cats, cows, and non-human primates (see Chapter 8).

The animal data associating the amygdala with fear fit well with observations in humans. When people are shown visual stimuli associated with pain or fear, blood flow to the amygdala increases (LaBar et al., 1998), *even if the stimulus is too brief for the person to be aware of it* (Pegna et al., 2005). People who suffer from temporal lobe seizures that include the amygdala commonly report that intense fear heralds the start of a seizure (Engel, 1992). Likewise, presurgical stimulation of temporal lobe sites may elicit feelings of fear in patients (Bancaud et al., 1994). Conversely, patients with damaged amygdalas do poorly at recognizing fear in human facial expressions (Adolphs et al., 2005).

BEFORE YOU DIE, YOU SEE
THE RING
★★★★★
"TERRIFYING"
GQ MAGAZINE
The countdown to your worst nightmare has begun.

Fear Factor People with damaged amygdalas report feeling little or no fear during even the scariest of movies.

The life of one woman, referred to as S.M., who suffers from a rare genetic disease that damaged both amygdalas, shows the value of being afraid (Feinstein et al., 2011). Not only is S.M. unafraid of snakes, spiders, and the pretend "monsters" jumping out of Halloween haunted houses, but she once walked right up to a knife-wielding drug addict who was trying to rob her. He was so disquieted by her strange response that *he* was the one who ran away. Once she was nearly killed in an act of domestic violence. While her

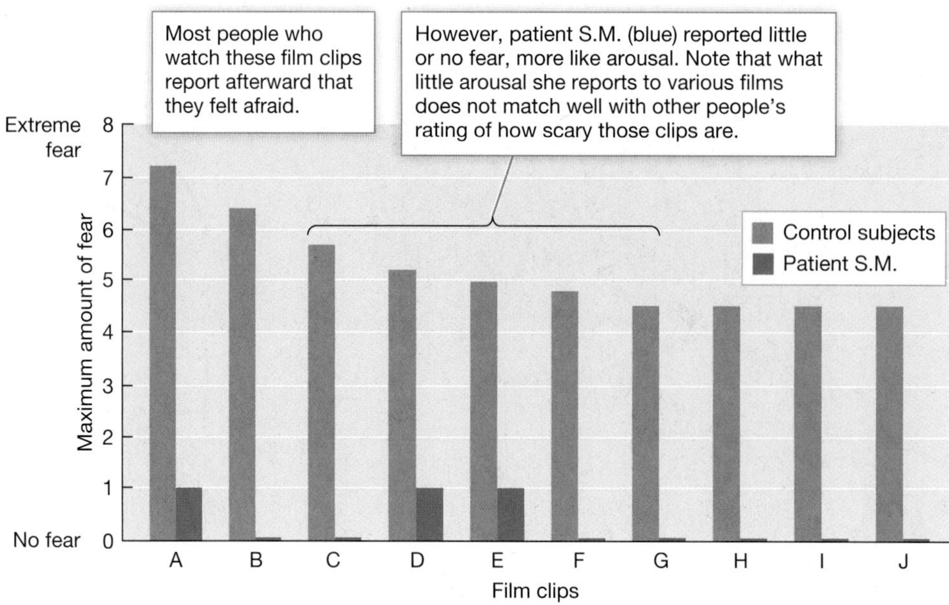

A – *The Ring* (2002) The ghost of a murdered child infiltrates the lives of her soon-to-be victims.
B – *Blair Witch Project* (1999) Campers are attacked by an unknown apparition at night.
C – *CSI* (2009) A man struggles to survive after being buried alive.
D – *The English Patient* (1996) A man is tortured by the Germans during World War II.
E – *Se7en* (1995) An apparent corpse suddenly awakes from the dead.
F – *Cry Freedom* (1987) Armed trespassers attack a woman who is home alone during the night.
G – *Arachnophobia* (1990) A large poisonous spider attacks a girl in the shower.
H – *Halloween* (1978) A woman is being chased by a murderer.
I – *The Shining* (1980) A young boy hears voices in the hallway of a haunted hotel.
J – *The Silence of the Lambs* (1991) A woman evades a serial killer in a dark basement.

Figure 13.14 The Woman Who Was Never Afraid (After Feinstein et al., 2011.)

behavioral responses and self-report appear typical for other emotions, S.M. shows very little sympathetic responses to fearful stimuli, and produces almost no startle response to a sudden, loud noise. Shown movie clips that other people find frightening, S.M. reports being unmoved (**Figure 13.14**). A mother of three children, S.M. is also very poor at recognizing the facial expressions of fear in other people (see Figure 13.8). Vietnam veterans who suffered traumatic events were much less likely to develop posttraumatic stress disorder if the event damaged their amygdala (Koenigs et al., 2008). We discuss this disorder further in **Box 13.2**.

Considerable evidence indicates that the amygdala is a crucial component of a brain circuit that both activates fear in ourselves and recognizes fear in others. Perhaps because fear is so crucial for survival, it is the only emotion so far that we know to be associated with a particular brain region. Still, scientists have identified other brain regions that are active during emotions, as we'll see next.

Affective neuroscience is revealing brain circuits for emotion

One approach to understanding the brain circuitry at work in emotions is to monitor brain activity while people do their best to experience a particular emotion. Such research suggests that several specific brain regions are often active when we experience emotions. For example, disgust appears to activate a

Psychology in Everyday Life

BOX 13.2

Posttraumatic Stress Disorder (PTSD)

Some people experience especially awful moments in life that seem etched in their memory forever, resulting in vivid impressions that persist. These events tend to be intense and usually associated with witnessing abusive violence and/or death. Precipitating events may be the sudden loss of a close friend, rape, torture, kidnapping, or profound social dislocation, such as in forced migration.

In these cases, memories of horrible events intrude into consciousness and produce the same intense visceral arousal—the fear and trembling and general sympathetic activation—that the original event caused. These traumatic memories are easily reawakened by stressful circumstances and even by seemingly benign stimuli that somehow prompt recollection of the original event. An ever-watchful and fearful attitude becomes the portrait of individuals afflicted with what is called **posttraumatic stress disorder (PTSD)**.

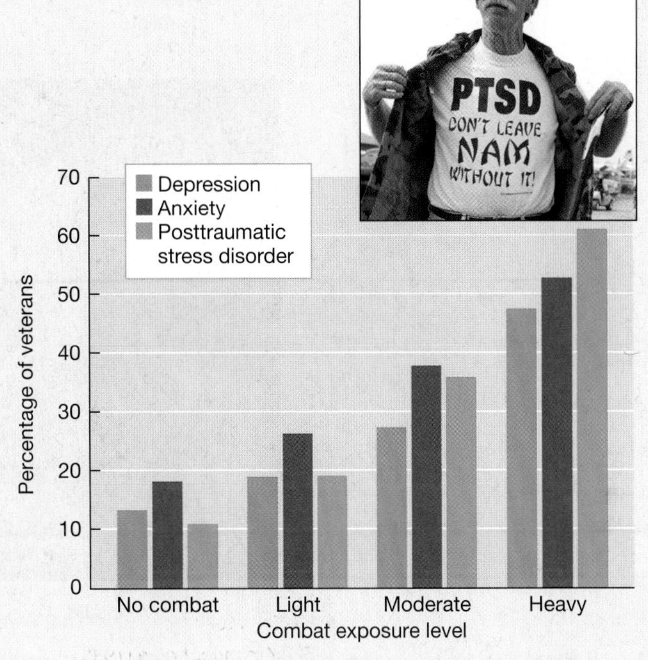

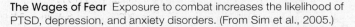

The Wages of Fear Exposure to combat increases the likelihood of PTSD, depression, and anxiety disorders. (From Sim et al., 2005.)

PTSD is common in soldiers who have seen combat, and indeed it was formerly called *combat fatigue*, *war neurosis*, or *shell shock*. About 19% of a random sample of Vietnam veterans had PTSD at some point after service. Among those exposed to high war-zone stressors, more than 35% developed PTSD at some point, and most of them were still suffering from the disorder decades later (Dohrenwend et al., 2006). A study of Australian veterans of the Korean War (Australian Institute of Health, 2005), conducted decades after the conflict, found a correlation between how much combat the soldiers had seen and their risk for PTSD and other disorders (see figure).

Genetic factors also affect vulnerability to PTSD, as shown in twin studies of Vietnam War veterans who had seen combat. Among twins who suffered from PTSD, monozygotic twins showed significantly greater concurrence for PTSD than dizygotic twins, and the specific contribution of inheritance to PTSD may account for one-third of the variance (Kremen et al., 2012). People who display combat-related PTSD show (1) memory changes such as amnesia for some war experiences, (2) flashbacks, and (3) deficits in short-term memory (Bremner et al., 1993). These memory disturbances suggest that the hippocampus may be involved, and indeed the volume of the right hippocampus is smaller in combat veterans with PTSD than in controls, with no differences in other brain regions (Bremner et al., 1995). It was once widely assumed that the stressful episode caused the hippocampus to shrink, but some veterans suffering PTSD left a monozygotic twin at home, and it turns out that the nonstressed twins without PTSD also tend to have a smaller hippocampus (Gilbertson et al., 2002). So an inherited tendency to have a small hippocampus may be what makes a person more susceptible to PTSD.

Nevertheless, effective therapy for PTSD is available. Unfortunately in the United States, Veterans' Administration hospitals are chronically underfunded and veterans with PTSD have long waits for treatment (Goodnough, 2014).

posttraumatic stress disorder (PTSD) A disorder in which memories of an unpleasant episode repeatedly plague the victim.

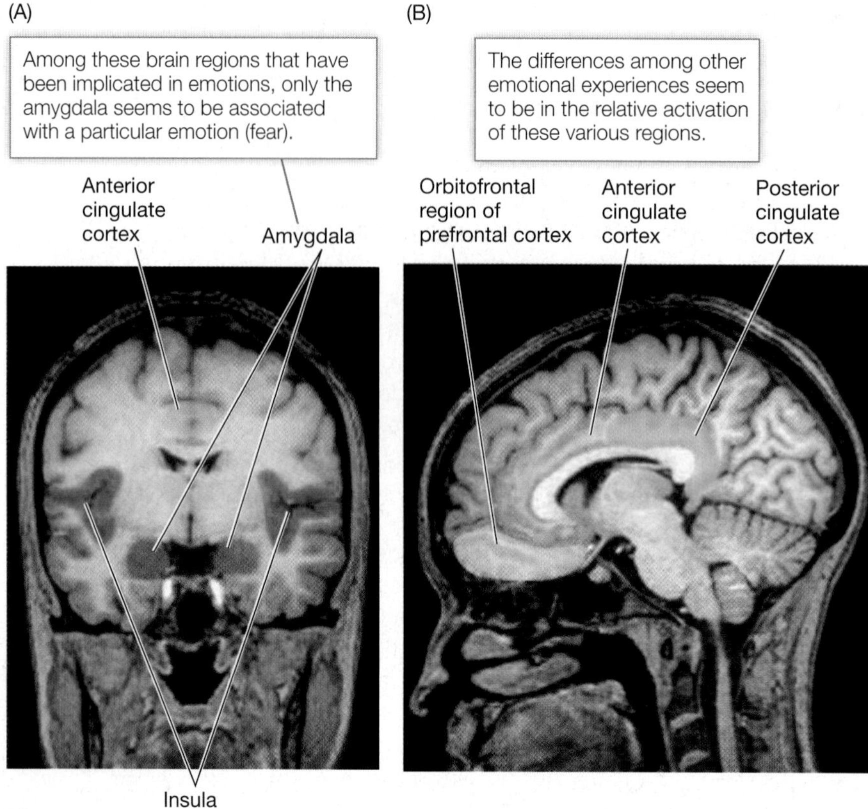
(A)
Among these brain regions that have been implicated in emotions, only the amygdala seems to be associated with a particular emotion (fear).
Anterior cingulate cortex
Amygdala
Insula
(B)
The differences among other emotional experiences seem to be in the relative activation of these various regions.
Orbitofrontal region of prefrontal cortex
Anterior cingulate cortex
Posterior cingulate cortex

Figure 13.15 The Emotional Brain (From Dolan, 2002.)

insula A region of enfolded cortex activated during several emotions.

cingulate cortex A region of cortex immediately above the corpus callosum that is activated during several emotions.

orbitofrontal cortex A portion of frontal cortex near the eyes that is activated in many emotional reactions.

cortical region called the **insula** (the portion of cortex that is folded inside the lateral fissure; **Figure 13.15**) and parts of the basal ganglia, but not the amygdala (Calder et al., 2000; Phillips et al., 1998). Sadness activates the insula and the **cingulate cortex** (the portion of cortex at the midline, lying just above the corpus callosum). Activation of the **orbitofrontal cortex** (the portion of frontal cortex just above and behind the eyes) is common in many emotional reactions (Montag et al., 2013).

Another study compared brain activation during four different kinds of emotion, and again the insula, cingulate cortex, and orbitofrontal cortex were among the regions activated. These studies indicate that *there is no simple, one-to-one relation between a specific emotion and changed activity of a brain region*. We have no "happy center" or "sad center." Instead, each emotion involves different patterns of activation across a network of brain regions associated with emotion. For example, activity of the cingulate cortex is altered in sadness, happiness, and anger, and the left somatosensory cortex is deactivated in both anger and fear. Feelings of regret over costly decisions involve activation of the amygdala and orbitofrontal cortex. Although different emotions are associated with different patterns of activation, there is a good deal of overlap among patterns for different emotions (Damasio et al., 2000).

What about love? In one study, researchers recruited volunteers who professed to be "truly, deeply, and madly in love" (Bartels & Zeki, 2000). Each participant furnished four color photographs: one of his or her boy- or girlfriend, and three of friends who were the same sex as the loved partner and were similar in age and length of friendship. Functional MRI brain scans were taken while each participant was shown counterbalanced sequences of the four photographs. Brain activity elicited by viewing the loved person was compared with that elicited by viewing friends. Love, compared with friendship, involved increased activity in the insula and anterior cingulate cortex (see Figure 13.15) and in the basal ganglia—all bilaterally (**Figure 13.16**). It also led to reduced activity in the posterior cingulate cortex and amygdala, and in the right prefrontal cortex. This combination of sites differs from those found in other emotional states, suggesting that a unique network of brain areas is responsible for the emotion of love.

The parts of the brain highlighted here become especially active when a person is looking at a photo of his or her romantic partner and thinking about their love for the partner.

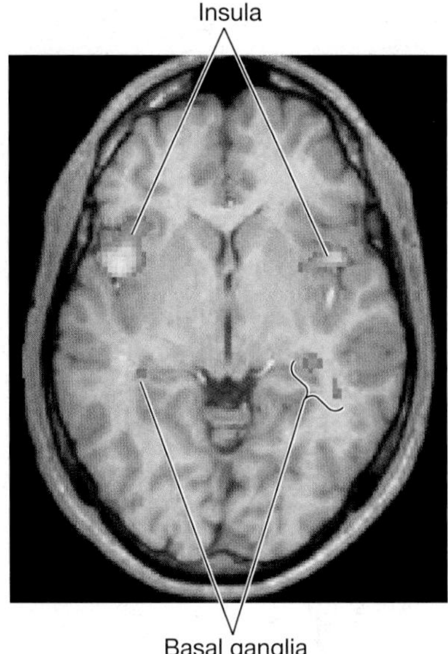

Figure 13.16 **"Tell Me Where Is Fancy Bred? Or in the Heart or in the Head?"** (From Bartels & Zeki, 2000.)

The left and right sides of the brain differ in emotional processing

Studying the results of brain damage offers another way to learn about brain circuits underlying emotion. Such studies indicate that the left and right sides of the brain may play different roles in emotion. For example, people who have suffered brain damage as a result of a stroke are more likely to be cheerful if the damage is to the right side of the brain rather than the left. This is an example of an **emotional syndrome**, when injury or disease has a general effect on emotional tone. In general, people who have suffered strokes involving the left cerebral hemisphere have the highest frequency of depressive symptoms. Damage to the left hemisphere is more likely to disrupt language ability, so you might think those with left hemisphere damage would be more depressed because they are more disabled. But in fact, injury-produced language deficits do not correlate with severity of depression (Starkstein & Robinson, 1994). In contrast, patients with lesions of the right parietal or temporal cortex are described as unduly cheerful and indifferent to their loss. Another indication that the two hemispheres differ in emotional tone comes from injection of a fast-acting anesthetic into either the left or right carotid artery supplying the brain, causing the entire cerebral hemisphere on that side to go to sleep for a short time (see Figure 10.11). Such injections into the left hemisphere produce a depressive aftereffect, whereas right-sided injections elicit smiling and a feeling of euphoria (Terzian, 1964).

Studies of how we detect emotions in other people also indicate that the left and right sides of the brain play separate roles. For example, people listening to two different recordings at the same time, one in the left ear and one in the right ear, have a hard time making out the information. They do a better job understanding the *meaning* of a message in the right ear and a better job detecting the *emotional tone* of a message in the left ear (Ley & Bryden, 1982). Because neurons from each ear project more strongly to the opposite hemisphere, these results indicate that the right hemisphere is better than the left at interpreting emotional aspects of vocal messages.

A similar difference is seen in the ability to detect emotional expressions on other people's faces. Emotional expressions presented to the left visual field (projecting to the right hemisphere) are more accurately identified than those presented to the right visual field (projecting to the left hemisphere; Bryden, 1982; Stone et al., 1996). Adults who were born with cataracts that blocked vision in their left visual field, therefore depriving them of stimulation to their right hemisphere during infancy, are poorer at recognizing facial expressions of emotions than are adults who had cataracts in the right visual field as babies, even after the cataracts have been removed (Le Grand et al., 2003). Perhaps visual experience is needed to teach the right hemisphere to become expert at deciphering facial expressions.

Not only is the right side of our brain better at detecting emotional expressions in other people, but it is also better at communicating our own emotional state. By cutting down the exact middle of the face in a photograph of a person who is displaying an emotion, we can create two new composite photos—one that combines two left sides of the face (one of which is printed in mirror image), and an-

emotional syndrome A syndrome in which injury or disease has a general effect on emotional tone.

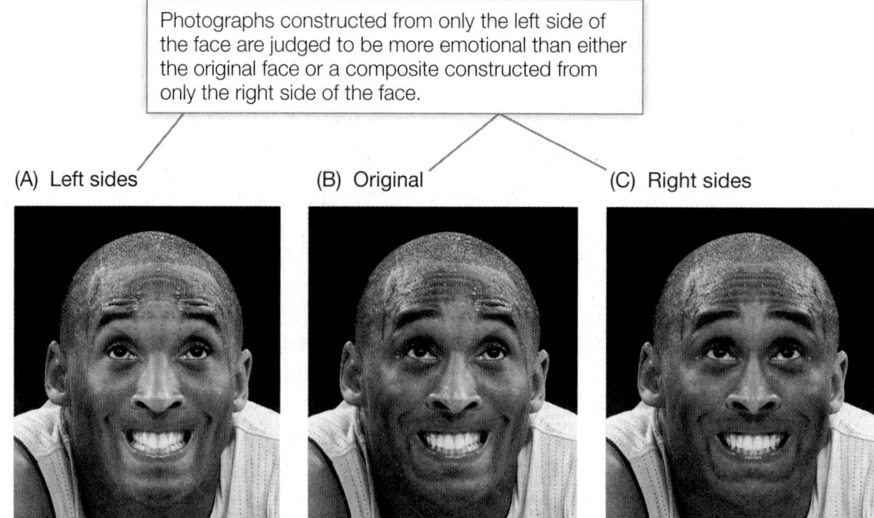

Photographs constructed from only the left side of the face are judged to be more emotional than either the original face or a composite constructed from only the right side of the face.
(A) Left sides
(B) Original
(C) Right sides

Figure 13.17 Emotions and Facial Asymmetry Composite faces reveal differences between left and right in the level of intensity of emotional expression.

other that combines two right sides. The results reveal that facial expressions are not symmetrical (**Figure 13.17**). Most observers judge the left-side photos as more emotional than the right-side photos. Because the left side of the face is controlled by the right hemisphere, this observation again suggests that the right hemisphere has a greater involvement than the left in emotional expression (Borod et al., 1997). This is true for both posed and spontaneous faces, for pleasant and unpleasant emotions, and for both sexes and all ages.

All told, it appears that the right hemisphere of the brain, which receives information from and controls the left side of the body, is better than the left hemisphere of the brain at communicating our emotions and detecting emotions in other people. But note that this is merely a difference in degree. The left hemisphere does express and detect emotions, just not quite as well as the right hemisphere.

13.1 SUMMARY

- *Emotion* is a subjective mental experience usually accompanied by involuntary physiological changes as well as distinctive behaviors. Involuntary physiological arousals are controlled by the *autonomic nervous system*, including the *sympathetic nervous system*, which prepares the body for action (so-called fight or flight responses), and the *parasympathetic nervous system*, which prepares the body to rest and recover.
- The *James–Lange theory* proposes that physiological response may come first, triggering our emotional experience.
- Schachter and Singer found that how we experience a particular pattern of autonomic arousal depends on context, such as our mental state before the arousal. In their classic experiment, people who were unknowingly given epinephrine to trigger sympathetic arousal were more likely to experience that arousal as anger if they were around an angry-acting person, or to experience the arousal as exhilaration if around an energetic, playful person.
- The *two-factor theory of emotion* says that autonomic arousal may intensify our emotional experience, but the emotion we experience depends on our cognitive interpretation of what's going on around us.
- At least eight different emotions can be detected in facial expressions. The emotions underlying most of these facial expressions can also be discerned by people from other cultures, suggesting that at

least some emotions may be universal across our species as a result of evolution.

- Aristotle's ancient notion of *catharsis*, that giving vent to our negative emotions can help diminish them, is not supported by research.
- The *facial feedback hypothesis* suggests that expressing an emotion causes us to feel it even more intensely. This hypothesis explains why activating the muscles for smiling can make us feel happier. Likewise, people who engage in strenuous physical activity while thinking aggressive thoughts are more aggressive afterward than people doing the same activity while thinking nonaggressive thoughts.
- People feel happiest when they are busily engaged in doing something, including working toward a goal.
- People living in poverty are not very happy, but outside of poverty, additional money does not necessarily bring additional day-to-day happiness.
- Having close personal relationships with other people, including a spouse, is consistently correlated with greater happiness, and people who strongly identify with a religion tend to be happier than nonreligious people.
- Fear is an unpleasant emotion that is adaptive and seems to have a specialized brain circuit that includes the *amygdala*. This brain region is active in animals during fear conditioning. People with damage to the amygdalas on both sides of the brain tend to have few fears and are poor at distinguishing fearful expressions on the faces of others.
- There is no known association of any other particular emotion with one particular brain region, but several brain regions tend to be active during emotion, including the *cingulate cortex*, *orbitofrontal cortex*, and *insula*.
- Emotional processing may differ in the two hemispheres of the brain. Damage to the right hemisphere may increase a person's cheerfulness, while damage to the left hemisphere is more likely to lead to depression.

REVIEW QUESTIONS

1. Compare the perspectives of folk psychology, the James–Lange theory, and the two-factor theory of emotion on the relationship between autonomic activity and the experience of emotional states.
2. Describe the results of the Schachter and Singer experiment and relate them to the role of cognitive factors and autonomic activity in emotions.
3. Describe the facial feedback hypothesis and discuss the various results that support it.
4. What factors seem to contribute to happiness?
5. Why does fear seem to be a special emotion, and what do we know about the brain regions involved in fear?

13.2 Stress and Health

We all experience stress, but what is it? Attempts to define stress tend to be rather vague. Hans Selye (1907–1982), whose work launched the modern field of stress research, broadly defined stress as "the rate of all the wear and tear caused by life" (Selye, 1956). Today, researchers try to sharpen their focus by treating **stress** as a multidimensional concept. Accordingly, we must consider three dimensions: **stressors**, the events and stimuli that threaten us; **stress evaluation**, the cognitive system that assesses those events; and the **stress response**, the body's physiological reaction.

stress The events and stimuli that threaten us, how we assess them, and our physiological reaction.

stressors The events and stimuli that threaten us.

stress evaluation The cognitive system that assesses events that threaten us.

stress response The physiological response of the body to the assessment of threat.

Food for Thought

In science fiction, several characters have been portrayed who have few or no emotions (robots, for example). What do you think it would be like to experience no emotions?

Things to Learn

- Physiology of stress response
- Limitations of "lie detectors"
- Early experience and adult stress response
- Importance of control and predictability in handling stress
- Reciprocal nature of mental health and bodily health
- Communication between brain, endocrine system, and immune system
- Negative consequences of long-term stress
- Strategies to deal with stress
- Social buffering hypothesis

Run for Your Life In nature, stressful events tend to be short-lived. Whatever the outcome, this chase will be over quickly.

We'll start this section describing the stress response, the physiological reactions that are remarkably similar across different species, including the release of several hormones that normally help us adapt to stress. Next we'll consider two factors that make a tremendous difference in whether we evaluate an experience as stressful: lack of control and unpredictability. We'll touch upon the field of health psychology and the remarkably consistent finding that what's good for our physical health is good for our mental health, and vice versa. We'll conclude the section by talking about ways to reduce stress and improve health. We can all expect to go through some tough times in our lives, but we'll see that there are things we can do, including building up a network of supportive friends and family, that help us weather the storms and preserve our health to enjoy a long, happy life.

Psychology in Everyday Life

BOX 13.3

"Lie Detector Tests" Detect Stress, not Lies

One of the most controversial attempts to apply psychological science is the so-called lie detector test. This test attempts to detect lying by measuring physiological responses during an interview. The test is based on the assumption that people have emotional responses when lying because they fear detection or feel guilt about lying. Emotions are usually accompanied by body responses that are difficult for a person to control, so a **polygraph** (Greek *poly*, "many"; *graphein*, "to write") monitors several different physiological measures, among them respiration, heart rate, blood pressure, and the electrical conductance of skin (basically, a measure of how much someone is sweating), at the same time (**Figure A**). The examiner asks many questions and tries to compare the physiological reactions when the participant is truthfully answering a "control question" ("What is your name?") versus answering an incriminating question. The theory is that a person truthfully denying an incriminating question will show the same physiological reactions as when truthfully answering a nonthreatening control question.

Proponents of polygraph examinations (primarily people who make a living selling or using polygraphs for "lie detection") claim that the tests are accurate 90% of the time. But the estimate from impartial research is an overall accuracy rate of about 65% (Nietzel, 2000), and many psychologists regard the technology as scientifically unproven (Iacono, 2000; Eriksson & Lacerda, 2007). A federally appointed panel of scientists noted that even if polygraphs were correct 80% of the time, then giving the test to 10,000 people that included 10 spies would condemn 1,600 innocent people and let 2 spies go free (National Academy of Sciences, 2003). Indeed, many criminals and spies have been able to pass the tests. For example, long-time CIA agent Aldrich Ames, who was sentenced to prison for espionage, successfully passed polygraph tests after becoming a spy. His countermeasures were not very sophisticated: get a good night's rest, relax, and be especially chatty and friendly with the polygraph operator (Weiner et al., 1995).

It is difficult to do convincing research on lie detection because most studies focus on only trivial attempts at deception that do not necessarily involve participants emotionally (Holden, 2001). One paper concluded, "It may, in fact, be impossible to conduct a proper validity study" (Saxe & Ben-Shakhar, 1999). In real-world situations, it's very difficult to know what the truth is. Because of these controversies, most American courts do not allow testimony about polygraph results in trials. However, such testimony is widely used in the initial stages of criminal investigations, often to convince suspects that they should confess (Nietzel, 2000). Unfortunately, even innocent

The physiology of the stress response is similar across all mammals

On the basis of his many studies of the impact of stressors on different organ systems of the body, Selye emphasized a close connection between stress and disease that he termed **general adaptation syndrome**. According to this scheme, the initial response to stress, called the **alarm reaction**, is followed by a second stage, called the **adaptation stage**, which attempts to reestablish balance. However, if stress is prolonged or frequently repeated, the **exhaustion stage** sets in, which is characterized by increased susceptibility to disease and eventually death.

The first step in the alarm reaction is activation of the sympathetic nervous system, part of the autonomic nervous system that we discussed above (see Figure 13.1). As we described there, this activation increases respiration, heart rate, and blood pressure, among other things. These physiological responses to stress provide the basis of so-called lie detector tests. As **Box 13.3** makes clear, these tests measure stress, not lying, which means that in typical use the number of innocent people they implicate vastly outnumbers the few guilty people they detect.

Close on the heels of these physiological responses to stress, a host of hormones are released. One classic study of stress followed a group of young recruits

general adaptation syndrome The system connecting stress and disease through a series of stages.

alarm reaction The activation of the sympathetic nervous system including a release of hormones as the initial response to stress.

adaptation stage The return to normal following an alarm reaction.

exhaustion stage The increased susceptibility to disease and possible death that follows prolonged or frequently repeated stress.

---

people may display emotional arousal when being questioned by the police.

Some scientists believe that modern neuroscience may someday provide new methods of lie detection. Conscious lying may involve unusual activation of control mechanisms of the prefrontal cortex (**Figure B**) (Abe et al., 2007). Fear results in activation of the amygdala (as we discussed earlier in this chapter), which might be visible with functional MRI. The anterior cingulate cortex becomes more active when subjects are lying (Langleben et al., 2002).

Initial results from brain imaging studies of deception are intriguing, but much more work will be required to establish that brain imaging can detect lies with enough reliability to be useful in making important decisions about individual people.

polygraph Also called *lie detector*. A device that monitors several physiological measures, such as respiration, heart rate, blood pressure, and electrical conductance of the skin.

(A)

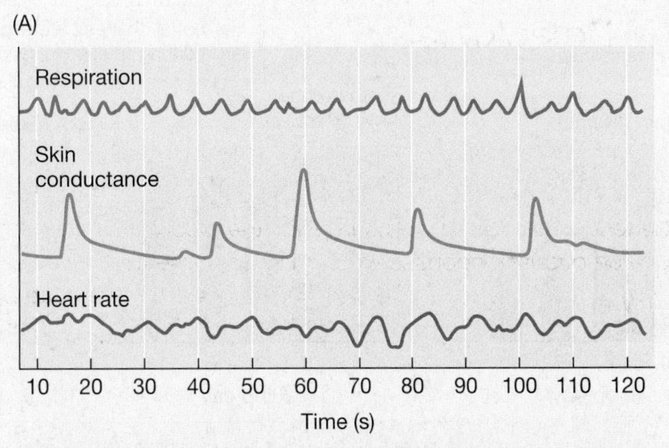

(B)

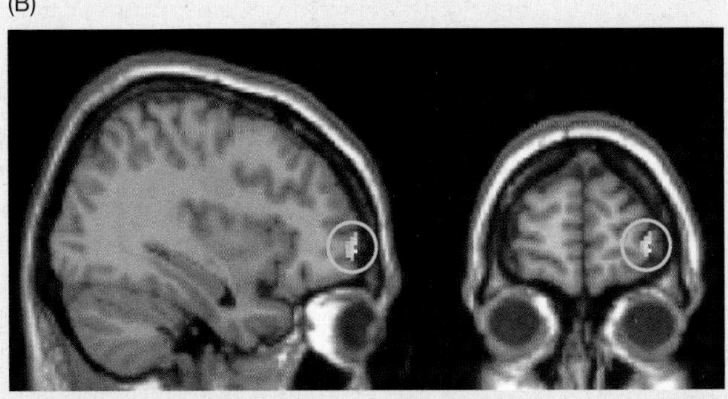

The Basis of Lie Detector Tests (A) The polygraph measures signs of arousal. But even an innocent person may feel alarmed if questioned about a crime. (B) These images reveal selective activation of the prefrontal cortex in a person who is lying (relative to a control scan). (Images courtesy of Nobuhito Abe.)

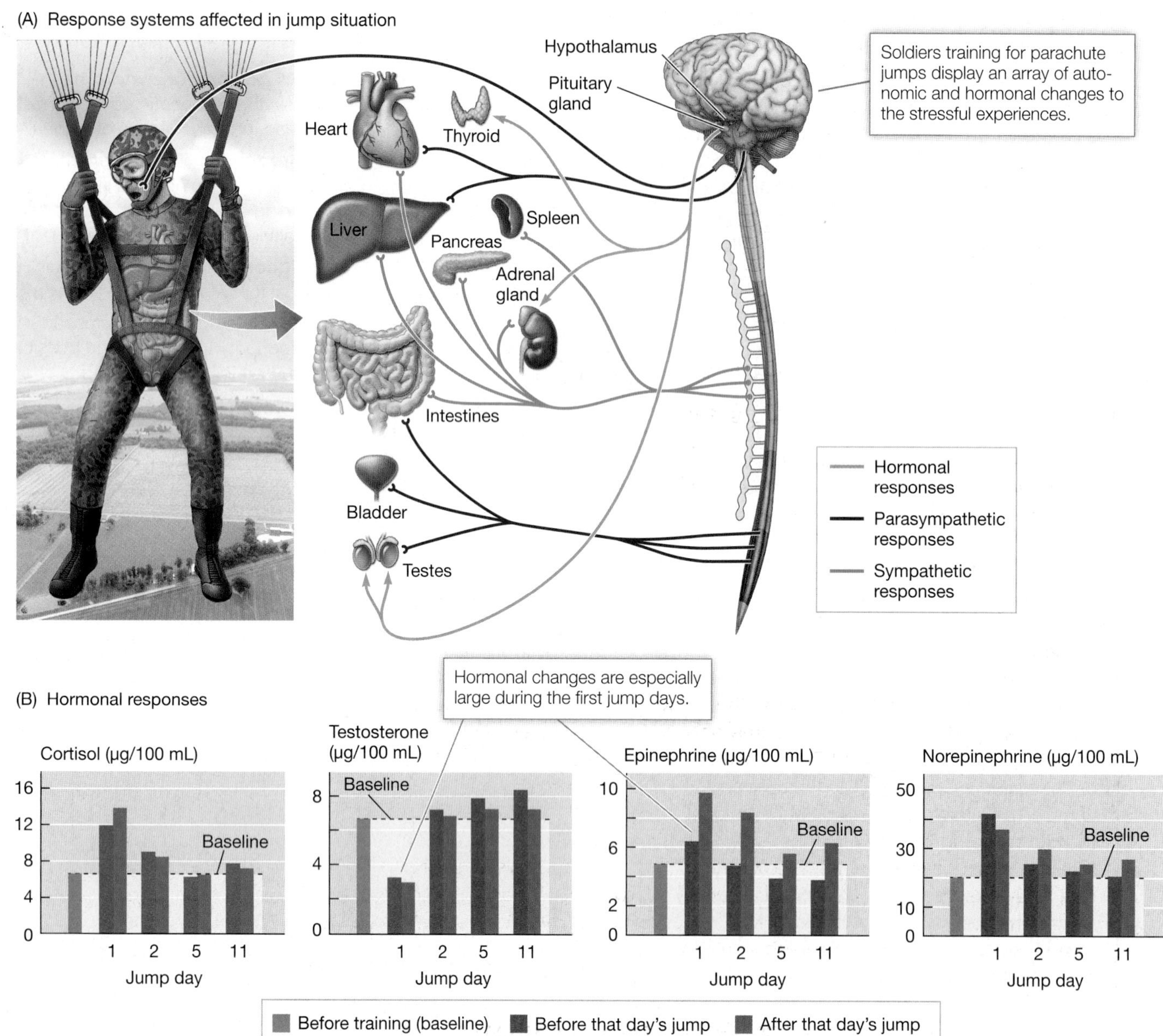

Figure 13.18 **Autonomic Activation during a Stress Situation** (After Ursin et al., 1978.)

cortisol A hormone from the adrenal gland released in response to stress.

adrenal gland An endocrine gland atop the kidney which releases hormones in response to stress.

in the Norwegian military both before and during parachute training (Ursin et al., 1978). During the training period, the men were propelled down a long sloping cable suspended from a four-story tower. At first the sense of danger was acute, even though the recruits knew they were not likely to lose their lives in this training.

On each jump day in this study, blood samples revealed release of hormones triggered by the sympathetic nervous system, including the hormone **cortisol** from the **adrenal gland** (**Figure 13.18**). Initially, cortisol levels were elevated in the blood, but successful jumps during training quickly led to a decrease in the jumpers' adrenal response. On the first jump, testosterone levels in the blood fell below those of controls, but these levels returned to normal with subsequent jumps. Other substances that showed marked increases in concentration at the initial jump included epinephrine (also known as adrenaline) and norepinephrine, both of which are also released from the adrenal gland when triggered by the sympathetic nervous system.

Less dramatic real-life situations also evoke clear hormonal responses (Frankenhaeuser, 1978). For example, riding in a commuter train provokes the release

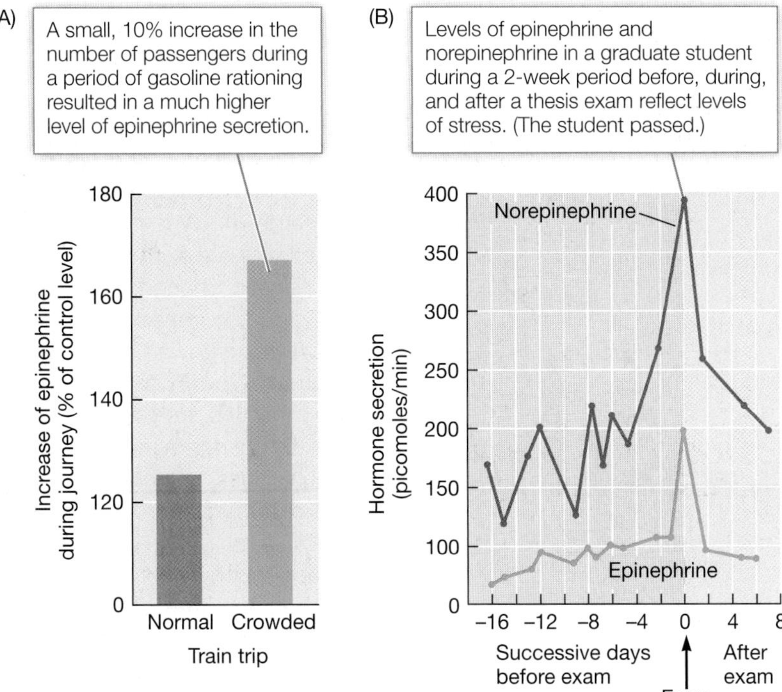
(A)
A small, 10% increase in the number of passengers during a period of gasoline rationing resulted in a much higher level of epinephrine secretion.
Increase of epinephrine during journey (% of control level)
180
160
140
120
0
Normal
Crowded
Train trip
(B)
Levels of epinephrine and norepinephrine in a graduate student during a 2-week period before, during, and after a thesis exam reflect levels of stress. (The student passed.)
Hormone secretion (picomoles/min)
400
350
300
250
200
150
100
0
Norepinephrine
Epinephrine
−16 −12 −8 −4 0 4 8
Successive days before exam
Exam
After exam

Figure 13.19 Hormonal Changes in Humans in Response to Social Stresses (After Frankenhaeuser, 1978.)

of epinephrine, and the longer the ride and the more crowded the train, the greater the hormonal response (**Figure 13.19A**). Factory work also leads to the release of epinephrine, and the shorter the work cycle—that is, the more frequently a person has to repeat the same operations—the higher the levels of epinephrine. The stress of a PhD oral exam also led to a dramatic increase in both epinephrine and norepinephrine (**Figure 13.19B**).

Not everyone responds to stress the same way

Why do individuals differ in their response to stress? One hypothesis focuses on early experience. Rat pups clearly find it stressful to have a human experimenter pick them up and handle them. Yet researchers found that rats that had been handled briefly as pups were less susceptible to adult stress than were rats that had been left alone as pups (Levine et al., 1967). For example, the previously handled rats secreted less *corticosteroid* (rat equivalent to cortisol) in response to a wide variety of adult stressors. This effect was termed **stress immunization** because a little stress early in life seemed to make the animals more resilient to later stress.

Follow-up research suggested an alternative explanation. It turned out that the pups being handled were benefitting not from the stressful handling itself, but from their *mothers' attention afterward.* When pups were returned to their mother after a separation, she spent considerable time licking and grooming them. In fact, she would lick the pups much longer if they were handled by humans during the separation. This gentle tactile stimulation from the mother was crucial for the stress immunization effect. Even among undisturbed litters, the offspring of mother rats that exhibited more licking and grooming behavior were more resilient in their response to adult stress than other rats were (Liu et al., 1997). Lack of maternal attention had a negative effect on rat pups, so that in adulthood they showed a greater stress response to novel stimuli, difficulty learning mazes, and reduced production of new neurons in the brain (Mirescu et al., 2004). In fact, the animals that recovered more rapidly from stress in adulthood were those that as pups had gotten lots of positive attention from their mothers.

Lack of maternal attention in early life appears to exert negative effects on adult stress responses by causing long-lasting changes in the expression of hormone

stress immunization The concept that mild stress early in life makes an individual better able to handle stress later in life. Research indicates early stress is only beneficial if the individual is comforted afterward.

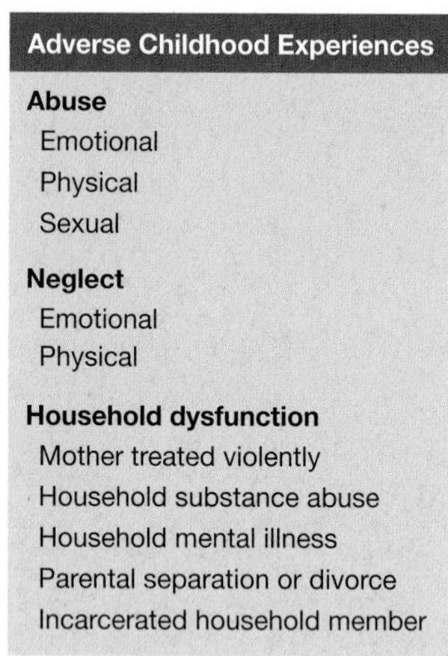

Adverse Childhood Experiences
Abuse
Emotional
Physical
Sexual
Neglect
Emotional
Physical
Household dysfunction
Mother treated violently
Household substance abuse
Household mental illness
Parental separation or divorce
Incarcerated household member

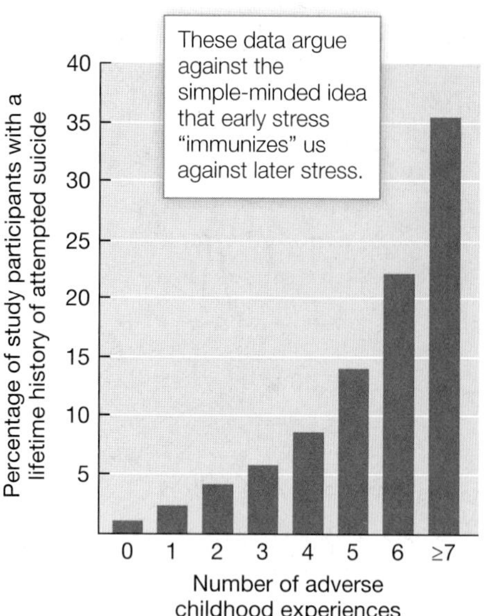

These data argue against the simple-minded idea that early stress "immunizes" us against later stress.

Figure 13.20 Adverse Experiences in Childhood Increase the Risk of Suicide in Adulthood (After Middlebrooks & Audage, 2008.)

receptors in the brain. This phenomenon is termed *epigenetic regulation* because the change in gene expression persists long after the original stimulus is gone. Epigenetic influences have been observed in humans (as well as in animals; see Chapter 4). When the brains of suicide victims were examined, for example, an epigenetic change in a certain hormone receptor gene was seen *only in those victims who had suffered abuse as children* (McGowan et al., 2009). Thus it may be that the early abuse caused the epigenetic change in the gene and left the individuals less resilient in response to stress, and therefore more susceptible to suicide.

In fact, much evidence clearly contradicts the idea that stress early in life makes it easier to withstand stress in adulthood. People who experience very stressful events in childhood are much more likely to become depressed and commit suicide (**Figure 13.20**; Middlebrooks & Audage, 2008). It appears that for childhood stress to be beneficial, it must be fairly mild stress, and it must be followed by positive attention from parents or guardians.

Lack of control and unpredictability make unpleasant events even more stressful

Unpleasant things happen to all of us once in a while, and those events can be stressful. Often how stressed we feel in response to some event depends on how we *perceive* that event. Research has identified two characteristics that make a tremendous difference in whether we perceive an event as stressful: lack of control and unpredictability. This information can be of practical value because if we can't avoid unpleasant events entirely, perhaps we can take steps to predict or control the events. The more control that individuals have over unpleasant events, the less stress they experience in response to those events. The story of how we came to understand the importance of control for minimizing stress is an interesting example of how a poor experimental design can lead scientists astray.

One of the most famous experiments in psychology, and one that has found its way into popular culture, is almost certainly incorrect. In the so-called executive monkey experiment, two monkeys were subjected to mild but unpleasant electrical shocks to the feet (Brady et al., 1958). The shocks came every 20 seconds unless one monkey, the "executive," pushed a button to avoid it. The other monkey had no button. Each pair of animals was *yoked*, meaning that when one monkey in a pair was shocked, they both were. Since the monkeys got exactly the same unpleasant shocks, you might think they would experience equal stress. But the monkeys that had some control, that could push the button to postpone shock, appeared to be more stressed, because several of them died of infections caused by *gastric ulcers* (open sores inside the stomach). The researcher's conclusion that it is stressful to be in control, like an executive, was quickly assimilated into our culture. But the conclusion was mistaken.

The experiment was flawed because the monkeys were not randomly assigned to the executive role. A total of four pairs of monkeys were tested. In pretraining, the four monkeys that learned the task best were selected to be the executives, while the other four monkeys became the yoked controls that got the same shocks as the executive monkey in each pair. The monkeys that learned the task fastest were probably the ones that were most stressed by the shocks. They may have been more sensitive to shocks, and to stressors in general, in the first place.

Noting this flaw in the executive monkey experiment, Weiss (1968) embarked on a series of well-designed experiments that led to conclusions exactly opposite of those from the executive monkey experiment, as we'll see next (**Figure 13.21**).

Researchers at Work

The value of control and predictability

Figure 13.21 Control Reduces the Stress from Electrical Shock (After Weiss, 1968.)

■ **Question:** Is it stressful to be an "executive," to have control over unwanted events in the environment?

■ **Hypothesis:** Alternatively, maybe having control over the environment will reduce the adverse effects of stressful events.

■ **Test:** Apply electrical shocks to the tails of pairs of rats. One rat in each pair, the executive, can turn off the shock for both rats by pressing a lever. The other rat in each pair is yoked and receives the same shock as the executive whenever the executive fails to push the lever.

■ **Result:** The animals that could control the shock developed *smaller* ulcers than the yoked animals. A third group of rats was put in the very same apparatus but did not receive any shocks: these rats had very few ulcers, so the apparatus itself was not very stressful.

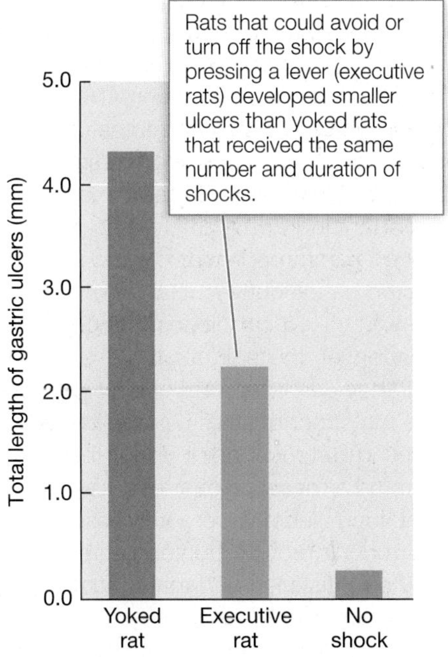
Rats that could avoid or turn off the shock by pressing a lever (executive rats) developed smaller ulcers than yoked rats that received the same number and duration of shocks.
Total length of gastric ulcers (mm)
5.0
4.0
3.0
2.0
1.0
0.0
Yoked rat
Executive rat
No shock

■ **Conclusion:** Since the two rats in each pair received the same amount of shock, it must have been the lack of control that caused the yoked rats to suffer more stress. Having control over stressful events appears to reduce the negative effects on health.

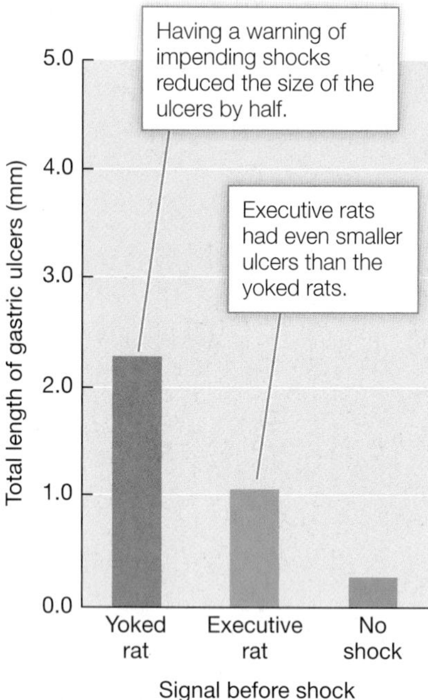
Having a warning of impending shocks reduced the size of the ulcers by half.
Executive rats had even smaller ulcers than the yoked rats.
Total length of gastric ulcers (mm)
5.0
4.0
3.0
2.0
1.0
0.0
Yoked rat
Executive rat
No shock
Signal before shock

Figure 13.22 Predictability Also Reduces the Stress from Electrical Shock

A separate experiment showed that predictability also makes a big difference in how stressful rats perceive events to be (Weiss, 1971a). Control rats were again put into the apparatus without receiving shocks, and they developed few ulcers. Two other groups of rats received shocks, and as in the first experiment, they were paired so that one executive rat could press a bar to avoid or stop the shock, while the yoked rat got the same shock as the executive. But this time, the rats were given a signal, an auditory tone, to let them know when the shock was coming. In these conditions, the yoked rats still got larger ulcers than the executive rats (**Figure 13.22**), but both groups had smaller ulcers than rats given no signal (see Figure 13.21).

Both factors, control and predictability, have been shown to matter in the way that humans respond to stress. For example, in some famous studies of British civil servants, people at the very top of the executive scale, who had the most control over what happened in their jobs, showed fewer signs of stress than the people under them, who had less control over their lives. In fact, the farther down the scale of authority people were, the more signs of stress they exhibited (Marmot et al., 1978). Not only that, the stress seemed to make a difference, as people at the lowest grade of employment (messengers, doorkeepers, etc.) were three times more likely to die in the following year than were people at the highest grade. Also, people who have a lot of control over their job (people at the top have the most control, the most flexibility in their jobs) are much less likely to develop heart disease (Kuper & Marmot, 2003; Nabi et al., 2013). So despite the urban myth that the executive monkey suffered because it had to make decisions, in humans we see that being in a position to make decisions about your work is good for your health.

By the way, one researcher found a way to replicate the outcome of the original executive monkey experiment in rats (Weiss, 1971b). He went back to his records and found those executive rats that were especially responsive, pushing the lever much more than was needed to turn off the shock. He reasoned that these hyperresponsive rats were like the hyperresponsive monkeys that had been selected to be executives in the original experiment. Indeed, these select executive rats had larger ulcers than the other executive rats.

Note that two things were going on here. First, these executive rats were *different from the start*. For whatever reason, they were especially eager to stop the shocks, and that seemed to reflect a more stressful response to the shocks. Second, because these executives were hyperresponsive, the rats to which they were yoked received far fewer shocks than the average yoked rat. So it appears that there are important individual differences in stress response, and the original executive monkey experiment was flawed because hyperresponsive animals had been selected as executives. But when animals are randomly assigned to the executive and yoked conditions (thereby controlling for individual differences in stress response), the animals that have control fare better than those that do not. And if they can't have control, being able to predict unpleasant events helps reduce the effect of stress on the body.

A different but interesting historical point about these experiments concerns their use of gastric ulcers as a measure of stress. Taken together, these studies convinced the world that such ulcers were purely "psychological." To some people this meant that ulcers could not be treated by "biological" or "medical" approaches. But eventually scientists learned that a bacterium (*Helicobacter pylori*) causes almost all ulcers in humans, so antibiotic treatment usually gets rid of the bacteria and the ulcers. There's little doubt that stress increases the severity of ulcers, and today we understand that stress impairs the immune system, as we'll discuss shortly. For this reason, bacteria that might have been kept in check by the immune system may proliferate under stressful conditions and cause an ulcer. So if you think you have an ulcer, it's a good idea both to see a doctor for antibiotic treatments and to reduce stress in your life.

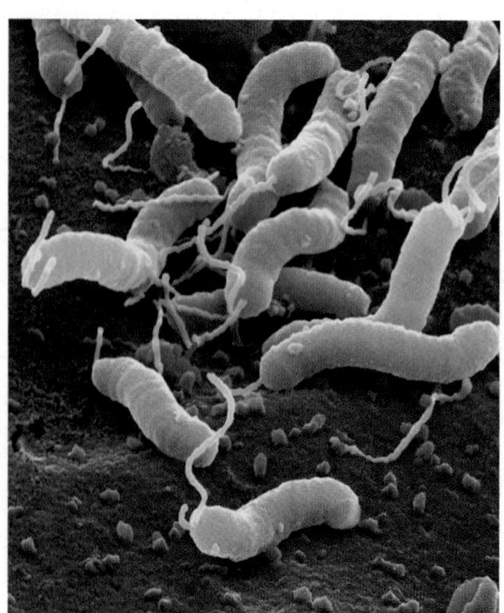

Gastric Ulcers The bacterium *Helicobacter pylori* is the most common cause of stomach ulcers.

This story about gastric ulcers is also one of my favorite examples of the mistake of thinking that if some process has a "psychological" component, then it must be beyond any "medical" intervention. In fact, an entire field of psychology is based on the idea that mental health and physical health are intertwined, as we'll see next.

health psychology The study of psychological, behavioral, and biological factors that influence physical and mental health.

Health psychology explores the relationship between physical and mental health

Health psychology examines the psychological, social, and biological factors that influence physical and mental health (Taylor, 1990). The overarching theme of health psychology is that what's good for the body is good for the mind, and vice versa. For this reason, it is a mistake to think there is some clear division between medical health and psychological health. We've already discussed how prolonged stress can damage our physical health. Research proves that the relationship between stress and health is reciprocal—psychological stress can damage the health of the body, and physical illness can take a toll on our minds.

For example, people who experience life events that are stressful are more likely to suffer physical ailments afterward. In the classic study of this type, researchers surveyed the medical records of thousands of people and asked the patients to report whether they had experienced any of a long list of stressful events in the years preceding their illness (Holmes & Rahe, 1967). There was a positive correlation between stressful life events and later illness. The researchers devised a Social Readjustment Rating Scale (SRRS), where people could check off various stressful life events. Each event has a number that indicates how stressful it is—death of a spouse or child was seen as the most stressful and given a score of 100, while divorce rated a 73, separation a 65, imprisonment a 63, etc. (**Table 13.1**). People with a score of over 300 were very likely to suffer an illness in the following year. This correlation between stressful life events and later illness was seen repeatedly (Andrews & Tennant, 1978). Another scale, called CUSS, gauging the stress associated with common events for college students, is presented in **Table 13.2**.

TABLE 13.1 Social Readjustment Rating Scale (SRRS)

Event	Score
Death of a spouse or child	100
Divorce	73
Marital separation	65
Imprisonment	63
Death of a close family member	63
Personal injury or illness	53
Marriage	50
Dismissal from work	47
Marital reconciliation	45
Retirement	45
Change in health of family member	44
Pregnancy	40
Sexual difficulties	39
Gain of a new family member	39
Business readjustment	39
Change in financial state	38
Death of a close friend	37
Change to different line of work	36
Change in frequency of arguments	35
Major mortgage	32
Foreclosure of mortgage or loan	30
Change in responsibilities at work	29
Child leaving home	29
Trouble with in-laws	29
Outstanding personal achievement	28
Spouse starts or stops work	26
Begin or end school	26
Change in living conditions	25
Revision of personal habits	24
Trouble with boss	23
Change in working hours or conditions	20
Change in residence	20
Change in schools	20
Change in recreation	19
Change in church activities	19
Change in social activities	18
Minor mortgage or loan	17
Change in sleeping habits	16
Change in number of family reunions	15
Change in eating habits	15
Vacation	13
Christmas	12
Minor violation of law	11

Source: Holmes & Rahe, 1967.

Remember: correlation does not prove causation; a correlation between stress and illness does not *prove* that the stressful events cause illness. Consider, for example, that some people may be more prone to stress than others. Of course people have no control over whether a spouse dies, but for most of the stressful events on the SRRS, the individual contributes to some degree to the stressful situation. For example, the person must have played some role in divorce, separation, imprisonment, dismissal from work, pregnancy, or having a mortgage. Is it possible that some people are genetically inclined to run into such difficulties, perhaps having genes that contribute to impulsiveness that make marital or legal problems and/or illness more likely? Indeed, one study found good evidence that relatives of a person prone to stress are more

TABLE 13.2 College Undergraduate Stress Scale (CUSS)

Event	Stress rating
Being raped	100
Finding out you are HIV-positive	100
Being accused of rape	98
Death of a close friend	97
Death of a close family member	96
Contracting a sexually transmitted infection (other than AIDS)	94
Concerns about being pregnant	91
Finals week	90
Concerns about your partner being pregnant	90
Oversleeping for an exam	89
Flunking a class	89
Going on a first date	57
Registration	55
Maintaining a steady dating relationship	55
Commuting to campus/work	54
Peer pressures	53
Being away from home for the first time	53
Getting sick	52
Concerns about your appearance	52
Getting straight A's	51
A difficult class that you love	48
Making new friends; getting along with friends	47
Fraternity or sorority rush	47
Falling asleep in class	40
Attending an athletic event	20

Source: Renner & Macklin, 1998.

likely to experience stress than the average person is (Kendler et al., 1999). But that study concluded that such heritable influences could not account entirely for the correlation between stressful events and illness. It concluded that the correlation reflects a causal relationship—that the events really did make illness more likely—in at least some cases.

What sorts of illnesses may be triggered by stressful events? You probably won't be surprised to learn that episodes of depression are more common after highly stressful events (Kendler & Gardner, 2010). It makes sense that experiencing stressful emotions and dealing with hardships in our everyday life would affect our minds and make us more susceptible to depression. In Chapter 16 we'll see that experiencing stress, especially early in life, also increases the likelihood of another major psychiatric disorder, schizophrenia.

But experiencing stressful events is also associated with disorders that we do not normally think of as "psychological." For example, cardiovascular problems such as heart disease and hypertension (high blood pressure) are commonly associated with stress (Abbott et al., 2014). People who perceive their lives as stressful are more likely to have a heart attack. Does this mean that heart disease should be classified as a "psychological" disorder, given that stress puts a burden on the heart, making it more susceptible to disease? Probably not, given that exercise, which also puts a burden on the heart, *reduces* the risk of heart disease.

And what about suffering infections from bacteria and viruses—would you consider these "psychological" disorders? Probably not. Nevertheless, there's good evidence that experiencing stress also makes us more susceptible to such infections (DeVries et al., 2007). In the study of British civil servants described earlier, researchers found that not only were people in the lowest pay grades more likely to have heart disease, but they were also more likely to suffer a wide variety of infections such as colds and the flu (Steptoe et al., 2007). This information suggests that the participants' immune systems did not function as effectively as those of the executives. How can the psychological experience of stress cause physical illness? We'll see next that the brain and immune system are in constant, reciprocal communication.

There is constant communication between the nervous system and the immune system

People sometimes think of the body's immune system as an automatic mechanism, attacking any invading virus or bacteria, independent of other body systems. But by the 1980s a new field, **psychoneuroimmunology**, arose to study psychological and neural influences on the immune system as well as immune system influences on behavior (Ader, 2001). For example, when researchers deliberately infected people with a cold virus, those who had happy social lives were less likely to come down with the cold (Cohen et al., 2006). Likewise, people who tend to feel positive emotions also produce more antibodies in response to a flu vaccination (Rosenkranz et al., 2003)—a response that should help them fight off sickness. These interactions go in both directions: the brain both monitors immune cells and their products, and can take steps to rein in the immune system to keep it from overreacting and damaging the body.

psychoneuroimmunology The study of psychological and neural influences on the immune system and its influences on behavior.

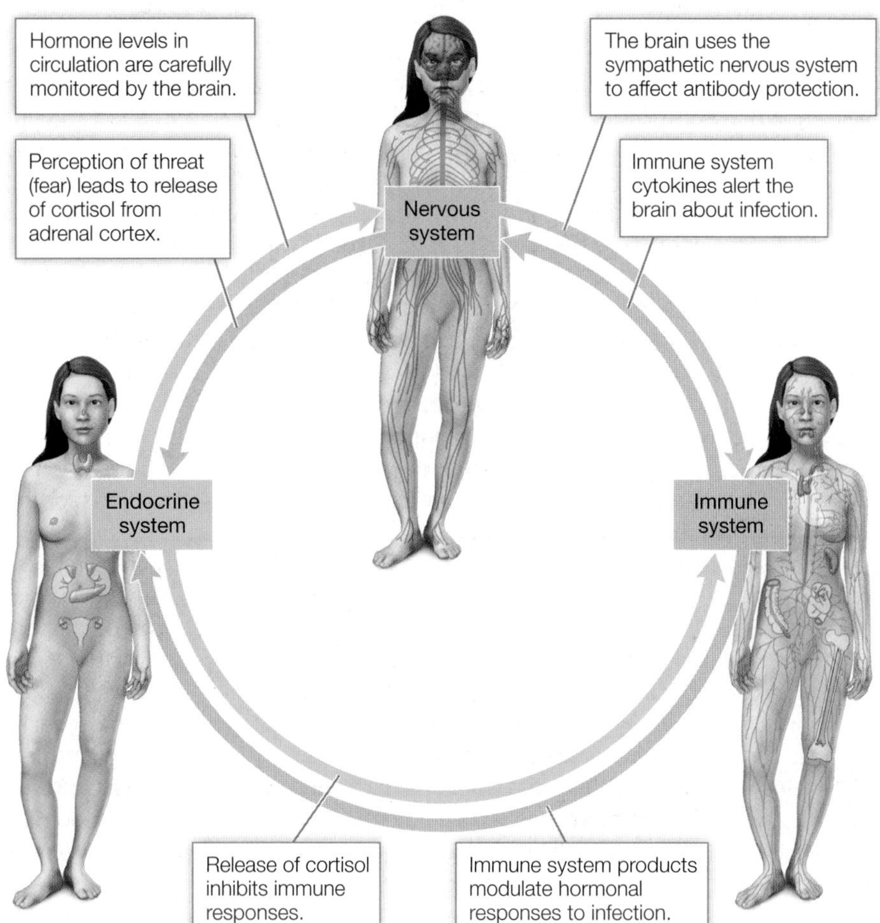

Hormone levels in circulation are carefully monitored by the brain.
Perception of threat (fear) leads to release of cortisol from adrenal cortex.
The brain uses the sympathetic nervous system to affect antibody protection.
Immune system cytokines alert the brain about infection.
Nervous system
Endocrine system
Immune system
Release of cortisol inhibits immune responses.
Immune system products modulate hormonal responses to infection.

Figure 13.23 The Brain Monitors and Controls Hormones and the Immune System

How does the brain keep tabs on the immune system? Neurons in the hypothalamus monitor the blood for proteins called **cytokines**, which the immune system uses to control the production of **white blood cells**, which attack invaders, and of **antibodies**, proteins that latch on to invaders to signal white blood cells to attack (Samad et al., 2001; Dantzer et al., 2008). This early-warning sensory system serves to alert the brain when microbes invade the body (Besedovsky & del Rey, 1992). In this way, the brain is directly informed about the actions of the immune system.

cytokines Proteins in the blood that control production of white blood cells and antibodies.

white blood cells Blood cells that attack microbes invading the body.

antibodies Proteins that latch on to invading microbes to signal white blood cells to attack.

There is an interesting theory about why our brains monitor the immune system so closely. Although that achy, lethargic feeling that we have with the flu is unpleasant, it is also adaptive because it forces us to rest and keep out of trouble until we recover (Hart, 1988). In other words, the discomfort might not be caused by the invading virus or bacteria themselves, but might be *imposed by the brain simply to force us to rest*. Perhaps high levels of cytokines signal the brain to impose that sick feeling. This suggestion has given rise to the idea that depression in some people may be caused by excessive amounts of cytokines in circulation, or by excessive brain sensitivity to those cytokines. Indeed, antidepressant drugs tend to reduce cytokine production (Maes et al., 1991; Dantzer et al., 2008).

We've just seen how the brain monitors the immune system, but how might the brain *control* the immune system? The autonomic nervous system provides nerves to all the organs of the immune system, including the spleen and lymph nodes, and can slow down their production of cytokines and white blood cells (**Figure 13.23**; Wang et al., 2003). Also, the brain controls the hormonal responses to stress that we described above (see Figure 13.18), and those hormones can also suppress immune responses.

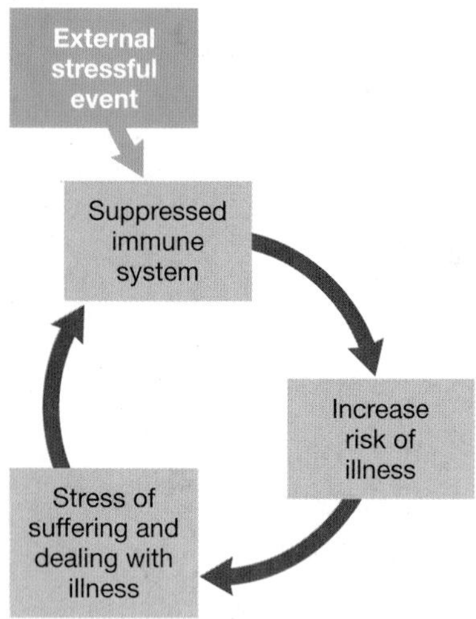

Figure 13.24 The Vicious Cycle of Prolonged Stress Stress suppresses the immune system, which is not a problem in the short run. But prolonged stress, which many humans experience, can lead to illness. Then the added stress of suffering from the illness and dealing with its consequences may suppress the immune system even further.

It has been repeatedly demonstrated that stress suppresses the immune system. This means that stress can lead to a vicious cycle—a suppressed immune system may lead to disease, which adds to the experience of stress, further weakening the immune system, and so on (**Figure 13.24**). To understand why stress suppresses the immune system, making us susceptible to this vicious cycle, let's consider the evolution of the stress response.

We are simply not adapted to handle prolonged stress

Under stressful conditions, as noted earlier, the brain causes the release of the steroid hormone cortisol from the adrenal glands. Cortisol suppresses immunological responses by inhibiting the division of some white blood cells and triggering the death of others. You might ask why, during times of stress, the brain causes cortisol to be released, if this hormone suppresses the immune system? Modern evolutionary theory offers some possible explanations for this seemingly maladaptive situation (Sapolsky, 2004).

When stress is a sudden emergency, the temporary suppression of immune responses makes sense because the stress response demands a rapid mobilization of energy, while immune responses take longer than the immediate, demanding situation. A zebra wounded by a lion must first escape and hide, and only then does infection of the wound pose a threat. So the stress of the encounter temporarily suppresses the immune system, saving resources until a safe haven is found. Later the zebra can afford to mobilize the immune system to heal the wound. The cortisol released as part of the stress response also suppresses swelling (inflammation) of injuries, especially of joints, which helps the zebra remain mobile long enough to find refuge. First the zebra runs away from the lion, then it lets the joint swell up and repair while it's safe.

In the wild, animals are under stress for only a short time, and any animal stressed for a prolonged period dies. So natural selection favored stress reactions as a drastic effort to deal with a short-term problem. What makes humans unique is that, with our highly social lives and keen minds, we are capable of experiencing stress for prolonged periods—months or even years. Some problems that we might worry about can last for years: Am I going to keep my job? Do people think I'm weird? In such cases, our large, sensitive brain causes us to have problems most other animals don't. Unfortunately, while our brain has evolved to make us capable of feeling stressed for long periods of time, the stress system still calls for changes that are only good for us in the short run. Those body reactions to stress, which evolved to benefit us in the face of short-term problems, become a problem when extended too long (Sapolsky, 2004). As Robert Sapolsky said, "For 99 percent of the beasts on this planet, stress is about three minutes of screaming in terror after which it's either over with or you're over with. …We turn [stress] on for 30-year mortgages." Humans suffering such long-term stress, lasting more than a month, are more likely to catch a cold (Cohen et al., 1998). People who are grieving the death of a relative, especially a spouse, also have a suppressed immune system for months or even years (Stein & Miller, 1993).

For students, stressful exam periods usually cause a decline in the number of immune cells and in levels of cytokines (Glaser et al., 1986). Importantly, a student's *perception* of the stress of the academic program is a predictor of the level of antibody in the blood: students who perceive the program as stressful show the lowest levels of antibodies. One experiment considered the effects of university examinations on wound healing in dental students (Marucha et al., 1998). Two small wounds were placed on the roof of the mouth of future dentists. The first wound was timed during summer vacation, and the second was made 3 days before the first major examination of the term. Not one student healed as rapidly during the exam period, when healing took 40% longer on average. One measure

■ **TABLE 13.3 The Stress Response and Consequences of Prolonged Stress**

Principal components of the stress response	Common negative consequences of prolonged stress
Suppression of immunity and of inflammatory response	Impaired disease resistance
Mobilization of energy at the cost of energy storage	Fatigue, muscle wasting, diabetes
Increased heart rate and blood pressure	Hypertension (high blood pressure)
Suppression of digestion	Ulcers
Suppression of growth	Psychogenic dwarfism
Suppression of reproduction	Loss of libido
Insensitivity to pain	Apathy
Enhanced sensory sensitivity, including altered cognition and sensory thresholds	Accelerated neural degeneration during aging

Source: Sapolsky, 1992.

of immunological response declined 68% during the exam period. So even something as transient, predictable, and relatively benign as examination stress can have significant consequences for wound healing. (Do you agree that examination periods are relatively benign?) This is a powerful example of how the stress system that helps us deal with short-term crises can wreak havoc with our bodies when it is prolonged. **Table 13.3** lists a variety of stress responses that are beneficial in the short term but are detrimental in the long term.

It's important to recognize that some people seem more prone to stress than others. In the 1970s, researchers identified two general behavior patterns—called type A and type B personalities—in the development of heart disease (Friedman & Rosenman, 1974). *Type A* behavior is characterized by excessive competitive drive, impatience, hostility, and accelerated speech and movements. In short, life is hectic and demanding for such individuals. In contrast, *type B* behavior patterns are more relaxed, with little evidence of aggressive drive or emphasis on getting things done fast. The type A and B terminology has entered our culture, but scientific support for this simple dichotomy has been spotty.

For example, some studies suggest that a tendency toward negative feelings, especially hostility, coupled with being socially inhibited, is more closely associated with heart disease than is the traditional type A personality (Kupper & Denollet, 2007). In Chapter 14 we'll see that one of the "big five" components of personality is neuroticism, the tendency to readily experience negative emotions such as anxiety or anger. Neuroticism is positively correlated with type A behavior (Bruck & Allen, 2003), so the greater susceptibility to heart disease found in earlier reports of type A people may reflect a greater neuroticism in these individuals. One strategy in the field of health psychology is to identify people who are especially prone to stress, and then intervene. Perhaps if we can get them to reduce the stress in their lives, they will enjoy better health.

What are some strategies for dealing with stress?

If being too brainy for our own good makes us humans prone to prolonged stress, can we harness our intelligence to reduce the impact of stress? This is the theme for the rest of this chapter: what can we do to reduce stress and improve our mental and physical health?

Relaxation Training Most versions of relaxation training involve attending to the moment and striving for deep relaxation of the entire body.

Although there are many different versions of it, **relaxation training** involves focusing your attention on something calming while becoming more aware of your body (McGuigan & Lehrer, 2007). The most common forms of relaxation training have two parts. The first part consists of going somewhere quiet to concentrate on a *soothing stimulus*, such as calming music or images, which can be either present or imagined. The second part is *progressive muscle relaxation*, when you deliberately tense the muscles in one part of your body and then strive to relax them as much as possible. You do this in first one part of the body and then another, with the goal of relaxing all the muscles in your body. Relaxation training, consisting of regular practice for 20–30 minutes per day, is often recommended for people suffering from anxiety disorders (discussed in detail in Chapter 16). For example, people suffering from posttraumatic stress disorder (PTSD), discussed in Box 13.2, may benefit from relaxation training (Vaughan et al., 1994; Committee on Treatment of Posttraumatic Stress Disorder, Institute of Medicine, 2008). It also seems likely that anyone who is feeling stressed now or might be in the future would benefit from such training. While some people employ *biofeedback*, the use of machines that measure physiological parameters such as heart rate or blood pressure, to monitor how well they are relaxing, such equipment is not necessary for relaxation training.

Many people find that **meditation**, the practice of mentally shutting out most of the outside world and cultivating an internal state of calmness and peace, helps reduce the experience of stress (see Chapter 7). There is a bewildering array of different types of meditation, associated with different cultures or religions, so it is difficult to generalize about the practice or to scientifically evaluate its effectiveness at reducing stress. Yet almost all meditation practices include relaxation, as seen in a reduction of heart rate, breathing rate, and blood pressure, during the meditation itself. There have been reports that some types of meditation can reduce the impact of stress, for example, by boosting the immune system (Davidson et al., 2003), but a review of the literature concluded that the evidence was mixed at best (Ospina et al., 2007). Furthermore, do the benefits of meditation come from the specific form of meditation itself or simply from the relaxation that typically accompanies meditation (Gillani & Smith, 2001)? In other words, meditation may simply provide a specific method of relaxation training. Interestingly, some people feel *more* anxious when they attempt meditation (Cramer et al., 2013), so it's not for everyone. If you are seeking to reduce stress, you might want to try meditation with an open mind. If it works, great, and if it doesn't, then try another form of relaxation training.

The University of Massachusetts Medical School has organized a program of therapy that was partially inspired by various meditation practices. **Mindfulness-based stress reduction** (**MBSR**) pairs relaxation with efforts to focus attention on the present moment, including current sensations, thoughts, and bodily states, in an open, nonjudgmental way. The idea is that much of the anxiety and depression experienced in response to stress comes from reliving past events or worrying about future problems. This same experience of "being in the present" is a goal of many schools of meditation. MBSR is focused on results and does not require practitioners to adopt any particular religious or spiritual views (Ludwig & Kabat-Zinn, 2008). Many studies indicate that MBSR indeed helps deal with stress, specifically by preventing relapses of anxiety disorders or depression (Hofmann et al., 2010). MBSR also reduces activity in the amygdala and other regions associated with negative emotions (Goldin & Gross, 2010). While the University of Massachusetts offers local MBSR training programs, considerable information about the programs, and on MBSR centers in other states and countries, is available on the Internet at www.umassmed.edu/cfm ("cfm" stands for Center for Mindfulness). The

relaxation training A technique that focuses attention on calming stimuli while relaxing the body, intended to reduce stress.

meditation The practice of focusing attention in order to relax the body and mind, and to reduce stress.

mindfulness-based stress reduction (MBSR) A technique that pairs relaxation with attention on the present moment.

TABLE 13.4 Mayo Clinic Top Seven Suggestions for Stress Relief

Recommendation	Examples
Get active	Virtually any form of exercise and physical activity can act as a stress reliever. Consider walking, jogging, gardening, house cleaning, biking, swimming, weightlifting, or anything else that gets you active.
Meditate	During meditation, you focus your attention and eliminate the stream of jumbled thoughts that may be crowding your mind and causing stress. Meditation instills a sense of calm, peace, and balance that benefits both your emotional well-being and your overall health.
Laugh	A good sense of humor can't cure all ailments, but it can help you feel better, even if you have to force a fake laugh through your grumpiness. So read some jokes, tell some jokes, watch a comedy, or hang out with your funny friends.
Connect	When you're stressed and irritable, your instinct may be to wrap yourself in a cocoon. Instead, reach out to family and friends and make social connections. Social contact is a good stress reliever because it can distract you and provide support.
Assert yourself	You might want to do it all, but you probably can't, at least not without paying a price. Learn to say no to some tasks or to delegate them.
Do yoga	With its series of postures and controlled-breathing exercises, yoga is a popular stress reliever. Yoga brings together physical and mental disciplines to achieve peacefulness of body and mind, helping you relax. Try yoga on your own or find a class.
Sleep	Stress often gives sleep the heave-ho. You have too much to do—and too much to think about—and your sleep suffers. If you have sleep troubles, make sure you have a quiet, relaxing bedtime routine, listen to soothing music, put clocks away, and stick to a consistent schedule.

Source: Ghoncheh & Smith, 2004.

Mayo Clinic also offers many suggestions for how to relieve stress, as summarized in **Table 13.4**.

Healthy living helps combat stress

We've already discussed how the psychological experience of stress can damage our physical health. This relationship between stress and health is reciprocal, meaning that attending to our physical health also helps counteract the physical damage caused by stress. Maintaining our physical health is also one of the best ways to reduce the mental toll of stress as well. First let's consider some of the things people may do in response to stress that are maladaptive—excessive drinking, smoking, and other drugs. These behaviors may alleviate the experience of stress in the short term, but they add to it in the long term. Then we'll look at the many findings indicating that taking care of our physical health helps us deal with the experience of stress, and helps us prevent one of the biggest psychological problems caused by stress—depression.

ALCOHOL One response to stress that humans have used since prehistoric times is drinking alcohol. Alcohol can help people relax, and studies consistently find that people who drink moderately—one or two drinks per day for men and one drink per day for women—have a reduced risk of many health problems, including heart disease, stroke, diabetes, and senile dementia (Di Castelnuovo et al., 2006). For women, there is a drawback to alcohol: even moderate drinking seems to increase the risk of breast cancer. Note that here "one drink" means a 5-ounce glass of wine, a 1.5-ounce shot of spirits, or a 12-ounce bottle of beer (each provides about 13 grams of alcohol).

alcoholism A disorder resulting from the excessive consumption of alcohol to the point that it interferes with a happy and productive life.

withdrawal Symptoms that occur when a drug is discontinued.

Not surprisingly, many of the health benefits of alcohol do not accrue if people drink to excess (more than two drinks in a bout), even if only occasionally. In fact, excessive drinking *increases* the risk of heart disease, stroke, and other problems. This brings us to another distinct risk of alcohol—**alcoholism**, a disorder caused when a person drinks so much alcohol that it interferes with leading a happy and productive life. It can be a slippery slope between moderate alcohol use that benefits our physical and mental health, and excessive alcohol use that can ravage our health and destroy our relationships with others. For this reason, most physicians and psychologists are reluctant to advise people to drink for their health, especially people with relatives who suffer from alcoholism. Only moderate drinking will benefit your health.

Finally, note that there are two cases where we are certain that even moderate alcohol use can be harmful. One is drinking by pregnant women. A mother's consumption of alcohol can have profoundly damaging effects on the fetus (including fetal alcohol syndrome, discussed in Chapter 5), and even moderate drinking in pregnancy seems to lower the IQ of the child later in life (Mattson et al., 1998). Put simply, there is no amount of alcohol consumption by a pregnant woman that is known to be safe for her fetus.

The other case is drinking and driving. Alcohol impairs our ability to drive safely. At least 16,000 Americans die each year—many of them college students—as a result of car accidents involving alcohol. Again, there is no level of alcohol consumption that is known *not* to affect driving ability.

DRUGS Some of the other things people do to cope with stress are clearly counterproductive. For example, people who are feeling stressed may resort to illegal drugs. In Chapter 7 we discussed the many dangers of illegal drugs, especially narcotics, such as heroin and cocaine, and amphetamines ("meth"). The main problem with this way of alleviating the experience of stress is that it only works for a short time, then leaves us worse off than we were before. To those dangers, add the danger of being arrested and imprisoned. Getting involved in the criminal justice system is not a good way to reduce the stress in your life!

SMOKING One of the most common responses to stress is known to be very harmful—smoking tobacco. In the short run, smoking a cigarette provides comfort by boosting mood and energy. But this way of dealing with stress is another example of a process that helps in the short run but makes the problem worse in the long run. Whatever comfort the cigarette provides now will be counterbalanced by additional stress in the future.

For one thing, the nicotine provided by cigarette smoking is remarkably addictive, meaning that once you're hooked, which can happen after just a few cigarettes (Brody et al., 2006), you will soon feel bad if you *don't* smoke. This is an example of **withdrawal**, when a person stops taking a drug and begins experiencing symptoms that are generally the opposite of the effects of the drug. In other words, the boost in energy and mood provided by the cigarette is followed by feelings of irritability, anxiety, and depression during withdrawal. Of course, a person addicted to cigarettes might simply keep on smoking to avoid withdrawal symptoms, and that's precisely what smokers do. This is one reason why cigarettes are among the most addictive drugs humankind has ever encountered—as addictive as heroin and cocaine. For people dealing with poverty and the stress that comes from not being able to make ends meet or take care of basic needs, cigarette addiction is especially counterproductive. The need to keep spending scarce funds on cigarettes simply adds to their stress.

"The Needle and the Damage Done"

But even smokers who can afford their addiction eventually suffer the long-term health consequences of smoking. In addition to causing shortness of breath, cigarette smoking increases the chances of almost every illness you can imagine: cancer of many kinds, heart disease, stroke, peptic ulcers, collapsed blood vessels (especially in the legs), erectile dysfunction in men, and reduced fertility in both sexes. Why are so many different health problems caused by smoking? Cigarette smoke contains an incredible mix of poisons, many of which haven't even been identified yet. Perhaps the most dramatic illustration of the terrible toxicity of cigarette smoke is its effect on facial skin. Comparing identical twins where only one twin smokes vividly illustrates how toxic cigarette smoke really is (Doshi et al., 2007). Once these health problems arise, the person who took up smoking to reduce stress becomes beset with even more stress.

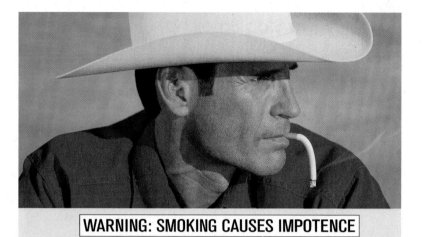

WARNING: SMOKING CAUSES IMPOTENCE

Cigarette Smoking Increases Your Stress in the Long Run Tobacco industry portrayals of the effects of cigarette smoking typically leave out the effect of erectile dysfunction in men, and of reduced fertility in both sexes.

I watched my mother slowly die of another consequence of smoking, and it makes a relatively rapid death from cancer look good by comparison. **Chronic obstructive pulmonary disorder** (**COPD**), which includes the condition called emphysema, results when the lungs are so damaged that respiration is impaired, and 85–90% of cases are due to smoking (Young et al., 2009). People with COPD have a hard time catching their breath, which is not so bad at first, but COPD is relentlessly progressive and there is no cure, or any treatment to reverse the damage. COPD is the fourth leading cause of death in the U.S., killing more people than breast cancer and diabetes combined (National Heart, Lung, and Blood Institute, 2010). It is a slow, painful death. You know how uncomfortable you feel when you're really short of breath from physical exertion? For COPD patients like my mother, that hunger for air never goes away, and they have to fight the panic of knowing it will only get worse.

When you tally up all the health consequences of cigarette smoking, perhaps it's not surprising that cigarette smoking is responsible for the death of millions of people. As one review pointed out, now that a billion humans smoke, hundreds of millions will be killed by the habit (Peto & Doll, 2006). Although smoking is a difficult addiction to beat, researchers have identified several measures that can help people stop smoking, as discussed in **Box 13.4**.

EXERCISE, DIET, AND SLEEP One common technique for dealing with stress—which millions of people use and, unlike smoking, really does help reduce stress and improve your health—is exercise. Surveys show that people who exercise regularly are less likely to suffer from depression (Harvey et al., 2010). Interpreting such correlations is difficult because people who, for other reasons, are resistant to depression may therefore be more open to exercising. But in studies where groups of adults were assigned to start an exercise regimen while others were given a control assignment, the people who exercised not only showed an improvement in memory, but also had a larger hippocampus, a brain region involved in memory (Erickson et al., 2011). The hippocampus has been implicated in depression, and one reason antidepressant drugs work is that they increase the production of new neurons in the hippocampus (Manev et al., 2001; Santarelli et al., 2003).

Perhaps the most effective form of exercise is whichever form you actually enjoy doing. Rather than making exercise one more thing you *have* to do, find a form of exercise that is something you *get* to do. Many people find yoga classes,

chronic obstructive pulmonary disorder (COPD) A progressive lung disease that impairs respiration due to lung damage, usually caused by smoking.

Psychology in Everyday Life

How to Stop Smoking

Tobacco use has brought premature death to more Americans than alcohol and all the illegal drugs combined. Cigarette smoking is a pernicious and highly addictive habit because it floods the blood supply with the stimulant nicotine (discussed in Chapter 7) at an incredibly rapid rate (see figure). Cigarette smoking is responsible for about 33% of all cancer deaths, including 90% of lung cancer deaths (Peto & Doll, 2006).

If you don't smoke, congratulate yourself. If you do smoke, you probably would like to quit. The fact that 76% of adult smokers *want* to quit proves how difficult it is to do, and some people never manage to give up cigarettes. Those who do quit often have to try more than once before they succeed. On the other hand, half of all adults who once smoked have managed to quit, so it can be done. In fact, the millions of adults who manage to quit smoking, added to the smokers who die, require the tobacco industry to generate "replacement smokers" to maintain profits. The tobacco industry's well-funded advertising campaigns to portray smoking as adventurous and cool are targeted at children, adolescents, and college students (Sepe et al., 2002). Health psychologists are particularly concerned about finding effective methods for people who want to stop smoking.

Some smokers try to reduce their cigarette smoking gradually, while others quit abruptly ("cold turkey"), and these strategies are about equally effective (Lindson et al., 2010). Nicotine replacement therapy (nicotine patches, gum, sprays, etc.) significantly improves the odds of quitting (Stead et al., 2008), in part by combating the withdrawal symptoms. Smokers who quit may become depressed, and indeed, antidepressants, such as bupropion, increase the odds of quitting (Hughes et al., 2007; Polosa & Benowitz, 2011). Counseling, either one-on-one or group therapy, is also effective (Stead & Lancaster, 2005), but exercise programs, acupuncture, cigarette substitutes, and hypnosis are not (Clinical Practice Guideline Treating Tobacco Use and Dependence, 2008; Barnes et al., 2010), despite the claims of practitioners offering those interventions. Whatever method a smoker uses, about half of those who manage to abstain for 6 months will never take up cigarettes again.

One effective aid to quit smoking has no pharmacological side effects: social support. Having family and friends cooperate—by doing things such as talking the smoker out of having a cigarette, expressing pleasure at the smoker's efforts, and predicting success—makes success in quitting more likely (Coppotelli & Orleans, 1985; Fiore et al., 2007). There's also strong evidence that one's social network can have a big impact on smoking (Park et al., 2004). Smokers are more likely than other people to socialize with other smokers, and the habit of smoking spreads through social ties, from friend to friend (ironically). Likewise, people are most likely to stop smoking if their friends and family stop too. *These effects are larger than any pharmacological intervention*. For example, if a spouse quits smoking, the other spouse also quits 67% of the time. Having a sibling, friend, or coworker quit also helps (Fratiglioni & Wang, 2008). It doesn't matter whether one's geographical neighbors quit, so these are not local effects of anti-smoking campaigns or laws. Rather, it's when friends or family members quit that smokers are most likely to stop. The closer the friend, the bigger effect he or she has. So if you want to stop smoking and you have friends or family who also want to quit, your best shot at shedding the habit is to try quitting together, and to offer each other encouragement and reinforcement.

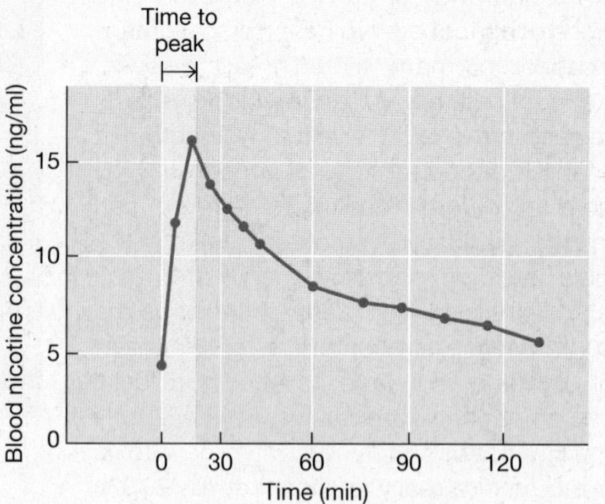

The Rush of Nicotine Cigarettes get nicotine into the blood at a remarkably fast rate, making cigarette smoking a highly addictive habit that is hard to quit (Bennett, 1983).

A scholarly resource for evaluating various programs to stop smoking is the Cochrane Library (www.cochrane.org/search/reviews/smoking). Authoritative tips to quit smoking can be found on the Centers for Disease Control and Prevention (CDC) "quit smoking" website (www.cdc.gov/tobacco/quit_smoking/index.htm) and the National Cancer Institute's "smokefree" website (www.smokefree.gov/), offering their START program: ***S***et a date, ***T***ell family and friends, ***A***nticipate and plan for challenges, ***R***emove all tobacco products and paraphernalia from home/car/work, and ***T***alk to a doctor about getting help.

which typically blend relaxation (Ghoncheh & Smith, 2004) and exercise, enjoyable and easy to maintain. Personally, I enjoy walking and loathe all other forms of exercise, so every day I take the time to walk a few miles.

It turns out that a healthy diet, which is good for your physical health and for avoiding obesity (as discussed in Chapter 12), is also good for your mental health. One study found that people who eat foods high in trans fats and saturated fats—the fats most common in industrially produced pastries and fast food—are more likely to suffer depression. The researchers started with more than 12,000 volunteers, none of whom had yet been diagnosed with depression. Those eating lots of fast food were 48% more likely to be diagnosed with depression over the next 6 years (Sánchez-Villegas et al., 2011). The more trans fats and saturated fats the people ate, the more likely they were to become depressed. Alternatively, those eating healthier fats, such as those found in fish, vegetable oil, and olive oil, were less likely to become depressed.

Likewise, sleep is good not only for your physical health, in part because it boosts the immune system (Besedovsky et al., 2012), but it's also good for your mental health. Several studies have found that young adults who do not get enough sleep are more susceptible to depression and suicide (Kahn-Greene et al., 2007; Wong et al., 2010).

By now you surely have noticed the theme in these studies—what's good for your physical health is good for your mental health. As noted earlier, that's a good summary of what health psychology has found. If you want a happy, healthy mental life, make a point of doing those things that will promote your physical health. Finally, there's excellent evidence that having social support also helps us withstand stress, as we will discuss next.

Friends and family provide us with a buffer from the cruel, cruel world

Researchers have consistently found that people who lack **social support**, in the form of friends or family, are more likely to suffer mental and physical illness. For example, people with low social support are not only more likely to suffer from depression and anxiety, but they are also more likely to suffer from cardiovascular disease and are more likely to die in the next few years (Uchino & Birmingham, 2010). As another example, people—especially men—who go through separation or divorce and then remain separated or divorced through subsequent decades are at a much increased risk of dying from heart disease than are people in other at-risk groups (Sbarra & Nietert, 2009). Such data gave rise to the **stress buffering hypothesis** that social support serves as a buffer between a person and the bumps in life, helping the person weather stressful events without developing physical or mental illness (Cohen & Wills, 1985).

The value of social support has also been demonstrated in the laboratory. Here, subjects given a demanding task that normally elevates cardiovascular measures, such as heart rate, show less of a response to the stress if a friend or family member is present. This reduced stress response in the presence of a friend may account for the greater ability of people with social support to be resilient and avoid mental and physical illness in response to stress.

Pets can also reduce our experience of stress. Researchers find that pet owners, on average, have significantly lower heart rate and blood pressure levels than non–pet owners, both at rest and when exposed to stress in the laboratory. What's more, for pet owners, having their pet physically present significantly lowers those measures in reaction to stress (Allen et al., 2002). In fact, having their pet with them lowers the stress response of pet owners better than having their spouse or friend there! It appears that having an animal friend can offer some of the same psychological benefits as family and human friends.

social support Friends and family that provide a network of resources.

stress buffering hypothesis The hypothesis that social support provides a buffer between a person and stressful events.

Figure 13.25 Life Is a Balancing Act

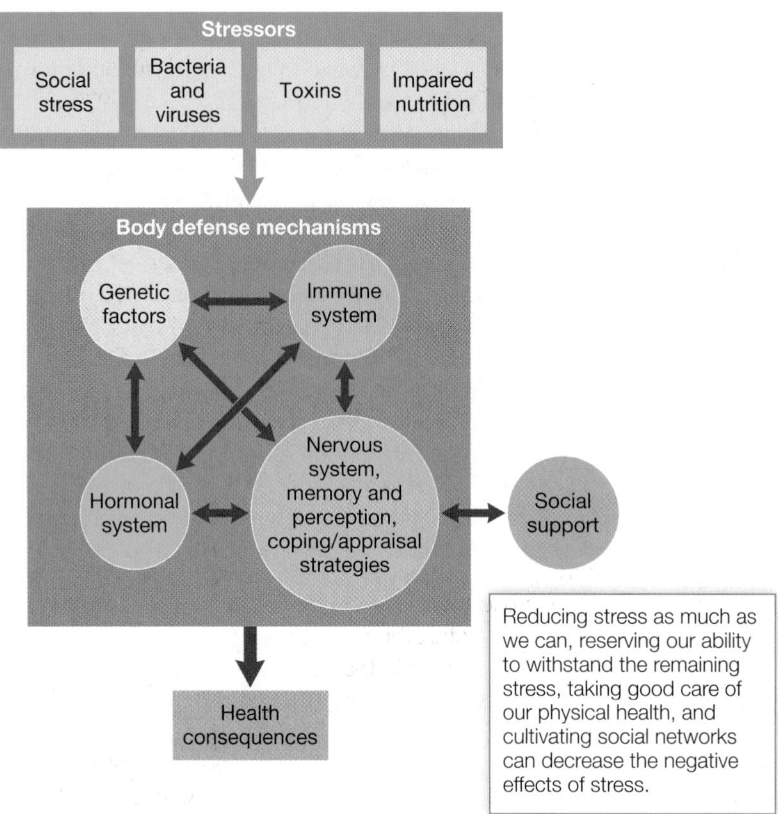

Our present-day understanding of the effects of stress on the interacting systems in the body, including our genes, brain, hormone system, and immune system, is summarized in **Figure 13.25**. While we can't control which genes we inherit, and may have little influence on some sources of stress that arrive at our door, there are many things we can do to reduce stress in our lives.

If you have any doubts about the rewards of having friendly relations (and friendly relatives), consider the Forest Troop of baboons we met at the start of this chapter. Recall that a group of especially aggressive males had made troop life particularly stressful. Perhaps it was fortunate that only these males—the meanest and most aggressive of the troop—got access to the food at the hunting lodge's dump site. It was only these males that ate the beef tainted with tuberculosis. They died horrible, agonizing deaths, but about half the males and most of the females and youngsters survived. The loss of the most aggressive males had a remarkable effect on the social life of the Forest Troop. The surviving males, which had always been a little easier to get along with than the more aggressive males, never ramped up their aggression to the levels that had been seen before in the troop. They occasionally tussled with one another, but hostilities usually ended before another baboon got hurt, and the males rarely took out their aggression on the innocent bystanders, the females and young. Now, all of the baboons spent much more time grooming each other, and otherwise spending "quality time" in peaceful pursuits.

Peaceful Baboons

As with humans, having friends appears to be calming and good for a baboon's health. Not surprisingly, members of the Forest Troop showed fewer physiological signs of stress after the aggressive males died. Even 20 years later, the Forest Troop remains a relatively peaceful place for a baboon. When new young males enter the Forest Troop, they might try the aggressive high jinks common to neighboring troops for a while, but the resident males don't engage. Within a month or so, the new males calm down and fit right into the more peaceful atmosphere of the Forest Troop.

Perhaps the most important lesson these animals have for us is that most of the stress we experience is avoidable. If we all treat each other better, everyone can benefit. These animals also make it clear that aggression, fighting, and stress are not inevitable consequences of biology. If baboons can, in a short time, convert from a fractious, stressed-out society to a more peaceful, nurturing society, and can maintain that new social order for generations, shouldn't we be able to follow suit?

The Cutting Edge

Fearless Parasites Manipulate Their Hosts

It's a good idea to be afraid in certain situations, such as when a predator is around. In an amazing story of adaptation, some parasites have evolved a way to reproduce by blocking fear in a mammal. *Toxoplasma gondii* is a single-celled microscopic organism that can infect many mammals and birds. But it can sexually reproduce only in the gut of cats, shedding millions of offspring in a cat's feces. How does the parasite get to the next cat to reproduce again? After all, cats don't normally eat the feces of other cats. But other animals, including mice, will eat cat feces. Although *Toxoplasma gondii* cannot sexually reproduce inside the mouse, it can still multiply, waiting for the next cat to eat the mouse and start the cycle over again.

The remarkable aspect of this story is that the parasite speeds up the cycle by infecting neurons in the mouse brain, which reduces the mouse's fear of cats. Mice that avoided the smell of cat urine *before* infection become unfazed by the odor, an effect that seems to be permanent (Ingram et al., 2013). By losing their fear of cats, the mice are much more likely to be eaten, and thereby to introduce *Toxoplasma* to another cat gut (**Figure 13.26**).

People who are around cat feces, as when cleaning a litter box, can become infected by the parasite and come down with a disease called toxoplasmosis, which usually causes achy, flu-like symptoms that may last for a month or more. In people with a compromised immune system, the effects can be serious, and there is particular concern about infection in pregnant women. Estimates are that as many as one-third of people worldwide have been infected with *Toxoplasma* at some point. That makes it sound like the disease can't be too serious. But there is growing concern that *Toxoplasma* may have previously unrecognized effects on human behavior. For example, people with schizophrenia are much more likely to have been infected with the parasite than the general population. This finding raises the possibility that toxoplasmosis may increase the risk of schizophrenia (Flegr, 2013). What's more, people who have been infected with *Toxoplasma* are more likely to be in traffic accidents (Flegr et al., 2009), which suggests that perhaps they were not as cautious as they should have been while driving. It's chilling to think that this parasite, which evolved a way to reduce fear in mice in order to spread, may also reduce fear in people, with sometimes fatal results. Will future research reveal other environmental factors that affect our emotions without our ever being aware of it?

Figure 13.26 Sometimes It's Not a Good Idea to Be Open to New Relationships (Courtesy of Wendy Marie Ingram and Adrienne Greene.)

13.2 SUMMARY

- *Stress* includes events and stimuli that threaten us (*stressors*), the cognitive system that assesses these events (*stress evaluation*), and the physiological response of the body to that assessment (*stress response*).
- There are two stages of normal stress response: the *alarm reaction*, when physiological systems activate the sympathetic nervous system and hormones, including *cortisol* from the *adrenal glands*, to prepare for action; followed by the *adaptation stage*, when everything returns to normal.
- Repeated or prolonged alarm reactions can lead to the *exhaustion stage*, when the stress responses that were beneficial in the short term become harmful in the long term.
- There are individual differences in how quickly a person recovers from stress. Positive attention from parents in childhood seems to make people more resilient in adulthood. In contrast, very stressful childhood events, including abusive parents, greatly increase the risk of suicide in adulthood.
- Animal experiments indicate that having control over stressors and being able to predict the arrival of stressors result in a less severe stress response. The same principles seem to apply to humans, as people with the most control over their workplace show the least evidence of stress and stress-related illness.
- *Health psychology* reveals that psychological stress can hurt the body and that physical illness can affect the mind.
- The brain monitors the immune system by detecting *cytokines*, proteins produced by *white blood cells*, the immune cells that attack invaders. Cortisol released during stress suppresses immune responses. These aspects of the stress response, which are beneficial in the short term, are harmful when prolonged.
- Posttraumatic stress disorder (PTSD) is especially harmful because it maintains the stress response long after the traumatic event.
- *Relaxation training*, such as *meditation* or *mindfulness-based stress reduction* (*MBSR*), focuses attention on calming stimuli while relaxing the body, which can help reduce stress.
- Healthy living practices, such as exercising, getting adequate sleep, and eating a healthy diet, improve mental as well as physical health.
- There is evidence that moderate intake of alcohol can improve physical and mental health, but it comes at the risk of *alcoholism*.
- Smoking, which may reduce the experience of stress in the short term, is highly addictive and has such a devastating effect on physical health that it increases stress in the long term.
- One of the most effective ways to minimize the impact of stress is to have a network of close friends and family. The *stress buffering hypothesis* says that *social support* helps people avoid the ill effects of stress.

REVIEW QUESTIONS

1. What are typical responses to stress, and how is it that those responses, which are beneficial in the short run, can be harmful in the long run?
2. How did our understanding of stress immunization in animals change, and what does our current understanding suggest concerning how children may grow up to be resilient adults?
3. How was the design of the executive monkey experiment flawed? How did experiments with rats indicate that control and predictability reduce the stress of unpleasant events?
4. What is health psychology, and what are some examples of how physical health affects mental health and vice versa?

Food for Thought

How many of the stressors listed on the College Undergraduate Stress Scale (CUSS) in Table 13.2 apply to you? How are you doing coping with these stresses?

Emotions, Stress and Health

The Stresses and Strains of Baboon Life

You might think the life of a baboon on the Serengeti plains of Africa would be sheer bliss. Baboons are highly social animals, meaning there are so many vigilant eyes that predators almost never manage to sneak up close, and if one does, it may regret it when an entire troop of adult baboons fights back. Food is relatively plentiful, so the baboons only need to work about 3 hours a day to get the calories they need. And yet, these baboons lead highly stressful lives. Why? Because as American researcher Robert Sapolsky (2008) puts it, if you only spend 3 hours a day working, then "you've got nine hours of free time every day to devote to making somebody else just *miserable*."

When Sapolsky first began studying a group of baboons that he named the Forest Troop, the animals' lives were dominated by the hyperaggressive young baboons. The behavior of these aggressive males required all the baboons in the troop to be constantly vigilant, not for lions or food but for other baboons.

Physiological examination of the baboons confirmed what behavioral observations suggested: the entire troop was *stressed out*. Their blood had high levels of hormones that are released from the adrenal glands during times of stress. The blood samples also revealed that these baboons had fewer immune system cells with which to produce antibodies to ward off illness (Sapolsky, 2002).

That lowered immunity may have played a role in the disaster that shattered the troop after a hunting lodge on the edge of their territory began dumping leftover food in the open. Of course, only the meanest, most aggressive males were getting food

Think Like a Psychologist:

Principles in Action

Whenever we encounter any interesting behavior we should consider the four principles. Here are some ways that the four principles relate to our opening story about baboon life.

MACHINE

The mind is a product of a physical machine, the brain.

The constant activation of a stress response in the baboons meant the release of high levels of stress hormones from the adrenal glands, which act on the brain and, among other things, made the animals cautious and over-reactive.

UNCONSCIOUS

We are consciously aware of only a small part of our mental activity.

Presumably baboons are like us and have no conscious control over the autonomic nervous system, so it is not easy to reduce the sympathetic nervous system's activation of the body and brain.

SOCIAL

We constantly modify our behavior, beliefs, and attitudes according to what we perceive about the people around us.

Virtually all the stress these animals experience is from their social interactions. Before the accident that killed the most aggressive males, the constant social tension took a toll on them all.

EXPERIENCE

Our experiences physically alter the structure and function of the brain.

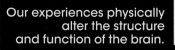

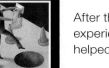

After the death of the most aggressive males, perhaps it was experiencing the relief of no longer living in constant stress that helped the animals get along.

KEY TERMS

adaptation stage, 573
adrenal gland, 574
alarm reaction, 573
alcoholism, 586
amygdala, 564
antibodies, 581
autonomic nervous system, 550
Cannon–Bard theory, 552
catharsis, 559
chronic obstructive pulmonary disorder (COPD), 587
cingulate cortex, 568
cortisol, 574
cultural display rules, 558
cytokines, 581
emotional syndrome, 569
emotion, 550
exhaustion stage, 573
facial feedback hypothesis, 559
general adaptation syndrome, 573
health psychology, 579
insula, 568
James–Lange theory, 552
meditation, 584
mindfulness-based stress reduction (MBSR), 584
orbitofrontal cortex, 568
parasympathetic nervous system, 551
polygraph, 573
posttraumatic stress disorder (PTSD), 567
psychoneuroimmunology, 580
relaxation training, 584
social support, 589
stress buffering hypothesis, 589
stress evaluation, 571
stress immunization, 575
stressors, 571
stress response, 571
stress, 571
sympathetic nervous system, 551
two-factor theory of emotion, 554
white blood cells, 581
withdrawal, 586

QUIZ YOURSELF

1. Which theory of emotion attributes the intensity of an emotion to the physiological arousal and the type of emotion to the cognitive interpretation?
   a. Two-factor theory
   b. Cannon–Bard theory
   c. James–Lange theory
   d. Cultural adaptation theory
2. Which of the following pairs of emotions is not part of the popular eight basic emotions classification system?
   a. Affection, disgust
   b. Anxiety, relaxation
   c. Fear, anger
   d. Happiness, sadness
3. What tool can be used to give a numerical rating to each of the stressful life events a person has experienced in the past year?
   a. Therapeutic index
   b. Neuroticism scale
   c. Hamilton Rating Scale for Depression
   d. Social Readjustment Rating Scale
4. According to the stress buffering hypothesis, which of the following is most important to help a person through stressful events without developing physical or mental illness?
   a. Wealth
   b. An engaging career
   c. Social support
   d. Periodic vacations
5. Which of the following is *not* monitored by a polygraph (lie detector)?
   a. Amygdala activation
   b. Respiration
   c. Heart rate
   d. Blood pressure
6. A subjective mental state that is usually accompanied by distinctive behaviors as well as involuntary physiological arousal is ________.
7. The amygdala is part of the specialized brain circuit for the emotion of ________.
8. Rat pups that had a little stress early in life seemed more resilient to later stress. This effect is termed ________.
9. Someone with ________ behavior patterns will typically be excessively competitive, impatient, hostile, and speak and move rapidly.
10. Lynette is trying to quit smoking. She is suddenly irritable, anxious, and depressed. These are symptoms of ________.

1. a; 2. b; 3. d; 4. c; 5. a; 6. emotion; 7. fear; 8. stress immunization; 9. type A; 10. withdrawal

U
SMITH
U
15
cutler

Personality

An Explosive Personality

Phineas Gage was a sober, efficient, capable young man of 25, respected by the workmen he supervised as they blasted rock to clear a path for a new railroad in Vermont in 1848. But something went wrong while Phineas was using an iron tamping rod to pack explosives at the bottom of a hole drilled into solid rock. The tamping rod—custom-made for him by a local blacksmith—was a cylinder an inch-and-a-fourth in diameter, about three-and-a-half feet long, flat at the bottom to tamp the charge, tapering to a point at the top. It resembled a javelin.

The iron rod must have struck a spark from the surrounding rock, because the charge went off unexpectedly, flinging the rod straight at Phineas's head. The rod pierced his left cheek, passed behind his left eye and out the top of his skull, landing some 60 feet away. From the force of the rod's path, Phineas was thrown onto his back, his limbs convulsing. Yet in a minute or two he spoke. With help from his men, he walked to a wagon, where he sat for the ride to town. There Phineas walked up a flight of stairs, unaided, to a doctor's office to have his wounds cleaned and bandaged. No one expected him to live; an undertaker made a coffin for him (Macmillan, 2000a).

Phineas survived the accident, but he worked at a series of menial jobs for another 12 years, one indication that he was a changed man (Harlow, 1868). After the accident he was moody, stubborn, boastful, prone to cursing, and "impatient of restraint or advice" (Macmillan, 2008, p. 829). Strangely enough, the explosion that forced an iron rod through his brain had left him with an explosive personality. Despite the miracle of his physical recovery, "his mind was radically changed, so decidedly that his friends and acquaintances said that he was 'no longer Gage'" (Macmillan, 2008, p. 829).

What happened to change Phineas Gage's personality?

Chapter Preview

personality The set of characteristics individuals possess that influence their thinking and behavior.

In this chapter we'll explore the concept of **personality**, the set of characteristics an individual possesses that influence his or her thinking and behavior. The term is derived from the Latin word for "mask," as in the masks that actors once wore to convey, to *personify*, a particular character. Similarly, a *persona* is a social role or character portrayed by an actor in a play. Even in real life, people may display more than one persona, such as the man who is an open, warm, caring father at home and a calculating, ruthless competitor in the office.

Given the observation that people behave very differently in various settings, you might wonder about the very concept of personality. Do you believe that a personality should be predictable? Can we count on someone with a given personality to behave more or less the same in many different situations? Can we predict the behavior of different people by their personalities? The overarching question is: How much of our behavior is due to our internal disposition, our *personality*, rather than the *situation* we're in?

We humans have struggled for centuries to understand the behaviors of other people. We have relied heavily on the idea that different people have different personalities that cause them to behave differently. So we'll begin by reviewing the history of ideas about personality, trying to identify concepts that have withstood the tests of time and science.

The psychoanalyst Sigmund Freud made an enormous impact on our culture's ideas about personality. But have his ideas stood the test of time? In Section 14.1, we'll introduce Freud's ideas and explain why most of them are no longer taken seriously. Section 14.2 introduces the much more empirical approach taken in personality studies today. You will learn about research that suggests there are a limited number of *traits,* or characteristics, making up each personality, including a group of traits known as the "big five" (no, this term does not refer to a tiny college football conference). In the third section we'll see that genes are an important influence, but not the only influence, on those traits. We'll conclude by discussing how culture and society contribute to our personality. While we focus on the degree to which personality influences behavior in this chapter, we'll consider how much the situation (the *social environment*) influences behavior in Chapter 15.

14.1 The Quest for Personality

Things to Learn

- Early ideas of personality types
- Freudian ego defense mechanisms
- Freudian psychosexual development model
- Unreliable projective tests
- Humanistic psychology and Rogerian therapy

In a story written over 4,000 years ago, the arrogant, fame-seeking hero *Gilgamesh* has a series of adventures with a comrade, Enkidu, who is energetic but without ambition. In a prelude to "bromance" movies still popular today, the dissimilar attitudes of the two men complement each other and help them get out of several scrapes with monsters. The story is a tribute to humans' long-held belief in the value of personality. Attempts to understand and catalog types of people have been made throughout history. While some of them, such as astrology, have been soundly discredited, others seem to have detected at least a kernel of truth about the different types of people we may encounter.

There is a long history of ideas about personality

Over 2,000 years ago the Greek physician Galen organized old ideas about the human body containing four fundamentally different types of fluids, or *humors.* Galen believed that an even balance of the four humors would make a person healthy and happy and that an imbalance would cause disease and affect a person's mood (**Figure 14.1**). These ideas were widely revered for many centuries, and provided the English language with several words, now obsolete, describing different personalities resulting from too much humor of one sort or another. Someone with an overabundance of *choler* (yellow bile) is energetic but dominating (like Gilgamesh), while a person with too much *sanguine* (blood) is outgoing but overly optimistic (like Gilgamesh's sidekick Enkidu). A *melancholic* (having an excess of black bile) person is a deep thinker who may be prone to depression, while a *phlegmatic* (having an excess of mucus) person is slow to anger and may be prone to shyness. Even today, a person who likes a good joke is said to have a sense of humor, and a tendency to brooding and sadness may be termed "melancholy."

Figure 14.1 Galen's Four Humors In ancient times, the human body was thought to possess four different fluids, or humors. A well-rounded person had the four humors in balance. Some people were thought to have an excess of one humor or another, giving them a particular personality. These medieval illustrations depict people who are, from upper left clockwise, either overly sluggish, energetic, depressed, or angry, depending on which humor was in excess.

While the notion that personality is influenced by four different bodily fluids was long ago discredited, there is no denying that some people are more inclined than others to sadness, while some people are more outgoing than others. Galen's observations about the various types of personalities came from his keen observation of people, even if his explanation for the causes of different personality types has not fared well.

Most of the personality theories that followed Galen incorporated his idea that there are a limited number of different **personality types**, and that particular combinations of behavioral characteristics tend to occur together. Personalities were commonly stereotyped. For example, people who tended toward deep thinking, a broody outlook, a tendency to depression, and an interest in poetry were said to have a "melancholic" personality type (or in today's stereotype, an "artistic type"). Theories on personality arising after Galen's differ primarily in the exact number of personality types proposed and the explanations for how a person came to have one type or another.

Today's psychologists tend not to think there are just a few personality types. Today's view is that while a small number of different personality *traits* can be defined, varying degrees of those traits can be combined in an almost infinite number of ways. In other words, today's psychologists tend to be skeptical of the notion that all personalities can be classified into just 4, 5, or even 16 different "types." We'll describe personality traits more thoroughly later in the chapter, but for now, keep in mind that there is a difference between personality *types* and personality *traits* as we review the older theories that embraced the notion that there are just a few personality types.

Astrology defines a limited number of personality types based on the idea that a person's birth at a particular time of the year endows them with one of 12 personalities that develop under the influence of the position of stars in the sky (the root of the word is *astro*, Latin for "star"). Not only is the position of the stars supposed to affect a person's personality at birth, but it supposedly continues to influence their mood and environment thereafter. Although astrology is widely regarded as a pseudoscience today (not to be confused with *astronomy*, the scientific study of the universe), millions of people regularly consult their horoscopes to get a prediction of what will happen to them each day. Despite this popularity, scientific tests have conclusively demonstrated that astrology does not work, either to predict a person's personality or what will happen to them this afternoon (**Box 14.1**). Many other theories of personality have fared no better but we have nonetheless learned from them.

personality types The particular combinations of behavioral characteristics that tend to occur together.

astrology A theory that a person's birth at a particular time of the year endows them with one of twelve personalities.

Skeptic at Large

BOX 14.1

Your Horoscope Today Says...

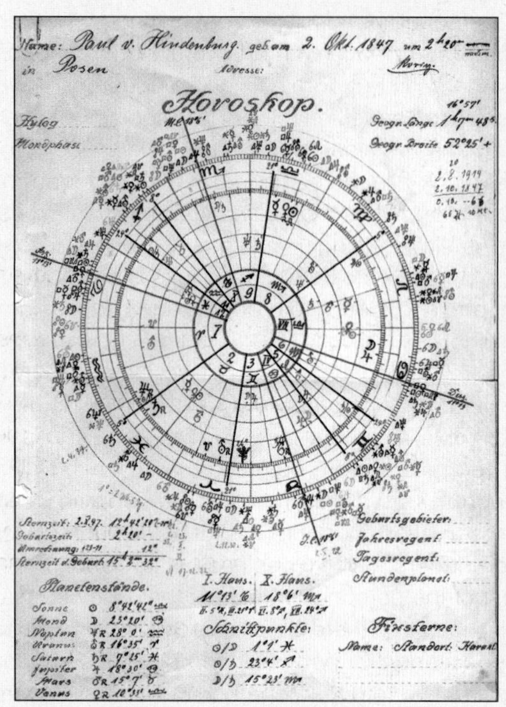

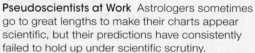

Pseudoscientists at Work Astrologers sometimes go to great lengths to make their charts appear scientific, but their predictions have consistently failed to hold up under scientific scrutiny.

Skeptics of astrology can readily offer many objections to horoscopes—predictions based on a person's birthday about personality traits and events that supposedly will happen on a certain day. For one, since there are only 12 signs of the zodiac, do we really think the same thing is going to happen to one-twelfth of the world's population today? And, if the planets affect us, how could astrology have been accurate before anyone knew about Uranus and Neptune? Why do horoscopes from different astrologers make different predictions? Whatever doubt these questions might raise, an open-minded person might still be interested in testing the claims of astrology, as has been done repeatedly. Unfortunately for astrologers, those various tests are uniformly negative—predictions about what will happen today are just as accurate for people who were not born under that sign as for people who were. Likewise, there is no correlation between astrologers' descriptions of the personality associated with each sign and someone's actual personality.

For example, astrologers claim that people with certain signs are incompatible with one another as marriage partners. Yet marriage records of thousands of couples in Michigan found no preponderance of one pairing of signs over another. Neither was there any correlation of signs in couples going through divorce (Silverman, 1971). People's self-descriptions are no more likely to fit their actual astrological sign description than would be expected by chance alone (Silverman & Whitmer, 1974). One famous study gave 28 "professional" astrologers the day and time of birth for 83 people so the astrologers could draw up more extensive horoscopes than just "Libra" and the like, keeping track of such factors as the position of the moon and so on when the participant was born (see

Freud focused on the unconscious

psychoanalysis The process, developed by Freud, of making a detailed analysis of a client's mind through open-ended discussions about thoughts and feelings.

While there is no denying the lasting impact that Sigmund Freud (1856–1939) has had on our culture, we'll see that his ideas have had, in the long run, little impact on psychology as a science. A brilliant Austrian physician, Freud firmly believed that all human behavior was rooted in the structure and function of the brain, but his training in neurology convinced him that too little was known about brain function to offer any insight into our day-to-day behavior. So instead he had long talks with his patients who had psychological problems, such as irrational fears (phobias) and anxiety attacks, trying to understand why they behaved in particular ways. Freud called this process **psychoanalysis**, the detailed analysis of a client's mind through open-ended discussions about his thoughts and feelings. The therapeutic approach of long, open-ended discussions based on the ideas of Freud or his followers is practiced by very few psychiatrists or psychologists today.

figure). Yet participants were no more likely to pick out their own chart than would be expected by chance alone, and the astrologers could not match the results of people's personality tests to the charts (Carlson, 1985).

Since scientific tests repeatedly show that the signs of the zodiac do not accurately describe a person's personality, why do so many people who read their horoscopes feel that they are accurate? Several factors are at work here. First, astrologers are careful to write flattering portraits of personality for every sign. We may feel the analysis fits us because it is flattering. One researcher sent out free horoscopes to thousands of people, 94% of whom replied that the description was accurate and insightful (Gauquelin, 1979). The problem is that they all got the same horoscope!

Second, there is the matter of **confirmation bias**, a tendency to remember events that fit our preconceptions and to dismiss or forget events that do not (see Section 10.3). Confirmation bias seems to be at work in the belief, quite common among emergency room doctors and nurses, that there are more accidents and violence around the time of the full moon. That idea has been repeatedly disproved. Yet people working at hospitals tend to recall especially bizarre or disturbing events that happen around the full moon, but don't recall those periods of the full moon when the ER is quiet (Kelly et al., 1996). With astrology, confirmation bias leads us to remember predictions that seem to unfold, and to downplay or forget predictions that fail.

A particular version of the confirmation bias that applies to personality is sometimes called **subjective validation**, our tendency to consider any description of our personality as correct because we read into vague descriptions a more specific, personal meaning. One researcher gave a personality test to students and, ignoring their answers completely, provided them all with the same "personality report," modified from a newspaper astrology column (Forer, 1949). When asked, the students rated the report as highly accurate! For example, the description included the sentence "At times you are extroverted, affable, sociable, while at other times you are introverted, wary, reserved," which would fit anyone. As we read this vague description, we may remember specific instances when we were indeed sociable, and specific instances when we were indeed reserved. This is sometimes called the *Forer effect*, after the researcher Bertram Forer. We read into each vague description specific details that fit our self-image (Dickson & Kelly, 1985). Of course, subjective validation is not just a concern when evaluating astrological descriptions of personality. Later, when we talk about how scientists evaluate personality tests, we will have to consider steps they must take to avoid being fooled by subjective validation.

confirmation bias A tendency to remember events that fit our preconceptions and to dismiss or forget events that do not.

subjective validation Also called the *Forer effect*. The tendency to pick out a specific, accurate meaning from an open-ended, vague personality description.

One lasting contribution to modern psychology was Freud's emphasis on the **unconscious**, the part of the mind that functions outside our conscious awareness. Freud was certainly not the first person to discuss or identify the unconscious, so we can't credit him with that. But he was the first to bring wide attention to the concept of unconscious processes and their effect on behavior. In everyday speech you may hear people refer to unconscious processes as *subconscious*, but Freud rejected this term (Freud, 1926/1990), and most psychologists do not use it. Freud did draw a distinction between the *conscious* mind, whatever thoughts we are presently aware of, and the *preconscious*, the information that we can call to mind when we want, such as memories of past events. The term *preconscious* is not widely used today but relates to what we call *long-term memory* (see Section 9.1), the information we can recall when needed. Freud believed that the vast majority of mental processes are unconscious. He likened the unconscious mind to the underwater

unconscious The part of the mind that functions outside our awareness.

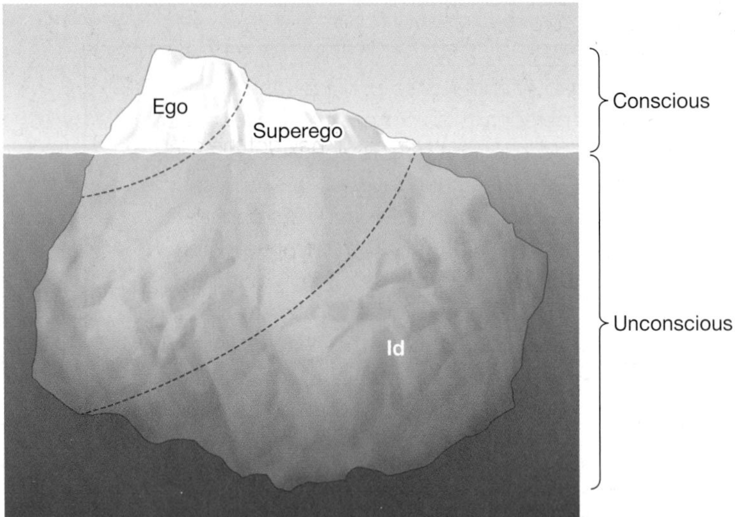

Figure 14.2 The Tip of the Iceberg Just as most of the body of an iceberg is submerged and out of sight, much of what goes on in our mind is not consciously accessible to us. This idea, underlying Sigmund Freud's ideas about psychological processes, has been well supported by scientific research. However, Freud's specific theories are untestable because they cannot be disproven (see Box 2.1).

bulk of an iceberg, and our conscious mind to the mere tip of the iceberg that can be seen (**Figure 14.2**).

Freud's primary distinction between conscious and unconscious processes, and the idea that much of our mental processes are unconscious, has been amply confirmed. Most of Freud's other ideas about the human mind, however, have not withstood scientific scrutiny, although they have left their mark on our culture. You've undoubtedly encountered—and perhaps have used—terms that Freud introduced, possibly without knowing exactly what he meant by them. Freud believed that babies come into the world following only the *pleasure principle*—seek pleasure and avoid pain. Freud named the part of the mind following the pleasure principle the **id**. As the baby grows, *reality* sets in; the child learns that it's not always possible to get what you want and avoid what you don't want. Freud suggested that a new part of the mind develops, called the **ego**—that tries to fulfill the goals of the id within the limits of reality. Noting that parents, teachers, and peers increasingly tell the child how she is *supposed* to behave in different situations, Freud imagined a part of the mind, which he called the **superego**, incorporating prescribed rules of behavior. As Freud saw it, throughout life the ego is shaped by the tension between the demands of the id to follow the pleasure principle, and the demands of the superego to do what society expects.

Freud's model of the superego inhibiting the id was shaped by the neurology of his day, which relied heavily on the case of Phineas Gage (Macmillan, 2000a,b), whom we met at the start of the chapter. Gage's accident caused him to lose many inhibitions—he tended to behave impulsively, selfishly. By the end of the 1800s, as Freud was receiving his neurology training, the field believed that rational behavior required inhibition of all but one particular thought or behavior. From that perspective, the damage to Gage's brain had affected his ability to inhibit his impulses (Macmillan, 2004). Freud incorporated the idea of inhibition into his theory in suggesting that one part of the mind, the superego, inhibits another part of the mind, the id. (Freud's writings cite many of the books that discussed Gage's case, so he must have been aware of it, but Freud never wrote directly about Gage.) One of the most central of Freud's beliefs was that the superego inhibits the id by forcing socially unacceptable desires beneath consciousness. He posited that by the time we are grown, the demands of the id are entirely unconscious and we are consciously aware of only our ego and superego.

Freud described several different ways the ego and superego could push unacceptable, id-driven desires out of consciousness. He used the term **defense mechanisms** to describe unconscious psychological processes that protect the ego from realizing and acting on the ugly, socially unacceptable urges of the id (**Table 14.1**). **Rationalization**—making excuses for why we behaved badly or want to behave badly—is an example of a defense mechanism. Sometimes when we rationalize our bad behavior ("I shouldn't have run that red light, but I'm really in a hurry"), we might be consciously aware of the rationalization, but might be unconscious of how flimsy the excuse really is.

id Freud's term for the part of the mind following the pleasure principle.

ego Freud's term for the part of the mind that tries to fulfill the goals of the id within the limits of reality.

superego Freud's term for the part of the mind that incorporates the rules of behavior that a person learns and accepts from other people.

defense mechanisms Unconscious psychological processes that protect the ego from realizing and acting upon socially unacceptable urges of the id.

rationalization The defense mechanism of making intellectual excuses for unacceptable behavior.

■ TABLE 14.1 A Sampling of Freudian Defense Mechanisms

Defense mechanism	Description	Example
Rationalization	Making intellectual excuses for unacceptable behavior	"Everyone cheats if they get the chance."
Repression	Suppression of socially unacceptable desires	Denying interest in money or popularity
Projection	Thinking others have your unacceptable desires	Perceiving a woman rival as promiscuous
Displacement	Redirecting desires from an unacceptable object to an acceptable one	A husband doting on his wife while desiring another woman
Sublimation	Redirecting energy from an unacceptable behavior to an acceptable one	Working out your aggressive feelings on the soccer field
Reaction formation	Acting exactly the opposite of your (unacceptable) desires	Avoiding any contact with the opposite sex
Regression	Reverting to immature behavior that would have been appropriate at a younger age	Having a temper tantrum
Denial	Refusing to see one's own weaknesses	"I never get angry!"

In Freud's thinking, ego defense mechanisms normally help us feel good about ourselves and so promote a healthy mental state. Freud believed, however, that sometimes defense mechanisms go too far, resulting in neurosis. He characterized a **neurosis** (plural *neuroses*) as a mental disorder characterized by anxiety or avoidance that interferes with everyday functioning (but is not accompanied by delusions or hallucinations). Freud might apply the term neurosis to, for example, a boy with an irrational fear of horses, or a woman afraid of having sexual relations with her husband, or a man obsessed with rats. We'll see in Chapter 16 that the term neurosis is no longer used by most psychologists or psychiatrists, who instead use more specific terms for the various conditions that used to be lumped under that term.

A specific Freudian defense mechanism that has been repeatedly challenged is that of repressed memories. Freud believed that memories of childhood sexual abuse were sometimes repressed, thereby protecting the ego from painful information, so that the person sincerely denied the abuse ever happened. This notion forms the basis of the idea that people can "recover" a traumatic memory to understand why they are unhappy today. The idea of recovered memories, which is still accepted in some clinical settings, has not been supported by scientific studies of memory, as we detailed in Sections 7.3 and 9.2 (Loftus & Davis, 2006). Many individual cases have proven that at least some so-called recovered memories were in fact false, resulting in innocent people being imprisoned. Thus the question of whether there really are recovered memories remains very uncertain.

Freud believed family dynamics during development affected personality

Freud's theories were popular in part because they seemed to be very comprehensive, covering many facets of human behavior. Freud didn't just propose a structure of the mind, he also purported to understand how these parts of the mind arise as humans grow up. Freud conceived of the human mind as growing through **psychosexual stages of development** from birth to adulthood. At each stage, different parts of the mind must reach some compromise between the demands of the id and the demands of the superego. In healthy development, the growing child recognizes and accepts the compromises between what he wants and what he can reasonably expect from life. Development of the mind

neurosis (pl. *neuroses*) Mental disorders characterized by anxiety or avoidance, that interfere with everyday functioning but are not accompanied by delusions or hallucinations.

psychosexual stages of development Freud's theory of how personality develops from birth to adulthood.

TABLE 14.2 Freud's Psychosexual Stages of Development

Stage	Age	Body focus	Conflict to resolve	Result if unresolved	Symptoms
Oral	0–2	Mouth, lips, tongue, feeding	Weaning from the breast	Overly passive, dependent, gullible	Smoking, overeating, nail-biting
Anal	2–3	Anus, elimination	Toilet training	Anal explosive	Overly messy
				Anal retentive (compulsive)	Overly neat, fussy
Phallic	3–6	Penis, clitoris	Masturbation; parental separation	Overly dependent on opposite-sex parent, overly hostile to same-sex parent	Promiscuity, impulsiveness, homosexuality
Latent	6–12	No particular focus	—	—	—
Genital	12+	Penis, vagina	Mature, socially acceptable sexual relationship	Unhappy sexual relationships	"Frigidity," "impotence"

may go awry if the child relies too heavily on defense mechanisms to shield the ego from the unreasonable demands of the id (**Table 14.2**).

In Freud's view, the newborn mind consists solely of the id, wanting nothing but pleasure, with no conscience or sense that anything else matters. He felt that babies derive the most pleasure from eating, specifically nursing at their mother's breast. Freud called this beginning of human personality the **oral stage**, when the baby pursues pleasurable sensations in the mouth, tongue, and lips. Eventually the child must be weaned, learning to forgo the instant pleasure of breast-feeding whenever he wants. If the baby accepts this necessity, he can then explore other pleasures the world has to offer. But if the child cannot accept the loss of the breast, he may continue to suck on his thumb or other objects, or eat inappropriate objects. When he grows up, he may chew on pens, smoke cigarettes, and so on to satisfy his unresolved oral urges.

As the baby grows, she enters the next phase, the **anal stage**, when the child derives pleasure from the sensation of defecating. Eventually the child is toilet trained and must resolve the conflict between the id, which wants to defecate as soon as the urge hits, and the superego (as developed by the parents), which tries to control when and where to defecate. If the child accepts that she must forgo defecation until she is in the right place at the right time, then she can fit into family life and progress to the next stages of life. If the child rebels against the restrictions of toilet training, she will eventually get with the program and use the potty like everyone else—but at a price. Freud saw people who are very messy and disorganized in their lives as "anal explosive," as not having adequately reconciled their transition out of the anal stage. And on the opposite end of the spectrum, he suggested that the child who is overly sensitive to parental concerns about toilet training may go too far, holding onto her feces too long until constipated, and eventually becoming overly fastidious about neatness, a personality trait Freudians term "anal retentive" or "anal compulsive." It is from this aspect of Freudian thought that people sometimes say that a highly fastidious and organized person is "really anal."

Freud called the next stage of childhood the **phallic stage**, a point at which he believed a drive for pleasure derived from masturbation was at work in the unconscious. People found the notion that young children might derive pleasure from their sexual organs rather shocking. However, this "shocking" aspect of Freud's theory may have provided enough titillation to propel people to discuss Freud and bring his ideas into the limelight. What issue does the child need to

oral stage The earliest phase in Freud's psychosexual stages of development, when the baby pursues pleasurable sensations in the mouth, tongue, and lips.

anal stage The second phase in Freud's psychosexual stages of development, when the child derives pleasure from the sensation of defecating.

phallic stage The third phase in Freud's psychosexual stages of development, when pleasure is derived from masturbation.

resolve at the phallic stage? You might think that the issue to be resolved is that the child needs to learn when masturbation is appropriate (alone in bed before going to sleep, say) and when it is not (while sitting at the dinner table with company, say). Indeed, Freud felt that failure to resolve the phallic stage would result in people who are reckless, vain, or driven to multiple sexual partners.

But Freud added a whole new level of titillation and complexity to the phallic stage by proposing that boys unconsciously want their mother for a sexual partner and wish their father were dead. Because the hero of the ancient Greek play *Oedipus Rex* (unknowingly) kills his father and (unknowingly) marries his mother, Freud coined the term **Oedipal complex** to describe the unconscious desire of boys to kill their father and become their mother's new mate. Likewise, Freud thought girls unconsciously want their father for a sexual partner and their mother dead. He also called this an Oedipal complex, but some of his followers called the female version an *Electra complex*. When the Oedipal complex is satisfactorily resolved, children accept that they cannot marry their opposite-sex parent, and will come to identify with their same-sex parent, modeling that parent's behaviors. A child who cannot reconcile feelings arising from the Oedipal complex may be overly hostile to the same-sex parent and/or overly close to the opposite-sex parent. For Freud, unresolved Oedipal complexes cause women to hate their mothers and/or dote excessively on their fathers, while causing men to hate their fathers and/or remain overly dependent on their mothers.

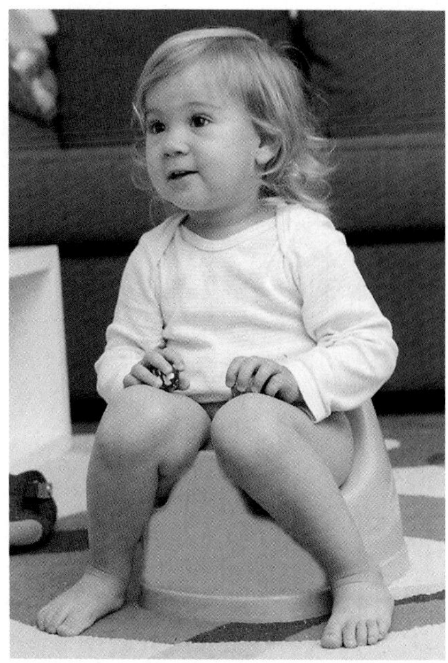

Potty Training Freud believed that the failure of a child to resolve the anal phase could lead to an overly messy or overly fastidious personality.

Freud called the next phase of psychosexual development the **latency stage**, which begins at about 6 years of age, when the child's superego represses most of the id-driven urges before sexual maturity arrives. The child has been weaned and potty trained and has learned not to masturbate in public, but is not yet mature enough to develop a sexual relationship. The final phase of psychosexual development, the **genital stage**, is characterized by healthy separation from the parents and greater interest in genitals (one's own and others') and, when successful, results in a mature, sexual partnership. Resolution of the genital phase includes greater understanding of the world and the development of loving relations and pride in accepting the responsibilities of adulthood.

A key criticism of Freud's ideas about psychosexual development, mirroring criticism of Freud's ideas in general, is the difficulty in testing whether they are true or not. Freud built up these notions, not by testing them, but by talking to adults about their childhoods and their relationships to their parents, and then using those reports to explain behavioral problems in adulthood. With his inventive and fertile mind, Freud was able to "explain" any patient's adult behavior, no matter what sort of childhood was described. Since he believed the patient has thoughts and desires that are *entirely* unconscious, then an infinite number of different unconscious processes could produce the present-day personality. And because the "evidence" of those unconscious processes is often subtle and subjective, a resourceful Freud could detect them all. He was fooled by his own confirmation bias.

A particular failure of Freud's conjectures concerns homosexuality. Although he explicitly stated that there was nothing immoral or shameful about homosexuality, Freud felt it resulted from atypical psychosexual development. For example, he thought a rejecting father and/or an overly indulgent mother could lead a boy to overly identify with his mother, and in modeling her behavior would end up being attracted to men. Despite extensive efforts to look for correlations between such early family relationships and adult sexual orientation, such correlations appear very weak if they are present at all (Bieber, 1962). Even for the weak correlations that are sometimes seen, there's the problem of cause and effect—do some sons become homosexual because they have a rejecting father, or did those fathers reject their sons as they grew up gay? In the meantime, growing evidence of genetic and hormonal influences on human sexual orientation (as we discussed in Section 12.3) do not fit with Freud's notions. Finally, al-

Oedipal complex Freud's term for the unconscious desire of boys to kill their father and become their mother's new mate.

latency stage The phase in Freud's psychosexual stages of development covering the ages 6–12, when the sexual conflicts are repressed.

genital stage The final phase in Freud's psychosexual stages of development, when the focus is on the penis and vagina and developing a mature, socially acceptable sexual relationship.

Skeptic at Large

BOX 14.2

Does Birth Order Affect Personality?

Freud emphasized the child's relationship to the parents as a force that shapes personality. Some of his followers, including the Austrian-born physician Alfred Adler (1870–1937), extended this notion by theorizing that the child's interaction with brothers and sisters also affects personality. The idea that a child's order of appearance in the family affects personality is known as the **birth-order effect**. For example, the oldest child may fear being "dethroned" from the parents' affection by the appearance of a younger sibling. Adler asserted that firstborns may feel inferior, question their importance, and have more problems adjusting to life. Later-born children are supposedly competitive, trying to pull their parents' attention away from the oldest child, while the pampering showered on the youngest child (or an only child) produces a charming but irresponsible personality. Other people spun elaborate theories about how each child's interactions with siblings would lead to one personality trait or another. Firstborns would become leaders with conservative values, middle-born children would be flexible and diplomatic, while last-borns would be risk-takers. Lots of popular books offer descriptions

Diluting Resources Each child in a large family is likely to receive less parental attention than a child with few or no siblings.

though Freud felt he could "cure" people of their homosexuality by helping them resolve conflicts in their psychosexual development, there is no evidence that anyone can actually change a person's sexual orientation (Lovett, 2013).

Psychoanalysts also suggested that the order in which children arrive in the family shapes personality, depending on whether the child is the oldest, youngest, or a middle child (Adler, 1964). These and related ideas about birth-order effects are remarkably widespread among parents and the popular press. But analysis of the thousands of articles that were published regarding birth-order effects provides virtually no support for any of them, as discussed in **Box 14.2**.

Freudians probe the unconscious to reveal conflicts in a client's personality

Because Freud believed unconscious processes play such a major role in controlling our behavior, he tried to develop methods to probe his patients' unconscious. One method was **free association**, when a therapist says a list of words or phrases and invites the client to reply to each one with whatever word or idea comes to mind. Freud believed that the person's unconscious would sometimes affect which word she would say, revealing her true feelings, which were being suppressed by defense mechanisms. It was up to the therapist to figure out what the words might reveal about the patient's unconscious desires.

free association A technique for probing a client's unconscious, when a client given a list of words or phrases replies to each with whatever comes to mind.

Freudian slips The utterance in spontaneous conversation of something that is socially unacceptable, but reveals the speaker's true feelings.

Closely related to free association are what came to be known as **Freudian slips**, when a person in spontaneous conversation says something that is socially unacceptable but reveals the speaker's true feelings (**Figure 14.3**). In everyday speech people might refer to any slip of the tongue that is embarrassing as of personalities based on birth order, and if you read one, you may feel it fits you well. But remember from the discussion in Box 14.1 that people who read horoscopes feel that those too fit them. Are we also reading ourselves into these birth-order descriptions?

When research psychologists began gathering data to test these ideas, there were some apparent trends in personality and intelligence across birth order, but the results were often inconsistent (Ernst & Angst, 1983). Many of those studies suffered a flaw in logic, because they failed to separate the effect of birth order from the effect of *family size*. Half the children from two-child families are firstborns, right? In four-child families, only one-fourth are firstborns and three-fourths are later-borns. This means that a group of kids who are firstborns will have come, on average, from smaller families than a group of later-borns. Why is family size important? Because a smaller family has fewer children among which to divide resources such as money and parental attention. In a larger family, each child gets a smaller share of these resources (see figure). Also, it turns out that highly educated, wealthy parents tend to have small families, so small families tend to have more resources, which are divided into larger portions for each child, than do large families. Put another way, a fourth-born child is more likely to have come from a poorer, less-educated family than a firstborn. So when a popular book notes that 21 of 23 astronauts were firstborns (Lehman, 2009), is that because they were firstborns or because they were from small families and benefitted from lots of resources while growing up? Most of the articles that claimed to find birth-order effects failed to control for family size, income, or social class.

This new perspective suggests that family size itself may matter, even if birth order does not. Indeed, there is a small but significant effect of family size on IQ—the more siblings a person has, the lower his IQ, as discussed in Chapter 11 (Kristensen & Bjerkedal, 2007). But as for clear demonstrations that birth order itself affects personality, studies indicate there is virtually no effect (Jefferson et al., 1998). So are you a firstborn, last-born, or middle child? It doesn't matter. Whether you want to be an astronaut, an accountant, or a personality researcher, go for it!

birth-order effect The hypothesis that the order of birth in a family affects each child's personality.

a Freudian slip, but a true Freudian slip is not just an embarrassing mistake, but a mistake that reveals unconscious desires. Consider the following statement made by former president George H. W. Bush: "For seven and a half years I've worked alongside President Reagan. We've had triumphs. Made some mistakes. We've had some sex... uh... setbacks." While this was certainly an embarrassing slip of the tongue, it was not a Freudian slip unless it revealed something about President Bush's unconscious desires.

Perhaps Freud's most famous method of divining the unconscious was his focus on dreaming. Freud believed that dreams resulted from demands of the id to behave in an entirely selfish fashion, and that all dreams depict wish fulfillment. But the ego and superego, disturbed by the selfish demands of the id, twist and distort dreams in an attempt to hide the potentially shocking desires of the person's unconscious. Freud would have patients describe in great detail the events in their dreams, which he

© Mike Baldwin / Cornered

Figure 14.3 Insert Foot in Mouth A Freudian slip is when we say something we did not mean to say, but which reveals our unconscious feelings.

called the *manifest content*. Then Freud would try to see past the tricks of the ego and superego to determine the true meaning, which he considered the *latent content*. This underlying, genuine meaning of the dream would reveal what the patient really wanted and, Freud hoped, help explain his or her irrational fears or maladaptive behavior. Freud proposed a number of different "tricks" the ego and superego might use to disguise the latent content. For example, if in the manifest content a close friend hurt the dreamer, Freud might say that in fact the dreamer wanted to hurt her friend, but was afraid to admit that to herself.

Again, Freud's fertile mind came up with so many different possible dream distortions that almost any latent content could be "uncovered," limited solely by the therapist's imagination. And again, none of the many possible interpretations of any given dream can ever be disproven. That's why few people studying sleep or dreaming today endorse Freud's ideas (see Section 7.2). This problem with Freud's system of interpreting dreams illustrates the core flaw in most of his ideas—they cannot be disproved. The science of psychology requires us to propose ideas that can be tested and, at least in theory, can be disproven. Science progresses as some ideas are disproven while others are retained, as discussed in Chapter 2.

This shortcoming of psychoanalysis—that its framework offers multiple "explanations," none of which can be disproven—is further illustrated by the problems of projective tests of the unconscious, which we'll take up next.

Projective tests are unreliable and their validity is difficult to determine

Freud's tremendous success in promoting the importance of the unconscious led several followers to develop other means to probe the unconscious. One such strategy is the use of **projective tests**, psychological tests where a client is asked to generate words or stories in response to a stimulus, with the assumption that unconscious processes will affect the person's response. The idea is that the client will "project" his or her unconscious thoughts onto the stimulus, making them accessible to the therapist.

Perhaps the most famous projective test is the **Rorschach test**, where a client's perceptions of a series of inkblots are recorded and analyzed to reveal unconscious processes (**Figure 14.4A**). Most clinical psychology programs still provided instruction in administering the Rorschach test at the start of this century (Viglione & Hilsenroth, 2001). Another projective test is the **thematic apperception test** (**TAT**), in which a person is shown a picture and asked to tell a story to describe what's happening in the picture, including what happened earlier and what the people in the picture are thinking and feeling (**Figure 14.4B**).

These projective tests are clever, and intuitively it seems like they should be able to tap into someone's unconscious. However, the Rorschach test and TAT have been widely criticized (Wood et al., 2003). To understand these criticisms, let's revisit some issues that arise in several areas in psychology and therefore several chapters in this book.

Trying to measure personality or any other psychological trait is a tricky business. In Section 11.1 we discussed this issue in the context of intelligence tests, but the same basic problems arise for tests of personality. The question of whether a test truly measures the trait of interest can be broken down into two separate questions—reliability and validity. The **reliability** of a test is the extent to which the test gives you the same answer, meaning that a particular participant scores about the same on the test if he takes it multiple times. Another indication of a test's reliability is if a particular participant scores about the same on the test no matter who is administering it. The **validity** of a test is the extent to which the test actually measures what you think it's measuring. In other

projective tests A method for probing the unconscious by asking a client to generate words or stories in response to a stimulus.

Rorschach test A projective test in which a client's perceptions of a series of inkblots is recorded and analyzed to reveal unconscious processes.

thematic apperception test (TAT) A projective test in which a person is shown a picture and asked to tell a story to describe what's happening in the picture. The response is analyzed to reveal unconscious processes.

reliability The degree to which a measurement tool produces consistent, repeatable results.

validity The extent to which a test, actually measures the trait it is intended to measure.

(A) Rorschach test

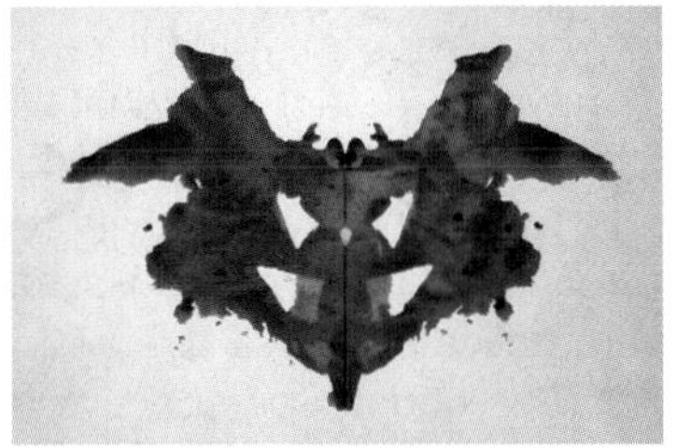
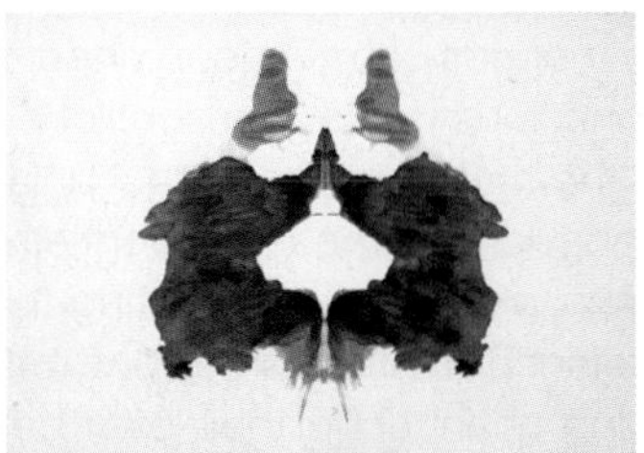
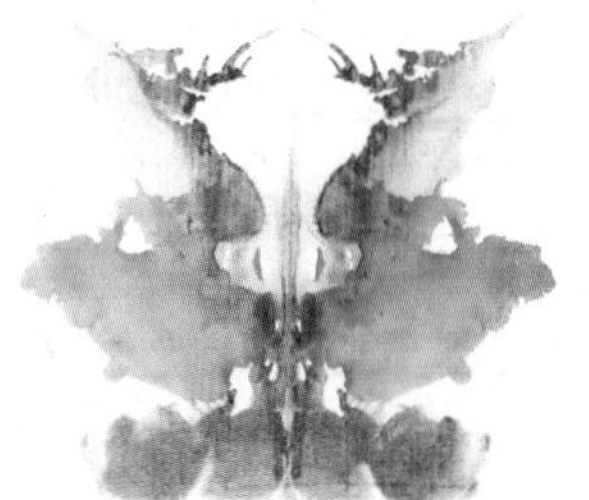

(B) TAT (thematic apperception test)

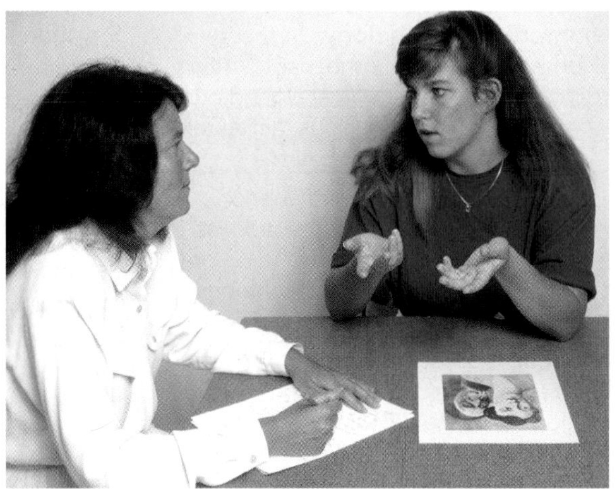

Figure 14.4 Projective Tests of the Unconscious (A) In the Rorschach test, participants report what they see in purposely ambiguous ink blots such as these. (B) In the thematic apperception test (TAT), participants relate stories explaining what's going on in drawings such as this one. For both projective tests, the therapist must interpret the responses to reveal the participant's unconscious feelings. Unfortunately, none of the infinite number of interpretations a therapist might propose could ever be disproved.

words, is the test that you think measures "an unresolved Oedipal complex" actually measuring that?

The projective Rorschach inkblot test and TAT are meant to reveal a person's unconscious feelings and motives, which might contribute to her personality. Criticism of these projective tests goes beyond the connection with psychoanalysis: critics say they are neither reliable nor valid. At least as originally used, neither test was *reliable* because, for a given set of answers from the client, different therapists would sometimes come to quite different conclusions. In other words, the *interpretations* of the test were very subjective, and seemed to depend almost as much on the personality of the tester as that of the client! Attempts have been made to standardize the tests, offering guidelines in interpreting responses so that different therapists come to similar conclusions about a particular client's responses. But it's not clear that those attempts have been successful or that practitioners in real life actually follow those guidelines. As we noted in Sections 2.2 and 11.1, a test that is not reliable cannot possibly be valid.

The *validity* of the projective tests as a way to explore Freudian notions of the unconscious has also been called into question. What is the point of determining whether a person has resolved his Oedipal complex if there's no such thing as an Oedipal complex? If the client denies having those unconscious urges, the psychoanalyst explains that away as the result of the client's ego defense mechanisms. In fact, the psychoanalyst can dismiss *anything* the client says, if the psychoanalyst believes the client has unconscious motives and urges. If the method were valid, different psychoanalysts presented with the same client should reach the same conclusions, but the history suggests psychoanalysts would differ. Various offshoots of psychoanalysis (*neo-Freudian* schools of thought) prospered alongside traditional Freudian psychoanalysis for decades because *none of them could be proven to be more effective than the other.* Thus the problems of projective tests of the unconscious, like the Rorschach and TAT, reflect the problems of psychoanalysis generally. Different therapists may offer very different interpretations of a client's responses. And if the diagnosis of the client's problem isn't accurate, how likely is it that the therapy will really help? Fortunately, an alternative vision of psychological therapy arose that had a more positive outlook than psychoanalysis and, more important, has proven more effective than psychoanalysis, as we'll see next.

humanistic psychology A theory that challenges psychoanalytic theory by emphasizing our free will and our ability to play a conscious, active role in shaping our own behavior.

self-actualization A humanistic psychology concept of the process by which a person lives up to his or her full potential, becoming the best and happiest human they can be.

Rogerian psychotherapy A method of treatment focusing on the client's goals, offering a nonjudgmental forum where the client can problem solve, with the therapist's cooperation.

Humanistic psychology challenged the psychoanalytic model

Psychoanalytic theories carry a deep undercurrent of pessimism, with their emphasis on unconscious urges, the conflict between what we want and what we can have, and the many defense mechanisms that keep us from understanding our own behavior. By the mid-twentieth century, several psychologists rebelled against this gloomy view, insisting that humans are not deluded victims of disguised defense mechanisms, but rather are active, effective agents for change, including changes in their own behavior. This counter-perspective to psychoanalysis, usually called **humanistic psychology**, emphasizes our free will and our ability to play a conscious, active role in shaping our own behavior. In Section 12.1 we discussed Maslow's humanistic concept of **self-actualization**, the process by which a person lives up to his or her full potential, becoming the best and happiest human he or she can be.

Humanistic psychology is constructively applied in psychotherapy by emphasizing that people can actively act as agents for shaping their own lives. Rather than focus on unconscious urges over which people have no control, humanistic psychotherapy focuses on how people can take charge of their lives and change their behaviors to be happy and fulfilled. The humanistic therapist's role is not to dredge up old conflicts, but to help clients find out what's missing from their lives and preventing their self-actualization, and so, in a practical way, help them plot a course of change, to grow into the life they want.

Carl Rogers (1902–1987), one of the founders of humanistic psychology, rejected traditional psychoanalysis and developed a new type of therapy known as "*client-centered*" or "person-centered" therapy. Sometimes called **Rogerian psychotherapy**, it focuses on what the client wants, both by having the client discuss whatever he or she wants, and by viewing the *client's* goals as the only legitimate goals of psychotherapy. Rogerian psychotherapy emphasizes providing clients with a comfortable, nonjudgmental environment to talk through their problems so that *they* can identify what they should do. The therapist should provide *unconditional positive regard* for the client and is in some ways acting more like a coach or facilitator than someone who is "curing" an "illness."

Rogers proposed several ways to test the effectiveness of client-centered psychotherapy, where the criterion was whether clients felt they had benefitted. These trials quickly confirmed the effectiveness of Rogerian psychotherapy and found that it was much more efficient than traditional psychoanalysis, because far fewer sessions were required for clients to feel their needs were satisfied. At least in terms of providing a welcoming, nonjudgmental environment and allowing clients to determine the course of discussions and the goal of the therapy, Rogerian psychotherapy lies at the heart of almost all clinical psychology today.

In the 1950s, the practice of psychoanalysis began to progressively decline. By casting doubt on the value of psychoanalysis, humanistic psychotherapy had cast doubt on Freud's theory of psychosexual stages, as well as his model of interactions between the id, the ego, and the superego. The field came to recognize Freudian notions of personality as overly elaborate, theory driven, and untestable. New approaches arose that emphasized the need to measure personality *empirically*, which we review in the next section.

Psychotherapy Session A Rogerian therapist provides the client with a chance to talk about her problems and to work out her own solutions.

14.1 SUMMARY

- Ancient theories that *personality* was made up of different combinations of four different body fluids, or humors, have been discarded.
- A person may think horoscopes are accurate because of *subjective validation*, or the Forer effect—the tendency to pick out a specific, accurate meaning from an open-ended, vague personality description.

- *Sigmund Freud* founded *psychoanalysis* and emphasized the importance of the *unconscious* for understanding our behavior. Freud proposed that the mind consists of the *id*, which seeks only pleasure; the *superego*, which incorporates society's restrictions on behavior; and the *ego*, which tries to fulfill the demands of the id within the confines of the superego.
- The ego keeps the selfish, unacceptable demands of the id from consciousness using *defense mechanisms* such as *rationalization*. Freud contended that overactive defense mechanisms could result in *neurosis*, a minor mental disorder such as anxiety or irrational fear (phobia).
- Freud proposed that different *personality types* form as a result of family interactions while the child passes through *psychosexual sta-ges of development*. If the child does not successfully resolve conflicts with his parents during the *oral*, *anal*, or *phallic stages*, he will be hampered in reaching a healthy psychological state in the adult *genital stage*.
- Freud relied heavily on the patient's report of dreams to probe the unconscious for clues to unresolved psychosexual issues. Later psychoanalysts developed *projective tests*, such as the *Rorschach test* and the *thematic apperception test* (*TAT*), to probe unconscious ideas. These tests have not, however, been found to be reliable or verifiable.
- Aside from its emphasis on the unconscious, modern psychology rejects the psychoanalytic system because it is unfalsifiable, offering many different explanations for whatever personality trait an individual might have.
- Psychoanalytic treatment has been abandoned in favor of *client-centered* therapies such as *Rogerian psychotherapy*, which focuses on the client's goals, offering a nonjudgmental forum where the client can solve problems with the cooperation of the therapist.

REVIEW QUESTIONS

1. What factors lead people to believe that horoscopes can accurately describe their personality or predict their future?
2. Describe the Freudian model of the mind, and of the role of defense mechanisms in the unconscious.
3. What are Freud's psychosexual stages of development, and what are the different personality types he believed might result from unresolved conflicts at each stage?
4. Contrast the methods and goals of psychoanalysis with Rogerian psychotherapy.

Food for Thought

Freudian concepts continue to heavily influence literature and culture, but have been abandoned by almost all research psychologists. Why has Freudian thinking been so unsuccessful in one domain (psychological science) and so successful in another (culture)?

14.2 The Rejection of Personality Types and the Pursuit of Traits

As the field of personality study moved away from Freudian thinking, psychologists began to explicitly reject preconceived theories of personality and determined instead to objectively catalog the characteristics of personality that can actually be observed in humans. In other words, psychologists began to take a purely practical, empirical approach to the study of personality. The idea was to gather a lot more information before articulating a theory, in the hopes that a more informed theory would be more likely to be correct.

Things to Learn

- Modern theories of personality traits
- Introversion and extraversion
- Factor analysis
- Big five personality traits
- MMPI tests of personality and disorders
- Unreliable Myers–Briggs test

Modern psychology emphasizes traits rather than types

As was mentioned earlier, most psychologists today reject the notion that there is a small number of personality "types"—that a small number of labels should

personality traits Particular aspects of behavioral characteristics that can be objectively measured in a quantitative fashion.

extravert Someone who likes being with other people and tends to be talkative and assertive.

introvert Someone who is less talkative and prefers solitary pursuits.

suffice to describe all people. Instead, personalities began to be viewed as a collection of characteristics, and a new generation of psychologists began to seek ways to measure various aspects of personality in a quantitative way.

The philosophy behind this fresh approach argued that if a given personality characteristic is *real*, then it should be possible to *measure* it, providing numbers to compare how strongly it is present in one person versus another. Psychologists began to use the term **personality traits** for particular aspects of personality that can be objectively measured in a quantitative fashion. This approach, sometimes called *trait psychology*, seeks to describe an individual's personality in terms of how much of several different personality traits he or she displays. As we'll see, this new approach launched a quest to determine exactly how many different personality traits contribute to human personalities. Psychologists felt that once they knew how many different personality traits are possible, they could describe each individual's personality, not in terms of a single label ("melancholy type" or "anal retentive type"), but in terms of how strongly he or she showed each of a number of different traits. By assigning numbers to indicate how strongly an individual displays a given trait, individuals and groups of individuals could be compared to see who showed more or less of that trait. An overall assessment of someone's personality would consist of several numbers, each reflecting how much he displayed one personality trait or another.

To demonstrate how this new approach was applied, we'll begin by examining a major personality trait—whether a person is outgoing. Then we'll talk about the twentieth-century program to catalog all human personality traits and attempt to boil them down into a few major categories—the so-called *big five traits.* We'll look, too, at the evidence that genes influence personality traits, and the issue of how personality interacts with different situations.

Introverts and extraverts offer a continuum of personalities

Probably people have always varied in how much they seek the company of others, and surely many people noticed this trait. Yet, surprisingly, it wasn't until the start of the twentieth century that specific terms were proposed to describe this aspect of personality. C. G. Jung (1875–1961), who studied with Freud but eventually developed a slightly different system of psychoanalysis, proposed terms to describe how people differ in their need to be around others—*introversion* versus *extraversion*. Today we might define an **extravert** (often spelled "extrovert" outside of psychology) as someone who likes being with other people and tends to be talkative and assertive. Jung created the term from the Latin roots for "outside" (*extra*) and "turning" (*vert*), and another way to characterize extraverts is to say their attention is turned outward, to others. You might think that Jung (1915) coined the term extravert to mirror the term outgoing, a term commonly used today to describe an extraverted person. But in fact Jung's term extravert entered the English language first—no record of the word outgoing to describe a very sociable person appeared in English until more than 40 years later ("Outgoing," 2014).

In contrast to an extravert, an **introvert** ("inward turning") is someone who is less talkative and less interested in the company of others. Introverts' attention is "turned inward" in the sense that they spend a lot of time with their own thoughts or doing solitary activities like reading, writing, or drawing. Introverts are not necessarily loners, as they may have intimate friends, but they tend to have fewer friends than extraverts. Although some introverts are shy around other people, that is not necessarily so. Many comedians who have no problem performing on stage or being talkative and funny in a small group are in fact introverts who seek and prize time alone. They are introverts because they prefer solitary activities, not because they are uncomfortable in social situations.

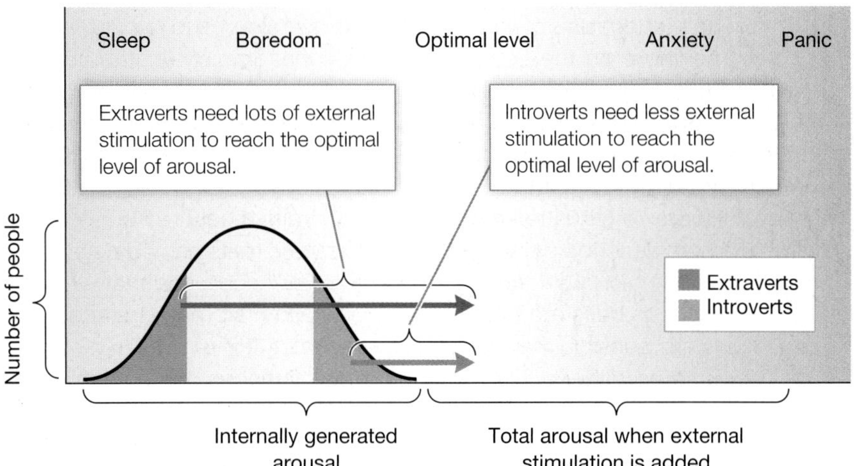

Figure 14.5 Eysenck's Two-Factor Theory of Personality Hans Eysenck's suggested explanation for differences in introversion-extraversion proposed that there is an optimal level of brain arousal that we all enjoy. He proposed that extraverts require lots of external stimulation to push their brains to an optimal level of arousal. In contrast, introverts are people whose brains tend to be more active, and therefore little external stimulation is needed to push them to the optimal level.

Psychologist Hans Eysenck (1916–1997) developed a theory of introversion and extraversion that relied heavily on notions of brain activity. Eysenck was also reacting strongly to psychoanalysis, which he believed was ineffective in helping people with behavioral problems. He hypothesized that introversion and extraversion resulted from some balance of inhibition and excitation in the brain and proposed that there may be an optimal level of brain excitation that we find pleasurable (**Figure 14.5**). In Eysenck's scheme, introverts are people whose brains are, when left alone, already fairly active so they only need a little outside stimulation to reach the optimal, pleasurable levels of brain activity. On the other hand, extraverts are people whose brains are not very active in isolation, so they learn to engage in behaviors to gather more stimulation. Thus they learn to seek other people's company and to engage in lots of lively, animated conversation.

Why do some people have higher levels of underlying brain excitation than others? Eysenck felt that heredity played an important role in this process. In a series of studies, including comparing identical and non-identical twins in ways we discussed in Section 4.4, Eysenck provided strong evidence of a hereditary influence on extraversion and introversion. Thus in contrast to Freud, who believed early family dynamics, the child's experience interacting with his or her parents, molded the child's personality, Eysenck believed that children are born with a predisposition to develop a particular personality. Eysenck did not dismiss early experience as playing a role, but argued that hereditary factors matter too.

Eysenck did not see introversion and extraversion as personality types but as a single trait that could be measured on a **continuum**, varying in degree from very, very introverted to very, very extraverted, with different people falling anywhere in between. While Freud described *qualitatively* different personality *types*, Eysenck described personality *traits* that differ *quantitatively.*

Building on this idea of quantitative traits, Eysenck proposed that another personality trait varies in a continuous fashion across individuals—*emotional instability* or **neuroticism**, how readily a person's emotional state is upset by the events of everyday life. Some people seem to keep an even keel in a range of situations, while other people are easily distressed by relatively minor events. Although clinicians no longer use the term *neurosis* (see Chapter 16), it was once applied to mental disorders characterized by anxiety, so an emotionally unstable person was said to be neurotic in the sense that he or she is more likely to become anxious, even about inconsequential things.

Eysenck believed that the two traits just described represent two independent measures of human personality. Each personality would fall somewhere

continuum When a trait varies in a continuous, gradual fashion.

neuroticism Also called *emotional instability*. How readily a person's emotional state is upset by the events of everyday life.

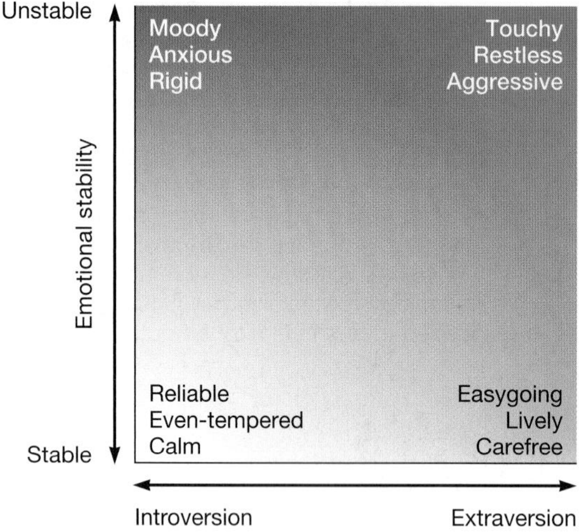

Figure 14.6 Personality Classified by Two Independent Traits By conceiving of introversion–extraversion as one continuously variable trait, and emotional stability–instability as another, we can understand each personality as falling somewhere along a continuum of these two independent traits. A stable introvert would be calm and even-tempered while being thoughtful and introspective. An unstable introvert would be moody and anxious while shunning the company of others. A stable extravert would be easygoing and sociable, maybe taking on a leadership role. An unstable extravert would be touchy and restless but also actively seeking human interactions, perhaps being impulsive in his relations. (After Eysenck & Eysenck, 1958.)

on the spectrum of introversion–extraversion, and would also fall somewhere on the spectrum of emotional stability–instability. Classification of a personality by two independent traits is depicted in **Figure 14.6**. Introversion–extraversion and emotional stability–instability are characterized as dimensions because they are not all-or-none characteristics.

Figure 14.6 illustrates how these two traits measured on a continuum help describe personality, but even more traits can come into play, three of which we'll talk about shortly. You'll soon see that when five continuous traits are taken into consideration, so many trait combinations are possible that defining a personality "type" is futile.

Eysenck's theory had two important influences on personality psychology. First, by insisting that there had to be a biological basis to any human personality trait (evidenced by his attempt to relate introversion-extraversion to brain activity and the influence of genes), he propelled the field to reconsider biological factors in addition to the family dynamics and experience factors that had dominated the field. Second, Eysenck was absolutely convinced that personality psychology should be subjected to scientific testing, which he felt was lacking in Freudian theory. He asserted that "what is true in Freud is not new," referring to the idea of the unconscious, and "what is new in Freud is not true," referring to his theory of psychosexual development (Eysenck, 1985). Eysenck championed efforts to quantitatively measure personality traits. Meanwhile, other personality psychologists were wrestling with the question of just how many personality traits there are.

How many personality traits are there?

In the 1930s, American psychologist Gordon Allport (1897–1967) realized that he could tap a rich and ancient source of information about personality types by turning to language. If a personality trait existed, then humans should have noticed it, and in that case there would likely be a word for that trait. Allport found that, if anything, language has too many such words—he catalogued over 4,000 English words describing different personality traits. Perhaps there really are 4,000 different human personality traits, but how would we ever measure them all for any one person?

British and American psychologist Raymond Cattell (1905–1998) saw a lot of overlap among those 4,000 traits, and tried to boil them down into a more manageable number by eliminating those that he felt were just two different words for the same underlying trait. Even then, he was left with over 170 words that appeared to describe at least partially different personality traits. Not trusting his own subjective judgment, Cattell turned to a statistical tool to winnow those 170-plus words down. He used **factor analysis**, a statistical method of examining many different measures to see whether some of those measures consistently covary with one another (we discuss correlation coefficients as a measure of covariation in Section 2.1). The reasoning is that if two different measures consistently covary, then they may represent two different ways of measuring the same underlying trait. For example, imagine I took five different measures from 100 people, say annual income, eye color, height, and their weight as measured by two different scales, one in pounds and the other in kilograms. Factor analysis of all those measures would reveal that weight in pounds and weight in kilograms, while not identical numbers, nevertheless covary across participants perfectly, suggesting that they are really two different measures of the same thing, which they are.

factor analysis A statistical method of examining many different measures to see whether some of those measures consistently covary with one another.

Similarly, Cattell (1946) asked a lot of people to describe the personalities of people they knew, using those 170-plus English words for personality traits. Then he used factor analysis of those reports to find which words describing

Low range	Trait	High range
Cool, distant, reserved	Warmth	Warm, outgoing
Concrete only, little abstract	Reasoning	Abstract thinker, quick learner
Stable, calm, hard to perturb	Emotional stability	Changeable, easily upset
Deferential, submissive	Dominance	Dominant, forceful
Serious, restrained	Liveliness	Lively, animated
Rule-conscious, dutiful	Rule-consciousness	Nonconforming, self-indulgent
Shy, timid, intimidated	Social boldness	Bold, venturesome, uninhibited
Objective, unsentimental	Sensitivity	Sensitive, sentimental
Trusting, unsuspecting	Vigilance	Vigilant, skeptical, distrustful
Grounded, practical	Abstractedness	Abstract, imaginative
Forthright, genuine, naïve	Privateness	Private, discreet, shrewd
Self-doubting, worried	Apprehension	Self-assured, unworried
Traditional, conservative	Openness to change	Experimental, liberal
Solitary, resourceful	Self-reliance	Group-oriented, a joiner
Organized, compulsive	Perfectionism	Flexible, lax, impulsive
Relaxed, tranquil	Tension	High energy, impatient

Figure 14.7 Cattell's 16 Source Traits of Personality Note that each trait can vary along a continuum from low to high. (After Conn & Rieke, 1994.)

different personality traits tended to covary. He ultimately concluded that the hundreds of terms for personality represent only 16 different underlying factors. Cattell called these 16 factors *source traits*, and suggested that they represented the foundation of human personality. What were these source traits? Cattell himself was uncomfortable giving them descriptive names, but source traits can be roughly described with English terms like *warmth*, *reasoning*, *dominance*, and so on (**Figure 14.7**). They include emotional stability, which Eysenck would later propose as an important factor in personality, as well as several different factors that roughly encompass introversion-extraversion.

Using factor analysis is a little like eating a potato chip—it's difficult to stop after just one. Later psychologists applied factor analysis further in an attempt to boil down those 16 personality factors into even fewer traits that make up human personality, as we'll discuss next.

Modern personality theory embraces the five-factor model

Following Cattell's example, other psychologists surveyed the personality traits of large samples of people, and tried to discern an even smaller number of factors that might represent an even more fundamental basis for personality. Cattell (1957) himself theorized that the 16 traits might in fact represent contributions from five different underlying factors for personality. Various psychologists pursued this line of thinking, each discerning five or sometimes four different underlying factors. While different labels were given to these four or five factors, by the late 1980s many personality psychologists realized that these different studies seemed to be converging on five basic factors. These factors became known as the **five-factor model**, five different traits that can each vary in degree from one person to another, and that together make up each individual's personality (Peabody & Goldberg, 1989). This view of personality is sometimes known as the *big five*.

These big five traits are *openness, conscientiousness, extraversion, agreeableness*, and *neuroticism* (**Figure 14.8**). An easy way to remember the big five traits is to use the mnemonic OCEAN (***O***penness, ***C***onscientiousness, ***E***xtraversion, ***A***greeableness, and ***N***euroticism). The order of the traits is not meant to reflect their importance to personality. Each is a relatively independent aspect of everyone's personality.

five-factor model The idea that five basic traits make up each individual's personality.

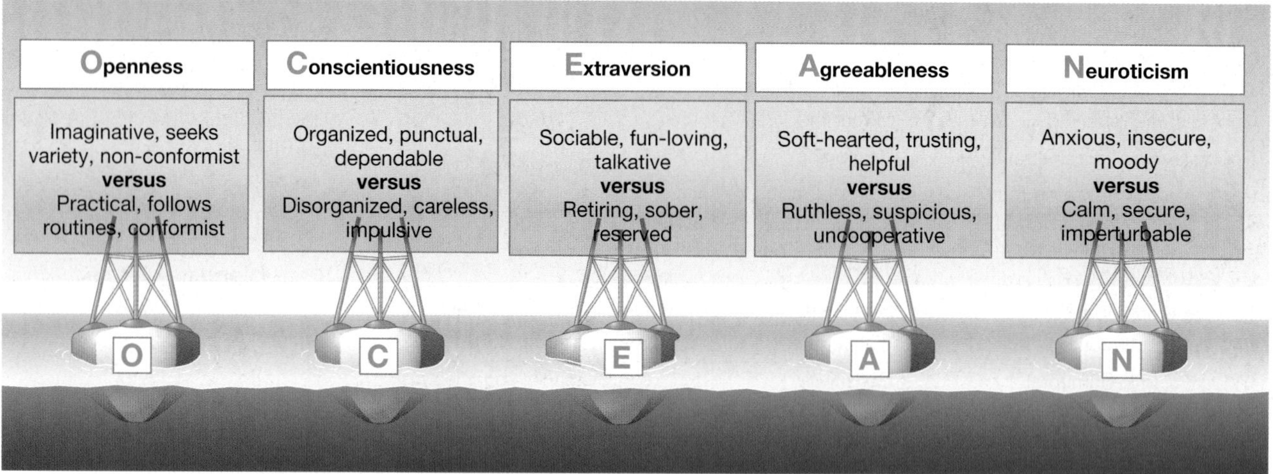

Figure 14.8 **The "Big Five" Personality Traits** The five-factor model proposes five relatively independent personality traits each of which can vary from low to high. A common memory device to remember them is "OCEAN."

Before we discuss each of the big five factors in detail, note two important points about this model. First, these are not particular traits that you either have or don't have. Everyone's personality is made up of each of the big five traits. What distinguishes different people is *how much* of each of the traits they have. Each of the big five traits is measured on a continuum, so your personality may be low in a particular trait, high in that trait, or anywhere in between. For this reason, tests of the big five traits usually report a quantitative score for the level of each trait. We'll see an example shortly.

Second, each of the five traits is considered to be at least partly independent of the others. In other words, knowing an individual's score in extraversion should not offer any prediction about what that person's score will be in neuroticism, or agreeableness, or any other of the big five. The idea is that these are five separate aspects of each personality. Some of the five traits may not be *entirely* independent; some traits tend to covary with others. For example, people who are high in extraversion tend to be low in neuroticism (in other words, extraverts are slightly more likely to be emotionally stable and cheerful than are introverts). But because there are plenty of exceptions to such trends—for example, there are introverts who are also very emotionally stable—we can say with reasonable confidence that the big five traits are at least somewhat independent.

Note that if each of five traits can vary on a scale from 1 to 5 across people, then there would be over 3,000 different personalities! Expand the scale from 1 to 10, and the five-factor model potentially embraces an enormous variety of personalities.

Now let's discuss these five traits in a bit more detail. One big five trait is our old friend extraversion, the tendency to seek out stimulation and the company of other people. A person high in extraversion is talkative and may indicate that "I am the life of the party" fits his personality. If you are an introvert, then you are low in extraversion. An introvert may report "I have little to say" and "I don't enjoy parties much." Most people fall somewhere in between the extremes of extraversion. The consistency with which extraversion has emerged as a critical aspect of personality over the years, from research with very different methods and examining many different groups of people, is striking. The durability of the concept of introversion-extraversion speaks well of C. G. Jung's insight in coining those terms—they represented a real trait and so emerged from the factor analysis approach. While Jung's career may have begun under Freud's guidance, Jung's work has had a more lasting impact on personality research than his mentor's.

Another big five trait that we discussed earlier is neuroticism, the degree to which a person is emotionally unstable or experiences negative emotions like anxiety or depression. A person high in neuroticism may say "I get stressed out easily." A person who is emotionally stable, meaning he or she is calm and not easily upset ("I am relaxed most of the time"), will have a low score in neuroticism. As mentioned earlier, extraverts tend to be low in neuroticism and introverts tend to be high in neuroticism, so these two traits may not be entirely independent of one another. On the other hand, many people are exceptions—emotionally stable introverts and neurotic extraverts—so the two traits are at least partially independent factors in personality.

A big five personality trait that we have not yet considered is **openness** to experience, an appreciation for art, imaginative pastimes, and unconventional, even unpopular ideas. People with high openness scores seek a variety of intellectual and physical experiences. They may report having a vivid imagination and an interest in abstract ideas. People low in openness tend to have more conventional ideas and prefer straightforward, concrete pursuits.

Conscientiousness refers to a tendency to be self-disciplined and reliable, and feel a need for achievement. People high in conscientiousness may report following a schedule and getting chores done right away. People low in conscientiousness may report procrastinating, leaving their belongings around, or shirking their duties.

Finally, **agreeableness** is the tendency to be compassionate and cooperative rather than suspicious and competitive. Someone high in agreeableness may report having a soft heart and taking time out for others. A person low in agreeableness will report little concern for other people and their problems, and will value self-interest more than getting along with other people.

The five-factor model is not without its critics. We already mentioned that the big five are not completely independent traits when we noted that people who are high in extraversion tend to be low in neuroticism, and vice versa. In addition, there are many personality traits, like snobbishness, religiosity, or a sense of humor, that don't seem to fit readily into any of the big five traits. Finally, some psychologists are uncomfortable with the lack of any theory to explain why there are 5 principle traits, rather than 4 or 20, or to explain what biological process underlies the five factors. Even if the big five don't capture every aspect of personality, there is wide consensus that they represent an important core of personality. So let's talk about how you measure these traits.

openness A personality trait that reflects a person's tendency to seek new experiences.

conscientiousness A personality trait that reflects a person's tendency to be self-disciplined and reliable, and feel a need for achievement.

agreeableness A personality trait that reflects a person's tendency to be compassionate and cooperative.

How do we assess personality traits?

Now that we've reviewed the history of the quest to determine the important traits underlying personality, we can talk about the practical matter of how to actually measure these traits. Many different tests have been developed over the years for one or another of the big five personality traits, even before they were recognized as the big five. Most personality tests simply ask people to report how they behave or feel in various situations. They indicate how well each statement does or does not describe their own experience. When we ask lots of different questions about how people feel or behave in many different situations, a pattern emerges that is presumed to reflect a personality. To assess another individual's personality, the test-taker can answer those questions about that person.

These days, the most common test of the big five personality traits in adults is the *NEO Personality Inventory, Revised edition* (*NEO PI-R*). *NEO* stands for ***N***euroticism-***E***xtraversion-***O***penness, but the original version of the test was revised to measure conscientiousness and agreeableness too (Costa & McCrae, 1992). The NEO PI-R consists of several hundred statements, such as "I'm pretty set in my ways" and "I like to have a lot of people around me." The participant indicates whether he or she strongly agrees, agrees, disagrees, or strongly disagrees with each statement. The participant can also choose to be neutral for each statement, if it is about equally true and false.

standardized When a test has been administered to many different people, so that the distribution of the scores are known.

The NEO PI-R test is **standardized**, which means that the responses of many, many people have been recorded, so that researchers know how most people score on the test, and which scores are unusually high or unusually low. This standardization is important because it enables the researcher to state with confidence that a particular score is higher or lower than the average in a comparison group, rather than relying on his or her subjective judgment about what constitutes a high score in a given trait.

While writing this chapter, I realized that I had never taken one of these personality tests, and decided that taking some tests might give me greater insight into how they work. So with the help of a colleague who is a clinical psychologist, I took the NEO PI-R. The test is fairly simple, and the version I took made it easy for me to decode the answers and tally up the results myself. The big five ratings are found by just adding up different numbers of points for particular subsets of the answers. Then I had five different numbers, which can vary from 0 to 192, one for each of the big five traits. But those raw numbers weren't very informative. Is a score of 86 on neuroticism high or low? Luckily, I could compare my score with those obtained from a large number of people in the appropriate comparison group, adult men. That comparison told me that about 55% of adult men have a lower neuroticism score than I do. In other words, my neuroticism score was at the 55th percentile of adult men, so I'm pretty average. If I were a female, I would have compared my score with a different comparison group, adult women. My score is even closer to the 50th percentile among women.

So how did I do? Compared with other men, I was in the average range, scoring between the 51st and 55th percentile, for three traits: neuroticism, extraversion, and agreeableness (**Figure 14.9**). So for those traits my personality seems to be pretty average. In fact, none of my scores were extreme, say higher or lower than 90% of men. Only two of my scores fell outside the middle of the distribution of men. My score for openness was higher than average, at the 66th percentile, while my conscientiousness score was low, at the 38th percentile (see Figure 14.9). Gee, 38th percentile for conscientiousness—that gave me a twinge. I admire conscientiousness, so I don't like to think I'm below average for that. Was this a fair measure of my personality? Do these scores accurately reflect who I am?

In other words, are big five tests reliable and valid, genuinely reflecting personality? Unlike the projective tests, Rorschach and TAT, which we discussed earlier, big five personality tests such as the NEO PI-R are quite *reliable*, meaning the various tests report similar scores for each individual, and people taking a test more than once tend to get the same scores. Once people reach the age of 30 or so, their scores on the big five tend to be quite stable (McCrae et al., 2000). But are the big five measures *valid*, reflecting genuine differences in personality? First, measures of big five traits based on an individual's self-report match pretty well what other people report about his or her personality. So to the extent that other people can judge someone's personality, that person's self-assessment on the big five test is accurate.

More important, several findings suggest that the five traits, as measured in personality tests, reflect many behaviors in real life (John et al., 2008). For example, people with low agreeableness are more likely to have heart attacks (Miller et al., 1996). People with high scores in extraversion have more friends and social support to deal with illness (Berkman et al., 2000), while highly neurotic people are less

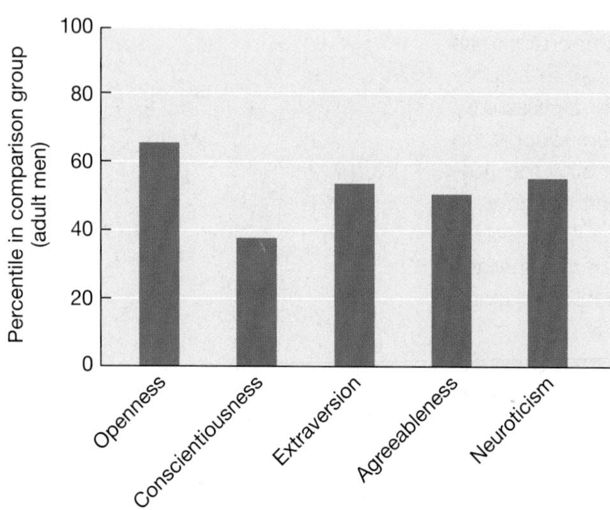

Figure 14.9 Big Five Personality Traits of a College Textbook Author Percentile scores, based on comparison with other adult men, for the author's personality as assessed by the NEO PI-R.

able to cope with illness, and are less likely to find their job satisfying (David & Suls, 1999). People with high levels of neuroticism are also more likely to have a particular version of a gene regulating the neurotransmitter serotonin (Lesch et al., 1996), and later we'll review other evidence of genetic influences on each of the big five traits. Taken together, these studies indicate that each of the big five personality traits, as measured by these tests, reflect genuine aspects of an individual's behavior and life outcomes. So assessing the five traits together should give a valid snapshot of someone's personality.

What about my two scores that differed a bit from average, high openness and low conscientiousness? If my personality is truly high in openness and low in conscientiousness, then those traits should reflect my behavior. What's more, other people with personalities high in openness and low in conscientiousness should have things in common with me. Well, studies indicate that people with high scores in openness are more likely to have liberal political views (McCrae, 1996), and presumably more likely to vote in a liberal manner, and I am politically liberal-ish. People who score high in openness tend to have more total years of education (Conard, 2006), and I have always loved school and learning. I went to school for 21 years. I have lots of different intellectual interests, including psychology, neuroscience, and statistics, and have taught them all. Plus, I willingly took a personality test that I didn't have to! So my behavior fits those trends in people high in openness.

What about conscientiousness? People with low conscientiousness scores are more likely to engage in risky behaviors like drug use and poor diet. While I do have a glass of wine at dinner sometimes, I've never smoked a cigarette or taken any illegal drug. So I'm not really a risk-taker (although I had no problem eating junk food when I was younger). People low in conscientiousness also tend to have lower college grade point averages (Conard, 2006), and I was never a straight-A student, despite my many years of education. So my personality fits some, but not all, of those trends. Where I really fit in with other people who are low in conscientiousness is in orderliness (I'm a messy person) and in attention deficit hyperactivity disorder (ADHD), which is more common in people who score low in conscientiousness (Nigg et al., 2002). I have always had many ADHD characteristics, but I never sought a diagnosis. I was very absentminded long before I became an "absentminded professor." I developed coping strategies, relying on pocket calendars and reminders, but they don't always work. If I don't meet all my obligations or meet all deadlines, it's not because I don't *care*, it's because I don't *remember*. By the way, high openness and low conscientiousness is also typical in stand-up comics (Greengross & Miller, 2009).

When it was all said and done, the NEO PI-R assessment that I'm average for most traits, a bit high in openness, and a bit low in conscientiousness, fits the me I think I know (and the me my wife and children report knowing). Of course, there's nothing mysterious at work if my big five scores fit my self-image, because I was the one who answered all those questions about myself. They *have* to reflect my self-image pretty well. But please note that if I am fooling myself about who I am, then I might, in all sincerity, give *untrue* answers to the questions. If I am hard to get along with, but don't think that about myself, then I'll answer questions in such a way that I will appear to be agreeable. That's why it's important that when *other* people assess an individual's personality via a big five test, it matches the individual's self-assessment fairly well. What might happen if I were deliberately dishonest in answering those questions? Could I cheat, answering the questions in such a way that I appear to be more conscientious than I really am? Of course I could. So a crucial requirement for any big five assessment to be accurate is that the individual has to be as honest as possible when answering the questions. Later we'll see that some other tests try to assess whether a person is being honest, but most big five tests do not.

Trait	Low end	Middle	High end
Openness	☐ Down-to-earth, practical, traditional, and pretty much set in your ways.	☐ Practical but willing to consider new ways of doing things. You seek a balance between the old and the new.	☒ Open to new experiences. You have broad interest and are very imaginative.
Conscientiousness	☒ Easygoing, not very well organized, and sometimes careless. You prefer not to make plans.	☐ Dependable and moderately well organized. You generally have clear goals but are able to set your work aside.	☐ Conscientious and well organized. You have high standards and always strive to achieve your goals.
Extraversion	☐ Introverted, reserved, and serious. You prefer to be alone or with a few friends.	☒ Moderate in activity and enthusiasm. You enjoy the company of others, but you also value privacy.	☐ Extraverted, outgoing, active, and high-spirited. You prefer to be around people most of the time.
Agreeableness	☐ Hardheaded, skeptical, proud, and competitive. You tend to express your anger directly.	☒ Generally warm, trusting, and agreeable, but you can sometimes be stubborn and competitive.	☐ Compassionate, good-natured, and eager to cooperate and avoid conflict.
Neuroticism	☐ Secure, hardy, and generally relaxed even under stressful conditions.	☒ Generally calm and able to deal with stress, but you sometimes experience feelings of guilt, anger, or sadness.	☐ Sensitive, emotional, and prone to experience feelings that are upsetting.

Figure 14.10 A Sample of NEO PI-R Evaluation We can describe the typical characteristics of people with low, average, or high percentile scores for each trait in words. I've marked with an "X" where I fall on the big five.

If we were to return to the old-fashioned idea that there are a limited number of personality types, we could ask how many types there are in terms of big five traits. For example, sometimes people who take the NEO PI-R are given a report telling them, for each trait, whether their score is about average, above average, or below average (**Figure 14.10**). Note that even with that simplified report of just three levels (above average, below average, about average) for each of the big five traits, nevertheless there are 243 different possible combinations. For all practical purposes, if there truly are 243 different personality types, then the concept of "types" really isn't useful anymore. That's one of the reasons most personality psychologists have abandoned the idea of *types* and instead think about individual *traits*, which can vary independently from one person to another. This large number of possible combinations of the big five traits indicates a tremendous diversity of human personalities.

Some tests are designed to screen for psychological disorders or career fit

Another long-standing and widely used personality test is the **Minnesota Multiphasic Personality Inventory** (**MMPI**). While the MMPI was originally designed to help diagnose people with mental illness, it is often taken by people who are just seeking counseling. The MMPI provides the therapist with a snapshot of the client's personality. Like the NEO PI-R, the MMPI consists of hundreds of statements that a person might make about himself ("I like children" or "I often hear voices without knowing where they come from"), for which the participant indicates whether each is true or false. The only options are true and false, so the test-taker must choose true if the statement is "mostly true" and false if it is "mostly false." The answers are tabulated to produce a numerical score for several different "scales."

Minnesota Multiphasic Personality Inventory (MMPI) A widely used personality test originally designed to screen for psychological disorders.

MMPI clinical scales Quantitative measures of a subject's responses to the MMPI, intended to detect different psychological problems.

After the participant has answered the 500-plus true-or-false questions about himself, those answers are analyzed to provide scores for different MMPI scales, quantitative measures of responses, each intended to reflect some aspect of the participant's behavior. The most basic MMPI scales are the ten **MMPI clinical scales**, most of which, as the name indicates, are intended to detect different psychological problems. For example, one MMPI scale is intended to detect **hypochondria**, a tendency to believe you are ill when you are not. Other scales reflect depression, schizophrenia, and paranoia (see Section 16.4). Other MMPI clinical scales measure other tendencies, which might be useful for a therapist to understand the client. For example, one scale measures our old friend introversion-extraversion, while another measures impulsivity.

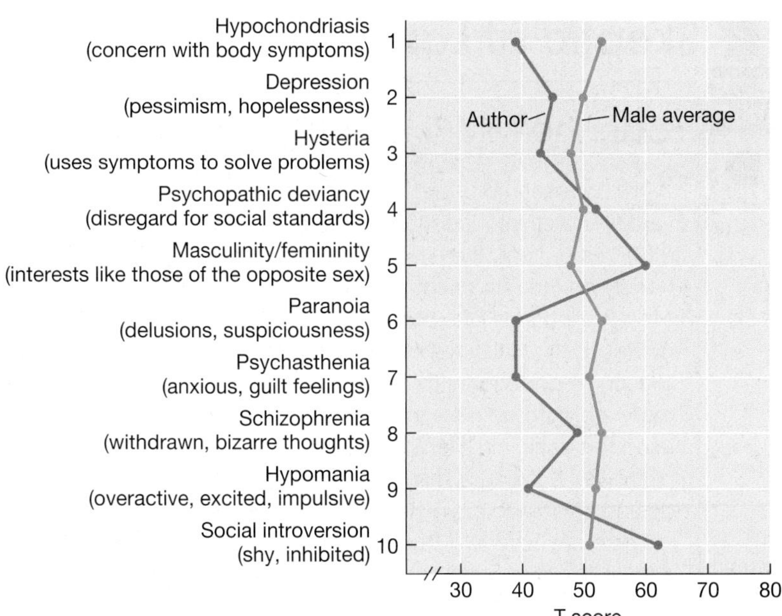

Figure 14.11 The Minnesota Multiphasic Personality Inventory, or MMPI
The blue line indicates my scores on the MMPI. (After Daliento et al., 2005.)

Like the NEO PI-R test we described earlier, the MMPI is standardized, so it's possible to compare a given person's scores with those of many people who have taken the test before. Of course, while an unusually high score on a given MMPI scale means you are not like most other people, it does not necessarily mean there is something wrong with you. Typically, a participant's score on the ten clinical scales is reported as a "T score," which can vary around an average of 50. Although there is no hard-and-fast rule, scores above 65 are generally considered "clinically significant," meaning a therapist should be alert for problems in that particular area, say depression.

hypochondria A tendency to believe you are ill when you are not.

To get a better idea of what taking the MMPI is like, I set aside about 90 minutes to answer the 500-plus questions, indicating whether each was true or false about myself. I tried to be as honest as possible, and gave the results to my colleague, who used a computer to calculate the various scales. You can see my results in **Figure 14.11**. Happily, none of my T scores were above 65, so there's no indication of psychological disorders, but of course I took the MMPI out of curiosity, not because I came to a therapist for help.

There are only two MMPI scales that we can compare to my NEO PI-R results: extraversion and neuroticism. In the MMPI's Social Introversion scale, my score indicated I'm slightly more introverted than the average man, while the NEO PI-R said I was about average for extraversion (see Figure 14.10), so they agree that I'm about average in introversion-extraversion. While the MMPI has no explicit neuroticism scale, my lower-than-65 T scores in scales measuring anxiety, hysteria, and depression match pretty well with my average neuroticism score on the NEO PI-R. So the results of the two tests coincide pretty well.

Of course some people taking a personality test may be motivated to cheat, hoping to portray themselves more positively. The MMPI analysis also provides several scales that are intended to reveal whether test-takers are lying, to present themselves as better (or worse) than they are. These scales primarily look for inconsistency in the answers. In case you're wondering, my scores on the "lie scales" of the MMPI were low, suggesting that I was not cheating, and my experience is that I was trying to be honest. But it's always possible that I might have unconsciously pushed the test in one direction or the other, and so too I might have unconsciously cheated to fool the lie scales as well.

The MMPI was originally designed to detect people who are suffering from psychological disorders, including depression and schizophrenia, but sometimes people suffering from these disorders may not want anyone else to know. They may be embarrassed by their symptoms, or they may be trying to avoid hospitalization. So the MMPI was also designed to try to tell when a

Skeptic at Large

BOX 14.3

Can the MMPI Reliably Detect Malingering?

While no research psychologist would regard the validity scales intended to measure dishonesty in the MMPI as perfect, there is one arena that has relied heavily on them to affect people's lives. One MMPI scale, called the "fake bad" scale, was developed by Paul Lees-Haley to detect people who are malingering—pretending to be sick, or sicker than they really are. Attorneys for insurance companies have used this scale in several court cases to argue that a person was faking symptoms and therefore should be denied insurance payments.

There are several disturbing issues about this scale and its use by the insurance industry. One problem is that Dr. Lees-Haley, who developed the scale, *paid* to have an article supporting his scale published in a medical journal. Not only that, but he works as an expert witness, usually for insurance companies, charging $600 an hour (Armstrong, 2008). This means he has a troubling economic incentive to find a test that accuses lots of people of "faking." Indeed, some psychologists feel the scale brands people as malingering when they are genuinely ill (Butcher et al., 2006). For example, one MMPI item used to calculate the Lees-Haley scale asks if the participant has lots of headaches. This is intended to detect a participant's tendency to complain. But many people who have suffered trauma from accidents actually do have frequent headaches. Perhaps it's not valid to compare the responses of accident victims to the frequency of response among the general population, most of whom have not been in an accident lately. In another test, the archived MMPI results of 20,000 people who had been admitted to psychiatric hospitals by psychiatrists over the years were analyzed, and almost half the patients met the Lees-Haley scale criterion for "possibly faking." It seems very unlikely that psychiatrists were wrong in half their diagnoses, suggesting that the scale has a lot of false positives in looking for fakers. As one psychologist said, the Lees-Haley fake bad scale is "great for insurance companies, but not great for people" (Armstrong, 2008).

person was "fudging" their answers. Just as there are ten clinical scales, scores to indicate the possibility of ten different psychological traits or disorders, there are several **validity scales**, intended to detect when participants are responding inconsistently or trying to hide or exaggerate psychological symptoms (**Box 14.3**).

There are several strategies to do this. One is to ask the same question in slightly different ways to see if the person gives the same answer. With over 500 questions to answer, it would be easy to lose track of what you said earlier, or even that you had answered a similar question. When the participant answers these planted questions inconsistently, then he may have been inconsistent for other questions too. So the test results may not be accurate. In other cases, the question is one that almost everyone, if honest, would answer in an unflattering way. Almost every adult has stolen something at some point in life, but a person trying to present a good image might deny ever stealing anything. Someone who answers too many such questions as though she has no shortcomings whatsoever will get a high score on the "lie scale," and the therapist will be leery about what the other scales say about the participant. There's even a scale that tries to detect if the participant has a tendency to always say "true" or always say "false."

As the name indicates, another test, the Myers–Briggs Type Indicator (MBTI), usually just called the **Myers–Briggs test**, emphasizes personality *types*, dividing people into 16 personality types, some of which are more common than others. By emphasizing personality types, it diverges from modern personality research, which emphasizes traits instead, as we've said.

validity scales Quantitative measures intended to detect when subjects are responding inconsistently or dishonestly.

Myers–Briggs test A personality test that categorizes people into 16 personality types.

In fact, the Myers–Briggs is founded on personality theories developed by psychoanalyst C. G. Jung in the 1920s, based on his clinical experiences. The Myers–Briggs test is very common, given to some 2 million people each year, typically to provide them with self-insight, perhaps to help choose a career. Unfortunately, research does not offer much support for the validity of the Myers–Briggs test; that is, there is some question about whether it measures personality traits accurately. Neither is it a particularly reliable test, as over one-third of participants, if retested more than 9 months later, are classified as a different personality "type" (Harvey, 1996; Pittenger, 1993). There's no evidence the MBTI actually predicts how well a person will do in one career or another (Druckman & Bjork, 1991). Comparing Myers–Briggs results with other personality tests suggests that the only personality trait among the big five that is reliably measured by the Myers–Briggs test is introversion-extraversion (Druckman & Bjork, 1991). Thus despite its popularity with some counselors and therapists, today the Myers–Briggs test is mostly ignored by researchers studying personality.

14.2 SUMMARY

- The eagerness with which someone seeks the company of others is the *personality trait* of extraversion—*extraverts* are talkative, assertive, and seek company, while *introverts* are less talkative and prefer solitary pursuits. Eysenck proposed that extraversion and *neuroticism* (emotional instability) are independent, continuously variable traits underlying personality.
- Cattell used *factor analysis* to boil down the thousands of English words used to describe personality to propose the existence of 16 different fundamental personality traits. Subsequent research by many different psychologists converged on the notion that these 16 traits in fact reflect the big five personality traits.
- The *five-factor model* asserts that *openness*, *conscientiousness*, *extraversion*, *agreeableness*, and *neuroticism* (OCEAN) are relatively independent, continuously variable traits that form the foundation of personality.
- Most big five personality tests, like the NEO PI-R, ask test-takers to agree or disagree with hundreds of statements about how they feel or behave in different situations. These tests are *standardized* so that researchers know how most people answer the questions, and can gauge how common or uncommon a person's scores are, typically by percentile, the percent of responses lower than the test-taker's score.
- The *Minnesota Multiphasic Personality Inventory* (*MMPI*), designed to screen for psychological disorders, also has *validity scales* to look for dishonest answers.
- While widely used, the *Myers–Briggs* test does not seem to measure personality well, or predict career success.

REVIEW QUESTIONS

1. What was the strategy of Cattell's factor analysis of English words for personality traits?
2. What are the big five traits, and what personality characteristics are typical of the low and high ends of each?
3. Why are research psychologists skeptical of the value of the Myers–Briggs test when so many businesses make use of it?

Food for Thought

Having learned about the big five, do you have a sense of whether you are low, high, or about average for each of the five traits?

14.3 Biological Influences on Personality

Things to Learn

- Genetic influences on the big five
- Temperament as a lifelong trait
- Person-situation debate
- Interactionists in personality

Once we accept the trait perspective and the strong evidence that there are five different traits that are reasonably independent of one another, an obvious question is: Why do people vary in any of these traits? In other words, why aren't we all more alike in our big five traits? As in most questions about variability in behavior, the two general classes of explanations are biological and social influences. In this section we'll see that there is ample evidence that one biological factor—genes—plays a role in the variability of big five traits across people. We'll also see that even newborn babies, who have had little or no social stimulation, vary in their response to the environment. So clearly there are biological influences on personality.

But the same data leave plenty of room for the environment to affect big five traits too. In fact, a debate arose that shook the foundations of personality psychology by suggesting that understanding environmental factors might offer a better prediction of how a person would behave than his or her personality would. As in most polarized debates, this one soon resolved into the recognition that both our environment and our personality affect our behavior.

There are genetic influences on personality traits

Psychologists have used twin studies, which we described in detail in Section 4.4, to determine how much genes contribute to the big five personality traits a person might display. Briefly, the reasoning is that if genes affect the various big five factors, then identical twins, who share the same genes and very similar environments growing up, should be more alike than non-identical twins, who also share similar environments growing up but share only half of their genes. That is exactly what has been found for each of the big five traits (Bouchard, 1994). Most important, identical twins who are raised apart are about as similar for the big five traits as are identical twins raised together (**Figure 14.12**). It is interesting how similar the five traits are in regard to heritability (recall from Section 4.4 that this is the statistical estimate of how much variation in the trait within a population is due to variation in genes). While the detailed numbers vary from study to study, they converge to indicate that differences in genes account for about 40–50% of the differences we see in human populations, for each of the big five factors.

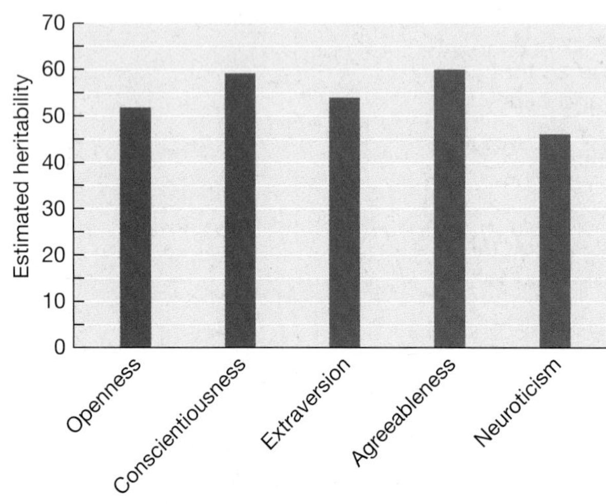

Figure 14.12 Heritability of the Big Five Personality Traits Various twin studies show good agreement, suggesting that 40–50% of the variability in each big five trait in the population is due to differences between people in their genes. Note that this leaves ample room for the environment to affect these traits. (After Bouchard, 1994.)

The evidence that genes influence the big five personality factors is also an important indication that they are indeed valid traits. If something as solid and objective as which genes you inherited affects your conscientiousness, neuroticism, and so on, then those are probably genuine differences in how people's brains, and therefore their minds, differ from one another. But do not take this to mean that genes alone determine personality, because we know that is not so. We will consider how the environment can affect personality in the next section.

Because genes can affect these personality traits in a measurable way, then presumably natural selection has been acting on those genes, and therefore those personality traits. The diversity of personalities suggests that there is more than one evolutionarily successful personality. The genetic influence on personality, and the notion that evolution favors a diversity of personalities in humans, raises the question of whether non-human animals also have personalities. This question, which was once seen as silly, has been addressed by several different researchers. Their findings indicate that animals also have personalities, and that as in humans, natural selection has favored a diversity of personalities within each species, as we'll discuss at the end of this chapter.

Temperament seems to be a lifelong characteristic

Most parents who have more than one child will tell you that the children behaved very differently from one another, right at birth. Despite being raised by the same parents, and in what must be fairly similar environments, the siblings may continue to display different personalities as they grow. Some of these differences are due to genes, because each child gets a unique combination of genes from his or her parents. That's why the personalities of identical twins are more alike than those of non-identical twins, as we discussed above. But even identical twins do not have identical personalities, so there's no denying that other factors, including the environment, have an effect on personality. Still, the personalities of non-identical twins are no more similar than those of ordinary, non-twin siblings, suggesting that being raised in the same place at the same time doesn't contribute that much to personality.

If we really want to get to the heart of genetic influences on personality, one strategy is to measure individual personalities before they've had a chance to be molded by other people. In other words, right after birth. When American psychologist Jerome Kagan and his colleagues (1998) examined newborn babies, they found that some seemed calm and easily soothed while other seemed irritable and hard to please. Eventually Kagan came up with a set of tests to estimate just how calm or irritable a baby is—dangling a new toy in front of his eyes, letting him hear a strange woman's voice, placing an alcohol-soaked cotton ball under his nose. Most babies show some sort of reaction to each stimulus, but they vary in how upset they get, whether they simply open their eyes wide, or yell and begin vigorously crying. They also vary in how quickly they recover from new stimuli. Kagan calls this variation in reaction to novel stimuli **temperament**, a person's emotional makeup, the way he or she generally responds to a variety of situations. While Kagan typically measured the babies' reactivity based on behaviors such as fretting and crying, it could also be monitored through physiological measures, such as accelerated heart rate, respiration, and blood pressure. About 20% of babies were highly reactive to the stimuli, fussing or crying easily for several minutes. Kagan refers to them as behaviorally uninhibited, or **high reactive** babies, but they are sometimes said to be "difficult" babies, as we discussed in Section 5.2. Another 40% of babies showed little reaction to novel stimuli, either not fussing at all or only for a short time. These are behaviorally inhibited, or **low reactive** or "easy" babies. About 40% of babies were somewhere in between in terms of their reaction to stimuli. These patterns of response were reliable, both across exposure to different stimuli and on repeated tests weeks apart. Kagan and colleagues conducted studies to track different temperaments, as we'll see next in **Figure 14.13**.

temperament A person's emotional makeup, the way the person generally responds to a variety of situations.

high reactive A baby who has a negative reaction to novel stimuli and takes longer to recover from that reaction.

low reactive A baby who shows little reaction to novel stimuli.

☑ Researchers at Work

Tracking different temperaments

Figure 14.13 The Continuity of Temperament (After Kagan et al., 1998.)

■ **Question:** Do behavioral differences present at birth persist to affect adult personality?

■ **Hypothesis:** High reactive and low reactive babies will grow up to show differences in personality.

Continued

Researchers at Work *Continued*

■ **Test:** Classify a large cohort of newborns as high reactive, low reactive, or in between. Assess the personalities of participants when they reach childhood and young adulthood to see if there are differences, on average, in their behavior.

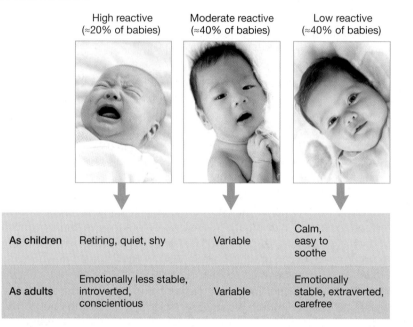

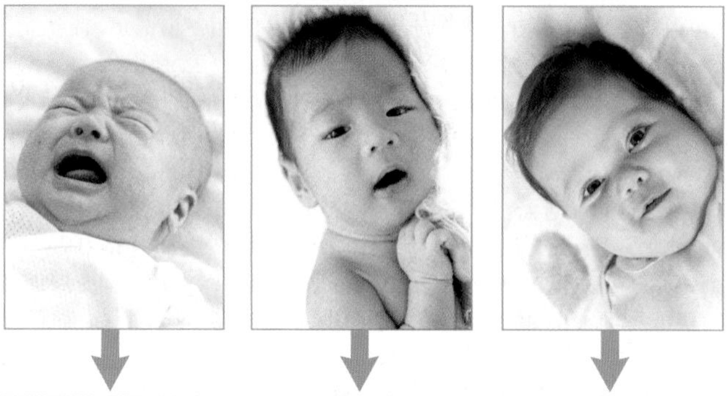

	High reactive (≈20% of babies)	Moderate reactive (≈40% of babies)	Low reactive (≈40% of babies)
As children	Retiring, quiet, shy	Variable	Calm, easy to soothe
As adults	Emotionally less stable, introverted, conscientious	Variable	Emotionally stable, extraverted, carefree

■ **Results:** When high reactive babies grow up, they tend to be reserved, quiet, and introverted. The low reactive babies grow up to be more adventurous, talkative, and extraverted. The moderate reactive babies showed a greater variability in behavior as children and adults.

■ **Conclusion:** Differences in temperament that are present at birth, before any extensive social interactions, persist into childhood and adulthood. These differences may reflect genetic or prenatal influences that help shape personality.

It's not easy to make predictions about those 40% of babies found in the middle, but the high and low reactive babies present a remarkably consistent picture as they grow up to be children and adults. When high reactive babies grow up, they tend to be reserved, quiet, and introverted. It is as though, finding encounters with the world upsetting, they have learned to keep their distance from new stimuli. The low reactive babies grow up to be more adventurous, talkative, and extraverted. Perhaps they are less upset by the bumps and bruises of life and so are more willing to explore. In longitudinal studies, following the same individuals from infancy on, these differences in temperament persist through adolescence and into young adulthood.

Many high reactive babies seem to get a grip on their fearfulness as they grow up, developing coping strategies to control when and where they are exposed to new stimuli. They may develop routines and work hard to complete school assignments thoroughly and well beforehand. Despite doing well in school, when asked, they are more likely to admit being tense and more uneasy than the kids who were low reactive babies. Indeed, some of the high reactive babies grow up to have more serious problems with anxiety. They may suffer from panic attacks or severe social phobia. When brought into the lab and shown photographs of angry faces, they will show a greater fear response than low reactives.

Whatever the basis of temperament, it must be reflected in some aspect of brain functioning. Kagan has suggested that what's reactive about high reactive babies is the amygdala, a part of the brain known to be involved in fearful responses. For Kagan, the different physiological responses of the babies—heart rate, blood pressure, and so on—reflect differences in how readily their amygdalas activate the autonomic nervous system.

How does temperament fit into the big five? Temperament seems to reflect a composite of at least three of the big five factors (Ahadi & Rothbart, 1994). Neuroticism, also known as emotional instability, is one factor in temperament—low reactive babies are emotionally stable, and high reactive babies are emotionally unstable. The greater prevalence of panic attacks and social phobia in high reactive individuals fits their higher neuroticism. Temperament also reflects extraversion, since low reactive babies tend to be more outgoing when they grow up. To a lesser extent, conscientiousness also reflects temperament. High reactive babies tend to display greater conscientiousness, which may reflect their attempt to control their exposure to unpleasant situations. After all, one way to avoid unpleasant surprises is by being vigilant, carefully seeing to all the details of life.

In short, temperament represents a broader categorization of personality, lumping together several distinct aspects of personality that can be measured independently when we assess adult personalities. In that sense, temperament does not give as fine-grained an analysis as the big five. You can also see temperament as a cruder measure of personality based on the fact that a large temperament group, those in between low and high reactive people, includes many different personalities, so you cannot readily predict what their behaviors will be like as they grow. Also, to the extent that temperament divides individuals into just three categories—high reactive, low reactive, and in-between—it represents a throwback to personality "types." In contrast, the concept of the big five, describing personality as a composite of five different traits, each representing a continuum, suggests there are hundreds of measurably different personalities.

Once you begin thinking of personality as something that can vary continuously across several different scales, it's easier to think that an individual's personality might change at least a little as he grows and experiences life. And let's not forget that the situation we find ourselves in matters too. We tend to be calmer in libraries than at some sporting event where long-term rivals are keeping the score close. How does the *situation* fit into our notions of personality?

Is personality stable across situations?

The American psychologist Walter Mischel (1968) lobbed a grenade at personality psychology by suggesting that people's behavior may be better explained by the *situations* they find themselves in than by their *personalities*. He asked, if situations are the prevailing determinant of behavior, is there any point in considering personality at all? In what came to be known as the **person-situation debate**, researchers argued over whether behavior could be better explained by a person's internal characteristics (sometimes referred to as the person's "disposition") or by the situation. For example, one researcher measured variability in the behavior that people showed in many different settings, and then compared those with measures of variability in behavior across people (Fleeson, 2004). He found more variability *within each individual* than *across people* (**Figure 14.14**). In other words, you could more accurately predict what a person would do if you

person-situation debate The question of whether behavior can be better explained by a person's internal characteristics, or by the surroundings.

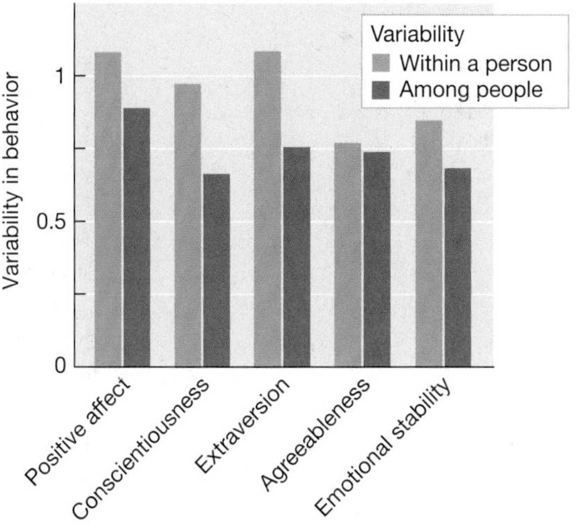

Figure 14.14 The Person-Situation Debate Psychologists observe considerable differences between people in how much they display various traits. Here the amount of variation for each trait is compared. However, the same person does not always behave the same, but rather shows different behaviors in different situations. That variability within a person is as great as the variability across people. Such data suggest that personality does not matter as much as the environment for predicting behavior. (After Fleeson, 2004.)

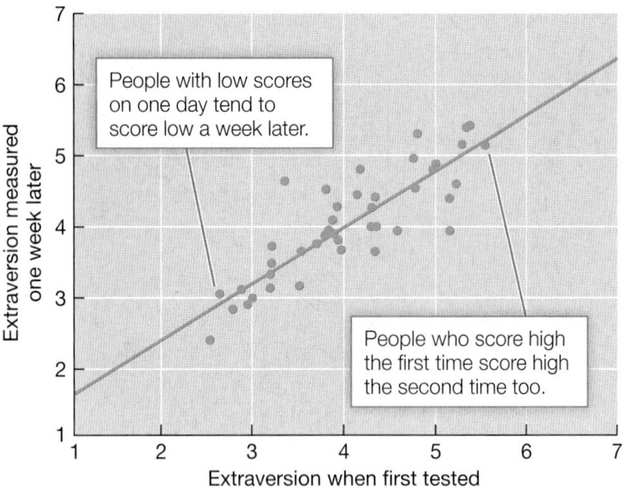

Figure 14.15 Some Personality Traits Are Consistently Seen Although situations influence behavior, people who are among the most extraverted in one situation will tend to be the most extraverted in another situation, too. (After Fleeson, 2004.)

knew the situation than if you knew who that person was. Such findings led to the *social learning* theory of situational specificity, that people act differently in different situations, as society has taught them to do, rather than acting consistently as a "personality" would have them do (Mischel & Shoda, 1999). By this theory, which we discuss in the next section, we each engage in constant self-monitoring of our own behavior, altering the behavior to better fit the role that society dictates for each situation.

Given such findings, is there any room for a personality to affect behavior? Apparently so, because if you observe someone in many different situations, you can find ways in which that person behaves consistently. For example, an extravert may not talk as much at a business meeting as he or she would at a party, which shows the importance of the situation for affecting behavior. But if someone is the *most* talkative person in *both* situations, that suggests that his personality, specifically his extraversion, matters too (**Figure 14.15**). Having established that genes influence each of the big five traits, it is clear that the situation can't explain all the ways in which we differ from one another. We may change our jeans when we go to a party, but we don't change our genes.

interactionists Personality psychologists who acknowledge the importance of the situation in assessing current behavior and the importance of personality in understanding someone's average behavior.

These days almost all personality psychologists agree that both the situation and personality are important. Personality psychologists today are **interactionists**, who assume that the situation is important for understanding the behavior that is displayed at the moment, but that personality is important for understanding someone's average behavior over days, weeks, and years. The interactionist perspective acknowledges that there are some situations in which almost everyone behaves the same—hostages on a hijacked plane, for example—and where personality counts for very little. But in situations where people show many different behaviors—in a shopping mall, for example—different personalities can explain why some people tend to browse many stores and take their time shopping, while others go only to one store, quickly do their shopping, and return home. In other words, while it is true that our behavior varies across situations, it is also true that we differ from one another in how we act in those situations. In fact, it was in response to the person–situation debate that psychologists knuckled down to test and confirm the validity of a core of traits that gave rise to the big five perspective.

Thus the person–situation debate has been more or less resolved, by acknowledging both the baseline effect of personality and the modulating effect of situations. It also acknowledges that social learning provides us with instruction about how we should behave in different situations. In the next section we'll consider further the ways the social environment affects personality, both as we grow and in adulthood.

14.3 SUMMARY

- Research suggests that about half the variation in each big five trait across the population is due to variation in genes.
- Newborn babies differ in *temperament*, how strongly they react to, and recover from, new stimuli. *High reactive* babies have a more negative reaction to stimuli and take longer to recover than *low reactive* babies. These differences are stable across time, as adults who were high reactive babies have personalities that are higher in neuroticism and

conscientiousness, and lower in extraversion, than adults who were low reactive babies.

- The *person–situation debate* focused on whether individuals' behavior is better explained by their personality or by their situation, and emphasized that social learning instructs us about how to behave in different situations.
- The debate was resolved by the *interactionist* model, accepted by nearly all personality psychologists today, which acknowledges the importance of the situation, but points out that two people with different personalities will consistently differ in how they respond to multiple situations. For example, extraverts talk more at parties than they do in libraries, but they also talk more than introverts do in either situation.

REVIEW QUESTIONS

1. What is the evidence that genes influence the big five traits?
2. Describe different temperaments in babies and the adult personality traits that tend to be associated with each.
3. What was the person–situation debate, and how was it resolved by the interactionist model?

Food for Thought

What if you one day have a child who, as a baby, is highly reactive, responding very negatively to little upsets and is difficult to soothe? As a parent, what could you do to help the child cope with the world while growing up and in adulthood?

14.4 Social Influences on Personality

Things to Learn

- Social learning
- Locus of control
- Bandura's reciprocal determinism
- Cross-cultural psychology

The ingenuity of research leading to the conclusion that five key traits can define personality is remarkable and has greatly accelerated our understanding of people. But our discussion of the trait perspective has not yet touched upon how a particular personality *develops* as a child grows up.

What shapes the development of the big five personality traits? We've seen that the temperament of babies offers some prediction of what their adult personality scores will be like for some of the big five, but not all. Yet for the babies with temperament between the low reactive and high reactive babies, we have no predictions at all. We know from twin studies that genes play a role in forming each of the big five, but those same data also make it clear that genes alone cannot account for any of the big five traits (see Figure 14.12). In other words, even if genes account for about half the variation in each big five trait, a complete understanding of how personality develops must also consider environmental influences. The most prominent environmental feature for a growing child is other people, so many researchers have explored social influences on personality.

This final section of the chapter concerns the **social learning** perspective on personality, which emphasizes how what we learn from other people helps form our personality. Sometimes called the *social learning theory* of personality development, it offers an explanation of how the big five traits might be shaped as a child grows.

This section looks at three perspectives to help understand social contributions to the developing personality. First we'll discuss the *behaviorist* perspective, which relies on learning theory to account for how the child's behavior is shaped by various rewards and punishments. This perspective emphasizes overt behaviors and how they are encouraged or discouraged, without much consideration of what the child is thinking. In contrast, the *cognitive* perspective focuses on the child's analysis of other people's behaviors, as she tries to understand the rules of social life, to develop her own style of thought and behavior. Finally, we'll discuss *cultural* influences, looking at ways in which growing up in a particular culture can influence the developing personality, resulting in a long-lasting mind-set affecting behavior.

social learning Changes in behavior brought about by interacting with other individuals.

response tendencies According to the behaviorist perspective, particular ways of reacting to various situations based on past learning experiences, which together form the personality.

locus of control The individual's perception about whether his or her efforts in life will be reinforced.

Behaviorism: Behavioral approaches emphasize overt behavior and rewards

The behaviorist explanation of personality development relies heavily on how parents interact with the child. For a strict behaviorist, the only acceptable object of study is observable behavior. To understand why a child behaves in a particular way, the behaviorist examines the events that preceded behavior. Using classical conditioning and operant conditioning as their model, behaviorists focus on how rewarding certain behaviors can make them more common, as we described in Section 8.2. Behaviorists examine *contingencies*, the events that happen after an individual displays a behavior, to determine whether it is being reinforced. From the behaviorist perspective, any behavior that is common must be getting reinforced. If the behavior is undesirable, then the trick is to determine what exactly is reinforcing the behavior and try to eliminate that reinforcement.

For example, if a child often misbehaves, he may do so because it gets his parents' attention, which he finds reinforcing, even if they are scolding him. If instead of scolding him the parents ignore him, his misbehavior may go away. Depending on which of these two tacks the parents take, the child's personality may develop differently. Concerning two of the big five traits, for example, the child may grow up to be either uncooperative or helpful with respect to agreeableness, and impulsive or dependable with respect to conscientiousness.

To American psychologist B. F. Skinner (1904–1990), whom we met in Section 8.2, personality was a constellation of **response tendencies**, particular ways of reacting to various situations based on past learning experiences. Although Skinner believed learning experiences during childhood shaped these response tendencies, he also believed it was always possible to learn new response tendencies, even as an adult. In other words, he did not conceive of personality as a lifelong unchanging characteristic of a person. Skinner saw consistency in an individual's personality as arising when contingencies in that person's life had not changed. Putting that person into an environment with very different contingencies, where behavior that had previously been rewarded was not, would change the person's response tendencies. An outsider observing the individual under these new contingencies might describe him as having a very different personality.

In the end, behaviorists lost the campaign to explain personality away as nothing more than learned response tendencies. For one thing, as evidence mounted that personality traits are heritable, behaviorists could offer little explanation for why genes should matter, if external rewards or punishments formed a personality. If the behaviorist theory of personality were true, then people exposed to the same reward contingencies should display the same response tendencies, no matter what genes they had. Also, behaviorism's disregard for mental processes meant it had little to say about how personality affects our *thinking*. Behaviorist theories of personality were soon replaced with theories that retained the notion of learning, but expanded to include cognitive processes, including the individual's perception of other people and the world.

Cognitive psychology: Perceptions of control and competency shape a developing personality

Today, nearly all psychologists agree with the behaviorist position that learning experience affects personality. Few psychologists who specialize in personality studies are considered behaviorists, however, because most also believe that cognitive processes also shape personality.

Some psychologists emphasize that cognitive processes, including perception, play a role in how we learn. **Locus of control** is the individual's *perception*

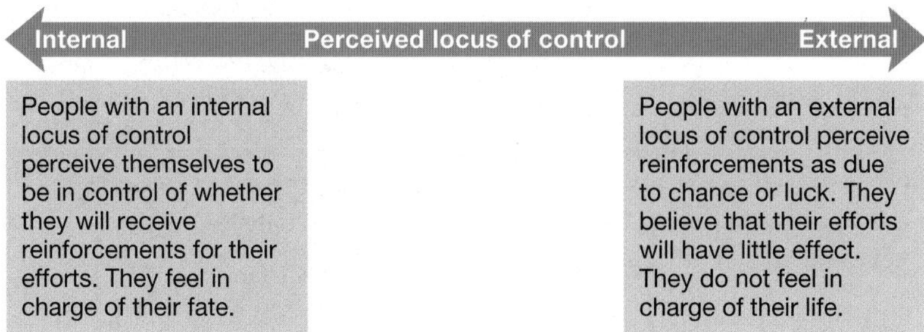

Figure 14.16 The Locus of Control

about whether his or her efforts in life will be reinforced (Rotter, 1966). *Locus* means "place," so the phrase refers to whether you perceive control to be inside yourself or outside yourself. People with an *internal locus of control* perceive that whether or not they get reinforced is up to them. In other words, they believe the efforts they make will be reinforced to improve their lives, so they feel in charge of their own destiny. In contrast, people with an *external locus of control* perceive that reinforcers in life are determined by other people, or by luck, not by their own efforts (**Figure 14.16**). They do not expect to be rewarded for their own efforts. Like other personality traits, locus of control is thought to vary continuously across individuals, from those with a very strong internal locus of control to those with a very strong external locus of control.

Closely related to the concept of locus of control is Canadian-born psychologist Albert Bandura's assertion that the cognitive processes going on while modeling other people's behavior could affect a child's developing personality. Bandura felt that one of the most important things a child can learn by observing others is **self-efficacy**, a term he coined to describe "beliefs in one's capabilities to organize and execute the courses of action required to manage prospective situations" (Bandura, 1995, p. 2). In other words, self-efficacy is the belief that you are effective, that you have the ability to succeed, and that you can master a particular situation. This requires the perception of an *internal* locus of control, because you have to believe your efforts matter in order to try. But self-efficacy isn't just having an internal locus of control; it is also the confidence that you will be *successful* as you tackle progressively greater challenges growing up.

For Bandura, an important part of personality development happens when the child observes other people, especially adults, and models their behaviors to succeed in various situations. As the child succeeds in this strategy in many different situations, at home, at the park, in restaurants, and in school, she gains self-efficacy. This self-efficacy, in turn, provides her with the confidence to tackle new situations, new problems, with the belief that she will succeed. Without self-efficacy, the child avoids new situations and challenges, and therefore fails to reach her full potential for a happy life. In other words, she is less likely to reach *self-actualization*, being the best and happiest human she can be, which we discussed in regard to Rogerian psychotherapy earlier in this chapter and in regard to Maslow's ideas in Section 12.1.

The theory of self-efficacy is a *social* theory since it hinges on social learning, which we discussed in Section 8.3. **Social modeling** is the tendency of individuals to mimic the behavior of others. Recall that social modeling is an example of observational learning, in this case, the individual learning by observing others and copying their behavior. You may also recall Albert Bandura's work showing that children who observe adults punching an inflatable doll are much more likely to punch the doll themselves when they get the chance (see Figure 8.27). There we focused on the conditions that promote learning through social modeling, but here we will focus on how social modeling affects personality.

self-efficacy The belief that you are capable: that you have the ability to succeed and to master a particular situation.

social modeling The tendency of individuals to mimic the behavior of others.

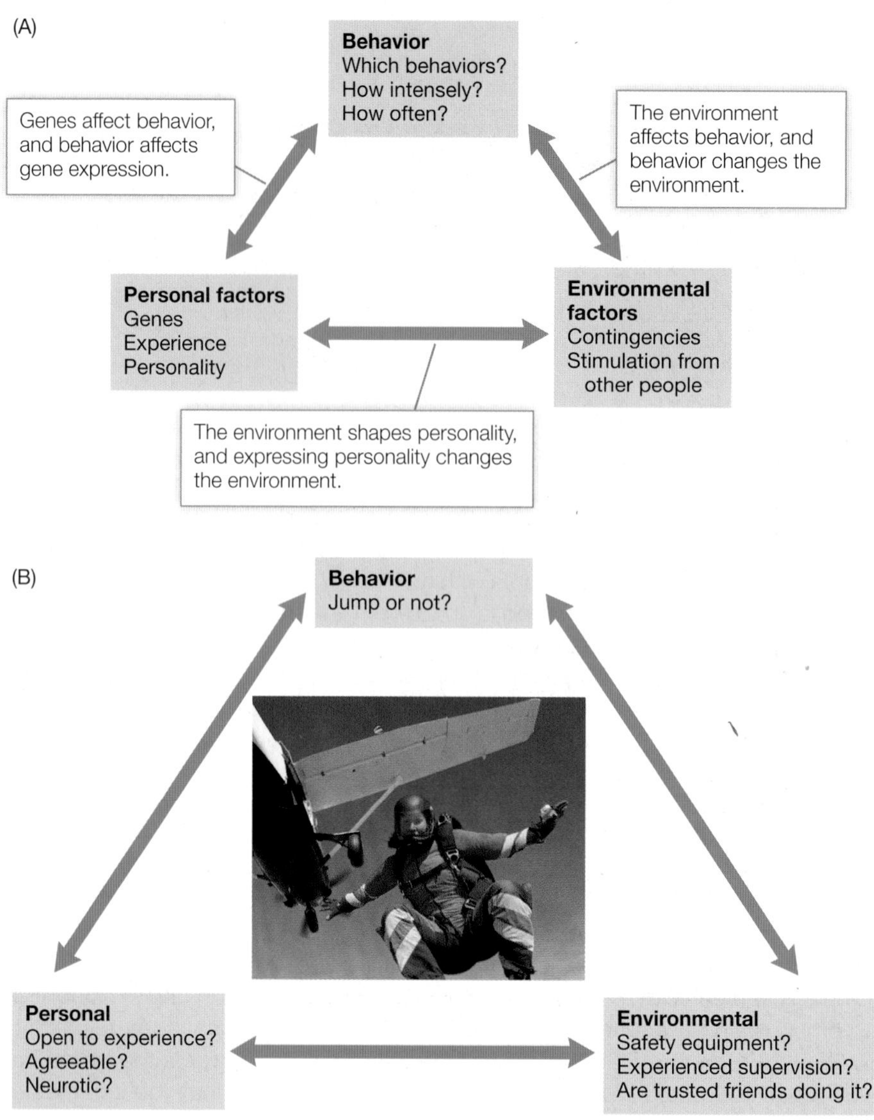
(A)
Behavior
Which behaviors?
How intensely?
How often?
Genes affect behavior, and behavior affects gene expression.
The environment affects behavior, and behavior changes the environment.
Personal factors
Genes
Experience
Personality
Environmental factors
Contingencies
Stimulation from other people
The environment shapes personality, and expressing personality changes the environment.
(B)
Behavior
Jump or not?
Personal
Open to experience?
Agreeable?
Neurotic?
Environmental
Safety equipment?
Experienced supervision?
Are trusted friends doing it?

Figure 14.17 Bandura's Model of Reciprocal Determinism

The concept of self-efficacy is not just a social theory but also a *cognitive* theory because the important question is not just whether the child becomes competent and successful but whether the child *perceives* herself to be competent and successful. If so, then she will also display more forethought when faced with a new situation, working out in her mind how to take on the new challenge. A child without self-efficacy, already expecting to fail, will avoid thinking out beforehand how to take on the challenge, and is therefore less likely to succeed. In other words, lack of self-efficacy produces a self-fulfilling prophecy that she will not succeed. Possessing self-efficacy also leads to a self-fulfilling prophecy—belief that she can succeed allows the forethought and persistence needed to succeed, which then strengthens self-efficacy. Thus the concept of self-efficacy is closely related to the notion of *self-esteem*, how competent and valuable a person feels himself to be.

In terms of the big five personality traits, people lacking self-efficacy will be less open to experience (avoiding new challenges), less extraverted (avoiding meeting new people in new situations), and more neurotic (less able to handle minor setbacks). People with low self-efficacy may or may not display those characteristics, depending on other factors, including the genes they inherit.

reciprocal determinism The theory that three different factors mutually influence one another: personal factors, environmental factors, and the individual's behavior.

Bandura also offered a theory to explain how genes and the social environment both affect, and are affected by, an individual's behavior. Called **reciprocal determinism**, it is the theory that three different factors mutually influence one another:

1. Personal factors, including the individual's genes, experience, and personality
2. Environmental factors, including contingencies that affect learning and other people
3. The individual's behavior

Reciprocal determinism acknowledges the importance of both genetic factors and social factors, but emphasizes that each has a reciprocal relationship with the person's behavior (**Figure 14.17A**). Yes, the way adults treat a child will influence her future behavior, but her behavioral reactions to those adults will also affect *their* behavior. Yes, biological characteristics, including the brain and genes, influence a person's behavior, but her behavior also affects her developing brain and which of those genes will become active, as we saw in Section 4.2. This reciprocal determinism, in shaping an individual's thinking and behavior, is also shaping her *personality*, which is, after all, a summation of her cognitive and behavioral tendencies.

An important aspect of reciprocal determinism is that the person is herself an active agent, bringing her personal characteristics to the environment and responding to that environment to build the life she wants, which includes actively shaping her personality, whether knowingly or not, by fulfilling those needs (**Figure 14.17B**). This perspective falls within the realm of humanistic psychology, particularly Rogerian psychotherapy, which we discussed earlier in this chapter. This idea also resonates with Abraham Maslow's concept of a hierarchy of human needs that culminates in the need for self-actualization, the human desire for fulfillment by becoming the best and most accomplished person possible. This striving for fulfillment includes developing the personality traits best suited for the life a person desires.

Cross-cultural psychology studies the role of culture in personality

As the name implies, *cross-cultural psychology* tries to compare different cultures, asking how people from one culture differ, on average, from people in another culture. If people from two different cultures reliably differ from one another in some behavior, then the difference in their behavior may in fact be caused by the differences in their cultures. In fact, researchers have found differences in personality in different cultures (McCrae et al., 2005). For example, in traditional cultures, such as Arab nations that follow strict Muslim laws, or hunter-gatherer societies such as the African bushmen, almost everyone scores low on "openness" compared with people in more Westernized cultures (Silverthorne, 2001).

An ardent believer in genetic influences on personality might suggest that perhaps different genes in the different cultures are responsible for their personality differences. But in North America, where many different ethnic groups have settled, the personalities of, say, people of Asian descent are significantly different from those of people raised in Asian cultures. Since the genetic pool is the same, the differences in personality must be due to differences in where the people were raised. In fact, when bilingual Hong Kong students moved to the United States, their big five traits became more in line with U.S. values every year they were there (**Figure 14.18**; McCrae et al., 1998).

Figure 14.18 Culture Clash Chinese business students tend to have lower scores on "openness to experience" than U.S. business students. But when Chinese business students immigrate to the United States, their openness scores tend to rise.

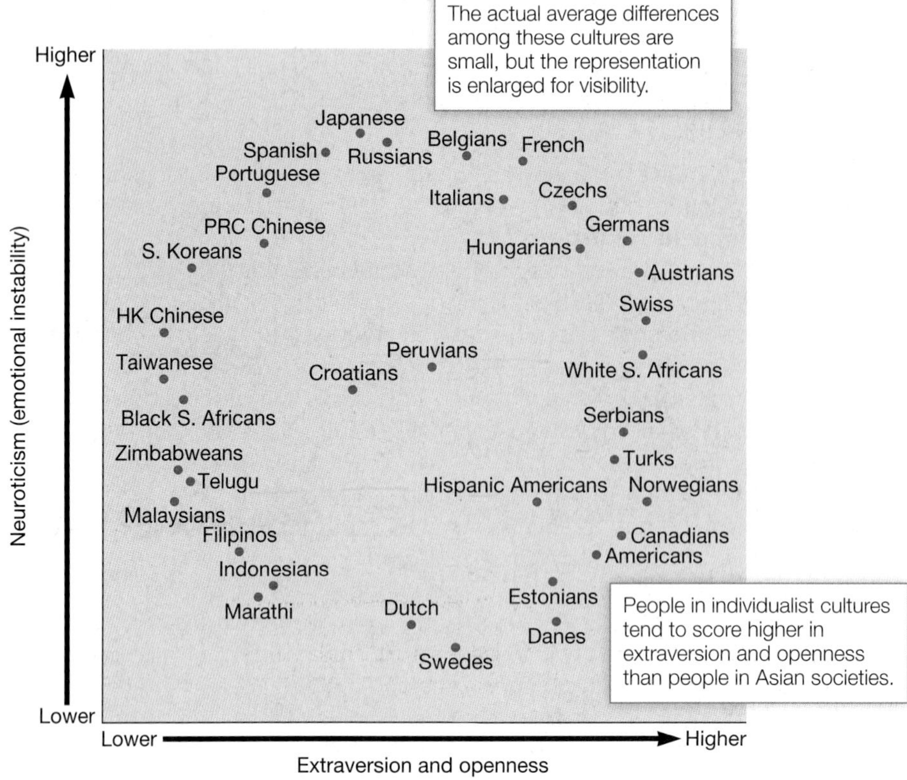

Figure 14.19 Comparing Cultures for the Big Five Traits In this graph the various cultures are plotted in terms of differences in average big five scores. The *x*-axis reflects a combination of extraversion and openness, while the *y*-axis reflects neuroticism. In fact, these average differences are small, but the representation is enlarged so you can see the labels. (After Allik & McCrae, 2004.)

We will take up the theme of cross-cultural differences in Section 15.1, where we will focus on cultural differences with regard to individualism, the idea that a single individual should strive for personal achievement. There is a very strong pro-individualism sentiment in U.S. culture, while many Asian cultures place greater emphasis on collectivism, the notion that people should work closely together to share the results and to share the credit for those efforts. Of course, it's not as though every culture is individualistic or collectivist; there is a continuum across cultures. Attitudes concerning individualism and collectivism are reflected primarily in the dimension of extraversion (Hofstede & McCrae, 2004). Specifically, people from individualist cultures tend to be more extraverted than people from collectivist cultures. This is one factor that contributes to the small but reliable differences seen between cultures in some big five traits (**Figure 14.19**). Could it be that people from individualist cultures have greater confidence in the value of what they have to say, and therefore speak up more than people from collectivist cultures? Turn to Chapter 15 to find out.

What Ever Happened to Phineas Gage?

In closing, let's take another look at the story of Phineas Gage, with which this chapter begins. Recall that Phineas was raised in nineteenth-century New England, where sobriety and industriousness were prized, and that before his accident his personality reflected those cultural values. After his accident, however, he became impulsive and irritable. The physician who attended him said he was "fitful, irreverent, indulging at times in the grossest profanity (which was not previously his custom), manifesting but little deference for his fellows, impatient of restraint or advice when it conflicts with his desires, at times pertinaciously obstinate, yet capricious and vacillating" (Harlow, 1868). With our understanding

(A)

(B)

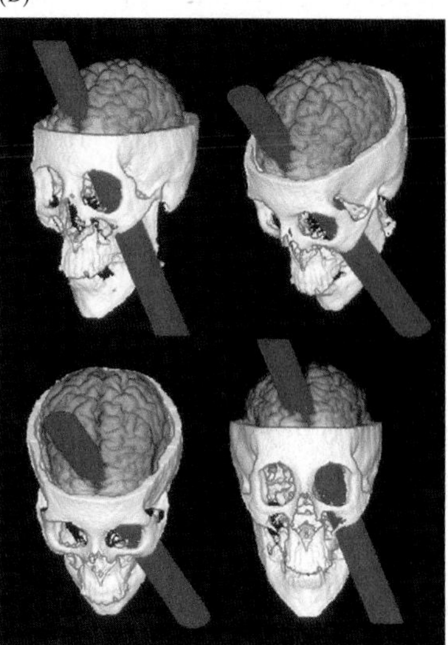

Figure 14.20 The Famous Phineas Gage (A) This photograph was probably made to advertise Phineas's paid appearances in various New England towns. He is holding the very bar that passed through his skull. (B) A twentieth-century reconstruction of the bar's path is based on analysis of Phineas's skull. These images indicate that the bar damaged the frontal lobes of the cortex. Today the frontal cortex is recognized as important for inhibiting impulsive behaviors.

of the big five personality traits, we can now characterize Phineas's personality as displaying less agreeableness and conscientiousness than it did before, and as more extraverted and neurotic. With these characteristics, Phineas no longer fit into his community very well, and was unable to hold down the job at which he had previously excelled. For a while, he toured locally, getting paid to appear with his famous iron bar (**Figure 14.20A**).

Today we have a somewhat better idea of how the bar accident affected Phineas's brain and, in turn, his personality. It is clear that the bar damaged the frontal lobes of his cortex (**Figure 14.20B**), which today neurologists recognize as important for inhibiting impulsive behavior. The frontal lobe is one of the last portions of the brain to mature, by the late teens (Gogtay et al., 2004), and this slow maturation may explain why teenagers can be so impulsive. Phineas's behavior after this region was damaged, as described above, may have been more like that of some teenagers than of a mature adult. Did his new, impatient, and changeable personality make it hard to get along with others? What we know for sure is that he left New England, working as a stagecoach driver in far-off Chile for several years. Perhaps he got on better with people in what was, in those days, still a frontier. He did not return to the United States until his health began failing 11 years after the accident, when he joined his mother and sister in San Francisco. They tended to him until his death from convulsions just short of his 37th birthday.

Phineas Gage's extraordinary case made a big impression on the world, including the scientific world. Some writers shamelessly sensationalized his case, exaggerating observed changes in his personality (Kean, 2014), but it is nevertheless clear from his physician's accounts that Phineas's personality changed significantly as a result of his accident. So it is no wonder that the case of Phineas Gage convinced the world that personality resides somewhere inside the brain. While we have a better grip today on at least some components of personality—such as the big five factors—we have yet to understand which parts of the brain mediate those traits, and how genes and the social environment during development shape those traits into myriad different human personalities.

The Cutting Edge

Do Non-Human Animals Have Personalities?

Most cat and dog owners think their pets have personalities—that individual animals behave in consistently different ways from one another. When owners are asked to evaluate their pets' personalities, the pets seem to vary in the way Eysenck described human personalities—how introverted they are, and how emotionally stable. Do the pets really have personalities, or are people simply projecting their own personalities onto the animals? Owners who rate their dogs as agreeable do tend to be agreeable themselves. On the other hand, different people rating an animal's personality agree pretty well. For example, four human caretakers' personality ratings of different spotted hyenas in a captive colony were quite consistent (Gosling, 1998).

What's more, if the animals really do have different personalities, then when they are put in a test situation, they should react differently, giving them a chance to display their personalities. Such individual differences displayed in test situations, consistent across time, sometimes for years, have been seen in many species (Gosling, 2008; Freeman & Gosling, 2010; Svartberg & Forkman, 2002). Perhaps the most common test is to see how readily the animal approaches unknown individuals of the same species, to get an idea of how "sociable" it is. This sociability, combined with ratings of how energetic the individual is, seems a lot like introversion-extraversion in humans. Researcher Samuel Gosling (2008) even sees consistent individual differences in introversion in fish and octopuses: "Whereas an introverted human will stay at home on a Saturday night or stand alone at a party, an octopus will stay in its den during feeding and attempt to hide itself by changing color." Another test is to expose the animal to a new object, rating whether the animal approaches or avoids it, to measure how fearful or curious the individual is. This seems a reasonable stand-in for neuroticism (emotional instability) in humans. More cognitively talented species show differences in more abstract personality traits, such as conscientiousness and impulsiveness.

These studies indicate that personality, like other behaviors, is subject to natural selection, so there is a continuum of personality across species, reflecting our descent from common ancestors. For example, by selectively breeding for calm behavior and sociability, researchers were able to produce tame foxes in the course of 40 years (Kukekova et al., 2008).

Figure 14.21 Extraverts or Introverts Are dogs natural extraverts while cats tend to be introverts?

No one's suggesting that lions and koalas are equally shy, or that otters and cows are equally curious, so natural selection has clearly provided different species with different overall behavioral tendencies (**Figure 14.21**). But the variation between individuals of the same species suggests that more than one personality can successfully reproduce. One individual might succeed by being extraverted and adventurous while another might reproduce by being introverted and cautious. In fact, individual differences in personality may help tailor an individual's chances of reproducing—a large and powerful male baboon may benefit by fighting off other males to get the attention of many females, while a male with a smaller body may be better off keeping a low profile, developing a reputation as being helpful to females, for a chance to copulate on the sly. Do these effects of personality on reproductive success apply to humans? Maybe, since surveys indicate that extraverted people have more sexual partners than introverted people. Unfortunately for the extraverts, they are also more likely to be hospitalized than introverts (Nettle, 2005).

Studies of animal personality confirm a role of both genetics and experience, suggesting that different personalities may have evolved both to provide behavioral flexibility (develop one personality under one set of conditions, another personality in other conditions) and to favor different reproductive strategies.

14.4 SUMMARY

- The *social learning* perspective emphasizes how other people shape our personality as we grow.
- Behaviorism emphasizes how the contingencies in life, whether behaviors are rewarded or punished, mold behavior into *response tendencies*, particular ways of reacting to situations, which an observer would describe as personality.
- While all psychologists agree that contingencies and learning affect behavior, most have moved beyond behaviorism to consider cognitive processes as well. For example, a person with an internal *locus of control* will be more likely to strive for reinforcements than a person with an external locus of control, who might attribute all reinforcements to luck or chance.
- In addition to an internal locus of control, Bandura believes a person can have *self-efficacy*—an ability to organize and execute ways to handle new situations.
- Achieving self-efficacy allows a person to reach self-actualization, the fulfillment of the individual's human potential.
- The development of personality is subject to *reciprocal determinism*, in which personal, environmental, and situational factors mutually influence one another.
- People from different cultures differ, on average, in terms of the big five personality traits.

REVIEW QUESTIONS

1. What term did behaviorists use to describe personality, and how did they think it came about?
2. What is the locus of control, and how does it relate to self-efficacy?
3. In what ways do the average big five traits differ in individuals from collectivist versus individualist societies?

Food for Thought

Which comes first, the cultural attitudes about individualism versus collectivism, or the underlying personality traits of the people living in that culture?

14

Personality

An Explosive Personality

Phineas Gage was a sober, efficient, capable young man of 25, respected by the workmen he supervised as they blasted rock to clear a path for a new railroad in Vermont in 1848. But something went wrong while Phineas was using an iron tamping rod to pack explosives at the bottom of a hole drilled into solid rock. The tamping rod—custom-made for him by a local blacksmith—was a cylinder an inch-and-a-quarter in diameter, about three-and-a-half feet long, flat at the bottom to tamp the charge, tapering to a point at the top. It resembled a javelin.

The iron rod must have struck a spark from the surrounding rock, because the charge went off unexpectedly, flinging the rod straight at Phineas's head. The rod pierced his left cheek, passed behind his left eye and out the top of his skull, landing some 60 feet away. From the force of the rod's path, Phineas was thrown onto his back, his limbs convulsing. Yet in a minute or two he spoke. With help from his men, he walked to a wagon, where he sat for the ride to town. There Phineas walked up a flight of stairs, unaided, to a doctor's office to have his wounds cleaned and bandaged. No one expected him to live; an undertaker made a coffin for him (Macmillan, 2000a).

Phineas survived the accident, but he worked at a series of menial jobs for another 12 years, one indication that he was a changed man (Harlow, 1868). After the accident he was moody, stubborn, boastful, prone to cursing, and "impatient of restraint or advice" (Macmillan, 2008, p. 829). Strangely enough, the explosion that forced an iron rod through his brain had left him with an explosive personality. Despite the miracle of his physical recovery, "his mind was radically changed, so decidedly that his friends and acquaintances said that he was 'no longer Gage'" (Macmillan, 2008, p. 829).

What happened to change Phineas Gage's personality?

Think Like a Psychologist:

Principles in Action

Whenever we encounter any interesting behavior we should consider the four principles. Here are some ways that the four principles relate to our opening story about Phineas:

MACHINE

The mind is a product of a physical machine, the brain.

When the bar destroyed parts of his prefrontal cortex, Phineas Gage's personality was altered. Loss of parts of the brain important for directing attention and inhibiting behavior left him impulsive in his action and speech.

UNCONSCIOUS

We are consciously aware of only a small part of our mental activity.

The brain has no pain receptors, so once his skin and scalp healed, Phineas would have no sensation of brain damage. Rather, his experience was simply that he felt more impatient with other people, more willing to curse and drink than he had before, and so he behaved accordingly.

SOCIAL

We constantly modify our behavior, beliefs, and attitudes according to what we perceive about the people around us.

Phineas Gage's impulsive behavior in action and speech affected his relationship with others. People who'd known him before found him changed and, apparently, not for the better. Eventually Phineas left everyone he knew behind to work in Chile, where the isolation of driving a stagecoach over mountainous routes may have been a better fit for his new nature.

EXPERIENCE

Our experiences physically alter the structure and function of the brain.

We have to consider the possibility that the experience of the accident may have contributed to the changes in Phineas Gage. After the explosion, he had to expect to die soon (everyone else thought he would) and probably knew a coffin was being built for him. That sort of near-death experience might also give a person more of a "you only live once" attitude.

KEY TERMS

agreeableness, 617
anal stage, 604
astrology, 599
birth-order effect, 607
confirmation bias, 601
conscientiousness, 617
continuum, 613
defense mechanisms, 602
ego, 602
extravert, 612
factor analysis, 614
five-factor model, 615
free association, 606
Freudian slips, 606
genital stage, 605
high reactive, 625
humanistic psychology, 610
hypochondria, 621
id, 602
interactionists, 628
introvert, 612
latency stage, 605
locus of control, 630
low reactive, 625
Minnesota Multiphasic Personality Inventory (MMPI), 620
MMPI clinical scales, 621
Myers-Briggs test, 622
neurosis, 603
neuroticism, 613
Oedipal complex, 605
openness, 617
oral stage, 604
personality, 598
personality traits, 612
personality types, 599
person-situation debate, 627
phallic stage, 604
projective tests, 608
psychoanalysis, 600
psychosexual stages of development, 603
rationalization, 602
reciprocal determinism, 632
reliability, 608
response tendencies, 630
Rogerian psychotherapy, 610
Rorschach test, 608
self-actualization, 610
self-efficacy, 631
social learning, 629
social modeling, 631
standardized, 618
subjective validation, 601
superego, 602
temperament, 625
thematic apperception test (TAT), 608
unconscious, 601
validity scales, 622
validity, 608

QUIZ YOURSELF

1. Which of the following is *not* one of Freud's defense mechanisms?
   a. Confirmation
   b. Repression
   c. Denial
   d. Sublimation
2. The personality trait that reflects how readily a person's emotional state is upset by the events of everyday life is
   a. extraversion.
   b. neuroticism.
   c. contentiousness.
   d. conformity.
3. The process by which a person lives up to his or her full potential, becoming the best and happiest human they can be is
   a. subjective validation.
   b. agreeableness.
   c. self-actualization.
   d. identity formation.
4. The Greek physician Galen thought the body contained four different types of fluids, or humors, and that different personalities resulted from too much of one sort of humor. What is the term for a person with too much black bile, who would be a deep thinker and prone to depression?
   a. Phlegmatic
   b. Choleric
   c. Sanguine
   d. Melancholic
5. What is the name of Bandura's theory positing that personal factors, environmental factors, and the individual's behavior mutually influence one another?
   a. Self-efficacy
   b. Reciprocal determinism
   c. Social learning
   d. Birth-order effect
6. If a test gives the same result each time it is administered to the same subject, it is ________. If it actually measures what it is supposed to measure, it is ________.
7. What are psychological tests where clients are asked to generate words or stories in response to a stimulus, with the assumption that unconscious processes will affect the person's response?
8. The tendency to remember events that fit our preconceptions and to forget events that do not is ________.
9. Babies show a variation in reaction to novel stimuli, such as when an alcohol-soaked cotton ball is placed under their noses. This variation is known as ________.

1. a; 2. b; 3. c; 4. d; 5. b; 6. reliable, valid; 7. projective tests; 8. confirmation bias; 9. temperament

Cutler

15 Social Psychology

The People's Temple

The Reverend Jim Jones had delivered thousands of people from "the devil's clutches" and gave them the discipline to put their lives in order. But there were also rumors of a dark side to his People's Temple. When government officials investigated complaints of violence and coercion, Jones and most of his followers left the United States and started a communal farm called Jonestown in Guyana, South America.

In 1978, in response to continued complaints from former temple members and their families, California congressman Leo Ryan took an investigative team to Guyana. Many members told him, in secret, that they wanted to leave but were afraid to say so because they would be punished. Eventually about 15 members asked to fly back to the United States with Ryan. At the airstrip, a group from Jonestown shot and killed Ryan and four others, severely wounding another dozen. Among those killed was an NBC cameraman who videotaped the shootings until he was murdered, providing footage that would shock America.

Back in Jonestown, Jim Jones assembled over 900 followers, telling them their church was doomed and that they should all commit "revolutionary suicide." He persuaded them to drink fruit-flavored punch with cyanide and sedatives. Almost all the members obeyed, parents giving the punch to their children and babies before taking it themselves. Jones himself died of a gunshot wound to the head, possibly self-inflicted, surrounded by the bodies of his dead and dying flock. You can learn more about this tragedy, including links to the chilling "death tape" of Jones persuading his flock to kill their wailing babies and themselves, at http://jonestown.sdsu.edu/.

When I read of the events that took place in Guyana that day, I imagine myself there and wonder what I would have done. Would I have seen past Jim Jones's doomsday rhetoric and refused to drink the poison? I might have been shot for the trouble, as several people apparently were, but surely it would have been better to hold out and give myself *some* chance to survive. But when I think harder, I realize that is a childish fantasy. I have to assume that I would have been like everyone else, or at least the vast majority, and would have meekly accepted death. What about you?

Jim Jones A charismatic leader, Jones helped many people change their lives for the better.

Chapter Preview

An important principle of social psychology is that we humans tend to do what those around us are doing. Much of the time that tendency works well; we follow cars around detours; we stand in line to buy tickets; we follow the rules. But sometimes the drive to be socially accepted leads people to behave in illogical, self-destructive, or even maniacal ways. This is not to say that everyone is alike, or that we'd all do the same thing in a given situation. The point is that we tend to underestimate how much we are influenced by the people around us.

Why are humans such intensely social animals? In our evolution on the African plains, skinny, hairless animals like us, without razor teeth or claws, survived by sticking together: hunting cooperatively, sharing resources, sleeping in groups so predators would have a harder time sneaking up on us. Our ancestors learned to pay close attention to others to predict what to do next and how to behave.

Our cultures evolved rules about how we should behave, and developed ways to teach those rules to our young as they grow up. When taught to follow the rules, and when everyone else seems to docilely do so, many people don't think twice about loyally lining up to go to war—or, as seen in the Jonestown case, even about drinking poison. In more ordinary situations, where conformity costs us nothing, we are even more likely to go along with the crowd.

To understand how the behavior of those around us affects our own thinking and behavior, we must analyze the behavior of individuals in groups, and the behavior of groups of individuals. This is the realm of **social psychology**: the study of how the "actual, imagined, or implied presence of other human beings" affects our behavior, beliefs, and attitudes (Allport, 1954, p. 5).

social psychology The study of how the real, implied, or imagined presence of other people affects our behavior, beliefs, and attitudes.

We can roughly divide social psychology into two processes: first, we observe the behavior of other people; then we decide, either consciously or unconsciously, how we will behave around those people (**Figure 15.1**).

We'll begin this chapter by observing some behaviors of people in groups and considering what psychological processes may influence those behaviors. Then we'll consider how our perceptions of other people's behavior may affect how we conduct ourselves. We'll wrap up by discussing several types of human interaction that are strongly influenced by the interplay of perception and choice: friendships and romantic relationships, aggression, and persuasion and authority.

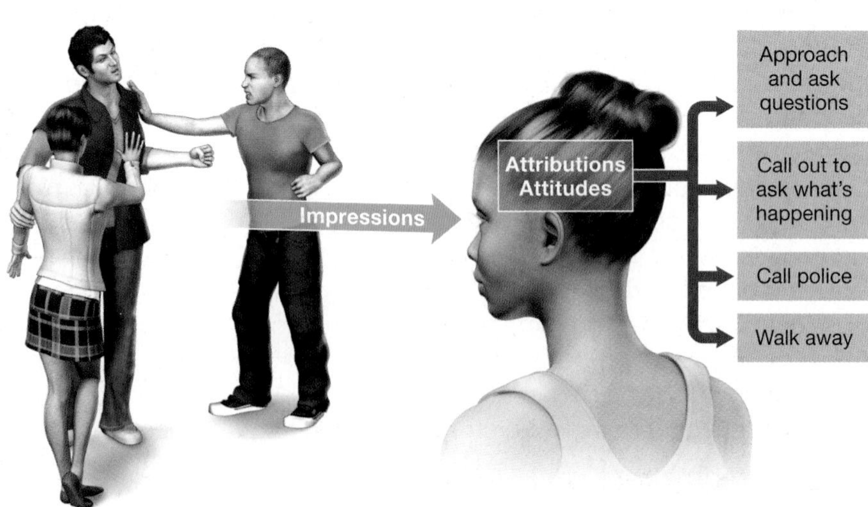

Figure 15.1 Processes of Social Psychology We can roughly divide social psychology into two parts: our perception of other people's behavior, and our decisions about how we will behave.

15.1 Social Perception

In many respects, the domain of social psychology begins the moment you try to make sense of another person's behavior. Why did she do that? What was he thinking? What sort of person is she? This is the process of **social perception**: perceiving the behavior and inferring motives of other people. In this section we'll discuss how a person's physical appearance shapes our initial impressions, and then we'll review the different kinds of explanations we use in trying to understand why a person behaves a particular way. We'll see that different cultures have very different ways of explaining a person's behavior, which may shape our attitudes about people. Finally, we'll discuss stereotyping and how widespread attitudes about different groups of people can have harmful, even deadly consequences.

Things to Learn

- Properties of attractive faces
- Fundamental attribution error
- Biases in attributing behavior
- Cultural differences in individualism
- Ways we avoid cognitive dissonance
- Racial discrimination in the death penalty
- Cognitive neuroscience measures of stereotypes
- Stereotype threat

Impressions and physical appearance affect social interactions

We spend much of our lives looking at people to decide if they are friendly or hostile, excited or sleepy, smart or dumb. A common theme of novels and movies is that appearances can be deceiving, yet experiments show that we consistently rely on physical appearance to help us predict another person's behavior. We judge physically attractive people to be healthier, more successful, and more socially skilled than unattractive people (Feingold, 1992; Principe & Langlois, 2013). We also imagine that attractive people are happier than unattractive people, and this seems a reasonable expectation. But when we ask people whether they are happy, it turns out that attractive people are generally no happier than unattractive people (Diener et al., 1995).

What makes a person look attractive? Surprisingly, one factor is whether the person looks "average." When researchers use computers to average photographs of 100 different men, they get a morphed face that is always judged to be attractive by participants (Langlois & Roggman, 1990). The same is true for morphed averages of women's faces (**Figure 15.2**). For the most part, the more faces that are averaged into an image, the more attractive it is rated.

social perception The process of perceiving the behavior and inferring the motives of other people.

(A) Original faces

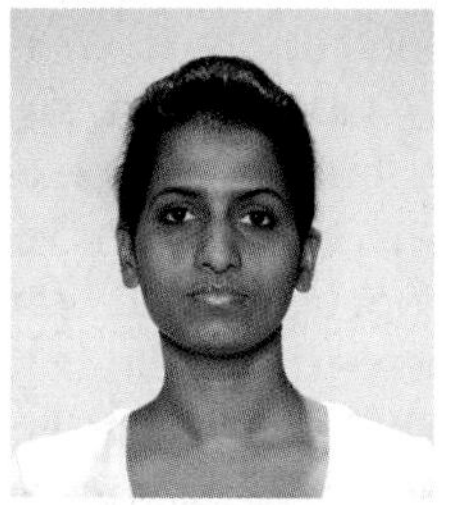
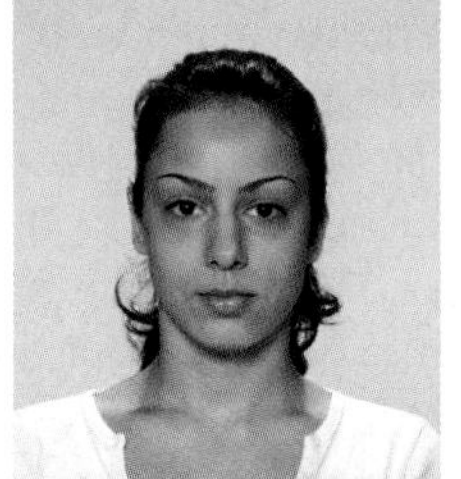
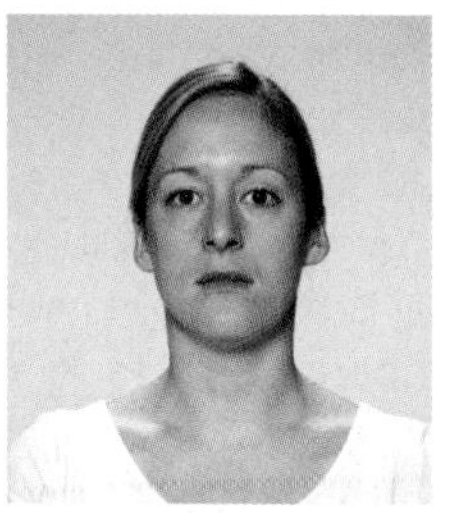

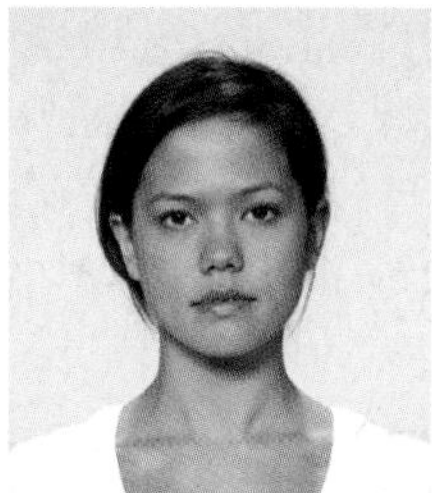

(B) Average of 5

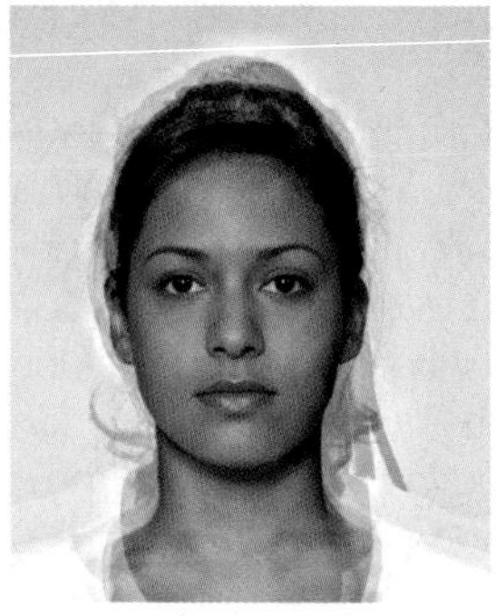

(C) Average of 20

Figure 15.2 Better When Averaged (A) Five individual women volunteered for this study. (B) By using a computer to average pictures of their faces, we get a face that is very symmetrical and attractive. (C) Averaging a lot of faces makes the final outcome even more symmetrical and even more attractive. (Courtesy of the Face Research Lab, faceresearch.org.)

facial symmetry The correspondence between the left and right side of the face.

evolutionary psychologists Psychologists who regard psychological traits as a result of evolution by natural selection.

One aspect of computer-averaged faces that makes them attractive is **facial symmetry**; a face is symmetrical if its left and right sides are perfect mirror images of one another. In most people, facial features on one side, like the eyes or cheeks, are different sizes or shapes than their counterparts on the other side. Other things being equal, we prefer symmetrical faces (Trujillo et al., 2013).

Why would we prefer symmetrical faces? **Evolutionary psychologists** try to explain psychological traits as adaptations that have evolved over time as a result of natural selection. This viewpoint suggests that a symmetrical face is a sign of good health. Accidents during development, such as nutrient shortages caused by an unhealthy diet, or exposure to diseases or parasites, may cause asymmetries. For example, an infection on the right side of a baby's face may make that side bigger or smaller than the left side. So having a symmetrical face suggests that a person experienced good nutrition growing up and didn't have too many run-ins with germs and worms and the like (Boothroyd et al., 2013b; Gray & Boothroyd, 2012). What's more, according to evolutionary psychologists, a person with a symmetrical face is likely to have inherited genes that were good enough to produce symmetry despite changes in nutrition or exposure to disease (Møller & Swaddle, 1998). Thus we may have evolved to find people with symmetrical faces attractive because they offer good genes to contribute to babies we might have together (Buss, 2005). We'll consider the evolutionary psychology perspective again in the next section of the chapter.

A second reason computer-averaged faces look attractive is *similarity*. In general we prefer faces that look more or less like our own. For this reason, people from Asia may regard Asian faces as more attractive than European faces, and vice versa. If you think about it, averaging a group of faces means that the end result will look similar to just about anyone who is looking at it.

A third quality that makes computer-averaged faces attractive is an artifact of the method: *absence of blemishes*. In general, we find smooth, unblemished skin to be attractive (Timms, 2013). Such skin is probably another indicator that a person is in good health and has had a healthy upbringing. Everyone has some facial blemishes, but no two people have blemishes in exactly the same spots. The result of averaging many faces is a final image with virtually no blemishes.

It may seem strange that a seemingly ancient preference like facial attractiveness can be produced by a technologically new device like a computer. Is it a coincidence that computer-averaged faces just happen to be attractive? Probably not, especially if you ask, How do we *learn* what is beautiful in a face? It turns out that babies also prefer looking at averaged faces (Rubenstein et al., 1999). Indeed, babies spend a lot of time looking at faces and much prefer looking at faces over just about any other object (see Figure 5.12). So it is possible that the baby brain is doing something like computer averaging, staring at each face, remembering that face, and then comparing it with the next face. In this way, the baby may "average" all these faces in order to recognize what a face is. We've seen that such averaging highlights qualities such as symmetry, similarity, and lack of blemishes that indicate what a good, healthy face should look like. For this reason, the baby may learn to regard symmetrical, unblemished faces as attractive. The same process might result in the baby's preferring Asian faces if most of the people taking care of the baby are Asians.

Another aspect of appearance that affects our judgment about people is whether a person has a "baby face," with prominent cheeks and eyes and a young-looking mouth. We judge such people to be immature and less competent than people with mature-looking faces (Zebrowitz & Montepare, 2005). There's evidence that these judgments of competence influence the decisions people make when they vote for political leaders. For example, in one election year, the more competent-looking candidates, as rated by voters who knew nothing else about them, won the election in 70% of the cases (**Figure 15.3**)

Figure 15.3 **Vote for Maturity!** In the race between these two political candidates, and in 70% of the other congressional races that year, the candidate who was judged to have the more mature face won the election.

(Todorov et al., 2005). Despite televised debates, political endorsements, and attack ads on television and radio, a major factor in deciding who will win an election is simply that split-second judgment about faces.

In politics, a lot of money and work go into carefully managing a candidate's image. But to some extent we are all engaged in **impression management**: things we do and say to try to make a certain impression on other people. Obvious examples of impression management center on our physical appearance: attention to hairstyle, using exercise and diet to control body shape, and choosing just the right clothes to wear. What other examples can you think of? We also use our *behavior* to manage the impression we make, hoping to pull off our best behavior when others are watching us.

Physical attraction also plays a big role in sexual behavior, a topic we covered in Section 12.3.

Attributions are easy to make and hard to shake

Attributions are judgments we make about the underlying cause of a particular event or process. We attribute daylight to the sun, and disease to bacteria or viruses. In social psychology, **attributions** are judgments we make about why a person behaves in a particular way.

According to **attribution theory**, we explain our own behavior and the behavior of others in two different ways (Heider, 1958). On the one hand, we may say a person behaved in a particular way because of the **situation** or the *environment* he was in: the myriad things that were going on around him before and during his behavior. From this perspective, we allow that almost anybody in the same situation would have behaved similarly. Situational explanations for behavior are sometimes referred to as *external attributions* because the causes are external to the person. On the other hand, we may attribute a particular behavior to a person's **disposition**, to certain behavioral traits specific to the individual, which tend to be displayed regardless of the situation. The perspective that personality plays a role in behavior—that *internal attributions* can influence behavior—suggests that different people will behave differently even if they are in the same situation.

Given that we are constantly attributing peoples' behavior either to the situation or to disposition, isn't it reasonable to suppose that *both* the situation and the individual's disposition affect a person's behavior? The question then becomes, *How much* should a certain behavior be attributed to the situation versus disposition? We attribute some behaviors largely to situational factors: peo-

impression management Things we do and say to try to present a favorable image to other people.

attributions Judgments we make about why a person behaves in a particular way.

attribution theory A set of ideas about how we explain our own behavior and the behavior of others.

situation The environment surrounding a person.

disposition A tendency to show a particular behavior, no matter what the situation is.

(A)

(B)

Figure 15.4 Attributions (A) When we make a mistake, behaving inappropriately, we may understand that our wrong behavior was caused by the *situation*: circumstances led us to do the wrong thing. (B) But when we see other people misbehave, we are more likely to blame their *disposition*.

fundamental attribution error The tendency to explain other people's behavior based on their dispositions rather than on the situation surrounding them.

ple at a party with a really great DJ may dance; destitute, hungry people may beg; a grieving widow may cry. Other behaviors are more dispositional in nature: hot-tempered people get angry; ambitious people seek the limelight; happy people whistle to themselves.

In making attributions about other people's behavior, we commonly make a particular type of mistake called **fundamental attribution error**—the tendency to attribute other people's behavior to their disposition rather than to the situation surrounding them (Ross, 1977). We tend to underestimate how important situational variables can be for other people. Why? Because most of the people we encounter we see only for short glimpses, and we tend to see them in the same situation—the classroom, bus stop, office, or basketball court. If we see people repeatedly in the same situation and they typically tend to act about the same each time, we may mistakenly think that the behavior we witness reflects their natural disposition *all* the time. As in so much of our behavior, most of us are unaware of how the fundamental attribution error affects our thinking (**Figure 15.4**).

When we make a friend, we tend to see that person in many different situations, and so we learn to appreciate how complicated that person is. She is very quiet in the classroom but loud and boisterous at home. He is aggressive and competitive on the basketball court but cooperative and helpful in his office. Great novelists understand this complexity of behavior, that we can be very different people in different contexts. So they portray heroes who sometimes behave badly, and villains who are admirable in some ways.

Our tendency to make the fundamental attribution error is so strong that we make it even when we're warned. For example, Jones and Harris (1967) had participants listen to people giving political speeches that were either in favor of or against Cuba's leader Fidel Castro. When the participants were asked to rate how the speakers felt about Castro, naturally they thought the pro-Castro speakers liked him and the anti-Castro speakers did not. But *even if the participants were told beforehand that each speaker was assigned randomly* to either the pro- or anti-Castro side, they *still* judged that the pro-Castro speakers liked him more! So even when we're told someone is acting as instructed, we still attribute his behavior to his disposition rather than the situation. The tendency to attribute people's behavior to varying degrees to either environmental or dispositional factors can be seen in political views, and there has been growing evidence of a genetic influence on these views (**Box 15.1**).

Psychology in Everyday Life

BOX 15.1

Inheriting Political Views

The political views of many people can often be categorized as either "mother-like" (nurturing, forgiving, sheltering) or "father-like" (favoring independence, demanding, punishing). In general, women's political attitudes are more mother-like and men's attitudes are more father-like. But there are plenty of people from each of the sexes on all sides of political debates, so clearly there's more to understanding people's beliefs than just which sex they happen to be.

Research has suggested that genes influence political views. Alford and colleagues (2005) asked twins how they felt about political issues such as prayer in schools, property taxes, unionization, women's rights, and the death penalty. They found that identical twins were more similar to each other in their political views than were non-identical twins and concluded that political views were indeed heritable. The scientists tried to break down these various political issues into basic attitudes that might be affected by genes. They concluded that suspicion of outsiders and a strong desire to be part of a group had a strong heritable component that would lead to similar political views, those that are generally considered conservative. On the other hand, inherited tendencies for tolerance for personal differences and suspicion of hierarchies and strong leaders might lead to liberal political views.

These findings in no way deny the importance of experience in shaping political views. In the United States, the political views of an entire generation were greatly affected by the Great Depression of the 1930s, and another generation was shaped by the Cold War between the United States and communist Russia. The idea is that genes provide an additional, dispositional influence, but not the only influence, on political views. So conservatism may tend to run in families, but political views change with time across groups and within individuals. There is a famous saying, often attributed to Winston Churchill, that if you're not a liberal at age 20, you have no heart, but if you're not a conservative by age 40, you have no brain. Whether he said it or not, young people do tend to be more liberal than older people, and as our genes remain the same throughout life, this observation suggests that life experience, including learning, also plays a big role.

There are times when we *under*estimate the effects of disposition, and that's when we think about our own mistakes. The **actor–observer bias** is the tendency to explain away our mistakes, when we are the *actor*, by attributing them to the environment rather than to our disposition (see Figure 15.4). "I'm not a bad person, events caused me to do that!" One reason we are willing to give ourselves a break, attributing errors to the situation rather than to ourselves, is because we know that we behave differently in different situations. The other aspect of the actor–observer bias is that when we are the *observer*, we revert to the fundamental attribution error, attributing other people's errors to their disposition—"That guy's a real jerk to behave that way." *My* bad behavior is dictated by the situation, but *your* bad behavior is determined by your disposition. "I'm a victim, you're a jerk." That's the actor–observer bias in a nutshell.

Conversely, when we perform well, we tend to congratulate ourselves (Miller & Ross, 1975). This is the **self-serving bias**: we attribute our successes to having a superior disposition ("I'm really good at math; that's why I did so well on that test") but attribute our failures to external forces ("That math test was really unfair").

Fundamental attribution error undoubtedly played a big role at Jonestown. The church members attributed evil motives to the congressman and his aides, the CIA, the FBI, almost the entire world outside the People's Temple (Moore, 1985). They minimized how the situation—the concern of families back in the United States—brought these outsiders to investigate. When Jones persuasively suggested to his followers that they do something really horrible—to kill their children and themselves—the actor–observer bias led them to believe that they were trapped by the situation, that they had no

actor–observer bias The tendency to explain away our own mistakes by attributing them to the environment, but to attribute the mistakes of others to their disposition.

self-serving bias The tendency to attribute our successes to our dispositions and attribute our failures to external factors.

Figure 15.5 Culture Influences Attribution When shown this drawing of a school of fish, people in China tend to assume that the front-most fish is being chased by the other fish, while Americans tend to assume that the front-most fish is leading the others. Does this difference reflect a cultural tendency in China to consider the larger picture and the importance of history, while American culture admires individuality and ambition? (After Aizenman, 2008.)

choice. They saw themselves as victims of circumstance, trapped in the *situation*, and saw the outsiders as bad people with a *disposition* hostile to Jones's mission. Yet it was the congressional visitors who were trying to help people, and the church members who murdered their children.

Different cultures foster different styles of attribution

Culture influences our attributions. Here is a simple experiment: Show someone a drawing of a school of fish and ask the viewer to speculate on what is taking place; some will attribute the behavior to internal, dispositional tendencies of the front-most fish ("It's leading the school") while others will attribute the behavior to external, situational tendencies ("The fish behind are urging the front-most fish forward") (**Figure 15.5**). Experimenters have introduced the same picture to viewers in different countries and have observed differences in behavior attribution across cultures. For example, there are differences, on average, in the attributions made by people in China versus the United States. Chinese participants are more likely to attribute the individual's behavior to the *situation*. "Those other fish are chasing him." Americans, on the other hand, are more likely to make attributions concerning the *disposition* of the fish in the picture (Choi et al., 2003). "He's leading them to some food."

individualism The tendency to put your own goals and wishes ahead of the goals and wishes of the group.

collectivism The tendency to put the goals of the group ahead of your own goals.

Another cultural difference in attributions about behaviors concerns the importance people place on individuals as distinctive and unique. Geert Hofstede (2005) has compared different cultures in terms of how much they embrace **individualism**: the tendency to put one's own goals and wishes ahead of the goals and wishes of a group. Individualism emphasizes a person's disposition, and values individual freedom. The opposite of individualism is **collectivism**: the tendency to put the goals of the group ahead of one's own goals, allowing less freedom to individuals and emphasizing the situation. Hofstede estimates that the United States values individualism more than any other country he's surveyed (**Figure 15.6**). We can all argue both sides about whether a culture em-

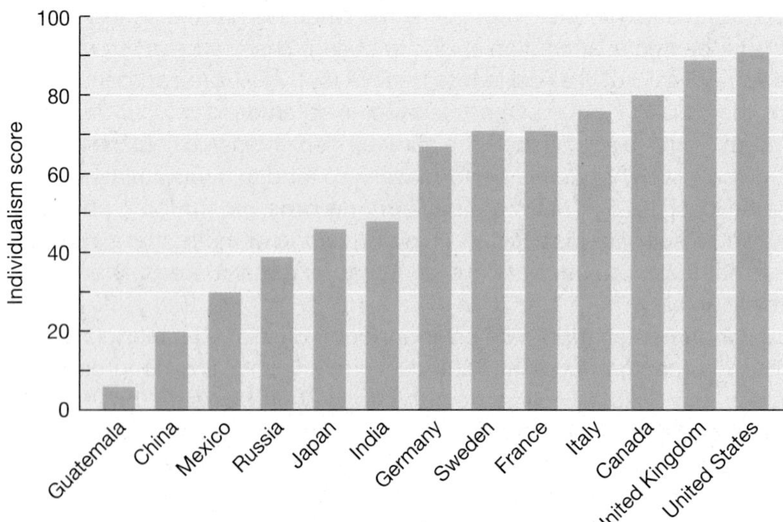

Figure 15.6 Cultural Differences in Attribution People in the United States and the United Kingdom value individualism, while people in China and Guatemala are more likely to value collectivism. (After http://geert-hofstede.com/countries.html.)

phasizing individualism or collectivism offers the happier life for its members. What is clear is that most of us are unaware of how being exposed to this pervasive attitude as we grow up affects our thinking. Note that many countries value individualism to an intermediate degree, between that of China and the United States.

Even within a culture there may be two fundamentally different styles of attribution. Psycholinguist George Lakoff (2008) has found dispositional and situational styles of attributions in almost all cultures. Why do these two styles appear in every culture? Lakoff suggests that patterns of attribution are learned within a fundamental unit of human existence—the family. Despite increases in the number of women seeking careers outside the home, most modern American families rely on a division of labor that was probably present in Africa millions of years ago. Men tend to travel away from the home to find food, while women tend to stay home to care for children and maintain the home. Why did that division of labor arise? Before the invention of baby bottles, only a mother could feed children, and in those days, when food was almost always scarce, children needed to be breast-fed for 4–6 years to have a good chance to reach adulthood.

Because of this division of labor that arose long ago, says Lakoff, most human families are subject to two different subcultures: the paternal culture of fathers, which emphasizes independence and dispositional attributions, and the maternal culture of mothers, which emphasizes nurturance and situational attributions. Imagine an angry father shouting to a mother about their son, "You're always making excuses for him." In that stereotype, the father is emphasizing the son's responsibility for his *disposition*, while the mother is emphasizing the *situation* that led the son to behave a certain way.

Attitudes affect behavior, and behaviors affect attitude

In most human institutions, people are expected to behave a certain way: we are quiet in church, loud at a party, subdued and studious in school, relaxed at the park. In some institutions, different groups of people are expected to behave very differently from one another. For example, in prisons, the guards and prisoners behave very differently from one another, there are strict rules about each role, and generally no one switches from one role to another.

In such situations, the fundamental attribution error flourishes. Each group of people attributes the behavior of the other group to a certain disposition, while attributing its own behavior to the particular situation. Over time, these attributions lead people in these situations to develop **social attitudes** (or, in this chapter, simply *attitudes*), which are evaluations about people, usually positive or negative, and a predisposition to act in a particular way toward them. Once social attitudes have developed, it can be very difficult to overcome them.

In 1971, Philip Zimbardo conducted an intriguing simulation regarding the power of attitudes and **social roles**, the behaviors and attitudes expected from someone with a particular social position, in the Stanford prison study (http://www.prisonexp.org). In this activity, male college students volunteered to be randomly assigned to play the role of either a prisoner or a guard in a mock prison. It began with a real police car arriving at the "prisoners'" homes, handcuffing them on the sidewalk, and driving them off, in some cases with the neighbors watching. The prisoners were put in cells that had steel bar doors, in the basement of the psychology building, with the "guards" assigned to enforce the rules. Guards wore khaki uniforms and sunglasses to disguise their emotions and to make them all look alike; the prisoners wore stocking caps (rather than having their hair shaved), making them all look similar too (**Figure 15.7**). The prisoners were also given numbers to replace their names, imparting even more anonymity (Haney et al., 1973).

social attitudes Our evaluations about people and a predisposition to act in a particular way toward them.

social roles The behaviors and attitudes expected from someone with a particular social position.

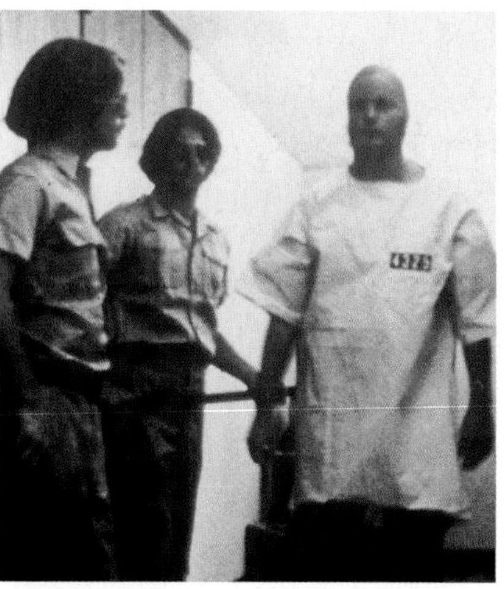

Figure 15.7 Stanford Prison Study Although assigned to their roles randomly, students in the social role of guard behaved differently, and had different attitudes, than did students in the social role of prisoner.

But on only the second day, the study began to break down. The prisoners, feeling genuinely oppressed and angry, started rebelling, pulling off their caps and refusing to follow directions. The guards, in turn, became upset with the rebelliousness of the prisoners and began calling for more order, more punishments (such as doing push-ups or being sprayed with icy blasts from a fire extinguisher). In other words, the participants began taking on the attitudes appropriate to their role, and as far as we can tell, they genuinely believed that their counterparts were mean, dangerous people. Even the researchers fell under the spell: when a prisoner complained of severe distress, they reacted like the "superintendents" they were supposedly only pretending to be. They really worried the prisoner was a "faker" trying to fool them. When one prisoner broke down in tears and begged to be allowed to leave, the other prisoners, punished for his "misdeed," began chanting that he was a "bad" prisoner.

The original plan was to run the simulation for 2 weeks, but within 6 days so many of the volunteers were stressed out that the researchers called it off. Once each member of the study, including the scientists, had played his *social role* a while, he began to actually adopt the *attitudes* appropriate to his make-believe role. What's more, once each participant had watched his counterpart playing whatever role he'd been assigned, he came to believe that the guards really were vicious people, or that the prisoners really were sneaky, "bad" people. These are attribution errors, of course. Having seen another participant act a particular way, it was hard for the prisoners not to believe he truly was "mean" or "sneaky" or "a faker."

Critics of the prison study felt that it was unrealistic in that people were assigned to be prisoners or guards at random and that the situation was too artificial to apply to real life (Gray, 2013). This is a concern, but there is a modern-day tragedy that seems remarkably similar. In the African nation of Rwanda there was a horrible murder of 800,000 people, mostly Tutsis killed by Hutus, in just 100 days in 1994 (**Figure 15.8**). This type of killing in which people are murdered based on race or ethnicity is often termed *genocide*. But the Tutsis and Hutus speak the same language, share the same religion, and have few physical differences. At one time the word *Tutsi* simply meant someone who was lucky enough to own cattle. A Hutu could become Tutsi if he could buy some cows. But in the early twentieth century, the Belgian colonists who ruled Rwanda issued ID cards that prominently identified everyone as either Tutsi or Hutu, and then put the minority Tutsis in charge, subjugating the Hutus (Prunier, 1999). There has been great enmity between these "peo-

Figure 15.8 A Chilling Death Toll This collection of skulls represents a fraction of the 800,000 Tutsis and their sympathizers who lost their lives in the 1994 Rwandan genocide.

ples" ever since, leading to this recent tragedy. Did the assignment of different roles to Rwandans, like the assignment of different roles in the Stanford simulation, make conflict more likely?

It is unlikely that any institutional review board today would allow this prison study to be repeated, and Zimbardo himself admits that he got too caught up in his role. For this reason it was never possible to follow up the study by trying to manipulate one variable, for example, allowing prisoners to use their names rather than assigned numbers, to see how each factor contributed to the hostility. But it is undeniable that we often attribute whatever behavior a person displays to his or her disposition. Surely this tendency was a big factor at the Abu Ghraib prison in Iraq where perfectly ordinary, normally reliable army guards ended up systematically torturing prisoners (**Figure 15.9**). It was probably easy for the guards to regard every prisoner as an evil terrorist. Similarly, the prisoners probably attributed the guards' misdeeds to an evil, Muslim-hating, power-hungry disposition, not to the circumstances of having been assigned the role of guard in a war zone 10,000 miles from home. Once the members of each group had played their role, they developed attitudes that made misunderstanding and conflict almost inevitable.

Figure 15.9 Abu Ghraib Iraqi prisoners probably attributed the misconduct of their U.S. guards to an evil disposition, but the guards probably attributed their own misconduct to the pressures of the situation.

Cognitive dissonance is the psychological discomfort of holding two conflicting beliefs

There is a conflict in the attitudes of prisoners and guards, both in the Stanford prison study and in real life. How do prisoners and guards explain why each regards the other as evil, while regarding themselves as victims? How can guards still regard themselves as victims after they have tortured prisoners?

If you sit at a piano and play two notes at once, sometimes they blend together and sometimes they sound unpleasant. That discomfort we feel when the two tones blend badly is called dissonance. **Cognitive dissonance** is the extension of this idea to thinking about our past behavior. It is the discomfort we feel if we are holding two different beliefs or attitudes that can't really be reconciled with one another (Festinger, 1957). For example, many people who smoke know that the habit is bad for them, yet they continue to smoke. They feel cognitive dissonance because the love of smoking really can't be reconciled with the fear of harm. Most of us deal with cognitive dissonance by trying to weasel our way out of it. The smoker may tell himself that he deserves to give himself a cigarette as a treat (yes, he really loves how it feels to pull in that smoke) or that he will have plenty of time to quit.

cognitive dissonance The psychological discomfort of simultaneously holding two conflicting beliefs, especially about oneself.

Festinger and Carlsmith (1959) performed a simple experiment to show how cognitive dissonance makes us uncomfortable and how we sometimes fool ourselves to avoid feeling that dissonance, as we discuss next (**Figure 15.10**).

☑ Researchers at Work

Getting paid to lie to others

Figure 15.10 Avoiding Cognitive Dissonance (After Festinger & Carlsmith, 1959.)

■ **Question:** Can our judgment be biased in order to keep a positive self-image?

■ **Hypothesis:** People who are paid a trivial amount to deceive others are more likely to convince themselves that they are not engaging in deception than are those who are well paid for the deceptive act.

Continued

Researchers at Work *Continued*

■ **Test:** Give students a boring task of putting spools on a rack and taking them off again. Then ask two-thirds of the participants to tell a waiting participant that the task was really interesting. Offer half of these students $1 for talking to the next participant, and offer the other half $20. Then, *after* each participant has talked to the next student, ask all participants how enjoyable the task *really* was.

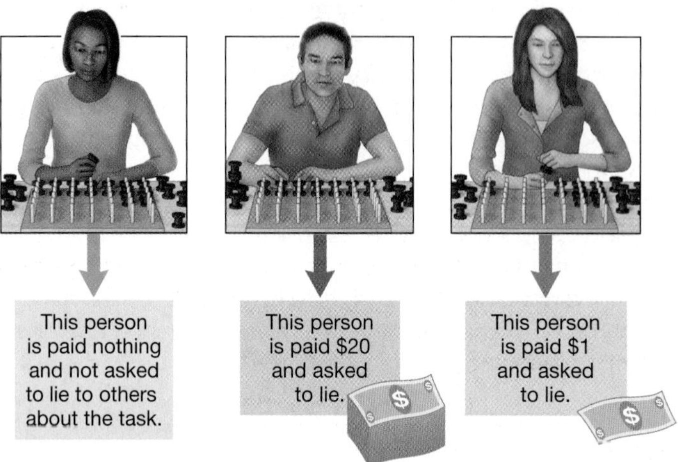
This person is paid nothing and not asked to lie to others about the task.
This person is paid $20 and asked to lie.
This person is paid $1 and asked to lie.

■ **Results:** Students in the control group who were not asked to lie said the task wasn't fun. Likewise, students who were paid $20 to tell the next participant that the task was enjoyable admitted that in fact it was not fun. But the students who were paid a measly $1 to lie about the task reported that they actually found the task enjoyable!

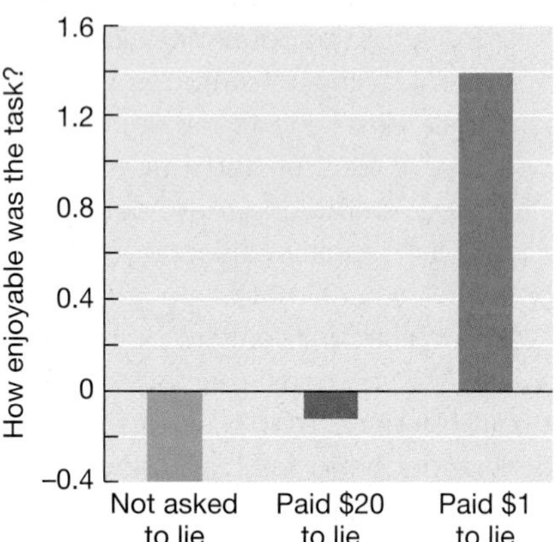
How enjoyable was the task?
1.6
1.2
0.8
0.4
0
−0.4
Not asked to lie
Paid $20 to lie
Paid $1 to lie

■ **Conclusion:** Assuming participants considered themselves generally truthful, knowingly deceiving someone for a mere dollar might cause uncomfortable cognitive dissonance. These students minimized that dissonance by coming to believe the task really was fun. The people paid $20 to lie had a strong incentive to lie ($20 was a lot of money in 1959) and thus experienced no cognitive dissonance even though what they told the next participant was inconsistent with what they really thought of the task.

Cognitive dissonance can also help explain the notorious behavior of a few American soldiers guarding prisoners at Abu Ghraib prison in Iraq. Some suggest that developing the attitude that the prisoners were almost subhuman

(Sherman, 2005) allowed the guards to avoid cognitive dissonance, to regard themselves as "good American soldiers" while mistreating Iraqis.

Cognitive dissonance is not solely associated with moral dilemmas; it is commonly encountered in everyday life. Let's say you're shopping for a new cell phone, for example. You're trying to weigh a lot of options and considering the many trade-offs between price and features. Should you pay $100 more for additional memory? Should you fork over the bucks to get a bigger screen? **Buyer's remorse**—the worry and doubt that we sometimes feel after a purchase—is a kind of cognitive dissonance. Buyer's remorse can be made worse if we learn new facts or hear more opinions from other people afterward. We may experience cognitive dissonance if we learn that the brand we bought is unreliable, or that the extra memory is unlikely to matter. If we accepted these new ideas as true, then we would conclude that our decision was wrong. To avoid this cognitive dissonance, we may discount the new facts and develop the attitude that other features are more important, so we can comfortably continue to think that we made the correct decision.

buyer's remorse The worry and doubt sometimes felt after a purchase.

effort justification The tendency to alter our evaluation of some object or process based on how much effort we made for it.

Have you ever found yourself in a restaurant where you've been a little shocked at the prices? Afterward did you feel the food was really outstanding? Well, maybe it was. Or maybe you avoided feeling cheated by the high prices by telling yourself the food was better than it really was. **Effort justification** is the tendency to alter our evaluation of some object or process based on how much effort we made. If we work hard for something, we are likely to value it more. So paying a lot for a meal may cause us to rate the food as better than we would do otherwise. This is a way to avoid cognitive dissonance. Aronson and Mills (1959) tested the idea of effort justification by giving participants tasks to do before they could become part of a "discussion group." Some participants were given a very easy task, some a very difficult task, and some a medium task. All then listened to the same boring tape of someone lecturing. The people who had to do a difficult task to earn the "privilege" of listening to the tape liked the lecture more than did the participants who had to do an easy task. The people who had to do a difficult task to hear the lecture changed their attitude about the lecture to justify their effort.

Here is an example of effort justification in the American marketplace. Toyota makes a sport utility vehicle that is sold under two different names: the Highlander is sold as a Toyota, but the RX 400 is sold under the luxury brand Lexus. According to *Consumer Reports* magazine, these are the same car, but the version with a Lexus name costs $7,000–$12,000 more. Yet when people are asked to rate how satisfied they are with the car they bought, those who bought a Lexus RX 400 are more satisfied than are those who bought the considerably less expensive Toyota Highlander. The Lexus owners appear to be benefiting from effort justification. "If it cost me that much money, then I must really love it!" Alternatively, maybe the Lexus owner loves proving to his neighbors that he has plenty of spare cash ("I bought this Lexus when I could have gotten the same car for thousands less"), and that gives him additional joy in the car.

Elliot Aronson (2011) offers a slightly different explanation for the behavior resulting from cognitive dissonance. For Aronson, the dissonance is between the person's behavior and her self-image. A person who thinks herself truthful but finds herself lying for something as trivial as a dollar may protect her self-image by shifting her attitude ("That task was sort of fun, some of the time"). A smoker who thinks of himself as a strong, independent thinker may protect this self-image by telling himself that smoking is an important adult pleasure that has just gotten "bad press."

These two ways of thinking about cognitive dissonance are probably equivalent. Whether we are protecting our minds from discomforting cognitive dissonance or protecting our self-image, the response is the same: we change our

Entrees
Baked Chicken Breast 60
Brown gravy, string beans, mashed potatoes
Atlantic Salmon 72
Rice pilaf, green peas, sour cream
Duck Breast 80
Carrots, turnips, roasted potatoes, brown gravy
BBQ Pork Loin 55
Corn bread, baked beans, cole slaw
Sirloin Steak 75
Potatoes with parsley, corn, worcestershire sauce

Wow, If It Costs This Much... Knowing a meal will be very expensive, we may resort to effort justification, judging the food more favorably to justify the price. That might also help us avoid feeling buyer's remorse.

self-handicapping Avoiding effort so that potential failure won't damage self-esteem. A way to avoid cognitive dissonance.

social prejudice An unfavorable stereotype about a large group of people.

discrimination Treating a person unfairly solely because he or she is part of some group.

attitudes or values about the task or object to make it easier to accept what we've done. We can continue to attribute our behavior to the situation, not our disposition. The actor–observer bias saves us from discomfort.

The self-image protection view of cognitive dissonance may explain a common problem of many college students (and others): **self-handicapping**, avoiding effort so potential failure won't damage self-esteem (Jones & Berglas, 1978). For example, some students (and some professors) may procrastinate because they are afraid they will not do well on some task such as writing a paper. So they make little effort, putting off the task until they do a rush job at the last minute. If it comes back with a poor grade, the student can avoid experiencing cognitive dissonance by telling himself, "Well, I would have done better if I'd spent more time at it" (Covington, 2000). Procrastinators protect their self-image ("I'm smart and a good writer") by exerting little effort ("I would have gotten a better grade if I'd tried harder"). In that sense, by self-handicapping, exerting little effort beforehand, they have ensured that a poor grade at the end won't hurt their self-image. If they get a good grade anyway, they feel even better ("Wow, I must really be great to do well with so little effort") and may procrastinate or do other things to put themselves at a disadvantage (skip lectures, or go bar-hopping the night before an exam) next time.

Does the concept of cognitive dissonance apply to the Jonestown tragedy? Might Reverend Jones have been a victim of cognitive dissonance? It's not clear whether some of Jones's followers decided on their own to kill the congressman and his party or whether Jones himself ordered it. But once the murders were committed, Jones likely experienced cognitive dissonance: "I'm a man of peace—who has taken part in murder." Shifting his attitude about the outsiders would have helped him reduce unpleasant dissonance and threat to his self-image. If Ryan's investigation could be perceived as part of a worldwide conspiracy, desperate measures like murder might be justified. In that state of mind, destroying his flock and himself may have seemed to Jones the only logical response to such a horrible conspiracy.

Stereotypes and racial prejudice live on

People are sometimes judged to have particular traits just because they belong to a certain racial, cultural, gender, or other group. That is, fairly or unfairly, people are often *stereotyped*. Some stereotypes are complimentary (all Asian students are good at math) but many are cast in a negative light. Thanks to jokes, books, television, and movies, we've all been exposed to portrayals of a gay man who behaves in a feminine fashion, a black man who is violent, a blonde woman who is empty-headed. Stereotypes result when we overgeneralize from these instances and come to believe that all gay men are feminine, all black men are violent, or all blonde women are stupid.

Stereotypes Abound "Chicken of the Sea Tuna… is this chicken… or is this fish?" Jessica Simpson

Holding a stereotyped belief will lead us to prejudge people, making a judgment about them when all we know, for example, is they are gay, or black, or female. **Social prejudice**, or more commonly *prejudice*, is an unfavorable stereotype, an attitude about a large group of people "which tends to be highly stereotyped, emotionally charged, and not easily changed by contrary information" (Krech et al., 1962). Because there are millions of African Americans, it is of course true that they display an enormous variety of characteristics. Yet some prejudiced people who see a stranger from a distance and can discern only that he has black skin may picture the man as aggressive, lazy, or unreliable. Sadly, in most instances prejudices are negative, leading to impressions of a person as inferior and as having undesirable characteristics.

Prejudices, like any other social attitude, affect our behavior toward others. Prejudice can lead to **discrimination**: putting a person at a disadvantage or treating a person unfairly solely because he or she is a member of a group. For example, when researchers sent identical e-mails purportedly from someone looking for an apartment to over 1,000 landlords in Los Angeles, those signed "Tyrell Jackson" got a positive reply only about 50% of the time. The same e-mail signed by "Patrick McDougall" got positive replies 89% of the time. E-mails from "Said Al-Rahman" got fewer positive responses than "Patrick" but more than "Tyrell." You can be discriminated against just for having a black-sounding or Middle-Eastern-sounding first name (Carpusor & Loges, 2006).

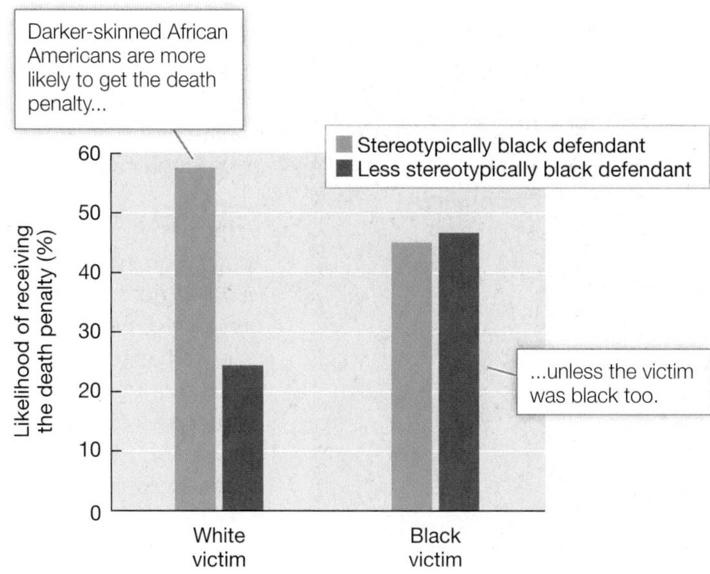

Figure 15.11 Odds of Receiving the Death Penalty, Classified by Race (After Eberhardt et al., 2006.)

Racial discrimination can have fatal consequences. An American man convicted of murder is much more likely to receive the death penalty if he is black. If you think this happens only in the South, maybe you've picked up a stereotype about Southerners. In Philadelphia, black men are four times more likely to receive the death penalty than are white men convicted of the same crime (Baldus et al., 1998). What's additionally cruel about the discrimination against African Americans in the death penalty is that it also applies to *victims*: if the victim is black, the murderer is *less* likely to get the death penalty.

Some people might think, "Well, maybe the murders committed by those particular black people really were more horrible than those committed by white men, so the difference in death sentencing is actually appropriate." Note that the person would have to be brave to say that out loud, for fear of being accused of being racist, but it's a valid scientific question. So let's explore it.

It turns out that there is a color continuum in death penalty discrimination: dark-skinned black men are even more likely to get the death penalty than are light-skinned black men (Eberhardt et al., 2006). In this study, photographs from a large pool of murder defendants were chosen at random and shown to a panel of white and Asian students who rated how "black-looking" the faces were. The students didn't know what the study was about. The researchers found that, for the same range of crimes, the men who had been rated as "stereotypically black" had gotten the death penalty more than twice as often as the "light-skinned" African Americans. Unless someone wants to propose that African American defendants who are "black-looking" really are more evil than those who are "light-skinned," it's hard to imagine how this could be anything but juries and judges being harder on defendants who look black.

Some people might say, "Well, maybe dark-skinned men really do commit more violent murders than light-skinned men." But this argument doesn't hold up when the *victim* is also black. When the victim is black, death penalty discrimination disappears (**Figure 15.11**). These observations suggest two possibilities: either dark-skinned men truly are more violent than light-skinned men—but only when they are killing white people—or the death penalty system in the United States is unfair to African Americans.

Whether you consider the murderer or the victim, the people imposing the death penalty in the United States value the lives of white people more than the lives of black people. Are the prosecutors, judges, and jurors who enforce this discrimination against African Americans doing it on purpose, or are they even aware of their prejudice? Quite likely, if we asked them, almost all would insist

Jesse Jackson Even African Americans such as Jackson, who has worked for many years to promote racial equality, have been exposed to many stereotypes about race, and it may affect their performance on the IAT.

that the skin color of the accused (or of the victim) had absolutely no effect on their decisions. Indeed, it is because these people are unaware of their prejudice, and the discrimination that results, that it does so much harm. Many don't bear any personal grudge or hatred against black people; they have simply absorbed the cultural stereotypes they grew up with.

Societal stereotypes are embedded deep in our brains

Are you prejudiced against white people, African Americans, or people from the Middle East? Just about everyone bristles at the accusation that he or she is prejudiced, but how would you know? One of the things that psychology as a science has revealed in recent years is that virtually everyone who has grown up in our culture displays evidence of having incorporated into their thinking certain stereotypes about different races. It's true even for people who are members of a racial minority who are suffering from discrimination themselves! The Reverend Jesse Jackson said, "There is nothing more painful to me at this stage in my life than to walk down the street and hear footsteps and start thinking about robbery—then look around and see someone white and feel relieved" (Johnson, 1993). The shock, for most of us, has been the realization that we can use cognitive neuroscience approaches to detect those prejudices.

There are many versions of the **Implicit Association Test** (**IAT**), which monitors reaction time to detect associations we might have with particular words and images (Greenwald & Banaji, 1995; Greenwald et al., 2002). In social psychology, the IAT has been used to detect how we unconsciously associate negative words and images with, for example, African American faces, as we'll see next (**Figure 15.12**).

Implicit Association Test (IAT) An assessment of reaction times used to detect associations between particular words or images.

☑ Researchers at Work

Implicit associations affect cognition

Figure 15.12 Implicit Association Test (IAT) (https://implicit.harvard.edu/implicit.)

■ **Question:** Do societal stereotypes affect our cognitive processing?

■ **Hypothesis:** Participants will take longer to associate positive words with people from various groups subject to negative stereotypes.

■ **Test:** Ask participants to rapidly sort words according to whether they are good or bad. For example, *wonderful* is a good word, *failure* is a bad word. Participants push a left button when the word is a good one, a right button when it's bad. They also sort photos of faces as either "African American" or "European American." Each of these tasks is fairly easy, and participants are asked to sort them as fast as possible without making mistakes. Then they are given a test where either black or white faces, or good or bad words pop up, and they continue to sort them as fast as they can.

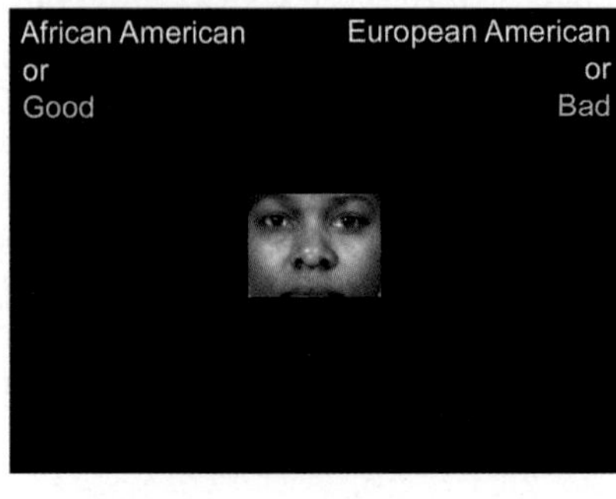

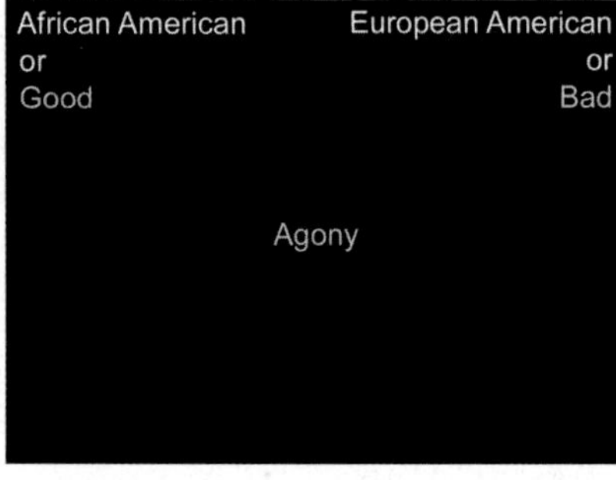

Now researchers switch the buttons, so participants are told to push the right button for "good" words and the left one for "bad" words. Again, they are presented with either faces or words and asked to sort them according to whether they are good or bad words, and whether they are black or white faces.

■ **Results:** Most people respond faster when the same key (say the left key) indicates "good" words and white faces than when the "good" key is associated with black faces.

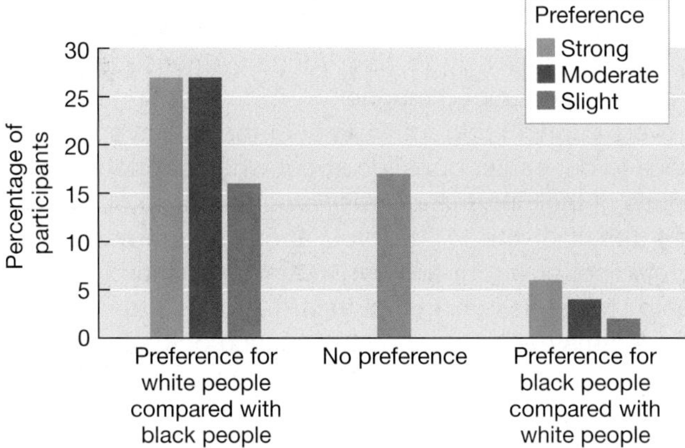

■ **Conclusion:** Participants readily associate white faces with good attributes and find it harder to associate black faces with good attributes. This bias is revealed because they need more time to properly sort the words and faces presented. The difficulty of associating "good" with black faces is interpreted to mean that people unknowingly harbor prejudice against black people. Over 50% of the people taking this test show a moderate to strong association bias favoring white people over black people.

Notice that the logic behind the IAT relies on thinking of the mind as a process going on in a machine. Because it takes longer to associate black faces with positive words than with negative words, some additional steps must be going on to make the decision. The additional steps are probably needed to reverse an inclination to associate black faces with negative words. Like any other machine, the brain needs more time if it must go through more steps to accomplish a task, in this case deciding how to sort the photo of a face. The same tests find that most people also have a strong association bias about gender roles (it's harder to associate female faces with high-level professional careers or with careers in science and technology) and about obese people (it's harder to associate pictures of obese people with positive words).

These tests show that racial and gender stereotypes common in our society become deeply embedded in our brain's function. Without our even being aware of it, our brain has a hard time associating characteristics that defy stereotypes. But does the IAT really reveal *prejudice*? That question is hotly debated. An alternative interpretation is that the IAT reveals that a person has been exposed to stereotypes about race. But that doesn't mean that the person in the real world, outside the IAT testing arena, would act on those stereotypes and behave in a prejudiced manner (Firmin, 2010; LaPiere, 1934). So perhaps the IAT is more a measure of the *culture* someone was raised in than of that individual as a *person* (Karpinski & Hilton, 2001).

If in fact it is cultural bias that the IAT detects, we may call into question the validity of the IAT as a measure of prejudice. Recall that *validity* is the extent to which a test actually measures what it is supposed to measure (see Sections 2.2 and 11.1. Supporters of the IAT point to numerous papers demonstrating that a person's IAT score is predictive of how that person will respond to other tests, so the IAT is measuring *something* in addition to just how quickly a person sorts items on a screen. But the more difficult question is whether the IAT predicts if that person will behave in a racially prejudiced manner in the real world. As some researchers pointed out, the Reverend Jesse Jackson would probably "fail" the IAT and show the same implicit bias in association that most of us do (Arkes & Tetlock, 2004). But in the real world Jackson has worked tirelessly to help African Americans, so he does not seem to behave in a prejudiced manner.

The controversy concerning the validity of the IAT as a measure of prejudice harks back to our earlier question about whether people behave the way they do because of their internal *disposition* or because of the external *situation*. Does the result of the IAT tell you about the participant's disposition (harboring prejudice) or about the participant's situation (growing up in our culture), or both? Might assuming that the IAT reveals internal prejudice rather than external circumstances be another instance of the fundamental attribution error: attributing the person's behavior to prejudice rather than to cultural influence?

Even so, it is troubling to think that cultural stereotypes about race are so pervasive that they affect our performance on a seemingly remote, abstract test. We saw another example in Section 1.3, where people more readily identified crime-related images if they had just seen a black face. Can we really incorporate those stereotypes so completely without it affecting our behavior in everyday life? Can we be sure that such stereotypes play no role in sentencing people to death? There are no definitive answers to these questions, but it would be wise for each of us to be vigilant, monitoring our behavior and attitudes for prejudices that lie beneath the surface.

Stereotype threat produces self-fulfilling prophecies

Social psychologists study a phenomenon that may serve to perpetuate stereotypes. **Stereotype threat** is experienced when exposure to a derogatory stereotype about a particular group (such as "African Americans are unintelligent" or "Females can't do math") causes group members to perform worse (Blascovich et al., 2001). The unflattering prediction about their performance becomes a self-fulfilling prophecy, seemingly confirming the stereotype. In Section 11.3 we saw how stereotype threat impairs the performance of African Americans on intelligence tests (see Figures 11.25 and 11.26).

Another well-studied instance of stereotype threat concerns the idea that girls are not as good as boys in math. There has been a lot of debate about whether the sex difference in scores on the math portion of the SAT and ACT is due to social factors, which we might be able to change, or to biological factors beyond our control. Thinkers have offered evolutionary arguments to explain why males might be better at math than girls, but even people who don't believe humans evolved at all still may believe that men and women are built differently, making boys better at math and girls better at social relations.

stereotype threat A phenomenon occurring when exposure to a derogatory stereotype about a particular group causes group members to perform worse.

These notions were widely known in our culture even before then-president of Harvard University Larry Summers announced his opinion that men have more "aptitude" for science and math than women, a statement that was widely reported in newspapers and on TV. An excerpt from Larry Summers's speech follows:

> *There are three broad hypotheses about the sources of the very substantial disparities...with respect to the presence of women in high-end scientific professions. One is what I would call the...high-powered job hypothesis. The second is what I would call different availability of aptitude at the high end, and the third is what I would call different socialization and patterns of discrimination... And in my own view, their importance probably ranks in exactly the order that I just described.*
>
> *(Summers, 2005)*

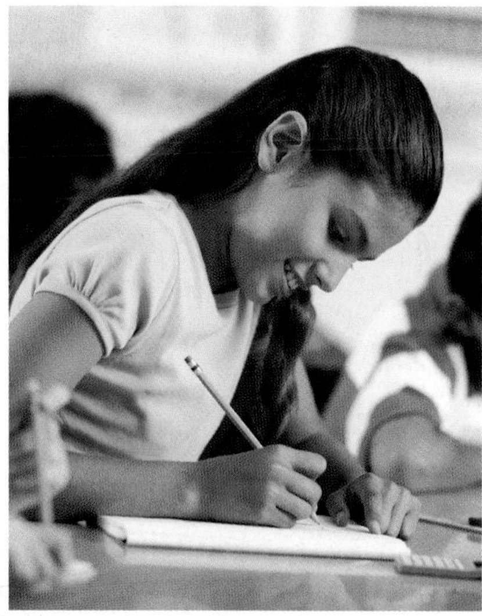

What Message Did This Girl Receive? When the media reported that the president of Harvard suggested that men have more "aptitude" for science and math than women, it was heard by millions of girls. Did the publicity provide a stereotype threat for this girl, worsening her performance in math and science?

But the next year, Dar-Nimrod and Heine (2006) published a study in which students were given mock versions of the SAT. Every version consisted of two math sections with a verbal section in between, but what differed was the reading content of the verbal section. In some versions, the verbal section had a reading in which the author argued that the sex difference in math scores was due to different experiences of boys and girls growing up. In another version, the reading argued that the sex difference in math was genetic. A third version argued that there were no sex differences in math test scores, and a fourth version talked about the biological basis of sex differences in human behavior without mentioning math. Men taking the test scored well on both math sections, no matter which essay they read in between. But women who read the essays favoring genetic or biological explanations of sex differences scored worse on the second math test than did women who read essays claiming there was no sex difference in math or that experience explained the sex difference.

In an earlier study, Spencer and colleagues (1999) found an even more dramatic effect. They gave young men and women a test with both easy and hard math problems. Some test-takers were told that there were gender differences in performance on this test (without saying which sex did better), and others were told that there were no gender differences on this particular test. Men scored the same in either condition, and women did just as well as the men on the easy questions in either condition. Women under stereotype threat (those told there was a gender difference in performance) did worse than men on the hard problems. But women who were told there was no gender difference on the test did so much better on the hard problems that the sex difference in performance disappeared (**Figure 15.13**)! Women seemed to try harder to solve the difficult math problems if they were told they could do as well as men. The supposedly "biological" sex difference in math performance did not surface when women were relieved of stereotype threat just before the test. In the meantime, the sex difference in performance on math exams has been shrinking over the last few decades; in some countries, the average score is higher for girls than for boys these days (**Figure 15.14**; Guiso et al., 2008).

	Women	Men
No stereotype threat presented ("There are no gender differences in performance on this test.")	Women performed as well as men.	Men performed well.
Stereotype threat presented ("There are gender differences in performance on this test.")	Women's performance declined.	Men's performance was unaffected.

Figure 15.13 Testing for the Effects of Stereotype Threat

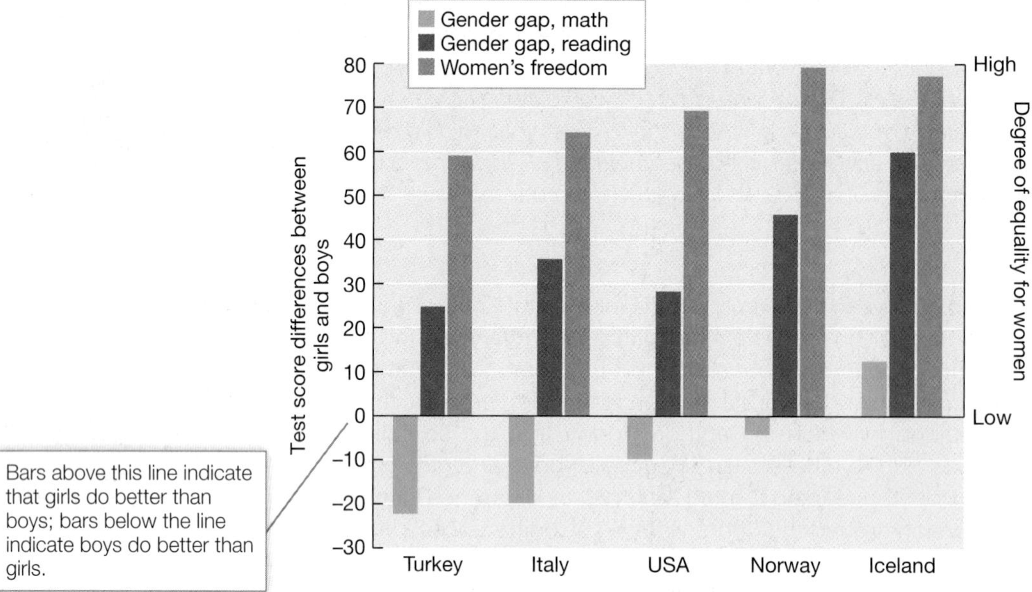

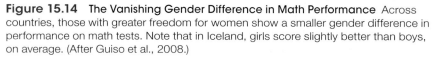

Figure 15.14 The Vanishing Gender Difference in Math Performance Across countries, those with greater freedom for women show a smaller gender difference in performance on math tests. Note that in Iceland, girls score slightly better than boys, on average. (After Guiso et al., 2008.)

15.1 SUMMARY

- *Social perception,* the process of perceiving the behavior and inferring motives of other people, may be unconsciously biased.
- We judge people who are more attractive, based on such factors as *facial symmetry* and absence of blemishes, to be more socially skilled and happier than other people, but they are not.
- We make the *fundamental attribution error* by overestimating how much a person's internal *disposition* guides behavior, rather than the external *situation.* When we see someone behaving badly, we are more likely to blame the person than the situation.
- The *self-serving bias* makes us more forgiving of ourselves, crediting our disposition when we do well and blaming the situation when we behave poorly.
- Attribution bias varies across cultures, as some emphasize *individualism* (the importance of a single individual's goals and achievements) while others emphasize *collectivism* (the importance of the group's goals ahead of personal goals).
- *Social attitudes*, our evaluations about people and a predisposition to act in a particular way toward them, are shaped by *social roles*, the behaviors and attitudes expected from someone with a particular social position, as in the Stanford prison study.
- *Cognitive dissonance* arises when we hold two conflicting attitudes about ourselves or our relationship to others. Without being aware of this influence, we may judge a boring task to be interesting if we've been paid a trivial sum to lie to someone else about it. Likewise, we may disregard new facts to avoid *buyer's remorse*, or value something more if we had to work really hard to get it (*effort justification*). We may *self-handicap* by making little effort on a task to avoid damaging our self-image if we do poorly.

- *Social prejudice*, holding an unfavorable stereotype about a large group of people, may lead to *discrimination*, treating people unfairly solely because they are part of some group.
- The *Implicit Association Test* (*IAT*), measuring the time it takes to accurately classify words or images, shows that most people need more time to associate black faces with positive terms, or female faces with high-power or high-tech jobs. While the IAT indicates that most of us have incorporated stereotypes about race or sex into our thinking, it is unclear whether this means we will be prejudiced in real life.
- Stereotypes may be self-fulfilling, as in the case of *stereotype threat*, when exposing members of a particular group to a derogatory stereotype about their performance in fact worsens their performance.

REVIEW QUESTIONS

1. What physical characteristics do most people find attractive in other people?
2. What is the fundamental attribution error?
3. What is the self-serving bias?
4. How do social roles affect our behavior?
5. What is the Implicit Association Test, and what does it suggest about the effects of stereotypes on our thinking?

Food for Thought

Would the sex difference in performance on the math section of the SAT disappear if we told test-takers the following lie: "You may have heard that there is a sex difference in math performance on tests like this, but we have found that this is no longer true"? Even if this manipulation did improve the girls' performance, how would you decide whether it would be ethical to tell such a lie to the students?

15.2 Social Influences on Behavior

Things to Learn

- Normative social influence
- Social facilitation and techniques for persuasion
- Ways we behave when part of a crowd or group
- Cooperation versus competition and the prisoner's dilemma
- Evolutionary psychology, inclusive fitness and altruism

So far we've talked about how we perceive other people as good, bad, friendly, hotheaded, or governed by disposition versus circumstance, and how stereotypes color those perceptions. By observing other people's behavior, we make conclusions about why they behave the way they do. But how does observing the behaviors of other people affect *our own behavior*? That question is the topic of this section.

We constantly waver between conformity and nonconformity

In any society there are certain rules about how people should behave, and most people obey those rules most of the time. **Social norms** (sometimes just *norms*) are the rules that a group uses to determine which behaviors, beliefs, attitudes, and values are appropriate or inappropriate. Some social norms are explicitly discussed in the home, classroom, or theme park. Don't talk with your mouth full, raise your hand to ask a question, keep your hands inside the roller coaster. Other social norms are implicit—not discussed out loud but implied by the structure of society (before 1968 only men were admitted to most of the Ivy League colleges) or by the behavior of others (when you get on an elevator, you should stand facing the doors).

Everyone feels pressure to abide by the social norms of the community. This pressure is the **normative social influence**, the pressure to behave and believe like everyone else, to be like most people. In U.S. culture we may be particularly aware of this pressure in our teenage years. Part of the normative social influence is probably inherent. We just don't like to be left out, and that may be left over from our evolution as creatures that must cooperate to survive. Even those disinclined to follow the crowd soon learn that it can be costly and painful to disregard social norms.

Solomon Asch (1956) performed a famous series of experiments illustrating the power of normative social influence. He assembled a group of students, showed them a line on one piece of paper, and then asked them to say out loud which of

social norms The widely agreed upon rules for what people should believe and how they should behave.

normative social influence The pressure to behave and believe like the rest of your community.

Figure 15.15 Solomon Asch's Demonstration of Normative Social Influence (A) Participants were shown the line on the left and then asked which of the lines on the right was the same length. (B) If the confederates first agreed that line B was the same length as the original line, most research participants also made that choice, but as the posture of the young man in the middle of the photograph indicates, they must have wondered how the confederates could be so wrong.

(A)

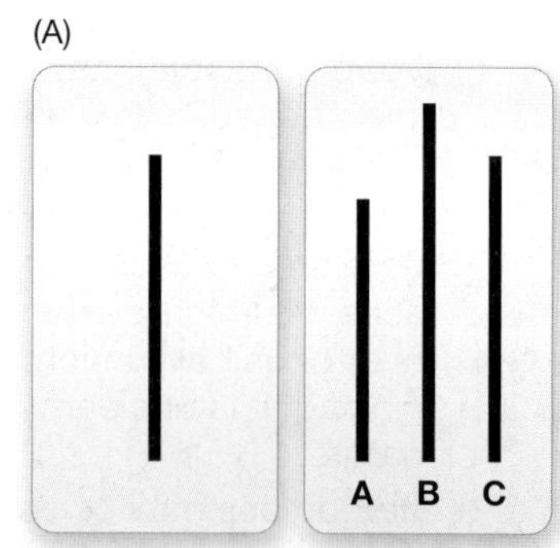

(B)

three lines on another sheet was the same length. Only one student in the group was a real participant of the experiment. The others were all *confederates* (people who are helping in a plot or plan; accomplices). Asch instructed the confederates to deliberately choose a wrong line. When all the confederates pointed first to a wrong line, about 75% of the participants went along with their rather obviously wrong choice. Surely the participants recognized that this was not the right line, but they tended to go along with the crowd (**Figure 15.15**). Interestingly, if even one confederate made the correct choice, the participant was much more likely to buck the majority and choose the correct line. Remember when we discussed how Americans emphasize individualism more than Asians? The tendency to give the popular but wrong answer in experiments is sometimes even stronger when the participants and confederates are Asian (Bond & Smith, 1996).

Normative social influences in small groups are seen in the **chameleon effect**: our tendency to mimic the postures, mannerisms, facial expressions, or other behaviors of the people around us (Chartrand & Bargh, 1999). Usually we are not even aware of our chameleon-like tendency to match the behavior of others. In my house the chameleon effect happens when I talk to my family in the Ozarks. My children laugh when I phone my relatives and unconsciously

chameleon effect The tendency to mimic the postures, mannerisms, facial expressions, or other behaviors of others.

revert to an Ozarks accent, start dropping the *gs* from the end of words, and drawl out words.

The chameleon effect can be easily tested. A participant is given some task that is actually just a distraction. Meanwhile, a confederate in the room, pretending to be another participant, starts either shaking her foot or rubbing her nose. Sure enough, if the confederate is rubbing her nose, the participant is more likely to rub his nose. Asked about it afterward, the participant might say he was unaware that he was doing that.

In another experiment, the confederate either deliberately mimics the posture of the participant or takes a neutral posture. Interestingly, the participants exposed to a mimicking confederate later report that they liked her more than did the participants exposed to a confederate who was not mimicking. You might conclude that if you want people to like you, you should mimic their posture, mannerisms, and ways of speaking. In fact, that probably would help them like you more. But you have to be subtle about it. If people *realize* you are deliberately imitating them, that turns them off. It turns out that people who are very *empathetic*, who are good at detecting another person's emotions and identifying with that person, are more likely to exhibit the chameleon effect. They tend to mimic other people without being aware that they're doing so. This may help people in a group to bond together.

You can also think of the chameleon effect as "social contagion": certain behaviors are catching. The most familiar example is yawning. Seeing someone yawn makes you much more likely to yawn, an effect that has been demonstrated in controlled laboratory settings. You don't even have to actually observe someone doing it to be susceptible. Even thinking about yawning may make you yawn. Are you yawning yet? By the way, no matter what you might have read or heard, the physiological function of a yawn is still unknown. The only known effect of yawning is to communicate to others that you're feeling tired or sleepy (see Box 13.1).

YOU ARE BEING WATCHED **Social facilitation** takes place when the presence of other people affects performance. Social psychologist Norman Triplett (1861–1910) noted that bicycle riders go faster when they are riding with others (Triplett, 1898). It seems just having people watch will cause you to do a task even better than when you are alone. Why does it help to have people watching? Part of the reason is probably a fairly simple case of *arousal*. When other people are around, we tend to be more aroused and that makes us more alert to the task at hand. Arousal probably explains why even cockroaches show social facilitation. That's right, cockroaches. Zajonc and colleagues (1969) studied how quickly cockroaches ran away from a light. If other cockroaches were visible, the subjects ran faster (**Figure 15.16**). It is unlikely that these critters are capable of complex thought ("Gosh, maybe if I run fast in front of those other cockroaches, one of them will give me a scholarship"). It seems more likely that the performing roaches were simply more aroused by the presence of their peers.

social facilitation The change in behavior brought about by the presence of others.

Many actors say they find it difficult to get into their role during rehearsals, but when they are in front of an audience, their performance may soar. Such actors may prefer live theater over television or movies, where the filming is done in front of only a handful of people, all of whom are busy doing their

Figure 15.16 Cockroaches Are Social Too Even a cockroach performs differently when other cockroaches are around. It will run faster in the presence of other cockroaches than by itself.

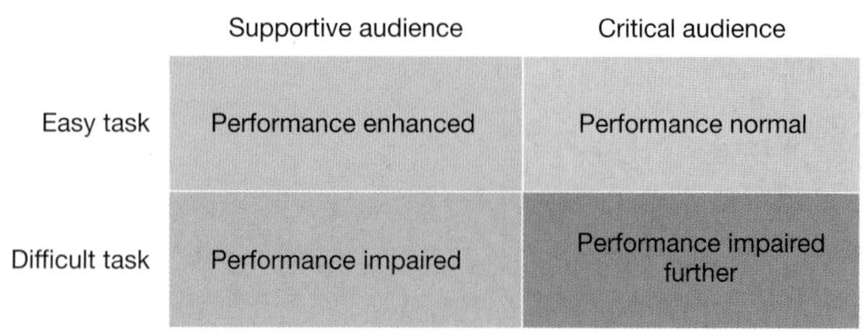

Supportive audience
Critical audience
Easy task
Performance enhanced
Performance normal
Difficult task
Performance impaired
Performance impaired further

Figure 15.17 Expectation of Evaluation Can Help or Hinder

job rather than enjoying the performance. These actors are probably enjoying some benefits beyond arousal. There's also the *expectation of evaluation*. They know that people will be judging them. Actors are well aware that the audience is watching them and evaluating them. So a second reason for social facilitation is the expectation that we are being evaluated. In the case of the actor immersed in her character, she is expecting approval, which boosts her confidence and performance.

But have you also been in situations where you felt the presence of an audience caused you to muff a performance, so-called choking under pressure? This is also a case of social "facilitation," even though in this case the audience makes it harder to do well. It turns out that having an audience improves our performance when we're doing something easy, or something we already do well. For example, Michaels and colleagues (1982) studied the effects of social facilitation on people playing pool. They noted that experienced pool players did better when they knew someone was watching them. But novice pool players did worse when they were watched. The experienced pool players were expecting approval ("Those spectators will see how good I am"), while the novices were expecting disapproval ("Those spectators will see I don't know what I'm doing"). So the expectation of evaluation *helps* us with easy or well-rehearsed tasks, but *hurts* us if we are beginners or some other factor makes the task hard for us (**Figure 15.17**).

In addition to the expectation of either approval or disapproval from the audience, what else can affect social facilitation? The *performer's perception of the audience's attitudes* will matter. Presumably this is one reason that sports teams tend to play better at home—they perceive the audience as ready to approve of them. When playing away, they perceive the audience as ready to disapprove. Part of the decreased test performance under stereotype threat, which we discussed earlier, is probably due to the people under stereotype threat feeling that the test administrators expect them to do poorly.

Past experience also matters as a performer tries to guess whether cheers or jeers will greet him. Comedians love to have a successful warm-up act before they take the stage. Once the audience is already laughing, it is likely to keep laughing. But notice how complex this situation is. If you're the star comedian, you don't want the act before you to be *too* funny. If that happens, you may start to worry that if the opening comic is much better than you are, the audience will be disappointed in your jokes. This expectation of disapproval will hinder your performance. Because so many factors affect social facilitation, performers have to avoid getting so worried about failing to please the audience that they end up doing badly.

In short, social facilitation improves our performance when the task is easy or one that we're already good at, but hurts our performance if the task is difficult or new. Indeed, this appears to be true even in the case of cockroaches. When the cockroaches in the study we mentioned earlier were given a harder task—solving a simple maze—having other cockroaches as spectators *hurt* their performance. The increased arousal that helped them solve a simple task (running) probably just got in their way when they had to learn something difficult.

USING SOCIAL FACILITATION FOR PERSUASION The **foot-in-the-door technique** is used to get people's attention or get them to provide a tiny favor in order to persuade them to make a bigger commitment. This technique is named after the now rare phenomenon of a door-to-door salesman trying to sell, say, a vacuum cleaner. Rather than actually stick his foot in the open doorway to prevent a homemaker from walking away from his sales pitch,

foot-in-the-door technique Asking someone to do something trivial before asking for a bigger favor.

the savvy salesman would say something intriguing or flattering to keep the woman's attention. If he could just get her to listen to his pitch, he had a chance of actually selling her something.

Any social interaction, even if it begins as a neutral one, facilitates more interaction, such as a sale. Many people use the foot-in-the-door technique: charities that send small gifts such as return address labels, car dealers who offer a test drive, and cult recruiters who first engage in small talk. For example, Cialdini and Schroeder (1976) sent teams of people out to solicit donations for a charity. Each team was given a specific script to follow at the door. The difference was that some of the teams added one more sentence: "Even a penny will help." Not only did the teams using this script get more people to donate, but they also gathered almost twice as much money total. Having asked for a tiny, trivial favor (give us a penny), they kept the resident's attention long enough to get significantly more money.

The foot-in-the-door technique is prevalent in an economy based on persuading people to spend money. When a store has a big sale, it sometimes sells an item for less than the store paid for it. But if a customer comes in to buy that item and then buys much more, the store will have come out ahead. An unethical variation of the foot-in-the-door technique is when the store advertises one item, but when the customer arrives, that item is no longer available and the sales person offers another as a substitute. It's hard to enforce laws against this "bait and switch" method, because sometimes stores legitimately run out of the best bargains.

A persuasion technique that is almost the opposite of foot-in-the-door is the **door-in-the-face technique**: first asking for some outrageous request (akin to having a door slammed in your face) and then changing the request to something more reasonable. In her exposé of the funeral industry, *The American Way of Death* (1963), Jessica Mitford found a trade magazine that recommended two variations of a door-in-the-face method to sell expensive coffins. After all, it's tough to get someone to spend a lot of money on something that will be seen only for a few hours and then be buried forever. One way to persuade a grieving relative to buy an expensive coffin is to first show him a *very* expensive coffin with a ridiculously high price. If the price tag takes his breath away, then offer a less expensive (but still costly) coffin, and the bereaved man may jump at the perceived "bargain." The other variation is to first show a cheap, shoddy-looking wooden box and say, "Well, you could bury your loved one in this thing for just a hundred bucks." Again, the shock of seeing the low end of coffins may lead the man to buy a more expensive version than he would have bought if he'd seen a middle-cost coffin first. In both cases, the shock of either a high price tag or the implication that he might have a callous attitude toward his loved one leads the man to try to repair his social status with the coffin salesman. How can he do that? By buying a coffin that is merely very expensive rather than ridiculously expensive.

door-in-the-face technique Making a very large request before asking for something more reasonable.

The Door-in-the-Face Technique Doesn't Always Work

social loafing Shirking responsibility because of being in a group.

diffusion of responsibility The tendency to be less likely to take action if others are available.

bystander effect The tendency of each person in an emergency to expect others to intervene, so the larger the group, the less likely each member is to help.

Sometimes being part of a group leads us to shirk our responsibilities

Several other phenomena illustrate how we behave differently around others than we do on our own. In some cases, we are less likely to act or exert ourselves, but in other cases we may find ourselves doing something that we would never do alone. Indeed, we might find ourselves doing something that would have been unimaginable before we were part of a group.

The clearest example of shirking responsibility in a group is **social loafing** or "free riding": those times when we slack off, exerting ourselves less than we might otherwise because we're with a group (Latane et al., 1979). For example, when you ask people to play tug-of-war, they will pull harder if they think they are alone on their side than if they think other people are pulling behind them (Ingham et al., 1974; Ringelmann, 1913). As the term *social loafing* suggests, when we think many people are involved, we tend to let the others do most of the work. This is not necessarily a conscious decision; usually it's not. We're just not as motivated to work hard when we're in a group because we know that all members of the group will share both success and blame.

This sharing of glory and blame is sometimes called **diffusion of responsibility**. For example, if you need help with something and you can think of five people who might be able and willing to help, you could e-mail them your request. But now the question arises, should you send one e-mail to all five people at once, letting each of them see that you've asked all five? Or should you send an individual e-mail to each person? Clearly it would be easier for you to send the same e-mail to all five. But if you do that, you are likely to get no responses at all. Psychologists conducting experiments of this type confirm that the proportion of people who respond to an e-mail is much greater if each person receives an e-mail sent only to that recipient (or at least *appears* to be sent only to that recipient) than if the e-mail is obviously sent to multiple addresses (Yechiam & Barron, 2003). When we get a group e-mail, the diffusion of responsibility leads us to loaf. We assume someone else will answer.

The term *social loafing* makes the practice seem unimportant, but there have been cases when social loafing has caused terrible harm. One night in 1964 a young woman named Kitty Genovese was murdered on the streets of a heavily populated area in New York City, but not in the quick fashion that you see on TV or in movies. Kitty screamed repeatedly when she was stabbed, and her attacker ran off, leaving her seriously wounded. Before she could crawl to her apartment, he returned, robbed her, stabbed her repeatedly, tried to rape her, and left her dying. The loud, bloody attack lasted over 30 minutes, but many people who heard the attack did nothing to help. Each person was sure that many other people were hearing the attack, and each assumed that someone else would intervene. Sensationalist reporting exaggerated the lack of neighbors' response (Manning et al., 2007). In fact, one woman came out after the attacks were over and held the dying Kitty (Cook, 2014). But no one who heard the first attack called the police, so diffusion of responsibility may have cost Kitty her life.

A Victim of the Bystander Effect? Kitty Genovese's murder in 1964 was shocking because so many neighbors did nothing to help her.

The tendency to expect others to intervene in an emergency has been called the **bystander effect**. In general, the more bystanders there are, the less likely each one is to try to help. As with the e-mail to five people, this is not a case of people being unhelpful, heartless, or callous. Rather, the expectation that "someone else will do it" causes each of us to stay out of it. Perhaps by knowing about this tendency, you and I will be more likely to call for help when we witness an emergency, even if many other people are around. Now that almost everyone carries a cell phone, are we more likely to make the call, or even more likely to assume that someone else already has?

Sometimes being part of a group leads us to do the wrong thing

In the case of social loafing, the diffusion of responsibility leads us to slack off. In other cases, the diffusion of responsibility becomes a license to act as we never would on our own. **Deindividuation** is the psychological process of losing one's own individual identity and coming to identify with the crowd (Festinger, 1952). The person who was an individual before is now deindividuated. When this happens in a group of people, the crowd may do things that the individuals would never consider doing alone.

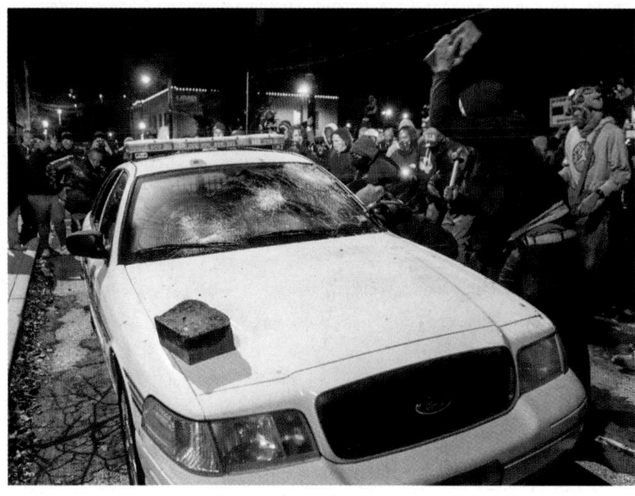

Angry Residents Ferguson, Missouri in the wake of a grand jury decision not to indict the officer who killed Michael Brown.

Several factors cause deindividuation. We've already mentioned the diffusion of responsibility—everyone's doing it, so it's not my fault, or not my fault alone. But there's also the factor of *anonymity*—no one knows who I am. If we feel little commonality with the crowd, however, we may resist deindividuation. A Yankees fan in the middle of a stadium of raving Red Sox fans is unlikely to go along with the crowd. In general, however, the larger the crowd, the more likely it is that deindividuation will take place. Any factors that favor anonymity, feelings of commonality, or increased crowd size will also favor deindividuation.

My university has a great basketball program and loads of enthusiastic fans. Sometimes after a game in the NCAA playoffs, a crowd of people gathers outside. Usually the crowd is boisterous but well behaved. But sometimes the crowd gets rowdy. In this state bad things happen: couches are dragged outside and set on fire, beer bottles are smashed, and shop windows may be broken. A big factor is alcohol. Drinking increases the diffusion of responsibility, feelings of commonality, and so on, and makes a person more likely to undergo deindividuation.

deindividuation The psychological process of losing your own individual identity and coming to identify with the crowd.

groupthink The tendency to agree with one another too readily and so make faulty decisions.

If the crowd is large enough, and if the emotional stakes are high, deindividuation can lead to a full-blown riot and mob violence. In 2014, in the wake of a grand jury clearing the officer in the Michael Brown shooting of any charges, a riot in Ferguson, Missouri caused considerable damage. Several police patrol cars and a dozen buildings were burned, and many windows were shattered.

Is deindividuation always a bad thing? It is a common part of basic military training, where it is considered important for coordinated action of individuals in emergency situations, including combat. In that case, whether deindividuation is a good thing depends on whether you view the military group's goals as good or bad.

Sometimes being part of a group leads us to make faulty decisions

Groupthink is the tendency of a group to make faulty decisions (Whyte, 1952). While several factors can lead to groupthink, the basic cause seems to be that the group of people is so eager to make a unanimous decision that they suppress their critical thinking (Janis, 1972). A famous and deadly example of groupthink in recent years, according to a 2004 bipartisan U.S. Senate report (Select Committee on Intelligence, 2004), was the conclusion of so many government intelligence analysts that Iraq possessed "weapons of mass destruction." The Senate committee unanimously agreed that the groupthink dynamic caused analysts to interpret ambiguous data as conclusively showing there were weapons of mass destruction in Iraq, and to ignore or minimize evidence that no such weapons existed. This was a case of groupthink costing billions of dollars and thousands of lives.

TABLE 15.1 Factors That Favor Teamthink or Help Avoid Groupthink

Groupthink	Teamthink
DESCRIPTION	
Group members striving to agree with one another; overwhelms adequate discussion of alternative courses of action. Defective decision making results.	Group members engage in effective synergistic thinking through the effective management of internal dialogue, mental imagery, and beliefs and assumptions. Enhanced decision making and team performance result.
DISTINGUISHING FEATURES	
Direct social pressure against divergent views	Encouragement of divergent views
Self-censorship of concerns	Open expression of concerns and ideas
Illusion of invulnerability to failure	Awareness of limitations and threats
Illusion of unanimity	Recognition of members' uniqueness
Excluding outside information	Recognition of views outside the group
Collective efforts to rationalize	Discussion of collective doubts
Stereotyped views of enemy leaders	Use of non-stereotypical views
Illusion of morality	Recognition of ethical and moral consequences of decisions

Source: Manz & Neck, 1995.

prisoner's dilemma An intellectual exercise used to study the roles of cooperation and competition.

It is easy to identify groupthink after the fact, to see how the decisions were faulty. But groupthink has certain characteristics, so when we see these at play in a group making a decision, we should be alert to the danger.

How can we avoid groupthink? Mainly by ensuring that minority and dissenting views get a full, fair hearing. For example, secret ballots during deliberation can help people with minority views be heard without identifying themselves, so they are not pressured by others. Likewise, anonymous "suggestion boxes" can help keep dissenting ideas alive. It may be helpful to ask members of the group to play "devil's advocate," to purposely defend as strongly as possible the dissenting viewpoint. But the most important safeguard is for the group to build a culture that respects all perspectives, avoids making dissenters feel guilty, and seeks out dissenting views (even if that means going outside the group). This perspective has been called *teamthink*, and **Table 15.1** offers ways to encourage such decision making (Manz & Neck, 1995).

What are the roles of cooperation and competition?

Sometimes what's best for one person is not best for another. There is an intellectual exercise that demonstrates a case of basic conflict in social relations. Described by mathematician Albert Tucker (1905–1995), it has been incorporated into many psychology experiments. In the **prisoner's dilemma** (Tucker, 1950), two people are arrested and each is interrogated separately, accused of a crime. Assume the crime is robbing a bank, and that both people are innocent. The logic of the situation is the same whether the people are guilty or innocent.

The dilemma arises when the police offer each prisoner, separately, the same deal:

> *If you confess to robbing the bank and your companion does not, then I'll use your testimony to send him away for 20 years, and you'll go free as our thanks for your testimony. The same goes for your accomplice: if he confesses and you don't, then he goes free and you go to jail. If you both confess, then you both go to jail but we'll see to it that you get early parole. If neither of you confess, then all we can really stick on you is jay-walking charges that will result in a fine.*

If both prisoners refuse to confess, they both benefit enormously because neither goes to jail. But if you put yourself in the place of a prisoner, you suddenly realize how much danger you're in. If you refuse to confess and your accomplice does, you go to jail for a long time, and you didn't even do anything. The dilemma is that, as you sit there alone, you will probably decide that, no matter what your accomplice does, you're better off confessing. If you confess and he doesn't, you go free. If you confess and he does too, at least you don't go to jail for as long a time (**Figure 15.18**). A famous joke reflects the crux of the prisoner's dilemma (Harrington, 2008). While Stalin is ruling Russia, the secret police arrest an orchestra conductor because they suspect the musical score he is studying of Tchaikovsky's violin concerto is really a secret code for some insurrection. They bring him in for questioning, where he insists it's a genuine music score and nothing else. But then another policeman enters and says, "You might as well confess; we've got Tchaikovsky in the next room and he's already talking."

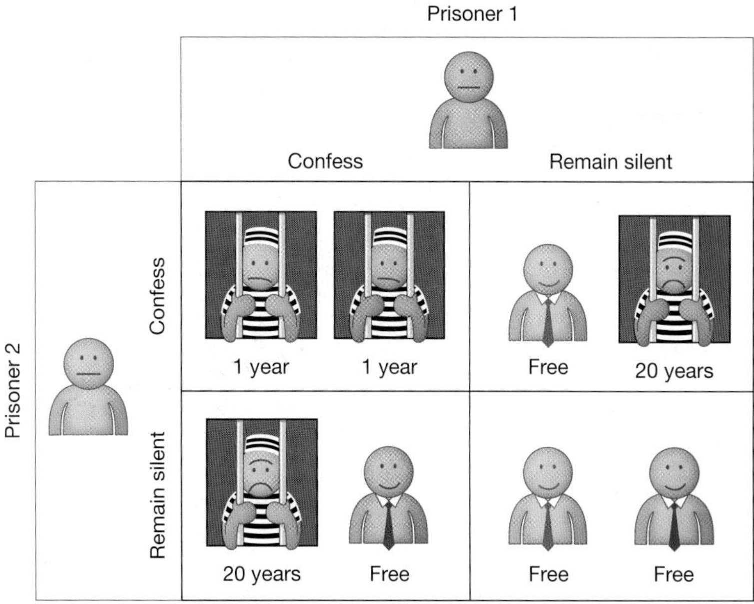

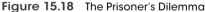

Figure 15.18 The Prisoner's Dilemma

By presenting these choices to people, asking what they would do, while adjusting the length of time in jail for the different outcomes, researchers can see how the consequence of each outcome affects the decision making. If you think it's too unrealistic to believe what people say they would do in such a situation, you can make it a bit more real. Bring people into the lab and give each of them $20. Then tell them that another participant in the next room has also been given $20 and now each of you has to decide whether to push a button in 5 minutes. If you push the button and the other person does not, then you keep your $20 and get a $10 bonus but he will lose all of his money. If you push the button and he does too, then you both lose $10. If you don't push the button and he does, you lose $20 and he gets the $10 bonus. If neither of you pushes the button, you *both* keep the $20 plus a $10 bonus. Both people would be better off not pushing the button (not "confessing"), but each has a strong motivation to push it to avoid losing money and to gain a shot at the additional $10 bonus. Whether in a police station or the lab, the prisoner's dilemma arises because the participants cannot communicate with each other. In most real-life situations, communicating to cooperate can benefit both parties.

Evolutionary psychology offers an explanation for altruism

A movement in psychology that we noted earlier in the chapter is evolutionary psychology, a field that regards psychological traits as a result of evolution by natural selection. Evolutionary biologists have documented many examples of how certain physical traits favor "fitness" and how certain genes that influence these traits have accumulated (that is, have been "conserved"). Evolutionary psychologists are likewise interested in *behavioral* traits that favor fitness, meaning behaviors that increase the probability that we will produce children, grandchildren, and so on. For example, if loving your children makes you more likely to protect them until they grow up, then you'll have more grandchildren someday. People behave this way, the theory goes, because genes favoring such behaviors resulted in more offspring, resulting in more people carrying those genes. On the other hand, people who didn't love and look after their

altruism The practice of putting others before oneself.

inclusive fitness How successful individuals are at spreading their own genes in *any* fashion, including benefitting relatives.

children were less likely to leave descendants, so their genes would be less and less frequently found in the human gene pool. In other words, evolutionary psychology assumes that human behavior evolves. From this perspective, we may surmise that some human behaviors that seem maladaptive today, which decrease the chance for a long life and many children, may have been adaptive long ago under different environmental circumstances.

Evolutionary psychologists are fascinated by **altruism**: the practice of putting others before oneself. When a person does something that is good for others but of no benefit to himself, or even harmful to himself, we say he is being altruistic. A person who runs into a burning building to save total strangers is displaying altruism. He is helping others even though he might be hurt or killed by doing so. Likewise, a squirrel that barks a warning about a hawk overhead is helping other squirrels survive, even though the squirrel might draw the hawk's attention.

From a strictly evolutionary point of view, there's something odd about altruism. If there are genes that contribute to making a person more likely to sacrifice her own good for the good of others, wouldn't you expect her to leave fewer descendants, and therefore those genes to disappear? Wouldn't genes promoting selfish behavior, doing whatever it takes to help oneself before all others, lead to lots of children and therefore spread? In general, the answer is yes. It is easy to find selfish people, so there may well be genes that contribute to selfish behavior. But, as you may have already surmised, there is an important exception: altruism that serves your children serves to conserve your genes for future generations.

Favoring yourself may help you reproduce, but your genes will be lost unless your children survive. Being altruistic toward your children would help spread your genes and is thus favored by natural selection.

Since all the people you are related to carry at least some of your genes, natural selection should also favor behaviors that help any of your relatives reproduce, as long as it doesn't hurt your own chances of reproduction too much. So evolutionary biologists and psychologists also speak of **inclusive fitness**: how successful an individual is at spreading her genes in *any* fashion, either by producing her own children or by helping her relatives produce children (who will share some of her genes).

Figure 15.19 Inclusive Fitness and Ground Squirrel Alarms It is dangerous for a ground squirrel to draw attention to itself by calling out a warning if a hawk is overhead. A ground squirrel is more likely to take that risk if it has relatives nearby. Selectively taking risks to save individuals that share some of its genes is a way for an individual to increase its inclusive fitness.

Inclusive fitness could explain why natural selection would favor altruism toward your relatives. The more closely related you are to a person, the more of your genes that person carries, and the more helping that person will help spread your genes. Your nieces and nephews will donate some of your genes to their children. As John Haldane (1955) said, "I would gladly lay down my life for two brothers…or eight cousins."

Animals certainly do not perform such complicated calculations, but it turns out that ground squirrels are much more likely to sound an alarm about a hawk overhead if they have relatives nearby (**Figure 15.19**). The more relatives they have around them, the more likely the squirrels are to behave altruistically (Sherman, 1985). So natural selection favors genes that make animals more likely to be altruistic toward their relatives. Of course, there may be times when non-relatives in the vicinity benefit too.

Are we just animals, looking after our relatives? If a scriptwriter wants to establish tension in a movie, he often puts the hero's child at risk, and the story consists of the hero taking extraordinary measures to save his child. But sometimes we help out other people who are not related to us. Does this sort of behavior offer a challenge to evolutionary psychology? No. Remember that humans are relatively long-lived with big brains and long memories. Evolutionary psychologists point out that sometimes helping out a non-relative is still good for your own genes. If you help your neighbor today, he may help you tomorrow. This **social exchange theory** says that sometimes when we help someone, we are expecting to gain something in return, a case of *reciprocal altruism*. For evolutionary psychologists this fact suggests that natural selection should also favor genes that make us more likely to help non-relatives, within reason.

Let's return to the prisoner's dilemma introduced earlier. Both prisoners have a strong incentive to confess, meaning both will go to jail. But what happens if the two prisoners face the dilemma more than once? Then, according to social exchange theory, each has an incentive to try to hold out. Why? Because if you and I are in this situation and you confess, going free and sending me to a long jail sentence, then I would remember that. Next time I would be likely to confess and send you to jail. But if you know we'll both be here again, then the smart move becomes not to confess, because you know that I may not confess and you will want to give me an incentive to hold out the next time we're arrested.

Mathematicians such as John Nash, portrayed in the movie *A Beautiful Mind*, worked out the complex probabilities for various situations of this sort as part of *game theory*. A crucial finding of their work is that when people have repeated exchanges, then both can benefit from helping each other. Importantly, these models indicate that *even if the two individuals are genetically unrelated*, natural selection can favor those who cooperate (Maynard Smith, 1982).

social exchange theory The notion that we help others, even if they are unrelated to us, because they may someday help us in return.

neuroeconomics The study of the neural basis of making economic decisions.

loss averse Characteristic of being very reluctant to do anything that might lead to loss.

Neuroeconomics offers a new way of studying human influence

Psychologists and economists are often interested in the same behavior: how people decide whether to buy something. For economists, knowing how consumers make buying decisions might help them predict future changes in the overall economy and predict demand for new products. For psychologists, studying economic decisions offers insight into decision making in an everyday, real-life context. People trained in each of these fields now collaborate to conduct research in **neuroeconomics**, the investigation of the neural basis of decision making, specifically in consumers.

One sign of this merger of interests was the award of the 2002 Nobel Prize in Economics to psychologist Daniel Kahneman. As with so many really powerful ideas, a main point of Kahneman's discoveries can be summarized readily and seems simple. It is this: We hate loss far more than we enjoy gain. In other words, if you lose $10, it lowers your mood much more than finding $10 raises your mood. That new car won't make you as happy as you think it will. But if a truck smashes that new car, you will feel really awful. Eventually we all learn this about ourselves and so we become **loss averse**: reluctant to do anything that might lead to loss. Loss aversion seems to play a role in the prisoner's dilemma: the fear of a great loss (long imprisonment) makes the prisoners more likely to make a false confession.

As we discussed in Section 10.3, a problem arises when our loss aversion causes us to make illogical decisions. Experimenters can chart this irrational behavior by either offering people money to play a gambling game or having people answer questions about hypothetical situations. For example, suppose you needed $10,000 to pay your tuition bill next year and you have two investments that your dearly departed Auntie Moneybags left to you when you were 10. One was $30,000 in General Motors stock that you've watched lose value until it's now worth $10,000. Bummer—$20,000 just gone. The other investment was $2,000 in

YouTube stock that has grown in value so it's now also worth $10,000. Which should you sell? Many people would choose the YouTube stock, hoping the General Motors stock would rise in value to get back some of that lost money. But that's an irrational decision—stock that's fallen is likely to continue to do so, while stock that's grown is likely to bring you more money. But most people hold onto the falling stock because they irrationally fear the loss of that $20,000 (that's probably gone for good). You can see why economists are interested in such behavior.

In fact, just as getting a new car won't make us as happy as we think it will, losing that new car won't make us as *un*happy as we think it will. The cornerstone of loss aversion is that when we *anticipate* events, we overestimate how bad a loss will make us feel. But if we actually *experience* the loss, it's often not as bad as we expected.

15.2 SUMMARY

- *Social norms*, the widely agreed upon rules for what people should believe and how they should behave, exert a *normative social influence*, pressuring us to behave and believe like everyone else. One example is the *chameleon effect*, when we unconsciously mimic others.
- *Social facilitation*, when the presence of observers changes our behavior, offers several other examples. Observers may improve our performance when the task is easy and we expect approval, but they may hurt our performance if we're doing something difficult or expect the observers to disapprove of us.
- The *foot-in-the-door technique*, asking someone to do something trivial before asking for more, exploits social facilitation to persuade other people to do what we want.
- *Social loafing* is caused by a perceived *diffusion of responsibility* and *deindividuation*, when each person identifies strongly with the crowd. An example of social loafing is the *bystander effect*, when individuals in a group fail to behave responsibly.
- Likewise, identification with others may lead to *groupthink*, when a group of people makes mistakes due to social pressures and self-censorship.
- In the *prisoner's dilemma*, a person may confess to a crime he did not commit to avoid a long prison sentence due to someone else's false confession. This tension between behaving selfishly and *altruism* (putting others before oneself) is studied by evolutionary psychologists as a trait that has evolved over time.
- Behaving altruistically toward people who are related to us improves our *inclusive fitness*, how good we are at getting some of our genes into the next generation by helping our relatives reproduce.
- The *social exchange theory* says we help others, even if they are unrelated to us, because they may someday help us in return.
- *Neuroeconomics*, the study of the neural basis of making economic decisions, reveals that humans tend to be risk averse: we are more afraid of loss than we are motivated to gain.

REVIEW QUESTIONS

1. What are social norms, and how do they affect our behavior?
2. How does the presence of an audience affect our performance?
3. In what ways may people behave differently when they are part of a crowd rather than by themselves?
4. What is the prisoner's dilemma, and how does it relate to our choosing between selfish behavior and altruistic behavior?

Food for Thought

Typically groupthink is regarded as a phenomenon seen in small to medium-sized groups: committees, commissions, and juries. But do the principles of groupthink apply to larger groups, say entire states or countries? What forces or measures can make groupthink more or less common when countries make decisions?

15.3 Friendship and Romance

Now that we've talked about the principles of social perception and social influence, we can apply them to different kinds of relationships, positive and negative. Before we discuss aggressive interactions and authority, which can lead to unpleasant outcomes, let's consider the important positive relationships of friendship and romance. As we discussed in Chapter 13, friends and mates can go a long way to buffer us from the stresses and strains of life. Having close friends or a supportive spouse appears to extend our lives (Holt-Lunstad et al., 2010). Friends are also important when we're growing up—having close friends appears to boost self-esteem and grades in middle school students (Jia et al., 2009). So it's worthwhile learning about how we make and keep friends and partners.

Things to Learn

- Characteristics of friendship
- Benefits of marriage
- Ways to strengthen a marriage
- Three components of romantic love

Friends have things in common and reciprocate

We have to meet someone before we can make friends, so it's no surprise that we tend to make friends with people who have things in common with us. After all, until relatively recently, this meant people we meet in person, which ensures we have some things in common such as where we live, work, or go to school. Even people we "meet" over the Web, who may live far away, probably share some of our interests—which Internet video games we play, or which Facebook pages we frequent. More than that, friends tend to share similar religious or moral values, and interests such as sports, art, or academics (Ledbetter et al., 2007).

Having such things in common may start a friendship, but the relationship deepens as we reveal more and more about ourselves. This is usually a gradual process as we get to know each other, and it must be at least somewhat reciprocal, as each friend grows comfortable revealing concerns and dreams to the other. Another characteristic of friends that we prize is that they seem to understand us, and most important, they are almost always supportive (Weisz & Wood, 2005), cheering us when we succeed and encouraging us when we have setbacks. As part of this process of getting to know each other, when a friend reveals a past mistake, we're better equipped to understand that he or she is a good person who got into a bad situation. In other words, we're less likely to make the fundamental attribution error about our friends.

Studies suggest that having common interests and a shared history is also important for friendships to endure. Having such things in common seems to facilitate ongoing communication, which is also typical of friendships that last, even when friends relocate far away (Ledbetter et al., 2007). Communication is important, but it's also good for friends to try to stay upbeat if the friendship is to continue. Of course friends share their worries and setbacks, but if either party comes to talk only about gripes and hardships, communication may become more sporadic and the friendship may fade (Wilson et al., 2011).

Likewise, it's important for both parties to make it clear that they value the friendship. Sometimes people you think are your friends may suddenly act uninterested in hearing from you, or be too busy to share what's happening in their lives. Worse, they may act snippy and say hurtful things seemingly out of the blue. People who display such ambivalence, acting very friendly at one time and then hostile at another, are sometimes referred to as *frenemies*, a mixture of *friend* and *enemy*. Such relationships can take a toll on your physical health (Holt-Lunstad et al., 2007) and don't usually last long.

"I love our nights in together, just you, me, and our 756 friends."

Facebook Attending to Facebook friends may limit the quality time spent with those around you.

These days many people use social media such as Facebook to keep up with friends (either distant or even next door), but face-to-face communication seems to be more rewarding and effective in keeping friendships alive (Schiffrin et al., 2010). We noted earlier that evolutionary psychologists have offered the social exchange theory that friendships were very adaptive among early humans—where the reciprocal altruism between friends might make the difference be-

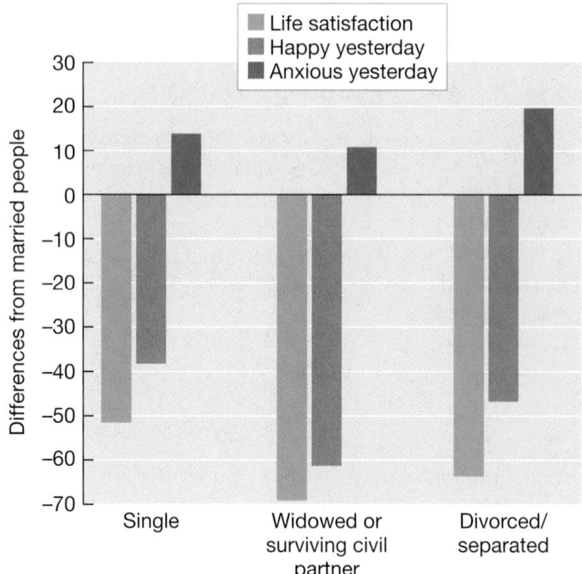

Figure 15.20 Single People Tend to Be Less Happy and More Anxious than Married People These data were gathered in the United Kingdom. (After Oguz et al., 2013.)

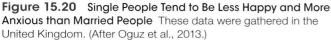

tween life and death. Thus we may have inherited genes that favor seeking out, prizing, and maintaining friends (Flora, 2013; Hruschka, 2010). Even in our civilized world, friends seem to be good for our health. Another relationship that makes our lives easier and longer is having a mate, which we'll consider next.

Married people tend to be happier and healthier than single people

Surveys consistently find that people who are married are happier than people who are unmarried (Gove, 1973). A recent survey in the United Kingdom confirmed this remarkably consistent finding (**Figure 15.20**). Of course these are correlational studies, so it's possible that people who have other advantages that will help them be happy and healthy are also more likely to get married and stay married. But studies that try to match people as closely as possible in terms of age, education, gender, and income indicate that married people *are happier than they would have been* if they had not married (Musick & Bumpass, 2012). This same study concluded that in the contemporary United States, couples who live together without getting married are about as happy as those who get married.

Of course, this doesn't mean that getting married or moving in with a partner will necessarily make you happier than you are now. In fact, the data suggest that getting married at a young age may not be a good idea. Young marriages are especially at risk for divorce—women who get married before they are 20 are more than twice as likely to get divorced as those who marry when they are 24 or older. As **Figure 15.21** indicates, women who get married as young adults are also more likely to be happy in their marriage. Waiting until you're older may give you a chance to learn what you want and prize in a partner, which may help the union last (Glenn et al., 2010).

More than a century ago, researchers established that married people are also less likely to die in the next few years than single people, and that when a spouse dies, the surviving partner is likely to die soon after (Farr, 1858). Modern studies amply confirm that married people have fewer health problems than single people (Proulx & Snyder-Rivas, 2013). As they grow older, married people are less likely to get pneumonia, have a heart attack, succumb to cancer (Aizer et al., 2013), or develop Alzheimer's disease (Lipnicki et al., 2013). So it's worthwhile for you to think about how to build a relationship that will last a lifetime.

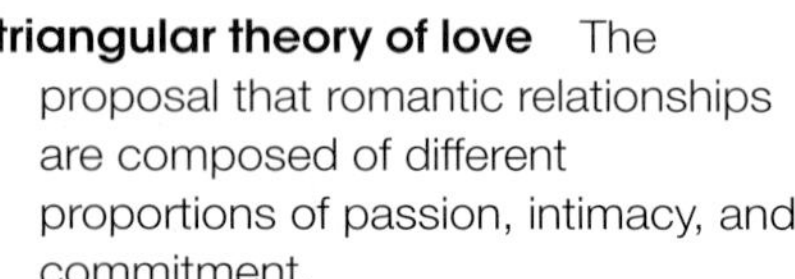
triangular theory of love The proposal that romantic relationships are composed of different proportions of passion, intimacy, and commitment.

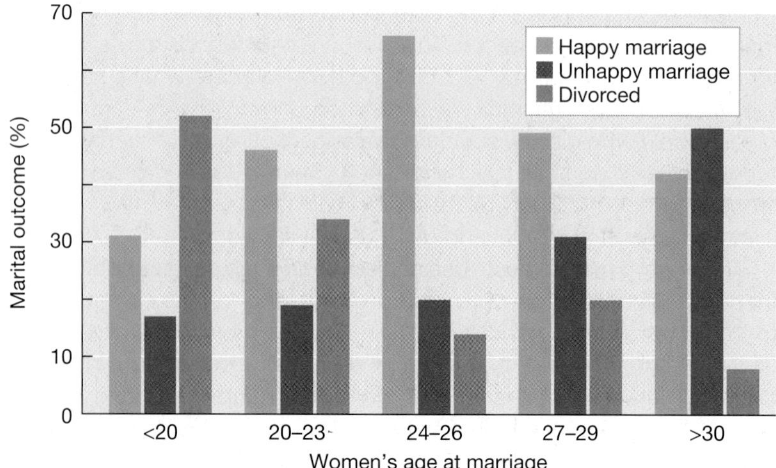

Figure 15.21 Marriages Early in Life Are Less Likely to Be Happy and Lasting Note that women who marry between the ages of 24 and 26 are most likely to report a happy marriage and are among the least likely to divorce. (After Hymowitz et al., 2013.)

TABLE 15.2 Seven Principles for Making Marriage Last

Principle	Examples
Enhance your love maps.	Know each other well. What does your partner like, dislike, hope for, dread?
Nurture fondness and admiration.	Respect and appreciate partners, and let them know it.
Turn toward each other rather than away.	Seek each other out when problems arise, so you can share emotional burdens. Share successes too.
Let your partner influence you.	Develop a teamwork mentality, considering each other's perspective and feelings.
Work together to solve conflicts and problems.	Develop strategies to calmly analyze problems and find ways to compromise.
Overcome gridlock.	Find out what feelings are getting in the way of solving problems, and learn acceptance.
Create shared meaning.	Develop a couple-culture—routines, rituals, family legends, and shared experiences.

Source: Gottman & Silver, 1999.

There are three components to romantic relationships

If you are married or in a relationship, what helps it to be happy and lasting? We can explore that question in several ways. For example, we can ask married people how satisfied they are with their lives in general and their marriage in particular and then probe for what their everyday interactions are like (Gottman & Silver, 1999). Such studies show that happy couples have more positive interactions (being affectionate, listening to each other, being playful) than negative interactions (criticizing, demanding, holding grudges). They argue sometimes, but have more positive than negative interactions. Researchers in this field have compiled a list of seven "principles" to help couples make their marriages happier and therefore more likely to last (**Table 15.2**).

When people first fall in love, they may feel an incredible rush of emotion when around their romantic partner. Unfortunately, that first rush of passion, however fulfilling at the time, may not last. Psychologist Robert Sternberg, whose ideas about multiple intelligences we discussed in Section 11.2, has also offered a way of thinking about the different aspects of romantic relationships. In his **triangular theory of love**, Sternberg (2007) asserts that *passion*, the exciting feelings of desire, is only one important part of romantic relationships. Romantic relationships may also include a sense of *commitment*, the decision to stay together and make plans together, and *intimacy*, a feeling of closeness and high regard for one another (**Figure 15.22A**).

Romantic relationships vary in how intimate, passionate, and committed the couple may be. Considering how much each of these three factors is present in a relationship offers a way of understanding different types of romance. For example, a relationship that consists of intimacy but not passion or commitment typifies a friendship more than a romance. A relationship built on passion only, without intimacy or commitment, typifies what we think of as infatuation, which is not likely to last (unless the relationship develops further). In fact, Sternberg of-

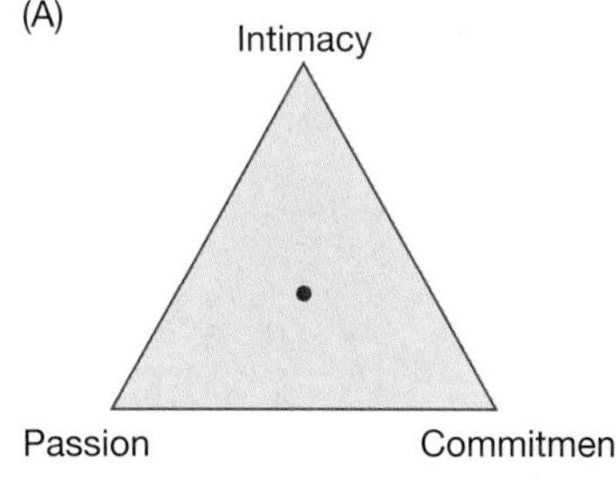
(A)
Intimacy
Passion
Commitment

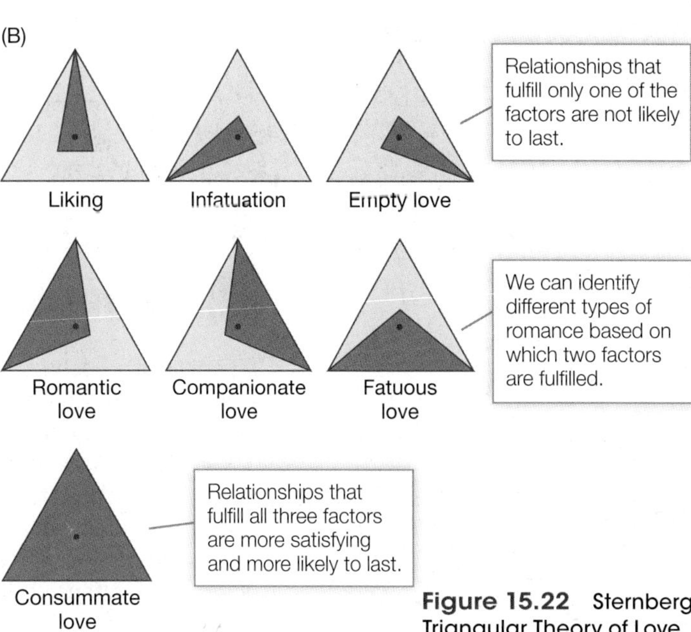
(B)
Liking
Infatuation
Empty love
Relationships that fulfill only one of the factors are not likely to last.
Romantic love
Companionate love
Fatuous love
We can identify different types of romance based on which two factors are fulfilled.
Consummate love
Relationships that fulfill all three factors are more satisfying and more likely to last.

Figure 15.22 Sternberg's Triangular Theory of Love

fers evidence that any romantic relationship built on just one of the three factors is not likely to last very long. Romances that include at least two of the factors appear to be more stable and lasting. He suggests that the most fulfilling romantic relationship, which he calls *consummate love*, is one that has all three characteristics: intimacy, commitment, and passion (**Figure 15.22B**).

Note that the principles for a strong marriage that we discussed earlier (see Table 15.2) are directed primarily toward building intimacy and commitment rather than passion. There is no simple way to ensure that passion will endure (if you learn how to sell passion in a bottle, you'll have plenty of customers). Sexual desire tends to fade with age, in both men and women, who as they age may find great satisfaction in simply cuddling (Heiman et al., 2011). Couples with long-term satisfaction in their sexual lives are good at communicating with one another (Smith et al., 2011). To the extent that efforts to build the commitment and intimacy of a relationship make it easier to communicate ways to please each other, they probably help keep the passion alive too.

15.3 SUMMARY

- Friends tend to have common interests and values, gradually share their dreams and concerns, and try to help each other. This *reciprocal altruism* may have been favored by natural selection.
- Friendships that last are characterized by mutual support and frequent communication that doesn't become dominated by negative emotions (gripe sessions).
- Our friends who make it clear that they value the friendship tend to last, while we tend to drift away from "frenemies," who act friendly on some occasions and indifferent or hostile on others.
- Married people tend to be happier and healthier than unmarried people, but people who marry when they are young are less likely to be happy in their marriage and more likely to divorce.
- Sternberg's *triangular theory of love* proposes that romantic relationships are composed of different proportions of passion, intimacy, and commitment. Relationships that are strong in at least two of these factors are more likely to be happy and lasting. Consummate love fulfills all three factors.

REVIEW QUESTIONS

1. What are the factors that lead people to become friends and to stay friends?
2. Describe Sternberg's triangular theory of love and how we might typify the different types of romances that embody one, two, or three of these factors.
3. What can couples do to strengthen their relationship so it will be happy and endure?

Food for Thought

Generally, married people are happier and healthier than single people. But many unmarried people lead long, happy lives. How do they do it?

15.4 Aggression

Things to Learn

- Role of male hormones in aggression
- Difference between controlled versus reactive aggression
- Role of genes, culture and video games in aggression
- Three rationales for punishment

It is difficult to estimate how many people have been hurt by **aggression**: behavior intended to cause physical or psychological harm or pain. Note that accidentally hurting someone is not aggression, because there was no *intent* to cause harm. Aggressive behaviors take so many different forms. Attacks on others are not always physical; many are verbal, aimed at causing psychological pain, such as insults, gossip, practical jokes. You could never count them all. The destruction caused by aggression is vast, and we will probably never be able to understand or abolish aggression entirely.

This section will discuss some of the causes and consequences of aggression, beginning with studies of animals that reveal how hormones can influence aggression. We'll discuss how genes and the environment play a large role in aggression as well. We'll wrap up by considering the use of punishment to control aggression.

aggression Behavior intended to cause physical or psychological harm or pain.

testosterone A steroid hormone secreted by the testes; the most prominent androgen.

androgens The primary steroid hormones produced by the testes, including testosterone.

Experiments in non-human animals offer a context for aggression

A fact of modern life is that most violent crimes are committed by men. As sex differences in behavior go, this one is notable. It is much larger than the sex difference in height, or the modest sex differences in scores on verbal tests (women do better on average) or math tests (men do better on average).

But the greater aggression of males isn't just typical of modern human life. It also existed in ancient life too, as history records. Many people consider the first Western historian to be Herodotus of ancient Greece, and the history he recorded was primarily a war in which men did almost all the fighting. The idea that there might be women warriors was so outlandish that Herodotus had to comment on the Amazons, women so fiercely devoted to war that they would cut off their right breast to make it easier to shoot a bow and arrow. Scholars dispute whether the Amazons ever existed, but even if they did, they were the exception that proves the rule. There are no other reports, confirmed or unconfirmed, of a society where only the women fight.

We observe the greater aggression in males in almost all other mammalian species as well. For non-human mammals, life can be tough. Most individuals born never reach adulthood. What's more, of those males that do reach adulthood, most never persuade any female to mate with them, even once (Aloise King et al., 2013; Le Boeuf, 1974). Mating is much easier for most female mammals: if they live to adulthood, they can almost always find a male that's willing to mate with them. In fact, there are so many willing males that a female can be very choosy, selecting only that male that will give her children the best genes she can get. Because females are very choosy about selecting a mate, so most males never make the cut, males often must fight one another to get access to a female. Of course, the male mice, deer, elephants, and aardvarks don't have to be *thinking* about all these consequences to behave this way. The males really, really want to mate with a female (natural selection has made sure of that), so if they must fight other males to get access to a female, they will.

In non-human animals, male–male aggression is driven by the same hormone that masculinizes the body and prepares it for reproduction as a male: testosterone. **Testosterone** is one of a class of steroid hormones called **androgens**, which are secreted by the testes. Before birth, these hormones cause the fetus to develop a male body, including a penis and scrotum (see Figure 12.23). Androgens also trigger many of the body changes at puberty, including growth of muscles. These same hormones also act on the brain, at least in non-human mammals, to trigger aggressive behavior toward other males. In seasonally breeding mammals such as deer, the testes release androgens before the mating season to promote antler growth. The androgens also induce the males to fight. When the breeding season is over, the flow of androgens from the testes slows, the antlers drop off, and the males stop fighting.

Did Amazons Really Exist? Supposedly each Amazon amputated her right breast so it wouldn't get in the way of her bowstring when she shot her arrows.

The effects of androgens on mammalian aggression have been studied in laboratory mice (**Figure 15.23**). Experiments indicate that androgens such as testosterone trigger aggression in animals by acting on a network of brain regions, especially in the hypothalamus (McCall & Singer, 2012). As these same brain regions in humans also have receptors to respond to androgens, the question arises: Does testosterone trigger aggression in men?

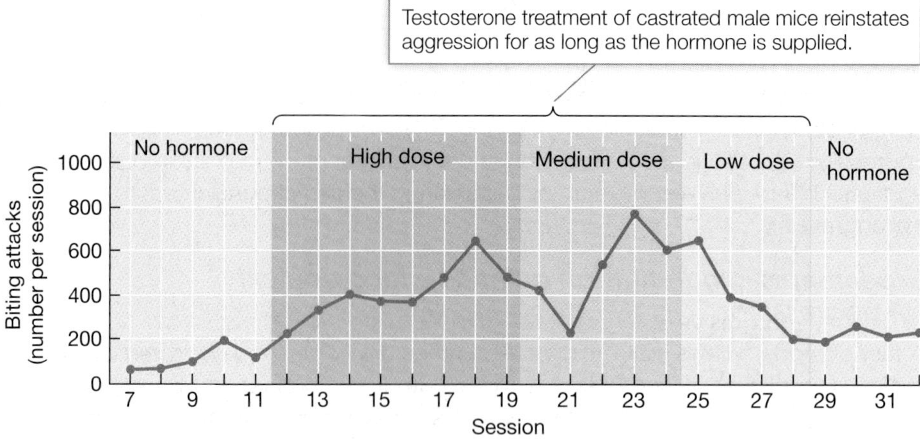

Figure 15.23 Testosterone Increases Aggression in Mice In this experiment, adult male mice were first castrated to remove androgens, which also reduced aggression. The researchers then measured aggression as they manipulated testosterone levels. (After Wagner et al., 1980.)

Hormones influence human aggression

As is often the case, it is difficult to know whether the same androgens that regulate aggression in other mammals also do so in humans. Most violent crimes are committed by men rather than women, and almost all men have more circulating testosterone than almost all women, but this doesn't mean that the higher testosterone causes the greater violence. There are other influences. For example, men are also raised in a culture that values physical aggression in males but not females. This socialization may be responsible for the sex difference in aggression.

In humans, testosterone seems more related to social dominance than to overt aggression. For example, athletes, actors, and con men tend to have higher levels of testosterone than do clerks or intellectuals, suggesting that high status is accompanied by high testosterone. Does high testosterone lead to high status or vice versa? The answer is both. Among men in athletic competitions, those who win increase testosterone secretion afterward while those who lose secrete less testosterone. This is not due to the physical exertion, because we see the same results in males competing in a chess tournament (Mazur & Booth, 1998). After the tourney, the winners have higher testosterone levels than the losers, although they did not differ before the competition. Furthermore, in *spectators* watching a soccer match, men rooting for the winning team increase testosterone release after the game, while boosters for the losing team decrease testosterone release (Bahrke et al., 1996; Bernhardt, 1997). So when men receive a boost in dominance, they will also boost their testosterone production for a while.

But there's reason to think androgens affect human aggression as well as dominance. Perhaps the strongest evidence comes from men who deliberately inject themselves with high doses of androgens—body builders and athletes. First there are many anecdotal reports of men and teenagers taking "anabolic steroids" who report inappropriate levels of irritability and aggression, so called "'roid rage." You might be skeptical of these reports since they are sometimes given as a defense for men who have been arrested for aggressive behavior. Surveys also indicate that men who have used anabolic steroids are more likely to have engaged in violent behavior (Beaver et al., 2008), but that is only a correlation—maybe people who have violent tendencies are also more likely to take steroids. There have been a few controlled laboratory studies, most of which indicate that men taking anabolic steroids do indeed experience greater levels of irritability and aggressive impulses than men given placebos (Pope et al., 2000). Given the millions of youth and men in the United States who take anabolic steroids, it seems clear that most of them don't come to the attention of police or psychiatrists. Nevertheless, this research, in conjunction with animal models, indicates that normal circulating levels of androgens probably play a role in making men more prone to violence and aggression than women.

Aggression can be planned or impulsive

Researchers have proposed that there are at least two different forms of aggression in humans. **Controlled/instrumental aggression** is carefully planned and usually intended to gain some goal, such as beating someone up to keep them from talking to authorities. Mass murder and genocide are examples of controlled/instrumental aggression. One reason they get so much attention is that they are relatively rare.

controlled/instrumental aggression An aggressive behavior carefully planned and usually intended to gain some goal.

reactive/impulsive aggression An aggressive behavior in response to some provocation.

Reactive/impulsive aggression occurs in response to some provocation, such as when you angrily shove someone who bumps into you (Vitiello & Stoff, 1997). This is the type of aggression that seems exacerbated by androgens. Sometimes referred to as *frustration-aggression*, it is more common and better studied than controlled/instrumental aggression. Reactive/impulsive aggression is accompanied by activation of the sympathetic nervous system, the so-called fight-or-flight reaction that speeds up breathing and heart rate, increases blood pressure, and so on, to prepare for action (see Figure 13.1). In animal models, applying electrical shock to the feet of rats will make them more likely to attack a cage mate. Even mild discomfort, such as applying a paper clip to the rat's tail, can trigger aggression.

In humans, several lines of evidence indicate that the *frontal lobes* of the brain are less active in people with a history of reactive aggression (Soloff et al., 2003). One hypothesis is that the frontal lobes serve to inhibit impulses, allowing us to reflect and consider before we do something we may regret. Some people may have less active frontal lobes, which may lead them to engage in more dustups and come to the attention of authorities.

There's also evidence that people with a history of reactive aggression are more fearful. For example, when people are shown pictures of angry faces, a center in the temporal lobe, called the *amygdala,* becomes activated in all people (see Figure 13.13). But people with a lifetime history of aggression show even more activation of the amygdala in these studies than do control participants (Coccaro et al., 2007). So perhaps they are more reactive because they are more fearful of sudden bumps and scares in everyday life.

Interestingly, treating people with the hormone oxytocin before they look at scary photos reduces amygdala activation (Kirsch et al., 2005). Would such a treatment help people with a history of reactive/impulsive aggression curb their behaviors? No one knows at present. If it did help, should certain people be forced to take hormones to control their behavior?

Angry Faces Activate Fear Centers in the Brain Even brief views of pictures of angry faces can activate the amygdala.

Genes and the environment influence aggression

As we noted, males are encouraged by our culture to be more aggressive than females. But clearly gender is not the whole story, because many men are never aggressive and some women can be violent. What other factors might influence aggression? As with all questions about the origins of human behavior, we must wrestle with the question of the relative contributions of genes and the environment.

Both twin studies and studies of adopted children demonstrate that there are genetic and environmental influences on antisocial behavior such as aggression. A literature review suggested that 30–40% of the variance in antisocial behavior is due to genetic influences (Rhee & Waldman, 2002). The exact proportions are subject to debate, but the bottom line is that both genes and environment matter for aggression and other antisocial behaviors. The next question is whether we can identify *particular* genes or *particular* environments that affect the probability that a person will be aggressive.

Several genes have been implicated in aggression. Usually the studies of these genes look at "impulsive behavior," the tendency to act immediately, without apparent reflection or control, in response to some stimulus. We considered this behavior when we described attention deficit hyperactivity disorder (ADHD) in Box 5.1. Studies of genetic influences on impulsive behavior tend to focus on ADHD or aggression, or both. The idea is that people who react swiftly to a stimulus, such as someone yelling at them, are more likely to "come out swinging" because they don't take the time to consider the consequences of aggression or the alternative ways of responding. In other words, they show the reactive/impulsive type of aggression we discussed earlier.

Why might there be genes in our population that favor impulsive behavior? One suggestion has been that impulsive behavior may be a very good trait for gathering food, especially small animal game (Stephens et al., 2004). Our ancestors in Africa who were struggling to survive by gathering food every day needed to be somewhat impulsive. If you saw a lizard scurrying away, your only chance of getting it was to shoot out your hand immediately. Also, if you think about it, in a precivilization culture in which there were no police or judges, being aggressive might not have been as maladaptive as it is today. Even early humans were social creatures, banding together to survive. Natural selection must have been constantly wavering between impulsive and restrained traits—resulting in individuals who are impulsive enough to survive, yet restrained enough to be tolerated by the group.

Genes that encode the **monoamine oxidase** (**MAO**) enzyme have been implicated in reactive/impulsive aggression. MAO normally breaks down neurotransmitters such as serotonin. Members of a large Dutch family with a history of reactive aggression had an unusual, mutant version of the MAO gene that caused a deficiency in the enzyme (Brunner et al., 1993). Another study suggested that high levels of MAO can increase aggression. In a group of boys with several common versions of an MAO gene, teachers and parents rated boys who were carrying a version of the gene that resulted in higher levels of MAO activity in the brain as aggressive (Beitchman et al., 2004). Genes that regulate MAO can also increase the probability that boys will respond to maltreatment by being aggressive when they grow up (Jaffee et al., 2005). Further understanding of the role of MAO in human aggression may someday bring prospects of intervening (along with difficult ethical questions that prospect may raise).

Social and cultural factors influence aggression

From the discussion so far, you might think that the basic biology of humans is responsible for human aggression, especially in men. But even if there are biological factors that predispose men to be aggressive, society has a big effect on how aggressive people will be. We observe a compelling demonstration of the effect of culture on human aggression on the North American continent. People in the

monoamine oxidase (MAO) The enzyme that normally inactivates the monoamines, including norepinephrine, dopamine, and serotonin.

United States are dramatically more violent than people in Canada, with nearly three times more intentional homicide per capita (United Nations Office on Drugs and Crime, 2014). For example, your chances of being killed by firearms are more than six times greater in the United States than in Canada. In an average year, 32 people in the United States are shot dead for every million inhabitants, while only 5 people per million inhabitants are killed by firearms in Canada (United Nations Office on Drugs and Crime, 2012).

Why does this difference in violence exist? There are several possible explanations. Guns are much easier to buy and keep in the United States than in Canada, and Canadian TV networks portray less violence than U.S. networks (Gosselin et al., 1997; Paquette, 2004). This difference in TV violence may be a contributing factor since there's evidence that exposure to video violence may make people more aggressive (**Box 15.2**). But whatever is responsible for the

Skeptic at Large

BOX 15.2

Video Violence and Aggression

For many years parents, teachers, and psychologists have been concerned about the portrayal of violence in movies, comic books, and television, and the possible effect those portrayals might have on people, especially children because they are more suggestible (Anderson et al., 2007). The concern accelerated with the development of computer games where the players make decisions about what the "avatars" who represent them on screen will do. As high-quality graphics became available, some games, such as *Dead Space, Resident Evil, Bulletstorm*, and the *Mortal Kombat* series, offered realistic depictions of people being dismembered and killed. These outcomes are rewarded as part of the game. The same graphic mayhem unfolds in multiplayer games over the Internet. Does exposure to such violence make people more violent?

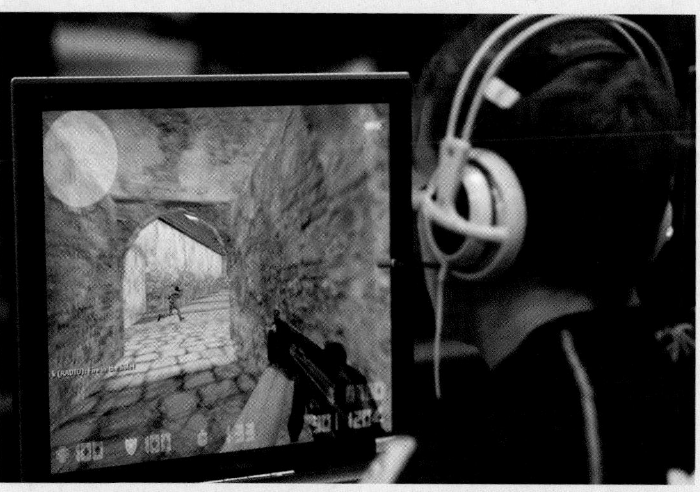

Shoot to Kill Point and shoot games reward players for quickly shooting their "enemies" in the head.

To determine effects of video game violence in the laboratory, investigators have exposed people to either violent or nonviolent movies and games and then asked them about their attitudes about violence or how they would act in a hypothetical situation. In those studies, exposure to violence definitely increases how aggressive a person is feeling, how aggressively he or she imagines behaving. It also increases physiological measures of arousal, suggesting the participant is more willing to behave aggressively. Exposure to violent video games also makes people more willing in a laboratory setting to behave aggressively, by blasting an air horn at someone playing as an opponent in the game (Carnagey & Anderson, 2005). Of course, blasting someone with an air horn is not the same thing as punching someone on the street, but the consistency with which exposure to violent video games affects substitute measures of aggression is impressive (Anderson & Bushman, 2001; Bushman et al., 2014).

There are even hints of the mechanism at work. Exposure to violent video games also desensitizes people to depictions of violence (Carnagey et al., 2007) and makes them less likely to empathize with portrayed victims of violence (Bartholow et al., 2006).

Continued

Skeptic at Large *Continued*

BOX 15.2

Having said that, we still have the question of whether fictional depictions of violence actually trigger violence in the real world. We know that most of the millions of people who play violent video games never become violent, so the question is whether there are a few people who, upon exposure to violent images, are more likely to be violent themselves. If only a few such people react this way, then it is difficult to study their reaction to violent video games in the laboratory, because we have no way, at present, to identify those few people.

However, there have been several incidents where people have played violent video games and then gone on to commit violent acts. For example, the young men behind the 1999 massacre at a high school in Columbine, Colorado, were devoted players of the violent video games *Doom* and *Quake* (Merritt & Brown, 2002). In a few cases, individuals have even carried out in real life the violence they'd done on screen. A 17-year-old British boy in 2004 was playing a game that awarded extra points for sneaking up behind a victim and bashing him in the head with a claw hammer. He then went to a friend's house and did exactly that to a 14-year-old boy.

These examples argue strongly that some people are very susceptible to video violence and that we need to find ways to identify such individuals before tragedy strikes. If now or in the future you have children, how will you feel about their playing video games with violent themes?

difference, it is clearly a cultural influence because the basic gene pool in the two countries is the same (both gene pools originated primarily from European settlers), and the patterns of immigration are basically the same. So we see that two groups of people carrying the same basic sets of genes can be either more violent or less, depending on their environment and culture.

What about sexual assault? While there has been some debate as to whether rape is a sexual act, there's never been disagreement that rape is an aggressive act. Some of the earliest recorded history includes descriptions of rape, although it is not always clear whether these early authors, who were men, entirely disapproved of rape (Deacy & Pierce, 1997).

Given the apparent relationship between video depictions of violence and aggression, it's natural to wonder whether film and TV depictions of sexual behavior lead to a greater incidence of sexual crimes such as rape. Indeed, in laboratory studies, exposing men to pornography may make them more likely to report negative attitudes about women. But interestingly, despite the intuitive expectation and the results of those laboratory studies, and despite the many people who oppose pornography on moral grounds, there is little or no evidence that increased access to pornography actually leads to more sexual crime (Diamond & Uchiyama, 1999). In fact, the evidence suggests the opposite: that as pornography becomes more widely available in a country, the incidence of sexual crimes actually *decreases* (Diamond, 2009). It may simply be that as pornography becomes available, some men who might have committed sexual crimes instead masturbate, without hurting anyone. These data suggest that sexual aggression may be fundamentally different from nonsexual aggression and that measures to control the one type may not be effective for the other.

How can punishment reflect the crime and serve society?

As a nation, Americans like to blame people and punish people. No civilization in history has ever imprisoned such a high proportion of its citizens as the United States today (**Figure 15.24**). If we correct for inflation, the United States has spent less on schools and more on prisons, year after year, for several decades (Liptak, 2008). The U.S. incarceration rate suggests a belief that a person's be-

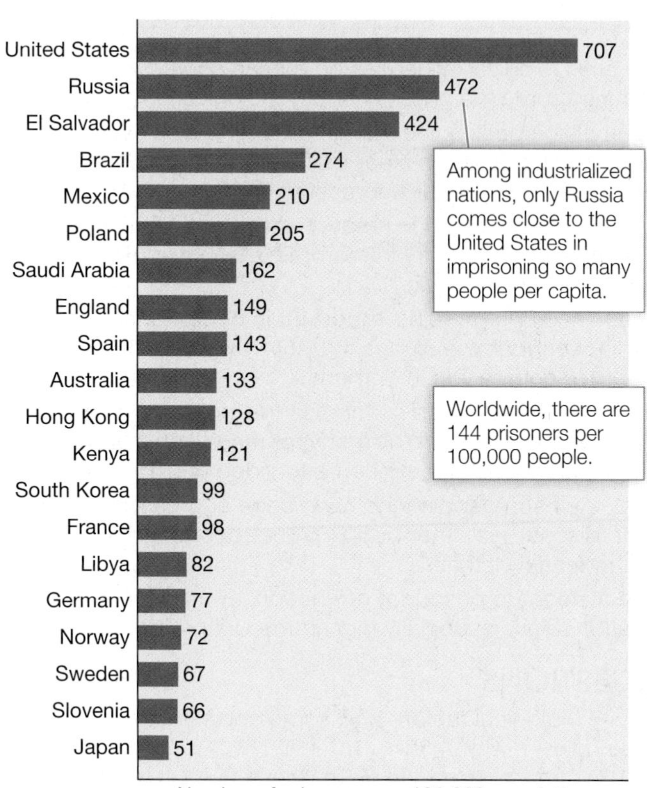

Figure 15.24 Proportions of Citizens in Prison The United States leads the world with the highest proportion of citizens imprisoned. (After Walmsley, 2012.)

havior is due to his or her disposition, rather than the situation he or she is in. Is this a countrywide example of fundamental attribution error? Indeed, that argument is going on in American politics all the time.

Both sides agree that punishment can persuade people not to display certain behaviors, such as stealing and killing. This function of punishment is **deterrence**, making the consequences of committing a crime so severe that people avoid committing the crime. The notion that punishment can deter crime makes no assumptions about whether people commit crimes because of their disposition. If anything, deterrence tries to provide an environment that discourages anyone, whatever his or her disposition, from doing the wrong thing.

Another function of putting people in jail, or even putting them to death, is **protection**, constraining the freedom of someone who is likely to hurt others. Note that this motive for punishment requires making a judgment about a person's *disposition*: Is this a person who will commit a crime no matter what's going on around him or her? In answering this question, judges and juries may make the fundamental attribution error, overemphasizing the person's disposition, and underestimating the importance of the context that led him to transgress.

The desires to deter future crime and to protect other people are both important, rational reasons to punish crime. But a third reason for punishment is **retribution**, the punishment of a person because he has been bad, giving him what he deserves. Social psychologists try to tease apart these three motives for punishment by asking people how long a prison term they would give hypothetical criminals and manipulating various "facts" about the crimes they committed. Such studies suggest that most people in the United States assign punishments primarily for purposes of retribution, not for deterrence or protection (Carlsmith, 2006).

deterrence The use of punishment to persuade people not to display certain behaviors.

protection The use of punishment to constrain a person's freedom so that he or she cannot hurt others.

retribution The punishment of a person beyond the need for deterrence or protection.

15.4 SUMMARY

- There are several biological influences on human *aggression*, behavior intended to cause someone physical or psychological pain or harm.
- In most mammalian species, including humans, males are more aggressive than females, and it is clear that *androgens* such as *testosterone* contribute to the greater aggression in males.
- *Reactive/impulsive aggression* in response to provocation has been associated with reduced activity in the brain's frontal lobes, which tend to inhibit impulsive behaviors.
- Several genes encoding proteins important in neurotransmitter signaling, including *monoamine oxidase* (*MAO*), have been implicated in reactive/impulsive aggression in humans.
- Widespread differences across cultures in the incidence of aggression make it clear that there are also environmental and cultural influences on aggression, such as exposure to video and TV violence.
- Societies may imprison people who have been aggressive, either as *deterrence*, to discourage other people from becoming violent, or as *protection* of potential victims.
- Many people are sent to prison for *retribution*, and this may be why the incarceration rate is especially high in the United States.

REVIEW QUESTIONS

1. What are some biological factors and some social factors that promote aggression?
2. What are the two types of aggression? Which one is better studied and why?
3. Should society punish people for aggressive behavior? If so, what factors can be considered in trying to make sure the punishment fits the crime?

Food for Thought

It seems likely that in the future we will identify more genes that predispose people to aggression or crime. Should people who have no control over the genes they inherited be punished less severely than people committing the same crime with different genes? Or should people carrying these genes get longer imprisonment to protect other people from future assault?

15.5 Persuasion and Authority

Things to Learn

- Milgram's famous study of authority
- Factors that make people more or less obedient
- Modern attempts to replicate findings on obedience

How can one person affect the behavior of another? That question is the topic of this final section of the chapter. In many cases, we persuade people to do something by appealing to their reason, listing off the advantages of doing as we suggest, or explaining why the disadvantages are minimal. But there are certain circumstances where one person has so much influence that he or she persuades people to do things that are not rational, such as hurting themselves or others. In these cases, there is a special aspect to the social interaction going on: either the circumstances are special, or the persuasive person is special, or both.

Sometimes the effects of persuasion can have serious consequences. For example, "experiments" in persuasion take place in courtrooms across the United States every weekday. A group of 6 to 12 people enters a room and has to strive to come to a unanimous decision, sometimes a decision that is a matter of life or death. These groups are juries. Although jurors may talk to each other during breaks in a trial, the judge instructs them not to talk about the case until all the evidence and testimony have been presented. That means that when the presentations are over and the jury shuffles into the room to make a decision, they begin talking to each other about the case for the first time.

Studies of laboratory simulations of juries (Nunez et al., 2011), and surveys of real jurors after they've deliberated (Neck & Moorhead, 1992), make it clear that groupthink is often at work in juries. And as in studies of groupthink, a single, strongly persuasive person may influence the outcome. The person will be especially effective at swaying other jurors if he or she is perceived as an authority. This undue influence of one person brings us to the most influential studies in social psychology—the influence of authority.

Stanley Milgram demonstrated the power of authority

authority The power or right to make decisions.

In a specific instance of social roles we discussed earlier, most societies grant some people **authority**, the power or right to make decisions, give orders. Stanley Milgram (1963, 1974) investigated the influence of authority in some of the most famous experiments in social psychology in 1961–1962 at Yale University. The results of these experiments on obedience surprised and alarmed most people. Every day we have to decide whether to obey various rules and conventions that we've been taught, and in general, a peaceful and productive society requires that most people obey most of the rules most of the time. But there have been many times when people have obeyed other people to cause great harm.

Intrigued by the many "good Germans" who quietly allowed millions of fellow citizens to be sent to the death camps during World War II, Milgram wanted to probe just how far an ordinary person would go to obey an authority figure. He recruited people from the surrounding community of New Haven, Connecticut, and brought them into the lab where an experimenter in a white lab coat explained what would happen. A pair of participants drew lots to decide which would be the "teacher." Then the experimenter went with them to the room next door to strap the other participant, designated the "learner," into a chair and attach wires to her or his wrist (**Figure 15.25**).

The teacher was brought to an adjacent room where she or he read one word ("slow") and then four more words ("walk," "truck," "dance," "music"). The learner was to report which of the four words was correct. If the learner got it wrong, the teacher was to flip switches on a big machine to deliver an electrical shock as punishment to the learner. The machine was very impressive (by 1960s standards), labeled "SHOCK GENERATOR, TYPE ZLB. DYSON INSTRUMENT COMPANY, WALTHAM, MASS." It had 30 switches, each labeled from 15 volts up to 450 volts, with the last two marked "XXX." The low end was also labeled "mild shock," and the high end was labeled "Danger: Severe Shock." Each time the learner made a mistake, the teacher was to increase the shock by another 15 volts. As you may have guessed, the learners seemed to make a lot of mistakes in this task, but that was because they were *confederates* who were deliberately making mistakes and were not really getting shocked at all (the drawing of lots to decide which person would be the "teacher" was rigged).

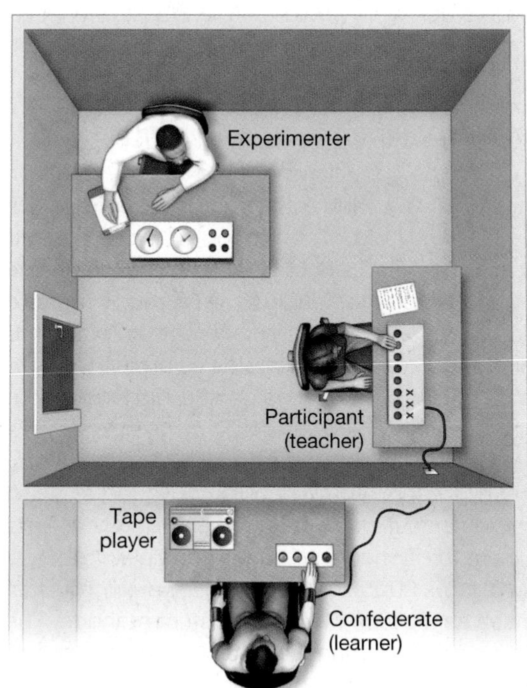

Figure 15.25 Teach Him a Lesson The participant was instructed to be a "teacher" administering electrical shock to a "learner" next door, who was actually a confederate, an actor. When the participant supposedly administered shocks, a tape player produced groans and screams from next door. Participants were more likely to administer high shocks if the experimenter was nearby.

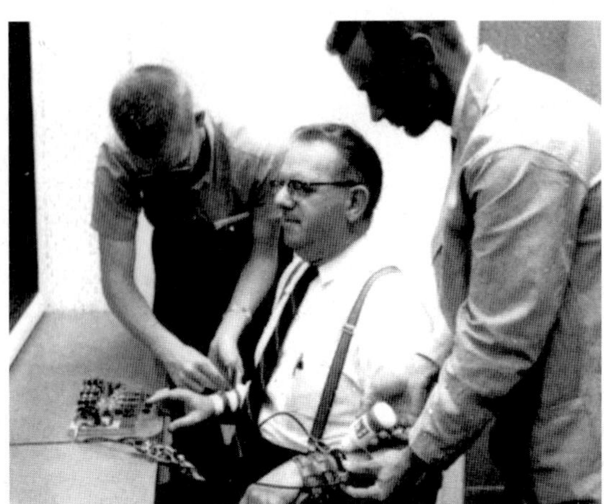

Getting Ready A confederate pretending to be a "learner" about to be shocked is strapped in by the participant and the experimenter.

The learners were actors, and when they received the "shocks," they triggered a tape recorder with prerecorded vocalizations, grunting at 45 volts, complaining at 120 volts. At 150 volts the learner loudly demanded to be released. As the punishment increased, the learner protested louder and louder, banging on the wall, eventually giving an "agonized scream" at 285 volts and soon stopped making any sound whatever, as if he had passed out from the pain. Whenever the teacher expressed concern about the other person, the experimenter, sitting at a desk behind the teacher, quietly instructed her or him to continue: "Please continue," "The experiment requires that you continue," "It is absolutely essential that you continue," or "You have no other choice, you *must* go on."

What would you do if you were the teacher? It's easy to think that we would stop once the learner began complaining, and a few participants did refuse to continue much past that point. But nearly two-thirds of participants from all walks of life—professionals, industrial workers, people who were unemployed—went all the way to 450 volts. The first experiments were done with undergraduate students as participants, presumably people much like you, and over 60% of them obeyed all the way to the maximum voltage.

Because this experiment is famous today, it's hard to evaluate how surprising these results were in 1963. Milgram had described the experiments to many social scientists beforehand, and all predicted that very few teachers would obey to the end, maybe 5%. The scientists felt that only a tiny fraction of humans could intentionally inflict harm on another person without a better reason than "following orders" or the token payment offered in the experiments. Remember that the experimenter offered no threats or additional incentives, or applied any other pressure on the teachers except his presence and his quiet, calm insistence that the experiment continue.

Did the teachers believe the experiment was real? Clearly, they did. At the start of the experiment, each was given a genuine mild electrical shock of 45 volts, supposedly to test that the machine was working. Every time a switch was flipped, a loud electrical buzzing sound was produced. What's more, most of the teachers were visibly upset and kept looking to the experimenter to discontinue. Sometimes the teacher would ask who would take responsibility for the consequences. "I will be responsible," said the experimenter, and usually the teacher administered the next shock.

Later variations of Milgram's experiment had surprising results

Stanley Milgram systematically varied the conditions of the experiment to learn more about what was going on. In this way, Milgram learned several important principles about this dangerous tendency of ordinary people to obey sadistic orders. For example, when Milgram repeated the study with the experimenter in another room, communicating by telephone, teachers were much more reluctant to continue. This showed Milgram that the *physical presence* of the "authority" figure increases his power of persuasion. This helps us understand that when Jim Jones of the People's Temple talked all those people into killing themselves, he was physically present, probably doing what he'd always done: walking among them, looking them in the eye, touching their hands and shoulders.

But notice that in Milgram's experiments, some people continued to shock the learner even when the experimenter was present only over the phone. Since 1995, several cruel pranksters have confirmed that some people will obey an authority figure over the phone (Wolfson, 2005). One prankster would call a fast-food restaurant and identify himself as a police officer or "district manager," using a calm, deliberative manner, and tell the manager that one employee was known to have stolen something or to be dealing illegal drugs. The manager was instructed to take the employee, almost always a woman, into a room and to remove each piece of clothing, one at a time, so the manager could search for the missing jewelry or illegal drugs or whatever. In some cases the naked victim was made to jump up and down "to see if anything fell out." Here the authority figure had two obedient victims: the manager and the employee, both of whom were traumatized by the hoax.

Remember that in Milgram's study the experimenter was a total stranger to the teachers, deriving his authority solely from his white lab coat, his behavior, and the setting: prestigious Yale University, where surely only important and ethical research went on. Milgram later repeated the experiment, this time having the participants meet at a rundown building in a busy part of town with no indications of an institutional affiliation. In this setting, the teachers were more reluctant to escalate the shocks and slightly fewer than half went all the way to 450 volts. Milgram concluded that one source of authority is affiliation with institutions such as universities, governments, armed forces, and businesses that the teachers respect. Similarly, the affiliation with an admired institution, the U.S. military, may have led officers and soldiers at Abu Ghraib prison to go too far.

In another version of the experiment, Milgram had two authority figures sit at the "command" desk, and the results were the same as with one experimenter *unless* one of them voiced doubts about continuing. Once teachers heard the disagreement, very few went on to give more shocks. Care was taken to make sure that the two experimenters would be perceived as having equal authority, but presumably if it had been a "lesser" authority who objected, the teachers might have gone on longer. Jim Jones had long insisted that he was the greatest human authority in his group, deriving this authority directly from God, so there was no chance of an "equal" authority disagreeing with him that last day.

In yet another Milgram variation, there were three teachers, but two were really actors. If the two actor-teachers refused to give another shock, very few participants, about 10%, could be induced to go any further. At that bitter end in Jonestown, one woman questioned whether they should obey Jones, killing their children and themselves. On tape recordings you can hear her voice, struggling to remain calm and persuasive, pleading for restraint. But most of the crowd was eager to obey Jim Jones's command. If only the woman had persisted in disobedience and others had joined her, then perhaps none of us would have ever heard of Jonestown. Instead, the majority ruled, and following the rules of groupthink, this woman and the others accepted their demise.

In Milgram's experiments, you might think that women, especially women in a 1960s America that emphasized traditional sex roles, would be more likely to take pity on the learner and stop. But Milgram found that men and women were equally obedient in administering shocks, a finding that has held up in several studies since (Blass, 2004). There was a sex difference, in that afterward the women were more *distressed* than the men. Despite the greater internal conflict, the women were as likely to go on.

Perhaps the most chilling variation of the experiment was when Milgram did not have the teachers actually flip the switch. Rather, they simply read the words while *someone else* dealt out the punishment. As Milgram pointed out, this situation seems much more analogous to everyday life, where our actions, or inactions, seem more remote from the outcome. Participants in this setting were, if anything, even *more* likely to go all the way to 450 volts. Predictably, the teachers in this version of Milgram's experiment excused themselves for their participation—they believed the person flipping the switch bore all the responsibility. Likewise, the many German citizens who ran the trains, kept utilities working, went to work in the factories supplying the war, surely felt they bore no responsibility for what happened in the death camps. Yet all their actions contributed to the slaughter.

At Jonestown, it is likely that those people who killed their children before committing suicide were as moral and sensitive as you are. We would be making the fundamental attribution error if we concluded that "they" were different from us. Rather than attribute their behavior to their disposition, as if their disposition were different from ours, we could attribute their behavior to the situation they were in. Milgram's research suggests that, in that same situation, most of us would have done the same thing.

The Cutting Edge

Aftermath of Milgram's Study

Today it seems unlikely that any research institution would allow a psychologist to repeat these experiments. Many of the participants were genuinely upset at the events that transpired, and it would be very difficult, maybe impossible, to predict beforehand how traumatic it might be for a given participant. One man, Milgram said, was "reduced to a twitching, stuttering wreck…approaching nervous collapse." There have been several attempts to re-create these studies without inflicting such harm (Dickinson et al., 2002). For example, one study repeated Milgram's procedure except they only let participants get as far as administering 150 volts before ending the study, and they replicated Milgram's results to that point (Burger, 2009).

In 2006, scientists repeated the entire Milgram experiments in a virtual environment (Slater et al., 2006), with the learner depicted on screen by a computer (**Figure 15.26**). The learner was always a woman, and it was made clear to the teachers that she was not real and that no one was getting shocked. There were two conditions: in one the virtual learner could be

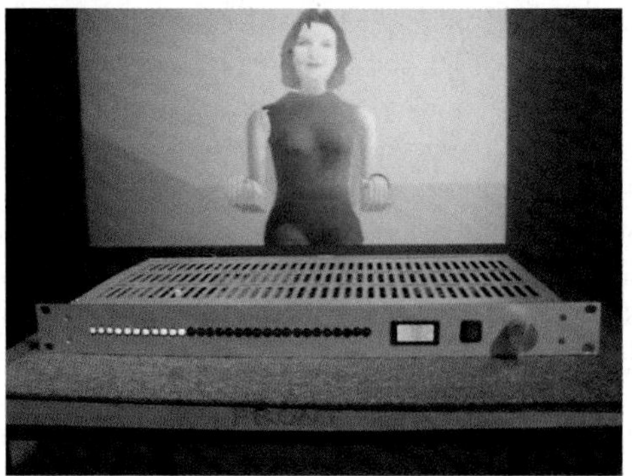

Figure 15.26 A Virtual Reprise of the Milgram Obedience Experiments
If the participant knows she is shocking an avatar rather than a real person in the Milgram experiment, will the results provide valid information about humans and authority?

seen and heard on screen, while in the other the learner's responses were communicated only through text on screen.

Although assured the shocks were not real, participants were slightly less likely to administer shocks when they could see and hear the learner rather than just read her responses. Most important, despite the virtual nature of the experiment, the teachers all reported experiencing stress. Their self-reports were confirmed by measuring heart rate, respiration rate, and how readily mild electrical current could pass through their skin (during stress, electricity passes more readily through skin, in part because more sweat is present). All teachers had higher than normal measures. What's more, these measures of stress were even higher in teachers who could see and hear the learner than in those who just read her responses. Note that what the participants physically did is the same in those two conditions, so it must have been hearing and seeing the learner that caused greater stress. Slater and colleagues suggest that this virtual version of Milgram's experiment might offer an ethically acceptable way to identify more of the factors that cause people to obey authority.

15.5 SUMMARY

- An important aspect of social roles is the position of *authority* granted to certain people.
- Stanley Milgram conducted experiments that showed that most people, in response to instructions from an authority figure, specifically a researcher in a white lab coat, would willingly administer painful shocks to another person.
- The physical presence of the authority figure increased the chances that participants would administer shocks, while any public disagreement among authority figures made it less likely that the participant would obey.
- Despite following the orders, many of the participants were distressed by their involvement in the experiments.

REVIEW QUESTIONS

1. Describe the basic experiment on authority and obedience that Stanley Milgram conducted.
2. What variations in the basic experiment were tried, and what did those outcomes indicate?

Food for Thought

In 1997, 39 members of the Heaven's Gate cult committed suicide in San Diego, believing that an approaching comet was bringing aliens who would pick up their liberated souls and reconstitute the cult members onboard a UFO. What, if any, responsibility does society have to "protect" people from ideas that seem absurd to the majority? Would that exercise of authority be any better or worse than Jones's use of his authority at Jonestown that fateful day?

Social Psychology

The People's Temple

The Reverend Jim Jones had delivered thousands of people from "the devil's clutches" and gave them the discipline to put their lives in order. But there were also rumors of a dark side to his People's Temple. When government officials investigated complaints of violence and coercion, Jones and most of his followers left the United States and started a communal farm called Jonestown in Guyana, South America.

In 1978, in response to continued complaints from former temple members and their families, California congressman Leo Ryan took an investigative team to Guyana. Many members told him, in secret, that they wanted to leave but were afraid to say so because they would be punished. Eventually about 15 members asked to fly back to the United States with Ryan. At the airstrip, a group from Jonestown shot and killed Ryan and four others, severely wounding another dozen. Among those killed was an NBC cameraman who videotaped the shootings until he was murdered, providing footage that would shock that they should all commit "revolutionary suicide." He persuaded them to drink fruit-flavored punch with cyanide and sedatives. Almost all the members obeyed, parents giving the punch to their children and babies before taking it themselves. Jones himself died of a gunshot wound to the head, possibly self-inflicted, surrounded by the bodies of his dead and dying flock. You can learn more about this tragedy, including links to the chilling "death tape" of Jones persuading his flock to kill their wailing babies and themselves, at http://jonestown.sdsu.edu/.

When I read of the events that took place in Guyana that day, I imagine myself there and wonder what I would have done. Would I have seen past Jim Jones's doomsday rhetoric and refused to drink the poison? I might have been shot for the trouble, as several people apparently were, but surely it would have been better to hold out and give myself some chance to survive. But when I think harder, I realize that is a childish fantasy. I have to assume that I

Think Like a Psychologist:

Principles in Action

Whenever we encounter any interesting behavior we should consider the four principles. Here are some ways that the four principles relate to our opening story about the Jonestown massacre.

MACHINE

The mind is a product of a physical machine, the brain.

Jim Jones had been abusing several drugs, including amphetamines to work late into the night and barbiturates to help him sleep. Habitual amphetamine use can lead to psychosis (see Chapter 7), including paranoid delusions, which may have played a role in Jones's reaction to Congressman Ryan's visit, and the decision to commit "revolutionary suicide."

UNCONSCIOUS

We are consciously aware of only a small part of our mental activity.

Jonestown had held several "dry runs" of a mass suicide, having members line up to drink a punch that Jones declared to be lethal when it was in fact harmless. Thus despite Jones's dark mood and fatalistic ramblings, some members may have unconsciously believed there was no poison in the punch.

SOCIAL

We constantly modify our behavior, beliefs, and attitudes according to what we perceive about the people around us.

Deindividuation surely played a part in so many of the people at Jonestown willingly drinking poison. Just as the visible presence of an experimenter led people in Milgram's study to inflict dangerous shocks, Jones's presence and monologue that day probably made the people more obedient.

EXPERIENCE

Our experiences physically alter the structure and function of the brain.

Most of the adults present at Jonestown had come from troubled backgrounds. Many others fled to Jonestown seeking a greater racial equality than in the United States. These experiences may have convinced them that there was nowhere to go if Jonestown ended, and that may have persuaded them to accept death.

KEY TERMS

actor-observer bias, 647
aggression, 677
altruism, 670
androgens, 677
attributions, 645
attribution theory, 645
authority, 685
buyer's remorse, 653
bystander effect, 666
chameleon effect, 662
cognitive dissonance, 651
collectivism, 648
controlled/instrumental aggression, 679
deindividuation, 667
deterrence, 683
diffusion of responsibility, 666
discrimination, 654
disposition, 645
door-in-the-face technique, 665
effort justification, 653
evolutionary psychologists, 644
facial symmetry, 644
foot-in-the-door technique, 664
fundamental attribution error, 646
groupthink, 667
Implicit Association Test (IAT), 656
impression management, 645
inclusive fitness, 670
individualism, 648
loss averse, 671
monoamine oxidase (MAO), 680
neuroeconomics, 671
normative social influence, 661
prisoner's dilemma, 668
protection, 683
reactive/impulsive aggression, 679
retribution, 683
self-handicapping, 654
self-serving bias, 647
situation, 645
social attitudes, 649
social exchange theory, 671
social facilitation, 663
social loafing, 666
social norms, 661
social perception, 643
social prejudice, 654
social psychology, 642
social roles, 649
stereotype threat, 658
testosterone, 677
triangular theory of love, 674

QUIZ YOURSELF

1. A baby-face has prominent cheeks and eyes and a young-looking mouth. When a political candidate has these features, voters who know nothing else about him judge him to be
   a. less competent.
   b. more energetic.
   c. more likely to do a good job.
   d. less attractive.
2. Even when subjects know beforehand that a speaker has been randomly assigned to a viewpoint, subjects still believe that the speech represents the speaker's own viewpoint and not the assignment. This is an example of ________.
3. Cultures differ in their emphasis on individuals as distinctive and unique. The tendency to put your own goals and wishes ahead of those of the group is ________. The tendency to put the goals of the group ahead of your own goals is ________.
4. Putting a person at a disadvantage or treating a person unfairly solely because he or she is a member of a group is ________.
5. One question related to the Implicit Association Test is whether the IAT is actually a measure of prejudice. This is a question of
   a. statistical significance.
   b. test validity.
   c. replicability.
   d. test reliability.
6. ________ is experienced when exposure to a derogatory, oversimplified idea of a group causes members of that group to perform worse.
7. Hannah, who was usually a shy, quiet person, was helping out at her club's food booth on campus. All the club members were wearing their club shirts and working to make sales. She joined in with calling out to strangers to encourage their participation. This loss of her own identity and becoming part of her group is known as
   a. the prisoner's dilemma.
   b. groupthink.
   c. deindividuation.
   d. altruism.
8. ________ is the investigation of the neural basis of decision making, specifically in consumers.
9. Evolutionary psychologists have suggested that friendships were highly adaptive among early humans, in part because they may be critical in difficult times. Helping someone who isn't related to you, and perhaps receiving help in return at a future time, is
   a. natural selection.
   b. the non-aggression principle.
   c. the chameleon effect.
   d. reciprocal altruism.
10. Compared with other people, those with a history of reactive aggression react to pictures of angry faces with more activation of the
    a. amygdala.
    b. hippocampus.
    c. occipital cortex.
    d. pineal gland.

1. a; 2. fundamental attribution error; 3. individualism, collectivism; 4. discrimination; 5. b; 6. Stereotype threat; 7. c; 8. Neuroeconomics; 9. d; 10. a

Clinical Psychology

"My Lobotomy"

Howard Dully's mother died when he was 4, and a few years later his father married a woman named Lucille. Howard and Lucille did not get along. Howard was rebellious in the way that many kids are—sassing back, breaking curfew, skipping out on church. But Howard was never violent with his stepmother or anyone else. He sometimes got in trouble at school, for not paying attention in class or smoking in the bathroom, but not for fighting or damaging school property. Howard's grades were erratic—an A on a test one day, an F on a test the next—but he was not flunking out.

Still, Lucille, frustrated with a headstrong boy in her house, took Howard to six different psychiatrists to find out "what was wrong with him." All concluded that his behavior was normal. But doctor number seven, the famous Walter Freeman, diagnosed the boy as schizophrenic. In 1960, Freeman gave 12-year-old Howard a lobotomy. First Freeman sedated the boy by giving him electroshocks—jolts of electricity across the skull that induce a seizure and render the patient unconscious. Then he lifted the boy's upper eyelids and used a hammer on an ice pick–like device to punch holes in the skull above each eye. He then inserted a device to cut off some of Howard's prefrontal cortex from the rest of his brain. Freeman was an old hand at the procedure, having lobotomized thousands of people, so the procedure took only 10 minutes. The total hospital charge was $200.

Family members said Howard acted like a zombie for several days, and then he was so lethargic and disinterested in the events around him that, according to Freeman's notes, they called Howard "lazy, stupid, dummy, and so on." One aunt said he acted like he was permanently tranquilized. And yet Lucille *still* wanted Howard out of her house. Soon Howard was institutionalized, and he would spend decades in various mental hospitals. Not until he was 50 was Howard able to find out what had happened to him as a child, a journey he recounts movingly in his memoir, *My Lobotomy*.

Chapter Preview

Deciding whether someone's behavior is normal or abnormal, and whether he needs treatment, is not easily done. Several famous cases, like that of Howard Dully, forced psychology to abandon the notion that unusual behavior is, by itself, a problem. Instead modern practitioners ask whether the person's behavior is interfering with his life or the lives of others. In this chapter we'll first consider the most common psychological problems, the mood disorders such as anxiety disorders and depression. We'll see that while there are drugs that can sometimes alleviate the symptoms of these disorders, counseling can be equally or even more helpful. The next section will discuss the more controversial topic of personality disorders, which are difficult to treat and which some people do not consider true disorders at all. Finally, we'll discuss schizophrenia, the diagnosis that was inappropriately applied to young Howard Dully. As we discussed in Chapter 4, it is the combination of particular genes and environmental stress that leads to this debilitating condition. In this chapter we'll learn also that, while far from perfect, antischizophrenia drugs have revolutionized psychiatry, relieving symptoms enough to allow some patients to return to society.

16.1 Modern Classification of Psychological Disorders

Things to Learn

- Modern history of diagnosing mental disorders
- Issues of reliability and validity in diagnosing disorders
- Distinction between whether behavior interferes with everyday life or is merely unusual
- Mental disorders are best understood as part of a continuum

In the distant past, a person who behaved strangely might be considered to suffer not from a disease but from possession by an evil spirit. Rather than being taken to a physician, the person might be taken to a religious leader, such as a priest or shaman, to drive out the evil spirit. In that atmosphere, the person might be blamed for his affliction, accused of not following religious practice properly to avoid possession, or of having sinned. Even in the early twentieth century, one severe mental disorder was said to result from "weak character," as we'll see in the section on schizophrenia. Today, some people still have the attitude that depression is simply a failure of willpower, and so they might avoid seeking help or discourage other people from seeking help.

It is undeniable that mental disorders take a toll on the lives of many people, as **Figure 16.1** makes clear. Modern health care practitioners don't blame people for having mental disorders—they are not regarded as a "choice" people have made, but as a problem that has beset them. That means it's appropriate to find some therapy to either change the behavior or help the patient find a way to have a happy life despite that behavior. Most modern therapists believe—unlike those in times past—that it isn't necessarily a problem if someone behaves in a strange manner. Unusual behavior warrants treatment if and only if the behavior interferes with the patient's pursuit of a happy, productive life or if it interferes with other people's lives. How did this new attitude about mental disorders come about?

Twentieth-century psychiatrists seeking standardization created the DSM

As Howard Dully's experience shows, different people may have different opinions about what is normal or abnormal. In retrospect, it seems that Howard was just a typical teenage boy—alternately compliant and rebellious, both at home and school. Several psychiatrists concluded that there was no problem that required psychiatric treatment. (At least not treatment for Howard—one psy-

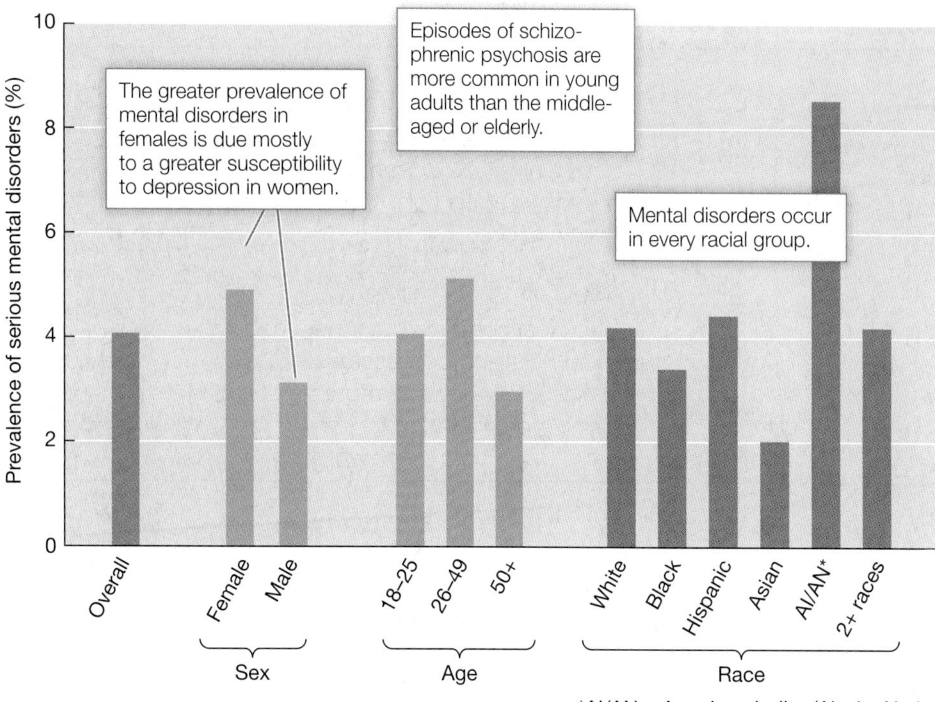
Prevalence is the percentage of people suffering from a disorder at any one point in time.
The greater prevalence of mental disorders in females is due mostly to a greater susceptibility to depression in women.
Episodes of schizophrenic psychosis are more common in young adults than the middle-aged or elderly.
Mental disorders occur in every racial group.
Prevalence of serious mental disorders (%)
10
8
6
4
2
0
Overall
Female
Male
18–25
26–49
50+
White
Black
Hispanic
Asian
AI/AN*
2+ races
Sex
Age
Race
*AI/AN = American Indian/Alaska Native

Figure 16.1 Prevalence of Serious Mental Disorders among U.S. Adults in 2012 (After National Institute of Mental Health, 2012.)

chiatrist thought his stepmother needed counseling about how to communicate with the boy.) Yet the seventh psychiatrist concluded not only that Howard suffered from a severe mental disorder, schizophrenia, but that he needed a drastic treatment—lobotomy.

How could different doctors come to such different conclusions? In the mid-twentieth century, different clinicians often gave very different diagnoses for the same patient. Plus, different doctors sometimes used different terms to refer to the same set of symptoms. These problems of subjective diagnosis and varying terminology became obvious during World War II as the U.S. Armed Forces had to deal with millions of soldiers, some of whom were, or became, behaviorally disturbed. To address this problem, the U.S. Army put together a manual that listed the various categories of mental disorders and the symptoms that accompany each one. Among other things, this manual was important for determining whether soldiers displaying behavioral problems could be treated (so they could be sent back to the front) or needed to be sent home. The idea was to provide **standardization**, establishing a common set of terms and definitions, to help different doctors reach the same diagnosis when examining a particular patient.

When the war ended, the psychiatrists discharged from the Army brought this new classification into civilian hospitals. The American Psychiatric Association revised the Army's manual (Grob, 1991) to publish the *Diagnostic and Statistical Manual of Mental Disorders*, soon known as *DSM-I*, in 1952. In the years since, it has been revised several times (*DSM-II*, *DSM-III*, *DSM-IV*), with the latest version, published in 2013, known as *DSM-5*. (Yes, a committee decided that this version should be referred to with the Arabic numeral 5 rather than the Roman numeral V.) Although revisions to the *DSM* are supervised under the leadership of an association of *psychiatrists*, clinical psychologists also participate in revision of the *DSM* and follow its guidelines. **Table 16.1** compares differences between psychiatrists, clinical psychologists, and research psychologists.

For the last several editions, the method the *DSM* offers for reaching a diagnosis has been the same. For each disorder, a menu of behavioral, cogni-

standardization Establishment of a common set of terms and definitions, to help different doctors reach the same diagnosis for a particular patient.

TABLE 16.1 Different Degrees, Different Roles

	Psychiatrist	Clinical psychologist	Research psychologist
Postgraduate education	Medical degree (MD or DO) and training in providing psychotherapy	Advanced degree in psychology, typically a PhD, and training in providing psychotherapy	Advanced degree in psychology, typically a PhD
Activities	Full medical examination, psychological testing and assessment, following *DSM* guidelines	Psychological testing and assessment, following *DSM* guidelines	Research and experimentation in particular subfields, such as developmental, personality, social, biological, or cognitive psychology
Treatments offered	May prescribe medication, such as antidepressants or antipsychotics; may also offer cognitive behavioral therapy or manage medication in conjunction with a psychologist	Psychotherapy, including cognitive behavioral therapy; in most jurisdictions, psychologists cannot prescribe medication because they do not have a medical degree	Typically does not provide psychotherapy; note that some psychiatrists and clinical psychologists also conduct research (your professor might be a research psychologist)

tive, and bodily symptoms is listed. Some of the behaviors on the list are those that many people might display, at least occasionally, so usually having just one of those symptoms is not enough to qualify someone for the diagnosis. Rather, it is only when a person displays a certain number of those symptoms that she is considered to have reached threshold to qualify for a diagnosis. For example, for **substance use disorder**, there are 11 different criteria (Hasin et al., 2013), listed in **Table 16.2**. If you look at the list, you can see that almost everyone displays some of those behaviors some of the time. Just because you show one of those behaviors doesn't mean you have a disorder. A client may be diagnosed with mild, moderate, or severe substance use disorder, depending on how many of these criteria are met. By the way, it is not uncommon for someone with a mental disorder to also have problems with drugs. Attempts to self-medicate, with cigarettes, alcohol, or illegal drugs, may lead to substance use disorder in addition to the underlying problem of depression, schizophrenia, or anxiety. Or alternatively, abuse of drugs may lead to symptoms of mental disorders, for example, amphetamine psychosis.

substance use disorder The official term for addiction, defined by meeting several criteria.

TABLE 16.2 Criteria for Substance Use Disorder

According to *DSM-5*, a client who meets two or three of the following criteria has a mild substance use disorder, one who meets four or five has a moderate substance use disorder, and a client meeting six or more has a severe substance use disorder.

1. Taking the substance in larger amounts or for longer than you meant to
2. Wanting to cut down or stop using the substance but not managing to
3. Spending a lot of time getting, using, or recovering from use of the substance
4. Cravings and urges to use the substance
5. Not managing to do what you should at work, home, or school, because of substance use
6. Continuing to use, even when it causes problems in relationships
7. Giving up important social, occupational, or recreational activities because of substance use
8. Using the substance again and again, even when it puts you in danger
9. Continuing to use, even when you know you have a physical or psychological problem that could have been caused or made worse by the substance
10. Needing more of the substance to get the effect you want (tolerance)
11. Development of withdrawal symptoms, which can be relieved by taking more of the substance

Source: American Psychiatric Association, 2013.

As we've discussed in previous chapters (see Chapters 11 and 14), the two major issues in evaluating any psychological classification system are *reliability* and *validity*. We have to deal with those same concerns about the process of determining whether someone has a mental disorder. By standardizing terminology, the original *DSM* helped improve **reliability**, the extent to which different clinicians reach the same diagnosis for any patient with a particular set of symptoms. Each revision of the *DSM* has attempted to improve the reliability of the manual, and most clinicians believe the revised editions have indeed become more reliable. While no one suggests that *DSM-5* is perfectly reliable, there is little controversy about whether if two different clinicians actually follow the guidelines, they are likely to reach the same diagnosis. The disagreements center on whether that diagnosis of a mental disorder is *valid*, as we'll see next.

Suffering a Disorder? *DSM-5* includes a diagnosis of gambling disorder for people who have persistent problems arising from gambling.

How do we define normal?

The controversies over the *DSM* have centered on **validity**, the extent to which a psychological test or process identifies a characteristic or disorder that really exists. For example, *DSM-5* offers a new diagnosis, *gambling disorder*. Does a person who repeatedly loses more than he can afford at casinos, gets fired for online gambling at work, and loses his home have a mental disorder, or is he simply very (very) irresponsible? Is he "sick" or reckless? Also, *DSM-5* controversially dropped what was called the "bereavement exclusion"—a 2-month "exception" that used to be made so as to not apply a diagnosis of a mental disorder based on behavior that might arise from grief. For example, if a woman's beloved partner dies, we expect her to show many signs of depression. According to *DSM-IV*, she was not said to have a mental disorder unless her depression symptoms persisted for more than 2 months. Following *DSM-5*, however, a clinician can diagnose that woman with depression even if her partner died only the week before. Is grief a mental disorder?

Critics of the *DSM* regard these trends in subsequent editions as turning perfectly normal human behavior into pathology (Frances, 2012). One concern is that turning more and more human conditions into "disorders" encourages physicians to prescribe pharmaceutical treatment, such as antidepressants for a grieving widow rather than letting time heal her psychological wounds. Should the widow suffer for a few months when faster relief may be offered through pharmacology? A second concern is that labeling behavior a "disorder" will free people with troublesome behaviors, such as compulsive gamblers, from taking stock of their actions and changing their behavior. Should the courts offer a more lenient sentence for someone convicted of embezzling funds from his workplace if he has been diagnosed with gambling disorder?

No matter how arguable the validity of some, or even all, of the diagnoses in *DSM-5* are, there is a powerful reason for designating someone as having a disorder—so he or she can receive treatment. Since the original *DSM*, medical care systems in much of the world have changed. Government-supported universal health care systems were set up in Canada and many European nations, and health insurance systems arose in the United States and other countries. Because there are always limits to the resources available to these systems, there is a need for a way to decide when it is appropriate to provide medical coverage to a particular person. For psychological disorders, health care providers have come to depend more and more on the latest edition of the *DSM* to decide whether a person qualifies for treatment. One new diagnosis added to *DSM-5* that makes it easier for people to get treatment is *tobacco use disorder*. Many people want to quit smoking and may need help to do so. Forty years ago, when the majority of American adults smoked, no one would have regarded them all as having a mental disorder. You see how slippery this notion of mental disorder can be.

reliability The extent to which different clinicians would reach the same diagnosis for any patient with a particular set of symptoms.

validity The extent to which a test actually measures the trait it is intended to measure.

Elyn Saks A Professor of Law, Psychology, and Psychiatry Sciences at USC, Elyn has schizophrenia.

Modern classification emphasizes the consequences for everyday life

Partly in reaction to earlier critics concerned about labeling normal behavior as a disorder, in 1994 *DSM-IV* required an additional criterion for about half the diagnoses: **clinical significance**, meaning the behavior causes "clinically significant distress or impairment in social, occupational, or other important areas of functioning." In other words, displaying unusual behavior, no matter how unusual, may not qualify a person as having a mental disorder. If he can still go about his everyday life, taking care of himself, interacting with friends, and performing well at work, then who's to say this person's unusual behavior reflects a disorder rather than a personal quirk?

For example, in *DSM-5* substance use disorder bypasses the issue of whether drugs are legal or illegal. That means no distinction is made whether the client uses legal drugs like alcohol or tobacco (or, in some states, marijuana), illegal drugs like cocaine and heroin, or prescription drugs that are used illegally. If you examine the 11 criteria listed in Table 16.2, you'll see that they center less on what the client *does* and more on what the client *regards as a problem* (the client wants to quit, the client has identified problems caused in a relationship, the client feels a missed social event was important).

Thus no matter how much alcohol a person might drink, if the person is happy drinking and happy with life in general, gets along well with others, holds down a job, and is otherwise healthy, alcoholism would not be considered a disorder by *DSM-5*. If this strikes you as reasonable, does it seem equally reasonable that *DSM-5* applies the same criteria to extensive use of *illegal* drugs, such as heroin? A person repeatedly arrested for drug use would probably begin to suffer from several of the problems listed in Table 16.2, and would then meet the criteria for a diagnosis.

In short, today we regard people as having a mental disorder not based solely on whether their behavior is typical or unusual, "normal" or "abnormal," but on whether their behavior is getting in the way of a productive, happy life. There are people who hear voices that they know are not real but who manage to function in a high-end job such as doctor, lawyer, or chief executive. One is Professor Elyn Saks, who won a "genius grant" from the MacArthur Foundation (Saks, 2013). Having delusions (irrational beliefs) and hallucinations (such as hearing voices that are not real) does not automatically classify someone as having a disorder. Many people report having, at least occasionally, thought they heard someone talking when they could not have. But people who are not able to hold down a job or maintain rewarding personal relationships because they have delusions and hallucinations (which is, sadly, often the case) would be classified as having a disorder. Symptoms of disorders range in intensity, leading to another growing perspective on mental disorders, which we'll discuss next.

Mental disorders may represent extremes on a continuum

Since an important function of *DSM-5* is to guide clinicians in deciding who does and does not qualify for treatment, by necessity it labels some people as having a disorder and other people as not having one. But there is something artificial about the notion that someone either has a disorder or does not. Unusual and maladaptive behaviors, like all behaviors, may be displayed only rarely by one person and often by another. Or the same person may display a troublesome behavior a lot in some situations and rarely in others. In other words, the frequency and severity of symptoms represent a continuum, from low to high, so it makes sense to think of disorders as also ranging from mild to severe. We've already seen how the *DSM* acknowledges this continuum in Table 16.2, where depending on the number of criteria a person shows, she may have no substance use disorder or may have one that is mild, moderate, or severe.

clinical significance An additional criterion for about half the diagnoses in *DSM*, requiring that there be clinically significant distress or impairment in social, occupational, or other important areas of functioning.

For one set of disorders, *DSM-5* made this idea of a continuum even more explicit. As the name indicates, **autism spectrum disorder (ASD)**, which is characterized by deficits in social communication and interaction accompanied by restricted, repetitive behaviors and interests, can be thought of as ranging from mild to severe. In a controversial move, *DSM-5* consolidated under this single diagnosis four separate disorders from *DSM-IV*. One of those was *autistic disorder*, which is what most people think of as autism, when a person uses almost no language and engages in solitary, repetitive behaviors. This condition can be thought of as one extreme of the spectrum in ASD. Now ASD also encompasses what was previously called *Asperger's syndrome*, which describes someone with good language communication skills who may nevertheless have trouble understanding other people's points of view and have restricted, highly specialized interests. We discussed autism and Asperger's syndrome in Section 5.2 when we noted that individuals with these disorders have deficits in discerning what other people think and feel. We may think of Asperger's as being at the mild end of a spectrum of autism disorders, as these individuals may function well enough to finish school, get a job, have a family, and so on. For this reason, the syndrome was sometimes referred to as "high-functioning autism." People with only a few social communication problems or highly specialized interests could be considered far enough on the mild side of the autism spectrum that they would not be diagnosed with ASD or (in previous editions of the *DSM*) Asperger's, but simply be considered "quirky." If we extend the analogy further, we could consider that we all fit on the autism spectrum somewhere.

Thinking in Pictures Professor Temple Grandin, who has autism, reports that she thinks in terms of pictures, not words, and that makes it easier for her to solve some problems.

The shift to considering autism as a spectrum brings us back to a central difficulty of any discussion about mental disorders, which is whether any behavior can be so unusual that it should be considered a sign of mental illness. The short answer is, no. For example, until 1973 the *DSM* considered homosexuality to be a mental disorder. It is true that less than 5% of the population is gay, meaning that this sexual orientation is rather "unusual," but so what? Most gay people function just fine in our society, especially now that public disapproval of homosexuality seems to be waning. In the years since 1973, the attitude that unusual or atypical behavior indicates mental illness has fallen out of favor.

The evolution of our perspective on disorders is one of the reasons that the term *abnormal psychology* has fallen out of use (despite the holdover of college courses using that title). Unless we mean *normal* to mean "what most people do," there's no objective way to decide whether a behavior is "abnormal." Today the focus of clinicians is on whether clients have feelings or behaviors that make them or other people unhappy. If so, then the goal of therapy is to help the clients deal with those behaviors, either reducing them or finding a way around them, to lead a happy, productive life.

autism spectrum disorder (ASD)
A disorder characterized by deficits in social communication and interaction accompanied by restricted, repetitive behaviors and interests, which can range from mild to severe.

16.1 SUMMARY

- The *Diagnostic and Statistical Manual of Mental Disorders* (*DSM*) arose after World War II to provide *standardization* of the definitions of psychiatric terms and mental disorders.
- Each subsequent edition of the *DSM*, including today's *DSM-5*, has increased the *reliability* of diagnosis, but there remains some controversy over the *validity* of various diagnoses.
- Most *DSM-5* diagnoses require the client to display some number of symptoms from a list to be considered to have a given disorder.
- For many diagnoses, the symptoms must be of *clinical significance*, meaning they cause significant distress or impairment in functioning, to be considered a disorder.

- There is growing recognition that mental disorders represent an extreme end of a continuum of behaviors, as in *autism spectrum disorder* (*ASD*).

REVIEW QUESTIONS

1. What was the main motive behind putting together the first *Diagnostic and Statistical Manual of Mental Disorders*?
2. What are the two biggest issues to consider when evaluating any psychological test or measurement, such as the *DSM*?
3. According to modern methods such as those in *DSM-5*, what is an important component of deciding whether someone has a mental disorder?

Food for Thought

If a close friend or relative died suddenly, you would feel terrible. If taking a pill could cause you to instantly feel happy, despite the loss, would you take it? Why or why not?

16.2 Anxiety Disorders, Obsessive-Complusive Disorder, and Depression

Things to Learn

- Different kinds of anxiety disorders
- Nature of obsessive-compulsive disorder (OCD)
- Treatments available for phobias and other anxiety disorders
- Nature and risks of depression
- Relative effectiveness of various treatment options for depression

Anxiety disorders and depression are the most common mental disorders, affecting millions of people every day. We will begin with anxiety disorders, such as phobias and panic attacks, which respond well to psychotherapy that directs clients to unlearn certain expectations and structure their lives to reduce the causes of anxiety. Then we'll consider obsessive-compulsive disorder, which is usually accompanied by marked anxiety and characterized by compulsive and repetitive actions, such as excessive hand washing, and irrational fears. Also in the category of anxiety disorders is posttraumatic stress disorder, which we covered in Chapter 13. We will close the section by discussing depression, which afflicts millions of people and can be deadly.

What are the roots of anxiety disorders?

All of us have at times felt apprehensive and fearful. But some people experience this state with an intensity that is overwhelming. The *DSM* distinguishes several major types of **anxiety disorders**, all of which are accompanied by intense, irrational anxiety that interferes with everyday functioning. Anxiety disorders include *panic disorder*, characterized by recurrent transient attacks of intense fearfulness, as well as *generalized anxiety disorder*, in which persistent, excessive anxiety and worry are experienced for months. *Phobic disorders* are intense, irrational fears that become centered on a specific object, activity, or situation that the person feels compelled to avoid. There is a genetic contribution to each of these disorders (Shih et al., 2004), but none appear to be caused by the simple effect of a single gene at work. Rather, there appear to be many genes involved, each affecting the risk for a disorder.

Panic disorder is characterized by recurrent *panic attacks*, sudden fear with no apparent cause, unusual body sensations such as dizziness, difficulty breathing, trembling, shaking, and a feeling of loss of control. It's estimated that within a given year nearly 2% of people in the United States may suffer from panic disorder, and as many as 5% over a lifetime (Kessler et al., 2005). Anxiety can be lethal: people with panic disorder are more likely than those without it to die from suicide (Coryell et al., 1986). **Generalized anxiety disorder** is characterized by excessive anxiety about otherwise common things or events, which lasts for at least 6 months and interferes with everyday life (Haller et al., 2014).

Treatment for panic disorder and generalized anxiety disorder usually consists of **cognitive behavioral therapy** (**CBT**)—structured, goal-oriented counseling, usually consisting of a limited number of sessions, that is directed more at education about the disorder and skills for managing current symptoms, including new ways to deal with various everyday situations, rather than extensive probing into early experience. CBT for panic disorder often consists of exposing clients to

anxiety disorders Several major types of disorders, all of which are accompanied by intense, irrational anxiety that interferes with everyday functioning.

panic disorder An anxiety disorder characterized by recurrent *panic attacks*, sudden fear with no apparent cause, unusual body sensations such as dizziness, difficulty breathing, trembling, and a feeling of loss of control.

generalized anxiety disorder (GAD) An anxiety disorder characterized by excessive anxiety about otherwise common things or events, which lasts for at least six months and interferes with everyday life.

cognitive behavioral therapy (CBT) Structured, goal-oriented counseling, usually of a limited number of sessions directed at education about the disorder and skills for managing symptoms in everyday life.

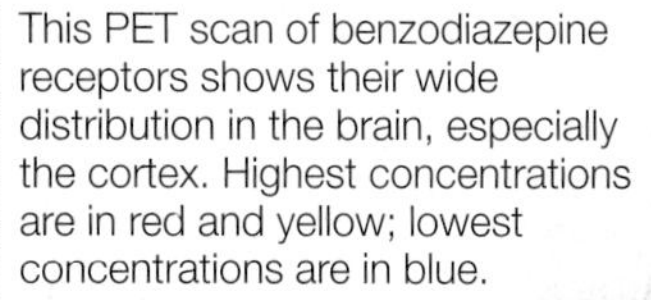

This PET scan of benzodiazepine receptors shows their wide distribution in the brain, especially the cortex. Highest concentrations are in red and yellow; lowest concentrations are in blue.

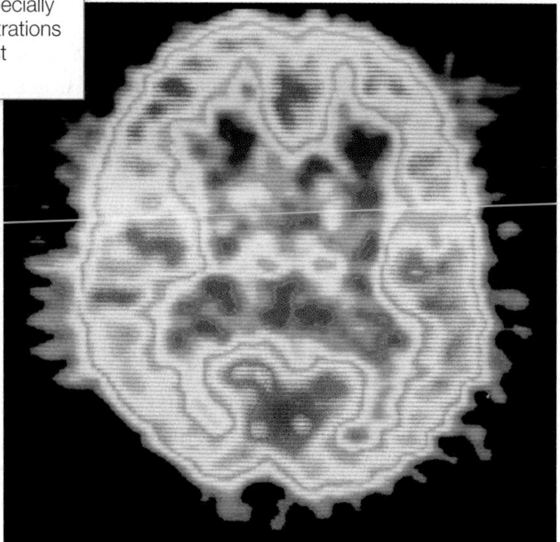

Front
Back

Figure 16.2 **Distribution of Benzodiazepine Receptors in the Human Brain** (Courtesy of Goran Sedvall.)

physical sensation and situations that remind them of the panic attack until they no longer react to the situation, and see that they won't die or be harmed. Then the goal is to learn new coping skills that enable the clients to relax if an attack happens. Relaxation techniques, as well as various mindfulness and meditation techniques that we discussed in Section 13.2, are often recommended for both panic disorder and generalized anxiety disorder.

CBT for anxiety disorders may be supplemented with medication to reduce anxiety. Drugs that relieve anxiety are called **anxiolytics** ("anxiety-dissolving"). Sometimes they are referred to informally as "minor tranquilizers." The most common ones are **benzodiazepines**, such as Valium and Xanax. They affect mood by boosting the effects of GABA receptors (see Chapter 3), which when stimulated normally inhibit neuronal activity throughout the cortex (**Figure 16.2**). This has a calming effect that kicks in very soon after taking the drug. Panic disorder and other anxiety disorders are also sometimes treated with antidepressants, which we will discuss later in this chapter, but these typically must be taken for several weeks before they affect mood. One disadvantage of anxiolytics such as the benzodiazepines is that they are potentially addictive and the client may become dependent on them to function at all.

Phobias can be unlearned

A **phobia** is a marked, long-lasting fear of an object or situation that is out of proportion to the real danger. In keeping with the overall philosophy of the *DSM*, a phobia is considered a disorder only if it interferes with normal functioning. Being unreasonably afraid of spiders may be a problem only infrequently and so would not be a disorder. But a fear of enclosed spaces, which might prevent a person from flying or using an elevator, may impair the client's ability to perform well or to pursue other activities. Estimates are that 9% of Americans suffer from a phobia of one kind or another at some point in life (Kessler et al., 2005). There is a heritable tendency to develop phobias (Van Houtem et al., 2013).

What are people afraid of? As you might have guessed, many people are afraid of spiders or snakes, but those fears don't have much influence on everyday life. A fear of dogs, on the other hand, may make it difficult to go out in public, where you might encounter someone walking a dog. Likewise, a fear of heights may be problematic if you need to go into tall buildings. Some people are so afraid of blood or injections that they may avoid going to the doctor or hospital.

As we saw in Chapter 8, some phobias probably result from an early experience where an encounter with the object now feared happened to coincide with

anxiolytics Drugs that relieve anxiety, sometimes informally called "minor tranquilizers."

benzodiazepines Common anxiolytics that affect mood by boosting the effects of GABA receptors, which normally inhibit neuronal activity throughout the cortex.

phobia A marked, long-lasting fear of an object or situation that is out of proportion to the real danger.

systematic desensitization The gradual exposure of a person to the feared object or situation until the person learns that there is no real danger; used as a treatment for phobias.

agoraphobia An irrational fear of certain environments.

obsessive-compulsive disorder (OCD) A disorder characterized by repeated, persistent thoughts or urges that are unwanted and repetitive, ritualistic behaviors and/or mental acts, which impair normal functioning.

some other, frightening experience. For example, a child who approaches a dog that suddenly barks and snaps may become overly afraid of all dogs, a type of learning called *fear conditioning.* Lab animals can be made afraid of almost any stimulus, such as a light or a sound tone, simply by repeatedly following presentation of the stimulus with some unpleasant event, such as a mild foot shock (see Figure 8.13). What we know from such laboratory studies is that the best way to unlearn fear conditioning is to present the stimulus repeatedly *without* the unpleasant event (for example, present the sound over and over again without the foot shock). In this sense, phobias tend to be self-maintaining—the person avoids exposure to the object or situation, so the opportunity never arises to learn that there is no reason to be afraid (or at least, not as afraid).

Thus one treatment for phobias is **systematic desensitization**, gradually exposing the person to the feared object or situation so that he can learn there is no real danger (Jones, 1924; Rutherford, 2006). Usually systematic desensitization is done over several sessions, but one option for phobias of animals, elevators, or darkness is called *one-session treatment*, which is not only abbreviated OST but was first described in detail by a Swedish psychologist named Öst (1989). The client is encouraged to approach the feared object and to stay there until his anxiety fades, then approach closer, and so on. OST has been shown to be effective for children and adolescents (Ollendick & Davis, 2013) and for adults (Zlomke & Davis, 2008).

Despite the name, **agoraphobia**—an irrational fear of certain environments, such as wide-open spaces, or places with lots of people, such as malls or airports—is not considered a phobia in *DSM-5*. Agoraphobia is classified as a separate disorder from phobias or panic disorder but has characteristics of each. People with this disorder are not so much afraid of the particular environment as they are afraid they will have a panic attack *in that environment*. In other words, people with agoraphobia often suffer from panic disorder too. CBT treatment for agoraphobia is typically a blend of that for phobias and panic disorder—gradual exposure to the environment or situation, so a fearful person can habituate to that environment and reduce the chance of a panic attack, and to realize that, even if a panic attack happens, she won't die or come to harm.

TABLE 16.3 Prevalence of Various Symptoms in OCD

Symptoms	Percentage of patients exhibiting symptoms
OBSESSIONS (THOUGHTS)	
Dirt, germs, or environmental toxins	40
Something terrible happening (e.g., fire, death, or illness of self or loved one)	24
Symmetry, order, or exactness	17
Religious obsessions	13
Body wastes or secretions (urine, stool, saliva, etc.)	8
Lucky or unlucky numbers	8
Forbidden, aggressive, or perverse sexual thoughts, images, or impulses	4
Fear of harming self or others	4
Household items	3
Intrusive nonsense sounds, words, or music	1
COMPULSIONS (ACTS)	
Performing excessive or ritualized hand washing, showering, bathing, toothbrushing, or grooming	85
Repeating rituals (e.g., going in or out of a door, getting up from or sitting down on a chair)	51
Checking (doors, locks, stove, appliances, emergency brake on car, paper route, homework, etc.)	46
Engaging in miscellaneous rituals (e.g., writing, moving, speaking)	26
Removing contaminants from objects	23
Touching	20
Counting	18
Ordering or arranging	17
Preventing harm to self or others	16
Hoarding or collecting	11
Cleaning household or inanimate objects	6

Source: Swedo et al., 1989.

Obsessive-compulsive disorder brings recurrent, unwanted thoughts and behaviors

Obsessive-compulsive disorder (**OCD**) is characterized by repeated, persistent thoughts or urges that are intrusive and unwanted and by repetitive, ritualistic behaviors (like hand washing or checking door locks) or mental acts (like praying or silently repeating a rhyme) that impair normal functioning. The name reflects the *obsessions* (unwanted thoughts) and *compulsions* (repeated, irrational behaviors). Generally, the person is made anxious by the obsessions and gains some relief by engaging in the compulsive behavior. For example, a person may find himself constantly thinking about germs, which makes him feel anxious

These MRIs show the brain of a patient who underwent a cingulotomy—the disruption of cingulate cortex connections—in an attempt to treat OCD.

(A) Horizontal view

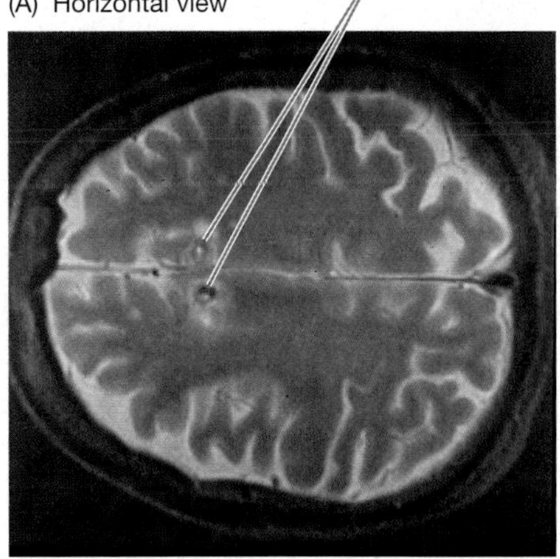

(B) Side view

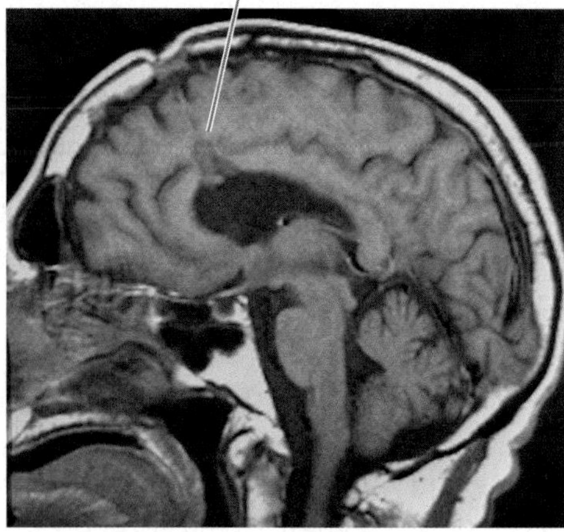

Figure 16.3 Neurosurgery to Treat Obsessive-Compulsive Disorder (From Martuza et al., 1990, courtesy of Robert L. Martuza.)

about contamination, so he repeatedly washes his hands. Often the person may be aware that his thoughts and anxiety are inappropriate and that his rituals are not rational responses. Yet still he finds himself thinking those thoughts, feeling that anxiety, and engaging in the compulsions. **Table 16.3** summarizes the more common symptoms of OCD.

Determining the number of people afflicted with OCD is difficult, especially because many people with this disorder tend to hide their symptoms. It is estimated that nearly 1% of adults will suffer from severe OCD in the United States in any given year (Kessler et al., 2005). In many cases, the initial symptoms of this disorder appear in childhood. The peak age group for onset of OCD, however, is 25 to 44 years.

Happily, OCD responds to treatment in most cases. It responds well to CBT (Olatunji et al., 2013) and also to several drugs. The most commonly prescribed medications are antidepressants (which we'll discuss in some detail when we describe depression). Why is it that antidepressants are useful in treating two such different disorders? For one thing, because depression often accompanies OCD, the two disorders may be related. Furthermore, functional brain imaging suggests that the same drugs alter the activity of the prefrontal cortex in people with OCD (Saxena et al., 2001) and in people with depression (as we'll discuss later in this chapter).

In cases of OCD that do not respond to CBT or to medication, clients may turn to controversial treatments, including deliberately destroying brain tissue (**Figure 16.3**)—although not nearly as much tissue as in the now discredited practice of lobotomy such as was experienced by Howard, whom we met at the start of this chapter. You can appreciate that this is a rather desperate step, and it is also difficult to evaluate the effectiveness of such surgery, not only because there are relatively few cases but also because it's impossible to conduct "blind" studies. Researchers can't ethically conduct a study where all the clients undergo brain surgery but only half of them have any brain tissue destroyed. Thus we don't know if the people who take this option, and who report a reduction in symptoms, benefitted because brain tissue was destroyed or because they expected the surgery to help (Gentil et al., 2014).

Many researchers believe that OCD is part of a spectrum of related disorders that involve repetitive behaviors, including *Tourette's syndrome* (Olson, 2004), which is characterized by involuntary, repetitive movements (like a grimace or eye blinking) and vocalizations (like throat clearing or sniffing), called *tics*. Tourette's and OCD are often **co-morbid** (occurring together), and both disorders involve abnormalities of the basal ganglia. However, drug therapy in Tourette's syndrome has typically focused on modifying the actions of dopamine rather than the serotonin systems targeted by antidepressants (as we'll see later).

co-morbid Occurring together, such as disorders.

OCD can run in families—that is, genetics plays a role in the appearance of the disorder. Several genes may contribute (Grados et al., 2003). There is evidence, too, that OCD can be triggered by infections. Upon observing that many children exhibiting OCD symptoms had recently been treated for strep throat, researchers found that many children with OCD produce antibodies to brain proteins (Dale et al., 2005; Esposito et al., 2014). The researchers theorize that in mounting an immune response to the streptococcal bacteria, these children also make antibodies that attack their own brains. The genetic link may be that some people are more likely than others to produce antibodies to the brain proteins.

Depression is a debilitating, potentially deadly disorder

Clinically, **depression** is characterized by an unhappy mood, loss of interests and energy, change of appetite, difficulty in concentration, and restless agitation. Pessimism seems to seep into every act (Solomon, 2001). Periods of such *unipolar depression* (depression that alternates with normal emotional states) can occur with no readily apparent stress. Without treatment, the depression often lasts several months. Depressive disorders of this sort are estimated to afflict 13–20% of the population at any one time (Cassens et al., 1990). *Bipolar disorder* (formerly known as *manic-depressive illness*) is characterized by repeated fluctuation between depressive periods and episodes of euphoric, sometimes grandiose, positive mood (or *mania*), which we will discuss later.

Depression can be lethal, as it may lead to suicide. About 80% of all suicide victims are profoundly depressed. Regardless of whether the person is depressed, many suicides appear to be impulsive acts. For example, one classic study found that of the more than 500 people who were prevented from jumping off the Golden Gate Bridge in San Francisco, only 6% later went on to commit suicide (Seiden, 1978). Suicide rates went down by a third in Britain when that country switched from using coal gas, which contains lots of deadly carbon monoxide, to natural gas for heating and cooking—thereby reducing the ease with which a person could impulsively commit suicide. The understanding that suicide is often an impulsive act is why society needs to erect barriers, either literally (on bridges) or metaphorically, to make it difficult for people suffering from depression and other mental disorders to kill themselves. We reviewed the warning signs of suicide in Table 5.2.

A remarkably enduring myth is that suicide and depression peak around the winter holidays. This is completely untrue, as we mentioned in Chapter 1 and discuss in **Box 16.1**. We have had solid data *for over a century* contradicting the notion that the winter holidays bring on depression, yet still the idea persists.

Genetic studies of depressive disorders reveal hereditary contributions. In twin studies, the concordance rate for depression (the percentage of time both twins have the disorder; see Chapter 4) is substantially higher in monozygotic twins (who share all the same genes) than in dizygotic twins (who share only half their genes) (Kendler et al., 1999). The concordance rate for monozygotic twins is similar whether the twins are reared apart or together. Adoption studies show higher rates of depression in the *biological* parents of a depressed patient than in the foster parents. Although several early studies implicated specific chromosomes as contributing to depression, subsequent studies failed to identify any particular gene (Risch et al., 2009). As is the case for schizophrenia, there probably is no single gene for depression. Rather, many genes contribute to make a person more or less susceptible, and environmental factors then determine whether depression results.

Descendants of people with severe depression have, on average, a thinner cortex across large swaths of the right hemisphere than do control participants (Peterson et al., 2009), which may increase vulnerability to depression. Many studies report that hippocampal volume is reduced in people with depression

depression A disorder characterized by an unhappy mood, loss of interests and energy, change of appetite, difficulty in concentration, and restless agitation.

Skeptic at Large

BOX 16.1

Does the Incidence of Depression Peak at the Holidays?

It has become a cliché in our culture to think that the holidays can be especially hard on people who are lonely. The pervasive talk about the holidays on the media combined with nostalgic memories of bygone childhood, so the folk mythology goes, conspires to depress those who are without close family. Hand in hand with this idea is the notion that suicide and suicide attempts are also clustered around December. This sounds like a persuasive case, but there's a big problem—it is completely false (Durkheim, 1897/1951). Statistical analyses have consistently found that the peaks in suicide attempts (**Figure A**; Ajdacic-Gross et al., 2005) and in hospital admissions for depression (Sato et al., 2006) occur in the spring and summer, not in December. In fact, the fewest suicides and new cases of depression in the United States happen in February each year, and rise after that as the weather improves. Could coming down from the excitement of the Christmas or Hanukkah holidays cause people to kill themselves? Interestingly, depression and suicide in the Southern Hemisphere peak during *its* springtime, which is September to November (Benedito-Silva et al., 2007), so the peak has nothing to do with any annual holiday.

(A)

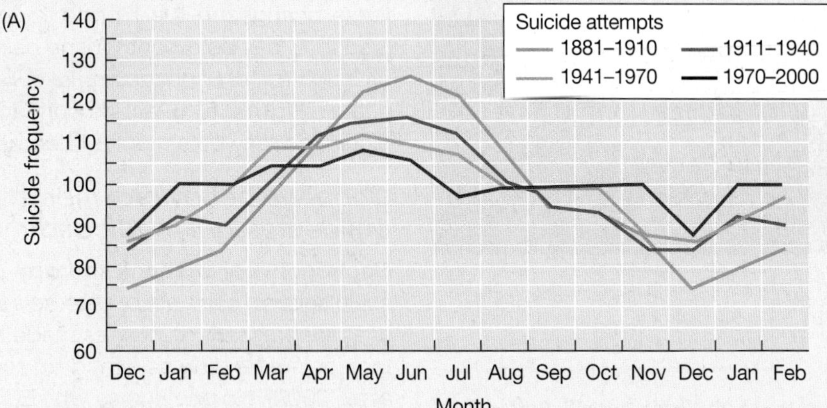

Seasonal Peak in Suicide The seasonal peak in suicide, first noted in 1897, is becoming less pronounced in the modern era. These data are from Switzerland. (After Ajdacic-Gross et al., 2005.)

Several explanations have been offered for the seasonal rhythms of suicide and depression. One explanation that you'll see online suggests that the dip in suicides during the December holidays occurs because it's a time of year when people are urged to help others and look forward to making the holidays joyous, so they avoid feeling sad (Wenz, 1977). This is a comforting idea, but it doesn't explain why the dip in depression in the Southern Hemisphere is around August (during that hemisphere's winter). Likewise, several explanations have been offered for the rise in depression as spring gives way to summer, but there's little data to support one notion over the other. One idea is that something about the increasing length of daylight as spring progresses affects some biological process that makes people vulnerable to depression and suicide. If indeed the seasonal transition from short days to long days makes some people vulnerable to suicide, perhaps the dampening of the seasonal variation in suicide over the past century (see Figure A) is due to our increasing reliance on indoor lighting.

There is one depressive disorder, however, that seems to be caused by too *little* daylight. **Seasonal affective disorder** (**SAD**) is diagnosed for people who report feeling transiently depressed every winter, when days grow short. Although by definition this is a depression that is relieved without treatment come springtime, many people report getting faster relief by exposing themselves to bright artificial lighting (**Figure B**).

seasonal affective disorder (**SAD**) A depressive disorder diagnosed in people who report feeling transiently depressed every winter.

(B)

Beating the Blues Some people report that exposing themselves to intense lighting in winter improves their mood.

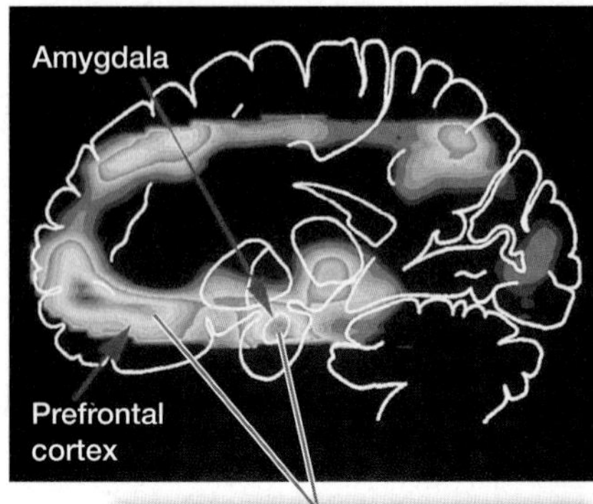

Amygdala
Prefrontal cortex
PET scans reveal increased activity in the prefrontal cortex and the amygdala of depressed patients.

Figure 16.4 Brain Activity Patterns in Depression (Courtesy of Wayne C. Drevets.)

electroconvulsive shock therapy (ECT) The intentional induction of a large-scale seizure, which is often effective in the relief of depression.

monoamine hypothesis The hypothesis that depression is caused by reduced activity of one or more monoamine transmitters, such as serotonin.

monoamine oxidase (MAO) The enzyme that normally inactivates the monoamines, including norepinephrine, dopamine, and serotonin.

tricyclics The second generation of antidepressants, which inhibit the reuptake of monoamines, prolonging their synaptic activity.

(Sexton et al., 2012), and there is reduced activation of the hippocampal region in depressed people during memory tasks (Young et al., 2011). But whether these changes in the hippocampus are present before the depression, and therefore may be a contributing *cause* of the disorder, or are a *result* of the depression remains unknown. Likewise, the localized brain activity in depressed people (**Figure 16.4**) differs from that of participants in control groups, but that difference may be a result of depression, not a cause of it.

Cognitive behavioral therapy is as effective as antidepressant medication

Electroconvulsive shock therapy (**ECT**)—the intentional induction of a large-scale seizure, can rapidly reverse severe depression (Weiner, 1994). The advent of antidepressant drugs has made ECT less common, but it remains an important tool for treating severe, drug-resistant depression (Fink & Taylor, 2007; Kim et al., 2009). No one knows why ECT helps depression, but as we'll see, no one knows why antidepressants work either.

Today, the most common treatment for depression is the use of drugs that affect monoamine neurotransmitters. The **monoamine hypothesis** (Schildkraut & Kety, 1967) was suggested by the first antidepressants, which were inhibitors of **monoamine oxidase** (**MAO**), the enzyme that normally inactivates the monoamines: norepinephrine, dopamine, and serotonin. While these drugs are seldom used today, the fact that MAO inhibitors raise the level of monoamines in synapses suggested that people with depression do not get enough stimulation at those synapses. Thus a second generation of antidepressants was developed, the **tricyclics** (named after their chemical structure), which inhibit the reuptake of monoamines, also prolonging their synaptic activity (see Figure 3.11).

Among the monoamines, serotonin may play the most important role in depression. A major class of modern antidepressants is the **selective serotonin reuptake inhibitors** (**SSRIs**), such as Prozac (**Table 16.4**). Closely related are drugs that inhibit reuptake at both serotonin and norepinephrine synapses (SNRIs, like Cymbalta). Both classes of drugs are more effective than MAO inhibitors and tricyclics, and have fewer side effects. However, there are problems with the theory that reduced serotonin stimulation causes depression. We know that SSRI drugs increase synaptic serotonin within hours of administration. Yet it typically takes several weeks of SSRI treatment before people feel better. This paradox suggests that it is the brain's *response* to increased synaptic serotonin that relieves the symptoms, and that this response takes time. So even though boosting serotonin helps some people, their depression may originally have been caused by other factors in the brain.

While SSRIs help many people who are depressed, they do not help everyone. In placebo-controlled trials, although a slightly higher proportion of people taking the drug rather than the placebo report relief (Turner et al., 2008), about a third of the people taking the *placebo* also feel better. This result suggests that some people helped by SSRI treatment are actually benefitting from a placebo effect (Berton & Nestler, 2006). One meta-analysis concluded that only a minority of depressed patients, the 13% constituting

TABLE 16.4 Drugs Used to Treat Depression

Drug class	Mechanism of action	Examples[a]
Monoamine oxidase (MAO) inhibitors	Inhibit the enzyme monoamine oxidase, which breaks down serotonin, norepinephrine, and dopamine	Marplan, Nardil, Parnate
Tricyclics	Inhibit the reuptake of norepinephrine, serotonin, and/or dopamine	Elavil, Wellbutrin, Aventyl, Ludiomil, Norpramin
Selective serotonin reuptake inhibitors (SSRIs)	Block the reuptake of serotonin, having little effect on norephinephrine or dopamine synapses	Prozac, Paxil, Zoloft

[a] The more commonly used trade names rather than chemical names are used.

the most severe cases, responded significantly better to SSRIs than to placebos (Fournier et al., 2010), as we discussed in Chapter 2. Furthermore, only about half of the people getting the drug are "cured," and about 20% show no improvement at all. Finally, there is little evidence that SSRIs or other antidepressant drugs work better than placebos when given to children or teenagers (Bower, 2006), yet millions of American children have been given prescriptions for SSRIs. The ineffectiveness of SSRIs in children and adolescents is tragic, because SSRIs increase the risk of suicide in people at these ages (Olfson et al., 2006), a finding that the drug companies tried to hide for years (Ramchandani, 2004).

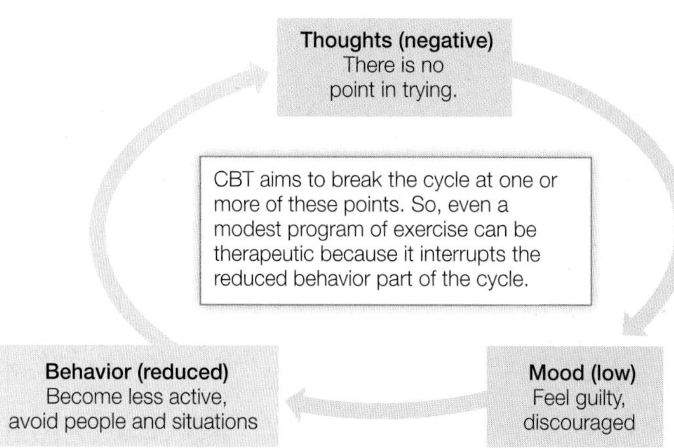

Figure 16.5 Depression's Endless Treadmill

Despite the overwhelming popularity of SSRIs for treating depression, 20 or so sessions of cognitive behavioral therapy (CBT), psychotherapy aimed at correcting negative thinking and improving interpersonal relationships, is about as effective as SSRI treatment (Butler et al., 2006). Furthermore, the rate of relapse is lower for CBT than for SSRI treatment (DeRubeis et al., 2008).

selective serotonin reuptake inhibitors (SSRIs) A major class of modern antidepressants, they increase availability of synaptic serotonin.

Interestingly, CBT and SSRI treatment together are more effective in combating depression than either one is alone (March et al., 2004). Typically, CBT helps the client recognize self-defeating modes of thinking and encourages breaking out of a cycle of self-fulfilling depression (**Figure 16.5**). SSRI treatment may help the client be more open to this CBT approach.

So if CBT is as effective as SSRIs, and less likely to lead to a return of the depression, why are most Americans suffering from depression treated with SSRIs alone, without CBT? A big factor is money—SSRIs are relatively inexpensive, so that treatment costs a lot less than paying a trained psychologist to provide CBT. Because SSRIs are inexpensive, health insurance companies typically make it easier to get the drugs than CBT. Also, the number of therapists in most areas is still low, so it can be difficult to get this treatment, even though it is the most effective for depression.

Finally, exercise is also an effective treatment for depression (Dunn et al., 2005; Wegner et al., 2014), especially when combined with other treatments (Mura et al., 2014), and it is available to most of us for free.

16.2 SUMMARY

- *Anxiety disorders* are characterized by intense, irrational anxiety that interferes with everyday life.
- *Panic disorder*, sudden undirected fear and physiological responses such as trembling and breathlessness, can be effectively treated with *cognitive behavioral therapy* (*CBT*) or *anxiolytics,* like the *benzodiazepines* such as Valium.
- The long-lasting, irrational fears characterizing *phobias* like *agoraphobia* can be treated by gradual exposure to the fearful situation or object.
- *Obsessive-compulsive disorder* (*OCD*), repetitive obsessive thoughts and ritualistic compulsive behaviors, can be treated with CBT and antidepressants.
- *Depression*, a long-lasting period of unhappy mood, apathy, and agitation, can be life-threatening because it may lead to impulsive acts of suicide.

- CBT is effective for depression, as are *selective serotonin reuptake inhibitors* (*SSRIs*), like Prozac and Zoloft. The combination of the two approaches is more effective than either alone. Exercise also helps combat depression.

REVIEW QUESTIONS

1. Lessons from learning studies have suggested what sort of therapy for people with phobias? How is it conducted?
2. What is the evidence that suicide is usually an impulsive act?
3. What are the two main classes of effective treatment for depression, and why is one more commonly used than the other?

Food for Thought

If a friend came to you asking for advice about whether to start taking SSRIs for depression, what would you say?

16.3 Personality Disorders

Things to Learn

- Six main kinds of personality disorders
- Various treatment approaches for personality disorders
- Difficulty treating borderline personality disorder
- Behaviors and attitudes of psychopaths

Personality disorders are enduring impairments in interacting with other people that cause the client significant distress. They are somewhat controversial diagnoses because it's not easy to see where the boundary is between someone who is simply disagreeable and someone who has a "disorder." The boundary seems even blurrier when you consider that behaviors that are considered bothersome in one culture, like being very self-centered, may be perfectly acceptable in others.

By definition, personality disorders do not include behaviors that are typical for people of a particular age (like crying in babies, or rebellious attitudes in teenagers) or in a particular culture, and they are not the direct result of some drug (like alcohol) or medical condition (like a fever or a lobotomy). Because personality may still be developing in children and adolescents, a *DSM-5* diagnosis of personality disorder can be applied only to people who are 18 or older (there is a possibility the child or teen will "grow out of it"). On the other hand, if a pattern of behaviors is really a disorder of *personality*, then the beginnings of the problem should have been present early in life, so *DSM-5* usually requires evidence that behaviors arose before adulthood. Personality disorders are not rare, affecting about 9% of U.S. adults in any 12-month period (Lenzenweger et al., 2007).

DSM-5 initially suggested a very different approach from *DSM-IV*, perhaps taking a cue from developments in personality research that emphasize personality *traits* rather than *types* (Hopwood et al., 2013), as we discussed in Chapter 14. The idea is that a client with a personality that is extreme in one or more traits (including the "big five"), such as introversion, neuroticism, and so on, may have difficulty getting along with others, which is the hallmark of personality disorders. After extensive discussion, *DSM-5* retained the ten personality disorders listed previously but suggested, as a "hybrid" model, collapsing them into six categories, which we discuss here.

personality disorders Enduring impairments in interacting with other people that cause the client significant distress.

schizotypal personality disorder A personality disorder that may resemble schizophrenia in the sense that the client may have very unconventional, even paranoid, beliefs and eccentric behavior that makes it difficult to maintain relationships.

obsessive-compulsive personality disorder (OCPD) A personality disorder in which behavior and thinking is characterized by a rigidity regarding order, organization, and notions of what is right or wrong.

Some personality disorders resemble mild versions of more serious disorders

Schizotypal personality disorder may resemble schizophrenia in the sense that the client may have very unconventional, even paranoid, beliefs, and eccentric behavior that makes it difficult to maintain relationships. Clients with schizotypal personality disorder are at risk for developing schizophrenia (Rosell et al., 2014).

A person with obsessive-compulsive disorder (OCD), which we discussed earlier, has *obsessions* (e.g., that some unknown person is going to hurt his mother) and *compulsions* to follow repetitive rituals (e.g., unlocking and locking every door three times) that are not rational. In contrast to people with OCD, people with **obsessive-compulsive personality disorder** (**OCPD**) do not experience obsessions or compulsions. But their behavior and thinking are characterized by a rigidity regarding order, organization, and notions of what is right and wrong (Starcevic & Brakoulias, 2014). People with OCPD are preoccupied with orderliness and perfectionism. Being super organized and strictly adhering to all rules isn't a problem in itself, but if such perfectionism keeps people from completing important tasks at work, or leads them to insist that others conform to their rigid ideas, it can take a toll on relationships and hence constitutes a personality disorder according to *DSM-5*.

Narcissistic personality disorder is characterized by a sense of self-importance requiring excessive admiration and a lack of empathy for others (Ronningstam, 2014). In everyday language we might characterize such a person as severely egotistical or having *megalomania* (a former clinical term for this disorder). Extreme self-centeredness has also long been called narcissism, after the Greek myth about the beautiful young man Narcissus, who fell in love with his own image in a pool of water.

Let's discuss in a bit more detail the remaining three personality disorders: borderline, avoidant, and antisocial–psychopathic.

Narcissus A handsome young man who loved his reflection in a pool of water so much he never left it.

Where are the borders for borderline personality disorder?

People who are emotionally unstable, experiencing frequent mood swings, identity disturbances, and impulsive behaviors that impair their relationships with other people may be diagnosed with **borderline personality disorder** (Lazarus et al., 2014). This term, which arose with *DSM-III* in 1980, was meant to suggest that the client is somewhere on the border between psychosis (referring to delusions about personal relationships, such as fear of abandonment) and neurosis (referring to irrational anxiety and overemotional behavior). While most clinicians today find the "borderline" concept of personality misleading, the term seems to have stuck. According to *DSM-5*, a person must display a certain number of traits from a checklist to be diagnosed with this disorder (**Table 16.5**). As with all *DSM-5* personality disorders, a borderline personality diagnosis is not made until a person is at least 18, but in many instances a pattern of behavior can be tracked to adolescence. This diagnosis is more common in women than in men, with estimates of overall prevalence in the population of about 1% (Lenzenweger et al., 2007).

narcissistic personality disorder A personality disorder characterized by a sense of self-importance requiring excessive admiration and a lack of empathy for others.

borderline personality disorder A personality disorder characterized by emotional instability, identity disturbances, and impulsive behavior that impairs relationships with others.

A central challenge for people with borderline personality disorder is difficulty regulating negative emotional feelings and anxiety-provoking thoughts, which leads to impulsive behaviors (including self-injurious behavior like wrist cutting) and recklessness. Not surprisingly, the intense, angry behavior of the borderline personality often interferes with relationships with other people. Ironically, in a kind of self-fulfilling prophecy, intense fear of being abandoned may lead people with borderline personality disorder to be clingy and demand so much reassurance that they actually do drive their friends away. This disorder is often accompanied by depression or bipolar disorder (discussed later in this chapter), as well as drug abuse, and as with those disorders, there is a danger of self-harm and suicide.

Psychotherapy can be effective for borderline personality disorder (Kliem et al., 2010), with the goal of helping clients regulate emotions. On the one hand, the therapist must accept clients' feelings as real but also provide feedback to offer a "reality check," helping clients be more mindful of their behaviors and the effects they

TABLE 16.5 Symptoms of Borderline Personality Disorder

According to *DSM-5*, five or more of the following symptoms should be present to reach criterion for this disorder.

1. Extreme emotional reactions to abandonment (real or imagined)
2. Intense, stormy relationships with others
3. Distorted self-image or sense of self
4. Impulsive, sometimes dangerous behavior (spending sprees, reckless driving, binge eating)
5. Suicidal behaviors or threats of self-harm (such as cutting)
6. Intense, highly changeable moods
7. Chronic feelings of emptiness or boredom
8. Inappropriate, intense anger
9. Stress-related paranoid thoughts or feeling cut off from oneself

Source: National Institute of Mental Health, n.d.

have on others (Dimeff & Linehan, 2001). Sometimes described as a "tough love" approach, the therapy may be difficult if clients exhibit the same maladaptive patterns of behavior with the therapist. A pattern of constantly demanding the therapist's attention, repeated talk of suicide, and emotional outbursts in therapy make these individuals difficult clients (Kröger et al., 2014). But it is important that the therapist serve as an emotional anchor, remaining nonjudgmental, calm, and stable in the face of a client's emotional instability (Sansone & Sansone, 2013). The goal is to teach clients to avoid self-injurious behavior and dramatic outbursts until they've had a chance to think more objectively about any given situation (Davidson & Tran, 2014). Medications are also used sometimes, typically mood stabilizers such as antidepressants. It is also important to get any drug abuse under control, both to help clients gain control of their emotions and to avoid legal entanglements that could derail therapy.

Avoidant personality disorder is characterized by social anxiety and feelings of inadequacy

It is a terrible burden to believe that you are socially inept and unappealing, and that strangers will immediately dislike and reject you. Such preoccupations typify people with **avoidant personality disorder**, who suffer from *social phobia* so they tend to be overly sensitive about negative comments or behaviors from other people. They therefore avoid interpersonal contact to such an extent that they may not be able to hold a job, develop friendships, or even leave their home. It is not easy to know the prevalence of this disorder, but estimates range from 5% of the population (Lenzenweger et al., 2007) to 7% (Kessler et al., 2005; Ruscio et al., 2008). Both sexes seem equally vulnerable to this disorder, and it affects all races.

Unfortunately, avoidant personality disorder tends to be self-reinforcing. Once someone has come to believe that he is inadequate for social interactions, or that people naturally dislike him, he is likely to withdraw from social life. Consequently, existing friendships tend to fade and the person forms no new friendships, affording himself no opportunity to learn that he *can* have fulfilling interactions with other people, that people *don't* automatically dislike him. Ironically, to the extent the person keeps to himself when in public, others may be reluctant to approach and befriend him.

CBT for a person with avoidant personality disorder centers on boosting the client's self-esteem, including confidence in interacting with others, and reducing oversensitivity to negative comments from others (Stein & Stein, 2008). This may be accomplished through teaching social skills (role-playing about how to make "small talk"), trying to gradually increase social interactions with others, or group therapy sessions. One difficulty of any such treatment is the client's extreme sensitivity to negative emotions in others, which may lead her to think the therapist dislikes her, or that the members of the therapy group will reject her. If this happens, the client may drop out of treatment. Sadly, such a failed therapeutic experience might reinforce the person's irrational beliefs about her social inadequacy.

The most common medicines prescribed for avoidant personality disorder are antidepressants, primarily the SSRIs that we discussed earlier. As when used to treat depression, SSRIs must be taken for several weeks before they affect mood.

avoidant personality disorder A personality disorder characterized by social phobia or extreme sensitivity about negative comments or behaviors from others such that interpersonal contact is avoided.

antisocial personality disorder (ASPD) A personality disorder characterized by a pattern of disregard for other peoples' rights, with little evidence of remorse for harm done to others.

Can we detect psychopaths in the modern world?

People who, starting in childhood or early adolescence, display a pattern of disregard for other peoples' rights, showing little evidence of remorse for harm done to others, may be diagnosed with **antisocial personality disorder (ASPD)**. People with ASPD tend to be impulsive and antagonistic, to lie, and to use superficial charm to manipulate other people. They may break the law repeatedly. ASPD is much more often diagnosed in men than in women. While *DSM-5* does not assign this diagnosis until a person is at least 18, it requires evidence of this disorder before that age. For example, people with ASPD may have gotten in trouble a lot at school, have a history of fighting, or have tortured animals or set fires when they were younger.

In extreme cases, people showing a pattern of ASPD behaviors, such as disregard for others and lack of remorse, may be described as *psychopaths* or *sociopaths* (the two terms are used interchangeably). *DSM-5* does not recognize psychopathy as a diagnosis, so no distinction is made between ASPD and psychopathy. But almost every clinician agrees that it is a matter of degree (Strickland et al., 2013). In other words, even though all psychopaths meet the criteria for a diagnosis of ASPD, not everyone with ASPD should be considered a psychopath. A widely used checklist for distinguishing psychopaths from people who "merely" have ASPD (Neumann et al., 2007) is described in **Table 16.6**, but as is so often the case with personality tests, it is difficult to gauge whether it really detects psychopaths (Skeem & Cooke, 2010).

■ **TABLE 16.6 Psychopathy Checklist**

Interpersonal/emotional traits	Lifestyle/antisocial traits
Superficial charm	Need for stimulation (easily bored)
Grandiose sense of worth	Parasitic lifestyle
Pathological lying	Lack of realistic goals
Manipulative/cunning	Impulsivity
Lack of remorse or guilt	Irresponsibility
Emotionally shallow	Poor behavioral control
Lack of empathy/callous	Early behavioral problems
Failure to take responsibility	Juvenile delinquency
Sexually promiscuous	Criminal versatility
Many short-term marital relationships	Revocation of conditional release

Source: Hare, 2003, and Harpur et al., 1989.

While a lack of empathy for other people is a hallmark of psychopaths (Deeley et al., 2006), there is evidence that these individuals can turn empathy on or off. When viewing emotionally laden videos, psychopaths show a different pattern of brain activation than do control participants. But when psychopaths are *instructed* to empathize with the character in the film, their brain activation pattern resembles that of control participants (Meffert et al., 2013).

ASPD is very difficult to treat because the afflicted people may not see any problem with their behavior, and generally seek treatment only when they are required to do so to avoid prison or stay out on parole. Plus, people with ASPD may use their well-practiced skills of deceit and charm to manipulate any therapist who tries to help them.

Table 16.7 summarizes the personality disorders we've discussed, with a brief reminder of behavior that typifies each. If you're wondering why we haven't talked about multiple personality, it's because that is a very controversial diagnosis, and may not exist, as we discuss in **Box 16.2**.

■ **TABLE 16.7 Personality Disorders**

DSM-IV personality disorders	*DSM-5* proposed simplification	Characteristic features	Estimated prevalence (%)
CHARACTERIZED BY ODD BEHAVIOR			
Schizotypal/paranoid/schizoid	Schizotypal	Odd beliefs and responses	4.7
CHARACTERIZED BY DRAMATIC, ERRATIC BEHAVIOR			
Borderline/histrionic/dependent	Borderline	Emotionally unstable, impulsive	3.1
Narcissistic	Narcissistic	Excessive self-importance, lack of empathy	1.4
Antisocial	Antisocial-psychopathic (ASPD)	Disregard for others, lack of remorse	1.3
CHARACTERIZED BY ANXIETY			
Avoidant	Avoidant	Extreme social phobia	3.0
Obsessive-compulsive personality disorder (OCPD)	Obsessive-compulsive personality disorder (OCPD)	Excessive tidiness and rigidity	2.5

Source: American Psychiatric Association, 2000, 2013; Lenzenweger, 2008.

Skeptic at Large

BOX 16.2

Multiple Personality Disorder: Myth or Reality?

Perhaps the most controversial disorder listed in *DSM-5* is **dissociative identity disorder (DID)**, previously known as *multiple personality disorder*, in which someone has at least two distinctive, enduring personalities that take turns controlling the person's behavior. Not only is there disagreement about how to recognize or treat the disorder, but many psychologists and psychiatrists also think it doesn't exist, or at most, is actually created by therapists.

One cause of skepticism is fueled by the history of DID. Virtually no one had ever heard of the idea of a single person with two very different personalities until 1957, when the book *The Three Faces of Eve* was published (Thigpen & Cleckley, 1957), quickly followed by a popular film. These portrayals set the mold of DID as resulting from a childhood trauma so distressing that the child creates a separate personality, which doesn't remember the trauma and is thereby protected from it. Eventually the patient in the book identified herself and published accounts (Sizemore & Pittillo, 1977) that so disagreed with her doctor's description that it's no longer clear what really happened (except that both patient and therapist sold books). While a few therapists reported similar cases after Eve's famous debut, the floodgates really opened after 1973 when the best-selling book *Sybil* (Schreiber, 1973) appeared, followed by a popular television movie. Upping the ante on Eve, Sybil supposedly had over a dozen personalities. Although thousands of cases of DID were diagnosed after *Sybil*, that presentation may have been entirely false. Before the book was even published, the real "Sybil" wrote her therapist that she did not have multiple personalities: "I have been lying in my pretense of them." But her therapist, already committed to writing the book with a journalist, dismissed the letter (Nathan, 2011). The therapist had used the controversial practice of drugging Sybil with sodium pentothal in an attempt to "recover memories," and clinicians listening to those tapes later concluded the therapist had suggested multiple personalities to Sybil (Lynn et al., 2012).

Two Faces of Sybil Shirley Mason (1923–1998) was the patient described as having multiple personalities in the book *Sybil*.

In the meantime, it has been difficult to find evidence that DID really exists independent of the claims of clinicians and patients. For example, do the different personalities really not all have access to the same memories? That is supposedly why DID happens, to protect one "self" from knowing something another "self" knows. But when put to the test, the self that claims not to remember something shows clear evidence of recognizing the event, as measured by cognitive methods (Huntjens et al., 2012). Given the deep doubts surrounding the famous early cases that defined DID for a generation of clinicians looking for other "Eves" or "Sybils," and that shaped the definition of the disorder in earlier versions of the *DSM*, it's not at all clear this disorder has *ever* existed. But then again, as there is also no consensus on how to treat DID if it does exist, maybe we don't need to worry about it. Most people diagnosed with DID also have other problems, like anxiety disorder, depression, or drug abuse, so perhaps the most appropriate conduct for a clinician encountering a client with symptoms of DID is to ignore it and try to treat the accompanying disorders. That may not lead to lucrative book deals or movie rights, but it might be in the client's best interests.

dissociative identity disorder (DID) A mental disorder diagnosed in a person who supposedly has at least two distinctive, enduring personalities that take turns controlling the person's behavior.

16.3 SUMMARY

- *Personality disorders*, enduring impairments in interacting with others, tend to be controversial diagnoses because everyone displays the symptoms at least occasionally.
- *Borderline personality disorder*, involving frequent mood swings and impulsive behaviors that damage relationships, may be challenging to treat if the client cannot maintain a relationship with the therapist.
- *Avoidant personality disorder* is the avoidance of interpersonal contact due to feelings of social inadequacy and irrational belief that others will automatically dislike you.
- Psychopaths represent extreme cases of *antisocial personality disorder* (*ASPD*), a disregard for others and lack of remorse.

REVIEW QUESTIONS

1. List some personality disorders and some of the symptoms common to each.
2. What sorts of behaviors are seen in borderline personality disorder, and how do they interfere with relationships?
3. Why is it that, if left untreated, avoidant personality disorder tends to be self-reinforcing?

Food for Thought

Do you think personality disorders have always been with us? Did our prehistoric ancestors have personality disorders? Why or why not?

16.4 Schizophrenia and Bipolar Disorder

Things to Learn

- Behavioral symptoms and brain correlates of schizophrenia
- Genes and environmental stress interact to affect the likelihood of schizophrenia
- Treatment and long-term outlook for people with schizophrenia
- Symptoms and treatment of bipolar disorder
- Risk of violence in people with schizophrenia or bipolar disorder

At the start of the twentieth century, thousands of patients in mental hospitals suffered from a disorder that began when middle-aged people suddenly began suffering from **delusions** (false beliefs strongly held in spite of contrary evidence), grandiosity (boastful self-importance), euphoria, poor judgment, and impulsive behavior. Their mental condition would deteriorate further into *dementia*, severe impairment in cognitive functions such as attention, memory, and language. Because these patients would also grow progressively weaker, eventually becoming bedridden, the disorder was called *paralytic dementia*.

Even before it was given this name, the disorder had been recognized for centuries and was often attributed to "weak character." But in 1911, microbiologist Hideyo Noguchi (1876–1928) discovered that the brains of people suffering from this disorder had been extensively damaged by syphilis, a sexually transmitted bacterial disease. The subsequent discovery of antibiotic drugs soon made this disorder a rarity. One course of penicillin treatment would prevent the mental symptoms from ever arising.

This early medical success story may have suggested to some that it was just a matter of time before we found the causes of other mental disorders, including schizophrenia, which, as we'll see, share some symptoms with syphilitic psychosis. But after more than a century, it is clear that there are no easy answers for what causes schizophrenia, or how to best treat it.

Diagnosis and classification of schizophrenia suggest many different disorders

The term *schizophrenia* (from the Greek *schizein*, "to split," and *phren*, "mind") was introduced by Eugen Bleuler (1857–1939) in 1911 (Bleuler, 1911/1950). Bleuler identified the key symptom as **dissociative thinking**, a major impairment in the logical structure of thought. Bleuler also described a mix of accompanying symptoms, including scattered thinking, emotional disturbance, delusions, and auditory hallucinations.

delusions False beliefs strongly held in spite of contrary evidence.

dissociative thinking A major impairment in the logical structure of thought.

TABLE 16.8 Symptoms of Schizophrenia

Positive symptoms (newly arisen behaviors or mental states)	Negative symptoms (loss of normal behaviors or mental states)
Hallucinations, most often auditory	Social withdrawal
Delusions of grandeur, persecution, etc.	Blunted affect (few emotional responses)
Disordered thought processes	Anhedonia (loss of pleasurable feelings)
Bizarre behaviors	Reduced motivation, poor focus on tasks
	Alogia (reduced speech output)
	Catatonia (reduced movement)

schizophrenia A disabling mental disorder characterized by hallucinations, delusions, disordered thinking, and emotional withdrawal.

positive symptoms Behavioral symptoms which are gained in schizophrenia; for example hallucinations, delusions, and agitation.

negative symptoms Behavioral functions that are lost in schizophrenia; for example slow and impoverished thought and speech, social withdrawal, or blunted affect.

Today, the symptoms considered to be indications of **schizophrenia** include the following:

- Auditory hallucinations
- Highly personalized delusions (false beliefs)
- Disorganized speech or behavior
- Cognitive impairments

Some investigators have proposed a major division of schizophrenic symptoms into two separate groups: positive and negative (**Table 16.8**) (Andreasen, 1991). The term **positive symptoms** refers to behavioral states that have been gained. Examples include hallucinations, delusions, and excited activity. The term **negative symptoms** refers to behavioral functions that have been lost—for example, slow and impoverished thought and speech, emotional and social withdrawal, and blunted affect (apparent poverty of emotions). Since people who suffer from schizophrenia report experiencing very strong emotions, the blunted emotions that are thought to characterize schizophrenia may be limited to emotional expression—facial and body signals (Kring & Caponigro, 2010). The fact that positive and negative symptoms respond differently to drug treatments suggests that they arise from different neural abnormalities.

There are probably several different kinds of schizophrenia, and in the past a lot of debate centered on how many kinds there are and what symptoms typify each one and what they should be called. Today, following the trend in clinical psychology to regard most disorders as part of a continuum of symptoms, most researchers see each person with schizophrenia as varying considerably in the *relative degree* of symptoms such as paranoia (delusion that others are persecuting you), blunted affect, and cognitive impairment (difficulty in understanding what's going on around you or in holding a coherent conversation). So some people with schizophrenia may be very articulate and observant, showing little sign of cognitive impairment and using that sharp mind to "discover" vast, elaborate conspiracies against them. Other people may have little paranoia and may function adequately in most situations, but show little emotional interest in their own cleanliness and safety. Yet others may be so cognitively impaired that they can't take care of themselves at all. Thus the evolving perspective is to regard "types" of schizophrenia as particular blends of positive and negative symptoms, which may shift with time.

Anatomical differences are seen in the brains of many people with schizophrenia

Because the symptoms of schizophrenia can be so marked and persistent, investigators hypothesized early in the twentieth century that the brains of people with this illness would show unusual differences in structure that are distinctive and measurable (Trimble, 1991). Only with the advent of CT and MRI scans,

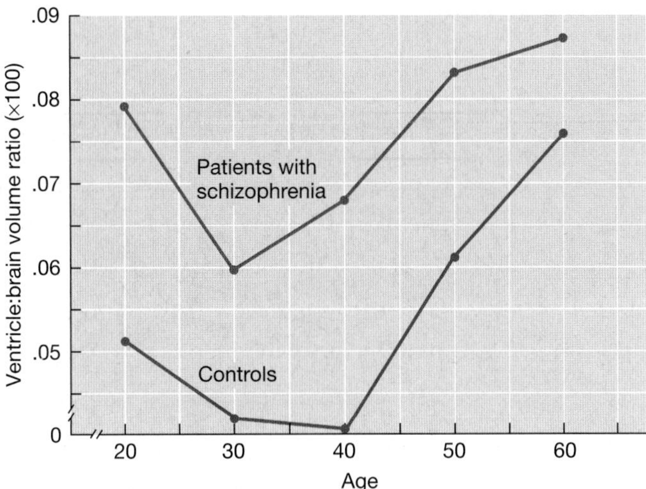

Figure 16.6 Ventricular Enlargement in Schizophrenia The volume of the cerebral ventricles, relative to overall brain volume, is greater in men with schizophrenia than in control patients. (After Hyde & Weinberger, 1990.)

however, has it become possible to study brain anatomy in living patients at all stages of their illness (Hyde & Weinberger, 1990). Such studies reveal the presence of significant anatomical differences in the brains of many patients with schizophrenia. The most reliable difference seen so far is that many patients with schizophrenia have enlarged cerebral ventricles, especially the lateral ventricles (**Figure 16.6**) (Hyde & Weinberger, 1990). This ventricular enlargement is not related to length of illness or to duration of hospitalization. In patients with ventricular enlargement, the extent of enlargement predicts how well the person will respond to medication for schizophrenia (Garver et al., 2000), which we'll discuss shortly.

Studies of identical twins have yielded startlingly clear results: if only one twin has schizophrenia, he or she has decidedly larger lateral ventricles than the twin who is well, whose ventricles are of normal size (**Figure 16.7**) (Torrey et al., 1994). What is the significance of enlarged ventricles? Because overall brain size does not seem to be affected in people with schizophrenia, the enlarged ventricles must come at the expense of neighboring brain tissue, including the hippocampus, which has been implicated in learning and memory, as we discussed

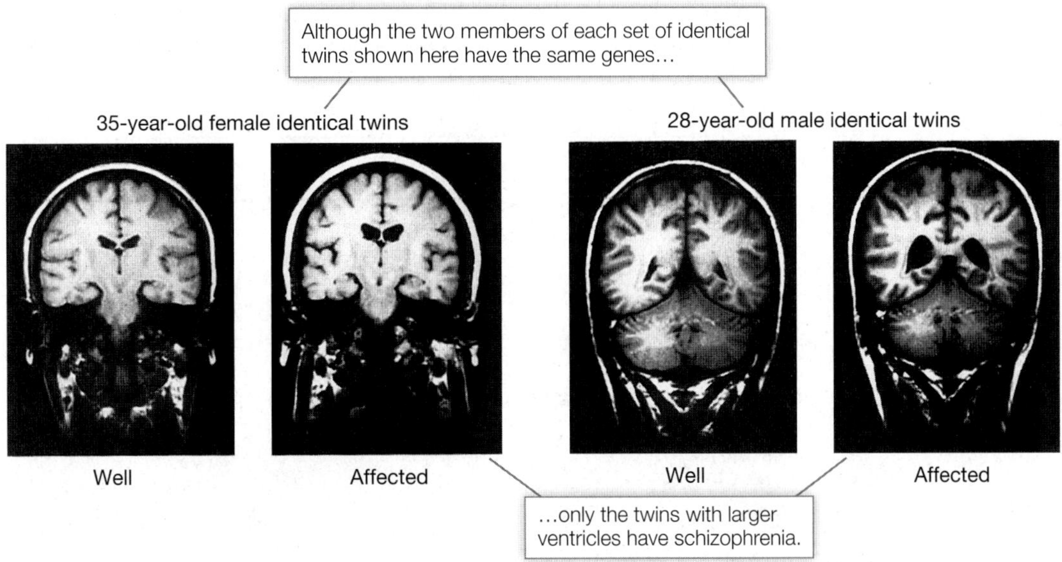

Figure 16.7 Identical Genes, Different Fates (After Torrey et al., 1994; MRI images courtesy of Dr. E. Fuller Torrey.)

in Chapters 8 and 9. Indeed, there are also differences between people with schizophrenia and control patients in the anatomical organization of cells within the hippocampus (Kovelman & Scheibel, 1984). Because these are physical differences between the brains of people with and without schizophrenia, it's easy to regard this as proof that schizophrenia is of "biological" origin. But in fact we still don't know whether being born with the anatomical differences causes schizophrenia, or whether suffering from schizophrenia causes the structural differences to develop.

There is a strong genetic component to schizophrenia

There is no doubt that there is a genetic component to schizophrenia. We discussed the evidence for a genetic influence on schizophrenia in some detail in Section 4.4, so here we will summarize those findings. The overall message is that the genes favoring schizophrenia do not act in an all-or-none fashion, but rather affect the *probability* that the disorder will arise. This is an important clue that environmental factors also affect the probability of schizophrenia.

Relatives of people with schizophrenia show a higher incidence of the disorder than is found in the general population, as we would expect if schizophrenia were heritable. Furthermore, the risk of schizophrenia among relatives increases with the closeness of the relationship, because closer relatives share a greater number of genes. Indeed, parents and siblings of people with schizophrenia have a higher risk of becoming schizophrenic than do people in the general population (see Figure 4.15) (Gottesman, 1991). In a few very rare cases, a single gene may be responsible for the appearance of schizophrenia in a particular family (Pletnikov et al., 2008). In that case, introducing this gene into mice causes them to develop enlarged ventricles (**Figure 16.8**), a common trait in people with schizophrenia, as we have seen. However, in the vast majority of cases of schizophrenia, the mode of inheritance of schizophrenia is not simple; that is, it does not involve a single recessive or dominant gene (Tamminga & Schulz, 1991). Rather, multiple genes play a role in the emergence of schizophrenia.

The strongest evidence of a genetic influence on schizophrenia comes from twin studies. As we detailed in Chapter 4, about 50% of monozygotic twins are concordant for schizophrenia, while the rate of concordance for dizygotic twins is only about 17% (see Figure 4.15) (Cardno & Gottesman, 2000; Gottesman, 1991). The significantly higher concordance rate among monozygotic twins is strong evidence of a genetic factor. After all, environmental variables like family

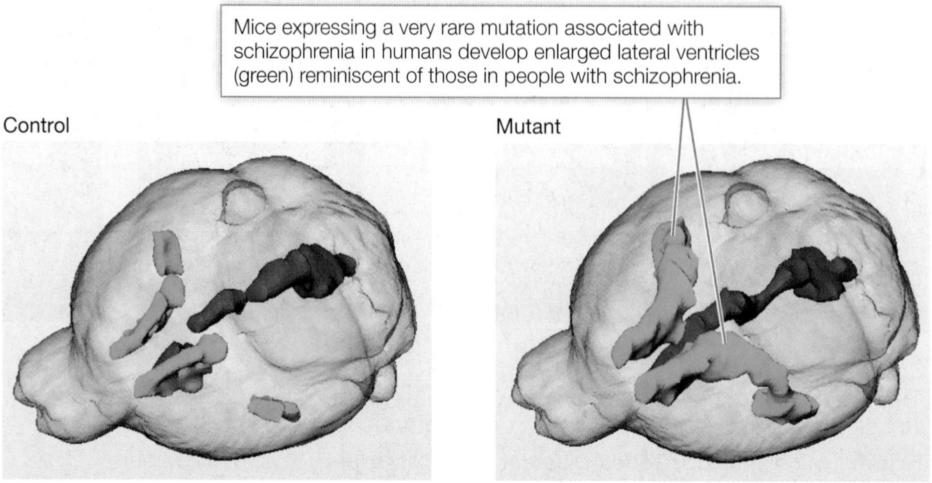

Mice expressing a very rare mutation associated with schizophrenia in humans develop enlarged lateral ventricles (green) reminiscent of those in people with schizophrenia.

Control

Mutant

Figure 16.8 Enlarged Ventricles in a Mouse Model (From Pletnikov et al., 2008.)

structure and socioeconomic stress would presumably be comparable for the two kinds of twins.

So even with identical twins, genes alone cannot fully explain whether a person will develop schizophrenia. What accounts for the discordance of the other 50% of monozygotic twins? The answer to this question could provide crucial clues about the environmental and developmental determinants of schizophrenia, and about which factors protect against its emergence in susceptible people. As we discussed in Chapter 4, the twin who goes on to develop schizophrenia tends to be the one who was less robust throughout life. The symptomatic twin frequently weighed less at birth and had an early developmental history that included more instances of physiological distress (Torrey et al., 1994). During development, this twin was more submissive, tearful, and sensitive than the identical sibling, and often was viewed by the twins' parents as being more vulnerable.

During childhood the developmental difficulties of twins who later suffer from schizophrenia are reflected in behavioral, cognitive, and other neurological signs, such as impairments in motor coordination (Torrey et al., 1994). Elaine Walker (1991) found that these early signs are sufficiently evident that observers watching home films of children can, with uncanny accuracy, pick out the child who went on to suffer from schizophrenia in adulthood (Schiffman et al., 2004). Although we certainly don't know all the environmental influences that make a difference, what we do know is that growing up in a stressful environment increases the chances of developing schizophrenia, as we'll discuss next.

Schizophrenia is an inherited susceptibility to stress, especially stress early in life

We've established that there is genetic influence on schizophrenia, but also that genes alone cannot fully account for the disorder. What environmental factors contribute to the probability of developing schizophrenia? Research suggests that a variety of stressful events significantly increase the risk. For example, schizophrenia usually appears during a time in life that many people find stressful—the transition from childhood to adulthood, when people deal with physical, emotional, and lifestyle changes (such as going away to college).

Prenatal stress—for example, if the mother has an infection while carrying the child—is also a risk factor. The baby of a pregnant woman who contracts influenza in the first trimester of pregnancy is seven times more likely to develop schizophrenia (Patterson, 2007). Several other maternal infections also increase chances that the fetus will develop schizophrenia one day (Brown, 2011). This correlation may be why people born in early spring are more likely to develop schizophrenia (Messias et al., 2004) (**Figure 16.9**): their mothers may be more likely to have gotten sick during the previous winter's flu season, at a fetal stage that is particularly vulnerable. Or perhaps some toxins, like pesticides, are more common at some times of the year than others. Likewise, if the mother and baby have incompatible blood types, or if the mother develops diabetes during pregnancy, or if for some reason there is a low birth weight (less than 5.5 pounds), the baby is more likely to develop schizophrenia (King et al., 2010). Birth complications that deprive the baby of oxygen also increase the probability of schizophrenia (Clarke et al., 2011). It is fascinating, and frightening, to think that events in the womb or at birth can affect an outcome 16 or 20 years later, when the schizophrenia appears. But please note, these are *statistical* trends across groups. For example, over 95% of people born in any particular month never have schizophrenia, so you can't use birthdays to predict whether any given *individual* will develop the disorder.

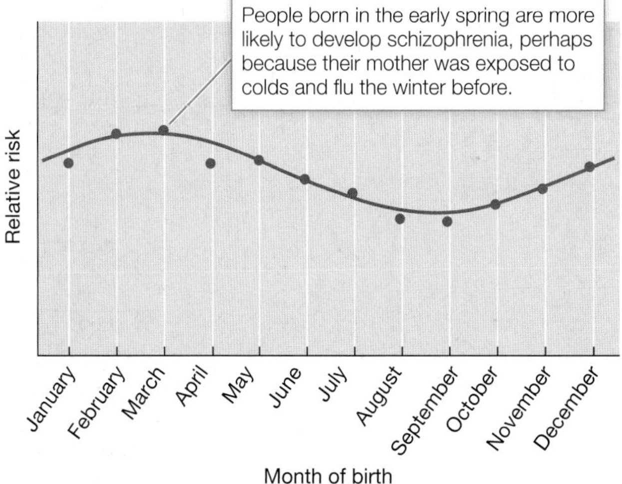
People born in the early spring are more likely to develop schizophrenia, perhaps because their mother was exposed to colds and flu the winter before.
Relative risk
January
February
March
April
May
June
July
August
September
October
November
December
Month of birth

Figure 16.9 Seasonal Birth Effect on Schizophrenia (After Mortensen et al., 1999.)

Another risk factor for schizophrenia seen in multiple studies is city life, as we'll consider next (**Figure 16.10**).

☑ Researchers at Work

The stress of city living

Figure 16.10 City Living Increases the Risk of Developing Schizophrenia (After Pedersen & Mortensen, 2001.)

■ **Question:** Does stress in early childhood increase the risk of developing schizophrenia?

■ **Hypothesis:** People growing up in the more stressful environment of big cities may be more likely to develop schizophrenia.

■ **Test:** Find a data set that lets you compare people from a relatively homogenous culture and genetic background, such as Denmark. Determine whether populations living in a big city (the capital), in smaller cities, or in rural areas differ in the proportion of people diagnosed with schizophrenia.

■ **Results:** People who are born and raised in a large city are twice as likely to develop schizophrenia as are people born and raised in a rural area.

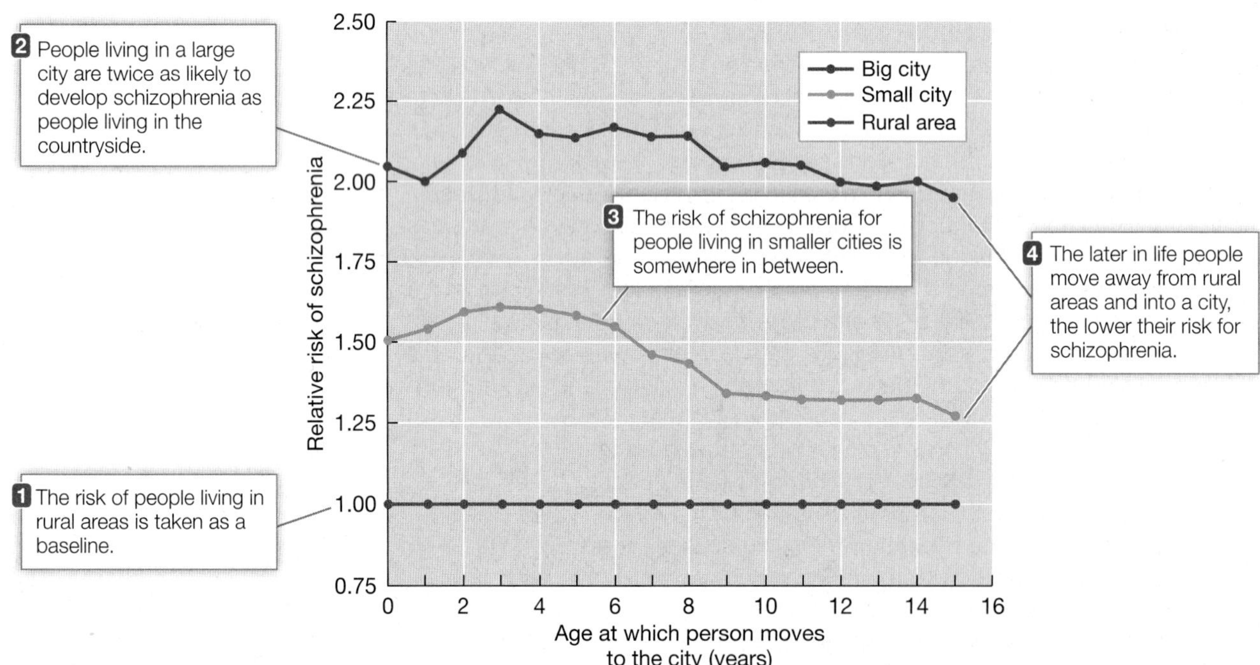
2 People living in a large city are twice as likely to develop schizophrenia as people living in the countryside.
1 The risk of people living in rural areas is taken as a baseline.
Relative risk of schizophrenia
2.50
2.25
2.00
1.75
1.50
1.25
1.00
0.75
Big city
Small city
Rural area
3 The risk of schizophrenia for people living in smaller cities is somewhere in between.
4 The later in life people move away from rural areas and into a city, the lower their risk for schizophrenia.
0
2
4
6
8
10
12
14
16
Age at which person moves to the city (years)

■ **Conclusion:** Some aspect of city living increases the probability that a person will develop schizophrenia (Pedersen & Mortensen, 2001).

It's interesting that the earlier in life people move to the city, the greater their risk of developing schizophrenia. Later studies have shown that children who move from the city to the country have a *reduced* risk of developing schizophrenia (van Os et al., 2010). We don't know what it is about living in a city that makes schizophrenia more likely to develop. Pollutants, greater exposure to minor diseases, crowded conditions, tense social interactions—all of these could be considered stressful.

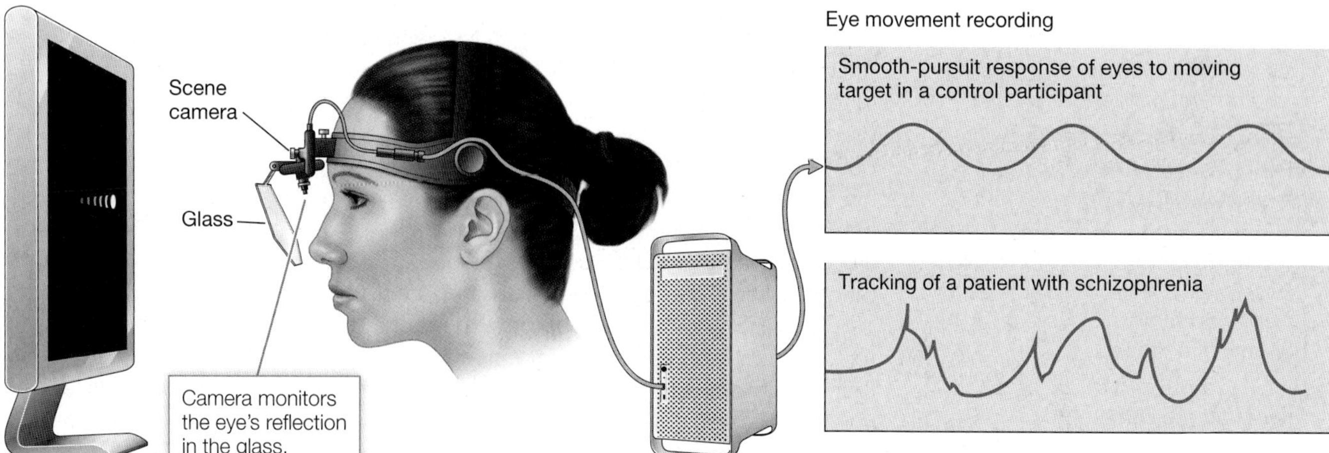

Figure 16.11 **Eye Tracking in Patients with Schizophrenia versus Control Participants** Patients with schizophrenia have greater difficulty making smooth-pursuit movements with their eyes than do control participants. Eye movement recordings indicate that the eyes of people who suffer from schizophrenia move in jerks and fits rather than smoothly tracking the moving object.

Studies of eye movements offer another promising way to identify people at risk for schizophrenia. When asked to keep their eyes on a moving object, people with schizophrenia often have difficulty making smooth eye movements, which can be recorded on a computer screen (Stuve et al., 1997). Instead, they show rapid, jerky eye movements (**Figure 16.11**), and no one understands why. We'll revisit the idea of tracking eye movements to identify people at risk for schizophrenia in The Cutting Edge at the end of this chapter.

For all these reasons, the modern view is that schizophrenia is caused by the interaction of genetic factors and stress. Each life stage has its own specific features that increase vulnerability to schizophrenia: infections before birth, complications at delivery, urban living in childhood, social stress in adolescence and adulthood (Powell, 2010). From this perspective, the emergence of schizophrenia depends on whether a person who is genetically susceptible to schizophrenia is subjected to environmental stressors. The models of genes interacting with environmental stressors also suggest that we may someday be able to identify a child at risk and reduce stress to avoid schizophrenia. New biological aids, such as functional brain imaging and genetic tools, might help us identify and understand the at-risk child early in life, when interventions to reduce stress might prevent schizophrenia later in life.

lobotomy The surgical separation of a portion of the frontal lobes from the rest of the brain.

Antipsychotic medications revolutionized the treatment of schizophrenia

Until the 1930s, there were no effective treatments for schizophrenia. Because patients were often unable to take care of themselves, they were placed in caregiving institutions. In many cases, the health and welfare of patients in these (poorly funded) institutions were badly neglected, leading to recurrent scandals. So perhaps it was in desperation that psychiatrists turned to **lobotomy**, the surgical separation of a portion of the frontal lobes from the rest of the brain, as a treatment for schizophrenia (**Figure 16.12**). Certainly there was little scientific evidence to think the surgery would be effective. But early practitioners reported nearly miraculous recoveries that, in retrospect, must be regarded as wishful thinking on the part of the physicians. The surgery may well have made the patients easier to handle, but they were rarely able to leave the mental institution. Used for almost any mental disorder, not just schizophrenia, lobotomies were performed on some 40,000 people in the United States alone (Kopell et al., 2005). The people given lobotomies came from all classes—poor people in state institutions and rich people in private clinics.

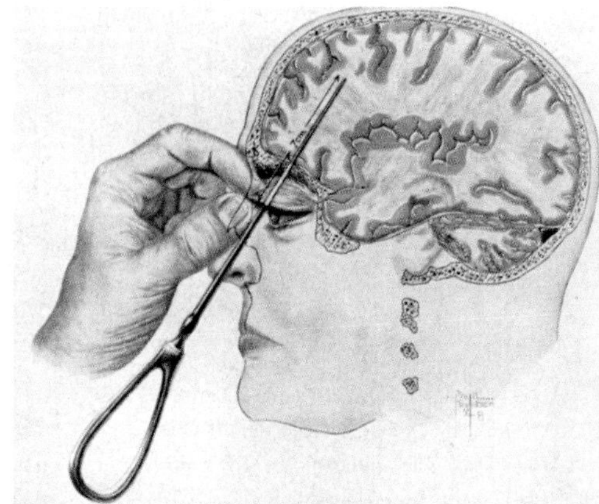

Figure 16.12 **Transorbital Lobotomy** By poking a hole in the skull just over each eye, physicians could damage the frontal lobes without having to cut any skin or leave stitches.

chlorpromazine The first drug that was effective in treating the positive symptoms of schizophrenia.

neuroleptics Antipsychotic drugs that traditionally function by blocking postsynaptic dopamine receptors.

dopamine hypothesis The hypothesis that people with schizophrenia suffer from an excess of either dopamine release or dopamine receptors.

typical neuroleptics Antipsychotic drugs that are D_2 receptor antagonists.

tardive dyskinesia A motor side effect of some neuroleptics that is characterized by involuntary movements, typically of the tongue, or difficulty walking, which may be debilitating.

atypical neuroleptics Antipsychotic drugs that don't have the selective high affinity for dopamine receptors but block other types of receptors, such as certain serotonin receptors.

By the 1950s, more and more physicians were skeptical that lobotomy was effective for any disorder, and a drug discovered in 1954—**chlorpromazine** (trade name Thorazine)—quickly replaced lobotomy as a treatment for schizophrenia. Chlorpromazine was originally developed as an anesthetic (Ban, 2007) but was accidentally observed to reduce the positive symptoms of schizophrenia, including auditory hallucinations, delusions, and disordered thinking. Ironically, the drug was first promoted as "a lobotomy in a bottle," because at the time that was viewed as a good thing! But chlorpromazine was much better than a lobotomy, not only because drug treatment is reversible while lobotomy is not, but because, unlike lobotomy, the drug actually worked. In fact, the symptoms of schizophrenia that responded to chlorpromazine were exactly those that kept people in mental institutions. The introduction of chlorpromazine truly revolutionized psychiatry, relieving symptoms for millions of sufferers and freeing them from long-term beds in psychiatric hospitals.

Poor Howard Dully, whom we met at the start of the chapter, was very unlucky to run into a physician still performing lobotomies as late as 1960 (**Figure 16.13**). Why didn't Dr. Freeman try giving Howard chlorpromazine? For one thing, the drug helps only positive symptoms, and Howard didn't have any of those—he wasn't hearing voices, experiencing delusions, or suffering disordered thinking at school. For that matter, there's little reason to think the boy had any symptoms of schizophrenia (six psychiatrists had declared him "normal"). Unfortunately for Howard, his stepmother just happened upon the wrong physician at the wrong time.

Chlorpromazine and other *antipsychotic* drugs, known as **neuroleptics**, that came along afterward were eventually found to share a specific action: they block postsynaptic dopamine receptors, particularly dopamine D_2 receptors. Because all of the earliest antipsychotic drugs blocked dopamine D_2 receptors, researchers proposed the **dopamine hypothesis**: that people with schizophrenia suffer from an excess of either dopamine release or dopamine receptors.

All of the various antipsychotic drugs that are now classified as **typical neuroleptics** are D_2 receptor antagonists. In fact, the clinically effective dose of the typical neuroleptic can be predicted from its affinity for D_2 receptors, as the dopamine hypothesis would predict (Castle et al., 2013; Seeman & Tallerico, 1998). For example, haloperidol, discovered a few years after chlorpromazine, has a greater affinity for D_2 receptors and quickly became the more widely used drug. Over the years, other clinical and experimental findings have bolstered the dopamine hypothesis. For example, treating patients who suffer from Parkinson's disease with L-dopa (the metabolic precursor of dopamine) may induce schizophrenia-like symptoms, presumably by boosting the synaptic availability of dopamine.

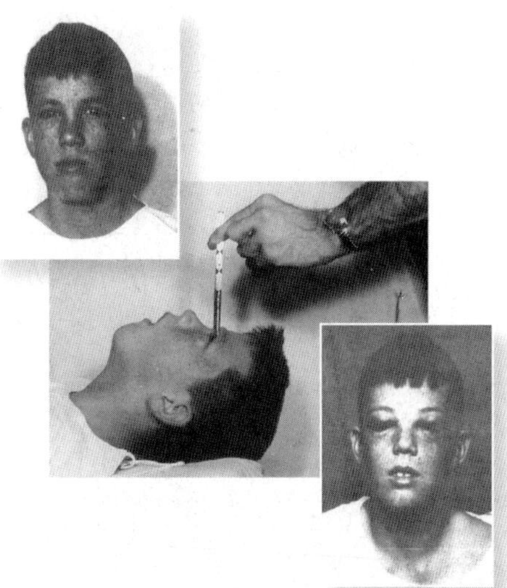

Figure 16.13 Twelve-Year-Old Howard Dully before, during, and after His Transorbital Lobotomy The swelling around his eyes eventually went away, but Howard would spend the next four decades in various mental institutions. These photographs appear in Mr. Dully's memoir, *My Lobotomy*.

Although some evidence supports the dopamine hypothesis of schizophrenia, there are also several problems with the hypothesis (Alpert & Friedhoff, 1980). For example, there is no correspondence between the speed with which drugs block dopamine receptors (quite rapidly—within hours) and how long it takes for the symptoms to diminish (usually on the order of weeks). Thus schizophrenia is more complex than just hyperactive dopamine synapses. Another weakness of the dopamine model of schizophrenia is that some people with schizophrenia don't respond to dopamine antagonists at all (Osser et al., 2013).

The search for new neuroleptics to avoid debilitating motor side effects such as **tardive dyskinesia**—characterized by involuntary movements, typically of the tongue, or difficulty walking (**Figure 16.14**)—led to the development of drugs called **atypical neuroleptics**. These drugs generally don't have the selective high affinity for dopamine receptors that is the hallmark of the typical neuroleptics, and they feature high affinity for other types of receptors, for example, selectively blocking certain serotonin receptors.

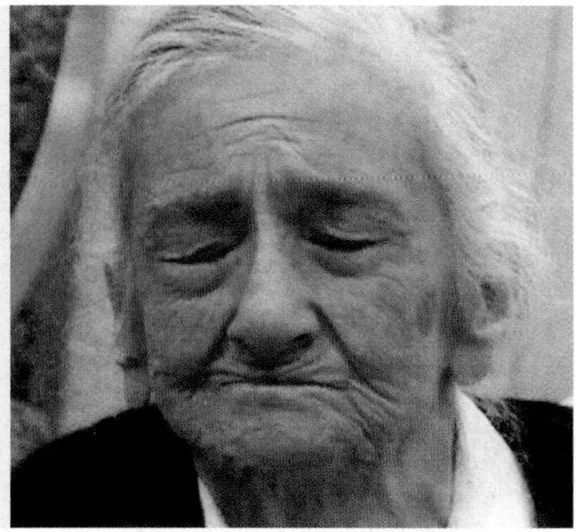

Figure 16.14 Tardive Dyskinesia This condition may include involuntary movements, often of the lower face. It can be caused by antipsychotic medications, and may persist even once the person has stopped taking the medicine.

Atypical neuroleptics are just as effective as the older generation of drugs for relieving the symptoms of schizophrenia. So if the problem is as simple as an overstimulation of dopamine receptors, why are the atypical neuroleptics effective? For example, some neuroleptics can *increase* dopamine release in frontal cortex (Hertel et al., 1999)—hardly what we would expect if excess dopaminergic activity causes schizophrenia. In fact, it seems that supplementing neuroleptic treatments with L-dopa (thereby increasing activity at synapses that use dopamine) actually helps reduce symptoms of schizophrenia (Jaskiw & Popli, 2004).

Until recently, almost all clinicians believed that atypical neuroleptics were more effective than typical antipsychotics for treating schizophrenia, especially for relieving negative symptoms. But a large British study comparing the outcome for patients who had been given the two types of drugs found no difference (Jones et al., 2006). Although the atypical neuroleptics are less likely than typical neuroleptics to cause side effects in motor function, they are more likely to cause weight gain (Sikich et al., 2008). So the overall outcome for quality of life appears similar for the two types of drugs (Heres et al., 2006), highlighting the need for better treatment options for people with schizophrenia.

Despite popular portrayals, most people who develop schizophrenia recover appreciably

Watching popular films and videos or reading popular fiction might give the impression that a person who develops schizophrenia will never recover. In fact, most people who develop schizophrenia do so as young adults, and then recover sufficiently that they get jobs, financially support themselves, and may even have a distinguished career (**Figure 16.15**). Why is there such a disconnect between reality and popular portrayals? Part of the answer is that, before the advent of neuroleptics, many people who developed schizophrenia were indeed likely to remain incapacitated for a long time. So despite the drawbacks and potential side effects of these drugs, they clearly have helped millions of people lead happier, more productive lives.

But even before neuroleptics were available, some people who had schizophrenic breakdowns as young adults later recovered (Bateson, 1962; Boltz, 1948). However, there was no systematic attempt to determine how many people with schizophrenia recovered. In the modern era after the arrival of antipsychotics, one follow-up 20 years after diagnosis found that about two-thirds of people who had been diagnosed with schizophrenia were considerably im-

Figure 16.15 Not So Beautiful Voices Mathematician John Nash's struggle with schizophrenia is depicted in the Academy Award–winning movie *A Beautiful Mind*. The movie portrays him having elaborate visual hallucinations, but in fact his hallucinations were exclusively auditory, consisting of taunting voices that fueled his paranoid thinking. Auditory hallucinations are common in schizophrenia; visual hallucinations are quite rare. Nash recovered from schizophrenia, stopped taking neuroleptics, and had a distinguished career as a professor at Princeton University.

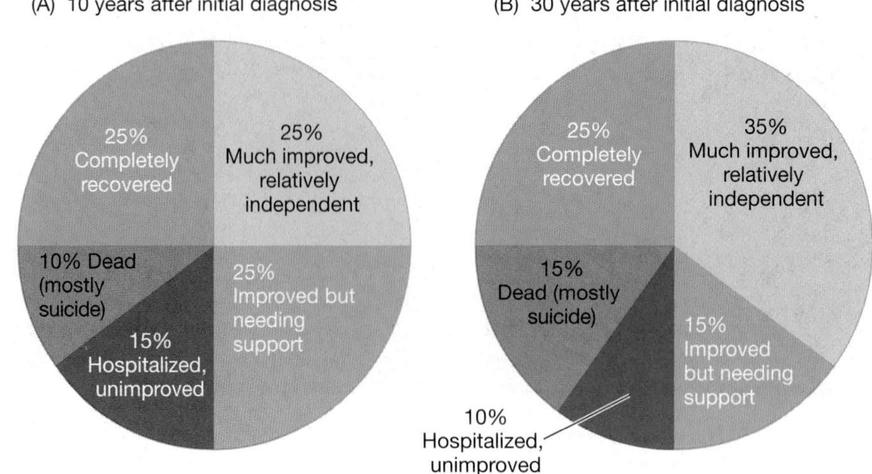

Figure 16.16 The Course of Schizophrenia

proved, and that about half of them (one-third of the original group) were "asymptomatic and living independently, had close relationships, were employed or otherwise productive citizens" (Harding et al., 1987). Interestingly, none of those who were completely recovered were taking antipsychotics (McGuire, 2000). So contrary to the impression that the media (and even some psychology textbooks) make, many people who have an episode of schizophrenia recover and have full, happy lives.

Those early follow-up studies have been confirmed many times. One widely respected guide for people with schizophrenia and their families (Torrey, 2006) summarizes the results of many different studies to offer the prospect presented in **Figure 16.16**. For example, one study reported that half the people with schizophrenia were working 7 years later, and about half of those employed people were symptom-free (Henry et al., 2010).

Several factors are associated with recovery from schizophrenia

When someone has a first episode of schizophrenia, several factors can help predict the likelihood of recovery. In general, the better the person was functioning prior to becoming ill, and the more suddenly his symptoms appeared, the more likely he is to recover (Rosen & Garety, 2005). Better outcome is also seen in people who are married, have more education, are older at the onset, and have close family and social networks.

Most clinicians agree that neuroleptics can be useful, especially in the first few weeks of an episode of schizophrenia, but there is less agreement about whether long-term use of the medication is beneficial, or worth the side effects. One study found that people diagnosed with schizophrenia who did not start taking antipsychotics were more likely to recover completely, but concluded that this was because these people were not as ill in the first place or had more resources, such as a supportive family, to help them recover (Harrow & Jobe, 2007).

Interestingly, people who develop schizophrenia are more likely to recover if they live in a more traditional, nonindustrialized nation than in an industrialized nation like the United States. When these statistics, gathered from the World Health Organization (WHO), were first reported (Sartorius et al., 1972), there was widespread skepticism, especially in the United States. How could people in poor countries, with hardly any doctors, possibly do better than Americans with their high standard of living, excellent health care, and effective drugs? But later follow-up studies came to the same conclusion (Jablensky et al., 1992; Leff et al., 1992). Skeptics nevertheless continued to probe the conclusion—perhaps there were differences in the criteria used to diagnose schizophrenia, or in judging recovery, or perhaps there were differences in the age or sex of the people sampled from different nations? But reanalysis of the data eliminated those possibilities (Hopper & Wanderling, 2000). More recent studies keep making the same point—if you become schizophrenic in a "developing" nation, you are twice as likely to recover than if you live in a "developed" nation (Myers, 2010).

Why do people recover more often in developing nations? One possibility is that, in developing nations, it is easier for people who have had an episode of schizophrenia to be reintegrated into society. If agriculture is the dominant way of earning a living, there's plenty of work that a recovered person can do to make a contribution and reenter society. In developed nations, where jobs are more technical and ongoing, people who have missed work for a month or more are unlikely to find their job still waiting for them. Even if they haven't been replaced, their employer may be leery of rehiring them.

One comparison supports the idea that reintegration into society is crucial for recovery from schizophrenia. The state of Vermont initiated a rehabilitation program for people with schizophrenia in the mid-1950s. The point of the program was to get the patients out of the hospital and back into the community. They were provided with community housing, social skills training, education, and job placements, as well as long-term follow-up visits. Twenty years later, these people were much more likely to be symptom-free and working than a closely matched set of patients in Maine, where a program had simply provided medication to stabilize the patients (DeSisto et al., 1995). In contrast, most of the recovered patients in Vermont had been off medication for years.

Bipolar disorder is more like schizophrenia than depression

Bipolar disorder is characterized by periods of depression alternating with periods of excessively expansive mood (or *mania*) that include sustained overactivity, talkativeness, strange grandiosity, and increased energy (**Figure 16.17**). The rate of alternation varies among individuals, with manic episodes that last for days and depressive episodes that typically last for weeks.

bipolar disorder A mental disorder characterized by periods of depression alternating with periods of excessively expansive mood.

(A) Manic phase

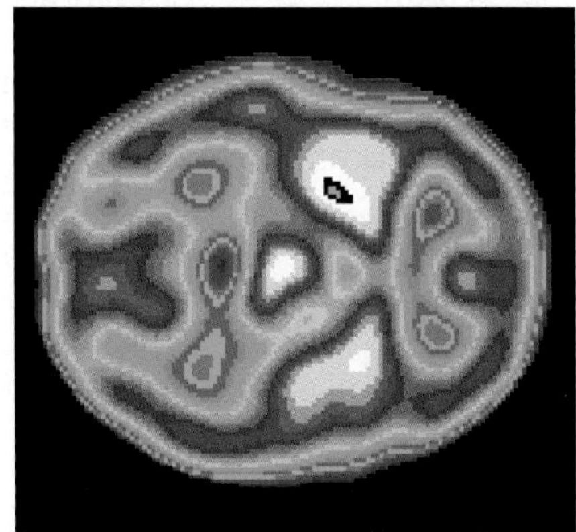

(B) Depressive phase

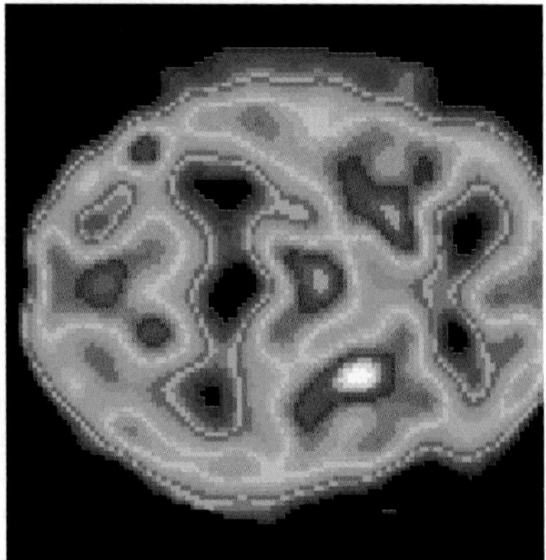

There are dramatic differences in brain activity between the manic (A) and depressive (B) phases of this person's bipolar disorder. White and red indicate the greatest brain activity, while blue indicates the lowest.

Figure 16.17 Functional Images of Bipolar Disorder (Courtesy of Dr. Robert G. Kohn, Brain SPECT, www.brainspect.com.)

Men and women are equally affected by bipolar disorder, and the age of onset is usually much earlier than for depression, typically before middle age. Bipolar disorder has a complex heritability: several different genes affect the probability of the disorder (Faraone et al., 2004; Green & Craddock, 2003; Smoller & Finn, 2003). The neural basis of bipolar disorder is not fully understood, but patients with bipolar disorder exhibit enlarged ventricles (Arnone et al., 2009), as is seen in schizophrenia (see Figures 16.7 and 16.8). The more manic episodes the person has experienced, the greater the ventricular enlargement, suggesting increasing brain tissue loss over time (Moorhead et al., 2007).

Because the changes in the brain seen in people with bipolar disorder are similar to those seen in people with schizophrenia, some researchers believe that bipolar disorder has more in common with schizophrenia than with depression. (This is one reason why old terms for bipolar disorder—*bipolar depression* and *manic depression*—have fallen out of favor.) For example, the self-aggrandizing ideas and extreme talkativeness of people in the manic phase of bipolar disorder ("The president called me this morning to thank me for my efforts") resemble the delusions of people who have schizophrenia. In addition, families in which some individuals have been diagnosed with bipolar disorder are more likely than other families to have individuals with a diagnosis of schizophrenia (Lichtenstein et al., 2009; van Os & Kapur, 2009). And although typical neuroleptics do not seem to help people with bipolar disorder, the newer, atypical neuroleptics may dampen the manic phase in people with bipolar disorder.

Most people suffering from bipolar disorder benefit from treatment with the element **lithium** (Howland, 2007; Kingsbury & Garver, 1998). The benefits of lithium for bipolar disorder were discovered by accident when it was intended as an inert control for another drug. In the 1940s, Australian psychiatrist John Cade speculated that people with bipolar disorder might suffer from a metabolic disorder that resulted in too much of the chemical *urea* in their urine. When he injected guinea pigs with human urine, he found that urine from people with bipolar disorder was indeed more toxic than urine from control participants. Was that because people with bipolar disorder had more urea in their urine? At the time, no one knew how to measure urea concentrations, so Cade began injecting guinea pigs with solutions of measured amounts of urea dissolved in water, to see if it would make the guinea pigs manic. When he had trouble getting the urea to dissolve in water, he accidentally found the beneficial effects of lithium, as we'll see next (**Figure 16.18**).

lithium A chemical element used for the treatment of bipolar disorder.

☑ Researchers at Work

The entirely accidental discovery of lithium therapy

Figure 16.18 Suprisingly Calm Guinea Pigs (After Cade, 1949.)

■ **Question:** Do people with bipolar disorder suffer from having too much urea in circulation?

■ **Hypothesis:** Injecting urea into guinea pigs will make them manic.

■ **Test:** Cade found that he could dissolve higher concentrations of urea into solution if he used a urea–lithium combination, lithium urate, rather than urea alone. Other guinea pigs got injections of lithium alone as a control group.

■ **Results:** Instead of the lithium urate making the guinea pigs manic, it calmed them. But in another surprise, the control injections of lithium alone were just as effective for calming the animals (Howland, 2007). Intrigued,

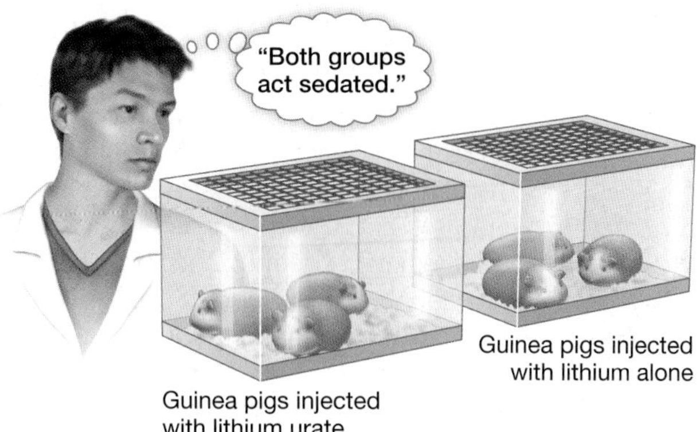

Cade took some lithium himself and, upon finding it harmless, tried giving it to patients with bipolar disorder (Cade, 1949). Almost all of the patients showed a remarkable recovery, and many who had been institutionalized for years could finally return home.

■ **Conclusion:** Lithium alone calms guinea pigs and relieves symptoms of bipolar disorder in humans. Note that this conclusion has nothing to do with the original question. This experiment demonstrates the importance of having a good control group. If Cade had not injected some guinea pigs with lithium alone, he might have wrongly concluded that urea has a calming effect.

Cade reported his remarkable results in an Australian medical journal in 1949, pointing out that lithium treatment would be preferred over lobotomies, which were being performed on people with bipolar disorder. Physicians in most of the world promptly began prescribing lithium to their patients, finding it very effective (Shorter, 2009). Unfortunately, that same year the United States had banned the addition of lithium to food and drinks (for example, lithium was an important ingredient in 7UP soda until 1950) because of toxic side effects, which in high concentrations can cause death. Lithium was not approved for the treatment of bipolar disorder in the United States until more than 20 years after Cade's publication.

The mechanism of action of lithium is not understood, but it has wide-ranging effects on the brain (Rowe & Chuang, 2004; Yin et al., 2006). Lithium occurs naturally in low levels in drinking water, and there's evidence that communities with more lithium in their water have a lower incidence of depression and suicide (Sugawara et al., 2013; Vita et al., 2014), which is consistent with the element affecting mood. Because there is real danger of a lithium overdose, care must be taken to avoid toxic side effects. Nevertheless, well-managed lithium treatment produces marked relief for many patients and even has been reported to increase the volume of gray matter in their brains (Moore et al., 2000). Supplementing lithium treatment with antidepressants is no more effective than using lithium alone (Sachs et al., 2007), which is further evidence that bipolar disorder is distinct from depression.

Despite lithium's effectiveness, some people with bipolar disorder stop taking the medication. One hypothesis is that the patient "misses" the often exhilarating manic episodes that are blocked by lithium. Unfortunately, however, without medication the depressive episodes return as well. Other drug treatments are available. As in unipolar depression, it appears that transcranial magnetic stimulation may provide a nonpharmacological treatment alternative in difficult cases of bipolar disorder (Michael & Erfurth, 2004). Furthermore, in some cases psychotherapy can be effective (Hollon et al., 2002) and perhaps can be beneficially combined with other forms of treatment.

7UP Keeps Me Mellow? Until 1950, 7UP contained lithium, which may have had a calming effect in some people.

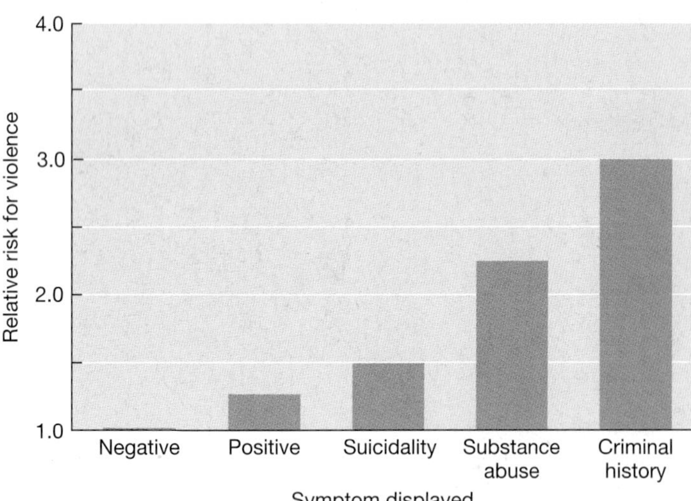

Figure 16.19 Risk Factors for Violence in Schizophrenia The presence of negative symptoms in schizophrenia did not predict the person would be any more likely to become violent than the general population. In contrast, a person with schizophrenia who had been violent in the past was three times more likely than the general population to be violent in the future. But note that, since the percentage of the general population who display violence is very low, the vast majority of people who have schizophrenia, even those who were violent in the past, are unlikely to be violent in the future. (After Witt et al., 2013.)

Are people with schizophrenia or bipolar disorder dangerous?

From time to time the media bombard us with news of a horrific act of violence, often with multiple victims, acts that are especially chilling because the targets seem to have been picked at random. The victims might be moviegoers at a late-night premiere, or people who happen to attend a "town hall meeting" with a local legislator. Usually the perpetrator is quickly found, and often he (it is usually a male) is found to be suffering from a mental condition such as schizophrenia. His choice of victims, which might seem logical in light of his delusions, is indeed arbitrary—it might have been any one of us. These tragic events unfold often enough that we all have the image of a person with a mental disorder who might suddenly turn violent. Indeed, in popular fiction, movies, and television, the mentally ill villain capable of bloodthirsty violence is a convenient shortcut that writers use to seize our attention. But are people with mental disorders dangerous in real life?

Compared with people chosen at random from the general population, people with schizophrenia, or people with bipolar disorder who are in a manic phase, are indeed more likely to display violent behavior (Volavka, 2013). But the *vast majority* of people with schizophrenia or bipolar disorder never behave violently. And because only about 1% of the population has schizophrenia, these people are responsible for only a tiny fraction of violent crimes (Walsh et al., 2002). In fact, because people with schizophrenia and bipolar disorder are at increased risk for suicide, they are much more likely to hurt themselves than someone else. The best predictor of whether a person with schizophrenia will become violent in the future is whether he has been violent in the past. If so, then that person is about three times more likely than a person chosen at random to be violent in the future (**Figure 16.19**). But let's put this in perspective. In one study, only 2% of people chosen at random were found to have committed a violent crime, while 8% of people with schizophrenia had done so, a fourfold difference (Wallace et al., 2004). But note that this indicates that *92% of people with schizophrenia had not committed a violent act.* This suggests that nine out of ten people with schizophrenia don't become violent.

In those few cases when a person with schizophrenia does become violent, it is usually because he stopped treatment (psychological treatment or medication that may have side effects) or has been abusing drugs (Witt et al., 2013). The basic pattern is that the person breaks some law, is arrested, is hospitalized and given treatment so he can function, but upon release stops seeing a therapist or taking medication (or self-medicates with illegal drugs or alcohol), only to start the cycle over again. Some researchers have urged that this small minority of people with schizophrenia who have been violent in the past should be carefully monitored, to be sure that they are getting treatment and avoiding drug abuse (Torrey, 2011). This proposal for so-called outpatient commitment raises difficult questions about impinging on the rights of individuals—should we force some people to get a monthly injection of an antischizophrenia drug? In 1999, the state of New York began requiring psychiatric patients who have broken the law to see caseworkers, who try to ensure that the patient continues therapy and takes prescribed medication. While paying for the caseworkers and therapy has been expensive, a 10-year follow-up found that total costs to the mental health care system and Medicaid for taking care of these patients were cut in half (Swanson et al., 2013). Perhaps more important, the patients were much less likely to commit a crime.

Unfortunately, there appears to be a cultural influence that may predispose people with schizophrenia in the United States to become violent. In America, people who hear voices that aren't really there often report that these voices are urging them to be violent ("Take their eyes out with a fork!"; "Why don't you end your life?"). In contrast, the hallucinated voices heard by people in India are much more likely to urge them to do some domestic task ("Go to the kitchen, prepare food") or focus on sex, as when a male voice screams vulgar words (Luhrmann, 2013). It's hard to understand these differences in the urgings of hallucinated voices in the two different countries unless they reflect the cultural surroundings. It is possible that growing up in a culture rich in the portrayal of violence in books, movies, television, and video games makes a person who develops schizophrenia more likely to imagine violent demands.

Because dramatic events are so memorable, they can have an exaggerated effect on our thinking and expectations about the future (the *availability heuristic* we discussed in Section 10.3). Rare and isolated real-life tragedies perpetrated by people with schizophrenia or bipolar disorder are emphasized even more graphically in fictional portrayals. Thus when we encounter someone with a mental disorder, the idea that he might become dangerous quickly comes to mind. We may become anxious and afraid, shunning the person rather than trying to direct him to seek help. Unfortunately, because many people with schizophrenia, especially those who are not getting treatment, become homeless, the stigma that they might be violent makes it even less likely that they will get treatment in the future. While of course we must all exercise caution in looking after ourselves, if we also remember that the vast majority of people with schizophrenia or bipolar disorder pose absolutely no threat to our safety, perhaps it will be easier for us to help them.

The Cutting Edge

Scanning for Schizophrenia Risk

The modern view of schizophrenia is that no inherited gene inevitably leads to the condition. Rather, some people inherit a susceptibility to schizophrenia that may be triggered by stress, especially in the transition from adolescence to adulthood. Thus there is a lot of interest in finding an **endophenotype**: a group of behavioral or physical characteristics that accompany an inherited susceptibility to a particular disorder.

We noted earlier that people with schizophrenia have difficulty making smooth eye movements. One research group devised a series of eye-tracking tasks. The participants' eye movements were monitored while they performed three tasks: (1) watching a cursor on a computer screen travel a complex weaving pathway (smooth pursuit), (2) freely viewing a series of photographs, and (3) trying to fix their gaze on one point while distracting stimuli appeared elsewhere on the screen. A set of 88 people with schizophrenia and 88 control participants performed the tasks, and as in previous studies, people with schizophrenia had a harder time controlling their eye movements.

Then the researchers used mathematical models based on the performance of the participants to determine whether some combination of measures would discriminate between those who did and those who did not have schizophrenia. They found one model that would indeed correctly classify every participant. But could this be a simple matter of picking up on the particular patterns of those particular participants? Perhaps some mathematical model could correctly discriminate between people randomly assigned to two groups. The big question was whether the model based on the training

endophenotype A group of behavioral or physical characteristics that accompany an inherited susceptibility to a particular disorder.

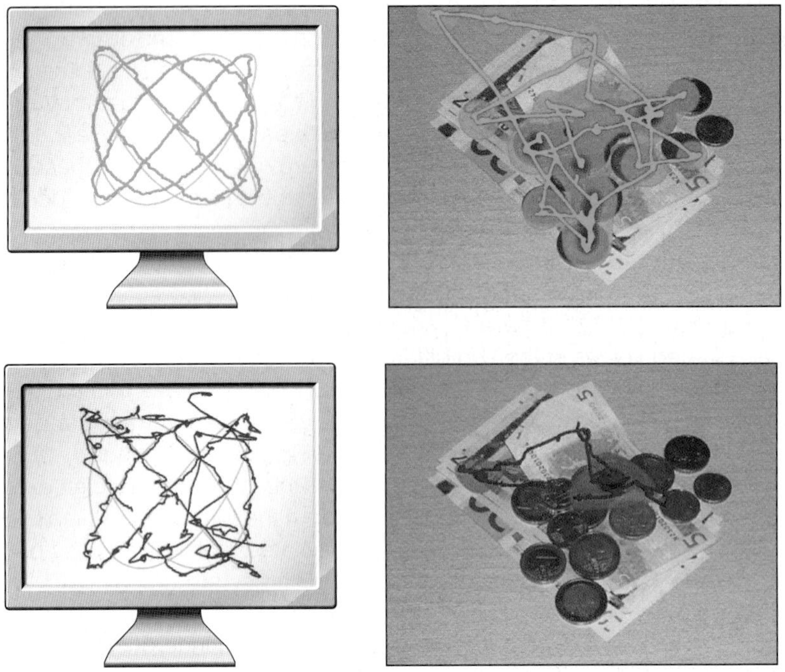

Smooth pursuit of moving cursor

Free viewing of a photograph

Control participants

People diagnosed with schizophrenia

Figure 16.20 Scanning for Schizophrenia People who have been diagnosed with schizophrenia have a more difficult time visually tracking moving objects than control participants do. Can this characteristic be used to identify people at risk of developing schizophrenia? (After Benson et al., 2012, courtesy of Philip Benson.)

set could correctly discriminate between people with and people without a diagnosis of schizophrenia in *another* set of participants. In fact, from a new data set of 298 total cases, the model identified those who had received a diagnosis of schizophrenia with 88% accuracy (Benson et al., 2012). When the researchers fine-tuned their mathematical model further, it discriminated the cases with 98% accuracy! No people diagnosed with schizophrenia were misclassified by the model. Five control participants showed abnormalities, but you have to wonder whether they were, in fact, at risk for schizophrenia. The differences in eye movement (**Figure 16.20**) were seen in both sexes and were not due to differences in whether the patients were in remission, or whether they were receiving antipsychotics, or any other factor examined.

If confirmed, this test could have a big impact on the diagnosis of schizophrenia, as the test itself takes only a few minutes and can be administered by a person who has had only a few hours of training. Thus it may one day be possible to quickly screen lots of people and see whether the test accurately predicts who might develop schizophrenia, and then to test interventions to avert the condition. We already know a key component of any intervention—try to buffer the person from physiological or psychological stress, especially in childhood. For example, CBT directed toward problem solving—helping clients remain integrated in their family and job and combating delusions that arise—has been shown to reduce the incidence of psychosis in people at risk for schizophrenia (Morrison et al., 2004). Of course, there are problems with any effort to screen lots of people to find those at risk for schizophrenia. For example, there is the thorny ethical issue of who should be permitted access to this information about a person.

16.4 SUMMARY

- *Schizophrenia* is characterized by *positive symptoms* such as auditory hallucinations and *delusions*, and *negative symptoms* such as blunted emotions and disordered thinking.
- People with schizophrenia tend to have enlarged brain ventricles, indicating some loss of surrounding brain tissue.
- There is a strong genetic contribution to schizophrenia, which can be viewed as a vulnerability to stress, especially early in life. For example, infections before birth, complications in the birth process, and growing up in a dense urban environment all increase the probability of developing schizophrenia.
- Antipsychotic drugs, including *typical neuroleptics* like *chlorpromazine*, which block D_2 dopamine receptors, and *atypical neuroleptics*, tend to reduce the positive symptoms of schizophrenia and have allowed many people to return to their family and community.
- Despite media portrayals, many people who develop schizophrenia recover to lead happy, productive lives, sometimes without continuing medication.
- *Bipolar disorder*, alternating periods of mania followed by depression, is poorly understood but usually responds well to treatment with *lithium*, for reasons no one understands.
- While people suffering the delusions of schizophrenia or bipolar disorder are more likely to be violent than the general population, the vast majority, over 90%, are never violent. These individuals are much more likely to hurt themselves than anyone else, as they are at risk for suicide.

REVIEW QUESTIONS

1. What are the positive and negative symptoms often seen in schizophrenia?
2. What is the major structural difference seen in the brains of people with schizophrenia compared with control participants?
3. What is the modern understanding of the role of genes in schizophrenia?
4. What medications are typically used to treat people with schizophrenia? Bipolar disorder?
5. What are the side effects of medications used to treat schizophrenia and bipolar disorder?

Food for Thought

Should people with schizophrenia who have been violent be required to take neuroleptics? How would you decide who should, or should not, be required to take such drugs?

Clinical Psychology

"My Lobotomy"

Howard Dully's mother died when he was 4, and a few years later his father married a woman named Lucille. For several reasons, Howard and Lucille did not get along. Howard was rebellious in the way that many kids are—sassing back, breaking curfew, skipping out on church. But Howard was never violent with his stepmother or anyone else. He sometimes got in trouble at school, for not paying attention in class or smoking in the bathroom, but not for fighting or damaging school property. Howard's grades were erratic—an A on a test one day, an F on a test the next—but he was not flunking out.

Still, Lucille, frustrated with a headstrong boy in her house, took Howard to six different psychiatrists to find out "what was wrong with him." All concluded that his behavior was normal. But doctor number seven, the famous Walter Freeman, diagnosed the boy as schizophrenic. In 1960, Freeman gave 12-year-old Howard a lobotomy. First Freeman sedated the boy by giving him electroshocks—jolts of electricity across the skull that induce a seizure and render the patient unconscious. Then he lifted the boy's upper eyelids and used a hammer on an ice pick–like device to punch holes in the skull above each eye. He then inserted a device to cut off some of Howard's prefrontal cortex from the rest of his brain. Freeman was an old hand at the procedure, having lobotomized thousands of people, so the procedure took only 10 minutes. The total hospital charge was $200.

Family members said Howard acted like a zombie for several days, and then he was so lethargic and disinterested in the events around him that, according to Freeman's notes, they called Howard "lazy, stupid, dummy, and so on." One aunt said he acted like he was permanently tranquilized. And yet Lucille *still* wanted Howard out of her house. Soon Howard was institutionalized, and he would spend decades in various mental hospitals. Not until he was 50 was Howard able to find out what had happened to him as a child, a journey he recounts movingly in his memoir, *My Lobotomy*.

Think Like a Psychologist:

Principles in Action

Whenever we encounter any interesting behavior we should consider the four principles. Here are some ways that the four principles relate to our opening story about Howard.

MACHINE

The mind is a product of a physical machine, the brain.

When Dr. Freeman disconnected parts of the prefrontal cortex from the rest of Howard's brain, the boy acted like a zombie for days. The brain damage immediately affected his behavior and probably had a lifelong effect on Howard's thinking.

UNCONSCIOUS

We are consciously aware of only a small part of our mental activity.

Dr. Freeman rendered Howard unconscious by using electroconvulsive shock, which also left Howard with no recall of what had happened in the days before and after the procedure. Howard reports that for decades afterward, he was angry without knowing why, becoming an alcoholic and homeless.

SOCIAL

We constantly modify our behavior, beliefs, and attitudes according to what we perceive about the people around us.

His stepmother's difficulty getting along with Howard resulted in the surgery. If her social skills had been better, Howard's life might have been quite different. Years afterward, Howard had a hard time getting along with other people or staying employed.

EXPERIENCE

Our experiences physically alter the structure and function of the brain.

Eventually, Howard was able to sober up, earn a college degree, get a job as a bus driver, and track down his medical records to see what had happened. Howard reports that the experience of finally learning what happened and talking to other people about his life has brought comfort. "I know my lobotomy didn't touch my soul. For the first time I feel no shame. I am, at last, at peace" (Dully, 2005).

KEY TERMS

agoraphobia, 702
antisocial personality disorder (ASPD), 710
anxiety disorders, 700
anxiolytics, 701
atypical neuroleptics, 720
autism spectrum disorder (ASD), 699
avoidant personality disorder, 710
benzodiazepines, 701
bipolar disorder, 723
borderline personality disorder, 709
chlorpromazine, 720
clinical significance, 698
cognitive behavioral therapy (CBT), 701
co-morbid, 703
delusions, 713
depression, 704
dissociative identity disorderDID, 712
dissociative thinking, 713
dopamine hypothesis, 720
electroconvulsive shock therapy (ECT), 706
endophenotype, 727
generalized anxiety disorder (GAD), 700
lithium, 724
lobotomy, 719
monoamine hypothesis, 706
monoamine oxidase (MAO), 706
narcissistic personality disorder, 709
negative symptoms, 714
neuroleptics, 720
obsessive-compulsive disorder (OCD), 702
obsessive-compulsive personality disorder (OCPD), 708
panic disorder, 700
personality disorders, 708
phobia, 701
positive symptoms, 714
reliability, 697
schizophrenia, 714
schizotypal personality disorder, 708
seasonal affective disorderSAD, 705
selective serotonin reuptake inhibitors (SSRIs), 707
standardization, 695
substance use disorder, 696
systematic desensitization, 702
tardive dyskinesia, 720
tricyclics, 706
typical neuroleptics, 720
validity, 697

QUIZ YOURSELF

1. The *DSM* system acknowledges that the frequency and severity of symptoms represent a ________, from low to high or a range of severity.
   a. continuum
   b. diagnosis
   c. significant difference
   d. dichotomy
2. Which of the following is not part of the cycle that cognitive behavioral therapy aims to break?
   a. Behavior
   b. Neurotransmitters
   c. Mood
   d. Thoughts
3. Bob feels he must touch the doorbell three times before he leaves the house. When he forgets, he goes home to do it even if it angers his boss. This touching of the doorbell is a(n)
   a. obsession.
   b. phobia.
   c. compulsion.
   d. symptom of depression.
4. A *DSM-5* diagnosis of a personality disorder has two requirements regarding age. The first is that the diagnosis cannot be made prior to age ________. The second is that relevant behaviors arose ________.
   a. 18; before adulthood
   b. 21; in infancy
   c. 12; earlier in childhood
   d. 25; during adolescence
5. If you become schizophrenic in a "developing" nation, you are ________ to recover than if you live in a "developed" nation.
   a. 50% more likely
   b. 20% more likely
   c. equally likely
   d. twice as likely
6. There are two major issues in evaluation of any psychology test or classification system. ________ is the extent to which the test or process identifies a characteristic or disorder that really exists. ________ is the extent to which different clinicians would reach the same diagnois for any patient with a particular set of symptoms.
7. ________ disorders involve apprehensive and fearful feelings that are overwhelming and interfere with daily life.
8. ________ personality disorder is characterized by excessive self-importance and lack of empathy. ________ personality disorder is also characterized by lack of empathy, but includes disregard for other people's rights.
9. ________, ________, and ________ are each effective treatments for depression. However, the most effective treatment would be a combination of all three.
10. ________ is the surgical separation of a portion of the frontal lobes from the rest of the brain, a surgery which was used as a treatment for schizophrenia before the use of the drug chlorpromazine.

1. a, 2. b, 3. c, 4. a, 5. d, 6. Validity; reliability 7. Anxiety, 8. Narcissistic; antisocial, 9. SSRI's; CBT; exercise, 10. Lobotomy

Answers to Review Questions

Chapter One

Section 1.1

1. Why did early humans need to pay careful attention to the behavior of others?

   Groups were better able to find food, notice predators, and provide protection. Early humans were better able to use the group if they paid attention to and remembered individual personalities and whether they'd been helpful or hurtful in the past.

2. What were the views of Plato and Descartes about the reliability of our senses for understanding the world?

   Plato was skeptical about the senses, which led him to rely, whenever possible, on logic and reasoning rather than observations alone, since they can be misleading. Descartes strove for a foundation of certain knowledge so he could build a system of knowing about reality that was not reliant on our fallible senses.

3. What does the phrase *tabula rasa* mean, and what philosopher is associated with applying this notion to the human mind?

   Tabula rasa means "blank slate." Philosopher John Locke believed that the mind of newborn babies was a blank slate that learns through the various senses what the world is like and how to behave.

4. What was Charles Darwin's contribution to the science of psychology?

   Darwin's chief contribution to the science of psychology was his book *The Expression of the Emotions in Man and Animals* (1872), in which he argued that all human behaviors, including our emotional behaviors, must have had beginnings in earlier ancestors.

Section 1.2

1. From psychology's beginnings, what were the three major schools of thought before the "cognitive revolution"? Who were some leaders of each school of thought?

   The first school after the beginnings of psychology as a field was the structuralist school, which used introspection to try to discover the various parts of the mind. Wilhelm Wundt and Edward Titchener were leaders of this school. The second major school of psychology was functionalism, the school of thought emphasizing the adaptive function of behavior as well as the careful measurement of the behavior of people and other animals. Two leaders in the functionalist school were William James and G. Stanley Hall. The third school, behaviorism, further emphasized the careful measurement of behavior, specifically when organisms are learning, and rejected the study of any mental phenomena, like emotions and consciousness, that could not be directly observed. This school was led by John B. Watson and B. F. Skinner.

2. In what ways do behaviorists and cognitive psychologists regard organisms as a "black box"? How did the arrival of computers affect the perspectives of cognitive psychologists?

   Behaviorists, such as Skinner, considered only what happened around an individual, and how that environment led to changes in his or her behavior, which was sometimes characterized as treating the individual as a "black box." Their concern was with what stimuli went in, and what behavior came out, not what was inside the organism itself. They felt the interior of the box was the concern of "brain science," not psychology. Cognitive psychologists study internal mental processes, specifically how we acquire and process information to gain knowledge, using an approach that involves gaining understanding of how this black box works by carefully varying inputs and monitoring outputs, without actually opening the box itself.

Cognitive psychologists saw computers to be also like a "black box," with information going in, being processed by the computer, then being sent out. Since they could understand how man-made computers work, it gave them hope that they could understand how the human mind works to also take in information, process it, and then produce behavior. Computers gave them an everyday confirmation that by varying the input and carefully noting the output, it was possible to understand how the program was operating inside the black box itself. If that black box happened to be the human brain, using the same approach would reveal how the mind works.

3. Who were some of the women who, despite many societal obstacles, managed to make important contributions to the early days of psychology?

   Mary Floyd Washburn was an early leader in the study of animal behavior, and she wrote the groundbreaking book *The Animal Mind*. The first woman president of the APA was Mary Whiton Calkins. Mary Cover Jones was inspired by the work of the behaviorist John B. Watson to develop a technique of treating phobias. Cover Jones also made contributions to developmental psychology.

Section 1.3

1. What are some of the persistent myths of psychology?

   Persistent myths in psychology include the following:

   - Sigmund Freud was a great pioneer in psychology who discovered the unconscious.
   - Scientific ability can be objectively assessed, so the best applicants get jobs in the lab.
   - We only use 10% of our brain.
   - Heritable traits, such as mental disorders and IQ, cannot be altered by experience.
   - Newborn babies can only focus their vision on objects that are nearby.
   - We use red, blue, and green detectors in our eye to distinguish colors.
   - Hypnosis is a fundamentally different state of consciousness that can be used to help recover memories.
   - A baby named Little Albert grew up to have phobias about furry objects.
   - People with amnesia don't remember their own name or recognize their family.
   - Subliminal messages can get you to buy things you wouldn't have bought.
   - Having kids listen to Mozart will make them smarter.
   - Some people choose to have a homosexual orientation.
   - The polygraph test can accurately detect when someone is lying.
   - Astrological signs provide a hint of a person's personality.
   - Many people heard and/or saw a woman named Kitty Genovese being murdered, but none of them tried to help her.
   - There is more crime and craziness around the full moon.
   - People who become schizophrenic never recover.
   - Taking introductory psychology is a waste of time because "all they teach you is stuff everybody already knows."

2. What four principles of psychology will be emphasized in this book (hint: MUSE)?

   The four principles of psychology that will be emphasized are these:

   a. The mind is a product of a physical machine, the brain.
   b. We are consciously aware of only a small part of our mental activity.
   c. We constantly modify our behavior, beliefs, and attitudes according to what we perceive about the people around us.
   d. Experience physically alters the structure and function of the brain.

3. Can you relate each of the four principles to some past behavior of your own? Or of someone you know?

   Answers to this question will be individual but should parallel the application of the four principles to Michael Brown's death.

Chapter Two

Section 2.1

1. Describe the major types of descriptive methods, identifying the strengths and concerns of each.

   The three methods used in descriptive studies are naturalistic observation, case studies, and surveys. Naturalistic observation involves describing and cataloging behavior of a species in its natural environment. Care must be taken to avoid having the presence of the observer affect the behavior and to ensure that the environment is truly representative of the species. A case study is a careful, intensive observation of one or a few individuals, typically people who display a particular behavior. If the case study involves treatment, it is not purely descriptive. Case studies may raise more questions than they answer. Surveys involve having people answer questions about their behavior, thoughts, or opinions and are another way to gather data about behavior. They may be done in a variety of ways, including on the Internet, on paper, by phone, and face-to-face. In surveys, people may not be honest in their responses and may not remember their past behavior and attitudes accurately.

2. What are correlations and why are they of limited value in understanding behavior?

   A correlation is a relationship between variables in which they fluctuate together. Correlation cannot demonstrate a causal relationship between two variables, so it is more useful as an observational tool or to suggest hypotheses rather than as a tool to explain behavior.

3. Describe experimentation in terms of independent and dependent variables, and in terms of experimental and control groups.

   Experimentation is a scientific approach of deliberately manipulating a variable to then observe whether and how other variables are altered in response. The variable that is manipulated is the independent variable, and the dependent variable is the variable that is expected to change as a result of the manipulation. The experimental group is the group of individuals for whom you have manipulated the independent variable. The control group is a group of individuals who closely resemble those in the experimental group but who did not receive the experimental treatment. To know what difference the independent variable makes, the measure from the experimental group needs to be compared with the measure from the control group.

4. What are the steps in strong inference? Is the aim to prove that a hypothesis is true?

   Strong inference consists of four steps:

   - Come up with alternative hypotheses to explain your observations.
   - Design an experiment that could have several different outcomes, some of which would disprove a hypothesis.
   - Carry out the experiment to see which outcome you get, and therefore which hypotheses have survived.
   - Then go back to the beginning.

   The aim of strong inference is to disprove as many plausible hypotheses as possible. While we can sometimes disprove a hypothesis, we can never prove it is true.

Section 2.2

1. Explain how random sampling improves our chances of drawing a representative sample.

   With random sampling, every member of the population has an equal chance of being selected, and the selection of one person has no influence on who is selected next. Since everyone has an equal likelihood of being selected, those who are selected should reflect the whole population being studied.

2. What are advantages and disadvantages of each of the three measures of central tendency?

   The mean, or arithmetic average, gives you an indication of where the scores cluster. However, the mean can be shifted a lot by one outlier and so may not be the best indicator of central tendency if there are outliers. The median indicates the score that is in the middle when all the scores are lined up by value. It is useful when there are outliers and you are interested in the typical value. However, the median may also be shifted considerably if the distribution is skewed. The most common score is the mode. It is often easy to determine. However, it may not be typical of all the scores and there may be several modes.

3. How do inferential statistics guide us in the process of testing hypotheses?

   When testing a hypothesis, an experiment is conducted and data about the two groups are gathered. Inferential statistics allows us to compare the two groups and determine whether the difference could be due to chance alone or is likely to represent a real difference between the groups.

4. Describe reliability and validity and how they apply to psychological measures.

   Reliability is the degree to which your measurement tool produces consistent, repeatable results. Validity is the degree to which your measurement tool actually measures what it's supposed to measure. A good measurement tool is both reliable and valid. The reliability of a psychological test is important because many psychological processes are not directly observable. After reliability is established, then validity can be examined. This is a difficult question in many areas of psychology, as there isn't agreement among psychologists on the meaning of different psychological process.

5. What is a placebo, and how do modern studies use placebos to evaluate the effectiveness of treatments?

   A placebo is a pill or other treatment that has no known medical effect. Placebos have powerful effects on many symptoms that might be considered physical. To determine whether a treatment is effective, the actual treatment must be compared with a placebo treatment. If the placebo is as effective as the treatment, then there is no point in administering the treatment.

6. What are the boards that must approve experiments on humans or other animals before they can begin, and what are the goals of that review process?

   Research on humans must be approved by an Institutional Review Board (IRB). IRBs strive to ensure the safety and privacy of any people being studied, and they require that participants provide informed consent. IRBs require that the participants be debriefed after the study about any information that was withheld, which informs the participants about what the study was about and reveals any deception used and why it was necessary. An Institutional Animal Care and Use Committee (IACUC) must review and approve any proposed research with animals. The goal is to evaluate the scientific rationale for the proposed study and to avoid or minimize any discomfort, stress, or pain to the animals.

Chapter Three

Section 3.1

1. What are the different parts of a neuron, and what do they do?

   The cell body contains the nucleus and cytoplasm. Dendrites are extensions off the cell body that receive information from other cells. The axon is the extension that sends information to other cells.

2. What are the three types of neurons, based on function, and what roles do they play? Which type is most common in the brain?

   The three types of neurons are motor neurons, sensory neurons, and interneurons. Motor neurons release their neurotransmitter onto muscles, making them contract to produce movement. Sensory neurons are sensitive to physical events and send information about those events to the brain. Interneurons send and receive signals from other neurons. Interneurons are far and away the most common type of neuron in the brain.

3. What is a neurotransmitter, and how does it send information from one neuron to another?

   A neurotransmitter is a chemical used to send information from one neuron to another. This occurs when the axon terminal of a neuron releases minute amounts of neurotransmitter into the synaptic cleft. The neurotransmitter reaches the other side of the synaptic cleft, where it binds briefly to receptors in the other neuron's dendrite. When the dendrite detects the neurotransmitter, it has received a signal from the first neuron.

4. What two processes halt the effect of neurotransmitter molecules once they've been released?

   The two processes are reuptake and degradation. First, the axon terminal that releases the neurotransmitter molecules also actively picks them up later to use again, a process called reuptake. Second, in the synaptic cleft itself there are chemicals called *degradative enzymes* that quickly dismantle transmitter molecules. Within a few milliseconds, most of the neurotransmitter molecules that were released by the axon terminal are gone from the synapse.

5. Name three neurotransmitters and give an example of a function each is known to play.

   Possible responses (any three):

   - Acetylcholine, the first neurotransmitter discovered, is used by many parts of the nervous system. Some neurons release acetylcholine onto the heart to slow its beating. Other neurons release acetylcholine onto muscles to make them contract.
   - Glutamate is one of the most common neurotransmitters in the brain. Glutamate is used in almost every system, from pain to vision, and almost always causes neurons to be more active.

- GABA (an acronym for ***g**amma **a**mino**b**utyric **a**cid*) is a neurotransmitter that usually induces neurons to reduce their activity.
- Endorphins are neurotransmitters that seem to act as "***endo**genous (internal) m**orphin**e*" to damp down pain signals.
- Serotonin is a neurotransmitter made by neurons in the base of the brain that send their axons throughout the brain and spinal cord. Serotonin excites some neurons and inhibits others.
- Norepinephrine (also known as noradrenaline) is a neurotransmitter used to speed heart rate, breathing, and neuronal activity as part of the "fight or flight" response.
- Dopamine is a neurotransmitter that is important in the brain's control of movement, and also in signaling pleasure from a wide variety of activities, including food, sex, and drugs.

Section 3.2

1. How does an individual neuron sum up all the synaptic input it receives?

   In neurons the voltage difference across the membrane changes constantly. Each time a neurotransmitter molecule attaches to a receptor, it opens an ion channel, a tiny tunnel or pore running through the cell membrane that allows ions to cross the membrane. Once the ion channel opens, positive or negative ions flow into the neuron, changing the voltage difference across the neuron's membrane. The ion channel only stays open for a few thousandths of a second. Then the channel closes again, allowing the neuron to return to its resting potential. A neuron's voltage fluctuates widely due to the combined effect of thousands of neurotransmitter molecules, at each of thousands of receptors, at each of thousands of synapses on the same neuron. In other words, the neuron is summarizing (or integrating) information from thousands of inputs (synapses) and continually updating that average to determine whether to send an action potential in response.

2. What changes in the membrane potential make a neuron more likely to produce an action potential? What changes in its membrane potential makes a neuron less likely to produce an action potential?

   An action potential can be triggered in a neuron by deliberately making the neuron less negative inside, or depolarizing it. The entry of positive ions at synapses depolarizes the neuron and brings it closer to the threshold for triggering an action potential. When negatively charged ions are allowed to enter the neuron, making the interior more negative, it becomes less likely to produce an action potential.

3. How does the neuronal production of action potentials resemble the flushing of a toilet? In what ways do the two processes differ?

   Neuronal production of action potentials resembles the function of a toilet through its all-or-none property, which is like a toilet that flushes the same regardless of the force on the lever. The neuron's action potential goes only in one direction down the axon, from the end attached to the cell body to the axon terminals. Similarly, the water in a toilet only goes in one direction. For a neuron, there is a brief refractory period after it fires, during which it cannot be fired again. Similarly, for a toilet there is a short period when it cannot be flushed again. Unlike a toilet, the outflow of which goes only to a single sewer line leaving a house, the action potential may flow down to many axon branches, allowing communication with hundreds of other neurons. Voltage-gated sodium channels on the axon branches ensure that the action potential is just as large in each branch, so it's not diminished by spreading out among branches. The outflow of a toilet would be diminished by spreading out among different pipes. A toilet has only one lever, but each neuron has hundreds or thousands of synapses, and some synapses make the neuron more likely to reach threshold, while others make it less likely. There is no comparable mechanism for a toilet to become less likely to flush, except perhaps Kaopectate.

Section 3.3

1. Describe the subdivisions of the CNS and PNS.

   The nervous system is divided into the central nervous system (CNS), made up of the brain and spinal cord, and the peripheral nervous system (PNS). The CNS gathers information and makes big decisions, and the PNS carries information between the body and the CNS. The PNS is composed of the somatic nervous system and the autonomic nervous system. The somatic nervous system consists of those millions of nerves that bring us the sensory information we are aware of plus the millions more nerves that we use to consciously control our muscles. The autonomic nervous system is an extensive network gathering information about our body and controlling countless internal processes *without* our being aware of it or being able to consciously direct it. The autonomic nervous system comprises the sympathetic nervous system, which prepares the body for action, and the parasympathetic nervous system, which triggers physiological responses to put the body at rest.

2. Name the major parts of the brain, including the four cortical lobes and some of the structures beneath them.

   The three main parts of the brain are the brainstem, the cerebellum, and the cerebrum. The brainstem is at the top of the spinal cord and is the stalk-like core of the brain that controls vital functions, such as breathing and heart rate, and transfers information between the cerebrum, cerebellum, and spinal cord. The cerebellum is on top of the brainstem, but tucked beneath and at the back of the cerebrum. The cerebellum controls balance and coordinates movements of the body. The cerebrum is the largest, most complicated part of the brain, sitting atop the rest of the nervous system in humans. It is responsible for all of our most complicated mental processes, including the analysis of sensory information, decision making, and language. The four lobes of the cerebral cortex are the frontal lobes, parietal lobes, occipital lobes, and temporal lobes.

3. Describe a function that is associated with each of the cortical lobes.

   The frontal lobes are involved in judgment, decision making, and body movement. The parietal lobes analyze pain and touch. The temporal lobes analyze sound and speech. The occipital lobes analyze vision.

Section 3.4

1. By what methods can a living human brain be examined without requiring surgery, and how do they differ?

   Transcranial magnetic stimulation allows scientists to temporarily inhibit a brain region through the skull, but without surgery. Electroencephalograms (EEGs) use electrodes on the surface of the scalp to detect electrical signals generated by the activation of synapses in the brain; they can detect different sleep states and epileptic seizures. Computed tomography (CT) and magnetic resonance imaging (MRI) scans offer detailed views of the human brain, while functional MRI (fMRI) and positron emission tomography (PET) show which brain regions are active when a person is performing a particular task.

2. We sometimes gain insight into the importance of a certain region of the brain by examining the behavior of a person who has suffered a stroke that has destroyed that region. This is an example of what type of method? What makes interpreting such reports tricky?

   One way to study brain function is to examine behavior after a *lesion*, or damage to an area of the brain. Lesion studies are tricky to interpret because loss of behavior following a lesion does not rule out the possibility that many other brain regions also normally play a role in that behavior.

3. How do modern studies of brain activity refute the myth that "we only use 10% of our brain"?

   Studies of functional activity in the brain rely on subtracting out the activity pattern of the brain when a person is doing a control task from the pattern of activity when doing the task of interest. Only by doing this can researchers determine where the *peaks* of activity are during different tasks, because there is widespread brain activity even when we are at rest.

Chapter Four

Section 4.1

1. How do genes carry information from parents to offspring?

   For each gene, you carry two different alleles, one from your mother and one from your father. Your genotype is determined by the alleles present in the egg and sperm that fused to form your first cell.

2. What are alleles, and why are some dominant while others are recessive?

   Alleles are one of two or more different forms of a gene. A dominant allele affects the individual's phenotype regardless of the other allele carried by the gene. A recessive allele affects the individual's phenotype only when it is present on both chromosomes.

3. Compare and contrast genotype and phenotype.

   The term *genotype* describes the genetic information you received from your parents. Your genotype was set at the instant of fertilization. Your phenotype is the sum total of all the physical characteristics and processes going on within you at a particular time. Note that while your genotype never changes, your phenotype never stays the same.

Section 4.2

1. Why do cells in some parts of the body, such as the liver, look and function differently than other types of cells, such as those in the brain?

   They express different subsets of genes and therefore make different sets of proteins, thereby taking on the structure and function appropriate to that particular type of cell.

2. Why is it important that different types of cells express different subsets of genes, and why do they need to carefully regulate how much of each kind of protein they make?

   While every cell carries a full set of genes, most cells use only a small subset of those genes. Each cell expresses the genes needed for the job it does. As conditions change in a day or during a life, each cell adjusts the genes it expresses to make the right mix of proteins for the present conditions.

3. Give examples of how the environment has influenced your genes and affected your behavior.

   Every sensory experience I have will cause cells to alter gene expression. This affects my neurons and changes the expression of their genes. This alters my phenotype, and subsequently my behavior. For example, if I read an article about the benefits of exercise, I may begin exercising, which will change my phenotype, which may affect my future behavior.

Section 4.3

1. How does a toxic allele lead to Huntington's disease?

   One allele of *huntingtin* works satisfactorily until middle age, when the abnormal, toxic protein it produces begins killing certain neurons in the brain. This death of cells in the striatum leads to abnormal involuntary movements, disordered thinking, and eventual death.

2. What is phenylketonuria, and how can the harmful consequences of this condition be avoided?

   Phenylketonuria (PKU) is a recessive hereditary disorder that at one time often resulted in mental impairment. Those afflicted with PKU lack a protein that breaks down phenylalanine, an amino acid that is present in many foods. Without a functional version of this protein, excess phenylalanine builds up in the blood and results in a disaster: brain cells die and mental functions falter. Today all babies are tested just a few days after birth to see if they have too much phenylalanine in their blood. Early detection is important because simply reducing phenylalanine in the diet prevents brain impairment. Food products containing phenylalanine are labeled so that people with PKU can avoid them. This dietary control is critical during the early years of life, especially before age 12.

3. Why is it that when two people who were both born deaf because of genetic disorders have children, their children usually can hear?

   Our ears use more than 100 different genes to work properly. If an individual inherits two dysfunctional alleles for any of these genes, that person will be born deaf. Most cases of inherited deafness are the result of recessive genes. Because there are so many different recessive genes that cause deafness, however, the children of two deaf people usually have normal hearing. This is because the parents generally carry two dysfunctional alleles, but for each parent it is for a different gene. Consequently, their offspring will inherit one functional and one dysfunctional allele for each of the two genes. That means they will have each of the proteins needed to make a functional ear. The children carry recessive alleles for deafness in two different genes and can pass these on to their children.

Section 4.4

1. What percentage of genes, on average, are shared between monozygotic twins? Between dizygotic twins?

   Monozygotic twins, who are derived from a single fertilized egg, have 100% of their genes in common. Dizygotic twins, who are derived from two separate eggs, have on average 50% of their genes in common. Dizygotic twins are no more genetically alike than any two siblings.

2. How does comparing concordance in monozygotic versus dizygotic twins give an estimate of heritability?

   A difference in the rate of concordance for a trait between monozygotic and dizygotic twins is a result of the closer genetic relation of the monozygotic twins. Generally, monozygotic twins are twice as related as dizygotic twins (have twice as many genes in common). So the difference in the rate of concordance times two gives an estimate of the variability in the trait that arises from the difference in the genes.

3. What is heritability? What is it not?

   Heritability is an estimate of the variation of a trait in a population that arises from differences in their genes. It is a statistical estimate of what percentage of variation for that trait is caused by the various genotypes. An estimate of heritability of a trait does not indicate what percentage of the population has that trait. Nor does it indicate what percentage of the people who have that trait have it because of genes. Because heritability estimates are derived from a particular population of people, they offer no predictive power about heritability in other populations, nor about any particular individual.

Section 4.5

1. Describe the evidence that stress plays a role in the development of schizophrenia.

   Many findings indicate that different kinds of stress, such as disease, malnutrition, and neglect, increase the probability that a person will develop schizophrenia. The proportion of people who develop schizophrenia rises during times of social upheaval such as war. Another clue that stress plays a role is the time of life when schizophrenia appears. Most people who develop the disorder start displaying symptoms at the age when they must make the stressful transition from adolescence to adulthood. Among the many cases of identical twins who are discordant for schizophrenia, the twin who developed schizophrenia was more often subjected to greater stress than the other twin. For example, the ill twin is more likely to have experienced complications during birth. The ill twin usually had a lower birth weight and is also more likely to have shown evidence of an infection at birth, such as fever.

2. What do old home movies of monozygotic twins tell us about the origins of schizophrenia?

   Evidence that the twin who developed schizophrenia was always the more vulnerable one come from home movies, in which observers can usually pick out which child, upon growing up, developed schizophrenia. This is the twin who shows more disorganized behavior. His or her movements are jerkier, less smooth. Even as a baby, the child who will develop schizophrenia shows more abnormal crawling behavior.

3. Does growing up in a big city increase or decrease the probability of developing schizophrenia?

   People who grow up in big cities are twice as likely to develop schizophrenia as people growing up in rural settings. The earlier in life they move to a big city, the greater their risk. This increased risk is probably because city life is more stressful than rural life.

Chapter Five

Section 5.1

1. What are the six stages of brain development, in order? (You can use logic to think about how some stages must precede others.)

   The first stage is neurogenesis, the division of cells that become neurons. It is followed by call migration, when neurons and other cells migrate to their final positions in the brain. Differentiation, the process by which individual cells become more and more different from one another, follows. Then synaptogenesis, the formation of synapses, occurs. The fifth stage is neuronal cell death, which is a normal stage of development when some cells, including some neurons, die. The final stage is synapse rearrangement, when new synapses form and old synapses retract.

2. Describe fetal alcohol syndrome.

   Fetal alcohol syndrome is a condition in which children prenatally exposed to alcohol from their mother's drinking are born with distinct facial features and varying degrees of mental impairment. The facial features include small eye openings, a thin upper lip, a low nasal bridge, a short nose, and an underdeveloped jaw. The brain may be smaller, have fewer wrinkles in the cortex, and lack a corpus callosum.

3. Which stage of brain development continues throughout life, and how does experience guide this stage?

   The reconfiguration of the synapses, part of synapse rearrangement (the sixth stage of cellular development in the brain), begins before birth and continues throughout life, serving to develop more efficient neural networks. Although they depend on the action of many genes, these cellular processes in brain development are also coordinated and guided by the environment and by experience. This is demonstrated by both sensitive periods and by the plasticity of the young brain.

Section 5.2

1. How do habituation techniques allow psychologists to measure sensory processes and learning in infants?

   Habituation techniques are methods of discerning individuals' recognition of a stimulus by determining whether they show evidence of habituating to that stimulus. In the case of sensory processes, the infant will habituate to a particular stimulus. That stimulus can than be changed slightly and if the infant can detect the change, the infant will show renewed interest in the stimulus. In this way the amount of variation in the stimulus needed for the infant to make the discrimination can be studied. Similarly, if an infant habituates to a picture and the picture is removed, the delay before the picture is shown again can be varied to give information about the infant's memory for that picture. If the infant doesn't recognize the picture, it will be given as much attention as a novel stimulus.

2. What are the four stages of cognitive development proposed by Piaget?

   The four stages in the cognitive development of children begin with the sensorimotor stage of the first few years when they learn about object permanence and a basic understanding of physics. This is followed by the preoperational stage when they learn language but tend to have egocentric thinking and have not yet learned about conservation. Young schoolchildren are in the concrete operational stage, and they understand conservation and many other logical principles but still tend to think in concrete rather than abstract terms. Later, starting at about age 11 or so, children reach the adult, formal operational stage of reasoning and are able to reason about abstract and theoretical principles.

3. How is temperament evaluated in infants?

   Temperament is a person's emotional makeup; the way he or she generally responds to a variety of situations. Infants can be evaluated by observation at about 2–3 months. About a third of the infants do not fit a specific classification in terms of emotional behavior, but the remaining infants show consistent patterns of response. Some babies are easy: they wake up and get hungry at regular, predictable times, react cheerfully to new environments, and rarely act fussy. Difficult babies fuss a good deal and respond irritably to new situations. These slow-to-warm-up babies are not very active and initially withdraw in response to new situations or people, but they slowly accept them with repeated exposure.

4. What are three types of attachment styles in young children, and how do those styles tend to correlate with later behaviors?

   Attachment is a strong emotional bond between the infant and his or her caregivers. Attachment is assessed using the strange situation. Secure attachment is the style of attachment in which the child is visibly upset when the caregiver leaves, rejects a stranger, and welcomes reunion with the caregiver. Avoidant attachment is the style of attachment in which the child shows little or no distress when the caregiver leaves, little or no response upon reunion, and interacts very little with a stranger. Ambivalent attachment is a style of attachment in which the child is upset when the caregiver leaves, may warm up to a stranger, and behave negatively toward the caregiver upon reuniting. Children who do not fit into any of these styles are classified as having a disorganized attachment style, which is a style of attachment in which the child shows an inconsistent pattern of response in the strange situation.

Children who showed the secure attachment style as infants have better social skills and more friends than do children who were avoidant or ambivalent. There's even evidence that the differing attachment styles of infants correlate with differences in their romantic relations as adults. Still, many infants who have a secure attachment grow up to be socially awkward, and many avoidant babies grow up to have warm, close friendships. Good interactions with peers while growing up increase the chances for positive adult relationships, even for people who were avoidant as children.

Section 5.3

1. What changes happen in the body and brain during adolescence?

   During adolescence, there is a brief but vigorous growth spurt of several inches per year, which is much more rapid than the inch or two a year that is gained after the first 2 years of life. Hormones, especially the gonadal hormones—estrogen from the ovaries and testosterone from the testes—drive the development of secondary sex characteristics: in girls, estrogens promote wide hips, soft skin, and breast development, whereas in boys, testosterone promotes muscle growth, change in facial structure (including a wider jaw and thicker brow), and beard growth. Hormones from the adrenal glands drive the development of pubic and underarm hair in both sexes.

   The changes in the brain during adolescence include myelination, which is completed by age 25 or so, and synapse rearrangement, which continues throughout life. As a result of these two changes, the top layer of cortex, which consists mostly of neuronal cell bodies, grows thinner. As there is little myelin in this region, the thinning of the top cortical layer reflects synapse rearrangement. This process is not complete until about age 20, with the greatest changes in frontal cortex.

2. What factors have been proposed to affect the age of menarche?

   Girls are reaching puberty earlier in Western nations, and a variety of factors have been proposed as an explanation. They include improved nutrition, improved medical treatment, exposure to human-made chemicals in the environment, and increases in body fat. The social experience of girls has also been proposed as an explanation. Girls who are raised with a father enter menarche later than girls with an absent or mostly absent father. Stress also affects the age of menarche in that the more stress a girl experiences, the more likely she is to reach menarche at a younger age. The modern world may be placing more stress on children. The absent father and stress factors may interact, as the absence of a father increases the stress on a family, and this may be why girls without a father present enter menarche sooner.

3. Describe Kohlberg's six stages of moral development.

   Kohlberg proposed three levels of moral reasoning, achieved in six stages. Young children use preconventional moral reasoning, which is based on personal consequences. This level consists of stage 1, which is about avoiding punishment, and stage 2, which centers on seeking reward. Kohlberg felt most adults develop to the level of conventional moral reasoning, which involves judging what's right and wrong based on society's expectations. The stages of this level are stage 3, centered on conformity, and stage 4, focused on social order. Kohlberg felt that few people achieve the third level, which is postconventional moral reasoning, in which rules are based on a social contract. In this level are stage 5, based on social contract, and stage 6, centered on universal principles. At the highest level of moral reasoning, a person may reject rules even when the majority of citizens disagree.

Section 5.4

1. Describe the tension between two ways of interacting with other people in Erikson's eight stages of psychosocial development.

   Erikson describes the stages of psychosocial development as being characterized by tension: we are often torn between opposing ways of interacting with other people. At the infant stage, a baby wavers between trusting and mistrusting her caregivers. At the second stage, the toddler is pulled between autonomy (self-guidance) and shame as she moves about and interacts with the world. In the third stage, preschoolers are torn between initiative and guilt as they interact with their family and people outside the family. Preadolescents, in the fourth stage, have to deal with feelings of industry and competence versus feeling inferior as they learn about their own strengths and weaknesses while interacting with their peers, who are engaging in the same self-evaluation, and family. Adolescents are in the fifth stage, torn between developing an identity, a consistent sense of who they are, and confusion about what they should be. In this stage, the most important relationships are with peers. In the sixth stage the young adult is torn between seeking intimacy and isolation. The seventh stage is middle adulthood, when the conflict is between generativity (generating new life material) and stagnation, staying stuck in unfulfilling relationships and careers. The eighth and final stage of life is to prepare for the inevitable end. The tension at this stage is between despair, giving up on life as we obsess over our coming death, versus integrity, learning to be satisfied with our life, accepting its inevitable decline and focusing on those aspects of life that still have meaning and purpose for us.

2. What do we lose, and gain, as we grow old?

   There are many changes in the body with aging, including loss of skin tone, graying and thinning of hair, loss of muscle, shutting down of reproductive systems, a dulling of the senses including vision and hearing, loss of perceptual speed, slowing of reaction times, a progressive decline in memory skills, and a gradual decline in fluid intelligence. However, there is continuous growth in crystallized intelligence and continued satisfaction with life. Even into old age, people continue to build on crystallized intelligence and are satisfied with their lives.

3. Describe the symptoms of Alzheimer's disease and the steps that have been shown to postpone the onset of those symptoms.

   Symptoms of Alzheimer's disease (AD) usually begin with forgetfulness, which is progressive; this is followed by impairment in language, perception, or judgment, or a change in personality. Having an active brain makes you less likely to develop AD. Physical activity, intellectual activity, and participation in social activities all serve to preserve cognitive function.

Chapter Six

Section 6.1

1. In psychology, what's the difference between sensation and perception?

   Sensation is the process by which the sensory cells detect the physical events going on around us or inside us. Perception is the experience we have as we further process and interpret information from sensory cells.

2. How do labeled lines help us interpret sensory input?

   When the brain receives an input in the form of an action potential, it identifies the sensory modality related to which nerves are propagating it.

3. Describe absolute threshold and how psychophysicists measure it.

   The absolute threshold is the lowest intensity of a stimulus that a person can detect half the time. The psychophysicists systematically vary a stimulus intensity and ask the subject to report the experience of the stimulus. Following many repetitions, psychophysicists are able to identify the stimulus intensity that is detectable half the time.

4. Draw a 2 × 2 table to describe the four possible outcomes of any signal detection task. The table needs to specify when the signal *really is* present or not, and when you *decide* the signal is present or absent.

	Signal status: Present	Signal status: Absent
Present	Hit	False alarm
Absent	Miss	Correct rejection

5. What is Weber's fraction and how does it relate to JNDs?

   Weber's fraction is the mathematical relationship between JNDs (just noticeable differences) and a stimulus. It is the smallest change in the magnitude of a stimulus that can be detected, expressed as a proportion of the original stimulus. The value of Weber's fraction varies among modalities.

Section 6.2

1. How are we able to perceive so many different kinds of stimuli (light touch, vibration, heat, cold, pain) from our skin?

   There are at least four different types of touch receptors found in every part of our skin. Each reports slightly different information.

2. Describe receptive fields and explain how a scientist can determine the receptive field of a neuron.

   The receptive field of a sensory cell is the total region of space where stimuli alter the cell's firing rate. The receptive field of a touch neuron is found by recording from the neuron and applying stimuli to the body to determine where stimuli affect the firing rate. After initially locating one point that makes the neuron fire faster or slower, the scientist can stimulate the area around that point and mark the boundaries of the receptive field.

3. Give some examples to demonstrate that "pain is in the brain" and not simply the result of nociceptor activity.

   When soldiers receive non-life-threatening wounds in combat, they report little or no pain. The same wounds would be perceived as very painful in another setting. The sensation in both cases is the same, but the perception is quite different. With phantom limb pain (pain in an amputated limb) the nociceptors are missing, but the brain perceives pain. Another example comes from the relief of phantom limb pain when the person uses a mirror box, virtual reality, or even imagination to simulate manipulating the missing limb.

Section 6.3

1. Describe the path of light entering each eye, and how information from the two retinas reaches the left and right cortex.

   Light enters the eye through the cornea, then passes through the lens, which focuses the image on the retina. Light from the left visual field strikes the right sides of both retinas (the nasal side of the left eye and the temple side of the right eye). Light from the right visual field strikes the left sides of both retinas (the temple side of the left eye and the nasal side of the right eye). The axons from left halves of both retinas pass to the left side of the brain. The axons from the right halves of both retinas pass to the right hemisphere.

2. What are the two main types of photoreceptors, and what does each contribute to our overall vision?

   Rods and cones are the two main types of photoreceptors. Rods are extremely sensitive, so they can function in very low levels of light. They respond the same to light of any wavelength so do not help in distinguishing colors. Cones are less sensitive, so they function only when there is plentiful light, but they are sensitive to lights of different wavelengths, enabling us to distinguish colors.

3. What are the binocular cues and monocular cues to distance vision?

   The difference in the visual images on the two eyes, or binocular disparity, provides binocular cues to the distance of objects, giving us information about the depth of objects in a view. Convergence, or the coming together of the lines of sight of the two eyes to focus on nearby objects, provides binocular cues to the brain about nearby objects.

   Monocular cues for depth include occlusion, or the blocking of more distant objects by nearby objects, and size cue, the property that objects appear smaller when farther away. The relative height of an object is another monocular depth cue: the farther away the object, the higher it appears on the retina. Parallel lines give the linear perspective monocular depth cue: the farther away they are, the more they converge. Distance fog is another cue. The scattering of light in air makes distant objects appear hazier. Motion parallax, or the shifting of a visual scene on the retina as you move your head, provides another monocular cue.

4. Describe the two processes that allow us to see over such a broad range of brightness. Which works faster? Which provides us with vision over a greater range of brightness?

   We see over an enormous range of light intensities because the pupil can quickly change size to control the amount of light entering the eye, but it can adjust over only a small range. To adjust to greater changes in light, we must rely on the adaptation of photoreceptors, which can vary enormously but work more slowly than changes in pupil size.

5. Describe how the visual system constructs our perception of color.

   Color perception depends on the ability of different cones to respond differentially to light of various wavelengths. Most people have three different types of cones, responding to short, medium, and long wavelengths, providing trichromatic vision. Our perception of color depends on the differential response of at least two different cones. In this way, the brain constructs for us the percept for every color, from red to violet, by comparing the mixture of activity from all three cone types. The rods also contribute to color perception, responding broadly to light of almost any color except extreme red. By reporting to the brain how much total light is present, the rods also inform us about how bright or dim a color is.

6. Describe what some optical illusions tell us about assumptions the brain makes in visual perception.

   If dots have a gradient of shading that starts light and gets progressively darker moving toward the bottom of the page within each dot, they appear to be bumps sticking out of the page. Dots that are shaded the opposite way appear to be dented into the page. This tells us that the brain assumes that lighting comes from above.

   When there is a slanted line on each side of two parallel horizontal lines, we see the upper horizontal line as longer than the lower line. This is an illusion because our brains are expecting linear perspective, so we perceive the upper line as being farther away and hence larger.

7. What are the Gestalt rules of perceptions? Sketch some examples of each.

   The rule of continuity means we see objects as unbroken, even when parts are occluded. The rule of proximity means that we see things close together as part of a whole. The rule of similarity means the more alike figures are, the more likely we are to see them as part of a whole. The rule of closure means we still see the shapes, even if there are breaks in their outlines. The rule of symmetry means we see symmetric lines as being part of the same object.

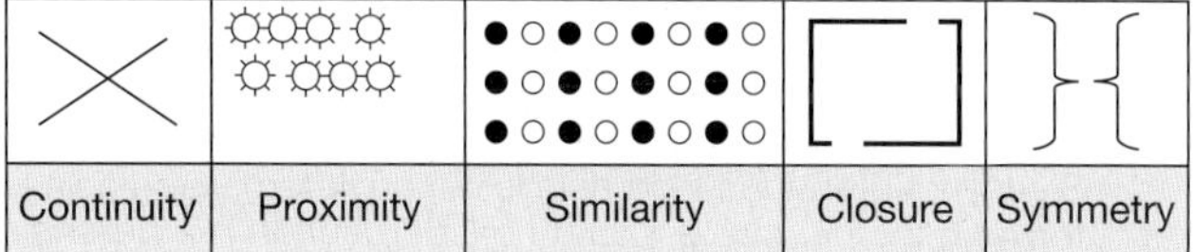

Section 6.4

1. Follow the path of vibrations from a firing cannon to the inner ear of someone 1,000 meters away. Be sure to note whether air molecules, membranes, bones, fluid, or cells are vibrating.

   The firing of the cannon sets air molecules around it into motion and they bump other air molecules. The bumping or vibrating molecules sets up sound waves. Eventually these vibrations reach the person's ear and are funneled into the ear to the tympanic membrane. The membrane begins to vibrate and transmits the vibration to the three little bones, called ossicles. The vibration of the ossicles is passed on to the oval window, causing it to vibrate. The cochlea receives the vibration from the oval window. This causes the fluid inside the cochlea to vibrate, which in turn causes the membranes that run the length of the cochlea to vibrate. The hair cells on the membrane detect the vibrations and transmit the information to the brain.

2. How does the cochlea analyze a mixture of sounds?

   Inside the cochlea, the vibrations cause the membranes to vibrate up and down. Sounds of different frequencies cause different parts of the cochlea to vibrate: high frequencies affect its narrow end close to the oval window, and low frequencies affect its wide end at the tip. Louder sounds cause larger vibrations. Upon the membrane, hair cells detect the movement and send signals about sound to the brain. The hair cells send on information about which frequencies are present and how loud each one is.

3. What are binaural cues for localizing the source of a sound?

   Binaural cures are found by comparing the latency and intensity of the sound arriving to the two ears. Sounds that arrive to the left ear first must have originated from somewhere on our left. Sounds that are louder in the right ear originated from somewhere on our right.

Section 6.5

1. What are the five basic kinds of taste receptors?

   Each taste bud cell contains one of the five different kinds of taste receptor cells that detect sweet, sour, salty, bitter, and meaty (umami) tastes.

2. Of the two chemosensory systems that contribute to flavors, which contributes most to the experience, and why?

   We have two chemosensory systems, the olfactory system in the nose for detecting odors, and the taste system on the tongue for detecting tastes. While we can detect only five tastes, we can detect at least 10,000 different odors. By combining our abilities to detect five tastes and thousands of odors, we can appreciate an amazingly wide range of flavors. The odors contribute the most to the experience.

3. Describe how the olfactory system is able to distinguish thousands of different odors.

   Olfactory receptor neurons detect odors and are embedded in a sheet of cells inside the nose. Odorants enter the nose and bind to receptor proteins on the olfactory receptor neurons. The binding either excites or inhibits the firing of each receptor neuron. This result is passed to the olfactory bulb of the brain. We make hundreds of different kinds of olfactory receptor proteins, each of which detects a particular odorant. By comparing the activity of hundreds of different kinds of olfactory receptors, the brain receives a distinct signal for each of the thousands of odors we can distinguish. The system compares the relative activity of the many receptor neurons. That allows us to distinguish more odors than we have distinct receptors for.

Chapter Seven

Section 7.1

1. What are the easy and hard problems of consciousness?

   The easy problem of consciousness, also called the mind–body problem, is finding out what particular pattern of brain activity underlies a particular conscious experience, such as being able to tell from brain activity whether a person is looking at a dog, listening to a song, or remembering a past event. The hard problem of consciousness is determining how brain processes result in our personal conscious experience, for example, the particular qualia that someone experiences, such as the experience of "red" versus "green."

2. What is confabulation, and how do instances of confabulation in humans seem to confirm Spinoza's speculation about a moving stone that gains consciousness?

   Confabulation is a person's filling in a gap in memory or understanding with a fabrication he or she believes to be true. Spinoza suggested that while we know what we want to do next, we are usually unaware of *why* we want to do that. Spinoza speculated that if he threw a stone through the air, and the stone suddenly became conscious, the stone would think, "I want to go over there," and it would believe it was going in that direction because of its desire. Spinoza's speculation is supported by the confabulated explanations given by split-brain patients for why their left hands (controlled by their right hemispheres) did things. Their left hemispheres, which control speech, did not know why but made up reasons. Similarly people who are induced into doing something by electrical brain stimulation usually confabulate explanations for their actions.

3. Describe split-brain patients and the evidence that they have two minds at work in one head?

   Split-brain patients have had the corpus callosum surgically cut so that the two halves of their brains do not communicate with each other. The left side of the body is controlled by the right hemisphere, which does not control speech, and the right side of the body is controlled by the left hemisphere, which is the verbal hemisphere. If a picture is presented to the right visual field, the patient can identify it. If a picture is presented to the left visual field, the patient cannot verbally identify it. However, if the patient is asked questions about the image that has been displayed in the left visual field, and is asked to choose a correct response with his or her left hand, the patient can to that. Since the left hemisphere is still unaware of the processing by the right hemisphere, there seem to be two minds.

4. What do experiments measuring brain activity before people make decisions suggest about the importance of consciousness and free will?

   Scientists monitoring brain recordings can predict when the participant is going to perform an act several seconds before he or she is aware of any such decision. These experiments call into question whether our conscious self is actually involved in our decisions or simply becomes aware of what other parts of our brain have decided. But these experiments neither prove nor disprove whether we have free will.

Section 7.2

1. What is the evidence that there is an internal biological clock in the brain?

   If you put animals or people in an environment without any cues about whether it is day or night, they will adopt a sleep–wake cycle of about 24 hours.

2. Describe the stages of sleep and how they tend to appear in the course of a night's sleep.

   Stage 1 sleep is characterized by the alpha rhythm in the EEG with by small, irregular waves and characteristic sharp waves. In stage 1 sleep, a person is easily awakened and may deny having been asleep. In stage 2 sleep the EEG shows characteristic trains of spikes called sleep spindles and large single spikes of activity called K complexes. The person is harder to rouse than in stage 1 sleep but may still deny having been asleep. Stage 3 sleep, which is deep sleep, is defined by the appearance of large-amplitude, very slow waves called delta waves (about one per second). REM (rapid-eye-movement) sleep is characterized by a pattern of desynchronized EEG, flaccid muscles, and rapid eye movements.

   During the course of a night's sleep, a person progresses from awake to stage 1 sleep, then to stage 2 sleep, and finally to stage 3 sleep. After a period in stage 3 sleep, the person comes up through stage 2 sleep, then into REM sleep. REM is followed by stage 2, then stage 3, in about 90-minute cycles. As the night goes on, there is a progressive lengthening of REM episodes and the loss of stage 3 sleep.

3. What major ideas have been offered to explain why we sleep?

   One important function of sleep is to force an individual to conform to a particular ecological niche for which it is well adapted, or niche adaptation. A second function of sleep is energy conservation. We require less energy during the time we are asleep. The amount of time an animal spends asleep is related to its size: small mammals sleep more than large mammals. Small mammals lose body heat at a higher rate than large mammals, so it is important that they conserve energy by spending more time inactive and asleep. Third, sleep is helpful for memory consolidation. There is evidence that material learned before a period of sleep will be better remembered than material learned but not followed by sleep. Finally, sleep restores the body in some way, probably related to the immune system.

4. Describe the brain regions that promote different stages of sleep and wakefulness, including the region that seems to switch between these states.

   Regions of the brain involved in stages of sleep and wakefulness include a slow-wave sleep (SWS) center in the basal forebrain, an arousal or waking center in the brainstem reticular formation, and a REM sleep center in the pons. A fourth center—a sleep-state control center, located in the hypothalamus—plays a pivotal role, activating one or another of the other three centers to determine whether we are in SWS, awake, or in REM sleep.

5. Describe the various sleep disorders.

   One sleep disorder, REM behavior disorder (RBD), is characterized by movement during REM sleep. People with this disorder are generally middle-aged men who begin acting out their dreams while in bed. They often dream of fighting or running away from some foe. Narcolepsy is a sleep disorder characterized by intense attacks of sleep that last from 5 to 30 minutes during usual waking hours. The person goes directly into REM sleep. Classic symptoms of narcolepsy include daytime sleepiness and cataplexy, the loss of muscle tone without loss of consciousness. Fatal familial insomnia (FFI) is a genetic disorder that eliminates sleep in middle age. The person sleeps less and less, and this eventually leads to death. Sleep-onset insomnia is difficulty in falling asleep. Sleep-maintenance insomnia is difficulty remaining asleep through the night. Sleep state misperception is a person's perception that he has not been asleep when he was actually sleeping. Sleep apnea is a sleep disorder in which respiration slows or stops periodically. Sudden infant deaths syndrome (SIDS) may be a form of sleep apnea in an infant with an immature brainstem. The infant suddenly stops breathing and dies for no apparent reason.

Section 7.3

1. Describe how one person might hypnotize another.

   The hypnotist, talking in a low, calm voice, asks you to look at a spot on a wall and to concentrate on that spot while listening to his voice. After a while the hypnotist may assert that your eyes are getting tired and that your eyelids feel heavy. He may encourage you to close your eyes. The hypnotist will then encourage you to relax deeply to induce a full hypnotic state. Continuing to speak in a calm, low voice, urging you to pay attention to him, the hypnotist may now suggest you do certain things or suggest a series of experiences you might feel.

2. What are the two major theories to describe what happens in hypnosis?

   The first of the two theories of what happens in hypnosis is the trance theory. It proposes that hypnosis is a genuinely altered state of consciousness that allows people to be more flexible in their experience and behavior. From this perspective, there is something special about the state of the participant's mind while in a hypnotic state, which allows the participant to ignore stimuli or break bad habits. The other theory is a social theory (or role-playing theory), in which the hypnotized participant is simply trying to accommodate another person, the hypnotist, whom the participant trusts, so they can together accomplish some mutual goal.

3. What, if any, benefits have been proven to result from hypnosis?

   Perhaps the most important use of hypnosis is in the control of pain. Hypnosis may be somewhat effective in helping people with obesity to eat less and exercise more to lose weight, but it must be used in conjunction with a behavioral weight management program of exercise and low-fat diet. It has limited effectiveness with addictions.

4. What is meditation and how might it benefit your health?

   Meditation is the practice of focusing attention in order to relax the body and mind, and to reduce stress. Attention is focused on a single, simple object or process to empty the mind of other content. Meditation has been shown to improve blood pressure, heart rate, and blood sugar levels.

Section 7.4

1. What are the main mechanisms by which psychoactive drugs can affect neurotransmitter receptors?

   Some drugs (agonists) deliver molecules that bind to the receptors as if they were molecules of the body's neurotransmitter, making neurons more or less likely to fire. Other drugs (antagonists) bind to the receptors but are sufficiently different from the neurotransmitters so the receptors doen't respond. This prevents any neurotransmitter from acting on the target neuron. A third type of drugs (neuromodulators) bind to a different part of the receptors and change how the receptors respond when neurotransmitters bind to it.

2. Describe the major classes of psychoactive drugs, and give at least one specific example of each.

   One major class of psychoactive drugs is depressants, or drugs that slow down mental processes and behavior. They tend to reduce how frequently neurons produce action potentials. Alcohol, barbiturates, and tranquilizers are depressants. A second major class of psychoactive drugs is stimulants. Stimulants increase neural activity and speed up cognition and behavior. Nicotine, caffeine, amphetamines, and cocaine are stimulants. A third class of psychoactive drugs is opiates, drugs that reduce pain sensitivity and can produce euphoria. They work by binding opioid receptors in the brain. Opium, morphine, and heroin are opiates. The final class of psychoactive drugs is hallucinogens, or drugs that alter sensory perceptions in dramatic ways and produce peculiar experiences. LSD, PCP, Ecstasy, and marijuana are hallucinogens.

3. What is the difference between psychological addiction and physical addiction?

   Psychological addiction is when someone continues using a drug that is causing problems, but is not continuing to use the drug to avoid withdrawal symptoms. Physical addiction is the continued use of a drug that is causing problems in part to avoid withdrawal symptoms.

4. What is our current understanding of how psychoactive drugs trigger pleasurable sensations and why they can lead to drug dependence?

   The release of dopamine into the nucleus accumbens creates pleasurable sensations. Many psychoactive drugs cause the release of large amounts of dopamine in this region. As unnaturally high levels of dopamine are released in the nucleus accumbens, the neurons there begin to reduce the number of dopamine receptors they provide. The same amount of dopamine then provides less pleasure than it did before. To have the same amount of pleasure as before, the dosage of the drug must be increased. Other pleasures in life that cause the release of dopamine still cause the same release, but they are less pleasurable because of the reduction in dopamine receptors. So while the drug gives you pleasure, you no longer get pleasure from other sources in your life.

Chapter Eight

Section 8.1

1. Describe the simplest types of learning and explain why they are adaptive.

   The three simplest forms of learning are habituation, dishabituation, and sensitization. In each, a response to a single stimulus is measured. Habituation takes place when repeated presentation of a stimulus elicits decreased response. It is adaptive because it allows unimportant events to be ignored. Dishabituation is a form of sensitization and is the sudden return of a response that had formerly been habituated. It is adaptive because at times what was an unimportant event becomes an important event. Sensitization takes place when a strong, aversive stimulus causes a subject to show an exaggerated response to other stimuli. This is adaptive because it promotes alertness to a changing environment.

2. Describe a typical example of classical conditioning as it might be done in a lab, being sure to include the specific terms for the various stimuli and responses. Now describe an instance of classical conditioning in everyday life, applying those same terms for the stimuli and responses.

   Pavlov's work with dogs is a typical example of classical conditioning. Meat powder placed on a dog's tongue naturally caused salivation. Then a bell was rung right before the meat powder was placed on the dog's tongue. After a number of instances of the two stimuli being paired, the dog's salivation would occur from the sound of the bell alone. The meat powder was the unconditioned stimulus (US), and salivation from the meat powder was the unconditioned response (UR). After the stimuli were repeatedly paired, the sound of the bell was the conditioned stimulus (CS), and the salivation following the sound of the bell alone was the conditioned response (CR).

   Jessica was coming down with the flu. At supper she tried out a new salad dressing that contained bleu cheese. Immediately after eating her salad, she was overcome by a wave of nausea. For the next several months, even the thought of the bleu cheese made her feel nauseous. The flu is the US and nausea is the UR. Bleu cheese flavor is the CS, and nausea following thoughts about bleu cheese is the CR.

3. What is conditioned taste aversion and how does it seem to violate some rules of classical conditioning?

   Conditioned taste aversion is the acquired repulsion to a taste or flavor that has been followed by nausea. When Garcia found this effect, it violated three ideas of classical conditioning. First, it violated the tenet that *all* stimuli could equally well be associated with a UR, because rats can more easily associate taste with nausea than associate sounds with nausea. Second, it violated the tenet that repeated pairings of the US and CS were necessary for an association to be formed, because rats can associate nausea with taste with just one pairing. Third, it violated the tenet that the US must immediately follow the CS for an association to be acquired, because rats can acquire the association of a taste with nausea that occurs even an hour later.

Section 8.2

1. What is Thorndike's law of effect and how does it explain the behavior of animals in a puzzle box?

   Thorndike's law of effect states that of the various responses a subject makes in a particular situation, those responses that are quickly followed by a satisfactory outcome are more likely to recur the next time the subject is in that situation. The law also predicts that any response quickly followed by an *unpleasant* outcome will be *less* likely to recur in the future.

When an animal is in a puzzle box, it displays many different behaviors and some of them result in release from the box. Only the behavior that leads to the opening of the box always precedes the opening. Over time, the animal learns to associate the response that opens the box with the pleasant outcome of being released.

2. Describe an example of operant conditioning in a Skinner box and in real life. How do different reinforcement schedules affect behavior in both instances?

An example of operant conditioning in a Skinner box is a pigeon learning to peck at a disk on the wall when the disk lights up. The pigeon is rewarded with a bit of food each time it completes the task successfully. The pigeon learns the behavior through shaping: it is rewarded for behaviors that are close to the desired response. A real-life example of operant conditioning is playing "Ring around the Rosie" with a small child if she picks up her toys promptly.

In each case, a fixed ratio (FR) reinforcement schedule would entail reinforcement after a certain number of responses. This would lead the pigeon to stop pecking and the child to stop picking up for a while after the reinforcement, since the next reinforcement would be a number of pecks or pick ups away. With a variable ratio (VR) reinforcement schedule, reinforcement would follow a varying number of responses. The pigeon would peck more times and the child would pick up her toys more times with this schedule. A fixed interval (FI) schedule would mean reinforcement after a set period of time. So the pigeon might be reinforced every 3 minutes, or the child every evening. With this schedule, the pigeon would be slow at responding right after the reward, then speed up before the next reward. Similarly, the child would not be as willing to pick up the toys in the morning but would be more eager to do that as evening approached. The response rate on a fixed interval schedule would be lower than on either of the ratio schedules. Finally, with a variable interval (VI) schedule, reinforcement would come at varying intervals. The response rate wouldn't peak as high as for fixed ratio (FR) and variable ratio (VR), but it would be steady. So pecking or picking up toys would occur at a steady rate.

3. What is active avoidance, why is it slow to extinguish and how might it be related to human behavior?

In active avoidance, the subject must perform the behavior to avoid an aversive stimulus. For instance, Pavlov's dogs learned to jump over a barrier to avoid the electric shock that followed a warning tone. It is difficult to extinguish this learning because the animal avoids the situation that would show it that the aversive stimulus is no longer occurring. This may be related to human phobias, or unreasonable fears of objects. For example, a child who is bitten by a dog may develop an irrational fear of dogs and, by avoiding any other dogs, has no opportunity to unlearn the phobia.

Section 8.3

1. What is latent learning, and how can you demonstrate that rats wandering about a maze without reward are nevertheless learning something?

Latent learning is learning that occurs without apparent reinforcement and which is not displayed right away. You can demonstrate latent learning in rats by making a maze with one-way doors. With one group of rats, you provide a food reward in the goal box each day beginning on the first day. With another group of rats, you do not provide a food reward for 10 days. These rats reach the goal box each day because they wander and once they've passed through a door they cannot go back. When you place a food reward in the goal box on the 11th day, the rats that have not previously been rewarded are just as fast in reaching the goal box as the rats that were rewarded all along, showing that they had been learning in the days prior.

2. Describe examples of observational learning in animals.

Observational learning in animals includes Japanese macaques learning to wash yams, then learning to dip them in seawater; blue tits in England learning to remove tinfoil tops from milk bottles to steal the cream; and male birds learning the specific song of their own neighborhood from their father. In each of these examples, the learner imitates the behavior of others.

3. What were the results of the Bobo doll studies, and what four-part model did Bandura propose to understand those results?

Results of the Bobo doll experiments included that children who had seen an adult behaving aggressively with the doll were more likely to play aggressively with Bobo. Boys were more aggressive than girls, especially if the adult model was a man. Children were equally likely to imitate behavior they saw on television as behavior they saw in person. They were more likely to imitate an adult with qualities they admired.

According to Bandura's four-part model for the results, the extent of social learning can vary depending on conditions at each stage. First, the person must be paying attention to the model's behavior. Second, the person must retain the information gained about the observed behavior. Third, the person must reproduce the behavior, and may get progressively better at imitating the behavior with practice. Fourth, the person must be motivated to reproduce the model's behavior.

Chapter Nine

Section 9.1

1. What are the stages of memory formation, and approximately how long is information retained at each stage?

The initial stage, the sensory buffer (iconic memory), stores sensory information for a second or so. If the sensory information is encoded so that we can make sense of it, it may be transferred to short-term memory (STM), or working memory, where we can consciously use that information. Without rehearsal, we retain information in STM for only a few seconds. Information from STM may be consolidated into long-term memory (LTM), which may be lifelong.

2. What are the two aspects of recall that result in the serial position curve of recall for a list of items? How does manipulating the time between presentation of the list and recall affect performance?

The U-shaped curve results from the primacy effect, or tendency to recall the first few items better, and the recency effect, or tendency to recall the last few items better. If the time between presentation and recall is very short, or if recall is requested immediately, the primacy effect is diminished. If the time between presentation and recall is long, the recency effect is reduced.

3. Why did scientists studying memory use nonsense syllables for memorization tasks?

Nonsense syllables were used rather than words to avoid the possibility that participants might associate a word with some object or event to help remember it. Because the information was basically irrelevant to real life, there would be no reason to make use of it in the course of a day. That meant the participant would have to rely solely on rehearsal to get the information into LTM.

Section 9.2

1. What phenomena indicate that most forgetting is due to a problem in retrieval of information rather than wholesale loss of information from LTM?

   Both the interference of an older memory with a new memory (proactive interference) and the interference of a new memory with an old memory (retroactive interference) are more likely to occur when the new information and old information are similar. This suggests that the old information is still there, but the incorrect memory is being accessed. Material learned right before sleep is better remembered, since there is less subsequent interference that can reduce retrieval. Relearning material that seems to be forgotten takes less time than learning the information initially, which indicates it wasn't lost entirely. Cued recall is better than free recall, indicating the material isn't lost and that it is made more accessible with the cue. Similarly, priming effect, or exposure to a stimulus related to a subsequent stimulus, also affects subsequent responses. Finally, the improved ability to retrieve information when the conditions of the original learning are reproduced, that is, context-dependent retrieval, also demonstrates that "forgotten" information in fact remains in LTM if context can be used to help retrieve it.

2. What are the two types of interference that impede our ability to retrieve information from LTM? Can you think of examples from your own experience?

   Proactive interference is the interference of an older memory with the formation of a new memory. Retroactive interference is the interference that the formation of a new memory causes to an old memory. An example of proactive interference is calling your new cat by the name of your old cat. An example of retroactive interference is finding it difficult to fill out a form requiring your last address because you can only think of your current address.

3. What are some ways you can improve your recall of information in school?

   In learning information, we should focus on understanding how it fits together. That will allow more ways for it to be activated within the semantic web. In those situations where we need to memorize a list of words or facts, mnemonic devices, such as cues based on the first letters, can be helpful. When information is chunked, the number of items to be remembered is reduced, and this can aid in learning. The method of loci, where the image of each item to be remembered is placed in a unique location, can be used for learning lists. Overlearning material will cement it in LTM.

Section 9.3

1. Name the two different subtypes of amnesia, and give an example of each.

   Retrograde amnesia is the loss of old memories formed prior to a trauma. For example, the chauffeur driving in the accident that killed Princess Diana says he cannot remember what happened in the final few minutes before the crash. Anterograde amnesia is the loss of the ability to form new memories after a trauma. For example, patient H.M. lost his ability to remember new material for more than a brief period, as he could not transfer declarative memory into LTM.

2. What are the different subtypes of memory, and what is the evidence that they are at least partially independent of one another?

   Long-term memory is composed of declarative and nondeclarative memory. Declarative memory is of things you know that you can tell others, and nondeclarative memory is of the things that you know that you can show by doing. Declarative memory is composed of episodic and semantic memory. Episodic memory is made up of detailed autobiographical memories, and semantic memory is made up of the memories for our huge store of knowledge. Nondeclarative memory is composed of skill learning, priming, and conditioning.

   Evidence that declarative memory and nondeclarative memory are independent comes from patient H.M. and from patients with Korsakoff's syndrome, who could form new nondeclarative memories but not new declarative memories.

   The evidence that episodic memory and semantic memory are independent comes from patient K.C., who has an intact semantic memory but has lost all of his autobiographical memory. Other evidence is from people like Jill Price, who have amazing autobiographical memories but only average semantic memories. Finally, brain imaging studies have found differences in the parts of the brain that are active when a person is engaged in retrieving semantic memories compared with episodic memories.

3. What is a Hebbian synapse, and how does LTP seem to represent this phenomenon?

   A Hebbian synapse is one that becomes stronger if it often causes the postsynaptic neuron to fire and that gets weaker if it rarely causes the postsynaptic cell to fire. Long-term potentiation was found where a barrage of action potentials in one part of the hippocampus caused a long-lasting increase in the strength of the synapses on another part of the hippocampus. LTP then behaved as a Hebbian synapse.

Chapter Ten

Section 10.1

1. What evidence indicates that animals are capable of understanding human words? Is there evidence that animals can come to understand syntax?

   Many domesticated animals, such as service dogs, can learn to respond in particular ways to spoken commands. But it is not clear that they distinguish between proper and improper syntax. The issues in this controversy include whether an animal can understand the meanings of words (semantics), understand the rules for combining words (syntax), produce human-like speech sounds (phonology), and produce novel strings of words (the generative quality of language). Different animals using different forms of communication have been able to do each of these. Another issue is whether any animal can show recursive logic.

2. What are some of the important stages in learning a first language?

   By 6 months most infants babble, producing meaningless sounds that are strung together so they resemble speech. At this stage, the child understands "no" and tries to repeat sounds. At about a year a child begins to use words, beginning with just one or two, then acquiring more and more. In this stage, the child uses telegraphic speech, using one word or two to convey a whole thought. At this time a child can follow simple commands and understand simple verbs. By 3 to 4 years of age, a child can be understood by a stranger. In this stage the child understands groupings of objects and colors. Finally, by 5 years of age a child has over 2,000 words and can engage in a conversation using complex sentences.

3. What are the different types of aphasia, and what do they tell us about brain organization of language?

   Broca's aphasia (nonfluent aphasia) results from damage to Broca's area at the bottom of the left frontal lobe. With this aphasia, the person has difficulty producing speech but has good comprehension of language. Wernicke's aphasia (fluent aphasia) results from damage to Wernicke's area at the top of the left temporal lobe. With this aphasia, the person produces speech, although it may be garbled, but has great difficulty understanding spoken or written language. Since over 90% of people with aphasia have damage in the left hemisphere, this tells us that for the vast majority of people, the left hemisphere is critical for language.

4. Describe some examples of studies indicating effects of linguistic relativism.

   Russian speakers may find it easier to discriminate among shades of blue that straddle the Russian words for "dark blue" and "light blue." People from cultures that relate to compass directions rather than left and right find it easier to identify north after moving around inside a building.

Section 10.2

1. How do we use categorization to build up prototypes about objects and processes in the world?

   Categorization is recognizing the similarities and differences between concepts. We categorize objects and events, and then we develop a prototype of a concept that fits in a particular category. While no single characteristic is necessary for membership in a category, the prototype is the best example of an object or process in that category. To categorize any particular object or event, we look to see how much it fits or does not fit the prototype for a category.

2. How did Donders add to the complexity of tasks to show that steps in mental processing take time?

   Donders first measured the participant's simple reaction time to a light, then introduced a second light. The participant was instructed to respond only if the red light was lit, but not the blue one. This took longer than simple reaction time. Donders then made the task more difficult with another two-light task. The participant was asked to press a button only if the light on the left was brighter than the light on the right. This task took longer to perform. Donders could then make the task even more difficult by making the lights more similar in brightness. As more steps were needed in mental processing, the reaction time increased.

3. What relationship did Shepard and Metzler find between the degree of rotation between two objects in certain tasks and time needed to respond?

   Shepard and Metzler found that the more degrees of rotation were required to line up the two images, the more time participants needed to complete the task. This was true whether the required rotation was in the plane of the paper or in the third dimension (depth) of the paper.

4. What are the stages in acquiring a skill?

   The first stage in learning a skill is the cognitive phase, in which the person is consciously aware of what she is doing. The performance is slow and there are frequent errors. The second stage is the associative phase, when there is faster performance with smoother movements and fewer errors than in the cognitive phase. In this stage the person still must concentrate on the task. The third stage is the autonomous phase, when the task seems automatic. Performance is smooth, rapid, and efficient. The person doesn't seem to be paying attention, just doing the task.

5. Give examples of findings illustrating change blindness and the attentional blink.

   Inattentional blindness studies show that when our attention is focused on one aspect of a video, such as counting basketball passes, we fail to notice other activity in the video, such as a gorilla walking through the scene. Change blindness is the failure of people to detect a change in a visual scene when there is a momentary interruption of vision. An example of this is the substitution of one experimenter for another when the first bends down behind a counter momentarily. Another aspect of attention in perception is the phenomenon of attentional blink, which is a brief lapse in attention that occurs shortly after we've detected a target.

Section 10.3

1. Give an example of how the anchoring effect can bias judgment.

   The anchoring effect has been demonstrated in an experiment in which participants spun a fortune wheel, which gave a supposedly random number. Participants were asked whether the percentage of the world's countries that are U.N. members from Africa was more or less that that supposedly random number, then they were asked to estimate the number of countries in Africa that were members of the U.N. Participants who spun a larger number had higher estimates than participants who spun a low number.

2. Suggest a way hindsight bias and confirmation bias could lead to belief persistence.

   Hindsight bias is the tendency to misremember our previous views to fit our current knowledge or beliefs. Confirmation bias is the tendency to detect and remember information that confirms our preconceptions, but forget exceptions. With each of these, we focus on information that agrees with our current knowledge or beliefs and ignore contradictory evidence. This leads to belief persistence.

3. What are some examples of how humans tend to be loss-averse?

   An example of being loss-averse is that when given two alternatives concerning mortality rates from a disease, people are willing to take a risk to avoid an alternative stated in terms of number of deaths, but they are unwilling to take such a risk if the alternative is stated in terms to how many people would be saved. This is in spite of the fact that the two alternatives are exactly equivalent. Similarly, given alternatives about gaining or losing money, people prefer the alternatives that are stated in terms of minimizing losses rather than those stated in terms of maximizing gains. Humans do not like to risk losing.

4. What are the various approaches that can help in solving problems?

   Some problems can be solved using an algorithm, which is a specific set of steps that can be followed that will always solve a particular problem. Other problems can be solved using heuristics, or "rules of thumb." A heuristic is an easy to follow set of rules that generally solves the problem. For problems with only one answer or outcome, working backward may be helpful. Working backward involves starting with the desired end result and reversing the steps needed to get there. Another approach to problem solving is to find a good way to represent the problem, perhaps using a graphical representation. Considering alternative representations of a problem may lead to insight, or the sudden understanding of the problem such that the solution is obvious.

Chapter Eleven

Section 11.1

1. Contrast the original meaning of intelligence quotient with the way modern IQ tests assess performance.

   Intelligence quotient was originally defined as the ratio of a child's mental age divided by his or her chronological age and then multiplied by 100. Modern IQ tests assess performance relative to other people of the same age. Modern tests are normalized, meaning they have been given to thousands of people so that both the average performance for any age and the amount of variability in performance are known.

2. How are modern IQ test scores distributed, and how does that distribution make it easy to use IQ scores to gauge a person's percentile ranking?

   Modern IQ test scores are distributed in a normal distribution with a mean of 100 and a standard deviation of 15. Because the mathematical properties of the normal distribution are known, for any IQ score, the percentile ranking is known.

3. What do psychologists mean by the reliability of a test, and what are the different means of assessing reliability?

   The reliability of a test is the consistency of the relative performance of various individuals on the test. Reliability may be assessed by administering the test on two different occasions (test–retest reliability), by having two different examiners administer the test (scoring reliability), or by giving two different versions of the test (cross-test reliability). Another means of assessing reliability is comparing the relative performance across the first and second halves of the same test (split-half reliability).

4. What does validity mean for a psychologist? Considering each of the three different types of validity of psychological tests, how valid are IQ tests?

   For a psychologist, validity means that a test actually measures what it is intended to measure. The three most important aspects of validity are convergent validity, content validity, and criterion-related validity. Convergent validity is the extent to which several different tests intended to measure the same psychological trait, like intelligence, give comparable results. There is good agreement among the results of different intelligence tests, so there is good convergent validity. Content validity is the ability of a test to measure all the various facets of the psychological trait in question. Since researchers disagree on what intelligence really is, there is disagreement about whether any particular test measures all aspects of intelligence. This means that there are questions about content validity of IQ tests. Criterion-related validity is the extent to which the scores on a psychological test predict someone's real-life performance, based on some standard. IQ tests have good criterion-related validity, as they correlate with such standards as measures of brain structure and function, performance in school and in the workplace, health, and income.

5. What are some aspects of life that correlate with IQ? Which of these aspects reflect something that you would consider intelligence?

   On average, children with higher IQ scores will grow up to get better grades in school, gain higher-paying jobs, and live longer, healthier lives than children with lower IQ scores.

Section 11.2

1. What do psychologists mean by *g* factor, and what are the two different aspects of *g* factor?

   The *g* factor is a reflection of pure mental ability that affects many different kinds of behavior and therefore will influence the results of tests of many different kinds of ability. The *g* factor is made up of fluid intelligence and crystallized intelligence. Fluid intelligence is the capacity to reason logically and solve new problems, independent of what you know already. Crystallized intelligence is the knowledge a person has acquired and the ability to use it appropriately.

2. Compare and contrast Sternberg's proposal of three kinds of intelligence with Gardner's proposal of eight or more different intelligences.

   Robert Sternberg suggests there are three intelligences: analytical intelligence of the type typically measured by IQ tests, practical intelligence to adapt to everyday life and accomplish practical tasks, and creative intelligence to deal with new and unusual situations by coming up with unique solutions. Howard Gardner proposes that there are at least eight different kinds of intelligence, including musical intelligence, bodily kinesthetic intelligence, naturalistic intelligence, and interpersonal and intrapersonal intelligence (which together constitute emotional intelligence). Sternberg's two intelligences that are in addition to analytical intelligence are based on existing knowledge and skill. Gardner would classify three of his eight intelligences (linguistic intelligence, logical-mathematical intelligence, and spatial intelligence) as comprising analytical intelligence. His five additional intelligences are similar to Sternberg's additional intelligences in that they are more skill-based, but they are more specific than Sternberg's.

3. What is the Flynn effect and what explanations have been offered to account for it?

   The Flynn effect is the gradually improved performance of people on IQ tests since they were developed. Explanations that have been offered include improvements in health and nutrition as well as response to growing up in a world with more experience in the type of logical, abstract reasoning that is measured by IQ tests.

Section 11.3

1. How do we estimate the heritability of a trait like IQ performance, and what do those estimates tell us about the influence of the environment on IQ?

   Heritability is a statistical estimate of the extent to which individual differences in genes contribute to individual differences in a trait, such as IQ performance, in a population. The simplest estimate is based on comparing the correlations of the IQ scores for genetically identical (MZ) twins with the correlations of the IQ scores for fraternal (DZ) twins, who have no more genes in common than any other siblings. Most estimates of the heritability of IQ are about 0.50. The other half of the variability in IQ scores of a population is due to experience and environmental factors.

2. Discuss some examples of the interaction of genes and the environment for both physical traits in plants and IQ scores in people.

   The interaction of genes and environment in plants may cause yarrow plant strains that do well at lower elevations to be different from those strains that flourish at higher elevations. For humans, an example of an interaction of genes and environment occurs when infants who are breast-fed grow up to have higher IQs, but only if they carry a particular version of one gene. For infants without that version, breast-feeding does not make a difference in IQ. Children with PKU will have normal intelligence only if they have a diet low in phenylalanine. Another example is that children from impoverished backgrounds who are adopted into middle-income families grow up to have higher IQs on average than their biological parents.

3. What is phenylketonuria, and how does it illustrate gene–environment interaction with respect to IQ?

   Phenylketonuria (PKU) is a genetic disorder caused by having a dysfunctional gene for an enzyme that normally helps digest the amino acid phenylalanine. A baby that inherits two dysfunctional copies of the gene will be unable to digest phenylalanine properly, which will lead to a buildup of toxic products that cause severe mental disability, including a very low IQ. However, if the baby is reared in an environment with little or no phenylalanine in the diet, the toxic buildup will be avoided and mental development will be normal, including a normal IQ score. For an infant with two dysfunctional copies of this gene, the effect of the gene depends on the environment.

4. Review the evidence that the difference in average IQ between black Americans and white Americans may be due to differences in their environments.

   The gap in average IQ between white Americans and African Americans has gotten much smaller during the twentieth century. This may be due to the improved economic and social conditions for black Americans, since it is too short a time for the genes to have changed. Other evidence that this IQ difference is due to environment comes from the IQ scores of the German children of American soldiers stationed in Germany. There is no difference in the average IQ scores of the children of black soldiers and white soldiers, even though there was a difference based on race in the soldiers' average scores. Additional evidence that the racial differences in average IQ may be caused by racial differences in economic status has come from heritability estimates of IQ in poor people. There is little evidence for heritability in impoverished families; for instance, average IQ scores for DZ twins are no more similar than the average IQ scores for MZ twins. An impoverished environment may be a limiting factor that does not allow us to see the contributions genes might have made.

5. What is stereotype threat, and how might it play a role in racial differences in average IQ?

   Stereotype threat is an emotional state experienced when exposure to a derogatory stereotype about a particular group causes its members to perform worse. Racial differences in IQ are widely known, and our society holds stereotypes suggesting that African Americans are less intelligent than other groups. It has been demonstrated that knowledge of such stereotypes and recollecting them during testing adversely affects test performance of African Americans, but not white Americans.

Chapter Twelve

Section 12.1

1. Describe the drive reduction model for understanding motivated behaviors.

   Each internal physiological need generates a drive, and the individual seeks out behavior that fulfills that need and reduces that drive.

2. How does negative feedback maintain set points, and how does that relate to the concept of homeostasis?

   Negative feedback turns off a process so that the system returns to its set point, or desired value. This results in homeostasis, or a constant internal environment.

3. Describe the reward pathway in the brain and how it might relate to motivated behavior.

   The reward pathway is interconnected sites in the brain where excitation of neurons leads to intense pleasure. Stimulation of any part of this circuit leads to the release of dopamine in the forebrain, which creates a pleasurable sensation. This may be related to motivated behavior through the reward system providing pleasure whenever a drive is being fulfilled. When the need is fulfilled, the behavior is no longer pleasurable.

4. In what ways are the various levels of human needs either "higher" or "lower" in Maslow's pyramid?

   Maslow's pyramid places the most basic needs at the bottom, and for an individual to attend to a higher-level need, all needs below that in the pyramid must be met. The lowest-level needs are basic for survival, while the need at the top, which few people achieve, is self-actualization, or fulfilling your potential. We are motivated to fulfill each of these needs.

Section 12.2

1. Describe some of the evidence that the brain enforces a body weight set point, using data from both non-human animals and humans.

   Lesions to the ventromedial hypothalamus (VMH) in rats cause animals that have always had constant access to unlimited supplies of food to suddenly eat more and gain weight. They subsequently reach a new, obese body weight, which becomes their new set point. If they are force-fed or food-deprived, they will gain additional weight or lose weight, but when allowed free access to food, they will return to their new (obese) set point. Similar results occur in humans suffering a stroke in that brain region. Lesions to the lateral hypothalamus in rats cause the rats to lose weight and acquire a set point lower than that of a normal rat. When we eat less, the brain reduces our basal metabolism so that more calories can be used to maintain the body weight set point.

2. What hormones inform the brain about body weight, and which part of the brain receives and integrates that information?

   Hormones reporting about body stores include insulin from the pancreas, two stomach hormones (one for decreasing appetite and one for increasing it), one from the intestines, and leptin from fat cells. These hormones are received and integrated in the arcuate nucleus region of the hypothalamus.

3. What behaviors can lead to a long-term reduction in body weight, and how do they compare to fad diets?

   Long-term loss of body weight results from permanent changes in diet and exercise. These changes include selecting smaller food portions, avoiding calorie-dense foods, eating more lower-calorie foods, eating breakfast, and becoming physically active every day. Fad diets are typically short-term changes in eating patterns, and any weight that is lost is regained when the dieting stops and normal eating patterns are resumed.

4. Describe the major eating disorders and evaluate the evidence that they may result from societal pressures to be thin.

   Anorexia nervosa is a condition in which people become obsessed with their body weight and display behaviors leading to extreme weight loss. Victims have a distorted body image and see themselves as fat. Bulimia is a condition where people of normal weight see themselves as fatter than they are and periodically gorge themselves, then vomit or take laxatives to avoid gaining weight. Evidence that these eating disorders are related to societal pressures to be thin includes the much higher rate in females than males and that the age of onset is typically adolescence to young adulthood. While young women are subject to more social pressure than young men to be thin, and the current ideal of feminine beauty includes thinness, anorexia was first described at a time when thinness was not emphasized. So while societal pressures for thinness may play a role in anorexia, there is likely a biological basis too.

Section 12.3

1. What is the role of gonadal steroids in the organization and activation of sexual behavior in non-human animals?

   The gonadal hormones function as coordinating agents, circulating throughout the body to have different effects in different regions. In general, androgens (produced by the testes) prepare the body for reproduction as a male, whereas estrogens and progesterone (produced by the ovaries) prepare the body for reproduction as a female. These same hormones also act on the brain to trigger reproductive behaviors.

2. Describe the role of hormones in sexual differentiation of the mammalian body, and the two conditions that result in a body that is masculine in some characteristics and feminine in others.

   Sexual differentiation depends on hormones produced by the gonads. If testes form, they begin to secrete androgens, resulting in the development of masculine structures, including a penis and scrotum. In the absence of androgens, feminine structures develop, including a clitoris, vagina, and labia. Congenital adrenal hyperplasia (CAH) and androgen insensitivity syndrome (AIS) both result in a body that has both masculine and feminine characteristics. A girl with CAH may have genitals that look both masculine and feminine because her adrenal glands have secreted more testosterone than is normal for a girl. A genetic male with AIS has testes and a clitoris, vagina, and labia because their body cannot respond to the testosterone secreted by the testes.

3. How does exposure to testosterone affect the size of the SDN-POA in rats?

   Female rats normally have a small SDN-POA, but exposure to testosterone during the sensitive period (first few days of life) causes the development of a large nucleus. When an adult female is exposed to testosterone, the size of the nucleus is unaffected. When androgens are removed from a newborn male rat, the SDN-POA is small in adulthood.

4. What is the evidence that prenatal exposure to testosterone affects sexual orientation in humans?

   A variety of measurements of the body in adults reflect prenatal testosterone exposure. These measurements indicate that lesbians were exposed to slightly higher levels of prenatal androgens.

5. Describe the fraternal birth order effect on sexual orientation in men, and weigh the evidence that it is due to social influences of brothers.

   The fraternal birth order effect is the finding that the more older brothers born to the same mother a boy has, the more likely he is to develop a homosexual orientation. The social influences of brothers may be discounted, since the effect only holds for bothers born to the same mother and not for other stepbrothers. Additionally, the effect holds when the brothers are raised apart.

Section 12.4

1. What are some of the basic social needs that people display?

   Social needs include the needs to interact, please, and gain recognition from others. Most people need affiliation, or establishing and maintaining relations with others. We also have a need for intimacy. We have needs for achievement and for power.

2. Describe how the Hawthorne effect was first noted and how it might relate to modern-day institutions.

   The Hawthorne effect was first noticed in studies that varied both physical and psychological variables in a factory with the goal of increasing productivity. While some of the results of the changes were unpredictable, a significant finding was that people behave differently when they know they are being studied. Many modern institutions have programs that show appreciation and recognition for individual workers and groups of workers. This carries with it the message that the individual is being monitored.

Chapter Thirteen

Section 13.1

1. Compare the perspectives of folk psychology, the James–Lange theory, and the two-factor theory of emotion on the relationship between autonomic activity and the experience of emotional states.

   The folk psychology notion of emotion is that when we perceive something, we have an emotional reaction, which is followed by the body responses. The James–Lange theory proposed that when we perceive something, the physiological reactions happen first, and then our mind, perceiving those reactions, experiences the emotions appropriate for those physiological changes. The two-factor theory says that physiological arousal tells us the intensity of the emotion while cognitive interpretation of what causes the arousal determines the type of emotion we experience.

2. Describe the results of the Schachter and Singer experiment, and relate them to the role of cognitive factors and autonomic activity in emotions.

   When people were unknowingly given epinephrine to trigger sympathetic arousal, they were more likely to experience the arousal as anger if they were around an angry-acting person, but they were more likely to experience the arousal as exhilaration if they were around an energetic, playful person. So while the autonomic activity was the same in both cases, the cognitive interpretation of the emotion experienced was affected by the environment.

3. Describe the facial feedback hypothesis, and discuss the various results that support it.

   This hypothesis suggests that the sensory feedback from our face actually affects our emotional experience. Participants who used their smiling muscles to hold a pencil in their teeth found a cartoon more amusing than did a control group. Participants using their frowning muscles to hold a pencil between their upper lip and nose found the cartoon less amusing than did the control group. In another study, adhesive bandages and rubber bands were used to either raise the cheeks, which made the participants feel happier, or lower the cheeks, which made them feel sadder. There is also evidence that people who have had Botox injections in their face to paralyze facial muscles do not feel emotions as fully as other people.

4. What factors seem to contribute to happiness?

   Factors that contribute to happiness include engaging in activity, working hard toward a goal, making progress toward that goal, having enough money not to be in poverty, having strong personal relationships, having a strong identification with a religion, and aging, particularly with for those with many strong personal relationships.

5. Why does fear seem to be a special emotion, and what do we know about the brain regions involved in fear?

   Fear is crucial for survival and it appears natural selection favored the evolution of fear. Fear is the only emotion that we know so far to be associated with a particular brain region. The key brain structure for producing fear is the amygdala.

Section 13.2

1. What are typical responses to stress, and how is it that those responses, which are beneficial in the short run, can be harmful in the long run?

   The initial responses to stress include activation of the sympathetic nervous system, which increases respiration, heart rate, and blood pressure, among other things. Hormones from the sympathetic nervous system are released, which may include cortisol, epinephrine, and norepinephrine. Prolonged stress can damage our physical health. Stress is associated with depression, cardiovascular problems such as heart disease and hypertension, and suppression of the immune system. When stress produces a short-term suppression of the immune system, it allows a rapid mobilization of energy. When stress is prolonged and the immune system is suppressed for a longer period, we become more susceptible to infection.

2. How did our understanding of stress immunization in animals change, and what does our current understanding suggest concerning how children grow up to be resilient adults?

   Originally it was thought that rats that were stressed by handling when they were pups became more resilient to stress as adults. This was superseded by the understanding that the stress of being handled as pups wasn't producing the resilience; it was the greater attention their mother paid to them after the handling that produced the resilience. Similarly, positive attention from parents in childhood makes people more resilient as adults.

3. How was the design of the executive monkey experiment flawed? How did experiments with rats indicate that control and predictability reduce the stress of unpleasant events?

   The executive monkey experiment was flawed because the monkeys were not randomly assigned to the executive role. The monkeys who were fastest at learning the task, and who may have been more stressed by the shocks, were made the executives. One rat experiment allowed the executive rats to avoid the shock by pressing a lever. The yoked rats received the same shocks as the executive rats, but they developed larger ulcers. The executive rats had more control in the situation than the yoked rats. In another experiment, an auditory signal preceded the shock. The executive rats could press a bar to avoid the shock. The yoked rats received the same shocks as the executive rats. In this case, the executive rats got fewer ulcers than the yoked rats, but both groups had fewer ulcers than rats given no signal and for whom the shock was unpredictable.

4. What is health psychology and what are some examples of how physical health affects mental health and vice versa?

   Health psychology examines the psychological, social, and biological factors that influence physical and mental health. Evidence that physical health affects mental health includes the monitoring, by the brain, of the immune system through the detection of cytokines and antibodies. When these signal the presence of illness, the discomfort of the illness may be from the brain, which may cause the unpleasant feelings that force us to rest. Evidence that mental health influences physical health includes the correlation between stressful life events and later physical illness such as heart disease and infections.

Chapter Fourteen

Section 14.1

1. What factors lead people to believe that horoscopes can accurately describe their personality or predict their future?

   Astrologers are careful to write flattering portraits of personality for every sign. We may feel the analysis fits us because it is flattering. With astrology, confirmation bias leads us to remember predictions that seem to unfold, and to downplay or forget predictions that fail. A person may think astrological horoscopes are accurate because of subjective validation, or the Forer effect, the tendency to pick out a specific, accurate meaning from an open-ended, vague personality description.

2. Describe the Freudian model of the mind and the role of defense mechanisms in the unconscious.

   Freud emphasized the importance of the unconscious for understanding our behavior. Freud proposed that the mind consisted of the id, which seeks only pleasure; the superego, which incorporates society's restrictions on behavior; and the ego, which tries to fulfill the demands of the id within the confines of the superego. According to Freud, the ego keeps the ugly, unacceptable demands of the id from consciousness by use of defense mechanisms.

3. What are Freud's psychosexual stages of development, and what are the different personality types he believed might result from unresolved conflicts at each?

   According to Freud, the beginning of human personality is the oral stage, when the baby pursues pleasurable sensations in the mouth, tongue, and lips. Unresolved conflicts in the oral stage can lead to being overly passive, dependent, and gullible. In the next stage, the anal stage, the child derives pleasure from the sensation of defecating. Unresolved conflicts in the anal stage can lead to being overly messy or overly neat. The third stage is the phallic stage, when pleasure is derived from masturbation. If children fail to resolve this stage, they may be overly dependent on the opposite-sex parent and overly hostile to the same-sex parent. Promiscuity, impulsiveness, and homosexuality may result. In the latent stage the child's superego represses most of the id-driven urges before sexual maturity arrives. There are no conflicts to be resolved in this stage. The final stage is the genital stage, characterized by healthy separation from the parents and greater interest in genitals (one's own and others'), leading to a mature, sexual partnership. Unresolved conflicts in this stage may result in unhappy sexual relationships.

4. Contrast the methods and goals of psychoanalysis with Rogerian psychotherapy.

   Freudian psychoanalysis can be summarized as many long, open-ended conversations with the client, including discussions of dreams and other insights into unconscious thoughts and desires, to get past defense mechanisms so the client can become aware of his or her internal conflicts. Once the client understands these internal conflicts, the idea is that he or she will be able to proceed with a life unencumbered by the internal conflicts that unconsciously make us unhappy. Rogerian psychotherapy focuses on what the client wants, both by having the client discuss whatever he or she wants and by viewing the client's goals as the only legitimate goals of psychotherapy. In contrast, a psychoanalytic therapist might feel it is important to get the client to remember or acknowledge something the client would rather not know. Rogerian psychotherapy emphasizes providing clients with a comfortable, nonjudgmental environment to talk through their problems so that they can identify what they should do. The therapist should provide unconditional positive regard for the client and is in some ways acting more like a coach or facilitator than someone who is "curing" an "illness." In distinction to Freud, Rogers proposed several ways to test the effectiveness of client-centered psychotherapy, where the criterion was whether the client felt he had benefitted.

Section 14.2

1. What was the strategy of Cattell's factor analysis of English words for personality traits?

   Gordon Allport had catalogued over 4,000 English words describing personality traits. Cattell reduced these to a more manageable number by eliminating those that he felt were just different words for the same underlying trait. Even then, he was left with over 170 words that appeared to describe at least partially different traits. He then used factor analysis to determine which of these terms covaried with each other. Following this analysis, he was left with 16 source traits that make up human personality.

2. What are the big five traits, and what personality characteristics are typical of the low and high ends of each?

   The big five traits are openness, conscientiousness, extraversion, agreeableness and neuroticism. A person on the low end of openness will be practical, follow routines, and be a conformist. A person on the high end of openness will be imaginative, seek variety, and be a nonconformist. A person on the low end of conscientiousness will be disorganized, careless, and impulsive. A person on the high end of conscientiousness will be organized, punctual, and dependable. A person on the low end of extraversion will be retiring, sober, and reserved. A person on the high end of extraversion will be sociable, fun loving, and talkative. A person on the low end of agreeableness will be ruthless, suspicious, and uncooperative. A person on the high end of agreeableness will be soft hearted, trusting, and helpful. A person on the low end of neuroticism will be calm, secure, and imperturbable. A person on the high end of neuroticism will be anxious, insecure, and moody.

3. Why are research psychologists skeptical of the value of the Myers–Briggs test when so many businesses make use of it?

   The Myers–Briggs emphasizes personality types, diverging from modern personality research, which emphasizes traits instead. There is little research evidence that the Myers–Briggs is a valid test for measuring personality traits or that it accurately predicts a person's success in one career or another. The Myers–Briggs is not a particularly reliable test, as over one-third of test-takers, if retested more than 9 months later, are classified as a different personality "type."

Section 14.3

1. What is the evidence that genes influence the big five traits?

   The evidence that genes influence personality comes from twin studies. Sets of identical twins, who have identical genes, are more alike in personality than sets of fraternal twins. This occurs even when each set of twins shares the same environment. A statistical estimate of heritability indicates that differences in genes account for about 40–50% of the differences we see in human populations, for each of the big five factors

2. Describe different temperaments in babies and the adult personality traits that tend to be associated with each.

   Babies who are highly reactive to novel stimuli, fussing or crying readily for several minutes, are referred to as behaviorally uninhibited, or high reactive babies. Babies who show little reaction to novel stimuli, either not fussing at all or only for a short time, are referred to as behaviorally inhibited, or low reactive babies. Most babies are somewhere in between in terms of their reaction to stimuli. Neuroticism is one factor in temperament: low reactive babies tend to grow up to be emotionally stable, and high reactive babies tend to be emotionally unstable. Temperament also reflects extraversion, since low reactive babies tend to be more outgoing when they grow up. To a lesser extent, conscientiousness also reflects temperament. High reactive babies tend to display greater conscientiousness, which may reflect their attempt to control their exposure to unpleasant situations.

3. What was the person–situation debate, and how was it resolved by the interactionist model?

   In the person–situation debate, the question was whether behavior could be better explained by a person's internal characteristics (sometimes referred to as the person's "disposition") or by the situation. Interactionists resolved this debate by demonstrating that the situation is important for understanding the behavior that is displayed at the moment, but personality is important for understanding someone's average behavior over days, weeks, and years.

Section 14.4

1. What term did behaviorists use to describe personality, and how did they think it came about?

   For behaviorists, personality was a constellation of response tendencies, or particular ways of reacting to situations based on past learning experiences. Learning experiences and related rewards and punishments shaped response tendencies. The response tendencies formed the personality.

2. What is the locus of control, and how does it relate to self-efficacy?

   Locus of control is the individual's perception about whether his or her efforts in life will be reinforced. People with an internal locus of control perceive that whether or not they get reinforced is up to them. People with an external locus of control perceive that reinforcers in life are determined by luck or chance, not by their own efforts. Bandura's term *self-efficacy* is the belief that you are effective, you have the ability to succeed, to master a particular situation. This requires the perception of an internal locus of control, because you have to believe your efforts matter in order to try. But self-efficacy isn't just having an internal locus of control; it is also the confidence that you will be successful as you tackle progressively greater challenges growing up.

3. In what ways do the average big five traits differ in individuals from collectivist versus individualist societies?

   People from more collectivist cultures tend to display less extraversion and openness to experience than people from more individualist cultures. This difference appears to be a cultural rather than genetic effect, because the big five traits of people who move to different cultures tend to shift to better match the new culture.

Chapter Fifteen

Section 15.1

1. What physical characteristics do most people find attractive in other people?

   Physical characteristics that most people find attractive in others are facial symmetry, similarity to their own face, and the absence of blemishes. All of these characteristics emerge when a computer averages many different faces. Such morphed faces are considered attractive by research participants.

2. What is the fundamental attribution error?

   This is the tendency to attribute other people's behavior to their disposition rather than to the situation surrounding them. It is the tendency to underestimate how important situational variables can be for other people.

3. What is the self-serving attribution bias?

   This is our tendency to attribute our successes to having a superior disposition, but attribute our failures to external forces.

4. How do social roles affect our behavior?

   Social roles are the behaviors and attitudes expected from people with particular social positions. They shape our social attitudes, which are our evaluations about people, usually positive or negative, and predispositions to act in particular ways toward them.

5. What is the Implicit Association Test, and what does it suggest about the effects of stereotypes on our thinking?

   The Implicit Association Test (IAT) monitors reaction time to detect associations we might have between particular words or images. The time to accurately classify words or images is measured, and classifications that take shorter times are thought to be more strongly associated. The test shows that racial and gender stereotypes common in our society become deeply embedded in our brain's function. Without even being aware of it, our brain has a hard time associating characteristics that defy stereotypes, such as positive attributes to African Americans, or scientific careers to women. The results suggest that we have been exposed to stereotypes about race and gender and incorporated them into our thinking.

Section 15.2

1. What are social norms and how do they affect our behavior?

   Social norms are the rules that a group uses to determine which behaviors, beliefs, attitudes, and values are appropriate or inappropriate. We feel the pressure to behave and believe like everyone else, which is known as the normative social influence.

2. How does the presence of an audience affect our performance?

   Social facilitation takes place when the presence of other people affects performance. Having an audience increases arousal. Having an audience improves our performance when we're doing something easy, or something we already do well, but it hurts our performance if the task is difficult or new. The expectation of evaluation, the perception of the audience's attitudes, and past experience all are factors in performing in front of an audience.

3. In what ways may people behave differently when they are part of a crowd rather than by themselves?

   Being in a group may lead to social loafing, which is shirking responsibility because you are in a group. When in a crowd, people may experience diffusion of responsibility and assume someone else will act. If this occurs in an emergency, it is known as the bystander effect. Generally the more bystanders there are, the less likely each one is to help out. Deindividuation, the process of losing your own identity and coming to identify with the crowd, is another way people behave differently, perhaps irresponsibly, in a crowd. Identification with others may lead to groupthink, which occurs when a group of people makes mistakes due to social pressures and self-censorship.

4. What is the prisoner's dilemma and how does it relate to our choosing between selfish behavior and altruistic behavior?

   In the prisoner's dilemma, two people are arrested and are interrogated separately, each accused of a crime. The police offer both prisoners the same deal: If you confess, your testimony will be used to send the other prisoner to jail and you will be released. If you both confess, you both will go to jail for a short time. If neither of you confesses, you will both go free. The selfish thing to do is to confess: one prisoner would go free if the other prisoner didn't confess, or both would have a short sentence if the other prisoner did confess. Altruistic behavior would have neither person confess so that they would both go free. Selfishness and altruism (putting others before oneself), and the tension between them, are studied by evolutionary psychologists as traits that have evolved over time.

Section 15.3

1. What are the factors that lead people to become friends and to stay friends?

   Friends have interests in common. Friendship deepens as we reveal more about ourselves. Friends understand each other and are supportive of each other. For enduring friendships there must be a shared history. Friends make it clear that they value the friendship.

2. Describe Sternberg's triangular theory of love and how we might typify the different types of romances that embody one, two, or three of these factors.

   Sternberg asserts that passion, the exciting feeling of desire, is only one important part of romantic relationships. Romantic relationships may also include a sense of commitment, the decision to stay together and make plans together, and also intimacy, a feeling of closeness and high regard for one another. A relationship that consists of intimacy but not passion or commitment typifies a friendship more than a romance. A relationship built on passion only, without intimacy or commitment, typifies infatuation, which is not likely to last (unless the relationship develops further). A relationship with commitment but not passion or intimacy typifies empty love. Relationships that are strong in at least two of these factors are more likely to be happy and lasting. Relationships with intimacy and passion but without commitment are typical of romantic love. Relationships with intimacy and commitment but without passion are typical of companionate love. Relationships with the combination of passion and commitment but without intimacy typify fatuous love. Consummate love includes all three factors.

3. What can couples do to strengthen their relationship so it will be happy and endure?

   Relationships are strengthened by knowing your partner well, nurturing your fondness and admiration for your partner, connecting with your partner, allowing your partner to influence you, solving your solvable problems, overcoming gridlock, and creating shared meanings.

Section 15.4

1. What are some biological factors and some social factors that promote aggression?

   In most mammalian species, including humans, males are more aggressive than females, and it is clear that androgens such as testosterone contribute to the greater aggression in males. Impulsive aggression, in response to some provocation, seems to reflect reduced activity in the brain's frontal lobes, which tend to inhibit impulsive behaviors. Several genes encoding proteins important in neurotransmitter signaling, including monoamine oxidase (MAO), have also been implicated in impulsive aggression in humans. Many cultures value physical aggression in males, which is a social factor promoting aggression. Widespread differences across cultures in the incidence of aggression make it clear that there are also environmental and cultural influences on aggression, such as exposure to video violence.

2. What are the two types of aggression? Which one is better studied and why?

   Controlled/instrumental aggression is a form of aggression that is carefully planned and usually intended to gain some goal. Reactive/impulsive aggression occurs in response to some provocation. Instrumental aggression is relatively rare, and reactive aggression is much more widely studied. Reactive aggression can be provoked in a laboratory-type study. Instrumental aggression, because it is a carefully planned type of aggression, is difficult to produce in a laboratory or for an experiment.

3. Should society punish people for aggressive behavior? If so, what factors can be considered in trying to make sure the punishment fits the crime?

   Societies may imprison people who have been aggressive, either as a deterrent, to discourage other people from becoming violent, or as a way to protect other victims. But another reason to imprison people is for retribution, punishing the individual beyond the need for deterrence or protection. This impulse may be responsible for the growing percentage of the U.S. population in prisons.

To fit the punishment to the crime, it is important to consider the context and type of the transgression. It is also important to cite the goal of the punishment: deterrent, protection, retribution, or rehabilitation. If the goal includes rehabilitation, then imprisonment by itself will not likely result in an improvement in impulse control, better anger management, or better social skills. These would require instruction.

Section 15.5

1. Describe the basic experiment on authority and obedience Stanley Milgram conducted.

   Stanley Milgram's basic experiment had three people: a participant, an experimenter in a white lab coat, and an actor, playing the part of another participant. The participant and the actor drew lots and, because the drawing was rigged, the participant was always given the role of the "teacher," while the actor took the role of the "learner." The learner was seated in an separate room with wires attached to his or her wrists. The teacher was seated in a larger room in front of a large machine with a series of 30 labeled switches on its front. The markings on the switches ranged from 15 volts to 450 volts, with labeling from "mild shock" to "severe shock" at the high end. In each trial, the teacher read one word followed by four words, and the learner was supposed to guess the correct word of the four. When the learner gave the wrong answer, the teacher was to punish the learner by throwing a switch to administer a shock. With each additional mistake, the voltage was increased. Recorded "responses" from the learner, who was not actually being shocked, were played and indicated increasing distress. If the teacher indicated an unwillingness to continue, the experimenter instructed him or her to continue. The outcome of interest in the experiment was how large a shock the teacher was willing to administer, reflecting his or her obedience to authority. The surprising result was that nearly two-thirds of the participants were willing to administer shocks up to 450 volts.

2. What variations in the basic Milgram experiment were tried, and what did those outcomes indicate?

   When Milgram repeated his experiment without the experimenter being physically present, but only giving instructions over the phone, teachers were much more reluctant to continue. This showed that the physical presence of an authority figure increases his power of persuasion. Milgram also repeated the experiment in a run-down building, rather than Yale University, and found that the teachers were more reluctant to continue administering shocks. This showed that a source of authority is affiliation with an admired institution. In another version, two authority figures sat at the "command" desk, and the results were the same as with one experimenter *unless* one of them voiced doubts about continuing. Then the teacher generally stopped administering shocks. The authority seemed to be diffused by the disagreement in this version. In another version, there were three teachers, with two of them actors. If one of the other teachers refused to continue, the participant also refused to continue. Milgram also used women as participants in the experiment and found that they were as likely as men to continue the shocks, but they were more distressed about it. Finally, in another version of the experiment, the teacher read the words while another person threw the switches. They were even more likely to continue to the highest voltages as the teachers in the classic version of Milgram's experiment.

Chapter Sixteen

Section 16.1

1. What was the main motive behind putting together the first *Diagnostic and Statistical Manual of Mental Disorders*?

   The *Diagnostic and Statistical Manual of Mental Disorders* (*DSM*) arose after World War II to standardize the definitions of psychiatric terms and mental disorders. This helped different doctors reach the same diagnosis when examining a particular patient.

2. What are the two biggest issues to consider when evaluating any psychological test or measurement, such as the *DSM*?

   The two major issues in evaluating any psychological test or classification system are reliability and validity. Reliability is the extent to which different clinicians would reach the same diagnosis for any patient with a particular set of symptoms. Validity is the extent to which a psychological test or process identifies a characteristic or disorder that really exists.

3. According to modern methods such as those in *DSM-5*, what is an important component of deciding whether someone has a mental disorder?

   Out of concern for labeling normal behavior as a disorder, about half the diagnoses have the additional criterion of asking whether the behavior causes "clinically significant distress or impairment in social, occupational, or other important areas of functioning." In other words, displaying unusual behavior, no matter how unusual, may not qualify a person as having a mental disorder. If she can still go about her everyday life, taking care of herself, interacting with friends, and performing well at work, then who's to say her unusual behavior reflects a disorder rather than a personal quirk?

Section 16.2

1. Lessons from learning studies have suggested what sort of therapy for people with phobias? How is it conducted?

   One treatment for phobias that was based on research in fear conditioning is systematic desensitization. This is done by gradually exposing the person to the feared object or situation so that he or she can learn that there is no real danger. This treatment is generally applied over several sessions, but it may be reduced to a single session.

2. What is the evidence that suicide is usually an impulsive act?

   One piece of evidence is that of more than 500 people who were prevented from jumping off the Golden Gate Bridge, only 6% went on to commit suicide. Another piece of evidence is that suicide rates went down by a third in Britain when that country switched from using coal gas, which contains lots of deadly carbon monoxide, to natural gas for heating and cooking—reducing the ease with which a person could impulsively commit suicide.

3. What are the two main classes of effective treatment for depression, and why is one more commonly used than the other?

   Selective serotonin reuptake inhibitors (SSRIs) are very popular for treating depression. A second form of treatment is 20 or so sessions of cognitive behavioral therapy (CBT), psychotherapy aimed at correcting negative thinking and improving interpersonal relationships. This is about as effective as SSRI treatment, and the rate of relapse is lower for CBT than for SSRI treatment. SSRI treatment alone is much more widely used than CBT. A big factor is money—SSRIs are relatively inexpensive, so that treatment costs a lot less than paying a trained psychologist to provide CBT. Because SSRIs are inexpensive, health insurance companies typically make it easier to get the drugs than CBT. Also, the number of CBT therapists in most areas is still low, so it can be difficult to get this treatment, even though it is the most effective for depression.

Section 16.3

1. List some common personality disorders and some of the symptoms common to each.

   Schizotypal personality disorder may resemble schizophrenia in the sense that the client may have very unconventional, even paranoid beliefs, along with eccentric behavior that makes it difficult to maintain relationships. While people with obsessive-compulsive personality disorder (OCPD) do not experience obsessions or compulsions that occur in OCD, their behavior and thinking is characterized by a rigidity regarding order, organization, and notions of what is right or wrong. People with OCPD are preoccupied with orderliness and perfectionism. Narcissistic personality disorder is characterized by a sense of self-importance requiring excessive admiration, along with a lack of empathy for others. Borderline personality disorder involves frequent mood swings, fear of abandonment, and impulsive behaviors that damage relationships. Avoidant personality disorder is the avoidance of interpersonal contact because of feelings of social inadequacy and an irrational belief that others will automatically dislike you. Antisocial personality disorder is a disregard for others and lack of remorse.

2. What sorts of behaviors are seen in borderline personality disorder, and how do they interfere with relationships?

   People who are emotionally unstable, experiencing frequent mood swings, identity disturbances, and impulsive behavior that impair their relationships with other people, may be diagnosed with borderline personality disorder. The intense, angry behavior of the borderline personality often interferes with relationships with other people. Ironically, in a kind of self-fulfilling prophecy, intense fear of being abandoned may lead people with borderline personality disorder to be clingy and to demand so much reassurance that they actually do drive their friends away.

3. Why is it that if left untreated, avoidant personality disorder tends to be self-reinforcing?

   Once someone has come to believe that he is inadequate in social interactions, or that people naturally dislike him, he is likely to withdraw from social life. Consequently, existing friendships tend to fade and the person forms no new friendships, affording him no opportunity to learn that he can have fulfilling interactions with other people and that people don't automatically dislike him. Ironically, to the extent the person keeps to himself when in public, others may be reluctant to approach and befriend him.

Section 16.4

1. What are the positive and negative symptoms often seen in schizophrenia?

   Positive symptoms are behavioral states that have been gained. Examples include hallucinations, delusions, and excited activity. Negative symptoms are behavioral functions that have been lost—for example, slow and impoverished thought and speech, emotional and social withdrawal, or blunted affect.

2. What is the major structural difference seen in the brains of people with schizophrenia compared with control participants?

   CT and MRI scans reveal the presence of significant, consistent anatomical differences in the brains of many patients with schizophrenia. The most reliable difference seen so far is that many patients with schizophrenia have enlarged cerebral ventricles, especially the lateral ventricles.

3. What is the modern understanding of the role of genes in schizophrenia?

   The genes favoring schizophrenia do not act in an all-or-none fashion, but rather they affect the probability that the disorder will arise. There is a strong genetic contribution to schizophrenia, which can be viewed as a vulnerability to stress, especially early in life. For example, infections before birth, complications in the birth process, or growing up in a dense urban environment all increase the probability of schizophrenia. Evidence of the genetic contribution includes that relatives of people with schizophrenia show a higher incidence of the disorder than is found in the general population. Furthermore, the risk of schizophrenia among relatives increases with the closeness of the relationship, because closer relatives share a greater number of genes. In a few very rare cases, a single gene may be responsible for the appearance of schizophrenia in a particular family. The strongest evidence of a genetic influence on schizophrenia comes from twin studies. About half of the monozygotic twins of people with schizophrenia are concordant for the disorder, while the rate of concordance for dizygotic twins is only about 17%. Although the significantly higher concordance rate among monozygotic twins is strong evidence of a genetic factor, many people who have a twin with schizophrenia never develop the disorder.

4. What medications are typically used to treat people with schizophrenia? Bipolar disorder?

   Antipsychotic drugs—including typical neuroleptics like chlorpromazine, which block D2 dopamine receptors, and atypical neuroleptics—tend to reduce the positive symptoms of schizophrenia and have allowed many people to return to their families and the community.

   Although typical neuroleptics do not seem to help people with bipolar disorder, the newer, atypical neuroleptics may dampen the manic phase in people with bipolar disorder. Most people suffering from bipolar disorder benefit from treatment with the element lithium.

5. What are the side effects of medicines used to treat schizophrenia and bipolar disorder?

   Typical neuroleptics can result in tardive dyskinesia, which is characterized typically by involuntary movements of the tongue or difficulty walking, and these are debilitating in some patients. Although the atypical neuroleptics are less likely than typical neuroleptics to cause side effects in motor function, they are more likely to cause weight gain. There is real danger of a lithium overdose, so care must be taken to avoid toxic side effects. It may be regarded as a side effect that some people with bipolar disorder stop taking the medication, and one hypothesis is that the person "misses" the often exhilarating manic episodes that are blocked by lithium.

Glossary

Numbers in brackets refer to the chapter(s) where the term is introduced.

A

absolute threshold The lowest intensity of a stimulus that can be detected half the time. [6]

accommodation In Piaget's theory of cognitive development, a change made in the mind as a result of taking in new information about the world. [5]

acetylcholine A neurotransmitter used by many parts of the nervous system. [3]

achievement tests Multiple-choice exams given to groups of students to assess readiness for college study. [11]

acid *See* lysergic acid diethylamide. [7]

acquisition In the context of classical conditioning, the gradual appearance of the CR in response to the CS alone. [8]

action potential Also called *nerve impulse*. The electrical message of a neuron that travels along the axon to the axon terminals. [3]

activation synthesis A theory that dreams result when the mind stitches together a narrative from images and sensations that were generated by random neural activity. [7]

activation In the context of sexual behaviors, the action of hormones in adulthood to make particular behaviors more likely to occur. [12]

active avoidance A response a subject has learned to avoid an aversive stimulus. [8]

actor-observer bias The tendency to explain away our own mistakes by attributing them to the environment, but to attribute the mistakes of others to their disposition. [15]

adaptation stage The return to normal following an alarm reaction. [13]

adaptation In Piaget's theory of cognitive development, the process by which an individual learns about the world and incorporates that information into his or her mental life. [5]

addiction The strong desire to self-administer a drug, even when it causes problems. [7]

adequate stimulus The type of stimulus for which a given sensory receptor organ is particularly adapted. [6]

ADHD *See* attention deficit hyperactivity disorder. [5]

adolescence The process of transition from childhood to adulthood. [5]

adoption studies Studies of identical twins separated at birth. [4]

adrenal gland An endocrine gland atop the kidney which releases hormones in response to stress. [13]

aggression Behavior intended to cause physical or psychological harm or pain. [15]

agonist A drug that activates a receptor in the same way as the normal neurotransmitter. [3, 7]

agoraphobia An irrational fear of certain environments. [16]

agreeableness A personality trait that reflects a person's tendency to be compassionate and cooperative. [14]

AIS *See* androgen insensitivity syndrome. [12]

alarm reaction The activation of the sympathetic nervous system including a release of hormones as the initial response to stress. [13]

alcohol The most common depressant, a neuromodulator that increases the responsiveness of GABA receptors. [7]

alcoholism A disorder resulting from the excessive consumption of alcohol to the point that it interferes with a happy and productive life. [13]

algorithm A specific set of steps that will always solve a particular problem. [10]

all-or-none property The fact that size of the action potential is independent of the size of the stimulus. [3]

alleles One of two or more different versions of a gene. [4]

alpha rhythm Brain waves of 8–12 Hz that occur during relaxed wakefulness. [7]

altruism The practice of putting others before oneself. [15]

Alzheimer's disease (AD) The most common cause of dementia in older people. [5]

ambivalent attachment Also called *resistant attachment*. A style of attachment in which the child is upset when the caregiver leaves, may warm up to a stranger, and behave negatively toward the caregiver upon reuniting. [5]

amino acids Subunits of proteins, strung together in a sequence that forms a particular protein molecule. [4]

amnesia A severe impairment of memory. [9]

amphetamines Powerful stimulants that increase the release of catecholamine neurotransmitters. [7]

amygdala A group of nuclei, one in each temporal lobe, that is key in producing and recognizing fear. [3, 13]

amyloid A protein that accumulates to cause plaques in AD. [5]

anal stage The second phase in Freud's psychosexual stages of development, when the child derives pleasure from the sensation of defecating. [14]

analgesic A substance that acts as a painkiller. [7]

anchoring effect The tendency to rely too heavily on an initial piece of information when making a judgment. [10]

androgen insensitivity syndrome (AIS) A condition in genetic males resulting from a mutation that makes the body insensitive to androgens. The genitals at birth resemble those of a girl. [12]

androgens The primary steroid hormones produced by the testes, including testosterone. [12, 15]

anesthesia A drug-induced loss of consciousness. [7]

angel dust *See* phencyclidine. [7]

anorexia nervosa A condition involving obsession with body weight that leads to extreme weight loss. [12]

antagonist A drug molecule that interferes with neuronal signaling by preventing a neurotransmitter from binding to its receptor. [3, 7]

anterograde amnesia Amnesia for events occurring after an event, such as a trauma. [9]

antibodies Proteins that latch on to invading microbes to signal white blood cells to attack. [13]

antisocial personality disorder (ASPD) A personality disorder characterized by a pattern of disregard for other peoples' rights, with little evidence of remorse for harm done to others. [16]

anxiety disorders Several major types of disorders, all of which are accompanied by intense, irrational anxiety that interferes with everyday functioning. [16]

anxiolytics Drugs that relieve anxiety, sometimes informally called "minor tranquilizers." [16]

aphasia An impairment of language after acquisition, often the result of a brain injury or disease. [10]

arcuate nucleus A hypothalamic region that receives hormonal signals about energy stores and stimulates other brain regions to trigger either hunger or satiety. [12]

Aristotle (384–322 BCE) An ancient Greek teacher who was a keen observer of animals and humans and was interested in sensory illusions. [1]

Army Alpha A written group test of intelligence used to place recruits in World War I. [11]

Army Beta An orally administered intelligence test used to place recruits in World War I. [11]

ASD *See* autism spectrum disorder. [16]

ASPD *See* antisocial personality disorder. [16]

Asperger's syndrome Also called *high functioning autism*. A part of the autism spectrum disorder in which individuals have no difficulty with verbal communication but still have difficulty discerning what others think and feel. [5]

assimilation In Piaget's theory of cognitive development, the process of taking in information about the external world. [5]

associative learning A type of learning in which a relationship is formed between two stimuli or between a stimulus and a behavior. [8]

associative phase The second stage of skill acquisition, in which performance is faster with fewer errors. [10]

astrology A theory that a person's birth at a particular time of the year endows them with one of twelve personalities. [14]

attachment A strong emotional bond or tie between the infant and caregivers. [5]

attention deficit hyperactivity disorder (ADHD) A problem in directing attention that is also accompanied by more physical activity and fidgeting. [5]

attention A concentration of the mind on a particular object or process. [10]

attentional blink A brief lapse of attention that occurs shortly after a person detects a target. [10]

attentional spotlight The ability to direct our attention to one part of our visual field. [10]

attribution theory A set of ideas about how we explain our own behavior and the behavior of others. [15]

attributions Judgments we make about why a person behaves in a particular way. [15]

atypical neuroleptics Antipsychotic drugs that don't have the selective high affinity for dopamine receptors but block other types of receptors, such as certain serotonin receptors. [16]

audition The process of hearing. [6]

authority The power or right to make decisions. [15]

autism spectrum disorder (ASD) A disorder characterized by deficits in social communication and interaction accompanied by restricted, repetitive behaviors and interests, which can range from mild to severe. [11, 16]

autism A spectrum of disorders characterized by impaired social interactions, problems communicating, and severely restricted behavior and interests. [5, 11]

autonomic nervous system A part of the nervous system that is not under our conscious control, consisting of the sympathetic and parasympathetic nervous systems. [3, 13]

autonomous phase The third stage of skill acquisition, during which performance seems automatic and requires no conscious attention. [10]

availability heuristic The tendency to rely on how readily an event comes to mind in judging its likelihood in the future. [10]

avoidant attachment A style of attachment in which the child shows little or no distress when the caregiver leaves, shows little or no response upon reunion, and interacts very little with a stranger. [5]

avoidant personality disorder A personality disorder characterized by social phobia or extreme sensitivity about negative comments or behaviors from others such that interpersonal contact is avoided. [16]

axon hillock The widest part of an axon where it originates from the cell body. [3]

axon terminal Also called *terminal button*. The end of an axon that passes information to other cells. [3]

axon A single extension from the nerve cell that carries nerve impulses from the cell body to other cells. [3]

B

B. F. Skinner (1904–1990) A behaviorist who rejected the study of any mental events and felt that the brain fell outside the field of psychology. [1]

babble The meaningless sounds strung together to resemble speech made by infants, typically before the age of 6 months. [10]

Baby X studies Investigations of the behavior of adults with babies as a function of their belief about the sex of the baby. [12]

barbiturates A class of depressant drugs. [7]

basal forebrain A region in the forebrain related to SWS sleep and insomnia. [7]

basal ganglia A collection of interconnecting nuclei under the cerebral cortex that help control movement of the body. [3]

basal metabolism The bodily processes that break down food for energy. [12]

behaviorism The perspective that psychologists should study only observable behavior and not subjective mental events. [1, 8]

belief persistence The tendency to hold on to a belief, even in the face of contradictory evidence. [10]

benzodiazepines Common anxiolytics that affect mood by boosting the effects of GABA receptors, which when stimulated normally inhibit neuronal activity throughout the cortex. [16]

bereavement The sense of loss and longing for someone who has died. [5]

beta activity *See* desynchronized EEG. [7]

bilingualism The ability to fluently use more than one language. [10]

binaural cues Information about the location of sound found by comparing input to the two ears. [6]

Binet–Simon scale An intelligence test developed by Binet and Simon for children that consists of 30 different tasks of increasing difficulty. [11]

binocular cues Information about distance provided by using two eyes. [6]

binocular disparity The difference in the views from two eyes; this provides one important visual clue for depth perception. [6]

biological clock A biological mechanism that keeps track of time. [7]

biological constraints on learning Also called *biological preparedness to learn*. The observation that some behaviors are more easily learned by one species than another. [8]

biological preparedness to learn *See* biological constraints on learning. [8]

bipolar disorder A mental disorder characterized by periods of depression alternating with periods of excessively expansive mood. [16]

birth-order effect The hypothesis that the order of birth in a family affects each child's personality. [14]

bisexuality Sexual orientation with attraction directed toward both sexes. [12]

bitter One of the five different tastes, detected by taste receptor proteins that respond to a wide range of chemicals. [6]

blind spots The parts of the visual fields that are missing because of the optic discs. [6]

BMI *See* body mass index. [12]

Bobo doll studies A set of social modeling experiments conducted by Albert Bandura. [8]

body mass index (BMI) A gauge of body weight based on the ratio of weight to height. [12]

body weight set point The body weight that is maintained by brain systems. [12]

borderline personality disorder A personality disorder characterized by emotional instability, identity disturbances, and impulsive behavior that impairs relationships with others. [16]

brain self-stimulation The repeated pressing of a bar to provide a small current of electricity to an area of the brain, producing a pleasurable sensation. [7]

brain The center of the nervous system that coordinates and regulates all body processes. [3]

brainstem The stalk-like core of the brain that controls vital functions and transfers information between the cerebrum, cerebellum, and spinal cord. [3]

Broca's aphasia Also called *nonfluent aphasia*. An impairment in speech production, but not in comprehension. [10]

Broca's area The bottom of the left frontal lobe, where Broca found damage producing nonfluent aphasia. [10]

bulimia A disorder in which people of normal weight see themselves as overweight and, following overeating, induce vomiting or take laxatives to avoid weight gain. [12]

buyer's remorse The worry and doubt sometimes felt after a purchase. [15]

bystander effect The tendency of each person in an emergency to expect others to intervene, so the larger the group, the less likely each member is to help. [15]

C

caffeine A stimulant found in many beverages, including coffee, tea, and many sodas. [7]

CAH *See* congenital adrenal hyperplasia. [12]

cannabinoids Naturally occurring neurotransmitters that normally stimulate the receptors that respond to THC in marijuana. [7]

Cannon–Bard theory The theory that our experience of emotion is independent of the simultaneous physiological changes that accompany it. [13]

case study A careful, intensive observation of one or a few individuals, typically people who display a particular behavior. [2]

castration The removal of the testes. [12]

categorization The process of recognizing the similarities and differences between concepts. [10]

catharsis A cleansing or purging of emotions. [13]

CBT *See* cognitive behavioral therapy. [16]

cell body Also called *soma*. The part of a cell surrounding the nucleus. [3]

cell migration The stage of development when neurons and other cells migrate to their final position in the brain. [5]

central nervous system (CNS) The brain and spinal cord. [3]

cerebellum A brain region attached to the brainstem that is involved in the regulation of movement. [3]

cerebral cortex Also called *cortex*. The outer covering of the cerebral hemispheres that consists largely of nerve cell bodies and their branches. [3]

cerebral hemispheres The left and right halves of the brain. [3]

cerebrum The brain region atop the brainstem that controls higher mental functions. [3]

chameleon effect The tendency to mimic the postures, mannerisms, facial expressions, or other behaviors of others. [15]

change blindness The failure to detect a change in a visual scene. [10]

Charles Darwin (1809–1882) The discoverer of evolution by natural selection who argued that all human behaviors must have had beginnings in earlier ancestors. [1]

chlorpromazine The first drug that was effective in treating the positive symptoms of schizophrenia. [16]

choice blindness The tendency of people not to notice when they have made a choice between two things and are subsequently told they had made the opposite choice. [10]

chromosomes Condensed strands of DNA and associated molecules found in the nucleus of cells. [4]

chronic obstructive pulmonary disorder (COPD) A progressive lung disease that impairs respiration due to lung damage, usually caused by smoking. [13]

chunking An encoding strategy that reduces the total number of items to be remembered by combining them into meaningful units. [9]

cingulate cortex A region of cortex immediately above the corpus callosum that is activated during several emotions. [13]

CIP *See* congenital insensitivity to pain. [6]

circadian rhythm Animals' active–rest cycle with a duration of about one day. [7]

classical conditioning Also called *Pavlovian conditioning*. A basic form of learning in which a neutral stimulus is repeatedly followed by another stimulus that normally elicits a response, until the formerly neutral stimulus now elicits that response. [8]

Clever Hans A horse in early-twentieth-century Berlin that seemed to understand mathematics, but was actually using cues from his owner to answer questions. [2]

clinical significance An additional criterion for about half the diagnoses in *DSM*, requiring that there be clinically significant distress or impairment in social, occupational, or other important areas of functioning. [16]

co-morbid Occurring together, such as disorders. [16]

cocaine A stimulant extracted from the leaves of the coca plant. [7]

cochlea A bony, fluid-filled, spiral-shaped tunnel of the inner ear that detects the vibrations transmitted from the tiny bones in the middle ear. [6]

cocktail party effect A hearing phenomenon when a person selectively attends to a particular conversation out of many. [10]

cognitive behavioral therapy (CBT) Structured, goal-oriented counseling, usually of a limited number of sessions directed at education about the disorder and skills for managing symptoms in everyday life. [16]

cognitive development The progressive increase in cognitive ability displayed by normally developing individuals. [5]

cognitive dissonance The psychological discomfort of simultaneously holding two conflicting beliefs, especially about oneself. [15]

cognitive map An internal representation of the layout of an area. [8]

cognitive phase The earliest stage of skill acquisition, during which there is conscious awareness of efforts. [10]

cognitive psychology The study of internal mental processes, specifically how we acquire and process information and gain knowledge. [1, 10]

coitus Also called *copulation* or *intromission*. The sexual act; occurs when the male's penis enters the female's vagina. [12]

collectivism The tendency to put the goals of the group ahead of your own goals. [15]

color constancy The visual perception that an object retains the same color, no matter what color light is shining on it. [6]

color opponent theory Also called *opponent–process theory*. The idea that color vision is based on a system of paired opposites of color. [6]

computed tomography (CT) A technique for examining brain structure through computer analysis of X-ray particles passing through the head from several different positions. [3]

concept An abstract idea or mental representation of an object or event. [10]

concordant Referring to any trait that is seen in both individuals of a pair of twins. [4]

concrete operational stage The cognitive stage at which children acquire formal logical skills ("operations"), but tend to be very concrete in their thinking. [5]

conditioned response (CR) The learned response to a previously neutral stimulus that was repeatedly paired with an US. [8]

conditioned stimulus (CS) The previously neutral stimulus that, after repeated pairing with the US, eventually triggers the response. [8]

conditioned taste aversion Also called *taste aversion* and *Garcia effect*. The acquired repulsion to a taste or flavor that was previously followed by nausea. [8]

conditioning Learning simple associations between stimuli. [9]

cone A class of photoreceptors in the retina that are responsible for color vision. [6]

confabulation Filling in a gap in memory or understanding with a fabrication that the person believes to be true. [7]

confirmation bias A tendency to remember events that fit our preconceptions and to dismiss or forget events that do not. [10, 14]

confounding variable A third factor that affects both variables of interest, causing them to covary even though neither has any causal effect on the other. [2, 4]

congenital adrenal hyperplasia (CAH) A condition caused by the secretion of excess testosterone by the adrenal glands before birth. At birth, the genitals may resemble those of a boy. [12]

congenital insensitivity to pain (CIP) A genetic condition that prevents the feeling of pain. [6]

conscientiousness A personality trait that reflects a person's tendency to be self-disciplined and reliable, and feel a need for achievement. [14]

consciousness Our perception of what is going on in our minds. [7]

conservation The physical laws that volume and mass of objects are conserved no matter how they might be rearranged. [5]

consolidation The process of transferring information from STM into LTM. [9]

constraints Rules that govern how you can get from the initial state to the goal state in a problem. [10]

constructivism The perspective that growing children are actively engaged in building their minds. [5]

content validity The ability of a test to measure all the various facets of the psychological trait in question. [11]

context-dependent retrieval The improved ability to retrieve information when the conditions of the original learning are reproduced. [9]

continuous reinforcement schedule The rewarding of a behavior every time it is displayed. [8]

continuum When a trait varies in a continuous, gradual fashion. [14]

control group A group of individuals who closely resemble those in the experimental group but did not receive the experimental manipulation. [2]

controlled/instrumental aggression An aggressive behavior carefully planned and usually intended to gain some goal. [15]

conventional moral reasoning Moral reasoning that weighs whether a behavior is "right" in terms of what society expects people to do. [5]

convergence The binocular cue from the coming together of the two eyes to focus on really close objects. [6]

convergent validity The extent to which several different tests intended to measure the same psychological trait give comparable results. [11]

COPD *See* chronic obstructive pulmonary disorder. [13]

copulation *See* coitus. [12]

cornea The round, transparent front of the eye. [6]

corpus callosum The main band of axons communicating between the two cerebral hemispheres. [3, 7]

correlation coefficient A quantitative, statistical measure of how closely two variables fluctuate together. [2]

cortex *See* cerebral cortex. [3]

cortisol A hormone from the adrenal gland released in response to stress. [13]

covary Vary together in a predictable fashion; generally said of two variables. [2]

CR *See* conditioned response. [8]

crib death *See* sudden infant death syndrome. [5]

criterion-related validity The extent to which the scores on a psychological test predict someone's real-life performance, based on some standard. [11]

cross-test reliability The extent to which two different tests thought to measure the same trait agree. [11]

crystallized intelligence (g_C) The knowledge a person has acquired and the ability to use it appropriately. [5, 11]

CS *See* conditioned stimulus. [8]

CT *See* computed tomography. [3]

cued recall The memory testing condition in which a participant is provided some hints about the information requested. [9]

cultural display rules How and when emotions are expressed in a particular culture. [13]

culturally biased Tests on which performance can be affected by the particular culture the test-taker has been exposed to. [11]

cytokines Proteins in the blood that control production of white blood cells and antibodies. [13]

D

decision making The cognitive process of assessing information to select a course of action among several alternatives. [10]

declarative memory Also called *explicit memory.* Facts or information acquired through learning that can be stated or described. [9]

deep structure The particular meaning beneath the surface structure of a sentence. [10]

defense mechanisms Unconscious psychological processes that protect the ego from realizing and acting upon socially unacceptable urges of the id. [14]

deindividuation The psychological process of losing your own individual identity and coming to identify with the crowd. [15]

delta waves Large amplitude brain waves of 1 Hz, characteristic of stage 3 sleep. [7]

delta-9-tetrahydrocannabinol (THC) The major active ingredient in marijuana. [7]

delusions False beliefs strongly held in spite of contrary evidence. [16]

dementia The progressive decline in cognitive function caused by damage or disease rather than normal aging. [5]

dendrite One of the extensions of a neuron's cell body that receives information. [3]

dependent variable The variable that you suspect might be affected when you manipulate the independent variable in an experiment. [2]

depolarizing Reducing the polarization of a neuron, making it more likely to fire. [3]

depressant A drug that tends to slow down mental processes and behavior. [7]

depression A disorder characterized by an unhappy mood, loss of interests and energy, change of appetite, difficulty in concentration, and restless agitation. [16]

depth perception The ability to perceive distance. [6]

descriptive method Making observations with the goal of accurately and impartially describing and cataloging behaviors without any attempt to influence them. [2]

desynchronized EEG Also called *beta activity.* A pattern of EEG activity comprising a mix of many different high frequencies, with no dominant frequency, and with low amplitude. [7]

deterrence The use of punishment to persuade people not to display certain behaviors. [15]

developmental psychology The study of how the mind and behavior progress as an individual grows up and ages. [5]

DID *See* dissociative identity disorder. [16]

difference threshold *See* just noticeable difference. [6]

differentiation The process by which individual cells become more and more different from one another. [5]

diffusion of responsibility The tendency to be less likely to take action if others are available. [15]

diffusion tensor imaging (DTI) A brain imaging technique that reveals axonal connections. [3]

discordant Referring to any trait that is seen in only one individual of a pair of twins. [4]

discrimination Treating a person unfairly solely because he or she is part of some group. [15]

dishabituation The sudden return of a response that had formerly been habituated. [8]

disorganized attachment A style of attachment in which the child shows an inconsistent pattern of response in the strange situation. [5]

disposition A tendency to show a particular behavior, no matter what the situation is. [15]

dissociative drug A drug that produces feelings of depersonalization and detachment from reality. [7]

dissociative identity disorder (DID) A mental disorder diagnosed in a person who supposedly has at least two distinctive, enduring personalities that take turns controlling the person's behavior. [16]

dissociative thinking A major impairment in the logical structure of thought. [16]

dizygotic twins Also called *fraternal twins* or *non-identical twins.* Twins derived from two separate eggs. [4, 11]

DNA A long molecule that encodes hereditary information, coiled up to form chromosomes in the nucleus of cells. [4]

dominant In the context of heredity, an allele that affects an individual's phenotype regardless of the other allele carried for that gene. [4]

door-in-the-face technique Making a very large request before asking for something more reasonable. [15]

dopamine hypothesis The hypothesis that people with schizophrenia suffer from an excess of either dopamine release or dopamine receptors. [16]

dopamine A neurotransmitter involved in movement and in signaling pleasure. [3, 12]

Down syndrome A condition caused by a third copy of chromosome 21, resulting in a characteristic facial pattern, short stature, and mild to severe intellectual disability. [11]

drive reduction model The concept that internal motivation is the result of a physiological need that generates a drive, leading to behaviors that fulfill the need to reduce that drive. [12]

DTI *See* diffusion tensor imaging. [3]

duplex theory The idea that both intensity differences and latency differences are used to localize sound. [6]

dyslexia Difficulty learning to read. [10]

DZ *See* dizygotic twins. [11]

E

easy problem of consciousness Also called the *mind–body problem*. The question of which particular pattern of brain activity underlies a particular conscious experience. [7]

ecstasy (MDMA) A hallucinogenic amphetamine. [7]

ECT *See* electroconvulsive shock therapy. [16]

Edward Thorndike (1874–1949) A behaviorist who studied how dogs and cats learn to escape from puzzle boxes. [1]

EEG *See* electroencephalogram. [3]

effort justification The tendency to alter our evaluation of some object or process based on how much effort we made for it. [15]

ego Freud's term for the part of the mind that tries to fulfill the goals of the id within the limits of reality. [14]

egocentrism In the context of cognitive development, the notion that everyone knows whatever you know. [5]

eidetic memory *See* photographic memory. [9]

ejaculation The forceful expulsion of semen from the penis. [12]

electroconvulsive shock therapy (ECT) The intentional induction of a large-scale seizure, which is often effective in the relief of depression. [16]

electroencephalogram (EEG) A recording of fluctuating potentials taking place in the brain, made by an electroencephalograph. [3, 7]

embryo An early developing individual, typically a sphere of dividing cells. [5]

emerging adulthood The transition from adolescence to full adulthood. [5]

emotion A subjective mental state that is usually accompanied by distinctive behaviors as well as involuntary physiological changes. [13]

emotional instability *See* neuroticism. [14]

emotional syndrome A syndrome in which injury or disease has a general effect on emotional tone. [13]

empiricist philosophers A group of British philosophers, including John Locke, who believed we are dependent on our unreliable senses to learn about the world. [1]

encoding The process of taking raw sensory information and converting it into a form that we can understand and report. [9]

endocannabinoids Neurotransmitters that normally act on the receptors that are activated by marijuana and related drugs. [7, 12]

endogenous opiates A class of neurotransmitters found in the brain, including endorphins. [7]

endophenotype A group of behavioral or physical characteristics that accompany an inherited susceptibility to a particular disorder. [16]

endorphins Neurotransmitters that seem to act as "*endo*genous (internal) m*orphin*e" to damp down pain signals. [3]

engram The physical encoding of a memory in the brain. [9]

epigenetics The study of factors that affect gene expression. [4]

episodic memory Detailed autobiographical declarative memory. [9]

escape conditioning A form of negative reinforcement in which the subject learns to perform a response to remove an aversive stimulus. [8]

estradiol The most common form of estrogen. [12]

estrogens One of two classes of ovarian hormones; both are crucial for female reproduction. [12]

evolutionary psychologists Psychologists who regard psychological traits as a result of evolution by natural selection. [15]

exhaustion stage The increased susceptibility to disease and possible death that follows prolonged or frequently repeated stress. [13]

experimental group The group of individuals for whom you have manipulated the independent variable in an experiment. [2]

experimentation A scientific approach of deliberately manipulating a variable to then observe whether and how other variables are altered in response. [2]

explicit memory *See* declarative memory. [9]

external motivating forces Factors originating outside the body that regulate behavior. [12]

extinction In classical conditioning, the loss of the conditioned response, caused by repeated presentation of the CS without the US. [8]

extravert Someone who likes being with other people and tends to be talkative and assertive. [14]

F

facial feedback hypothesis The hypothesis that sensory feedback from our face contributes to our emotional experience. [13]

facial symmetry The correspondence between the left and right side of the face. [15]

factor analysis A statistical method of examining many different measures to see whether some of those measures consistently covary with one another. [14]

fade The gradual disappearance of a memory based on its physical loss from the brain. [9]

family-based treatment For anorexia, a follow-up treatment to hospitalization that involves a family member in constant attendance who insists that the patient eat. [12]

FAS *See* fetal alcohol syndrome. [4]

fat Also called *lipid*. Our long-term reservoir for glucose. [12]

fatal familial insomnia (FFI) A fatal genetic human disorder that eliminates sleep at some point in midlife. [7]

fear conditioning A type of classical conditioning, in which a previously neutral stimulus is repeatedly paired with a painful stimulus until the subject shows fearful responses to the first stimulus. [8]

fertilization The fusion of sperm and egg. [4]

fetal alcohol syndrome (FAS) A condition in which children exposed to alcohol from their mother's drinking are born with distinct facial features and varying degrees of mental impairment. [5, 11]

fetus A developing individual at the stage where major organs and structures have formed. In humans, about the ninth week of development. [5]

FFI *See* fatal familial insomnia. [7]

FI *See* fixed interval. [8]

five-factor model The idea that five basic traits make up each individual's personality. [14]

fixed interval (FI) A schedule in which a reinforcement is provided for the first response after a fixed length of time since the last reinforcement. [8]

fixed ratio (FR) A schedule in which every nth response is rewarded. [8]

flashback The experience, long after taking LSD, that a dose of drug had just been taken, even though the person is drug-free. [7]

flashbulb memories Vivid, detailed memories of a momentous event. [9]

flavor The combined stimulation provided to taste receptors in the mouth and olfactory receptors in the nose while eating something. [6]

flow The experience of being wholly involved in some activity, just for its own sake, and time flies by and you seem to know what to do without conscious effort. [10]

fluent aphasia *See* Wernicke's aphasia. [10]

fluid intelligence (g_F) The capacity to reason logically and solve new problems, independent of what you know already. [5, 11]

Flynn effect The substantial increase in average scores on IQ tests that has taken place since they were developed. [11]

fMRI *See* functional MRI. [3]

foot-in-the-door technique Asking someone to do something trivial before asking for a bigger favor. [15]

Forer effect *See* subjective validation. [14]

forgetting The inability to retrieve information from LTM. [9]

formal operational stage The cognitive stage at which children are able to consider many different theoretical possibilities for a condition, so they can solve complex, hypothetical problems using abstract ideas. [5]

FR *See* fixed ratio. [8]

fragile X syndrome An intellectual disability due to a dysfunctional gene on the X chromosome, resulting in an elongated face and prominent ears, as well as extreme shyness. [11]

framing effect A cognitive bias that occurs when the way information is presented makes a significant difference in what people will decide. [10]

Francis Sumner (1895–1954) The first African American awarded a doctorate in psychology, in 1920 from Clark University. He went on to chair the psychology department at Howard University. [1]

fraternal birth order effect The finding that the more older brothers a boy has, the more likely he is to grow up to be gay. [12]

fraternal twins *See* dizygotic twins. [4]

free association A technique for probing a client's unconscious, when a client given a list of words or phrases replies to each with whatever comes to mind. [14]

free recall The memory testing condition in which the person must retrieve the information without any hints or guides. [9]

free will The power to make choices that are not constrained by supernatural, nonphysical forces. [7]

frequency distributions Graphs in which a score is noted on the *x*-axis while the number of people who have each score is noted on the *y*-axis. [2, 11]

Freudian slips The utterance in spontaneous conversation of something that is socially unacceptable, but reveals the speaker's true feelings. [14]

frontal lobes The section of the cerebrum in front, just above and behind the eyes. [3]

functional MRI (fMRI) Magnetic resonance imaging that detects changes in blood flow and oxygen content, identifying regions of the brain that are particularly active during a given task. [3]

functionalism A broad school of thought in psychology that insisted that mental processes like consciousness must serve a practical, adaptive purpose. [1]

fundamental attribution error The tendency to explain other people's behavior based on their dispositions rather than on the situation surrounding them. [15]

G

g *See* generalized intelligence. [11]

GABA An acronym for *gamma-aminobutyric acid*. A neurotransmitter that usually reduces the activity of neurons. [3]

GAD *See* generalized anxiety disorder. [16]

gambler's fallacy The belief that the outcome of random events up to this point will affect the probability of future random events. [10]

Garcia effect *See* conditioned taste aversion. [8]

gender constancy The concept that sex categories are permanent and not affected by variations in appearance. [12]

gender identity The sense, developed in childhood, of whether one is male or female. [12]

gene expression A process by which a cell directs a gene to make its protein. [4]

gene-environment interaction The effect of the environment on gene expression. [4]

gene A length of DNA that encodes the information for making a protein. [4]

general adaptation syndrome The system connecting stress and disease through a series of stages. [13]

generalized anxiety disorder (GAD) An anxiety disorder characterized by excessive anxiety about otherwise common things or events, which lasts for at least six months and interferes with everyday life. [16]

generalized intelligence (*g* factor, *g*) A general ability that reflects an overall mental ability. [11]

generative Term used to describe the capacity of a language to produce an infinite number of sentences. [10]

genetic determinism The belief that genes determine everything about us, including our behavior. [4]

genital stage The final phase in Freud's psychosexual stages of development, when the focus is on the penis and vagina and developing a mature, socially acceptable sexual relationship. [14]

genotype All the genetic information that one specific individual has inherited. [4]

Gestalt psychologists A group of German psychologists who insisted that the entire perception we experience is more than just the sum of the parts. [6]

Gestalt psychology A German school of psychology that emphasizes that the whole perception is more than just the sum of separate sensations. [6]

Gestalt rules of perception Tenets to explain many instances where vision organizes images. [6]

g_F *See* fluid intelligence. [10]

glia Also called *glial cells*. Brain cells that regulate the strength of connections between neurons. [3]

glial cells *See* glia. [3]

glucose A simple sugar used by brain and body cells for energy. [12]

glutamate A common neurotransmitter in the brain that usually causes neurons to be more active. [3]

goal state The desired outcome of a problem. [10]

gonads The reproductive organs that make either sperm (testes in males) or eggs (ovaries in females). [12]

groupthink The tendency to agree with one another too readily and so make faulty decisions. [15]

H

habituation technique A method of discerning individuals' recognition of a stimulus by determining whether they show evidence of habituating to that stimulus. [5]

habituation A simple type of learning in which repeated presentation of a stimulus elicits a weaker and weaker response. [5, 8]

hair cells Specialized receptor cells inside the cochlea. [6]

hallucinogens Drugs that alter sensory perceptions in dramatic ways and produce peculiar experiences. [7]

hard problem of consciousness The question of how brain processes result in our personal conscious experience (qualia). [7]

Hawthorne effect The phenomenon that people may behave differently when they know they are being studied. [12]

health psychology The study of psychological, behavioral, and biological factors that influence physical and mental health. [13]

Hebbian synapse A synapse that becomes stronger if it often causes the postsynaptic neuron to fire, and gets weaker if it rarely causes the postsynaptic cell to fire. [9]

hemispheric lateralization *See* hemispheric specialization. [3]

hemispheric specialization Also called *hemispheric lateralization*. The tendency for one side of the brain or the other to perform certain complex tasks. [3]

heritability A statistical estimate of the extent to which individual differences in genes in a population contribute to individual differences in a trait. [4, 11]

heritable A trait that is influenced by one or more genes inherited from one's parents. [4]

heroin A chemically altered form of morphine that is even more powerful and addictive. [7]

heterosexuality Sexual orientation with attraction directed toward members of the opposite sex. [12]

heuristic A relatively easy-to-follow set of rules that often, but not always, solves the problem. [10]

hierarchies Organizational structures where items have some relationship to one another. [9]

high functioning autism *See* Asperger's syndrome. [5]

high reactive A baby who has a negative reaction to novel stimuli and takes longer to recover from that reaction. [14]

hindsight bias The tendency to misremember our previous views to fit our current knowledge or beliefs. [10]

hippocampus Part of the limbic system that is crucial in the formation of permanent memories. [3, 9]

homeostasis The process of keeping a constant, stable internal environment in the body. [12]

homosexuality Sexual orientation with attraction directed toward members of the same sex. [12]

hormones (1) Chemicals released from one part of the body that enter the bloodstream and affect other parts of the body. [3, 12] (2) In the context of adolescent development, gonadal hormones such as estrogens and testosterone that drive sexual development. [5]

humanistic psychology A theory that challenges psychoanalytic theory by emphasizing our free will and our ability to play a conscious, active role in shaping our own behavior. [14]

Huntington's disease A progressive genetic disorder characterized by abrupt, involuntary movements and profound changes in mental functioning. [4]

hyperpolarizing Increasing the polarity of a neuron, making it less likely to fire. [3]

hypnosis A process at work when one person, the hypnotist, suggests that another person will experience particular perceptions or engage in particular behaviors. [7]

hypochondria A tendency to believe you are ill when you are not. [14]

hypocretin A neuropeptide found almost exclusively in the hypothalamus, it coordinates the transition from one sleep state to another. [7]

hypothalamus A part of the brainstem beneath the thalamus that regulates many physiological processes, including hunger, thirst, and temperature. [3, 12]

hypothesis A tentative explanation for a relationship between two or more variables. [2]

hysteria A mental disorder diagnosed until the 1930s, believed to be caused by a malfunctioning uterus. [1]

I

I/O psychology *See* industrial and organizational psychology. [12]

IACUC *See* Institutional Animal Care and Use Committee. [2]

IAT *See* Implicit Association Test. [15]

id Freud's term for the part of the mind following the pleasure principle. [14]

identical twins *See* monozygotic twins. [4]

identity In the context of adolescent development, a consistent sense of who one is and should be. [5]

Implicit Association Test (IAT) An assessment of reaction times used to detect associations between particular words or images. [15]

implicit bias *See* unconscious bias. [2]

implicit memory *See* nondeclarative memory. [9]

impression management Things we do and say to try to present a favorable image to other people. [15]

imprinting The behavior by which birds are predisposed to follow any moving object that they see shortly after hatching. [5, 8]

inattentional blindness The phenomenon of appearing to be blind to things that we aren't attending to. [10]

inclusive fitness How successful individuals are at spreading their own genes in *any* fashion, including benefitting relatives. [15]

independent variable The variable that is deliberately manipulated in an experiment. [2]

indifferent gonads The unformed gonads in a fetus, which resemble a mix of testes and ovaries. [12]

individualism The tendency to put your own goals and wishes ahead of the goals and wishes of the group. [15]

industrial and organizational psychology (I/O psychology) The study of factors affecting performance in the workplace. [12]

infant A young child that has not yet learned to talk. [5]

infantile amnesia Relative inability of adults to recall events of their early childhood. [5]

inferential statistics Mathematical procedures to help infer what the population is like based on a sample. [2]

informed consent The process of informing participants in a study about what they'll be doing and any risks they face, then getting their active agreement beforehand. This is required by IRBs. [2]

initial state The situation at the beginning of a problem. [10]

inner cell mass A clump of cells inside a mammalian embryo that will form the body. [5]

inner ear The tiny snail-shaped cochlea, and some similar organs that are important for balance. [6]

insight A sudden understanding of a problem that leads to a solution. [8, 10]

insomnia Difficulty getting the amount of sleep needed. [7]

Institutional Animal Care and Use Committee (IACUC) A group of individuals convened by an institution to review and approve the proposed research with animals before it can begin. [2]

Institutional Review Board (IRB) A group of individuals convened by an institution to ensure studies involving humans meet ethical standards. [2]

instrumental learning *See* operant conditioning. [8]

insula A region of enfolded cortex activated during several emotions. [13]

intellectual disabilities Also called *mental disabilities*. A diverse group of lifelong conditions that impair intellectual development. [11]

intelligence quotient (IQ) Originally, the ratio of a child's mental age divided by his or her chronological age and then multiplied by 100. Today, a measure of a person's performance relative to a comparison group of people on intelligence tests. [11]

intelligence The ability to acquire, retain, and apply knowledge. [11]

interactionists Personality psychologists who acknowledge the importance of the situation in assessing current behavior and the importance of personality in understanding someone's average behavior. [14]

intermittent reinforcement schedule *See* partial reinforcement schedule. [8]

internal dialogue The words and sentences passing through your mind as a form of self-talk or inner speech. [7]

internal motivating forces Factors originating inside the body that regulate behavior. [12]

interneuron A neuron that receives input from and sends output to other neurons. [3]

intromission *See* coitus. [12]

introvert Someone who is less talkative and prefers solitary pursuits. [14]

IQ *See* intelligence quotient. [11]

IRB *See* Institutional Review Board. [2]

iris The colored disc sitting just in front of the lens of the eye and that controls the amount of light entering the eye. [6]

Ivan Pavlov (1849–1936) A Russian physiologist who described classical conditioning, such as how ringing a bell before giving food to a dog would eventually result in the dog learning to salivate at just the sound of the bell. [1]

J

James-Lange theory The theory that our experience of emotion is a response to the physiological changes that accompany it. [13]

jet lag The disruption of circadian rhythms caused by rapid travel across time zones. [7]

JND *See* just noticeable difference. [6]

John B. Watson (1878–1958) A behaviorist who insisted that psychology should be an objective experimental branch of natural science concerned only with observable behavior. [1]

John Locke (1632–1704) A seventeenth-century British empiricist philosopher who believed that the mind of a newborn baby is a *tabula rasa* that is molded by experience. [1]

judgment The cognitive process of forming an opinion or making an evaluation by comparing possible actions. [10]

just noticeable difference (JND) Also called *difference threshold*. The smallest change in magnitude of a stimulus that can be detected. [6]

K

K complexes Large single spikes in the EEG. [7]

Kenneth Clark A pioneering African American psychologist who developed the Clark Doll Test along with his wife, Mamie Phipps Clark. [1]

Korsakoff's syndrome A memory disorder, characterized by retrograde amnesia, anterograde amnesia, and confabulation, that is generally caused by thiamine deficiency. [9]

L

L cones *See* long-wavelength cones. [6]

labeled lines The concept that specific nerves are dedicated to relaying specific types of sensory information to the brain. [6]

latency stage The phase in Freud's psychosexual stages of development covering the ages 6–12, when the sexual conflicts are repressed. [14]

latent content According to Freud, the real wishes that underlie a dream. [7]

latent learning Learning that occurs without being immediately apparent and often without reinforcement. [8]

lateral hypothalamus (LH) A brain region related to the body weight set point. Damage to this region results in a new, lower set point. [12]

lateralization The tendency for the right and left cerebral hemispheres to differ in their specializations. [10]

law of effect The notion, proposed by Thorndike, that any behavior that results in a satisfactory outcome is more likely to recur in the future. [8]

learned helplessness A type of learning in which the subject learns that an aversive stimulus cannot be avoided. [8]

learning The acquisition of knowledge, skill, attitudes, or understanding as a result of experience. [8]

lens The flexible, transparent structure in the eye that helps focus an image on the back of the eye's interior. [6]

leptin A hormone secreted by fat cells that signals the arcuate nucleus about energy stores. [12]

lesion An area of tissue damage. [3]

LH *See* lateral hypothalamus. [12]

libido The motivation to have sex. [12]

lie detector *See* polygraph. [13]

limbic system A collection of brain nuclei under the cerebral cortex that play a key role in learning, emotions, and sensory processing. [3]

linear perspective The depth cue from parallel straight lines that converge with distance. [6]

linguistic relativism The hypothesis that the language we speak influences the way we think. [10]

linguists Scientists who study language. [10]

lipid *See* fat. [12]

lithium A chemical element used for the treatment of bipolar disorder. [16]

lobotomy The surgical separation of a portion of the frontal lobes from the rest of the brain. [16]

locus of control The individual's perception about whether his or her efforts in life will be reinforced. [14]

long-term memory (LTM) The nearly limitless store of memories that last more than a few minutes. [9]

long-term potentiation (LTP) The stable and long-lasting enhancement of synaptic transmission. [9]

long-wavelength cones Also called *L cones*. Cone photoreceptors that are best at detecting light of long wavelengths, such as red. [6]

loss averse Characteristic of being very reluctant to do anything that might lead to loss. [10, 15]

low reactive A baby who shows little reaction to novel stimuli. [14]

LSD *See* lysergic acid diethylamide. [7]

LTM *See* long-term memory. [9]

LTP *See* long-term potentiation. [9]

lysergic acid diethylamide (LSD) Also called *acid*. A hallucinogen that tends to alter or distort visual experiences. [7]

M

M cones *See* medium-wavelength cones. [6]

magic mushrooms *See* psilocybin. [7]

magnetic resonance imaging (MRI) A technique that uses magnetic fields to generate images revealing structural details in the living brain. [3]

Mamie Phipps Clark (1917–1983) A pioneering African American psychologist who developed the Clark Doll Test along with her husband, Kenneth Clark. [1]

mammillary bodies A pair of structures in the brainstem that receive inputs from the hippocampus; they are damaged in Korsakoff's patients. [9]

manifest content According to Freud, what a dream seems to depict. [7]

MAO *See* monoamine oxidase. [16]

Margaret Floy Washburn (1871–1939) A psychologist who described the behavior of many animals, relating them to the human mind. [1]

marijuana Drug obtained from the *Cannabis sativa* plant, generally ingested via smoking. [7]

Mary Cover Jones (1897–1987) An early psychologist who studied the development of children and pioneered the technique of desensitization for phobias. [1]

Mary Whiton Calkins (1863–1930) The first female president of the American Psychological Association and a professor at Wellesley College. She completed the requirements for a doctorate at Harvard but was never awarded the degree. [1]

Max Wertheimer (1880–1943) An influential pioneer in Gestalt psychology. [1]

MBSR *See* mindfulness-based stress reduction. [13]

MDMA *See* ecstasy. [7]

mean The average measure for a group calculated by adding up all the scores and dividing that sum by the number of individuals in the group. [2]

measure of central tendency An indication of where the scores in a sample cluster. [2]

medial temporal lobe The innermost portion of the temporal lobe, which includes the hippocampus and neighboring cortex. [9]

median A measure of central tendency that is the value that falls in the middle of all the scores, such that half the scores are higher and half are lower. [2]

meditation The practice of focusing attention in order to relax the body and mind, and to reduce stress. [7, 13]

medium-wavelength cones Also called *M cones*. Cone photoreceptors that are best at detecting light of intermediate wavelengths, such as yellows and greens. [6]

memory trace The physical record of a memory made in the brain by a learning experience. [9]

memory The ability to store and retrieve information we have learned. [9]

menarche The time at which a girl has her first menstrual period. [5]

menopause The time a woman's menstrual periods stop, around age 50. [5, 12]

mental age The intellectual abilities commonly found in children of a particular age. [11]

mental disabilities *See* intellectual disabilities. [11]

mental imagery The ability to visualize images or events in our mind. [10]

mescaline Also called *peyote*. A hallucinogenic drug that affects visual experience by way of neural systems that use norepinephrine as a neurotransmitter. [7]

meta-analysis A careful review of many studies that tries to gauge whether there really is an effect of the manipulation on the behavior of interest. [2]

method of loci A mnemonic device where each item of a list is imagined in a separate location in a familiar place. [9]

methylphenidate Also called *Ritalin*. A nervous system stimulant used to treat ADHD. [5]

middle ear The eardrum and the three tiny bones for conducting sound. [6]

mind-body problem *See* easy problem of consciousness. [7]

mind A process going on in the brain that includes all thoughts and feelings. [3]

mindfulness-based stress reduction (MBSR) A technique that pairs relaxation with attention on the present moment. [13]

Minnesota Multiphasic Personality Inventory (MMPI) A widely used personality test originally designed to screen for psychological disorders. [14]

mirror neuron Neuron that is active both when an individual makes a particular movement and when that individual sees another individual make that same movement. [3]

misinformation effect The susceptibility of our memory to incorporate false details that fit in. [9]

MMPI clinical scales Quantitative measures of a subject's responses to the MMPI, intended to detect different psychological problems. [14]

MMPI *See* Minnesota Multiphasic Personality Inventory. [14]

mnemonic devices Methods of helping to memorize information. [9]

mode A measure of central tendency that is the single score that is most commonly found among the participants. [2]

monoamine hypothesis The hypothesis that depression is caused by reduced activity of one or more monoamine transmitters, such as serotonin. [16]

monoamine oxidase (MAO) The enzyme that normally inactivates the monoamines, including norepinephrine, dopamine, and serotonin. [15, 16]

monocular cues Depth cues that are available even to one eye. [6]

monozygotic twins Also called *identical twins*. Twins derived from a single fertilized egg. [4, 11]

Monty Hall problem An example of an error in decision making in which someone fails to properly estimate the probability of an outcome after being given additional information. [10]

morality A set of rules determining whether conduct is right or wrong. [5]

morphemes The basic units of meaning in a language. They are composed of phonemes. [10]

morphine The major active substance in opium, noted for its painkilling properties. [7]

motherese The singsong, high-pitched speech with slow, exaggerated pronunciation that parents use with babies. [10]

motion parallax A monocular depth cue from the shifting of a visual scene on the retina from head movement. [6]

motivation Forces that regulate behavior toward a goal. [12]

motor cortex The backmost strip of the frontal cortex; it controls movement. [3]

motor development The progressive increase in motor abilities displayed by growing babies. [5]

motor neuron A type of neuron that sends commands to make muscles move, using acetylcholine as a neurotransmitter. [3]

MRI *See* magnetic resonance imaging. [3]

multiple intelligences Models of intelligence that extend beyond the aspects measured by traditional intelligence tests. [11]

mutation A change in the nucleotide sequence of a gene as a result of unfaithful replication. [4]

myelin The fatty insulation around an axon, formed by glial cells, which increases the speed of conduction of nerve impulses. [3]

Myers–Briggs test A personality test that categorizes people into 16 personality types. [14]

MZ *See* monozygotic twins. [6]

N

***n*-back task** A procedure where participants are given a sequence of items and must report whenever the current item is identical to the one "*n*" items before. [11]

narcissistic personality disorder A personality disorder characterized by a sense of self-importance requiring excessive admiration and a lack of empathy for others. [16]

narcolepsy An unusual disorder causing a person to have intense attacks of sleep that last from 5 to 30 minutes during usual waking hours. [7]

natural selection The process by which mutations that improve survival and reproduction accumulate in subsequent generations, changing a species over time. [1, 4]

nature One side of a philosophical debate that attributes our behavior to genetics. [4]

need for achievement The motivation to take on challenging tasks that can be done successfully. [12]

need for affiliation The motivation to establish and maintain relationships. [12]

need for power Also called the *power motive*. The motivation to be in charge. [12]

negative feedback A signal to a system to decrease activity. [12]

negative punishment The removal of a stimulus following a response, decreasing the likelihood of that behavior. [8]

negative reinforcement The removal of a stimulus following a behavior, increasing the likelihood of that behavior. [8]

negative symptoms Behavioral functions that are lost in schizophrenia; for example slow and impoverished thought and speech, social withdrawal, or blunted affect. [16]

nerve impulse *See* action potential. [3]

nerves Bundles of axons that carry information to and commands from the central nervous system (CNS) to the rest of the body. [3]

nervous system The complex communication network of the body that is composed of all the neurons. [3]

neural network A wide-ranging scattering of many interneurons communicating with one another to process information. [3]

neural plasticity *See* plasticity. [3]

neural tube An early stage of the developing nervous system, which will eventually form the brain and spinal cord. [5]

neuritic plaques Abnormal clumps of dead and dying neurons seen in brains of people with AD. [5]

neuroeconomics The study of the neural basis of making economic decisions. [15]

neurogenesis The division of cells that become neurons. [5]

neuroleptics Antipsychotic drugs that traditionally function by blocking postsynaptic dopamine receptors. [16]

neuromodulator A drug molecule that affects neurotransmitter–receptor signaling without displacing the normal neurotransmitter. [7]

neuronal cell death A normal stage of development when some cells, including some neurons, die. [5]

neurons Also called *nerve cells*. Cells specialized to process information, making up the nervous system. [3]

neuropathic pain Pain caused by a damaged or malfunctioning nervous system. [6]

neuroscience The study of the nervous system, which includes the brain and spinal cord and all of their connections to the body. [1, 3]

neurosis (pl. *neuroses*) Mental disorders characterized by anxiety or avoidance, that interfere with everyday functioning but are not accompanied by delusions or hallucinations. [14]

neuroticism Also called *emotional instability*. How readily a person's emotional state is upset by the events of everyday life. [14]

neurotransmitter receptors Also called *receptors*. Large protein molecules, embedded in the cell membrane, to which neurotransmitters can bind. [3]

neurotransmitter Also called *transmitter*. The chemical used by a neuron to transmit information to another cell. [3]

nicotine A stimulant found in tobacco that acts as an agonist at many acetylcholine receptors. [7]

nociceptors Free nerve endings that are specialized pain receptors. [6]

nodes of Ranvier Regularly spaced breaks in the myelin sheath of an axon. [3]

noise The firing of a sensory cell without a stimulus or to an irrelevant stimulus. [6]

non-associative learning Simple forms of learning involving changes in the response to a single stimulus. [8]

non-identical twins *See* dizygotic twins. [4]

non-matching-to-sample test A task where the subject demonstrates recognition of an object by not touching it; used to demonstrate declarative memory. [9]

non-REM (NREM) sleep Sleep stages 1, 2, and 3. [7]

nondeclarative memory Also called *implicit memory*. Memory about perceptual or motor procedures that is demonstrated by performance. [9]

nonfluent aphasia *See* Broca's aphasia. [10]

nonsense syllables Short combinations of letters intended to be meaningless. [9]

norepinephrine A neurotransmitter that speeds heart rate, breathing, and neuronal activity as part of the "fight or flight" response. [3]

norm-referenced *See* normalized. [11]

normal distribution A bell-shaped curve describing the distribution of scores around a mean. [11]

normalized Also called *norm-referenced*. A test that has been administered to many people so that the performance average and variability are established. [11]

normative social influence The pressure to behave and believe like the rest of your community. [15]

NREM *See* non-REM sleep. [7]

nucleotides Four subunits of DNA that combine in different ways to specify which protein the cell will make. [4]

nucleus accumbens A region at the base of the forebrain that is part of the reward pathway. [7, 12]

nucleus (1) The term used by anatomists to refer to any collection of neuron cell bodies in the brain or spinal cord. [3] (2) The spherical central structure of a cell that contains the chromosomes. [4]

nurture One side of a philosophical debate that attributes our behavior to environmental influences. [4]

O

obese Overweight such that it is unhealthy. [12]

object permanence The concept that objects continue to exist even if we no longer perceive them. [5]

observation The careful noting and recording of events that occur over time. [2]

observational learning Learning that occurs when one individual imitates the behavior of another individual. [8]

obsessive-compulsive disorder (OCD) A disorder characterized by repeated, persistent thoughts or urges that are unwanted and repetitive, ritualistic behaviors and/or mental acts, which impair normal functioning. [16]

obsessive-compulsive personality disorder (OCPD) A personality disorder in which behavior and thinking is characterized by a rigidity regarding order, organization, and notions of what is right or wrong. [16]

Occam's razor A principle that when choosing between competing hypotheses, the simpler one, requiring the fewest assumptions, is usually better. [2]

occipital lobes Also called *visual cortex*. Regions of cortex at the back of the brain, which receive information from the eyes. [3]

OCD *See* obsessive-compulsive disorder. [8]

OCPD *See* obsessive-compulsive personality disorder. [8]

odorants Molecules that can be smelled. [6]

Oedipal complex Freud's term for the unconscious desire of boys to kill their father and become their mother's new mate. [14]

olfaction The process of smelling odors. [6]

olfactory bulb The part of the brain that receives impulses from the axons of the olfactory receptor neurons. [6]

olfactory epithelium The sheet of cells lining the inside of the nose, in which the olfactory receptor neurons are embedded. [6]

olfactory receptor neurons Sensory neurons that detect odors and are found embedded in a sheet of cells lining the nose. [6]

openness A personality trait that reflects a person's tendency to seek new experiences. [14]

operant conditioning chambers Also called *Skinner boxes*. Cages in which animals can learn to do a simple task, such as press a bar, to obtain a reward. [8]

operant conditioning Also called *instrumental learning*. A form of associative learning in which the likelihood that an act will be performed depends on the consequences that follow it. [8]

opioid receptors A receptor that responds to endogenous and/or exogenous opioids. [7]

opium An extract of the seedpod of the poppy flower; it has painkilling properties. [7]

opponent-process theory *See* color opponent theory. [6]

optic disc The round area on the retina, lacking rods and cones, where axons exit the eye. [6]

optimal arousal model The concept that individuals have an internal motivation to maintain the right amount of arousal. [12]

oral stage The earliest phase in Freud's psychosexual stages of development, when the baby pursues pleasurable sensations in the mouth, tongue, and lips. [14]

orbitofrontal cortex A portion of frontal cortex near the eyes that is activated in many emotional reactions. [13]

organizational hypothesis The proposal that the brain is permanently masculinized by exposure to androgens during development. [12]

ossicles The three tiny bones in the middle ear that amplify sounds. [6]

outer ear Also called *pinna*. The visible part of the ear and the canal leading to the eardrum. [6]

outlier A score that is either much greater or much smaller than the others. [2]

oval window The opening from the middle ear to the cochlea of the inner ear. [6]

ovaries The female gonads, which produce eggs for reproduction. [12]

P

***p*-value** The probability that the difference between two samples could occur by chance alone. [2]

panic disorder An anxiety disorder characterized by recurrent *panic attacks*, sudden fear with no apparent cause, unusual body sensations such as dizziness, difficulty breathing, trembling, and a feeling of loss of control. [16]

paradoxical sleep *See* rapid-eye-movement (REM) sleep. [7]

parasympathetic nervous system The part of the autonomic nervous system that prepares the body to relax and recuperate. [3, 13]

parietal lobes Regions of cortex behind the frontal lobes; they are involved in touch, pain, and sense of body position. [3]

partial reinforcement schedule Also called *intermittent reinforcement schedule*. The rewarding of a behavior only some of the time it is displayed. [8]

passive avoidance A response a subject has learned to refrain from displaying, to avoid an aversive stimulus. [8]

patient H.M. Henry Molaison, a patient who, because of bilateral medial temporal lobe damage, could not form new explicit memories. [9]

patient K.C. A patient who, because of damage to his cortex, lost all memory for personal information but retained his memory for general knowledge. [9]

Pavlovian conditioning *See* classical conditioning. [8]

PCP *See* phencyclidine. [7]

percentiles A way of comparing scores on a test using the percentage of the comparable population that scores below a given score. [11]

percept The final interpretation of a stimulus. [6]

perception The experience we have as we process and interpret information from sensory cells. [6]

perceptual speed How quickly we can detect and process stimuli. [5]

peripheral nervous system (PNS) The portion of the nervous system that includes all the nerves and neurons outside the brain and spinal cord. [3]

person–situation debate The question of whether behavior can be better explained by a person's internal characteristics, or by the surroundings. [14]

personality disorders Enduring impairments in interacting with other people that cause the client significant distress. [16]

personality traits Particular aspects of behavioral characteristics that can be objectively measured in a quantitative fashion. [14]

personality types The particular combinations of behavioral characteristics that tend to occur together. [14]

personality The set of characteristics individuals possess that influence their thinking and behavior. [14]

PET *See* positron emission tomography. [7]

peyote *See* mescaline. [7]

phallic stage The third phase in Freud's psychosexual stages of development, when pleasure is derived from masturbation. [14]

phantom limb pain The perception of pain in a missing appendage. [6]

phencyclidine (PCP) Also called *angel dust*. A drug developed as a potent analgesic and anesthetic agent. [7]

phenotype The sum of an individual's physical characteristics at one particular time. [4]

phenylketonuria (PKU) An inherited disorder of protein metabolism in which the absence of an enzyme leads to a toxic buildup of certain compounds, causing intellectual disability. [4, 11]

phobia A marked, long-lasting fear of an object or situation that is out of proportion to the real danger. [8, 16]

phonemes The basic speech sounds that make up languages. [10]

photographic memory Also called *eidetic memory*. The supposed ability to recall entire images with extreme detail. [9]

photon The smallest particle of light. [6]

photoreceptor adaptation The ability of rods and cones to change their sensitivity. [6]

photoreceptors Light-sensitive receptor cells in the retina. [6]

pinna *See* outer ear. [6]

pituitary gland An endocrine gland that releases hormones that affect virtually all other endocrine glands. [3]

PKU *See* phenylketonuria. [7]

placebo A pill or other treatment that has no known medical effect. [2]

plasticity Also called *neural plasticity*. The ability of the brain to change in structure or function. [3, 5]

Plato (428–347 BCE) An ancient Greek philosopher who was skeptical of our senses and stressed reliance on logic and reasoning. [1]

PNS *See* peripheral nervous system. [3]

polarized Having a positive or negative charge. [3]

polygraph Also called *lie detector*. A device that monitors several physiological measures, such as respiration, heart rate, blood pressure, and electrical conductance of the skin. [13]

population The entire set of individuals we want to understand. [2]

positive punishment The addition of a stimulus following a response, decreasing the likelihood of that behavior. [8]

positive reinforcement The addition of a stimulus following a behavior, increasing the likelihood of that behavior. [8]

positive symptoms Behavioral symptoms which are gained in schizophrenia; for example hallucinations, delusions, and agitation. [16]

positron emission tomography (PET) A technique for examining brain function using injections of radioactive substances used by the brain. Particle detectors and computers are used to find where most of the radioactive markers gather in the brain. [3]

postconventional moral reasoning Moral reasoning, sometimes called the "principled level," in which rules and laws are part of a social contract, or that certain rules are universal, to be followed even if most people don't agree. [5]

posttraumatic stress disorder (PTSD) A disorder in which memories of an unpleasant episode repeatedly plague the victim. [13]

potential difference in charge The measure of the tendency for charged particles to move from one place to another, usually reported in volts. [3]

power motive *See* need for power. [12]

preconventional moral reasoning Moral reasoning that weighs whether a behavior is "right" in terms of personal consequences. [5]

prefrontal cortex The frontmost part of the frontal lobes, which is involved in many of our most complex behaviors. [3]

preoperational stage The stage at which children learn to use language to represent objects and actions. [5]

presbyopia A condition in which most people over 40 find it difficult to focus on nearby objects. [5]

primacy effect The improved recall of items from the beginning of the list in a recall task. [9]

primary reinforcer A stimulus that fills a biological need or that the subject already finds unpleasant. [8]

primary visual cortex (V1) The region of the occipital cortex where most visual information first arrives. [6]

priming The ability of information presented at one time to affect a person's response at a later time. [9]

prisoner's dilemma An intellectual exercise used to study the roles of cooperation and competition. [15]

proactive interference The type of interference when an existing memory interferes with formation of a new memory. [9]

progesterone One of two ovarian hormones that are crucial for female reproduction. [12]

projective tests A method for probing the unconscious by asking a client to generate words or stories in response to a stimulus. [14]

protection The use of punishment to constrain a person's freedom so that he or she cannot hurt others. [15]

protein A long string of amino acids. The basic building material of organisms. [4]

prototype The best example of a concept that fits a particular category. [10]

psilocybin Also called *magic mushrooms*. A hallucinogenic drug that affects visual experience. [7]

psychoactive drugs Drugs (chemical substances) that alter mental function, affecting consciousness. [7]

psychoanalysis The process, developed by Freud, of making a detailed analysis of a client's mind through open-ended discussions about thoughts and feelings. [14]

psychological test A way of measuring a psychological event or process. [2]

psychology The scientific study of the mind and behavior. [1]

psychoneuroimmunology The study of psychological and neural influences on the immune system and its influences on behavior. [13]

psychophysics The study of how physical events, such as lights and sounds, affect our senses. [1, 6]

psychosexual stages of development Freud's theory of how personality develops from birth to adulthood. [14]

PTSD *See* posttraumatic stress disorder. [7]

puberty The landmark event when an individual becomes capable of reproducing. [5]

pupil The opening at the center of the iris. [6]

puzzle box A cage equipped with levers and latches so that an animal must open a door to escape. [8]

Q

qualia The entirely subjective experience a person has with a perception. [7]

R

random samples Samples in which every member of the population has an equal chance of being selected, and the selection of one person has no influence on who is selected next. [2]

randomized, double-blind, placebo-controlled trial The best form of assessment for evaluating drug effectiveness, in which patients are randomly assigned to either the drug or placebo treatment, and neither the patient nor the person evaluating his progress knows which group he is in. [2]

range The highest and lowest scores, a rough gauge of variability. [2]

rapid-eye-movement (REM) sleep Also called *paradoxical sleep*. A stage of sleep characterized by desynchronized EEG, flaccid muscles, and rapid eye movements. [7]

rationalization The defense mechanism of making intellectual excuses for unacceptable behavior. [14]

RBD *See* REM behavior disorder. [7]

reaction time The amount of time it takes a subject to initiate some action after a predetermined signal. [5, 10, 11]

reactive/impulsive aggression An aggressive behavior in response to some provocation. [15]

recency effect The improved recall of the items at the end of the list in a recall task. [9]

receptive field The region of space where stimuli affect the activity of a cell in a sensory system. [6]

receptors *See* neurotransmitter receptors. [3]

receptors *See* sensory receptor cells. [6]

recessive In the context of heredity, an allele that affects an individual's phenotype only when it is present on both chromosomes. [4]

reciprocal determinism The theory that three different factors mutually influence one another: personal factors, environmental factors, and the individual's behavior. [14]

reflex A simple behavior that is automatically triggered by a particular stimulation, without our conscious effort. [3]

refractory period The time following a male orgasm, during which stimulation cannot produce an erection. [12]

refractory phase A period during and immediately after a nerve impulse when a neuron cannot produce another action potential. [3]

rehearsal The conscious repetition of information. [9]

reinforcement schedule The rules determining the frequency with which an operant conditioning subject is reinforced. [8]

reinforcer A stimulus that appears in response to behavior and increases the probability of that behavior recurring. [8]

relaxation training A technique that focuses attention on calming stimuli while relaxing the body, intended to reduce stress. [13]

reliability (1) The degree to which a measurement tool produces consistent, repeatable results. [2, 11, 14] (2) The extent to which different clinicians would reach the same diagnosis for any patient with a particular set of symptoms. [16]

REM behavior disorder (RBD) A syndrome, primarily found in middle-aged men, that involves movements during REM sleep that seem to correspond to movements taking place in the current dream. [7]

REM *See* rapid-eye-movement sleep. [7]

René Descartes (1596–1650) A Renaissance philosopher who built a system of knowing about reality that does not rely on our fallible senses. [1]

replication The repeating of an experiment to determine if results are comparable to the original finding. [2]

representative sample A sample that accurately reflects the total population of interest. [2]

resistant attachment *See* ambivalent attachment. [5]

response tendencies According to the behaviorist perspective, particular ways of reacting to various situations based on past learning experiences, which together form the personality. [14]

resting potential The membrane potential of a neuron when it is not being stimulated. [3]

reticular formation The area running through the middle of the brainstem, from medulla to midbrain, which is related to arousal from sleep. [7]

retina The surface at the back of the eye where the image from the lens and cornea is focused. [6]

retribution The punishment of a person beyond the need for deterrence or protection. [15]

retrieval The act or process of accessing information from LTM. [9]

retroactive interference The type of interference when forming a new memory interferes with retrieval of an old memory. [9]

retrograde amnesia Amnesia for events occurring prior to an event, typically a trauma. [9]

reuptake The process by which axon terminals take back neurotransmitter molecules from the synaptic cleft. [3]

reward pathway A pathway from the midbrain to the frontal cortex that produces pleasurable sensations when stimulated electrically. [7, 12]

Ritalin *See* methylphenidate. [5]

rod A class of photoreceptors in the retina that can detect very low levels of light. [6]

Rogerian psychotherapy A method of treatment focusing on the client's goals, offering a nonjudgmental forum where the client can problem solve, with the therapist's cooperation. [14]

role-playing theory *See* social theory of hypnosis. [7]

Rorschach test A projective test in which a client's perceptions of a series of inkblots is recorded and analyzed to reveal unconscious processes. [14]

S

S cones *See* short-wavelength cones. [6]

SAD *See* seasonal affective disorder. [16]

Sally and Anne test A test to probe whether a child has a theory of other people's minds. [5]

saltatory conduction The form of conduction in which the action potential "jumps" from one node of Ranvier to the next. [3]

salty One of the five different tastes, detected by taste receptor proteins that allow positively charged sodium ions to enter the cell. [6]

sample The subset of the population selected for actual study. [2]

savant syndrome A very rare condition in which a mentally disabled person also exhibits exceptional ability in some limited field, such as memory, mathematics, or music. [9, 11]

schema In the context of Piaget's theory of cognitive development, a cognitive structure inside the mind. [5]

schizophrenia A disabling mental disorder characterized by hallucinations, delusions, disordered thinking, and emotional withdrawal. [4, 16]

schizotypal personality disorder A personality disorder that may resemble schizophrenia in the sense that the client may have very unconventional, even paranoid, beliefs and eccentric behavior that makes it difficult to maintain relationships. [16]

SCN *See* suprachiasmatic nucleus. [16]

scoring reliability The extent to which two different scorers report the same score for the subject. [11]

seasonal affective disorder (SAD) A depressive disorder diagnosed in people who report feeling transiently depressed every winter. [16]

second-order conditioning Also called *secondary conditioning*. Learning in which a previously learned CS, which elicits a CR, repeatedly follows another neutral stimulus so that that second neutral stimulus also comes to elicit a CR. [8]

secondary conditioning *See* second-order conditioning. [8]

secondary reinforcer A stimulus the subject comes to associate with one or more primary reinforcers. [8]

secondary sex characteristics Physical characteristics that are typical of adults of one sex or the other. [5]

secure attachment A style of attachment in which the child is visibly upset when the caregiver leaves, rejects a stranger, and welcomes reunion with the caregiver. [5]

selective serotonin reuptake inhibitors (SSRIs) A major class of modern antidepressants, they increase availability of synaptic serotonin. [16]

self-actualization A humanistic psychology concept of the process by which a person lives up to his or her full potential, becoming the best and happiest human they can be. [12, 14]

self-efficacy The belief that you are capable: that you have the ability to succeed and to master a particular situation. [14]

self-handicapping Avoiding effort so that potential failure won't damage self-esteem. A way to avoid cognitive dissonance. [15]

self-serving bias The tendency to attribute our successes to our dispositions and attribute our failures to external factors. [15]

semantic memory Generalized declarative memory. [9]

semantic webs Large networks of words with meanings that have different degrees of connection to one another. [9]

semantics The study of the meanings of words. [10]

semen A mixture of fluid, including sperm, that is released during ejaculation. [12]

sensation The process by which the nervous system detects the physical events around or inside us. [6]

sensitive period A time during development when exposure to a stimulus has the greatest effect on a particular behavior. [5, 10, 12]

sensitization A simple form of learning in which a strong, aversive stimulus causes a subject to show an exaggerated response to other stimuli. [8]

sensorimotor stage The first stage of cognitive development in which individuals learn to use sensory and motor systems. [5]

sensory adaptation The progressive loss of responsiveness in sensory cells exposed to a constant stimulus. [6]

sensory buffer Also called *sensory memory*. A very brief type of memory for sensory information. [9]

sensory code The relationship between stimuli and the action potentials they produce in sensory cells. [6]

sensory cortex Several different regions of cortex devoted to analyzing sensory information. [3]

sensory memory *See* sensory buffer. [9]

sensory modalities The different types of senses. For example, vision, hearing, taste, touch, and smell. [6]

sensory neuron A type of neuron that is sensitive to physical events and sends information to the brain about them, typically using glutamate as a neurotransmitter. [3]

sensory receptor cells Also called *receptors*. Specialized sensory cells that detect stimuli. [6]

sensory receptor organ A clump of receptor cells, all detecting a particular kind of stimulus. [6]

serial position curve A U-shaped curve showing the likelihood of remembering an item in a list based on its position in that list. [9]

serotonin A neurotransmitter made by neurons in the base of the brain that send their axons throughout the brain and spinal cord. [3]

set point A particular value that a system keeps returning to. [12]

sexual differentiation The process in fetal development, controlled by the hormones produced by the gonads, of forming either male or female structures. [12]

sexual orientation The direction of a person's sexual interest. [12]

shape constancy The visual perception that an object retains the same shape, no matter what angle we happen to see it from. [6]

shaping The process by which a subject is readily provided with a reinforcer whenever the subject comes close to showing the desired behavior, and then is required to come closer and closer to that desired behavior before receiving the reinforcer. [8]

short-term memory (STM) A type of memory of limited capacity and duration of only seconds. [9]

short-wavelength cones Also called *S cones*. Cone photoreceptors that are best at detecting light of short wavelengths, such as violet. [6]

SIDS *See* sudden infant death syndrome. [16]

signal detection theory A way to measure how well a real stimulus (a signal) is detected in the midst of irrelevant stimuli (noise). [6]

simple reflexes Unlearned, automatic responses to specific stimuli. [5]

situation The environment surrounding a person. [15]

size constancy The visual perception that an object does not change size, regardless of its distance away. [6]

size cue The property that objects appear smaller when they are farther away. [6]

skill learning Learning to perform a challenging task. [9]

skill The ability to perform very well with a minimum of effort. [10]

Skinner boxes *See* operant conditioning chamber. [8]

sleep apnea A sleep disorder in which respiration slows or stops periodically, waking the sufferer. Excessive daytime sleepiness may result from the frequent nocturnal awakening. [7]

sleep debt The increased feelings of sleepiness and tendency to sleep longer after a period of losing sleep. [7]

sleep paralysis The temporary inability to move or talk either just before dropping off to sleep or just after waking. [7]

sleep spindles A train of spikes in the EEG. [7]

sleep state misperception A disorder in which people report not having been asleep when they actually were. [7]

slow-wave sleep (SWS) Sleep that is defined by the presence of slow-wave EEG activity (delta waves). [7]

social attitudes Our evaluations about people and a predisposition to act in a particular way toward them. [15]

social exchange theory The notion that we help others, even if they are unrelated to us, because they may someday help us in return. [15]

social facilitation The change in behavior brought about by the presence of others. [15]

social learning Changes in behavior brought about by interacting with other individuals. [8, 14]

social loafing Shirking responsibility because of being in a group. [15]

social modeling The tendency of individuals to mimic the behavior of others. [14]

social motivation The drive to interact, please, and gain recognition from others. [12]

social norms The widely agreed upon rules for what people should believe and how they should behave. [15]

social perception The process of perceiving the behavior and inferring the motives of other people. [15]

social prejudice An unfavorable stereotype about a large group of people. [15]

social psychology The study of how the real, implied, or imagined presence of other people affects our behavior, beliefs, and attitudes. [15]

social roles The behaviors and attitudes expected from someone with a particular social position. [15]

social support Friends and family that provide a network of resources. [13]

social theory of hypnosis Also called *role-playing theory.* Theory that the hypnotized participant is simply trying to accommodate another person, the hypnotist, whom the participant trusts. [7]

soma *See* cell body. [3]

somatic nervous system The part of the PNS that carries sensory information from the body to the CNS and motor commands from the CNS to the body. [3]

somatosensory cortex The frontmost strip of parietal cortex that receives touch information. [3]

sound localization The ability to perceive the source of a sound. [6]

sour One of the five different tastes, detected by taste receptor proteins that allow positively charged hydrogen ions to enter the cell. [6]

spinal cord A cylindrical bundle of neurons and axons connected to the base of the brain. [3]

split brain The result of a surgery that destroys the pathways of communication between the two cerebral hemispheres. [7]

split-half reliability The extent to which different parts of the exam produce a similar score. [11]

spontaneous recovery The return of a previously extinguished CR in response to the CS after a period of rest. [8]

spreading activation The idea that memories are somehow linked to one another based on characteristics they share, so that recalling one word is likely to lead us to recall another, related word. [9]

spurious correlations Instances when two variables covary not because there is any causal relationship between them, but because they are both being affected by some other variable. [2]

SSRI *See* selective serotonin reuptake inhibitor. [16]

stage 1 sleep The initial stage of sleep in which the EEG shows small, irregular waves and characteristic sharp waves called vertex spikes. [7]

stage 2 sleep A stage of sleep that is defined by sleep spindles and K complexes. [7]

stage 3 sleep A stage of sleep that is defined by the presence of large-amplitude slow waves (delta waves). [7]

stages of psychosocial development Erik Erikson's proposed progressive stages of human development in which we decide how to behave with regard to others. [5]

standard deviation The average amount that each individual score falls above or below the mean, used to express variance. [2, 11]

standardization Establishment of a common set of terms and definitions, to help different doctors reach the same diagnosis for a particular patient. [16]

standardized (1) A test administered according to a set of instructions intended to control the conditions of the test. [11] (2) When a test has been administered to many different people, so that the distribution of the scores are known. [14]

Stanford hypnotic susceptibility test A tool used to estimate how readily a person can be hypnotized. [7]

Stanford-Binet test An intelligence test for American children developed by Terman of Stanford University, based on the Binet–Simon scale. [11]

statistically significant A *p*-value chosen by convention as indicating that the differences are not likely due to chance. In psychology, this is generally that *p* is less than 0.05. [2]

stereotype threat A phenomenon occurring when exposure to a derogatory stereotype about a particular group causes group members to perform worse. [11, 15]

stereotyped In the context of sexual behaviors, the species-specific unvarying form of sexual behavior in non-human animals. [12]

stimulants Drugs that tend to increase neural activity and also speed up cognition and behavior. [7]

stimulus generalization When the subject displays a CR to stimuli that are similar to, but not exactly identical to, the CS used in training. [8]

stimulus (pl. *stimuli*) (1) Any physical event that affects a sensory receptor cell. [6] (2) In the context of learning, a sensory event that an individual can detect. [8]

STM *See* short-term memory. [16]

strange situation A test of the attachment as revealed by a child's reaction to a temporary separation from the caregiver. [5]

stranger anxiety The negative response of infants toward unfamiliar people. [5]

stress buffering hypothesis The hypothesis that social support provides a buffer between a person and stressful events. [13]

stress evaluation The cognitive system that assesses events that threaten us. [13]

stress immunization The concept that mild stress early in life makes an individual better able to handle stress later in life. Research indicates early stress is only beneficial if the individual is comforted afterward. [13]

stress response The physiological response of the body to the assessment of threat. [13]

stress The events and stimuli that threaten us, how we assess them, and our physiological reaction. [13]

stressors The events and stimuli that threaten us. [13]

strong inference A prescribed method for conducting scientific inquiry that consists of repeatedly disproving hypotheses. [2]

structuralism The introspective analysis of the human mind by breaking it down into the simplest kinds of experience, and then asking how these simple experiences come together to produce more complex experiences. [1]

study population The group from which we can actually draw our sample. [2]

subcoeruleus A region in the brainstem that inhibits motor neurons during REM sleep. [7]

subjective validation Also called the *Forer effect*. The tendency to pick out a specific, accurate meaning from an open-ended, vague personality description. [14]

subliminal perception When a participant shows evidence of having perceived a stimulus without being consciously aware of it. [10]

subliminal Referring to a stimulus that a person is unaware of having perceived. [1]

substance use disorder The official term for addiction, defined by meeting several criteria. [7, 16]

sudden infant death syndrome (SIDS) Also called *crib death*. Death that occurs when a baby less than a year old simply stops breathing while asleep. [5, 7]

superego Freud's term for the part of the mind that incorporates the rules of behavior that a person learns and accepts from other people. [14]

superstition The false belief that a particular behavior will bring about a stimulus or event. [8]

suprachiasmatic nucleus (SCN) A small region of the hypothalamus that controls circadian rhythm. [7]

surface structure The particular string of words that are put together in a sentence. [10]

surveys A means of gathering data about behavior by having people answer questions about their behavior, thoughts, or opinions. [2]

sweet One of the five different tastes, detected by taste receptor proteins that respond to sugar molecules. [6]

SWS *See* slow-wave sleep. [16]

sympathetic nervous system The part of the autonomic nervous system that activates the body for action (the "fight or flight" response). [3, 13]

synapse rearrangement The phenomenon of new synapses forming and old synapses retracting, especially prominent early in life. [5]

synapse A specialized junction where the axon terminal of a neuron communicates with another cell. [3]

synaptic cleft The tiny, fluid-filled gap between the a neuron's axon terminal and another cell. [3]

synaptogenesis The formation of synapses. [5]

syntax The rules for constructing phrases and sentences in a language. [10]

systematic desensitization The gradual exposure of a person to the feared object or situation until the person learns that there is no real danger; used as a treatment for phobias. [16]

T

Tan A man who had lost the ability to utter more than the single syllable "tan," but seemed to understand language, as reported by Broca. [10]

tardive dyskinesia A motor side effect of some neuroleptics that is characterized by involuntary movements, typically of the tongue, or difficulty walking, which may be debilitating. [16]

tastant A chemical that encounters the taste receptor cell and excites it. [6]

taste aversion *See* conditioned taste aversion. [8]

taste buds Collections of 50–150 cells, including taste receptor cells and support cells, on the surface of the tongue, back of the mouth, and roof of the mouth. [6]

taste pore An opening in a taste bud on the surface of the tongue, where chemicals in the mouth encounter the surface of taste receptor cells. [6]

taste receptor cells Cells on the surface of the tongue that produce taste receptor proteins, which actually detect one of the five tastes. [6]

TAT *See* thematic apperception test. [16]

telegraphic speech Communication form in young children, in which a few words are used to express an idea. [10]

temperament A person's emotional makeup, the way the person generally responds to a variety of situations. [5, 14]

temporal lobes Regions of cortex on the sides of the brain, which receive information about smell, taste, sound, and are critical for understanding language. [3]

teratogen Any substance that reaches an embryo or fetus and disrupts prenatal development. [5]

terminal button *See* axon terminal. [3]

test-retest reliability The quality of giving similar results when a test is administered more than once to the same person. [11]

testes The male gonads, which produce sperm for reproduction. [12]

testosterone A steroid hormone secreted by the testes, the most prominent androgen. [12, 15]

thalamus The brain region at the top of the brainstem that trades information with the cerebrum. [3]

THC *See* delta-9-tetrahydrocannabinol. [7]

thematic apperception test (TAT) A projective test in which a person is shown a picture and asked to tell a story to describe what's happening in the picture. The response is analyzed to reveal unconscious processes. [14]

theory of mind The understanding that other people may have different information, including inaccurate ideas. [5]

theory A group of hypotheses about a particular phenomenon that have survived all current testing and that are all compatible with one another. [2]

threshold (1) The size of depolarization necessary to trigger an action potential. [3] (2) The weakest possible stimulus that still affects a sensory cell's firing. [6]

tip-of-the-tongue phenomenon When we feel that we can almost say aloud the word we are trying to remember. [9]

TMS *See* transcranial magnetic stimulation. [16]

tolerance The phenomena in which a person must take a higher and higher dose of a drug to get the same effect. [7]

Tower of Hanoi A problem in which you transfer a series of different-sized disks from one spindle to another following a specific set of rules. [10]

trait A physical or behavioral characteristic feature displayed by an individual. [4]

trance theory of hypnosis A theory that hypnosis is a genuinely altered state of consciousness that allows people to be more flexible in their experience and behavior. [7]

tranquilizer A depressant that typically makes people feel less anxious. [7]

transcranial magnetic stimulation (TMS) The temporary, localized disruption of the functioning of a brain region produced by the application of strong magnetic fields. [3]

transmitter *See* neurotransmitter. [3]

triangular theory of love The proposal that romantic relationships are composed of different proportions of passion, intimacy, and commitment. [15]

trichromatic theory The idea that color vision is based on receptors for three different colors. [6]

tricyclics The second generation of antidepressants, which inhibit the reuptake of monoamines, prolonging their synaptic activity. [16]

Tuskegee syphilis study A study in which the U.S. Public Health Service and the Centers for Disease Control followed the progression of syphilis in hundreds of poor African American men in Tuskegee, Alabama, without providing them with a known cure for the disease. [2]

twin study Study of identical twins; used to estimate heritability of certain traits. [4]

two-factor theory of emotion A theory that physiological arousal determines the intensity of the emotion while cognitive interpretation determines the type of emotion experienced. [13]

typical neuroleptics Antipsychotic drugs that are D_2 receptor antagonists. [16]

U

umami One of the five different tastes, detected by taste receptor proteins that respond to amino acids. [6]

unconditioned response (UR) The specific response that is naturally evoked by that US. [8]

unconditioned stimulus (US) A stimulus that naturally evokes a specific response. [8]

unconscious bias Also called *implicit bias*. An inclination to prefer one type of person, object, or idea over others without being consciously aware of that preference. [2]

unconscious The part of the mind that functions outside our awareness. [14]

UR *See* unconditioned response. [16]

US *See* unconditioned stimulus. [16]

V

V1 *See* primary visual cortex. [7]

validity scales Quantitative measures intended to detect when subjects are responding inconsistently or dishonestly. [14]

validity The extent to which a test actually measures the trait it is intended to measure. [2, 11, 14, 16]

variable interval (VI) A schedule in which reinforcement for the response is provided at some variable interval of time after the last response. [8]

variable ratio (VR) A schedule in which the number of responses required to obtain a reward changes. [8]

variables Factors, either events in the environment or other behaviors, that often change along with the behavior of interest. [2]

variance A statistical measure of the amount of variability in a population or sample. [2]

ventromedial hypothalamus (VMH) A brain region related to the body weight set point. Damage to this region results in a new, higher set point. [12]

vesicles Microscopic spheres in a neuron that contain neurotransmitter molecules to be released into the synaptic cleft. [3]

VI *See* variable interval. [16]

visual cliff An apparently steep drop in the floor that is actually covered by a clear surface. [5]

visual cortex *See* occipital lobe. [3]

visual field The part of space that we can see at any one time. [6]

VMH *See* ventromedial hypothalamus. [16]

VR *See* variable ratio. [16]

W

Wada test A test in which a short-lasting anesthetic is delivered into one brain hemisphere or the other to determine which hemisphere principally mediates language. [10]

WAIS *See* Wechsler Adult Intelligence Scale. [16]

Weber's fraction The smallest change in the magnitude of a stimulus that can be detected, expressed as a proportion of the original stimulus. [6]

Wechsler Adult Intelligence Scale (WAIS) An intelligence test designed for adults, 16 to 89 years of age. [11]

Wechsler Intelligence Scale for Children (WISC) An intelligence test designed for children 6 to under 16 years of age. [11]

Wernicke's aphasia Also called *fluent aphasia*. An impairment in understanding what is heard or read accompanied by fluent speech, which may be garbled. [10]

Wernicke's area The area at the top of the temporal lobe that is damaged in fluent aphasia. [10]

white blood cells Blood cells that attack microbes invading the body. [13]

Wilhelm Wundt (1832–1920) A German physiologist who established the first research laboratory in psychology and wrote the first psychology textbook. [1]

William James (1842–1910) An American psychologist who emphasized the adaptive function of behaviors and mental processes to help survival and reproduction. [1]

Williams syndrome A genetic disorder characterized by normal verbal abilities but severe deficits in spatial reasoning. [10]

withdrawal symptoms The unpleasant sensations that occur when a person stops using a drug. [7]

Wolfgang Köhler (1887–1967) An influential pioneer in Gestalt psychology. [1]

working backward The problem-solving strategy of starting with the desired end result and reversing the steps needed to get there. [10]

working memory A system that keeps memories available for ready access during performance of a task. [9]

Z

zygote A fertilized egg. [5]

Illustration Credits

Cover and chapter opener illustrations:
© Dave Cutler, www.davecutlerstudio.com.

Chapter 1 1.1: © CLSI. 1.5B: Courtesy of Olly Moss, Ollymoss.com. p. 4: © Jeff Roberson/AP/Corbis. p. 5: Illustrations by John Gould, from Birds of New Guinea and the Adjacent Papuan Islands. p. 7: George Richmond, late 1830s. p. 10: © Bettmann/Corbis. p. 11: © Underwood & Underwood/Corbis. p. 17: © Robert Maass/Corbis. p. 20 *Scientist*: © Neustockimages/istock. p. 20 *Scan*: Courtesy of Jamie Eberling. p. 20 *Quadruplets*: © The Genain Quadruplets. p. 20 *Peekaboo*: © James Brey/ istock. p. 20 *Balloons*: © Tim Clayton/Corbis. p. 20 *Hypnosis*: © BSIP SA/Alamy. p. 20 *Amnesiac*: © Krysten Kellum/Zuma Press/Corbis. p. 21 *Coke*: © Corbis. p. 21 *Mozart*: Anonymous painting, possibly by Pietro Antonio Lorenzoni (1721-1782). p. 21 *Homosexuals*: © Muskoka Stock Photos/Shutterstock. p. 21 *Polygraph*: © Tek Image/Science Source. p. 21 *Astrology*: © Interfoto/ Alamy. p. 21 *Genovese*: © The New York Times/Redux. p. 21 *Moon*: Courtesy of NASA. p. 21 *Saks*: © Damian Dovarganes/AP/Corbis. p. 21 *Cartoon*: © Nicholson, from *The Australian*, www.nicholsoncartoons.com.au.

Chapter 2 2.8: © Mary Evans Picture Library/Alamy. 2.12C: © Justin Kase zsixz/Alamy. 2.12D: © Christopher Futcher/istock. 2.18: National Archives. Box 2.1: © Everett Collection/Alamy. Box 2.2: © Popartic/Shutterstock. p. 31: © Richard Levine/Alamy. p. 32: © Angela Hampton Picture Library/Alamy. p. 37: © Wiley Ink, inc./ CartoonStock. p. 56 *top*: © RGB Ventures/SuperStock/ Alamy. p. 56 *bottom*: © The Photolibrary Wales/Alamy.

Chapter 3 3.16A: © Interfoto/Alamy. 3.16B: © Guy Croft SciTech/Alamy. 3.17B, 3.18: Photographs courtesy of S. Mark Williams and Dale Purves, Duke University Medical Center. 3.23: © BSIP SA/Alamy. 3.24: © AJ Photo/BSIP/Corbis. 3.26A: © Scott Camazine/Alamy. 3.26B: © Science Photo Library/Alamy. 3.26C: Courtesy of Jamie Eberling. 3.28B: © Simon Fraser/Science Source. Box 3.1B: © Moviestore collection Ltd/Alamy. p. 103: © Kate Mitchell/Corbis.

Chapter 4 4.11B: © Andrew Francis Wallace/ The Toronto Star/Zuma Press. 4.13A: Photo by David McIntyre; simulation created using software from Vischeck (www.vischeck.com). 4.13B: © Brand X Pictures/Alamy. 4.17: © The Genain Quadruplets. Box 4.1A: Screenshot from the Daily Mail Online, www. dailymail.co.uk. Box 4.1B: © Dr. Ken Greer/Visuals Unlimited, Inc. p. 113: © Splash News/Corbis. p. 114: © Associated Press. p. 116: © Bailey-Cooper Photography 2/Alamy. p. 127: © Noah Goodrich/Caters News/Zuma Press. p. 128: © Brian Mitchell/Corbis. p. 134: © Trinity Mirror/Mirrorpix/Alamy. p. 135: © Mark Peterson/Corbis.

Chapter 5 5.1 *bottom*: © CNRI/Science Source. 5.4A: © Rick's Photography/Shutterstock. 5.5: © Florence Low.

5.6A: © Tom Grill/Corbis. 5.6B: © Bubbles Photolibrary/Alamy. 5.6C: © Christine Hanscomb/Science Source. 5.7: © Queerstock, Inc./Alamy. 5.9: © James Brey/istock. 5.10: © Mark Richards/PhotoEdit. 5.14A: © Michael Newman/PhotoEdit. 5.15: © Farrell Grehan/Corbis. 5.21: © Jeffrey Phelps/Aurora Photos/Corbis. 5.22: © Nina Leen/The LIFE Picture Collection/Getty Images. Box 5.1: After Shaw et al., 2007. Box 5.3: © Picture Partners/Alamy. p. 166: © A. Ramey/PhotoEdit. p. 168: © Gavin Hellier/Robert Harding World Imagery/Corbis. p. 172: © Bettmann/Corbis. p. 177: © Image Source/Alamy. p. 180: © Elena Tiniakou/Demotix/Corbis. p. 182: © B Christopher/Alamy. p. 183: © Michael Keller/Corbis.

Chapter 6 6.13: © Sinauer Associates. 6.15: Photo by Culver Pictures, Inc. 6.20: Courtesy of R. W. Rodieck. 6.29: © Jon Arnold Images Ltd/Alamy. 6.33A: © Peter Hermes Furian/Shutterstock. 6.43A: © Tetra Images/Alamy. Box 6.1: David McIntyre. p. 209: © George S de Blonsky/Alamy. p. 226: © Tim Clayton/Corbis.

Chapter 7 7.3: © Craig Stephen/Alamy. 7.11: © Philippe Garo/Science Source. 7.18A: © San Diego History Center. 7.19: Courtesy of Ray Meddis. Box 7.1: DILBERT © 1993 Scott Adams. Used by permission of UNIVERSAL UCLICK. All rights reserved. p. 248: © Jolanda Cats & Hans Withoos/Corbis. p. 251: CALVIN AND HOBBES © 1988 Watterson. Reprinted with permission of UNIVERSAL UCLICK. All rights reserved. p. 261: © www.BibleLandPictures.com/Alamy. p. 268 *top*: © Tomo Jesenicnik/istock. p. 268 *bottom*: © Ira Bachinskaya/istock. p. 272: Henry Fuseli, *The Nightmare*, 1791. p. 273 *top*: © ariwasabi/istock. p. 273 *bottom*: © Steve Maslowski/Visuals Unlimited, Inc. p. 274: © Hoberman Collection/Alamy. p. 276: Courtesy of H. Budka. p. 279: Courtesy of Joanne Delphia. p. 280: © Christopher Nash/Alamy. p. 282: © Hulton-Deutsch Collection/Corbis. p. 283: © The Print Collector/Alamy. p. 284: © BSIP SA/Alamy. p. 287 *left and right*: © Associated Press. p. 290: © Werli Francois/Alamy.

Chapter 8 8.4: Bettmann/Corbis. 8.6: © Corbis. 8.11: © Lincoln P. Brower. 8.12: © Nina Leen/Time & Life Pictures/Getty Images. 8.16: Courtesy of Med Associates. 8.19: © Carlos Osorio/AP/Corbis. 8.25A: © Cyril Ruoso/JH Editorial/Minden Pictures/Corbis. 8.25B: © Roger Wilmshurst/Alamy. 8.26 *inset*: © Double Brow Imagery/Shutterstock. 8.30: © Dr. Thomas Deerinck/Visuals Unlimited, Inc. Box 8.1: © Robert McGouey/Wildlife/Alamy. Box 8.2: © Zuma Press, Inc./Alamy. p. 316: Courtesy of the Neuroscience History Archives, Brain Research Institute, University of California, Los Angeles. p. 321: © New Line Cinema/AF archive/Alamy.

Chapter 9 9.11: © Sara K. Schwittek/Reuters/Corbis. 9.14: Courtesy of Dr. Suzanne Corkin, MIT. 9.16: From Corkin et al., 1997; courtesy of Suzanne Corkin. 9.20: Courtesy of D. P. Agamanolis, neuropathology-web.org. Box 9.2: Kathleen Turley/Tri-Valley Herald/Zuma Press. Box 9.4: © Krysten Kellum/Zuma Press/Corbis. p. 367: © Blend Images/Alamy. p. 371: © MBI/Alamy.

Chapter 10 10.4A: © Gorilla Foundation/Associated Press. 10.4B: © Frans Lanting Studio/Alamy. 10.5: © Rick Friedman/Corbis. 10.14 *left*: © PaulShlykov/istock. 10.14 *all others*: © GlobalP/istock. 10.20, 10.21: Figures provided by Daniel Simons. 10.27: © Larry Lilac/Alamy. 10.30: Still from "Choice blindness for the taste of Jam," on ChoiceBlindnessLab's YouTube channel, tinyurl.com/jam-choice. Box 10.1: © Tampa Bay Times/Zuma Press. p. 400: © Christopher Felver/Corbis. p. 401: David McIntyre. p. 402: © Balazs Mohai/epa/Corbis. p. 409: © UpperCut Images/Alamy. p. 411 *Cher*: © Frank Trapper/Corbis. p. 411 *Branson*: © James Leynse/Corbis. p. 417: Courtesy of Ted Gibson. p. 425: © dmac/Alamy. p. 428 *Ma*: © Alex Grimm/Reuters/Corbis. p. 428 *Fischer*: © Bettmann/Corbis. p. 428 *Williams*: © Marcio Jose Sanchez/AP/Corbis. p. 431: © Homer Sykes/Alamy. p. 437: David McIntyre. p. 439: Cartoon by Nicholson, from *The Australian*, www.nicholsoncartoons.com.au. p. 442: © gemphotography/istock.

Chapter 11 11.3: © Photo Researchers, Inc. 11.4: © Richard T. Nowitz/Corbis. 11.16A: Courtesy of the National Fragile X Foundation. 11.16B: © moodboard/Corbis. 11.17A: © Then Chih Wey/Xinhua Press/Corbis. 11.17B: © Bettmann/Corbis. 11.17C: © Henning Kaiser/dpa/Corbis. 11.18: © Daniel Tammet. 11.27: Screenshot from www.memory-improvement-tips.com. Box 11.2: Anonymous painting, possibly by Pietro Antonio Lorenzoni (1721-1782). p. 463: © New Line Cinema. p. 471: © Bob Daemmrich/Alamy. p. 489: © Bob Ebbesen/Alamy.

Chapter 12 12.12: © John Sholtis/Rockefeller University. 12.15A: © Ash Knotek/Zuma Press. 12.15B: Kunsthistorisches Museum, Vienna. 12.26: © The Wellcome Photo Library. 12.27: Courtesy of Kimberly Saviano/AISSG-USA. 12.30A: © Sinauer Associates. 12.35: © Reuters NewMedia Inc./Corbis. 12.37: © nevodka/istock. p. 514: © Zuma Press, Inc./Alamy. p. 516: © ClassicStock/Alamy. p. 518: © Quinn Palmer/Demotix/Corbis. p. 523: © Bettmann/Corbis. p. 540 *left*: © Cydney Conger/Corbis. p. 540 *right*: © Horizon International Images Limited/Alamy. p. 543: © vario images GmbH & Co.KG/Alamy.

Chapter 13 13.8: © Sinauer Associates. 13.10: © Ken Cedeno/Corbis. 13.11A: © Richard Green/Commercial/Alamy. 13.11B: Courtesy of Jennifer Basil-Whitaker. 13.17: © Lucy Nicholson/Reuters/Corbis. 13.26: Courtesy of Wendy Marie Ingram and Adrienne Greene. Box 13.2: © Jeremy Hogan/Alamy. p. 550: © blickwinkel/Alamy. p. 558: © STR/Reuters/Corbis. p. 560 *Rourke*: © Frank Trapper/Corbis. p. 561: © Steve Skjold/Alamy. p. 563: © Daily Mail/Rex/Alamy. p. 565: © Dreamworks/AF archive/Alamy. p. 572: © Gallo Images/Alamy. p. 578: © Juergen Berger/Science Source. p. 585: © nicolesy/istock. p. 586: © ejwhite/Shutterstock. p. 587: © California Department of Health Services. p. 590: © Richard Garvey-Williams/Alamy.

Chapter 14 14.1: © Science Source. 14.3: © Mike Baldwin/CartoonStock. 14.4B: © Lewis J. Merrim/Science Source. 14.13 *left*: © leungchopan/Shutterstock. 14.13 *center*: © hin255/Shutterstock. 14.13 *right*: © Drpixel/Shutterstock. 14.17: © Oliver Furrer/cultura/Corbis. 14.18: © Lou Linwei/Alamy. 14.20A: From the collection of Jack and Beverly Wilgus. 14.20B: Courtesy of Hanna Damasio. 14.21: © Juniors Bildarchiv GmbH/Alamy. Box 14.1: © Interfoto/Alamy. Box 14.2: © Beth Hall/AP/Corbis. p. 605: © MitarArt/Alamy. p. 610: © Wavebreak Media/AGE Fotostock.

Chapter 15 15.2: Courtesy of the Face Research Lab at the University of Glasgow Institute of Neuroscience and Psychology, faceresearch.org. 15.3 Courtesy of the U.S. House of Representatives. 15.7: Courtesy of Philip G. Zimbardo. 15.8: © Yannick Tylle/Corbis. 15.15: From Asch, S. E., 1955. Opinions and Social Pressure. *Scientific American* 193: 31. 15.16: © Alessandro Mancini/Alamy. 15.26: From Slater et al. 2006. Box 15.2: © Jochen Tack/Alamy. p. 642: © Bettmann/Corbis. p. 654: © David Acosta/Celebrity Monitor/Splash News/Corbis. p. 656: © John Gress/Corbis. p. 659: © Tim Pannell/Corbis. p. 665: CALVIN AND HOBBES © 1985 Watterson. Reprinted with permission of UNIVERSAL UCLICK. All rights reserved. p. 666: © The New York Times/Redux. p. 667: © Tannen Maury/epa/Corbis. p. 673: © Gary Cook/CartoonStock. p. 677: © Bettmann/Corbis. p. 679 *left*: © georgemuresan/istock. p. 679 *center*: © Maridav/istock. p. 679 *right*: © Creatista/istock. p. 687: Courtesy of Alexandra Milgram.

Chapter 16 16.6: © Bettmann/Corbis. 16.12: From Oltman et al., 1949. Frontal Lobotomy. *Am. J. Psychiatry* 105: 742. 16.13: Courtesy of Howard Dully. 16.14: Courtesy of Steven J. Frucht. 16.15: © EFE/Zuma Press. Box 16.1: Courtesy of Uplift Technologies. Box 16.2: © Associated Press. p. 697: © Melvyn Longhurst/Alamy. p. 698: © Damian Dovarganes/AP/Corbis. p. 699: © Nancy Kaszerman/Zuma Press/Corbis. p. 709: Painting by Michelangelo Caravaggio, c. 1595.

References

A

Abbot, N. C., Stead, L. F., White, A. R., Barnes, J., & Ernst, E. (2000). Hypnotherapy for smoking cessation. *Cochrane Database of Systematic Reviews*, *2*, CD001008. [7]

Abbott, A. (2007, April 13). Mozart doesn't make you clever. *Nature*. doi:10.1038/news070409-13. [11]

Abbott, R. A., Whear, R., Rodgers, L. R., Bethel, A., Thompson Coon, J., Kuyken, W., et al. (2014). Effectiveness of mindfulness-based stress reduction and mindfulness based cognitive therapy in vascular disease: A systematic review and meta-analysis of randomised controlled trials. *Journal Psychosomatic Research*, *76*, 341–351. [13]

Abe, N., Suzuki, M., Mori, E., Itoh, M., & Fujii, T. (2007). Deceiving others: Distinct neural responses of the prefrontal cortex and amygdala in simple fabrication and deception with social interactions. *Journal of Cognitive Neuroscience*, *19*, 287–295. [13]

Adelmann, P. K., & Zajonc, R. B. (1989). Facial efference and the experience of emotion. *Annual Review Psychology*, *40*, 249–280. [13]

Ader, R. (2001). Psychoneuroimmunology. *Current Directions in Psychological Science*, *10*, 94–98. [13]

Adler, A. (1964). *Problems of neurosis*. New York: Harper and Row. [14]

Adler, J. (2012). Erasing painful memories. *Scientific American*, *306*(5), 56–61. [9]

Adolphs, R., Gosselin, F., Buchanan, T. W., Tranel, D., Schyns, P., & Damasio, A. R. (2005). A mechanism for impaired fear recognition after amygdala damage. *Nature*, *433*, 68–72. [13]

Ahadi, S., & Rothbart, M. (1994). Temperament, development, and the big five. In, C. F. Halverson, G. A. Kohnstamm, & R. Martin (Eds.). *The developing structure of temperament and personality from infancy to adulthood* (pp. 189–207). Hillsdale, NJ: Erlbaum. [14]

Ainsworth, M. D. S., Blehar, M. C., Waters, E., & Wall, S. (1978). *Patterns of attachment: A psychological study of the strange situation*. Hillsdale, NJ: Erlbaum. [5]

Aizenman, N.C. (2008, February 29). The high cost of incarceration. *Denver Post*. Retrieved from http://www.denverpost.com/ci_8400051 [15]

Aizer, A. A., Chen, M. H., McCarthy, E. P., Mendu, M. L., Koo, S., Wilhite, T. J., et al. (2013). Marital status and survival in patients with cancer. *Journal of Clinical Oncology*, *31*, 3869–3876. [15]

Ajdacic-Gross, V., Bopp, M., Sansossio, R., Lauber, C., Gostynski, M., Eich, D., et al. (2005). Diversity and change in suicide seasonality over 125 years. *Journal of Epidemiology & Community Health*, *59*, 967–972. [16]

Aldrich, M. A. (1993). The neurobiology of narcolepsy-cataplexy. *Progress in Neurobiology*, *41*, 533–541. [7]

Alexander, G. M., & Hines, M. (2002). Sex differences in response to children's toys in nonhuman primates (*Cercopithecus aethiops sabaeus*). *Evolution and Human Behavior*, *23*, 467–479. [12]

Alford, J. R., Funk, C. L., & Hibbing, J. R. (2005). Are political orientations genetically transmitted? *American Political Science Review*, *99*, 153–167. [15]

Allen, K. M., Blascovich, J., & Mendes, W. B. (2002). Cardiovascular reactivity and the presence of pets, friends, and spouses: The truth about cats and dogs. *Psychosomatic Medicine*, *64*, 727–739. [13]

Allik, J., & McCrae, R. R. (2004). Towards a geography of personality traits: Patterns of profiles across 36 cultures. *Journal of Cross-Cultural Psychology*, *35*, 13–28. [14]

Allison, D. B., & Faith, M. S. (1996). Hypnosis as an adjunct to cognitive-behavioral psychotherapy for obesity: A meta-analytic reappraisal. *Journal of Consulting and Clinical Psychology*, *64*, 513–516. [7]

Allison, T., Gerber, S. D., Breedlove, S. M., & Dryden, G. L. (1977). A behavioral and polygraphic study of sleep in the shrews *Suncus murinus*, *Blarina brevicauda* and *Cryptotis parva*. *Behavioral Biology*, *20*, 354–366. [7]

Allport, G. W. (1954). The historical background of social psychology. In G. Lindzey (Ed.). *The Handbook of Social Psychology*, (pp. 3–56). Cambridge, MA: Addison-Wesley. [15]

Almas, A. N., Degnan, K. A., Radulescu, A., Nelson, C. A., 3rd, Zeanah, C. H., & Fox, N. A. (2012). Effects of early intervention and the moderating effects of brain activity on institutionalized children's social skills at age 8. *Proceedings of the National Academy of Sciences, USA*, *109*(Suppl 2), 17228–17231. [11]

Almy, M., Chittenden, E., & Miller, P. (1966). *Young children's thinking: Studies of some aspects of Piaget's theory.* New York: Teacher's College Press. [5]

Aloise King, E. D., Banks, P.B. & Brooks, R. C. (2013). Sexual conflict in mammals: consequences for mating systems and life history. *Mammal Review*, *43*, 47–58. [15]

Alpert, M., & Friedhoff, A. J. (1980). An un-dopamine hypothesis of schizophrenia. *Schizophrenia Bulletin*, *6*, 387–389. [16]

American Psychiatric Association. (2000). *Diagnostic and statistical manual of mental disorders 4th edition, text revision: DSM-IV-TR*. Washington, DC: American Psychiatric Association. [16]

American Psychiatric Association. (2013). *Diagnostic and statistical manual of mental disorders 5th edition: DSM-5*. Washington, DC: American Psychiatric Association. [16]

American Psychological Association. (2010). *Publication manual of the American Psychological Association* (*6th ed.*). Washington, DC: American Psychological Association. [2]

American Speech–Language–Hearing Association. (n.d.) How does your child hear and talk? Retrieved from http://www.asha.org/public/speech/development/chart.htm [10]

Andersen, E. (2012, March 23). True fact: The lack of pirates is causing global warming. *Forbes.* Retrieved from http://www.forbes.com/sites/erikaandersen/2012/03/23/true-fact-the-lack-of-pirates-is-causing-global-warming/ [2]

Anderson, C. A., & Bushman, B. J. (2001). Effects of violent video games on aggressive behavior, aggressive cognition, aggressive affect, physiological arousal, and prosocial behavior: A meta-analytic review of the scientific literature. *Psychological Science*, *12*, 353–359. [15]

Anderson, C. A., Gentile, D. A., & Buckley, K. E. (2007). *Violent video game effects on children and adolescents: Theory, research, and public policy.* New York: Oxford University Press. [15]

Anderson, J. R., Myowa-Yamakoshi, M., & Matsuzawa, T. (2004). Contagious yawning in chimpanzees. *Proceedings of the Royal Society of London. Series B: Biological Sciences*, *271*: S468–S470. [13]

Andreasen, N. C. (1991). Assessment issues and the cost of schizophrenia. *Schizophrenia Bulletin*, *17*, 475–481. [16]

Andreasen, N. C., Flaum, M., Swayze, V., 2nd, O'Leary, D. S., Alliger, R., Cohen, G., et al. (1993). Intelligence and brain structure in normal individuals. *American Journal of Psychiatry*, *150*, 130–134. [11]

Andrews, G., & Tennant, C. (1978). Life event stress and psychiatric illness. *Psychological Medicine*, *8*, 545–549. [13]

Angier, N. (2004, April 13). No time for bullies: Baboons retool their culture. *The New York Times*, p. F2. [13]

Annie E. Casey Foundation, KIDS COUNT Data Center. (2014). Children in single-parent families by race. Retrieved from http://datacenter.kidscount.org/data/acrossstates/Rankings.aspx?ind=107 [11]

Archer, J., & McCarthy, B. (1988). Personal biases in student assessment. *Educational Research*, *30*, 142–145. [10]

Arkes, H., & Tetlock, P. E. (2004). Attributions of implicit prejudice, or "Would Jesse Jackson 'fail' the implicit association test?" *Psychological Inquiry*, *15*, 257–278. [15]

Armstrong, D. (2008, March 5). Malingerer test roils personal-injury law: 'Fake bad scale' bars real victims, its critics contend. *The Wall Street Journal*. Retrieved from http://online.wsj.com/news/articles/SB120466776681911325 [14]

Arnett, J. J. (1999). Adolescent storm and stress, reconsidered. *American Psychologist, 54*, 317–326. [5]

Arnett, J. J. (2000). Emerging adulthood: A theory of development from the late teens through the twenties. *American Psychologist*, *55*, 469–480. [5]

Arnett, J. J. (2004). *Emerging adulthood: The winding road from the late teens through the twenties.* New York: Oxford University Press. [5]

Arnold, K., & Zuberbühler, K. (2006). Language evolution: Semantic combinations in primate calls. *Nature*, *441*, 303. [10]

Arnone, D., Cavanagh, J., Gerber, D., Lawrie, S. M., Ebmeier, K. P., & McIntosh, A. M. (2009). Magnetic resonance imaging studies in bipolar disorder and schizophrenia: Meta-analysis. *British Journal of Psychiatry*, *195*, 194–201. [16]

Aronson, E. (2011). *The social animal* (11th ed.). New York: Worth. [15]

Aronson, E., & Mills, J. (1959). The effect of severity of initiation on liking for a group. *Journal of Abnormal and Social Psychology*, *59*, 177–181. [15]

Asch, S. E. (1956). Studies of independence and conformity: I. A minority of one against a unanimous majority. *Psychological Monographs*, *70*(9, Whole No. 416), 1–70. [15]

Aserinsky, E., & Kleitman, N. (1953). Regularly occurring periods of eye motility, and concomitant phenomena, during sleep. *Science*, *118*, 273–274. [7]

Asmar, R., Safar, M., & Queneau, P. (2001). Evaluation of the placebo effect and reproducibility of blood pressure measurement in hypertension. *American Journal of Hypertension*, *14*, 546–552. [2]

Atkinson, R. C., & Shiffrin, R. M. (1968). Human memory: A proposed system and its control processes. In K. W. Spence & J. T. Spence, *The psychology of learning and motivation* (Vol. 2, pp. 89–195). New York: Academic Press. [9]

Atkinson, R. C., & Shiffrin, R. M. (1971, August). The control of short-term memory. *Scientific American*, *225*(2), 82–90. [9]

Australian Institute of Health. (2005). *The health study 2005: Australian veterans of the Korean war.* Melbourne, Australia: Monash University Press. [13]

B

Baddeley, A. (2003). Working memory: Looking back and looking forward. *Nature Reviews. Neuroscience*, *4*, 829–839. [9]

Baddeley, A. D., & Warrington, E. K. (1970). Amnesia and the distinction between long- and short-term memory. *Journal of Verbal Learning and Verbal Behavior*, *9*, 176–189. [9]

Bahrke, M. S., Yesalis, C. E., & Wright, J. E. (1996). Psychological and behavioural effects of endogenous testosterone and anabolic-androgenic steroids. An update. *Sports Medicine (Auckland)*, *22*, 367–390. [15]

Baldus, D., Woodworth, G., Zuckerman, D., Weiner, N. A., & Broffitt, B. (1998). Race discrimination and the death penalty in the post-*Furman* era: An empirical and legal overview, with preliminary findings from Philadelphia. *Cornell Law Review*, *83*, 1638–1770. [15]

Ban, T. A. (2007). Fifty years chlorpromazine: A historical perspective. *Neuropsychiatric Disease and Treatment*, *3*, 495–500. [16]

Bancaud, J., Brunet-Bourgin, F., Chauvel, P., & Halgren, E. (1994). Anatomical origin of deja vu and vivid "memories" in human temporal lobe. *Brain*, *117*, 71–90. [13]

Bandura, A. (1986). *Social foundations of thought and action: A social cognitive theory.* Englewood Cliffs, NJ: Prentice Hall. [8]

Bandura, A. (Ed.). (1995). *Self-efficacy in changing societies.* United Kingdom: Cambridge University Press. [14]

Bandura, A., Ross, D., & Ross, S. A. (1961). Transmission of aggression through imitation of aggressive models. *Journal of Abnormal and Social Psychology*, *63*, 575–582. [8]

Barnes, J., Dong, C. Y., McRobbie, H., Walker, N., Mehta, M., & Stead, L. F. (2010). Hypnotherapy for smoking cessation. *Cochrane Database of Systematic Reviews*, *10*, CD001008. doi:10.1002/14651858.CD001008.pub2 [13]

Barnett, T. D., Barnard, N. D., & Radak, T. L. (2009). Development of symptomatic cardiovascular disease after self-reported adherence to the Atkins diet. *Journal of the American Dietetic Association*, *109*, 1263–1265. [12]

Baron-Cohen, S., Leslie, A. M., & Frith, U. (1985). Does the autistic child have a 'theory of mind'? *Cognition*, *21*, 37–46. [5]

Barrie, J. M. (1902). *The admirable Crichton.* Retrieved from http://www.gutenberg.org/ebooks/3490 [11]

Bartels, A., & Zeki, S. (2000). The neural basis of romantic love. *Neuroreport*, *11*, 3829–3834. [13]

Bartholow, B. D., Bushman, B. J., & Sestir, M. A. (2006). Chronic violent video game exposure and desensitization to violence: Behavioral and event-related brain potential data. *Journal of Experimental Social Psychology*, *42*, 532–539. [15]

Bartlett, T. (2014, June 2). The search for psychology's lost boy. *Chronicle of Higher Education.* Retrieved from http://chronicle.com/article/The-Search-for-Psychologys/146747 [8]

Bartoshuk, L. M. (1993). Genetic and pathological taste variation: What can we learn from animal models and human disease? In D. Chadwick, J. Marsh, and J. Goode (Eds.), *The molecular basis of smell and taste transduction* (pp. 251–267). New York: Wiley. [6]

Bateson, G. (1962). *Perceval's narrative: A patient's account of his psychosis 1830–1832.* London: The Hogarth Press. [16]

Batty, G. D., Wennerstad, K. M., Smith, G. D., Gunnell, D., Deary, I. J., Tynelius, P., et al. (2008). IQ in early adulthood and mortality by middle age: Cohort study of 1 million Swedish men. *Epidemiology*, *20*, 100–109. [11]

Bauer, P. J. (2005). Developments in declarative memory decreasing susceptibility to storage failure over the second year of life. *Psychological Science, 16,* 41–47. [5]

Baumeister, R. F., & Leary, M. R. (1995). The need to belong: Desire for interpersonal attachments as a fundamental human motivation. *Psychological Bulletin*, *117*, 497–529. [12]

Bavelier, D., Green, C. S., Pouget, A., & Schrater, P. (2012). Brain plasticity through the life span: Learning to learn and action video games. *Annual Review of Neuroscience*, *35*, 391–416. [2]

Beaver, K. M., Vaughn, M. G., Delisi, M., & Wright, J. P. (2008). Anabolic-androgenic steroid use and involvement in violent behavior in a nationally representative sample of young adult males in the United States. *American Journal of Public Health*, *98*, 2185–2187. [15]

Beck, H. P., Levinson, S., & Irons, G. (2009). Finding little Albert: A journey to John B. Watson's infant laboratory. *American Psychologist*, *64*, 605–614. [8]

Beecher, H. K. (1956). Relationship of significance of wound to pain experienced. *JAMA*, *161*, 1609–1613. [6]

Beitchman, J. H., Mik, H. M., Ehtesham, S., Douglas, L., & Kennedy, J. L. (2004). MAOA and persistent, pervasive childhood aggression. *Molecular Psychiatry*, *9*, 546–547. [15]

Belleville, G., Foldes-Busque, G., Dixon, M., Marquis-Pelletier, E., Barbeau, S., Poitras, J., et al. (2013). Impact of seasonal and lunar cycles on psychological symptoms in the ED: An empirical investigation of widely spread beliefs. *General Hospital Psychiatry*, *35*, 192–194. [10]

Bellinger, D. C., Stiles K. M., & Needleman, H. L. (1992). Low-level lead exposure, intelligence and academic achievement: A long-term follow-up study. *Pediatrics*, *90*, 855–861. [11]

Belluck, P. (2008, December 4). Strangers may cheer you up, study says. *The New York Times.* Retrieved from http://www.nytimes.com/2008/12/05/health/05happy-web.html?pagewanted=all&_r=0 [13]

Belsky, J. (2002). Quantity counts: Amount of child care and children's socioemotional development. *Journal of Developmental and Behavioral Pediatrics*, *23*, 167–170. [5]

Belsky, J., & Braungart, J. M. (1991). Are insecure-avoidant infants with extensive day-care experience less stressed by and more independent in the strange situation? *Child Development, 62*, 567–571. [5]

Belsky, J., Vandell, D. L., Burchinal, M., Clarke-Stewart, K. A., McCartney, K., & Tresch Owen, M. (2007). Are there long-term effects of early child care? *Child Development*, *78*, 681–701. [5]

Benbow, C. P., & Stanley, J. C. (1980). Sex differences in math ability: Fact or artifact? *Science*, *210*, 1262–1264. [11]

Benedetti, F. (1986). Tactile diplopia (diplesthesia) on the human fingers. *Perception*, *15*, 83–91. [6]

Benedito-Silva, A. A., Pires, M. L. N., & Calil, H. M. (2007). Seasonal variation of suicide in Brazil. *Chronobiology International*, *24*, 727–737. [16]

Bennett, W. (1983). The nicotine fix. *Rhode Island Medical Journal*, *66*, 455–458. [13]

Bensafi, M., Porter, J., Pouliot, S., Mainland, J., Johnson, B., Zelano, C., et al. (2003). Olfactomotor activity during imagery mimics that during perception. *Nature Neuroscience*, *6*, 1142–1144. [10]

Benson, P. J., Beedie, S. A., Shephard, E., Giegling, I., Rujescu, D., & St. Clair, D. (2012). Simple viewing tests can detect eye movement abnormalities that distinguish schizophrenia cases from controls with exceptional accuracy. *Biological Psychiatry*, *72*, 716–724. [16]

Berenbaum, S. A., & Hines, M. (1992). Early androgens are related to childhood sex-typed toy preference. *Psychological Science, 3*, 203–206. [12]

Berenbaum, S. A., & Snyder, E. (1995). Early hormonal influences on childhood sex-typed activity and playmate preferences: Implications for the development of sexual orientation. *Developmental Psychology, 31,* 31–42. [12]

Berkman, L. F., Glass, T., Brissette, I. & Seeman, T. E. (2000). From social integration to health. *Social Science & Medicine*, *51*, 843–857. [14]

Berlin, B., & Kay, P. (1969). *Basic color terms: Their universality and evolution*. Berkeley: University of California Press. [10]

Bernhardt, P. C. (1997). Influences of serotonin and testosterone in aggression and dominance: Convergence with social psychology. *Current Directions in Psychological Science*, *2*(6), 44–48. [15]

Berridge, C. W., & Arnsten, A. F. (2013). Psychostimulants and motivated behavior: Arousal and cognition. *Neuroscience & Biobehavioral Reviews*, *37*(9 Pt. A), 1976–1984. [7]

Berthold, A. (1849). Transplantation der hoden. *Archiv für Anatomie, Physiologie und Wissenschaftliche Medicin*, *16*, 42–46. [1]

Berton, O., & Nestler, E. J. (2006). New approaches to antidepressant drug discovery: Beyond monoamines. *Neuroscience*, *7*, 137–151. [16]

Besedovsky, H. O., & del Rey, A. (1992). Immune-neuroendocrine circuits: Integrative role of cytokines. *Frontiers of Neuroendocrinology*, *13*, 61–94. [13]

Besedovsky, L., Lange, T., & Born, J. (2012). Sleep and immune function. *Pflügers Archiv European Journal of Physiology*, *463*, 121–137. [13]

Beyerstein, B. L. (1999). Whence cometh the myth that we only use ten percent of our brains? In S. Della Sala (Ed.), *Mind myths: Exploring popular assumptions about the mind and brain* (pp. 1–24). Chichester, UK: John Wiley & Sons, Ltd. [1]

Bialystok, E., & Martin, M. M. (2004). Attention and inhibition in bilingual children: Evidence from the dimensional change card sort task. *Developmental Science*, *7*, 325–339. [10]

Bialystok, E., Luk, G., & Kwan, E. (2005). Bilingualism, biliteracy, and learning to read. *Scientific Studies of Reading*, *9*, 43–61. [10]

Bieber, I. (1962). *Homosexuality: A psychoanalytic study of male homosexuals*. New York: Basic Books. [14]

Binet, A. (1916). New methods for the diagnosis of the intellectual level of subnormals (E. S. Kite, Trans.). *The development of intelligence in children*. Vineland, NJ: Publications of the Training School at Vineland. (Original work published 1905) Retrieved from http://psychclassics.yorku.ca/Binet/binet1.htm [11]

Binet, A. (1984). *Modern ideas about children* (S. Heisler, Trans.). Menlo Park, CA: Stanford University. (Original work published 1909) [11]

Blanchard, R., Cantor, J. M., Bogaert, A. F., Breedlove, S. M., & Ellis. L. (2006). Interaction of fraternal birth order and handedness in the development of male homosexuality. *Hormones and Behavior, 49*, 405–414. [12]

Blanton, H., Jaccard, J., Klick, J., Mellers, B., Mitchell, G., & Tetlock, P. E. (2009). Strong claims and weak evidence: Reassessing the predictive validity of the IAT. *Journal of Applied Psychology*, *94*, 567–582. [1]

Blascovich, J., Spencer, S. J., Quinn, D., & Steele, C. (2001). African Americans and high blood pressure: The role of stereotype threat. *Psychological Science*, *12*, 225–229. [11, 15]

Blass, E. M., Jobaris, R., & Hall, W. G. (1976). Oropharyngeal control of drinking in rats. *Journal of Comparative and Physiological Psychology*, *90*, 909–916. [12]

Blass, T. (2004). *The man who shocked the world: The life and legacy of Stanley Milgram*. New York: Basic Books. [15]

Bleuler, E. (1950). *Dementia praecox; or, The group of schizophrenias* (J. Zinkin, Trans.). New York: International Universities Press. (Original work published 1911) [16]

Bliss, E. L., & Branch, C. H. (1960). *Anorexia nervosa: Its history, psychology, and biology*. New York: Hoeber. [12]

Bliss, T. V. P., & Lømo, T. (1973). Long-lasting potentiation of synaptic transmission in the dentate area of the anaesthetized rabbit following stimulation of the perforant path. *Journal of Physiology (London)*, *232*, 331–356. [9]

Bliwise, D. L. (1989). Neuropsychological function and sleep. *Clinics in Geriatric Medicine*, *5*, 381–394. [7]

Block, J. H. (1983). Differential premises arising from differential socialization of the sexes: Some conjectures. *Child Development*, *54*, 1335–1354. [12]

Blum, D. (2002). *Love at Goon Park: Harry Harlow and the science of affection*. Cambridge, MA: Perseus Publishing. [5]

Blumstein, A. (1995). Youth violence, guns, and the illicit drug industry. *Journal of Criminal Law and Criminology*, *86*, 10–36. [5]

Boas, F. (1911). The handbook of North American Indians. Introduction. *Smithsonian Institution, Bureau of Ethnology Bulletin*, *40*(1), 1–84. Retrieved from http://www.biodiversitylibrary.org/bibliography/37959#/summary [10]

Bogaert, A. F. (2006). Biological versus nonbiological older brothers and men's sexual orientation. *Proceedings of the National Academy of Sciences, USA*, *103*, 10771–10774. [12]

Boltz, O. H. (1948). A report of spontaneous recovery in two cases of advanced schizophrenic organismic stagnation. *American Journal of Psychiatry*, *105*, 339–345. [16]

Bond, R., & Smith, P. B. (1996). Culture and conformity: A meta-analysis of studies using Asch's line judgment task. *Psychological Bulletin*, *119*, 111–137. [15]

Boothroyd, L. G., Craig, P. S., Crossman, R. J., & Perrett, D. I. (2013a). Father absence and age at first birth in a western sample. *American Journal of Human Biology*, *25*, 366–369. [5]

Boothroyd, L. G., Scott, I., Gray, A. W., Coombes, C. I., & Pound, N. (2013b). Male facial masculinity as a cue to health outcomes. *Evolutionary Psychology*, *11*, 1044–1058. [15]

Borgstein, J., & Grootendorst, C. (2002). Half a brain. *Lancet*, *359*, 473. [10]

Bornstein, M., Kessen, W., & Weiskopf, S. (1976). The categories of hue in infancy. *Science*, *191*, 201–202. [10]

Borod, J. C., Haywood, C. S., & Koff, E. (1997). Neuropsychological aspects of facial asymmetry during emotional expression: A review of the normal adult literature. *Neuropsychology Review*, *7*, 41–60. [13]

Boroditsky, L. (2011). How language shapes thought. *Scientific American*, *304*(2), 63–65. [10]

Boroditsky, L., & Gaby, A. (2010). Remembrances of times east: Absolute spatial representations of time in an Australian aboriginal community. *Psychological Science*, *21*, 1635–1639. [10]

Borrow, S. J., Adam, K., Chapman, K., Oswald, I., Hudson, L., & Idzikowski, C. J. (1980). REM sleep and normal intelligence. *Biological Psychiatry*, *15*, 165–169. [7]

Bosman, J., & Goode, E. (2014, August 12). FBI steps in amid unrest after police kill Missouri youth. *The New York Times*, p. A1. [1]

Bouchard, T. J. (1994). Genes, environment and personality. *Science*, *264*, 1700–1701. [14]

Bouchard, T. J. (2002). Genetic influence on human psychological traits: A survey. *Current Directions in Psychological Science*, *13*, 148–151. [4]

Bouchard, T. J., Jr., & McGue, M. (1981). Familial studies of intelligence: A review. *Science, 212,* 1055–1059. [11]

Bourget D., & Whitehurst, L. (2007). Amnesia and crime. *Journal of the American Academy of Psychiatry and the Law*, *35*, 469–480. [9]

Bower, B. (2000). Genes to grow on. *Science News*, *157*(9), 142. [10]

Bower, B. (2006). Prescription for controversy: Medications for depressed kids spark scientific dispute. *Science News*, *169*, 168–172. [16]

Bower, G. H., Clark, M. C., Lesgold, A. M. & Winzenz, D. (1969). Hierarchical retrieval schemes in recall of categorized word lists. *Journal of Verbal Learning and Verbal Behavior*, *8*, 323–343. [9]

Bowlby, J. (1969–1980). *Attachment and loss*. (Vols. 1–3). New York: Basic Books. [5]

Bowman, M. L. (1997). *Individual differences in posttraumatic response*. Mahway, NJ: Erlbaum. [6]

Boyd, R. (2008, February 7). Do people only use 10 percent of their brains? *Scientific American*, Retrieved from http://www.scientificamerican.com/article/do-people-only-use-10-percent-of-their-brains/ [1]

Boynton, P. M. (1998). People should participate in, not be subjects of, research. *The BMJ*, *317*, 1521. [2]

Boysson-Bardies, B. (2001). *How language comes to children*. Cambridge, MA: MIT Press. [10]

Braddick, O., & Atkinson, J. (2011). Development of human visual function. *Vision Research*, *51*, 1588–1609. [5]

Brady, J. V., Porter, R. W., Conrad, D. G., & Mason, J. W. (1958). Avoidance behavior and the development of gastroduodenal ulcers. *Journal of the Experimental Analysis of Behavior*, *1*, 69–72. [13]

Braun, K. A., Ellis, R., & Loftus, E. F. (2002). Make my memory: How advertising can change our memories of the past. *Psychology and Marketing*, *19*, 1–23. [9]

Bray, G. A. (1969). Effect of caloric restriction on energy expenditure in obese patients. *Lancet, 2,* 397–398. [12]

Breedlove, S. M. (2010). Minireview: Organizational hypothesis: Instances of the fingerpost. *Endocrinology, 151,* 4116–4122. [12]

Breitner, J. C., Wyse, B. W., Anthony, J. C., Welsh-Bohmer, K. A., Steffens, D. C., Norton, M. C., et al. (1999). APOE-epsilon4 count predicts age when prevalence of AD increases, then declines: The Cache county study. *Neurology, 53,* 321–331. [5]

Brémer, F. (1938). L'activité électrique de l'écorce cérébrale. *Actualités Scientifiques et Industrielles*, *658*, 3–46. [7]

Bremner, J. D., Randall, P., Scott, T. M., Bronen, R. A., Seibyl, J. P., Southwick, S. M., et al. (1995). MRI-based measurement of hippocampal volume in patients with combat-related posttraumatic stress disorder. *American Journal of Psychiatry*, *152*, 973–981. [13]

Bremner, J. D., Scott, T. M., Delaney, R. C., Southwick, S. M., Mason, J. W., Johnson, D. R., et al. (1993). Deficits in short-term memory in posttraumatic stress disorder. *American Journal of Psychiatry*, *150*, 1015–1019. [13]

Brickman, P., Coates, D., & Janoff-Bulman, R. (1978). Lottery winners and accident victims: Is happiness relative? *Journal of Personality and Social Psychology*, *36*, 917–927. [13]

Brizendine, L. (2006). *The female brain*. New York: Morgan Road/Broadway Books. [10]

Broberg, D. J., & Bernstein, I. L. (1987). Candy as a scapegoat in the prevention of food aversions in children receiving chemotherapy. *Cancer*, *60*, 2344–2347. [8]

Broder, D. S. (1996, March 31). Remembering Ed Muskie, a man of civility and vision. *The Seattle Times*. Retrieved from http://community.seattletimes.nwsource.com/archive/?date=19960331&slug=2321781 [13]

Brody, A. L., Mandelkern, M. A., London, E. D., Olmstead, R. E., Farahi, J., Scheibal, D., et al. (2006). Cigarette smoking saturates brain alpha 4 beta 2 nicotinic acetylcholine receptors. *Archives of General Psychiatry*, *63*, 907–915. [13]

Brody, N. (1997). Intelligence, schooling, and society. *American Psychologist*, *52*, 1046–1050. [11]

Brooker, R. J., Buss, K. A., Lemery-Chalfant, K., Aksan, N., Davidson, R. J., & Goldsmith, H. H. (2013). The development of stranger fear in infancy and toddlerhood: Normative development, individual differences, antecedents, and outcomes. *Developmental Science*, *6*, 864–878. [5]

Brooks, S. J., O'Daly, O. G., Uher, R., Schiöth, H. B., Treasure, J., & Campbell, I. C. (2012). Subliminal food images compromise superior working memory performance in women with restricting anorexia nervosa. *Consciousness & Cognition*, *21*, 751–763. doi:10.1016/j.concog.2012.02.006. [12]

Brown, A. S. (2011). Exposure to prenatal infection and risk of schizophrenia. *Frontiers in Psychiatry*, *2*, 63. [16]

Brown, J. (1958). Some tests of the decay theory of immediate memory. *Quarterly Journal of Experimental Psychology*, *10*, 12–21. [9]

Browne, H. A., Gair, S. L., Scharf, J. M., & Grice, D. E. (2014). Genetics of obsessive-compulsive disorder and related disorders. *Psychiatric Clinics of North America*, *37*, 319–335. [4]

Bruck, C. S., & Allen, T. D. (2003). The relationship between big five personality traits, negative affectivity, type A behavior, and work–family conflict. *Journal of Vocational Behavior*, *63*, 457–472. [13]

Brudevoll, J. E., Liestøl, K., & Walløe, L. (1979). Menarcheal age in Oslo during the last 140 years. *Annals of Human Biology*, *6*, 407–416. [5]

Brunner, H. G., Nelen, M., Breakefield, X. O., Ropers, H. H., & van Oost, B. A. (1993). Abnormal behavior associated with a point mutation in the structural gene for monoamine oxidase A. *Science*, *262*, 578–580. [15]

Bryan, W. L., & Harter, N. (1899). Studies on the telegraphic language: The acquisition of a hierarchy of habits. *Psychology Review*, *8*, 345–375. [10]

Bryant, R. A., & McConkey, K. M. (1989). Hypnotic blindness: A behavioral and experiential analysis. *Journal of Abnormal Psychology*, *98*, 71–77. [7]

Bryden, M. P. (1982). *Laterality: Functional asymmetry in the intact brain*. New York: Academic Press. [13]

Buckalew, L. W., & Ross, S. (1981). Relationship of perceptual characteristics to efficacy of placebos. *Psychological Reports*, *49*, 955–961. [2]

Burger, J. M. (2009). Replicating Milgram: Would people still obey today? *American Psychologist*, *64*, 1–11. [15]

Burns, J. M., Cronk, B. B., Anderson, H. S., Donnelly, J. E., Thomas, G. P., Harsha, A., et al. (2008). Cardiorespiratory fitness and brain atrophy in early Alzheimer disease. *Neurology*, *71*, 210–216. [5]

Bushman, B. J. (2002). Does venting anger feed or extinguish the flame? Catharsis, rumination, distraction, anger, and aggressive responding. *Personality and Social Psychology Bulletin*, *28*, 724–731. [13]

Bushman, B. J., Baumeister, R. F., & Stack, A. D. (1999). Catharsis, aggression, and persuasive influence: Self-fulfilling or self-defeating prophecies? *Journal of Personality and Social Psychology*, *76*, 367–376. [13]

Bushman, B. J., Gollwitzer, M., & Cruz, C. (in press). There is broad consensus: Media researchers agree that violent media increase aggression in children, and pediatricians and parents concur. *Psychology of Popular Media Culture*, doi:10.1037/ppm0000046 [15]

Buss, D. M. (2005). *The handbook of evolutionary psychology*. New York: Wiley. [15]

Butcher, J. N., Hamilton, C. K., Rouse, S. V., & Cumella, E. J. (2006). The deconstruction of the Hy scale of MMPI-2: Failure of RC3 in measuring somatic symptom expression. *Journal of Personality Assessment*, *87*, 186–192. [14]

Butler, A. C., Chapman, J. E., Forman, E. M., & Beck, A. T. (2006). The empirical status of cognitive-behavioral therapy: A review of meta-analyses. *Clinical Psychology Review*, *26*, 17–31. [16]

Byers-Heinlein, K., Burns, T. C., & Werker, J. F. (2010). The roots of bilingualism in newborns. *Psychological Science*, *21*, 343–348. [10]

Byington, E. & Felps, W. (2010). Why do IQ scores predict job performance? An alternative, sociological explanation. *Research in Organizational Behavior*, *30*, 175–202. doi:10.1016/j.riob.2010.08.003 [11]

Byne, W., Tobet, S., Mattiace, L. A., Lasco, M. S., Kemether, E., Edgar, M. A., et al. (2001). The interstitial nuclei of the human anterior hypothalamus: An investigation of variation with sex, sexual orientation, and HIV status. *Hormones & Behavior*, *40*, 86–92. [12]

C

Cabeza, R., Anderson, N. D., Locantore, J. K., & McIntosh, A. R. (2002). Aging gracefully: Compensatory brain activity in high-performing older adults. *Neuroimage*, *17*, 1394–1402. [5]

Cade, J. F. (1949). Lithium salts in the treatment of psychotic excitement. *Medical Journal of Australia*, *2*, 349–352. [16]

Calder, A. J., Keane, J., Manes, F., Antoun, N., & Young, A. W. (2000). Impaired recognition and experience of disgust following brain injury. *Nature Neuroscience*, *3*, 1077–1078. [13]

Calkins, M. W. (1901). *An introduction to psychology*. New York: Macmillan. Retrieved from https://archive.org/details/introductiontops00calk [1]

Campbell, F. A., & Ramey, C. T. (1995). Cognitive and school outcomes for high-risk African-American students at middle adolescence: Positive effects of early intervention. *American Educational Research Journal*, *32*, 743–772. [11]

Campos, J. J., Langer, A., & Krowitz, A. (1970). Cardiac responses on the visual cliff in prelocomotor human infants. *Science*, *170*, 196–197. [5]

Cannon, W. B. (1932). *The wisdom of the body*. New York: W. W. Norton. [12]

Cannon, W. B., & Washburn, A. L. (1912). An explanation of hunger. *American Journal of Physiology*, *29*, 441–454. [12]

Cappella, J. N. (1993). The facial feedback hypothesis in human interaction: Review and speculation. *Journal of Language and Social Psychology*, *12*, 13–29. [13]

Cardno, A. G., & Gottesman, I. I. (2000). Twin studies of schizophrenia: From bow-and-arrow concordances to star wars Mx and functional genomics. *American Journal of Medical Genetics*, *97*, 12–17. [16]

Carey, B. (2007, September 11). Brainy parrot dies, emotive to the end. *The New York Times*. Retrieved from http://www.nytimes.com/2007/09/11/science/11parrot.html [10]

Carlsmith, K. M. (2006). The roles of retribution and utility in determining punishment. *Journal of Experimental Social Psychology*, *42*, 437–451. [15]

Carlson, S. (1985). A double-blind test of astrology. *Nature*, *318*, 419–425. [14]

Carmichael, L., Hogan, H. P., & Walter, A. A. (1932). An experimental study of the effect of language on the reproduction of visually perceived forms. *Journal of Experimental Psychology*, *15*, 73–86. [9]

Carnagey, N. L., & Anderson, C. A. (2005). The effects of reward and punishment in violent video games on aggressive affect, cognition, and behavior. *Psychological Science*, *16*, 882–889. [15]

Carnagey, N. L., & Anderson, C. A. (2007). Changes in attitudes towards war and violence after September 11, 2001. *Aggressive Behavior*, *33*, 118–29. [13]

Carnagey, N. L., Anderson, C. A., & Bushman, B. J. (2007). The effect of video game violence on physiological desensitization to real-life violence. *Journal of Experimental Social Psychology*, *43*, 489–496. [15]

Carpusor, A., & Loges, W. E. (2006). Rental discrimination and ethnicity in names. *Journal of Applied Social Psychology*, *36*, 934–952. [15]

Carstensen, L. L. (2006). The influence of a sense of time on human development. *Science*, *312*, 1913–1915. [5]

Cartwright, R. D. (1979). The nature and function of repetitive dreams: A survey and speculation. *Psychiatry*, *42*, 131–137. [7]

Caruso, O. R., Taylor, J. J., & Detterman, D. K. (1982). Intelligence research and intelligent policy. In D. K. Detterman & R. J. Sternberg (Eds.), *How and how much can intelligence be increased.* Norwood, NJ: Ablex Publishing. [11]

Casey, B. J., Getz, S., & Galvan, A. (2008). The adolescent brain. *Developmental Review*, *28*, 62–77. [5]

Caspi, A. (2000). The child is father of the man: Personality continuities from childhood to adulthood. *Journal of Personality and Social Psychology, 78*, 158–172. [5]

Caspi, A., Moffitt, T. E., Cannon, M., McClay, J., Murray, R., Harrington, H., et al. (2005). Moderation of the effect of adolescent-onset *Cannabis* use on adult psychosis by a functional polymorphism in the catechol-O-methyltransferase gene: Longitudinal evidence of a gene X environment interaction. *Biological Psychiatry*, *57*, 1117–1127. [7]

Caspi, A., Williams, B., Kim-Cohen, J., Craig, I. W., Milne, B. J., Poulton, R., et al. (2007). Moderation of breastfeeding effects on the IQ by genetic variation in fatty acid metabolism. *Proceedings of the National Academy of Sciences, USA*, *104*, 18860–18865. Retrieved from http://www.ncbi.nlm.nih.gov/pmc/articles/PMC2141867/?tool=pubmed [11]

Cassens, G., Wolfe, L., & Zola, M. (1990). The neuropsychology of depressions. *Journal of Neuropsychiatry and Clinical Neurosciences*, *2*, 202–213. [16]

Castle, D., Keks, N., Newton, R., Schweitzer, I., Copolov, D., Paoletti, N., et al. (2013). Pharmacological approaches to the management of schizophrenia: 10 years on. *Australasian Psychiatry*, *21*, 329–334. [16]

Cattell, R. B. (1946). *Description and measurement of personality*. New York: World Book. [14]

Cattell, R. B. (1957). *Personality and motivation structure and measurement*. New York: World Book. [14]

Cattell, R. B. (1987). *Intelligence: Its structure, growth and action*. Amsterdam, Netherlands: Elsevier. [11]

Cech, E., Rubineau, B., Silbey, S., & Serond, C. (2011). Professional role confidence and gendered persistence in engineering. *American Sociological Review, 76,* 641–666. [12]

Ceci, S. J., & Williams, W. M. (1997). Schooling, intelligence, and income. *American Psychologist*, *52*, 1051–1058. [11]

Cecil, M., Brubaker, J.. Adler, M.. Dietrich, N.. Altaye, M., Egelhoff, C., et al. (2008). Decreased brain volume in adults with childhood lead exposure. *PLoS Medicine*, *5*, e112. [11]

Center for Mental Health Services. (2006). *Mental health, United States, 2004*. DHHS Pub. No. (SMA)-06-4195. Rockville, MD: Substance Abuse and Mental Health Services Administration. [5]

Centers for Disease Control and Prevention (2014, April 17). Alcohol use in pregnancy. Retrieved from http://www.cdc.gov/ncbddd/fasd/alcohol-use.html. [11]

Centers for Disease Control and Prevention. (2013). *U.S. Public Health Service syphilis study at Tuskegee*. Retrieved from http://www.cdc.gov/tuskegee/index.html [2]

Centerwall, B. S, & Criqui, M. H. (1978). Prevention of the Wernicke-Korsakoff syndrome: A cost-benefit analysis. *The New England Journal of Medicine*, *299*, 285–289. [9]

Chalmers, D. J. (2010). *The character of consciousness*. Oxford, UK: Oxford University Press. [7]

Chandrashekar, J., Hoon, M. A., Ryba, N. J., & Zuker, C. S. (2006). The receptors and cells for mammalian taste. *Nature*, *444*, 288–294. [6]

Chang, B. S., Ly, J., Appignani, B., Bodell, A., Ravenscroft, R. S., Sheen, V. L., et al. (2005). Reading impairment in the neuronal migration disorder of periventricular nodular heterotopia. *Neurology, 64*, 799–803. [10]

Charles, E. P., & Rivera, S. M. (2009). Object permanence and method of disappearance: Looking measures further contradict reaching measures. *Developmental Science, 12,* 991–1006. [5]

Charles, S. T., & Carstensen, L. L. (2010). Social and emotional aging. *Annual Review Psychology*, *61*, 383–409. [13]

Chartrand, T. L., & Bargh, J. A. (1999). The chameleon effect: The perception-behavior link and social interaction. *Journal of Personality and Social Psychology*, *76*, 893–910. [15]

Chemelli, R. M., Willie, J. T., Sinton, C. M., Elmquist, J. K., Scammell, T., Lee, C., et al. (1999). Narcolepsy in orexin knockout mice: Molecular genetics of sleep regulation. *Cell*, *98*, 437–451. [7]

Chen, A., Dietrich, K. N., Ware, J. H., Radcliffe, J., & Rogan, W. J. (2005). IQ and blood lead from 2 to 7 years of age: Are the effects in older children the residual of high blood lead concentrations in 2-year-olds? *Environmental Health Perspectives*, *113*, 597–601. [11]

Chen, X., & French, D. C. (2008). Children's social competence in cultural context. *Annual Review of Psychology, 59,* 591–616. [5]

Chennaoui, M., Arnal, P. J., Sauvet, F., & Léger, D. (in press). Sleep and exercise: A reciprocal issue? *Sleep Medicine Reviews*. doi:10.1016/j.smrv.2014.06.008. [7]

Cheyne, J. A. (2002). Situational factors affecting sleep paralysis and associated hallucinations: Position and timing effects. *Journal of Sleep Research*, *11*, 169–177. [7]

Chiang, M.-C., Barysheva, M., Shattuck, D. W., Lee, A. D., Madsen, S. K., Avedissian, C., et al. (2009). Genetics of brain fiber architecture and intellectual performance. *Journal of Neuroscience*, *29*, 2212–2224. [11]

Chodoff, P., & Roy, A. (1982). *Hysteria*. New York: Wiley. [1]

Choi, I., Dalal, R., Kim-Prieto, C., & Park, H. (2003). Culture and judgment of causal relevance. *Journal of Perssonality and Social Psychology*, *84*, 46–59. [15]

Chomsky, N. (1957). *Syntactic structures*. The Hague, Netherlands: Mouton. [10]

Chooi, W-T, & Thompson, L. A. (2012). Working memory training does not improve intelligence in healthy young adults. *Intelligence*, *40*, 531–542. Retrieved from http://www.sciencedirect.com/science/article/pii/S0160289612000839 [11]

Chumlea, W. C., Schubert, C. M., Roche, A. F., Kulin, H. E., Lee, P. A., Himes, J. H., et al. (2003). Age at menarche and racial comparisons in US girls. *Pediatrics, 111,* 110–113. [5]

Cialdini, R. B., & Schroeder, D. A. (1976). Increasing compliance by legitimizing paltry contributions: When even a penny helps. *Journal of Personality and Social Psychology, 34*, 599–604. [15]

Clark, K. B., & Clark, M. P. (1947). Racial identification and preference among negro children. In E. L. Hartley (Ed.), *Readings in Social Psychology*. (pp. 169–178). New York: Holt, Reinhart, and Winston. [1]

Clark, R. D., & Hatfield, E. (1989). Gender differences in receptivity to sexual offers. *Journal of Psychology and Human Sexuality, 2*, 39–55. [12]

Clarke, M. C., Tanskanen, A., Huttunen, M., Leon, D. A., Murray, R. M., Jones, P. B., et al. (2011). Increased risk of schizophrenia from additive interaction between infant motor developmental delay and obstetric complications: Evidence from a population-based longitudinal study. *American Journal of Psychiatry*, *168*, 1295–1302. [4, 16]

Cleveland, W., & Alvarez, M. (2011). *Yo, Millard Fillmore!* Westport, CT: Prospecta Press. [9]

Clinical Practice Guideline Treating Tobacco Use and Dependence 2008 Update Panel, Liaisons, & Staff. (2008). A clinical practice guideline for treating tobacco use and dependence: 2008 update: A U.S. public health service report. *American Journal of Preventative Medicine*, *35*, 158–176. [13]

Coccaro, E. F., McCloskey, M. S., Fitzgerald, D. A., & Phan, K. L. (2007). Amygdala and orbitofrontal reactivity to social threat in individuals with impulsive aggression. *Biological Psychiatry*, *62*, 168–178. [15]

Cohen, G. L., Garcia, J., Apfel, N., & Master, A. (2006). Reducing the racial achievement gap: A social-psychological intervention. *Science*, *313*, 1307–1310. [11]

Cohen, N. J., & Squire, L. R. (1980). Preserved learning and retention of pattern-analyzing skill in amnesia: Dissociation of knowing how and knowing what. *Science*, *210*, 207–210. [9]

Cohen, S., & Wills, T. A. (1985). Stress, social support, and the buffering hypothesis. *Psychological Bulletin*, *98*, 310–357. [13]

Cohen, S., Alper, C. M., Doyle, W. H., Treanor, J. J., & Turner, R. B. (2006). Positive emotional style predicts resistance to illness after experimental exposure to rhinovirus or influenza A virus. *Psychosomatic Medicine*, *68*, 809–815. [13]

Cohen, S., Frank, E., Doyle, W. J., Skoner, D. P., Rabin, B. S. & Gwaltney, J. M., Jr. (1998). Types of stressors that increase susceptibility to the common cold. *Archive of Internal Medicine, 169*, 62–67. [13]

Colapinto, J. (2000). *As nature made him: The boy who was raised as a girl.* New York: Harper Perennial. [12]

Colapinto, J. (2007, April 16). The interpreter. *The New Yorker.* Retrieved from http://www.newyorker.com/magazine/2007/04/16/the-interpreter-2[1]

Colom, R., Burgaleta, M., Román, F. J., Karama, S., Alvarez-Linera, J., Abad, F. J., et al. (2013). Neuroanatomic overlap between intelligence and cognitive factors: Morphometry methods provide support for the key role of the frontal lobes. *Neuroimage*, *72*, 143–152. [11]

Colom, R., Lluis-Font, J. M., & Andrés-Pueyo, A. (2005). The generational intelligence gains are caused by decreasing variance in the lower half of the distribution: Supporting evidence for the nutrition hypothesis. *Intelligence*, *33*, 83–91. [11]

Committee on Treatment of Posttraumatic Stress Disorder, Institute of Medicine (2008). *Treatment of posttraumatic stress disorder: An assessment of the evidence.* Washington, DC: National Academy of Sciences Press. [13]

Committee on Women in Psychology. (2006). *Committee on women in psychology 2006 annual report.* Retrieved from http://www.apa.org/pi/women/committee/annual-report-2006.pdf [1]

Conard, M. A. (2006). Aptitude is not enough: How personality and behavior predict academic performance. *Journal of Research in Personality*, *40*, 339–346. [14]

Conel, J. L. (1939). *The postnatal development of the human cerebral cortex: Vol. 1. The cortex of the newborn.* Cambridge, MA: Harvard University Press. [5]

Conel, J. L. (1947). *The postnatal development of the human cerebral cortex: Vol. 3. The cortex of the three-month infant.* Cambridge, MA: Harvard University Press. [5]

Conel, J. L. (1959). *The postnatal development of the human cerebral cortex: Vol. 6. The cortex of the twenty-four-month infant.* Cambridge, MA: Harvard University Press. [5]

Conn, S. R., & Rieke, M. L. (1994). *The 16PF fifth edition technical manual.* Champaign, IL: Institute for Personality and Ability Testing. [14]

Conte, A., Khan, N., Defazio, G., Rothwell, J. C., & Berardelli, A. (2013) Pathophysiology of somatosensory abnormalities in Parkinson disease. *Nature Reviews. Neurology*, *9*, 687–697. [6]

Cook, K. (2014). *Kitty Genovese: The murder, the bystanders, the crime that changed America.* New York: Norton. [1, 15]

Cooke, B. M., Chowanadisai, W., & Breedlove, S. M. (2000). Post-weaning social isolation of male rats reduces the volume of the medial amygdala and leads to deficits in adult sexual behavior. *Behavioural Brain Research*, *117*, 107–113. [8]

Cooper, H., Nye, B., Charlton, K., Lindsay, J., & Greathouse, S. (1996). The effects of summer vacation on achievement test scores: A narrative and meta-analytic review. *Review of Educational Research*, *66*, 227–268. [11]

Cooper, R. M., & Zubek, J. P. (1958). Effects of enriched and restricted early environments on the learning ability of bright and dull rats. *Canadian Journal of Psychology*, *12*, 159–164. [4, 11]

Coppotelli, H. C., & Orleans, C. T. (1985). Partner support and other determinants of smoking cessation maintenance among women. *Journal of Consulting and Clinical Psychology*, *53*, 455–460. [13]

Corballis, M. C. (2002). *From hand to mouth: The origins of language.* Princeton, NJ: Princeton University Press. [10]

Corbett, B. A., Shickman, K., & Ferrer, E. (2008). Brief report: The effects of Tomatis sound therapy on language in children with autism. *Journal of Autism Developmental Disorders*, *38*, 562–566. [11]

Corkin, S. (2002). What's new with the amnesic patient H.M.? *Nature Reviews. Neuroscience*, *3*, 153–159. [9]

Corkin, S., Amaral, D. G., Gonzalez, R. G., Johnson, K. A., & Hyman, B. T. (1997). H.M.'s medial temporal lobe lesion: Findings from magnetic resonance imaging. *Journal of Neuroscience*, *17*, 3964–3979. [9]

Coryell, W., Noyes, R., Jr, & House, J. D. (1986). Mortality among outpatients with anxiety disorders. *American Journal of Psychiatry*, *143*, 508–510. [16]

Cosentino, S., Scarmeas, N., Helzner, E., Glymour, M. M., Brandt, J., Albert, M., et al. (2008). APOE epsilon 4 allele predicts faster cognitive decline in mild Alzheimer disease. *Neurology, 70*, 1842–1849. [5]

Costa, P. T., & McCrae, R. R. (1992). *Revised NEO personality inventory (NEO-PI-R) and NEO five-factor inventory (NEO-FFI) professional manual.* Odessa, FL: Psychological Assessment Resources. [14]

Council, J. R., Kirsch, I., & Grant, D. L. (1996). Imagination, expectancy, and hypnotic responding. In: R. G. Kunzendorf, N. P. Spanos and B. Wallace (Eds.), *Hypnosis and Imagination* (pp. 41–65). New York: Baywood. [7]

Covington, M. V. (2000). Goal theory, motivation, and school achievement: An integrative review. *Annual Review of Psychology*, *51*, 171–200. [15]

Cowan, N., Rouder, J. N., Blume, C. L., & Saults, J. S. (2012). Models of verbal working memory capacity: What does it take to make them work? *Psychological Review*, *11*, 480–499. [9]

Cox, G. R., Callahan, P., Churchill, R., Hunot, V., Merry, S. N., Parker, A. G., et al. (2012). Psychological therapies versus antidepressant medication, alone and in combination for depression in children and adolescents. *Cochrane Database of Systematic Reviews, 11*, CD008324. doi:10.1002/14651858.CD008324.pub2 [5]

Cox, J. J., Reimann, F., Nicholas, A. K., Thornton, G., Roberts, E., Springell, K., et al. (2006). An SCN9A channelopathy causes congenital inability to experience pain. *Nature, 444*, 894–898. [6]

Craik, F. I., Bialystok, E., & Freedman, M. (2010). Delaying the onset of Alzheimer disease: Bilingualism as a form of cognitive reserve. *Neurology, 75*, 1726–1729. [10]

Cramer, H., Lauche, R., Langhorst, J., Paul, A., Michalsen, A., & Dobos, G. (2013). Predictors of yoga use among internal medicine patients. *BMC Complementary and Alternative Medicine, 13*, 172. [13]

Crystal, D. (2010). *The Cambridge encyclopedia of language* (3rd ed.), Cambridge: Cambridge University Press. [10]

Csíkszentmihályi, M. (1998). *Finding flow: The psychology of engagement with everyday life.* New York: Basic Books. [10]

Cunha, F., & Heckman, J. J. (2009). The economics and psychology of inequality and human development. *Journal of the European Economic Association, 7*, 320–364. [11]

Currie, J., & Thomas, D. (1995). Does Head Start make a difference? *American Economic Review, 85*, 341–341. [11]

Curtiss, S. (1977). *Genie: A psycholinguistic study of a modern-day wild child.* San Diego: Academic Press. [5]

Curtiss, S. (1989). The independence and task-specificity of language. In M. H. Bornstein & J. S. Bruner (Eds.), *Interaction in human development* (pp. 105–137). Hillsdale, NJ: Erlbaum. [10]

D

D'Esposito, M., & Postle, B. R. (2014, September 19). The cognitive neuroscience of working memory. *Annual Review of Psychology.* Advance online publication. [6]

Dale, R. C., Heyman, I., Giovannoni, G., & Church, A. W. (2005). Incidence of anti-brain antibodies in children with obsessive-compulsive disorder. *British Journal of Psychiatry, 187*, 314–319. [16]

Daliento, L., Mapelli, D., Russo, G., Scarso, P., Limongi, F., Ianizzi, P., et al. (2005). Health related quality of life in adults with repaired tetralogy of Fallot: Psychological and cognitive outcomes. *Heart, 91*, 213–218. [14]

Damasio, A. R., Grabowski, T. J., Bechara, A., Damasio, H., Ponto, L. L., Parvizi, J., et al. (2000). Subcortical and cortical brain activity during the feeling of self-generated emotions. *Nature Neuroscience, 3*, 1049–1056. [13]

Damasio, H. (1995). *Human brain anatomy in computerized images.* New York: Oxford University Press. [10]

Dantz, B., Edgar, D. M., & Dement, W. C. (1994). Circadian rhythms in narcolepsy: Studies on a 90 minute day. *Electroencephalography and Clinical Neurophysiology, 90*, 24–35. [7]

Dantzer, R., O'Connor, J. C., Freund, G. G., Johnson, R. W., & Kelley, K. W. (2008). From inflammation to sickness and depression: When the immune system subjugates the brain. *Nature Reviews. Neuroscience, 9*, 46–56. [13]

Dar-Nimrod, I., & Heine, S. J. (2006). Exposure to scientific theories affects women's math performance. *Science, 314*, 435. [11, 15]

Dark, J., Forger, N. G., & Zucker, I. (1984). Rapid recovery of body mass after surgical removal of adipose tissue in ground squirrels. *Proceedings of the National Academy of Sciences, USA, 81*, 2270–2272. [12]

Darwin, C. (1872). *The expression of the emotions in man and animals.* London: J. Murray. [13]

David, J., & Suls, J. (1999). Coping efforts in daily life: Role of big five traits and problem appraisal. *Journal of Personality, 67*, 119–140. [14]

Davidson, J. M., Camargo, C. A., & Smith, E. R. (1979). Effects of androgen on sexual behavior in hypogonadal men. *Journal of Clinical Endocrinology and Metabolism, 48*, 955–958. [12]

Davidson, K. M., & Tran, C. F. (2014). Impact of treatment intensity on suicidal behavior and depression in borderline personality disorder: A critical review. *Journal of Personality Disorders, 28*, 181–197. [16]

Davidson, R. J., & Irwin, W. (1999). The functional neuroanatomy of emotion and affective style. *Trends in Cognitive Science, 3*, 11–21. [13]

Davidson, R. J., Kabat-Zinn, J., Schumacher, J., Rosenkranz, M., Muller, D., Santorelli, S. F., et al. (2003). Alterations in brain and immune function produced by mindfulness meditation. *Psychosomatic Medicine, 65,* 564–570. [13]

Davis, B. E., Moon, R. Y., Sachs, H. C., & Ottolini, M. C. (1998). Effects of sleep position on infant motor development. *Pediatrics, 102*, 1135–1140. [5]

Davis, J. I., Senghas, A., & Ochsner, K. N. (2009). How does facial feedback modulate emotional experience? *Journal of Research in Personality, 43*, 822–829. [13]

Davis, J. I., Senghas, A., Brandt, F., & Ochsner, K. N. (2010). The effects of BOTOX injections on emotional experience. *Emotion, 10*, 433–440. [13]

de Luis, O., Valero, M. C., & Jurado, L. A. (2000). WBSCR14, a putative transcription factor gene deleted in Williams-Beuren syndrome: Complete characterisation of the human gene and the mouse ortholog. *European Journal of Human Genetics, 8*, 215–222. [10]

de Waal, F. B. M. (2003). Darwin's legacy and the study of primate visual communication. *Annals of the New York Academy of Sciences, 1000*, 7–31. [13]

Deacy, S., & Pierce, K. F. (Eds.). (1997). *Rape in antiquity.* London: Duckworth. [15]

Dearborn, G. V. N. (1932). A case of congenital general pure analgesia. *Journal of Nervous and Mental Disease, 75*, 612–615. [6]

Deary, I. (2008). Why do intelligent people live longer? *Nature, 456*, 175–176. [11]

Deary, I., & Der, G. (2005). Reaction time explains IQ's association with death. *Psychological Science, 16*, 64–69. [11]

Deci, E. L. (1971). Effects of externally mediated rewards on intrinsic motivation. *Journal of Personality and Social Psychology, 18*, 105–115. [12]

Deconinck, F. J., Smorenburg, A. R., Benham, A., Ledebt, A., Feltham, M. G., & Savelsbergh, G. J. (2014, August 26). Reflections on mirror therapy: A systematic review of the effect of mirror visual feedback on the brain. *Neurorehabilitation and Neural Repair.* Advance online publication. [6]

Deeley, Q., Daly, E., Surguladze, S., Tunstall, N., Mezey, G., Beer, D., et al. (2006). Facial emotion processing in criminal psychopathy. Preliminary functional magnetic resonance imaging study. *British Journal of Psychiatry, 189*, 533–539. [16]

Dehaene, S. (1996). The organization of brain activations in number comparison: Event-related potentials and the additive-factors method. *Journal of Cognitive Neuroscience, 1*, 47–68. [10]

Demicheli, V., Rivetti, A., Debalini, M. G., & Di Pietrantonj, C. (2012). Vaccines for measles, mumps and rubella in children. *Cochrane Database of Systematic Reviews, 15*, CD004407. doi:10.1002/14651858.CD004407.pub3 [5]

DePaulo, B. M., & Kashy, D. A. (1998). Everyday lies in close and casual relationships. *Journal of Personality and Social Psychology, 74*, 63–79. [12]

DeRubeis, R. J., Siegle, G. J., & Hollon, S. D. (2008). Cognitive therapy versus medication for depression: Treatment outcomes and neural mechanisms. *Nature Reviews. Neuroscience, 9*, 788–796. [16]

DeSisto, M. J., Harding, C. M., McCormick, R. V., Ashikaga, T., & Brooks, G. W. (1995). The Maine and Vermont three-decade studies of serious mental illness. I. Matched comparison of cross-sectional outcome. *British Journal of Psychiatry, 167*, 331–338. [16]

Devane, W. A., Dysarz, F. A., Johnson, M. R., Melvin, L. S., & Howlett, A.C. (1988). Determination and characterization of a cannabinoid receptor in rat brain. *Molecular Pharmacology, 34*, 605–613. [7]

Devane, W. A., Hanus, L., Breuer, A., Pertwee, R. G., Stevenson, L.A., Griffin, G. et al. (1992). Isolation and structure of a brain constituent that binds the cannabinoid receptor. *Science, 258*, 1946–1949. [7]

DeVoogd, T. J. (1994). Interactions between endocrinology and learning in the avian song system. *Annals of the New York Academy of Sciences, 1000*, 7–31. [10]

DeVries, A. C., Craft, T. K., Glasper, E. R., Neigh, G. N., & Alexander, J. K. (2007). Social influences on stress responses and health. *Psychoneuroendocrinology, 32*, 587–603. [13]

Di Castelnuovo, A., Costanzo, S., Bagnardi, V., Donati, M. B., Iacoviello, L., & de Gaetano, G. (2006). Alcohol dosing and total mortality in men and women: An updated meta-analysis of 34 prospective studies. *Archives of Internal Medicine, 166*, 2437–2445. [13]

Diamond, M. (2009). Pornography, public acceptance and sex related crime: A review. *International Journal of Law and Psychiatry, 32*, 304–14. [15]

Diamond, M., & Sigmundson, H. K. (1997). Management of intersexuality. Guidelines for dealing with persons with ambiguous genitalia. *Archives of Pediatric and Adolescent Medicine, 151*, 1046–1050. [12]

Diamond, M., & Uchiyamam A. (1999). Pornography, rape, and sex crimes in Japan. *International Journal of Law and Psychiatry, 22*, 1–22. [15]

Diamond, M. C. (1967). Extensive cortical depth measurements and neuron size increases in the cortex of environmentally enriched rats. *Journal of Comparative Neurology, 131*, 357–364. [9]

Diamond, M. C., Lindner, B., Johnson, R., Bennnett, E. L., & Rosenzweig, M. R. (1975). Differences in occipital cortical synapses from environmentally enriched, impoverished, and standard colony rats. *Journal of Neuroscience Research, 1*, 109–119. [9]

Dickens, W. T., & Flynn, J. R. (2006). Black Americans reduce the racial IQ gap: Evidence from standardization samples. *Psychological Science, 17*, 913–920. [11]

Dickinson, R. (with Edler, G., and Rushton, S.). (2002). The Milgram re-enactment. Retrieved from http://www.rod-dickinson.net/pages/milgram/project-synopsis.php [15]

Dickson, D. H., & Kelly, I. W. (1985). The 'Barnum effect' in personality assessment: A review of the literature. *Psychological Reports, 57*, 367–382. [14]

Diener, E., & Seligman, M. E. (2002). Very happy people. *Psychological Science, 13*, 81–84. [13]

Diener, E., Wolsic, B., & Fujita, F. (1995). Physical attractiveness and subjective well-being. *Journal of Personality and Social Psychology, 69*, 120–129. [15]

Digdon, N., Powell, R. A., & Harris, B. (2014, July 28). Little Albert's alleged neurological impairment. Watson, Rayner, and historical revision. *History of Psychology.* Advance online publication. Retrieved from http://www.ncbi.nlm.nih.gov/pubmed/25068585 [8]

Dimeff, L., & Linehan, M. M. (2001). Dialectical behavior therapy in a nutshell. *The California Psychologist, 34*, 10–13. [16]

Dohrenwend, B. P., Turner, J. B., Turse, N. A., Adams, B. G., Koenen, K. C., & Marshall, R. (2006). The psychological risks of Vietnam for U.S. veterans: A revisit with new data and methods. *Science, 313*, 979–982. [13]

Dolan, R. J. (2002). Emotion, cognition, and behavior. *Science, 298*, 1191–1194. [13]

Domjan, M., & Purdy, J. E. (1995). Animal research in psychology: More than meets the eye of the general psychology student. *American Psychologist, 50*, 496–503. [1]

Donders, F. C. (1869). On the speed of mental processes (W. G. Koster, Trans.). *Acta Psychologica, 30*, 412–431. [10]

Donoho, C. L. (2003). The "top-of-the-line" influence on the buyer-seller relationship. *Journal of Business Research, 56*, 303–309. [10]

Doshi, D. N., Hanneman, K. K., & Cooper, K. D. (2007). Smoking and skin aging in identical twins. *Archives of Dermatology, 143*, 1543–1546. [13]

Doty, R. L., Shaman, P., Applebaum, S. L., Giberson, R., Siksorski, L., & Rosenberg, L. (1984). Smell identification ability: Changes with age. *Science, 226*, 1441–1443. [5]

Dronkers, N. F., Plaisant, O., Iba-Zizen, M. T., & Cabanis, E. A. (2007). Paul Broca's historic cases: High resolution MR imaging of the brains of Leborgne and Lelong. *Brain, 130*, 1432–1441. [10]

Druckman, D., & Bjork, R. A. (Eds.). (1991). *In the mind's eye: Enhancing human performance*. Washington, DC: National Academy Press. [7, 14]

Druckman, D., & Bjork, R. A. (Eds.). (1994). *Learning, remembering, believing: Enhancing human performance.* Washington, DC: National Academy Press. [7]

Dully, H. (Narrator). (2005, November 16). My lobotomy [Radio broadcast episode]. In D. Isay & P. Kochhar (Producers), *All Things Considered*. Brooklyn, NY: Sound Portraits Productions. [16]

Dunbar, R. I. (2012). Social cognition on the internet: Testing constraints on social network size. *Philosophical Transactions of the Royal Society. Series B: Biological Sciences. 367*, 2192–2201. [1]

Dunbar, R. I., & Shultz, S. (2007). Evolution in the social brain. *Science, 317*, 1344–1347. [1]

Duncker, K. (1945). On problem solving. *Psychological Monographs: General and Applied, 58*(5, Whole No. 270), 1–113. [8]

Dunn, A. L., Trivedi, M. H., Kampert, J. B., Clark, C. G., & Chambliss, H. O. (2005). Exercise treatment for depression: Efficacy and dose response. *American Journal of Preventative Medicine*, *28*, 1–8. [16]

Durkheim, E. (1951). *Suicide: A study in sociology* (J. A. Spaulding, & G. Simpson, Trans.). Glencoe, IL: Free Press. (Original work published 1897) [16]

Dush, C. M. K., & Amato, P. R. (2005). Consequences of relationship status and quality for subjective well-being. *Journal of Social and Personal Relationships*, *22*, 607–627. [13]

Duyme, M., Dumaret, A. C., & Tomkiewicz, S. (1999). How can we boost IQs of "dull children"? A late adoption study. *Proceedings of the National Academy of Sciences, USA*, *96*, 8790–8794. [11]

E

Easterlin, R. A., McVey, L. A., Switek, M., Sawangfa, O., & Zweig, J. S. (2010). The happiness-income paradox revisited. *Proceedings of the National Academy of Sciences, USA*, *107*, 22463–22468. [13]

Eaton, R. F., & Sleigh, M. J. (2002). The need for comparative textbooks: A review and research in developmental evaluation. *Teaching of Psychology 29*, 101–105. [1]

Ebbinghaus, H. (1913). *Memory: A contribution to experimental psychology* (H. A. Ruger & C. E. Bussenius, Trans.). New York: Teachers College Press. (Original work published 1885). Retrieved from http://psychclassics.yorku.ca/Ebbinghaus/index.htm [9]

Eberhardt, J. L., Davies, P. G., Purdie-Vaughns, V. J., & Johnson, S. L. (2006). Looking deathworthy: Perceived stereotypicality of black defendants predicts capital-sentencing outcomes. *Psychological Science*, *17*, 383–386. [15]

Eberhardt, J. L., Goff, P. A., Purdie, V. J., & Davies, P. G. (2004). Seeing black: Race, crime, and visual processing. *Journal of Personality and Social Psychology*, *87*, 876–893. [1]

Ebstein, R. P., Israel, S., Chew, S. H., Zhong, S., & Knafo, A. (2010). Genetics of human social behavior. *Neuron*, *65*, 831–844. [4]

Edwards, G., & Gross, M. M. (1976). Alcohol dependence: Provisional description of a clinical syndrome. *British Medical Journal*, *1*, 1058–1061. [7]

Eimas, P. D., Siqueland, E. R., Jusczyk, P., & Vigorito, J. (1971). Speech perception in infants. *Science*, *171*, 303–306. [10]

Ellenbogen, J. M., Hu, P. T., Payne, J. D., Titone, D., & Walker, M.P. (2007). Human relational memory requires time and sleep. *Proceedings of the National Academy of Sciences, USA*, *104*, 7317–7318. [7]

Ellins, J. (2006). *John Garcia: Life of a neuroethologist and history of taste aversion*. Parker, CO: Outskirts Press. [8]

Else-Quest, N. M., Hyde, J. S., & Linn, M. C. (2010). Cross-national patterns of gender differences in mathematics: A meta-analysis. *Psychological Bulletin*, *136*, 103–127. [11]

Enard, W., Khaitovich, P., Klose, J., Zöllner, S., Heissig, F., Giavalisco, P., et al. (2002). Intra- and interspecific variation in primate gene expression. *Science*, *296*, 340–343. [10]

Engel, J., Jr. (1992). Recent advances in surgical treatment of temporal lobe epilepsy. *Acta Neurologica Scandinavica. Supplementum*, *140*, 71–80. [13]

Epstein, C. M., Woodard, J. L., Stringer, A. Y., Bakay, R. A., Henry, T. R., Pennell, P. B., et al. (2000). Repetitive transcranial magnetic stimulation does not replicate the Wada test. *Neurology*, *55*, 1025–1027. [10]

Erdheim, J. (1904). Uber Hypophysenganggeschwulste und Hirncholestcatome. *Sitzungsberichte der Akademie der Wissenschaften in Wien*, *113*, 537–726. [12]

Erickson, K. I., Voss, M. W., Prakash, R. S., Basak, C., Szabo, A., Chaddock, L., et al. (2011). Exercise training increases size of hippocampus and improves memory. *Proceedings of the National Academy of Sciences, USA*, *108*, 3017–3022. [13]

Ericsson, K. A. (1998). The scientific study of expert levels of performance: General implications for optimal learning and creativity. *High Ability Studies*, *9*, 75–100. [10]

Ericsson, K. A. (2000). How experts attain and maintain superior performance: Implications for the enhancement of skilled performance in older individuals. *Journal of Aging and Physical Activity*, *8*, 346–352. [10]

Erikson, E. H. (1950). *Childhood and society.* New York: Norton. [5]

Eriksson, A., & Lacerda, F. (2007). Charlantry in forensic speech science: A problem to be taken seriously. *International Journal of Speech Language and the Law*, *14*, 169–193. [13]

Ernst, C., & Angst, J. (1983). *Birth order: Its influence on personality.* Berlin, Germany: Springer-Verlag. [14]

Ernst, T., Chang, L., Leonido-Yee, M., & Speck, O. (2000). Evidence for long-term neurotoxicity associated with methamphetamine abuse: A 1H MRS study. *Neurology*, *54*, 1344–1349. [7]

Esposito, S., Bianchini, S., Baggi, E., Fattizzo, M., & Rigante, D. (2014). Pediatric autoimmune neuropsychiatric disorders associated with streptococcal infections: An overview. *European Journal of Clinical Microbiology & Infectious Diseases*, *33*, 2105–2109. [16]

Estes, W. K. (1997). Processes of memory loss, recovery, and distortion. *Psychological Review*, *104*, 148–169. [9]

Estók, P., Zsebõk, S., & Siemers, B. M. (2010). Great tits search for, capture, kill and eat hibernating bats. *Biology Letters*, *6*, 59–62. [8]

Etcoff, N. L., Ekman, P., Magee, J. J., & Frank, M. G. (2000). Lie detection and language comprehension. *Nature*, *405*, 139. [10]

Everett, C., & Madora, K. (2012). Quantity recognition among speakers of an anumeric language. *Cognitive Science*, *36*, 130–141. [10]

Everitt, B. J. (2014). Neural and psychological mechanisms underlying compulsive drug-seeking habits. *European Journal of Neuroscience*, *40*, 2163–2182. [7]

Everson, C. A. (1993). Sustained sleep deprivation impairs host defense. *American Journal of Physiology*, *265*, R1148–R1154. [7]

Everson, C. A., Bergmann, B. M., & Rechtschaffen A. (1989). Sleep deprivation in the rat: III. Total sleep deprivation. *Sleep*, *12*, 13–21. [7]

Eyferth, K. (1961). Leistungen verschidener Gruppen von Besatzungskindern in Hamburg-Wechsler Intelligenztest fur Kinder (HAWIK) [Performance of different groups of occupation children on the Hamburg-Wechsler Intelligence Test for Children]. *Archhiv fur die gesamte Psychologie*, *113*, 222–241. [11]

Eysenck, H. J. (1985). *Decline and fall of the Freudian empire.* Washington, DC: Scott-Townsend. [14]

Eysenck, H. J., & Eysenck, M. W. (1958). *Personality and individual differences*. New York: Plenum. [14]

F

Falk, D. (2004). Prelinguistic evolution in early hominins: Whence motherese? *Behavioral and Brain Science*, *27*, 491–503. [10]

Fantz, R. L. (1964). Visual experience in infants: Decreased attention to familiar patterns relative to novel ones. *Science*, *146*, 668–670. [5]

Fantz, R. L. (1965). Visual perception from birth as shown by pattern selectivity. *Annals of New York Academy of Science, 118*, 793–814. [5]

Faraone, S. V., Glatt, S. J., Su, J., & Tsuang, M. T. (2004). Three potential susceptibility loci shown by a genome-wide scan for regions influencing the age at onset of mania. *American Journal of Psychiatry*, *161*, 625–630. [16]

Farr, W. (1858). The influence of marriage on the mortality of the French people. In: G. W. Hastings (Ed.). *Transactions of the national association for the promotion of social science* (pp. 504–513). London: John W. Parker and Son. [15]

Fazio, R. H., Jackson, J. R., Dunton, B. C., & Williams, C. J. (1995). Variability in automatic activation as an unobtrusive measure of racial attitudes: A bona fide pipeline? *Journal of Personality and Social Psychology, 69*, 1013–1027. [1]

Fechner, G. T. (1966). *Elements of psychophysics*. Volume I. (H. E. Adler, Trans.) New York: Holt, Rinehart and Winston. (Original work published 1860)[6]

Federal Bureau of Investigation. (2009). Table 1. In *Crime in the United States*. Retrieved from http://www2.fbi.gov/ucr/cius2009/data/table_01.html [10]

Feingold, A. (1992). Good-looking people are not what we think. *Psychological Bulletin*, *111*, 304–341. [15]

Feinstein, J. S., Adolphs, R., Damasio, A., & Tranel, D. (2011). The human amygdala and the induction and experience of fear. *Current Biology*, *21*, 34–38. [13]

Festinger, L. (1952). Some consequences of de-individuation in a group. *Journal of Abnormal and Social Psychology*, *47*(Suppl.), 382–389. [15]

Festinger, L. (1957). *A theory of cognitive dissonance*. Stanford, CA: Stanford University Press. [15]

Festinger, L., & Carlsmith, J. M. (1959). Cognitive consequences of forced compliance. *Journal of Abnormal and Social Psychology*, *58*, 203–210. [15]

Finger, S. (1994). *Origins of neuroscience: A history of explorations into brain function.* New York: Oxford University Press. [10]

Fink, M., & Taylor, M. A. (2007). Electroconvulsive therapy: Evidence and challenges. *JAMA*, *298*, 330–332. [16]

Finn, E. S., Shen, X., Holahan, J. M., Scheinost, D., Lacadie, C., Papademetris, X., et al. (2013). Disruption of functional networks in dyslexia: A whole-brain, data-driven analysis of connectivity. *Biological Psychiatry*, *76*, 397–404. doi:10.1016/j.biopsych.2013.08.031. [10]

Fiore, M. C., Keller, P. A., & Curry, S. J. (2007). Health system changes to facilitate the delivery of tobacco-dependence treatment. *American Journal of Preventative Medicine*, *33*(6 Suppl.), S349–S356. [13]

Firmin, M. W. (2010). Commentary: The seminal contribution of Richard LaPiere's attitudes vs actions (1934) research study. *International Journal of Epidemiology, 39*, 18–20. [15]

Fischer, C., Hatzidimitriou, G., Wlos, J., Katz, J. & Ricaurte, G. (1995). Reorganization of ascending 5-HT axon projections in animals previously exposed to the recreational drug (+/–) 3,4-methylenedioxymethamphetamine (MDMA, "ecstasy"). *Journal of Neuroscience, 15,* 5476–5485. [7]

Fischhoff, B., & Beyth, R. (1975). "I knew it would happen": Remembered probabilities of once-future things. *Organizational Behavior and Human Performance*, *13*, 1–16. [10]

Fisher, S. E., & Marcus, G. F. (2005). The eloquent ape: Genes, brains and the evolution of language. *Nature Reviews. Genetics, 7*, 9–20. [10]

Fitts, P. M., & Posner, M. I. (1967). *Human performance*. Belmont, CA: Brooks/Cole. [10]

Fleeson, W. (2004). Moving personality beyond the person-situation debate. *Current Directions in Psychological Science*, *13*, 83–87. [14]

Flegal, K. M., Carroll, M. D., Ogden, C. L., & Johnson, C. L. (2002). Prevalence and trends in obesity among US adults, 1999–2000. *Journal of the American Medical Association*, *288*, 1723–1727. [12]

Flegr, J. (2013). How and why *Toxoplasma* makes us crazy. *Trends in Parasitology*, *29*, 156–163. doi:10.1016/j.pt.2013.01.007. [13]

Flegr, J., Klose, J., Novotná, M., Berenreitterová, M., & Havlícek, J. (2009). Increased incidence of traffic accidents in *Toxoplasma*-infected military drivers and protective effect RhD molecule revealed by a large-scale prospective cohort study. *BMC Infectious Diseases*, *26*, 72. doi:10.1186/1471-2334-9-72. [13]

Flora, C. (2013). *Friendfluence: The surprising ways friends make us who we are*. New York: Anchor. [15]

Flum, D. R., Salem, L., Elrod, J. A., Dellinger, E. P., Cheadle, A., & Chan, L. (2005). Early mortality among Medicare beneficiaries undergoing bariatric surgical procedures. *JAMA*, *294*, 1903–1908. [12]

Flynn, J. R. (1987). Massive IQ gains in 14 nations: What IQ tests really measure. *Psychological Bulletin*, *101*,171–191. [11]

Flynn, J. R. (1998). IQ gains over time: Toward finding the causes. In U. Neisser (Ed.), *The rising curve: Long-term gains in IQ and related measures*. (p. 37) Washington, DC: American Psychological Association. [11]

Flynn, J. R. (2009). *What is intelligence: Beyond the Flynn effect*. Cambridge, MA: Cambridge University Press. [11]

Foell, J., Bekrater-Bodmann, R., Diers, M., & Flor, H. (2013). Mirror therapy for phantom limb pain: Brain changes and the role of body representation. *European Journal of Pain*, *18*, 729–739. doi:10.1002/j.1532-2149.2013.00433.x [6]

Forer, B. R. (1949). The fallacy of personal validation: A classroom demonstration of gullibility. *Journal of Abnormal and Social Psychology*, *44*, 118–123. [14]

Fournier, J. C., DeRubeis, R. J., Hollon, S. D., Dimidjian, S., Amsterdam, J. D., Shelton, R. C., et al. (2010). Antidepressant drug effects and depression severity: A patient-level meta-analysis. *JAMA*, *303*, 47–53. [2, 16]

Fowler, J. H., & Christakis, N. A. (2008). Dynamic spread of happiness in a large social network: Longitudinal analysis over 20 years in the Framingham Heart Study. *The BMJ*, *338*, a2338. doi:10.1136/bmj.a2338. [13]

Frances, A. (2012, May 11). Diagnosing the D. S. M. *The New York Times*, p. A19. [16]

Francis, D. D., Szegda, K., Campbell, G., Martin, W. D., & Insel, T. R. (2003). Epigenetic sources of behavioral differences in mice. *Nature Neuroscience*, *6*, 445–446. [4]

Frank, M. C., Everett, D. L., Fedorenko, E., & Gibson, E. (2008). Number as a cognitive technology: Evidence from Pirahã language and cognition. *Cognition*, *108*, 819–24. [10]

Frankenburg, W. K., Dodds, J., Archer, P., Shapiro, H., & Bresnick, B. (1992). The Denver II: A major revision and restandardization of the Denver Developmental Screening Test. *Pediatrics*, *89,* 91–97. [5]

Frankenhaeuser, M. (1978). Psychoneuroendocrine approaches to the study of emotion as related to stress and coping. *Nebraska Symposium on Motivation*, *26*, 123–162. [13]

Franklin, T. R., Acton, P. D., Maldjian, J. A., Gray, J. D., Croft, J. R., Dackis, C. A., et al. (2002). Decreased gray matter concentration in the insular, orbitofrontal, cingulate, and temporal cortices of cocaine patients. *Biological Psychiatry*, *51*, 134–142. [7]

Fratiglioni, L., & Wang, H. X. (2008). The collective dynamics of smoking in a large social network. *The New England Journal of Medicine*, *358*, 2249–2258. [13]

Freeman, H. D., & Gosling, S. D. (2010). Personality in nonhuman primates: A review and evaluation of past research. *American Journal of Primatology*, *72*, 653–671. [14]

French, C. A., & Fisher, S. E. (2014). What can mice tell us about *Foxp2* function? *Current Opinion in Neurobiology*, *28*, 72–79. doi:10.1016/j.conb.2014.07.003. [10]

Freud, S. (1901). *Psychopathology of everyday life*. New York: W.W. Norton. Retrieved from http://psychclassics.yorku.ca/Freud/Psycho/ [9]

Freud, S. (1990). *The question of lay analysis*. (J. Strachey, Trans.) New York: W. W. Norton. (Original work published 1926) [14]

Fridlund, A. J., Beck, H. P., Goldie, W. D., & Irons, G. (2012). Little Albert: A neurologically impaired child. *History of Psychology*, *15*, 302–327. [8]

Friedman, M., & Rosenman, R. H. (1974). *Type A behavior and your heart.* New York: Knopf. [13]

Friend, A., DeFries, J. C., & Olson, R. K. (2008). Parental education moderates genetic influences on reading disability. *Psychological Science*, *19*, 1124–1130. [11]

Frisby, J. P. (1980). *Seeing: Illusion, brain and mind*. Oxford, UK: Oxford University Press. [6]

Fritz, C., Curtin, J., Poitevineau, J., Borsarello, H., Wollman, I., Tao, F. C., et al. (2014). Soloist evaluations of six old Italian and six new violins. *Proceedings of the National Academy of Sciences, USA*, *111*, 7224–7229. [2]

Fritz, C., Curtin, J., Poitevineau, J., Morrel-Samuels, P., & Tao, F. C. (2012). Player preferences among new and old violins. *Proceedings of the National Academy of Sciences, USA*, *109*, 760–763. [10]

Fudge, D. S. (2014). Fifty years of J. R. Platt's strong inference. *The Journal of Experimental Biology*, *217*, 1202–1204. [2]

Fukuda, K., Ogilvie, R. D., Chilcott, L., Vendittelli, A.-M., & Takeuchi, T. (1998). The prevalence of sleep paralysis among Canadian and Japanese college students. *Dreaming*, *8*, 59–66. [7]

Furumoto, L. (1980). Mary Whiton Calkins (1863–1930). *Psychology of Women Quarterly*, *5*, 55–68. [1]

G

Galaburda, A. M. (1994). Developmental dyslexia and animal studies: At the interface between cognition and neurology. *Cognition*, *56*, 833–839. [10]

Galanter, E. (1962). Direct measurement of utility and subjective probability. *American Journal of Psychology, 75,* 208–220. [6]

Galton, F. (1869). *Hereditary genius: An inquiry into its laws and consequences*. London: Macmillan/Fontana. Retrieved from http://galton.org/books/hereditary-genius/ [11]

Gaoni, Y., & Mechoulam, R. (1964). Isolation, structure, and partial synthesis of an active constituent of hashish. *Journal of the American Chemical Society*, *86*, 1646–1647. [7]

Garber, H. L. (1988). *The Milwaukee project: Preventing mental retardation in children at risk*. Washington, DC: American Association on Mental Retardation. [11]

Garcia, J., & Koelling, R. A. (1966) Relation of cue to consequence in avoidance learning. *Psychonomic Science*, *4*, 123–124. [8]

Gardner, C. D., Kiazand, A., Alhassan, S., Kim, S., Stafford, R. S., Balise, R. R. et al. (2007). Comparison of the Atkins, Zone, Ornish, and LEARN diets for change in weight and related risk factors among overweight premenopausal women. The A to Z weight loss study: A randomized trial. *JAMA, 297,* 969–977. [12]

Gardner, H. (1993). *Multiple intelligences: The theory in practice*. New York: Basic Books. [11]

Gardner, H. (1999). *Intelligence reframed: Multiple intelligences for the 21st century*. New York: Basic Books. [11]

Gardner, R. A., & Gardner, B. T. (1969). Teaching sign language to a chimpanzee. *Science*, *165*, 664–672. [10]

Gardner, R. A., & Gardner, B. T. (1984). A vocabulary test for chimpanzees (*Pan troglodytes*). *Journal of Comparative Psychology*, *98*, 381–404. [10]

Garver, D. L., Holcomb, J. A., & Christensen, J. D. (2000). Heterogeneity of response to antipsychotics from multiple disorders in the schizophrenia spectrum. *Journal of Clinical Psychiatry*, *61*, 964–972. [16]

Gauquelin, M. (1979). *Dreams and illusions of astrology*. New York: Stein and Day. [14]

Gazzaniga, M. S. (2005). Forty-five years of split-brain research and still going strong. *Nature Reviews. Neuroscience*, *6*, 653–659. [3]

Gazzaniga, M. S., & Hillyard, S. A. (1971). Language and speech capacity of the right hemisphere. *Neuropsychologia*, *9*, 273–280. [10]

Gazzaniga, M. S., & LeDoux, J. E. (2013). *The integrated mind*. New York: Springer. [7]

Gentil, A. F., Lopes, A. C., Dougherty, D. D., Rück, C., Mataix-Cols, D., Lukacs, T. L., et al. (2014). Hoarding symptoms and prediction of poor response to limbic system surgery for treatment-refractory obsessive-compulsive disorder. *Journal of Neurosurgury*, *121*, 123–130. [16]

Gershoff, E. T. (2002). Corporal punishment by parents and associated child behaviors and experiences: A meta-analytic and theoretical review. *Psychological Bulletin*, *128*, 539–579. [8]

Ghoncheh, S., & Smith, J. C. (2004). Progressive muscle relaxation, yoga stretching, and ABC relaxation theory. *Journal of Clinical Psychology*, *60*, 131–136. [13]

Gibbs, W. W. (2002). From mouth to mind. *Scientific American*, *287*(2), 26. [10]

Gibson, J. J. (1966). *The senses considered as perceptual systems.* Boston: Houghton Mifflin. [6]

Gilbertson, M. W., Shenton, M. E., Ciszewski, A., Kasai, K., Lasko, N. B., Orr, S. P., et al. (2002). Smaller hippocampal volume predicts pathologic vulnerability to psychological trauma. *Nature Neuroscience*, *5*, 1242–1247. [13]

Gillani, N. B., & Smith, J. C. (2001). Zen meditation and ABC relaxation theory: An exploration of relaxation states, beliefs, dispositions, and motivations. *Journal of Clinical Psychology*, *57*, 839–846. [13]

Gilligan, C. (1982). *In a different voice: Psychological theory and women's development.* Cambridge, MA: Harvard University Press. [5]

Gilman, S. L., King, H., Porter, R., Rousseau, G. S., & Showalter, E. (1993). *Hysteria beyond Freud*. Berkeley: University of California Press. Retrieved from http://ark.cdlib.org/ark:/13030/ft0p3003d3/ [1]

Giraux, P., & Sirigu, A. (2003). Illusory movements of the paralysed limb restore motor cortex activity. *Neuroimage*, *20*, S107–S111. [6]

Glaser, R., Rice, J., Speicher, C. E., Stout, J. C., & Kiecolt-Glaser, J. K. (1986). Stress depresses interferon production by leukocytes concomitant with a decrease in natural killer cell activity. *Behavioral Neuroscience*, *100*, 675–678. [13]

Glei, D. A., Landau, D. A., Goldman, N., Yi-Li, C., Rodriguez, G., & Weinstein, M. (2005). Participating in social activities helps preserve cognitive function: An analysis of a longitudinal, population-based study of the elderly. *International Journal of Epidemiology, 34*, 864–871. [5]

Glenn, N. D., Uecker, J. E., & Love, R. W. B., Jr. (2010). Later first marriage and marital success. *Social Science Research*, *39*, 787–800. [15]

Gogtay, N., Giedd, J. N., Lusk, L., Hayashi, K. M., Greenstein, D., Vaituzis, A. C., et al. (2004). Dynamic mapping of human cortical development during childhood through early adulthood. *Proceedings of the National Academy of Sciences, USA, 101*, 8174–8179. [5, 14]

Goldberg, Y. P., Pimstone, S. N., Namdari, R., Price, N., Cohen, C., Sherrington, R. P., et al. (2012). Human Mendelian pain disorders: A key to discovery and validation of novel analgesics. *Clinical Genetics, 82*, 367–373. [6]

Goldin, C., & Rouse, C. (2000). Orchestrating impartiality: The impact of "blind" auditions on female musicians. *American Economic Review*, *90*, 715–741. [2]

Goldin, P. R., & Gross, J. J. (2010) Effects of mindfulness-based stress reduction (MBSR) on emotion regulation in social anxiety disorder. *Emotion*, *10*, 83–91. [13]

Goldin-Meadow, S. (2006). Talking and thinking with our hands. *Current Directions in Psychological Science*, *15*, 34–39. [10]

Goldstein, A., & Hilgard, E. R. (1975). Failure of the opiate antagonist naloxone to modify hypnotic analgesia. *Proceedings of the National Academy of Sciences, USA*, *72*, 2041–2043. [7]

Golomb, J., de Leon, M. J., George, A. E., Kluger, A., Convit, A., Rusinik, H., et al. (1994). Hippocampal atrophy correlates with severe cognitive impairment in elderly patients with suspected normal pressure hydrocephalus. *Journal of Neurology, Neurosurgery and Psychiatry*, *57*, 590–593. [5]

Golombok, S., & Fivush, R. (1994). *Gender development.* New York: Cambridge University Press. [12]

Gonzales, K., Roeber, J., Kanny, D., Tran, A., Saiki, C., Johnson, H., et al. (2014). Alcohol-attributable deaths and years of potential life lost—11 States, 2006–2010. *Morbidity and Mortality Weekly Report*, *63*(10), 213–216. [7]

Goodnough, A. (2014, May 31). Many veterans praise care, but all hate the wait. *The New York Times*, p. A1. Retrieved from http://www.nytimes.com/2014/06/01/us/many-veterans-praise-health-care-but-all-hate-the-wait.html [13]

Gopnik, A., Meltzoff, A. N., & Kuhl, P. K. (2000). *The scientist in the crib: What early learning tells us about the mind.* New York: William Morrow. [5]

Gordon, P. (2004). Numerical cognition without words: Evidence from Amazonia. *Science*, *306*, 496–499. [10]

Gorski, R. A., Harlan, R. E., Jacobson, C. D., Shryne, J. E., & Southam, A. M. (1980). Evidence for the existence of a sexually dimorphic nucleus in the preoptic area of the rat. *Journal of Comparative Neurology*, *193*, 529–539. [12]

Gosling, S. D. (1998). Personality dimensions in spotted hyenas (*Crocuta crocuta*). *Journal of Comparative Psychology*, *112*, 107–118. [14]

Gosling, S. D. (2008). Personality in non-human animals. *Social and Personality Psychology Compass*, *2*, 985–1001. [14]

Gosselin, A., Deguise, J., Pacquette, G., & Benoit, L. (1997). Violence on Canadian television and some of its cognitive effects. *Canadian Journal of Communication*, *22*(2). Retrieved from http://www.cjc-online.ca/index.php/journal/article/view/992/89 [15]

Gottesman, I. I. (1991). *Schizophrenia genesis*: *The origins of madness*. New York: Freeman. [4, 16]

Gottfredson, L. S. (1997). Intelligence. *Scientific American*, *24*(1), January/February. [11]

Gottman, J. M., & Silver, N. (1999). *The seven principles for making marriage work*. New York: Crown Publishers. [15]

Gould, S. J. (1979). Species are not specious. *New Scientist*, *83*, 374–376. [1]

Gould, S. J. (1981). *The mismeasure of man*. New York: W. W. Norton. [11]

Gove, W. R. (1973). Sex, marital status, and mortality. *American Journal of Sociology*, *79*, 45–67. [15]

Gracely, R. H., Dubner, R., Deeter, W. R., & Wolskee, P. J. (1985). Clinicians' expectations influence placebo analgesia. *Lancet*, *1*, 43. [2]

Grados, M. A., Walkup, J., & Walford, S. (2003). Genetics of obsessive-compulsive disorders: New findings and challenges. *Brain & Development*, *25*(Suppl. 1), S55–S61. [16]

Graffin, N. F., Ray, W. J., & Lundy, R. (1995). EEG concomitants of hypnosis and hypnotic susceptibility. *Journal of Abnormal Psychology*, *104*, 123–131. [7]

Grandjean, P., & Landrigan, P. J. (2006). Developmental neurotoxicity of industrial chemicals. *Lancet*, *368*, 2167–2178. [11]

Granier-Deferre, C., Bassereau, S., Ribeiro, A., Jacquet, A. Y., & Decasper, A. J. (2011). A melodic contour repeatedly experienced by human near-term fetuses elicits a profound cardiac reaction one month after birth. *PLoS ONE, 6*(2): e17304. doi:10.1371/journal.pone.0017304 [5]

Graves, F. C., & Wallen, K. (2006). Androgen-induced yawning in rhesus monkey females is reversed with a nonsteroidal anti-androgen. *Hormones and Behavior*, *49*, 233–236. [13]

Gray, A. W., & Boothroyd, L. G. (2012). Female facial appearance and health. *Evolutionary Psychology*, 10, 66–77. [15]

Gray, M. (2009, April 2). New York's Rockefeller drug laws. *Time.* Retrieved from http://www.time.com/time/nation/article/0,8599,1888864,00.html [7]

Gray, P. (2013). *Why Zimbardo's prison experiment isn't in my textbook* [blog post]. Retrieved from http://www.psychologytoday.com/blog/freedom-learn/201310/why-zimbardo-s-prison-experiment-isn-t-in-my-textbook [15]

Green, D. M., & Swets, J. A. (1966). *Signal detection theory and psychophysics*. New York: Wiley. [6]

Green, E., & Craddock, N. (2003). Brain-derived neurotrophic factor as a potential risk locus for bipolar disorder: Evidence, limitations, and implications. *Current Psychiatry Reports*, *5*, 469–476. [16]

Greengross, G., & Miller, G. F. (2009). The big five personality traits of professional comedians compared to amateur comedians, comedy writers, and college students. *Personality and Individual Differences*, *47*, 79–83. [14]

Greenough, W. T. (1976). Enduring brain effects of differential experience and training. In M. R. Rosenzweig and E. L. Bennett (Eds.), *Neural mechanisms of learning and memory* (pp. 255–278). Cambridge, MA: MIT Press. [9]

Greenough, W. T., & Volkmar, F. R. (1973). Pattern of dendritic branching in occipital cortex of rats reared in complex environments. *Experimental Neurology*, *40*, 491–504. [9]

Greenwald, A. G., & Banaji, M. R. (1995). Implicit social cognition: Attitudes, self-esteem, and stereotypes. *Psychological Review*, *102*, 4–27. [15]

Greenwald, A. G., Banaji, M. R., Rudman, L. A., Farnham, S. D., Nosek, B. A., & Mellott, D. S. (2002). A unified theory of implicit attitudes, stereotypes, self-esteem, and self-concept. *Psychological Review*, *109*, 3–25. [15]

Greenwald, A. G., Poehlman, T. A., Uhlmann, E. L., & Banaji, M. R. (2009). Understanding and using the implicit association test: III. Meta-analysis of predictive validity. *Journal of Personality and Social Psychology, 97*, 17–41. [1]

Grill, H. J. (1985). Introduction: Physiological mechanisms in conditioned taste aversions. In N.S. Braveman & P. Bronstein, *Environmental assessments and clinical applications of conditioned food aversions* (pp. 67–88). New York: New York Academy of Sciences. [8]

Grob, G. N. (1991). Origins of *DSM-I*: A study in appearance and reality. *American Journal of Psychiatry*, *148*, 421–431. [16]

Grossmann, K., Grossmann, K. E., & Kindler, H. (2005). Early care and the roots of attachment and partnership representation in the Bielefeld and Regensburg Longitudinal studies. In K.E Grossmann, K. Grossmann, & E. Waters (Eds.), *Attachment from infancy to adulthood: The major longitudinal studies* (pp. 98–136). New York: Guilford Press. [5]

Grunt, J. A., & Young, W. C. (1953). Consistency of sexual behavior patterns in individual male guinea pigs following castration and androgen therapy. *Journal of Comparative and Physiological Psychology, 46*, 138–144. [12]

Guiso, L., Monte, F., Sapienza, P., & Zingales, L. (2008). Culture, gender, and math. *Science*, *320*, 1164–1165. [11, 15]

Gulevich, G., Dement, W., & Johnson, L. (1966). Psychiatric and EEG observations on a case of prolonged (264 hours) wakefulness. *Archives of General Psychiatry*, *15*, 29–35. [7]

Gustavson, C. R., Jowsey, J. E., & Milligan, D. N. (1982). A three-year evaluation of taste aversion coyote control in Saskatchewan. *Journal of Range Management*, *35*, 57–59. [8]

Guthrie, E. R. (1952). *The psychology of learning.* New York: Harper and Row. [10]

Gutiérrez-García, J. M., & Tusell, F. (1997). Suicides and the lunar cycle. *Psychological Reports*, *80*, 243–250. [10]

H

Hackman, D. A., Farah, M. J., & Meaney, M. J. (2010) Socioeconomic status and the brain: Mechanistic insights from human and animal research. *Nature Reviews. Neuroscience*, *11*, 651–659. [4]

Hackney, C. H., & Sanders, G. S. (2003). Religiosity and mental health: A meta-analysis of recent studies. *Journal for the Scientific Study of Religion*, *42*, 43–55. [13]

Haesler, S., Rochefort, C., Georgi, B., Licznerski, P., Osten, P., & Scharff, C. (2007). Incomplete and inaccurate vocal imitation after knockdown of FoxP2 in songbird basal ganglia nucleus Area X. *PLoS Biology*, *5*, e321. [10]

Haldane, J. B. S. (1955). Population genetics. *New Biology*, *18*, 34–51. [15]

Hall, L., Johansson P., Tärning, B., Sikström, S., & Deutgen, T. (2010). Magic at the marketplace: Choice blindness for the taste of jam and the smell of tea. *Cognition*, *117*, 54–61. [10]

Hall, L., Strandberg, T., Pärnamets, P., Lind, A., Tärning, B., & Johansson, P. (2013). How the polls can be both spot on and dead wrong: Using choice blindness to shift political attitudes and voter intentions. *PLoS ONE*, *8*, e60554. [10]

Haller, H., Cramer, H., Lauche, R., Gass, F., & Dobos, G. J. (2014). The prevalence and burden of subthreshold generalized anxiety disorder: A systematic review. *BMC Psychiatry*, *14*, 128. [16]

Hamilton, A. F. (2013). Reflecting on the mirror neuron system in autism: A systematic review of current theories. *Developmental Cognitive Neuroscience, 3*, 91–105. [3]

Han, X., Chen, M., Wang, F., Windrem, M., Wang, S., Shanz, S., et al. (2013). Forebrain engraftment by human glial progenitor cells enhances synaptic plasticity and learning in adult mice. *Cell Stem Cell*, *12*, 342–353. [8]

Hanchar, H. J., Dodson, P. D., Olsen, R. W., Otis, T. S., & Wallner, M. (2005). Alcohol-induced motor impairment caused by increased extrasynaptic GABA(A) receptor activity. *Nature Neuroscience*, *8*, 339–345. [7]

Haney, C., Banks, C., & Zimbardo, P. (1973). Interpersonal dynamics in a simulated prison. *International Journal of Criminology & Penology*, *1*, 69–97. [15]

Hänig, D. P. (1901). Zur Psychophysik des Geschmackssinnes. *Philosophische Studien*, *17*, 576–623. [6]

Hannula-Jouppi, K., Kaminen-Ahola, N., Taipale, M., Eklund, R., Napola-Hemmi, J., Käärläinen, H., et al. (2005). The axon guidance receptor gene ROBO1 is a candidate gene for developmental dyslexia. *PLoS Genetics*, *1*, e50. [10]

Harding, C. M., Brooks, G. W., Ashikaga, T., Strauss, J. S., & Breier, A. (1987). The Vermont longitudinal study of persons with severe mental illness, II: Long-term outcome of subjects who retrospectively met *DSM-III* criteria for schizophrenia. *American Journal of Psychiatry*, *144*, 727–735. [16]

Hare, R. D. (2003). *The Hare psychopathy checklist-revised* (2nd ed). Toronto, ON: Multi-Health Systems. [16]

Harlow, H. F. (1959). Love in infant monkeys. *Scientific American*, *200*, 68–74. [5]

Harlow, H. F., & Suomi, S. J. (1971). Social recovery by isolation-reared monkeys. *Proceedings of the National Academy of Sciences, USA*, *68*, 1534–1538. [5, 8]

Harlow, H. F., Dodsworth, R. O., & Harlow, M. K. (1965). Total social isolation in monkeys. *Proceedings of the National Academy of Sciences, USA*, *54*, 90–97. [5]

Harlow, J. M. (1868). Recovery from the passage of an iron bar through the head. *Massachusetts Medical Society Medical Communications*, *2*, 327–347. [14]

Harold, D., Paracchini, S., Scerri, T., Dennis, M., Cope, N., Hill, G., et al. (2006). Further evidence that the KIAA0319 gene confers susceptibility to developmental dyslexia. *Molecular Psychiatry*, *11*, 1085–1091. [10]

Harper, D. E., & Hollins, M. (2014). Coolness both underlies and protects against the painfulness of the thermal grill illusion. *Pain*, *155*, 801–807. [6]

Harpur, T. J., Hare, R. D., & Hakstian, A. R. (1989). Two-factor conceptualization of psychopathy: Construct validity and assessment implications. *Psychological Assessment*, *1*, 6–17. [16]

Harrington, J. (2008). *Games, strategies and decision making*. New York: Worth. [15]

Harrow, M., & Jobe, T. H. (2007). Factors involved in outcome and recovery in schizophrenia patients not on antipsychotic medications: A 15-year multifollow-up study. *Journal of Nervous and Mental Disease*, *195*, 406–414. [16]

Hart, B. L. (1988). Biological basis of the behavior of sick animals. *Neuroscience and Biobehavioral Reviews*, *12*, 123–137. [13]

Harvey, R. J. (1996). Reliability and validity. In A. L. Hammer (Ed.), *MBTI Applications: A decade of research on the Myers-Briggs type indicator* (pp. 5–29). Palo Alto, CA: Consulting Psychologists Press. [14]

Harvey, S. B., Hotopf, M., Overland, S., & Mykletun, A. (2010). Physical activity and common mental disorders. *The British Journal of Psychiatry*, *197*, 357–364. [13]

Hasin, D. S., O'Brien, C. P., Auriacombe, M., Borges, G., Bucholz, K., Budney, A., et al. (2013). *DSM-5* criteria for substance use disorders: Recommendations and rationale. *American Journal of Psychiatry*, *170*, 834–851. doi:10.1176/appi.ajp.2013.12060782. [16]

Hauser, R. M. (2002, August). *Meritocracy, cognitive ability, and the sources of occupational success*. Paper presented at the meeting of the American Sociological Association, Chicago, IL. [11]

Hawkins, R. D. (2013). Possible contributions of a novel form of synaptic plasticity in *Aplysia* to reward, memory, and their dysfunctions in mammalian brain. *Learning & Memory*, *20*, 580–591. [1]

Hawkins, R. M. F. (2001). A systematic meta-review of hypnosis as an empirically supported treatment for pain. *Pain Reviews*, *8*, 47–73. [7]

Hayes, D. P., & Grether, J. (1969). *The school year and vacations: When do students learn?* New York: Eastern Sociological Association. (ERIC Document Reporduction Service No. ED037322) [11]

Hayward, V. (2008). A brief taxonomy of tactile illusions and demonstrations that can be done in a hardware store. *Brain Research Bulletin*, *75*, 742–745. [6]

Headey, B., Muffels, R., & Wagner, G. G. (2010). Long-running German panel survey shows that personal and economic choices, not just genes, matter for happiness. *Proceedings of the National Academy of Sciences, USA*, *107*, 17922–17926. [13]

Heath, R. G. (1972). Pleasure and brain activity in man. *Journal of Nervous and Mental Diseases*, *154*, 3–18. [7]

Hebb, D. O. (1949). *The organization of behavior.* New York: Wiley. [9]

Heckert, J. (2012, November 18). The hazards of growing up painlessly. *The New York Times, Sunday Magazine*, p. MM26. [6]

Heider, F. (1958). *The psychology of interpersonal relations*. New York: Wiley. [15]

Heiman, J. R., Long, J. S., Smith, S. N., Fisher, W. A., Sand, M. S., & Rosen, R. C. (2011). Sexual satisfaction and relationship happiness in midlife and older couples in five countries. *Archives of Sexual Behavior*, *40*, 741–753. [15]

Helzner, E. P., Scarmeas, N., Cosentino, S., Portet, F., & Stern, Y. (2007). Leisure activity and cognitive decline in incident Alzheimer disease. *Archives of Neurology, 64,* 1749–1754. [5]

Henig, R. T. (2004, April 4). The quest to forget. *New York Times Magazine*. Retreived from http://www.nytimes.com/2004/04/04/magazine/04MEMORY.html?pagewanted=all [9]

Hennenlotter, A., Dresel, C., Castrop, F., Ceballos-Baumann, A. O., Wohlschläger, A. M., & Haslinger, B. (2009). The link between facial feedback and neural activity within central circuitries of emotion—New insights from botulinum toxin-induced denervation of frown muscles. *Cerebral Cortex*, *19*, 537–542. [13]

Henrichson, C., & Delaney, R. (2012). *The price of prisons: What incarceration costs taxpayers.* New York: Vera Institute of Justice. [7]

Henry, L. P., Amminger, G. P., Harris, M. G., Yuen, H. P., Harrigan, S. M., Prosser, A. L., et al. (2010). The EPPIC follow-up study of first-episode psychosis: Longer-term clinical and functional outcome 7 years after index admission. *Journal of Clinical Psychiatry*, *71*, 716–728. doi:10.4088/JCP.08m04846yel. [16]

Herculano-Houzel, S. (2012). The remarkable, yet not extraordinary, human brain as a scaled-up primate brain and its associated cost. *Proceedings of the National Academy of Sciences, USA*, *109*(Suppl. 1), 10661–10668. [3, 5]

Herdt, G., & Boxer, A. (1993). *Children of horizons*. New York: Beacon Press. [5]

Herdt, G., & McClintock, M. (2000). The magical age of 10. *Archives of Sexual Behavior*, *29*, 587–606. [12]

Heres, S., Davis, J., Maino, K., Jetzinger, E., Kissling, W., & Leucht, S. (2006). Why olanzapine beats risperidone, risperidone beats quetiapine, and quetiapine beats olanzapine: An exploratory analysis of head-to-head comparison studies of second-generation antipsychotics. *American Journal of Psychiatry*, *163*, 185–194. [16]

Hertel, P., Fagerquist, M. V., & Svensson, T. H. (1999). Enhanced cortical dopamine output and antipsychotic-like effects of raclopride by alpha2 adrenoceptor blockade. *Science*, *286*, 105–107. [16]

Hewes, G. (1973). Primate communication and the gestural origin of language. *Current Anthropology*, *14*, 5–24. [10]

Higbee, K. L., & Clay, S. L. (1998). College students' beliefs in the ten-percent myth. *The Journal of Psychology, 132*, 469–476. [1]

Hilgard, E. R. (1948). *Theories of learning*. London: Methuen. [1]

Hilgard, E. R., Morgan, A. H., & Macdonald, H. (1975). Pain and dissociation in the cold pressor test: A study of hypnotic analgesia with "hidden reports" through automatic key pressing and automatic talking. *Journal of Abnormal Psychology*, *84*, 280–289. [7]

Hines, M. (2011). Prenatal endocrine influences on sexual orientation and on sexually differentiated childhood behavior. *Frontiers in Neuroendocrinology*, *32*, 170–182. [12]

Hingson, R. W., Heeren, T., Zakocs, R. C., Kopstein, A., & Wechsler, H. (2002). Magnitude of alcohol-related mortality and morbidity among U.S. college students ages 18–24. *Journal of Studies on Alcohol and Drugs*, *63*, 136–144. [7]

Hobson, J. A., & Friston, K. J. (2012) Waking and dreaming consciousness: Neurobiological and functional considerations. *Progress in Neurobiology*, *98*, 82–98. doi:10.1016/j.pneurobio.2012.05.003. [7]

Hoeft, F., Hernandez, A., McMillon, G., Taylor-Hill, H., Martindale, J. L., Meyler, A., et al. (2006). Neural basis of dyslexia: A comparison between dyslexic and nondyslexic children equated for reading ability. *Journal of Neuroscience*, *26*, 10700–10708. [10]

Hofmann, S. G., Sawyer, A. T., Witt, A. A., & Oh, D. (2010). The effect of mindfulness-based therapy on anxiety and depression: A meta-analytic review. *Journal of Consulting and Clinical Psychology. 78*, 169–183. [13]

Hofstede, G. (2005). *Cultures and organizations: software of the mind* (2nd ed.). New York: McGraw-Hill. [15]

Hofstede, G., & McCrae, R. R. (2004). Personality and culture revisited: Linking traits and dimensions of culture. *Cross-Cultural Research*, *38*, 52–88. [14]

Hohmann, G. W. (1966). Some effects of spinal cord lesions on experienced emotional feelings. *Psychophysiology*, *3*, 143–156. [13]

Holden C. (2001). Polygraph screening. Panel seeks truth in lie detector debate. *Science*, *291*, 967. [13]

Hollon, S. D., Thase, M. E., & Markowitz, J. C. (2002). Treatment and prevention of depression. *Psychological Science in the Public Interest*, *3*, 39–77. [16]

Holman, B. L., Mendelson, J., Garada, B., Teoh, S. K., Hallgring, E., Johnson, K.A., et al. (1993). Regional cerebral blood flow improves with treatment in chronic cocaine polydrug users. *Journal of Nuclear Medicine*, *34*, 723–727. [7]

Holmes, D. S. (1987). The influence of meditation versus rest on physiological arousal. In M. West (Ed.), *The Psychology of Meditation* (pp. 81–103). Oxford, UL: Clarendon Press. [7]

Holmes, T. H., & Rahe, R. H. (1967). The social readjustment rating scale. *Journal of Psychosomatic Research*, *11*, 213–218. [13]

Holowka, S., Brosseau-Lapré, F., & Petitto, L. A. (2002). Semantic and conceptual knowledge underlying bilingual babies' first signs and words. *Language Learning*, *52*, 205–262. [10]

Holsen, L. M., Dalton, K. M., Johnstone, T., & Davidson, R. J. (2008). Prefrontal social cognition network dysfunction underlying face encoding and social anxiety in fragile X syndrome. *NeuroImage*, *43*, 592–604. [11]

Holt-Lunstad, J., Smith, T. B., & Layton, J. B. (2010). Social relationships and mortality risk: A meta-analytic review. *PLoS Medicine*, 7(7): e1000316. doi:10.1371/journal.pmed.1000316 [13, 15]

Holt-Lunstad, J., Uchino, B. N., Smith, T. W., & Hicks, A. (2007). On the importance of relationship quality: The impact of ambivalence in friendships on cardiovascular functioning. *Annals of Behavioral Medicine*, *33*, 278–90. [15]

Honig, W. K., & Urcuioli, P. J. (1981). The legacy of Guttman and Kalish (1956): Twenty-five years of research on stimulus generalization. *Journal of the Experimental Analysis of Behavior*, 36, 405–445. [8]

Hopper, K., & Wanderling, J. (2000). Revisiting the developed versus developing country distinction in course and outcome in schizophrenia: Results from ISoS, the WHO collaborative followup project. International Study of Schizophrenia. *Schizophrenia Bulletin*, *26*, 835–846. [16]

Hopwood, C. J., Wright, A. G., Krueger, R. F., Schade, N., Markon, K. E., & Morey, L. C. (2013). *DSM-5* pathological personality traits and the personality assessment inventory. *Assessment*, *20*, 269–285. [16]

Horn, J. L. (1970). Organization of data on life-span development of human abilities. In L. R. Goulet & P. B. Baltes (Eds.), *Life-span developmental psychology: Theory and research*. (pp. 424–467) New York: Academic Press. [5]

Horn, J. L., & Cattell, R. B. (1967). Age differences in fluid and crystallized intelligence. *Acta Psychologica*, *26*, 107–129. [11]

Horne, J. (2011). The end of sleep: 'Sleep debt' versus biological adaptation of human sleep to waking needs. *Biological Psychology*, *87*, 1–14. [7]

Howland, R. H. (2007). Lithium: Underappreciated and underused? *Psychiatric Annals*, *37*, 618–621. [16]

Hruschka, D. (2010). *Friendship: Development, ecology and evolution of a relationship*. Berkeley: University of California Press. [15]

Hubel, D. H., & Wiesel, T. N. (1965). Binocular interaction in striate cortex kittens reared with artificial squint. *Journal of Neurophysiology*, *28*, 1041–1059. [5]

Huedo-Medina, T. B., Kirsch, I., Middlemass, J., Klonizakis, M., & Siriwardena, A. N. (2012). Effectiveness of non-benzodiazepine hypnotics in treatment of adult insomnia: Meta-analysis of data submitted to the Food and Drug Administration. *The BMJ*, *345*, e8343 doi:10.1136/bmj.e8343 [2]

Hughes, J. R., Stead, L. F., & Lancaster, T. (2007). Antidepressants for smoking cessation. *Cochrane Database of Systematic Reviews*, *1*, CD000031. doi:10.1002/14651858.CD000031.pub4 [13]

Hull, C. L. (1943). *Principles of behavior.* New York: Appleton-Century-Crofts. [12]

Hunt, E. (1995). The role of intelligence in modern society. *American Scientist*, *83*, 356–368. [11]

Hunt, E. (2010). *Human intelligence*. Cambridge: Cambridge University Press. [11]

Huntjens, R. J., Verschuere, B., & McNally, R. J. (2012). Inter-identity autobiographical amnesia in patients with dissociative identity disorder. *PLoS ONE*, *7*, e40580. [16]

Hurley, A. M., Tadrous, M., & Miller, E. S. (2010). Thimerosal-containing vaccines and autism: A review of recent epidemiologic studies. *Journal of Pediatric Pharmacology and Therapeutics*, *15,* 173–181. [5]

Hurley, D. (2012, April 18). Can you make yourself smarter? *The New York Times Magazine*, p. MM38. Retrieved from http://www.nytimes.com/2012/04/22/magazine/can-you-make-yourself-smarter.html?pagewanted=all&_r=1& [11]

Huttenlocher, P. R., deCourten, C., Garey, L. J., & Van der Loos, H. (1982). Synaptogenesis in human visual cortex—Evidence for synapse elimination during normal development. *Neuroscience Letters*, *33*, 247–252. [5]

Hyde, J. S., Lindberg, S. M., Linn, M. C., Ellis, A. B., & Williams, C. C. (2008). Diversity. Gender similarities characterize math performance. *Science*, *321*, 494–495. [11]

Hyde, T. M., & Weinberger, D. R. (1990). The brain in schizophrenia. *Seminars in Neurology*, *10*, 276–286. [16]

Hymowitz, K., Carroll, J. S., Wilcox, W. B., & Kaye, K. (2013). *Knot yet: The benefits and costs of delayed marriage in America*. Charlottesville: University of Virginia, National Marriage Project. [15]

Hypnosis, no anesthetic, for man's surgery. (2008, April 22). Retrieved from http://www.cbsnews.com/news/hypnosis-no-anesthetic-for-mans-surgery/ [7]

I

Iacono, W. G. (2000). Forensic 'lie detection': Procedures without scientific basis. *Journal of Forensic Psychology Practice*, *1*, 75–86. [13]

Ingham, A. G., Levinger, G., Graves, J., & Peckham,V. (1974). The Ringelmann effect: Studies of group size and group performance. *Journal of Experimental Social Psychology*, *10*, 371–384. [15]

Ingram, W. M., Goodrich, L. M., Robey, E. A., & Eisen, M. B. (2013). Mice infected with low-virulence strains of *Toxoplasma gondii* lose their innate aversion to cat urine, even after extensive parasite clearance. *PLoS ONE*, 8(9): e75246. doi:10.1371/journal.pone.0075246 [13]

Insley, S. J. (2000). Long-term vocal recognition in the northern fur seal. *Nature*, *406*, 404–405. [10]

International Human Genome Sequencing Consortium. (2004). Finishing the euchromatic sequence of the human genome. *Nature*, *431*, 931–945. [4]

Isaacowitz, D. M., & Blanchard-Fields, F. (2012). Linking process and outcome in the study of emotion and aging. *Perspectives on Psychological Science*, *7*, 3–17. [5]

Isaacson, R. L. (1972). Hippocampal destruction in man and other animals. *Neuropsychologia*, *10*, 47–64. [9]

Iverson, J. M., & Goldin-Meadow, S. (1998). Why people gesture when they speak. *Nature*, *396*, 228. [10]

Izawa, M. R., French, M. D., & Hedge, A. (2011). Shining new light on the Hawthorne illumination experiments. *Human Factors*, *53*, 528–547. [12]

J

Jablensky, A., Sartorius, N., Ernberg, G., Anker, M., Korten, A., Cooper, J. E., et al. (1992). Schizophrenia: Manifestations, incidence and course in different cultures. A World Health Organization ten-country study. *Psychological Medicine. Monograph Supplement*, *20*, 1–97. [16]

Jaeggi, S. M., Buschkuehl, M., Jonides, J., & Perrig, W. J. (2008). Improving fluid intelligence with training on working memory. *Proceedings of the National Academy of Sciences, USA, 105*, 6829–6833. [5, 11]

Jaeggi, S. M., Studer-Luethi, B., Buschkuehl, M., Su, Y.-F., Jonides, J., & Perrig, W. J. (2010). The relationship between n-back performance and matrix reasoning—Implications for training and transfer. *Intelligence*, *38*, 625–636. Retrieved from http://www.sciencedirect.com/science/article/pii/S0160289610001091 [11]

Jaffee, S. R., Caspi, A., Moffitt, T. E., Dodge, K. A., Rutter, M., Taylor, A. et al. (2005). Nature X nurture: Genetic vulnerabilities interact with physical maltreatment to promote conduct problems. *Development and Psychopathology*, *17*, 67–84. [15]

Jakicic, J. M., Marcus, B. H., Lang, W., & Janney, C. (2008). Effect of exercise on 24-month weight loss maintenance in overweight women. *Archives of Internal Medicine*, *168*, 1550–1559. [12]

Jakubowicz, D., Maman, D., & Essah, P. (2008, June). *Effect of diet with high carbohydrate and protein breakfast on weight loss and appetite in obese women with metabolic syndrome*. Poster session presented at the annual meeting of the Endocrine Society, San Francisco. [12]

James, W. (1890). Attention. In *The principles of psychology* (Vol. 1., pp. 403–404). Cambridge, MA: Harvard University Press. [10]

James, W. (1890). *Principles of psychology.* New York: Holt. [1, 9, 13]

Janis, I. L. (1972). *Victims of groupthink: A psychological study of foreign-policy decisions and fiascoes*. Boston: Houghton Mifflin. [15]

Jantz, R. L. (2001). Cranial change in Americans: 1850–1975. *Journal of Forensic Sciences*, *46*, 784–787. [11]

Jaschik, S. (2007). Fooling the College Board. *Inside Higher Education*, *3*, 26. Retrieved from https://www.insidehighered.com/news/2007/03/26/writing [10]

Jaskiw, G. E., & Popli, A. P. (2004). A meta-analysis of the response to chronic L-dopa in patients with schizophrenia: Therapeutic and heuristic implications. *Psychopharmacology (Berlin)*, *171*, 365–374. [16]

Jefferson, T., Herbst, J. H., & McCrae, R. R. (1998). Associations between birth order and personality traits: Evidence from self-reports and observer ratings. *Journal of Research in Personality*, *32*, 498–509. [14]

Jenkins, J., & Dallenbach, K. (1924). Oblivescence during sleep and waking. *American Journal of Psychology*, *35*, 605–612. [7, 9]

Jensen, A. R. (1999). *The g factor: The science of mental ability*. Westport, CT: Praeger. [11]

Jia, Y., Way, N., Ling, G., Yoshikawa, H., Chen, X., Hughes, D., et al. (2009). The influence of student perceptions of school climate on socioemotional and academic adjustment: A comparison of Chinese and American adolescents. *Child Development*, *80*, 1514–1530. [15]

Johansson, P., Hall, L., Sikström, S., & Olsson, A. (2005). Failure to detect mismatches between intention and outcome in a simple decision task. *Science*, *310*, 116–119. [10]

Johansson, R. S., & Flanagan, J. R. (2009). Coding and use of tactile signals from the fingertips in object manipulation tasks. *Nature Reviews. Neuroscience*, *10*, 345–358. [6]

John, O. P., Naumann, L. P., & Soto, C. J. (2008). Paradigm shift to the integrative big-five trait taxonomy: History, measurement, and conceptual issues. In O. P. John, R. W. Robins, & L. A. Pervin (Eds.), *Handbook of personality: Theory and research* (pp. 114–158). New York: Guilford Press. [14]

Johnson, D. M. (1939). Confidence and speed in the two-category judgment. *Archives of Psychology*, *241*, 1–52. [10]

Johnson, J. S., & Newport, E. L. (1989). Critical period effects in second language learning: The influence of maturational state on the acquisition of English as a second language. *Cognitive Psychology*, *21*, 60–99. [10]

Johnson, M. A. (1993, November 29). Crime: New frontier—Jesse Jackson calls it top civil-rights issue. *Chicago Sun-Times*, p. 4. [15]

Johnson, S. R. (2008). The trouble with QSAR (or how I learned to stop worrying and embrace fallacy). *Journal of Chemical Information and Modeling, 48*, 25–26. [2]

Johnson, W., Turkheimer, E., Gottesman, I. I., & Bouchard, T. J. (2010). Beyond heritability: twin studies in behavioral research. *Current Directions in Psychological Science*, *18*, 217–220. [11]

Johnston, L. D., O'Malley, P. M., Miech, R. A., Bachman, J. G., & Schulenberg, J. E. (2014). *Monitoring the future national results on drug use: 1975-2013: Overview, Key Findings on Adolescent Drug Use*. Ann Arbor: Institute for Social Research, The University of Michigan. Retrieved from http://www.monitoringthefuture.org//pubs/monographs/mtf-overview2013.pdf [7]

Joly-Mascheroni, R. M., Senju, A., & Shepherd, A. J. (2008). Dogs catch human yawns. *Biology Letters*, *4*, 446–448. [13]

Jones, E. E., & Berglas, S. (1978). Control of attributions about the self through self-handicapping strategies: The appeal of alcohol and the role of underachievement. *Personality and Social Psychology Bulletin*, 4, 200–206. [15]

Jones, E. E., & Harris, V. A. (1967). The attribution of attitudes. *Journal of Experimental Social Psychology*, *3*, 1–24. [15]

Jones, M. C. (1924). A laboratory study of fear: The case of Peter. *The Pedagogical Seminary*, *31*, 308–315. Retrieved from http://psychclassics.yorku.ca/Jones/ [1, 8]

Jones, P. B., Barnes, T. R., Davies, L., Dunn, G., Lloyd, H., Hayhurst, K. P., et al. (2006). Randomized controlled trial of the effect on quality of life of second- vs first-generation antipsychotic drugs in schizophrenia: Cost utility of the latest antipsychotic drugs in schizophrenia study (CUtLASS 1). *Archives of General Psychiatry*, *39*, 1079–1087. [16]

Joy, J. E., Watson, S. J., Jr., & Benson, J. A., Jr. (1999). *Marijuana and medicine: Assessing the science base*. Washington, DC: National Academy Press. [7]

Jung, C. G. (1915). On psychological understanding. *The Journal of Abnormal Psychology*, *9*, 385–399. [14]

Jung, C. G. (1919). *Studies in word-association* (M. D. Eder, Trans.). New York: Moffat, Yard & Co. (Original work published 1906) Retrieved from http://openlibrary.org/books/OL23343062M/Studies_in_word-association [10]

Jusko, T. A., Henderson, C. R., Jr., Lanphear, B. P., Cory-Slechta, D. A., Parsons, P. J., & Canfield, R. L. (2008). Blood lead concentrations < 10 μg/dL and child intelligence at 6 years old. *Environmental Health Perspectives*, *116*, 243–248. [11]

K

Kagan, J. (2002). Childhood predictors of states of anxiety. *Dialogues in Clinical Neuroscience, 4*, 287–293. [5]

Kagan, J., Snidman, N., & Arcus, D. (1998). Childhood derivatives of high and low reactivity in infancy. *Child Development*, *69*, 1483–1493. [14]

Kahn-Greene, E. T., Killgore, D. B., Kamimori, G. H., Balkin, T. J., & Killgore, W. D. (2007). The effects of sleep deprivation on symptoms of psychopathology in healthy adults. *Sleep Medicine*, *8*, 215–221. [13]

Kahneman, D. (2011). *Thinking, fast and slow.* New York: Farrar, Straus and Giroux. [10]

Kahneman, D., & Deaton, A. (2010). High income improves evaluation of life but not emotional well-being. *Proceedings of the National Academy of Sciences, USA*, *107*, 16489–16493. [13]

Karama, S., Ad-Dab'bagh, Y., Haier, R. J., Deary, I. J., Lyttelton, O. C., Lepage, C., et al. (2009). Positive association between cognitive ability and cortical thickness in a representative US sample of healthy 6 to 18 year-olds. *Intelligence*, *37*, 145–155. [11]

Karpicke, J. D., & Roediger, H. L., III. (2008). The critical importance of retrieval for learning. *Science*, *319*, 966–968. [9]

Karpinski, A., & Hilton, J. L. (2001). Attitudes and the implicit association test. *Journal of Personality and Social Psychology*, *81*, 774–788. [15]

Kaufman, A. S. (2001). WAIS-III IQs, Horn' s theory, and generational changes from young adulthood to old age. *Intelligence*, *29*, 131–167. [11]

Kaufman, A. S., & Kaufman, J. C. (2001). Emotional intelligence as an aspect of general intelligence: What would David Wechsler say? *Emotion*, *1*, 258–264. [11]

Kawai, M. (1965). Newly-acquired pre-cultural behavior of the natural troop of Japanese monkeys on Koshima islet. *Primates*, *6*, 1–30. [8]

Kay, K. N., & Gallant, J. L. (2009) I can see what you see. *Nature Neuroscience*, *12*, 245. [7]

Kay, K. N., Naselaris, T., Prenger, R. J., & Gallant, J. L. (2008). Identifying natural images from human brain activity. *Nature*, *452*, 352–355. [7]

Kean, S. (2014). *The tale of the dueling neurosurgeons: The history of the human brain as revealed by true stories of trauma, madness, and recovery*. New York: Little, Brown. [14]

Keenan, J. P., Nelson, A., O'Connor, M., & Pascual-Leone, A. (2001). Self-recognition and the right hemisphere. *Nature*, *409*, 305. [10]

Keesey, R. E., & Boyle, P. C. (1973). Effects of quinine adulteration upon body weight of LH-lesioned and intact male rats. *Journal of Comparative and Physiological Psychology, 84*, 38–46. [12]

Keith, M. (2010). *Not a wake: A dream embodying π's digits fully for 10000 decimals*. Princeton, NJ: Vinculum Press. [9]

Kelly, I. W., Rotton, J., & Culver, R. (1996). The moon was full and nothing happened: A review of studies on the moon and human behavior and human belief. In J. Nickell, B. Karr & T. Genoni (Eds.), *The outer edge: Classic investigations of the paranormal* (pp. 16–35). Amherst, NY: Committee for the Scientific Investigation of Claims of the Paranormal. [10, 14]

Kendler, K. S., & Gardner, C. O. (2010). Dependent stressful life events and prior depressive episodes in the prediction of major depression. *Archives of General Psychiatry*, *67*, 1120–1127. [13]

Kendler, K. S., Gardner, C. O., & Prescott, C. A. (1999). Clinical characteristics of major depression that predict risk of depression in relatives. *Archives of General Psychiatry*, *56*, 322–327. [16]

Kendler, K. S., Karkowski, L. M., & Prescott, C. A. (1999). Causal relationship between stressful life events and the onset of major depression. *The American Journal of Psychiatry*, *156*, 837–841. [13]

Keogh, B. K., Bernheimer, L. P., & Guthrie, D. (2004). Children with developmental delays twenty years later: Where are they? How are they? *American Journal of Mental Retardation, 109*, 219–230. [11]

Kesner, R. P., & Novak, J. M. (1982). Serial position curve in rats: Role of the dorsal hippocampus. *Science, 218*, 173–175. [9]

Kessler, R. C., Chiu, W. T., Demler, O., & Walters, E. E. (2005). Prevalence, severity, and comorbidity of twelve-month *DSM-IV* disorders in the National Comorbidity Survey Replication (NCS-R). *Archives of General Psychiatry, 62*, 617–627. [16]

Khan, A., Faucett, J., Lichtenberg, P., Kirsch, I., & Brown, W. A. (2012). A systematic review of comparative efficacy of treatments and controls for depression. *PLoS ONE, 7*, e41778. doi:10.1371/journal.pone.0041778. [2]

Killingsworth, M. A., & Gilbert, D. T. (2010). A wandering mind is an unhappy mind. *Science, 330*, 932. [13]

Kim, A. (2006). Wilhelm Maximilian Wundt. In E. N. Zalta (Ed.), *The Stanford Encyclopedia of Philosophy* (Spring 2014 ed.). Retrieved from http://plato.stanford.edu/archives/spr2014/entries/wilhelm-wundt/ [1]

Kim, D. R., Pesiridou, A., & O'Reardon, J. P. (2009). Transcranial magnetic stimulation in the treatment of psychiatric disorders. *Current Psychiatry Reports, 11*, 447–452. [16]

Kim, K. H., Relkin, N. R., Lee, K. M., & Hirsch, J. (1997). Distinct cortical areas associated with native and second languages. *Nature, 388*, 171–174. [10]

Kindt, M., Marieke, S., & Vervliet, B. (2009). Beyond extinction: Erasing human fear responses and preventing the return of fear. *Nature Neuroscience, 12*, 256–258. [9]

King, B. D., Woody, W. D., & Viney, W. (2013). *A history of psychology: Ideas and context*. New York: Pearson. [1]

King, B. M. (2006). The rise, fall, and resurrection of the ventromedial hypothalamus in the regulation of feeding behavior and body weight. *Physiology & Behavior, 87*, 221–244. [12]

King, J. L. (1998). The effects of gender bias and errors in essay grading. *Educational Research Quarterly, 22*, 13–25. [10]

King, S., St-Hilaire, A., & Heidkamp, D. (2010). Prenatal factors in schizophrenia. *Current Directions in Psychological Science, 19*, 209–213. [16]

Kingsbury, S. J., & Garver, D. L. (1998). Lithium and psychosis revisited. *Progress in Neuro-Psychopharmacology & Biological Psychiatry, 22*, 249–263. [16]

Kinsey, A. C., Pomeroy, W. B., & Martin, C. E. (1948). *Sexual behavior in the human male*. Philadelphia: Saunders. [12]

Kinsey, A. C., Pomeroy, W. B., Martin, C. E., & Gebhard, P. H. (1953). *Sexual behavior in the human female*. Philadelphia: Saunders. [12]

Kirsch, P., Esslinger, C., Chen, Q., Mier, D., Lis, S., Siddhanti, S., et al. (2005). Oxytocin modulates neural circuitry for social cognition and fear in humans. *The Journal of Neuroscience, 25*, 11489–11493. [15]

Kleitman, N., & Engelmann, T. (1953). Sleep characteristics of infants. *Journal of Applied Physiology, 6*, 269–282. [7]

Kliem, S., Kröger, C., & Kossfelder, J. (2010). Dialectical behavior therapy for borderline personality disorder: A meta-analysis using mixed-effects modeling. *Journal Consulting Clinical Psychology, 78*, 936–951. [16]

Klump, K. L., Bulik, C. M., Kaye, W. H., Treasure, J., & Tyson, E. (2009). Academy for Eating Disorders (AED) position paper: Eating disorders are serious mental lilnesses. *International Journal of Eating Disorders, 42*, 97–103. [12]

Klüver, H., & Bucy, P. C. (1938). An analysis of certain effects of bilateral temporal lobectomy in the rhesus monkey, with special reference to "psychic blindness." *Journal of Psychology, 5*, 33–54. [13]

Knibestol, M., & Valbo, A. B. (1970). Single unit analysis of mechanoreceptor activity from the human glabrous skin. *Acta Physiologica Scandinavica, 80*, 178–195. [6]

Knobloch-Westerwick, S., & Meng, J. (2009). Looking the other way: Selective exposure to attitude-consistent and counterattitudinal political information. *Communication Research, 36*, 426–448. [10]

Koenigs, M., & Tranel, D. (2008). Prefrontal cortex damage abolishes brand-cued changes in cola preference. *Social Cognitive and Affective Neuroscience, 3*, 1–6. [2]

Koenigs, M., Huey, E. D., Raymont, V., Cheon, B., Solomon, J., Wassermann, E. M., et al. (2008). Focal brain damage protects against post-traumatic stress disorder in combat veterans, *Nature Neuroscience, 11*, 232–237. [13]

Koestler, A. (1959). *The sleepwalkers: A history of man's changing vision of the universe.* New York: Macmillan. [2]

Koestner, R., & McClelland, D. C. (1992). The affiliation motive. In C. P. Smith (Ed.), *Motivation and personality: Handbook of thematic content analysis* (pp. 205–210). New York: Cambridge University Press. [12]

Kohlberg, L. (1963). The development of children's orientations toward a moral order: I. Sequence in the development of moral thought. *Vita Humana*, 6, 11–33. [5]

Köhler, W. (1925). *The mentality of apes*. New York: Harcourt and Brace. [8]

Kopell, B. H., Machado, A. G., & Rezai, A. R. (2005). Not your father's lobotomy: Psychiatric surgery revisited. *Clinical Neurosurgery, 52*, 315–330. [16]

Korenbrot, J. I. (2012). Speed, sensitivity, and stability of the light response in rod and cone photoreceptors: Facts and models. *Progress in Retinal and Eye Research*, 31: 442–466. [6]

Korman, M., Doyon, J., Doljansky, J., Carrier, J., Dagan, Y., & Karni, A. (2007). Daytime sleep condenses the time course of motor memory consolidation. *Nature Neuroscience, 10*, 1206–1213. [7]

Kosslyn, S. M. (1994). *Image and brain: The resolution of the imagery debate*. Cambridge, MA: MIT Press. [7]

Kosslyn, S. M., Thompson, W. L., & Ganis, G. (2006). *The case for mental imagery.* Oxford, UK: Oxford University Press. [10]

Kosslyn, S. M., Thompson, W. L., Kim, I. J., & Alpert, N. M. (1995). Topographic representations of mental images in primary visual cortex. *Nature, 378*, 496–498. [10]

Kovelman, J. A., & Scheibel, A. B. (1984). A neurohistological correlate of schizophrenia. *Biological Psychiatry, 19*, 1601. [16]

Krauss, R. M. (1998). Why do we gesture when we speak? *Current Directions in Psychological Science, 7*(2), 54–60. [10]

Krebs, V. (2000). Working in the connected world: Book network. *International Human Information Resource Management Journal, 4*, 87–90. [10]

Krech, D., Crutchfield, R. S., & Ballachey, E. L. (1962). *Individual in society.* New York: McGraw-Hill. [15]

Kremen, W. S., Jacobson, K. C., Xian, H., Eisen, S. A., Waterman, B., Toomey, R., et al. (2005). Heritability of word recognition in middle-aged men varies as a function of parental education. *Behavior Genetics*, *35*, 417–433. [11]

Kremen, W. S., Koenen, K. C., Afari, N., & Lyons, M. J. (2012). Twin studies of posttraumatic stress disorder: Differentiating vulnerability factors from sequelae. *Neuropharmacology*, *62*, 647–653. [13]

Kril, J., Halliday, G., Svoboda, M., & Cartwright, H. (1997). The cerebral cortex is damaged in chronic alcoholics. *Neuroscience*, *79*, 983–998. [7]

Kring, A. M., & Caponigro, J. M. (2010). Emotion in schizophrenia: Where feeling meets thinking. *Current Directions in Psychological Science*, *19*, 255–259. [16]

Kristensen, P., & Bjerkedal, T. (2007). Explaining the relation between birth order and intelligence. *Science*, *316*, 1717. [11, 14]

Kröger, C., Röepke, S., & Kliem, S. (2014). Reasons for premature termination of dialectical behavior therapy for inpatients with borderline personality disorder. *Behavior Research and Therapy*, *60*, 46–52. [16]

Kruger, J., Galuska, D., Serdula, M., & Jones, D. (2004). Attempting to lose weight: Specific practices among U.S. adults. *American Journal of Preventive Medicine, 26*, 402–406. [12]

Kruglinski, S. (2006). *Amnesia: A new look at the forgotten past*. Retrieved from Columbia University, Graduate School of Journalism Web site: http://web.jrn.columbia.edu/studentwork/misc/amnesia.asp [9]

Kuhl, B. A., Dudukovic, N. M., Kahn, I., & Wagner, A. D. (2007). Decreased demands on cognitive control reveal the neural processing benefits of forgetting. *Nature Neuroscience*, *10*, 908–914. [9]

Kuhl, P. K., Stevens, E., Hayashi, A., Deguchi, T., Kiritani, S., & Iverson, P. (2006). Infants show a facilitation effect for native language phonetic perception between 6 and 12 months, *Developmental Science*, *9*, F13–F21. [10]

Kuhle, B. X., Barber, J. M., & Bristol, A. S. (2009). Predicting students' performance in introductory psychology from their psychology misconceptions. *Journal of Instructional Psychology, 36*, 1–6. [1]

Kühn, S., Gleich, T., Lorenz, R. C., Lindenberger, U., & Gallinat, J. (2013). Playing Super Mario induces structural brain plasticity: Gray matter changes resulting from training with a commercial video game. *Molecular Psychiatry*, *19*, 265–271. [2]

Kuhn, T. (1962). *The structure of scientific revolutions.* Chicago: University of Chicago Press. [2]

Kukekova, A. V., Trut, L. N., Chase, K., Shepeleva, D. V., Vladimirova, A. V., Kharlamova, A. V., et al. (2008). Measurement of segregating behaviors in experimental silver fox pedigrees. *Behavior Genetics*, *38*, 185–194. [14]

Kunnapas, T. M. (1955). An analysis of the "vertical-horizontal illusion." *Journal of Experimental Psychology*, *49*, 134–140. [1]

Kuper, H., & Marmot, M. (2003). Job strain, job demands, decision latitude, and risk of coronary heart disease within the Whitehall II study. *Journal of Epidemiology and Community Health*, *57*, 147–153. [13]

Kupper, N., & Denollet, J. (2007). Type D personality as a prognostic factor in heart disease: Assessment and mediating mechanisms. *Journal of Personality Assessment*, *89*, 265–276. [13]

L

LaBar, K. S., Gatenby, J. C., Gore, J. C., LeDoux, J. E., & Phelps, E. A. (1998). Human amygdala activation during conditioned fear acquisition and extinction: A mixed-trial fMRI study. *Neuron*, *20*, 937–945. [13]

Lai, C. S. L., Fisher, S. E., Hurst, J. A., Vargha-Khadem, F., & Monaco, A. P. (2001). A forkhead-domain gene is mutated in a severe speech and language disorder. *Nature*, *413*, 519–523. [10]

Lakoff, G. (2008). *The political mind: Why you can't understand 21st-century American politics with an 18th-century brain.* New York: Viking Adult. [15]

LaMarre, H. L., Landreville, K. D., & Beam, M. A. (2009). The irony of satire: Political ideology and the motivation to see what you want to see in *The Colbert Report*. *The International Journal of Press/Politics*, *14*, 212–231. [10]

Lang, E. V., Benotsch, E. G., Fick, L. J., Lutgendorf, S., Berbaum, M. L., Berbaum, K. S., et al. (2000). Adjunctive non-pharmacological analgesia for invasive medical procedures: A randomised trial. *Lancet*, *355*, 1486–1500. [7]

Langleben, D. D., Schroeder, L., Maldjian, J. A., Gur, R. C., McDonald, S., Ragland, J. D., et al. (2002). Brain activity during simulated deception: An event-related functional magnetic resonance study. *Neuroimage*, *15*, 727–732. [13]

Langlois, J. H., & Roggman, L. (1990). Attractive faces are only average. *Psychological Science*, *1*, 115–121. [15]

Lango Allen, H., Estrada, K., Lettre, G., Berndt, S. I., Weedson, M. N., Rivadeneira, F., et al., (2010). Hundreds of variants clustered in genomic loci and biological pathways affect human height. *Nature*, *467*, 832–838. [11]

Lansink, J. M., & Richards, J. E. (1997). Heart rate and behavioral measures of attention in six-, nine-, and twelve-month-old infants during object exploration. *Child Development, 68*, 610–620. [5]

LaPiere, R. T. (1934). Attitudes vs. actions. *Social Forces*, *13*, 230–237. [15]

Larroche, J.-C. (1977). *Developmental pathology of the neonate.* Amsterdam: Excerpta Medica. [5]

Larzelere, R. E., & Kuhn, B. R. (2005). Comparing child outcomes of physical punishment and alternative disciplinary tactics: A meta-analysis. *Clinical Child and Family Psychology Review*, *8*, 1–37. [8]

Latane, B., Williams, K., & Harkins, S. (1979). Many hands make light the work: The causes and consequences of social loafing. *Journal of Personality and Social Psychology*, *37*, 822–832. [15]

Laumann, E. O., Gagnon, J. H., Michael, R. T., & Michaels, S. (1992). *National Health and Social Life Survey, 1992: (United States)* [Data file]. Ann Arbor, MI: Inter-university Consortium for Political and Social Research. [12]

Lautenschlager, N. T., Cox, K. L., Flicker, L., Foster, J. K., van Bockxmeer, F. M., Xiao, J., et al. (2008). Effect of physical activity on cognitive function in older adults at risk for Alzheimer disease: A randomized trial. *JAMA, 300*, 1027–1037. [5]

Lavie, P. (1996). *The enchanted world of sleep* (A. Berris, Trans.). New Haven, CT: Yale University Press. (Original work published 1993) [7]

Lawlor, D. A., Clark, H., & Leon, D. A. (2006). Associations between childhood intelligence and hospital admissions for unintentional injuries in adulthood: The Aberdeen children of the 1950s cohort study. *American Journal of Public Health*, *97*, 291–297. [11]

Lazarsfeld, P. F. (1949). The American soldier: An expository review. *Public Opinion Quarterly*, *13*, 377–404. [10]

Lazarus, S. A., Cheavens, J. S., Festa, F., & Zachary Rosenthal, M. (2014). Interpersonal functioning in borderline personality disorder: A systematic review of behavioral and laboratory-based assessments. *Clinical Psychology Review*, *34*, 193–205. [16]

Le Boeuf, B. J. (1974). Male-male competition and reproductive success in elephant seals. *American Zoologist*, *14*, 163–176. [15]

Le Grand, R., Mondloch, C. J., Maurer, D., & Brent, H. P. (2003). Expert face processing requires visual input to the right hemisphere during infancy. *Nature Neuroscience*, *6*, 1108–1112. [13]

Le Grange, D. (2005). The Maudsley family-based treatment for adolescent anorexia nervosa. *World Psychiatry*, *4*, 142–146. [12]

Leary, M. R., Twenge, J. M., & Quinlivan, E. (2006). Interpersonal rejection as a determinant of anger and aggression. *Personality and Social Psychology Review*, *10*, 111–132. [12]

Ledbetter, A. M., Griffin, E. M., & Sparks, G. G. (2007). Forecasting "friends forever": A longitudinal investigation of sustained closeness between best friends. *Personal Relationships*, *14*, 343–350. [15]

LeDoux, J. E. (1994). Emotion, memory and the brain. *Scientific American*, *270*(6), 50–57. [13]

LeDoux, J. E. (1995). Emotion: Clues from the brain. *Annual Review of Psychology*, *46*, 209–235. [13]

LeDoux, J. E. (1996). *The emotional brain: The mysterious underpinnings of emotional life*. London: Simon & Schuster. [13]

Lee, V. E., & Loeb, S. (1995). Where do Head Start attendees end up? One reason why preschool effects fade out. *Educational Evaluation and Policy Analysis*, *17*, 62–82. [11]

Leff, J., Sartorius, N., Jablensky, A., Korten, A., & Ernberg, G. (1992). The international pilot study of schizophrenia: Five-year follow-up findings. *Psychological Medicine*, *22*, 131–145. [16]

Lehman, K. (2009). *Birth order book: Why you are the way you are*. Ada, MI: Revell Books. [14]

Lenzenweger, M. F. (2008). Epidemiology of personality disorders. *Psychiatric Clinics of North America*, *31*, 395–403. [16]

Lenzenweger, M. F., Lane, M. C., Loranger, A. W., & Kessler, R. C. (2007). *DSM-IV* personality disorders in the National Comorbidity Survey Replication. *Biological Psychiatry*, *62*, 553–564. [16]

Lepage, M., Habib, R., Cormier, H., Houle, S., & McIntosh, A. R. (2000). Neural correlates of semantic associative encoding in episodic memory. *Cognitive Brain Research*, *9*, 271–80. [9]

Leroi, A. M. (2003). *Mutants: On the form, variety and errors of the human body*. London: Penguin Books. [4]

Leroi, I., Sheppard, J. M., & Lyketsos, C. G. (2002). Cognitive function after 11.5 years of alcohol use: Relation to alcohol use. *American Journal of Epidemiology*, *156*, 747–752. [7]

Lesch, K. P., Bengel, D., Heils, A., Sabol, S., Greenberg, B., Petri, S., et al. (1996). Association of anxiety-related traits with a polymorphism in the serotonin transporter gene regulatory region. *Science*, *274*, 1527–1530. [14]

LeVay, S. (1991). A difference in hypothalamic structure between heterosexual and homosexual men. *Science*, *253*, 1034–1037. [12]

Levenson, R. W. (1992). Autonomic nervous system differences among emotions. *Psychological Science*, *3*, 23–27. [13]

Levine, M. W., & Shefner, J. M. (1981). *Fundamentals of sensation and perception*. New York: Random House. [6]

Levine, S., Haltmeyer, G. C., & Karas, G. G. (1967). Physiological and behavioral effects of infantile stimulation. *Physiology & Behavior*, *2*, 55–59. [13]

Levinson, S. C., & Haviland, J. B. (1994). Spatial conceptualization in Mayan languages. *Linguistics*, *32*(4/5), 613–622. [10]

Levitin, D. J. (2006). *This is your brain on music: The science of a human obsession*. New York: Dutton/Penguin. [10]

Levy, F. (2010, July 14). The world's happiest countries. *Forbes*. Retrieved from http://www.forbes.com/2010/07/14/world-happiest-countries-lifestyle-realestate-gallup.html [13]

Lewis, R. (2013). *The forever fix: Gene therapy and the boy who saved it*. New York: St. Martin's Griffin. [4]

Ley, R. G., & Bryden, M. P. (1982). A dissociation of right and left hemispheric effects for recognizing emotional tone and verbal content. *Brain and Cognition*, *1*, 3–9. [13]

Libet, B., Gleason, C. A., Wright, E. W., & Pearl, D. K. (1983). Time of conscious intention to act in relation to onset of cerebral activity (readiness-potential): The unconscious initiation of a freely voluntary act. *Brain*, *106*, 623–642. [7]

Lichtenstein, P., Yip, B. H., Björk, C., Pawitan, Y., Cannon, T. D., Sullivan, P. F., et al. (2009). Common genetic determinants of schizophrenia and bipolar disorder in Swedish families: A population-based study. *Lancet*, *373*, 234–239. [16]

Lidstone, S. C., Schulzer, M., Dinelle, K., Mak, E., Sossi, V., Ruth, T. J., et al. (2010). Effects of expectation on placebo-induced dopamine release in Parkinson disease. *Archives of General Psychiatry*, *67*, 857–865. [2]

Liégeois, F., Baldeweg, T., Connelly, A., Gadian, D. G., Mishkin, M., & Vargha-Khadem, F. (2003). Language fMRI abnormalities associated with FOXP2 gene mutation. *Nature Neuroscience*, *6*, 1230–1237. [10]

Lilienfeld, S. O., Lynn, S. J., Ruscio, J., & Beyerstein, B. L. (2009). *50 great myths of popular psychology: Shattering widespread misconceptions about human behavior*. New York: Wiley-Blackwell. [1]

Lin, L., Faraco, J., Li, R., Kadotani, H., Lin, X., Qiu, X., et al. (1999). The sleep disorder canine narcolepsy is caused by a mutation in the hypocretin (orexin) receptor 2 gene. *Cell*, *98*, 365–376. [7]

Lindberg, L. D., Boggess, S., Porter, L., & Williams, S. (2000). *Teen risk-taking: A statistical portrait*. Washington, DC: Urban Institute, Health and Human Services. [5]

Lindson, N., Aveyard, P., & Hughes, J. R. (2010). Reduction versus abrupt cessation in smokers who want to quit. *Cochrane Database of Systematic Reviews*, *3*, CD008033. doi:10.1002/14651858.CD008033.pub2 [13]

Lipnicki, D. M., Sachdev, P. S., Crawford, J., Reppermund, S., Kochan, N. A., Trollor, J. N., et al. (2013). Risk factors for late-life cognitive decline and variation with age and sex in the Sydney Memory and Ageing Study. *PLoS ONE*, *8*(6), e65841. [15]

Lippa, R. A. (2010). Sex differences in personality traits and gender-related occupational preferences across 53 nations: Testing evolutionary and social-environmental theories. *Archives of Sexual Behavior, 39*, 619–636. doi:10.1007/s10508-008-9380-7. [12]

Liptak, A. (2008, April 23). U. S. prison population dwarfs that of other nations. *The New York Times*. Retrieved from http://www.nytimes.com/2008/04/23/world/americas/23iht-23prison.12253738.html?pagewanted=all&_r=0 [15]

Lisdahl, K. M., Gilbart, E. R., Wright, N. E., & Shollenbarger, S. (2013). Dare to delay? The impacts of adolescent alcohol and marijuana use onset on cognition, brain structure, and function. *Frontiers in Psychiatry, 4*, 53. doi:10.3389/fpsyt.2013.00053 [7]

Liu, D., Diorio, J., Tannenbaum, B., Caldji, C., Francis, D., Freeman, A., et. al. (1997). Maternal care, hippocampal glucocorticoid receptors, and hypothalamic-pituitary-adrenal responses to stress. *Science, 277*, 1659–1662. [4, 13]

Lock, J., Le Grange, D., Agras, W. S., Moye, A., Bryson, S. W., Jo, B. (2010). Randomized clinical trial comparing family-based treatment with adolescent-focused individual therapy for adolescents with anorexia nervosa. *Archives of General Psychiatry, 67*, 1025–1032. doi:10.1001/archgenpsychiatry.2010.128. [12]

Loewi, O. (1921). Über humorale Übertragbarkeit der Herznervenwirkung. I. Mittei-Lung. *Pfluegers Archiv fuer die Gesamte Physiologie des Menschen und der Tiere, 189*, 239–242. [3]

Loftus, E. F. (1997). Creating false memories. *Scientific American, 277*(3), 70–75. [7]

Loftus, E. F. (2003). Make-believe memories. *American Psychologist, 58*, 867–873. [9]

Loftus, E. F., & Davis, D. (2006). Recovered memories. *Annual Review of Clinical Psychology, 2*, 469–498. [14]

Loftus, E. F., & Palmer, J. C. (1974). Reconstruction of automobile destruction: An example of the interaction between language and memory. *Journal of Verbal Learning and Verbal Behavior, 13*, 585–589. [10]

Lothian, J. A. (2011). Lamaze breathing: What every pregnant woman needs to know. *The Journal of Perinatal Education, 20*, 118–120. [7]

Lovett, I. (2013, June 20). After 37 years of trying to change people's sexual orientation, group is to disband. *The New York Times*, p. A12. [14]

Löw, K., Crestani, F., Keist, R., Benke, D., Brünig, I., Benson, J. A., et al. (2000). Molecular and neuronal substrate for the selective attenuation of anxiety. *Science, 290*, 131–134. [9]

Loy, C. T., Schofield, P. R., Turner, A. M., & Kwok, J. B. (2013). Genetics of dementia. *The Lancet, 383*, 828–840. doi:10.1016/S0140-6736(13)60630-3. [5]

Ludwig, D. S., & Kabat-Zinn, J. (2008). Mindfulness in medicine. *JAMA, 300*, 1350–1352. doi:10.1001/jama.300.11.1350 [13]

Luhrmann, T. M. (2013, September 19). The violence in our heads. *The New York Times*, p. A31. [16]

Luria, A. R. (1987). *The mind of a mnemonist: A little book about a vast memory*. Cambridge: Harvard University Press. [9]

Lyamin, O. I., Manger, P. R., Ridgway, S. H., Mukhametov, L. M., & Siegel, J. M. (2008). Cetacean sleep: An unusual form of mammalian sleep. *Neuroscience & Biobehavioral Reviews, 32*, 1451–1484. [7]

Lyn, H., Greenfield, P. M., Savage-Rumbaugh, S., Gillespie-Lynch, K., & Hopkins, W. D. (2011). Nonhuman primates do declare! A comparison of declarative symbol and gesture use in two children, two bonobos, and a chimpanzee. *Language & Communication, 31*, 63–74. [10]

Lynn, R., & Vanhanen, T. (2002). *IQ and the wealth of nations*. Westport, CT: Praeger. [11]

Lynn, S. J., Lilienfeld, S. O., Merckelbac, H., Giesbrecht, T., & van der Kloet, D. (2012). Dissociation and dissociative disorders: Challenging conventional wisdom. *Current Directions in Psychological Science, 21*, 48–53. [16]

M

Maccoun, R. J. (2013). The puzzling unidimensionality of DSM-5 substance use disorder diagnoses. *Frontiers in Psychiatry, 25*, 153. [7]

MacDonald, G., & Leary, M. R. (2005). Why does social exclusion hurt? The relationship between social and physical pain. *Psychological Bulletin, 131*, 202–223. [12]

MacKenzie, M. J., Nicklas, E., Waldfogel, J., & Brooks-Gunn, J. (2013, October 21). Spanking and child development across the first decade of life. *Pediatrics, 132*, e1118–e1125. doi:10.1542/peds.2013-1227 [8]

Mackintosh, N. (2011). IQ and human intelligence (2nd ed.). Oxford, UK: Oxford University Press. [11]

Macmillan, M. (2000a). *An odd kind of fame: Stories of Phineas Gage*. Cambridge, MA: MIT Press. [14]

Macmillan, M. (2000b). Nineteenth-century inhibitory theories of thinking: Bain, Ferrier, Freud (and Phineas Gage). *History of Psychology, 3*, 187–217. [14]

Macmillan, M. (2004). Inhibition and Phineas Gage: Repression and Sigmund Freud. *Neuropsychoanalysis, 6*, 181–192. [14]

Macmillan, M. (2008). Phineas Gage – Unravelling the myth. *The Psychologist (The British Psychological Society), 21*, 828–831. [14]

Macnamara, B. N., Hambrick, D. Z., & Oswald, F. L. (2014). Deliberate practice and performance in music, games, sports, education, and professions. A meta-analysis. *Psychological Science, 25*, 1608–1618. [10]

Madrigal, A. (2008, April 28). Forget brain age: Researchers develop software that makes you smarter. *Wired*. Retrieved from http://archive.wired.com/science/discoveries/news/2008/04/smart_software [11]

Maes, M., D'Hondt, P., Martin, M., Claes, M., Schotte, C., Vandewoude, M., et al. (1991). L-5-hydroxytryptophan stimulated cortisol escape from dexamethasone suppression in melancholic patients. *Acta Physiologica Scandinavica, 83*, 302–306. [13]

Main, M., & Solomon, J. (1986). Discovery of a new, insecure-disorganized/disoriented attachment pattern. In T. B. Brazelton & M. Yogman (Eds.), *Affective development in infancy* (pp. 95–124). Norwood, NJ: Ablex. [5]

Mair, W. G. P., Warrington, E. K., & Wieskrantz, L. (1979). Memory disorder in Korsakoff's psychosis. *Brain, 102*, 749–783. [9]

Majnemer, A., & Barr, R. G. (2005). Influence of supine sleep positioning on early motor milestone acquisition. *Developmental Medicine and Child Neurology, 47*, 370–376. [5]

Maldonado, R., & Rodríguez de Fonseca, F. (2002). Cannabinoid addiction: Behavioral models and neural correlates. *Journal of Neuroscience*, *22*, 3326–3331. [7]

Malnic, B., Godfrey, P. A., & Buck, L. B. (2004). The human olfactory receptor gene family. *Proceedings of the National Academy of Sciences, USA*, *101*, 2584–2589. [6]

Mamtani, R., & Cimino, A. (2002). A primer of complementary and alternative medicine and its relevance in the treatment of mental health problems. *Psychiatric Quarterly*, *73*, 367–381. [7]

Manev, H., Uz, T., Smalheiser, N. R., & Manev, R. (2001). Antidepressants alter cell proliferation in the adult brain in vivo and in neural cultures in vitro. *European Journal of Pharmacology*, *411*(1-2): 67–70. [13]

Manning, R., Levine, M., & Collins, A. (2007). The Kitty Genovese murder and the social psychology of helping: The parable of the 38 witnesses. *American Psychologist*, *62*, 555–562. [15]

Mannuzza, S., Klein, R. G., & Moulton, J. L., III. (2008). Lifetime criminality among boys with attention deficit hyperactivity disorder: A prospective follow-up study into adulthood using official arrest records. *Psychiatry Research*, *160*, 237–246. [5]

Manz, C. C., & Neck, C. P. (1995). Teamthink: Beyond the groupthink syndrome in self-managing work teams. *Journal of Managerial Psychology*, *10*, 7–15. [15]

Marcel, A. J. (1983). Conscious and unconscious perception: An approach to the relations between phenomenal experience and perceptual processes. *Cognitive Psychology*, *15*, 238–300. [10]

March, J., Silva, S., Petrychi, S., Curry, J., Wells, K., Fairbank, J., et al. (2004). Fluoxetine, cognitive-behavioral therapy, and their combination for adolescents with depression: Treatment for adolescents with depression study (TADS) randomized controlled trial. *Journal of the American Medical Association*, *292*, 807–820. [16]

Marchione, M. (2007, April 5). Disease underlies Hatfield-McCoy feud. *The Washington Post*. Retrieved from http://www.washingtonpost.com/wp-dyn/content/article/2007/04/05/AR2007040501135.html [4]

Marcus, G. (2009, March 23). Total recall: The woman who can't forget. *Wired Magazine*, *17*. Available from http://archive.wired.com/wired/issue/17-04 [9]

Marcus, G. F., Vijayan, S., Bandi Rao, S., & Vishton, P. M. (1999). Rule learning by seven-month-old infants. *Science*, *283*, 77–80. [10]

Marler, P. (1970). Birdsong and speech development: Could there be parallels? *American Scientist*, *58*, 669–673. [10]

Marler, P., & Slabbekoorn, H. (2004). *Nature's Music: The Science of Birdsong*. San Diego: Elsevier Academic Press. [8]

Marmot, M. G., Rose, G., Shipley, M., & Hamilton, P. J. (1978). Employment grade and coronary heart disease in British civil servants. *Journal of Epidemiology and Community Health*, *32*, 244–249. [13]

Marsicano, G., Goodenough, S., Monory, K., Hermann, H., Eder, M., Cannich, A., et al. (2003). CB1 cannabinoid receptors and on-demand defense against excitotoxicity. *Science*, *302*, 84–88. [7]

Martin, L. (1986) Eskimo words for snow: A case study in the genesis and decay of an anthropological example. *American Anthropologist*, *88*, 418–423. [10]

Martuza, R. L., Chiocca, E. A., Jenike, M. A., Giriunas, I. E., & Ballantine, H. T. (1990). Stereotactic radiofrequency thermal cingulotomy for obsessive compulsive disorder. *Journal of Neuropsychiatry and Clinical Neurosciences*, *2*, 331–336. [16]

Marucha, P. T., Kiecolt-Glaser, J. K., & Favagehi, M. (1998). Mucosal wound healing is impaired by examination stress. *Psychosomatic Medicine*, *60*, 362–365. [13]

Maslow, A. H. (1943). A theory of human motivation. *Psychological Review*, *50*, 370–396. [12]

Mast, F. W., Preuss, N., Hartmann, M., & Grabherr, L. (2014). Spatial cognition, body representation and affective processes: The role of vestibular information beyond ocular reflexes and control of posture. *Frontiers in Integrative Neuroscience*, *8*, 44. Retreived from http://www.ncbi.nlm.nih.gov/pmc/articles/PMC4035009/ [6]

Masters, W. H., & Johnson, V. E. (1966). *Human sexual response*. Boston: Little, Brown. [12]

Matsuda, Y. T., Okanoya, K., & Myowa-Yamakoshi, M. (2013). Shyness in early infancy: Approach-avoidance conflicts in temperament and hypersensitivity to eyes during initial gazes to faces. *PLoS ONE*, *8*(6), e65476. doi:10.1371/journal.pone.0065476. [5]

Mattes, R. D. (1994). Prevention of food aversions in cancer patients during treatment. *Nutrition and Cancer*, *21*, 13–24. [8]

Mattson, S. N., Riley, E. P., Gramling, L., Delis, D. C., & Jones, K. L. (1998). Neuropsychological comparison of alcohol-exposed children with or without physical features of fetal alcohol syndrome. *Neuropsychology*, *12*, 146–153. [13]

Maxwell, J. C., & Brecht, M. L. (2011). Methamphetamine: Here we go again? *Addictive Behaviors*, *36*, 1168–1173. [7]

Mayer, J. D., Roberts, R. D., & Barsade, S. G. (2008). Human abilities: Emotional intelligence. *Annual Review of Psychology*, *59*, 507–536. [11]

Mayes, R., Bagwell, C., & Erkulwater, J. (2008). ADHD and the rise in stimulant use among children. *Harvard Review of Psychiatry*, *16*, 151–166. [5]

Maynard Smith, J. (1982). *Evolution and the theory of games*. United Kingdom: Cambridge University Press. [15]

Mayo, E. (1933). *The human problems of an industrial civilization*. New York: Macmillan. [12]

Mazur, A., & Booth, A. (1998). Testosterone and dominance in men. *Behavioral and Brain Sciences*, *21*, 353–363. [15]

McCall, C., & Singer, T. (2012). The animal and human neuroendocrinology of social cognition, motivation and behavior. *Nature Neuroscience*, *15*, 681–688. [15]

McCall, W. V., & Edinger, J. D. (1992). Subjective total insomnia: An example of sleep state misperception. *Sleep*, *15*, 71–73. [7]

McClelland, D. C., Atkinson, J. W., Clark, R. A., & Lowell, E. L. (1953). *The achievement motive*. Princeton, NJ: Van Nostrand. [12]

McClure, S. M., Li, J., Tomlin, D., Cypert, K. S., Montague, L. M., & Montague, P. R. (2004). Neural correlates of behavioral preference for culturally familiar drinks. *Neuron*, *44*, 379–387. [2]

McCormick, Z., Chang-Chien, G., Marshall, B., Huang, M., & Harden, R. N. (2013). Phantom limb pain: A systematic neuroanatomical-based review of pharmacologic treatment. *Pain Medicine*, *15*, 292–305. doi:10.1111/pme.12283. [6]

McCrae, C. S., Rowe, M. A., Tierney, C. G., Dautovich, N. D., Definis, A. L., & McNamara, J. P. (2005). Sleep complaints, subjective and objective sleep patterns, health, psychological adjustment, and daytime functioning in community-dwelling older adults. *Journals of Gerontology. Series B, Psychological Sciences and Social Sciences*, *60*, 182–189. [7]

McCrae, R. R. (1996). Social consequences of experiential openness. *Psychological Bulletin*, *120*, 323–337. [14]

McCrae, R. R., Costa, P. T., Jr., del Pilar, G. H., Rolland, J. P., & Parker, W. D. (1998). Cross-cultural assessment of the five-factor model: The revised NEO personality inventory. *Journal of Cross-Cultural Psychology*, *29*, 171–188. [14]

McCrae, R. R., Costa, P. T., Jr., Ostendorf, F., Angleitner, A., Hřebíčková, M., Avia, M. D., et al. (2000). Nature over nurture: Temperament, personality, and life span development. *Journal of Personality and Social Psychology*, *78*, 173. [14]

McGowan, P. O., Sasaki, A., D'Alessio, A. C., Dymov, S., Labonté, B., Szyf, M., et al. (2009). Epigenetic regulation of the glucocorticoid receptor in human brain associates with childhood abuse. *Nature Neuroscience*, *12*, 342–348. [4, 13]

McGuigan, F. J., & Lehrer, P. M. (2007). Progressive relaxation: Origins, principles and clinical application. In P. M. Lehrer, R. L. Woolfolk & W. E. Sime (Eds.), *Principles and Practices of Stress Management* (pp. 57–87). New York: Guilford Press. [13]

McGuire, P. A. (2000). New hope for people with schizophrenia. *Monitor on Psychology*, *31*, *24*. Retrieved from http://www.apa.org/monitor/feb00/schizophrenia.aspx [16]

McLaughlin, S. K., McKinnon, P. J., Spickofsky, N., Danho, W., & Margolskee, R. F. (1994). Molecular cloning of G proteins and phosphodiesterases from rat taste cells. *Physiology & Behavior*, *56*, 1157–1164. [6]

McLay, R. N., Daylo, A. A., & Hammer, P. S. (2006). No effect of lunar cycle on psychiatric admissions or emergency evaluations. *Military Medicine*, *171*, 1239–1242. [10]

McMahon, E., Wintermark, P., & Lahav, A. (2012). Auditory brain development in premature infants: The importance of early experience. *Annals of the New York Academy of Sciences*, *1252*, 17–24. [5]

McNally, R. J. (2003). Recovering memories of trauma: A view from the laboratory. *Current Directions in Psychological Science*, *12*, 32–35. [9]

Meddis, R. (1977). *The sleep instinct.* London: Routledge & Kegan Paul. [7]

Meffert, H., Gazzola, V., den Boer, J. A., Bartels, A. A., & Keysers, C. (2013). Reduced spontaneous but relatively normal deliberate vicarious representations in psychopathy. *Brain*, *136*, 2550–2562. [16]

Meguerditchian, A., & Vauclair, J. (2006). Baboons communicate with their right hand. *Behavioural Brain Research*, *171*, 170–174. [10]

Mehl, M. R., Vazire, S., Ramírez-Esparza, N., Slatcher, R. B., & Pennebaker, J. W. (2007). Are women really more talkative than men? *Science*, *317*, 82. [10]

Mekemson, C., & Glantz, S. A. (2002). How the tobacco industry built its relationship with Hollywood. *Tobacco Control*, *11*, 81–91. doi:10.1136/tc.11.suppl_1.i81 [10]

Meng, H., Smith, S. D., Hager, K., Held, M., Liu, J., Olson, R. K., et al. (2005). DCDC2 is associated with reading disability and modulates neuronal development in the brain. *Proceedings of the National Academy of Sciences, USA*, *102*, 17053–17058. [10]

Mennella, J. A. (2008). The sweet taste of childhood. In A. I. Basbaum, A. Kaneko, G. M. Shepherd, & G. Westheimer (Eds.), *The senses: A comprehensive reference: Vol. 4. Olfaction and taste* (pp. 183–188). San Diego: Academic Press. [6]

Mennella, J. A., Pepino, M. Y., Duke, F. F., & Reed, D. R. (2010) Age modifies the genotype-phenotype relationship for the bitter receptor TAS2R38. *BMC Genetics*, *11*, 60. doi:10.1186/1471-2156-11-60. [6]

Merikle, P. M., & Daneman, M. (1996). Memory for unconsciously perceived events: Evidence from anesthetized patients. *Consciousness and Cognition*, *5*, 525–541. [10]

Merritt, J. O. (1979). None in a million: Results of mass screening for eidetic ability. *Behavioral and Brain Sciences*, *2*, p. 612. [9]

Merritt, R., & Brown, B. (2002). *No easy answers: The truth behind death at Columbine.* New York: Lantern Books. [15]

Messias, E., Kirkpatrick, B., Bromet, E., Ross, D., Buchanan, R. W., Carpenter, W. T., Jr., et al. (2004). Summer birth and deficit schizophrenia: A pooled analysis from 6 countries. *Archives of General Psychiatry*, *61*, 985–989. [16]

Meyer-Bahlburg, H. F., Dolezal, C., Baker, S. W., Ehrhardt, A. A., & New, M. I. (2006). Gender development in women with congenital adrenal hyperplasia as a function of disorder severity. *Archives of Sexual Behavior, 35*, 667–684. [12]

Michael, N., & Erfurth, A. (2004). Treatment of bipolar mania with right prefrontal rapid transcranial magnetic stimulation. *Journal of Affective Disorders*, *78*, 253–257. [16]

Michaels, J. W., Blommel, J. M, Brocato, R. M., Linkous, R. A., & Rowe, J. S. (1982). Social facilitation and inhibition in a natural setting. *Replications in Social Psychology*, *2*, 21–24 [15]

Michel, J. B., Shen, Y. K., Aiden, A. P., Veres, A., Gray, M. K., Google Books Team, et al. (2011). Quantitative analysis of culture using millions of digitized books. *Science*, *331*, 176–182. [10]

Middlebrooks, J. S., & Audage, N. C. (2008). *The effects of childhood stress on health across the lifespan.* Atlanta, GA: Centers for Disease Control and Prevention, National Center for Injury Prevention and Control. [13]

Miles, L. E., & Dement, W. C. (1980). Sleep and aging. *Sleep*, *3*, 1220. [7]

Milgram, S. (1963). Behavioral study of obedience. *Journal of Abnormal and Social Psychology*, *67*, 371–378. [15]

Milgram, S. (1974). *Obedience to authority: An experimental view.* New York: Harper Collins. [15]

Milkman, K. L., Akinola, M., & Chugh, D. (2014, July 11). *What happens before? A field experiment exploring how pay and representation differentially shape bias on the pathway into organizations* (Retrieved from http://ssrn.com/abstract=2063742). New York: Social Science Research Network. [2]

Miller, D. T., & Ross, M. (1975). Sell-serving biases in the attribution of causality: Fact or fiction? *Psychological Bulletin*, *82*, 213–225. [15]

Miller, G. A. (1956). The magical number seven, plus or minus two: Some limits on our capacity for processing information. *Psychological Review*, *63*, 81–97. Retrieved from http://psychclassics.yorku.ca/Miller/ [1, 9]

Miller, G. A. (2003). The cognitive revolution: A historical perspective. *Trends in Cognitive Sciences*, *7*, 141–144. [1]

Miller, T. Q., Smith, T. W., Turner, C. W., Guijarro, M. L., & Hallet, A. J. (1996). A meta-analytic review of research of hostility and physical health. *Psychological Bulletin*, *119*, 322–348. [14]

Milner, B. (1965). Memory disturbance after bilateral hippocampal lesions. In P. M. Milner & S. E. Glickman (Eds.), *Cognitive processes and the brain; an enduring problem in psychology* (pp. 97–111). Princeton, NJ: Van Nostrand. [9]

Milner, B. (1970). Memory and the medial temporal regions of the brain. In D. H. Pribram & D. E. Broadbent (Eds.), *Biology of memory* (pp. 29–50). New York: Academic Press. [9]

Mirescu, C., Peters, J. D., & Gould, E. (2004). Early life experience alters response of adult neurogenesis to stress. *Nature Neuroscience*, *7*, 841–846. [13]

Mirsky, A. F., Bieliauskas, L. A., French, L. M., Van Kammen, D. P., Jönsson, E., & Sedvall, G. (2000). A 39-year followup of the Genain quadruplets. *Schizophrenia Bulletin*, *26*, 699–708. [4]

Mischel, W. (1968). *Personality and assessment*. New York: Wiley. [14]

Mischel, W., & Shoda, Y. (1999). Integrating dispositions and processing dynamics within a unified theory of personality: The cognitive affective personality system (CAPS). In L. A. Pervin & O. John (Eds.), *Handbook of personality: Theory and research* (2nd ed., pp. 197–218). New York: Guilford. [14]

Mitford, J. (1963). *The American way of death*. New York: Buccaneer Books. [15]

Miura, I. T., Okamoto, Y., Kim, C. C., Steere, M., & Fayol, M. (1993). First graders' cognitive representation of number and understanding of place value: Cross-national comparisons—France, Japan, Korea, Sweden and the United States. *Journal of Educational Psychology*, *85*, 24–30. [10]

Miyawaki, Y., Uchida, H., Yamashita, O., Sato, M. A., Morito, Y., Tanabe, H. C., et al. (2008). Visual image reconstruction from human brain activity using a combination of multiscale local image decoders. *Neuron*, *60*, 915–929. [7]

Møller, A. P., & Swaddle, J. P. (1998). *Asymmetry, developmental stability, and evolution*. New York: Oxford University Press. [15]

Monks, T. J., Jones, D. C., Bai, F., & Lau, S. S. (2004). The role of metabolism in 3,4-(+)-methylenedioxyamphetamine and 3,4-(+)-methylenedioxymethamphetamine (ecstasy) toxicity. *Therapeutic Drug Monitoring*, *26*, 132–136. [7]

Montag, C., Reuter, M., Jurkiewicz, M., Markett, S., & Panksepp, J. (2013). Imaging the structure of the human anxious brain: a review of findings from neuroscientific personality psychology. *Reviews in the Neurosciences*, *24*, 167–190. doi:10.1515/revneuro-2012-0085. [13]

Montague, C. T., Farooqi, I. S., Whitehead, J. P., Soos, M. A., Rau, H., Wareham, N. J., et al. (1997). Congenital leptin deficiency is associated with severe early-onset obesity in humans. *Nature*, *387*, 903–908. [12]

Moorcroft, W. H. (2013). *Understanding sleep and dreaming*. Boston: Springer. [7]

Moore, D. S. (1993). *The basic practice of statistics telecourse study guide*. San Francisco: Freeman. [2]

Moore, G. J., Bebchuk, J. M., Wilds, I. B., Chen, G., & Manji, H. K. (2000). Lithium-induced increase in human brain grey matter. *Lancet*, *356*, 241–242. [16]

Moore, M. M. (1985). Nonverbal courtship patterns in women: Context and consequences. *Ethology and Sociobiology*, *64*, 237–247. [2]

Moore, R. (1985). *A sympathetic history of Jonestown*. Lewiston, NY: Edwin Mellen Press. [15]

Moorhead, T. W., McKirdy, J., Sussmann, J. E., Hall, J., Lawrie, S. M., Johnstone, E. C., et al. (2007). Progressive gray matter loss in patients with bipolar disorder. *Biological Psychiatry*, *62*, 894–900. [16]

Moran, J. M. (2013). Lifespan development: The effects of typical aging on theory of mind. *Behavioural Brain Research*, 237, 32–40. [5]

Moreno, F. A., Wiegand, C. B., Taitano, E. K., & Delgado, P. L. (2006). Safety, tolerability, and efficacy of psilocybin in 9 patients with obsessive-compulsive disorder. *Journal of Clinical Psychiatry*, *67*, 1735–1740. [7]

Mori, K., & Mori, H. (2009). Another test of the passive facial feedback hypothesis: When your face smiles, you feel happy. *Perceptual and Motor Skills*, *109*, 76–78. [13]

Morris, B. (2002, May 13). Overcoming dyslexia. *Fortune*, *145*(10), 1–7. [10]

Morris, D. H., Jones, M. E., Schoemaker, M. J., Ashworth, A., & Swerdlow, A. J. (2010). Determinants of age at menarche in the UK: Analyses from the breakthrough generations study. *British Journal of Cancer*, *103*, 1760–1764. [5]

Morrison, A. P., French, P., Walford, L., Lewis, S. W., Kilcommons, A., Green, J., et al. (2004). Cognitive therapy for the prevention of psychosis in people at ultra-high risk: Randomised controlled trial. *British Journal of Psychiatry*, *185*, 291–297. [16]

Morrison, A. R. (1983). A window on the sleeping brain. *Scientific American*, *248*(4), 94–102. [7]

Mortensen, P. B., Pedersen, C. B., Westergaard, T., Wohlfahrt, J., Ewald, H., Mors, O., et al. (1999). Effects of family history and place and season of birth on the risk of schizophrenia. *New England Journal of Medicine*, *340*, 603–608. [16]

Moser, E., & Moser, M. B. (2014). Mapping your every move. *Cerebrum*, *2014*, 4. [8]

Moskowitz, T. J., & Wertheim, L. J. (2011). *Scorecasting: The hidden influences behind how sports are played and games are won*. New York: Crown Archetype. [10]

Moss-Racusin, C. A., Dovidio, J. F., Brescoll, W. L., Graham, M. J., & Handelsman, J. (2012). Science faculty's subtle gender biases favor male students. *Proceedings of the National Academy of Sciences, USA*, *109*, 16474–16479. [2]

Mukamal, K. J., Conigrave, K. M., Mittleman, M. A., Camargo, C. A., Jr., Stampfer, M. J., Willett, W. C., et al. (2003). Roles of drinking pattern and type of alcohol consumed in coronary heart disease in men. *New England Journal of Medicine*, *348*, 109–118. [7]

Mukhametov, L. M. (1984). Sleep in marine mammals. In A. Borbely and J. L. Valatx (Eds.), *Experimental Brain Research series: Suppl. 8. Sleep mechanisms (pp. 227–238).* Berlin: Springer. [7]

Müller, J. (1843). *Elements of physiology*. Philadelphia: Lea and Blanchard. [6]

Mumby, D. G., Gaskin, S., Glenn, M. J., Schramek, T. E., & Lehmann, H. (2002). Hippocampal damage and exploratory preferences in rats: Memory for objects, places and contexts. *Learning & Memory*, *9*, 49–57. [9]

Münsterberg, H. (1893). Psychological laboratory of Harvard University. [A catalogue of equipment and readings, prepared for the World's Columbian Exposition in Chicago.] http://psychclassics.yorku.ca/Munster/Lab/[1]

Mura, G., Moro, M. F., Patten, S. B., & Carta, M. G. (2014). Exercise as an add-on strategy for the treatment of major depressive disorder: A systematic review. *CNS Spectrums*, *3*, 1–13. [16]

Murray, C. (2007). The magnitude and components of change in the black–white IQ difference from 1920 to 1991: A birth cohort analysis of the Woodcock–Johnson standardizations. *Intelligence*, *35*, 305–318. [11]

Murray, E. A., & Wise, S. P. (2012). Why is there a special issue on perirhinal cortex in a journal called hippocampus? The perirhinal cortex in historical perspective. *Hippocampus*, *22*, 1941–1951. [9]

Murray, L., de Rosnay, M., Pearson, J., Bergeron, C., Schofield, E., Royal-Lawson, M., et al. (2008). Intergenerational transmission of social anxiety: The role of social referencing processes in infancy. *Child Development, 79*, 1049–1064. [5]

Murray, R. M., Morrison, P. D., Henquet, C., & Di Forti, M. (2007). *Cannabis*, the mind and society: The hash realities. *Nature Reviews. Neuroscience*, *8*, 885–895. [7]

Musick, K., & Bumpass, L. (2012). Reexamining the case for marriage: Union formation and changes in well-being. *Journal of Marriage and Family*, *74*, 1–18. [13, 15]

Myers, N. L. (2010). Culture, stress and recovery from schizophrenia: Lessons from the field for global mental health. *Culture, Medicine and Psychiatry*, *34*, 500–528. [16]

N

Nabi, H., Kivimäki, M., Batty, G. D., Shipley, M. J., Britton, A., Brunner, E. J., et al. (2013). Increased risk of coronary heart disease among individuals reporting adverse impact of stress on their health: The Whitehall II prospective cohort study. *European Heart Journal*, *34*, 2697–2705. doi:10.1093/eurheartj/eht216. [13]

Nader, K., & Hardt, O. (2009). A single standard for memory: The case for reconsolidation. *Nature Reviews. Neuroscience*, *10*, 224–234. [9]

Nash, M. (1987). What, if anything, is regressed about hypnotic age regression? A review of the empirical literature. *Psychological Bulletin*, *102*, 42–52. [7]

Nassar, M. A., Stirling, L. C., Forlani, G., Baker, M. D., Matthews, E. A., Dickenson, A. H., et al. (2004). Nociceptor-specific gene deletion reveals a major role for Nav1.7 (PN1) in acute and inflammatory pain. *Proceedings of the National Academy of Sciences, USA*, *101*, 12706–12711. [6]

Nathan, D. (2011). *Sybil exposed*. New York: Free Press. [16]

National Academy of Sciences. (2003). *The Polygraph and Lie Detection*. Washington, DC: National Academy Press. Retrieved from: http://www.nap.edu/openbook.php?isbn=0309084369. [13]

National Center for Health Statistics. (2007). *Health, United States, 2007 with chartbook on trends in the health of Americans*. Hyattsville, MD: U. S. Government Printing Office. Retrieved from http://www.cdc.gov/nchs/data/hus/hus07.pdf [12]

National Commission on Terrorist Attacks upon the United States. (2011). The 9/11 commission report: Final report of the National Commission on Terrorist Attacks upon the United States (pp. 261–262). Washington, DC: U. S. Government Printing Office. Retrieved from http://www.gpo.gov/fdsys/pkg/GPO-911REPORT/pdf/GPO-911REPORT.pdf [10]

National Heart, Lung, and Blood Institute (2010, November 9). New NIH data shows gains in COPD awareness. Retrieved from http://www.nhlbi.nih.gov/news/press-releases/2010/new-nih-data-show-gains-in-copd-awareness.html. [13]

National Institute of Mental Health. (2012). Serious mental illness (SMI) among adults. Retrieved from http://www.nimh.nih.gov/health/statistics/prevalence/serious-mental-illness-smi-among-us-adults.shtml [16]

National Institute of Mental Health. (n.d.). *Borderline personality disorder*. Retrieved from http://www.nimh.nih.gov/health/topics/borderline-personality-disorder/index.shtml. [16]

National Institutes of Health. (2014, February). *Speech and language developmental milestones* (NIH Pub. No. 13-4781). Bethesda, MD. Retrieved from http://www.nidcd.nih.gov/health/voice/Pages/speechandlanguage.aspx [10]

National Science Foundation, National Center for Science and Engineering Statistics. (2013). Table 5-13: Bachelor's degrees awarded in engineering, by sex, race/ethnicity, and citizenship: 1990–2010. In *Women, minorities, and persons with disabilities in science and engineering*. Special report NSF 13-304. Retrieved from http://www.nsf.gov/statistics/wmpd/2013/pdf/tab5-13.pdf [12]

National Science Foundation. (2012). Table 23. U.S. citizen and permanent resident doctorate recipients, by race, ethnicity, and broad field of study: Selected years, 1992–2012. Retrieved from http://www.nsf.gov/statistics/sed/2012/pdf/tab23.pdf [1]

Neck, C. P., & Moorhead, G. (1992). Jury deliberations in the trial of U.S. v. John Delorean: A case analysis of gloupthink avoidance and an enhanced framework. *Human Relations*, *45*, 1091–1099. [15]

Neisser, U. (1967). *Cognitive psychology*. Englewood Cliffs, NJ: Prentice Hall. [1]

Neisser, U. (1997). Rising scores on intelligence tests. *American Scientist*, *85*, 440–447. [11]

Neisser, U., & Hyman, I. (2000). *Memory observed: remembering in natural contexts*. New York: Worth. [9]

Neisser, U., Boodoo, G., Bouchard, T. J., Jr., Boykin, A. W., Brody, N., Ceci, S. J., et al. (1996). Intelligence: Knowns and unknowns. *American Psychologist*, *51*, 77–101. [11]

Nettle, D. (2005). An evolutionary approach to the extraversion continuum. *Evolution and Human Behavior, 26*, 363–373. [14]

Neubauer, A., & Fink, A. (2009). Intelligence and neural efficiency: Measures of brain activity versus measures of functional connectivity in the brain. *Intelligence, 37,* 223–229. [11]

Neumann, C. S., Hare, R. D., & Newman, J. P. (2007). The super-ordinate nature of the psychopathy checklist-revised. *Journal of Personality Disorders*, *21*, 102–117. [16]

New survey finds Americans care about brain health, but misperceptions abound. (2013). Retrieved from http://www.harrisinteractive.com/vault/MichaelJFoxFoundRelease_9.25.13.pdf [1]

Newman, A. J., Bavelier, D., Corina, D., Jezzard, P., & Neville, H. J. (2002). A critical period for right hemisphere recruitment in American sign language processing. *Nature Neuroscience*, *5*, 76–80. [10]

NICHD Early Child Care Research Network. (2006). Child-care effect sizes for the NICHD Study of Early Child Care and Youth Development. *The American Psychologist, 61*, 99–116. [5]

NICHD Early Child Care Research Network. (2008). Social competence with peers in third grade: Associations with earlier peer experiences in child care. *Social Development, 17*, 419–453. [5]

Nichols, M. J., & Newsome, W. T. (1999). The neurobiology of cognition. *Nature, 402*, C35–C38. [1]

Nicolaus, L. K. (1987). Conditioned aversions in a guild of egg predators: Implications for aposematism and prey defense mimicry. *The American Midland Naturalist, 117*, 405–419. [8]

Nielsen, J. A., Zielinski, B. A., Ferguson, M. A., Lainhart, J. E., & Anderson, J. S. (2013). An evaluation of the left-brain vs. right-brain hypothesis with resting state functional connectivity magnetic resonance imaging. *PLoS ONE, 8*(8), e71275. [10]

Nietzel, M. T. (2000). Police psychology. In A. E. Kazdin (Ed.), *Encyclopedia of psychology* (Vol. 6, pp. 224–226). Washington, DC: American Psychological Association. [13]

Nigg, J. T., John, O. P., Blaskey, L. G., Huang-Pollock, C. L., Willcutt, E. G., Hinshaw, S. P., et al. (2002). Big five dimensions and ADHD symptoms: Links between personality traits and clinical symptoms. *Journal of Personality and Social Psychology, 83*, 451–469. [14]

Niraj, S., & Niraj, G. (2014). Phantom limb pain and its psychologic management: A critical review. *Pain Management Nursing, 15,* 349–364. [6]

Nisbett, R. E. (2005). Heredity, environment, and race differences in IQ. *Psychology, Public Policy, and Law, 11*, 302–310. [11]

Nishida, M., & Walker, M. P. (2007). Daytime naps, motor memory consolidation and regionally specific sleep spindles. *PLoS ONE, 2*, e341. [7]

Nishimoto, S., Vu, A. T., Naselaris, T., Benjamini, Y., Yu, B., & Gallant, J. L. (2011). Reconstructing visual experiences from brain activity evoked by natural movies. *Current Biology, 21*(19), 1641–1646. [7]

Nixon, H. K. (1925). Popular answers to some psychological questions. *American Journal of Psychology, 36*, 418–423. [1]

Noad, M. J., Cato, D. H., Bryden, M. M., Jenner, M.-N., & Jenner, K. C. (2000). Cultural revolution in whale songs. *Nature, 408*, 537–538. [10]

Northcraft, G. B., & Neale, M. A. (1987). Experts, amateurs, and real estate: An anchoring-and-adjustment perspective on property pricing decisions. *Organizational Behavior and Human Decision Processes, 39*, 84–97. [10]

Nottebohm, F. (1980). Brain pathways for vocal learning in birds: A review of the first 10 years. *Progress in Psychobiology and Physiological Psychology, 9*, 85–124. [10]

Nudel, R., & Newbury, D. F. (2013). FOXP2. *Wiley Interdisciplinary Reviews: Cognitive Science, 4*, 547–560. [10]

Nuland, S. B. (2004). *The doctors' plague: Germs, childbed fever and the strange story of Ignac Semmelweis.* New York: Norton. [2]

Nunez, N., McCrea, S. M., & Culhane, S. E. (2011) Jury decision making research: Are researchers focusing on the mouse and not the elephant in the room? *Behavioral Sciences & the Law, 29*, 439–451. [15]

O

O'Connell, D. N., Shor, R. E., & Orne, T. (1970). Hypnotic age regression: An empirical and methodological analysis. *Journal of Abnormal Psychology, 76*, 1–32. [7]

O'Connor, S. C., & Rosenblood, L. K. (1996). Affiliation motivation in everyday experience: A theoretical comparison. *Journal of Personality and Social Psychology, 70*, 513–522. [12]

O'Keefe, J., & Dostrovsky, J. (1971). The hippocampus as a spatial map. Preliminary evidence from unit activity in the freely-moving rat. *Brain Research, 34*, 171–175. [8]

O'Keefe, J., Burgess, N., Donnett, J. G., Jeffery, K. J., & Maguire, E. A. (1998). Place cells, navigational accuracy, and the human hippocampus. *Philosophical Transactions of the Royal Society B: Biological Sciences, 353*, 1333–1340. [8]

O'Keefe, J. H., Bhatti, S. K., Patil, H. R., DiNicolantonio, J. J., Lucan, S. C., & Lavie, C. J. (2013). Effects of habitual coffee consumption on cardiometabolic disease, cardiovascular health, and all-cause mortality. *Journal of the American College of Cardiology, 62*, 1043–1051. [7]

Oberauer, K., & Hein, L. (2012). Attention to information in working memory. *Current Directions in Psychological Science, 21*, 164–169. [9]

Oberndorfer, T. A., Frank, G. K., Simmons, A. N., Wagner, A., McCurdy, D., Fudge, J. L., et al. (2013). Altered insula response to sweet taste processing after recovery from anorexia and bulimia nervosa. *American Journal of Psychiatry, 170*, 1143–1151. doi:10.1176/appi.ajp.2013.11111745 [12]

Oesterle, E. C. (2013). Changes in the adult vertebrate auditory sensory epithelium after trauma. *Hearing Research, 297*, 91–98. [6]

Oguz, S., Merad, S., Snape, D., & Office for National Statistics. (2013). *Measuring national well-being—What matters most to personal well-being?* Retrieved from http://www.ons.gov.uk/ons/dcp171766_312125.pdf [15]

Olatunji, B. O., Davis, M. L., Powers, M. B., & Smits, J. A. (2013). Cognitive-behavioral therapy for obsessive-compulsive disorder: A meta-analysis of treatment outcome and moderators. *Journal of Psychiatric Research, 47*, 33–41. [16]

Olds, J., & Milner, P. (1954). Positive reinforcement produced by electrical stimulation of septal area and other regions of rat brain. *Journal of Comparative and Physiological Psychology, 47*, 419–427. [7, 8, 12]

Olfson, M., Marcus, S. C., & Shaffer, D. (2006). Antidepressant drug therapy and suicide in severely depressed children and adults: A case-control study. *Archives of General Psychiatry, 63*, 865–872. [16]

Ollendick, T. H., & Davis, T. E., 3rd. (2013). One-session treatment for specific phobias: A review of Öst's single-session exposure with children and adolescents. *Cognitive Behavioral Therapy, 42*, 275–283. [16]

Olson, P. L. (1991). Driver perception response time. *Accident Reconstruction Journal, 3*, 16–21, 29. [5]

Olson, S. (2004). Making sense of Tourette's. *Science, 305*, 1390–1392. [16]

Olsson, A., & Phelps, E. A. (2007). Social learning of fear. *Nature Neuroscience, 10*, 1095–1102. [13]

Orne, M. T. (1979). The use and misuse of hypnosis in court. *International Journal of Clinical and Experimental Hypnosis, 27*, 311–341. [7]

Ospina, M. B., Bond, K., Karkhaneh, M., Tjosvold, L., Vandermeer, B., Liang, Y., et al. (2007). *Meditation practices for health: State of the research* (AHRQ Publication No. 07-E010). Rockville, MD: Agency for Healthcare Research and

Quality. Retrieved from http://archive.ahrq.gov/downloads/pub/evidence/pdf/meditation/medit.pdf [13]

Osser, D. N., Roudsari, M. J., & Manschreck, T. (2013). The psychopharmacology algorithm project at the Harvard South Shore Program: An update on schizophrenia. *Harvard Review of Psychiatry*, *21*, 18-40. [16]

Öst, L. G. (1989). One-session treatment for specific phobias. *Behavioral Research & Therapy*, *27*, 1–7. [16]

Ouattara, K., Lemasson, A., & Zuberbühler, K. (2009). Campbell's monkeys concatenate vocalizations into context-specific call sequences. *Proceedings of the National Academy of Sciences, USA*, *22*, 22026–22031. [10]

Outgoing. (2014). In *Oxford English online dictionary*. Retrieved from http://www.oed.com [14]

P

Padgett, S. (2002, July 30). Unbeaten birds: Fowl play. *Las Vegas Review-Journal*, p. 1E. [8]

Pagnoni, G. & Cekic, M. (2007). Age effects on gray matter volume and attentional performance in Zen meditation. *Neurobiology of Aging*, *28*, 1623–1627. [7]

Pakkenberg, B., Pelvig, D., Marner, L., Bundgaard, M. J., Gundersen, H. J., Nyengaard. J. R., et al. (2003) Aging and the human neocortex. *Experimental Gerontology*, *38*(1-2), 95–99. [3]

Panksepp, J. (2005). Beyond a joke: From animal laughter to human joy? *Science*, *308*, 62–63. [10]

Panksepp, J. (2007). Can PLAY diminish ADHD and facilitate the construction of the social brain? *Journal of the Canadian Academy of Child and Adolescent Psychiatry, 16,* 57–66. [5]

Paquette, G. (2004). Violence on Canadian television networks. *The Canadian Child and Adolescent Psychiatry Review*, *13*, 13–15. [15]

Park, E. W., Schultz, J. K., Tudiver, F. G, Campbell, T., & Becker, L. A. (2004). Enhancing partner support to improve smoking cessation. *Cochrane Database of Systematic Reviews*, *3*, CD002928. doi:10.1002/14651858.CD002928.pub2 [13]

Parker, E. S., Cahill, L., & McGaugh, J. L. (2006). A case of unusual autobiographical remembering. *Neurocase*, *12*, 35–49. [9]

Partlicius, S. (1654). *A new method of physick: or, A short view of Paracelsus and Galens practice; in 3 treatises*. (Culpeper, trans.). London: Peter Cole in Leaden Hall. [1]

Pashler, H. E. (1988). Familiarity and visual change detection. *Perception & Psychophysics*, *44*, 369–378. [10]

Paterson, S. J., Brown, J. H., Gsödl, M. K., Johnson, M. H., & Karmiloff-Smith, A. (1999). Cognitive modularity and genetic disorders. *Science*, *286*, 2355–2358. [10]

Patterson, D. R., & Jensen, M. P. (2003). Hypnosis and clinical pain. *Psychological Bulletin*, *129*, 495–521. [7]

Patterson, F., & Linden, E. (1981). *The education of Koko.* New York: Holt, Rinehart, and Winston. [10]

Patterson, P. H. (2007). Maternal effects on schizophrenia risk. *Science*, *318*, 576–578. [16]

Paul-Labrador, M., Polk, D., Dwyer, J. H., Velasquez, I., Nidich, S., Rainforth, M., et al. (2006). Effects of a randomized controlled trial of transcendental meditation on components of the metabolic syndrome in subjects with coronary heart disease. *Archives of Internal Medicine*, *166*, 1218–1224. [7]

Pavloff. (1923, July 23). *Time, The Weekly News-Magazine*, *1*(21), pp. 20–21. [8]

Peabody, D., & Goldberg, L. R. (1989). Some determinants of factor structures from personality-trait descriptors. *Journal of Personality and Social Psychology*, *57*, 552–567. [14]

Pedersen, C. B., & Mortensen, P. B. (2001). Evidence of a dose-response relationship between urbanicity during upbringing and schizophrenia risk. *Archives of General Psychiatry*, *58*, 1039–1046. [4, 16]

Pegna, A. J., Khateb, A., Lazeyras, F., & Seghier, M. L. (2005). Discriminating emotional faces without primary visual cortices involves the right amygdala. *Nature Neuroscience*, *8*, 24–25. [13]

Pelham, W. E., Jr., & Fabiano, G. A. (2008). Evidence-based psychosocial treatments for attention-deficit/hyperactivity disorder. *Journal of Clinical Child and Adolescent Psychology, 37,* 184–214. [5]

Pellegrini, R. J. (1977). Mate separation and emotional attachment in romantic love relationships: Does absence make the heart grow fonder? *Psychological Reports*, *41*, 1175–1178. [2]

Perner, J., Frith, U., Leslie, A., & Leekam, S. (1989). Exploration of the autistic child's theory of mind: Knowledge, belief and communication *Child Development, 60,* 689–700. [5]

Péron, F., Thornberg, L., Gross, B., Gray, S., & Pepperberg, I. M. (2014). Human–grey parrot (*Psittacus erithacus*) reciprocity: A follow-up study. *Animal Cognition*, *17*, 937–944. [10]

Peschansky, V. J., Burbridge, T. J., Volz, A. J., Fiondella, C., Wissner-Gross, Z., Galaburda, A. M., et al. (2010). The effect of variation in expression of the candidate dyslexia susceptibility gene homolog Kiaa0319 on neuronal migration and dendritic morphology in the rat. *Cerebral Cortex, 20, 884–897.* [10]

Petanjek, Z., Judaš, M., Šimic, G., Rasin, M. R., Uylings, H. B. M., Rakic, P., et al. (2011). Extraordinary neoteny of synaptic spines in the human prefrontal cortex. *Proceedings of the National Academy of Sciences, USA*, *108*, 13281–13286. [5]

Peterson, B. S., Warner, V., Bansal, R., Zhu, H., Hao X., Liu, J., et al. (2009). Cortical thinning in persons at increased familial risk for major depression. *Proceedings of the National Academy of Sciences, USA*, *106*, 6273–6278. [16]

Peterson, L. R., & Peterson, M. J. (1959). Short-term retention of individual verbal items. *Journal of Experimental Psychology*, *58*, 193–198. [9]

Peto, R., & Doll, R. (2006). The hazards of smoking and the benefits of stopping. In G. Bock & J. Goode (Eds.), *Novartis Foundation Symposium: Vol. 275. Understanding nicotine and tobacco addiction* (pp. 3–16). Chichester, UK: Wiley. [13]

Pettit, H. O., & Justice, J. B., Jr. (1991). Effect of dose on cocaine self-administration behavior and dopamine levels in the nucleus accumbens. *Brain Research*, *539*, 94–102. [7]

Pettman, T. L., Misan, G. M., Owen, K., Warren, K., Coates, A. M., Buckley, J. D., et al. (2008). Self-management for obesity and cardio-metabolic fitness: Description and evaluation of the lifestyle intervention program of a randomised controlled trial. *International Journal of Behavioral Nutrition and Physical Activity*, *5*, 53. [12]

Pew Center on the States. (2008, February). *One in 100: Behind bars in America 2008*. Washington, DC: Pew Charitable Trusts. [7]

Pew Research Center (2011, May 16). *Is college worth it?* (Retrieved from http://www.pewsocialtrends.org/files/2011/05/higher-ed-report.pdf). Washington, DC: Cohn, D. [2]

Pew Research Center (2013, June 4). *The global divide on homosexuality: Greater acceptance in more secular and affluent countries*. (Retrieved from http://www.pewglobal.org/2013/06/04/the-global-divide-on-homosexuality/) Washington, DC. [2]

Pfefferbaum, A., Sullivan, E. V., Mathalon, D. H., Shear, P. K., Rosenbloom, M. J., & Lim, K. O. (1995). Longitudinal changes in magnetic resonance imaging brain volumes in abstinent and relapsed alcoholics. *Alcoholism: Clinical and Experimental Research*, *19*, 1177–1191. [7]

Pfungst, O. (1911). *Clever Hans (The horse of Mr. von Osten): A contribution to experimental animal and human psychology* (Trans. C. L. Rahn). New York: Henry Holt. (Original work published 1907). Retrieved from http://www.gutenberg.org/files/33936/33936-h/33936-h.htm [2]

Phillips, M. L., Young, A. W., Scott, S. K., Calder, A. J., Andrew, C., Giampietro, V., et al. (1998). Neural responses to facial and vocal expressions of fear and disgust. *Proceedings of the Royal Society of London. Series B: Biological Sciences*, *265*, 1809–1817. [13]

Phoenix, C. J., Goy, R. W., Gerall, A. A., & Young, W. C. (1959). Organizing action of prenatally administered testosterone propionate on the tissues mediating mating behavior in the female guinea pig. *Endocrinology, 65*, 369–382. [12]

Piaget, J. (1954). *The construction of reality in the child* (M. Cook, Trans.). New York: Ballantine. (Original work published 1937) [5]

Pinker, S. (1994). *The language instinct.* New York: Morrow. [10]

Pitman, R. K., Sanders, K. M., Zusman, R. M., Healy, A. R., Cheema, F., Lasko, N. B, et al. (2002). Pilot study of secondary prevention of posttraumatic stress disorder with propranolol. *Biological Psychiatry*, *51*, 189–192. [9]

Pittenger, D. J. (1993). Measuring the MBTI...And coming up short. *Journal of Career Planning & Employment*, *54*, 48–52. [14]

Pittler, M. H., & Ernst, E. (2005). Complementary therapies for reducing body weight: A systematic review. *International Journal of Obesity*, *29*, 1030–1038. [7]

Platt, J. R. (1964). Strong inference. *Science*, *146*, 347–353. [2]

Pletnikov, M. V., Ayhan, Y., Nikolskaia, O., Xu, Y., Ovanesov, M. V., Huang, H., et al. (2008). Inducible expression of mutant human DISC1 in mice is associated with brain and behavioral abnormalities reminiscent of schizophrenia. *Molecular Psychiatry*, *13*, 13–186. [16]

Plous, S. (1993). *The psychology of judgment and decision making*. New York: McGraw-Hill. [10]

Plutchik, R. (1994). *The psychology and biology of emotion.* New York: HarperCollins. [13]

Polosa, R., & Benowitz, N. L. (2011). Treatment of nicotine addiction: Present therapeutic options and pipeline developments. *Trends in Pharmacological Sciences*, *32*, 281–289. [13]

Poole, J. H., Tyack, P. L., Stoeger-Horwath, A. S., & Watwood, S. (2005). Animal behaviour: Elephants are capable of vocal learning. *Nature*, *434*, 455–456. [10]

Pope, H. G., Kouri, E. M., & Hudson, J. I. (2000). Effects of supraphysiologic doses of testosterone on mood and aggression in normal men. *Archives of General Psychiatry*, *57*, 133–140. [15]

Popper, K. R. (1959). *The logic of scientific discovery.* London: Hutchinson. [2]

Portenoy, R. K., Jarden, J. O., Sidtis, J. J., Lipton, R. B., Foley, K. M., & Rottenberg, D. A. (1986). Compulsive thalamic self-stimulation: A case with metabolic, electrophysiologic and behavioral correlates. *Pain, 27*, 277–290. [12]

Posner, M. I. (1978). *Chronometric explorations of mind.* Hillsdale, NJ: Erlbaum, 1978. [10]

Posner, M. I. (2005). Timing the brain: Mental chronometry as a tool in neuroscience. *PLoS Biology*, *3*, e51. [10]

Powell, R. A., Digdon, N., Harris, B., & Smithson, C. (2014). Correcting the record on Watson, Rayner, and Little Albert: Albert Barger as "psychology's lost boy." *American Psychologist*, *69*, 600–611. [8]

Powell, S. B. (2010). Models of neurodevelopmental abnormalities in schizophrenia. *Current Topics in Behavioral Neurosciences*, *4*, 435–481. [16]

Pratkanis, A. R. (1992). The cargo-cult science of subliminal persuasion. *Skeptical Inquirer*, *16.3*, 260–272. Retrieved from http://www.csicop.org/si/show/cargo-cult_science_of_subliminal_persuasion/ [10]

Pratkanis, A., Eskenazi, J., & Greenwald, A. (1994). What you expect is what you believe (but not necessarily what you get): A test of the effectiveness of subliminal self-help audiotapes. *Basic and Applied Social Psychology*, *15*, 251–276. [10]

Premack, D. (1971). Language in a chimpanzee? *Science*, *172*, 808–822. [10]

Press, C., Catmur, C., Cook, R., Widmann, H., Heyes, C., & Bird, G. (2012). FMRI evidence of 'mirror' responses to geometric shapes. *PLoS ONE*, *7*(*12*), e51934. [3]

Price, J., & Davis, B. (2008). *The woman who can't forget*. Free Press: New York. [9]

Price, J., Kerr, R., Hicks, M., & Nixon, P. F. (1987). The Wernicke-Korsakoff syndrome: A reappraisal in Queensland with special reference to prevention. *Medical Journal of Australia*, *147*, 561–565. [9]

Principe, C. P., & Langlois, J. H. (2013). Children and adults use attractiveness as a social cue in real people and avatars. *Journal of Experimental Child Psychology*, *115*, 590–597. [15]

PRO-ED Inc. (1999). Speech and language milestone chart. Retrieved from http://www.ldonline.org/article/6313 [10]

Proal, A. C., Fleming, J., Galvez-Buccollini, J. A., & DeLisi, L. E. (2014). A controlled family study of *Cannabis* users with and without psychosis. *Schizophrenia Research*, *152*, 283–288. [7]

Proulx, C. M., & Snyder-Rivas, L. A. (2013). The longitudinal associations between marital happiness, problems, and self-rated health. *Journal of Family Psychology*, *27*, 194–202. [15]

Provine, R. R. (2005). Yawning. *American Scientist*, *93*(6), 532–540. [13]

Provine, R. R., Tate, B. C., & Geldmacher, L. L. (1987). Yawning: No effect of 3-5% CO_2, 100% O_2, and exercise. *Behavioral and Neural Biology*, *48*, 382–392. [13]

Pruett, D., Waterman, E. H., & Caughey, A. B. (2013). Fetal alcohol exposure: Consequences, diagnosis, and treatment. *Obstetrical & Gynecological Survey, 68*, 62–69. [5]

Prunier, G. (1999). *The Rwanda crisis: History of a genocide* (2nd ed.). Kampala, Uganda: Fountain. [15]

Pugh, K. R., Mencl, W. E., Shaywitz, B. A., Shaywitz, S. E., Fulbright, R. K., Constable, R. T., et al. (2000). The angular gyrus in developmental dyslexia: Task-specific differences in functional connectivity within posterior cortex. *Psychological Science*, *11*, 51–56. [10]

Pullum, G. (1991). *The great Eskimo vocabulary hoax*. Chicago: University of Chicago Press. [10]

Purves, D., & Lotto, R. B. (2010). *Why we see what we do redux: A wholly empirical theory of vision*. Sunderland, MA: Sinauer. [6]

Puts, D. A., Apicella, C. L., & Cárdenas, R. A. (2012). Masculine voices signal men's threat potential in forager and industrial societies. *Proceedings of the Royal Society of London. Series B: Biological Sciences*, *279*, 601–609. [2]

Q

Qian, M., Wang, D., Watkins, W. E., Gebski, V., Yan, Y. Q., Li, M. et al. (2005). The effects of iodine on intelligence in children: A meta-analysis of studies conducted in China. *Asia Pacific Journal of Clinical Nutrition*, *14*, 32–42. [11]

Quignon, P., Giraud, M., Rimbault, M., Lavigne, P., Tacher, S., Morin, E., et al. (2005). The dog and rat olfactory receptor repertoires. *Genome Biology*, *6*, R83. [6]

Quoidbach, J., Dunn, E. W., Petrides, K. V., & Mikolajczak, M. (2010). Money giveth, money taketh away: The dual effect of wealth on happiness. *Psychological Science*, *21*, 759–763. [13]

R

Raine, A., Venables, P. H., Dalais, C., Mellingen, K., Reynolds, C., & Mednick, S. A. (2001). Early educational and health enrichment at age 3–5 years is associated with increased autonomic and central nervous system arousal and orienting at age 11 years: Evidence from the Mauritius Child Health Project. *Psychophysiology*, *38*, 254–266. [9]

Rainville, P., Duncan, G. H., Price, D. D., Carrier, B., & Bushnell, M. C. (1997). Pain affect encoded in human anterior cingulate but not somatosensory cortex. *Science*, *277*, 968–71. [7]

Ramachandran, V. S., & Hubbard, E. M. (2001). Synaesthesia—A window into perception, thought and language. *Journal of Consciousness Studies*, *8*, 3–34. [7]

Ramachandran, V. S., & Rogers-Ramachandran, D. (1996). Synaesthesia in phantom limbs induced with mirrors. *Proceedings of the Royal Society of London. Series B: Biological Sciences*, *263*, 377–286. [6]

Ramachandran, V. S., & Rogers-Ramachandran, D. (2000). Phantom limbs and neural plasticity. *Archives of Neurology*, *57*, 317–320. [6]

Ramchandani, P. (2004). A question of balance: How safe are the medicines that are prescribed to children? *Nature*, *430*, 401–402. [16]

Ramey, C. T., & Ramey, S. L. (1998). Prevention of intellectual disabilities: Early interventions to improve cognitive development. *Preventative Medicine*, *27*, 224–232. [11]

Rampon, C., & Tsien, J. Z. (2000). Genetic analysis of learning behavior-induced structural plasticity. *Hippocampus*, *10*, 605–609. [9]

Ramus, F., Hauser, M. D., Miller, C., Morris, D., & Mehler, J. (2000). Language discrimination by human newborns and by cotton-top tamarin monkeys. *Science*, *288*, 349–351. [10]

Rasmussen, T., & Milner, B. (1975). Clinical and surgical studies of the cerebral speech areas in man. In: K. J. Zulch, O. Creutzfeldt, & G. C. Galbraith (Eds.), *Cerebral localization* (pp. 238–255). New York: Springer. [10]

Rauscher, F. H., Shaw, G. L., & Ky, K. N. (1993). Music and spatial task performance. *Nature*, *365*, 611. [11]

Ravenscroft, I. (2010). *Folk psychology as a theory*. Retrieved from Stanford University, Encyclopedia of Philosophy's Web site: http://plato.stanford.edu/entries/folkpsych-theory/ [2]

Raymond, J. E., Shapiro, K. L., & Arnell, K. M. (1992). Temporary suppression of visual processing in an RSVP task: An attentional blink? *Journal of Experimental Psychology: Human Perception & Performance*, *18*, 849–860. [10]

Recht, L. D., Lew, R. A., & Schwartz, W. J. (1995). Baseball teams beaten by jet lag. *Nature*, *377*, 583. [7]

Reder, L. M., Oates, J. M., Dickison, D., Anderson, J. R., Gyula, F., Quinlan, J. J. et al. (2007). Retrograde facilitation under midazolam: The role of general and specific interference. *Psychonomic Bulletin & Review*, *14*, 261–269. [9]

Redick, T. S., Shipstead, Z., Harrison, T. L., Hicks, K. L., Fried, D. E., Hambrick, D. Z., et al. (2013). No evidence of intelligence improvement after working memory training: A randomized, placebo-controlled study. *Journal of Experimental Psychology: General*, *142*, 359–379. [11]

Renner, J., Stafford, D., Lawson, A., McKinnon, J., Friot, E., Kellogg, D., et al. (1976). *Research, teaching, and learning with the Piaget model*. Norman, OK: University of Oklahoma Press. [5]

Renner, M. J., & Macklin, R. S. (1998). CUSS: A life stress instrument for classroom use. *Teaching of Psychology*, *25*, 46–48. [13]

Renner, M. J., & Rosenzweig, M. R. (1987). *Enriched and impoverished environments: Effects on brain and behavior*. New York: Springer. [9]

Rescorla, R. A. (1968). Probability of shock in the presence and absence of CS in fear conditioning. *Journal of Comparative and Physiological Psychology*, *66*, 1–5. [8]

Resnik, D., & Bond, C. (2007). Use of 'subjects' should not be subjective. *Association for Psychological Science, Observer*, *20*(5), 4. [2]

Reyna, V. F., & Brainerd, C. J. (2011). Dual processes in decision making and developmental neuroscience: A fuzzy-trace model. *Developmental Review, 31*(2–3), 180–206. [5]

Rhee, S. H., & Waldman, I. D. (2002). Genetic and environmental influences on antisocial behavior: A meta-analysis of twin and adoption studies. *Psychological Bulletin*, *128*, 490-529. [15]

Ringelmann, M. (1913). Recherches sur les moteurs animés: Travail de l'homme [Research on animate sources of power: The work of man]. *Annales de l'Institut National Agronomique 2nd series*, *12*, 1–40. [15]

Rinomhota, A. S., Bulugahapitiya, D. U., French, S. J., Caddy, C. M., Griffiths, R. W., & Ross, R. J. (2008). Women gain weight and fat mass despite lipectomy at abdominoplasty and breast reduction. *European Journal of Endocrinology*, *158*, 349–352. [12]

Risch, N., Herrell, R., Lehner, T., Liang, K.-Y., Eaves, L., Hoh, J., et al. (2009). Interaction between the serotonin transporter gene (5-HTTLPR), stressful life events, and risk of depression: A meta-analysis. *JAMA*, *301*, 2462–2471. [16]

Risley, T. R., & Hart, B. (1995). Meaningful differences in the everyday experience of young American children. Baltimore: Paul Brookes Pub Co. [11]

Rizzolatti, G., Fogassi, L., & Gallese, V. (2006). Mirrors of the mind. *Scientific American*, *295*(5), 54–61. [3]

Robertson, R. (2011). Supine infant positioning—Yes, but there's more to it. *The Journal of Family Practice, 60*, 605–608. [5]

Robinson, J. P., & Martin, S. (2008). What do happy people do? *Social Indicators Research*, *89*, 565–571. [13]

Rodríguez-Martínez, A. B., Alfonso-Sánchez, M. A., Peña, J. A., Sánchez-Valle, R., Zerr, I., Capellari, S., et al. (2008). Molecular evidence of founder effects of fatal familial insomnia through SNP haplotypes around the D178N mutation. *Neurogenetics*, *9,* 109–118. [7]

Roenneberg, T., Kuehnle, T., Pramstaller, P. P., Ricken, J., Havel, M., & Merrow, M. (2004). A marker for the end of adolescence. *Current Biology*, *14*, R1038–R1039. [5, 7]

Roethlisberger, F. J., & Dickson, W. J. (1939). *Management and the worker: An account of a research program conducted by the Western Electric Company, Hawthorne Works, Chicago*. Cambridge, MA: Harvard University Press. [12]

Roffwarg, H. P., Muzio, J. N., & Dement, W. C. (1966). Ontogenetic development of the human sleep-dream cycle. *Science*, *152*, 604–619. [7]

Ronningstam, E. (2014). Introduction to the special series on "Narcissistic personality disorder—New perspectives on diagnosis and treatment". *Journal of Personality Disorders*, *5*, 419–421. [16]

Rosch, E. (1975b). Cognitive representations of semantic categories. *Journal of Experimental Psychology: General*, *104*, 192–233. [10]

Rosch, R. H. (1975a). Cognitive reference points. *Cognitive Psychology*, *7*, 532–547. [10]

Rosell, D. R., Futterman, S. E., McMaster, A., & Siever, L. J. (2014) Schizotypal personality disorder: A current review. *Current Psychiatry Reports*, *16*, 452. [16]

Roselli, C. E., & Stormshak, F. (2009). The neurobiology of sexual partner preferences in rams. *Hormones and Behavior*, *55*, 611–620. [12]

Rosen, K., & Garety, P. (2005). Predicting recovery from schizophrenia: A retrospective comparison of characteristics at onset of people with single and multiple episodes. *Schizophrenia Bulletin*, *31*, 735–750. [16]

Rosenbaum, R. S., Köhler, S., Schacter, D. L., Moscovitch, M., Westmacott, R., Black, S. E., et al. (2005). The case of K.C.: Contributions of a memory-impaired person to memory theory. *Neuropsychologia*, *43*, 989–1021. [9]

Rosenkranz, M. A., Jackson, D. C., Dalton, K. M., Dolski, I., Ryff, C. D., Singer, B. H., et al. (2003). Affective style and in vivo immune response: Neurobehavioral mechanisms. *Proceedings of the National Academy of Sciences, USA*, *100*, 11148–11152. [13]

Rosenthal, D. (1963). *Genain quadruplets: A case study and theoretical analysis of heredity and environment in schizophrenia*. New York: Basic Books. [4]

Rosenzweig, M. R., Krech, D., & Bennett, E. L. (1961). Heredity, environment, brain biochemistry, and learning. In W. Dennis (Ed.) *Current trends in psychological theory* (pp. 87–110). Pittsburgh, PA: University of Pittsburgh Press. [9]

Rosenzweig, M. R., Krech, D., Bennett, E. L., & Diamond, M. C. (1962). Effects of environmental complexity and training on brain chemistry and anatomy: A replication and extension. *Journal of Comparative and Physiological Psychology*, *55*, 429–437. [9]

Ross, L. (1977). The intuitive psychologist and his shortcomings: Distortions in the attribution process. In L. Berkowitz, *Advances in experimental social psychology* (Vol. 10, pp. 173–220). New York: Academic Press. [15]

Rosser, J. C., Jr., Lynch, P. J., Cuddihy, L., Gentile, D. A., Klonsky, J., & Merrell, R. (2007). The impact of video games on training surgeons in the 21st century. *Archives of Surgery*, *142*, 181–186. [2]

Rossi, E. L. (2002). A conceptual review of psychosocial genomics of expectancy and surprise. *American Journal of Clinical Hypnosis*, *2*, 103–118. [7]

Rothschild, A. J. (1992). Disinhibition, amnestic reactions, and other adverse reactions secondary to triazolam: A review of the literature. *Journal of Clinical Psychiatry*, *53*, 69–79. [7]

Rotter, J. B. (1966). Generalized expectancies of internal versus external control of reinforcements. *Psychological Monographs*, *80*(1, Whole No. 609), 1–28. [14]

Rovee-Collier, C. (2002). The development of infant memory. *Current Directions in Psychological Science*, *8,* 80–85. [5]

Rowe, M. K., & Chuang, D. M. (2004). Lithium neuroprotection: Molecular mechanisms and clinical implications. *Expert Reviews in Molecular Medicine*, *18*, 1–18. [16]

Rubenstein, A. J., Kalakanis, L., & Langlois, J. H. (1999). Infant preferences for attractive faces: A cognitive explanation. *Developmental Psychology*, *35*, 848–855. [15]

Rumbaugh, D. M. (Ed.) (1977). *Language learning by a chimpanzee: The Lana project*. New York: Academic Press. [10]

Ruppenthal, G. C., Arling, G. L., Harlow, H. F., Sackett, G. P., & Suomi, S. J. (1976). A 10-year perspective of motherless-mother monkey behavior. *Journal of Abnormal Psychology*, *85*, 341–349. [5]

Ruscio, A. M., Brown, T. A., Chiu, W. T., Sareen, J., Stein, M. B., & Kessler, R. C. (2008). Social fears and social phobia in the USA: Results from the National Comorbidity Survey Replication. *Psychological Medicine*, *35*, 15–28. [16]

Rush, B. (1789). Account of a wonderful talent for arithmetical calculation, in an African slave, living in Virginia. *The American Museum*, 5(1): 62–63 (article 20). [11]

Rushton, J. P., & Jensen, A. R. (2005). Thirty years of research on race differences in cognitive ability. *Psychology, Public Policy, and Law*, *11*, 235–294. [11]

Russell, J. A. (1994). Is there universal recognition of emotion from facial expressions? A review of the cross-cultural studies. *Psychological Bulletin*, *115*, 102–141. [13]

Russo, E. B., Jiang, H. E., Li, X., Sutton, A., Carboni, A., del Bianco, F., et al. (2008). Phytochemical and genetic analyses of ancient *Cannabis* from central Asia. *Journal of Experimental Botany*, *59*, 4171–4182. [7]

Rutherford, A. (2006). Mother of behavior therapy and beyond: Mary Cover Jones and the study of the "whole child." In D. Dewsbury, L. T. Benjamin, & M. Wertheimer (Eds.), *Portraits of pioneers in psychology, Vol. VI* (pp. 189–206). Washington, DC: American Psychological Association. [1]

Ryan, J. J., Sattler, J. M., & Lopez, S. J. (2000). Age effects on Wechsler Adult Intelligence Scale-III subtests. *Archives of Clinical Neuropsychology*, *15*, 311–317. [11]

S

Sachs, G. S., Nierenberg, A. A., Calabrese, J. R., Marangell, L. B., Wisniewski, S. R., Gyulai, L., et al. (2007). Effectiveness of adjunctive antidepressant treatment for bipolar depression. *New England Journal of Medicine, 356,* 1711–1722. [16]

Sacks, O. (1996). *An anthropologist on Mars*. New York: Vintage. [11]

Saks, E. (2013, January 25). Successful and schizophrenic. *The New York Times*, p. SR5. Retrieved from http://www.nytimes.com/2013/01/27/opinion/sunday/schizophrenic-not-stupid.html?_r=0 [16]

Saksida, L. M., Bussey, T. J., Buckmaster, C. A., & Murray, E. A. (2006). No effect of hippocampal lesions on perirhinal cortex-dependent feature-ambiguous visual discriminations. *Hippocampus, 16*, 421–430. [9]

Salisbury, J. J., & Rowland, N. E. (1990). Sham drinking in rats: Osmotic and volumetric manipulations. *Physiology & Behavior, 47*, 625–630. [12]

Salkever, D. S. (2014). Assessing the IQ-earnings link in environmental lead impacts on children: Have hazard effects been overstated? *Environmental Research, 131*, 219–230. [11]

Samad, T. A., Moore, K. A., Sapirstein, A., Billet, S., Allchorne, A., Poole, S., et al. (2001). Interleukin-1β-mediated induction of Cox-2 in the CNS contributes to inflammatory pain hypersensitivity. *Nature, 410*, 471–475. [13]

Samson, S., & Zatorre, R. J. (1994). Contribution of the right temporal lobe to musical timbre discrimination. *Neuropsychologia, 32*, 231–240. [10]

Sánchez-Villegas, A., Verberne, L., De Irala, J., Ruíz-Canela, M., Toledo, E., Serra-Majem, L., et al. (2011). Dietary fat intake and the risk of depression: The SUN project. *PLoS ONE, 6*, e16268. [13]

Sanders, L. (2014, September 24). The debate over spanking is short on science, high on emotion. *Science News*. Retrieved from https://www.sciencenews.org/blog/growth-curve/debate-over-spanking-short-science-high-emotion [8]

Sansone, R. A., & Sansone, L. A. (2013). Responses of mental health clinicians to patients with borderline personality disorder. *Innovations in Clinical Neuroscience, 10*(5–6), 39–43. [16]

Santarelli, L., Saxe, M., Gross, C., Surget, A., Battaglia, F., Dulawa, S., et al. (2003). Requirement of hippocampal neurogenesis for the behavioral effects of antidepressants. *Science, 301*, 805–809. [13]

Saper, C. S., Chou, T. C., & Scammell, T. E. (2001). The sleep switch: Hypothalamic control of sleep and wakefulness. *Trends in Neuroscience, 24*, 726–731. [7]

Sapolsky, R. M. (1992). Neuroendocrinology of the stress response. In J. B. Becker, S. M. Breedlove, and D. Crews (Eds.), *Behavioral endocrinology* (pp. 287–324). Cambridge, MA: MIT Press. [13]

Sapolsky, R. M. (2002). *A primate's memoir.* New York: Scribner. [13]

Sapolsky, R. M. (2004). *Why zebras don't get ulcers* (3rd ed.). New York: Holt. [13]

Sapolsky, R. M. (Actor) (2008, September 24). Stress: Portrait of a killer [Television series episode]. In J. Hemingway (Producer), *National Geographic Special*, United States: Public Broadcasting Service. [13]

Sartorius, N., Shapiro, R., Kimura, M., & Barrett, K. (1972). WHO international pilot study of schizophrenia. *Psychological Medicine, 2*, 422–425. [16]

Sato, T., Bottlender, R., Sievers, M., & Möller, H. (2006). Distinct seasonality of depressive episodes differentiates unipolar depressive patients with and without depressive mixed states. *Journal of Affective Disorders, 90*, 1–5. [16]

Saul, S. (2006, March 8). Some sleeping pill users range far beyond bed. *The New York Times*. Retrieved from http://www.nytimes.com/2006/03/08/business/08ambien.html?pagewanted=all&_r=0 [7]

Savage-Rumbaugh, E. S. (1993). *Language comprehension in ape and child.* Chicago: University of Chicago Press. [10]

Savage-Rumbaugh, E. S., & Lewin, R. (1994). *Kanzi: The ape at the brink of the human mind.* New York: Wiley. [10]

Saxe, L. & Ben-Shakhar, G. (1999). Admissibility of polygraph tests: The application of scientific standards post-Daubert. *Psychology, Public Policy and the Law, 5,* 203–223. [13]

Saxena, S., Brody, A. L., Ho, M. L., Alborzian, S., Ho, M. K., Huang, S. C., et al. (2001). Cerebral metabolism in major depression and obsessive-compulsive disorder occurring separately and concurrently. *Biological Psychiatry, 50,* 159–170. [16]

Sbarra, D. A., and Nietert, P. J. (2009). Divorce and death: Forty years of the Charleston Heart Study. *Psychological Science, 20*, 107–113. [13]

Scarborough, E. (2000). Margaret Floy Washburn. In A. Kazdin (Ed.), *Encyclopedia of Psychology* (Vol. 8, pp. 230–232). New York: Oxford University Press. [1]

Schachter, S. (1959). *The psychology of affiliation: Experimental studies of the sources of gregariousness*. Stanford, CA: Stanford University Press. [12]

Schachter, S., & Singer, J. E. (1962). Cognitive, social, and physiological determinants of emotional state. *Psychological Review, 69,* 379–399. [13]

Schacter, D. L. (2001). *The seven sins of memory: How the mind forgets and remembers*. New York: Houghton Mifflin. [9]

Schaie, K. W., & Willis, S. L. (1993). Age difference patterns of psychometric intelligence in adulthood: Generalizability within and across ability domains. *Psychology and Aging, 8,* 44–55. [5]

Schaie, K. W., & Zanjani, F. A. K. (2006). Intellectual development across adulthood. In C. H. Hoare (Ed.) *Handbook of adult development and learning* (pp. 99–122). New York: Oxford University Press. [11]

Schaler, J. (Ed.) (2006). *Howard Gardner under fire*. Peru, IL: Open Court Publishing. [11]

Schalock, R. L., Borthwick-Duffy, S. A., Bunitnx, W. H. E., Coulter, D. L., & Craig, E. M. (2009). *Intellectual disability: Definition, classification, and systems of supports* (11th ed). Washington, DC: American Association on Intellectual and Developmental Disabilities. [11]

Scheibe, S., & Carstensen, L. L. (2010). Emotional aging: Recent findings and future trends. *The Journals of Gerontology: Series B, Psychological Sciences & Social Sciences, 65B*, 135–144. [5]

Schenck, C. H., Bundlie, S. R., Ettinger, M. G., & Mahowald, M. W. (1986). Chronic behavioral disorders of human REM sleep: A new category of parasomnia. *Sleep, 9*, 293–308. [7]

Schiff, M. A., Reed, S. D., & Daling, J. R. (2004). The sex ratio of pregnancies complicated by hospitalisation for hyperemesis gravidarum. *BJOG*, *111*, 27–30. [1]

Schiffman, J., Walker, E., Ekstrom, M., Schulsinger, F., Sorensen, H., & Mednick, S. (2004). Childhood videotaped social and neuromotor precursors of schizophrenia: A prospective investigation. *American Journal of Psychiatry*, *161*, 2021–2027. [16]

Schiffrin, H., Edelman, A., Falkenstern, M., & Stewart, C. (2010). The associations among computer-mediated communication, relationships, and well-being. *Cyberpsychology, Behavior, and Social Networking*, *13*, 299–306. [15]

Schildkraut, J. J., & Kety, S. S. (1967). Biogenic amines and emotion. *Science*, *156*, 21–30. [16]

Schino, G., & Aureli, F. (1989). Do men yawn more than women? *Ethology and Sociobiology*, *10*, 375–378. [13]

Schmidt, F. L., & Hunter, J. E. (1998). The validity and utility of selection methods in personnel psychology: Practical and theoretical implications of 85 years of research findings. *Psychological Bulletin*, *124*, 262–274. [11]

Schmolck, H., Buffalo, E. A., & Squire, L. R. (2000). Memory distortions develop over time: Recollections of the O.J. Simpson trial verdict after 15 and 32 months. *Psychological Science*, *11*, 39–45. [9]

Schreiber, F. R. (1973). *Sybil*. Chicago: Regnery. [16]

Schulz, H. (2008). Rethinking sleep analysis. *Journal of Clinical Sleep Medicine*, *4*, 99–103. [7]

Schulz-Stübner, S., Krings, T., Meister, I. G., Rex, S., Thron, A., & Rossaint, R. (2004). Clinical hypnosis modulates functional magnetic resonance imaging signal intensities and pain perception in a thermal stimulation paradigm. *Regional Anesthesia and Pain Medicine*, *29*, 549–556. [7]

Schürmann, M., Hesse, M. D., Stephan, K. E., Saarela, M., Zilles, K., Hari, R., et al. (2005). Yearning to yawn: The neural basis of contagious yawning. *Neuroimage*, *24*, 1260–1264. [13]

Schwartz, J. (1994). Low-level lead exposure and children's IQ: A meta-analysis and search for a threshold. *Environmental Research*, *65*, 42–55. [11]

Sclafani, A., Springer, D., & Kluge., L. (1976). Effects of quinine adulteration on the food intake and body weight of obese and nonobese hypothalamic hyperphagic rats. *Physiology & Behavior, 16*, 631–640. [12]

Scoboria, A., Mazzoni, G., Kirsch, I., & Milling, L. S. (2002). Immediate and persisting effects of misleading questions and hypnosis on memory reports. *Journal of Experimental Psychology: Applied*, *8*, 26–32. [7]

Scoville, W. B., & Milner, B. (1957). Loss of recent memory after bilateral hippocampal lesions. *Journal of Neurology, Neurosurgery and Psychiatry*, *20*, 11–21. [9]

Seavey, C., Katz, P., and Zalk, S. R. (1975). Baby X: The effects of gender labels on adult responses to infants. *Sex Roles*, *2*, 103–109. [12]

Seeman, P., & Tallerico, T. (1998). Antipsychotic drugs which elicit little or no parkinsonism bind more loosely than dopamine to brain D2 receptors, yet occupy high levels of these receptors. *Molecular Psychiatry*, *3*, 123–134. [16]

Segal, N. (2000). *Entwined lives: Twins and what they tell us about human behavior.* New York: Plume. [4]

Segal, N. L. (2001). Genain quadruplets: Variations on the schizophrenic syndrome. *Twin Research*, *4*, 57–59. [4]

Seiden, R. H. (1978). Where are they now? A follow-up study of suicide attempters from the Golden Gate Bridge. *Suicide and Life Threatening Behavior*, *8*, 203–216. [5, 16]

Select Committee on Intelligence. (2004). Overall conclusions—Weapons of mass destruction: Conclusion 3. In *U. S. intelligence community's pre-war intelligence assessments on Iraq* (Senate Report No. 108-301, p. 18). Washington, DC: U.S. Government Printing Office. [15]

Seligman, M. E. P. & Maier, S. F. (1967). Failure to escape traumatic shock. *Journal of Experimental Psychology*, *74*, 1–9. [8]

Seltzer, M. M., Floyd, F., Greenberg, J., Lounds, J., Lindstromm, M., & Hong, J. (2005). Life course impacts of mild intellectual deficits. *American Journal of Mental Retardation*, *110*, 451–468. [11]

Selvin, S. (1975). A problem in probability. *American Statistician*, *29*, 67. [10]

Selye, H. (1956). *The stress of life.* New York: McGraw-Hill. [13]

Senju, A., Maeda, M., Kikuchi, Y., Hasegawa, T., Tojo, Y., & Osanai, H. (2007). Absence of contagious yawning in children with autism spectrum disorder. *Biology Letters*, *3*, 706–708. [13]

Sepe, E., Ling, P. M., & Glantz, S. A. (2002). Smooth moves: Bar and nightclub tobacco promotions that target young adults. *American Journal of Public Health*, *92*, 414–419. [13]

Sexton, C. E., Mackay, C. E., & Ebmeier, K. P. (2012). A systematic review and meta-analysis of magnetic resonance imaging studies in late-life depression. *American Journal of Geriatric Psychiatry*, *21*, 184–195. [16]

Shaver, P. R., Collins, N., & Clark, C. L. (1996). Attachment styles and internal working models of self and relationship partners. In G. J. O. Fletcher & J. Fitness (Eds.), *Knowledge structures in close relationships: A social psychological approach* (pp. 25–62). Mahwah, NJ: Lawrence Erlbaum. [5]

Shaw, P., Eckstrand, K., Sharp, W., Blumenthal, J., Lerch, J. P., Greenstein, D., et al. (2007). Attention-deficit/hyperactivity disorder is characterized by a delay in cortical maturation. *Proceedings of the National Academy of Sciences, USA, 104*, 19649–19654. [5]

Shaywitz, S. E., Shaywitz, B. A., Fulbright, R. K., Skudlarski, P., Mencl, W. E., Constable, R. T., et al. (2003). Neural systems for compensation and persistence: Young adult outcome of childhood reading disability. *Biological Psychiatry*, *54*, 25–33. [10]

Shelbourne, P. F., Keller-McGandy, C., Bi, W. L., Yoon, S. R., Dubeau, L., Veitch, N. J., et al. (2007). Triplet repeat mutation length gains correlate with cell-type specific vulnerability in Huntington disease brain. *Human Molecular Genetics*, *16*, 1133–1142. [4]

Shepard, R. N., & Metzler, J. (1971). Mental rotation of three-dimensional objects. *Science*, *171*, 701–703. [10]

Sherman, N. (2005). *Stoic warriors: The ancient philosophy behind the military mind.* New York: Oxford University Press. [15]

Sherman, P. W. (1985). Alarm calls of Belding's ground squirrels to aerial predators: Nepotism or self-preservation? *Behavioral Ecology and Sociobiology*, *17*, 313–323. [15]

Sherwin, B. B. (2002). Randomized clinical trials of combined estrogen-androgen preparations: Effects on sexual functioning. *Fertility and Sterility, 77*(Suppl. 4), 49–54. [12]

Sherwin, B. B., & Gelfand, M. M. (1987). The role of androgen in the maintenance of sexual functioning in oophorectomized women. *Psychosomatic Medicine, 49,* 397–409. [12]

Shih, R. A., Belmonte, P. L., & Zandi, P. P. (2004). A review of the evidence from family, twin and adoption studies for a genetic contribution to adult psychiatric disorders. *International Review of Psychiatry, 16*, 260–283. [16]

Shipstead, Z., Redick, T. S., Hicks, K. L., & Engle, R. W. (2012). The scope and control of attention as separate aspects of working memory. *Memory, 20*, 608–628. [9]

Shorter, E. (2009). The history of lithium therapy. *Bipolar Disorders, 11* (Suppl. 2), 4–9. [16]

Shu, W., Cho, J. Y., Jiang, Y., Zhang, M., Weisz, D., Elder, G. A., et al. (2005). Altered ultrasonic vocalization in mice with a disruption in the Foxp2 gene. *Proceedings of the National Academy of Sciences, USA, 102*, 9643–9648. [10]

Shurkin, J. N. (2006). *Broken genius: The rise and fall of William Shockley, creator of the electronic age.* New York: Palgrave Macmillan. [11]

Siegel, J. M. (2001). The REM sleep–memory consolidation hypothesis. *Science, 294*, 1058–1063. [7]

Siegel, J. M., Tomaszewski, K. S., & Nienhuis, R. (1986). Behavioral states in the chronic medullary and midpontine cat. *Electroencephalography and Clinical Neurophysiology, 63*, 274–288. [7]

Siener, R. (2006). Impact of dietary habits on stone incidence. *Urological Research, 34*, 131–133. [12]

Sikich, L, Frazier, J. A., McClellan, J., Findling, R. L., Vitiello, B., Ambler, D., et al. (2008). Double-blind comparison of first- and second-generation antipsychotics in early-onset schizophrenia and schizo-affective disorder: Findings from the treatment of early-onset schizophrenia spectrum disorders (TEOSS) study. *American Journal of Psychiatry, 165*, 1420–1431. [16]

Sileno, A. P., Brandt, G. C., Spann, B. M., & Quay, S. C. (2006). Lower mean weight after 14 days intravenous administration peptide YY_{3-36} (PYY_{3-36}) in rabbits. *International Journal of Obesity (Lond), 30*, 68–72. [12]

Silverman, B. I. (1971). Studies of astrology. *The Journal of Psychology, 77,* 141–149. [14]

Silverman, B. I., & Whitmer, M. (1974). Astrological indicators of personality. *The Journal of Psychology, 87,* 89–95. [14]

Silverthorne, C. (2001). Leadership effectiveness and personality: A cross cultural evaluation. *Personality and Individual Differences, 30*, 303–309. [14]

Sim, M., Ikin, J., & McKenzie, D. (2005). *Health study 2005: Australian veterans of the Korean War.* Melbourne, Australia: Monash University Press. [13]

Simcock, G., & Hayne, H. (2003). Age-related changes in verbal and nonverbal memory during early childhood. *Developmental Psychology, 39*, 805–814. [5]

Simm, P. J., & Werther, G. A. (2005). Child and adolescent growth disorders—An overview. *Australian Family Physician, 34*, 731–737. [5]

Simmons, R. (2002). *Odd girl out: The hidden culture of aggression in girls.* Harcourt Brace: New York. [12]

Simon, G. T. (1967). *The big bands* (p. 261). New York: Macmillan. [2]

Simons, D. J., & Chabris, C. F. (1999). Gorillas in our midst: Sustained inattentional blindness for dynamic events. *Perception, 28*, 1059–1074. [10]

Simons, D. J., & Levin, D. T. (1998). Failure to detect changes to people during a real-world interaction. *Psychonomic Bulletin & Review, 5*, 644–649. [10]

Simons, D. J., & Rensink, R. A. (2005). Change blindness: Past, present, and future. *Trends in Cognitive Sciences, 9*, 16–20. [10]

Simos, P. G., Fletcher, J. M., Bergman, E., Breier, J. I., Foorman, B. R., Castillo, E. M., et al. (2002). Dyslexia-specific brain activation profile becomes normal following successful remedial training. *Neurology, 58*, 1203–1213. [10]

Simpson, J. A., Winterheld, H. A., Rholes, W. S., & Oriña, M. M. (2007). Working models of attachment and reactions to different forms of caregiving from romantic partners. *Journal of Personality and Social Psychology, 93*, 466–477. [5]

Sizemore, C. C., & Pittillo, E. S. (1977). *I'm Eve.* New York: Doubleday. [16]

Skeem, J. L., & Cooke, D. J. (2010). Is criminal behavior a central component of psychopathy? Conceptual directions for resolving the debate. *Psychological Assessment, 22*, 433–445. [16]

Skinner, B. F. (1969). *Contingencies of reinforcement: A theoretical analysis.* New York: Appleton-Century-Crofts. [8]

Skinner, B. F. (1989). The origins of cognitive thought. *American Psychologist, 44*, 13–18. [1]

Slama, F., Courtet, P., Golmard, J. L., Mathieu, F., Guillaume, S., Yon, L., et al. (2009). Admixture analysis of age at first suicide attempt. *Journal of Psychiatric Research, 43*, 895–900. [5]

Slater, M., Antley, A., Davison, A., Swapp, D., Guger, C., Barker, C., et al. (2006). A virtual reprise of the Stanley Milgram obedience experiments. *PLoS ONE, 1*, e39. [15]

Sloan, C. A., & McGinnis, I. (1982). The effect of handwriting on teachers' grading of high school essays. *Journal of the Association for the Study of Perception, 17,* 15–21. [10]

Smith, A., & Sugar, O. (1975). Development of above normal language and intelligence 21 years after hemispherectomy. *Neurology, 25*, 813–818. [10]

Smith, A., Lyons, A., Ferris, J., Richters, J., Pitts, M., Shelley, J., et al. (2011). Sexual and relationship satisfaction among heterosexual men and women: The importance of desired frequency of sex. *Journal of Sex and Marital Therapy, 37,* 104–115. [15]

Smith, C., & Lloyd, B. (1978). Maternal behavior and perceived sex of infant: Revisited. *Child Development, 49*, 1263–1265. [12]

Smith, K. H., & Rogers, M. (1994). Effectiveness of subliminal messages in television commercials: Two experiments. *Journal of Applied Psychology, 79*, 866–874. [10]

Smith, M. J., Cobia, D. J., Wang, L., Alpert, K. I., Cronenwett, W. J., Goldman, M. B., et al. (2014). *Cannabis*-related working memory deficits and associated subcortical morphological differences in healthy individuals and schizophrenia subjects. *Schizophrenia Bulletin, 40*, 287–299. [7]

Smith, R. (2000). A good death; An important aim for health services and for us all. *British Medical Journal, 320*, 129–130. [5]

Smith, S. (1997, September 2). Dreaming awake Part 1: Living with narcolepsy. *Minnesota Public Radio News. Retrieved from* http://news.minnesota.publicradio.org/features/199709/02_smiths_narcolepsy/narco_1.shtml [7]

Smith, T. B., McCullough, M. E., & Poll, J. (2003). Religiousness and depression: Evidence for a main effect and the moderating influence of stressful life events. *Psychological Bulletin, 129*, 614–636. [13]

Smoller, J. W., & Finn, C. T. (2003). Family, twin, and adoption studies of bipolar disorder. *American Journal of Medical Genetics. Part C, Seminars in Medical Genetics, 123*, 48–58. [16]

Snoep, L. (2008). Religiousness and happiness in three nations: A research note. *Journal of Happiness Studies, 9*, 207–211. [13]

Soloff, P. H., Meltzer, C. C., Becker, C., Greer, P. J., Kelly, T. M., & Constantine, D. (2003). Impulsivity and prefrontal hypometabolism in borderline personality disorder. *Psychiatry Research, 123*, 153–163. [15]

Solomon, A. (2001). *The noonday demon: An atlas of depression.* New York: Scribner. [16]

Somerville, M. J., Mervis, C. B., Young, E. J., Seo, E. J., del Campo, M., Bamforth, S., et al. (2005). Severe expressive-language delay related to duplication of the Williams-Beuren locus. *New England Journal of Medicine, 353*, 1694–1701. [10]

Sood, B., Delaney-Black, V., Covington, C., Nordstrom-Klee, B., Ager, J., Templin, T., et al. (2001). Prenatal alcohol exposure and childhood behavior at age 6 to 7 years: I. Dose-response effect. *Pediatrics, 108*, e34. doi:10.1542/peds.108.2.e34. [5]

Soon, C. S., Brass, M., Heinze, H. J., & Haynes, J. D. (2008). Unconscious determinants of free decisions in the human brain. *Nature Neuroscience, 11*, 543–545. [7]

Sound Research Laboratories. (1991). Noise control in industry. Taylor & Francis. [5]

Soussignan, R. (2002). Duchenne smile, emotional experience, and autonomic reactivity: A test of the facial feedback hypothesis. *Emotion, 2*, 52–74. [13]

Spalding, D. A. (1872). On instinct. *Nature, 6*, 485–486. [8]

Spanos, N. P. (1996). *Multiple identities & false memories: A sociocognitive perspective.* Washington, DC: American Psychological Association. [7]

Spanos, N. P., Burnley, M. C., & Cross, P. A. (1993). Response expectancies and interpretations as determinants of hypnotic responding. *Journal of Personality and Social Psychology, 65*, 1237–1242. [7]

Spanos, N. P., Jones, B., & Malfara, A. (1982). Hypnotic deafness: Now you hear it-now you still hear it. *Journal of Abnormal Psychology, 91*, 75–77. [7]

Spanos, N. P., Quigley, C. A., Gwynn, M. I., Glatt, R. L., & Perlini, A. H. (1991). Hypnotic interrogation, pretrial preparation, and witness testimony during direct and cross-examination. *Law and Human Behavior, 15*, 639–653. [7]

Spearman, C. (1904). General intelligence, objectively determined and measured. *American Journal of Psychology, 15*, 201–293. [11]

Spearman, C. (1927). *The abilities of man: Their nature and measurement.* New York: Macmillan. [11]

Spencer, S. J., Steele, C. M., & Quinn, D. M. (1999). Stereotype threat and women's math performance. *Journal of Experimental Social Psychology, 35*, 4–28. [11, 15]

Sperling, G. (1960). Negative afterimage without prior positive image. *Science, 131*, 1613–1614. [9]

Sperry, R. W. (1977). Forebrain commissurotomy and conscious awareness. *Journal of Medicine and Philosophy, 2*, 101–126. [7]

Squire, L. R. (2009) Memory and brain systems: 1969–2009. *The Journal of Neuroscience, 29*, 12711–12716. [9]

Squire, L. R., & Zola-Morgan, S. (1991). The medial temporal lobe memory system. *Science, 253*, 1380–1386. [9]

Staddon, J. E. R. (1993). *Behaviorism: Mind, mechanism, and society.* London: Duckworth. [1]

Standing, L. G. (1973). Learning 10,000 pictures. *Quarterly Journal of Experimental Psychology, 25*, 207–222. [9]

Starcevic V., & Brakoulias, V. (2014). New diagnostic perspectives on obsessive-compulsive personality disorder and its links with other conditions. *Current Opinion in Psychiatry, 27*, 62–67. [16]

Starkstein, S. E., & Robinson, R. G. (1994). Neuropsychiatric aspects of stroke. In C. E. Coffey, J. L. Cummings, M. R. Lovell, and G. D. Pearlson (Eds.), *The American Psychiatric Press textbook of geriatric neuropsychiatry* (pp. 457–477). Washington, DC: American Psychiatric Press. [13]

Statistics Canada (2010). *Survey methods and practices* (Catalogue no. 12-587-X). Retrieved from http://www.statcan.gc.ca/pub/12-587-x/12-587-x2003001-eng.pdf [2]

Stead, L. F., & Lancaster, T. (2005). Group behaviour therapy programmes for smoking cessation. *Cochrane Database of Systematic Reviews, 2*, CD001007. doi:10.1002/14651858.CD001007.pub2 [13]

Stead, L. F., Perera, R., Bullen, C., Mant, D., & Lancaster, T. (2008). Nicotine replacement therapy for smoking cessation. *Cochrane Database of Systematic Reviews, 1*, CD000146. [13]

Steele, C. M., & Aronson, J. (1995). Stereotype threat and the intellectual test performance of African Americans. *Journal of Personality and Social Psychology, 69*, 797–811. [11]

Steele, K. M., Dalla Bella, S., Peretz, I., Dunlop, T., Dawe, L. A., Humphrey, G. K., et al. (1999). Prelude or requiem for the 'Mozart effect'? *Nature, 400*, 827 [11]

Stein, M., & Miller, A. H. (1993). Stress, the hypothalamic-pituitary-adrenal axis, and immune function. *Advances in Experimental Medicine and Biology, 335*, 1–5. [13]

Stein, M. B. & Stein, D. J. (2008). Social anxiety disorder. *Lancet, 371*, 1115–1125. [16]

Steinberg L. (2013). Does recent research on adolescent brain development inform the mature minor doctrine? *Journal of Medicine and Philosophy, 38*, 256–67. [5]

Stephens, D. W., Kerr, B., & Fernández-Juricic, E. (2004). Impulsiveness without discounting: The ecological rationality hypothesis. *Proceedings of the Royal Society of London. Series B: Biological Sciences, 271*, 2459–2465. [15]

Steptoe, A., Shameal-Tonsi, A., Gylge, A., Henderson, B., Bergström, S., & Marmot, M. (2007). Socioeconomic status, pathogen burden, and cardiovascular disease risk. *Heart, 93*, 1567–1570. [13]

Stern, M., & Karraker, K. H. (1989). Sex stereotyping of infants: A review of gender labeling studies. *Sex Roles, 20*, 501–522. [12]

Stern, W. (1914). The psychological methods of testing intelligence (G. M. Whipple, Trans.). *Educational Psychology Monographs*, No. 13. Baltimore: Warwick & York. (Original work published 1912) Retrieved from https://archive.org/details/psychologicalmet00ster [11]

Sternberg, R. J. (1988). *The triarchic mind: A new theory of intelligence.* New York: Viking Press. [11]

Sternberg, R. J. (2005). There are no public-policy implications. A reply to Rushton and Jensen. *Psychology, Public Policy and Law, 11*, 295–301. [11]

Sternberg, R. J. (2007). Triangulating love. In T. J. Oord (Ed.), *The altruism reader: Selections from writings on love, religion, and science* (pp. 332–347). West Conshohocken, PA: Templeton Foundation. [15]

Stoelb, B. L., Molton, I. R., Jensen, M. P., & Patterson, D. R. (2009). The efficacy of hypnotic analgesia in adults: A review of the literature. *Contemporary Hypnosis*, *26*, 24–39. [7]

Stone, V. E., Nisenson, L., Eliassen, J. C., & Gazzaniga, M. S. (1996). Left hemisphere representations of emotional facial expressions. *Neuropsychologia*, *34*, 23–29. [13]

Stout, J. G., Dasgupta, N., Hunsinger, M., & McManus, M. A. (2011). STEMing the tide: Using in-group experts to inoculate women's self-concept in science, technology, engineering, and mathematics (STEM). *Journal of Personality and Social Psychology, 100*, 255–270. [12]

Strack, F., Martin, L., & Stepper, S. (1988). Inhibiting and facilitating conditions of the human smile: A nonobtrusive test of the facial feedback hypothesis. *Journal of Personality and Social Psychology*, *54*, 768–777. [13]

Streissguth, A. P., Landesman-Dwyer, S., Martin, J. C., & Smith, D. W. (1980). Teratogenic effects of alcohol in humans and laboratory animals. *Science, 209*, 353–361. [1]

Strickland, C. M., Drislane, L. E., Lucy, M., Krueger, R. F., & Patrick, C. J. (2013). Characterizing psychopathy using *DSM-5* personality traits. *Assessment*, *20*, 327–338. doi:10.1177/1073191113486691. [16]

Stromeyer, C. F., 3rd, & Psotka, J. (1970). The detailed texture of eidetic images. *Nature*, *225*, 346–349. [9]

Stronks, H. C., & Dagnelie, G. (2014) The functional performance of the Argus II retinal prosthesis. *Expert Review of Medical Devices*, *11*, 23–30. Retreived from http://www.ncbi.nlm.nih.gov/pubmed/24308734 [6]

Sturm, R. A., & Larsson, M. (2009). Genetics of human iris colour and patterns. *Pigment Cell & Melanoma Research*, *22*, 544–562. [4]

Stuve, T. A., Friedman, L., Jesberger, J. A., Gilmore, G. C., Strauss, M. E., & Meltzer, H. Y. (1997). The relationship between smooth pursuit performance, motion perception and sustained visual attention in patients with schizophrenia and normal controls. *Psychological Medicine*, *27*, 143–152. [16]

Substance Abuse and Mental Health Services Administration. (2013). *Results from the 2012 national survey on drug use and health: Summary of national findings* (NSDUH Series H-46, HHS Publication No. SMA 13 4795). Rockville, MD. Substance Abuse and Mental Health Services Administration. [7]

Sugawara, N., Yasui-Furukori, N., Ishii, N., Iwata, N., & Terao, T. (2013). Lithium in tap water and suicide mortality in Japan. *International Journal of Environmental Research and Public Health*, *10*, 6044–6048. [16]

Sullivan, P. F., Kendler. K. S., & Neale, M. C. (2003). Schizophrenia as a complex trait: Evidence from a meta-analysis of twin studies. *Archives of General Psychiatry*, *60*, 1187–1192. [4]

Summers, L. H. (2005). *Remarks at NBER conference on diversifying the science & engineering workforce* [Speech transcript]. Available from Harvard University Web site, Office of the President, http://harvard.edu [15]

Suomi, S. J., Delizio, R., & Harlow, H. F. (1976) Social rehabilitation of separation-induced depressive disorders in monkeys. *American Journal of Psychiatry*, *133*, 1279–1285. [5]

Surbey, M. K. (1990). Family composition, stress, and the timing of human menarche. In T. E. Zeigler & F. B. Bercovitch (Eds.), *Socioendocrinology of primate reproduction.* (pp. 11–32). New York: Wiley. [5]

Sutcliffe, J. G., & de Lecea, L. (2002). The hypocretins: Setting the arousal threshold. *Nature Reviews. Neuroscience*, *3*, 339–349. [7]

Suzuki, D. T., Griffiths, A. J. F., & Lewontin, R. C. (1981). *An introduction to genetic analysis*. San Francisco: Freeman. [11]

Svartberg, K., & Forkman, B. (2002). Personality traits in the domestic dog (*Canis familiaris*). *Applied Animal Behaviour Science*, *79*, 133-155. [14]

Swanson, J. W., Van Dorn, R. A., Swartz, M. S., Robbins, P. C., Steadman, H. J., McGuire, T. G., et al. (2013). The cost of assisted outpatient treatment: Can it save states money? *American Journal Psychiatry*, *170*, 1423–1432. [16]

Swedo, S. E., Rapoport, J. L., Leonard, H., Lenane, M., & Cheslow, D. (1989). Obsessive-compulsive disorder in children and adolescents. Clinical phenomenology of 70 consecutive cases. *Archives General Psychiatry*, *46*, 335–341. [16]

T

Taglialatela, J. P., Cantalupo, C., & Hopkins, W. D. (2006). Gesture handedness predicts asymmetry in the chimpanzee inferior frontal gyrus. *Neuroreport*, *17*, 923–927. [10]

Taipale, M., Kaminen, N., Nopola-Hemmi, J., Haltia, T., Myllyluoma, B., Lyytinen, K., et al. (2003). A candidate gene for developmental dyslexia encodes a nuclear tetratricopeptide repeat domain protein dynamically regulated in brain. *Proceedings of the National Academy of Sciences, USA*, *100*, 11553–11558. [10]

Talarico, J. M., & Rubin, D. C. (2003). Confidence, not consistency, characterizes flashbulb memories. *Psychological Science*, *14*, 455–461. [9]

Talma, H., Schönbeck, Y., van Dommelen, P., Bakker, B., van Buuren, S., & HiraSing, R. A. (2013). Trends in menarcheal age between 1955 and 2009 in the Netherlands. *PLoS ONE, 8*(4), e60056. doi:10.1371/journal.pone.0060056. [5]

Tamminga, C. A., & Schulz, S. C. (1991). *Schizophrenia research.* New York: Raven. [16]

Tanner, J. M., Whitehouse, R. H., & Takaishi, M. (1966). Standards from birth to maturity for height, weight, height velocity, and weight velocity: British children, 1965. II. *Archives of Disease in Childhood, 41*, 613–635. [5]

Tavosanis, G. (2012). Dendritic structural plasticity. *Developmental Neurobiology*, *72*, 73–86. [9]

Taylor, S. E. (1990). Health psychology. *American Psychologist*, *45*, 40–50. [13]

Taylor, S. E., Klein, L. C., Lewis, B. P., Gruenewald, T. L., Gurung, R. A. R., & Updegraff, J. A. (2000). Biobehavioral responses to stress in females: Tend-and-befriend, not fight-or-flight. *Psychological Review*, *107*, 411–429. [12]

Temple, E., Deutsch, G. K., Poldrack, R. A., Miller, S. L., Tallal, P., Merzenich, M. M., et al. (2003). Neural deficits in children with dyslexia ameliorated by behavioral remediation:

Evidence from functional MRI. *Proceedings of the National Academy of Sciences, USA*, *100*, 2860–2865. [10]

Terrace, H. S. (1979). *Nim.* New York: Knopf. [10]

Terzian, H. (1964). Behavioural and EEG effects of intracarotid sodium amytal injection. *Acta Neurochirurgica*, *12*, 230–239. [13]

Thannickal, T. C., Moore, R. Y., Nienhuis, R., Ramanathan, L., Gulyani, S., Aldrich, M., et al. (2000). Reduced number of hypocretin neurons in human narcolepsy. *Neuron*, *27*, 469–474. [7]

Thigpen, C. H., & Cleckley, H. M. (1957). *The three faces of Eve.* New York: Popular Library [16]

Thomas, A., & Chess, S. (1984). Genesis and evolution of behavioral disorders: From infancy to early adult life. *American Journal of Psychiatry*, *141*, 1–9. [5]

Thomas, R. K. (1994). Pavlov's rats "dripped saliva at the sound of a bell." *Psycoloquy*, *5*(80). Retrieved from http://www.cogsci.ecs.soton.ac.uk/cgi/psyc/newpsy?5.80 [8]

Thomas, S. G., Daniel, R. T., Chacko, A. G., Thomas, M., & Russell, P. S. (2010). Cognitive changes following surgery in intractable hemispheric and sub-hemispheric pediatric epilepsy. *Child's Nervous System*, *26*, 1067–1073. [10]

Thompson, R. A. (1991). Infant day care: Concerns, controversies, choices. In J. V. Lerner and N. L. Galambos, (Eds.), *Employed mothers and their children* (pp. 9–36). New York: Garland. [5]

Thorndike, E. L. (1911). *Animal intelligence: Experimental studies.* New York: Macmillan. Retrieved from http://www.archive.org/details/animalintelligen00thor [8]

Thorndike, E. T. (1898). Some experiments on animal intelligence. *Science*, *7*, 818–824. [1]

Timms, R. M. (2013). Moderate acne as a potential barrier to social relationships: Myth or reality? *Psychology, Health & Medicine*, *18*, 310–20. [15]

Todorov, A., Mandisodza, A. N., Goren, A., & Hall, C. C. (2005). Inferences of competence from faces predict election outcomes. *Science*, *308*, 1623–1626. [15]

Tolman, E. C. (1948). Cognitive maps in rats and men. *Psychological Review*, *55*, 189–208. Retrieved from http://psychclassics.yorku.ca/Tolman/Maps/maps.htm [8]

Tolman, E. C., & Honzik, C. H. (1930a). Insight in rats. *University of California Publications in Psychology*, *4*, 215–232. [8]

Tolman, E. C., & Honzik, C. H. (1930b). Introduction and removal of reward and maze performance in rats. *University of California Publications in Psychology*, *4*, 257–275. [8]

Tomatis, A. (1991). *Pourquoi Mozart?* Paris: Diffusion Hachette. [11]

Torrey, E. F. (2006). *Surviving schizophrenia: A manual for families, patients and providers* (5th ed). New York: Harper. [4, 16]

Torrey, E. F. (2011). Stigma and violence: Isn't it time to connect the dots? *Schizophrenia Bulletin*, *37*, 892–896. [16]

Torrey, E. F., Bowler, A. E., Taylor, E. H., & Gottesman, I. I. (1994). *Schizophrenia and manic depressive disorder.* New York: Basic Books. [16]

Trachtenberg, F. L., Haas, E. A., Kinney, H. C., Stanley, C., & Krous, H. F. (2012). Risk factor changes for sudden infant death syndrome after initiation of Back-to-Sleep campaign. *Pediatrics*, *129*, 630–638. [5]

Travis, F., Tecce, J., Arenander, A., & Wallace, R. K. (2002). Patterns of EEG coherence, power, and contingent negative variation characterize the integration of transcendental and waking states. *Biological Psychology*, *61*, 293–319. [7]

Treffert, D. A. (2013). Savant syndrome 2013—Myths and realities. Retrieved from https://www.wisconsinmedicalsociety.org/professional/savant-syndrome/resources/articles/savant-syndrome-2013-myths-and-realities/ [11]

Treffert, D. A. & Christensen, D. D. (2005). Inside the mind of a savant. *Scientific American*, *293*(6), 108–113. Retrieved from http://www.pleasanton.k12.ca.us/avhsweb/emersond/appsych/ch11_development/savant.pdf [9]

Treyster, Z., & Gitterman, B. (2011). Second-hand smoke exposure in children: Environmental factors, physiological effects, and interventions within pediatrics. *Reviews on Environmental Health*, *26*(3), 187–195. [5]

Trimble, M. R. (1991). Interictal psychoses of epilepsy. *Advances in Neurology*, *55*, 143–152. [16]

Triplett, N. (1898). The dynamogenic factors in pacemaking and competition. *American Journal of Psychology*, *9*, 507–533. [15]

Trujillo, L. T., Jankowitsch, J. M., & Langlois, J. H. (2013). Beauty is in the ease of the beholding: A neurophysiological test of the averageness theory of facial attractiveness. *Cognitive, Affective, & Behavioral Neuroscience.* doi:10.3758/s13415-013-0230-2. [15]

Tryon, R. C. (1940). Genetic differences in maze-learning ability in rats. *Yearbook of the National Society for the Study of Education*, *39*, 111–110. [4]

Tucker, A. (1950). A two-person dilemma. Unpublished manuscript, Stanford University, Redwood City, CA. [15]

Tulving, E. (1972). Episodic and semantic memory. In E. Tulving and W. Donaldson (Eds.), *Organization of memory* (pp. 381–403). New York: Academic Press. [9]

Tulving, E. (1989). Memory: Performance, knowledge, and experience. *European Journal of Cognitive Psychology*, *1*, 3–26. [9]

Tulving, E., Schacter, D. L., & Stark, H. A. (1982). Priming effects in word fragment completion are independent of recognition memory. *Journal of Experimental Psychology: Learning, Memory and Cognition*, *8*, 336–342. [9]

Turiel, E. (2002). *The culture of morality: Social development, context, and conflict.* Cambridge, UK: Cambridge University Press. [5]

Turkheimer, E., Haley, A., Waldron, M., D'Onofrio, B., & Gottesman, I. I. (2003). Socioeconomic status modifies heritability of IQ in young children. *Psychological Sciences*, *14*, 623–628. [11]

Turner, E. H., Matthews, A. M., Linardatos, E., Tell, R. A., & Rosenthal, R. (2008). Selective publication of antidepressant trials and its influence on apparent efficacy. *New England Journal of Medicine*, *358*, 252–260. [16]

Tversky, A., & Kahneman, D. (1974). Judgments under uncertainty: Heuristics and biases. *Science*, *185*, 1124–1131. [10]

Tversky, A., & Kahneman, D. (1981). The framing of decisions and the psychology of choice. *Science*, *211*, 453–458. [10]

Tyack, P. L. (2003). Dolphins communicate about individual-specific social relationships. In F. de Waal & P. L. Tyack (Eds.), *Animal social complexity: Intelligence, culture, and individualized societies* (pp. 342–361). Cambridge, MA: Harvard University Press. [10]

U

Uchino, B. N., & Birmingham, W. (2010). Stress and support processes. In R. J. Contrada, & A. Baum (Eds.), *The hand-*

book of stress science: Biology, psychology, and health (pp. 110–122). New York: Springer. [13]

Umiltà, M. A., Kohler, E., Galiese, V., Fogassi, L., Kysers, C., & Rizzolatti, G. (2001). I know what you are doing: A neurophysiological study. *Neuron, 31*, 155–165. [3]

United Nations Office on Drugs and Crime. (2012). Global study on homicide. Retreived from http://www.unodc.org/unodc/en/data-and-analysis/homicide.html [15]

United Nations Office on Drugs and Crime. (2014). *Global study on homicide 2013*. Vienna, Austria: United Nations Publications. Retrieved from https://www.unodc.org/documents/gsh/pdfs/2014_GLOBAL_HOMICIDE_BOOK_web.pdf [15]

Ursin, H., Baade, E., & Levine, S. (1978). *Psychobiology of stress: A study of coping men.* New York: Academic Press. [13]

Uylings, H. B., & de Brabander, J. M. (2002). Neuronal changes in normal human aging and Alzheimer's disease. *Brain and Cognition, 49*, 268–276. [5]

V

Van Houtem, C. M., Laine, M. L., Boomsma, D. I., Ligthart, L., van Wijk, A. J., & De Jongh, A. (2013). A review and meta-analysis of the heritability of specific phobia subtypes and corresponding fears. *Journal of Anxiety Disorders, 27*, 379–388. [16]

van Os, J., & Kapur, S. (2009). Schizophrenia. *Lancet, 374*, 635–645. [16]

van Os, J., Kenis, G., & Rutten, B. P. (2010). The environment and schizophrenia. *Nature, 468*, 203–212. [16]

van Praag, H., Kempermann, G., & Gage, F. H. (2000). Neural consequences of environmental enrichment. *Nature Reviews. Neuroscience, 1*, 191–198. [9]

Vance, D. E. (1995). Belief in lunar effects on human behavior. *Psychological Reports, 76*, 32–34. [10]

Vaughan, K., Armstrong, M. S., Gold, R., O'Connor, N., Jenneke, W., & Tarrier, N. (1994). A trial of eye movement desensitization compared to image habituation training and applied muscle relaxation in post-traumatic stress disorder. *Journal of Behavior Therapy and Experimental Psychiatry, 25*, 283–291. [13]

Vaughan, W., & Greene, S. L. (1984). Pigeon visual memory capacity. *Journal of Experimental Psychology: Animal Behavior Processes, 10*, 256–271. [9]

Veenhoven, R. (2010). Capability and happiness: Conceptual difference and reality links. *Journal of Socio-Economics, 39*, 344–350. [11]

Verplanck, W. S. (1956). The operant conditioning of human motor behavior. *Psychological Bulletin. 53*, 70–83. Available from http://cogprints.org/ [8]

Viglione, D. J., & Hilsenroth, M. J. (2001). The Rorschach: facts, fictions, and future. *Psychological Assessment, 13*, 452–471. [14]

Vita, A., De Peri, L., & Sacchetti, E. (2014, July 14). Lithium in drinking water and suicide prevention: A review of the evidence. *International Clinical Psychopharmacology.* Advance online publication. [16]

Vitiello, B., & Stoff, D. M. (1997). Subtypes of aggression and their relevance to child psychiatry. *Journal of the American Academy of Child and Adolescent Psychiatry, 36*, 307–315. [15]

Volavka, J. (2013). Violence in schizophrenia and bipolar disorder. *Psychiatria Danubina, 25*, 24–33. [16]

Volkow, N. D., Wang, G. J., Fowler, J. S., Tomasi, D., & Telang, F. (2011). Addiction: Beyond dopamine reward circuitry. *Proceedings of the National Academy of Sciences, USA, 108*, 15037–15042. [12]

Von Neumann, J. (1951). The general and logical theory of automata. In L. A. Jeffress (Ed.), *Cerebral mechanisms in behavior–Hixon Symposium* (pp. 1–31). New York: Wiley. [1, 8]

W

Waber, R. L., Shiv, B., Carmon, Z., & Ariely, D. (2008). Commercial features of placebo and therapeutic efficacy. *JAMA, 299*, 1016–1017. [2]

Wada, J., & Rasmussen T. (1960). Intracarotid injection of sodium amytal for the lateralization of cerebral speech dominance. *Journal of Neurosurgery, 17*, 266–282. [10]

Wagner, G. C., Beuving, L. J., & Hutchinson, R. R. (1980). The effect of gonadal hormone manipulations on aggressive target-biting in mice. *Aggressive Behavior, 6*, 1–7. [15]

Waldrop, M. M. (2012). Computer modelling: Brain in a box. *Nature, 482*, 456–458. [3]

Walker, E. F. (1991). *Schizophrenia: A life-course developmental perspective.* San Diego, CA: Academic Press. [16]

Walker, E., & Lewine, R. J. (1990). Prediction of adult-onset schizophrenia from childhood home movies of the patients. *American Journal of Psychiatry, 147*, 1052–1056. [4]

Wallace, C., Mullen, P. E., & Burgess, P. (2004). Criminal offending in schizophrenia over a 25-year period marked by deinstitutionalization and increasing prevalence of comorbid substance use disorders. *American Journal of Psychiatry, 161*, 716–727. [16]

Wallis, C. (2009, November 2). A powerful identity, a vanishing diagnosis. *The New York Times*, p. D1. [5]

Walmsley, R. (2012). World prison population list (10th ed.). Retrieved from http://www.prisonstudies.org/sites/prisonstudies.org/files/resources/downloads/wppl_10.pdf [15]

Walsh, E., Buchanan, A., & Fahy, T. (2002). Violence and schizophrenia: Examining the evidence. *British Journal of Psychiatry, 180*, 490–495. [16]

Walton, G. M., & Spencer, S. J. (2009). Latent ability: Grades and test scores systematically underestimate the intellectual ability of negatively stereotyped students. *Psychological Science, 20*, 1132–1139. [11]

Wang, H., Yu, M., Ochani, M., Amella, C. A., Tanovic, M., Susarla, S., et al. (2003). Nicotinic acetylcholine receptor $\alpha 7$ subunit is an essential regulator of inflammation. *Nature, 421*, 384–388. [13]

Wansink, B., Kent, R. J., & Hoch, S. J. (1998). An anchoring and adjustment model of purchase quantity decisions. *Journal of Marketing Research, 35*, 71–81. [10]

Washburn, M. F. (1908). *The animal mind: A text-book of comparative psychology.* New York: Macmillan. [1]

Watanabe, M., Liao, J. H., Jara, H., & Sakai, O. (2013). Multispectral quantitative MR imaging of the human brain: Lifetime age-related effects. *Radiographics, 33*, 1305–1319. [10]

Waterhouse, L. (2006). Multiple intelligences, the Mozart effect, and emotional intelligence: A critical review. *Educational Psychologist, 41*, 207–225 [11]

Watkins, M. W., Lei, P. W., & Canivez, G. L. (2007). Psychometric intelligence and achievement: A cross-lagged panel analysis. *Intelligence, 35*, 59–68. [11]

Watson, J. B. (1913). Psychology as the behaviorist views it. *Psychological Review*, *20*, 158–177. Retrieved from http://psychclassics.yorku.ca/Watson/views.htm [1, 8]

Watson, J. B. (1924). *Behaviorism*. New York: People's Institute Publishing Company. [8]

Watson, J. B. (1928). What is behaviorism? *The Golden Book Magazine*, *7*(40), 507–515. [1]

Watson, J. B. & Rayner, R. (1920). Conditioned emotional reactions. *Journal of Experimental Psychology*, *3*, 1–14. [8]

Weaver, I. C., Champagne, F. A., Brown, S. E., Dymov, S., Sharma, S., Meaney, M. J., et al. (2005). Reversal of maternal programming of stress responses in adult offspring through methyl supplementation: Altering epigenetic marking later in life. *Journal of Neuroscience*, *25*, 11045–11054. [4]

Webb, W. B. (1992). *Sleep, the gentle tyrant.* Bolton, MA: Anker. [7]

Wegner, M., Helmich, I., Machado, S., Nardi, A. E., Arias-Carrión, O., & Budde, H. (2014). Effects of exercise on anxiety and depression disorders: Review of meta-analyses and neurobiological mechanisms. *CNS & Neurological Disorders - Drug Targets*, *13*, 1002–1014. [16]

Weiner, R. D. (1994). Treatment optimization with ECT. *Psychopharmacology Bulletin*, *30*, 313–320. [16]

Weiner, T., Johnston, D., & Lewis, N. A. (1995). *Betrayal: The story of Aldrich Ames, an American spy.* New York: Random House [13]

Weiss, J. M. (1968). Effects of coping responses on stress. *Journal of Comparative and Physiological Psychology*, *65*, 251–260. [13]

Weiss, J. M. (1971a). Effects of coping behavior with and without a feedback signal on stress pathology in rats. *Journal of Comparative and Physiological Psychology*, *77*, 22–30. [13]

Weiss, J. M. (1971b). Effects of punishing the coping response (conflict) on stress pathology in rats. *Journal of Comparative and Physiological Psychology*, *77*, 14–21. [13]

Weisz, C., & Wood, L. F. (2005). Social identity support and friendship outcomes: A longitudinal study predicting who will be friends and best friends 4 years later. *Journal of Personal and Social Relationships*, *22*, 416–432. [15]

Weitzenhoffer, A. M. (2000). *The practice of hypnotism* (2nd ed.). New York: Wiley. [7]

Weitzenhoffer, A. M., & Hilgard, E. R. (1959). *Stanford hypnotic susceptibility scales, forms A & B*. Palo Alto, CA: Consulting Psychologists Press. [7]

Weitzman, E. D. (1981). Sleep and its disorders. *Annual Review of Neurosciences*, *4*, 381–417. [7]

Wenz, F. V. (1977). Seasonal suicide attempts and forms of loneliness. *Psychological Reports*, *40*, 807–810. [16]

Werker, J. F., Gilbert, J. H. V., Humphrey, K., & Tees, R. C. (1981). Developmental aspects of cross-language speech perception. *Child Development*, *52*, 349–355. [10]

Whalley, L. J., & Deary, I. J. (2001). Longitudinal cohort study of childhood IQ and survival up to age 76. *The BMJ*, *322*, 819 [11]

Whitehouse, W. G., Orne, E. C., Dinges, D. F., Bates, B. L., Nadon, R., & Orne, M. T. (2005). The cognitive interview: Does it successfully avoid the dangers of forensic hypnosis? *American Journal of Psychology*, *118*, 213–234. [7]

Why women musicians are inferior? (1938, February). *Down Beat*. [2]

Whyte, W. H., Jr. (1952). Groupthink. *Fortune*, pp. 114–117, 142, 146. [15]

Wickström, G., & Bendix, T. (2000). The "Hawthorne effect" —What did the original Hawthorne studies actually show? *Scandinavian Journal of Work, Environment & Health*, *26*, 363–367. [12]

Will, B., Galani, R., Kelche, C., & Rosenzweig, M. R. (2004). Recovery from brain injury in animals: Relative efficacy of environmental enrichment, physical exercise or formal training (1990–2002). *Progress in Neurobiology*, *72*, 167–182. [9]

Williams, T. J., Pepitone, M. E., Christensen, S. E., Cooke, B. M., Huberman, A. D., Breedlove, N. J., et al. (2000). Finger-length ratios and sexual orientation. *Nature, 404*, 455–456. [12]

Wilson, K., Mattingly, B. A., Clark, E. M., Weidler, D. J., & Bequette, A. W. (2011). The gray area: Exploring attitudes toward infidelity and the development of the perceptions of dating infidelity scale. *Journal of Social Psychology*, *151*, 63–86. [15]

Wilson, T. D., & Gilbert, D. T. (2005). Affective forecasting knowing what to want. *Current Directions in Psychological Science*, *14*, 131–134. [13]

Wilson, T. D., Meyers, J., & Gilbert, D. T. (2003). How happy was I, anyway? *Social Cognition*, *6*, 421–446. [13]

Wimmer, H., & Perner, J. (1983). Beliefs about beliefs: Representation and constraining function of wrong beliefs in young children's understanding of deception. *Cognition, 13*, 103–128. [5]

Winawer, J., Witthoft, N., Frank, M. C., Wu, L., Wade, A. R., & Boroditsky, L. (2007). Russian blues reveal effects of language on color discrimination. *Proceedings of the National Academy of Sciences, USA*, *104*, 7780–7785. [10]

Winerip, M. (2005, May 4). SAT essay test rewards length and ignores errors. *The New York Times*. Retrieved from http://www.nytimes.com/2005/05/04/education/04education.html?pagewanted=all&position= [10]

Wines, M., & Robles, F. (2014, August 22). Key factor in police shootings: Reasonable fear. *The New York Times*, p. A1. [1]

Wise, R. A. (1996). Neurobiology of addiction. *Current Opinion in Neurobiology, 6*, 243–251. [7]

Wise, R. A. (2006). Role of brain dopamine in food reward and reinforcement. *Philosophical Transactions of the Royal Society of London. Series B: Biological Sciences*, *29*, 1149–1158. [12]

Wise, R. A., Bauco, P., Carlezon, W. A., Jr., & Trojniar, W. (1992). Self-stimulation and drug reward mechanisms. *Annals of the New York Academy of Sciences*, *28,* 192–198. [12]

Witt, K., van Dorn, R., & Fazel, S. (2013). Risk factors for violence in psychosis: Systematic review and meta-regression analysis of 110 studies. *PLoS ONE*, *8*, e55942. [16]

Wolfe, J. E., Kluender, K. R., & Levi, D. M. (2012). *Sensation & perception*. Sunderland, MA: Sinauer. [6]

Wolfe, U., Maloney, L., & Tam, M. (2005). Distortions of perceived length in the frontoparallel plane: Tests of perspective theories. *Perception & Psychophysics*, *67*, 967–979. [1]

Wolfson, A. (2005, October 9). A hoax most cruel: Caller coaxed McDonald's managers into strip-searching a worker. *The Courier-Journal*. Available from http://www.courier-journal.com [15]

Wolk, R., & Somers, V. K. (2003). Cardiovascular consequences of obstructive sleep apnea. *Clinics in Chest Medicine, 24*, 195–205. [7]

Wong, M. M., Brower, K. J., & Zucker, R. A. (2010). Sleep problems, suicidal ideation, and self-harm behaviors in adolescence. *Journal of Psychiatric Research, 45*, 505–511. [13]

Wood, D. C. (1988). Habituation in *Stentor* produced by mechanoreceptor channel modification. *Journal of Neuroscience, 8*, 2254–2258. [8]

Wood, J. M., Nezworski, M. T., Lilienfeld, S. O., & Garb, H. N. (2003). *What's wrong with the Rorschach?* San Francisco: Jossey-Bass. [14]

Woolfolk, M. E., Castellan, W., & Brooks, C. I. (1983). Pepsi versus Coke: Labels, not tastes, prevail. *Psychological Reports*, *52*, 185–186. [2]

World Health Organization (2010a). *Childhood lead poisoning*. Retrieved from http://www.who.int/ceh/publications/leadguidance.pdf [11]

World Health Organization, (2010b). *ICD-10: Total statistical classification of diseases and related health problems*. Retrieved from http://www.who.int/classifications/icd/ICD10Volume2_en_2010.pdf [11]

Worthen, J. B., & Wade, C. E. (1999). Direction of travel and visiting team athletic performance: Support for a circadian dysrhythmia hypothesis. *Journal of Sport Behavior, 22*, 279–287. [7]

Wright, A. A., Santiago, H. C., Sands, S. F., Kendrick, D. F., & Cook, R. G. (1985). Memory processing of serial lists by pigeons, monkeys, and people. *Science*, *229*, 287–289. [9]

Wright, E. (2008). *The case for qualia*. Cambridge, MA: MIT Press. [7]

Wuethrich, B. (2000). Learning the world's languages—Before they vanish. *Science*, *288*, 1156–1159. [10]

Wundt, W. M. (1893). *Grundzüge der physiologischen Psychologie* (Vol. II, 4th ed.). Leipzig: Engelmann. [1]

Y

Yechiam, E., & Barron, G. (2003). Learning to ignore online help requests. *Computational & Mathematical Organization Theory, 9*, 327–339. [15]

Yerkes, R. (1919). Report of the psychology committee of the national research council. *The Psychological Review, 26*, 83–149. [11]

Yerkes, R. M., & Dodson, J. D. (1908). The relation of strength of stimulus to rapidity of habit-formation. *Journal of Comparative Neurology and Psychology, 18*, 459–482. [12]

Yin, L., Wang, J., Klein, P. S., & Lazar, M. A. (2006). Nuclear receptor Rev-erbα is a critical lithium-sensitive component of the circadian clock. *Science, 311*, 1002–1004 [16]

Yin, R. K. (2013). *Case study research: Design and methods* (5th ed). Beverly Hills, CA: Sage Publishing. [2]

Young, K. D., Erickson, K., Nugent, A. C., Fromm, S. J., Mallinger, A. G., Furey, M. L., et al. (2011). Functional anatomy of autobiographical memory recall deficits in depression. *Psychological Medicine*, *29*, 1–13. [16]

Young, R. P., Hopkins, R. J., Christmas, T., Black, P. N., Metcalf, P., & Gamble, G. D. (2009). COPD prevalence is increased in lung cancer, independent of age, sex and smoking history. *European Respiratory Journal*, *34*, 380–386. [13]

Z

Zago, S., Sartori, G., & Scarlato, G. (2004). Malingering and retrograde amnesia: The historic case of the Collegno amnesic. *Cortex*, *40*, 519–532. [9]

Zagorsky, J. L. (2007). Do you have to be smart to be rich? The impact of IQ on wealth, income and financial distress. *Intelligence*, *35*, 489–501. [11]

Zajonc, R. B., Heingartner, A., & Herman, E. M. (1969). Social enhancement and impairment of performance in the cockroach. *Journal of Personality and Social Psychology, 13*, 83–92. [15]

Zammit, S., Lewis, G., Dalman, C., & Allebeck, P. (2010). Examining interactions between risk factors for psychosis. *The British Journal of Psychiatry, 197*, 207–211. [7]

Zargar, M., Khaji, A., Kaviani, A., Karbakhsh, M., Masud, M., & Abdollahi, M. (2004). The full moon and admission to emergency rooms. *Indian Journal of Medical Sciences*, *58*, 191–195. [10]

Zarkin, G. A., Dunlap, L. J., Belenko, S., & Dynia, P. A. (2006). Benefit-cost analysis of the Kings County district attorneys office Drug Treatment Alternative to Prison (DTAP) program. *Justice Research and Policy*, *7*, 1–25. [7]

Zatorre, R. J., Evans, A. C., & Meyer, E. (1994). Neural mechanisms underlying melodic perception and memory for pitch. *Journal of Neuroscience*, *14*, 1908–1919. [10]

Zebrowitz, L. A., & Montepare, J. M. (2005). Appearance DOES matter. *Science*, *308*, 1565–1566. [15]

Zecevic, N., & Rakic, P. (1976). Differentiation of Purkinje cells and their relationship to other components of developing cerebellar cortex in man. *Journal of Comparative Neurology, 167*, 27–47. [5]

Zhang, W., Robertson, J., Jones, A., Dieppe, P., & Doherty, M. (2008). The placebo response and its determinants in osteoarthritis – Meta-analysis of randomised controlled trials. *Annals of the Rheumatic Diseases*, *67*, 1716–1723. [2]

Zhang, Y., Proenca, R., Maffei, M., Barone, M., Leopold, L., & Friedman, J. M. (1994). Positional cloning of the mouse obese gene and its human homologue. *Nature*, *372*, 425–432. [12]

Zlomke, K., & Davis, T. E., III. (2008). One-session treatment of specific phobias: A detailed description and review of treatment efficacy. *Behavior Therapy*, *39*, 207–223. [16]

Zucker, I. (1988). Seasonal affective disorders: Animal models non fingo. *Journal of Biological Rhythms, 3*, 209–223. [12]

Name Index

T

U

V

W

Y

Z

Subject Index

Entries with an f next to the page number indicate that the information will be found in a figure. Entries with a t next to the page number indicate that the information will be found in a table.

A

B

D

G

M

N

O